THE OXFORD

Essential Dictionary of the U. S. Military

Oxford Titles Available
from Berkley Books

THE OXFORD AMERICAN DESK DICTIONARY AND THESAURUS, 2ND EDITION
THE OXFORD ESSENTIAL DESK REFERENCE
THE OXFORD ESSENTIAL GUIDE TO PEOPLE & PLACES OF THE BIBLE
THE OXFORD ESSENTIAL DICTIONARY OF THE U.S. MILITARY
THE OXFORD ESSENTIAL DICTIONARY OF DIFFICULT WORDS
THE OXFORD DICTIONARY OF AMERICAN USAGE AND STYLE
THE OXFORD ESSENTIAL DICTIONARY
THE OXFORD ESSENTIAL GUIDE FOR PUZZLE SOLVERS
THE OXFORD ESSENTIAL GUIDE TO THE U.S. GOVERNMENT
THE OXFORD ESSENTIAL GUIDE TO WRITING
THE OXFORD ESSENTIAL QUOTATIONS DICTIONARY
THE OXFORD ESSENTIAL SPELLING DICTIONARY
THE OXFORD ESSENTIAL THESAURUS
THE OXFORD FRENCH DICTIONARY
THE OXFORD GERMAN DICTIONARY
THE OXFORD GREEK DICTIONARY
THE OXFORD ITALIAN DICTIONARY
THE OXFORD RUSSIAN DICTIONARY
THE OXFORD NEW SPANISH DICTIONARY

Essential Dictionary of the U. S. Military

BERKLEY BOOKS, NEW YORK

THE OXFORD ESSENTIAL DICTIONARY
OF THE U.S. MILITARY

A Berkley Book / published by arrangement with
Oxford University Press, Inc.

PRINTING HISTORY
Berkley edition / July 2001

The Penguin Putnam Inc. World Wide Web site address is
www.penguinputnam.com

ISBN: 0-425-18069-7

BERKLEY®
Berkley Books are published by
The Berkley Publishing Group, a division of Penguin Putnam Inc.,
375 Hudson Street, New York, New York 10014.
BERKLEY and the "B" design are trademarks
belonging to Penguin Putnam Inc.

PRINTED IN THE UNITED STATES OF AMERICA

10 9 8 7 6 5 4 3 2 1

Contents

Staff

Managing Editor:	Elizabeth J. Jewell
Acquisitions Editor:	Christine A. Lindberg
Senior Editor:	Erin McKean
Staff Project Editors:	Matthew Z. Brown Suzanne Burke Martin Coleman Conrad C. Crane Spencer Downing Jerilyn Seife Famighetti Orin K. Hargraves Ethan Kytle Mark LaFlaur Nancy LaRoche John R. Leech Jennifer Levasseur Martha B. Mayou Joseph Patwell Julia Penelope Charles Reginald Shrader Srdjan Smajic Mark Whitaker Steven T. Wuhs
Pronunciation Editors:	Linda Costa John K. Bollard Sharon Goldstein Ellen Johnson William A. Kretzschmar Rima McKinzey Katherine Sietsema
Researcher and Proofreader:	Sandra Ban
Data Entry:	Kimberly Roberts

Preface

The *Oxford Essential Dictionary of the U.S. Military* is intended as a quick-reference, compact guide for the student of American military history and for members of the U.S. armed services. The dictionary covers essential terms, biographies, and battles, with features that include clear, concise definitions, derivatives and inflected forms, word origin information, and special additional information presented in text boxes for further reading.

Special Reference Sections at the back of the book provide charts of useful information, including ranks, the terms of Secretaries of War and Defense, and casualty information for American battles.

This handy "essential" dictionary is an excellent yet economical choice for those who need quick reference to specialized military terms and the people and events of American military history. The *Oxford Essential Dictionary of the U.S. Military*, with its attention to quality, thoroughness, and currency, continues the tradition of Oxford—the world's most trusted name in dictionaries.

Introduction

The *Oxford Essential Dictionary of the U.S. Military* provides concise information on more than 8600 military terms, including short encyclopedic entries for battles, important people, weapons, planes, ships, and other transport, military slang, and political and geographic terms closely related to the military history of the United States.

The selection of terms for inclusion in the *Oxford Essential Dictionary of the U.S. Military* was done with careful attention to the entire span of U.S. military history, from colonial times to the present.

HOW TO USE THIS BOOK

The "entry maps" below explain the different parts of typical entries in this dictionary.

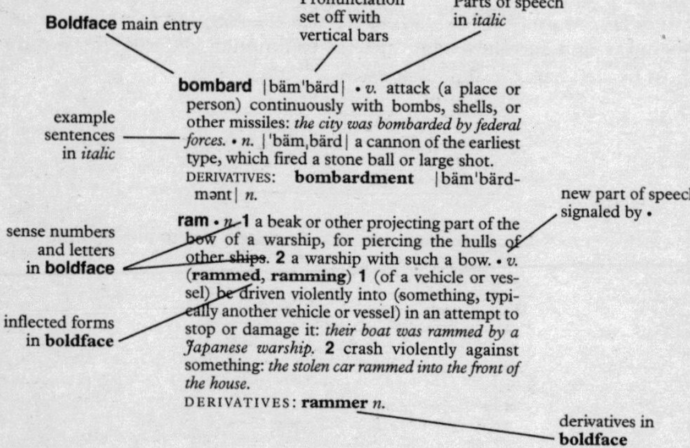

Main entries and other boldface forms

Main entries appear in boldface type, as do inflected forms, idioms and phrases, and derivatives.

Pronunciation

Pronunciations are given for words thought to be especially difficult or unfamiliar to most Americans. For more details on pronunciation, including a complete pronunciation key, see the pages that follow this Introduction.

Cross-references

Cross-references appear in small capitals, for example, in the entry **Breed's Hill, Battle of**, a cross reference is given in small type to **Bunker Hill, Battle of**.

> **Breed's Hill, Battle of** • see BUNKER HILL, BATTLE OF.

Special Features

Additional information is provided for hundreds of entries, especially biographical entries. These special boxed features highlight the some of the most surprising or unusual information about the lives of American military men and women, as well as for planes, ships, weapons, and other terms.

> **Adams, Charles** (1845–95) • Union army officer and diplomat, born Karl Adam Schwanbeck. . . . and prevented their extermination by the Colorado militia.
>
> Adams insisted that Colorado print its laws in German as well as in English and Spanish, and had some political influence with the naturalized Germans in the territory.

> **Agent Orange** • a defoliant used by the United States in the VIETNAM WAR. . . . liver failure, and chloracne. See also OPERATION RANCH HAND.
>
> The United States also used the herbicides and defoliants Agent White and Agent Blue, so called because of the color of the labels on the shipping containers.

Selected entries also have usage notes and etymologies to aid in complete understanding of the term.

> **nuclear** • *adj.* **1** denoting, relating to, or powered by the energy released in nuclear fission or fusion: *nuclear submarines.* **2** denoting, possessing, or involving weapons using this energy: *a nuclear bomb | nuclear nations.*
>
> USAGE: The standard pronunciation of the word **nuclear** rhymes with **clear**. A variant pronunciation exists, famously used by Presidents EISENHOWER and CARTER, which pronounces the second part of the word like **-ular** in **circular** or **particular**. This pronunciation is not acceptable in standard English although it is still widely heard.

> **asdic** |ˈæzˌdik| (also **ASDIC**) • *n.* chiefly Brit. an early form of sonar used to detect submarines.
>
> ORIGIN: World War II: acronym from *Allied Submarine Detection Investigation Committee.*

Key to the Pronunciations

This book uses a respelling system and several special symbols, as described below, to show how entries are pronounced:

æ *as in* **cavalry** /ˈcævəlrē/
ä *as in* **kamikaze** /ˌkämiˈkäzē/
ā *as in* **napalm** /ˈnāpä(l)m/
CH *as in* **Chaffee** /ˈCHæfē/
e *as in* **clandestine** /klænˈdestin/
ē *as in* **Riyadh** /rēˈyäd/
er *as in* **air** /er/; **aerospace** /ˈerōˌspās/
ə *as in* **guerrilla** /gəˈilə/
g *as in* **grapnel** /ˈgræpnəl/
i *as in* **interdiction** /ˌintərˈdikSHən/
ī *as in* **Geiger** /ˈgīgər/
ir *as in* **ear** /ir/; **Iroquois** /ˈirəˌkwoi/
j *as in* **Sturgis** /ˈstərjis/
KH *as in* **Reich** /rīKH/
N *as in* **Clemenceau** /ˌklāˌmäNˈsō/
NG *as in* **Bangalore** /ˌbæNGgəˈlôr/
ô *as in* **war** /wôr/
ō *as in* **aerodrome** /ˈerəˌdrōm/
o͝o *as in* **foot** /fo͝ot/; **Schurz** /SHo͝orts/
o͞o *as in* **Rousseau** /ro͞oˈsō/
oi *as in* **Burgoyne** /ˈbərˌgoin/
ow *as in* **Osterhaus** /ˈästərˌhows/
SH *as in* **Schroeder** /ˈSHrōdər/
t̲ *as in* **stratosphere** /ˈstræt̲əˌsfir/
TH *as in* **Oglethorpe** /ˈōgəlˌTHôrp/
T̲H̲ *as in* **northern** /nôrT̲H̲ərn/
y *as in* **Ewell** /ˈyo͞owəl/
Y *as in* **Utrecht** /ˈYˌtreKHt//
ZH *as in* **sabotage** /ˈsæbəˌtäZH/

Variants

More than one acceptable pronunciation may be given, with semicolons between the variants; for example:

defilade /ˈdefəˌlād; ˌdefəˈlād/

If the pronunciations of the word differ only in part, then the syllable or syllables affected are shown as cutbacks:

rendezvous /ˈrändiˌvo͞o -dā-/

Stress

The part of the word that carries the main stress is preceded by a high primary stress mark (ˈ). In some words with more than one syllable, the part of a word that carries a lesser degree of stress is preceded by a secondary stress mark (ˌ).

kamikaze /ˌkämiˈkäzē/

Abbreviations

AFB	Air Force Base
adj.	adjutant, adjective
adv.	adverb
brig.	brigadier
Brit.	British
c.	circa
CIA	Central Intelligence Agency
col.	colonel
e.g.	for example
etc.	et cetera ("and so on")
exclam.	exclamation
fl.	flourished
gen.	general
i.e.	that is to say
imper.	imperative
int.	interjection
km	kilometer
kph	kilometers per hour
lt.	lieutenant
maj.	major
mi	miles
mph	miles per hour
n.	noun
n.pl.	noun plural
NASA	National Aeronautics and Space Administration
NATO	North Atlantic Treaty Organization
part.	participle
past part.	past participle
perf.	perfect (tense)
pl.	plural
prep.	preposition
sing.	singular
U.S.	United States (of America)
UK	United Kingdom (Great Britain)
UN	United Nations
USSR	Union of Soviet Socialist Republics (Soviet Union)
v.	verb

Note on proprietary status

This book includes some words that are, or are asserted to be, proprietary names or trademarks. Their inclusion does not imply that they have acquired for legal purposes a nonproprietary or general significance. In cases where the editor has some evidence that a word is used as a proprietary name or trademark, this is indicated by the designation TRADEMARK, but no judgment concerning the legal status of such words is made or implied thereby.

Essential Dictionary of the U. S. Military

Aa

A-1 • see SKYRAIDER.
A-3 • see SKYWARRIOR.
A-4 • see SKYHAWK.
A-4 missile • see SKYHAWK.
A-5 • see VIGILANTE.
A-6 • see INTRUDER.
A-7 • see CORSAIR II.
A-10 • see THUNDERBOLT II.
A-10A • a heavily armored plane designed to destroy tanks and constructed around its powerful 30 mm gun and enormous munitions drum. Its wide combat radius and short takeoff and landing ability enable it to operate in and out of locations near front lines.
A-12 • see BLACKBIRD.
A-20 • see BOSTON II.
A-26 • see INVADER.
AA • *abbr.* antiaircraft.
AAA • *abbr.* antiaircraft artillery.
Aachen, Battle of • (October 1944) a WORLD WAR II battle in which Aachen became the first German city to fall to Allied forces. U.S. forces encircled Aachen and entered to find bitter resistance, despite having subjected the defenders to a prolonged aerial and artillery bombardment that destroyed about two-thirds of the city. The garrison surrendered on October 21.
AADC • *abbr.* area air defense commander.
AAF • *abbr.* Army Air Force(s).
Aardvark • (**F-111**) a two-seat twin-engine aircraft used as an attack/strike plane.
AB • *abbr.* able seaman; able-bodied seaman.
aback • *adv.* (of a sail) pressed backward against the mast by a headwind.
abaft • *adv.* in or behind the stern of a ship. • *prep.* nearer the stern than; behind: *the yacht has a shower just abaft the galley.*
abatis • *n.* (also **abattis**) (pl. same, **abatises**, or **abattises**) a defense made of felled trees placed lengthwise over each other with the boughs pointing outwards.
Abbot, Henry Larcom (1831–1927) • Union army officer and topographical engineer, born in Beverly, Massachusetts. Wounded in 1861 at FIRST BULL RUN, Abbot was rewarded for his "gallant and meritorious service" with a promotion to brevet captain. From November 1862 to February 1863, Abbot served as chief topographical engineer for Maj. Gen. NATHANIEL P. BANKS's expedition to New Orleans and the lower Mississippi region. From 1864 to 1865 he commanded the siege artillery of the ARMY OF THE JAMES, which was then involved in operations against PETERSBURG and RICHMOND. His work earned him the brevet rank of major general, U.S. volunteers, by the war's conclusion.

As a consulting engineer on the PANAMA CANAL, Abbot was influential in convincing the government to accept the consulting board's minority report favoring a lock-canal over the sea-level canal recommended by the majority.

ABC warfare • the use or threat of use of atomic, biological, or chemical weapons in war.
abeam • *adv.* **1** on a line at right angles to a ship's or an aircraft's length. **2** (**abeam of**) opposite the middle of (a ship or aircraft): *she was lying almost abeam of us.*
abeam replenishment • the transfer at sea of personnel or supplies by rigs between two or more ships proceeding side by side.
Abercrombie, James (also **Abercromby**) (1706–81) • British general, born in Scotland. In the FRENCH AND INDIAN WAR (1754–63), Abercrombie commanded the British in their attack on the French fort of TICONDEROGA (1758); he withdrew after heavy losses to the Marquis DE MONTCALM's smaller force. He was relieved of command by Sir JEFFREY AMHERST that same year and recalled to England.
Aberdeen Proving Ground • (**APG**) site of the U.S. Army's oldest active testing area for weapons and munitions. Known as the "Home of Ordnance," it was established in October 1917, shortly after the United States entered WORLD WAR I. Like other proving grounds, Aberdeen Proving Ground is used for testing and development of ordnance material (weaponry and munitions), laboratory research, and training of military personnel.
Abert, John James (1788–1863) • military engineer, born in Frederick City, Maryland. Abert persistently lobbied Congress to form a Corps of Topographical Engineers separate from the U.S. ARMY CORPS OF ENGINEERS. In 1838 a separate U.S. ARMY CORPS OF TOPOGRAPHIC ENGINEERS was established, and Abert was promoted to colonel and named commander of the new corps on July 7, 1838.

Abert was a friend of the naturalist John James Audubon, who named a squirrel after him (the *Sciurus aberti.*).

---

able-bodied seaman • (also **able seaman**) a merchant seaman qualified to perform all routine duties.
ABM • *abbr.* antiballistic missile.
abolition • *n.* the action or an act of abolishing a system, practice, or institution: *the abolition of slavery.*
abolitionist • *n.* a person who favors the abolition of a practice or institution, especially capital punishment or (formerly) slavery.
DERIVATIVES: **abolitionism** *n.*
abort • *v.* **1** to terminate a mission for any reason other than enemy action. **2** to discontinue aircraft takeoff or missile launch.
about face • in dismounted drill, a pivoting turn to the rear executed by an individual in formation when halted.
Abrams • (**M1; M-1A1**) the main U.S. battle tank, the M1 was delivered to the U.S. Army in February 1980 and named for the late Gen.

CREIGHTON ABRAMS. Its successor, the M-1 A1, first delivered in August 1985, is considered to be the world's best battle tank, in part because of its improved armor—similar to the ceramic-and-steel Chobham armor developed in the United Kingdom—but also because of its M256 smooth-bore Rheinmetall main gun produced and developed in West Germany. Although it weighs 63 tons, the M-1A1 can travel at a speed of 45 mph, but its turbine engine consumes a lot of gas and its electronic system is delicate. Nevertheless, it was the most important U.S. tank used in the PERSIAN GULF WAR (1991). In March 1988, the development of a new armor plate made of depleted uranium (a nonradioactive substance) began. Also called MAIN BATTLE TANK.

Abrams, Creighton Williams, Jr. (1914–74) • general and Army Chief of Staff (1972–74), born in Springfield, Massachusetts. During WORLD WAR II Abrams became a legendary figure as a tank commander. His unit was the first to crack the fabled MAGINOT LINE. During the BATTLE OF THE BULGE in December 1944, it was the first to reach the embattled 101st Airborne Division at BASTOGNE. He received the DISTINGUISHED SERVICE CROSS for destroying a German antitank gun that was holding up the advance. Between May 1967 and June 1972 Abrams served in VIETNAM. His first assignment was as deputy to his WEST POINT classmate Gen. WILLIAM C. WESTMORELAND, commander of the U.S. MILITARY ASSISTANCE COMMAND, Vietnam. In that capacity Abrams assumed responsibility for the pacification program and for training the South Vietnamese Army (ARVN). During the TET OFFENSIVE of 1968 he commanded U.S. and South Vietnamese forces in the northern provinces of South Vietnam.

At the Battle of the Bulge, he is reported to have exclaimed of the Germans, "They've got us surrounded again, the poor bastards."

---

abreast • *adv.* **1** side by side and facing the same way: *the path was wide enough for two people to walk abreast | they were riding three abreast.* **2** alongside or level with something: *the cart came* ***abreast of*** *the Americans in their rickshaw.* **3** figurative up to date with the latest news, ideas, or information: ***keeping abreast of*** *developments.*

absent without leave • (**AWOL**) absent from one's military post or duty without the permission of proper authority, but not intending to desert.

AC • Brit. *abbr.* aircraftman.

AC-47 • the first aerial gunship developed for combat support. It grew out of specific needs for a more effective weapon system to defend the strategic hamlets and small forts throughout the countryside in the VIETNAM WAR. It was capable low-altitude cruising and hovering. The more sophisticated AC-119 and AC-130 eventually supplanted it.

AC-119 • see AC-47.

AC-130 • see HERCULES, def. 1.

AC-130H • see SPECTRE.

AC-130U • see SPOOKY.

ACCHAN • *abbr.* Allied Command Channel.

accidental attack • an unintended attack that occurs not by deliberate national design, but rather as a direct result of a random event, such as mechanical failure, human error, or unauthorized action by a subordinate.

accolade • *n.* **1** an award or privilege granted as a special honor or as an acknowledgment of merit: *the ultimate accolade of a visit by the president.* **2** an expression of praise or admiration. **3** a touch on a person's shoulders with a sword at the bestowing of a knighthood.

accommodation ladder • a ladder or stairway up the side of a ship allowing access, especially to and from a small boat.

accountability • *n.* the legal or regulatory obligation imposed on an officer or other person for keeping accurate record of property, documents, or funds. The person having this obligation may or may not have actual possession of the property, documents, or funds. See also RESPONSIBILITY.

accoutrement |əˈko͞otərmənt; -trə-| (also **accouterment**) • *n.* (usually **accoutrements**) a soldier's outfit other than weapons and garments.

accuracy of fire • the precision of fire expressed by the closeness of a grouping of shots at and around the center of the target.

ace • *n.* a military aviator who has shot down more than five enemy aircraft.

ACE industries • those firms in the aircraft, communications, and electronics industries which in the post-WORLD WAR II period continued to focus on the development and production of defense materiel.

Acheson, Dean Gooderham |ˈæchəsən| (1893–1971) • lawyer, statesman, and secretary of state, born in Middletown, Connecticut. Acheson served in President FRANKLIN D. ROOSEVELT's administration as assistant secretary of state for economic affairs. He was also undersecretary of state (1945–1947) and secretary of state under President HARRY S. TRUMAN (1949–53). Acheson was a chief architect (with GEORGE F. KENNAN) of the COLD WAR policy of CONTAINMENT and a shaper of the TRUMAN DOCTRINE (1947). He assisted with the MARSHALL PLAN (1947–48), and presided over final diplomatic negotiations for the NORTH ATLANTIC TREATY (1949), and advocated a nuclear arms control agreement with the USSR. Acheson advocated a policy of developing "situations of strength" before entering into negotiations with the Soviet Union. He was an informal adviser to Presidents JOHN F. KENNEDY and LYNDON B. JOHNSON, urging Kennedy to bomb Cuba during the CUBAN MISSILE CRISIS and advising Johnson not to continue the VIETNAM WAR after the TET OFFENSIVE in 1968.

ack-ack • *n.* **1** an antiaircraft gun or regiment. **2** antiaircraft gunfire: *a burst of ack-ack fire.* ORIGIN: World War II: signalers' name for the letters *AA*.

ACLU • *abbr.* American Civil Liberties Union.

ACM • *abbr.* (**AGM-29**) advanced cruise missile; an air-launched missile that is designed to evade air and ground-based defenses in order to strike heavily defended, hardened targets. It is normally carried by a B-52 bomber.

acorn • *n.* a U.S. Navy unit comprised of the personnel and equipment needed to construct, maintain, and operate an advanced naval air base, particularly in the Pacific theater in WORLD WAR II.

acoustic • *adj.* (of an explosive mine or other weapon) able to be set off by sound waves.

acoustical surveillance • employment of electronic devices, including sound-recording, -receiving, or -transmitting equipment, for the collection of information.

acoustic jamming • the deliberate radiation or reradiation of mechanical or electroacoustic signals with the objectives of obliterating or obscuring signals that the enemy is attempting to receive and of deterring enemy weapon systems.

acoustic mine • (also **sonic mine**) a naval mine that is activated by the acoustic field of a ship or sweep while ignoring typical noise frequencies and sounds of marine life.

acoustic warfare • action involving the use of underwater acoustic energy to determine, exploit, reduce, or prevent hostile use of the underwater acoustic spectrum and actions which retain friendly use of the underwater acoustic spectrum.

acquire • *n.* **1** (for acquisition radars) the process of detecting the presence and location of a target in sufficient detail to permit identification. **2** (for tracking radars) the process of positioning a radar beam so that a target is in that beam.

acting pilot officer • a rank in the RAF above warrant officer and below pilot officer.

acting rank • a temporary rank assigned to a person who is performing the duties normally performed by someone of higher rank.

action • *n.* **1** armed conflict. **2** a military engagement: *a rearguard action.* **3** a manner or style of doing something, typically the way in which a mechanism works or a person moves.
PHRASES: **go into action** start battle. **in action** engaged in battle.

action agent • in intelligence usage, one who has access to, and works against, the target.

action deferred • expression used to designate or notify that tactical action on a specific track is being withheld for better tactical advantage and that weapons are available and commitment is pending.

action stations • chiefly Brit. the positions taken up by military personnel in preparation for action (often as a command or signal to prepare for action).

activate • *v.* **1** to put into existence by official order a unit, post, camp, station, base, or shore activity which has previously been constituted and designated by name or number, or both, so that it can be organized to function in its assigned capacity. **2** to prepare for active service a naval ship or craft which has been in an inactive or reserve status.

active aircraft • aircraft that are currently and actively engaged in supporting flying missions either through direct assignment to operational units or in preparation for such assignment (or reassignment) through any of the logistic processes of supply, maintenance, and modification.

active air defense • direct defensive action taken to nullify or reduce the effectiveness of hostile air action. Active air defense includes such measures as the use of aircraft, air defense weapons, weapons not used primarily in an air defense role, and electronic warfare.

active defense • the employment of limited offensive action and counterattacks to deny a contested area or position to the enemy.

active duty • (**AD**) the playing of a direct role in the operational work of the armed forces as opposed to doing administrative work.

Active Guard and Reserve • (**AGR**) those members of the NATIONAL GUARD and Reserve who have volunteered for active duty and provide full-time support for the National Guard, Reserve, and active duty organizations in order to recruit, organize, administer, instruct, or train the Reserve components.

active homing guidance • a system of homing guidance wherein both the source for illuminating the target and the receiver for detecting the energy reflected from the target as the result of the illumination are carried within the missile.

active list • a list of the officers in an armed service who are liable to be called on for duty.

active sealift forces • the MILITARY SEALIFT COMMAND active COMMON-USER SEALIFT and the AFLOAT PREPOSITIONING FORCE, which includes all the necessary cargo-handling and delivery systems and operating personnel.

active sector • a designated area in which active military operations are taking place.

active service • direct participation in warfare as a member of the armed forces.

act of hostility • an unfriendly or belligerent act on the part of one nation toward another.

act of war • an act by one nation intended to initiate or provoke a war with another nation; an act considered sufficient cause for war.

ACTS • *abbr.* Air Corps Tactical School.

actual ground zero • the point on the surface of the earth at, or vertically below or above, the center of an actual nuclear detonation.

actual range • the horizontal distance an aerial bomb travels from the moment it is released until the moment it strikes the target.

actuate • *v.* to operate a mine-firing mechanism in such a way that all the requirements of the mechanism for firing, or for registering a target count, are met.
DERIVATIVES: **actuation** *n.*

acute radiation dose • the total ionizing radiation dose received at one time and over so short a period of time that biological recovery cannot occur.

ACV • *abbr.* air-cushion vehicle.

ACW • *abbr.* Aircraftwoman.

AD • *abbr.* active duty.

Adams, Charles (1845–95) • Union army officer and diplomat, born Karl Adam

Schwanbeck in Anclam, Pomerania, Germany. In the CIVIL WAR, Adams served in the 6th Massachusetts Regiment and was wounded twice. Adams was appointed brigadier general of Colorado territorial militia in 1870 and in 1879 he negotiated a peaceful settlement with the Ute Indians and prevented their extermination by the Colorado militia.

Adams insisted that Colorado print its laws in German as well as in English and Spanish, and had some political influence with the naturalized Germans in the territory.

Adams, John (1735–1826) • 2nd president of the United States, diplomat, and member of the Continental Congress, born in Braintree (now Quincy), Massachusetts; father of 6th president JOHN QUINCY ADAMS. In the Continental Congress Adams nominated GEORGE WASHINGTON for commander in chief (1775), was instrumental in the establishment of the U.S. Navy and Marines, chaired the Congress's BOARD OF WAR AND ORDNANCE (1776–77), and negotiated the peace with Britain (1782). Under Washington he was the nation's first vice president (1789–97) and was elected president in 1796 as a FEDERALIST (1797–1801). He built up the navy, but his refusal to declare war on France and his signing of the ALIEN AND SEDITION ACTS (1798) turned the Federalist party against "His Rotundity."

The first president to live in the White House, Adams was defeated in the election of 1800 by THOMAS JEFFERSON; both men died on July 4, 1826, the fiftieth anniversary of the DECLARATION OF INDEPENDENCE that Adams recommended and Jefferson wrote.

Adams, John Quincy (1767–1848) • 6th president of the United States, diplomat, secretary of state, and U.S. congressman, born in Braintree (now Quincy), Massachusetts, the son of 2nd President JOHN ADAMS. He conceived the MONROE DOCTRINE (1823). As president, he strove to launch a vast program of national public works, such as road and canal construction.

In the close three-way election of 1824, neither Adams, HENRY CLAY, nor ANDREW JACKSON received an electoral majority; the election was decided in the House of Representatives, and, with Clay's support, Adams was made president. With only 31 percent, he holds the record for the lowest percentage of the popular vote.

Adams-Onís Treaty • an agreement made between the United States and Spain in 1819, in which Spain ceded Florida to the United States and relinquished its claims to Oregon, and the United States acknowledged Spanish sovereignty over Texas and paid $5 million of American financial claims against Spain. It established the western boundaries for the LOUISIANA PURCHASE and an official U.S. boundary from the Atlantic to the Pacific Ocean, the latter boundary extending north from the mouth of the Sabine River, then west at 42° north latitude. Its main negotiators were Don Luis de Onís, the Spanish minister to the United States, and JOHN QUINCY ADAMS, the U.S. Secretary of State. Also known as the TRANSCONTINENTAL TREATY.

Adams, Samuel (1722–1803) • revolutionary politician, signer of the DECLARATION OF INDEPENDENCE, and governor of Massachusetts (1793–97), born in Boston, Massachusetts. A cousin of JOHN ADAMS, Samuel Adams served on the Board of War of the Second Continental Congress. A spokesperson for the SONS OF LIBERTY, he took part in the BOSTON TEA PARTY.

ADC • *abbr.* aide-de-camp.

ADCON • *abbr.* administrative control.

adj. • *abbr.* adjutant.

adjust fire • in artillery and naval gunfire support: **1** an order or request to initiate an ADJUSTMENT OF FIRE. **2** a method of control transmitted in the call for fire by the observer or spotter to indicate that they will control the adjustment.

adjustment of fire • process used in artillery and naval gunfire to obtain correct bearing, range, and height of burst when engaging a target by observed fire.

adjutant |ˈæjət̮ənt| • *n.* **1** a military officer who acts as an administrative assistant to a senior officer. **2** a person's assistant or deputy.

Adjutant General |ˈæjədənt; ˈæjətnt ˈjen(ə)rəl| • (pl. **Adjutant Generals**) **1** (in the U.S. Army) the chief administrative officer. **2** (in the British army) a high-ranking administrative officer.

Adm. • *abbr.* Admiral.

administrative airlift service • the airlift service usually provided by specific identifiable aircraft that have been assigned to military organizations or commands for internal administration.

administrative control • (**ADCON**) the direction or exercise of authority over subordinate or other organizations in respect to administration and support, including organization of service forces, control of resources and equipment, personnel management, unit logistics, individual and unit training, readiness, mobilization, demobilization, discipline, and other matters not included in the operational missions of the subordinate or other organizations.

administrative escort • a warship or a merchant ship that carries a naval convoy commodore and his staff. It serves as a platform for simultaneous communication with control authority and a coastal convoy.

administrative order • an order covering traffic, supplies, maintenance, evacuation, personnel, and other administrative details.

administrative troops • military personnel in units providing administrative and logistical support to combat forces.

admiral • *n.* **1** a commander of a fleet or naval squadron, or a naval officer of very high rank. **2** a commissioned officer of very high rank in the U.S. Navy or Coast Guard, ranking above a vice admiral.

DERIVATIVES: **admiralship** *n.*

Admiral of the Fleet • the highest rank of admiral in the ROYAL NAVY.

admiralty • *n.* (pl. **-ies**) **1** the rank or office of an admiral. **2** (**Admiralty**) the department of the British government that once administered the ROYAL NAVY.

Admiralty Board • the department in the British Defense Ministry in charge of administering and planning for the Royal Navy.

advance • *v.* **1** to move forward; to attack. **2** a request from a spotter to indicate the desire that the illuminating projectile burst earlier in relation to the subsequent bursts of high explosive projectiles.

Advance Base School • a U.S. Navy submarine school in New London, Connecticut. The Navy made it a submarine base (SUBASE) in 1916. Since then, it has been called Naval Submarine Base New London (SUBASE NLON). It occupies more than 500 acres of land on the east side of the Thames River in Groton, Connecticut. The base supports twenty-one attack submarines, the Navy's nuclear research deep submersible (NR-1), the Navy's Submarine School, the Naval Submarine Facility, the Submarine Force Tactical Development Group, and the Commander Submarine Development Squadron 12. All submarines in the Navy are stationed here for training, and the base provides support and housing facilities for 10,000 active duty personnel as well as for civilian workers and their families.

advanced base • a base located in or near a theater of operations whose primary mission is to support military operations.

advanced fleet anchorage • a safe place to anchor for a large number of naval ships and mobile auxiliary support units, located in or near a theater of operations.

advanced landing field • an airfield, usually having minimum facilities, in or near an objective area.

Advanced Research Projects Agency • see DEFENSE ADVANCED RESEARCH PROJECTS AGENCY.

advance force • a temporary organization within the amphibious task force that precedes the main body to the objective area. Its function is to participate in preparing the objective for the main assault by conducting such operations as reconnaissance, seizure of supporting positions, minesweeping, preliminary bombardment, underwater demolitions, and air support.

advance guard • a detachment sent ahead of the main force. Its functions are to ensure the main body's uninterrupted advance, to protect the main body against surprise, facilitate the advance by removing obstacles and repairing roads and bridges, and to cover the deployment of the main body if it is committed to action.

advance guard reserve • the second of the two main parts of an ADVANCE GUARD, the other being the ADVANCE GUARD SUPPORT. It protects the main force and is itself protected by the advance guard support. Small advance guards do not have reserves.

advance guard support • the first of the two main parts of an ADVANCE GUARD, the other being the ADVANCE GUARD RESERVE. It is made up of three smaller elements (in order, from front to rear): the advance guard point, the advance party, and the support proper. The advance guard supports the advance guard reserve.

advance rate • the speed at which a military force advances, usually expressed in miles or kilometers per a given period of time.

advance to contact • an offensive operation designed to gain or reestablish contact with the enemy.

ADVENT, Project • U.S. Army program to develop and launch into synchronous orbit an instantaneous repeater satellite for military communications. The project was cancelled in May 1962.

AEC • *abbr.* Atomic Energy Commission.

AEF • *abbr.* **1** American Expeditionary Forces. **2** air expeditionary force. **3** Allied Expeditionary Force.

Aegis (or **AEGIS**) | 'ējis | • a totally integrated shipboard weapon system that combines computers, radars, and missiles to prove a defense umbrella for surface shipping. The Aegis system is capable of automatically detecting, tracking, and destroying airborne, seaborne, and land-launched weapons.

aerial dart • see FLECHETTE.

aerial gunner • a U.S. Air Force enlisted specialty assigned to personnel trained to operate flexible guns mounted on aircraft.

aerial port • an airfield that has been designated for the sustained air movement of personnel and materiel, and to serve as an authorized port for entrance into or departure from the country in which it is located.

aerial reconnaissance • reconnaissance undertaken with an airplane or other flying device in order to secure information about the enemy, the terrain, or the weather.

aerodrome | 'erəˌdrōm | • *n.* an area prepare d for the accommodation (including any buildings, installations, and equipment), landing, and takeoff of aircraft.

aerodynamic missile • a missile that uses aerodynamic forces to maintain its flight path.

aerodynamics • *n.* **1** the study of the properties of moving air, and especially of the interaction between the air and solid bodies moving through it. **2** the properties of a solid object regarding the manner in which air flows around it.

aerographer • *n.* **1** a student of the atmosphere and its phenomena. **2** a U.S. Navy warrant officer specialty for personnel who study weather patterns and prepare weather forecasts, especially forecasts of flying conditions.

aeromedical evacuation • the movement of patients under medical supervision to and between medical treatment facilities by air transportation.

aeronautical chart • a specialized representation of mapped features of the earth, or some part of it, produced to show selected terrain, cultural and hydrographic features, and supplemental information required for air navigation and pilotage, or for planning air operations.

aerospace |ˈerō,spās| • *adj.* of, or pertaining to, the earth's envelope of atmosphere and the space above it. These two separate entities are considered as a single realm for activity in launching, guidance, and control of vehicles that will travel in both entities.

AEW • *abbr.* air expeditionary wing.

AF • *abbr.* air force.

AFB • *abbr.* air force base.

AFC • *abbr.* automatic frequency control, a system in radios and television that keeps them tuned on to an incoming signal.

AFCRM • *abbr.* Air Force Combat Readiness Medal.

AFLC • *abbr.* Air Force Logistics Command.

afloat prepositioning force • (**APF**) shipping of military equipment and supplies that is maintained in full operational status to support commanders' battle plans. It consists of the three maritime prepositioning ship squadrons in addition to the afloat prepositioning ships.

afloat prepositioning ships • (**APS**) merchant ships positioned near a front line to support military forces and loaded with tactical equipment and supplies.

AFRC • *abbr.* Air Force Reserve.

Afrika Korps • (also the **Deutsches Afrika Korps** or **DAK**) the German forces commanded by Gen. Erwin Rommel in North Africa from February 1941 to March 1943, when it became a part of the Italian First Army. The Afrika Korps fought the British forces in North Africa to a standstill and defeated unseasoned American forces at the Kasserine Pass in February 1943 before being forced to surrender in Tunisia in May 1943.

AFRTS • *abbr.* Armed Forces Radio and Television Service.

AFSC • *abbr.* Air Force Systems Command.

AFSOC • *abbr.* Air Force Special Operations Command.

aft • *adv.* & *adj.* at, near, or toward the stern of a ship or tail of a aircraft: *he made his way to the aft cargo compartment.*

after • *adj.* nearer the stern: *the after cabin.*

afterburning • *n.* **1** the integral feature of some rocket motors to continue burning irregularly for some period after the main burning and thrust have stopped. It increases the thrust of a jet engine by using the uncombined oxygen in the exhaust gases to burn additional fuel. **2** the process of fuel injection or combustion of unburned or partially burned carbon compounds in the exhaust gases of a turbojet engine.

afterdeck • *n.* an open deck toward the stern of a ship.

after-flight inspection • following a flight, the general examination of an aircraft for the discovery of obvious defects, the correction of defects reported by aircraft crews, the replenishment of consumable or expendable stores, and the securing of aircraft.

aftermost • *adj.* nearest the stern of a ship or tail of an aircraft.

afterwinds • *n.* wind currents occurring in the vicinity of a nuclear explosion directed toward the burst center, resulting from the updraft accompanying the rise of the fireball.

AFV • *abbr.* armored fighting vehicle.

AG • *abbr.* Adjutant General.

Agency, the • see Central Intelligence Agency.

agent • *n.* in intelligence usage, one who is authorized or instructed to obtain or to assist in obtaining information for intelligence or counterintelligence purposes.

Agent Orange • a defoliant used by the United States in the Vietnam War to destroy the Vietcong's forest cover and food supply. Agent Orange was a 50/50 mixture of two herbicides, 2,4-D and 2,4,5-T, which formed the highly toxic compound dioxin. Between 1965 and 1970, the U.S. Air Force sprayed more than 40 million pounds of Agent Orange over 5 million acres of forest in Vietnam and Cambodia. The herbicide was later found to cause birth defects and such serious illnesses as cancer, adult-onset diabetes, liver failure, and chloracne. See also Operation Ranch Hand.

The United States also used the herbicides and defoliants Agent White and Agent Blue, so called because of the color of the labels on the shipping containers.

AGER • a U.S. Navy designation denoting environmental research ships.

aggression • *n.* **1** hostile or violent behavior or attitudes toward another; readiness to attack or confront. **2** the action of attacking without provocation, especially in beginning a quarrel or war: *the dictator resorted to armed aggression.* **3** forceful and sometimes overly assertive pursuit of one's aims and interests.

aggressor force • **1** a friendly military force using enemy uniforms, equipment, and doctrine for the purpose of opposing friendly troops in training exercises. **2** a force that initiates combat action, especially the invasion of another nation.

AGM-28A • see Hound Dog.

AGM-28B • see Hound Dog.

AGM-29 • see ACM.

AGM-45 • see Shrike.

AGM-53 • see Condor.

AGM-65 • see Maverick.

AGM-69 • see short range attack missile.

AGM-78 • see Standard ARM.

AGM-84 • see Harpoon.

AGM-114 • see Hellfire.

AGM-122 • see Sidearm.

AGM-123 • see Skipper II.

AGM-129 • see ACM.

AGOR • a U.S. Navy designation denoting oceanographic research ships.

AGR • *abbr.* Active Guard and Reserve.

Agreement on Measures to Reduce the Risk of Outbreak of Nuclear War • a document signed in 1971 by the United States and the USSR, under the direction of the two countries' SALT delegations, to improve measures against accidental use of nuclear weapons and to require immediate notification of a risk of nuclear war. It was established to facilitate communication and to prevent misinterpretation of either side's intentions in the event of a nuclear incident.

Agreement on the Prevention of Incidents at Sea • a document signed in Moscow on May 25, 1972, by U.S. Secretary of the Navy John Warner and Soviet Admiral of the Fleet Sergei Gorshkov to address potentially threatening U.S. and Soviet naval maneuvers begun in the late 1960s. It was established to increase communication of military activities, thereby preventing miscalculations and avoiding armed conflicts that might arise from a misinterpretation of one side's intentions as hostile.

aground • *adj.* & *adv.* (with reference to a ship) on or onto the bottom in shallow water: *the ships must slow to avoid* ***running aground.***

agroville • *n.* a fortified settlement in South Vietnam in the Agroville Program (1959–60) of President NGO DINH DIEM. Peasants were forcibly relocated to agrovilles, where they were guarded by the army in an effort to suppress any Communist activity.

Agua Dulce Creek, Battle of • in the TEXAS WAR OF INDEPENDENCE (1836), a battle on March 2, 1836, about 25 miles below San Patricio, in which a small band of Texas volunteers were defeated by about 550 Mexican troops led by Gen. JOSÉ DE URREA.

Aguinaldo, Emilio (1869–1964) • Filipino revolutionary leader, statesman, and national hero, born near Cavite, Luzon, Philippines. Aguinaldo commanded the Filipino rebellion against Spain (1896–98). After he was elected president by revolutionary assembly, he led an insurrection against U.S. authority (1899–1901) following the SPANISH-AMERICAN WAR (1898). He was captured by Brig. Gen. FREDERICK FUNSTON and compelled to take an oath of allegiance to the United States in 1901.

AH-1 • see HUEYCOBRA.

AH-1J • see SDB-1 SEA COBRA.

AH-64 • see APACHE.

ahoy • *exclam.* a call used in hailing: *ahoy there!*
PHRASES: **land ahoy!** an exclamation announcing the sighting of land from a ship.

aide • *n.* short for aide-de-camp.

aide-de-camp |ˈād də ˈkæmp| • *n.* (pl. **aides-de-camp** |ˈādz|) a military officer acting as a confidential assistant to a senior officer.

aiguillette |ˌāgwəˈlet| • *n.* an ornament on some military and naval uniforms, consisting of braided loops hanging from the shoulder and on dress uniforms ending in points that resemble pencils.

aim • *v.* point or direct (a weapon or camera) at a target: *he aimed the rifle again.* • *n.* the directing of a weapon or object at a target: *his aim was perfect, and the guard's body collapsed backward.*
PHRASES: **take aim** point a weapon or camera at a target.

AIM-7 • see SPARROW.

AIM-9 • see SIDEWINDER.

AIM-54A • see PHOENIX.

aimed fire • fire in which the target can be seen and the fire adjusted, either by the gun crew or by an observer in communication with the gun crew.

aiming point • the point on which the sight of a weapon is laid for direction.

aiming posts • marked stakes placed in the ground to assist in aligning a weapon on a target.

air alert • **1** warning of imminent enemy air attack. **2** a state of readiness of combat aircraft, either airborne or on the ground, to take immediate action against an enemy air threat.

Air America • a proprietary airline of the CIA acting as an ordinary civilian air transport firm in Southeast Asia during the VIETNAM WAR. Air America supported the U.S. Air Force in dangerous, covert operations (often at night or with cloud cover) within enemy-occupied areas of Vietnam, Laos, Thailand, and Cambodia. The CIA shut it down in 1976.

Air America grew out of the Civil Air Transport (CAT), founded in China in 1948 by Gen. CLAIRE L. CHENNAULT and Whiting Willauer, and purchased by the CIA in 1950.

---

air and space expeditionary task force • (**ASETF**) a deployed numbered air force (NAF) or command group of a military or naval force that is immediately subordinate to an NAF supplied as the U.S. Air Force component committed to a joint operation.

air assault • rapid tactical deployment of infantry troops by helicopter.

air atomic age • the period since 1945 in which national security and strategy have been dominated by the existence of nuclear weapons and the ability to deliver them by manned bomber or missile.

air attack • **1** (**coordinated air attack**) a combination of two or more types of air attack (dive, glide, low-level) in one strike, using one or more types of aircraft. **2** (**deferred air attack**) a procedure in which attack groups rendezvous as a single unit. It is used when attack groups are launched from more than one station with their departure on the mission being delayed pending further orders. **3** (**divided air attack**) a method of delivering a coordinated air attack that consists of holding the units in close tactical concentration up to a point, then splitting them to attack an objective from different directions.

airboat • *n.* a shallow-draft boat powered by an aircraft engine, for use in swamps.

airborne force • a force made up of both ground and air combat units, brought together, equipped, and trained to engage in airborne missions.

airborne land forces • land forces delivered to a combat zone or brought into a region for covert operations by aircraft.

airborne operation • an operation involving the air movement into an objective area of combat forces and their logistic support for execution of a tactical or strategic mission. The means employed may be any combination of airborne units, air transportable units, and types of transport aircraft, depending on the mission and the overall situation.

Airborne Warning and Control Systems • (**AWACS**) a long-range aircraft equipped with radar and other sensors and employed to track enemy air, sea, and land forces and to direct friendly aircraft.

air-breathing • *adj.* of a missile or other airborne delivery system, requiring air intake for combustion of its propellant fuel and needing to remain within the earth's atmosphere.

air-burst • *n.* a bomb burst that occurs in the air at a distance from its target, which is typically a large, reflecting, solid object like the earth's surface.

air-capable ship • any ship, other than an aircraft carrier, from which aircraft can take off, be recovered, or receive and transfer logistic support. Such ships include: nuclear aircraft carriers, amphibious assault ships (used as landing platforms for helicopters), or general purpose amphibious assault ships. See also AVIATION SHIP.

air cavalry • heliborne combat maneuver force trained to locate the enemy and delay their attack on friendly forces.

air command • a major subdivision of the U.S. Air Force. For operational purposes, it normally consists of two or more air forces.

Air Command and Staff College • a post-graduate service school at Maxwell AFB in Alabama.

This school was called the Air Corps Tactical School from 1932 to 1942 and was the Air Command and Staff School from 1946 to 1954, when it received its current name.

Air Corps • see ARMY AIR CORPS.

Air Corps Reserve • the reserve component of the ARMY AIR CORPS, before it was reorganized as the Air Force.

Air Corps Tactical School • a command and staff service school for midcareer officers, located at Maxwell AFB in Alabama from 1932 to 1942. Formerly known as the Air Service Field Officers' School, it was established at Langley Field, Virginia, when the ARMY AIR CORPS replaced the Air Service under the Air Corps Act of 1926. It was moved to Maxwell in 1932 and became the Army Air Forces of Applied Tactics in 1942. It became part of AIR UNIVERSITY in 1946.

air corridor • a restricted air route of travel specified for use by friendly aircraft and established for the purpose of preventing friendly aircraft from being fired on by friendly forces.

air cover • protection from aircraft for land-based or naval operations in war situations.

aircraft • *n.* (pl. **aircraft**) an airplane, a helicopter, a glider, or a dirigible that can fly through the air.

aircraft arresting barrier • (also called **barricade** or **emergency barrier**) a device, not dependent on an aircraft arresting hook, used to stop an aircraft by absorbing its forward momentum in an emergency landing or an aborted takeoff.

aircraft arresting hook • a device fitted to an aircraft to engage arresting gear. Also called TAIL HOOK.

aircraft carrier • a large warship equipped to serve as a base for aircraft that can take off from and land on its deck.

aircraft commander • the aircrew member designated by competent authority as being in command of an aircraft and responsible for its safe operation and accomplishment of the assigned mission.

aircraftman • *n.* (pl. **-men**) the lowest male rank in the RAF, below leading AIRCRAFTMAN.

aircraft scrambling • the directing of the immediate takeoff of aircraft from a ground alert condition of readiness.

aircraft torpedo • a torpedo fired from a low-flying aircraft and targeted at surface shipping.

aircrew • *n.* (pl. **aircrews**) [treated as sing. or pl.] **1** the crew manning an aircraft. **2** (pl. same) a member of such a crew: *each aircraft carried three aircrew.*

aircrewmen • see AIRCREW.

air-cushion vehicle • (**ACV**) a vehicle, usually driven by a propeller, that can travel over land or water with its weight, including its payload, wholly or mostly supported on a continuously generated, slowly moving cushion of low-pressure air.

air defense • collectively, all defensive measures designed to destroy attacking enemy aircraft or missiles in the earth's envelope of atmosphere, or to nullify or reduce the effectiveness of such attack.

air defense warning conditions • a degree of air raid probability according to the following code (the term "air defense division/sector" referred to herein may include forces and units afloat and/or deployed to forward areas, as applicable): **1** (**air defense warning yellow**) attack by hostile aircraft and/or missiles is probable. **2** (**air defense warning red**) attack by hostile aircraft and/or missiles is imminent or is in progress. **3** (**air defense warning white**) attack by hostile aircraft and/or missiles is improbable. This warning may be called either before or after air defense warning yellow or red. The initial declaration of air defense emergency will automatically establish a condition of air defense warning other than white for purposes of security control of air traffic.

airdrop • *n.* an act of dropping supplies, troops, or equipment by parachute from an aircraft. • *v.* (**-dropped, -dropping**) drop (such things) by parachute.

air-dropped torpedo • a torpedo that is launchable only from a helicopter or microplane and is fired from very near the surface of the water.

air echelon • in joint air-ground operations, the air component of the operation as distinguished from the ground forces which it supports or accompanies.

air expeditionary force • (**AEF**) U.S. Air Force wings, groups, and squadrons in readiness for combat and committed to a joint operation. See also AIR AND SPACE EXPEDITIONARY TASK FORCE.

air expeditionary wing • (**AEW**) a wing or part of a wing that is under the administrative control of an air and space expeditionary task force or air and space task force by the Department of the Air Force in order to carry out a joint operation. See also AIR AND SPACE EXPEDITIONARY TASK FORCE.

air force • (**AF**) **1** the branch of a nation's armed forces responsible for air warfare as well as transporting personnel and equipment by air. **2** a unit larger than a division and smaller than a command in the U.S. Air Force.

Air Force Academy • an undergraduate service school at Colorado Springs, Colorado. Candidates are appointed by political nomination. Founded by Congress in 1954, it officially opened in 1955 at Lowry Air Force Base in Denver, Colorado, and has been at Colorado Springs since 1958. Female cadets were first admitted in 1976.

Air Force Association • an independent, not-for-profit, civilian group that promotes the importance of a well-equipped and well-trained Air Force to the security of the United States and its allies as well as the relevance of U.S. military strength to global peace to the general public in the United States. The group was formed after WORLD WAR II and has almost 150,000 members and 300 chapters. Its daily business is carried out by headquarters staff in Arlington, Virginia.

Air Force Chief of Staff • the chief officer of the U.S. Air Force. The Air Force Chief of Staff reports to the secretary of the Air Force and to the President.

Air Force Combat Readiness Medal • (**AFCRM**) U.S. decoration awarded to Air Force personnel who have for a period of two years sustained individual combat or mission readiness or preparedness for direct weapons system deployment.

Air Force Cross • U.S. military decoration for "extraordinary heroism in connection with military operations against an armed enemy." Established in 1960, the Air Force Cross may be awarded to personnel serving with the U.S. Air Force and is the equivalent of the DISTINGUISHED SERVICE CROSS.

Air Force Institute of Technology • a postgraduate service school at Wright-Patterson AFB in Ohio.

Founded 1919, when the Air School of Application was established at McCook Field in Dayton, Ohio, it was moved to Wright Field in 1927, and received its current name in 1947.

Air Force Logistics Command • (**AFLC**) in 1926, the Materiel Division, under the Office of the Chief of the AIR CORPS, served four major functions: research and development (R&D), procurement, supply, and maintenance. In 1941, these four functions were split between two organizations, the Materiel Command (R&D and procurement) and the Air Service Command (supply and maintenance). In 1944, the R&D function was allocated to the newly established Research and Development Command, with the logistics group responsible for procurement, supply, and maintenance. After several name changes, the Air Force Logistics Command was inactivated on July 1, 1992, with the creation of the Air Force Materiel Command, which integrated the functions of the former AIR FORCE SYSTEMS COMMAND and the Air Force Logistics Command.

Air Force Museum • located at Wright-Patterson AFB in Dayton, Ohio, the AF Museum maintains aircraft galleries, with more than 300 aircraft and missiles on display. It provides guided tours to the public, and has special displays at specific times of the year.

Air Force Reserve Command • (**AFRC**) located at Robins Air Force Base in Georgia, established as the Air Force Reserve on April 14, 1948. It supports the Air Force mission to defend the United States by controlling and exploiting airspace and providing global power and extending the reach of that power. The AFRC has thirty-seven flying wings and more than 440 aircraft assigned to it. Of these aircraft, 99 percent are always mission-ready and can be deployed within seventy-two hours.

Air Forces in Europe • see U.S. AIR FORCES IN EUROPE.

Air Force Space Command • one of the eight major commands of the U.S. Air Force. It is responsible for the operation of space satellites, and it provides missile warning, monitors weather in space, ensures global communication and navigation, and tracks space debris. The Command was established at Peterson Air Force Base in Colorado Springs, Colorado, in 1982.

Air Force Systems Command • (**AFSC**) a now-defunct Air Force Command responsible primarily for engineering research and development. When the Air Force was restructured in 1961, Systems Command acquired the materiel procurement functions from AF LOGISTICS COMMAND. When the Air Force was again reorganized in 1992, the functions of the Systems Command were again merged with those of the Logistics Command, and it was inactivated on July 1, 1992. See also AIR FORCE LOGISTICS COMMAND.

Air Force Special Operations Command • a unified command of all air force special operations that was created in 1990 and first deployed extensively in the PERSIAN GULF WAR (1991).

Air Force, U.S. • (**USAF**) the part of the U.S. armed forces with primary responsibility for air warfare, military space research, and air defense. It also provides air services to other branches of the armed services. Created as an independent service in 1947, the Air Force is part of the Department of Defense and is headquartered at the Pentagon.

Military air activities began as part of the Army, with the use of reconnaissance balloons in the Civil War and the Spanish-American War (1898). Previous names have included the Air Service (1920–1926); Air Corps (1926–1941), and Army Air Forces.

---

airframe • *n.* **1** the structural components of an airplane, including the framework and skin of such parts as the fuselage, empennage, wings, landing gear (minus tires), and engine mounts. **2** the framework, envelope, and cabin of an airship. **3** the assembled principal structural components of a missile, not including the propulsion system, control system, electronic equipment, and payload.

air front • in air operations, the approximate line along which contact between friendly and enemy aircraft is expected.

air-ground (team) • a team of personnel from aviation and ground combat elements formed to direct and coordinate close air support operations. The term is also used to refer to coordinated air-ground operations in general.

air gun • a gun that fires pellets using compressed air.

airhead • *n.* a base secured in enemy territory where supplies and troops can be received and evacuated by air.

ORIGIN: World War II: on the pattern of *bridgehead.*

air intercept (also **air interception**) • the process of effecting visual or electronic contact by a friendly aircraft with another aircraft.

Air intercept typically is conducted in five phases: **climb phase** (airborne to cruising altitude); **maneuver phase** (receipt of initial vector to target until beginning the transition to attack speed and altitude); **transition phase** (increase or decrease of speed and altitude required for the attack); **attack phase** (turn to attack heading, acquire target, complete attack, and turn to breakaway heading); and **recovery phase** (breakaway to landing).

---

air interdiction • air operations conducted to destroy, neutralize, or delay the enemy's military potential before it can be brought to bear effectively against friendly forces.

AirLand battle • U.S. Army doctrine for the conduct of operations on a non-linear battlefield and emphasizing continuous operations in depth and the integration of nuclear, chemical, and conventional forces and close cooperation between air and ground forces.

airlift • *n.* an act of transporting supplies by aircraft, typically in a blockade or other emergency. • *v.* transport (troops or supplies) by aircraft, typically when transportation by land is difficult: *helicopters were employed to airlift the troops out of danger.*

airman • *n.* (pl. **-men**) **1** a pilot or member of the crew of an aircraft, especially in an air force. **2** a male member of the RAF below commissioned rank. **3** a member of the U.S. Air Force of the lowest rank, below sergeant.

Airman Basic • the lowest enlisted rank in the U.S. Air Force corresponding to Recruit in the U.S. Army, Seaman Recruit in the U.S. Navy and Coast Guard, and Private in the U.S. Marine Corps; pay grade E-1.

Airman First Class • an enlisted rank in the U.S. Air Force corresponding to a Corporal or Specialist-4 in the U.S. Army, Corporal in the U.S. Marine Corps, and Petty Officer Third Class in the U.S. Navy and Coast Guard; pay grade E-4.

Airman's Medal • U.S. military decoration awarded for "heroism not involving actual conflict with an armed enemy." The Airman's Medal may be awarded to any person serving with the U.S. Air Force and is the equivalent of the Army's SOLDIER'S MEDAL.

Air Medal • U.S. military decoration awarded for "meritorious achievement while participating in aerial flight." Established by Executive Order on May 11, 1942, the Air Medal may be awarded to members of any branch of service.

airmobile |ˈerˌmōbəl| • *adj.* (of troops) moved about by helicopters.

airmobile forces • the ground combat and supporting air vehicle units necessary for an airmobile operation.

Air National Guard • (**ANG**) a separate reserve component of the U.S. Air Force, its mission is to provide ready units at the national level (to support national security objectives), state level (to protect life and property; to preserve peace, order, and the public safety), and at the community level (to participate in local, state, and national programs).

air offensive • sustained operations by strategic and/or tactical air weapon systems against hostile air forces or surface targets.

air pistol • a pistol that fires pellets using compressed air.

air plot • **1** a continuous plot used in air navigation of a graphic representation of true headings steered and air distances flown. **2** a continuous plot of the position of an airborne object represented graphically to show true headings steered and air distances flown. **3** within ships, a display that shows the positions and movements of an airborne object relative to the plotting ship.

air power • airborne military forces.

air raid • an attack in which bombs are dropped from aircraft onto a ground target.

air raid reporting control ship • a ship that performs the air warning radar and air raid reporting delegated to it by the air defense ship.

air reconnaissance • the acquisition of intelligence information by employing visual observation and/or sensors in air vehicles.

air rifle • a rifle that fires pellets using compressed air.

air room • the space around an aircraft in flight which separates it from the ground and other aircraft; the space available for aerial maneuvering.

airship • *n.* a craft that weighs less than the air it displaces and has its own means of propulsion and directional control surfaces. Also called DIRIGIBLE.

airspeed • *n.* the speed of an aircraft relative to the air through which it is moving. Compare with GROUND SPEED.

air station • an airfield operated by a navy or marine corps.

air strike • an attack made by aircraft.

air strip • an unimproved surface which has been adapted for takeoff or landing of aircraft, usually having minimum facilities.

air superiority • the degree of dominance in the air battle of one force over another which permits the conduct of operations by the former and its related land, sea, and air forces at a given time and place without prohibitive interference by the opposing force.

air support • assistance given to ground or naval forces in an operation by their own or allied aircraft.

air supremacy • the degree of air superiority wherein the opposing air force is incapable of effective interference.

air surveillance • the systematic observation of airspace by electronic, visual, or other means, primarily for the purpose of identifying and determining the movements of aircraft and missiles, friendly and enemy, in the airspace under observation.

air-to-air missile • a missile fired from an aircraft and directed at other aircraft or at other missiles.

air-to-ground • *adj.* directed or operating from an aircraft in flight to the land surface.

air-to-surface missile • a missile fired from an aircraft and directed at a ground water surface target.

air traffic controller • an individual especially trained for and assigned to the duty of airspace management and traffic control (by use of radio, radar, or other means) of airborne objects.

air transport • **1** the movement of personnel and cargo by air. **2** an aircraft designed to move personnel and/or cargo.

air transport group • a task group of transport aircraft units that provides transport for landing forces or provides logistic support.

Air University • a postgraduate service school with headquarters at Maxwell AFB in Alabama. It consists of several colleges, academies, and training centers at Maxwell AFB in Alabama, Maxwell's Gunter Annex, and Patterson AFB in Ohio.

Originally the Army Air Forces School of Applied Tactics, it was moved to Maxwell in 1945 and received its current name in 1946.

Air War College • a postgraduate senior service school at Maxwell AFB in Alabama. Established in 1946 when the Army Air Forces School became AIR UNIVERSITY, it is the highest-level school in the Air Force professional military education system. It is one of several component schools of AIR UNIVERSITY.

air wing • a U.S. Air Force, Navy, or Marine Corps aviation unit consisting of one or more squadrons and their supporting elements usually organized to perform one primary type of mission (bomber, fighter, interceptor, etc.). In the U.S. Air Force, two or more air wings make up an air division.

airwoman • *n.* (pl. **-women**) **1** a woman pilot or member of the crew of an aircraft, especially in an air force. **2** a female member of the U.S. Air Force of the lowest rank, below staff sergeant. **3** a female member of the U.S. Navy whose general duties are concerned with aircraft. **4** a female member of the RAF below commissioned rank.

Aitape • a town on the northern coast of New Guinea, one of many sites captured by Gen. DOUGLAS MACARTHUR during the final year of WORLD WAR II in the Pacific. Aitape was invaded on April 22, 1944, and was under U.S. control by April 24.

Aix-la-Chapelle, Peace of |ˌeks lä SHä'pel; ˌāks| • on October 18, 1748, the Treaty of Aix-la-Chapelle ended the War of the Austrian Succession, which was fought in North America between France and Britain as KING GEORGE'S WAR. It restored the possessions of both warring countries and served as a truce, but it failed to resolve disputes over dominance of North America.

AK-47 • an automatic rifle, originally of Russian manufacture, that is one of the most widely used assault weapons in the world today. It is reliable under adverse conditions, inexpensive to manufacture, and reasonably accurate. Also called KALASHNIKOV.

***Alabama*, CSS** • a screw sloop-of-war built in 1862 for the CONFEDERACY and the most famous ship of the Confederate navy, commanded by Capt. RAPHAEL SEMMES. In its first year at sea, this raider, often called the "ghost ship," captured, and sometimes burned, *Yankee* merchant ships in the North Atlantic. Continuing the destruction through the West Indies, the *Alabama* attacked and sank the USS *Hatteras* along the coast of Texas. After visiting Cape Town, South Africa, the ship headed for the East Indies, where it spent six months and destroyed seven more ships before heading off to Europe. In June 1864, the CSS *Alabama* was attacked and destroyed while docked at Cherbourg, France, by the *Kearsarge,* a U.S. sloop-of-war. During its two-year career, the *Alabama* claimed sixty-five U.S. ships valued at almost $6 million.

***Alabama*, USS** • commissioned on August 16, 1942, a South Dakota Class battleship (BB60), the *Alabama* was used in both the European and Pacific theaters during WORLD WAR II. It protected British convoys and, in the Pacific, was used to protect U.S. amphibious assault forces and to defend allied carriers with intense antiaircraft fire.

The USS *Alabama* is now located in Mobile and serves as a memorial to all Alabama veterans of WORLD WAR II, and has hosted nearly 10 million paid visitors.

Alamance, Battle of • (May 16, 1771) a defeat, by the North Carolina militia, of 2,000 REGULATORS charging corruption, inordinate taxation, and inadequate representation. Nine men on each side were killed; fifteen rebels were tried for treason, and six were hanged. The Regulator rebellion, or WAR OF THE REGULATION, was the most serious in the English colonies since BACON'S REBELLION in 1676.

Alamo, Battle of the • (February 23–March 6, 1836) a siege during the TEXAS WAR OF INDEPENDENCE. Despite orders to withdraw from San Antonio, a group of 187 Texans vainly attempted to hold a small fortified mission there against an army of 4,000 under Mexican Gen. ANTONIO LÓPEZ DE SANTA ANNA. Texans who died there included DAVY CROCKETT, JAMES BOWIE, and WILLIAM TRAVIS. News of Santa Anna's "no prisoners" order and the burning of the dead Texans' bodies, along with reports of the tremendous casualties inflicted upon the Mexican army, rallied the Texans fighting to secede from Mexico.

ALCM • an air-launched cruise missile.

Alden, James (1810–77) • Union naval officer, born in Portland, Maine (then part of Massachusetts). At the battle of MOBILE BAY (1864), Alden commanded the ironclad steam sloop *Brooklyn.* Mistaking buoys for torpedoes (mines), Alden indecisively and overcautiously stopped and then backed the *Brooklyn.* The ironclad turned broadside in the channel, confusing the other ships in the column and driving Adm. DAVID FARRAGUT, aboard the *Hartford,* to swear, "Damn the torpedoes. Go ahead!"

alee |ə'lē| • *adv. & adj.* **1** on the side of a ship that is sheltered from the wind. **2** (of the helm) moved around to leeward in order to tack a vessel or to bring its bows up into the wind.

alert • *n.* **1** readiness for action, defense, or protection. **2** a warning signal of a real or threatened danger, such as an air attack. **3** the period of time during which troops stand by in response to an alarm. **4** a warning, received by a unit or a headquarters, that forewarns of an impending operational mission. • *v.* forewarn; prepare for action.

alert force • specified forces maintained in a special degree of readiness.

Alexander, Edward Porter (1835–1910) • Confederate army officer, born in Washington, Georgia. Alexander was the chief signal officer and chief of ordnance under generals P.G.T. BEAUREGARD, JOSEPH E. JOHNSTON, and ROBERT E. LEE (1861–62). He coordinated the delivery of ordnance during the SEVEN DAYS', SECOND BULL RUN, and ANTIETAM (all 1862) campaigns, and was tactical chief of Gen. JAMES LONGSTREET's artillery at FREDERICKSBURG (1862), CHANCELLORSVILLE, and GETTYSBURG (both 1863). Alexander commanded Lee's guns during the siege of PETERSBURG (1864) and the APPOMATTOX (1865) campaigns and was, as Jefferson Davis noted, among the very few officers "whom Gen. Lee would not give to anybody."

Alexander, William (1726–83) • Revolutionary army officer, born in New York City. Alexander prepared New York City for a threatened British assault until GEORGE WASHINGTON came down from Boston to take command. His relations with Washington were warm and his war experience varied and useful, though not exceptional. He was taken prisoner at New York (1776) but released; he fought at WHITE PLAINS and TRENTON (1776); he was promoted to major general, fought under Washington at BRANDYWINE and GERMANTOWN (both 1777), and encamped at VALLEY FORGE (1777–78).

Algerine War • see BARBARY WARS.

Alien Act • a restriction passed in 1918, after U.S. entry into WORLD WAR I, that mandated the deportation of any alien who was a proven member of an anarchist organization upon entering the United States. It allowed for the prosecution of aliens through an administrative process and was an attempt to control public discourse during the war.

Alien and Sedition Acts • four security laws signed by President JOHN ADAMS and passed by the U.S. FEDERALIST Congress in 1798 during the QUASI-WAR WITH FRANCE of 1798–1800. The three laws restricting aliens were the Naturalization Act, Alien Friends Act, and Alien Enemies Act. The Sedition Act diminished freedom of speech and press and was the first federal law that punished as a crime any statement made against the government or its members.

alignment |ə'līnmənt| • *n.* a position of agreement or alliance.

Allan, John (1746–1805) • Revolutionary army officer, born in Edinburgh Castle, Edinburgh, Scotland. Commissioned a colonel in the CONTINENTAL ARMY, Allan was appointed the superintendent of eastern Indians and he cultivated Indian support for the patriot cause. He occupied and defended Machias, on the far eastern frontier of Maine, against British attack from Nova Scotia, resulting in the eastern boundary of the United States being fixed at the St. Croix River (farther east) rather than at the Kennebeck.

Allen, Ethan (1738–89) • frontier revolutionary leader and hero, born in Litchfield, Connecticut. In the first offensive victory of the REVOLUTIONARY WAR, Allen led his GREEN MOUNTAIN BOYS in a bold surprise attack on FORT TICONDEROGA (1775), becoming an instant hero by taking control of Lake Champlain within two days without a single casualty. In a daring effort to capture a weakly defended Montréal, he was taken prisoner by the British and held for two years in brutal captivity.

Allen, Henry Watkins (1820–66) • Confederate army officer and governor of Louisiana, born in Prince Edward County, Virginia. In 1862 he was a lieutenant colonel in command of the 4th Louisiana Regiment at SHILOH; and he fought in defense of VICKSBURG (1863) and accompanied JOHN C. BRECKINRIDGE in a failed expedition to retake Baton Rouge, where he was severely wounded. Unable to serve in the field, Allen was promoted to brigadier general and ordered to serve in the Confederate TRANS-MISSISSIPPI DEPARTMENT (1863). He was elected governor of Louisiana in 1864. Allen is credited not only with greatly improving the war-weakened economy in Louisiana and Texas, but with saving Louisiana from destruction by an all-out UNION invasion by having persuaded Trans-Mississippi commander Gen. E. KIRBY SMITH not to send a letter in 1865 defiantly answering the Union's demand for surrender. After the war he fled to Mexico.

Allen, William Henry (1784–1813) • naval officer, born in Providence, Rhode Island. In January 1807 Allen was ordered to the frigate *Chesapeake* as third lieutenant. Among the sailors recruited for the *Chesapeake* were several deserters from the British navy. As the unprepared *Chesapeake* left Norfolk, the frigate was attacked by the HMS *Leopard,* a much more powerful ship, which was determined to take the deserters away by force. After three destructive broadsides the *Chesapeake* surrendered. The only shot fired by the *Chesapeake* in return was fired by Allen, who took a live coal from the galley to touch off a gun in his division.

all hands • all of the officers and sailors aboard a ship.

alliance • *n.* a union or association formed for mutual benefit, especially between countries or organizations: *a defensive alliance between Australia and New Zealand | divisions within the alliance.*

Allied Coalition • the military coalition of thirty-six countries against Iraq in the PERSIAN GULF WAR (1991). It consisted of Afghanistan, Argentina, Australia, Bahrain, Bangladesh, Belgium, Canada, Czechoslovakia, Denmark, Egypt, France, Germany, Greece, Hungary, Honduras, Italy, Kuwait, Morocco, the Netherlands, New Zealand, Niger, Norway, Oman, Pakistan, Poland, Portugal, Qatar, Saudi Arabia, Senegal, South Korea, Spain, Syria, Turkey, the United Arab Emirates, the United Kingdom, and the United States.

Allied Command Channel • (**ACCHAN**) a NATO command with headquarters at Northwood in the United Kingdom. ACCHAN is always commanded by a British admiral (CINCHAN), who is responsible for the defense and control of merchant shipping in the area from the North Sea through the English Channel.

allied commander • see NATO COMMANDER.

Allied Expeditionary Air Force • all of the military personnel (the armies, navies, and air forces), equipment and weaponry, medical staff, support and maintenance supplies, and so on brought together by the ALLIED POWERS during WORLD WAR II, under Supreme Allied Commander DWIGHT D. EISENHOWER.

Allied Expeditionary Force • (**AEF**) official designation of the Allied forces assembled in England to carry out the mission of invading the European continent and undertaking operations to defeat Germany and her allies. Supreme Headquarters, Allied Expeditionary Forces (SHAEF), commanded by U.S. Gen. DWIGHT D. EISENHOWER, was created on February 15, 1944, and (having successfully completed its mission) was inactivated on July 16, 1945. The WORLD WAR II-era Allied Expeditionary Force should not be confused with the AMERICAN EXPEDITIONARY FORCES led by Gen. JOHN J. PERSHING in WORLD WAR I.

Allied Force, Operation • seventy-eight-day NATO air campaign in the Kosovo region to protect the ethnic Albanian population from the Serbian/Yugoslav military and police forces of Slobodan Milosevic. Operation Allied Force, which began on March 24, 1999, and ended on June 20, 1999, involved nineteen NATO nations and over 38,000 air combat sorties. It was the largest combat operation in NATO history.

Allied High Command • (in WORLD WAR I and WORLD WAR II) the highest combined headquarters of the Allied forces and/or the Allied military and civilian leadership in general.

Allied Powers • **1** (in WORLD WAR I) the countries opposed to the CENTRAL POWERS; the major Allied Powers were France, the British Empire, and the Russian Empire, formally joined by the Treaty of London, signed on September 5, 1914. Other Allies, linked by treaty to one or more of the Allied Powers, included Portugal, Japan, and Italy, but not the United States, even after its entry into the war in April 1917. The United States, and other countries opposed to the Central Powers, were called "Associated Powers." See also CENTRAL POWERS. **2** (in WORLD WAR II) the countries opposed to the AXIS POWERS; the major Allied Powers were Great Britain, France, the Soviet Union, the United States, and China. In general, the Allies included all the nations that had signed the Declaration of the UNITED NATIONS on January 1, 1942. See also AXIS POWERS.

Allies, the • see ALLIED POWERS.

All-Volunteer Force • term used to refer to the U.S. armed forces in general after the elimination of compulsory military service in the 1970s.

all-weather air defense fighter • a fighter plane equipped with weapons that enable it to engage airborne targets in all weather conditions, both day and night.

ally |əˈlī; ˈælī| • *n.* (pl. **-ies**) **1** a state formally cooperating with another for a military or other purpose, typically by treaty: *debate continued on greater burden sharing among NATO allies.* **2** a person or organization that cooperates with or helps another in a particular activity: *he was forced to dismiss his closest political ally.* **3** (**the Allies**) a group of nations taking military action together, in particular the countries that fought with the United States in WORLD WAR I and WORLD WAR II.

alow |əˈlō| • *adv.* in or into the lower part of a ship.

altitude chamber • see HYPOBARIC CHAMBER.

Al Wafrah • (**Al-Wafrah**) a small city in southern Kuwait of strategic importance in the PERSIAN GULF WAR (1991). The U.S. MARINE EXPEDITIONARY FORCE attacked the Iraqi Army in this area from the nearby Saudi Arabian border beginning on January 20, 1991. The 6th Marine Regiment secured Al Wafrah on January 30, 1991.

AM • *abbr.* amplitude modulation.

ambient noise • sounds, other than those emitted by a target, surrounding a listener or mechanical sound detection system (such as sonar) that interfere with hearing or locating the sounds emitted by a target.

ambulance corps • (usually singular) the military personnel, their vehicles, equipment, and medical supplies necessary for the safe removal of the wounded from a battlefield and the transportation of them to better-equipped medical facilities behind the front lines.

ambuscade |ˈæmbəˌskād; ˌæmbəˈskād| • *n.* dated an ambush. • *v.* archaic attack from an ambush.

ambush • *n.* a surprise attack by people lying in wait in a concealed position: *seven members of a patrol were killed in an ambush* | *terrorists waiting* ***in ambush***. • *v.* (often **be ambushed**) make a surprise attack on (someone) from a concealed position: *they were ambushed and taken prisoner by the enemy.*

AMEDD • *abbr.* Army Medical Department.

America First Committee • an isolationist group organized in September 1940 to fight President FRANKLIN D. ROOSEVELT's policies. The group conducted its own polls, showing, in contrast to official polls, that the American public disapproved of the declaration of war on the AXIS POWERS.

American Articles of War • a code of military law adopted by the Continental Congress in 1775, at the outbreak of the REVOLUTIONARY WAR, to govern discipline and justice in the army. It was written by JOHN ADAMS, along with the Rules for the Regulation of the Navy of the United Colonies, and both were based on the codes governing the Royal Navy and the British army. After several revisions, it was replaced in 1950 by the UNIFORM CODE OF MILITARY JUSTICE.

American Civil Liberties Union • (**ACLU**) a non-profit organization formed in 1920 that sought to ensure the freedoms guaranteed in the Bill of Rights. One of its earliest targets was unfair treatment against antiwar propagandists. During WORLD WAR II it stood almost alone in denouncing the federal government's roundup and internment in camps of more than 110,000 Japanese Americans. In 1989 it was successful in defeating attempts by Congress to ban flag-burning, defending it as a form of free speech; this had been a common activity during protests of the VIETNAM WAR.

American Defense Preparedness Association • an association of American manufacturers formed in the post-WORLD WAR II period for the purpose of influencing the Congress and the American public to support a sustained high level of public spending on advanced weapons systems and other defense needs.

American Expeditionary Forces • (**AEF**) all of the military personnel (the armies, navies, and air forces), equipment and weaponry, medical staff, support and maintenance supplies, and so on sent to the Western front by President WOODROW WILSON after his declaration of war in April 1917, under the command of Gen. JOHN J. PERSHING. Pershing arrived in Paris in June 1917 to take up his command, two months after the United States had entered WORLD WAR I. Although more than two million U.S. troops reached Europe, many arrived too late to see combat. Nevertheless, the AEF had 264,000 casualties, including 50,554 killed in battle and 25,000 by disease.

American Legion • an organization of U.S. war veterans, founded in Paris on March 15–17, 1919, by delegates from the combat and service units of the AMERICAN EXPEDITIONARY FORCES, and given a national charter by Congress on September 16, 1919. Over the years, the charter has been amended to admit veterans of succeeding wars: in 1942 to admit WORLD WAR II veterans; in 1950 to admit veterans of the KOREAN WAR; in 1966 to admit veterans of the VIETNAM WAR. Its national headquarters is in Indianapolis, Indiana.

American North Russian Expeditionary Force • more than 5,000 American soldiers, including the 339th Infantry, the 337th Ambulance Company, the 337th Field Hospital Company, and a battalion of the 310th Engineers, sent to Archangel, Russia, in September 1918, on an unclear mission, although in part it was hoped they would thwart the Russian revolution. The soldiers arrived expecting friendly Allies but found instead hostile Bolsheviks and a frigid landscape stripped of food and supplies. The "Polar Bears," as they were called, were left in Russia until May 15, 1919, long after other American soldiers had been called home. The group lost more than 200 members during the expedition.

American Party • a political party established in 1972 by a faction of the American Independent Party of Alabama governor George Wallace. The American Party backed concepts of free enterprise, a free market economy, reduction of federal intervention in personal matters, a sound currency, and a return to the gold standard, as well as eliminating many rights of labor unions and minimum-wage laws. The party effectively came to an end after the 1980 election.

American Peace Society • a pacifist group founded in 1828 that was the first nationally based secular peace organization in American history. Based in Boston, the society organized peace conferences and published a periodical entitled *Advocate of Peace*. Its most famous leader was Benjamin Franklin Trueblood (1847–1916), a Quaker who in his book *The Federation of the World* (1899) called for the establishment of an international state to bring about lasting peace in the world. The group is now based in Washington, D.C.

American Revolution • see REVOLUTIONARY WAR.

American Society of Naval Engineers • (**ASNE**) an organization founded in 1888 committed to advancing the knowledge and practice of naval engineering in diverse applications and operations, enhancing the professionalism of its members, and promoting naval engineering as a career. It admits to membership a wide range of military and civilian professionals and students associated with naval engineering in its many aspects.

American Southern Army • an army organized to fight for the Colonists during the

Revolutionary War. They had a famous victory in the battle of Cowpens. The British captured the entire 5,400-man army when they took Charleston in May 1780.

American Union Against Militarism • a pacifist group founded in 1915 and dissolved in 1922. Initially known as the American League for the Limitation of Armaments, the organization changed its name to American Union Against Militarism in 1916. Members lobbied in Washington, D.C., and established a Civil Liberties Bureau, which later became the American Civil Liberties Union. The group, whose theme song, "I Didn't Raise My Boy to Be a Soldier," became a national hit, was part of the successful effort to avoid war with Mexico in 1916.

American Veterans Committee • (**AVC**) a veterans service organization chartered by Congress in 1944. It has a membership of about 15,000, and headquarters in Bethesda, Maryland.

American Volunteer Group • see Flying Tigers.

Ames, Adelbert (1835–1933) • Union army officer, born in Rockland, Maine. He was awarded the Congressional Medal of Honor for heroic service at First Bull Run (1861), where he refused to leave his post despite a serious wound. As brigadier general of volunteers in the Spanish-American War (1898), he participated in the siege of Santiago and the Battle of San Juan Hill.

When Ames died he was the last surviving Civil War general.

Amherst, Sir Jeffrey (**Jeffery, Baron Amherst**) (1717–97) • British general, born at Riverhead, Kent, England. Amherst was governor general of British North America (1760–63) and commander in chief of the British army (1772–95). In the French and Indian War (1754–63), Amherst commanded the 14,000–man British seige of the French fortress of Louisbourg on Cape Breton Island (1758) and captured the forts of Ticonderoga and Crown Point (1759).

amidships (also **amidship**) • *adv. & adj.* in the middle of a ship: *the destroyer rammed her amidships | an amidships engine.*

Amity and Commerce, Treaty of • a document signed by Benjamin Franklin and the French foreign minister, on February 6, 1778, during the Revolutionary War. It was used by France to weaken Britain by giving America special trading privileges and recognition as a country.

Ammen, Daniel (1819–98) • Union naval officer, author, and inventor, born in Brown County, Ohio. In the Civil War, he commanded blockade ships around southern ports and led assaults in several important engagements, including the attack on Forts Walker and Beauregard at Port Royal (1861). He was promoted to commander in 1863 and was given command of the monitor vessel *Patapsco.* With this vessel he participated in the attack on Fort Sumter (1863). Commanding naval recruits aboard the passenger steamer *Ocean Queen* bound for Panama, he suppressed a mutinous uprising (1864). After the war, Ammen was the director of the Bureau of Navigation (1871–78) and the secretary of the Isthmian Canal Commission (1872–76).

As a boy in Ohio, Ammen saved his friend Ulysses S. Grant from drowning.

---

ammo • *n.* informal term for ammunition.

ammunition • *n.* a supply or quantity of bullets and shells.

ammunition consumption • **1** the expenditure of ammunition by firing. **2** the rate at which ammunition is used up, usually expressed in terms of the number of rounds or tons of ammunition expended per a given period of time.

ammunition supply point • a designated location or facility for the distribution of ammunition to using units.

amnesty |ˈæmnistē| • *n.* (pl. **-ies**) **1** an official pardon for people who have been convicted of political offenses: *an amnesty for political prisoners | the new law granted amnesty to those who illegally left the country.* **2** an undertaking by the authorities to take no action against specified offenses or offenders during a fixed period: *a month-long weapons amnesty | under a temporary amnesty, a group of wounded guerrillas was allowed to leave.* • *v.* (**-ies, -ied**) grant an official pardon to: *the guerrillas would be amnestied and allowed to return to civilian life.*

amphibian • *n.* a small craft capable of moving on land or water driven by propellers and wheels or air cushion.

amphibious |æmˈfibēəs| • *adj.* **1** relating to, living in, or suited for both land and water: *amphibious habitats | an amphibious vehicle.* **2** (of a military operation) involving forces landed from the sea: *an amphibious assault.* **3** (of forces) trained for such operations.

amphibious assault • an amphibious operation that involves establishing a force on a hostile or potentially hostile shore.

amphibious assault ship • (**LHA**) a naval ship designed to carry and land assault troops by helicopters, landing craft, or other amphibious vehicles.

amphibious command ship • (**LCC**) a naval ship used by a commander to control amphibious operations.

amphibious force • **1** a naval force and landing force, together with supporting forces that are trained, organized, and equipped for amphibious operations. **2** in naval usage, the administrative title of the amphibious type command of a fleet.

amphibious group • a command within the amphibious force, consisting of the commander and staff, designed to exercise operational control in executing all phases of a division-size amphibious operation.

Amphibious Landing Ships • World War II requirements prompted the development by the Allies of a wide variety of amphibious landing ships and landing craft, many of which were based on British designs. Perhaps the best known was the **Landing Ship, Tank**

(LST), designed to transport tanks and other combat vehicles and land them on a beach or dock through clam-shell doors in the bow. The first LSTs, developed in 1942, were converted Maracaibo oil tankers. Over 1,000 of the 300-foot, 2,286-ton LST Mark II were built, and they played a central role in World War II amphibious operations. An American variant, the LST Mark VII, began construction in 1944, and was known as the **Landing Ship, Medium** (LSM). The 203-foot LSM had a speed of 12 knots. A variant of the LSM, the **Landing Ship, Medium (Rocket)** (LSM[R]), was designed to provide fire support for amphibious landings. Equipped with launchers for up to 1,040 rockets, the LSM(R), which was first employed in the landings on OKINAWA in March 1945, had the firepower of a pre-World War II cruiser. Based on the LST/LSM design, the **Landing Ship, Vehicle** (LSV) was designed specifically to transport and land wheeled vehicles. Another well-known amphibious landing ship developed during World War II was the **Landing Ship, Dock** (LSD), which was designed as a combination troop carrier and floating dry dock. The LSD was capable of carrying the largest landing craft in its well deck, which could be flooded to launch the loaded landing craft at sea through a stern gate. Both the LST and the LSD continue to provide the U.S. Navy with significant amphibious shipping capability.

amphibious operation • an attack launched from the sea by naval and landing forces, embarked in ships or craft involving a landing on a hostile or potentially hostile shore. An amphibious operation involves five phases: planning, embarkation, rehearsal, movement, and assault.

amphibious ship • a ship capable of traveling and maneuvering on land or water.

amphibious shipping • ships designed to carry, land, and support assault forces and capable of being loaded or unloaded in the objective area by Navy personnel without external assistance.

amphibious task force • (**ATF**) a task force organized to conduct an amphibious operation. Such a task force always includes Navy forces and a landing force, with their air support, and can also include ships provided by the MILITARY SEALIFT COMMAND and aircraft provided by the Air Force.

amphibious transport group • a subdivision of a larger amphibious task force, made up primarily of transport ships. The transport unit is usually formed to load and unload troops and equipment over a specific beach. The ships in such a group are combat-ready in order to support the landing force as it maneuvers onshore.

amphibious vehicle • a vehicle capable of moving on land and water that has wheels or tracks.

amphibious warfare • warfare consisting of attacks launched from the sea by naval and landing forces embarked in ships or craft and involving the landing and establishing of forces on a hostile shore.

Amphibious Warfare School • a postgraduate marine specialist training school at Quantico, Virginia. Established in 1921, it is one of several component schools of the MARINE CORPS UNIVERSITY.

amputate |ˈæmpyəˌtāt| • *v.* cut off (a limb), typically by surgical operation: *the wounded had to **have** legs or arms **amputated**.*

DERIVATIVES: **amputation** |ˌæmpyəˈtāSHən| *n.*

AMRAAM |ˈæmˌræm| • *abbr.* advanced medium range air-to-air missile.

amtrac |ˈæmˌtræk| (also **amtrack**, **amtrak**) • *n.* an amphibious tracked vehicle used for landing assault troops on a shore.

ORIGIN: World War II: blend of AMPHIBIOUS and *tractor*.

AMVETS |ˈæmˌvets| • a federally chartered service and support organization whose membership consists of veterans of all U.S. armed forces. It was formed in 1947.

Anaconda Plan • a military strategy to defeat the CONFEDERACY proposed in 1861 by the Commanding General of the UNION Army, Gen. WINFIELD SCOTT. Scott's plan was to employ Union army and navy forces to blockade the southern ports, split the Confederacy in half by seizing the line of the Mississippi River, and establish strong Federal positions all around the periphery of the Confederate States. The "Anaconda Plan" was intended to force surrender without prolonged and bloody combat. It was not adopted formally, but the subsequent Union strategy for conducting the war was largely an active, aggressive form of the general plan to surround the Confederacy and "squeeze it to death."

anchor • *n.* a heavy object attached to a rope or chain and used to moor a vessel to the sea bottom. • *v.* moor (a ship) to the sea bottom with an anchor: *we anchored in the harbor.*

PHRASES: **at anchor** (of a ship) moored by means of an anchor. **drop anchor** (of a ship) let down the anchor and moor. **weigh** (or **raise** or **heave**) **anchor** (of a ship) take up the anchor when ready to start sailing.

anchorage • *n.* a place where a ship may be anchored.

anchor cable • in air transport, a cable in an aircraft to which the parachute static lines or strops are attached.

Anchors Aweigh • the official song of the U.S. Navy, written in 1906. Charles A. Zimmerman composed the tune, and Alfred H. Miles wrote the lyrics.

anchor watch • a detail of a ship's crew keeping watch while the ship is at anchor.

Anderson, George Thomas (1824–1901) • Confederate brigadier general, born in Covington, Georgia, known as "Tige." In the MEXICAN WAR (1846–48), he was a second lieutenant in the Georgia Mounted Volunteers (1847) and served in the occupation of MEXICO CITY. In the CIVIL WAR, he commanded an infantry brigade at MALVERN HILL, the SEVEN DAYS' battles around Richmond, SECOND BULL RUN, and ANTIETAM (all 1862), and earned a reputation as an intrepid fighter. At GETTYSBURG (1863), until he was severely wounded, he led his brigade in valiant fighting at DEVIL'S DEN and LITTLE ROUND TOP. He fought with Gen. JAMES LONGSTREET in the BATTLE OF THE WILDERNESS. He was a brigade commander at SPOTSYLVANIA, COLD HARBOR, and the PETERSBURG campaign (all 1864), and was present at the surrender at APPOMATTOX (1865).

Anderson, Joseph Reid (1813–92) • industrialist and Confederate army officer, born in Botetourt County, Virginia. Commissioned a brigadier general, he was briefly commander of the Department of North Carolina and was wounded during the SEVEN DAYS' battles (1862). More a businessman than a soldier, Anderson was the owner of Tredegar Iron Works (also referred to as J. R. Anderson & Co.), Richmond, largest supplier of cannon, armor plate for Confederate ironclads, railroad rails, and other war materiel to the Confederate government.

Anderson, Patton (1822–72) • Confederate major general, born James Patton Anderson in Winchester, Tennessee. Anderson commanded a volunteer battalion in the MEXICAN WAR (1846–48), but his unit saw no action. He fought at SHILOH (1862) with the ARMY OF TENNESSEE, and at STONES RIVER with BRAXTON BRAGG and Maj. Gen. JOHN C. BRECKINRIDGE and led the Mississippi division at GETTYSBURG (1863), after which he was promoted to major general.

Anderson, Richard Heron (1821–79) • Confederate general, born near Statesburg, South Carolina. Anderson served in the U.S. Army on the frontier and in the MEXICAN WAR (1846–48). At the start of the CIVIL WAR, family pressure led Anderson to resign his Federal commission and accept a commission as colonel of the 1st South Carolina Regular Regiment, although he was personally opposed to slavery. During the Confederate retreat from Yorktown, Anderson checked the Union pursuit at the battle of WILLIAMSBURG (1862); his younger brother Mackenzie died in that battle. After Gen. James Longstreet was severely wounded in the battle of the WILDERNESS (1864), Maj. Gen. Anderson was placed in temporary command of the 1st Corps until Longstreet's return in that fall. His rapid march of the corps from the Wilderness battlefield to Spotsylvania Court House on the night of May 7 prevented the Union army from cutting Gen. ROBERT E. LEE's army off from Richmond.

After the war, Anderson tried to work his family's plantation but failed. He went to work as a laborer for the South Carolina railroad and lived in a boardinghouse.

Anderson, Robert (1805–71) • Union army officer and hero of FORT SUMTER, born in Jefferson County, Kentucky. A slaveholder who was nonetheless devoted to the idea of the Union, Anderson was assigned to command three forts in Charleston, South Carolina in 1860. After succession, having moved from the less defensible FORT MOULTRIE to FORT SUMTER, he refused Confederate Gen. P.G.T. BEAUREGARD's demand for surrender and held the fort for two days under bombardment, finally surrendering on April 14, 1861, with full honors of war. He returned to Fort Sumter on April 14, 1865, to raise the flag he had lowered there four years earlier.

Robert Anderson was said to have sworn in ABRAHAM LINCOLN, who saw brief service during the BLACK HAWK WAR (1832).

Andersonville Prison • the largest military prison of the Confederate army during the CIVIL WAR, located near Andersonville, Georgia, officially known as Camp Sumter. Some 52,300 Federal enlisted men were detained there between February 1864 and April 1865, and more than 13,200 died from disease, exposure, and lack of medicines. After the war, the commander of the camp, Capt. Henry Wirz, was convicted and hanged for the maltreatment and death of Union POWs. He was the only Confederate official to be executed.

André, John (1750–80) • British officer, actor, playwright, and spy, born in London. He was an aide-de-camp to Gen. Sir HENRY CLINTON and in charge of correspondence between the commander in chief and British secret agents in America. When André was caught by American militiamen with BENEDICT ARNOLD's treasonous correspondence about the plan to surrender WEST POINT to British, he was tried as spy by a military tribunal, found guilty, and hanged.

Andrews, Frank Maxwell (1884–1943) • Army officer and ARMY SIGNAL CORPS aviator, born in Nashville, Tennessee. Andrews was a strong advocate for a modern air force within the army and believed in the strategic potential of bomber aircraft. He helped develop and acquire weapons such as the B-17 Flying Fortress. In 1943 he succeeded Gen. DWIGHT D. EISENHOWER as supreme commander of American forces in Europe and helped to plan OPERATION OVERLORD. He died in a plane crash near Iceland.

In 1949 the newly independent U.S. Air Force named Andrews Air Force Base, Maryland, in his honor.

Andrews, George Leonard (1828–99) • Union army officer, civil engineer, and educator, born in Bridgewater, Massachusetts. Andrews led the Second Massachusetts regiment during the SHENANDOAH VALLEY campaign of 1862; after the battles of CEDAR MOUNTAIN and ANTIETAM (both 1862) he was promoted to brigadier general of volunteers. As chief of staff to Gen. NATHANIEL P. BANKS, Andrews played a prominent role in the 1863 campaign to sever the CONFEDERACY into east and west segments along a Union-controlled Mississippi River. He accepted the surrender of the starving Confederate garrison at PORT HUDSON, and courteously returned Maj. Gen. Frank Gardner's sword, signifying an honorable surrender. Andrews was a key officer in the Union's program to recruit, train, and employ black troops, a program known as the CORPS D'AFRIQUE.

Andros, Sir Edmund |ˈændrəs| (1637–1714) • royal governor of the province of New York and New Jersey (1674–81), born in London. Andros was also the royal governor-general of the Dominion of New England (1686) and the governor of the provinces of Virginia (1692–98) and of Maryland (1693–94). In the service of James Stuart, duke of York, Andros came to New York following England's defeat of the Netherlands (1674) to claim the duke's lands from the Dutch (including Manhattan, Long Island, Staten Island, the Hudson valley to Albany, and the Jersies). He transformed the administration of New York from the Dutch to an English model and negotiated stabilizing treaties with the IROQUOIS.

ANG • *abbr.* Air National Guard.

Angell, Israel (1740–1832) • Revolutionary army officer, born in Providence, Rhode Island. Angell was colonel of the 2nd Rhode Island Regiment at the battles of BRANDYWINE (1777) and MONMOUTH (1778). Under Gen. NATHANAEL GREENE, Angell won distinction for bravery and skill under fire at the battle of Springfield (June 23, 1780). Angell and Maj. HENRY "LIGHT-HORSE HARRY" LEE commanded 1,000 CONTINENTAL troops and militia in an effort to stop the advance of 5,000 British and Hessian troops toward the Rahway River, until forced to withdraw.

Anglo-American Arcadia Conference • a conference begun on December 22, 1941, in Washington D.C. to address issues of WORLD WAR II. It was held between British Prime Minister WINSTON CHURCHILL and U.S. President FRANKLIN D. ROOSEVELT. It established the ANGLO-AMERICAN COMBINED CHIEFS OF STAFF. On January 1, 1942, during the conference, the ALLIES signed the Declaration of the United Nations.

Anglo-American Combined Chiefs of Staff • the British Chiefs of Staff and the U.S. JOINT CHIEFS OF STAFF acting together in WORLD WAR II to advise Prime Minister WINSTON CHURCHILL and President FRANKLIN D. ROOSEVELT on the conduct of the war and to issue directives to the commanders-in-chief of the various theaters of war.

Anglo-Dutch Wars • (1652–54, 1664–67) early wars for control of the colonies in North America. British desire to halt Dutch trade with British colonies led to the first war, which ended in a stalemate. In the second war the British took New Netherland. Gov. PETER STUYVESANT surrendered, and New Amsterdam became New York in 1664, after the August 25 landing of the first British regulars on North American soil.

Anglo-French War • **1** (1689–97) see KING WILLIAM'S WAR. **2** (1702–12) see QUEEN ANNE'S WAR. **3** (1744–48) see KING GEORGE'S WAR. **4** (1755–63) see FRENCH AND INDIAN WAR.

An Loc, Battle of • (also **Anloc**) in the Vietnam War, a three-month siege (April 13–July 11, 1972) of the capital of Binh Long Province in South Vietnam, about 65 miles north of Saigon, in which South Vietnamese (ARVN) troops, aided by massive U.S. bombing sorties, held their ground against three divisions of VIETCONG and North Vietnamese Army (NVA) forces surrounding and shelling the city. The North Vietnamese withdrew on July 11. The South Vietnamese army's 5,400 casualties included 2,300 dead or missing, while the NVA forces' estimated losses were about twice that high.

The ARVN's resistance blunted the North Vietnamese EASTER OFFENSIVE and prevented a direct assault on Saigon.

Annapolis • city in Maryland that is home to the U.S. NAVAL ACADEMY.

Annapolis Royal • see PORT ROYAL.

annihilate |əˈnīəˌlāt| • *v.* **1** destroy utterly; obliterate: *a simple bomb of this type could annihilate them all* | *a crusade to annihilate evil.* **2** defeat utterly: *the stronger force annihilated its opponent virtually without loss.*

DERIVATIVES: **annihilator** |-ˌlātər| *n.* **annihilation** |əˌnīəˈlāsHən| *n.*

ANSCOL • *abbr.* Army and Navy Staff College.

antebellum |ˌænteˈbeləm| • *adj.* occurring or existing before a particular war, especially the CIVIL WAR: *the conventions of the antebellum South.*

ORIGIN: mid 19th cent.: from Latin, from *ante* 'before' and *bellum* 'war.'

antenna mine • a submersible contact mine that is fitted with antennae which, when touched by a steel ship, initiate a galvanic action that activates the mine.

anteroom |ˈænteˌro͞om; -ˌro͞om| • *n.* a sitting room in an officers' mess.

anthrax |ˈænˌTHræks| • *n.* a serious bacterial disease, causing severe skin ulcerationor, a form of pneumonia. Anthrax spores can survive for long periods of time in harsh conditions, making anthrax a possible biological weapon.

antiaircraft • *adj.* (especially of a gun or missile) used to attack enemy aircraft.

antiaircraft artillery • artillery designed for actively combating air targets from the ground.

antiair warfare • action required to destroy or reduce to an acceptable level the enemy air and missile threat. Antiair warfare includes both active (interceptors, bombers, antiaircraft guns, surface-to-air and air-to-air missiles, and electronic measures/countermeasures) and passive (cover, concealment, dispersion, deception, and mobility) means and methods.

antiarmor helicopter • (also *antitank helicopter*) a helicopter used primarily to attack and destroy armored vehicles.

Anti-Ballistic Missile Treaty • an agreement signed in 1972 by the United States and the USSR as part of the SALT I TREATY. It limited each country's defensive ballistic missile system to two sites with 100 ABM launchers per site. In 1974 it was altered to limit each country to one ABM site and to allow only fixed, land-based ABM systems.

Antietam, Battle of • (also known as the **Battle of Sharpsburg**) (September 17, 1862) the bloodiest one-day conflict in U.S. military history, with more than 3,500 killed and more than 20,000 total casualties. Maj. Gen. George B. McClellan, who possessed a copy of Gen. Robert E. Lee's battle orders, attacked Lee's positions near Sharpsburg, Maryland, while many Confederate forces were still at Harpers Ferry. Union forces induced sufficient casualties to halt Lee's invasion of the North, but, erroneously believing Lee's forces four times their actual size, McClellan held back, allowing the Confederates to withdraw. Recognizing the missed opportunity to destroy Lee's army, President Abraham Lincoln later relieved McClellan of his command.

antifouling • *n.* **1** treatment of a boat's hull with a paint or similar substance designed to prevent fouling. **2** an antifouling substance.

anti-G suit • a device worn by aircrew to counteract the effects on the human body of positive acceleration.

anti-intervention • *adj.* opposed to interference, especially military interference, by the state in another's affairs.

antimilitarism • *n.* the belief that war is unjustifiable, that the role played by the military in fostering injustice should be opposed, and that the causes of war should be eliminated by nonviolent action.

antinuclear (or **anti-nuclear**) • *adj.* |ˈˌænˌtī ˈn(y)o͞okli(ə)r; ˈˌæn(t)ē ˈn(y)o͞okli(ə)r; ˈˌæn(t)ə ˈn(y)o͞okli(ə)r| opposed to the development of nuclear weapons or nuclear power.

antipersonnel • *adj.* designed to kill or injure people rather than to damage buildings or equipment.

antipersonnel mine • a contact mine designed to kill or maim the person stepping on it.

antiradar missile • a missile designed to home in on a ground-based radar installation and destroy it.

antiradiation missile • a missile that seeks out and destroys a heat source.

antisatellite weapon • a weapon designed to destroy an object in space.

antiship missile • a missile designed for use against ships.

antislavery • *adj.* opposed to slavery and dedicated to working for its abolition.

antisubmarine rocket • (**ASROC**) a nuclear depth charge or homing torpedo that is launched from a surface ship.

antisubmarine torpedo • (**ASTOR**) a submarine-launched long-range high-speed wire-guided wakeless torpedo capable of carrying a nuclear warhead for use in antisubmarine and antisurface ship operations.

antisubmarine warfare • operations conducted with the intention of denying the enemy the effective use of submarines.

antisubmarine warfare forces • the forces organized primarily to engage in antisubmarine action. Such a force may be composed of surface ships, aircraft, submarines, or some combination of these, along with their supporting systems.

antitank • *adj.* for use against enemy tanks: *new antitank missiles.*

antitank artillery • artillery designed to destroy tanks, including armor-piercing artillery.

antitank gun • a gun capable of disabling or impairing a tank, typically one that uses armor-piercing ammunition.

antitank weapon • any weapon designed to destroy a tank. These may include guns of various sizes, guided missiles, rockets and their delivery systems, grenades, mines, and other obstacle systems.

antiwar movement • a campaign to end a war or a state's involvement in a war, especially the 1963–73 effort to end U.S. involvement in the Vietnam War.

Antwerp, Liberation of • (September 1944) the World War II retaking of a major Belgian port by Allied forces under British Gen. Bernard Law Montgomery on September 4, 1944, for the purpose of using Antwerp as a major supply port for an Allied drive into Germany for a quick end to the war. See also Operation Market-Garden.

Anvil, Operation • (also known as **Operation Dragoon**) (August 15–September 1944) the code name for the Allied landing on the French Riviera in World War II. It was originally intended to prevent Germans from focusing solely on Allies at Normandy, and by advance of those troops into France, to cut off the retreat of German units in southern France. Allied forces took more than 100,000 prisoners and joined with Allies advancing from Normandy on September 2.

Anzio, Battle of • (also known as **Operation Shingle**) (January–May 1944) a World War II battle to maintain positions after an amphibious landing at Anzio on the Italian coast. On January 22, 36,000 Allied troops under U.S. VI Corps Maj. Gen. John Lucas landed nearly unopposed on this beach thirty miles south of Rome and eighty miles north of the Gustav Line. Pausing to reinforce the beachhead, Lucas missed his chance to push forward to the controlling Alban Hills, and arriving German artillery, and eventually the entire German 145th Army, pinned down the Allies. A breakout was engineered on May 23, after the capture of Cassino on the Gustav Line.

Apache • (**AH-64**) an attack helicopter designed to destroy tanks and to provide battlefield support. It carries a 30 mm chain gun under the nose and clusters of four anti-tank missiles under its stub wings.

Apache Wars • a protracted campaign in the American Southwest, beginning in the 1870s under U.S. Gen. George Crook and Brig. Gen. Nelson A. Miles. The United States fought against bands of Chiricahua Apache Indians led by such fierce and elusive fighters as Geronimo and the chief Cochise. Cavalry pursuits and Indian skirmishes continued till the end of the 19th century.

Ap Bac, Battle of • (January 2, 1963) a Vietnam War battle in which a 320-man Vietcong battalion checked an Army of the Republic of Vietnam (South Vietnamese) force of approximately 3,000, at Ap Bac southwest of Saigon. The failure of the ARVN forces, supplied with American-manufactured planes, helicopters, and armored personnel carriers, provoked doubts about the South Vietnamese government's military leadership and its soldiers' ability and willingness to fight.

APC • *abbr.* armored personnel carrier.

APF • *abbr.* afloat prepositioning force.

APG • *abbr.* Aberdeen Proving Ground.

apogee |'æpəjē| • *n.* the point at which a missile trajectory or a satellite orbit is farthest from the center of the gravitational field of the controlling body or bodies.

Applied Physics Laboratory • a technical and scientific research facility at The Johns Hopkins University in Laurel, Maryland. A collaboration between the U.S. government and the university, it began conducting wartime defense research for the government in 1942. It is credited for the development of a proximity fuse first used by the U.S. military during WORLD WAR II. It currently maintains ninety specialized research facilities.

applied research • research concerned with the practical application of knowledge, material, and/or techniques directed toward a solution to an existent or anticipated military requirement.

Appomattox Campaign • (March 29–April 9, 1865) the name given to the final operations of the CIVIL WAR, including the battles of FORT STEDMAN and FIVE FORKS. It began with Confederate Gen. ROBERT E. LEE's attempt to break out of his defensive position in Petersburg, Virginia, and ended with his surrender at Appomattox on April 9, 1865.

Appomattox Court House • a CIVIL WAR battle on April 9, 1865, in which Gen. ROBERT E. LEE decided to make one last try to escape the Union forces and reach the supply depot at Lynchburg. Union infantry arrived and surrounded Lee on three sides, and he surrendered to Gen. ULYSSES S. GRANT.

appreciation of the situation • see ESTIMATE OF THE SITUATION.

approach • *v.* (of an aircraft) descend toward and prepare to land on (an airfield, runway, etc.): *the single-seater plane hit a post as it was approaching the runway.* • *n.* the part of an aircraft's flight in which it descends gradually toward an airfield or runway for landing.

apron • a defined area, on an airfield, intended to accommodate aircraft for purposes of loading or unloading passengers or cargo, refueling, parking, or maintenance.

APS • *abbr.* afloat prepositioning ships.

APSD • *abbr.* armor-piercing discarding sabot.

Aquatone, Project • code name given to the secret contract given by the U.S. government in the early 1950s to the LOCKHEED Aircraft Corporation to develop the U-2 spy plane.

AR-15 • an assault rifle, originally developed in the 1950s and similar to the M-16, but lighter and able to use a number of different ammunition clips and modifying devices.

Arapaho • a nomadic Algonquian-speaking Southern Plains Indian tribe located on the eastern slope of the Rocky Mountains in Wyoming and on reservations in Oklahoma. The Arapaho were often allied with the CHEYENNE, SIOUX, Comanche, and KIOWA in opposition to white expansion.

Archer, James Jay (1817–64) • Confederate brigadier general, born in Harford County, Maryland. As a field commander of the Tennessee brigade under A. P. HILL in 1862, Archer fought at MECHANICSVILLE, GAINES' MILL, CEDAR MOUNTAIN, SECOND BULL RUN, and ANTIETAM, where he was so ill he arrived on the field in an ambulance. He played a key role at CHANCELLORSVILLE (1863) where his brigade seized an artillery emplacement that was the key to the entire battlefield. He was taken prisoner at GETTYSBURG (1863) and held for one year in broken health; he rejoined his command at PETERSBURG (1864), but died that year of illness at Richmond.

Archer was in command of a post on the Pacific coast at the outbreak of the war. He resigned and handed over command of his station to Lt. PHILIP H. SHERIDAN. Archer made his way across the continent to Richmond and accepted a captaincy in the Confederate army.

Arc Light • a code name given to the use of U.S. Air Force B-52 bombers, beginning in June 1965, to provide pre-planned and on-call close air support bombing strikes against VIETCONG and North Vietnamese units. The strikes were much feared both for their destructiveness and the fact that, since the bombers flew so high, there was usually no prior warning of an incoming strike.

Area 51 • a military installation at the Nellis Range near Groom Lake in northwest Nevada. It is a subject of intense speculation due to its secrecy. Believed to have been a U.S. Air Force testing site for high-level stealth aircraft such as the F-117 NIGHTHAWK, Area 51 was photographed from space and widely discussed in the media. It may no longer be in use. Speculation exists that Area 51 is connected with UFO sightings. The installation may have been relocated to another site.

area air defense commander • within a unified command, subordinate unified command, or joint task force, the commander assigned overall responsibility for AIR DEFENSE.

area bombing • the bombing of a target that is in effect a general area rather than a small or pinpoint target.

area command • a command that is composed of those organized elements of one or more of the armed services, designated to operate in a specific geographical area, and placed under a single commander.

area defense • a defense against air attack organized to protect a large area as distinguished from a point or line defense.

area of operations • **1** the portion of an area of war necessary for military operations and for the administration of such operations. **2** the area of the theater of war allocated to a given military unit for the purpose of conducting operations.

Argentan, Battle of • see FALAISE-ARGENTAN GAP.

Argonne Forest • see MEUSE-ARGONNE OFFENSIVE.

Argonne National Laboratory • a laboratory in Argonne, Illinois, under the direction of the U.S. DEPARTMENT OF ENERGY. Founded in 1946 to conduct basic atomic research and to explore possible peacetime uses for nuclear energy, its research now covers a broad range of science and engineering concerns.

Arista, Mariano (1802–55) • Mexican general and president of Mexico (1851–53). Arista fought in the Mexican army against the TEXAS WAR OF INDEPENDENCE (1836). In the MEXICAN WAR (1846–48), as commander of the Mexican Army of the North, he was defeated by ZACHARY TAYLOR at PALO ALTO and routed at RESACA DE LA PALMA (1846).

***Arizona*, USS** • commissioned on October 17, 1916, a Pennsylvania Class battleship, served as a gunnery training ship during WORLD WAR I and was part of the honor escort for the transport *George Washington* that carried President WOODROW WILSON to the PARIS PEACE CONFERENCE in December 1918. When the Japanese attacked PEARL HARBOR on December 7, 1941, the *Arizona* was in drydock for repairs to its hull (damaged during exercises with the *Oklahoma* and *Nevada*). At about 8:10 A.M., the ship was hit by an 800-kilogram bomb and sank. More than 1,100 men died on the ship.

In 1962 a memorial to the *Arizona* was dedicated. In 1980 a visitor center was opened on shore and the Navy turned the memorial over to the National Park Service.

Arleigh Burke Class • a class of U.S. Navy destroyers equipped with the AEGIS air defense system. The *Arleigh Burke* (DDG-51) was the first of its class and the first U.S. ship to incorporate shaping techniques that reduce radar cross-section, thereby reducing the likelihood that this class can be detected and targeted by enemy weapons and sensors. Originally intended to defend against enemy aircraft, cruise missiles, and nuclear-attack submarines, Arleigh Burke destroyers are used in high-threat areas for anti-air, antisubmarine, antisurface, and strike missions.

The USS *Cole,* the ship rammed by a small boat carrying explosives off the coast of Yemen on October 12, 2000, was an Arleigh Burke-class destroyer.

Arlington National Cemetery • a national burial ground at the Potomac River, in Arlington County, Virginia. It became a military cemetery in 1864 by order of the secretary of war, and on May 13, 1864, a Confederate prisoner was the first soldier buried there. Since then, some soldiers from all subsequent wars in which the United States has participated have been buried in the cemetery, including a few officers of the REVOLUTIONARY WAR. Memorials located at the site include the TOMB OF THE UNKNOWN SOLDIER.

arm • *v.* **1** supply or provide with weapons: *both sides* ***armed themselves with*** *grenades and machine guns.* **2** activate the fuse of (a bomb, alarm, or other device) so that it is ready to explode: *the bomb would be quite safe until it was armed.* • *n.* see ARMS.

armada |är'mädə| • *n.* **1** a fleet of warships. **2** any fleet of boats: *an armada of inflatable rafts.*

Armageddon |ˌärmə'gedn| • **1** (in the New Testament) the last battle between good and evil before the Day of Judgment. **2** a dramatic and catastrophic conflict, typically seen as likely to destroy the world or the human race: *nuclear Armageddon.*

ORIGIN: Greek, from Hebrew *har mĕgiddōn* 'hill of Megiddo' (Rev. 16:16.)

Armalite |'ärməˌlīt| • *n.* trademark a type of light automatic rifle.

armament |'ärməmənt| • *n.* **1** (also **armaments**) military weapons and equipment: *chemical weapons and other unconventional armaments.* **2** the process of equipping military forces for war: *instruments of disarmament rather than of armament.*

armed forces (also **armed services**) • a country's military forces, especially its army, navy, and air force.

armed forces censorship • the examination and control of personal communications to or from persons in the armed forces and persons accompanying or serving with the armed forces.

Armed Forces Leave Act of 1946 • a bill signed by President HARRY S. TRUMAN on August 9, 1946, to increase benefits for WORLD WAR II veterans and to democratize the military service system. It gave officers and enlisted troops equal amounts of annual leave and paid them accrued leave through maturity bonds when their term of service ended.

Armed Forces Policy Council • a U.S. government council which advises the Secretary of Defense on broad policy regarding the armed forces. Its composition includes the Secretary of Defense (as Chairman), the Deputy Secretary of Defense, the Service secretaries, and the chairman and members of the JOINT CHIEFS OF STAFF.

Armed Forces Radio and Television Service • (**AFRTS**) a DEPARTMENT OF DEFENSE activity, the successor to the Armed Forces Radio Service (AFRS) formed in August 1942 to provide information, education, and entertainment to U.S. military forces world-wide. The various AFRTS radio and television broadcasting stations carry commercial programs as well as programs produced by AFRTS itself.

Armed Forces Reserve Act • an act passed on July 9, 1952, to reorganize the reserve forces into the categories of ready, standby, and retired, and to restrict the use of KOREAN WAR veterans in future service. It allowed Reservists and Guardsmen to volunteer for active duty, thereby enabling the armed forces to use them in peacetime operations and to avoid mobilizations. It was amended by the RESERVE FORCES ACT of 1955.

Armed Forces School of Music • a DEPARTMENT OF DEFENSE activity at the NAVAL AMPHIBIOUS BASE LITTLE CREEK, Norfolk, Virginia, is the world's largest military music school and provider of multi-level instruction for some 350 students annually.

Armed Forces Staff College • located two miles south of the Norfolk Navy Base in Norfolk, Virginia, a part of the NATIONAL DEFENSE UNIVERSITY that prepares mid-career U.S. military officers and selected allied officers for duty on joint and combined staffs.

Founded in 1943 as the ARMY-NAVY STAFF COLLEGE, it received its current name in 1946.

---

armed mine • a mine from which all safety devices have been withdrawn and that will explode on receipt of a target signal, influence, or contact.

armed neutrality • a wartime condition in which a neutral country arms itself to defend against aggression on the part of either belligerent.

armed reconnaissance • a mission with the primary purpose of locating and attacking targets of opportunity (that is, enemy materiel, personnel, and facilities) in assigned general areas or along assigned ground communications routes, and not for the purpose of attacking specific briefed targets.

Armed Services Committee, House • see HOUSE ARMED SERVICES COMMITTEE.

Armed Services Committee, Senate • see SENATE ARMED SERVICES COMMITTEE.

armed sweep • a sweep fitted with cutters or other devices to increase its ability to cut mine moorings.

Armistead, James • see LAFAYETTE, JAMES.

Armistead, Lewis Addison (1817–63) • Confederate general, born in New Bern, North Carolina. At GETTYSBURG (1863), while leading one of three brigades in PICKETT'S CHARGE on CEMETERY HILL, with his hat on the tip of his raised sword, Armistead was hit by a FEDERAL volley in the midst of the northern position.

Lewis entered WEST POINT in 1834 but was forced to resign in February 1836 for "imprudence" and "disorderly conduct." Tradition has it that the "disorderly conduct" was when Armistead broke a mess-hall plate on the head of fellow cadet JUBAL A. EARLY.

---

armistice |'ärmistis| • *n.* an agreement made by opposing sides in a war to stop fighting for a certain time; a truce

Armistice Day • the anniversary of the WORLD WAR I armistice of November 11, 1918, now replaced by VETERANS DAY.

armor |'ärmər| (Brit. **armour**) • *n.* **1** the metal coverings formerly worn by soldiers or warriors to protect the body in battle: *knights in armor | a suit of armor.* **2** (also **armor plate**) the tough metal layer covering a military vehicle or ship to defend it from attack. **3** military vehicles collectively: *the contingent includes infantry, armor, and logistic units.*

armored (Brit. **armoured**) • *adj.* **1** (of a military vehicle or ship) covered with a tough metal layer as a defense against attack: *armored vehicles.* **2** (of troops) equipped with such vehicles: *the 2nd Armored Division.* **3** (of a soldier) wearing armor.

armored ground vehicle • (also **armored land vehicle**) a vehicle designed with heavy external armor to protect it from enemy fire.

armored land vehicle • see ARMORED GROUND VEHICLE.

armored personnel carrier • a highly mobile full-tracked vehicle with light armor. Capable of AMPHIBIOUS travel, it can also be dropped into a target area. It is used primarily for moving personnel and their equipment during tactical operations, and can be modified, either by modifications during production or the use of special kits, making it suitable for use as a mortar carrier, command post, flame thrower, antiaircraft artillery chassis, or limited recovery vehicle.

armored reconnaissance airborne assault vehicle • a full-tracked vehicle with light armor that serves as the primary reconnaissance vehicle during infantry and airborne operations and as the main assault weapon of airborne troops.

armored vehicle • any land vehicle made with heavy or light external armor that protects its crew and structural integrity.

armorer (Brit. **armourer**) • *n.* an official in charge of the arms of a military unit.

armor-piercing ammunition • ammunition made of extremely hard alloys that is designed to penetrate armor.

armor-piercing discarding sabot • (**APSD**) an ammunition round made from an extremely hard alloy that is smaller than the bore of the gun firing it. It is encased in a metal ring matching the bore (the sabot) that falls away after leaving the bore. The small diameter of the projectile concentrates all of its kinetic energy on a small spot of enemy armor, increasing chances of penetration.

armor unit • a unit of armored vehicles, such as tanks and/or armored personnel carriers.

armory (Brit. **armoury**) • *n.* (pl. **-ies**) **1** a place where arms are kept; an arsenal. **2** a place where military Reservists are trained or headquartered, sometimes used for public functions: *National Guard members standing by in an armory.* **3** a supply of arms: *the most powerful weapon in our armory.* **4** a place where arms are manufactured.

arms • *n.* weapons and ammunition; armaments: *arms exports.*

PHRASES: **lay down (one's) arms** cease fighting. **take up arms** begin fighting. **under arms** equipped and ready for war or battle: *one million men under arms.*

arms control • *n.* international disarmament or arms limitation, especially by mutual consent.

Arms Control and Disarmament Agency • an executive branch agency of the U.S. Government established by President JOHN F. KENNEDY in September 1961 for the development, implementation, and support of arms control and disarmament policies and negotiations regarding the same with foreign powers.

arms export • the export of weapons, ammunition, and other military goods from one country to another, usually in exchange for a monetary payment.

Arms Export Control Act of 1976 • an act passed on June 30, 1976, (after President GERALD R. FORD had vetoed an earlier and stronger version of the bill) that expanded congressional authority over control of U.S. arms sales and exports. It emphasized public disclosure and review procedures. It was the most significant piece of arms transfer legislation since the MUTUAL SECURITY ACT of 1951.

arms race • a competition between nations for superiority in the development and accumulation of weapons, especially between the U.S. and the former USSR during the COLD WAR.

arms transfer • the transfer of weapons, ammunition, and other military goods from one entity to another (usually between governments), either with or without payment or other reimbursement.

Armstrong, John (1717–95) • surveyor, soldier, member of the Continental Congress, and Revolutionary army officer, born in County Fermanagh, Ulster, Ireland. In Pennsylvania, as Penns's surveyor and agent, he helped survey and cut supply routes across the mountains for British general EDWARD BRADDOCK (1755) and persuaded the Quaker colony to establish its first chain of frontier forts from Maryland to the Susquehanna. Armstrong commanded Pennsylvania troops during PONTIAC'S REBELLION (1763–66); he was brigadier general of the Pennsylvania militia; and was elected to the Continental Congress (1779–80). In the FRENCH AND INDIAN WAR, Armstrong achieved fame as the "Hero of Kittanning" when he planned and executed the destruction of Kittanning (September 8, 1756), a major Delaware Indian stronghold on the Allegheny River north of FORT DUQUESNE, where he killed the Delaware war leader in the first offensive action against the Indians following BRADDOCK'S defeat near Fort Duquesne (1755).

Armstrong, John (1755–1816) • REVOLUTIONARY WAR officer, born in New Jersey. In 1790 he and thirty of his men were sent to accompany 150 Kentucky militia in an attack against an Indian settlement on the Eel River. When the Indians ambushed Armstrong's men and the militia, many of the militiamen threw away their guns without firing a shot (including their commander, Col. JOHN HARDIN) and ran through his men, throwing them in disorder. Armstrong lost his sergeant and twenty-one of his men.

Armstrong, John, Jr. (1758–1843) • soldier, senator, and secretary of war, born in Carlisle, Pennsylvania. Armstrong was the son of JOHN ARMSTRONG, the "hero of Kittanning." During the REVOLUTIONARY WAR, Armstrong wrote anonymously the controversial "Newburgh Addresses," intended to pressure Congress into redressing the army's grievances, especially concerning the lack of pay, which were perceived as challenging GEORGE WASHINGTON's authority, but he was eventually forgiven. As a brigadier general, he was assigned the defense of New York harbor in 1812. As war secretary during the WAR OF 1812, Armstrong infused new energy into the department, but treated his officers imperiously, was known to interfere in matters belonging to the commanders, failed to coordinate his activities with President JAMES MADISON, and was blamed for insufficient defense of Washington, D.C., that led to its burning by British troops after the BATTLE OF BLADENSBURG in 1814. He resigned that year.

army • *n.* (pl. **-ies**) **1** an organized military force equipped for fighting on land: *the two armies were in position.* **2** (**the army** or **the Army**) the branch of a nation's armed services that conducts military operations on land: *enlisted men in the army | army officers.*

Army Adjutant General School • recently relocated to Fort Jackson, South Carolina, from Fort Benjamin Harrison, Indiana and part of the U.S. ARMY SOLDIER SUPPORT INSTITUTE, this school provides instruction for U.S. Army Adjutant General Corps personnel and oversees the development of doctrine and organization for Army personnel and administrative operations.

Army Air Armor Center and School • a U.S. ARMY TRAINING AND DOCTRINE COMMAND activity, located at Fort Knox, Kentucky.

Army Air Corps • the successor to the U.S. ARMY AIR SERVICE, authorized by an act of Congress of July 2, 1926. Responsible in the interwar period for all Army aviation activities, notably the development of strategic bombing doctrine, technological advances in aircraft and supporting equipment, and large scale training of aviators beginning in 1930, the Army Air Corps achieved semi-independent status as the U.S. ARMY AIR FORCES (USAAF) on June 1, 1941. Commanded during WORLD WAR II by Gen. HENRY H. "HAP" ARNOLD, the USAAF planned and carried out the strategic bombing of Germany and Japan and provided air superiority, close air support, interdiction, troop carrier, and air transport support for the Army. With the passage of the NATIONAL SECURITY ACT of July 1947, the old Army Air Corps/Army Air Forces became an independent service as the U.S. Air Force.

Army Air Defense Artillery Center and School • a U.S. ARMY TRAINING AND DOCTRINE COMMAND activity at Fort Bliss, Texas, the focal point for U.S. Army air defense artillery training and the development of air defense artillery organization, equipment, and doctrine. The installation occupies some 1.2 million acres and employs some 12,000 military and 7,500 civilian personnel.

Army Air Forces • see AIR FORCE.

Army Air Forces Training Command • a formal training program for army air forces technicians and crews. Established in 1941, it was created in response to an increase of pilots and equipment in the ARMY AIR CORPS as authorized by Congress in the National Defense Act of 1940.

Army Air Service • an early U.S. military aviation service, created in May 1918. During WORLD WAR I, the U.S. Army had more than 11,000 planes and 190,000 personnel.

Army and Air Force Vitalization and Retirement Act • a 1948 law that established a retirement system for Reserve and NATIONAL GUARD career personnel, and allowed Army and Air Force officers to retire with a minimum of twenty years service.

Army and Navy Staff College • (**ANSCOL**) established in Washington, D.C., in 1943, under the JOINT CHIEFS OF STAFF. It became the NATIONAL WAR COLLEGE in 1946.

Army aviation • see U.S. AIR FORCE.

Army Aviation Center and School • a training center and school for U.S. Army personnel in both fixed and rotary wing aviation at both the primary and advanced level, which oversees the development of U.S. Army aviation doctrine at FORT RUCKER, Alabama. Some 5,300 military and 6,000 civilian personnel are assigned to the Army Aviation Center and other activities on the 63,232-acre installation.

Army Aviation Logistics School • a school at FORT EUSTIS, Virginia, that provides training in Army aviation maintenance and supply operations and oversees the development of Army aviation maintenance and supply doctrine.

army brat • the child of a soldier raised in a military environment. Army brats are traditionally characterized as "precocious, ubiquitous, underfoot, and insubordinate." The equivalent Navy term is "navy junior."

Army Cadet Command • a subordinate of the U.S. ARMY TRAINING AND DOCTRINE COMMAND, responsible for management of the ARMY RESERVE OFFICERS TRAINING CORPS (ROTC) program at high schools, colleges, and universities in the United States.

Army Chaplain School • recently relocated to FORT JACKSON, South Carolina, from Fort Hamilton, New York, and part of the U.S. ARMY SOLDIER SUPPORT INSTITUTE, this school provides training for U.S. Army chaplains and religious activities personnel and oversees the development of doctrine and organization for Army chaplain operations.

Army Chemical Corps • a U.S. Army Corps that provides nuclear, biological, chemical, smoke, and flame operations on the battlefield as well as being responsible for combat operations, logistics, training, intelligence, personnel management, research and development, and analysis.

Army Chemical School • recently relocated to FORT LEONARD WOOD, Missouri, from Fort McClellan, Alabama, this U.S. ARMY MANEUVER SUPPORT CENTER school provides training for U.S. Army personnel in chemical and biological defense operations and oversees the development of doctrine and organization for Army chemical and biological defense operations.

Army Chief of Staff • the chief officer of the U.S. Army. The Army Chief of Staff reports to the secretary of the Army and to the President.

Army Combined Arms Center • the focal point for the development of Army doctrine and organization for combined arms warfare, at Fort Leavenworth, Kansas. Some 3,000 military and 2,100 civilian personnel are assigned to the Combined Arms Center and other activities on the 5,600-acre installation.

Army Combined Arms Support Command • located at FORT LEE, Virginia, this command coordinates instruction and doctrinal development for the logistical and administrative support of Army units in the field. Some 3,000 military and 3,000 civilian personnel are assigned to the Combined Arms Support Command and other activities at the 5,575-acre installation.

Army Command and General Staff College • a postgraduate service school at Fort Leavenworth, Kansas. Founded in 1882 as the School of Application for Infantry and Cavalry at Fort Leavenworth, it received its current name in 1946 and has consisted of several specialized schools since 1987. It grants the degree of Master of Military Arts and Science.

Army Corps of Engineers • (**USACE**) an organization of the U.S. Army, headquartered in Washington, D.C., with approximately 34,600 civilian and 650 military men and women, responsible for providing responsive engineering services, including the planning, design, construction, and operation of water resources and other civil works projects; designing and managing the construction of military facilities for the Army and the Air Force; and providing design and construction management support for other Defense and federal agencies.

Army Corps of Topographic Engineers • one of eight laboratories of the U.S. Army, under the Engineer Research and Development Center, responsible for mapping and terrain analysis, providing the armed forces with superior knowledge of the battlefield. It also supports both civil and environmental initiatives through research, development, and the application of such expertise in the topographic and related sciences.

Army, Department of the • the executive branch of the U.S. Army, including all the field headquarters, troops and forces, reserve organizations, bases, installations, and their activities and functions under the command or supervision of the secretary of the Army.

Army Electronic Proving Ground • (**EPG**) a U.S. Army testing ground for electronic systems located at FORT HUACHUCA, Arizona, that has been in operation since 1954. It conducts technical tests of communications, intelligence, and electronic warfare equipment, often in conjunction with nearby WHITE SANDS MISSILE RANGE in New Mexico. It serves as the headquarters for other electronic proving grounds throughout the country.

Army Engineer School • a part of the U.S. ARMY MANEUVER SUPPORT CENTER, located at Fort Leavenworth, Missouri, it provides training for U.S. Army combat engineers and oversees the development of doctrine for combat engineer operations, including such functions as the construction of field fortifications, barriers, bridges, and other facilities; mine warfare; and water supply operations.

Army Europe/Seventh U.S. Army • see U.S. ARMY EUROPE/SEVENTH U.S. ARMY.

Army Field Artillery Center and School • a U.S. ARMY TRAINING AND DOCTRINE COMMAND activity located at Fort Sill, Oklahoma, this school is the focal point for U.S. Army field artillery training and the development of field artillery organization, equipment, and doctrine. The installation occupies some 93,828 acres and employs some 14,300 military and 6,100 civilian personnel.

Army Finance School • a part of the U.S. ARMY SOLDIER SUPPORT INSTITUTE and recently relocated to FORT JACKSON, South Carolina, from Fort Benjamin Harrison, Indiana, it provides training for U.S. Army Finance Corps personnel and oversees the development of doctrine and organization for Army finance operations.

Army Forces Command • (**FORSCOM**) the Army's largest major command, headquartered at Fort McPherson, Georgia, and consisting of more than 760,000 active Army, Army Reserve, and A soldiers.

Army Green-44 • the U.S. Army Shade 44 general duty (Class A) uniform adopted on October 1, 1957, and consisting of a coat (blouse) and trousers in a dark blue-green color.

Army Industrial College • a postgraduate service school at Fort McNair, Washington, D.C. Established in 1924, it became a joint service program after WORLD WAR II and was renamed the INDUSTRIAL COLLEGE OF THE ARMED FORCES in 1946.

Army Infantry Center and School • a U.S. ARMY TRAINING AND DOCTRINE COMMAND activity, located at Fort Benning, Georgia, the focal point for U.S. Army infantry training and the development of infantry organization, equipment, and doctrine. The installation, which occupies some 184,000 acres and employs some 25,000 military and 6,100 civilian personnel.

Army Intelligence Center and School • a U.S. ARMY TRAINING AND DOCTRINE COMMAND activity, located at Fort Huachuca, Arizona, the focal point for U.S. Army intelligence training and the development of intelligence organization, equipment, and doctrine. The installation occupies some 73,242 acres and employs some 5,900 military and 2,400 civilian personnel.

army issue • equipment or clothing supplied by the army: *an army issue sleeping bag.*

Army List • the official roster maintained by Headquarters, Department of the Army, of all living U.S. Army commissioned officers, arranged by rank and date of rank. The Army List is in fact divided into separate lists for REGULAR ARMY officers on active duty, retired Regular Army officers, officers of the Reserve components, retired officers of the Reserve components, and officers retired for medical disability.

Army Logistics Management College • a U.S. ARMY TRAINING AND DOCTRINE COMMAND activity, located at Fort Lee, Virginia, responsible for providing training in logistics management subjects for U.S. military and civilian personnel and selected foreign military personnel.

Army Management Staff College • this college, at FORT BELVOIR, Virginia, provides instruction in organizational management theory and methods for selected Army uniformed and civilian personnel as well as for personnel from other services.

Army Maneuver Support Center • (**MANSCEN**) a U.S. Army Training and Doctrine Command activity located at Fort Leonard Wood, Missouri, responsible for integrating training and the development of doctrine, organization, and materiel at the U.S. Army CHEMICAL, ENGINEER, and MILITARY POLICE Schools.

Army Medical Department • (**AMEDD**) an organization of the U.S. Army responsible for operating the Army's fixed hospitals and dental facilities, providing preventive health services carrying on medical research, development, and training institutions, as well as providing food inspection and animal care for the entire DEPARTMENT OF DEFENSE through its veterinary command. Its field hospitals are usually deployed to provide humanitarian assistance, peacekeeping, and other support operations, not in support of conventional battlefield situations, although the department does provide trained medical specialists to the Army's combat medical units. Although the Continental Congress had created a medical service on July 27, 1775, it was not until 1818, after the WAR OF 1812 (when the Army had no medical department per se), that the U.S. Congress included the creation of a permanent Army medical service in a military reorganization act. At the beginning of the twentieth century, AMEDD was again restructured, and new branches were added, including the NURSING CORPS. In 1911, a Dental Corps was created, and, in 1917, their pay, benefits, and military status were made equal with Army doctors.

Army Medical Service • an organization of AMEDD, the Medical Service's mission is to support the Army's health care system by providing the skilled personnel for the clinical, scientific, administrative, command, and support services. These professionals serve in eight major groupings: health care administration, aviation, optometry, pharmacy; the behavioral, laboratory, and preventive medicine sciences, and audiology.

Army Military Police School • a U.S. ARMY TRAINING AND DOCTRINE COMMAND activity located at Fort Leonard Wood, Missouri, responsible for the training of U.S. Army military police personnel and the development of military police organization, equipment, and doctrine.

Army Museum System • an organization that collects, preserves, and displays information about important people and events that have shaped the development of the U.S. Army. In order to carry out its mission, the System maintains thirty-four separate museums, including two sites each for the 82nd Airborne Division and the Medical Department, in addition to museums dedicated to the NATIONAL GUARD and the Army Reserve.

army-navy • *adj.* denoting the type of store that specializes in military surplus equipment, or the goods sold there.

Army-Navy Staff College • see NATIONAL WAR COLLEGE, ARMED FORCES STAFF COLLEGE.

Army Nurse Corps • see NURSING CORPS.

Army of Northern Virginia • the main Confederate army in the East during the CIVIL WAR, the Army of Northern Virginia was commanded from June 1, 1962, by Gen. ROBERT E. LEE. At its peak in 1863, it numbered some 75,000 men. Under Lee's command the Army of Northern Virginia participated in the SEVEN DAYS', SECOND BULL RUN, ANTIETAM, and FREDERICKSBURG campaigns of 1862; the CHANCELLORSVILLE and GETTYSBURG campaigns in 1863 and the WILDERNESS, SPOTSYLVANIA, and COLD HARBOR battles in 1864. Lee surrendered the Army of Northern Virginia to Union Gen. ULYSSES S. GRANT at Appomattox, Virginia, on April 9, 1865.

Army of Tennessee • the main Confederate army in the West during the CIVIL WAR, assembled at Corinth, Mississippi, by Gen. ALBERT SIDNEY JOHNSTON in March 1862 and commanded successively by Gens. JOSEPH E. JOHNSTON, P.G.T. BEAUREGARD, BRAXTON BRAGG, JOSEPH E. JOHNSTON, and JOHN B. HOOD. The Army of Tennessee, again under the command of Joseph E. Johnston, surrendered to Union forces on April 26, 1865, near Durham, North Carolina, having participated in the battles of SHILOH, PERRYVILLE (1862), STONES RIVER (1862–63), CHICKAMAUGA (1863), MISSIONARY RIDGE (1863), ATLANTA (1864), FRANKLIN (1864), NASHVILLE (1864), and BENTONVILLE (1865). The Confederate Army of Tennessee should not be confused with its principal opponent, the Union Army of the Tennessee, created October 16, 1862, and commanded successively by Gens. ULYSSES S. GRANT, WILLIAM T. SHERMAN, JAMES B. MCPHERSON, JOHN A. LOGAN, and OLIVER O. HOWARD. The Union Army of the Tennessee was mustered out of service on August 1, 1865, having served in the winter campaign in northern Mississippi in 1862, the VICKSBURG campaign of 1863, the ATLANTA campaign of 1864, Sherman's MARCH TO THE SEA (1864–65), and the Carolinas campaign of 1865.

Army of the Cumberland • a CIVIL WAR division of the Union army. Organized after FORT SUMTER and first commanded by GEORGE THOMAS, the army was reorganized as the ARMY OF THE OHIO in late 1861. Another Army of the Cumberland was organized under WILLIAM S. ROSECRANS in October of 1862, and fought in the battles of STONES RIVER (1862–63), CHICKAMAUGA, CHATTANOOGA (both 1863), NASHVILLE (1864), and others.

Army of the James • a force of 33,000 men led by Maj. Gen. JUDAH BENJAMIN at Bermuda Hundred, May 6–7, 1864, in conjunction with Gen. ULYSSES S. GRANT'S WILDERNESS TO PETERSBURG CAMPAIGN. The Union forces succeeded in driving Confederate brigades from the depot and cut the Richmond–Petersburg Railroad at Port Walthall Junction, Virginia.

Army of the Ohio • a Union CIVIL WAR military force, organized in October 1861 as the ARMY OF THE CUMBERLAND under the command of WILLIAM T. SHERMAN, and a month later reorganized as the Army of the Ohio under the command of Maj. Gen. DON CARLOS BUELL.

Army of the Potomac • a Union CIVIL WAR military force, that, under Maj. Gen. GEORGE B. MCCLELLAN attempted to take Richmond, Virginia, from the CONFEDERACY. He shipped the army, with all of its supplies and weaponry, to FORT MONROE in March 1862, and then began his PENINSULAR CAMPAIGN in June. Although the Army of the Potomac eventually repulsed Gen. ROBERT E. LEE'S ARMY OF NORTHERN VIRGINIA, Lee's forces held Richmond, and the Peninsular Campaign ended in failure. After the Union's defeat at CHANCELLORSVILLE, Gen. GEORGE G. MEADE assumed command of the Army in 1863 and accomplished what the Army of the Potomac's five previous leaders had been unable to manage: he defeated Robert E. Lee and his Army at GETTYSBURG.

Army of the Tennessee • see ARMY OF TENNESSEE.

Army Ordnance Center and School • a U.S. ARMY TRAINING AND DOCTRINE COMMAND activity, located at ABERDEEN PROVING GROUND, Maryland. It is the focal point for U.S. Army ordnance training and the development of ordnance organization, equipment, and doctrine. The installation occupies some 72,500 acres and employs some 3,600 military and 7,200 civilian personnel.

Army Ordnance Missile and Munitions School • a U.S. ARMY TRAINING AND DOCTRINE COMMAND activity at REDSTONE ARSENAL, Alabama, responsible for the training of U.S. Army missile and munitions training and the development of Army organization, equipment, and doctrine with respect to missiles and munitions.

Army Quartermaster Center and School • a U.S. ARMY TRAINING AND DOCTRINE COMMAND activity, at FORT LEE, Virginia. It is the focal point for U.S. Army quartermaster (supply) training and the development of quartermaster organization, equipment, and doctrine.

Army Rangers • small groups of soldiers trained to make surprise raids behind enemy lines. Although units called "Rangers" were operating in the U.S. West as early as 1670, and the Rangers commanded by Cap. Benjamin Church played a significant role in ending King Philip's War (1675–76), it was Maj. Robert Rogers who organized nine companies of colonists to fight for the British in the French and Indian War (1754–63) in 1756 and codified and developed the concept of such a military group. He published a list of twenty-eight common sense combat rules as well as a set of standing orders that stressed operational preparedness, security, and tactics. Rogers set up a training program for his ranger units, and, in June 1758, was using live-fire exercises. On June 14, 1775, the Continental Congress established six companies of expert riflemen—two in Pennsylvania, two in Maryland, and two in Virginia—the organization George Washington called the "Corps of Rangers." Francis Marion, known as the "Swamp Fox," had learned how to use swamps and forests for cover from the Cherokees, and he and his rangers terrorized the British in South Carolina using Native American techniques of surprise attack and sudden disappearance. The most famous rangers of the Civil War were those serving in the Confederate Army under Col. John S. Mosby, which began as a three-man scouting unit and grew to eight companies by 1865. There were rangers active in the Union Army as well, in particular Mean's Rangers, who captured Confederate Gen. James Longstreet's ammunition train and a portion of Mosby's Rangers. In 1942, the War Department decided to organize a unit of soldiers similar to the British Commandos and authorized the activation of the First U.S. Army Ranger Battalion, activated on June 19, 1942. They served with distinction in the campaigns of Northern Africa and the invasion of Italy. There were six Ranger battalions active in World War II that carried out dangerous missions in the Omaha Beach landings of the Normandy Invasion in 1944, fought through the difficult Central Europe Campaign, and engaged the Japanese in the Pacific theater in battles in the Philippines, rescuing 500 survivors of the Bataan Death March. Perhaps the most well-known Ranger outfit is Merrill's Marauders, named after its commander Brig. Gen. Frank Merrill, the U.S. ground unit charged with spearheading the mission behind enemy lines in Burma and the destruction of Japanese communications and supply lines. In 1944, this unit was merged with the 475th Infantry, and, in 1974, the 475th became the modern 75th Infantry Regiment. In 1950, as a result of their successes, airborne Ranger infantry became an integral part of every U.S. infantry division. Numerous units of the Army Rangers have fought in all the major wars and conflicts of the United States, including Korea, Vietnam, and the Persian Gulf War. Most notable, however, was the failed attempt to rescue the Iran hostages in 1980, a mission carried out by the 1st Battalion of the 75th Infantry. In 1984, the Department of the Army recognized the effectiveness of its Ranger Battalions by increasing the size of the active duty force and establishing a Ranger Regimental Headquarters.

Army Reorganization Act • **1** (1866) an act passed by Congress on July 28, 1866, after the Civil War, to allocate six regiments, the 9th and 10th Cavalry and the 38th, 39th, 40th, and 41st Infantry Regiments, for enlisted black men. It signified the first inclusion of black units in the regular army. Commissioned officers of black units were predominately white. Around 1870 the Cheyenne began calling the 10th Regiment the "Buffalo" soldiers, a name that eventually referred also to the infantrymen. **2** (1950) a law passed to reorganize and coordinate the army after World War II and in response to the National Security Act of 1947 and the Joint Chiefs of Staff, which was initialized in 1947. It recognized Infantry, Artillery, and Armor as components of the army, allowed the Army General Staff to expand, and increased the responsibilities of the secretary of the army.

Army Satellite Communications Agency • an agency of the U.S. Army created at Fort Monmouth, New Jersey, in 1962 that limited the participation of the U.S. Army, as an organization, to ground terminals and providing ground support for space systems, both functions that it continues to perform.

Army School of the Americas • an army training school for U.S. and Latin American military personnel, located at Fort Benning, Georgia. In 1946, it was established as the Latin American Training Center-Ground Division at Fort Amador, Panama, and in 1950 it was moved to Fort Gulick and renamed The U.S. Army Caribbean School. It received its current name in 1963 and was moved to Fort Benning in 1984. Closed in December 2000 because of public protests over atrocities committed in South and Central America by its graduates, it reopened in January 2001 under the name Western Hemisphere Institute for Security Cooperation. Its official academic language is Spanish.

Army Signal Center and School • a U.S. Army Training and Doctrine Command activity, located at Fort Gordon, Georgia, the focal point for U.S. Army signal training and the development of signal organization, equipment, and doctrine. The installation, which occupies some 55,597 acres, employs some 11,000 military and 4,700 civilian personnel.

Army Signal Corps • created in 1860, when the Army adopted Maj. Albert Myer's visual communications system. In 1863, Congress authorized the regular Signal Corps for the remainder of the Civil War. In addition to visual signaling, the Corps became responsible for the electric telegraph in 1867, and, in 1870, was authorized by Congress to establish a national weather service. By 1907, an Aeronautical Division had been established under the command of the Chief Signal Officer, and the Corps assumed responsibility for Army aviation until 1918, when it became the Army Air Service. Numerous technological innovations in radio and telegraph communications came out of the Corps's laboratories at FORT MONMOUTH in the early years of the twentieth century, and the Corps remains the "information manager" of the U.S. Army.

Army Soldier Support Institute • (**USASSI**) established in July 1973 at Fort Benjamin Harrison, Indiana, as the U.S. Army Administration Center, a U.S. ARMY TRAINING AND DOCTRINE COMMAND activity given its current name in August 1984 and that underwent several reorganizations before moving to FORT JACKSON, South Carolina, in September 1995. USASSI integrates the training and doctrinal development activities of the U.S. Army Adjutant General, Finance, and Recruiting and Retention Schools, the U.S. ARMY NON-COMMISSIONED OFFICERS ACADEMY, and the U.S. Army element of the SCHOOL OF MUSIC.

Army Special Forces • founded at FORT BRAGG, North Carolina, in June 1952 as the SPECIAL FORCES GROUP, the U.S. Army organization recruited, trained, and equipped to carry out special warfare operations. Also called the GREEN BERETS.

Army Staff College • a postgraduate army service school at FORT LEAVENWORTH, Kansas. Established in 1904 as the second year course offered by the General Service and Staff College, it admitted the most distinguished graduates of the INFANTRY AND CAVALRY SCHOOL. It became the ARMY COMMAND AND GENERAL STAFF COLLEGE in 1928.

army surplus • goods and equipment that are in excess of the army's requirements: *an army surplus store.*

Army Training and Doctrine Command Analysis Center • (**TRAC**) the center responsible for providing relevant, credible analysis to assist in computer-modeling and decision-making for the U.S. ARMY TRAINING AND DOCTRINE COMMAND, the Department of the Army, the Office of the Secretary of Defense, the Joint Staff, and the commanders in chief of the unified commands, headquartered at FORT LEAVENWORTH, Kansas.

Army Training Center • a U.S. ARMY TRAINING AND DOCTRINE COMMAND activity responsible for basic training of Army enlisted personnel and some advanced individual training.

Army Transportation Center and School • a U.S. ARMY TRAINING AND DOCTRINE COMMAND activity, located at FORT EUSTIS, Virginia, the focal point for U.S. Army transportation training and the development of transportation organization, equipment, and doctrine. The installation, occupies some 8,228 acres and employs some 9,300 military and 4,100 civilian personnel.

Army Transport Service • a fleet of warships organized under the U.S. Army in late 1898 as an integral part of the Army Quartermaster Department. It was alternatively expanded and contracted according to needs until 1942, when it was absorbed into the Army's TRANSPORTATION CORPS.

Army, U.S. • the principal land force of the United States, entrusted with defending the country and preserving peace. The first regulary fighting force was the **Continental army**, founded June 14, 1775, to replace local militias. The DEPARTMENT OF THE ARMY is organized as part of the DEPARTMENT OF DEFENSE and is headed by the Secretary of the Army.

Army War College • a postgraduate senior service school at CARLISLE BARRACKS, Pennsylvania. It grants the degree of Master of Strategic Studies. Founded in 1901 in Washington, D.C. by Secretary of War ELIHU ROOT, it was closed in 1940 and reestablished in 1950 at Fort Leavenworth. It moved to Carlisle Barracks in 1951.

Army Warrant Officer Career Center • this center, located at Fort Rucker, Alabama, is responsible for the education, training, and professional development of U.S. Army warrant officers and the development of related doctrine and management procedures.

Arnhem • during OPERATION MARKET-GARDEN (September 1944), a town on the lower Rhine in the eastern Netherlands where 16,500 British paratroopers from the 1st Airborne Division and 3,500 glider-borne troops sought to seize bridges from remnants of Germany's 9th and 10th SS PANZER Divisions (Garden), while the American 82nd and 101st Airborne divisions captured bridges between Eindhoven and Veghel (Market). The American effort succeeded (with about 3,500 casualties), but because the British Guards Armoured Division could not reinforce the 1st Airborne quickly enough, the paratroopers were forced to withdraw. About 1,000 were killed in the battle, 2,000 escaped, and 6,000 were taken prisoner.

Arnhem was the Germans' first big success since the invasion of NORMANDY in June 1944.

Arnold, Benedict (1741–1801) • REVOLUTIONARY WAR general and traitor, born in Norwich, Connecticut. With ETHAN ALLEN, he captured FORT TICONDEROGA in 1775. He was wounded in a failed assault on Quebec late that same year. Arnold was appointed military governor of Philadelphia in 1778 and was soon charged with corruption and reprimanded in a court-martial, after which he resigned. He was given command of WEST POINT in 1780, claiming to be too lame and ill to take the active command GEORGE WASHINGTON planned for him. Arnold is infamous for his treasonous offer to British Gen. HENRY CLINTON to turn over West Point and 3,000 rebel troops in exchange for £10,000 for defection and £20,000 for the delivery of West Point. The mission misfired when go-between JOHN ANDRÉ was caught by American troops with compromising documents (he was later hanged). Arnold fled downriver, leaving his wife to convince Washington that she knew nothing of the plot. In New York, where his wife later joined him, he was shunned by British officers as a traitor. He saw service in the British army as a brigadier general, routing the Virginia militia in 1780 and sacking and burning New London, Connecticut, in 1781.

Arnold also volunteered in three campaigns of the FRENCH AND INDIAN WAR (1754–63), but deserted to be with his dying mother.

Arnold, Henry Harley (**"Hap"**) (1886–1950) • aviation pioneer and general, born in Gladwyne, Pennsylvania. As chief of the Army Air Force, he oversaw expansion of ARMY AIR FORCES in WORLD WAR II. He joined the JOINT CHIEFS OF STAFF in 1942, and was promoted to four-star general in 1943 and to five-star general of the army in 1944. He was made the first general of the Air Force by special Act of Congress in 1949. As five-star general of the Army, he directed B-29 operations of the Twentieth Air Force from his PENTAGON office, culminating in the atomic bombings of HIROSHIMA and NAGASAKI (1945). Arnold's greatest contribution was in orchestrating the creation of the world's largest air force and leading it to victory. Under his aegis in World War II the Army Air Forces grew from 22,000 men and 3,900 aircraft to 2.5 million personnel and 63,715 planes arrayed in 243 combat groups.

Aroostook War • (February–May 1839) a border conflict between the United States and Canada concerning disputed territory in the valley of the Aroostook River between Maine and New Brunswick. Maine farmers and Canadian lumbermen both sought to use the land, and each asked its government for military backing. Gen. WINFIELD SCOTT was sent with a small detachment and worked with the governor of Maine and the lieutenant governor of New Brunswick to calm tensions until the dispute could be settled. The boundary was defined by the WEBSTER-ASHBURTON TREATY of 1842.

ARPA • see DEFENSE ADVANCED RESEARCH PROJECTS AGENCY.

ARPAnet • a network of computers, organized in the 1960s by the DEPARTMENT OF DEFENSE, that linked U.S. scientific and academic researchers. It was the forerunner of today's Internet.

array • *n.* an arrangement of troops.

Arrears Act of 1879 • a measure passed in January 1879 to increase pensions for Union CIVIL WAR veterans. It called for the payment of pensions to the disabled from the date of discharge from the army, instead of from the time of the last claim. Political pressure from union veterans and the GRAND ARMY OF THE REPUBLIC helped enact the law. By 1880 it had nearly doubled prior annual pension expenditure.

arrival • *n.* slang (WORLD WAR I) the sound of an approaching shell.

arsenal • *n.* **1** a collection of weapons and military equipment stored by a country, person, or group: *Britain's nuclear arsenal.* **2** a place where weapons and military equipment are stored or made.

arsenal of democracy • a term used to describe the role played by American industry during WORLD WAR II, in which the United States outproduced both Germany and Japan by almost twofold and equipped not only the world's largest navy and air force and one of the world's largest armies but also contributed significantly to the arming of America's allies, particularly Great Britain and the Soviet Union.

Arthur, Chester Alan (1829–86) • 21st president of the United States (1881–85); born in Fairfield, Vermont. Vice president under James A. Garfield, Arthur took office upon Garfield's assassination (1881). Arthur endorsed creation of a modern navy and signed two bills authorizing construction of the nation's first steel ships. He was denied Republican renomination in 1884.

In the CIVIL WAR, Brig. Gen. Arthur was appointed acting quartermaster general of New York, given the complex task of feeding, housing, clothing, and equipping thousands of troops pouring into New York City on their way to combat.

Articles for the Government of the Navy • a code of military law passed by the Continental Congress in 1800, after an expansion of the U.S. Navy, to govern discipline and justice in the navy. It replaced the 1799 *Act for the Government of the Navy,* which followed the 1775 *Rules for the Regulation of the Navy of the United Colonies.* After another naval expansion during the CIVIL WAR, the articles were revised and remained in effect as amended through WORLD WAR II. In 1950 military law for all of the armed forces was combined in the UNIFORM CODE OF MILITARY JUSTICE.

artificer |är'tifisər| • *n.* a skilled mechanic in the armed forces.

artificial daylight • illumination of an intensity greater than the light of a full moon on a clear night.

artificial moonlight • illumination of an intensity between that of starlight and that of a full moon on a clear night.

artillery • *n.* (pl. **-ies**) **1** large-caliber guns used in warfare on land: *tanks and heavy artillery* | *artillery shells.* **2** a military detachment or branch of the armed forces that uses such guns: *two regiments of field artillery.*

DERIVATIVES: **artillerist** *n.* **artilleryman** *n.*

Artillery School of Practice • an army service school at Fortress Monroe, Virginia. Established in 1824, it became the model for the subsequent army service schools, including the SCHOOL OF APPLICATION FOR INFANTRY AND CAVALRY, established in 1882, and the U.S. ARMY COMMAND AND GENERAL STAFF COLLEGE, established in 1946.

ARVN • an English acronym for the army of South Vietnam during the VIETNAM WAR, abbreviating Army of the Republic of Vietnam. See also NATIONAL LIBERATION FRONT, VIETCONG.

ASAT |'a,sæt| • *abbr.* antisatellite weapon.

Asboth, Alexander Sandor (1811–68) • Union army officer and diplomat, born in Keszthely, Hungary. In the CIVIL WAR, he was a brigadier general of volunteers and commanded a division at PEA RIDGE (1862). He fought at CORINTH (May 1862) under Gen. JOHN POPE's army of the Mississippi. As commander of the District of West Florida in

1863, headquartered at Fort Pickens, Asboth sought to recruit regiments from among the pro-Union whites and freedmen of the area. He was badly wounded (his left arm and cheekbone were shattered) during a reconnaissance near Marianna, Florida, in September 1864, and he never fully recovered. He was minister resident to the Argentine Republic (1866–68) after traveling to Paris in the hopes of finding surgeons who could remove the bullet lodged in his neck. Several operations were unsuccessful.

ASCM • *abbr.* antiship cruise missile.

asdic |ˈæzˌdik| (also **ASDIC**) • *n.* chiefly Brit. an early form of sonar used to detect submarines. ORIGIN: World War II: acronym from *Allied Submarine Detection Investigation Committee.*

ASETF • *abbr.* air and space expeditionary task force.

A Shau Valley • a valley in the Thua Thien Hue Province, Vietnam, that was of strategic importance during the VIETNAM WAR. Known as "Death Valley" by the helicopter pilots of the 101st Airborne Division, the A Shau Valley was the site of numerous battles, including the infamous battle for HAMBURGER HILL (Hill 937) in June 1969.

Ashby, Turner (1828–62) • Confederate army officer, born in Fauquier County, Virginia. Brig. Gen. Ashby commanded the various cavalry units attached to Gen. STONEWALL JACKSON in the 1862 SHENANDOAH VALLEY campaign, where he was noted for daring but not for the discipline of his troops. A member of Jackson's staff observed that Ashby's "service to the army was invaluable, but had he been as full of discipline as he was of leadership his successes would have been more fruitful and his reputation still greater."

In 1861 Ashby disguised himself as an itinerant horse-doctor and traveled as far as Chambersburg, Pennsylvania, to get information on Union troops, positions, and planned movements.

Ashe, John (1720?-81) • Revolutionary army officer, born in the Albemarle Sound region of North Carolina. In the REVOLUTIONARY WAR, Ashe led a force of rangers that defeated the British at Moore's Creek Bridge, North Carolina. In a surprise British attack at Briar Creek, Georgia (March 3, 1779), Ashe's Georgians stood their ground until overwhelmed, while the North Carolinians broke and ran, some without having fired a shot. Ashe's defeat crushed the hopes of Lincoln and other patriots to recover Georgia and left the state firmly in British hands. This battle ended his career.

Ashe, John Baptista (1748–1802) • Revolutionary army officer, and member of the Continental Congress and U.S. Congress, born in Rocky Point, North Carolina. As a lieutenant in the New Hanover militia in North Carolina's WAR OF THE REGULATION (1768–71), he was captured and beaten by REGULATORS. He served at VALLEY FORGE during the harsh winter of 1777–78. As a lieutenant colonel under Maj. Gen. NATHANAEL GREENE, Ashe commanded a battalion at EUTAW SPRINGS (1781), where his unit's mauling of a British regiment drew praise from Greene.

Ashe's Island in North Carolina was named for John Baptista Ashe; Asheville, Asheboro, and Ashe County, North Carolina were all named for his father, Samuel Ashe.

Asiatic Fleet • the successor to the U.S. Navy's ASIATIC SQUADRON established in the 19th century, the U.S. Asiatic Fleet was commanded in December 1941 by Adm. Thomas C. Hart from headquarters in Manila. Assigned the mission of defending the Philippine Islands, the Asiatic Fleet consisted of one heavy and two light cruisers, thirteen old destroyers, twenty-nine submarines, six motor torpedo boats, and thirty-two amphibious aircraft as well as six gunboats and the 4th U.S. Marine Regiment recently transferred from China. Having suffered heavy losses in the operations following the Japanese INVASION OF THE PHILIPPINES on December 8, 1941, the remnants of the Asiatic Fleet were then withdrawn to Australia and the Dutch East Indies. The U.S. Asiatic Fleet was subsquently absorbed into the U.S. PACIFIC FLEET.

ASM • *abbr.* air-to-surface missile.

ASNE • *abbr.* American Society of Naval Engineers.

aspect change • the difference in appearance of an object viewed from various directions by radar.

Aspin, Les, Jr. (1938–95) • U.S. congressman and secretary of defense, born in Milwaukee, Wisconsin. Aspin was a policy analyst for Defense Secretary ROBERT S. MCNAMARA (1966–68); a U.S. congressman (1971–93); and the chairman of the House Armed Forces Committee (1985–93). The first defense secretary under President BILL CLINTON (1993–94), his brief term was troubled by controversies about the president's policy on gays in the military, the U.S. intervention in Somalia, and a BOTTOM UP REVIEW of defense structure and strategy.

ASROC • *abbr.* antisubmarine rocket.

assault • *n.* **1** the climax of an attack, closing with the enemy in hand-to-hand fighting. **2** in an amphibious operation, the period of time between the arrival of the major assault forces of the amphibious task force in the objective area and the accomplishment of the amphibious task force mission. **3** a phase of an airborne operation beginning with delivery by air of the assault echelon of the force into the objective area and extending through attack of assault objectives and consolidation of the initial airhead. • *v.* to make a short, violent, but well-ordered attack against a local objective, such as a gun emplacement, a fort, or a machine gun nest.

assault aircraft • an aircraft that delivers troops and/or cargo to the area of a military objective.

assault craft • a landing craft or amphibious vehicle used primarily to land troops and equipment during an amphibious assault.

assault fire • **1** the fire delivered by attacking

troops as they close with the enemy. **2** in artillery, extremely accurate, short-range destruction fire at point targets.

assault phase • **1** in an amphibious operation, the period of time between the arrival of the major assault forces of the amphibious task force in the objective area and the accomplishment of their mission. **2** in an airborne operation, a phase beginning with delivery by air of the assault echelon of the force into the objective area and extending through attack of assault objectives and consolidation of the initial airhead.

assault wave • a formation of forces, landing ships, craft, amphibious vehicles, or aircraft constituting the initial attack increment of an amphibious assault.

assembly • *n.* (pl. **-ies**) (usually **the assembly**) a signal for troops to assemble, given by drum or bugle.

assembly anchorage • an anchoring place for the assembly and routing of ships.

assembly area • **1** an area in which a command is assembled preparatory to further action. **2** in a supply installation, the gross area used for collecting and combining components into complete units, kits, or assemblies.

asset • *n.* any piece of materiel that can be deployed advantageously against an enemy, or if belonging to an enemy, whose destruction will result in an advantage.

Association of the United States Army • (**AUSA**) a private organization founded in 1950 by the merger of the Infantry and Field Artillery Associations, the purpose of which is to support the U.S. Army by providing information to the Congress and the public, lobbying for the passage of bills favorable to the Army and to both active and retired Army personnel, and generally facilitating the interaction of Army leaders with the civilian community.

astern • *adv.* **1** behind or toward the rear of a ship or aircraft: *the engine rooms lay astern.* **2** (of a ship) backward: *the lifeboat was carried astern by the tide.*

ASTOR • *abbr.* antisubmarine torpedo.

astronaut |ˈæstrəˌnôt| • *n.* a person who is trained to travel in a spacecraft.

ASW • *abbr.* antisubmarine warfare.

AT-1 • (**Snapper**) an antitank guided missile used by WARSAW PACT forces. It is a wire guided missile with a HEAT warhead capable of penetrating 380 millimeters of armor and a range of 2,000 meters.

AT-2 • (**Swatter**) a radio-guided antitank missile used by WARSAW PACT forces. It carries a HEAT warhead capable of penetrating 500 millimeters of armor, with a variable range of 500 to 4000 meters.

AT-3 • (**Sagger**) a wire-guided antitank missile used by WARSAW PACT forces. It carries a shaped-charge HEAT warhead capable of penetrating 400 millimeters of armor, with a variable range of 400 to 3000 meters.

ATF • *abbr.* amphibious task force.

Atkinson, Henry (1782–1842) • army officer, born in Person County, North Carolina. As a colonel in command of the 6th Infantry, he supervised construction of JEFFERSON BARRACKS, Missouri, the first army infantry school. He led the 6th Infantry against Sauks, Mesquakies, and Kickapoos in the BLACK HAWK WAR in Illinois and Wisconsin (1832).

Atlacatl Battalion • the first Salvadoran unit trained by the U.S. ARMY'S SPECIAL FORCES advisors early in 1981, a counter-insurgency group deployed on search-and-destroy missions, a key element in President RONALD REAGAN's drive to ensure the ability of El Salvador's military to suppress rebellions. It was commanded by Lt. Col. Domingo Monterrosa, well known as a rabid fighter and directly responsible for the slaughter of 733 Salvadoran peasants at El Mozote in December 1981. Salvadorans called the battalion "The Yankees' Battalion."

Atlanta, Battle of • (June 22, 1864) a CIVIL WAR battle in which Gen. JOHN B. HOOD's Confederate forces gained the rear of Union army Maj. Gen. WILLIAM T. SHERMAN's left flank and launched a coordinated attack with troops assaulting from before the lines. The vicious battle resulted in heavy casualties on both sides and forestalled the fall of Atlanta, which was held by beseiged Confederates until evacuated on September 2, 1864.

Atlanta Campaign • (May 1–September 8, 1864) the name given to the series of engagements fought by Union forces in Gen. WILLIAM T. SHERMAN's march across Georgia. The march was an attempt to destroy the Confederate ARMY OF TENNESSEE, initially under Gen. JOSEPH E. JOHNSTON, replaced in July by the more aggressive Gen. JOHN B. HOOD. Sherman was unable to achieve his main objective, though he did capture Atlanta, among other distinctions. The campaign ended when Hood headed west and Sherman began his MARCH TO THE SEA across Georgia and South Carolina.

Atlantic, Battle of the • (1941–45) the general name given to military maritime activities in the Atlantic during WORLD WAR II. It was primarily an ongoing effort to keep open supply lines to the British Isles by thwarting German surface and submarine raiders' attempts to sink cargo and troop transports. The German surface threat was essentially eliminated soon after the United States became a belligerent, but their submarines continued to present a threat throughout most of the war.

Atlantic Charter, the • a declaration of post-WORLD WAR II aims issued by British Prime Minister WINSTON CHURCHILL and U.S. President FRANKLIN D. ROOSEVELT on August 14, 1941, prior to U.S. entry into the war. It was created during a five-day conference held between the two men aboard ship in the North Atlantic. It was the predecessor of the UNITED NATIONS DECLARATION.

Atlantic Command • see U.S. ATLANTIC COMMAND.

Atlantic Fleet • see MAJOR FLEET.

Atlantic Torpedo Flotilla • a fleet of seven of the U.S. Navy's largest destroyers, the *Whipple* (D-15, the flagship of the Torpedo Flotilla), the *Truxtun* (D-14), the *Stewart*

(D-13), the *Lawrence* (D-8), the *Hull* (D-7), the *Hopkins* (D-6), and a tender ship, the *Arethusa*, chosen to accompany the GREAT WHITE FLEET for the first part of its cruise, from Norfolk, Virginia, to San Francisco. The ships were detached from the Fleet at San Francisco and redesignated the Pacific Torpedo Flotilla. In 1919, they were all decommissioned and sold.

Atlantic Wall • name given by ADOLF HITLER to the series of German-built fortifications stretching some 1,670 miles along the Atlantic coast of Europe from the Netherlands to Spain. The wall was a key part of Hitler's defenses, but failed to stop the Allied landings in NORMANDY in June 1944.

Atlas • the first intercontinental ballistic missile built by the United States, tested in 1958 and deployed in 1959. See also MINUTEMAN.

atmosphere • *n.* the air enveloping the earth.

atom bomb (also **atomic bomb**) • a bomb that derives its destructive power from the rapid release of nuclear energy by fission of heavy atomic nuclei, causing damage through heat, blast, and radioactivity. In such a bomb two pieces of a fissile material are brought together by a conventional explosion to form a super critical mass. Neutrons then cause an uncontrolled fission chain reaction that quickly releases large amounts of energy.

Atomic Energy Commission • (**AEC**) a U.S. federal agency created by the Atomic Energy Act of August 1, 1946, charged with controlling the development and manufacture of nuclear weapons and overseeing the research and development of peaceful uses of nuclear energy. It assumed control of the nation's nuclear program when it replaced the Manhattan Engineer District of the U.S. ARMY CORPS OF ENGINEERS on December 31, 1946. Headed by a five-member board, the Commission used most of its resources to develop and produce weapons during the late 1940s and early 1950s, but also built a few small nuclear-power plants, primarily for research. After the Atomic Energy Act was revised in 1954 to allow private industry to construct nuclear reactors for the production of electric power, and under the direction of GLENN T. SEABORG, the AEC's chairman from 1961 to 1971, commercially profitable nuclear facilities proliferated during the 1970s. In 1974, the U.S. government, recognizing the conflict of interest between the AEC's military and civilian commitments—regulating the nuclear industry in order to insure the health and safety of the U.S. public on the one hand, and supporting military uses of nuclear weapons on the other—disbanded the AEC in the Energy Reorganization Act of 1974 and split its functions between the Nuclear Regulatory Commission, which regulates the nuclear-power industry, and the Energy Research and Development Administration, which oversaw the development of nuclear weapons by the military. The latter agency was dissolved in 1977 and its function taken up by the newly created DEPARTMENT OF ENERGY.

atomic war • a war involving the use of nuclear weapons.

atrocity |ə'träsitē| • *n.* (pl. **-ies**) an extremely wicked or cruel act, typically one involving physical violence or injury: *forces were reported to have committed* ***atrocities against*** *the civilian population | war atrocities.*

attach • *n.* **1** the placement of units or personnel in an organization where such placement is relatively temporary. **2** the detailing of individuals to specific functions where such functions are secondary or relatively temporary.

attack aircraft carrier • (**CV** or **CVN**) a warship that supports and operates aircraft, attacks targets on land or water, and supports other military forces.

attack cargo ship • (**LKA**) a ship designed or converted as a transport for combat-loaded cargo in an assault landing. Its speed, armament, ability to carry landing craft, as well as the size of its hatches and booms are greater than comparable cargo ships.

attack carrier striking force • a naval force that has as its most important weapon carrier-based aircraft. Other ships protect and screen carriers from submarine, air, and surface threats.

attack group • a subordinate task organization of the navy forces of an amphibious task force. It is composed of assault shipping and supporting naval units designated to transport, protect, land, and initially support a landing group.

attention • *n.* **1** a position assumed by a soldier, standing very straight with the feet together and the arms straight down the sides of the body: *the squadron* ***stood to attention*** *when we arrived | midshipmen standing* ***at attention.*** **2** an order to assume such a position.

attitude • *n.* the position of a body as determined by the inclination of the axes to some frame of reference.

Attlee, Clement Richard (1883–1967) • British statesman. As Labour prime minister (1945–51), Attlee replaced Churchill midway through the POTSDAM CONFERENCE (1945), attended also by President HARRY S. TRUMAN and JOSEF STALIN, and established Britain as a close ally with the United States early in the cold war confrontation with the Soviet Union.

attrit • *v.* (**attritted, attritting**) informal wear down (an enemy) by sustained action.

attrition • *n.* the reduction of the effectiveness of a force caused by loss of personnel and materiel.

attrition and exhaustion, strategy of • a strategy emphasizing the gradual and often indirect erosion of the enemy's military power and will to resist. Such a strategy may be adopted when a nation is unable or unwilling to apply the force necessary to achieve its objectives through annihilation of the enemy but risks high casualties and materiel losses and a protracted war, either of which may be politically unacceptable.

attrition reserve aircraft • aircraft purchased specifically to replace anticipated losses in peacetime and/or during wartime.

augmentation forces • combat forces transferred from a supporting commander to a combat commander in order to strengthen the combatant forces or the operational control of such forces while executing an operation order already approved.

Augur, Christopher Colon |'ôgər| (1821–98) • Union army officer, born in Kendall, New York. In mid-January 1863 Augur took command of a three-brigade division at Baton Rouge, a force of reserve troops backing NATHANIEL P. BANKS's campaign (May–July 1863) to capture PORT HUDSON on the Mississippi. With 3,000 men, Augur advanced from Baton Rouge and beat the Confederates in a battle at Plains Store on May 21, then led assaults on PORT HUDSON from the south as Banks struck from the north. After a six-week siege, the garrison surrendered on July 9.

Aurora • a hypersonic reconnaissance aircraft (replacing the canceled SR-71 BLACKBIRD spyplanes) rumored to be a project of the Lockheed Advanced Development Co. ("the SKUNK WORKS") for the U.S. Air Force still being secretly developed at Groom Dry Lake (AREA 51) in the Nevada desert. This project has come to be called "Aurora" because that name appeared below the SR-71 and U-2 aircraft in the PENTAGON's 1985 budget request, but, if this were the aircraft's name at the time, it has since been changed to maintain secrecy.

AUSA • *abbr.* Association of the United States Army.

Auschwitz |'owsнvits| • a Nazi concentration camp in World War II, near the town of Oświęcim (Auschwitz) in Poland.

automatic • *adj.* (of a firearm) self-loading and able to fire continuously until the ammunition is exhausted or the pressure on the trigger is released. • *n.* a gun that continues firing until the ammunition is exhausted or the pressure on the trigger is released.

automatic pilot • a feature of a flight control system that provides altitude stabilization with respect to internal references.

Automatic Secure Voice Communications Network • (**AUTOSEVOCOM**) a worldwide, switched, secure voice network developed to fulfill the long-haul, secure voice requirements of the DEPARTMENT OF DEFENSE.

automatic throttle • a feature of a flight control system that actuates an aircraft throttle system based on its own computation and feedback from appropriate data sources.

Automatic Voice Network • (**AUTOVON**) a major subsystem of the Defense Switched Network, which replaced the Automatic Voice Network as the principal long-haul, nonsecure voice communications network within the DEPARTMENT OF DEFENSE's communications system.

autonomous operation • in air defense, the mode of operation assumed by a unit after it has lost all communications with higher echelons. The unit commander assumes full responsibility for control of weapons and engagement of hostile targets.

AUTOSEVOCOM • *abbr.* Automatic Secure Voice Communications Network.

AUTOVON • *abbr.* Automatic Voice Network.

auxiliary • *adj.* (of troops) engaged in the service of a nation at war but not part of the regular army, and often of foreign origin. • *n.* **1** (**auxiliaries**) troops engaged in the service of a nation at war but not part of the regular army, and often of foreign origin. **2** a naval vessel with a supporting role, not armed for combat.

auxiliary force • a force established to back up or reinforce regular forces already engaged in combat or to undertake combat or support functions which regular forces cannot or do not wish to undertake, such as scouting, handling supplies, or policing rear areas.

AV-8 • see HARRIER.

AV-8B • see HARRIER II.

avast • *exclam.* stop; cease: *you, young man, avast there!*

ORIGIN: early 17th cent.: from Dutch *hou'-vast, houd vast* 'hold fast!'

AVC • *abbr.* American Veterans Committee.

Averell, William Woods (1832–1900) • Union army officer, born in Cameron, New York. Averell was noted more for training and organizing troops than for aggressiveness in combat. Averell's most successful venture in the war came when he led West Virginia volunteers in a series of cavalry raids directed at Confederate strongholds in the SHENANDOAH VALLEY, in particular a raid against the Virginia and Tennessee Railroad depot in Salem, Virginia (December 1863), in which, with small loss to his own force, his troopers captured 200 prisoners and 150 horses and destroyed a large quantity of enemy supplies.

On September 22, 1864, while Averell was under the command of Maj. Gen. PHILIP H. SHERIDAN, Sheridan's forces drove the Confederates off Fisher's Hill. When Sheridan learned that Averell's cavalry had gone into camp that night instead of supporting the infantry's fifteen-mile chase, Sheridan summarily dismissed Averell, who struggled for twenty-four years to prove that Sheridan's dismissal was politically motivated. In 1888 he was reinstated in the Army by special act of Congress and placed on the retired list.

---

aviation • *n.* the flying or operating of aircraft: *the aviation industry* | *aviation engineering.*

aviation ship • a nuclear or non-nuclear aircraft carrier. See also AIR-CAPABLE SHIP.

aviator • *n.* dated a pilot.

AWACS |'ā,wæks| • **1** a long-range airborne radar system for detecting enemy aircraft and missiles and directing attacks on them. **2** an aircraft equipped with this radar system.

ORIGIN: 1960s: acronym from *airborne warning and control system.*

aweigh • *adj.* (of an anchor) raised just clear of the sea or riverbed.

AWOL |'ā,wôl| • absent from where one should be but without intent to desert.

ORIGIN: 1920s: acronym from *absent without (official) leave.*

axis of advance • a line of advance assigned for purposes of control; often a road or a group of roads, or a designated series of locations, extending in the direction of the enemy.

Axis Powers • name given to the alliance of Germany, Italy, Japan, Romania, Bulgaria, and Hungary before and during WORLD WAR II. The name is taken from the 1936 treaty between Germany and Italy which formed the so-called "Rome-Berlin Axis".

Ayres, Romeyn Beck (1825–88) • Union artillery officer, born in Montgomery County, New York. Ayres was a captain of artillery at FIRST BULL RUN (1861) and was the chief of artillery in the PENINSULAR and MARYLAND campaigns (both 1862). He was also the chief of artillery for the 6th Army Corps at FREDERICKSBURG (1862). He suffered heavy losses at GETTYSBURG (1863) and was sent to quell New York City draft riots. In May and June 1864, Ayres's brigade was heavily engaged and suffered severe losses in the battles of the WILDERNESS, SPOTSYLVANIA, and COLD HARBOR; in a month the brigade's losses numbered more than 2,000.

azimuth • *n.* direction, expressed in degrees or mils of a circle computed from true or magnetic North (0° or 0 mils) and increasing in a clockwise direction.

AZON • *abbr.* Azimuth Only, denoting a guidance system for vertical bombs used in WORLD WAR II. In clear weather one bombardier could guide up to five VB-1 Azon bombs at once.

Bb

B-1B • see LANCER.

B-2 • see STEALTH BOMBER.

B-2A • see SPIRIT.

B-10 • an all-metal monoplane bomber developed for the U.S. Army by the Glenn L. Martin Company of Baltimore in the mid1930s. It was used for coastal defense around the United States mainland and also by Army bombardment squadrons until the development of the B-17.

B-17 • see FORTRESS.

B-17B • see FORTRESS.

B-17C • see FORTRESS.

B-24 • see LIBERATOR.

B-25 • see MITCHELL.

B-26 • see MARAUDER.

B-29 • see SUPERFORTRESS.

B-36 • a series of bomber aircraft developed in the late 1940s by Convair that was the largest bomber ever built at that time. It had six retractable gun turrets and carried a normal crew of fifteen. It was phased out by the mid-1950s, to be replaced by B-52s.

B-45 • the first operational jet bomber to be used by the U.S. Air Force, starting in 1948. It was also the first bomber to allow air refueling and the first jet bomber to carry a nuclear payload. It was completely phased out by the end of the KOREAN WAR.

B-47 • (**Stratojet**) a jet bomber developed for the Air Force by Boeing in the late 1940s that was the mainstay of the medium-bombing strength of the STRATEGIC AIR COMMAND all throughout the 1950s. It carried a crew of only three but was difficult to land. Improvements in training eventually enhanced its safety record. It was completely phased out by the mid-1960s.

B-52 • see STRATOFORTRESS.

B-57 • see CANBERRA.

B-58 • see HUSTLER.

B-66 • see SKYWARRIOR.

B-70 • (**Valkyrie**) an experimental long-range strategic bomber, first developed in the 1950s, that was originally planned to be the replacement for the B-52. Because of its high cost and vulnerability to SAMs, the aircraft never went into production and was completely phased out even as a research project by the late 1960s.

Babcock, Orville Elias (1835–84) • soldier, engineer, and presidential secretary, born in Franklin, Vermont. Babcock graduated third in his class at the U.S. MILITARY ACADEMY in 1861. He fought at the siege of VICKSBURG (1863). In 1865, he was an aide to Gen. ULYSSES S. GRANT, was wounded, and was responsible for selecting Wilmer McLean's house as the site of Gen. ROBERT E. LEE's surrender at APPOMATTOX COURT HOUSE.

As Grant's secretary, Babcock was involved in several controversies, including exceeding his authority on a trip in 1869 to the Dominican Republic and returning with a treaty of annexation.

---

back • *v.* **1** supplement in order to reinforce or strengthen: *U.S. troops were* ***backed up*** *by forces from European countries.* **2** (of the wind) change direction counterclockwise around the points of the compass: *the wind had backed to the northwest.* The opposite of VEER. **3** put (a sail) aback in order to slow the vessel down.

backchannel *adj.* • held or done in secret or indirectly, often concerning sensitive information; clandestine: *backchannel negotiations.*

backfire bomber • the Western designation for a long-range Soviet aircraft (TU-22) capable of performing nuclear strikes as well as conventional attacks and antiship and reconnaissance missions. It is capable of in-flight refueling with modification. It was considered a threat against the contiguous United States on high-altitude subsonic missions, and against European and Asian targets with its low-altitude supersonic dash capabilities. It was first developed in the 1960s and remains in use today in Russia and some other former Soviet countries.

back-scattering • *n.* radio wave propagation in which the direction of the incident and scattered waves, resolved along a reference direction (usually horizontal), are oppositely directed.

A signal received by back-scattering is often referred to as a **back-scatter**.

backsight • *n.* the sight of a rifle or other weapon that is nearer the eye.

backstay • *n.* a stay on a sailing ship leading downward and aft from the top or upper part of a mast.

backup aircraft authorization • additional aircraft authorized over and above primary aircraft in order to insure that primary aircraft can receive scheduled and unscheduled maintenance, modifications, inspections, and repair without reducing the number of aircraft available for operational missions. There are no operating funds allocated for such aircraft in the Defense budget. See also PRIMARY AIRCRAFT AUTHORIZATION.

backup aircraft inventory • the specific aircraft designated to fill the backup authorization. See also PRIMARY AIRCRAFT INVENTORY.

backup force • an organized military force prepared to back up or reinforce units already engaged in a military operation.

backwash • *n.* **1** the motion of receding waves. **2** a backward current of water or air created by the motion of an object through it.

backwind • *v.* (of a sail or vessel) deflect a flow of air into the back of (another sail or vessel). • *n.* a flow of air deflected into the back of a sail.

Bacon's Rebellion • (1676) a civil revolt in Virginia that sprang from colonial disagreement over response to an Indian uprising. Nathaniel Bacon (1647–76), a member of the Virginia Council, organized forces that violated Gov. Sir WILLIAM BERKELEY's orders and took indiscriminate offensive actions against neighboring Indian tribes, friendly or otherwise. When Berkeley removed Bacon from his council seat, Bacon's forces marched on Jamestown, burned it, and drove Berkeley out of town. The rebellion ended following Bacon's death from dysentery. After the episode, British regulars were stationed permanently in the colony.

Bad Aibling • site in southern Germany of a U.S.-operated ground station for control and downlink of communications intelligence satellites.

Badeau, Adam |bəˈdō| (1831–95) • Union army officer and author, born in New York City. As a lieutenant colonel, he was military secretary to ULYSSES S. GRANT (1864–65). Badeau wrote a three-volume *Military History of Ulysses S. Grant* (1868, 1881) with Grant's full cooperation. When Grant decided to write his own memoirs, Badeau, fearing rightly that this would hurt the sales of his own works on Grant, offered to work as a research assistant (though he appears to have desired greater credit) for the general's memoirs in 1884 and 1885, for $10,000. Grant severed their working relationship when newspapers accused him of letting Badeau write the manuscript. After Grant's death, Badeau sued for the remainder of his fee and won, going on to write a history of Grant's administration, *Grant in Peace, from Appomattox to Mount McGregor* (1887).

badge • *n.* a distinctive emblem worn as a mark of office, membership, achievement, licensed employment, etc.

Badge of Military Merit • see PURPLE HEART.

baggage train • a train of vehicles, used to carry baggage, especially following an army: *the trail made by Custer's baggage train is to this day a well-known landmark.*

Bailey, Ann Hennis Trotter (1742–1825) • frontier scout and REVOLUTIONARY WAR spy, born in Liverpool, England. In 1791, Bailey singlehandedly saved FORT LEE (now Charleston, West Virginia) from certain destruction by hostile Indians with a three-day, 200-mile round trip to obtain resupply of gunpowder from Fort Savannah. She was known to the Shawnee as "the White Squaw of the Kanawha" and to settlers as "Mad Ann Bailey" because she supposedly knew no fear.

Bailey bridge • a temporary bridge of lattice steel designed for rapid assembly from prefabricated standard parts, used especially in military operations.

ORIGIN: World War II: named after Sir D. Bailey (1901–85), the English engineer who designed it.

Bailey, Joseph (1825–67) • Union army officer and military engineer, born probably in Pennsville, Ohio. During the RED RIVER CAMPAIGN (1864), Bailey ingeniously conceived and directed a ten-day, 3,000-man construction of a dam across the Red River near Alexandria, Louisiana, permitting Rear Adm. DAVID D. PORTER's thirty-three-vessel fleet to pass.

Bailey, Theodorus (1805–77) • U.S. Navy rear admiral, born at Chateaugay near Plattsburg, New York. Considered one of the ablest naval commanders during the CIVIL WAR, Bailey was second in command under Adm. DAVID FARRAGUT of the attacking force against Fort Jackson, New Orleans (1862), and was sent ashore by Farragut to demand New Orleans's surrender. In 18 months, his ships captured 150 Confederate blockade runners off the Florida coast.

The U.S. Navy has named three ships USS *Bailey* after him: a torpedo boat (1899–1918), and two destroyers, the USS *Bailey*: (1919–40) and (1942–46).

Baird, Absalom (1824–1905) • Union army officer and inspector general of the army, born in Washington, Pennsylvania. In the CIVIL WAR, under Gen. WILLIAM T. SHERMAN in the ATLANTA CAMPAIGN, Baird personally led the charge of a brigade at JONESBORO (September 1, 1864), routing the entrenched Confederates and ensuring Union victory, for which he was awarded the Confederate MEDAL OF HONOR in 1896.

Baker, Edward Dickinson (1811–61) • Union army officer, born in London, England. As a political associate and longtime friend of President ABRAHAM LINCOLN, Baker introduced Lincoln at the presidential inauguration in March 1861. In the CIVIL WAR, he was nominated by Lincoln as brigadier general in the U.S. Volunteers and given command of the California Regiment. He was killed in action at BALL'S BLUFF on the Potomac River.

The Lincolns held such regard for Baker that they named their second son Edward in his honor.

Baker, Newton Diehl (1871–1937) • secretary of war during WORLD WAR I. The Reform mayor of Cleveland (1912–16), and a member of the AMERICAN UNION AGAINST MILITARISM, he was chosen by President WOODROW WILSON as secretary of war. Baker's support for the draft was important in convincing antimilitarist associates that it was necessary in a war for democracy.

Bakers Creek, Battle of • see CHAMPION HILL.

balance • *n.* the ability of a boat to stay on course without adjustment of the rudder.
PHRASES: **balance of power 1** a situation in which nations of the world have roughly equal power. **2** the power held by a small group when larger groups are of equal strength.

Balangiga massacre • massacre of a U.S. infantry company during an insurrection by Filipino guerrillas on September 28, 1901, at Balangiga, Samar, the Philippines. The massacre provoked swift and brutal retribution by U.S. Brig. Gen. JACOB H. SMITH and Brig. Gen. JAMES FRANKLIN BELL. To destroy the Filipino resistance, Bell arrested all local Filipino officials, moved the entire population into garrisoned enclaves dubbed "concentration camps," and began large-scale operations in the countryside that did not cease until the insurrection leader, Gen. Miguel Malvar, surrendered on April 16, 1902.

balisage • *n.* the nighttime marking of a route with dim lighting to maintain blackout conditions.

ball • *n.* for small arms ammunition, a solid core bullet for use against targets not requiring armor-piercing or incendiary capability.

ballast • *n.* **1** heavy material, such as gravel, sand, iron, or lead, placed low in a vessel to improve its stability. **2** a substance of this type carried in an airship or on a hot-air balloon to stabilize it, and jettisoned when greater altitude is required. • *v.* (usually **be ballasted**) give stability to (a ship) by putting a heavy substance in its bilge: *the vessel has been ballasted to give the necessary floating stability.*
PHRASES: **in ballast** (of a ship) laden only with ballast.

ball cartridge • a rifle cartridge intended for use against personnel and light armored targets with competition or sniper rifles.

Ball, George Wildman (1909–94) • lawyer, diplomat, and undersecretary of state, born in Des Moines, Iowa. As President JOHN F. KENNEDY'S undersecretary of state, Ball promoted the European Economic Community and did not have the confidence ROBERT S. MCNAMARA, MCGEORGE BUNDY, and DEAN RUSK had in the U.S. involvement in Vietnam. He issued dire and accurate predictions but failed to dissuade President LYNDON B. JOHNSON from escalating U.S. involvement.

ballistic • *adj.* of or relating to projectiles or their flight.
DERIVATIVES: **ballistically** *adv.*

ballistic missile • a missile with a high, arching trajectory, that is initially powered and guided but falls under gravity onto its target.

Ballistic Missile Defense Organization • a DEPARTMENT OF DEFENSE organization in charge of the Ballistic Missile Defense Program and established to implement the missile defense program set forth in the BOTTOM-UP REVIEW. It traces its history back to the STRATEGIC DEFENSE INITIATIVE program begun in 1983 by President RONALD REAGAN. It received its current name on May 13, 1993.

ballistic missile early warning system • an electronic system for providing detection and early warning of attack by enemy intercontinental ballistic missiles.

ballistics • *n.* **1** the science of projectiles and firearms. **2** the study of the effects of being fired on a bullet, cartridge, or gun.

ballistics, external • the branch of applied physics which deals with the actions and characteristics of missiles or projectiles in flight.

ballistics, internal • the branch of applied physics which deals with the actions and characteristics of missiles or projectiles as they are expelled from the barrel of the propelling weapon.

ballistics, terminal • the branch of applied physics which deals with the actions and characteristics of missiles or projectiles as they approach the target.

ballistic trajectory • the trajectory (of a missile, etc.) traced after the propulsive force is terminated and the body is acted upon only by gravity and aerodynamic drag.

balloon |bəˈlo͞on| • *n.* a large bag filled with hot air or gas to make it rise in the air, typically carrying a basket for passengers: *a hot-air balloon.*
PHRASES: **when** (or **before**) **the balloon goes up** informal when (or before) the action or trouble starts. *we've got to get our man out of there before the balloon goes up.*

Ball's Bluff, Battle of • (sometimes also known as **Balls Bluff**) (October 21, 1861) a repulsed Union attempt to cross the Potomac River into Virginia. The Union brigade under Col. EDWARD BAKER landed on the Virginia shore but was met by Confederate Gen. NATHAN EVANS's troops. The Union brigade, unable to maintain a defensive line, was forced to evacuate after losing about half its strength and its commander. Confederate losses were less than ten percent.

ball turret • a rotating aircraft gun turret in the shape of a ball, usually mounted on the belly of an aircraft and enclosing the gunner.

Baltimore Affair • see CHILEAN CRISIS.

BAMBI |'bæmbē| • *abbr.* ballistic missile boost interceptor, a late 1950s idea for a missile defense system in which satellite-launched, hit-to-kill rockets would home in on the heat of enemy missiles in the boost phase and destroy them within five minutes of launching. See also NIKE ZEUS.

BAMBI overlapped with the Nike-Zeus program, and was canceled in 1968.

Bancroft, Edward (1744–1821) • physician, scientist, spy, and double agent, born in Westfield, Massachusetts. During the REVOLUTIONARY WAR, Bancroft, sympathetic to the colonies' cause, was recruited as a spy for Americans. He was officially employed as a "secretary" for the American delegation in Paris, but also spied for British secret service, mainly for money. Bancroft often used his inside information to profit in the stock market.

Bancroft, George (1800–91) • navy secretary, scholar, and diplomat, born in Worcester, Massachusetts. As the secretary of the navy under President JAMES K. POLK (1845–46), Bancroft was a founder of the U.S. NAVAL ACADEMY at *Annapolis* and tried to streamline the navy department. Bancroft was instrumental in the acquisition of California, ordering the Pacific Naval Squadron in June 1845 to occupy San Francisco and other ports in case of war.

banderole |'bændə,rōl| (also **banderol**) • *n.* a long, narrow flag with a cleft end, flown at a masthead.

bandit • *n.* (pl. **bandits** or **banditti** |bæn'ditē|) **1** a robber or outlaw belonging to a gang and typically operating in an isolated or lawless area. **2** slang an enemy aircraft.
DERIVATIVES: **banditry** |-trē| *n.*

bandolier |,bændə'lir| (also **bandoleer**) • *n.* a shoulder-belt with loops or pockets for cartridges.

Bangalore torpedo |,bæNGgə'law(ə)r tawr'pēdō| • a tube containing explosives used by infantry for blowing up wire entanglements or other barriers.

Banks, Nathaniel Prentiss (1816–94) • congressman and Union general, born in Waltham, Massachusetts. In the CIVIL WAR, Maj. Gen. Banks arrived in New Orleans in December 1862 with orders to help reopen the Mississippi River and pacify the local Confederates infuriated by the administration of the radical BENJAMIN BUTLER. Banks captured PORT HUDSON (July 9, 1863) after a six-week siege and heavy losses that could have been avoided had he been quicker in following orders to coordinate with ULYSSES S. GRANT, who was busy besieging VICKSBURG.

banquette |bæNG'ket| • *n.* a raised step behind a rampart.

banzai attack • a suicidal infantry assault, usually associated with the Japanese in WORLD WAR II.

baptism of fire • a soldier's first battle; by extension any first encounter with a dangerous or difficult situation.

BAR • *abbr.* Browning automatic rifle.

Barbary pirates • North African sea raiders sponsored by the governments of Morocco, Algiers, Tunis, and Tripoli in the late 18th and early 19th century. The seizure of American ships by the so-called Barbary pirates led first to the payment of tribute by the U.S. government, but in the first years of the 19th century the fledgling U.S. Navy was sent into the Mediterranean Sea to cooperate with other nations in suppressing the pirates, which was done by 1815. The efforts of the U.S. Navy and Marine Corps to suppress the Barbary pirates were generally weak and ineffective but were very popular at home and produced a lasting impact on popular patriotic culture, including the line in the MARINE CORPS HYMN, "...to the shores of Tripoli...."

Barbary Wars • (1801-5, 1815), armed naval conflicts with the Barbary States of Morocco, Algiers, Tunis, and Tripoli. After losing the benefits of British naval protection, the United States agreed to pay tribute to the Barbary States for passage into and through the Mediterranean. Seizures of American sailors and vessels in attempts to collect ransom led to both conflicts. An American siege of Tripoli from 1803 to 1805 produced a reinstatement of the status quo ante, which did not solve the problem from the American perspective. Action during this period was marked by the first use of marines in 1804. In 1815, ten ships under Commodore STEPHEN DECATUR seized the Algerian flagship, freed American hostages, and exacted a new treaty establishing America's right of safe passage in the Mediterranean. (The first conflict is also known as the **Tripolitan War**; the second, the **Algerine War.**)

barbed wire • wire with clusters of short, sharp spikes set at intervals along it, used to make fences or in warfare as an obstruction.

Barber, Francis (1750–83) • Revolutionary army officer, born in Princeton, New Jersey. Barber was a lieutenant colonel (later colonel) in command of the 3rd New Jersey Regiment, served as deputy adjutant general for the Western (Gen. JOHN SULLIVAN's) army, served under Gen. NATHANAEL GREENE at WEST POINT, and as an aide-de-camp to Gen. LAFAYETTE at the siege of YORKTOWN (1781).

Barber was on his way to pick up his wife for a visit with Martha Washington when a tree fell on him and killed him instantly.

---

barbette |bär'bet| • *n.* **1** a fixed armored housing at the base of a gun turret on a warship or armored vehicle. **2** a platform on which a gun is placed to fire over a parapet.

barge • *n.* **1** a flatbed vessel capable of navigating in shallow water. It has no structures on its surface, and is used to transport cargo, ships' supplies, or for general utility purposes, typically on canals and rivers, either under its own power or towed by another. **2** a boat used by the chief officers of a warship.

bargeman • *n.* a person in charge of or employed on a barge.

bargemaster • *n.* the person in charge of a barge, either self-propelled or non-self-propelled, or of a collection of barges.

bargepole • *n.* a long pole used to propel a barge and fend off obstacles.

bark • *n.* (also **barque**) a sailing ship, typically with three masts, in which the foremast and mainmast are square-rigged and the mizzenmast is rigged fore-and-aft.

barkentine | 'bärkən,tēn | (Brit. **barquentine**) • *n.* a sailing ship similar to a bark but square-rigged only on the foremast.

Barksdale, William (1821–63) • Confederate army officer and U.S. congressman (1852–60), born in Rutherford County, Tennessee. In the CIVIL WAR, Barksdale was colonel (eventually brigadier general) of the 13th Mississippi Infantry Regiment at FIRST BULL RUN (1861) and in the PENINSULAR CAMPAIGN (1862). He led the attack on MALVERN HILL (1862), carrying the flag when his standard bearer fell. With STONEWALL JACKSON at ANTIETAM (1862), Barksdale's regiment sustained heavy casualties; they made courageous stands at FREDERICKSBURG (1862) and CHANCELLORSVILLE (1863). He fought alongside JAMES LONGSTREET at GETTYSBURG (1863) and died on CEMETERY RIDGE.

Barlow, Francis Channing (1834–96) • Union army officer and New York secretary of state (1865), born in Brooklyn, New York. Barlow was lieutenant colonel of the 61st New York Volunteer Infantry in the PENINSULAR and SEVEN DAYS' campaigns (1862). As brigadier general, Barlow commanded the 1st Division, 2nd Corps in the Virginia campaigns of 1864, leading an assault on the Confederate salient known as the "BLOODY ANGLE" (May 12, 1864), an attack resulting in more than 5,000 Confederate casualties, most of whom were captured. He was brevetted major general (August 1, 1864) for his conduct at the Bloody Angle, at COLD HARBOR (1864), and during the PETERSBURG TO RICHMOND CAMPAIGN (1864). After Gen. ROBERT E. LEE's surrender (1865), Barlow was promoted to major general.

Barnard, John Gross (1815–82) • Union army officer, military engineer, and Superintendent of WEST POINT (1855–56), born in Sheffield, Massachusetts. In the CIVIL WAR, Barnard was appointed by ULYSSES S. GRANT as chief engineer of the armies in the field. He finished the war as a brevet major general and colonel in the Corps of Engineers; he was also the author of *A Report on the Defenses of Washington* (1871). During the Civil War, Barnard built the defenses of Washington, D.C., encompassing Washington, Georgetown, and Alexandria, and consisting of sixty forts and ninety-three batteries, totaling 25,799 yards, with 35,711 yards of infantry covered way and emplacements for 1,447 guns—one of the great engineering feats of American military history.

Barnes, James (1801–69) • Union army officer, born in Boston, Massachusetts. Barnes was the colonel of the 18th Massachusetts Infantry in the PENINSULAR, BULL RUN, and MARYLAND campaigns (1861–62). He was promoted to brigadier general of volunteers in 1862 and commanded a brigade in the Fifth Corps at FREDERICKSBURG (1862) and CHANCELLORSVILLE (1863). At GETTYSBURG (1863), Barnes led his division into the "wheatfield" on July 2, where it saw severe fighting.

Barnes, Joseph K. (1817–83) • U.S. Army medical officer and surgeon general, born in Philadelphia, Pennsylvania. In the CIVIL WAR, Barnes was favored by war secretary EDWIN M. STANTON and was promoted to brigadier general (1864) and appointed surgeon general (1864–82). He sought to protect the Army Medical Department from congressional cutbacks. Barnes attended President ABRAHAM LINCOLN after he was shot (1865), and he made the official announcement of the president's death; he struggled to save President JAMES A. GARFIELD (1881), also assassinated.

Barney, Joshua (1759–1818) • Revolutionary War naval officer, born in Baltimore, Maryland. In 1794 President GEORGE WASHINGTON nominated him one of six captains in the new navy. Disappointed at being ranked only third, Barney declined the nomination and instead accepted a commission in the French navy. He returned to the United States in 1802. Early in the WAR OF 1812, on a ninety–day privateer cruise, he captured four ships, eight brigs, three schooners, and three sloops valued at over $1.5 million. He defended the Chesapeake Bay area, then joined the ill-fated defense of Washington, D.C., at the BATTLE OF BLADENSBURG (1814).

Barnitz, Albert Trorillo Siders | 'bärnits | (1835–1912) • Union army officer and poet, born at Bloody Run, Bedford County, Pennsylvania. In the CIVIL WAR, Barnitz commanded the 2nd Ohio Cavalry; in the PLAINS INDIANS WARS (1854–90), he was the captain and company commander of the 7th Cavalry against the *Cheyenne* Indians of the Central Plains. Barnitz was brevetted a full colonel for distinguished gallantry in Gen. GEORGE ARMSTRONG CUSTER's charge on BLACK KETTLE's Cheyenne village on the Washita (1868).

In the Civil War, under Gen. George Armstrong Custer, Barnitz led the 2nd Ohio Cavalry in taking Confederate arms and prisoners near APPOMATTOX and wrote a twenty-five-stanza epic poem, "With Custer at Appomattox," which he often read at veterans' meetings. His initial adulation of Custer turned to contempt, and in May 1867 he wrote "(Custer) spares no effort to render himself generally obnoxious" and added, "He is the most complete example of a petty tyrant that I have ever seen."

Barnwell, John (c. 1671–1724) • colonial agent, militiaman, Indian fighter, born in Ireland. As a colonel in the Tuscarora War (1711–12), Barnwell led the South Carolina expedition of 1711–12 to quell the uprising, earning a reputation as South Carolina's foremost Indian fighter and the nickname "Tuscarora Jack." As a representative of the colony in London (1720), he convinced the Board of Trade to accept South Carolina as a royal colony. He constructed Fort King George on the Altamaha River at Darien, the (sands biblical) beginning of the state of Georgia.

barquentine • *n.* British spelling of BARKENTINE.

barrack • *v.* (often **be barracked**) provide (soldiers) with accommodations in a building or set of buildings: *the granary in which the platoons were barracked.*

barracks • *n.* a large building or group of buildings used to house soldiers.

barrage |bə'räzh| • *n.* a concentrated artillery bombardment over a wide area.

barrage, aerial • a barrier of barrage balloons put up as a defense against air attack.

barrage balloon • a large balloon anchored to the ground by cables and typically with netting suspended from it, serving as an obstacle to low-flying aircraft in the vicinity of a military installation or a city. They were first used toward the end of WORLD WAR I to protect London against German bombers.

barrage, box • a curtain of artillery fire laid down in the shape of a box to impede enemy movements and protect friendly troops.

barrage, electronic • intensive jamming of enemy radio or radar frequencies or other electronic emissions so as to disrupt enemy communications and electronic surveillance.

barrage jamming • simultaneous electromagnetic jamming over a broad band of frequencies.

barrel • *n.* a tube forming part of a gun: *I saw two flashes from the barrel of the gun.*
PHRASES: **with both barrels** informal with unrestrained force or emotion.

Barrel Roll, Operation • the campaign of bombing in Laos in the VIETNAM WAR, approved in December 1964 on the recommendation on the JOINT CHIEFS OF STAFF. It was intended to disrupt critical supply trains and infiltration routes of the VIETCONG.

barricade • *n.* another term for AIRCRAFT ARRESTING BARRIER.

barrier combat air patrol • one or more divisions or units of fighter planes used to create a barrier, across a probable direction from which an enemy attack might come, between a force and a target area. The divisions are deployed as far from the attacking force as control conditions permit, and provide additional protection against attacks that use the most direct approach paths.

barrier forces • all air, surface, and submarine units and their supporting systems that have been positioned in order to provide early detection and warning regarding the most likely route of enemy forces as well to block their progress and destroy them.

barrier minefield • a minefield laid to protect a friendly position by blocking an enemy attack or forcing the attacker into certain areas where he can be more effectively engaged.

Barringer, Rufus (1821–95) • Confederate army officer, born in Cabarrus County, North Carolina. As a captain in the 1st North Carolina Cavalry, he served in the PENINSULAR, SECOND BULL RUN, ANTIETAM, FREDERICKSBURG (all 1862), and CHANCELLORSVILLE (1863) campaigns. As a brigadier general, he received Gen. ROBERT E. LEE's compliments for a rout at REAM's (1864). During the war, Barringer participated in seventy-six actions, had two horses shot from under him, and was wounded three times.

When Barringer was captured near PETERSBURG (1865), he was introduced to President ABRAHAM LINCOLN, who, as a former fellow congressman with Barringer's brother, wrote a note requesting special consideration.

Barry, John (1745?–1803) • ship captain and REVOLUTIONARY WAR naval hero, born in County Wexford, Ireland. Barry is considered the patriarch of the American navy. He was appointed the senior captain of the U.S. Navy when it was created by Congress in 1794. In the Americans' first naval victory in the Revolutionary War, Barry, captain of the brig *Lexington,* captured the British sloop *Edward* near the Virginia Capes (1776). Congress awarded him command of its finest vessel, *Alliance* (1780), which he used to capture many British ships. During the QUASI-WAR WITH FRANCE (1798) he commanded the frigate *United States,* flagship of the West Indies squadron.

Barry, William Farquhar (1818–79) • Union army officer, born in New York City. Barry was the coauthor (with HENRY J. HUNT and WILLIAM H. FRENCH) of *Instruction for Field Artillery* (1860), which was widely used in both the Union and Confederate ranks. He was chief of artillery for the ARMY OF THE POTOMAC and the chief of artillery under Gen. WILLIAM T. SHERMAN in the ATLANTA CAMPAIGN (1864).

Barton, Clara (1821–1912) • CIVIL WAR nurse, relief worker, and founder of the AMERICAN RED CROSS, born Clarissa Harlowe Barton in North Oxford, Massachusetts. Barton tended wounded Union soldiers and ran medical supply lines at ANTIETAM, FREDERICKSBURG (both 1862), the WILDERNESS campaign (1864), and other battles. Barton publicized the work of the International Red Cross, lobbied tirelessly for Senate ratification of the GENEVA CONVENTIONS (signed in 1882), and was the American National Red Cross's first president (1882–1904).

Clara Barton was an early feminist; in her work as a teacher and clerk at the Patent Office, she demanded—and got—pay equal to what men in the same position were getting.

Barton, William (1748–1831) • Revolutionary army officer, born in Warren, Rhode Island. Barton planned and led an abduction raid of a British general from Newport,

Rhode Island (1777), for which he was thanked by Congress, promoted to lieutenant colonel, and presented with a ceremonial sword. He later served as an aide-de-camp to Gen. NATHANAEL GREENE.

base • *n.* **1** a locality from which operations are projected or supported. **2** an area or locality containing installations that provide logistic or other support. **3** a home airfield or home carrier.

base altitude • an altitude maintained during a given aerial mission especially on the flight to the target or aerial assembly point.

base camp • a camp from which expeditions or other activities set out or from which they can be carried out.

base command • an area containing a military base or group of such bases organized under one commander.

base defense • the local military measures, both normal and emergency, required to nullify or reduce the effectiveness of enemy attacks on, or sabotage of, a base, to ensure that the maximum capacity of its facilities is available to friendly forces.

base fuze • a fuze located in the base of a projectile or bomb.

base hospital • a military hospital situated at some distance from the area of active operations during a war.

base line • **1** in surveying, a surveyed line established with more than usual care, to which surveys are referred for coordination and correlation. **2** in photogrammetry, the line between the principal points of two consecutive vertical air photographs, usually measured on one photograph after the principal point of the other has been transferred. **3** in radio navigation systems, the shorter arc of the great circle joining two radio transmitting stations of a navigation system. **4** in triangulation, the side of one of a series of coordinated triangles the length of which is measured with prescribed accuracy and precision and from which lengths of the other triangle sides are obtained by computation.

base of operations • an area or facility from which a military force begins its offensive operations, to which it falls back in case of reverse movement, and in which supply facilities are organized.

base pay • the annual or monthly compensation (salary) due military personnel on the basis of rank and length of service, exclusive of allowances (for quarters, rations, etc.), specialty pay (for aviation duty, diving, parachuting, etc.), combat service, or other extra pay.

base point • in gunnery, a well-defined point on the terrain which is used as a reference point for direction and range.

basic intelligence • fundamental intelligence concerning the general situation, resources, capabilities, and vulnerabilities of foreign countries or areas that may be used as reference material in the planning of operations at any level and in evaluating subsequent information relating to the same subject.

basic load • the quantity of supplies required to be on hand within, and which can be moved by, a unit or formation. The basic load is expressed according to the wartime organization of the unit or formation and maintained at the prescribed level.

basic (military) training • instruction given to new recruits to provide them with essential military knowledge and skills (dismounted drill, the use of weapons, first aid, field craft, etc.).

basin • *n.* an enclosed area of water where vessels can be moored: *a yacht basin.*

basket case • informal a person or thing regarded as useless or unable to cope.
ORIGIN: early 20th cent.: originally slang denoting a soldier who had lost all four limbs, thus unable to move independently.

basket leave • an informal procedure whereby an officer planning to be away from his assigned post or station on a weekend or holiday is permitted to submit to his commander a signed but otherwise blank leave form. If the officer returns to his assigned post or station on time, the leave form is destroyed and the officer is not charged for leave taken. If the return of the officer is delayed, the commander fills in and approves the leave form and the officer is charged for the appropriate number of days of leave.

bastion |ˈbæsCHən| • *n.* a projecting part of a fortification built at an angle to the line of a wall, so as to allow defensive fire in several directions.

Bastogne • town in Belgium, near the border with Luxembourg. In WORLD WAR II, during the BATTLE OF THE BULGE (1944–45) it was held by the 101st U.S. Airborne division against overwhelming German bombardment, until relieved by the U.S. 3rd Army. Nearby there are several military cemeteries and a monument to fallen U.S. soldiers.

Bataan, Battle of • (December 1941–April 1942) a defeat of U.S. forces attempting to withstand the Japanese INVASION OF THE PHILIPPINES at the beginning of WORLD WAR II. On December 24, 1942, Gen. DOUGLAS MACARTHUR ordered U.S. troops to withdraw to the Bataan Peninsula and Corregidor Island, which he believed defensible until reinforced. Over the following two weeks, more than 80,000 made it to the peninsula. Supply shortages led to malnutrition and disease, but the Americans managed to hold a stable line by the end of January. American forces were unable to send help, however, and President FRANKLIN D. ROOSEVELT ordered MacArthur to escape, which he did on March 11, 1942. A Japanese offensive begun on April 3 led to the unconditional surrender of the remaining U.S. forces on April 9.

Bataan Death March • (April 1942) the ruthless forced march of American and Filipino POWs to Japanese prison camps after the fall of Bataan. Some 75,000 surviving defenders of Bataan, most of them ill and severely malnourished, were marched approximately 60 miles to a rail center where they were sent to their ultimate destinations. The Japanese were unprepared to deal with such numbers, and their commanders tolerated any cruelty exercised on the captives, including execution for falling out of line, regardless of reason. Some 600 to 700 Americans died before reaching the camp, as did 5,000 to 10,000 Filipinos. Thousands more died in the camps.

Bate, William Brimage (1826–1905) • Confederate general, governor, and U.S. senator, born in Bledsoe's Lick (now Castalian Springs), Tennessee. Bate served in the MEXICAN WAR (1846–48) as a first lieutenant in the 3rd Tennessee Volunteer Infantry and in the CIVIL WAR as a colonel in the 2nd Tennessee Volunteer Regiment. He was a division commander at MISSIONARY RIDGE (1863). In 1864 he was promoted to major general and fought with the ARMY OF TENNESSEE in the ATLANTA CAMPAIGN, and the FRANKLIN AND NASHVILLE that same year. A courageous front-line commander who reportedly had six horses killed under him, Bate declined the nomination for the governorship of Tennessee in June 1863, saying that while an armed force threatened Tennessee, he would rather defend his state than govern it. He was eventually elected governor in 1882 and reelected in 1884.

bathyscaphe |ˈbæTHəˌskæf| • *n.* a manned submersible vessel of a kind used by the French deep-sea explorer Auguste Piccard (1884–1962).
ORIGIN: 1940s: coined in French by its inventor, from Greek *bathus* 'deep' + *skaphos* 'ship.'

bathysphere |ˈbæTHəˌsfir| • *n.* a manned spherical chamber for deep-sea observation, lowered by cable from a ship.
ORIGIN: 1930s: from Greek *bathus* 'deep' + *sphere*.

baton • *n.* a short stick or staff or something resembling one, in particular: **1** a long stick carried and twirled by a drum major. **2** a police officer's club. **3** a staff symbolizing office or authority, especially one carried by a field marshal.

battalion • *n.* a large body of troops ready for battle, especially an infantry unit forming part of a brigade typically commanded by a lieutenant colonel.

battalion landing team • (also **BLT**) in an amphibious operation, an infantry battalion normally reinforced by necessary combat and service elements; the basic unit for planning an assault landing.

battering ram • **1** a heavy object swung or rammed against a door to break it down. **2** a heavy beam, originally with an end in the form of a carved ram's head, used in breaching fortifications.

battery • *n.* (pl. **-ies**) **1** a fortified emplacement for heavy guns. **2** an artillery subunit of guns, men, and vehicles.

battle • *n.* **1** a sustained fight between large, organized armed forces: *the Battle of Shiloh* | *he died* ***in battle***. For battles not entered here, look under the placename or other identifier. For the *Battle of the Alamo*, see *Alamo, Battle of the*. **2** a lengthy and difficult conflict or struggle: *the battle over the future shape of Europe* | *the battle against aging*. • *v.* **1** fight or struggle tenaciously to achieve or resist something. **2** engage in a fight or struggle against.

Battle above the Clouds • see LOOKOUT MOUNTAIN, BATTLE OF.

battle casualty • any casualty incurred as the direct result of hostile action, sustained in combat or relating thereto or sustained going to or returning from a combat mission.

battlecruiser • *n.* a large warship of a type built in the early 20th century, carrying similar armament to a battleship but faster and more lightly armored.

battle cry • a word or phrase shouted by soldiers going into battle to express solidarity and to intimidate the enemy.

Battle, Cullen Andrews (1829–1905) • Confederate army officer, born in Powelton, Georgia. In the CIVIL WAR, as a lieutenant colonel in the 3rd Alabama Infantry, Battle was wounded at SEVEN PINES, participated in heavy fighting at SOUTH MOUNTAIN and ANTIETAM (all 1862), and was commended for "brilliant and valuable service" at GETTYSBURG (1863). Promoted to colonel, he and the 3rd Alabama were engaged in fierce fighting in the BATTLE OF THE WILDERNESS and at SPOTSYLVANIA (both 1864).

Battle Dress Uniform • the camouflage-patterned U.S. combat and fatigue uniform introduced in the 1970s.

battle drill • combat training exercises designed to replicate as nearly as possible the sights, sounds, and other sensory impacts of battle so as to accustom troops to combat conditions and to respond automatically in certain combat situations.

battle fatigue • combat fatigue; shell shock.

battlefield • *n.* the terrain on which a battle is fought.

battlefield illumination • the lighting of the battle area by artificial light, either visible or invisible to the naked eye.

battlefield surveillance • systematic observation of the battle area for the purpose of providing timely information and combat intelligence.

battle force • a permanent operational naval task force comprised of carriers, surface combatants, and submarines that are assigned to numbered fleets. These battle forces are divided into battle groups.

battle formation • the deployment of a military force in the relative positions which the commander intends that they should maintain upon entering combat.

battle group • **1** a permanent naval task force comprised of a carrier or a battleship, surface combatants, and submarines assigned as direct support and providing mutual support. These groups are expected to destroy enemy air, surface, and submarine forces that come within its operational area as well as to strike at targets on enemy shorelines and to provide covering firepower inland. **2** a military force created to fight together, typically consisting of several different types of troops.

Battle Hymn of the Republic • a CIVIL WAR-era hymn written in November 1861 for Union soldiers by Julia Ward Howe. She composed the lyrics after touring army camps near Washington, D.C., and hearing "John

Brown's Body." It was published in 1862 in *The Atlantic Monthly*, whose editor, James T. Field, is credited for naming the song. Its predecessors are "Say, Brothers, Will You Meet Us" (1858), "John Brown" (July 1861), and "Glory, Hallelujah" (July 1861), to which it was set and with which it was first printed in 1862.

battle jacket • a tailored waist-length woolen jacket that was formerly worn as part of the Army service uniform. Adaptations of it have appeared in civilian fashions.

battlement |ˈbætlmənt| • *n.* (usually **battlements**) a parapet at the top of a wall, usually of a fort or castle, that has regularly spaced, squared openings for shooting through.

battle reserves • reserve supplies accumulated by an army, detached corps, or detached division in the vicinity of the battlefield, in addition to unit and individual reserves.

battleship • *n.* a heavy warship of a type built chiefly in the late 19th and early 20th centuries, with extensive armor protection and large-caliber guns.
ORIGIN: late 18th cent.: shortening of *line-of-battle ship*, originally with reference to the largest wooden warships.

battleship gray • a dull bluish gray that is the traditional color of U.S. battleships.

battle station • the place of duty of a member of a ship's crew during actual or simulated combat.

Bayard, Nicholas |ˈbāyərd| (1644–1711?) • alleged traitor, born in the Netherlands. Bayard, a former Dutch nationalist mayor of New York City under English rule (appointed 1685), was related to PETER STUYVESANT. He was a commanding officer of the New York County militia in LEISLER'S REBELLION (1689–91), during which he urged the governor to execute JACOB LEISLER, a militia captain and leader of the rebellion, under an act passed by the general assembly making it high treason to attempt to "disturb the peace, good, and quiet" of the government. Ironically, Bayard was sent to trial in 1702 on the same charge of high treason after he presented a petition to the Dutch Leislerian government (returned to power in 1701), accusing them of being corrupt and discriminating against the English. He escaped the gallows since the Leislerians were afraid to act decisively against him.

Bay of Pigs Invasion • (April 17–19, 1961) a CIA-sponsored invasion by 1,300 Cuban exiles of the Bahía de los Cochinos (Bay of Pigs), Cuba, intended to foment rebellion and overthrow of FIDEL CASTRO's communist regime, but crushed by 20,000 Cuban militiamen in a one-day battle. The long-planned covert operation, unanimously approved by the JOINT CHIEFS OF STAFF, was presented to President JOHN F. KENNEDY for authorization in his first week in office by CIA director ALLEN DULLES. Kennedy reluctantly gave the go-ahead, and the operation promptly fell apart. The president refused to authorize air support—the U.S. government supposedly was not involved—and most of the exiles were either killed or captured. The invasion provoked international outrage, humiliated the new president and intensified his determination to overthrow Castro, and led to the removal of Dulles from the CIA.

bayonet • *n.* **1** slang (in the CIVIL WAR and WORLD WAR I) a soldier. **2** a swordlike stabbing blade that may be fixed to the muzzle of a rifle for use in hand-to-hand fighting. • *v.* (**bayoneted, bayoneting**) stab (someone) with a bayonet.

bazooka • *n.* a short-range tubular rocket launcher used against tanks.

beach • *v.* run or haul up (a boat or ship) onto a beach: *crews would not beach for fear of damaging crafts.*

beach group • another term for SHORE PARTY.

beachhead • *n.* a defended position on a beach taken from the enemy by landing forces, from which an attack can be launched.
ORIGIN: WORLD WAR II (originally U.S.): formed on the pattern of *bridgehead*.

beach minefield • a minefield in the shallow water approaches to a possible amphibious landing beach.

beach party • the naval component of a shore party.

beach support area • in amphibious operations, the area of the rear of a landing force or elements thereof, established and operated by shore party units, which contains the facilities for the unloading of troops and materiel and the support of the forces ashore; it includes facilities for the evacuation of wounded, enemy prisoners of war, and captured materiel.

beacon • *n.* **1** a fire or light set up in a high or prominent position as a warning, signal, or celebration. **2** a light or other visible object serving as a signal, warning, or guide, especially at sea or on an airfield. **3** a radio transmitter whose signal helps to fix the position of a ship, aircraft, or spacecraft.

bead • *n.* a small knob forming the front sight of a gun.
PHRASES: **draw** (or **get**) **a bead on** take aim at.

beam • *n.* **1** the direction of an object visible from the port or starboard side of a ship when it is perpendicular to the center line of the vessel: *there was land in sight* ***on the port beam.*** **2** a ship's breadth at its widest point: *a cutter with a beam of 16 feet.* **3** the shank of an anchor. **4** a series of radio or radar signals emitted to serve as a navigational guide for ships or aircraft. • *v.* **1** transmit (a radio signal or broadcast) in a specified direction: *beaming a distress signal into space.*
PHRASES: **on her** (or **its**) **beam-ends** (of a ship) heeled over on its side; almost capsized.

beam rider • a missile guided by an electronic beam.

beam sea • a sea that is running at approximately right angles to a vessel's heading.

bear • *v.* (past **bore**; past part. **borne**) (of a vehicle or boat) convey (passengers or cargo).
PHRASES: **bear arms** carry firearms. **bring to bear** aim (a weapon): *bringing his rifle to bear on a distant target.* **bear off** change course away from the wind.

beat • *v.* (past **beat**; past part. **beaten** |ˈbētn|) sail into the wind, following a zigzag course with repeated tacking: *we beat southward all that first day.*

beaten zone • the area on the ground upon which the cone of fire falls.

Beatty, David (1871–1936) • British admiral in WORLD WAR I and first earl. Adm. Beatty led early naval operations in World War I and led a squadron against the German fleet in the BATTLE OF JUTLAND.

Beatty, John (1749–1826) • Revolutionary army officer and U.S. representative, born in Warwick, Pennsylvania. In the REVOLUTIONARY WAR Beatty was a major and company commander of the 5th Pennsylvania Battalion; he was captured at Fort Washington, Manhattan, in 1776 and exchanged in 1778. After his release, Beatty was promoted to colonel and named commissary general to supply the needs of captured enemy prisoners. For permitting trade with British, however, he was subjected to a general court-martial and reprimanded by GEORGE WASHINGTON (1780). He resigned that year.

Beauregard, Pierre Gustave Toutant |ˈbōri̦gärd| (1818–93) • Confederate general, born in St. Bernard Parish, Louisiana. Beauregard was the commander of the Department of South Carolina and Georgia and of the Military Division of the West; he was nicknamed "Old Bory." Beauregard is best known for having ordered the bombardment of FORT SUMTER; he received its surrender on April 14, 1861. He was promoted to full general after leading (with Gen. JOSEPH E. JOHNSTON) the Confederate victory at the battle of FIRST BULL RUN (1861).

Beaver Wars • (1640s–1680s), a series of conflicts between IROQUOIS and Algonquin tribes living near the Great Lakes. Involvement in the fur trade destabilized Native American cultures by introducing European diseases and by imparting economic stresses on natural resources. When demand for beaver furs led to the animals' being hunted out in traditional Iroquois land, tribal groups began expanding into Algonquin territories, leading to an escalating cycle of warfare.

becalm • *v.* (usually **be becalmed**) leave (a sailing vessel) unable to move through lack of wind.

Beckwith, Charles Alvin (1929–94) • SPECIAL FORCES officer and first commander of DELTA FORCE, born in Atlanta, Georgia. Beckwith was a U.S. ARMY RANGER, and a veteran of KOREA and VIETNAM, nicknamed "Chargin' Charlie." After many years of lobbying the army to establish an antiterrorist unit, Beckwith was promoted to colonel and given the go-ahead in the mid 1970s to form the DELTA FORCE, which he trained at FORT BRAGG, North Carolina. Lt. Col. Beckwith was the organizer of Delta Force counterterrorist Operation EAGLE CLAW (April 24, 1980), a complex, ill-fated, ultimately aborted attempt to rescue hostages held by Iranians at the American embassy in Teheran, in which eight U.S. servicemen died.

Bedaux, Charles Eugene |bəˈdō| (1886–1944) • scientific manager, entrepreneur, and fascist collaborator, born near Paris, France. In 1940 Bedaux became actively involved with NAZI rulers of France and the VICHY government; he was captured by the ALLIES in 1942 and brought to the United States for trial on charges of treason. He committed suicide in prison in Miami.

Beehive projectile • an anti-personnel projectile loaded with fléchettes and fired from an artillery piece or tank gun.

BEF • *abbr.* British Expeditionary Force.

before-flight inspection • a preflight check to ensure general aircraft safety and that disposable loads, including fuel, armament, and equipment, are stowed correctly.

before the wind |wind| • with the wind blowing more or less from astern.

belay |biˈlā| • *v.* **1** fix (a running rope) around a cleat, pin, rock, or other object, to secure it. **2** slang stop; enough!: *"Belay that, mister. Man your post."*

belaying pin • a pin or rod, typically of metal or wood, used on board ship to secure a rope fastened around it.

bell • *n.* (preceded by a numeral) the time as indicated every half hour of a watch by the striking of the ship's bell one to eight times: *at five bells in the forenoon of June 11.*

Bell 47 • (**H-13** or **HTL**) the first helicopter certified for nonmilitary service. As the H-13 military model, it was used by the U.S. Army as the first air ambulance during the KOREAN WAR. As the HTL, the U.S. Navy used it as a trainer helicopter.

bellbuoy |ˈbel̦bo͞oē; -̦boi| • *n.* a buoy equipped with a bell rung by the motion of the sea, warning nearby vessels of shoal waters.

Belleau Wood, Battle of • (June 6–26, 1918) an American victory in WORLD WAR I, and the Marine Corps' bloodiest battle to that date, fought against the Germans near Château Thierry, France. Assigned to clear a woodland and take the town of Bourches, a 2nd Division brigade began the battle by advancing in formation. With poor artillery support to offset the heavy automatic fire they were taking, the brigade continued to advance in small groups, engaging in hand-to-hand combat, and continued to press on until the woods had been cleared. Total casualties for the Marines were over 50 percent.

Belle Isle • a Confederate military prison in the James River at Richmond, Virginia. Belle Isle became a prison after FIRST BULL RUN (1861). There were no barracks, only tents designed to hold about 3,000 prisoners, although the prison eventually held more than twice that many. Belle Isle was in the middle of the rapids of the James River, making escape dangerous. Most who tried drowned.

belligerent • *adj.* engaged in a war or conflict, as recognized by international law: *a conference of socialists from all belligerent countries | both belligerent powers.* • *n.* a nation or person engaged in war or conflict, as recognized by international law: *ships and goods captured at sea by a belligerent | the movement of belligerents into threatening positions.*

DERIVATIVES: **belligerently** *adv.*

Bell, James Franklin (1856–1919) • brigadier general, born near Shelbyville, Kentucky. Bell wrote the first U.S. Army manual on the conduct of maneuvers. Bell was the commandant of the General Service and Staff College at FORT LEAVENWORTH and was appointed by President THEODORE ROOSEVELT as fourth chief of staff of the U.S. Army (1906). In the SPANISH-AMERICAN WAR (1898), Bell was chief of military intelligence for the PHILIPPINE EXPEDITIONARY FORCE (later VIII Corps), commanded the 36th Volunteer Infantry, and conducted negotiations with EMILIO AGUINALDO. He won the CONGRESSIONAL MEDAL OF HONOR near Porac, Luzon, Philippines (1899). In the guerrilla war that followed, as the army's premier counterinsurgency expert, Bell crushed Filipino resistance in the northern Philippines (1902).

Bell is also noteworthy for having convinced Roosevelt that the navy should locate its main Pacific base at PEARL HARBOR rather than in the Philippines.

Bell UH-1 • see IROQUOIS.

Belo, Alfred Horatio (1839–1901) • Confederate army officer and newspaper manager-publisher, born in Salem, North Carolina. In the CIVIL WAR, Belo was the organizer and captain of the Forsyth County Riflemen and commanded a battalion in the 55th North Carolina Regiment. He was one of the youngest Confederate colonels and was severely wounded at GETTYSBURG (1863) and COLD HARBOR (1864).

below decks (also **below, below deck**) • *adj.* & *adv.* in or into the space below the main deck of a ship: *the sleeping quarters were below decks | nuclear weapons stored below decks.* • *n.* (**belowdecks**) the space below the main deck of a ship.

Bemis Heights, Battle of • (also known as **Second Battle of Saratoga**) (October 7, 1777) a conclusive American REVOLUTIONARY WAR victory that resulted in the capture of more than 5,800 British troops, the first time this had happened on American soil. This battle was notable for the heroism displayed by Gen. BENEDICT ARNOLD. American troops led by Maj. Gen. HORATIO GATES repulsed British forces under Maj. Gen. JOHN BURGOYNE marching to push through the American line on Bemis Heights. Taking the fight to the enemy, the Americans successfully assaulted the British line, forcing them into a retreat toward Saratoga, where Burgoyne sought terms of surrender ten days later.

bend • *v.* attach (a sail or rope) by means of a knot: *sailors were **bending** sails **to** the spars.* • *n.* (**the bends**) decompression sickness, especially in divers.

Bendire, Charles Emil (1836–97) • Union army officer and naturalist, born Karl Emil Bender in Hesse-Darmstadt (now Germany). In the CIVIL WAR, Bendire was commissioned a second lieutenant in the 2nd Infantry (1864); he transferred to the 1st Cavalry, and was breveted first lieutenant "for gallant and meritorious services" at the battle of Trevilian Station, Virginia. He became a captain in 1873, and for most of his army life he served at isolated posts in the western territories. He retired in 1886; in 1890 he was breveted major for gallant services in an 1877 action against the NEZ PERCÉ at Canyon Creek, Montana.

Benjamin, Judah Philip (1811–84) • U.S. senator, Confederate cabinet member, and lawyer, born at Christiansted, St. Croix, West Indies. The first (acknowledged) Jew elected to the U.S. Senate (1852), Benjamin became known as "the brains of the Confederacy" by serving not only as its attorney general, secretary of war, and secretary of state, but also as a close adviser and confidant to President JEFFERSON DAVIS and Varina Howell Davis. As secretary of state, Benjamin arranged the ERLANGER LOAN from a Paris bank to the Confederacy (1863), the only significant European loan of the war, and drew up instructions for Confederate peace commissioners who met with President ABRAHAM LINCOLN and WILLIAM H. SEWARD at the HAMPTON ROADS CONFERENCE (1865).

Bennett, Floyd (1890–1928) • naval aviator, born at Truesdale Hill, Town of Caldwell (now Lake George), New York. As an enlisted pilot serving on the cruiser *USS Richmond* in 1925, he applied for and was assigned to the Navy-MacMillan expedition to Greenland (1925). Bennett was a winner of the DISTINGUISHED SERVICE MEDAL and the CONGRESSIONAL MEDAL OF HONOR, and was promoted to warrant officer by act of Congress. Bennett was chosen as pilot by Lt. Commander RICHARD E. BYRD for a flight to the North Pole (May 1926), with Byrd navigating, in a Fokker trimotor—a flight of 1,360 miles.

Bennett collapsed, suffering from double pneumonia, on a rescue flight to the Gulf of St. Lawrence. CHARLES LINDBERGH flew through a severe blizzard to bring him serum, but unfortunately it was the wrong kind for his type of pneumonia, and a few days later he died. In 1929, Byrd flew to the South Pole in a plane named the *Floyd Bennett* and at the pole they dropped an American flag from Bennett's grave.

Benning, Henry Lewis (1814–75) • Confederate army officer, born in Columbia County, Georgia. In the CIVIL WAR, Benning organized and was elected colonel of 17th Georgia Infantry; he fought in the PENINSULAR CAMPAIGN (1862). Benning was known as "Old Rock" for his tenacity as a field commander. Benning won praise for "coolness, courage, and skill" in holding his position at SECOND BULL RUN and at ANTIETAM (both 1862). Under Maj. Gen. JOHN B. HOOD at GETTYSBURG (1863), he dislodged Union forces from DEVIL'S DEN and and held ground against repeated counterattacks. Benning maintained high troop morale and had one of the lowest desertion rates in the army.

Bennington, Battle of • (August 16, 1777) an American victory in the REVOLUTIONARY WAR. New Hampshire militiamen under Brig.

Gen. JOHN STARK defeated and captured the majority of a large British expeditionary force. The force, with the goal of raiding the militia's stores in Bennington, Vermont, was detached from the main body of Maj. Gen. JOHN BURGOYNE's army.

Bent, George (1843–1918) • frontiersman, soldier, and Indian interpreter, born at Bent's Old Fort on the Arkansas River in present-day southeastern Colorado. In the CIVIL WAR, Bent fought with a Confederate cavalry regiment at PEA RIDGE (1862) and in EARL VAN DORN's campaigns in Arkansas and Mississippi. He was captured at the siege of CORINTH (1862) and paroled at St. Louis. Bent married BLACK KETTLE's niece, Magpie, in 1866 and was an interpreter for Black Kettle. After the Civil War, Bent went to live with fellow CHEYENNES (on his mother's side) in the upper Arkansas Valley. He was severely wounded in JOHN M. CHIVINGTON's attack at the SAND CREEK MASSACRE (1864) but escaped and later took part in numerous attacks on U.S. cavalry.

Bentley, Elizabeth Terrill (1908–63) • Communist party activist and government witness, born in New Milford, Connecticut. In the early 1940s, Bentley collected information from U.S. government employees in numerous agencies for two espionage rings; fearing Soviet reprisal, she provided the FBI with information and names. She testified at four trials, including that of JULIUS AND ETHEL ROSENBERG.

Bentonville, Battle of • a CIVIL WAR battle fought in March 1865 in Johnston County, North Carolina between Union forces under Gen. WILLIAM T. SHERMAN and Confederate forces under Gen. JOSEPH E. JOHNSTON. It was a victory for the Union and forced the Confederates to retreat to Raleigh, where Johnston later signed an armistice with Sherman, formally surrendering his army.

Bentonville, Battle of • (March 19-21, 1865), a series of encounters between Confederate troops under Gen. JOSEPH E. JOHNSTON and the left wing of Maj. Gen. WILLIAM T. SHERMAN's Union Army of Georgia near Bentonville, North Carolina. Several skirmishes were punctuated by direct attacks that never evolved into the decisive battle Johnston sought in order to keep Sherman's army from linking with ULYSSES S. GRANT's.

beret |bəˈrā| • *n.* a round flattish cap of felt or cloth.

Bergepanzer • WORLD WAR II-era German tank recovery vehicle. The Bergepanzer "PANTHER" (Sd. Kfz. 179), of which some 297 were built, was equipped for the recovery of armored vehicles of up to 50 tons. It was armed with a 20 mm gun and a 7.92 mm machine gun.

Bering Sea Patrol • in 1895, the Revenue Cutter Service officially established a Bering Sea Patrol under the command of Captain Calvin L. Hooper. Because the cutters became the only government known to those who lived in the Bering Sea and coastal arctic regions, they came to perform other duties as well, including rescue missions. Perhaps the most unusual duty performed by the Bering Sea Patrol was the Court Cruise. A cutter would transport a judge, a public defender, a court clerk, and a Deputy U.S. Marshall to hear criminal cases at various places; those cases often involved poaching, murder, assault with a deadly weapon, arson, and selling liquor to the native peoples in the region. Once the cutter, now turned into a floating jail, had left its prisoners at Valdez, it returned to the Bering Sea Patrol Headquarters at Unalaska for reassignment. After World War II, light aircraft were able to reach many isolated villages that had previously only been accessible to ships, and the duties of the Patrol became law enforcement and conservation missions. On September 4, 1964, the U.S. Coast Guard changed the Patrol's name to the Alaska Patrol, officially ending more than ninety years of duty.

Berkeley, Sir William (1606–77) • royal governor (1641–52, 1660–77) and captain general of Virginia, born in or near London. Berkeley's second term was strained by economic hardships in the colony, accusations of favoritism toward elite inner circle, deprivation of freemen's rights, and neglect of frontiersmen against Indian attacks. Widespread discontent exploded in BACON'S REBELLION (1676). After NATHANIEL BACON died and the insurrection collapsed, Berkeley, disregarding a royal commission to pardon the rebels, ordered many of them hanged; summoned back to London, he died there before meeting with the king.

Berlin Airlift • (June 22, 1948–May 12, 1949) a combined effort by the U.S. Air Force and the RAF to evade the Soviet blockade of the occupation zones. The airlift brought in the 4,500 tons Berlin needed daily to support its industry and the city's population of two million. The airlift planes (two-thirds American and one-third British) were harassed by Soviet planes, but were not shot at.

The time for loading the planes was a mere hour and 25 minutes, while unloading in Berlin took only 49 minutes. By the end of the blockade, 1,783,000 tons had been lifted, with thirty-one lives lost in 12 fatal accidents.

Berlin Crises • heightened periods of tension between the United States and the USSR over the status of West Berlin. The first crisis, in 1958, came about when Soviet premier NIKITA KHRUSHCHEV campaigned to reduce the Allied presence in West Berlin and to encourage the West to recognize the German Democratic Republic (GDR). Kruschchev declared he would turn over border control West Berlin and West Germany to the GDR. The United States responded only by authorizing CINCEUR to create a secret planning group (named "Live Oak," and active until 1990) to prepare for possible military confrontation. The second crisis, in 1962, involved the massing of tanks on either side of CHECKPOINT CHARLIE after the East German leader closed the sector borders with barbed wire and, later, concrete (the BERLIN WALL CRISIS, 1961).

Berlin Wall Crisis • a heightened period of tension between the United States and the USSR, after the Soviet premier NIKITA KHRUSHCHEV supported the efforts of East Germany's leader to close the sector borders between East and West Berlin, first with barbed wire and then with a concrete wall.

berm |bərm| • *n.* **1** an artificial ridge or embankment, e.g., as a defense against tanks. **2** a narrow space, especially one between a ditch and the base of a parapet.

Bermuda Triangle • an area of the western Atlantic Ocean where a large number of ships and aircraft are said to have mysteriously disappeared.

Bernard, Simon (1779–1839) • military engineer, born in France. Once a maréchal de camp under Napoleon, he was recruited to the WAR DEPARTMENT to draft plans for a system of forts to defend the U.S. coastline from seaborne attacks.

Bernard was the most prominent of several Napoleonic veterans who contributed to the reform of the American military establishment after the WAR OF 1812. His principal role was as chief architect of the system of seacoast fortifications that long remained a central component of U.S. defense policy.

---

berth • *n.* **1** a ship's allotted place at a wharf or dock. **2** a fixed bed or bunk on a ship, train, or other means of transport. • *v.* **1** moor (a ship) in its allotted place: *these modern ships can almost berth themselves.* **2** (of a ship) dock: *the Dutch freighter berthed at the Brooklyn docks.* PHRASES: **give a wide berth** steer (a ship) well clear of something while passing it.

berthing • *n.* **1** the action of mooring a ship: *as soon as the berthing was complete, they went ashore.* **2** mooring position; accommodation in berths.

best bower • anchor carried on the starboard bow.

Betty Crocker • slang (in the VIETNAM WAR) a serviceman assigned to (usually desk) duty in Saigon, a comparatively safe and domestic role.

Béxar • a siege and battle from October 3 to December 11, 1835, that marked a turning point in the TEXAS WAR OF INDEPENDENCE. San Antonio de Béxar, as the city was then known, was a Mexican stronghold. Texas troops laid siege to it for two months, and when they were about to retreat in frustration, leader Ben Milam rallied the troops for an attack with the now-famous phrase, "Who will go with old Ben Milam into San Antonio?" on December 5. The desperate, house-to-house fighting lasted for four days, until the Mexican commander sued for peace. Although the Mexicans would regain the city within months, this battle redefined the war, because the Mexicans were now the invaders.

BFV • *abbr.* Bradley Fighting Vehicle.

BGM-71 • a portable, tube-launched, optically-tracked, wired-guided (TOW) missile.

BGM-109 • see TOMAHAWK.

Biak Island • (also **Wiak Island**) an island off the northern coast of Irian Jaya. In WORLD WAR II, Biak was taken by the Japanese in April 1942, and retaken May 27–July 22 by Allied forces.

bicorne • *n.* a brimmed hat with two opposing sides turned up so as to form two points, worn by both army and navy officers in the 18th and 19th centuries and as part of the full-dress uniform of some military forces today.

Biddle, Clement (1740–1814) • Revolutionary army officer, born in Philadelphia. In the REVOLUTIONARY WAR, Gen. NATHANAEL GREENE appointed him as volunteer aide-de-camp (1776). He was also commissary general of forage (1777–80) under Greene. As a successful merchant from a prominent Philadelphia family, Biddle was well placed to provide for the material needs of the Continental Army. Upon Greene's recommendation, Biddle was named quartermaster general and colonel of the Pennsylvania militia (1781), his position until the end of the war.

Biddle, Nicholas (1750–78) • Revolutionary naval officer, born in Philadelphia. As a captain in the Continental navy, he commanded the *Andrea Doria* (1776) and joined ESEK HOPKINS, the colonies' naval commander in chief, in capturing British forts in the Bahamas and raiding British shipping in the North Atlantic. Commanding the 32-gun warship *Randolph* (1776), he captured the 20-gun *True Briton,* along with 3 accompanying merchantmen. He died in a sea battle with the 64-gun British ship of the line *Yarmouth*, 60 leagues east of Barbados.

Big Bertha • a 420-mm howitzer used in WORLD WAR II that fired a 1,764 lb. (800 kilogram) shell about 6 miles (10 kilometers).

Big Bethel, Battle of • (June 10, 1861), the first land battle of the CIVIL WAR, fought at Big Bethel church, near Hampton, Virginia. A predawn attack on Confederate positions by Federal troops went awry from the start. The Confederates were able to hold their field-works in a contest of little consequence, save for making known the southern commander, Col. JOHN B. MAGRUDER.

Big Red One, the • unofficial name for the 1st Infantry Division, the oldest continuously serving division in the U.S. Army (since 1917). Their patch is a large red numeral "1".

The Big Red One fought at MEUSE-ARGONNE (1918), OMAHA BEACH (1944), and the BATTLE OF THE BULGE (1944–45), and were the first division to fight in VIETNAM.

Big Round Top • see ROUND TOP.

Big Three, The • in WORLD WAR II, the United States, Britain, and the USSR. Also, the GRAND ALLIANCE.

big wing • an aerial defense tactic proposed by RAF Squadron Leader Douglas Bader in 1940 to oppose LUFTWAFFE attacks during the BATTLE OF BRITAIN. Bader proposed that German air raids be met straight away with two-five squadrons of interceptors so as to overwhelm the attacking force. The RAF commander, Air Chief Marshal Sir HUGH DOWDING, preferred the existing tactic of deploying one squadron or less to intercept the enemy formations and determine their probable target before deploying additional aircraft to engage the attackers.

Bikini atoll • the site in the Marshall Islands where the United States conducted twenty-three tests of nuclear weapons. Testing took place from 1946 to 1958 and involved weapons totaling 77 megatons. In the earliest tests, in July 1946, the United States exploded two atomic devices to test their effects on naval forces. The first device, which was exploded above the water's surface, sank five of about seventy ships arranged for the test, and the second device, exploded underwater, sank nine ships. In March 1954 a 15-megaton device named Bravo yielded a larger-than-expected explosion, and radiation contaminated several of the atoll's populated islands. Controversy over the effects of radiation on the islands' people and ecology continues to the present day.

bilge • *n.* **1** the area on the outer surface of a ship's hull where the bottom curves to meet the vertical sides. **2** (**bilges**) the lowest internal portion of the hull.

bilge keel • each of a pair of plates or timbers fastened under the sides of the hull of a ship to provide lateral resistance to the water, prevent rolling, and support its weight in dry dock.

bill • *n.* **1** the point of an anchor fluke. **2** a stiff brim at the front of a cap.

billet • *n.* **1** a shelter for troops. **2** a personnel position or assignment that may be filled by one person. • *v.* to quarter troops.

Billings, John Shaw (1838–1913) • Union army medical officer, library organizer, and public health activist, born near Allensville, Indiana. In the CIVIL WAR, he was a first lieutenant and assistant surgeon in the U.S. Army (1862). After the war, he conducted a survey (1869–70) of the far-flung national network of marine hospitals; the supervisory agency that resulted evolved into today's U.S. Public Health Service. Billings's most lasting military medical contribution was his work as officer-in-charge of the library of the surgeon general's office, by 1895 the largest medical library in the Americas if not in the world; he initiated two pioneering finding guides to the collection, the *Index Catalogue* (16 vols., 1880–87) and the *Index Medicus* (1879–95).

bill of health • a certificate relating to the incidence of infectious disease on a ship or in the port from which it has sailed.

Billy Yank • a Union soldier in the CIVIL WAR.

biological agent • a microorganism that causes disease in personnel, plants, or animals or causes the deterioration of materiel.

biological ammunition • a type of ammunition, the filler of which is primarily a biological agent.

biological defense • the methods, plans, and procedures involved in establishing and executing defensive measures against attacks using biological agents.

biological operation • **1** the employment of biological agents to produce casualties in personnel or animals and damage to plants or materiel. **2** the defense against such employment.

biological warfare • warfare involving the use of bacteria, viruses, and other biological agents to kill, sicken, or disorient the enemy.

biological weapon • a weapon that projects, disperses, or disseminates a biological agent with the power to kill or incapacitate personnel.

Biological Weapons Convention • a convention, proposed in 1972 and ratified by the United States in 1975, that countries involved would not develop, produce, stockpile, or acquire biological agents or toxins for weapons or the means of delivery for biological weapons. It was agreed to by 22 governments, including the Soviet Union and the United Kingdom.

biplane • *n.* an airplane that has two pairs of wings attached at different levels, especially one pair of wings above the fuselage and one pair below.

bipod • *n.* a two-legged collapsible support for mortars and other weapons that are too heavy to fire while holding.

Birney, David Bell (1825–64) • Union major general. Birney was born in Huntsville, Alabama, but moved to Cincinatti with abolitionist father. He was the younger brother of WILLIAM BIRNEY. In the CIVIL WAR, as brigadier general, he led a brigade of Maine and New York troops under PHILIP KEARNY's division of the 3rd Corps in the PENINSULAR campaign, SEVEN DAYS' battles, and SECOND BULL RUN (all 1862). He commanded the division after Kearny's death (1862). As major general, he led a division in the 2nd Corps in the bloody WILDERNESS TO PETERSBURG CAMPAIGN (1864), distinguishing himself during the fighting at SPOTSYLVANIA. Birney was named by ULYSSES S. GRANT as commander of the 10th Corps in the Army of the James (1864), and led it in maneuvers against RICHMOND; he fell ill with malaria.

Birney, William (1819–1907) • Union army officer, born in Alabama, the son of an abolitionist leader. William is the older brother of DAVID BELL BIRNEY. He supervised recruiting of U.S. COLORED TROOPS (USCTs) and was assigned a brigade of USCTs in the Department of the South. He was active in raiding outposts, railroads, mills, etc. and led a division in the all-black XXV Army Corps, Army of the James, in pursuit of Gen. ROBERT E. LEE's ARMY OF NORTHERN VIRGINIA retreating from PETERSBURG (1864). He was stripped of command by Maj. Gen. EDWARD ORD when Birney accused him of trying to deny his black troops a role in Lee's defeat.

Bismarck Sea, Battle of the • (March 3, 1943) a WORLD WAR II naval battle in which combined Allied sea and air forces destroyed a Japanese convoy near New Guinea. Eight troop transports and eight destroyers were attacked as they carried a Japanese army division to reinforce positions in New Guinea and the Solomon Islands. Low-level bombing and strafing runs by U.S. and Australian B-25s, followed by torpedo attacks from U.S. PT BOATS, sunk all the transports and four destroyers.

bivouac |ˈbivo͞oˌæk; ˈbivwæk| • *n.* a temporary camp without tents or cover, used especially by soldiers. • *v.* (**bivouacked, bivouacking**) stay in such a camp.
ORIGIN: early 18th cent. (denoting a night watch by the whole army): from French, probably from Swiss German *Bîwacht* 'additional guard at night,' apparently denoting a citizens' patrol supporting the ordinary town watch.

black • *adj. & adv.* in intelligence, a term used to indicate reliance on illegal concealment rather than on cover.

Blackbird • (**SR-71**) a tactical and strategic reconnaissance aircraft built by LOCKHEED for the CENTRAL INTELLIGENCE AGENCY. The Blackbird was supposed to have a higher service ceiling (85,000 feet) and a greater maximum speed (Mach 3) than the U-2. It is possible that approximately fifteen A-12s were delivered to the CIA beginning in 1962, and these were used by the U.S. Air Force until the SR-71 came into use in 1964.

Black Chamber, the • a covert code-breaking and intelligence gathering activity within the MILITARY INTELLIGENCE DIVISION of the WAR DEPARTMENT during the 1920s. The Black Chamber's activities were taken over by the U.S. ARMY SIGNAL CORPS' SIGNAL INTELLIGENCE SERVICE in 1929.

Black Eagles, the • commissioned on April 29, 1967, as an aircraft squadron and deployed one week later to WESTPAC (Western Pacific command) aboard the *USS Constellation*, flying E-2As ("Hawkeyes"). The squadron served in VIETNAM from 1967 to 1975, and it played a vital role in the evacuation of U.S. forces from South Vietnam in May 1975. Since 1987, the squadron has been deployed several times to Mediterranean trouble spots, and was one of the first units deployed after the Iraqi invasion of KUWAIT. The Black Eagles spent three months in the Gulf of Oman in support of OPERATION DESERT SHIELD. Also called CARRIER AIRBORNE EARLY WARNING SQUADRON 113 (VAW-113).

black flag • a pirate's ensign, typically thought to feature a white skull and crossbones on a black background; Jolly Roger.

Black Hawk • (**HH-60G; MH-60G; UH-60**) a light transport helicopter used by air assault, air cavalry, and aeromedical evacuation units, it is one of eighty-two combat search-and-rescue helicopters received by the U.S. Air Force when its Night Hawk (HH-60D) was canceled after the completion of a single prototype. Its protective armor can withstand hits from 23 mm shells. Also called PAVE HAWK.

Black Hawk War • (1832) the final armed resistance of the Indian tribes of the Old Northwest to the encroachment of white settlers on their lands east of the Mississippi River. The conflict began in April 1832 when some 2,000 Sauk (Sac) and Mesquakie (Fox) Indians led by the Sauk chief, BLACK HAWK, disavowed an 1804 treaty and moved from Iowa east across the Mississippi into northwestern Illinois. The movement of Black Hawk's band led to the mobilization of militia forces and the deployment of the U.S. 6th Infantry, commanded by Col. HENRY ATKINSON, from JEFFERSON BARRACKS, Missouri, into Illinois in pursuit of the Indians. Fighting began on May 14, 1832, when the Indians trying to parley were attacked by militiamen. Throughout the summer of 1832, Black Hawk's followers raided white settlements and were pursued by the Army and the militia. They were finally cornered and decisively defeated at the mouth of the Bad Axe River on August 2.

Black Kettle (1807?–68) • Cheyenne chief. Black Kettle (Me-tu-ra-to or Moka-ta-va-tah in Cheyenne) served as a scout and warrior in combat with neighboring tribes. He was the principal chief during the 1861 treaty negotiations at Fort Wise, Colorado, where he accepted an American flag during the negotiations, symbolically accepting the notion of peace with white America. After the SAND CREEK MASSACRE in 1864, where Black Kettle was shot more than eight times and more than 100 Cheyenne were murdered and mutilated, the remaining Cheyenne (and especially the CHEYENNE DOG SOLDIERS) were distrustful of Black Kettle, who still called for peace with whites. He continued to negotiate with whites, returning hostages, and worked to achieve full agreement of his tribe to another treaty in 1867 which restricted the Cheyenne to a reservation in INDIAN TERRITORY. The U.S. Army continued to violate the treaty and ignore Black Kettle's peacemaking efforts; Black Kettle and his wife were killed nearly four years to the day after the Sand Creek massacre. They were shot in the back while trying to flee Gen. GEORGE AMSTRONG CUSTER's dawn attack of their village.

The day after the battle, survivors hid Black Kettle's body; in 1934, a skeleton wearing his jewelry was found by Works Progress Administration workers trying to stabilize a bridge over the Washita River.

---

black list • in intelligence, a list of persons suspected or confirmed as security risks. A black list is an official counterintelligence listing of actual or potential enemy collaborators, sympathizers, intelligence suspects, and other persons whose presence menaces the security of friendly forces.

black magic • Slang M-16 assault rifle, so called because of its black plastic and steel construction. (The M-16 was also nicknamed the **Black Rifle, Widow Maker,** and **Mattel Toy Rifle.**)

Rumors have circulated that the Mattel toy company actually produced the weapon for the U.S. Army. In fact Mattel manufactured a nearly lifesize and realistic "M-16 Marauder" toy gun in 1966.

---

black propaganda • propaganda that purports to emanate from a source other than the true one.

Black Sheep • the nickname for Marine Attack Squadron 214, first commissioned in early 1942 at Ewa, Hawaii. Its mission is to provide close-air support, and conduct armed reconnaissance and limited air defense for Marine expeditionary forces. It was active in the Pacific theater in WORLD WAR II and has seen action in every major conflict since.

Black Widow • (**P-61**) a large twin-engine twin-boom attack aircraft, the only aircraft designed to be a night fighter during WORLD WAR II. The P-61 entered service very late in the war, when the allied forces had gained air superiority, so it was used mostly as a night intruder and attack plane.

Bladensburg, Battle of • a fight during the WAR OF 1812 between 5,000 British forces and 500 American troops, as well as 1,000 citizen soldiers, that took place on August 25, 1814, near the town of Bladensburg, Maryland. The Americans unsuccessfully tried to stop the British from marching on nearby Washington, D.C. Finding the WASHINGTON NAVY YARD set ablaze by Americans and thereby rendered useless, the British retaliated by setting fire to the Capitol, the WHITE HOUSE, and the War and Treasury Department offices.

Blair, Francis Preston, Jr. (1821–75) • Union army officer, U.S. congressman and senator, born in Lexington, Kentucky. A congressman from Missouri, the only Free Soiler from a slave state, he was appointed brigadier general in the U.S. Army, raised seven Missouri infantry regiments, and led a brigade in battle at VICKSBURG (1863) under Gen. WILLIAM T. SHERMAN. He was then promoted to major general and commanded an infantry corps through the remainder of the war.

Bland, Theodorick (1742–90) • Revolutionary army officer, born in Prince George County, Virginia. Bland took part (with JAMES MONROE and BENJAMIN HARRISON) in a 26–man raid of the Virginia governor's mansion, distributing confiscated weapons to Whig partisans (1775). As a colonel of the 1st Regiment of Continental Light Dragoons in the Continental army under Washington, he fought in the battle of BRANDYWINE (1777).

blank • *adj.* (also **blank cartridge**) a cartridge containing gunpowder but no bullet, used for training or as a signal. • *v.* cover up, obscure, or cause to appear blank or empty: *electronic countermeasures* ***blanked out*** *the radar signals.*

blanket • *v.* take wind from the sails of (another craft) by passing to windward.

Bleeding Kansas • (1854-58), a term referring to violent encounters between pro-slavery and antislavery factions in the Kansas territory. The KANSAS-NEBRASKA ACT of 1854 allowed that self-determination would resolve the question of slavery in these territories. Pro-slavery settlers burned the town of Lawrence on May 21, 1856, an act followed by the murder of five pro-slavery settlers by JOHN BROWN and accomplices. Ensuing raids and retaliations caused the death of hundreds, and the territory was declared in open insurrection. U.S. troops sent in by President FRANKLIN PIERCE were able to assert control by dispersing the pro-slavery militia.

Bletchley Park • the Buckinghamshire, England, center of operations for the British Foreign Office's Government Code and Cypher School. Beginning in 1939, a staff of several thousand mathematicians, engineers, clerks, and others secretly worked at Bletchley Park to decipher encoded communications of German and other enemy forces. The first decryptions of the German "Enigma" encryption device were produced in the summer of 1940, and by January 1941 information about German plans for attacking Greece played a significant part in British tactics. By 1944 a worldwide intelligence network was in place to intercept and decode messages and to distribute the information to operational theater commanders and back to Bletchley Park for an overview of the war. In addition to contributing to the war effort, devices and ideas developed at Bletchley Park led to the world's first electronic computers.

blimp • *n.* a small airship or barrage balloon; dirigible. • *v.* slang (aviation) to quickly open and close a throttle, as when coming in for a landing, so that if necessary the engine will be ready for a rapid pickup.

blind bombing zone • a restricted area (air, land, or sea) established for the purpose of permitting air operations, unrestricted by the operations or possible attack of friendly forces.

blind pig • slang (in WORLD WAR I) a large shell from a trench mortar.

blip • *n.* the display of a received pulse on a radar screen.

blister gas • poison gas that causes blisters on and intense irritation to the skin.

blitz • *n.* **1** an intensive or sudden military attack. **2** (**the Blitz**) the German air raids on Britain in 1940.

ORIGIN: abbreviation of BLITZKRIEG.

Blitzkrieg |ˈblitsˌkrēg| • the integration of infantry, armor, artillery, and aircraft in a highly mobile team to quickly drive through and defeat enemy forces arrayed in a linear or positional defense. Originally applied to the German conquest of Poland in 1939 and France in 1940, the term "Blitzkrieg" has come to be use for any rapid, violent, and successful military action involving combined arms.

ORIGIN: WORLD WAR II: from German, literally 'lightning war.'

blockade • *n.* an act of sealing off a place to prevent goods or people from entering or leaving.

PHRASES: **run a blockade** (of a ship) manage to enter or leave a blockaded port.

DERIVATIVES: **blockader** *n.*

Blockade Proclamation • an 1861 declaration by President ABRAHAM LINCOLN that called for a blockade on the ports of South Carolina, Georgia, Alabama, Florida, Mississippi, Louisiana, and Texas, on the grounds that these states were insurgent. It was an inciting incident in the CIVIL WAR. Officially titled the PROCLAMATION OF BLOCKADE.

blockade-runner • *n.* a vessel that runs or attempts to run into or out of a blockaded port.

blockbuster • *n.* a huge aerial bomb capable of destroying targets within a wide area.

blockhouse • *n.* a building constructed for military defense, made of logs, stone, or other sturdy material, with loopholes for firing weapons and observation. It is usually square or angular and is often built with a projecting upper story.

blockship • *n.* a ship which is moored or grounded in a channel in order to block it for purposes of war or to provide shelter.

blood chit • a card or small cloth chart depicting an American flag and a statement in several languages to the effect that anyone assisting the bearer to safety will be rewarded.

Bloody Angle • the center of the Confederate forces at the CIVIL WAR BATTLE OF SPOTSYLVANIA (1864), the site of the the bloodiest fighting of the battle.

Bloody Lane • a sunken farm road that was the site of a twelve-hour confrontation during the BATTLE OF ANTIETAM (1862). The fight at Bloody Lane took place on September 17 between Confederate Gen. ROBERT E. LEE's forces and Union Gens. GEORGE B. MCCLELLAN's and AMBROSE BURNSIDE's troops near Antietam Creek, outside Sharpsburg, Maryland. The Confederates were defeated, leading to Gen. Lee's retreat back south. The road was called "Bloody Lane" because 23,000 men were killed or wounded that day, making it the single bloodiest day in U.S. history.

Bloody Ridge, Battle of • see EDSON's RIDGE, BATTLE OF.

Bloomfield, Joseph (1753–1823) • Revolutionary army officer, born in Woodbridge, New Jersey. In the REVOLUTIONARY WAR, he was a captain in the 3rd New Jersey Regiment, stationed in New York's Mohawk Valley to keep the IROQUOIS from aiding the British, and then in the Philadelphia area, where the regiment participated in the battles of BRANDYWINE and MONMOUTH (1778). He was wounded at Brandywine (1777). In the WAR OF 1812, he was a brigadier general stationed at Plattsburgh, New York, awaiting the British invasion of Canada that never came.

blowback • *n.* **1** the escape, to the rear and under pressure, of gases formed during the firing of a weapon. Blowback may be caused by a defective breech mechanism, a ruptured cartridge case, or a faulty primer. **2** a type of weapon operation in which the force of expanding gases acting to the rear against the face of the bolt furnishes all the energy required to initiate the complete cycle of operation.

BLT • *abbr.* battalion landing team.

bludgeon |ˈbləjən| • *n.* a thick stick with a heavy end, used as a weapon.

Blue Bark • **1** U.S. military personnel, U.S. citizen civilian employees of the DEPARTMENT OF DEFENSE, and the dependents of both categories who travel in connection with the death of an immediate family member. It also applies to designated escorts for dependents of deceased military members. **2** the personal property shipment of a deceased member.

blue coat • a soldier in a blue uniform, especially a Union soldier during the CIVIL WAR.

blue ensign • Brit. a blue flag with the UNION JACK in the top corner next to the flagstaff, flown chiefly by British naval auxiliary vessels.

blue forces • forces used in a friendly role during NATO exercises.

blue helmet • a member of a UNITED NATIONS peacekeeping force.

bluejacket • *n.* informal a sailor in the navy.

Blue Peter • a blue flag with a white square in the center, raised by a ship about to leave port.

blue water • the high seas; open ocean. A **blue water navy** is one organized, trained, and equipped for operations on the high seas; a **brown water navy** is one organized, trained, and equipped for coastal or riverine operations.

bluff • *adj.* (of a cliff or a ship's bow) having a vertical or steep broad front.

blunderbuss |ˈbləndərˌbəs| • *n.* a short large-bored gun firing balls or slugs.

ORIGIN: mid 17th cent.: alteration (by association with blunder) of Dutch *donderbus*, literally 'thunder gun.'

Blunt, James Gillpatrick (1826–81) • Union army officer, physician, and politician, born in Trenton, Hancock County, Maine. Given (and often removed from) a series of commands in the frontier departments of Kansas, Arkansas, and the INDIAN TERRITORY, Maj. Gen. Blunt lived up to his name through frequent quarrels and insubordination (as by charging JOHN C. FRÉMONT with incompetence and questioning HENRY W. HALLECK's loyalty), but proved an aggressive fighter. He was unquestionably (even fanatically) loyal to the Union and the cause of abolition.

BMEWS |bēˈmyo͞oz| • *abbr.* Ballistic Missile Early Warning System, the first operational missile detection radar system, designed to provide immediate, long-range warning of a missile attack over the polar region, established in the late 1950s. See also NORAD.

Part of the North American Aerospace Defense Command (NORAD) created in 1957–58, BMEWS sites were established at Thule Air Base, Greenland, and Clear Air Force Station, Alaska, and in 1958–60 at the Royal Air Force Station at Fylingdales-Moor in the United Kingdom.

Bn. • *abbr.* Battalion.

board • *n.* a distance covered by a vessel in a single tack. • *v.* get on or into (a ship, aircraft, or other vehicle).

Board of Economic Warfare • a body formed by President FRANKLIN D. ROOSEVELT in 1941 to coordinate international economic and defense policy. It was abolished in 1943 amid criticism that it was an attempt to export the New Deal.

Board of Navy Commissioners • created in 1815 by Congress, the Board acted as advisors and assistants to the SECRETARY OF THE NAVY. At first, their authority was limited to procurement of stores and the supervision of vessel construction. In 1832, Congress requested that they devise rules to bring about uniformity of vessels and equipment.

Board of War and Ordnance • a committee created by Congress in June 1776 to oversee the Continental army and the conduct of the REVOLUTIONARY WAR.

boat • *n.* **1** a small vessel propelled on water by oars, sails, or an engine: *a fishing boat* | *a boat trip.* **2** (in general use) a ship of any size.

boat deck • the deck from which a ship's lifeboats are launched.

boathook |'bōt,ho͝ok| • *n.* a long pole with a hook and a spike at one end, used for fending off or pulling a boat.

boat lane • a lane for amphibious assault landing craft, which extends seaward from the landing beaches to the line of departure. The width of a boat lane is determined by the length of the corresponding beach.

boatswain |'bōsən| (also **bo'sun** or **bosun**) • *n.* a ship's officer in charge of equipment and the crew.

boatswain's chair • a seat suspended from ropes, used for work on the body or masts of a ship or the face of a building.

boatyard • *n.* a place where boats are built, repaired, or stored.

bobstay • *n.* a rope used to hold down the bowsprit of a ship and keep it steady.

Bockscar Nagasaki • the B-29 that transported and dropped the atomic bomb on NAGASAKI.

body armor • clothing worn by army and police personnel to protect against gunfire.

body bag • slang (also called **rubber bag**) a zippered green or black plastic bag used in the VIETNAM WAR for return to the United States of bodies of U.S. soldiers killed in action. See also HUMAN REMAINS POUCH.

body count • the number of enemy dead remaining on a battlefield after a combat action.

body snatcher • slang **1** a stretcher-bearer who retrieves the wounded from the battlefield. **2** (in WORLD WAR I) a sniper at the front lines.

Boelcke, Oswald (1891–1916) • WORLD WAR I aviator, born in Giebichenstein near Halle, Germany. Boelcke was noted as the developer of seven rules of aerial combat; including surprise the enemy; maintain offensive advantage; use formation flying; and avoid flying in "lone eagle" patrols. He died in a midair collision with another German pilot after forty successful dogfights.

The British RFC sent a wreath to his grave, with the message "To the memory of Captain Boelcke, our brave and chivalrous opponent."

bogey • *n.* slang an air contact that is unidentified but assumed to be an enemy. Compare with UNKNOWN.

bolt-action (also **bolt action**) • *adj.* (of a gun) having a breech that is opened by turning a bolt and sliding it back.

bolt rope • a rope sewn round the edge of a vessel's sail to prevent tearing.

bomb • *n.* **1** a container filled with explosive, incendiary material, smoke, gas, or other destructive substance, designed to explode on impact or when detonated by a time mechanism, remote-control device, or lit fuse. **2** an explosive device fitted into a specified object: *a package bomb.* **3** (**the bomb**) nuclear weapons considered collectively as agents of mass destruction: *she joined the fight against the bomb.* • *v.* attack (a place or vehicle) with a bomb or bombs: *London was bombed, night after night.*

bombard |bäm'bärd| • *v.* attack (a place or person) continuously with bombs, shells, or other missiles: *the city was bombarded by federal forces.* • *n.* |'bäm,bärd| a cannon of the earliest type, which fired a stone ball or large shot.
DERIVATIVES: **bombardment** |bäm'bärdmənt| *n.*

bombardier |,bämbə(r)'dir| • *n.* **1** a member of a bomber crew in the U.S. Air Force responsible for sighting and releasing bombs. **2** a rank of noncommissioned officer in certain Canadian and British artillery regiments, equivalent to corporal.

bomb bay • a compartment in the fuselage of an aircraft in which bombs are held and from which they may be dropped.

bomb disposal • the defusing or removal and detonation of unexploded and delayed-action bombs.

bomb disposal unit • another term for EXPLOSIVE ORDNANCE DISPOSAL UNIT.

bomber • *n.* **1** an aircraft designed to carry and drop bombs. **2** a person who plants, detonates, or throws bombs in a public place, especially as a terrorist. **3** short for BOMBER JACKET.

Bomber Command • a subordinate element of the British ROYAL AIR FORCE assigned the mission of strategic bombardment. In the early years of WORLD WAR II the RAF Bomber Command engaged in both daylight and night bombardment of the AXIS POWERS.

bomber jacket • a short jacket, usually zipping up the front, gathered with tight knit bands at the cuffs and waist.

bomb impact plot • a graphic representation of the target area, usually a pre-strike air photograph, on which prominent dots are plotted to mark the impact or detonation points of bombs dropped on a specific bombing attack.

bombing run • the part of the flight path of a bomber that brings it into position to release its weapons.

bombproof • *adj.* strong enough to resist the effects of blast from a bomb.

bombsight • *n.* a mechanical or electronic device used in an aircraft for aiming bombs.

Bonham, Milledge Luke (1813–90) • Confederate general, U.S. congressman, and governor of South Carolina (1862–64), born in South Carolina's Edgefield District. In the CIVIL WAR, he was the brigadier general of

South Carolinian troops at FIRST BULL RUN (1861) and defending RICHMOND (1864).

Bonhomme Richard*, USS** • **1** a converted 900-ton East Indiaman that sank the more heavily armed frigate HMS *Serapis* off the English coast on September 23, 1779. Although the damaged American vessel floated only one day longer, the victory became a signal of American naval success and was the occasion of JOHN PAUL JONES's famous response to the British commander's invitation to surrender: "I have not yet begun to fight." **2** (Bon Homme Richard***) (**CV-31**) the second *Bon Homme Richard* was launched in April 1944, commissioned in November 1944, and left Norfolk for PEARL HARBOR in March 1945, where it joined the PACIFIC FLEET. After being converted for troop transport duty, the ship made several trans-Pacific crossings, returning armed service personnel to the United States, then was decommissioned at Puget Sound in January 1947. *Bon Homme Richard* was recommissioned in January 1951 and sent to Korea, where it was involved in heavy air strikes against North Korea. Again decommissioned in May 1953 in order to undergo modernization, the *Bon Homme Richard* completed conversion in October 1955 and continued to serve with the Pacific Fleet.

Bonneville, Benjamin Louis Eulalie de (1796–1878) • Union army officer, born in or near Paris. Bonneville is the subject of Washington Irving's *Adventures of Captain Bonneville* (1837). Some historians speculate that Bonneville may have been a government agent sent to spy on the British in Oregon, based on the army's willingness to grant him a leave of absence in 1832 to engage in the fur trade in the northern Rockies, the ease of his reinstatement, and various statements he made to his superiors in letters.

Bonus Army • a group of over 20,000 WORLD WAR I veterans who marched on Washington, D.C., to receive their World War I bonus during the summer of 1932. Most of the veterans, unemployed and in desperate circumstances, demanded the passage of a bill providing immediate payment of their bonus. They called themselves the BONUS EXPEDITIONARY FORCE and peacefully camped and rallied in parks and military bases. When the Senate defeated the bill on June 17, 1932, the veterans refused to leave. Troops ordered by President HERBERT HOOVER and led by Gen. DOUGLAS MACARTHUR entered several buildings and the main camp, setting tents on fire and forcing an evacuation on July 29, 1932. A smaller group of veterans remained in Washington and marched in May 1933, but were not successful in pressuring Congress. Nevertheless, the bonus was finally paid in 1936.

bonus damage • slang destruction beyond the intended target. See also COLLATERAL DAMAGE.

Bonus Expeditionary Force • see BONUS ARMY.

booby trap • an explosive or nonexplosive device or other material, deliberately placed to cause casualties when an apparently harmless object is disturbed or a normally safe act is performed. • *v.* (**booby-trap**) to set or place a booby trap in or on an object or area.

boom • *n.* **1** a pivoted spar to which the foot of a vessel's sail is attached, allowing the angle of the sail to be changed. **2** a floating beam used to contain oil spills or to form a barrier across the mouth of a harbor or river.

boondocks • *n.* **1** a remote, sparsely populated place; the sticks. **2** (also, **the boonies, bush**) in the VIETNAM WAR, a jungle, a remote area far from base camp or city, or Vietnam generally.

ORIGIN: a term first used by Marines fighting guerrillas in the Philippines (1899–1902) in reference to the isolated mountain terrain.

booster • *n.* **1** a high-explosive element sufficiently sensitive so as to be actuated by small explosive elements in a fuze or primer and powerful enough to cause detonation of the main explosive filling. **2** an auxiliary or initial propulsion system that travels with a missile or aircraft and that may or may not separate from the parent craft when its impulse has been delivered. A booster system may contain, or consist of, one or more units.

boost phase • that portion of the flight of a ballistic missile or space vehicle during which the booster and sustainer engines operate.

boot camp • a military training camp for new recruits, with harsh discipline.

Booth, John Wilkes (1838–65) • actor and assassin of President ABRAHAM LINCOLN, born in Harford County, Maryland. Booth was the first assassin of a U.S. president. An accomplished Shakespearean actor from a family of actors, Booth plotted to kidnap or assassinate Abraham Lincoln to avenge the South. He shot Lincoln at Ford's Theatre in Washington on April 14, 1865, shouting, "Sic semper tyrannis (thus always to tyrants)! The South is avenged!"

boot top • the part of a ship's hull just above the waterline, typically marked by a line of contrasting color.

bore • *v.* hollow out (a gun barrel or other tube). • *n.* **1** the hollow part inside a gun barrel or other tube. **2** the diameter of this; the caliber: *a small-bore rifle*. **3** a gun of a specified bore: *he was shot in the leg with a twelve-bore*.

Boscawen, Edward (1711–61) • British admiral and naval hero, popular for the taking of Porto Bello (1739) and the siege of Cartagena (1741). In the FRENCH AND INDIAN WAR (1754–63), Boscawen intercepted a French squadron near Newfoundland, capturing two ships and 1,500 men (1755). Made admiral in 1758, "Old Dreadnought" helped Gen. JEFFREY AMHERST besiege and capture the French fortress of Louisbourg, Cape Breton Island (1758).

bo's'n • *n.* variant spelling of BOATSWAIN.

Bosnian Crisis • in the 1990s, the disintegration of the former Yugoslavia led to a NATO-led peacekeeping mission that was the largest military operation in Europe since WORLD WAR II. After ethnic Serbs extended their control to 70 percent of Bosnia, and reports reached the West of massacres, mass rapes, and ETHNIC CLEANSING, there were public demands for intervention. At first, the United States, under President BILL CLINTON, supported an arms embargo but declined to commit United States forces. After the Bosnian Serb offensive in 1995, which included the capture of alleged "safe havens" Sebrenica and Zepa, the U.S. committed NATO airpower against the Serbs. On October 5, 1995, a cease-fire was declared, and the three Balkan presidents traveled to DAYTON, Ohio, for peace talks. A treaty was signed in Paris on December 14, 1995, ending the four-year civil war. However, U.S. troops remained in Bosnia and Yugoslavia as peacekeepers, especially between the Serbs and ethnic Albanians in the province of KOSOVO.

Boston, Evacuation of • see DORCHESTER HEIGHTS.

Boston II • (**A-20**) an attack bomber—originally produced to the order of the French government and called DB-7—it was taken over by the British government after France fell to the NAZIS and was designated Boston. The A-20 was the first of the DB-7 type to be built according to U.S. Army specifications; later, with the British name Havoc (a name now abandoned), it was converted into a night fighter.

Boston Massacre • (March 5, 1770) a so-called massacre in which a small band of British Army regulars, who were members of a garrison stationed in Boston to protect customs agents, fired a volley into a crowd of townspeople they had been unable to disperse. Five townspeople died. The troops were removed from Boston by Gen. THOMAS GAGE, and all but two redcoats involved were acquitted by a local jury.

Boston Naval Shipyard • see CHARLESTOWN NAVY YARD.

Boston Navy Yard • see CHARLESTOWN NAVY YARD.

Boston Tea Party • (December 16, 1773) an organized refusal by Boston merchants to accept a shipment of tea, in protest against tea taxes retained after the British Parliament's repeal of the TOWNSHEND ACTS. Patriots known as SONS OF LIBERTY, led by SAMUEL ADAMS, PAUL REVERE, and others, dressed as Mohawks, boarded several British East India Company vessels and dumped 300 chests of tea into Boston Harbor.

bosun (also **bo'sun**) • *n.* variant spelling of boatswain.

bottom • *n.* **1** the ground under a sea, river, or lake: *the liner plunged to the bottom of the sea.* **2** the keel or hull of a ship, especially the relatively flat portion on either side of the keel. • *v.* (of a ship) reach or touch the ground under the sea: *nuclear submarines cannot bottom.*

Bottom-Up Review • a study of U.S. defense programs in the post-COLD WAR era released in 1993 by President BILL CLINTON's administration and used to establish the Ballistic Missile Defense Program. It detailed a three-part missile defense program, which included theater and national missile defense technology programs, and a third program to support the requirements of both theater and national missile defenses.

Bougainville • the largest of the Solomon Islands group, eastern New Guinea. Bougainville was controlled by Japanese forces during WORLD WAR II, until U.S. troops landed on November 1, 1943. Allied airstrips were built on Bougainville by January 1944, for use in attacking the Japanese strongholds throughout the South Pacific. Although Japanese forces were essentially defeated on Bougainville by March 1944, intermittent Japanese resistance on the island continued through the end of the war.

bouncing betty • a bounding fragmentation (shrapnel-filled) type of antipersonnel land mine, first used in the PERSIAN GULF WAR (1991), that springs up a few feet from the ground and explodes at stomach level. They can also be fired from howitzers.

bounding mine • (also called **bouncing mine**) a mine, first developed by East Germany in the 1950s, that springs into the air to waist level or higher when detonated and sprays its charge of red-hot metal pieces in all directions.

bounty • *n.* (pl. **-ies**) a monetary gift or reward, typically given by a government, especially a sum paid to army or navy recruits upon enlistment.

bounty jumper • a person who enlists for a cash bounty and then deserts. The term became popular late in the CIVIL WAR, although the practice had existed for several centuries.

Bouquet, Henry |bo͞oˈkā| (1719–65) • British army officer, born in Rolle, Switzerland. In the FRENCH AND INDIAN WAR, (1754–63) he was second in command under Gen. JOHN FORBES in successful attack on FORT DUQUESNE (Pittsburgh) in 1758. In PONTIAC'S REBELLION, he defeated the Indian war party at Bushy Run near Pittsburgh (August 1763). Without shooting, he negotiated the Indians' surrender and an end to the war (1764).

bouquet mine • a mine in which a number of buoyant mine cases are attached to the same sinker, so that when the mooring of one mine case is cut, another mine rises from the sinker to its set depth.

bow |bow| (also **bows**) • *n.* the front end of a ship: *water sprayed high over her bows.*
PHRASES: **on the bow** within 45° of the point directly ahead.

bower (also **bower anchor**) • *n.* each of two anchors carried at a ship's bow.

bower cable • a bow anchor cable.

Bowie, James (1796–1836) • soldier, frontiersman, and hero of the TEXAS WAR OF INDEPENDENCE (1836), born in Tennessee (probably), or Logan County, Kentucky. Bowie is credited with the invention of the BOWIE KNIFE. Bowie settled in Texas in 1828 and became the leader of the Americans in Texas opposing Mexican government. He fought in the battle of Nacogdoches, one of the Disturbances of 1832 that began the process of revolution in Texas, and participated in skirmishes leading up to the siege of San Antonio (1835–36). After a command dispute with

WILLIAM B. TRAVIS, Bowie died at the Alamo, under attack by Gen. ANTONIO LÓPEZ DE SANTA ANNA.

Bowie knife • a hunting knife, used extensively on the American frontier in the early 19th century, with a long steel blade and a handle of horn.

bowknot |ˈbōˌnät| • *n.* a double-looped knot in a ribbon, tie, or other fastening.

bowline |ˈbōlin; ˈbōˌlīn| • *n.* a rope attached to the weather leech of a square sail and leading forward, thus helping the ship sail nearer the wind.

bowsprit |ˈbowˌsprit; ˈbō-| • *n.* a spar extending forward from a ship's bow, to which the forestays are fastened.

bow wave • a wave or system of waves set up at the bows of a moving ship.

box • *v.* (in phrase **box the compass**) **1** recite the compass points in correct order. **2** make a complete change of direction.

Boxer Rebellion • see CHINA RELIEF EXPEDITION.

Boyd, Belle (1844–1900) • Confederate spy, born Isabelle Boyd in Martinsburg, Virginia (now West Virginia). A courier, nurse, blockade runner and smuggler, she was the courier for Gens. P.G.T. BEAUREGARD and STONEWALL JACKSON, and was captured and imprisoned several times. She wrote a memoir, *Belle Boyd in Camp and Prison* (1865).

Boyd, John Parker (1764–1830) • army officer, born in Newburyport, Massachusetts. Boyd fought in a Massachusetts infantry regiment suppressing SHAYS'S REBELLION (1786–87) and fought against American Indian uprisings. In the WAR OF 1812, he was criticized for a loss to a smaller British force at the battle of Crysler's Farm (1813) during a two-pronged offensive against Montreal. Boyd was ordered to Indiana Territory for service against the Indian confederation led by TECUMSEH in 1811, where he was second in command to Gov. WILLIAM HENRY HARRISON. When attacked by Indians, he won the battle of TIPPECANOE (1811).

Boyington, Gregory (1912–88) • Marine Corps aviator, born in Coeur d'Alene, Idaho. In WORLD WAR II, Boyington was a fighter pilot with the AMERICAN VOLUNTEER GROUP (AVG) (the famous "FLYING TIGERS") in air combat over Burma and China (1942), and with Marine Fighter Squadron 214, (the legendary "BLACK SHEEP" 1943–44). With twenty-eight victories he was the top marine ace of World War II and, the top marine ace ever. He was awarded the MEDAL OF HONOR and the NAVY CROSS. He wrote an autobiography, *Baa Baa Black Sheep*, in 1958.

Boyle, Jeremiah Tilford (1818–71) • Union army officer, born in Mercer County, Kentucky. In the CIVIL WAR, Boyle was assigned by Secretary of War EDWIN M. STANTON to Louisville to command "peacekeeping" forces in western Kentucky. In this bitterly divided border state, Boyle trampled civil liberties (and exasperated President ABRAHAM LINCOLN) with countless arrests on suspicion of disloyalty, censorship, interference in local elections, and frequent executions of suspected guerrillas. Further, he continually overestimated the numbers of Confederate raiders, dispatched garbled and inaccurate intelligence of enemy movements, and pursued slowly if at all.

Boyle, Thomas (1776?–1825) • ship captain and privateer, born (reputedly) at Marblehead, Massachusetts. During the WAR OF 1812, in two privateer ships, the *Comet* and the *Chasseur,* Boyle amassed a phenomenal record in battle with British ships in the Atlantic, between the West Indies and South America, and in the English Channel: in two years he secured eighty prizes valued at more than a million dollars.

Bozeman Trail • a gold-rush trail created in 1862 by U.S. explorer John Bozeman, extending approximately 400 miles (644 km) from Laramie, Wyoming, to Bannack, Montana. The trail cut through the Powder River Basin, which was prime hunting area guaranteed to the SIOUX by the FORT LARAMIE TREATY in 1851. After Bozeman's parties were repeatedly attacked by the Sioux along the trail from 1862 to 1865, federal troops were assigned to guard it. On December 21, 1866, Chief RED CLOUD led his allies in the Fetterman Massacre, in which eighty U.S. soldiers were killed at Fort Kearny. This defeat caused the United States to agree to a second treaty in 1868, which abandoned the Bozeman Trail to the Sioux and guaranteed Sioux lands in South Dakota.

BQM-34 • see FIREBEE.

brace • *n.* a device that clamps things tightly together or that gives support, especially a rope attached to the yard of a ship for trimming the sail.

bracket • *n.* the distance between two artillery shots fired either side of the target to establish range. • *v.* (**bracketed, bracketing**) establish the range of (a target) by firing two preliminary shots, one short of the target and the other beyond it.

Bradburn, Juan Davis (1787–1842) • military adventurer and officer of the Republic of Mexico, born John Davis Bradburn in Virginia. (He was known as Juan from 1817 until his death.) Bradburn was sent in 1830 to open a new garrison on Galveston Bay and establish the town of Anahuac; as lieutenant colonel in Mexican army, he was sworn to enforce the law, and was in frequent conflict with Anglo settlers (such as WILLIAM B. TRAVIS) on Mexican land.

Braddock, Edward (1695–1755) • British major general and commander in chief of British forces in North America, born in London. Early in the FRENCH AND INDIAN WAR (1754–63), Braddock was assigned (1755) to take the newly built French stronghold at the forks of the Ohio, FORT DUQUESNE, and then to sweep the French from the Ohio Valley and pursue them back into Canada (BRADDOCK'S EXPEDITION), which ended in ambush and where Braddock was mortally wounded.

Braddock's Expedition • (also **Braddock's Defeat**) the ambush and defeat of the army of

Edward Braddock near Fort Duquesne in the French and Indian War (1754–63) in 1755. The combined French and Native American attackers, though numbering just over 800, quickly overcame the surprised army of 1,400. Braddock and all other officers present were killed in the battle or its aftermath, except for George Washington.

Bradley Fighting Vehicle • (**M2A3** and **M3A3**) a fully armored, fully tracked tank developed in the 1990s that is designed to carry mechanized infantry into close contact with the enemy. It is also equipped to provide fire support to cover its dismounted operations, and to destroy enemy tanks and other vehicles. Also called **BFV**.

Bradley, Omar Nelson (1893–1981) • World War II commander and the first chairman of the Joint Chiefs of Staff, born in Clark, Missouri. Bradley was the head of the Veterans Administration (1945–47); army chief of staff (1948); the first permanent chairman of the Joint Chiefs of Staff (1949–53); and a four-star general (1950). Bradley supported President Harry S. Truman's decision to replace Gen. Douglas MacArthur (1951). Bradley, well trusted by Dwight D. Eisenhower, was given a series of large, crucial assignments. He commanded the II Corps in the North Africa campaign and Sicily (1943) and led the 1st Army in the Normandy invasion (1944). He was the commander of the 12th Army Group, comprising four U.S. armies, forty-three divisions, and 1.3 million men, the largest ground force ever commanded by a U.S. general. Advising against expanding Korean War against Chinese or Soviets, warned it would be "the wrong war, at the wrong place, at the wrong time, and with the wrong enemy."

Bragg, Braxton (1817–76) • Confederate general, born in Warrenton, North Carolina. Bragg was the fifth ranking officer in the Confederacy. He fought in the Seminole Wars (1855–58) and in the Mexican War (1846–48), distinguishing himself at Buena Vista (1847). In the Civil War, Bragg was promoted to full general and given permanent command of the Western Department (1862). Reinforced by James Longstreet, he defeated William S. Rosecrans at Chickamauga (1863), the largest battle in western theater, but failed to retake Chattanooga (1863). Relieved of field command after losing Missionary Ridge to Ulysses S. Grant (1863), he became a military adviser to Jefferson Davis (1864–65).

Bragg, Edward Stuyvesant (1827–1912) • Union army officer, U.S. congressman, and diplomat, born in Unadilla, Otsego County, New York. In the Civil War, as a colonel, Bragg commanded the "Iron Brigade," the Army of the Potomac, from Fredericksburg (1862) until the war's end (but not at Gettysburg). In the Petersburg to Richmond Campaign (1864), he was promoted to brigadier general of volunteers.

brail • *n.* (**brails**) small ropes that are led from the leech of a fore-and-aft sail to pulleys on the mast for temporarily furling it. • *v.* (**brail a sail up**) furl (a sail) by hauling on such ropes.

brainwash • *v.* make (someone) adopt radically different beliefs by using systematic and often forcible pressure: *the organization could brainwash young people.*

branch • *n.* **1** a subdivision of any organization. **2** a geographically separate unit of an activity that performs all or part of the primary functions of the parent activity on a smaller scale. Unlike an annex, a branch is not merely an overflow addition. **3** an arm or service of the army.

Brandy Station, Battle of • (June 9, 1863) a Civil War battle, the largest cavalry battle in the history of North America. As Gen. Robert E. Lee's Confederate troops prepared to push north out of Virginia, Brig. Gen. Alfred Pleasonton led a Union cavalry corps in a surprise attack on Maj. Gen. J.E.B. Stuart's Confederate horse and artillery. Pleasonton's men were unable to disperse Stuart's forces and eventually retreated after inflicting 500 casualties and suffering 900 of their own.

Brandywine (Creek), Battle of • (September 11, 1777) a Revolutionary War battle in which British troops under Sir William Howe broke through American positions, along a Pennsylvania creek, chosen by George Washington to block the British march toward Philadelphia. Though plagued by poor communications and intelligence, Washington's men, suffering heavy casualties, managed to avoid a catastrophic defeat.

Brannan, John Milton (1819–92) • Union army officer, born in Washington, D.C. In the Mexican War (1846–48), Brannan was awarded a captain's brevet for courageous performance at the battles of Contreras and Churubusco (both 1847). In the Civil War, the regular army brevetted Brannan a full colonel after Chickamauga (1863), where his division in Gen. George Thomas's XIV Corps covered William S. Rosecrans's panicked retreat, a stand that helped establish Thomas's reputation as the "Rock of Chickamauga."

Brant, Joseph (1742–1807) • (also known as **Thayendanegea**) Mohawk Indian chief, commissioned captain in British army, and war leader of the pro-British Iroquois, born in the Ohio country. A protégé of the British superintendent of Indian affairs Sir William Johnson, Brant served the British in the French and Indian War (1754–63)and Pontiac's Rebellion (1763–66). In the Revolutionary War, he led Mohawk and Loyalist followers in Lt. Col. Barry St. Leger's expedition to besiege Fort Stanwix. With intelligence from his sister Mary Brant, he ambushed American rebel forces at the Battle of Oriskany (1777). After the war, he obtained the Six Nations Reserve for the resettlement of Mohawk and others of the Six Nations on the Grand River near Brantford, Ontario. Nearly 2,000 Indians followed Brant there in 1785.

brass • *n.* slang **1** high-ranking officers. **2** the metal casings of expended small arms ammunition.

brassard |brəˈsärd; ˈbræsärd| • *n.* **1** a band worn on the sleeve, typically having an identifying mark and worn with a uniform. **2** a piece of armor for the upper arm.

brass hat • Brit. informal a high-ranking officer in the armed forces.

ORIGIN: late 19th cent.: so named because of the gilt insignia on the caps of such officers.

Brazos River • a river that starts its course in eastern New Mexico and western Texas and flows southeast to the Gulf of Mexico. The river valley was a region where Anglo-Americans first settled in Texas. Texans declared their independence from Mexico on March 2, 1836, at the settlement of Washington-on-the-Brazos, a ferry landing along the river. In 1842, President SAM HOUSTON moved the capital briefly to Washington-on-the-Brazos, which is known today as the "birthplace of the Texas Republic."

breach • *n.* **1** an act of breaking or failing to observe a law, agreement, or code of conduct: *a breach of confidence.* **2** a break in relations: *a sudden* ***breach between*** *members of the alliance.* **3** a gap in a wall, barrier, or defense, especially one made by an attacking army. • *v.* **1** make a gap in and break through (a wall, barrier, or defense): *the river breached its bank.* **2** break or fail to observe (a law, agreement, or code of conduct).

break • *v.* (past **broke**; past part. **broken**) **1** separate or cause to separate into pieces as a result of a blow, shock, or strain. **2** unfurl (a flag or sail). **3** succeed in deciphering (a code). **4** open (a shotgun or rifle) at the breech. **5** (chiefly of a military force) make a rush or dash in a particular direction: *the flight broke to the right and formed a defensive circle.* **6** fail to observe (a law, regulation, or agreement). **7** crush the emotional strength, spirit, or resistance of: *the idea was to hold the prisoners of war, not to break them.* **8** destroy the power of (a movement or organization). • *n.* **1** an interruption of continuity or uniformity: *airstrikes have continued without a break for over a week.* **2** a breakout, especially from prison.

PHRASES: **break camp** see CAMP. **break cover** emerge into the open. **break ranks** see RANK. **break step** see STEP.

break out (of war, fighting, or similarly undesirable things) start suddenly: *forest fires have broken out across Indonesia.*

break through make or force a way through (a barrier): *the infantry attempted to break through enemy lines.*

breakaway • *n.* **1** the onset of a condition in which the shock front moves away from the exterior of the expanding fireball produced by the explosion of a nuclear weapon. **2** after completion of an attack, the turn to one's heading as directed.

breaker • *n.* **1** a heavy sea wave that breaks into white foam on the shore or a shoal. **2** a person or thing that breaks something: *a codebreaker.*

Brearly, David |ˈbrer,le| (1745–90) • REVOLUTIONARY WAR officer, jurist, and framer and defender of the U.S. Constitution, born near Maidenshead (now Lawrenceville), New Jersey. In the Revolutionary War, as a lieutenant colonel of the 1st New Jersey Regiment, he served at the battles of BRANDYWINE (1777), GERMANTOWN (1777), and MONMOUTH (1778). Brearly resigned from the army when he was elected chief justice of the New Jersey Supreme Court in 1779.

breasthook • *n.* a large piece of shaped timber fitted horizontally in the bows of a ship, used to connect the sides to the stem.

breastwork • *n.* a low temporary defense or parapet.

Breckinridge, John Cabell (1821–75) • Confederate general, U.S. congressman (1851–55), and vice president of the United States, born in Lexington, Kentucky. Breckinridge, a likable border-state moderate, was elected vice president under JAMES BUCHANAN (1857–61); as vice president, he worked unsuccessfully for a sectional compromise. He was nominated as a presidential candidate by the Democratic party's southern wing; he swept the South but lost nationally to ABRAHAM LINCOLN. As a brigadier general in the Confederate army, Breckinridge was involved in the heaviest fighting in the western theater, at SHILOH (1862), CHICKAMAUGA (1863), and MISSIONARY RIDGE (1863). As JEFFERSON DAVIS's last war secretary, Breckinridge worked to ensure an honorable defeat, counseling Gen. JOSEPH E. JOHNSTON in armistice negotiations with Gen. WILLIAM T. SHERMAN in North Carolina and opposing continuation of war with guerrilla bands. He also struggled to preserve official Confederate government records from destruction.

breech • *n.* **1** the part of a cannon behind the bore. **2** the back part of a rifle or gun barrel.

breechblock • *n.* a metal block that closes the aperture at the back part of a rifle or gun barrel.

breeches buoy • a lifebuoy with canvas breeches attached that, when suspended from a rope, can be used to transfer a passenger to safety from a ship.

breeching • *n.* a thick rope used to secure the carriages of cannon on a ship and to absorb the force of the recoil.

breech-loader • *n.* a gun designed to have ammunition inserted at the breech rather than through the muzzle.

DERIVATIVES: **breech-loading** *adj.*

Breed's Hill, Battle of • see BUNKER HILL, BATTLE OF.

Bren (also **Bren gun**) • *n.* a lightweight quick-firing machine gun used by the ALLIED FORCES in WORLD WAR II.

ORIGIN: blend of *Brno* (a town in the Czech Republic where it was originally made) and *Enfield* in England (site of the Royal Small Arms Factory where it was later made).

Brest-Litovsk, Peace of • a series of peace negotiations begun on December 22, 1917, between the CENTRAL POWERS, the Ukranian Republic, and Soviet Russia to resolve WORLD WAR I hostilities. The Central Powers and the nationalist Ukrainian Republic signed a treaty on February 9, 1918. The Soviet government signed the Treaty of Brest-Litovsk on March

3, 1918, to accept Germany's demands and after Germany began new eastward invasions that threatened the Bolshevik Revolution. Russia lost Ukraine, its Polish-Baltic territories, and Finland.

Bretton Woods Conference • a WORLD WAR II meeting attended by representatives from forty-four nations, held at Bretton Woods, New Hampshire, on July 1–2, 1944. It established the International Bank for Reconstruction and Development, which was established in 1945, and the International Monetary Fund, which was established in 1946. Both were established to provide postwar economic assistance to governments in need.

brevet |brə'vet; 'brevit| • *n.* a former type of military commission conferred especially for outstanding service by which an officer was promoted to a higher rank without the corresponding pay: *a brevet lieutenant.* • *v.* (**breveted** or **brevetted**, **breveting** or **brevetting**) confer a brevet rank on.

brevity code • a code that provides no security but that has as its sole purpose the shortening of messages rather than the concealment of their content.

Brewer, Lucy • allegedly the first woman Marine, who supposedly served, disguised as a man, on the *USS Constitution* during the WAR OF 1812.

Brezhnev Doctrine • a policy promoted by Soviet leader LEONID BREZHNEV that asserted that the Soviet Union had the right to use military force to maintain the strict rule of the Communist Party in nearby socialist countries. The Brezhnev Doctrine was used to justify the invasion of Czechoslovakia in 1968 after Alexander Dubçek introduced political reforms there. The policy was maintained through 1989.

Brezhnev, Leonid (Ilich) |'brezH,nef; 'brezHnyif| (1906–82) • Soviet statesman. General Secretary of the Communist Party of the Soviet Union from 1966 to 1982 and President from 1977 to 1982. His period in power was marked by intensified persecution of dissidents at home and by attempted détente followed by renewed cold war in 1968; he was largely responsible for the invasion of Czechoslovakia (1968).

bridge • *n.* the elevated, enclosed platform on a ship from which the captain and officers direct operations.

bridgehead • *n.* a strong position secured by an army inside enemy territory from which to advance or attack.

Bridge, Horatio (1806–93) • Union naval officer and author, born in Augusta, Maine. Bridge was the paymaster general of the U.S. Navy. He wrote *The Journal of an African Cruiser* (1845) and *Personal Recollections of Nathaniel Hawthorne* (1893).

bridle • *n.* **1** the headgear used to control a horse, consisting of buckled straps to which a bit and reins are attached. **2** a mooring cable.

briefing • *n.* the act of giving in advance specific instructions or information, normally in oral form.

brig • *n.* **1** a two-masted, square-rigged ship with an additional gaff sail on the mainmast. **2** informal a prison, especially on a warship.

Brig. • *abbr.* Brigadier.

brigade • *n.* **1** a subdivision of an army, typically consisting of a small number of infantry battalions and/or other units and often forming part of a division: *he commanded a brigade of 3,000 men.* **2** an organization with a specific purpose, typically with a military or quasi-military structure: *the local fire brigade.* • *v.* (often **be brigaded**) rare form into a brigade.

brigade major • the principal staff officer to the brigadier in command at the headquarters of a brigade.

Brigade of the American Revolution • an international historical organization, founded in 1962, dedicated to recreating the lives of the common soldiers who fought in the REVOLUTIONARY WAR. It has more than 2,500 members organized into 130 units. Each unit represents one of the military units that fought in the Revolution.

brigadier |'brigə,di(ə)r| • *n.* a rank of officer in the British army, above colonel and below major general.

brigadier general • an officer in the U.S. Army, Air Force, or Marine Corps ranking above colonel and below major general.

brigantine |'brigən,tēn| • *n.* a two-masted sailing ship with a square-rigged foremast and a fore-and-aft-rigged mainmast.

brig of war • a two-masted warship that carries two or more headsails.

Brilliant Pebbles • 1,000 space-based, hit-to-kill interceptors (anti-missile missiles), orbiting 200 to 300 miles above the earth, designed to be effective against missiles with ranges greater than 375 miles. These were to be a component of the GLOBAL PROTECTION AGAINST LIMITED STRIKES (GPALS) missile defense system proposed in 1991 by President GEORGE H. BUSH. See also STRATEGIC DEFENSE INITIATIVE.

bring • *v.* (past and past part. **brought** |brôt|) **bring something about** cause a ship to head in a different direction. **bring someone off** be rescued from a ship in difficulties.

brinksmanship • *n.* the practice of pressing military or diplomatic demands right up to the point of starting a war. The term, coined in the 1950s, is used particularly to describe those actions which risk igniting a general nuclear war.

The first recorded use of this COLD WAR term was in a Febuary 25, 1956, speech by Democratic presidential candidate Adlai E. Stevenson in reference to JOHN FOSTER DULLES, Dwight D. Eisenhower's Secretary of State.

Brisbin, James Sanks (1837–92) • Union army officer, born in Boalsburg, Pennsylvania. Brisbin, who served in twenty-eight pitched battles during the CIVIL WAR, was a strong advocate of increased enlistment of black soldiers. He was appointed a colonel of U.S. COLORED TROOPS, and raised nearly 20,000 Colored Troops in Kentucky.

Britain, Battle of • (August–October 1940) a series of air battles over southern England between the ROYAL AIR FORCE and the German LUFTWAFFE during WORLD WAR II. German bombers attacked British coastal defenses, radar stations, and shipping in preparation for an invasion, then began a campaign of night bombings over London, Coventry, and other cities (the BLITZ). The RAF lost about 900 planes, and the Luftwaffe some 2,300; the battle was Germany's first major setback of World War II, and invasion plans were abandoned.

broach • *v.* (also **broach to**) (of a ship with the wind on the quarter) veer and pitch forward because of bad steering or a sea hitting the stern, causing it to present a side to the wind and sea, losing a steerage, and possibly suffer serious damage: *we had broached badly, side on to the wind and sea* • *n.* a sudden and hazardous veering of a ship having such consequences.

broad pennant (also **broad pendant**) • a short swallow-tailed pennant distinguishing the commodore's ship in a squadron.

broad reach • *n.* a point of sailing in which the wind blows over a boat's quarter, between the beam and the stern: ***on a broad reach*** *they are magnificent craft.* • *v.* (**broad-reach**) sail with the wind in this position.

broadside • *n.* **1** a nearly simultaneous firing of all the guns from one side of a warship. **2** the set of guns that can fire on each side of a warship. **3** the side of a ship above the water between the bow and quarter.

PHRASES: **broadside on** (also **broadside to**) sideways on: *the canoe was broadside to the waves.*

Brodhead, Daniel (1736–1809) • Revolutionary army officer, born in Albany, New York. In the REVOLUTIONARY WAR, Brodhead served at the siege of Boston (1775), the battles of NEW YORK (1776), BRANDYWINE (1777), and GERMANTOWN (1777), and wintered at VALLEY FORGE (1777–78) with GEORGE WASHINGTON. He was sent by Washington to FORT PITT and appointed commander of the Western Department.

Despite being known as an Indian hater, Brodhead amicably concluded a treaty with the Delawares, who gave him the ceremonial name "Great Moon."

Bronco • (**OV-10**) a night surveillance aircraft procured by the U.S. Navy in the early 1960s for counter-insurgency operations.

Bronze Star Medal • U.S. military decoration awarded for "heroic or meritorious achievement or service not involving aerial flight" during operations against an armed enemy of the United States or while serving with friendly foreign forces engaged in armed conflict. The Bronze Star Medal was established by an Executive Order in February 1944 (superseded by Executive Order 11046 of 1962). The Bronze Star Medal may be awarded to members of any branch of service.

Brooke Army Medical Center • an organization of the U.S. ARMY MEDICAL DEPARTMENT (AMEDD) and located at Fort Sam Houston. It is the principal group responsible for delivering health care to members of the Army under the command of the surgeon general.

Brooke, John Mercer (1826–1906) • Confederate naval officer, scientist, and inventor, born at Fort Brooke, Tampa Bay, Florida. At the NAVAL OBSERVATORY (1851–53), Brooke invented a deep-sea sounding apparatus that permitted the first accurate mapping of bottom topography. In the CIVIL WAR, he devised a plan for reconstructing the USS *Merrimac* into an ironclad, and oversaw production of armor and guns for the ship, renamed CSS *Virginia.* While chief of the NAVY BUREAU OF ORDNANCE (1863–65), he invented the "Brooke" gun, a rifled cannon made of cast iron, the most powerful weapon produced by the Confederate government.

Brooke rifle • a rifle used by the Confederate Army in the CIVIL WAR that had a wrought-iron reinforcing bands around the breech end of the rifle.

Brooklyn Navy Yard • the popular name for the New York Navy Yard, a shipyard that was first established on the East River in the 1700s. Naval ships for all major U.S. conflicts were built there, including torpedo boats, destroyers, coast guard cutters, battleships, and aircraft carriers. It reached the height of its productivity in WORLD WAR II. It closed on June 30, 1966.

***Brooklyn*, USS** • (**CA-3**) an armored "heavy" cruiser commissioned in December 1896 and flagship of the **"Flying Squadron"** during the SPANISH-AMERICAN WAR (1898). Inactive between 1908 and 1915, the *Brooklyn* served in WORLD WAR I, mostly in the Pacific, and, in 1921, was decommissioned and sold.

Brooks, John (1752–1825) • Revolutionary army officer and governor of Massachusetts, born in Medford, Massachusetts. In the REVOLUTIONARY WAR, he served in most battles, from CONCORD (1775) on. At MONMOUTH (1778), he was adjutant to Gen. CHARLES LEE, and testified on his behalf at the court-martial of Lee for insubordination and needless retreat before the enemy. Brooks also defended GEORGE WASHINGTON at the time of the NEWBURGH CONSPIRACY (1783), and was one of three officers selected to present complaints to Congress.

Brooks, William Thomas Harbaugh (1821–70) • Union army officer, born in New Lisbon, Ohio. In the 3rd U.S. Infantry, "Bully" Brooks served in the SEMINOLE WAR (1842–43) and saw action in the MEXICAN WAR (1846–48) at PALO ALTO, RESACA DE LA PALMA, MONTERREY, VERACRUZ, CERRO GORDO, CONTRERAS, and MEXICO CITY. He won brevets of captain and major for conspicuous service at Monterrey and Contreras. In the CIVIL WAR, Brooks was commander, 1st Division, IV Corps, ARMY OF THE POTOMAC, at FREDERICKSBURG (1862) and praised for "gallant and spirited" leadership at CHANCELLORSVILLE (1863). He was briefly major general, commander of the Department of the Monongahela, but suffered political reprisals for friendship with the deposed Gen. GEORGE

B. McClellan and for criticism of Gens. Ambrose Burnside and Joseph Hooker, favorites of President Abraham Lincoln administration.

brow • *n.* **1** a gangway from a ship to the shore. **2** a hinged part of a ferry or landing craft forming a landing platform or ramp.

Brown Bess • a nickname for an 18th century flintlock gun, the first to become a standardized military firearm. The name is probably from the acid treatment of its barrel that gave it a brown color. The first models had a smooth bore with accuracy up to about 60 to 70 yards. Later rifling improved accuracy.

Brownell, Henry Howard (1820–72) • Civil War poet and naval officer, born in Providence, Rhode Island. Brownell composed patriotic verses commemorating Union naval actions, with such titles as "General Orders," "The River Fight," and "The Bay Fight." In "Bury Them," commemorating Col. Robert Gould Shaw's ill-conceived but brave attack on Fort Wagner (July 18, 1863), Brownell remarks that the Union dead, flung into a "horrible Pit," will—like fabled "Dragon's Teeth"—emerge a "crop of steel."

Brown, George Scratchley (1918–78) • Air Force chief of staff (1973–74) and Joint Chiefs of Staff (JCS) chairman (1974–78), born in Montclair, New Jersey. In World War II, Brown was a squadron commander, group operations officer, and executive officer of the 93rd Bombardment Group; he was awarded the Distinguished Service Cross. In the Office of the Secretary of Defense (1959–63), he proved particularly adept at smoothing interservice rivalries and buffering relations between Secretary Robert S. McNamara and the JCS, and played a similar role as assistant to JCS chairman Gen. Earle Wheeler (1966–68). In the Vietnam War, he commanded the 7th Air Force in South Vietnam (1968–70) and was air deputy for Gen. Creighton Abrams, commander of American forces in Vietnam. As JCS chairman he effected the first major reorganization of the JCS since 1958.

Brown, Harold (1927–) • nuclear weapons designer, secretary of the Air Force, and Secretary of Defense. Brown was the first scientist to become Secretary of Defense. As the director of the Lawrence Livermore National Laboratory (1960), he took a leading role in the design of the Polaris missile warhead. As secretary of the air force (1965–68), he was a drafter of the Vietnam War bombing program, but came to favor deescalation. Brown was a member of the SALT I delegation under President Richard M. Nixon; as the defense secretary under President Jimmy Carter (1977–81), he was involved with the MX missile, SALT II, and nuclear strategy.

Browning automatic rifle • (**BAR**) a .30-06 caliber gas-operated automatic rifle. The BAR was the U.S. Army's main squad automatic rifle in World War II and Korea.

Browning, John Moses (1855–1926) • American inventor, born in Ogden, Utah. Browning was the leading American designer of automatic arms in the early 20th century. Browning patented a breech-loading single-shot rifle (1879) and a gas-operated Colt machine gun (1895), and designed firearms for Colt, Winchester, Stevens, and Remington gunmakers. He was the inventor of the **Browning automatic pistol** (1911; standard issue until the 1980s), the **Browning machine gun** (1917), and the automatic rifle, or BAR (1918).

Brown, Jesse Leroy (1926–50) • naval aviator, born in Hattiesburg, Mississippi. Brown was the first black aviation trainee in the U.S. Navy (graduated 1948), and was assigned to Fighter Squadron 32 in January 1949. He flew about twenty combat missions early in the Korean War. While flying close air support in the Chosin Reservoir campaign (1950), Brown's Corsair was hit, and he was forced to make a crash landing behind enemy lines. Rescue attempts failed. He was awarded the Distinguished Flying Cross and the Purple Heart posthumously.

Brown was the first black naval aviator, the first black aviator to die in combat, and the first black U.S. naval officer to be killed in combat. As a recognition of his service, on Febuary 17, 1973, the navy commissioned the USS *Jesse L. Brown,* Destroyer Escort 1089.

Brown, John (1800–59) • abolitionist, born in Torrington, Connecticut. Driven by at first a fervent, then a fanatical devotion to the abolition of slavery, Brown led killings of five proslavery activists in Pottawatomie, Kansas (1856), during the Bleeding Kansas skirmishes between proslavery and abolitionist guerrillas. He also led a raid into Missouri, where his men seized eleven slaves and several horses and killed a slaveowner, and conceived plans to attack slavery in the southern states. On October 16, 1859, Brown led twenty-one volunteers in a raid on the federal arsenal at Harpers Ferry, Virginia (now West Virginia), intending to seize weapons and incite a nationwide slave revolt. Brown was taken by a storming party of U.S. Marines commanded by Col. Robert E. Lee. In his trial, Brown claimed he was an instrument of God to free the slaves, and said, before he was hanged, "I, John Brown, am now quite certain that the crimes of this guilty land will never be purged away but with Blood."

Brown, John • Revolutionary War army officer, born in Haverhill, Massachusetts. Brown assisted in campaigns with Ethan Allen and Benedict Arnold and led a recapture of Fort Ticonderoga from Gen. John Burgoyne (1777). During the seige of Quebec (1775), Brown had a public dispute with Benedict Arnold, openly declaring that he did not trust Arnold, and resigned from the army (February 1777), refusing to serve any longer under Arnold. Recalled to help Gov. George Clinton fend off attacks by Sir John Johnson, Brown was killed, along with forty-five of his men, in an ambush in the Mohawk Valley.

Brownshirts • see Sturmabteilung.

Brown, Thomas (1750–1825) • REVOLUTIONARY WAR soldier and superintendent of the Southern Indian Department, born in Whitby, England. A conspicuous LOYALIST, Brown was an early target of the Georgia Whigs. He promoted the strategy of recruiting Indian allies to fight revolutionaries, and recruited corps of rangers in east Florida. Brown led raids along southern Georgia frontier. He constructed Fort Cornwallis on the Savannah River (surrendered June 6, 1781) and defended Savannah (surrendered July 11, 1781).

Brown Water Navy • the Mobile Riverine Force (Task Force 117 [TF-117]) established to provide support for U.S. Army infantry of the 9th Infantry Division in the MEKONG Delta during the VIETNAM WAR. Although activated on January 7, 1967, not until 1968 did the MRF have its full complement of 180 river assault craft. After the TET OFFENSIVE early in 1968, the MRF continued to expand. During the four years of its existence, the Brown Water Navy fought thousands of small battles for control of Vietnam's rice bowl and major enemy supply routes among the inland waterways. As a result of the VIETNAMIZATION PROGRAM, the end of the MRF came when the U.S. Navy transferred the last 125 combat boats to the Vietnamese Navy on December 10, 1970. See also BLUE WATER.

Broz, Josip • see TITO.

Bruce anchor • a modern type of anchor made in one piece, with three flukes forming a scoop.

Bryan, William Jennings (1860–1925) • DEMOCRATIC PARTY leader, U.S. congressman (1891–95), and secretary of state, born in Salem, Illinois. In the SPANISH-AMERICAN WAR (1898), Bryan was a colonel of the 3rd Nebraska Volunteer Regiment. He was the most prominent leader of the Democratic party from 1896 to 1912. As the first secretary of state under WOODROW WILSON (1913–15), Bryan hoped to promote world peace by means of bilateral conciliation treaties through which the participating nations agreed, in event of a dispute, to observe a "cooling off" period. Bryan negotiated such treaties with 30 nations. He resigned rather than sign Wilson's note to Germany after the sinking of the LUSITANIA. Remaining loyal to the president, he continued to demand neutrality and opposed preparedness, which, he said, "provokes war." Bryan supported the LEAGUE OF NATIONS in 1919, and when it was blocked in the Senate, he recommended compromise in 1920 to save it.

Brzezinski, Zbigniew K. |brəˈzHinskē; -ˈzin| (1928–) • national security adviser and professor, born in Warsaw, Poland. Brzezinski was national security adviser to President JIMMY CARTER (1977–81), and was awarded the Presidential Medal of Freedom for his role in the normalization of U.S.-Chinese relations and for contributions to the human rights and national security policy.

Buchanan, Franklin (1800–74) • U.S. and Confederate naval officer, born in Baltimore, Maryland. Buchanan was the first superintendent of the U.S. NAVAL ACADEMY (1845–47). He commanded the sloop *Germantown* in the MEXICAN WAR (1846–48), the steam frigate *Susquehanna* on MATTHEW C. PERRY's expedition to Japan (1852), and commanded the WASHINGTON NAVY YARD (1859–61). In the CIVIL WAR, he resigned his U.S. commission and was commissioned a captain in the Confederate Navy. Commanding the ironclad *Virginia,* he attacked and destroyed the wooden frigates *Congress* and *Cumberland* (March 8, 1862). He commanded the naval defenses of MOBILE BAY, which he surrendered to Adm. DAVID FARRAGUT (August 5, 1864).

Buchanan, James (1791–1868) • fifteenth president of the United States (1857–61); born near Mercersburg, Pennsylvania. As the last "antebellum" president, Buchanan sought to defuse the sectional crisis, but made decisions that only inflamed tensions. His greatest challenge was to settle the Kansas controversy and remove the issue of slavery's expansion from national politics. Buchanan isolated himself from dissenting views, disliked confrontation, never understood northern feelings against slavery, and was excessively pro-southern in his views, qualities that eventually destroyed his political influence and wrecked his presidency.

Buchenwald |ˈbo͝okən,wôld| • a NAZI concentration camp in WORLD WAR II, near the village of Buchenwald in eastern Germany.

Bucher, Lloyd Mark (1928–) • U.S. naval officer, born in Pocatello, Idaho. Bucher was the commander of the first U.S. Navy vessel seized since the *Chesapeake* in 1807. A longtime submarine officer, Bucher was given command of the USS *Pueblo,* an NSA-Naval Security Group SIGINT vessel fired upon and seized by North Korea on January 23, 1968, during an intelligence-gathering mission in the Sea of Japan. Bucher surrendered, and the eighty-two-man crew was imprisoned and tortured to admit to spying. After their release on December 22, 1968, in exchange for an official U.S. admission of espionage, a navy court of inquiry recommendation that Bucher be court-martialed was vetoed by Navy Secretary JOHN H. CHAFEE. Bucher retired from the navy in 1973.

Buckner, Simon Bolivar (1886–1945) • general, born in Munfordville, Kentucky, the son of Confederate general SIMON BOLIVAR BUCKNER and the highest-ranking American general killed in WORLD WAR II. In World War I, Buckner was a trainer of army units and a commandant of cadets at WEST POINT (1933–36). He was promoted to brigadier general in 1940 and to lieutenant general in 1944. Troops under Buckner's command defeated a Japanese attempt to gain a strong foothold in the Aleutian Islands in 1942 and 1943. He was killed at the invasion of OKINAWA and was posthumously awarded the DISTINGUISHED SERVICE CROSS for his "outstanding leadership, tactical genius, and personal courage."

Buckner, Simon Bolivar (1823–1914) • Confederate general and governor of Kentucky (1887–91), born in Hart County, Kentucky. In the MEXICAN WAR (1846–48), Buckner was breveted captain for gallant and meritorious conduct. He was appointed Kentucky's inspector general of state militia in 1860. Brig. Gen. Buckner surrendered FORT DONELSON (February 1862) on the famous "unconditional surrender" terms of Gen. ULYSSES S. GRANT. Released after five months' imprisonment, Buckner was promoted to major general and participated in numerous battles, most notably at PERRYVILLE (1862) and CHICKAMAUGA (1863). He was promoted to lieutenant general in the Trans-Mississippi Department under Gen. E. KIRBY SMITH (1864) and, after APPOMATTOX, negotiated the surrender of troops late in 1865.

Buell, Don Carlos |'byo͞oəl| (1818–98) • soldier and businessman, born near Marietta, Ohio. Buell fought in the SEMINOLE WAR (1855–57) and the MEXICAN WAR (1846–48), and commanded the ARMY OF THE OHIO (1861–62). He reinforced ULYSSES S. GRANT at SHILOH (April 6–7, 1862), and attacked Confederates at PERRYVILLE, Kentucky (October 8, 1862), who then withdrew from the state. ABRAHAM LINCOLN and Secretary ofWar EDWIN M. STANTON blamed Buell for not forcing a decisive battle and crushing the Confederate forces.

Buena Vista, Battle of • (February 22–23, 1847) an American victory during the MEXICAN WAR (1846–48). Mexican general ANTONIO LÓPEZ DE SANTA ANNA, after capturing a U.S. courier, marched his dwindling army, initially 21,000 soldiers, across 200 miles of desert to fight Maj. Gen. ZACHARY TAYLOR's force of 5,000 mainly untested men. U.S. troops, directed by Brig. Gen. JOHN WOOL, took a stand across a road between two mountains, and, taking advantage of superior artillery and the timely arrival of reinforcements, managed to hold off the Mexicans, whose losses were estimated at 2,000 to 3,500. American casualties were approximately 700.

Buffalo soldiers • the first black regiments in the regular army, established by Congress on July 1866. Originally the 9th and 10th Calvary and the 38th, 39th, 40th, and 41st Infantry Regiments, in 1869 the 38th and the 41st were merged into the 24th Infantry Regiment and the 39th and 40th were merged into the 25th Infantry Regiment. They served mostly at the frontier, but also fought in Cuba, in the PHILIPPINE WAR, and in Mexican border skirmishes.

The name "Buffalo" was first applied to the 10th Calvary Regiment about 1870 by the CHEYENNE. Supposedly the Cheyenne of the time thought the curly-haired, dark-skinned soldiers resembled buffalo.

Buford, Abraham (1749–1833) • Revolutionary War officer, born in Culpeper County, Virginia. Buford served in the northern states during the first three years of the REVOLUTIONARY WAR; then he transferred to South Carolina in 1778 where in May 1780 he fought against the forces of Lt. Col. BANASTRE TARLETON at the WAXHAWS. The result was a complete British victory: 300 American soldiers were killed. American survivors believed that Tarleton's men deliberately slaughtered men who were trying to capitulate.

Buford, Abraham (1820–84) • Confederate cavalry officer, born in Woodford County, Kentucky. Buford fought in the STONES RIVER campaign (1862–63) and at the battle of CHAMPION HILL (1863). In March 1864, under Maj. Gen. NATHAN BEDFORD FORREST, Buford commanded a cavalry division and led raids in the spring campaign in western Tennessee and Kentucky; he was praised by Forrest in June 1864, when Forrest routed a Union force double the size of his own. After fighting in JOHN B. HOOD'S NASHVILLE campaign (1864), Buford was given command of the Confederate cavalry remaining in Alabama (Febuary 1865) and surrendered on May 9 at Gainesville, Alabama.

Buford, John (1826–63) • Union army officer, born in Woodford County, Kentucky. During the CIVIL WAR, Buford commanded a cavalry brigade under Maj. Gen. JOHN POPE, and was appointed chief of cavalry in the ARMY OF THE POTOMAC. In 1863, he distinguished himself at GETTYSBURG. At the request of President ABRAHAM LINCOLN, Buford was promoted to major general shortly before his death.

bug • *n.* a concealed microphone or listening device or other audiosurveillance device. • *v.* install such means for audiosurveillance: *the embassy had been bugged for several months.*

buildup • *n.* the process or act of attaining the prescribed strength of units and levels of vehicles, equipment, stores, and supplies.

bulge • *n.* a piece of land that projects outward from an otherwise regular line: *the advance created an eastward-facing bulge in the line.*

Bulge, Battle of the • (also known as **Battle of the Ardennes**) (December 16, 1944–January 28, 1945) the largest WORLD WAR II land battle on the WESTERN FRONT, and the last major German counteroffensive of the war. Allied forces were able to halt the drive with the loss of about 80,000 men, mainly Americans. German losses are estimated to have topped 100,000. ADOLF HITLER himself ordered 250,000 men to attempt to cut Allied forces in half and to retake the crucial port of Antwerp. Secretly massed PANZER-led units launched their assault into the thinnest part of the Allied lines and began pressing through the Ardennes with the initial goal of seizing the road and communication center of Bastogne, Belgium, on their way to Antwerp. Though surprised and suffering tremendous losses, Allied units were able to slow the Germans and hold an almost completely encircled Bastogne. American armor moved swiftly to counterattack and cut German supply lines. The Germans' forward motion, a bulge 70 miles deep into Allied lines, was essentially checked by Christmas, but it took another month before the Allies could push back to the original line. Both sides suffered, but the Germans' losses were fatal, as the troops and equipment lost were irreplaceable.

bulkhead • *n.* a dividing wall or barrier between compartments in a ship, aircraft, or other vehicle.

Bulletin of the Atomic Scientists • a publication of the nonprofit Educational Foundation for Nuclear Science whose mission is to educate the public about issues relating to war and peace. It is best known for its DOOMSDAY CLOCK.

Bull Run, First Battle of • (also known as **First Manassas**) (July 21,1861) the first major battle of the CIVIL WAR, won by the Confederates. Some 28,000 Union troops led by Gen. IRVIN MCDOWELL marched under presidential order to Manassas, Virginia, 25 miles southwest of Washington, where Gen. P.G.T. BEAUREGARD's 32,000 Confederate soldiers straddled the Washington-Richmond rail line. Since his men were undisciplined for combat, McDowell paused to give his troops additional training before attacking the rebels on the far side of Bull Run, a tributary of the Potomac. A fierce defensive stand, which earned Maj. Gen. THOMAS "STONEWALL" JACKSON his nickname, followed by a Confederate counterattack, broke the Union forces, which fled to Washington. Union losses totaled upwards of 2,600; the Confederates, nearly 2,000.

Bull Run, Second Battle of • (also known as **Second Manassas**) (August 29–30, 1862) the third of the battles known as the Second Bull Run Campaign, in which the Confederate forces repulsed an offensive drive into Virginia by Union forces under Maj. Gen. JOHN POPE, and during which the total losses for both sides approached 25,000. On August 29, knowing the Confederate armies had divided, and in possession of 75,000 troops, Pope took the initiative to attack the defensive positions of Maj. Gen. THOMAS "STONEWALL" JACKSON's 18,000 men. Unknown to Pope, Gen. JAMES LONGSTREET was already moving to support Jackson's right with 30,000 men. Advancing his divisions piecemeal, Pope was unable to use his advantage; and his units were driven back by Jackson's troops, who took the ground offered by the Union retreat. Jackson's men withdrew to their original positions under the cover of darkness, leading Pope, unaware of Longstreet's arrival on Jackson's right the previous day, to assume the enemy was retreating and to order a pursuit on August 30. Union forces ran into the center of the artillery-supported Confederate line. The battle continued until dark and a heavy rain made fighting impossible, after which the Union troops began to withdraw.

bull's-eye • *n.* (also **bullseye**) **1** the center of a target in sports such as archery, shooting, and darts. **2** a shot that hits such a target center.

bully beef • slang (in WORLD WARS I and II) canned corned beef. See also MONKEY MEAT.

bulwark | 'bo͝ol,wərk | • *n.* **1** a defensive wall. **2** (usually **bulwarks**) an extension of a ship's sides above the level of the deck.

Bundy, McGeorge (1919–96) • historian, educator, and government official. As the special assistant to Presidents JOHN F. KENNEDY and LYNDON B. JOHNSON for national security affairs (1961–66), Bundy supervised the NATIONAL SECURITY COUNCIL staff and played a key role in foreign policy. He supported the BAY OF PIGS invasion (1961), counseled the president during the CUBAN MISSILE CRISIS (1962), and joined Defense Secretary ROBERT S. MCNAMARA in urging increased U.S. involvement in Vietnam, advocating "sustained reprisals" against the North Vietnamese.

bunker | 'bəNGkər | • *n.* **1** a large container or compartment for storing fuel: *a coal bunker.* **2** a reinforced underground shelter, typically for use in wartime. • *v.* fill the fuel containers of (a ship); refuel.

Bunker Hill, Battle of • (June 17, 1775) the first major battle of the REVOLUTIONARY WAR, and a defeat of militiamen who had fortified Breed's and Bunker Hills on the Charlestown Peninsula north of Boston. Though many of the colonial forces fought bravely, and British regulars required three costly assaults to achieve the ground, only later did general colonial sentiment regard the decision to fight here as more than a misguided adventure.

bunt • *n.* **1** the baggy center of a sail or fishing net. **2** an act of flying an aircraft in part of an outside loop.

buntline | 'bənt,līn | • *n.* a line for restraining the loose center of a sail while it is furled.

buoy | bo͞o-ē; boi | • *n.* an anchored float serving as a navigation mark, to show reefs or other hazards, or for mooring. • *v.* mark with an anchored float: (**buoyed**) *a buoyed channel.*

buoyage • *n.* the provision of buoys.

BUR • see BOTTOM-UP REVIEW.

bureaucrat | 'byo͝orə,kræt | • *n.* an official in a government department.

DERIVATIVES: **bureaucratic** | ,byo͝orə 'krætik | *adj.* **bureaucratically** | ,byo͝orə 'krætik(ə)lē | *adv.*

bureaucratese • *n.* derisive term for the jargon of military and civilian government officials.

Bureau of Colored Troops • a bureau established on May 22, 1863, in the Adjutant General's Office of the U.S. War Department to handle all matters relating to the recruitment and organization of African American soldiers.

Bureau of Navigation • one of five formerly independent federal agencies united under the U.S. Coast Guard. It was established under the control of the Treasury Department on July 5, 1884, merged with the Steamboat Inspection Service to form the Bureau of Navigation and Steamboat Inspection in 1932, which was renamed the Bureau of Marine Inspection and Navigation in 1936, and made a permanent part of the Coast Guard on July 16, 1946.

Bureau of Public Relations, Army • the department of the army that handled public relations and propaganda during WORLD WAR II.

Burgoyne, John (1723–92) • British general and dramatist, born in London. Burgoyne achieved a brilliant record for military daring as a lieutenant colonel in the FRENCH AND INDIAN WAR (1754–63). As a general, Burgoyne in May 1777 led a British army from Canada up Lake Champlain and quickly seized FORT TICONDEROGA. After suffering a serious check at BENNINGTON that same year, he arrived at BEMIS HEIGHTS in September. In two major battles on September 19 and October 7, he was halted and then forced to retreat to Saratoga. Burgoyne surrendered to Maj. Gen. HORATIO GATES on October 17, 1777.

Burke, Arleigh Albert (1901–96) • admiral, born near Boulder, Colorado. In WORLD WAR II, he won the nickname "31 Knot Burke" in the Battle of Cape St. George in the Solomon Islands (November 1943) when his Destroyer Squadron 23 defeated a Japanese force. During the 1949 REVOLT OF THE ADMIRALS Burke helped prepare the navy's congressional testimony on defense unification. Burke was appointed chief of naval operations in 1955 by DWIGHT D. EISENHOWER (skipping ninety-two higher-ranked admirals), and, while serving an unprecedented three terms (six years), advocated development of POLARIS submarine-based ballistic missile program.

Burke, Michael (1918–87) • intelligence operative born in Enfield, Connecticut. Burke served in the OFFICE OF STRATEGIC SERVICES (OSS) in Europe under WILLIAM J. DONOVAN. He landed behind enemy lines in France and Italy several times during WORLD WAR II; as a JEDBURGH TEAMS operative, helped to plan the D-DAY invasion of France. Burke was decorated with a NAVY CROSS, a SILVER STAR, and the French MÉDAILLE DE LA RÉSISTANCE.

Burma Supply Road • a route linking Lashio in Burma to Kunming in China, covering 717 miles (1,154 km). Completed in 1939, it was built by the Chinese in response to the Japanese occupation of the Chinese coast, to serve as a supply route to the interior.

burn • *v.* to deliberately expose the true status of a person under cover. • *n.* the legitimate destruction and burning of classified material, usually accomplished by the custodian of the material, as prescribed in regulations.

burned • *adj.* **1** of a clandestine operator, having been exposed to the operation (especially in a surveillance) **2** of a source of information, having its reliability compromised.

burn notice • an official statement by one intelligence agency to other agencies, domestic or foreign, that an individual or group is unreliable for any of a variety of reasons.

Burnside, Ambrose Everett (1824–81) • Union general, governor of Rhode Island (1866–69), and U.S. senator (1875–81), born in Liberty, Indiana. As a brigadier general of volunteers, Burnside captured Roanoke Island and New Bern on North Carolina coast; while commanding the left wing at ANTIETAM (1862), his failure to move quickly contributed to Gen. GEORGE B. MCCLELLAN's defeat. He replaced McClellan as commander of the ARMY OF THE POTOMAC (a position he had twice declined earlier), but was relieved of command in early 1863 after the unsuccessful FREDERICKSBURG campaign against Gen. ROBERT E. LEE (December 1862). During the siege of PETERSBURG, Burnside's corps in the Army of Potomac was badly defeated at the BATTLE OF THE CRATER (1864); he was blamed for the defeat by a Court of Inquiry and resigned in April 1865.

Sideburns is an alternation of Burnsides' name; he had very large sideburns himself.

Burns, Otway, Jr. (1775–1850) • privateer, shipbuilder, and state legislator, born on Queen's Creek, Onslow County, North Carolina. Burns was North Carolina's most famous privateer; during the WAR OF 1812 he commanded the fast schooner *Snap Dragon* on three successful voyages, raiding British shipping from Nova Scotia to Brazil.

burp gun • **1** a submachine gun, especially a Russian or German one used in World War II. **2** an automatic pistol.

Burr, Aaron (1756–1836) • U.S. senator (1791–97), vice president of the United States, and Revolutionary army officer, born in Newark, New Jersey. In the REVOLUTIONARY WAR, as aide-de-camp to Maj. Gen. ISRAEL PUTNAM in New York City, Burr played a central role in rescuing American troops trapped at Brooklyn Heights as British troops were landing north of the city (September 1776). In the election of 1800, Burr tied with THOMAS JEFFERSON, but was defeated on the thirty-sixth ballot; he served as vice president under Jefferson (1801–04). Burr is infamous for mortally wounding the Federalist leader ALEXANDER HAMILTON in a duel at Weehakwen, New Jersey (July 11, 1804), for Hamilton's part in depriving Burr of the presidency in 1800 and the New York governorship in 1804.

Burrows, William Ward (1758–1805) • first commandant of the U.S. Marine Corps, born in Charleston, South Carolina. From its establishment by Congress (1798), Burrows recruited, trained and led the corps during his six-year tenure as commandant, laying the foundations of excellence and esprit de corps essential to military identity. Burrows was the only commandant to lead the marines in two major conflicts: the QUASI-WAR WITH FRANCE (1798) and the BARBARY WARS (1801–05, 1815) He established headquarters at Marine Barracks in the new capital and created the Marine Corps Band.

Bush, George Herbert Walker (1924–) • forty-first president of the United States (1989–93), born in Milton, Massachusetts. Bush, a Navy fighter pilot in WORLD WAR II, was shot down over the Pacific, rescued at sea, and awarded the DISTINGUISHED FLYING CROSS. Bush was a U.S. congressman (1966–70); ambassador to the UNITED NATIONS (1971–73); chairman, Republican National Committee (1973–74); chief of U.S. Liaison Office in China (1974–75); director of

Central Intelligence Agency (1976–77); and was elected vice president under Ronald Reagan (1980, 1984). In 1988, he became the first sitting vice president elected president in 150 years. He ordered the U.S. invasion of Panama (1989). After the Iraqi invasion of Kuwait (August 1990), Bush forged an international coalition of forces to liberate Kuwait, called Operation Desert Storm (1991). He signed a nuclear arms reduction agreement with Soviet leader Mikhail Gorbachev (1991) and sought serious Mideast peace talks.

Bush, George Walker (1946–) • 43rd president of the United States, born in New Haven, Connecticut. During the Vietnam War, Bush served two years in the Texas Air National Guard. He was Governor of Texas from 1994 to 2001. Bush, son of the 41st president, defeated Vice President Al Gore (winner of the popular vote by over 500,000 votes) in one of the closest elections in U.S. history. He won 271 electoral votes, just one more than the minimum; five weeks after election day, Bush was awarded Florida's twenty-five electoral votes by a (contested) margin of 537 out of 6 million cast.

Bush, Vannevar (1890–1974) • science administrator and engineer, born in Everett, Massachusetts. Bush was the chair of the National Research Council's Division of Engineering and Industrial Research (1936–40) and the chief adviser to President Franklin D. Roosevelt on military technology. As the director of the Office of Scientific Research and Development, Bush coordinated civilian research on military projects and oversaw the Manhattan Project and the development of many kinds of military technology, including radar and the proximity fuse.

bushwhacker • *n.* a guerrilla fighter.

The term was coined during the Civil War after William C. Quantrill led a band of 450 men in an attack on Lawrence, Kansas, on August 21, 1863. In the raid 150 people were killed, shot, or burned to death. Known as "Quantrill's Raiders" or "Quantrill's Bushwhackers," Quantrill's men were considered outlaws by Union forces, but they became an official Confederate troop in August 1862.

butcher shop • slang (in World War I) an operating room or surgical department.

Butler, Benjamin Franklin (1818–93) • Union general, U.S. congressman (1867–75, 1877–79), and governor of Massachusetts (1882–84), born in Deerfield, New Hampshire. Early in the Civil War, Maj. Gen. Butler caused a stir by refusing to return three runaway slaves, whom he called "contraband of war," and employing them instead as freedmen; in August 1861 Congress passed the first Confiscation Act, in effect making Butler's solution U.S. policy. Butler is perhaps best known as the controversial administrator of New Orleans (captured May 1862). He executed a man who had torn down the U.S. flag, arrested the mayor and other vocal Confederate supporters, and outraged the city with his famous General Order No. 28, which threatened to treat all females who abused Union troops as "women of the town plying their avocation."

Butler, Matthew Calbraith (1836–1909) • Confederate general and U.S. senator, born in Greenville, South Carolina. Butler was a major general of volunteers in the Spanish-American War (1898). In the Civil War, he fought at First Bull Run (1861), Second Bull Run (1862), Antietam (1862), and Brandy Station (1863). He commanded brigades and divisions under generals J.E.B. Stuart and Wade Hampton in the heavy Virginia fighting of 1864.

Butler, Richard (1743–91) • Revolutionary army officer and Indian commissioner, born in Dublin, Ireland. In the Revolutionary War, Butler fought under Daniel Morgan and Anthony Wayne; he fought at Monmouth (1778) and Yorktown (1781). He was brevetted brigadier general in 1783. Appointed an Indian commissioner (1784), Butler (with his colleagues) extracted vast territorial concessions. In 1791, under Arthur St. Clair, he campaigned against the Ohio Indians. On November 4, a force led by the Miami warrior Little Turtle surprised and overwhelmed Butler and St. Clair's troops. Butler died from a tomahawk blow to the head, one of some 600 white soldiers killed in this greatest single defeat suffered by a U.S. military force at the hands of Native Americans.

Butler, Smedley Darlington (1881–1940) • U.S. Marine Corps major general and Congressional Medal of Honor recipient, born in West Chester, Pennsylvania. Butler fought in the Spanish-American War (1898) as a 2nd lieutenant in the Marine Corps. In the China Relief Expedition in 1900, he was wounded twice, cited for bravery, and promoted to the brevet rank of captain. He participated in interventions in Honduras (1903), the Philippines (1905–07), Nicaragua (1912), Panama (1913), Mexico (1914), and Haiti (1915–16). In World War I, for his excellent command of a vast American camp in Brest, France, Butler was awarded the Distinguished Service Medal of both the army and the navy and was promoted to brigadier general at age thirty-seven. As marine base commander at Quantico, Virginia. (1920–24, 1929–31), he protected the Marine Corps from critics in the army and Congress who argued that the army could do the marines' job.

Butler, William O. (1759–1821) • Revolutionary War soldier and congressman, born in Prince William County, Virginia. Butler joined the South Carolina militia in 1775 at age fifteen. He fought, under several commanders, at Great Canebrake on Reedy Creek (December 1775), at Stono (June 1779), the siege of Savannah, Georgia (1779), and the siege of Augusta, Georgia (1780). During the War of 1812, he was a major general of the South Carolina militia.

butt • *n.* (also **butt end**) the thicker end, especially of a tool or a weapon: *a rifle butt.*

Butterfield, Daniel (1831–1901) • soldier and businessman, born in Utica, New York. A brigadier general of volunteers under Gen. George B. McClellan, Butterfield was chief of staff to generals Joseph Hooker and George G. Meade. At Gaines' Mill, he rescued the colors of an embattled regiment and led the outfit in a counterattack (June 1862); for which he was awarded the Congressional Medal of Honor. As chief of staff to Meade at Gettysburg (1863), he later claimed Meade had ordered him to draw up a plan to retreat even after the battle began.

Butterfield was famed for revising the lights-out bugle call into "Taps," the haunting melody that beckons soldiers, living and dead, to their rest.

butty • *n.* (pl. **-ies**) (also **butty boat**) an unpowered freight barge intended to be towed.

buzz bomb • nickname for the German V-1 bomb, the first successful guided missile, used against targets in Holland and London in World War II.

Byrd, Richard Evelyn (1888–1957) • naval aviator and polar explorer, born in Winchester, Virginia. Byrd commanded the naval air party that accompanied the Donald B. MacMillan expedition to Greenland (1925); in 1926, with pilot Floyd Bennett, made flight from Spitsbergen to the North Pole and back again, for which he was awarded the Congressional Medal of Honor and the Distinguished Service Medal. Byrd was promoted to rear admiral in 1930.

Cc

C2V • *abbr.* Command and Control Vehicle.

C-5 • see Galaxy.

C-17 • see Globemaster III.

C-46 • see Commando.

C-47 • see Dakota.

C-53 • see Skytrooper.

C-54 • see Skymaster.

C-82 • see Packet.

C-119 • see Flying Boxcar.

C-121 • see Constellation.

C-123 • a twin-engine STOL assault transport manufactured for the U.S. Air Force by Fairchild beginning in 1954 and known as the "Provider." The C-123, which could carry sixty-one troops and had a range of about 1,035 miles, was used extensively in Vietnam to resupply isolated outposts.

C-130 • see Hercules.

C-141 • see Starlifter.

CA-3 • see *Brooklyn*, USS.

CA-44 • see *Vincennes*, USS.

Cabell, Samuel Jordan (1756–1818) • Revolutionary War soldier and congressman, born in Amherst County, Virginia. He raised and captained the Amherst Rifles. Cabell crossed the Delaware River with George Washington on Christmas night 1776, and helped capture 1,400 Hessian mercenaries at Trenton.

Cabell, William Lewis (1827–1911) • Confederate general, nicknamed "Old Tige," born in Danville, Virginia. With P.G.T. Beauregard and Joseph E. Johnston, he designed the Confederate battle flag to provide the southern troops with a banner more easily distinguishable from the Union's "stars and stripes" than the Confederacy's original national flag, the "stars and bars."

cable • *n.* **1** a thick rope of wire or nonmetallic fiber, typically used for construction, mooring ships, and towing vehicles. **2** the chain of a ship's anchor. **3** a length of 200 yards (182.9 m) or (in the United States) 240 yards (219.4 m).

cable tier • a place in a ship for stowing a coiled cable.

caboose |kəˈbo͞os| • *n.* **1** a railroad car with accommodations for the train crew, typically attached to the end of the train. **2** archaic a kitchen on a ship's deck.

cadet |kəˈdet| • *n.* **1** a young trainee in the armed services or police force: *an air force cadet.* **2** a student in training at a military school. DERIVATIVES: **cadetship** |-ˌship| *n.*

Cadwalader, John |kædˈwälədər| (1742–86) • Revolutionary War soldier, born in Philadelphia. Appointed brigadier general of the Pennsylvania militia, Cadwalader fought in the battle of Princeton and as a volunteer at Brandywine and Germantown (all 1777).

Cadwalader fought a duel on July 4, 1778, with Thomas Conway, who had been accused of plotting to remove Washington from command (the "Conway Cabal").

Cadwalader, Lambert |kædˈwälədər| (1743–1823) • Revolutionary War soldier, born in Trenton, New Jersey. In August 1776 he rushed with his battalion (the Third Pennsylvania) to assist George Washington in the battle of New York (1776), but arrived after the battle had been lost.

Cairo Conference • the meetings of world leaders held in Cairo, Egypt, in November and December 1943, during World War II. The first conference was held November 22–

26, 1943, with President FRANKLIN D. ROOSEVELT, British Prime Minister WINSTON CHURCHILL, and Chinese President Chiang Kai-shek. They discussed their goal of winning unconditional Japanese surrender and the return of territories Japan had captured, as well as Korea's independence. Roosevelt and Churchill also talked about plans for the invasion of NORMANDY. During the second conference, held December 2–7, Roosevelt and Churchill attempted to win Turkish President Ismet Inönü over to the Allied cause.

caisson |'kaˌsän; 'kāsən| • *n.* **1** a large watertight chamber, open at the bottom, from which the water is kept out by air pressure and in which construction work may be carried out under water. **2** a floating vessel or watertight structure used as a gate across the entrance of a dry dock or basin. **3** a chest or wagon for holding or conveying ammunition.

Calhoun, John Caldwell (1782–1850) • U.S. legislator, Secretary of War, Vice President, and Secretary of State, born near Abbeville, South Carolina. As Secretary of War (1817–25) under President JAMES MONROE, Calhoun was instrumental in improving the administration and professionalism of the U.S. Army. He oversaw improvement of the army ration, reorganized the army's pay and pension system, supported the reform of the WEST POINT curriculum, and backed the construction of a system of coastal and frontier fortifications. In 1822, Calhoun also proposed the so-called "expansible Army" plan whereby a small peacetime army could be rapidly expanded in time of crisis. He served as Vice President from 1825 to 1832 under Presidents JOHN QUINCY ADAMS and ANDREW JACKSON. He resigned in 1832 to take a seat in the Senate where he served until 1843. He was a leading advocate of "states rights," and developed the so-called "nullification" theory by which the states could "nullify" national laws they considered inimical to state interests. Calhoun subsequently served as U.S. Secretary of State (1844–45) and signed the treaty annexing Texas, but upon his return to the Senate in 1846, he opposed the MEXICAN WAR (1846–48).

caliber |'kæləbər| (Brit. **calibre**) • *n.* **1** the internal diameter or bore of a gun barrel: *a .22 caliber repeater rifle.* **2** the diameter of a bullet, shell, or rocket.

DERIVATIVES: **calibered** *adj.*

calibrate • *v.* **1** (often **be calibrated**) mark (a gauge or instrument) with a standard scale of readings. **2** correlate the readings of (an instrument) with those of a standard in order to check the instrument's accuracy. **3** adjust (experimental results) to take external factors into account or to allow comparison with other data.

DERIVATIVES: **calibrator** *n.*

Calley, William L. (1943–) • army officer, born in Miami. Calley was in command of the U.S. Army Americal Division, charged in the MY LAI incident in which Vietnamese civilians, including women and children, were massacred on March 16, 1968 (the Army's final estimate of the number killed was 347). In the fall of 1969, letters written by a former soldier to government officials forced the Army to act. Several soldiers and veterans were charged with murder, and several officers were charged with dereliction of duty because they covered up the massacre. Special investigations by both the U.S. Army and the House of Representatives determined that a massacre had, in fact, occurred. Of the soldiers originally charged, only five were court-martialed. Of those, only Calley was convicted. On March 29, 1971, he was found guilty of the premeditated murder of at least twenty-two Vietnamese civilians and was sentenced to life imprisonment. Later, Calley's sentence was reduced to ten years, and, in 1974, a federal district court overturned his conviction and he was released.

call fire • fire delivered by a supporting unit on a specific target in response to a request from the supported unit.

call up • *n.* an act of summoning someone or of being summoned to serve in the armed forces: *my call up papers.*

calm |kä(l)m| • *adj.* (of the sea) not disturbed by large waves. • *n.* (often **calms**) an area of the sea without wind.

caltrop |'kæltrəp; 'kôl-| (also **caltrap**) • *n.* a spiked metal ball thrown on the ground to impede wheeled vehicles or (formerly) cavalry horses.

Cambodia, invasion of • in April 1970, during the VIETNAM WAR, President RICHARD M. NIXON authorized the incursion of U.S. military forces (accompanied by Republic of South Vietnam forces) into Cambodia in order to disrupt the supply lines of the VIETCONG and to destroy their bases in Cambodia being used to support operations in South Vietnam. The incursion, which lasted until the end of June 1970, had limited tactical success but aroused strong opposition among anti-Vietnam War groups in the United States and led to several large demonstrations.

Camden, Battle of • a battle of the REVOLUTIONARY WAR in Camden, South Carolina, on August 16, 1780. It was a victory for Britain against ill and poorly-trained Americans. It helped to effectively end military resistance in South Carolina and gave the British temporary control of the entire South.

camel • *n.* an apparatus for raising a sunken ship, consisting of one or more watertight chests to provide buoyancy.

Cam Lo • a mountain refuge in Vietnam and a Marine base camp along Highway 9, 9 miles (14 km) west of Dong Ha in Quang Tri Province. Located 9 miles (14 km) south of the demilitarized zone, it was the southwestern part of "Leatherneck Square," (a nickname for a quadrilateral area bounded by the bases at Con Thien, Gio Linh, Cam Lo, and Dong Ha along the Cam Lo River). The river was an important supply route for the U.S. Marines and Army and was a frequent target of the North Vietnamese Army and Vietcong.

camo |'kæmō| • *n.* informal short for CAMOUFLAGE: *a camo jacket.*

camouflage | ˈkæməˌfläZH; -ˌfläj | • *n.* **1** the disguising of military personnel, equipment, and installations by painting or covering them to make them blend in with their surroundings: *camouflage nets.* **2** the clothing or materials used for such a purpose: *figures dressed in army camouflage.* • *v.* (often **be camouflaged**) hide or disguise the presence of (a person, animal, or object) by means of camouflage: *the van was camouflaged with netting and branches from trees.*
ORIGIN: WORLD WAR I: from French, from *camoufler* 'to disguise' (originally thieves' slang), from Italian *camuffare* 'disguise, deceive,' perhaps by association with French *camouflet* 'whiff of smoke in the face.'

camouflet | ˈkæməˌflā | • *n.* the resulting cavity in a deep underground burst when there is no rupture of the surface. Compare with CRATER .

camp • *n.* **1** a group of tents, huts, or other shelter set up for troops temporarily, but more permanent than a bivouac. **2** any military post, temporary or permanent.

campaign • *n.* a series of military operations intended to achieve a particular objective, confined to a particular area, or involving a specified type of fighting: *a desert campaign* | *the army set off* **on campaign.**
DERIVATIVES: **campaigner** *n.*

campaign plan • a plan for a series of related military operations aimed at accomplishing a strategic or operational objective within a given time and space.

Campbell, Arthur (1743–1811) • frontiersman, soldier, and politician, born in Augusta County, Virginia. He was a cousin of WILLIAM CAMPBELL. Among the first pioneers of southwest Virginia, Campbell protected settlers' interests as their elected representative and militia commander. He led troops during LORD DUNMORE'S WAR (1774) and the REVOLUTIONARY WAR.

Campbell, John (4th Earl of Loudoun) • a Scottish nobleman who was the Commander in Chief of the British armed forces in America in the early stages of the FRENCH AND INDIAN WAR (1754–63) (a post he lost after Braddock's defeat), and titular Governor of Virginia from 1756 to 1758. Loudoun County in Virginia is named after him, though he never visited North America.

Campbell, William (1745–81) • REVOLUTIONARY WAR militia officer. Born in Augusta County, Virginia, Campbell became prominent in the state militia during LORD DUNMORE'S WAR against the Indians in 1774. In 1776 he joined a patriot force commanded by Patrick Henry, his brother-in-law, and helped expel the royal governor. After serving in a number of Virginia militia positions, he was promoted to colonel in 1780, and led a Washington County force to join units gathering to stop Maj. PATRICK FERGUSON'S Loyalist raid into North Carolina. Campbell was chosen to lead the patriot march which caught Ferguson at KINGS MOUNTAIN. Campbell played a key role in the decisive American victory that destroyed Ferguson's force and finished Gen. CHARLES CORNWALLIS'S North Carolina campaign. Campbell took part in the BATTLE OF GUILFORD COURT HOUSE in 1781, served a brief period in the state legislature, and was appointed brigadier general of militia.

Camp David Accords • two parallel but separate agreements signed on September 17, 1978, by President JIMMY CARTER, who mediated the negotiations, Israeli prime minister Menachem Begin, and Egyptian president Anwar Sadat, after a two-week conference at Camp David, Maryland, to establish a Middle East peace. In the first agreement, Sadat pledged to recognize Israel and sign a peace treaty if Begin promised to withdraw Israeli troops from the Sinai. In the second, Begin agreed to suspend Israeli settlements on the West Bank until further negotiations with Palestinian representatives. The West Bank negotiations were unfulfilled, largely because of each country's interpretation of the Palestinian clauses in the agreements.

camp follower • a civilian who works in or is attached to a military camp.

Camp Grant Massacre • the murder near Camp Grant, Arizona, in 1871 of more than 100 Apaches, mostly women and children, who had been given asylum there. The perpetrators were members of the Tucson Committee of Public Safety, aided by a force of Papago Indians, the Apaches' long-time enemies.

Cam Ranh Bay • a sheltered inlet off the South China Sea, Vietnam. The Japanese controlled the bay during WORLD WAR II from 1941 to 1945. During the VIETNAM WAR, the U.S. military constructed airfields and a large supply base at Cam Ranh Bay, which was relinquished to the South Vietnamese in 1972. The North Vietnamese Army seized Cam Ranh Bay in April 1975, and it was taken over by the Soviet Union in 1979.

Canberra • **(B-57)** a twin-jet aircraft used by the Air Force for more than twenty-five years, starting in the KOREAN WAR. It was a nuclear and conventional weapons platform and also used for reconnaissance, weather, and electronic countermeasures.

Canby, Edward Richard Sprigg (1817–73) • Union army officer, born in Piatt's Landing, Kentucky. He fought in the SEMINOLE WAR (1840–42), the MEXICAN WAR (1846–48), and the Mormon rebellion (1847–48). In the CIVIL WAR, Canby commanded Union forces in New Mexico, turning aside Confederate invaders. As an assistant to Secretary of War EDWIN M. STANTON, he helped maintain peace in New York City after draft riots (1863). He commanded the Military Division of West Mississippi (including Gulf states), captured Mobile, Alabama (Apr. 1865), and accepted the surrender of Gen. E. KIRBY SMITH (May 1865).

As commander of the Department of Columbia, Canby became the first U.S. general to die at the hands of American Indians when he was shot and killed by Modoc leader Keintpoos, a.k.a. "Captain Jack," during an extended parley in California.

---

canister • *n.* **1** a cylinder of pressurized gas, typically one that explodes when thrown or fired from a gun: *riot police fired tear-gas canisters into the crowd.* **2** small bullets packed in cases that fit the bore of an artillery piece or gun: *another deadly volley of canister.*

cannelure |ˈkænlˌ(y)o͝or| • *n.* a groove around the cylindrical part of a bullet.

cannon • *n.* (pl. usually same) **1** a large, heavy piece of artillery, typically mounted on wheels, formerly used in warfare. **2** an automatic heavy gun that fires shells from an aircraft or tank.

cannonade |ˌkænəˈnād| • *n.* a period of continuous, heavy gunfire. • *v.* discharge heavy guns continuously: (**cannonading**) *the daily cannonading continued.*

cannonball • *n.* a round metal or stone projectile fired from a cannon.

cannoneer • *n.* an artilleryman who positioned and fired a cannon.

cannon fodder • soldiers regarded merely as material to be expended in war.

can opener • slang **1** (in WORLD WAR II) an aircraft equipped with antitank or anti-armored vehicle weaponry, especially the ROYAL AIR FORCE's HURRICANES equipped with a 40mm gun on each wing, capable of firing a 2.5-lb. shell, used in the North Africa campaign in early 1943. **2** a bayonet. **3** a cook.

cant • *v.* (of a ship) swing round: *the ship canted to starboard.*

canteen • *n.* **1** a restaurant provided by a military camp for its personnel. **2** a small water bottle, as used by soldiers or campers.

Cantigny, Battle of • a capture by the American 1st Division on May 28, 1918, and the first American attack of WORLD WAR I. To test the Americans' offensive ability in their first active sector, the French command ordered the new division, a reinforced U.S. regiment of about 4,000 men, to capture Cantigny, a village located near Montdidier in the Somme region. Assisted by French tanks, the division captured the town in forty-five minutes and took over 200 prisoners. The Americans withstood a series of counterattacks over the next two days.

cantonment |kænˈtōnmənt; -ˈtän-| • *n.* a military camp, especially a permanent military station in British India.

CAP • *abbr.* **1** combat air patrol. **2** crisis action planning.

capability • *n.* forces or resources giving a country or state the ability to undertake a particular kind of military action: *their nuclear weapons capability.*

Capers, Ellison (1837–1908) • Confederate soldier and Episcopal clergyman, born in Charleston, South Carolina. Capers served as major, lieutenant colonel, and colonel of the 24th South Carolina Infantry, and inspired distinguished service at FORT SUMTER (1861), CHICKAMAUGA (1863), and MISSIONARY RIDGE (1863).

capital ship • a large warship such as a battleship or aircraft carrier.

cap'n |ˈkæpm| • *n.* informal contraction of CAPTAIN, used in representing speech.

caponier |ˌkæpəˈnir| • *n.* a covered passage across a ditch around a military fort.

capstan |ˈkæpstən| • *n.* a revolving cylinder with a vertical axis used for winding a rope or cable, powered by a motor or pushed around by levers.

Capt. • *abbr.* Captain.

captain • *n.* **1** the person in command of a ship. **2** a naval officer of high rank, in particular (in the U.S. Navy or Coast Guard) an officer ranking above commander and below commodore. **3** an army officer of high rank, in particular (in the U.S. Army, Marine Corps, or Air Force) an officer ranking above first lieutenant and below major. • *v.* be the captain of (a ship).

DERIVATIVES: **captaincy** *n.*

captain general • an honorary rank of senior officer in the British army, most commonly in an artillery regiment.

Captain of the Fleet • an officer holding the rank of Captain or Commodore in the ROYAL NAVY serving on the staff of a flag officer.

Captain's Mast • an occasion, often an assembly of a ship's crew, at which the captain awards non-judicial punishment, listens to requests, or commends individual crewmen for meritorious actions. Known in the U.S. Marine Corps as OFFICE HOURS.

carabineer |ˌkerəbəˈnir| (also **carabinier**) • *n.* a cavalry soldier whose principal weapon was a carbine.

carbine |ˈkärˌbīn; -ˌbēn| • *n.* **1** a light automatic rifle. **2** a short rifle or musket used by cavalry.

car-bombing • *n.* a terrorist act involving the detonation of a bomb in or under a parked car.

careen |kəˈrēn| • *v.* **1** turn (a ship) on its side for cleaning, caulking, or repair. **2** (of a ship) tilt; lean over: *a heavy flood tide caused my vessel to careen dizzily.*

Carley float |ˈkärlē| • *n.* a large emergency raft carried on board ship, typically consisting of a buoyant canvas ring with a wooden grid deck inside it.

ORIGIN: early 20th cent.: named after Horace S. *Carley*, American inventor.

carline (also **carlin** or **carling**) • *n.* (usually **carlines**) any of the pieces of squared timber fitted fore and aft between the deck beams of a wooden ship to support the deck planking.

Carlisle Barracks • the second oldest continuously active U.S. Army installation (after WEST POINT, New York), located in the town of Carlisle some 30 miles west of Harrisburg, Pennsylvania. Established in 1757 as an assembly point and logistical base for British and colonial forces in the FRENCH AND INDIAN WAR (1754–63), Carlisle Barracks served as a logistical base for Gen. GEORGE WASHINGTON's army during the REVOLUTIONARY WAR and was the home of the U.S. Army cavalry in the mid-19th century. Burned by Confederate forces in 1863 during the GETTYSBURG campaign, the small installation subsequently served as the home of the U.S. Army Medical Field Service School, the U.S. Army Civil Affairs and Military Government School, and other Army training and education activities. In 1951, Carlisle Barracks became the home of the U.S. ARMY WAR COLLEGE. Some 600 military and 900 civilian personnel work on the 458-acre installation.

Carlson, Evans Fordyce (1896–1947) • army and Marine Corps officer and writer, born in Sidney, New York. As an adviser and patrol leader in Nicaragua he developed night-fighting tactics and was awarded the NAVY CROSS. As an intelligence officer in Shanghai, Peking, in the late 1930s, he observed Chinese Communist army operations, and accompanied guerrillas behind Japanese lines. In WORLD WAR II, he commanded the "Carlson's Raiders" marine battalion, launching raids behind enemy lines in the Makin Atoll (conducted in rubber boats launched from submarines) and on GUADALCANAL (1942).

Carnegie Endowment for International Peace • an institution for research on peace and public education on world affairs founded by philanthropist ANDREW CARNEGIE (1835–1919) in 1910. Carnegie donated ten million dollars to the Endowment to "hasten the abolition of war, the foulest blot upon our civilization." The organization is headquartered in Washington, D.C., and has worked to study the causes and impact of war, promote international understanding, and aid in the development of international law and dispute settlement.

Carney, William Harvey (1840–after 1901) • Union army sergeant, born in Norfolk, Virginia. As a sergeant in Col. ROBERT GOULD SHAW's 54th Massachusetts Regiment, he participated in an assault on FORT WAGNER, South Carolina (July 1863). Col. Shaw and the color sergeant were shot; Carney planted the national flag on the crest. Although severely wounded and pinned down by heavy fire, he kept it aloft. Eventually reaching a hospital tent, he said, "Boys, the old flag never touched the ground." He was awarded the Congressional Medal of Honor, in 1900, the first African American to win this honor.

Caroline Affair • the destruction by burning and casting adrift on the Niagra river of the U.S.S. *Caroline* in 1838 by loyal Canadians. The ship had been dispatched with supplies and ammunition to aid rebel Canadians. The incident increased Anglo-American tensions until the WEBSTER-ASHBURTON TREATY.

carpet-bomb • *v.* (**carpet-bombing**) bomb (an area) intensively.

carpet bombing • the intensive bombing of a designated area in a close pattern by many aircraft, usually B-52s, as though laying a wall-to-wall carpet. In WORLD WAR II the term denoted bombing campaigns designed to clear wide areas for advancing troops. (Also called saturation bombing).

Carr, Eugene Asa (1830–1910) • Union army officer, born in Concord, Erie County, New York. A decorated CIVIL WAR general, Carr was ranked among the army's most effective American-Indian fighters. He campaigned against the Apache, SIOUX, Utah, Comanche, and Kiawa. Wounded at PEA RIDGE, he held his position despite heavy losses and was promoted to brigadier general of volunteers (1865) and was awarded the CONGRESSIONAL MEDAL OF HONOR (1894) for gallantry. He commanded a division during the VICKSBURG and Mobile campaigns (1865). After the Civil War, in one of the army's most decisive victories, he routed the Cheyenne DOG SOLDIERS at Summit Springs, Colorado (July 1869).

Carrier Airborne Early Warning Squadron 113 • (**VAW-113**) see BLACK EAGLES, THE.

carrier air group • two or more aircraft squadrons formed under one commander for administrative and tactical control of operations from a carrier.

carrier striking force • a naval task force composed of aircraft carriers and supporting combatant ships capable of conducting strike operations.

Carrington, Henry Beebee (1824–1912) • Union army officer and author, born in Wallingford, Connecticut. He served as adjutant general of Ohio and brigadier general of volunteers and as colonel of the 18th Infantry.

As adj. general of Ohio, his most controversial act was to suppress antiwar and COPPERHEAD agitation in Ohio and Indiana. He had the agitators arrested and tried by military tribunals. His actions were later overturned by a Supreme Court decision (*Ex Parte Milligan* 1866), but by then the war was over.

Carroll, Samuel Sprigg (1832–93) • Union army officer, born in Washington, D.C. As a colonel in the volunteer army, he fought STONEWALL JACKSON's forces in the SHENANDOAH VALLEY, at KERNSTOWN, PORT REPUBLIC, and CEDAR MOUNTAIN (1862). He commanded brigades at FREDERICKSBURG and CHANCELLORSVILLE (1863), and later at WILDERNESS and SPOTSYLVANIA (1864). He effectively reinforced CEMETERY HILL at GETTYSBURG (July 2, 1863), and briefly commanded a division at war's end. In 1864 he was commended by Gen. OLIVER O. HOWARD for "fearlessness and energetic action" as a commander.

His flaming red hair earned him the nickname "Bricktop" with his men.

carronade |ˌkærəˈnād| • *n.* a short large-caliber cannon, formerly in naval use.

carry • *v.* (**-ies, -ied**) **1** support and move (someone or something) from one place to another: *medics were carrying a wounded man on a stretcher.* **2** transport: *the train service carries 20,000 passengers daily.* **3** support the weight of: *the bridge is capable of carrying even the heaviest loads.* **4** (of a gun or similar weapon) propel (a missile) to a specified distance. • *n.* (pl. **-ies**) **1** the action of keeping something, especially a gun, on one's person: *this pistol is the right choice for on-duty or off-duty carry.* **2** the range of a gun or similar weapon. ▸**carry something away** lose (a mast or other part of a ship) through breakage.

cartel |kär'tel| • *n.* **1** an association of manufacturers or suppliers with the purpose of maintaining prices at a high level and restricting competition: *the Columbian drug cartels.* **2** chiefly historical a coalition or cooperative arrangement between political parties intended to promote a mutual interest.

Carter Doctrine • on January 23, 1980, after a series of events in 1979 threatening American interests in the Persian Gulf region, President JIMMY CARTER announced that the United States would use military force if necessary to defend those interests, which included oil resources. He created a RAPID DEPLOYMENT JOINT TASK FORCE to provide military aid and to assist in emergency situations in the gulf.

Carter, Jimmy (1924–) • 39th president of the United States (1977–81), born James Earl Carter, Jr., in Plains, Georgia. After graduation from the U.S. NAVAL ACADEMY, Carter served in the navy under Adm. HYMAN RICKOVER in the nuclear submarine program (1946–53). He was Governor of Georgia (1970–74) and defeated incumbent President GERALD R. FORD (1976). Carter's initiatives included transportation deregulation, environmental protection, new departments of energy and education, efforts toward long-term national energy policy, and attention to international human rights. Carter obtained the PANAMA CANAL Treaties (1977), signed the SALT II TREATY with Soviet Union (1979), announced the CARTER DOCTRINE, asserting U.S. protection of the Persian Gulf, and mediated the CAMP DAVID ACCORDS between Israel and Egypt (1979). After the 1979 Soviet invasion of Afghanistan, he ordered an embargo of grain sales to the USSR and a U.S. boycott of the 1980 Summer Olympic Games in Moscow. Carter was paralyzed by the Iran hostage crisis (1979–81) and humiliated by a failed rescue attempt (see OPERATION EAGLE CLAW). He suffered a bitter challenge for Democratic nomination by Sen. Edward Kennedy and was defeated in a landslide by RONALD REAGAN (1980).

Carter, Samuel Powhatan (1819–91) • Union naval and army officer, born in Elizabethton, Tennessee. From the Kentucky mountain base, he recruited and commanded a volunteer brigade of East Tennesseans. On "Carter's Raid," he led almost 1,000 cavalrymen over a torturous mountain route in brutal winter weather to destroy bridges on the East Tennessee and Virginia Railway (1862–63). He was commandant of U.S. NAVAL ACADEMY from 1870 to 1873 and retired as rear admiral in 1881.

cartridge • *n.* a casing containing a charge and a bullet or shot for small arms or an explosive charge for blasting.

cartridge belt • a belt with pockets or loops for cartridges of ammunition, typically worn over the shoulder.

CAS • *abbr.* close air support.

Casablanca Conference • a meeting held in Casablanca on January 12–23, 1943, during WORLD WAR II, between Prime Minister WINSTON CHURCHILL and President FRANKLIN D. ROOSEVELT to plan military strategy. After the meeting, Roosevelt publicly announced the Allied policy of UNCONDITIONAL SURRENDER for Germany, Italy, and Japan.

Case-Church Amendment • an amendment finally passed by the Senate on June 29, 1973, after the signing of the PARIS PEACE AGREEMENTS, to prohibit any future use of U.S. forces in the VIETNAM WAR, specifically in Vietnam, Laos, and Cambodia, without congressional authorization. Presented by Senators Clifford Case and Frank Church, it was initially passed on June 14 but subsequently modified to allow the continuation of bombing in Cambodia until August 15.

President RICHARD M. NIXON secretly promised South Vietnam's president NGUYEN VAN THIEU that the United States would resume bombing in North and South Vietnam if he determined it necessary.

---

casemate • *n.* **1** an armored enclosure for guns on a warship. **2** a small room in the thickness of the wall of a fortress, with embrasures from which guns or missiles can be fired.

case shot • bullets or pieces of metal in an iron case fired from a cannon.

casevac |'kazɪvak, 'kaẕhɪ-| SLANG • *n.* evacuation of casualties by air. • *v.* (**casevaced, casevacing**) evacuate (a casualty) by air.
ORIGIN: 1950s: blend of *casualty* and *evacuation.*

Casey, Silas (1807–82) • soldier, born in East Greenwich, Rhode Island. As a captain, he led a storming party of 250 men as a "forlorn hope" against CHAPULTEPEC castle in the MEXICAN WAR (1847). In the CIVIL WAR, he organized and trained Union volunteers in 1861, then commanded a division under GEORGE B. MCCLELLAN in 1862. In the PENINSULAR CAMPAIGN, he was routed at SEVEN PINES with more than 1,800 casualties (1862), and he was deposed as field commander and sent back to Washington, D.C.

Casey, Thomas Lincoln (1831–96) • military engineer, born at Madison Barracks, Sackett's Harbor, New York. A graduate of WEST POINT, during the CIVIL WAR Casey oversaw the construction of defenses and forts along the Maine coast.

Casey, William Joseph (1913–87) • intelligence officer, lawyer, and CIA director (1981–87), born in New York City. During WORLD WAR II, Casey was the chief of the OFFICE OF STRATEGIC SERVICES (OSS), overseeing secret intelligence operations for Europe (1944). After serving as RONALD REAGAN'S 1980 campaign manager, Casey was appointed as CIA director and became the longest-serving DCI since ALLEN DULLES in the 1950s. With the freedoms permitted by the 1980 INTELLIGENCE REFORM ACT, Casey presided over an "unleashed" CIA with an increased budget and an emphasis on clandestine operations, especially in Afghanistan, Angola, and Nicaragua.

Casey's worst embarrassment came in the IRAN-CONTRA AFFAIR (1986); in the hearings that resulted, witnesses claimed that Casey had been involved in the affair; Casey gave false testimony to Congress under oath, but was disabled by a stroke and brain tumor from completing his testimony.

CASF • *abbr.* Composite Air Strike Force.

Cash-and-Carry policy • name given to the policy on arms sales to foreign governments followed by the United States in WORLD WAR II during its period of neutrality before the adoption of the LEND-LEASE program. Under the "Cash-and-Carry" policy the United States agreed to sell armaments to Britain and other nations opposed to the AXIS POWERS, but only on the condition that the arms were paid for in advance and transported from the United States in foreign shipping.

cashier • *v.* (usually **be cashiered**) dismiss someone from the armed forces in disgrace because of a serious misdemeanor: *he was found guilty and cashiered* | (**cashiered**) *a cashiered National Guard major.*

Cassino, Battle of • a long-running battle (January–May 1944) in and around the abbey at Monte Cassino, Italy. Germans had captured the town and strategic lookout point afforded by the hill on which the abbey stands. American and British troops were repeatedly repelled and withdrew in their attempts to take it. After after three weeks of fierce fighting in mountain terrain the position was won for the ALLIES by the Polish 2nd Corps.

cast off (or **cast something off**) **1** set a boat or ship free from its moorings: *the boatmen cast off and rowed downriver* | *Jack cast off our moorings.* **2** (of a boat or ship) be set free from its moorings.

Castillo de San Marcos |kə'stēyō də sæn 'märkōs| • the oldest masonry fort in the country, in ST. AUGUSTINE, Florida. It was built by Spain between 1672 and 1696 in order to fend off attacks from the north.

Castle Bravo • one of a series of thermonuclear weapon design tests carried out in 1954. Castle Bravo was the first solid-fuel H-BOMB and the largest bomb ever tested by the United States. It also created the worst radiological disaster in U.S. history, exposing scores of Marshall Islanders as well as others to dangerous levels of radiation.

Castro, Fidel (1927–) • a Cuban statesman, Prime Minister from 1959 to 1976, and President since 1976, born near Birín, Cuba. In 1953 he organized a rebel force to remove Gen. Fulgencio Batista from office, and he was arrested when the force attacked the Moncada military barracks in Santiago de Cuba on July 26. He was sentenced to a fifteen-year imprisonment but was released in 1955 in a political amnesty. In December 1956 he landed on the coast of Oriente province, Cuba, with an armed expedition, most of whom were killed or captured. Castro and the remaining force retreated to the mountains of the Sierra Maestra, where they organized a guerilla campaign that eventually overthrew the Batista regime on January 1, 1959. Castro became the commander in chief of the armed forces of the new Cuban government, and in February 1959 he became premier. In April 1961 at the BAY OF PIGS INVASION, Castro defeated an attack by Cuban exiles equipped by the U.S. government to overthrow his government. In the CUBAN MISSILE CRISIS (1962–63), the Soviet Union withdrew its nuclear weapons from the island in exchange for a U.S. pledge that included and end to attempts to overthrow Castro's regime.

casualty • *n.* any person who is lost to the organization by having been declared "dead," "missing," "ill," "injured," or "duty status-whereabouts unknown."

Caswell, Richard (1729–89) • REVOLUTIONARY WAR militia general and first governor of North Carolina, born in Baltimore County, Maryland. An effective wartime executive, Caswell devoted extraordinary effort to raising and equipping troops for the field. As major general of the state militia, he supported Gen. HORATIO GATES at the disastrous BATTLE OF CAMDEN, South Carolina (1780).

cat • *n.* **1** short for cat-o'-nine-tails. **2** short for cathead. • *v.* (**catted, catting**) raise (an anchor) from the surface of the water to the cathead.

catalytic attack • an attack designed to bring about a war between two major powers through the disguised machinations of a third power.

catapult • *n.* a device in which accumulated tension is suddenly released to hurl an object some distance, in particular: **1** a military machine worked by a lever and ropes for hurling large stones or other missiles. **2** a mechanical device for launching a glider or other aircraft, especially from the deck of a ship. • *v.* hurl or launch (something) in a specified direction with or as if with a catapult: *the plane was refueled and catapulted back into the air again.*

cathead • *n.* a horizontal beam extending from each side of a ship's bow, used for raising and carrying an anchor.

cat-o'-nine-tails • *n.* a rope whip with nine knotted cords, formerly used (especially at sea) to flog offenders.

caulk |kôk| (also **calk**) • *n.* (also **caulking**) a waterproof filler and sealant, used in building work and repairs. • *v.* **1** seal (a gap or seam) with such a substance. **2** stop up (the seams of a boat) with oakum and waterproofing material, or by driving plate-junctions together; make (a boat) watertight by this method.

DERIVATIVES: **caulker** *n.*

Causeway, Battle of the • see RUMAILA, BATTLE OF.

cavalry |'kævəlrē| • *n.* (pl. **-ies**) [usually treated as pl.] **1** soldiers who fought on horseback. **2** a branch of an army made up of such soldiers. **3** modern soldiers who fight in armored vehicles.

DERIVATIVES: **cavalryman** *n.* (pl. **-men**).

CAVU • *abbr.* ceiling and visibility unlimited, the ideal flying conditions in which there are neither large clouds or haze.

Cayuse • (**OH-6A**) a light observation helicopter built by Hughes. More than 1,400

Cayuse helicopters were built throughout the 1960s. The helicopter was thought to give crew members a better chance of survival in a crash, as the egg-shaped body tended to roll into a ball.

CD • *abbr.* **1** civil defense. **2** corps diplomatique.

C-day • the unnamed day on which a deployment operation commences or is to commence. The deployment may be movement of troops, cargo, weapon systems, or a combination of these elements utilizing any or all types of transport.

Cdr. (also **CDR**) • *abbr.* Commander.

Cdre • *abbr.* Commodore.

cease engagement • in air defense, a fire control order used to direct units to stop the firing sequence against a designated target. Guided missiles already in flight will continue to intercept.

cease-fire • *n.* **1** a temporary suspension of fighting, typically one during which peace talks take place; a truce. **2** an order or signal to stop fighting.

cease loading • in artillery and naval gunfire support, the command used during the firing of two or more rounds to indicate the suspension of inserting rounds into the weapon.

Cedar Creek, Battle of • a major CIVIL WAR battle in the SHENANDOAH VALLEY on October 19, 1864. The Confederate Army made a surprise attack on the Union encampment there, and though they held an early advantage, the North was eventually victorious under the leadership of Gen. PHILIP H. SHERIDAN.

Cedar Falls, Operation • an offensive in January 1967 against the IRON TRIANGLE region of Vietnam with the goal of routing the VIET-CONG base camps there. Both U.S. and ARVN divisions totaling 30,000 troops took part. The operation uncovered large caches of arms and other equipment, with minimal U.S. and ARVN casualties.

Cedar Mountain • the Virginia site of a CIVIL WAR battle fought on August 9, 1862. The battle occurred during the Northern Virginia campaign of 1862 and involved over 24,000 men. Maj. Gen. THOMAS J. JACKSON led Confederate troops to Gordonsville, Virginia, in July and was reinforced with another division. Union forces led by Maj. Gen. NATHANIEL P. BANKS were deployed to Culpeper County, Virginia, to seize the rail junction in Gordonsville. While Union forces dominated the early stages of the battle at Cedar Mountain, a counterattack by the Confederates changed the tide of the encounter, and the Confederates won. (Also called Slaughter's Mountain and Cedar Run.)

ceiling • *n.* **1** the maximum altitude that a particular aircraft can reach. **2** the altitude of the base of a cloud layer. **3** the inside planking of a ship's bottom and sides.

celestial guidance • the guidance of a missile or other vehicle by reference to celestial bodies.

cell • *n.* a small group of individuals who work together for clandestine or subversive purposes.

Céloron de Blainville, Pierre-Joseph (1693–1759) • French army officer and explorer, born in Montreal, Canada. A captain in the French colonial regulars, he commanded various forts throughout the Great Lakes region. His Ohio expedition and report of 1749 paved the way for the French occupation of the upper Ohio in 1753, which precipitated the FRENCH AND INDIAN WAR (1754–63).

Cemetery Hill • a prominent terrain feature at GETTYSBURG (1863), Cemetery Hill marked the right (northern) flank of the Union position and was held despite determined Confederate assaults.

Cemetery Ridge • a ridge south of GETTYSBURG where Union forces held against "PICKETT'S CHARGE" on July 3, 1863. Cemetery Ridge and the adjacent CEMETERY HILL were Union strongholds against Confederate attacks commanded by Gen. ROBERT E. LEE. Union Gen. GEORGE G. MEADE's defeat of Gen. GEORGE E. PICKETT at Gettysburg is considered the turning point of the Civil War.

censorship • *n.* the practice of officially examining books, films, etc., and suppressing unacceptable parts.

centerfire • *adj.* **1** (of a gun cartridge) having the primer in the center of the base. **2** (of a gun) using such cartridges. • *n.* a gun using such a cartridge.

Center for Defense Information • a private research organization that analyzes military activity, located in Washington, D.C. Founded in 1972 by GENE LA ROCQUE, it is funded by contributions and grants and staffed by retired military officers in collaboration with experienced civilians. It attempts to provide unbiased evaluations of and alternatives for U.S. defense programs.

Center for International Security Affairs • (**CISA**) established in 1995 to coordinate LOS ALAMOS NATIONAL LABORATORY's increasing interactions with emerging states, China, and other countries. The principal objective of the Center's programs is the reduction of weapons of mass destruction, and it seeks to stabilize three important aspects of nuclear weaponry: the materials needed to build nuclear weapons, the information about how to build a nuclear weapon, and institutions that control nuclear weapons.

Center for Strategic and International Studies • a private, nonpartisan institution that evaluates global policy issues, located in Washington, D.C. Founded in 1962, it attempts to affect global policies through strategic analysis and action commissions.

centigray • *n.* a unit of absorbed dose of radiation (equal to one rad).

Central Intelligence Agency • (**CIA**) an independent U.S. agency responsible to the president through its Director and to the people of the United States through Congressional intelligence oversight committees. It was officially created by President HARRY S. TRUMAN in 1947 when he signed the NATIONAL SECURITY ACT, but its history is usually traced back to the OFFICE OF STRATEGIC

SERVICES active during WORLD WAR II. The NATIONAL SECURITY ACT charged the **Director of Central Intelligence** (DCI) with coordinating U.S. intelligence activities, as well as correlating, analyzing, and providing that information to the president, the NATIONAL SECURITY COUNCIL, and all the officials responsible for formulating and carrying out U.S. national security policy.

Central Intelligence Group • name borne from January 20, 1946 to July 25, 1947 by the organization which became the CENTRAL INTELLIGENCE AGENCY.

Central Powers • the nations opposed to the ALLIED POWERS in WORLD WAR I: Germany, Austria-Hungary, and Turkey.

CEP • *abbr.* circular error probable.

Cerro Gordo, Battle of • an 1847 battle in the MEXICAN WAR (1846–48) during Gen. WINFIELD SCOTT's campaign to take Mexico City. The U.S. victory resulted in the occupation of Xalapa, a position that the Mexican forces under ANTONIO LÓPEZ DE SANTA ANNA had thought impregnable. Both ULYSSES S. GRANT and ROBERT E. LEE took part, and they are assumed to have gained experience that would serve them in the Civil War.

CFC • *abbr.* Combined Forces Command.

CFE • (**The Conventional Forces in Europe**) a series of negotiations officially begun on March 9, 1989, and that concluded with the signing of the CFE Treaty in Paris on November 19, 1990. The treaty proposed to establish "a secure and stable balance of conventional armed forces in Europe at lower levels" than before. It resulted in large reductions of Soviet armed forces, but few in NATO armed forces. (Also known as the **Treaty on Conventional Armed Forces in Europe**.)

CG • *abbr.* guided missile cruiser.

CG-47 • see GUIDED MISSILE CRUISER; *Ticonderoga*, USS, DEF. 2.

CGS • *abbr.* (in the UK) Chief of General Staff.

CH-3 • see JOLLY GREEN GIANT.

CH-46 • see SEA KNIGHT.

CH-47 • see CHINOOK.

CH-53A • see SEA STALLION.

CH-53E • see SEA STALLION.

CH-54 • see SKYCRANE.

Chafee, John H. (1922–99) • born in Providence, Rhode Island, a Rhode Island Republican senator and chairman of the Environmental and Public Works Committee. He graduated from Yale University in 1947 and afterwards joined the Marine Corps. After WORLD WAR II, he earned a law degree from Harvard University in 1950 and then returned to service in the KOREAN WAR, in which he was placed in command of a rifle company. After the war, he entered politics and in 1962 was elected as governor of Rhode Island, to which he was twice re-elected. He lost re-election in 1968 and was appointed Secretary of the Navy by President RICHARD M. NIXON in 1969. He resigned as Secretary in 1972.

chaff • *n.* strips of metal foil or metal filings released in the atmosphere from aircraft, or deployed as missiles, to obstruct radar detection or confuse radar-tracking missiles.

Chaffee, Adna Romanza (1842–1914) • Union army officer, born in Orwell, Ohio. Chaffee enlisted in the 6th Cavalry in 1861, and by the end of the CIVIL WAR had taken part in at least fifty-four battles and skirmishes. After 1867 he gained a reputation as a peerless Indian fighter on the southwestern frontier. He fought the Comanches at Paint Creek, Texas (1868), and commanded the San Carlos Indian Reservation (1879–1880) In the SPANISH-AMERICAN WAR (1898), he led a brigade at Santiago, capturing the stronghold of El Caney. While commanding American forces in China during the CHINA RELIEF EXPEDITION (1900), he gained praise for skill in battle and tactful treatment of inhabitants. In 1904 he served as chief of the army general staff and lieutenant general.

Chaffee was the only American soldier to have risen to lieutenant general from the rank of private.

Chaffee, Adna Romanza, Jr. (1884–1941) • U.S. army officer, born in Junction City, Kansas. He graduated from WEST POINT in 1906 shortly after his father stepped down as ARMY CHIEF OF STAFF. The younger Chaffee rose to the rank of colonel during WORLD WAR I, seeing action in both the 1918 ST. MIHIEL and MEUSE-ARGONNE offensives. In 1927 he was assigned to the GENERAL STAFF, where he promoted the development of a new mechanized armored striking force based on tanks. He earned the title "father of the Armored Force" for his strong advocacy for the new weaponry and leadership of the movement to incorporate it into the American Army. In 1931 he oversaw the mechanization of the 1st Cavalry and conducted pioneering experimentation with it. He finally won approval for the organization of his Armored Force in 1940, and was deservedly named its chief. By the end of the year he had already organized two armored divisions. He was promoted to the permanent rank of major general in August 1941, but unfortunately died in Boston that same month.

Cancer prevented Chaffee from ever leading his troops into battle.

Chaffee tank • (**M-24 light tank**) U.S. light tank which entered service late in WORLD WAR II and also saw service in the KOREAN WAR. Named for Maj. Gen. ADNA CHAFFEE, JR., the first commander of U.S. armored forces, the Chaffee light tank had a gross weight of some 19 tons and was armed with a 75-mm gun with coaxially mounted .30 caliber machine gun, a .50 caliber anti-aircraft machine gun mounted on the turret, and a .30 caliber flexible machine gun mounted in the bow. It had a crew of four men.

chain • *n.* (**chains**) a structure of planks projecting horizontally from a sailing ship's sides abreast of the masts, used to widen the basis for the shrouds.

chain gun • a machine gun that uses a motor-driven chain to power all moving parts.

chain of command • the succession of commanding officers from a superior to a subordinate through which command is exercised. Also called COMMAND CHANNEL.

chainplate • *n.* a strong link or plate on a sailing ship's side, to which the shrouds are secured.

chain reaction • the self-sustaining fission reaction spread by neutrons that occurs in nuclear reactors and bombs.

chain shot • pairs of cannonballs or half balls joined by a chain, fired from cannons in sea battles in order to damage masts and rigging.

chain-wale • *n.* a wooden strip or plank mounted horizontally on the side of a sailing ship, abreast of a mast, to which the shrouds are attached.

Chalmers, James Ronald (1831–98) • Confederate general and U.S. congressman, born in Halifax County, Virginia. Chalmers commanded an infantry brigade at SHILOH (1862), cavalry in BRAXTON BRAGG's Kentucky campaign, and fought at STONES RIVER (December 1862–January 1863). Chalmers also commanded a division under Gen. NATHAN BEDFORD FORREST, and participated in the military action that led to the massacre of surrendering black and Tennessee Union soldiers at FORT PILLOW (1864), although his role in this infamous affair is still unclear.

chamber • *n.* the part of a gun bore that contains the charge or bullet. • *v.* place (a bullet) into the chamber of a gun.

Chamberlain, (Arthur) Neville (1869–1940) • prime minister of England, (1937–40) born in Birmingham. At the beginning of WORLD WAR II, he tried to maintain peaceful relations with ADOLF HITLER and BENITO MUSSOLINI through a policy of appeasement, engineering the Munich Pact in 1938, which gave Hitler the Sudeten (an area of Czechoslovakia, one fifth of the country and rich in natural resources) in addition to other areas that went to Hungary and Poland. When he returned to England in triumph, he proclaimed, "I believe it is peace in our time," but his optimism had no basis and the failure of appeasement became obvious when Hitler invaded and conquered Czechoslovakia in 1939. After Germany's annexation of Czechoslovakia, Chamberlain guaranteed Poland against a similar fate, but, when Germany invaded Poland only months later, he declared war. His own party turned against him, and he was forced to resign when British forces were defeated in Norway.

Chamberlain, Joshua Lawrence (1828–1914) • Union soldier, politician, and educator, born in Brewer, Maine. Chamberlain commanded the 20th Maine Infantry at GETTYSBURG, holding the extreme left flank of the ARMY OF THE POTOMAC, resting on LITTLE ROUND TOP, against repeated assaults (1863), for which he was awarded the CONGRESSIONAL MEDAL OF HONOR in 1893. He also commanded brigades at NORTH ANNA and COLD HARBOR, PETERSBURG, and APPOMATTOX (1864–65).

Champion, Henry (1723–97) • political and military leader who played an important role in provisioning the CONTINENTAL ARMY, born in East Haddam, Connecticut. Appointed supply commissioner, he specialized in procuring beef. He relieved a severe meat shortage at VALLEY FORGE (1778).

After the Continental Congress stopped issuing currency in 1779, Champion had to rely on taxes paid in meat for supplying the army for the rest of the war.

Champion Hill • (**Bakers Creek**) the site in Mississippi of a CIVIL WAR battle that took place on May 16, 1863. The battle was part of Maj. Gen. ULYSSES S. GRANT's operations against VICKSBURG in 1863. Following the Union capture of Jackson, Mississippi, Lieut. Gen. JOHN C. PEMBERTON was ordered to attack the Federals at Clinton, Mississippi, but he felt that this plan was too dangerous. Instead, he decided to attack Union supply trains moving from Grand Gulf to Raymond. However, on May 16 he was reordered to attack at Clinton and began reversing direction at Champion Hill. As a result, the rear, which included a number of supply wagons, was made into the lead force. Union forces caught up with the Confederates at Champion Hill and deployed another line of troops toward the enemy's left flank. Confederate units were posted at the top of Champion Hill to watch for these Union troops. Both Union forces and artillery attacks caused the Rebels to scatter in disorder. After attacks and counterattacks, the Confederates were in full retreat toward VICKSBURG.

Chancellorsville, Battle of • a week-long CIVIL WAR battle in May 1863, in and around Chancellorsville, Virginia. It was a major victory for the Confederacy, and sometimes considered to be ROBERT E. LEE's greatest victory. There were heavy casualties on both sides, including generals. It was at this battle that Gen. STONEWALL JACKSON was mortally wounded by his own men.

chandler • *n.* (also **ship chandler**) a dealer in supplies and equipment for ships and boats.

change step • *v.* (in marching) alter one's step so that the opposite leg marks time.

chantey |'SHæntē| (also **chanty, shanty,** or **sea chantey**) • *n.* a song with alternating solo and chorus, of a kind originally sung by sailors while working together.

ORIGIN: mid 19th. cent.: probably from French *chantez!* 'sing!'

Chantilly, Battle of • (also called **Ox Hill**) a CIVIL WAR battle that took place in Fairfax County, Virginia, where Confederate Maj. Gen. "STONEWALL" JACKSON cut off Union forces retreating from SECOND BULL RUN. On September 1, 1862, during a severe thunderstorm, Jackson defeated Union forces at the price of huge casualties on both sides, including Union Maj. Gens. PHILIP KEARNY and ISAAC STEVENS.

CHAOS, Operation • a CIA program in the

1960s and 1970s for surveillance of domestic opponents of the VIETNAM WAR. Although ordered by President LYNDON B. JOHNSON and later by President RICHARD M. NIXON, Operation CHAOS was subsequently determined to be a violation of the CIA's charter and thus illegal.

Chaparral |ˌSHæpəˈræl| • (**MIM-72**) a short-range low-altitude surface-to-air missile, consisting of a turret mounted on a tracked vehicle carrying four ready-to-fire missiles. The air-to-air equivalent is the SIDEWINDER.

chaplain |ˈCHæplən| • *n.* a member of the clergy attached to a private chapel, institution, ship, branch of the armed forces, etc. DERIVATIVES: **chaplaincy** |ˈCHæplənsē| *n.*

Chaplain School • see ARMY CHAPLAIN SCHOOL.

Chapultepec, Battle of • a decisive battle near the end of the MEXICAN WAR (1846–48) on September 12, 1847, in which Mexico City fell to U.S. forces.

charge • *n.* **1** the amount of propellent for a fixed-, semifixed-, or separate-loading projectile, round, or shell. It may also refer to the quantity of explosive filling contained in a bomb, mine, or the like. **2** in combat engineering, a quantity of explosive, prepared for demolition purposes.

Charles F. Adams-class • a class of 23 4,-500-ton missile destroyers based on the FORREST SHERMAN CLASS and launched on September 10, 1960.

Charleston Harbor • a city in South Carolina that, during the CIVIL WAR, was the site of the capture by Confederates of FORT SUMTER in April 1861, and the site of the Union blockade from 1863 to 1865. On September 7–8, 1863, Federal advances forced Confederate troops to evacuate FORT WAGNER and Battery Gregg, but further Federal attacks were repulsed. The city held out until February 1865 and was finally evacuated when Gen. WILLIAM T. SHERMAN's advanced northward from Savannah after his MARCH TO THE SEA.

Charleston, siege of • a REVOLUTIONARY WAR battle, this was Sir HENRY CLINTON's greatest victory for the British. He succeeded in occupying Charleston, South Carolina, in May 1780. The city had been defended by continentals under the leadership of BENJAMIN LINCOLN, who surrendered in the face of superior power and urging from local civic leaders, who wanted to spare the city from further damage.

Charlestown Navy Yard • one of six navy yards authorized by Congress in 1799, the Boston site of the yard was not purchased until two years later. The yard was used primarily for storage until the WAR OF 1812, when the Navy's first ship-of-the-line, the USS *Independence*, was built there. The shipyard built over 200 warships, and maintained or repaired thousands of ships. The frigate USS *Constitution*, known as "Old Ironsides," inaugurated the drydock in 1833. From 1837 until the yard closed in 1975, most of the rope and cordage used by Navy ships was made there. During WORLD WAR II, more than 50,000 people worked at the yard. The yard is now part of the Boston National Historical Park. Also called BOSTON NAVAL SHIPYARD or BOSTON NAVY YARD.

Charlie • **1** a code word representing the letter C, used in radio communication. **2** slang a member of the Vietcong or the Vietcong collectively.
ORIGIN: shortening of *Victor Charlie*, radio code for *VC*, representing *Vietcong*.

chart • *n.* a geographical map or plan, especially one used for navigation by sea or air. • *v.* **1** make a map of (an area). **2** plot (a course) on a chart: *the pilot found his craft taking a route he had not charted.*

chase |CHās| • *n.* the part of a gun enclosing the bore.

Chase, Salmon Portland (1808–73) • statesman, antislavery leader, and chief justice of the United States, born in Cornish, New Hampshire. A founder of the Republican party, Chase was a four-time presidential candidate, a U.S. senator (1849–55, 1860–1), and governor of Ohio (1855–61). Chase advocated freed slaves' use as soldiers, access to land, and right to vote. As ABRAHAM LINCOLN's secretary of the Treasury (1861–64), Chase was responsible for financing a war of unprecedented scale. During his tenure he introduced paper money, established a national banking system, and regulated trade between the Union and the Confederacy. Appointed chief justice by ABRAHAM LINCOLN (1864–73), Chase supported universal male suffrage and opposed military government in the South.

In 1837 he became interested in the antislavery movement after defending in court the freedom of Matilda, whose master had brought her to Ohio. Chase maintained that slavery depended on local law for its enforcement because the framers of the Constitution had sought *not* to support it at the national level. On the basis of this analysis, he argued that no law outside of a slave state could support the enslavement of an individual; that is, that once a person had entered free territory, as Matilda had, that person reverted to his or her natural state of freedom. Because of his commitment to the legal defense of slaves, he became known as the "attorney general for fugitive slaves."

---

chasseur |SHæˈsər| • *n.* a soldier, usually in the light cavalry, equipped and trained for rapid movement, especially in the French army.

Château Thierry, Battle of • see MARNE, SECOND BATTLE OF THE.

Chattanooga, Battle of • a decisive battle fought at Chattanooga, on the Tennessee River, from November 23–25, 1863, during the CIVIL WAR. In September 1863, a Southern army commanded by Gen. BRAXTON BRAGG besieged a Federal army led by Gen. WILLIAM S. ROSECRANS at Chattanooga, a vital Confederate railroad junction. In the following month, Gen. ULYSSES S. GRANT took charge of the campaign and seized the offensive. He opened a new and protected line of supply, via Brown's Ferry, and reinforcements from Gen. JOSEPH HOOKER and Gen. WILLIAM T. SHERMAN arrived. Hooker captured LOOKOUT MOUNTAIN (November 24) on the left of Bragg's line; and the next day, Grant attacked all along the line, defeating the Confederate center on MISSIONARY RIDGE and thereby lifting the siege. The Confederate Army retreated to Georgia by the end of the month. Union losses numbered some 6,000; Confederate some 7,000.

CHB • *abbr.* Navy Cargo Handling Battalion.

Cheatham, Benjamin Franklin |ˈCHētəm| (1820–86) • Confederate general, born near Nashville, Tennessee. At STONES RIVER (1862–63), Cheatham was reportedly drunk and incapable of directing his division. That same year, at SPRING HILL, he allowed the army of JOHN M. SCHOFIELD to slip by and suffered heavy casualties in the subsequent battle of FRANKLIN.

checkerboard tactics • tactical method developed, along with the PENTOMIC DIVISION, by military forces in the early 1950s. Checkerboard tactics emphasized dispersal and rapid concentration of units on a nuclear battlefield. The basic concept was that ground combat units would not defend or attack on a single continuous line but would be dispersed in small groups which did not present a lucrative target for a nuclear strike. As required, the combat units would take advantage of superior mobility and communications to mass for defense or attack at key points.

checkpoint • *n.* **1** a predetermined point on the surface of the Earth used as a means of controlling movement, a registration target for fire adjustment, or reference for location. **2** center of impact; a burst center. **3** geographical location on land or water above which the position of an aircraft in flight may be determined by observation or by electrical means. **4** a place where military police check vehicular or pedestrian traffic in order to enforce circulation control measures and other laws, orders, and regulations.

Checkpoint Charlie • a border crossing operated by the Allied military between East and West Berlin that became a symbol of the COLD WAR. The name "Charlie" represents the letter 'c' in the military alphabet, after the Alpha and Bravo checkpoints on the outskirts of Berlin. Allied military, diplomats, and foreigners used the crossing. Checkpoint Charlie was the site of the famous "tank confrontation" of late 1961. On October 22, the East German border police denied entrance to U.S. representatives after their refusal, in accordance with Allied law, to submit to checks. Tanks were subsequently deployed on both sides of the checkpoint. After several days, Moscow and East Berlin capitulated. It was the first time that Soviet and American tanks had faced each other directly since WORLD WAR II, and it was the only time during the Cold War that they did so.

chemical • *adj.* relating to, involving, or denoting the use of poison gas or other chemicals as weapons of war: *the manufacture of chemical weapons.*

DERIVATIVES: **chemically** *adv.*

chemical agent • a chemical substance that is intended for use in military operations to kill, seriously injure, or incapacitate personnel through its physiological effects.

Riot-control agents, herbicides, smoke, and flame are *not* classified as chemical agents.

chemical mine • a mine that releases a chemical weapon, typically mustard gas or nerve gas, when activated.

Chemical School • see ARMY CHEMICAL SCHOOL.

chemical warfare • all aspects of military operations involving the employment of lethal and incapacitating munitions/agents and the warning and protective measures associated with such offensive operations.

Chemical Warfare Service • an organization of the U.S. WAR DEPARTMENT, created in May 1918 by presidential executive order, and charged with the exclusive jurisdiction and control of the manufacture and production of toxic gases, gas-defense applicances, including gas-shell filling plants, and all research in connection with gas warfare. During WORLD WAR II, the Service was responsible for training not only its own troops but also the entire U.S. Army and civilians for defense against the use of chemical, mortar, smoke generator, and chemical air operations in case of enemy attack. In 1946, the Service became the Chemical Corps of the U.S. Army.

chemical warfare weapons • lethal and incapacitating munitions/agents, usually of either chemical or biological origin.

Chemical Weapons Convention • a multinational agreement concluded in 1992 and entered into force in 1997 to reduce chemical weapons stockpiles and to establish provisions for compliance inspections. It was created after negotiations at the Conference of Disarmament and succeeded both the GENEVA PROTOCOL ON CHEMICAL WARFARE of 1925 and the BIOLOGICAL WEAPONS CONVENTION of 1972. A new Chemical Weapons Convention was signed on January 13, 1993, and entered into force on April 29, 1997, to prohibit the production, storage, and use of poison gas and to establish provisions for compliance inspections.

Cheney, Richard (1941–) • U.S. congressman, secretary of defense, and vice president, born in Lincoln, Nebraska. In the House of Representatives (1979–89) and as minority whip, he supported President RONALD REAGAN's military buildup and aid to the Nicaraguan CONTRAS. Despite lack of military service, he was appointed by President GEORGE H. BUSH as secretary of defense (1989–93) after Congress rejected nominee John Tower. Cheney reformed procurement, curtailed some weapons programs, and followed orders to downsize the U.S. military. Following Iraq's invasion of KUWAIT (August 2, 1990), Cheney helped persuade Saudi Arabia to permit basing of U.S. military forces and to join the ALLIED COALITION in the PERSIAN GULF WAR (1991) against SADDAM HUSSEIN's Iraqi army. In 2000 he was elected vice president on the Republican ticket with GEORGE W. BUSH.

Chennault, Claire Lee (1890–1958) • U.S. army officer and aviator. Born in Texas, Chennault attended Officers' Training Camp in 1917 and was commissioned first lieutenant in the infantry. He did not get into WORLD WAR I but did transfer into the SIGNAL CORPS and become a pilot. He became one of the Air Service's premier experts on pursuit aviation while an instructor at the AIR CORPS TACTICAL SCHOOL in the 1930s, but retired as a lieutenant colonel in 1937 because of deafness. Hired by Madame Chiang Kai-shek to organize Chinese air defenses against Japan, he established and led the AMERICAN VOLUNTEER GROUP, which became known as the "Flying Tigers" and compiled a remarkable record in air combat. In April 1942 he was recalled to active duty as a colonel, and he soon became chief of Army Air Forces in China. In March 1943 he was promoted to major general in command of the 14th Air Force, providing tactical support to American and Chinese ground forces. He commanded that unit until the end of the war, and retired again in October 1945.

When he retired, he formed Civil Air Transport (CAT), the predecessor firm to AIR AMERICA. CAT carried arms, munitions, and troops for the Chinese Nationalist regime. (After a secret purchase by the CIA in 1950, CAT airdropped agents and supplies into China, supported anti-Communist forces in Burma, and provided the pilots to fly resupply missions for the French at DIEN BIEN PHU, VIETNAM, in 1954.)

Cherbourg, Battle of • a battle fought in western Normandy as part of OPERATION OVERLORD on June 25, 1944, during WORLD WAR II. It was an Allied victory against German defenses, which surrendered Cherbourg on June 27.

Cherokee Mounted Rifles • military units of the U.S. Confederacy from 1861 to 1865, organized under the leadership of STAND WATIE, who was commissioned by Brig. Gen. BEN MCCULLOCH to raise a regiment and, at a meeting of the southern sympathizers of the FIVE CIVILIZED TRIBES on July 27, 1861, the First Cherokee Regiment was organized. On October 7, 1861, the day the treaty between the Cherokee Nation and the CONFEDERACY was signed, the regiment was almost full, with 1,214 men on its rolls.

Cherokee War • (1759–61) three campaigns mounted by the white colonists of the Carolinas against the Cherokee Indians. The first campaign, in 1759, was ended by an outbreak of smallpox among the colonial forces. The second, in 1760, was led by British regulars but was successfully turned back by the Cherokees. The third, in 1761, was also led by British regulars and resulted in some concessions by the Cherokees. The war arose from the greed for land of the colonists and misunderstandings between the colonists and the Cherokees, and took place in the context of the greater FRENCH AND INDIAN WAR (1754–63) being fought to the north.

cherry • *adj.* slang new to battle.

Chesapeake affair • the seizure and searching, off the coast of Virginia, of the USS *Chesapeake* in 1807 by the HMS *Leopard*, whose commander suspected that British deserters might be aboard. Four of the *Chesapeake*'s crew were impressed. The incident was an inciting factor in the WAR OF 1812.

chevron |ˈsHevrən| • *n.* a line or stripe of cloth or metal in the shape of a V or an inverted V worn on the sleeve of a uniform to indicate the rank of enlisted personnel.

Cheyenne • an Algonquian-speaking Plains Indian tribe located in Wyoming, Nebraska, and the western Dakotas, and later in Montana and Oklahoma. Together with the LAKOTA SIOUX, the two branches of the Cheyenne, the Northern and the Southern, resisted westward expansion of white settlers on the Great Plains. In 1878, the Northern Cheyenne, led by Dull Knife and Little Wolf, fled their reservation in Oklahoma and trekked north to their homeland in Montana, pursued by U.S. Army troops. After many hardships, they were permitted to remain there on a reservation on the Tongue River.

Cheyenne Dog Soldiers • a company of Cheyenne warriors who were the military elite of the Cheyenne Nation. They were active initially with other Native tribes and later with U.S. forces, in conflicts and raids in the areas that are now Kansas, Colorado, and Wyoming from the 1830s. They consistently refused to enter into treaties with the United States. They suffered a decisive defeat in a battle with U.S. cavalry at Summit Springs, Colorado, in 1869.

***Cheyenne*, USS** • (**SSN 773**) the last of the Los Angeles-class attack submarines to be commissioned, it is capable of various operations, including antisubmarine warfare, intelligence gathering, the landing of special forces, strike missions, mining, and search and rescue. Its armament includes MK-48 advanced-capability torpedoes, TOMAHAWK and HARPOON missiles, and mobile mines. With version "I" of the 688 model of Los Angeles-class submarines (the "I" stands for 'improved'), the *Cheyenne* is quieter, carries an advanced BSY-1 sonar suite combat system, can lay mines from its torpedo tubes, and is configured for under-ice operations.

Chiang Kai-shek |ˌCHæNG ˌkī ˈsHek| (1887-1975) • (also **Jiang Jie Shi**) Chinese general and political leader, President of China from 1928 to 1931 and from 1943 to 1949, and of Taiwan from 1950 to 1975, born in Fenghua, Zhejiang Province. As the Second SINO-JAPANESE WAR merged with WORLD WAR II, Chiang rose in international prestige, becoming the supreme commander of the Allied forces in the China theater in 1942 and attending the CAIRO CONFERENCE in 1943. By 1950 the Communists had forced Chiang and the Nationalist government to retreat to the island of Taiwan (Formosa). With U.S. military and economic assistance, Chiang reorganized his military forces and instituted limited democratic political reforms, promising the reconquest of the Chinese mainland. He contributed to Taiwan's economic development, political stability, and land reform. In 1971 the UNITED NATIONS expelled his regime and accepted the Communist government of China.

Chickamauga, Battle of • the largest CIVIL WAR battle of the Western theater, which took place September 18–20, 1863, near Chattanooga, Tennessee. Nearly 130,000 troops, about equally divided between the sides, participated, and there were casualties of over 30,000. It is marked as a Confederate victory, but did not result in any territorial or tactical gains.

Chickasaw Bayou, Battle of • a Confederate victory in December 1862 that frustrated ULYSSES S. GRANT's attempts to take VICKSBURG by the direct approach. Forces under WILLIAM T. SHERMAN, after some preparations, made a frontal assault on the heavily defended Walnut Hills area of Warren County, Mississippi, which was rebuffed with heavy Union casualties.

chief master sergeant • a non-commissioned officer in the U.S. Air Force ranking above senior master sergeant and below warrant officer.

Chief Master Sergeant of the Air Force • the highest ranking non-commissioned officer in the U.S. Air Force and the principal enlisted adviser to the Air Force Chief of Staff.

chief officer • (**chief naval officer**) the officer second in command of a naval vessel.

Chief of Naval Operations • the senior officer of the U.S. Navy, responsible for the administration and support of all U.S. naval forces. The Chief of Naval Operations sits as a member of the JOINT CHIEFS OF STAFF.

chief of staff • the senior staff officer of a service or command.

chief petty officer • a senior non-commissioned officer in a navy, in particular an NCO in the U.S. Navy or Coast Guard ranking above petty officer and below senior chief petty officer.

chief technician • a rank of noncommissioned officer in the RAF, above sergeant and below flight sergeant.

chief warrant officer • a member of the U.S. armed forces ranking above warrant officer and below the lowest-ranking commissioned officer.

Chien Thang • see "WILL TO VICTORY" PROGRAM.

Chieu Hoi • see OPEN ARMS PROGRAM.

Chilean Crisis • a naval incident in 1891 in which sailors from the USS *Baltimore*, standing in the port of Valparaiso, Chile, became involved in a barroom brawl that left two of them dead. Military repercussions were obviated when the Chilean government acquiesced to an ultimatum from President BENJAMIN HARRISON for an apology and restitution. Also called the BALTIMORE AFFAIR.

China-Burma-India theater • (also **CBI theater**) the least influential and least prominent area that saw major military action in WORLD WAR II. Although the United States had an objective of building up China as a source of manpower and a possible base for an eventual invasion of JAPAN, other Allies were largely preoccupied with the more dramatic events in other theaters. A joint British and American operation reopened the strategic BURMA SUPPLY ROAD in 1945, which had been blocked by the Japanese.

China Clipper • (**Martin M-130**) a transoceanic flying boat used by Pan American Airways between the world wars. It made the first commercial double crossing of the Pacific between November 22, 1935 and December 6, 1935, and regular trans-Pacific service began on October 21, 1936. In 1942, the remaining pair of M-130s were impressed for war service as U.S. Navy transports, but neither was given a Naval designation. In early 1945, shortly after the tenth anniversary of its first flight, the China Clipper was wrecked when it struck an unlit boat during a night landing.

China Lobby • the U.S. policy toward China from the mid-1940s until RICHARD M. NIXON's presidency. Henry Luce, the publisher of *Time*, was one of the more powerful and visible proponents of the China Lobby. From 1945 to 1949, he and other anti-communist conservatives pressured Congress and the Administration for military and economic aid to support CHIANG KAI-SHEK against MAO TSE-TUNG's forces and the Japanese. This powerful lobby group, composed of members of Congress, members of the media, and labor unions, suppressed criticism of Chiang Kai-shek and raised approximately $3 billion in aid from the government for him. When the army was defeated, several statesmen were accused by the Lobby of being responsible for "losing China" to Mao and communism. U.S.-China relations remained hostile, consisting of no diplomatic relations, trade, or contact, and these relations were seen as contributing to conflicts that erupted between both nations during the KOREAN and VIETNAM WARS. It is believed that the Lobby backed Gen. DOUGLAS MACARTHUR's interest in invading China during the Korean War. Such anti-China sentiment began to diminish with DWIGHT D. EISENHOWER and JOHN F. KENNEDY's presidencies and with Nixon's interest in resuming contact with China.

China Relief Expedition • a multinational expeditionary force under overall British command in the summer of 1900 whose aim was to put down the BOXER REBELLION and break the siege of the foreign Legation Quarter in Beijing. It succeeded on both fronts. The multimillion dollar indemnity secured by the United States from this was used mostly to educate Chinese students in the United States.

Chinese People's Volunteers • (**CPV**) Chinese Communist military forces which intervened in the KOREAN WAR. Officially known as the Chinese People's Volunteers in the War to Resist U.S. Aggression and Aid Korea, the CPV maintained the fiction that it was a force of volunteers eager to aid their North Korean Communist brethren, but in reality the CPV was formed principally from infantry units of the 4th Field Army of the (Chinese Communist) PEOPLE'S LIBERATION ARMY. The CPV entered Korea in October 1950, and inflicted heavy blows on the UNITED NATIONS forces before being forced into a stalemate which eventually produced the armistice agreements of July 1953. The CPV remained in Korea until October 1958.

Chinook • (**CH-47**) a helicopter used for the U.S. Army's airborne divisions to airlift artillery and other heavy equipment after infantry landings. A variant of the Chinook, with armor, armament, and advanced avionics and electronics (designated MH-47E), it is used by the Army for clandestine operations. The Chinook was the Army's main transport helicopter, able to carry thirty-three soldiers or three to four tons of cargo and fly 150 mph.

Chippewa, Battle of • a victory for Gen. WINFIELD SCOTT over the British in the WAR OF 1812, near Fort Erie, Ontario in 1814. Scott's army wore gray uniforms that the British commander mistakenly took for the gray coats of untrained levies. The gray uniforms worn at WEST POINT to this day commemorate this victory.

Chisolm, Alexander Robert (1834–1910) • Confederate soldier and financier, born in Beaufort, South Carolina. Chisolm was an aide-de-camp to Gen. P.G.T. BEAUREGARD at FORT SUMTER and throughout the CIVIL WAR. An efficient and resourceful staff officer, he supervised troop dispositions, acted as liaison, and carried dispatches. At FIRST BULL RUN (1861), he singlehandedly rallied a demoralized Virginia regiment, then led a cavalry force in harassing retreating Federals near Cub Run bridge. He served at SHILOH and the defense of CHARLESTON (both 1862); at Gen. JOSEPH E. JOHNSTON's surrender at Greensboro, Chisolm signed the parole of its troops (1864).

Chittenden, Hiram Martin (1858–1917) • a WEST POINT graduate who served in the SPANISH-AMERICAN WAR (1898) and later in the ARMY CORPS OF ENGINEERS. He was instrumental in the development of Yellowstone National Park and wrote several books of history about the American West.

Chivington, John Milton (1821–94) • U.S. army officer and clergyman. Born in Warren County, Ohio, Chivington became a Methodist preacher in 1844. He left Ohio in 1848 to become a frontier missionary, and earned the nickname of "Fighting Parson" for his involvement with antislavery forces in Kansas. He was commissioned major in the 1st Colorado Volunteers when the CIVIL WAR began, and was promoted to colonel in 1862. He distinguished himself in combat actions in New Mexico during Col. EDWARD R.S. CANBY's campaign to turn back the invasion of Gen. HENRY H. SIBLEY, particularly at Apache Canyon. In 1863 Chivington was appointed commander of the military district of Colorado, where he was responsible for dealing with Indians taking advantage of the absence of federal troops. On November 29, 1864, he led a force of Colorado militia against a group of Indians camped along Sand Creek led by BLACK KETTLE, who believed they had peacefully surrendered to the federal commander at nearby Fort Lyon. Three separate hearings were conducted that examined Chivington's role at what became known as the SAND CREEK MASSACRE (1864), but no official action was taken. Chivington escaped court-martial by resigning from the service.

chlorine gas • gaseous chlorine, a chemical weapon that acts as a choking agent, searing the lining of the respiratory tract. It was first used extensively in WORLD WAR I.

chock • *n.* a support on which a rounded structure, such as a cask or the hull of a boat, may be placed to keep it steady. • *v.* support (a boat, cask, etc.) on chocks.

choke • *n.* a narrowed part of a shotgun bore, typically near the muzzle and serving to restrict the spread of the shot.

Chongqing (**Chungking**) • a city in Sichuan province in central China. It was the capital of China from 1938 to 1946. Chongqing was the capital of the Nationalist Government during WORLD WAR II. After the Japanese invaded Nanjing in November 1937, CHIANG KAI-SHEK moved the Nationalist Government to Chongqing. The capital was returned to Nanjing in 1946, but moved to Chongqing again in October 1949 with the outbreak of fighting with the Communists. Chongqing fell under Communist control on November 30, 1949.

chop • *n.* the broken motion of water, typically due to the action of the wind against the tide: *we started our run into a two-foot chop.*

Chosin Reservoir, Battle of the • a battle late in the KOREAN WAR (December 1950) in the campaign begun by Gen. DOUGLAS MACARTHUR to bring the war to an end. The battle was fought largely by and won by the Marines, though there were heavy casualties and nearly all of them suffered frostbite in temperatures that reached -25° F.

Christie, J. Walter (1865–1944) • American tank designer, born in River Edge, New Jersey. A self-taught mechanical engineer, Christie improved the turret track for naval guns during the SPANISH-AMERICAN WAR (1898), and by the early years of the 20th century had developed his own designs for a front-wheel drive car, which he raced in the Grand Prix in France. In 1916 he tried his hand at a prototype four-wheeled gun carriage for the military ordnance branch, but he chafed at their requirements. After submitting many designs, in 1928 he was able to demonstrate his "Model 1940" high-speed tank chassis at Fort Meyer. The model was well-received (and praised by then Lt. Col. GEORGE S. PATTON), but the purchase was revoked by the secretary of war because the price was too high. Christie then looked to sell his designs to Poland and Russia, but was unable to receive full State Department approval.

Christie did live to see the Russians develop a series of tanks based on his designs, which fought well against the Germans advances in 1941. His ideas were also used by British tank designers.

Christmas bombings • see LINEBACKER II.

Christmas tree • slang **1** a nuclear missile onboard a submarine. **2** a control room or cockpit's panel of indicator lights, green (good) and red (bad).

chronic radiation dose • a dose of ionizing radiation received either continuously or intermittently over a prolonged period of time.

A chronic radiation dose may be high enough to cause radiation sickness and death, but if received at a low-dose rate, a significant portion of the acute cellular damage will be repaired.

chu-hoi |ˈCHōō ˈhoi| • slang (in the PERSIAN GULF WAR) surrendering enemy troops.
ORIGIN: from the Vietnamese word for "surrender," picked up by U.S. troops in the VIETNAM WAR.

Chungking • see CHONGQING.

Church, Benjamin (1639–1718) • soldier, born in Plymouth, Massachusetts. Church was captain of the Plymouth Colony militia in KING PHILIP'S WAR (1675) between the colonists and the WAMPANOAGS and allied tribes. Dismissing "the fancy of a Mighty Conquest," he warned fellow colonists that "they must make a business of the War, as the Enemy did." A friend of local tribes, Church made effective use of Indian troops and led units that included both captured enemies and Christianized natives. His company tracked down and killed PHILIP (1676). Church later fought in KING WILLIAM'S WAR (1689–97)/(1702–13) and QUEEN ANNE'S WAR. He recounted his military exploits in *Entertaining Passages Relating to King Philip's War* (1716).

Church, Benjamin (1734–78?) • physician, poet, and traitor, born in Newport, Rhode Island. Despite patriotic poetry and fiery speeches against British rule, Church "carried on a criminal Correspondence with the Enemy." He informed Gen. THOMAS GAGE of colonial troop strengths and allocations. Interception of a letter (September 1775) led to his arrest, military trial, and expulsion from the Massachusetts House of Representatives.

Churchill, Sir Winston S. (1874–1965) • British prime minister during WORLD WAR II, born Winston Leonard Spencer Churchill at Blenheim, Oxfordshire, England. He served as a soldier during WORLD WAR I, and returned to serve in Parliament as minister of munitions under DAVID LLOYD GEORGE. Following the end of the war, he was secretary for war from 1918 to 1921. Out of office for ten years (1929–39), he became a vocal critic of Conservative policy on India, and was fiercely opposed to Chamberlain's attempt to appease ADOLF HITLER and BENITO MUSSOLINI. Churchill returned to his post at the Admiralty when World War II began, and, when ARTHUR NEVILLE CHAMBERLAIN had to resign, he was asked to form a coalition government, and did so in May 1940, becoming its prime minister. He and President FRANKLIN D. ROOSEVELT were close friends, and Churchill signed the ATLANTIC CHARTER in 1941, which declared the Allies' war strategy. He also met with Allied leaders in CASABLANCA, Washington, CAIRO, Moscow, and TEHRAN, and with JOSEF STALIN and Roosevelt in the Crimea in 1945 to plan for the coming victory over the AXIS POWERS. He announced the surrender of Germany on May 8, 1945 and, within two weeks, his coalition government collapsed. Churchill lost in a general election in July 1945, and became the opposition leader until October 1951, when he again became prime minister. He served in that capacity until April 1955 when he resigned to take up writing and painting. In 1953, he won the Nobel Prize for literature for his six-volume history of World War II (1948–54), and also wrote the four-volume *History of the English-Speaking Peoples* (1956–58).

Churchill, Thomas James (1824–1905) • Confederate army officer and politician, born in Jefferson County, Kentucky. He fought in the MEXICAN WAR (1846–48) as lieutenant general of the First Kentucky Mounted Riflemen. In the CIVIL WAR, Churchill raised the First Arkansas Mounted Riflemen. Assigned to defend Fort Hindman on the Arkansas River, he was forced to surrender (January 1863) when some of his troops raised unauthorized white flags. In the TRANS-MISSISSIPPI DEPARTMENT under Gen. E. KIRBY SMITH, he attacked and drove back Maj. Gen. FREDERICK STEELE's forces in the battle of Jenkins's Ferry (April 30, 1864), incurring significant Confederate casualties. He was promoted to major general in 1865.

Churubusco, Battle of • one in the series of battles in the MEXICAN WAR (1846–48) between Gen. WINFIELD SCOTT and ANTONIO LÓPEZ DE SANTA ANNA, on Scott's campaign toward Mexico City. The American victory on August 20, 1847, along with the victory at CONTRERAS earlier in the day, led to Santa Anna agreeing an armistice the next day.

chute • *n.* informal a parachute.

CI • *abbr.* counterintelligence.

CIA • *abbr.* Central Intelligence Agency.

CIC • *abbr.* **1** combat information center **2** Counter Intelligence Corps.

Cilley, Joseph (c. 1734–99) • REVOLUTIONARY WAR soldier and politician, born in Nottingham, New Hampshire. In 1774 he was a member of a patriot group that raided British cannons, muskets, and other ammunition stores from Fort William and Mary (later Fort Constitution) near Portsmouth shortly before British vessels entered the harbor. During the war he was major, and later colonel, of the 2nd New Hampshire Infantry.

CINC |ˌsē-inˈsē| • *abbr.* Commander in Chief. The title generally reserved in the U.S.

military services to senior (four-star) commanders of joint or combined commands, particularly the unified commands under the JOINT CHIEFS OF STAFF. The President of the United States is the commander in chief of all U.S. military forces. For a specific CINC see the discussion under the entry for the command concerned. CINC is sometimes added to other letters to form a longer acronym, as in CINCENT.

CINCAAFCE • *abbr.* Commander in chief, NATO's Allied Air Forces Central Europe (CINCAAFCE). The Commander is responsible for providing air force support to NATO in the European theater and U.S. forces in parts of Africa and the Middle East. See U.S. EUROPEAN COMMAND (USEUCOM).

CINCAF |ˈsiNGkˌæf| • *abbr.* Commander in Chief, U.S. Asiatic Fleet. Obsolete (pre-WORLD WAR II) title of the U.S. Navy admiral commanding U.S. naval forces in the waters contiguous to China and the Philippine Islands.

CINCAFLANT |ˈsiNGkˌæfˌlænt| • *abbr.* Commander in Chief, U.S. Air Forces, Atlantic Command. Title of the U.S. Air Force four-star general commanding the Air Force component of the unified U.S. ATLANTIC COMMAND from headquarters at Langley AFB, Virginia.

CINCARLANT |ˈsiNGkˌärˌlænt| • *abbr.* Commander in Chief, U.S. Army Forces, Atlantic Command. Title of the U.S. Army four-star general commanding the Army component of the unified U.S. Atlantic Command from headquarters at Fort McPherson, Georgia. The position of CINCARLANT is normally held concurrently by the Commanding General, U.S. Army Forces Command (CGFORSCOM).

CINCCFC • *abbr.* Commander in Chief, Combined Forces Command.

CINCENT |ˈsinsent| • *abbr.* Commander in Chief Central Command.

CINCEUR • *abbr.* Commander in Chief, Europe.

CINCHAN |ˈsiNGkˌCHæn| • *abbr.* Commander in Chief Channel.

Cincinnati, Society of the • a veterans' organization for officers of the REVOLUTIONARY WAR, founded in 1783 in Newburgh, New York. It was established with the aim of preserving ties between the officers and pressuring the national government to honor their pension claims. Membership to the society could be passed to the eldest male descendent, and excluded enlisted men. The organization had chapters in all thirteen states and was one of the country's earliest national institutions. However, by the 1830s, with the passing of the Revolutionary generation, interest in the group had waned and many state chapters closed. Around the Centennial of 1876, several dormant state chapters were revived in the East and new ones created in the West.

CINCJFCOM |ˈsiNGkˌjefˌkäm| • *abbr.* Commander in Chief, U.S. Joint Forces Command.

CINCLANT |ˈsiNGkˌlænt| • *abbr.* Commander in Chief, Atlantic. Obsolete but commonly used title for the Commander in Chief, U.S. Atlantic Command (CINCUSLANTCOM).

CINCLANTFLT |ˈsiNGkˌlæntˌflēt| • *abbr.* Commander-in-Chief, U.S. Atlantic Fleet.

CINCNET |ˈsiNGkˌnet| • *abbr.* CINC's Network. Name given to the network of computer linkages among the commanders in chief (CINCs) of the U.S. unified commands.

CINCNORAD |ˈsiNGkˌnôrˌæd| • *abbr.* Commander in Chief, North American Aerospace Defense Command.

CINCPAC |ˈsiNGkˌpæk| • *abbr.* Commander in Chief, Pacific. Obsolete but commonly used title for the Commander in Chief, U.S. Pacific Command (CINCUSPACOM).

CINCPACAF |ˈsiNGkˌpækˌæf| • *abbr.* Commander in Chief, U.S. Pacific Air Forces. Title of the four-star U.S. Air Force general commanding the Air Force component of U.S. Pacific Command.

CINCPACFLT |ˈsiNGkˌpækˌflēt| • *abbr.* Commander-in-Chief, U.S. Pacific Fleet.

CINCPOA |ˈsiNGkˌpōə| • *abbr.* Commander in Chief, Pacific Ocean Area. Title of the commander in chief of the WORLD WAR II-era U.S. theater command in the Central Pacific, a position held by U.S. Navy Admiral CHESTER W. NIMITZ from 1942 to 1945. As CINCPOA Admiral Nimitz conducted naval, air, and amphibious operations in the Central Pacific area including the Aleutian, GILBERT, Marshall, and Mariana islands; the PHILIPPINE SEA and LEYTE GULF; IWO JIMA; and OKINAWA.

CINCSWPA |ˈsiNGkˌswäpə| • *abbr.* Commander in Chief, Southwest Pacific Area. The title of the commander in chief of the WORLD WAR II-era Allied combined theater command in the Southwestern Pacific, a position held by Gen. DOUGLAS MACARTHUR from April 18, 1942 to September 2, 1945. The primary mission for which the American, Australian, British, and Dutch forces under CINCSWPA were responsible was the defense of certain strategic bases in Australia; the preparation and conduct of operations aimed at recapturing the Philippine Islands and other objectives; and the support of friendly operations in the Pacific Ocean Area and the CHINA-BURMA-INDIA theaters. As CINCSWPA Gen. MacArthur conducted naval, air, and amphibious operations in New Guinea, the Solomon Islands, and the Philippine Islands.

CINCUNC |ˈsiNGˌkəNGk| • *abbr.* Commander in Chief, United Nations Command.

CINCUS |ˈsiNGˌkəs| • *abbr.* Commander in Chief, U.S. Fleet. Obsolete (pre-WORLD WAR II) title of the U.S. Navy admiral commanding U.S. naval forces afloat.

The title was changed in part because of the unfortunate pronunciation, which was not considered auspicious as the title for a Navy admiral.

CINCUSACOM |ˈsiNGkˌyo͞osəˌkäm| • *abbr.* see U.S. ATLANTIC COMMAND (USLANTCOM aka USACOM).

CINCUSAFE |ˈsiNGkˌyo͞osəˌfē| • *abbr.* Commander in Chief, U.S. Air Forces in Europe.

CINCUSAREUR |ˈsiNGkˌyo͞oˌsärˌyŏr| • *abbr.* Commander in Chief, U.S. Army Europe/7th U.S. Army. Obsolete title for the Commanding General, USAREUR/7th U.S. Army.

CINCUSARLANT • *abbr.* Commander in Chief, U.S. Army Forces Atlantic Command.

CINCUSEUCOM |ˈsiNGkˌyo͞oˌkäm| • *abbr.* Commander in Chief, U.S. European Command; also known as U.S. Commander in Chief, Europe (USCINCEUR).

CINCUSLANTCOM • *abbr.* Commander in Chief, U.S. Atlantic Command, a U.S. four-star flag officer commanding from headquarters in Norfolk, Virginia. CINCUSLANTCOM also serves as NATO's Supreme Allied Commander Atlantic (SACLANT).

CINCUSNAVEUR |ˈsiNGkˌnævˌyo͝or| • *abbr.* Commander in Chief, U.S. Naval Forces Europe.

CINCUSSPACECOM |ˈsiNGkˌspāˌskäm| • *abbr.* Commander in Chief, U.S. Space Command.

CINCUSSTRATCOM • *abbr.* Commander in Chief, U.S. Strategic Command.

cipher |ˈsīfər| • *n.* any cryptographic system in which arbitrary symbols or groups of symbols represent units of plain text of regular length, usually single letters, or in which units of plain text are rearranged, or both, in accordance with certain predetermined rules. Ciphers involve the substitution of a letter or number for each letter or number of the message, such substitutes being taken from a prepared printed list (a **book-based cipher**) or generated by a machine or computer (**machine-generated cipher**).

circular error probable • (**CEP**) an indicator of the delivery accuracy of a weapons system, used as a factor in determining probable damage to a target. The circular error probable is the radius of a circle within which half of a missile's projectiles are expected to fall.

CISA • *abbr.* Center for International Security Affairs.

citadel • *n.* a fortress, typically on high ground, protecting or dominating a city.

Citadel, The • an undergraduate and graduate private military school in Charleston, South Carolina. Established in 1842 by the South Carolina General Assembly, it formed the South Carolina Military Academy with the Arsenal in Columbia. It is state-funded and first admitted female cadets in 1996.

Occupied by Union forces from 1865 to 1879, it was closed during the RECONSTRUCTION and reopened in 1881.

---

citizen-sailor • *n.* a draftee serving in the navy or a naval Reservist.

citizen-soldier • *n.* **1** a National Guardsman or Army Reservist. **2** a draftee. Usually used in a positive sense. See also WEEKEND WARRIOR.

city buster • a nuclear weapon powerful enough to destroy a city. See also COUNTRY BUSTER.

civil censorship • the censorship of civilian communications (such as messages, printed matter, and film) entering, leaving, or circulating within areas or territories occupied or controlled by armed forces.

civil defense • the organization and training of civilians for the protection of lives and property during and after attacks in wartime.

civil defense intelligence • the product resulting from the collection and evaluation of information concerning all aspects of the situation in the United States and its territories that are potential or actual targets of any enemy attack including, in the preattack phase, the emergency measures taken and estimates of the civil populations preparedness.

civil disobedience • the refusal to comply with certain laws or to pay taxes and fines, as a peaceful form of political protest.

civil disturbance • group acts of violence and disorder prejudicial to public law and order.

civilian |səˈvilyən| • *n.* a person not in the armed services or the police force. • *adj.* of, denoting, or relating to a person not belonging to the armed services or police: *military agents in civilian clothes.*

civilian internee • **1** a civilian who is interned during armed conflict or occupation for security reasons or for protection, or because they have committed an offense against the detaining power. **2** any civilian interned and protected in accordance with the terms of the GENEVA CONVENTION.

Civilian Internee Information Center • the U.S. national center that provides information to enemy and U.S. civilian internees.

Civil Rights Act • a law passed by the Republican-dominated Congress on April 9, 1866, during RECONSTRUCTION to protect the rights of freed slaves and to guarantee equal rights to blacks. It was passed over a March 27 veto by President ANDREW JOHNSON. The FOURTEENTH AMENDMENT to the U.S. Constitution, which guaranteed the civil rights of all citizens regardless of race, was subsequently passed in 1868.

civil war • a war between citizens of the same country that have divided over ideological, political, or religious conflict.

Civil War, American (April 1861–April 1865) • costing more than 600,000 American lives, the Civil War consolidated the REVOLUTIONARY WAR of 1776 by ensuring that the United States would remain a single republic rather than a collection of potentially independent states. The Civil War brought enormous changes to the United States, most notably in the THIRTEENTH and FOURTEENTH AMENDMENTS, which abolished slavery and gave citizenship to African Americans. The war also made use of several military innovations. Longer-range and more destructive ammunition, primarily the minié rifle bullet, made casualty rates much higher than in previous wars. The Civil War also was the first to make use of the draft and ironclad warships, and extensive use of rail transport and military telegraph lines, and it was first to be widely documented by photographers. Prompted by sectional disputes between slaveholding southern states and northern states, the Civil War began following the election of Republican ABRAHAM LINCOLN, whose party was committed to free labor ideology. Rather than accepting Lincoln's leadership, seven southern states, led by South Carolina and comprising Alabama, Georgia, Florida, Louisiana, Mississippi, and Texas elected to secede from the Union and form the CONFEDERATE STATES OF AMERICA (CSA) in February 1861. The CONFEDERACY elected MEXICAN WAR (1846–48) hero and former Secretary of War JEFFERSON DAVIS as their president, and began organizing an independent government modeled on the U.S. Constitution, with caveats guaranteeing slavery. On April 12, the Confederacy began fighting to assert its independence when Confederate troops fired on FORT SUMTER in the Charleston, South Carolina harbor. Soon after, Arkansas, North Carolina, Tennessee, and Virginia joined the Confederacy. Union commander Gen. WINFIELD SCOTT's strategic response was to blockade and encircle the Confederacy in a strategy dubbed the ANACONDA PLAN. Nevertheless, the first two years of fighting favored Confederate armies. Despite the superiority in men and supplies held by the Union's ARMY OF THE POTOMAC, the ARMY OF NORTHERN VIRGINIA led by ROBERT E. LEE won or dramatically stopped U.S. armies in a series of battles fought in northern Virginia and Maryland. Notable among these were the 1861 FIRST BATTLE OF BULL RUN, in which southern armies won the war's first major contest; a series of dramatic raids conducted in the SHENANDOAH VALLEY by troops under Gen. THOMAS "STONEWALL" JACKSON; the SEVEN DAYS' BATTLE (1862), in which Lee, at high cost, drove Union general GEORGE B. MCCLELLAN back from the Confederate capital at Richmond; the 1862 SECOND BATTLE OF BULL RUN, in which Lee virtually crushed Union armies fighting under JOHN POPE; ANTIETAM, that same year, where McClellan failed to capitalize on a costly victory that stopped Lee's advance into the heart of Maryland; and FREDERICKSBURG (also 1862), which witnessed well-defended Confederates cutting down 13,000 Union troops with only 5,000 losses of their own. While Lee stymied Union armies in the East, federal forces under ULYSSES S. GRANT chipped away at the South's western defenses. In February 1862 Grant launched joint army-navy attacks that took FORT HENRY and FORT DONELSON in Kentucky and Tennessee, piercing the center of the Confederacy's western defenses. As Union armies began moving into the Confederacy from the West, Gen. ALBERT SIDNEY JOHNSTON counterattacked near SHILOH (1862) on the Tennessee River. Grant's unprepared troops suffered heavy casualties, but managed to repel the attack. The Union then began a long push into the South. The year 1863 proved crucial in many ways. After Antietam, Lincoln had issued the EMANCIPATION PROCLAMATION stating that the federal government considered all slaves still in Confederate territory to be free, which went into effect on January 1, 1863. The proclamation had two important consequences. For many in the North it transformed the war into a crusade against slavery. It also dissuaded Britain from officially recognizing and aiding the Confederacy. That year, the United States accepted African American enlistments to the army for the first time since 1820. By war's end, over 179,000 African-American men served in the U.S. armed forces. The year 1863 also witnessed two of the most crucial Confederate military defeats. Lee attempted to bring the Union to negotiate a peace by making an offensive strike. Federal armies under Gen. GEORGE G. MEADE stopped that advance in the BATTLE OF GETTYSBURG, Pennsylvania in July—the war's largest and most consequential battle. In the west, on July 4, Grant took the city of VICKSBURG, the Confederacy's last major stronghold on the Mississippi. In 1864, Lincoln promoted Grant to general-in-chief. As Grant pushed against Lee's armies toward the Confederate capital at Richmond, Gen. WILLIAM T. SHERMAN assailed Atlanta and then conducted his infamous MARCH TO THE SEA (1864–65). Aiming to undercut the Confederacy's ability to sustain warfare in terms of both material and morale, Sherman's forces cut a sixty-mile wide trail through Georgia from Atlanta to the Atlantic, earning him the longstanding enmity of many southerners, despite his own personal regard for the region and its people. These two offensives combined with a concerted Union press to shatter the Confederacy. The war effectively ended on April 9, 1865, when Lee surrendered the Army of Northern Virginia at APPOMATTOX, Virginia. In something of an anticlimax, Gen. JOSEPH E. JOHNSTON handed over the last Confederate army to Sherman near Durham, North Carolina, on April 26. The RECONSTRUCTION that followed in its wake was fraught, a situation only made worse by Abraham Lincoln's death on April 15, 1865.

civvy informal • *n.* **1** a civilian, as distinct from a member of the police force or armed services. **2** (**civvies**) civilian clothes, as opposed to a uniform.

CL-41 • see *Philadelphia*, USS.

Claghorn, George (1748–1824) • Revolutionary army officer and shipwright, born in Chilmark, Massachusetts. Claghorn constructed the frigate *Constitution*, the most famous warship in American history. One of the most celebrated shipwrights of the early national period, Claghorn built a carefully crafted masterpiece, much larger and stouter than contemporary warships. He was an officer in Massachusetts regiments during the REVOLUTIONARY WAR and a colonel of militia afterward.

clandestine |klænˈdestən; -ˌtīn; -ˌtēn; ˈklændəs-| • *adj.* kept secret or done secretively, especially because illicit: *she deserved better than these clandestine meetings.*

DERIVATIVES: **clandestinely** *adv.*

clandestine operation • an operation sponsored or conducted by governmental departments or agencies in such a way as to assure secrecy or concealment. A clandestine operation differs from a COVERT OPERATION in that emphasis is placed on concealment of the operation rather than on concealment of the identity of the sponsor. In special operations, an activity may be both covert and clandestine and may focus equally on operational considerations and intelligence-related activities.

Clark, Charles (1811–77) • Confederate general and governor of Mississippi. During the MEXICAN WAR (1846–48) he raised a volunteer company and served as colonel of the 2nd Mississippi Infantry. He was appointed JEFFERSON DAVIS's replacement as major general of Mississippi state troops in 1861. In 1863 Clark was elected Mississippi's second and last Confederate governor. He formally surrendered Mississippi to Union forces on May 22, 1865.

Clarke, Elijah (1742?–99) • Georgia patriot, born in Edgecombe County, South Carolina. Clark led a resistance movement during the British occupation that kept Georgia from falling entirely under British control.

Clark, George Rogers (1752–1818) • REVOLUTIONARY WAR general and "conqueror of the Northwest," born in Albemarle County, Virginia. In the Revolutionary War, he led Kentucky riflemen, obtaining gunpowder and his militia commission from Virginia governor Patrick Henry. He raided British outposts south and west of Detroit. He captured Kaskaskia on the Mississippi (1778) and, in a daring winter assault, Vincennes on the Wabash (1779), securing American claims to the Northwest. He led an expedition against the Shawnee Indians in Ohio (1782).

The financial records of Clark's raids were burnt by BENEDICT ARNOLD's troops in a 1781 attack on Richmond, Virginia. As a result, he was never paid for his expenditures and finished his life in poverty.

Clark, Mark Wayne (1896–1984) • U.S. army officer. Clark was born in New York and graduated from WEST POINT in April 1917. During WORLD WAR I he was wounded as an infantry battalion commander. At the beginning of WORLD WAR II he served as chief of staff of Army Ground Forces under Gen. LESLEY J. MCNAIR, helping to organize the expanding American army. In November 1942 he was made a lieutenant general and deputy commander of Allied forces in NORTH AFRICA under DWIGHT D. EISENHOWER. Clark soon moved on to take over the 5th Army, which he landed at Salerno, Italy, in September 1943. He commanded that organization through the difficult campaign up the Italian boot, until being promoted to take command of 15th Army Group in December 1944. After accepting the German surrender in Italy as a full general in May 1945 he became Allied High Commissioner for Austria, gaining valuable experience negotiating with Communists that would prove very useful when he succeeded MATTHEW B. RIDGWAY as supreme commander of UNITED NATIONS forces in KOREA in May 1952. Clark held that post until an armistice was signed in July 1953, and retired from the army in October that year, moving on to become president of THE CITADEL.

Clarkson, Matthew (1758–1825) • REVOLUTIONARY WAR soldier, businessman, politician and philanthropist, born in New York City. Clarkson was aide-de-camp to BENEDICT ARNOLD at SARATOGA (1777) and in Philadelphia, and to BENJAMIN LINCOLN at CHARLESTON (1780) and YORKTOWN (1781).

Clark, Wesley K. (1944–) • U.S. army officer and NATO supreme commander during OPERATION ALLIED FORCE (KOSOVO CRISIS, 1999), born in Little Rock, Arkansas. Clark graduated first in his class at WEST POINT (1966) and was a Rhodes scholar (1966–68). He led military negotiations for the Bosnian Peace Accords at DAYTON (1995), was the commander in chief of the U.S. Southern Command, Panama (1996–97), served as Supreme Allied Commander Europe (1997–2000), was in overall command of NATO's military forces in Europe, and led approximately 75,000 troops from thirty-seven NATO and other nations in operations in BOSNIA-HERZEGOVINA and KOSOVO.

Clark, William Thomas (1831–1905) • Union army officer and politician, born in Norwalk, Connecticut. Clark helped to raise the 13th Iowa Infantry Regiment at Davenport in 1861, and, serving with the ARMY OF THE TENNESSEE, he fought in many major western battles, including SHILOH and CORINTH in 1862, and VICKSBURG in 1863. He was brevetted major general in 1865.

clasp • *n.* a silver bar on a medal ribbon, inscribed with the name of the battle at which the wearer was present.

classification • *n.* the determination that official information requires, in the interests of national security, a specific degree of protection against unauthorized disclosure, coupled with a designation signifying that such a determination has been made.

classified |ˈklæsəˌfīd| • *adj.* (of information or documents) designated as officially secret and to which only authorized people may have access: *classified information on nuclear experiments.*

Clausewitz, Karl Maria von (1780–1831) • Prussian general and military theorist.

Clausewitz, who fought in the Napoleonic wars, is most famous for his unfinished treatise *On War* (*Vom Kriege*), published posthumously in 1832 (an English translation was published in 1873). His most famous dictum is that war is "merely the continuation of politics by other means." Clausewitz wrote that a war, though theoretically boundless, is limited by the political objectives of the belligerents and by "friction" (errors, chance, fatigue). He viewed the defensive as the stronger form of war, and advocated that offensive operations be swift, overwhelming, and decisive.

claw |klô| • *v.* (of a sailing ship) beat to windward: *the ability to* ***claw off*** *a lee shore.*

Clay, Green (1757–1828) • pioneer and soldier, born in Powhatan County, Virginia. As a major general in the WAR OF 1812, he led 3,000 Kentucky volunteers and relieved the siege of Fort Meigs (1813).

Clay, Henry (1777–1852) • Speaker of the House of Representatives (1811–14, 1815–21, 1823–25), secretary of state (1825–29), U.S. senator (1806–07, 1810–11, 1831–42, 1849–1852), and Whig candidate for president (1832, 1844), born in Hanover County, Virginia. Clay was known as the "Great Pacificator" and the "Great Compromiser" for his role in resolving the MISSOURI COMPROMISE and COMPROMISE OF 1850 crises. Clay signed the treaty ending the WAR OF 1812.

In 1806, Clay was chosen to serve out the unexpired Senate term of John Adair. No one noticed that he was not yet thirty, and thus ineligible to serve in the Senate.

Clay, Lucius DuBignon (1897–1978) • army engineer and general, born in Marietta, Georgia. Clay was a leader in mobilization for WORLD WAR II, overseeing army production and procurement. In 1944 he was put in command of supply bases in NORMANDY for the Allied thrust into Germany. Clay initiated the BERLIN AIRLIFT (1948–49), and was President JOHN F. KENNEDY's representative to West Berlin during the BERLIN WALL CRISIS (1961–62).

Clay, Lucius DuBignon, Jr. (1919–94) • air force general, born in Alexandria, Virginia. Clay was a bomber pilot, a squadron commander (at age twenty-three), and a group commander in WORLD WAR II. He flew more than sixty combat missions in support of the D-DAY LANDING (1944), the breakout at ST. LÔ (1944), and the BATTLE OF THE BULGE 1944–45). As an Air Force brigadier general he commanded the 12th Air Force, and he commanded the 7th Air Force in Vietnam. He was the deputy commander for operations, U.S. MILITARY ASSISTANCE COMMAND, VIETNAM. Clay played a pivotal role in the establishment of the U.S. Air Force and the development of American airpower.

claymore • *n.* a type of antipersonnel mine.

clear • *v.* **1** approve or authorize, or obtain approval or authorization for: **a** a person or persons with regard to their actions, movements, duties, etc. **b** an object or group of objects, as equipment or supplies, with regard to quality, quantity, purpose, movement, disposition, etc. **c** a request, with regard to correctness of form, validity, etc. **2** give one or more aircraft a clearance. **3** give a person a security clearance. **4** fly over an obstacle without touching it. **5** pass a designated point, line, or object. The end of a column must pass the designated feature before the feature is cleared. **6 a** operate a gun so as to unload it or make certain no ammunition remains. **b** free a gun or stoppages. **7** open the throttle of (an idling engine) to free it from carbon. **8** clear the air to gain either temporary or permanent air superiority or control in a given sector.

clearway • *n.* a defined rectangular area on the ground or water at the end of a runway in the direction of takeoff and under controls of the competent authority, selected or prepared as a suitable area over which an aircraft may make a portion of its initial climb to a specified height.

cleat |klēt| • *n.* a T-shaped piece of metal or wood, especially on a boat or ship, to which ropes are attached.

Cleburne, Patrick Ronayne |'klēbərn| (1828–64) • Confederate army officer, born in Ireland. Cleburne fought at SHILOH (1862) and, after promotion by JEFFERSON DAVIS to major general that same year, at STONES RIVER (1862–63) and CHICKAMAUGA (1863). He was killed at the BATTLE OF FRANKLIN (1864).

Cleburne is best remembered for advocating the enlistment of slaves in the army and rewarding service with emancipation; Cobb believed the Confederate patriot should "give up the negro slave rather than be a slave himself." His position, however, prevented further career advancements.

Clemenceau, Georges (1841–1929) • French statesman, journalist, premier (1906–09, 1917–20), and minister of war, nicknamed "the Tiger." For several years before WORLD WAR I broke out, Clemenceau wrote against Germany and advocated French military preparedness. Becoming prime minister in 1917 after three years of war, Clemenceau restored France's morale and will to win, and advocated a unified allied command. After the armistice, he led the French delegation at the PARIS PEACE CONFERENCE, where he pressed for German disarmament. He opposed President WOODROW WILSON and DAVID LLOYD GEORGE's plans for a LEAGUE OF NATIONS, preferring instead an anti-German alliance. He was dissatisfied with the TREATY OF VERSAILLES, but succeeded in persuading Wilson to continue U.S. and Allied military occupation of the Rhineland.

Clemenceau regarded Wilson as too idealistic and is reported to have quipped about Wilson's FOURTEEN POINTS, "The good Lord had only ten."

Cleveland, Benjamin (1738–1806) • frontiersman and REVOLUTIONARY WAR militia officer, born in Prince William County, Virginia. As a militia captain in North Carolina, he campaigned ruthlessly against Loyalists and the Cherokee. Later, as colonel of the Wilkes County militia, he led a column of about 900 "overmountain men" in an utter defeat of Maj. PATRICK FERGUSON's force of about 125 British regulars and 1,000 Tories at KINGS MOUNTAIN (1780).

Cleveland, Grover (1837–1908) • 22nd and 24th president of the United States (1885–89, 1893–97), born Stephen Grover Cleveland in Caldwell, New Jersey. As governor of New York (1883–85), Cleveland reorganized the militia, promoted efficient government, and opposed corrupt Tammany Hall. In the tight, mud-spattered presidential election of 1880, he was elected as a reform Democrat. Cleveland supported lower tariffs and civil service reform, reduced CIVIL WAR pensions, and signed the Interstate Commerce Act (1887).

Cleveland lost to BENJAMIN HARRISON in 1888 (though he won the popular vote), but retook the WHITE HOUSE from Harrison in 1892, thereby becoming the only U.S. president to serve two nonconsecutive terms.

clew |klo͞o| • *n.* **1** the lower or after corner of a sail. **2** (**clews**) the cords by which a hammock is suspended. • *v.* **1** (**clew a sail up**) draw the lower ends of a sail to the upper yard or the mast ready for furling. **2** (**clew a sail down**) let down a sail by the clews in unfurling.

Clifford, Clark McAdams (1906–98) • presidential adviser and secretary of defense, born in Fort Scott, Kansas. In WORLD WAR II, he served in the navy (1944–46). As special adviser to HARRY S. TRUMAN, he helped craft the TRUMAN DOCTRINE (1947) and the NATIONAL SECURITY ACT OF 1947, which created the DEPARTMENT OF DEFENSE and the NATIONAL SECURITY COUNCIL. As a foreign policy adviser to JOHN F. KENNEDY (1961–63) and as chairman of the PRESIDENT'S FOREIGN INTELLIGENCE ADVISORY BOARD under Kennedy and LYNDON B. JOHNSON, Clifford supervised U.S. espionage operations and helped shape policy on VIETNAM.

clinch • *v.* fasten (a rope or angling line) with a clinch knot. • *n.* (also **clinch knot**) a knot used to fasten ropes or angling lines, using half hitch with the end seized back on its own part.

clinker-built • *adj.* another term for LAPSTRAKE.

Clinton, Bill (1946–) • 42nd president of the United States (1993–2001), born William Jefferson Blythe III, in Hope, Arkansas. Clinton was governor of Arkansas (1979–81, 1983–93). Clinton's relationship with the military was strained at best. During the 1992 campaign it was revealed that he evaded service in the VIETNAM WAR, which he had protested against while a Rhodes Scholar at Oxford, and soon after inauguration his administration was embroiled in a controversy about ending a ban on homosexuals in the military; he settled for a compromise policy, dubbed the "DON'T ASK, DON'T TELL, DON'T PURSUE" POLICY, that satisfied no one.

Military actions during Clinton's two terms included periodic air strikes against Iraq and OPERATION ALLIED FORCE, a U.S.-led NATO air campaign to stop Serbian aggression in Kosovo, Yugoslavia, the largest military operation in Europe since WORLD WAR II.

Clinton, George (1686–1761) • colonial governor of New York. Clinton commanded the British Mediterranean fleet (1737). Commissioned as governor of New York in 1741, he did not arrive to take office until 1743. He warned the government that a stamp tax would cause much trouble in the colonies. With Sir WILLIAM JOHNSON, he secured the Iroquois as allies in the FRENCH AND INDIAN WAR (1754–63) and placed Johnson in charge of Indian relations. Lengthy border disputes with New Jersey, New Hampshire, and Massachusetts led to a new governor being appointed in 1753. After returning to England in 1754, Clinton bought a seat in Parliament (1754–61); he was named admiral of the fleet in 1757.

Clinton, George (1739–1812) • soldier, governor of New York, and vice president of the United States, born in Little Britain, New York. He fought in the FRENCH AND INDIAN WAR (1754–63) as a young subaltern, and was a brigadier general of militia in the REVOLUTIONARY WAR. He directed the futile defense of Fort Montgomery (1777), hindering British major general Sir HENRY CLINTON from joining JOHN BURGOYNE at SARATOGA (1777). He served six successive terms as governor. Clinton was elected vice president under THOMAS JEFFERSON (1804) on the Democratic-Republican ticket.

Clinton, James (1736–1812) • REVOLUTIONARY WAR officer, born in Little Britain, New York. As a brigadier general in the Continental army, he erected fortifications for defense of the Highlands along the Hudson River. He was severely wounded defending Forts Montgomery and Clinton (1777).

Clinton, Sir Henry (1730–95) • British general, born in Newfoundland, son of colonial governor GEORGE CLINTON. Clinton was present at the battle of BUNKER HILL (1775) and later conducted an ineffectual campaign in the south before returning to New York and thence to England where he was knighted. After serving under Sir WILLIAM HOWE at the battles of NEW YORK and WHITE PLAINS (1776) and the occupation of New York, and heading the British occupation of Rhode Island, Clinton replaced Howe, whom he regarded as overly cautious, as the commander in chief of British forces in North America (1778–82). Clinton, once full of bold plans for Howe, quickly acquired his own reputation for cautiousness. He failed to trap the Marquis de LAFAYETTE at Barren Hill, Pennsylvania (1778), and evacuated Philadelphia. After engaging the Continental army at MONMOUTH (1778) and capturing CHARLESTON (1780), Clinton was replaced by Lord CHARLES CORNWALLIS and ordered back to New York, where he was blamed for the defeat at YORKTOWN (1781) for having failed to come to Cornwallis's aid.

clip • *n.* a metal holder containing cartridges for an automatic firearm.

close to the wind |klōs| • (of a sailing vessel) pointed as near as possible to the direction from which the wind is blowing while still making headway.

close air support |klōs| • (**CAS**) air action by fixed- and rotary-wing aircraft against hostile targets which are in close proximity to friendly surfaces forces and which require detailed integration of each air mission with the fire and movement of those forces.

closed area • a designated area in or over which passage of any kind is prohibited.

close-hauled |klōs| • *adj.* & *adv.* (of a ship) close to the wind.

close reach |klōs| • *n.* a point of sailing in which the wind blows from slightly forward of the beam: *we sailed* ***on a close reach*** *directly for Sharp's Island.* • *v.* (**close-reach**) sail with the wind in this position.

close support |klōs| • the action of the supporting force against targets or objectives that are sufficiently near the supported force as to require detailed integration or coordination of the supporting action with the fire, movement, or other actions of the supported force.

clove hitch • a knot by which a rope is secured by passing it twice around a spar or another rope that it crosses at right angles in such a way that both ends pass under the loop of rope at the front.

cluster • *n.* **1** a fireworks signal in which a group of stars burns at the same time. **2** a group of bombs released together. A bomb cluster usually consists of fragmentation or incendiary bombs. **3** two or more parachutes for dropping light or heavy loads. **4** in land-mine warfare, a component of a pattern-laid minefield. It may be antitank, antipersonnel, or mixed. It consists of one to five mines and no more than one antitank mine. **4** two or more engines coupled together so as to function as one power unit. **6** in naval-mine warfare, a number of mines (of like or mixed types) laid in close proximity to each other as a pattern or coherent unit. **7** in minehunting, a group of minelike contacts.

cluster bomb • a bomb that releases a number of projectiles on impact to injure or damage personnel and vehicles.

CM • *abbr.* command module.

CMC • *abbr.* Commandant of the Marine Corps.

Cmdr. • *abbr.* Commander.

Cmdre or **Cmdre.** • *abbr.* Commodore.

CMSgt • *abbr.* Chief Master Sergeant.

CNN effect • the impact of worldwide television news broadcasts on government decision-making in crises and wars. The ubiquity and timeliness of broadcasts by the *Cable News Network* (CNN) and other television news services can influence, for good or ill, the assessment of the intentions and capabilities of one potential or actual belligerent by another.

CNO • *abbr.* **1** chief naval officer. **2** Chief of Naval Operations.

CO • *abbr.* **1** Commanding Officer. **2** conscientious objector.

coalition |ˌkōəˈlisHən| • *n.* an alliance for combined action, esapecially a temporary alliance of political parties forming a government or of states: *a coalition of conservatives and disaffected Democrats.*

DERIVATIVES: **coalitionist** |-nist| *n.*

Coalition, Allied • see ALLIED COALITION.

coalition warfare • warfare conducted by an alliance of states.

coastal frontier defense • the organization of the forces and materiel of the armed forces assigned to provide security of the coastal frontiers of the continental United States and its overseas possessions.

Coast Guard Academy • an undergraduate service school at New London, Connecticut. Entrance to the academy is based on competitive examination, and not political appointment as with the three other major service schools. Founded by Congress in 1876 as the School of Instruction for the Revenue Marine, near New Bedford, Massachusetts, it was the REVENUE CUTTER SERVICE SCHOOL OF INSTRUCTION from 1914–15. It has been at its present site in New London since 1932, and first admitted female cadets in 1975.

Coast Guard, U.S. • part of the U.S. Armed Forces, the Coast Guard has seven peacetime missions: the enforcement of boating safety regulations, search and rescue, maintenance of aids to navigation, enforcement of Merchant Marine safety regulations, environmental protection, enforcement of customs, fisheries, and immigration laws, and port safety. The Coast Guard is supported by a **Coast Guard Reserve** and a **Coast Guard Auxiliary**, which assists in search and rescue missions, teaches boating courses, and conducts pleasure boat inspections. In wartime, the Coast Guard performs port security, ship escort, and transport duty as part of the U.S. Navy. In peacetime, the Coast Guard is part of the U.S. Department of Transportation.

Cobb, Thomas Reade Rootes (1823–62) • lawyer, Confederate congressman and military officer born in Jefferson County, Georgia. Cobb was the younger brother of Treasury secretary Howell Cobb. Cobb was the author of *An Inquiry into the Law of Negro Slavery* (1858) and *A Historical Sketch of Slavery from the Earliest Periods* (1859). In the CIVIL WAR he organized "Cobb's Legion" and was promoted to brigadier general in 1862. He died at FREDERICKSBURG (1862).

Cobb claimed slavery was divinely ordained, and celebrated South Carolina's secession with a motto he had spread across the front of his house: "Resistance to Abolition is Obedience to God."

---

co-belligerent • *n.* any of two or more nations engaged in war as allies.

DERIVATIVES: **co-belligerence** *n.*

Cobra, Operation • **1** in WORLD WAR II, the code name for the American First Army's July 1944 breakout operation, preceded by carpet bombing, to penetrate German defenses around ST. LÔ and secure Coutances, France. **2** during the PERSIAN GULF WAR, the 101st Airborne Division's deep air assault by 15,000 paratroopers behind enemy lines on Febuary 24, 1991, that helped cut off the highway linking the Iraqi front to Baghdad.

Cochise (1810?–74) • legendary Chiricahua Apache chief, born probably in southeastern Arizona. Cochise participated in raids on Mexican settlements in the 1830s and 1840s, and became the principal chief of the Chokonen band in 1856. During the mid-1850s he alternated allegiances between the United States and Mexico.

Cochise War (1861–72) • began after Lt. George Bascom hanged COCHISE's brother and two nephews in a dispute over a boy kidnapped by Apaches. Cochise's antipathy toward the Americans became legendary: he waged guerrilla warfare until he was forced to agree to a peace treaty in 1872, after which he settled with his warriors on a reservation.

Cochran, Jacqueline (1910–80) • pioneer aviator and business executive, born in Muscogee, Florida. An aviation enthusiast, Cochran in 1941 became the first woman to ferry a B-17 bomber to Britain. She recruited twenty-five other women for the job, thus freeing male pilots to fly front-line missions. In 1943 she was appointed head of the Woman's Airforce Service Pilots (WASP). The first woman to break the sound barrier, Cochran held more aviation records at the time of her death than any other U.S. pilot. She was awarded the army's DISTINGUISHED SERVICE MEDAL in 1945.

Cochran was also the owner of a successful cosmetics company and was voted Woman of the Year in Business in 1953 and 1954.

---

cocked hat • **1** a brimless triangular hat pointed at the front, back, and top. **2** a hat with a wide brim permanently turned up toward the crown, such as a tricorne.

cockpit | 'käk,pit | • *n.* a compartment for the pilot and sometimes also the crew in an aircraft or spacecraft.

Cockrell, Francis Marion (1834–1915) • Confederate general and U.S. senator, born in Johnson County, Missouri. In the CIVIL WAR, Cockrell was involved in the major battles of the VICKSBURG campaign (1862–63), after which he was promoted to brigadier general.

COCOM • *abbr.* combatant command (command authority).

code • *n.* **1** any system of communication in which arbitrary groups of symbols represent units of plain text of varying length. Codes may be used for brevity or for security. **2** a crypto-system in which the cryptographic equivalents (usually called "code groups") typically consisting of letters or digits (or both) in otherwise meaningless combinations are substituted for plain text elements which are primarily words, phrases, or sentences.

codebreaking • *n.* the decrypting of code or cipher messages by unauthorized persons (the enemy). See CODING AND DECODING.

code of honor • a set of standards for behaving honorably, usually unwritten but understood generally by the group to which it pertains.

code word • **1** a word that has been assigned a classification and a classified meaning to safeguard intentions and information about a classified plan or operation. **2** a cryptonym used to identify sensitive intelligence data.

coding and decoding • the process of encrypting messages in code or cipher for transmission and decrypting by authorized persons of such messages at the receiving end. The decrypting of code or cipher messages by unauthorized persons (the enemy) is known as CODEBREAKING.

Coercive Acts • four measures passed by the British Parliament in 1774 as retribution for American colonial defiance and the BOSTON TEA PARTY. The acts closed the Boston port until colonists paid for the destroyed tea, subjected the colony to a military government, allowed convicted royal officials and soldiers to be tried outside the colony, and authorized housing for British troops in private American homes.

Coeur d'Alene War • see SPOKANE WAR.

coffin • *n.* slang an old and unsafe aircraft or vessel.

Cohan, George Michael (1878–1942) • performer; writer of songs, musicals, and plays, and producer; born in Providence, Rhode Island. Cohan was a patriarch of popular musical entertainment and a significant contributor to the country's wartime fighting spirit. He was awarded a special CONGRESSIONAL MEDAL OF HONOR for "OVER THERE" and "It's a Grand Old Flag."

Cohen, William S. (1940–) • defense secretary and U.S. senator, born in Bangor, Maine. Cohen was a three-term U.S. congressman (1973–79) and a three-term senator (1979–97). Cohen was a member of the Senate Armed Services and Governmental Affairs Committees (1979–97) and the Senate Select Committee on Intelligence (1983–91, 1995–97). As defense secretary (1997– 2000), Cohen has presided over U.S. military operations worldwide, including air strikes against Iraq and suspected terrorist targets, including the U.S. component of OPERATION ALLIED FORCE (March–June 1999), the seventy-eight-day bombing campaign to drive Yugoslav President SLOBODAN MILOSEVIC's forces out of the Serbian province of KOSOVO, which was the largest military operation in Europe since WORLD WAR II. Cohen urged the U.S. Senate to ratify the COMPREHENSIVE TEST BAN TREATY (rejected October 13, 1999) and led an initiative to streamline and improve DEPARTMENT OF DEFENSE infrastructure and support activities.

cohort • *n.* a group of people banded together or treated as a group: ***a cohort of*** *civil servants patiently drafting legislation.*

COI • *abbr.* Office of Strategic Services.

Col. • *abbr.* Colonel.

Cold Harbor, Battle of • the final battle in ULYSSES S. GRANT's WILDERNESS to PETERSBURG Campaign in June 1864. It was won by the Union under Grant's command, though with heavy casualties, and Grant noted in his memoirs that this was the only attack order he wished he had never given. Following the battle, in Hanover County, Virginia, Grant began the advance of his army to PETERSBURG.

cold launch • a technique for launching ballistic missiles from submarines or land silos by using compressed gas or steam to propel them into the air before the main engine is ignited once the missile has cleared the launcher. A cold launch presumably delays enemy detection of the launch by delaying the characteristic heat signature of the missile's engines.

cold war • **1** a state of international tension wherein political, economic, technological, sociological, psychological, paramilitary, and military measures short of overt armed conflict involving regular military forces are employed to achieve national objectives. **2** (**the Cold War**) the state of political hostility that existed between the Soviet bloc countries and the U.S.-led Western powers from 1945 to 1990.

collateral damage • inadvertent casualties and destruction in civilian areas in the course of military operations.

collective security • the cooperation of several countries in an alliance to strengthen the security of each.

College of Naval Command and Staff • a postgraduate service school for mid-grade officers at Newport, Rhode Island. It emphasizes teaching the operational and tactical elements of command, in addition to a core class on international relations, international law, military management, economics, and comparative cultures. Established in the 1960s, it is co-located with the NAVAL WAR COLLEGE, which is the Navy's senior service school.

College of Naval Warfare • a postgraduate service school for senior officers at Newport, Rhode Island. It stresses the policy, administrative, and strategic questions of command, including war games and a seapower and national planning study. In addition, students take a core class on international relations, international law, military management, economics, and comparative cultures. Established in the 1960s, it is co-located with the NAVAL WAR COLLEGE, which is the Navy's senior service school.

Collins, Napoleon (1814–75) • Union naval officer, born in Fayette County, Pennsylvania. In the MEXICAN WAR (1846–48), Collins joined Commodore MATTHEW C. PERRY's expedition up the Tuxpan River (1847). During the CIVIL WAR, he helped capture several Confederate forts and British and Confederate ships. Collins is best remembered for his capture of the Confederate ship *Florida* off the coast of Brazil, a bold violation of Brazilian neutrality that earned him both praise and criticism; he was court-martialed but ordered back to service in 1866.

colonel |ˈkərnl| • *n.* **1** an army officer of high rank, in particular (in the U.S. Army, Air Force, and Marine Corps) an officer above a lieutenant colonel and below a brigadier general. **2** informal short for lieutenant colonel.
DERIVATIVES: **colonelcy** |ˈkərnlsē| *n.* (pl. **-ies**).

colonel general • title once used to designate an officer who had supreme command of an army.

colonel-in-chief • *n.* (pl. **colonels-in-chief**) a title given to the honorary head of a regiment in the British army.

color • *n.* **1** the flag of a regiment or ship. **2** a national flag. **3** the armed forces of a country, as symbolized by its flag: *he was* ***called to the colors*** *during the war.*

Colored Troops • segregated units of the U.S. Army comprised of black soldiers, usually serving under white officers. Segregation was U.S. Army policy from the CIVIL WAR until 1945, when the Gillem Report recommended expansion of opportunities for black military personnel. In 1950, the Army issued special regulations governing the treatment of black personnel, and abolished the ten percent quota that had previously limited the numbers of African Americans in the military.

color guard • a small detachment of enlisted personnel whose ceremonial duty it is to carry and escort the colors.

colour sergeant • a rank of noncommissioned officer in the ROYAL MARINES, above sergeant and below warrant officer.
ORIGIN: with reference to the sergeant's responsibility for carrying one of the regiment's colors in an honor guard.

Colquitt, Alfred Holt (1824–94) • Confederate army officer and politician, born in Walton County, Georgia. Colquitt was a major in the MEXICAN WAR (1846–48). During the CIVIL WAR, Colquitt quickly rose to the rank of major general; his greatest military success was as an infantry commander in the victory at Olustee, Florida, in 1864, over superior Union forces.

Colt • trademark a type of revolver.

colting • a beating with a knotted rope (a "colt") formerly employed as a punishment aboard a naval vessel.

Colton, Walter (1797–1851) • clergyman, naval chaplain, journalist, and author, born in Rutland County, Vermont. Colton was appointed naval chaplain by President ANDREW JACKSON in 1831. He accompanied ROBERT F. STOCKTON to Monterey, California, in 1845, and was appointed alcalde (chief justice) of Monterey in 1846.

Colton founded the first newspaper in California, the *Californian,* in 1846. Colton also ordered the people he convicted to build their own prison, which they did so well that he pardoned several of the ablest workers.

Colt, Samuel (1814–62) • inventor and industrialist, born in Hartford, Connecticut. Colt, who created firearms, pyrotechnics, and explosives, invented the revolver and his manufacturing techniques became known all over the world as the "American system." He devised a system for electrically detonating mines under hostile ships entering a harbor, but the government wouldn't purchase it because he was so secretive about how it worked. Colt revolvers, much favored by the TEXAS RANGERS, were adopted by governments around the world. Turkey bought 5,000 of his revolvers and in gratitude Colt topped his factory with an onion dome.

Columbiad • a heavy artillery gun developed in the early 19th century and used primarily for seacoast defense. It had a bore up to 10 inches. See also RODMAN GUN.

column • *n.* **1** one or more lines of people or vehicles moving in the same direction: *a column of tanks moved northwest.* **2** a narrow-fronted deep formation of troops in successive lines. **3** a military force that might deploy in such a formation. **4** a similar formation of ships in a fleet or convoy. **5** an upright shaft forming part of a machine and typically used for controlling it: *a Spitfire control column.*

column formation • a formation in which elements are placed one behind the other.

column gap • the space between two consecutive elements proceeding on the same route. It can be calculated in units of length or in units of time measured from the rear of one element to the front of the following element.

Colvocoresses, George Musalas (1816–72) • Union naval officer, born on the Greek island of Chios. In 1856, he commanded a party that captured the barrier forts in the Canton River, below Canton, China. On blockade duty in the CIVIL WAR, Colvocoresses captured the Confederate blockade runner *Stephen Hart.*

combat |ˈkämˌbæt| • *n.* **1** fighting between armed forces: *killed* ***in combat*** | *pilots reenacted the aerial combats of yesteryear.* **2** nonviolent conflict or opposition: *intellectual combat.*

combat air patrol • an aircraft patrol provided over an objective area, over the force protected, over the critical area of a combat zone, or over an air defense area, for the purpose of intercepting and destroying hostile aircraft before they reach their target.

combatant |kəmˈbætnt; ˈkämbəṭənt| • *n.* **1** a person engaged in fighting during a war. **2** a nation at war with another. **3** a person engaged in conflict or competition with another. • *adj.* engaged in fighting during a war: *all the combatant armies had machine guns.*

combatant command • **1** (also called **command authority**; **COCOM**) nontransferable command authority exercised only by commanders of unified or specified combatant commands unless otherwise directed by the president or the secretary of defense. Operational control is inherent in combatant command. **2** a unified or specified command with a broad continuing mission under a single commander, established and so designated by the president, through the secretary of defense and with the advice and assistance of the chairman of the JOINT CHIEFS OF STAFF. Combatant commands typically have geographic or functional responsibilities.

combatant commander • **1** a commander in chief of one of the unified or specified combatant commands established by the President of the United States. **2** the commander of a combat unit.

combat area • a restricted area (air, land, or sea) that is established to prevent or minimize mutual interference between friendly forces engaged in combat operations.

combat camera • visual information documentation covering air, sea, and ground actions of armed forces in combat and combat support operations, and in related peacetime training activities such as exercises, war games, and operations.

combat dress • uniform of a type intended to be worn by soldiers in actual combat: *a hulking first lieutenant in combat dress.*

combat effectiveness • **1** the quality of being effective in combat. **2** the abilities and fighting qualities of a combat unit.

combat fatigue • **1** more recent term for SHELL SHOCK. **2** (**combat fatigues**) a uniform of a type to be worn into combat.

combat forces • those forces whose primary missions are to participate in combat.

combat information center • the agency in a ship or aircraft manned and equipped to collect, display, evaluate, and disseminate tactical information for the use of the embarked flag officer, commanding officer, and certain control agencies.

combat intelligence • that knowledge of the enemy, weather, and geographical features required by a commander in the planning and conduct of combat operations.

combat jacket • see FIELD JACKET.

combat load • the total warlike stores carried by an aircraft.

combat loading • the arrangement of personnel and the stowage of equipment and supplies in a manner designed to conform to the anticipated tactical operation of the organization embarked. Each individual item is stowed so that it can be unloaded at the required time.

combat motivation • the combination of social and psychological factors which impels soldiers to engage in combat. Such factors include fear of the consequences of defeat, hatred of the enemy (real or induced), and the desire to sustain and protect comrades.

combat readiness • synonymous with OPERATIONAL READINESS, with respect to missions or functions performed in combat.

DERIVATIVES: **combat ready** *adj.*

combat service support • the essential capabilities, functions, activities, and tasks necessary to sustain all elements of operating forces in theater at all levels of war. Combat service support includes, but is not limited to, supply, maintenance, transportation, and health services.

combat stress • the physical and psychological stress felt by the soldier before, during, and after active combat.

combat support • fire support and operational assistance provided to combat elements, including artillery, air defense artillery, engineer, military police, signal, and military intelligence support.

combat surveillance • a continuous, all-weather, day-and-night, systematic watch over the battle area in order to provide timely information for tactical combat operations.

Combat Talon • (**MC**) versions of the C-130 cargo transport aircraft designed specifically for use by U.S. SPECIAL FORCES, and equipped for low-altitude deep-penetration missions.

combat trauma • psychological damage incurred as a result of participation in active combat.

combat zone • **1** the area required by combat forces for the conduct of operations. **2** the territory forward of the army's rear area boundary.

combined arms • the integrated use of several combat branches (infantry, armor, artillery, aviation, etc.) during operations.

Combined Arms and Services Staff School • a postgraduate army service school at FORT LEAVENWORTH, Kansas. Established in 1980, it is one of several schools that make up the U.S. ARMY COMMAND AND GENERAL STAFF COLLEGE.

Combined Arms Center • see U.S. ARMY COMBINED ARMS CENTER.

Combined Arms Support Command • see U.S. ARMY COMBINED ARMS SUPPORT COMMAND.

combined force • a military force composed of elements of two or more allied nations.

Combined Forces Command • (**CFC**) the combined Republic of Korea/U.S. command in Korea, established on November 7, 1978, and commanded by a U.S. Army four-star general (CINCCFC) from headquarters in Seoul. CINCCFC serves concurrently as Commander in Chief, United Nations Command (CINCUNC); Commander, U.S. Force Korea; and Commanding General, 8th U.S. Army.

Combined Japanese Fleet • senior administrative command of the Imperial Japanese Navy during WORLD WAR II with responsibility for almost all of Japan's naval combatant vessels of aircraft carriers.

combined operation • an operation conducted by forces of two or more allied nations acting together for a single mission.

come about • (of a ship) change direction.

COMINT • *abbr.* communications intelligence.

command • *v.* **1** give an authoritative order. **2** have authority over; be in charge of (a unit): *he commanded a battalion at Normandy.* **3** dominate (a strategic position) from a superior height: *the two castles commanded the harbor.* **4** be in a strong enough position to secure: *no party commanded a majority.* **5** deserve and receive: *a moral force that commanded respect.* • *n.* **1** an authoritative order: *it's unlikely they'll obey your commands.* **2** authority, especially over armed forces: *an officer* ***took command*** | *who's* ***in command****?* | *thirty thousand people* ***under*** *our* ***command****.* **3** a group of officers exercising control over a particular group or operation. **4** a body of troops or a district under the control of a particular officer.

command and control • the running of an armed force or other organization: *a command-and-control bunker.*

Command and Control Vehicle • (**C2V**) a tracked armored vehicle used as an automated tactical command post during mobile armored operations. Also called **M-4**.

commandant |ˈkämənˌdænt; -ˌdänt| • *n.* an officer in charge of a particular force or institution: *the West Point commandant of cadets.*

Commandant of the Marine Corps • (**CMC**) the chief officer of the U.S. Marine Corps.

command authority • see COMBATANT COMMAND.

command channel • see CHAIN OF COMMAND.

command chief master sergeant • the senior noncommissioned officer in any U.S. Air Force unit larger than a squadron.

commandeer |ˌkämənˈdir| • *v.* officially take possession or control of (something), especially for military purposes: *telegraph and telephone lines were commandeered by the generals.*

commander • *n.* **1** a person in authority, especially over a body of troops or a military operation: *the commander of a paratroop regiment.* **2** a naval officer of high rank, in particular (in the U.S. Navy or Coast Guard) an officer ranking above lieutenant commander and below captain.

DERIVATIVES: **commandership** *n.*

commander in chief (also **Commander in Chief**) • (pl. **commanders in chief**) **1** a head of state or officer in supreme command of a country's armed forces. **2** an officer in charge of a major subdivision of a country's armed forces, or of its forces in a particular area.

commander's concept • see CONCEPT OF OPERATIONS.

Commando • (**C-46**) an aircraft originally designed for civil transport but built only for military use.

commando • *n.* (pl. **-os**) **1** a soldier specially trained to carry out raids: *the commando unhooked a grenade from his belt.* **2** a unit of such troops. **3** a group forming part of a larger organization, typically an illegal or secret one, and carrying out attacks on its behalf.

Commando Hunt, Operation • a bombing campaign in the VIETNAM WAR running from 1968 to 1972 that was intended to delay and disorganize the enemy. Targets included supply and storage areas along the HO CHI MINH TRAIL, as well as supply areas in Cambodia and Laos.

commando knife • a long, slender knife suitable for hand-to-hand combat.

command post • **1** the place from which a military unit is commanded. **2** any headquarters for communication.

command sergeant major • the senior noncommissioned officer in any U.S. ARMY unit larger than a company.

commerce raiding • the use of fast, well-armed naval vessels to attack enemy merchant shipping, especially raiding done by Confederate vessels during the CIVIL WAR.

commissariat |ˌkäməˈserēət| • *n.* a department for the supply of food and equipment.

commissary |ˈkäməˌserē| • *n.* (pl. **-ies**) **1** a restaurant in a military base, prison, or other institution. **2** a store that sells food and drink to members of an organization, especially a large grocery store on a military base.

DERIVATIVES: **commissarial** |ˌkäməˈserēəl| *adj.*

commission • *n.* **1** the authority to perform a task or certain duties. **2** an instruction, command, or duty given to a person or group of people: *he received a commission to act as an informer.* **3** a warrant conferring the rank of officer in an army, navy, or air force: *he has resigned his commission.* **4** a group of people officially charged with a particular function: *the United Nations High Commission for Refugees.* • *v.* **1** give an order for or authorize the production of (something such as a building or piece of equipment). **2** bring (a warship) into readiness for active service: *the aircraft carrier* Midway *was commissioned in 1945.* **3** (usually **be commissioned**) appoint (someone) to the rank of officer in the armed services: *he was commissioned after attending midshipman school* | (**commissioned**) *a commissioned officer.*

PHRASES: **in commission** (of a ship, vehicle, machine, etc.) in use or in service.

DERIVATIVES: **commissionable** *adj.*

Committee of Safety • (also **Council of Safety**) any of a number of committees organized in the American colonies that were authorized to oversee public safety and to call up militias.

Committee on Military Affairs • a committee of the U.S. House of Representatives established in 1822 to manage the military establishment and address issues of public defense. It was replaced by the HOUSE ARMED SERVICES COMMITTEE in 1946.

Committee on Public Information • a federal agency established under President WOODROW WILSON, after U.S. entry into WORLD WAR I in April 1917, to enforce censorship and to run a propaganda campaign promoting the war.

Committee on the Present Danger • a conservative lobbying group formed in 1976 to promote a policy of military containment, in response to the perceived threat of the Soviet Union.

commodore |'kämə,dôr| • *n.* a naval officer of high rank, in particular an officer in the U.S. Navy or Coast Guard ranking above captain and below rear admiral, generally given temporarily to an officer commanding a squadron or division of a fleet.

Common Sense • a pamphlet written in America by Englishman THOMAS PAINE, published on January 10, 1776. It called for American independence and a union of the American colonies, and as propaganda, it influenced colonists to pursue both in the REVOLUTIONARY WAR. Paine's "Crisis" papers, issued from 1776 to 1783, were each signed "Common Sense."

common soldier • see SOLDIER (sense 1).

common-user sealift • sealift services provided for all DEPARTMENT OF DEFENSE agencies and, when authorized, for other U.S. agencies by the MILITARY SEALIFT COMMAND, a component of the U.S. TRANSPORTATION COMMAND.

communication • *n.* **1** the imparting or exchanging of information or news: *direct communication between the two countries will produce greater understanding.* **2** a letter or message containing such information or news. **3** (**communications**) means of connection between people or places, in particular: **a** the means of sending or receiving information, such as telephone lines or computers: *satellite communications* | *a communications network.* **b** the means of traveling or of transporting goods, such as roads or railroads: *excellent road and rail communications.*

PHRASES: **lines of communication** the connections between an army in the field and its bases.

DERIVATIVES: **communicational** *adj.*

communications intelligence • technical and intelligence information derived from foreign communications by other than the intended recipients.

communications satellite • one of two types of orbiting vehicle that relays signals between communications stations: **1** (**active communications satellite**)) a satellite that receives, regenerates, and retransmits signals between stations. **2** (**passive communications satellite**) a satellite that reflects communications signals between stations.

communications security • (**COMSEC**) the protection resulting from all measures designed to deny unauthorized persons information of value which might be derived from the possession and study of telecommunications, or to mislead unauthorized persons in their interpretation of the results of such possession and study.

communism • *n.* (often **Communism**) a theory or system of social organization in which all property is vested in the community and each person contributes and receives according to his or her ability and needs.

DERIVATIVES: **communist** *n.* & *adj.* **communistic** *adj.*

The most familiar form of communism is that established by the Bolsheviks after the Russian Revolution of 1917, and it has generally been understood in terms of the system practiced by the former Soviet Union and its allies in Eastern Europe, in China in 1949, and in some developing countries such as Cuba, Vietnam, and North Korea.

---

community of nations • an idea advocating peace and mediation, rather than policies of militarism and imperialism, and based on the interests of all nations.

Commutation Act of 1783 • an act passed by the Congress at the end of the REVOLUTIONARY WAR to provide officers who served in the war with five years' full pay in the form of government certificates bearing 6 percent interest. It replaced the half-pay pensions for life that had been granted in 1780.

commutation fee • a sum of money provided to an individual by the government in lieu of authorized quarters or rations in kind or by an individual to the government in lieu of performing military service.

compact • *n.* a formal agreement or contract between two or more parties. • *v.* make or enter into (a formal agreement) with another party or parties: *the Democratic Party compacted an alliance with dissident groups.*

companion • *n.* **1** a covering over the hatchway leading below decks. **2** a raised frame with windows on the quarterdeck of a ship to allow light into the decks below. **3** short for COMPANIONWAY.

companion hatchway • see COMPANIONWAY HATCH.

companion ladder • another term for COMPANIONWAY.

Companion of Honour • a member of a British order of knighthood founded in 1917.

companionway • *n.* a set of steps leading from a ship's deck down to a cabin or lower deck.

companionway hatch • the entry to a set of steps from a ship's deck to a cabin or lower deck.

company • *n.* (pl. **-ies**) **1** a body of soldiers, especially the smallest subdivision of an infantry battalion, typically commanded by a major or captain: *the troops of C Company.* **2** (**the Company**) informal the Central Intelligence Agency.

PHRASES: **ship's company** the entire crew of a ship.

company officer • an army officer serving within an infantry company.

company sergeant major • the highest-ranking noncommissioned officer of an infantry company.

compartment • *n.* **1** a space within a larger space, separated from the rest by partitions, such as in an aircraft, railroad car, wallet, or desk. **2** a watertight division of a ship: *the aft cargo compartment.*

compartmentation • *n.* **1** establishment and management of an organization so that information about the personnel, internal organization, or activities of one component is made available to any other component only to the extent required for the performance of assigned duties. **2** effects of relief and drainage upon avenues of approach so as to produce areas bounded on at least two sides by terrain features such as woods, ridges, or ravines that limit observation or observed fire into the area from points outside the area.

Composite Air Strike Force • (**CASF**) a fighting unit first envisioned by the TACTICAL AIR COMMAND that was designed to incorporate all elements of a modern tactical air force—counterair fighters, ground-attack aircraft, tankers, and transports—that could be deployed on short notice to any part of the world. It was operational between 1955 and 1973.

Comprehensive Test Ban Treaty • an agreement to prohibit "any nuclear weapon test explosion or any other nuclear explosion" anywhere. Negotiated at the 1996 Geneva Conference on Disarmament, it extended the LIMITED TEST BAN TREATY. All forty-four states that formally participated in the Conference on Disarmament must sign and ratify the treaty in order for it to enter into force.

On September 24, 1996, President BILL CLINTON became the first leader to sign it.

Compromise of 1850 • a series of measures adopted by the Congress on September 9, 1850, prior to the CIVIL WAR, to address slavery and territory issues and to avert secession by the South. Proposed largely by Senator HENRY CLAY of Kentucky, it included several measures to ensure a balance between free and slave states. It admitted California to the Union as a free state, and from the remaining land acquired in the MEXICAN WAR (1846–48), it established Utah and New Mexico as territories with an open status of slavery, a measure that overruled the MISSOURI COMPROMISE.

computer simulation • the use of computers to simulate battlefield or other military situations and conditions, usually for the purpose of developing and testing operational plans or training.

comrade • *n.* **1** (also **comrade-in-arms**) a fellow soldier or serviceman. **2** a fellow socialist or communist (often as a form of address).

COMSEC • *abbr.* communications security.

Comstock, Cyrus Ballou (1831–1910) • military engineer, born in West Wrentham, Massachusetts. During the CIVIL WAR Comstock served with the construction of defenses for Washington, D.C., on the engineering staff of the ARMY OF THE POTOMAC, and then as senior engineer at the siege and capture of VICKSBURG (1862–63). From 1864–70 he served as an aide-de-camp for Gen. ULYSSES S. GRANT.

Conant, James Bryant (1893–1978) • educator and scientist, born in Boston, Massachusetts. Conant chaired the National Defense Research Council, the weapons research and development group of the federal OFFICE OF SCIENTIFIC RESEARCH AND DEVELOPMENT (1939–46). He coordinated the federal effort to develop the atomic bomb and other scientific war-related programs. An advocate of total war, he authorized the "all-out" development of an atomic weapon in December 1940. As high commissioner and ambassador in Germany (1953–57), he managed occupying military forces, coordinated relief efforts, and provided diplomatic leadership.

concentrated fire • **1** the fire of the batteries of two or more ships directed against a single target. **2** fire from a number of weapons directed at a single point or small area.

concentration • *n.* **1** an assembly of troops in a given area. **2** the simultaneous firing of a number of artillery pieces or mortars on a common, usually prearranged, area or target.

concept of operations • (also called **commander's concept**) a verbal or graphic statement, in broad outline, of a commander's assumptions or intent in regard to an operation or series of operations. The concept is designed to give an overall picture of the operation and is included primarily for additional clarity of purpose.

Concord, Battle of • an early battle of the REVOLUTIONARY WAR on April 19, 1775, between British forces and American militiamen. The British had marched to Concord with the intention of seizing military supplies, but the colonial leaders, with advance warning of their approach, removed them. See also LEXINGTON, BATTLE OF.

Condor • (**AGM-53**) a rocket-powered TV-guided missile, related to the WALLEYE, that was cancelled before completion.

conduct sheet • a military form designed to record someone's offenses and punishments.

conduct unbecoming • in full, "Conduct unbecoming an officer and a gentleman"; acts punishable under the UNIFORM CODE OF MILITARY JUSTICE which, while not necessarily criminal in nature, nevertheless reflect adversely on the government, the military service, and the officer corps. For example, excessive use of profanity or engaging in a drunken brawl might be considered "conduct unbecoming."

Cone, Hutchinson Ingham (1871–1941) • naval engineer and naval officer, born in Brooklyn, New York. Cone served on the USS *Baltimore* during Commodore GEORGE DEWEY's victory over the Spanish at the battle of MANILA BAY in 1898. Cone supervised the shift from coal to oil fuel to increase the operational radius of the navy, and was involved in trials of a turbo-electric propulsion system. He commanded the USS *Dixie* from April 1914 until July 1915, when he became marine superintendent of the PANAMA CANAL, and commanded naval air forces in Europe during WORLD WAR I. Cone was wounded while freeing lifeboats on the RMS *Leinster*, on which he was a passenger; for his lifesaving actions he was made an honorary commander of the ORDER OF THE BRITISH EMPIRE. Cone retired from the Navy in 1922 as engineer-in-chief, with rank of rear admiral.

CONELRAD |ˈkänl,ræd| • short for *control of electromagnetic radiation:* a radio-based national security alert system established by order of President HARRY S. TRUMAN in September 1951. In the event of a Soviet attack on the United States, all commercial radio stations would stop transmitting in order to prevent Soviet bombers from using radio stations as navigation beacons. Instead, selected CONELRAD stations would broadcast public emergency information at 604 kHz or 1240 kHz. The CONELRAD system was replaced by the Emergency Broadcast System in 1963.

After 1953, all radios sold in the United States were required to indicate the CONELRAD frequencies (640/1240 kHz) with small Civil Defense triangles.

---

cone of silence • an inverted cone-shaped space directly over the aerial towers of some forms of radio beacons in which signals are unheard or greatly reduced in volume.

Confederacy, The • collective term for those states which seceded from the UNION in 1860 and 1861 and joined the CONFEDERATE STATES OF AMERICA. Eleven Confederate states actually seceded and two other states, Missouri and Kentucky, sent delegates to the Confederate Congress, raised military forces for the Confederate Army, and from time to time had state governments which favored the Confederacy but did not formally secede from the Union.

Confederate battle flag • the flag most often associated with the Confederacy, consisting of a blue St. Andrew's cross edged in white on a red field, with a white star representing each Confederate state set in the cross. The design was suggested by Gen. P.G.T. BEAUREGARD, and although accepted by the Confederate War Department on October 1, 1861, the familiar battle flag was never formally adopted by the Confederate Congress.

Confederate Memorial Day • a day (generally May 30) set aside to remember those soldiers and sailors of the armed forces of the CONFEDERATE STATES OF AMERICA who died during the CIVIL WAR.

Confederate Secret Service • the intelligence, counterintelligence, and sabotage service of the CONFEDERATE STATES OF AMERICA during the CIVIL WAR.

Confederate States of America • the eleven southern states (Alabama, Arkansas, Florida, Georgia, Louisiana, Mississippi, North Carolina, South Carolina, Tennessee, Texas, and Virginia) that seceded from the United States in 1860 and 1861, thus precipitating the CIVIL WAR. (Also called the **Confederacy**.)

Conference on Security and Cooperation in Europe • a series of negotiations held by thirty-three European states, Canada, and the United States to address the security and stability of Europe. On August 1, 1975, it culminated in the signing of the CSCE Final Act, also called the HELSINKI ACCORDS, which established diplomacy for the remainder of the COLD WAR, including the inviolability of existing borders, nonintervention in the internal affairs of other states, and respect for human rights. In 1994 it was renamed the ORGANIZATION FOR SECURITY AND COOPERATION IN EUROPE.

confidential • *adj.* intended to be kept secret: *confidential information.*

DERIVATIVES: **confidentiality** *n.*

conflict • *n.* a prolonged armed struggle: *overseas conflicts.*

confusion agent • an individual whose primary purpose is confounding the intelligence or counterintelligence apparatus of another country rather than collecting and transmitting information.

Congressional Medal of Honor • a gold medal occasionally awarded by Congress for exceptional achievement not involving armed combat. Often confused with the MEDAL OF HONOR, a military decoration, the Congressional Medal of Honor may be awarded to any U.S. citizen.

congressional oversight • the supervision by the Congress of governmental agencies and other bodies, such as the military. Congressional review is conducted mainly by standing committees of the House and Senate, but also by panels convened for a special purpose, such as the one that held hearings on the IRAN-CONTRA AFFAIR. In such committees members of Congress gather information and dictate the preferred course of action.

***Congress*, USS** • one of six frigates authorized by the U.S. Congress, including the USS *Constitution*, and launched on August 15, 1799. The *Congress* participated in a

QUASI-WAR WITH FRANCE (escorting U.S. merchant ships to the East Indies), the BARBARY WAR (1804), and the WAR OF 1812. In 1829, it was a receiving ship at the Norfolk Navy Yard, Virginia, and, in 1834, judged unfit for repair and broken up.

conn (also **con**) • *v.* direct the steering of (a ship): *he hadn't conned anything bigger than a Boston whaler.* • *n.* (**the conn**) the action or post of conning a ship: *I quickly took the conn and restored the channel course.*

conning tower |ˈkäniNG ˈˌtow(ə)r| • the superstructure of a submarine, from which it can be commanded when on the surface, and containing the periscope.

Connor, Patrick Edward (1820–91) • soldier, entrepreneur, and politician, born Patrick Edward O'Connor in County Kerry, Ireland. Connor was the captain of "Connor's Company" of Texas Volunteers at BUENA VISTA (1847). At the start of the CIVIL WAR he was in the 3rd Regiment, California Infantry; they were sent to Salt Lake City, where he founded Fort Douglas (1862).

conscientious objector • a person who for reasons of conscience objects to serving in the armed forces.

conscribe • *v.* to enlist or enroll, particularly by signing one's name or mark to a roster.

conscript • *v.* |kənˈskript| (often **be conscripted**) enlist (someone) compulsorily, typically into the armed services: *they were* ***conscripted into*** *the army.* • *n.* |ˈkänˌskript| a person enlisted compulsorily.

conscription • *n.* compulsory enlistment for state service, typically into the armed forces.

Conscription Act of 1917 • see SELECTIVE SERVICE ACT of 1917.

Conscription Law of 1862/1864 • the first national draft law in American history, enacted by the Confederate Congress on April 16, 1862, during the CIVIL WAR. All able-bodied unmarried white men eighteen to thirty-five years of age, and later seventeen to fifty years of age, were eligible for a three-year service under the draft, but the law's effectiveness was weakened by its exemptions and provisions for substitution. On January 5, 1864 an order was approved to eliminate substitution and to enroll men formerly exempted under the provision.

consort • *n.* |ˈkänˌsôrt| a ship sailing in company with another.

Constellation • (**C-121**) used primarily as a transport aircraft for very important people, the C-121 is best known in its EC-121 version as a radar aircraft. Another version, the C-121J, was an airborne television studio used during the VIETNAM WAR.

Constitutional Union party • a political party organized in Baltimore in May 1860 by the WHIG and KNOW NOTHING parties. The Constitutional Union party criticized sectional politics and was supported by states in the middle of the United States along the North/South division. It was believed that this part of the country would become the main battleground in a civil war.

***Constitution*, USS** • one of six frigates, including the USS *Congress*, authorized by an act of Congress in 1794, and, more heavily armed than standard frigates, formidable naval opponents. In a battle with the British ship *Guerriere* during the WAR OF 1812, the British saw that their shot seemed to bounce harmlessly off the *Constitution*'s hull and nicknamed it "Old Ironsides." The *Constitution* served well from 1798 until early in the 20th century, establishing U.S. superiority at sea, and was saved twice from scrapping by public sentiment. In 1925 it was restored using funds donated by schoolchildren and patriotic groups. In 1931, it was recommissioned and, under tow, toured ninety port cities along the U.S. coasts in the course of three years. Placed in permanent commission in 1941, a 1954 act of Congress made the Secretary of the Navy responsible for the *Constitution*'s upkeep.

consul • *n.* an official appointed by a government to live in a foreign city and protect the government's citizens and interests there.
DERIVATIVES: **consular** *adj.* **consulship** *n.*

consumption rates, battlefield • the average quantity of an item consumed or expended during a given time interval under active combat conditions.

contact mine • a mine detonated by physical contact, typically concealed near the surface of the ground.

containment, strategy of • U.S. strategy developed during the early 1950s designed to discourage or prevent the territorial expansion and/or expansion of influence of the Soviet Union and other Communist states.

contamination • *n.* **1** the deposit, absorption, or adsorption of radioactive material, or of biological or chemical agents on or near structures, areas, personnel, or objects. **2** the condition of food and/or water made unfit for consumption by humans or animals because of the presence of environmental chemicals, radioactive elements, bacteria or organisms, the byproduct of the growth of bacteria or organisms, decomposing material (to include the food substance itself), or waste in the food or water.

continental • *n.* **1** (**Continental**) a member of the colonial army in the American Revolution: *twenty-two Continentals were killed and scalped.* **2** (also **Continental**) a piece of paper currency used at the time of the REVOLUTION WAR: *the redemption of Continentals by the government.* • *adj.* (also **Continental**) pertaining to the thirteen original colonies of the United States.: *in 1783 the officers and men of the continental forces had little to celebrate.*

Continental Army • see U.S. ARMY.

Continental Navy • see U.S. NAVY.

Continental United States • (**CONUS**) the territory of the United States that is within North America between Canada and Mexico, and the adjacent territorial waters.

Continental United States Intelligence • U.S. Army intelligence command located at Fort Holabird, Maryland, created in the 1960s to monitor civilian civil rights and antiwar organizations, infiltrate radical groups, and sometimes to act as agent-provocateurs in order to discredit radical organizations.

contingency plan • a plan for major possible circumstances that can reasonably be anticipated in the principal geographic subareas of the command.

contingent • *adj.* **1** subject to chance: *the contingent nature of the job.* **2** (of losses, liabilities, etc.) that can be anticipated to arise if a particular event occurs. **3** (**contingent on/upon**) occurring or existing only if (certain other circumstances) are the case; dependent on: *resolution of the conflict was contingent on the signing of a cease-fire agreement.* • *n.* a body of troops or police sent to join a larger force in an operation: *a contingent of 2,000 marines.*
DERIVATIVES: **contingently** *adv.*

continuous fire • **1** fire conducted at a normal rate without interruption for application of adjustment corrections or for other causes. **2** in field artillery and naval gunfire support, loading and firing at a specified rate or as rapidly as possible, consistent with accuracy within the prescribed rate of fire for the weapon. Firing will continue until terminated by the command "end of mission" or temporarily suspended by the command "cease loading" or "check firing."

contraband • *n.* **1** goods that have been imported or exported illegally. **2** trade in smuggled goods. **3** (also **contraband of war**) goods forbidden to be supplied by neutrals to those engaged in war. **4** during the CIVIL WAR, a black slave, especially a fugitive or captured slave.

contract labor • labor acquired from nongovernmental sources on a contractual basis. Such labor has often been used by the U.S. armed forces to supplement the efforts of uniformed personnel.

Contras, the • (also, **contras**) the guerrilla force in Nicaragua that opposed the left-wing SANDINISTA government (1979–90), and was supported by the United States for much of that time. It was officially disbanded in 1990, after the Sandinistas' electoral defeat.
ORIGIN: plural of *contra*, an abbreviation of Spanish *contrarevolucionario* 'counterrevolutionary.'

Contreras, Battle of • one in the series of battles in the MEXICAN WAR (1846–48) between Gen. WINFIELD SCOTT and ANTONIO LÓPEZ DE SANTA ANNA, on Scott's campaign toward Mexico City. Won on the same day as the shorter battle of CHURUBUSCO, this American victory on August 20, 1847, led to Santa Anna agreeing to an armistice the next day.

control • *n.* **1** authority that may be less than full command exercised by a commander over part of the activities of subordinate or other organizations. **2** in mapping, charting, and photogrammetry, a collective term for a system of marks or objects on the earth or on a map or a photograph, whose positions or elevations, or both, have been or will be determined. **3** physical or psychological pressures exerted with the intent to assure that an agent or group will respond as directed. **4** an indicator governing the distribution and use of documents, information, or material. Such indicators are the subject of intelligence community agreement and are specifically defined in appropriate regulations.

controllable mine • a mine that, after laying, can be controlled by the user, to the extent of making the mine safe or live, or to fire the mine.

controlled airspace • an airspace of defined dimensions within which air traffic control service is provided to controlled flights.

CONUS • *abbr.* Continental United States.

conventional forces • armed forces capable of conducting operations using nonnuclear weapons.

conventional war • warfare, other than guerrilla/counterinsurgent warfare, conducted without the use of nuclear, biological, or chemical weapons.

conventional weapons • weapons which are not nuclear, biological, nor chemical.

Convention on the Prohibition of the Development, Production and Stockpiling of Bacteriological (Biological) and Toxin Weapons • an agreement completed in 1972 by the Conference of the Committee on Disarmament and entered into force in 1975 to restrict biological and toxin warfare stocks. The international community condemned the use of such warfare in the VIETNAM WAR as a violation of the GENEVA PROTOCOL. U.S. President RICHARD M. NIXON ordered the destruction of America's biological weapons stockpile in 1969 and of its toxin stocks in 1970.

convoy |ˈkänˌvoi| • *n.* a group of ships or vehicles traveling together, typically accompanied by armed troops, warships, or other vehicles for protection. • *v.* |ˈkänˌvoi; kən ˈvoi| (of a warship or armed troops) accompany (a group of ships or vehicles) for protection.
PHRASES: **in convoy** (of traveling vehicles) as a group; together: *the army trucks had passed through in convoy the previous evening.*

convoy escort • **1** one (or more) naval ship(s) or aircraft traveling with a convoy and responsible for its protection. **2** an escort that protects a convoy of vehicles from being scattered, destroyed, or captured. See also ESCORT.

convoy through escort • those ships of the close escort which normally remain with the convoy from its port of assembly to its port of arrival.

Conway, Thomas (1735–1800?) • soldier, born in Ireland. A colonel in the French army, Conway volunteered his services to the United States. He was commissioned a brigadier general by Congress and fought at BRANDYWINE and GERMANTOWN (both 1777). His correspondence with Gen. HORATIO GATES, highly critical of GEORGE WASHINGTON, was taken by Washington and others as apparently fomenting a plot to remove Washington from command of the Continental army and replace him with Gates (called the "Conway Cabal"). Shunned by the MARQUIS DE LAFAYETTE and others loyal to Washington, he resigned his commission. After being severely wounded in duel with JOHN CADWALADER (July 4, 1778) he wrote an apology to Washington.

Conyngham, Gustavus |ˈkäniNG,hæm| (1747–1819) • naval officer, born in County Donegal, Ireland. In 1775 Conyngham sailed to Holland to purchase military supplies for the Continental army, but British pressure prevented him from acquiring any cargo. Stranded in France, Conyngham was given a commission by American representatives, including Benjamin Franklin, who were in Paris seeking aid from the French. Conyngham was commissioned captain of the lugger *Surprise* in 1777 and within a week of sailing had captured two British vessels. Ordered by the French (who seized his commission) to return the ships, Conyngham went back to sea a few months later in the cutter *Revenge* and captured or destroyed at least sixty vessels in twenty-two months.

Conyngham spent most of his time after the REVOLUTIONARY WAR trying to win recognition of and compensation for his services during the war from Congress. Because his original commission had been seized and never returned, his case was difficult to prove, and suffered from Congress's impatience with the number and quality of commissions Benjamin Franklin had given out in Paris, and Congress denied his petition. The commission turned up shortly before WORLD WAR I in a print shop in Paris and was bought by an American collector.

Cooke, Philip St. George (1809–95) • cavalry officer and author, born in Leesburg, Virginia. Cooke was a veteran commander and author of the manual *Cavalry Tactics* (1861). During the MEXICAN WAR (1846–48), Cooke commanded a battalion of Mormon volunteers in New Mexico and led them on a notable cross-desert march to southern California (1846). In the CIVIL WAR, Cooke helped GEORGE B. MCCLELLAN organize the ARMY OF THE POTOMAC and he commanded the Cavalry Reserve under McClellan. During the PENINSULAR CAMPAIGN, Cooke failed to prevent his son-in-law J.E.B. STUART from leading the Confederate cavalry of Gen. ROBERT E. LEE's ARMY OF NORTHERN VIRGINIA completely around the Union army (1862).

Cooke's decision to remain loyal to the Union was complicated when his son and both of his sons-in-law chose Virginia over the Union and became Confederate officers. His son, John Rogers Cooke, became a Confederate brigadier general. His son-in-law J. E. B. Stuart's fame as Robert E. Lee's renowned cavalry commander provoked rumors that Cooke did not enthusiastically favor prosecuting the war, and eventually contributed to Cooke's professional decline.

---

cookhouse • *n.* a kitchen in a military camp.

Cook, Philip (1817–94) • Confederate general and politician, born in Twiggs County, Georgia. Cook was a regimental and brigade commander in the ARMY OF NORTHERN VIRGINIA. As an officer in, then colonel of, the 4th Georgia Infantry, he fought with distinction at MALVERN HILL and at ANTIETAM (both 1862), where he was wounded. In the BATTLE OF THE WILDERNESS (1864), Cook helped lead STONEWALL JACKSON's offensive against the right flank of the ARMY OF THE POTOMAC. There, Cook overwhelmed a sector of the XI Corps line, captured six cannon, and pursued the Federals to a second defensive line, suffering a broken leg from a minié ball (1863). After recuperating while serving in the Georgia state senate, Cook returned to the field, commanding a brigade. He was promoted to brigadier general in 1864 and fought at CEDAR CREEK and FORT STEDMAN, where he was severely wounded a third time (1865).

Coolidge, Calvin (1872–1933) • 30th president of the United States (1923–29), born John Calvin Coolidge in Plymouth, Vermont. He was elected lieutenant governor of Massachusetts (1915) and governor (1918). He gained national reknown through a tough stand against a Boston police strike in 1919. Elected vice president under WARREN G. HARDING (1920), he took office on Harding's death in 1923 and was reelected in 1924. "Silent Cal" was noted for efficient administration, fiscal prudence, tax cuts, and debt reduction; he had a limited interest in foreign affairs. The Coolidge administration's best-known foreign policy initiative was the multilateral KELLOGG-BRIAND TREATY of 1928.

Coontz, Robert Edward (1864–1935) • naval officer, born in Hannibal, Missouri. Coontz was chief of naval operations (1919–23), commander of the U.S. Fleet (1923–25), and commander of the naval district at Norfolk, Virginia (1925–28). As chief of naval operations, Coontz guided the development of the U.S. Navy during the postwar period of demobilization and reduced appropriations. He supported naval aviation, and worked to give that arm a near-independent status. Coontz also supported the building of aircraft carriers and established the basis of the powerful U.S. naval air armada of the 1940s.

Cooperative Threat Reduction • a DEPARTMENT OF DEFENSE program implemented in November 1991, at the end of the COLD WAR, as a measure to reduce the threat of nuclear weapons systems. It was established to assist the new independent states of the former Soviet Union in the storage, transportation, dismantlement, and elimination of nuclear weapons from the Soviet era.

Cooper-Church Amendment • an amendment passed by the Senate on June 30, 1970, during the VIETNAM WAR, to prohibit the use of U.S. forces in the war after June 30, 1970, and the reintroduction of forces without congressional approval. Introduced by Senators John Sherman Cooper and Frank Church, it was modified in December by the House of Representatives after attempts by President RICHARD M. NIXON's administration to allow presidential discretion. It was the first time that the Congress had restricted the deployment of U.S. troops during a war.

Cooper, Joseph Alexander (1823–1910) • Union army officer and farmer, born near Cumberland Falls, Kentucky. Cooper commanded volunteer infantry in eastern Kentucky and Tennessee, and fought at STONES RIVER (1862–63). Cooper was a brigade commander under JOHN M. SCHOFIELD in the ATLANTA campaign, and played a key role in the defense of Tennessee (1865), defeating invading forces under JOHN B. HOOD at Franklin and Nashville.

Cooper, Samuel (1798–1876) • Confederate army officer, born in Fishkill, New York. Cooper was military assistant to the secretary of war in the MARTIN VAN BUREN, JAMES K. POLK, and ZACHARY TAYLOR administrations. He was the author of *A Concise System of Instructions and Regulations for the Militia and Volunteers of the United States...* (1836), which was very popular with state militias. He served as adjutant general of the army from 1852 until he resigned his commission in 1861. Cooper, a close friend and confidant of JEFFERSON DAVIS, had strong ties to the South and owned a farm in Virgina. Upon secession, Cooper traveled to the Confederate capital in Montgomery, Alabama, and offered his services to Davis. Davis appointed Cooper adjutant and inspector general of the Confederate army. Made a full general later in 1861, he remained throughout the CIVIL WAR the highest ranking officer of the Confederate army. Although Davis referred to him as chief of staff of the army, Cooper confined his office to administrative support.

coordinated attack • a carefully planned attack in which all participating elements have been fully informed as to the overall plan and the planned actions of other attacking and supporting elements.

Coordinator of Information • see OFFICE OF STRATEGIC SERVICES.

Copperhead • the U.S.-produced M712 laser-guided antiarmor artillery round.

Coral Sea, Battle of the • the first confrontation between American and Japanese aircraft carriers in WORLD WAR II, on May 7–8, 1942. Apprised by intelligence of an impending Japanese invasion of New Guinea and the Solomon Islands, Adm. CHESTER W. NIMITZ of the Pacific fleet dispatched the carriers *Yorktown* and *Lexington*. The Japanese ships *Shokaku* and *Zuikaku* were involved. The *Lexington* was lost, but the planned Japanese invasion was cancelled, and neither of its two ships made it to the battle of MIDWAY later that year, where the *Yorktown* played a decisive role.

Corbin, Margaret Cochran (1752–c. 1800) • REVOLUTIONARY WAR heroine, born in Franklin County, Pennsylvania. Corbin married John Corbin, an artilleryman, who was killed at the battle of Fort Washington (November 16, 1776). Corbin, according to official reports, was "wounded and utterly disabled by three Grape shott, while she filled with distinguished Bravery the post of her Husband, who was Killed by her side, serving a piece of Artillery at Fort Washington." Disabled by her war wounds, she became a pensioner of Congress, who awarded her half of a regular soldier's pay and a complete suit of clothes annually. Enrolled in the CORPS OF INVALIDS, she performed garrison duties at WEST POINT, where she lived thereafter, becoming known as "Captain Molly."

cordage • *n.* cords or ropes, especially in a ship's rigging.

CORDS • (It is an acronym for **Civil Operations and Revolutionary (or Rural) Development Support.**) a program developed during the VIETNAM WAR that integrated military and civilian efforts to destroy the VIETCONG infrastructure and at the same time build stronger support for the South Vietnamese government in the countryside.

corduroy • *n.* (or **corduroy road**) tree trunks and branches laid across a swamp or marshy area to create a road.

Corinth, Battle of • a CIVIL WAR battle in Mississippi that was fought October 3–4, 1862. Confederate troops wanted to recapture Corinth and march into Middle Tennessee. Since the Union takeover of Corinth, Union forces had reinforced the city, which was an important transportation center. However, Confederate troops pushed the Federals back and passed into the city through a gap in Union forces. Since Maj. Gen. EARL VAN DORN felt confident that he could defeat Union forces the next day, and heat, fatigue, and water shortages were taking a toll on the troops, he halted fighting for the day. Before resuming fighting the next day, Maj. Gen. WILLIAM S. ROSECRANS regrouped defenses, and Union artillery caused heavy casualties, forcing the Confederates into retreat. Van Dorn was defeated at Hatchie Bridge, Tennessee, the following day.

cornet • *n.* the fifth grade of commissioned officer in a cavalry troop, who carried the colors. It is still used in some British cavalry regiments for officers of the rank of second lieutenant.

DERIVATIVES: **cornetcy** *n.* (pl. **-ies**)

Cornwallis, Charles (1738–1805) • commanding general of British forces in the southern campaign in the REVOLUTIONARY WAR, born in London. He was the 2nd earl Cornwallis, later marquis. In the Revolutionary War, Cornwallis was victorious at NEW YORK and WHITE PLAINS (both 1776) but unsuccessful at TRENTON (1776), PRINCETON (1777), and MONMOUTH (1778). More outstanding as a field commander than as a strategist, he defeated American forces at BRANDYWINE (1777). Invading South Carolina, he defeated Gen. HORATIO GATES at CAMDEN (1780); and was defeated in turn by NATHANAEL GREENE at GUILFORD COURT HOUSE (1781). Ordered by HENRY CLINTON to establish a defensive base, he marched into Virginia. Despite reinforcements and fortifications at YORKTOWN, Cornwallis was forced to surrender his besieged army to GEORGE WASHINGTON (1781), effectively ending the war in America.

Corona, Project • code name for the CIA's first photographic satellite reconnaissance system. Project Corona was approved in February 1958 and consisted of three main subprograms: the Discoverer satellite program with some thirty-eight satellites launches between February 1959 and February 1962; the U.S. Air Force Sentry reconnaissance satellite program, later renamed the Satellite and Missile Observation System (SAMOS) with thirty satellite launches between October 1960 and November 1963; and the U.S. Air Force Missile Alarm Defense System (MIDAS) designed to detect Soviet ballistic missile launches.

Corp. |kawrp| • *abbr.* (also **Corp**) informal Corporal: *been abroad before, Corp?*

corporal • *n.* a low-ranking noncommissioned officer in the armed forces, in particular (in the U.S. Army) an NCO ranking above private first class and below sergeant or (in the U.S. Marine Corps) an NCO ranking above lance corporal and below sergeant.

corps |kôr| • *n.* (pl. **corps** |kôrz|) **1** a main subdivision of an armed force in the field, consisting of two or more divisions: *the 5th Army Corps.* **2** a branch of a military organization assigned to a particular kind of work: *the Army Medical Corps.*

Corps D'Afrique • the CIVIL WAR regiments, first formed in 1862, consisting of freed slaves who fought for the Union. Their pay and benefits were inferior to those supplied to white regiments and strict segregation was enforced.

Corps of Invalids • a continental regiment whose organization was authorized by Congress on June 20, 1777, during the REVOLUTIONARY WAR. It was composed of men who were injured in service and no longer fit for field duties, but who were found capable of light garrison duty.

Corregidor, Battle of • a battle for the island fortress of Corregidor in Manila Bay in early 1942, between the Japanese and forces under the command of Gen. DOUGLAS MACARTHUR. Dangerously short of food, medicine, and ammunition after some questionable tactical gambits, the Americans eventually surrendered. See also BATAAN, BATTLE OF.

Corsair • (**F4U**) a fast single-seat single-engine fighter aircraft of the 1940s and one of the most successful fighters of WORLD WAR II.

Corsair II • (**A-7**) an all-weather single-seat, light attack aircraft having one turbofan engine. It is designed to operate from an aircraft carrier, and is armed with cannon. It can carry an assortment of nuclear and/or conventional ordnance as well as air-to-air and air-to-ground missiles.

Corse, John Murray (1835–93) • Union general, born in Pittsburgh, Pennsylvania. Corse was the commander of Union volunteers under JOHN POPE, WILLIAM T. SHERMAN, and ULYSSES S. GRANT, and major of the 6th Iowa. Promoted to brigadier general of volunteers, at CHATTANOOGA Corse captured the heavily defended advance position at MISSIONARY RIDGE and was seriously wounded (1863). He was a division commander in ATLANTA campaign and on the MARCH TO THE SEA (1864–1865).

Defending Allatoona Pass, outnumbered and virtually surrounded, Corse was enjoined by Sherman to hang on until reinforcements arrived (a plea later corrupted into the phrase "Hold the fort!"

Cortina, Juan Nepomuceno |kôr'tēnə| ("Cheno") • (1824–92) Mexican revolutionary, general, governor, and rancher, born in Camargo, Tamaulipas, Mexico. Cortina, a champion of Mexican-American rights, shot an Anglo city marshal who was brutally beating a Mexican ranch hand in 1859. Seeking revenge for mistreatment of Tejanos, Cortina conducted the decade-long "Cortina War"; raiding south Texas from Brownsville to Rio Grande City, eluding pursuers, including ROBERT E. LEE. He was arrested as a cattle thief and court-martialed in 1875.

corvette |kôr'vet| • *n.* **1** a small warship designed for convoy escort duty. **2** a sailing warship with one tier of guns.

COSSAC • *abbr.* Chief of Staff, Supreme Allied Commander; an office established in WORLD WAR II and tasked with the planning of OPERATION OVERLORD.

cotton diplomacy • diplomatic measures undertaken by the Confederate States of America to gain the support of Great Britain and other foreign nations during the CIVIL WAR. It was so called because the Confederacy's principal negotiating leverage was the export of cotton required by European mills.

Couch, Darius Nash (1822–97) • Union army officer, born in town of Southeast, Putnam County, New York. As a lieutenant of artillery in the MEXICAN WAR (1846–48), Couch fought at BUENA VISTA (1847). In the CIVIL WAR, he commanded a division during GEORGE B. MCCLELLAN'S PENINSULAR CAMPAIGN and fought well at WILLIAMSBURG, FAIR OAKS, and MALVERN HILL (all 1862). As a corps commander at FREDERICKSBURG (1862), he crossed the Rappahannock River by pontoon boats under enemy fire. Couch commanded the withdrawal of JOSEPH HOOKER'S army from CHANCELLORSVILLE (1863).

Cougar • (**F9F-6**) a single-engine fighter with swept-back wings, built in large numbers from 1952 on, even though other available fighter aircraft performed better. It had little in common with the PANTHER (F9F-5), and the two fighters share the same designation only for political reasons.

Council of Safety • see COMMITTEE OF SAFETY.

council of war • a gathering of military officers in wartime.

Council on National Defense • see WAR INDUSTRIES BOARD.

countdown • *n.* the step-by-step process leading to the initiation of missile testing, launching, and firing. It is performed in accordance with a predesignated time schedule.

counter • *n.* the curved part of the stern of a ship projecting aft above the waterline.

counter air • air operations conducted to attain and maintain a desired degree of air superiority by the destruction or neutralization of enemy forces. Both air offensive and air defensive actions are involved.

counterattack • *n.* an attack by part or all of a defending force against an enemy attacking force, for such specific purposes as regaining lost ground or cutting off or destroying enemy advance units, and with the general objective of denying to the enemy the attainment of their purpose in attacking.

counterbattery fire • fire delivered for the purpose of destroying or neutralizing indirect fire weapon systems.

counterespionage • *n.* the aspect of counterintelligence designed to detect, destroy, neutralize, exploit, or prevent espionage activities through identification, penetration, manipulation, deception, and repression of individuals, groups, or organizations conducting or suspected of conducting espionage activities.

counterfire • *n.* fire (including counterbattery, counterbombardment, and countermortar fire) intended to destroy or neutralize enemy weapons systems.

counterforce option • the employment of strategic air and missile forces in an effort to destroy, or render impotent, military capabilities of an enemy force, particularly the enemy's nuclear capable forces.

counterguerrilla operations • operations and other activities conducted by armed forces, paramilitary forces, or non-military agencies to neutralize or destroy anti-government guerrilla forces.

counterinsurgency • *n.* the military, paramilitary, political, economic, psychological, and civic actions taken by a government to defeat insurgency.

counterintelligence • (**CI**) *n.* information gathered and activities conducted to protect against espionage, other intelligence activities, sabotage, or assassinations conducted by or on behalf of foreign governments or elements thereof, foreign organizations or foreign persons, or international terrorist activities.

Counter Intelligence Corps • WORLD WAR II-era U.S. Army counterespionage and security organization. Its functions were subsumed by the U.S. Army Military Intelligence and Security Corps (later the MILITARY INTELLIGENCE branch) in the 1950s.

countermand • *v.* **1** revoke (an order): *an order to arrest the strike leaders had been countermanded.* **2** revoke an order issued by (another person): *he countermanded the captain.*

countermarch • *v.* march in the opposite direction or back along the same route.

countermeasure • *n.* an action taken to counteract a danger or threat.

countermine • *n.* an excavation dug to intercept another dug by an enemy. • *v.* dig a countermine against.

counteroffensive • *n.* an attack made in response to one from an enemy, typically on a large scale or for a prolonged period.

countersabotage • *n.* the aspect of counterintelligence designed to detect, destroy, neutralize, or prevent sabotage activities through identification, penetration, manipulation, deception, and repression of individuals, groups, or organizations conducting or suspected of conducting sabotage activities.

counterscarp • *n.* the outer wall of a ditch in a fortification. Compare with SCARP.

countersign • *n.* archaic a signal or password given in reply to a soldier on guard.

counter-stealth • *n.* the measures undertaken to defeat or degrade stealth (radar avoidance) technology.

countersubversion • *n.* the aspect of counterintelligence designed to detect, destroy, neutralize, or prevent subversive activities through the identification, exploitation, penetration, manipulation, deception, and repression of individuals, groups, or organizations conducting or suspected of conducting subversive activities.

countersurveillance • *n.* passive and active measures taken to prevent observation by the enemy.

counterterrorism • *n.* offensive measures taken to prevent, deter, and respond to terrorism.

countervalue option • in nuclear strategy, a choice to attack an opponent's civilian population and general economic centers rather than only it's military installations.

country buster • a nuclear weapon (theoretically) powerful enough to destroy an entire nation.

coup d'état | ˌkoo͞ dä'tä | • (pl. **coups d'état** | -'tä(z) | pronunc. same) (also **coup**) a sudden, violent, and illegal seizure of power from a government: *he was overthrown in an army coup d'état.*

ORIGIN: mid 17th cent.: French, literally 'blow of state.'

course | kôrs | • *n.* the route or direction followed by a ship, aircraft, road, or river: *the new fleet* ***changed course*** *to join the other ships.*

court-martial • *n.* (pl. **courts-martial** or **court-martials**) a judicial court for trying members of the armed services accused of offenses against military law: *they appeared before a court-martial | he was found guilty by court-martial.* • *v.* (**-martialed, -martialing**; Brit **-martialled, -martialling**) try (someone) by such a court.

Court of Appeals for the Armed Forces • a federal court established by Congress in the UNIFORM CODE OF MILITARY JUSTICE enacted on May 5, 1950. It was designed to ensure a military judicial system that gave members of the armed services accused of crimes rights that parallel those given to civilians accused of crimes. In 1994, it was redesignated the U.S. Court of Appeals for the Armed Forces by the NATIONAL DEFENSE AUTHORIZATION ACT.

Court of Military Appeals • former name of the U.S. COURT OF APPEALS FOR THE ARMED FORCES.

cover • *n.* **1** the action by land, air, or sea forces to protect by offense, defense, or threat of either or both. **2** those measures necessary to give protection to a person, plan, operation, formation, or installation from the enemy intelligence effort and leakage of information. **3** the act of maintaining a continuous receiver watch with transmitter calibrated and available, but not necessarily available for immediate use. **4** shelter or protection, either natural or artificial: *the sirens wailed and people ran for cover.* **5** photographs or other recorded images that show a particular area of ground. **6** a code meaning, "keep fighters between force/base and contact designated at distance stated from force/base": *cover bogey 27-30 miles.* **7** an identity or activity adopted by a person, typically a spy, to conceal their true activities: *he was worried that their cover was blown.* **8** military support given when someone is in danger from or being attacked by an enemy: *they agreed to provide additional naval cover.* **9** an activity or organization used as a means of concealing an illegal or secret activity: *the organizations often use their philanthropy as a* ***cover for*** *subsidies to terrorists.* • *v.* **1** aim a gun at (someone) in order to prevent them from moving or escaping. **2** protect (an exposed person) by shooting at an enemy: (**covering**) *the jeeps retreated behind spurts of* ***covering fire.*** **3** (of a fortress, gun, or cannon) have (an area) within range.

PHRASES: **break cover** suddenly leave a place of shelter, especially vegetation, when being hunted or pursued. **cover one's ass** (or **back**) informal foresee and avoid the possibility of attack or criticism. **take cover** protect oneself from attack by ducking down into or under a shelter: *if the bombing starts, take cover in the basement.* **under cover of 1** concealed by: *the yacht made landfall under cover of darkness.* **2** while pretending to do something: *Moran watched every move under cover of reading the newspaper.*

▸**cover something up 1** put something on, over, or around something, especially in order to conceal or disguise it. **2** try to hide or deny the fact of an illegal or illicit action or activity.

DERIVATIVES: **coverable** *adj.*

covering fire • **1** fire used to protect troops when they are within range of enemy small arms. **2** in amphibious usage, fire delivered prior to the landing in order to cover preparatory operations such as underwater demolition or minesweeping.

covert action • action so planned and executed as to conceal the identity of, or permit plausible denial by, the sponsor.

covert operation • an operation planned and executed as to conceal the identity of, or permit plausible denial by, the sponsor. A covert operation differs from a CLANDESTINE OPERATION in that emphasis is placed on concealment of the identity of the sponsor rather than on concealment of the operation.

Cowpens, Battle of • a battle at Cowpens, South Carolina, in the REVOLUTIONARY WAR on January 17, 1781. It was a decisive victory for DANIEL MORGAN and his Virginia, Maryland, and Delaware continentals against British forces under BANASTRE TARLETON.

cox |käks| • *n.* a coxswain, especially of a racing boat.

Cox, Jacob Dolson (1828–1900) • Union general and politician, born in Montreal, Canada. As a brigadier general in the CIVIL WAR, Cox fought at SOUTH MOUNTAIN and ANTIETAM (both 1862), where he commanded the 9th Corps in its assault on the Burnside Bridge. Cox took part in the ATLANTA campaign, the MARCH TO THE SEA, and the battles of FRANKLIN and NASHVILLE (1864–65). Cox was promoted to major general in 1864.

coxswain |ˈkäksən| • *n.* the steersman of a ship's boat, lifeboat, or other boat.

DERIVATIVES: **coxswainship** |-ˌSHip| *n.*

Cox, William Ruffin (1832–1919) • Confederate army officer and politician, born at Scotland Neck, North Carolina. Cox served in the U.S. House of Representatives (1880–86) and as secretary of the Senate (1893–1900). One of ROBERT E. LEE's generals, Cox began as a major during the PENINSULAR CAMPAIGN (1862). He fought in the SEVEN DAYS' battles; at SOUTH MOUNTAIN, ANTIETAM, and FREDERICKSBURG (all 1862). Cox received eleven wounds during the CIVIL WAR, including five at CHANCELLORSVILLE (1863) when his regiment suffered 75 percent casualties in fifteen minutes. Cox led the army's last attack before Lee's surrender at APPOMATTOX COURT HOUSE (1865).

Coy Brit. • *abbr.* Company.

Cpl. • *abbr.* Corporal.

CPO • *abbr.* Chief Petty Officer.

CPOS • *abbr.* Civilian Personnel Occupation Standard; a classification system for civilian jobs in the armed forces.

CPV • *abbr.* Chinese People's Volunteers.

crack |kræk| • *v.* informal find a solution to; decipher or interpret: *he cracked the codes used in the message.* • *adj.* very good, especially at a specified activity or in a specified role: *he is a crack shot* | *crack troops.*

crackerjack |ˈkrækərˌjæk| informal • *adj.* exceptionally good: *a crackerjack eye surgeon.* • *n.* the traditional Navy uniform, especially the black wool pants with bell bottoms. The pants have thirteen buttons for the original thirteen states and are tied in the back with string. This uniform is worn on formal occasions.

Craig, Isaac (1742–1826) • REVOLUTIONARY WAR officer, Pittsburgh business and civic leader, born in Hillsborough, Ireland. Craig took part in the capture of the Hessians at TRENTON on Christmas night 1776, and fought in the battles of PRINCETON, BRANDYWINE, and GERMANTOWN (all 1777); he wintered at VALLEY FORGE (1777–78). Commanding FORT PITT, Craig led troops to assist GEORGE ROGERS CLARK in the Detroit expedition (1781). Craig was deputy quartermaster general and military storekeeper of Pittsburgh (1791), led federal troops during the WHISKEY REBELLION (1794), and helped prepare munitions during WAR OF 1812.

Craig, Malin (1875–1945) • chief of staff of the U.S. Army (1935–39), born in St. Joseph, Missouri. In WORLD WAR I, Craig served in the MARNE (1914), ST. MIHIEL, and MEUSE-ARGONNE campaigns (both 1918). As the "Father of World War II mobilization planning," Craig rebuilt military preparedness, advocating motorization, mechanization, and modernization.

Craik, James (1730–1814) • physician and military surgeon, born near Dumfries, Scotland. Craik was a friend and physician to GEORGE WASHINGTON. As a Virginia regimental surgeon during the FRENCH AND INDIAN WAR (1754–63), Craik became friends with George Washington. He cared for EDWARD BRADDOCK at his death (July 9, 1755), and cared for the wounded, including the MARQUIS DE LAFAYETTE, in many ofWashington's major battles. Craik informed Washington of the CONWAY Cabal, and was a founding member of the SOCIETY OF THE CINCINNATI (1783).

Washington's "man of choice in all cases of sickness," Craik attended the first president at his deathbed. Craik used every method he knew of, futilely administering blistering, bleeding, and purgatives, to try to save Washington from what may have been strep throat.

Crampton's Gap, Battle of • a CIVIL WAR conflict in Maryland that took place on September 14, 1862, a part of the BATTLE OF SOUTH MOUNTAIN. The Battle of Crampton's Gap occurred during the MARYLAND CAMPAIGN in 1862. Gen. ROBERT E. LEE advanced on HARPERS FERRY after invading Maryland. The ARMY OF THE POTOMAC under Maj. Gen. GEORGE B. MCCLELLAN followed the Confederates to Frederick, Maryland, where battles were fought within mountain passes, including Crampton's Gap through South Mountain. While the Confederates were driven back, McClellan did not follow up with attacks, giving Lee time to gather together his dispersed troops and capture Harper's Ferry.

Crane, John (1744–1805) • soldier and patriot, born in Braintree, Massachusetts. Crane volunteered in the FRENCH AND INDIAN WAR (1754–63), replacing his father, who had been drafted. He was one of the SONS OF LIBERTY and hosted preparations for the BOSTON TEA PARTY (1773). He commanded an artillery company during the siege of Boston and at BUNKER HILL (1775). He commanded an artillery regiment at GERMANTOWN, BRANDYWINE (both 1777), and MONMOUTH (1778).

During the Boston Tea Party, Crane was knocked unconscious when a tea chest fell on him. Believing him dead, his companions left him buried underneath a pile of wood shavings in a nearby carpenter's shop, but he recovered.

crank • *adj.* archaic (of a sailing ship) easily keeled over, especially by wind or sea through improper design or loading.

crap hat • vulgar slang (in the British army) a term used by paratroopers and commandos to refer to a soldier from a regiment in the rest of the army.

ORIGIN: probably with derogatory reference to the standard khaki-colored (now dark blue) berets, in contrast to the prized red and green berets of the special regiments.

crash-dive • *v.* **1** (of a submarine) dive rapidly and steeply to a deeper level in an emergency. **2** (of an aircraft) plunge steeply downward into a crash. • *n.* (**crash dive**) a steep dive of this kind by a submarine or aircraft.

crater • *n.* the pit, depression, or cavity formed in the surface of the earth by an explosion. In the case of a deep underground burst, no rupture of the surface may occur See CAMOUFLET.

Crater, Battle of the • a CIVIL WAR battle on July 30, 1864, when forces under Gen. ULYSSES S. GRANT exploded a huge mine under a Confederate earthwork that was part of the fortification of PETERSBURG. The explosion left a crater 30 feet deep.

C rations • prepared food in cans, provided to troops where fresh food is unavailable or cooking impossible.

Craven, Thomas Tingey (1808–87) • Union naval officer, born in the District of Columbia, and brother of TUNIS AUGUSTUS MACDONOUGH CRAVEN. In 1850 Craven was appointed commandant of midshipmen at ANNAPOLIS. In the CIVIL WAR, he commanded the Potomac River flotilla. As captain of the steam frigate *Niagara* in 1865, Craven failed to execute orders to engage in combat the Confederate iron ram *Stonewall* at El Ferrol, Spain; he was consequently court-martialed, suspended for two years, and gained the reputation of being overly cautious.

Craven, Tunis Augustus MacDonough (1813–64) • Union naval officer, born in Portsmouth, New Hampshire, and brother of Adm. THOMAS TINGEY CRAVEN. One of the navy's most distinguished surveyors and hydrographers, Craven was chosen in 1857 to command an expedition to survey a projected ship canal route from the Atlantic to the Pacific through the Isthmus of Panama. In 1863 Craven was given command of the newly built ironclad *Tecumseh*, which struck a Confederate mine the following year in the attack on Fort Morgan near Mobile, Alabama. Craven sacrificed his life to save a fellow naval officer.

Crawford, Samuel Johnson (1835–1913) • Union army officer, politician, born in Lawrence County, Indiana. In the CIVIL WAR, Crawford recruited a company of soldiers as part of the 2nd Kansas Volunteer Infantry. He was later colonel of the 2nd Kansas Colored Infantry. As governor of Kansas after the war, Crawford opposed the federal government's "soft" Indian policy, claiming that the Indians "will neither improve nor cultivate the lands, and their occupancy prevents others from doing it."

Crawford, William (1732–82) • REVOLUTIONARY WAR soldier, born in Frederick County, Virginia. A surveyor, land speculator, and personal friend of GEORGE WASHINGTON, Crawford's loyalty to his birthplace led him to enlist in the Continental troops raised by Virginia early in the Revolution. He served under Washington at the battles of NEW YORK, TRENTON (both 1776), and PRINCETON (1777). As commander of an expedition into the Ohio country in 1782, Crawford was captured by Native American and British forces and was burned at the stake in retaliation for the massacre of a party of Christian Delaware Indians.

Crawford, William Harris (1772–1834) • U.S. senator (1807–12), cabinet member, and presidential candidate, born in Amherst County, Virginia. Crawford was President JAMES MADISON's minister to France during the WAR OF 1812, then secretary of war under Madison (1815–16). He improved the quality of education at WEST POINT by requiring cadets to pass an entrance examination.

Crazy Horse (c.1840–77) • legendary Oglala LAKOTA war chief, born near Butte in present-day South Dakota. He led warriors during RED CLOUD'S WAR (1866–67). He rejected the FORT LARAMIE TREATY (1868) and led the resistance of nontreaty Lakota. A courageous warrior who commanded the respect of both his own people and his enemies, Crazy Horse was a Lakota head warrior, or "shirt wearer," who came to prominence in the mid-1870s by resisting the migration of white settlers and gold prospectors in the Black Hills. In 1876, with SITTING BULL, he emerged as the most conspicuous leader of the Lakota-Cheyenne alliance and was a central figure in the GREAT SIOUX WAR that year. In battle with 7th Cavalry at the LITTLE BIGHORN, Crazy Horse led the charges that destroyed GEORGE ARMSTRONG CUSTER and his immediate command (June 25, 1876). He surrendered at Camp Robinson, Nebraska, on May 7, 1877, and resigned himself to reservation life, but rumors that he was planning to escape led to his arrest and death.

credibility gap • **1** an apparent difference between what is said or promised and what happens or is true. **2** a lack of trust in a person's or institution's statements and motives: *the Army's worst enemy is a continuing credibility gap.*

Creek War • a war fought from 1811 to 1814 in the Southeast between the Creek nations and white settlers from Georgia, Alabama, Kentucky and Tennessee under the leadership of ANDREW JACKSON. Creek resistance dwindled by attrition until the decisive BATTLE OF HORSESHOE BEND that ended the war.

creeping barrage • a barrage in which the fire of all units participating remains in the same relative position throughout and which advances in steps of one line at a time.

creeping mine • in naval mine warfare, a buoyant mine held below the surface by a weight, usually in the form of a chain, which is free to creep along the seabed under the influence of stream or current.

Cresap, Michael (1742–75) • frontiersman and REVOLUTIONARY WAR soldier, born in Old Town, Maryland. As captain of a rifle company from Frederick County, Maryland, Cresap marched with "Cresap's Rifles" 550 miles in twenty-five days, joining the Continental army at Boston (1775). Cresap was blamed by Virginians for beginning LORD DUNMORE'S WAR (1774). Near Wheeling, he attacked and scalped two warriors, one Delaware and the other Shawnee. At the treaty conference, he was charged with the murder of the family of the Mingo war chief JAMES LOGAN (Tah-gah-jute).

Thomas Jefferson in his *Notes on the State of Virginia* also blamed the Yellow Creek massacre on Cresap.

---

crib • *n.* an underground ditch or trenchlike structure designed for the discharge of low- and intermediate-level liquid nuclear wastes directly into the ground. A crib is about 20 feet deep and up to 1,400 feet long, lined with rock and soil.

crime • *n.* **1** an action or omission that constitutes an offense and is punishable by law: *shoplifting was a serious crime.* **2** an action or activity that, although not illegal, is considered to be evil, shameful, or wrong: *apartheid was a* ***crime against*** *humanity.*

crisis action planning • (**CAP**) **1** the process involving the time-sensitive development of joint operation plans and orders in response to an imminent crisis. Crisis action planning follows prescribed crisis action procedures to formulate and implement an effective response within the time frame permitted by the crisis. **2** the time-sensitive planning for the deployment, employment, and sustainment of assigned and allocated forces and resources that occurs in response to a situation that may result in actual military operations. Crisis action planners base their plan on the circumstances that exist at the time planning occurs.

crisis relocation planning • (**CRP**) a civil defense plan devised in the 1970s for evacuating civilians from the site of an expected nuclear strike and directing them to "host areas" a safe distance (at least 10 miles) away.

critical intelligence • intelligence which is crucial and requires the immediate attention of the commander so as to enable the commander to make decisions that will provide a timely and appropriate response to actions by the potential or actual enemy.

critical mass • for nuclear weapons, the minimum amount of fissionable material capable of supporting a chain reaction under precisely specified conditions.

critical zone • the area over which a bombing plane engaged in horizontal or glide bombing must maintain straight flight so that the bomb sight can be operated properly and bombs dropped accurately.

Crittenden Compromise • an amendment presented to Congress in December 1860 by Senator John J. Crittenden of Kentucky. An attempt to avert the CIVIL WAR, it allowed for the continuation of slavery where it already existed and compensation for the owners of fugitive slaves. It also proposed to reenact the MISSOURI COMPROMISE of 1820 and extend the boundary to the Pacific, prohibiting slavery north of the line but allowing slavery south of the line. It was defeated in the Senate on March 2, 1861.

Crittenden, George Bibb (1812–80) • Confederate army officer, born in Russellville, Kentucky. Crittenden fought in the BLACK HAWK WAR (1832), but resigned from with garrison duty to study law. Bored with the law, he volunteered for service in the border war with Mexico in 1842, and was captured that same year. He was released due to the intervention of his father, a U.S. senator. Crittenden was captain of a company of mounted riflemen in the MEXICAN WAR (1846–48), and fought at CONTRERAS and CHURUBUSCO (both 1847). Appointed major but court-martialed for drinking, he was reinstated, again due to the influence of his father, then governor of Kentucky. In the CIVIL WAR, Crittenden joined the Confederate army despite his father's wishes, and was made a major general and commander of Confederate forces in southeastern Kentucky. Defeated by GEORGE H. THOMAS at Mill Springs, or Logan's Crossroads (1862), he was accused of being drunk at the time, and was arrested and tried by a military court of inquiry, but finally released. He resigned his commission, and rejoined as a volunteer.

While imprisoned in Mexico, he and his fellow inmates were compelled to draw lots to decide who would be shot in retaliation for a failed escape attempt. Crittenden drew two favorable beans and was able to save himself and a friend.

Crittenden, Thomas Leonidas (1819–93) • Union army officer and lawyer, born in Russellville, Kentucky. As an aide to the staff of Gen. ZACHARY TAYLOR during the MEXICAN WAR (1846–48), Crittenden was selected to carry the news of the victory at BUENA VISTA (1847) to President JAMES K. POLK. In the CIVIL WAR, he commanded and reorganized Kentucky's state militia. He was promoted to major general in 1862 and brevetted brigadier general after his performance at STONES RIVER. Directing the 21st Corps during the campaign leading to CHICKAMAUGA (1863), Crittenden retreated, thinking the battle lost; a court inquiry found his conduct "most credible," but his military usefulness after that was permanently impaired.

Crockett, Davy (1786–1836) • frontiersman, U.S. congressman, and folk hero, born David Crockett in Greene County, Tennessee. Crockett was a volunteer in the Indian wars in the southeast (1813–15) and a militia officer. As a state legislator (1821–25), he took an active interest in public land policy regarding the West. He was elected to the U.S. House of Representatives (1827–31, 1833–35), campaigning as a "straight shooter." Crockett was the hero of tall tales in *Sketches and Eccentricities of Col. David Crockett of West Tennessee* (1833) and *Crockett Almanacs* (1835–1856), and he published an autobiography, *A Narrative of the Life of David Crockett of the State of Tennessee* (1834). Defeated in a reelection bid, remarked, "you may all go to hell and I will go to Texas." In Texas, Crockett joined Col. WILLIAM B. TRAVIS in the defense of the ALAMO, "animating the men to do their duty" (1836).

Croghan, George |ˈkrō-ən| (1791–1849) • inspector general of the U.S. Army (1825–45), born near Louisville, Kentucky. Croghan fought at TIPPECANOE (1811). In the WAR OF 1812, he defended Fort Stephenson, in defiance of Gen. WILLIAM HENRY HARRISON's orders to evacuate and burn the fort; and he repulsed a much larger British and Indian force (August 1–2, 1813). On yearly inspection tours as inspector general, Croghan gained a reputation for intoxication and gambling and was court-martialed in 1845.

Croix de Guerre • a French civilian and military honor consisting of a Maltese cross with superimposed crossed swords, instituted in 1915, and again in 1939. It was awarded to French soldiers and to soldiers of other armies for their services to France in WORLD WARS I AND II. The VICHY government issued a Croix de Guerre in 1941 that was later ruled to be invalid.

Crook, George (1828–90) • Union army officer, born near Taylorsville, Ohio. A prominent Union officer during the CIVIL WAR, Crook fought at ANTIETAM (1862), CHICKAMAUGA (1863), and in the SHENANDOAH VALLEY campaign (1864); he rose to the rank of brigadier general and commanded the cavalry of the ARMY OF THE POTOMAC from February 1865 until the end of the war. Crook's finest military accomplishment was in 1883, when he led Apache scouts and U.S. troops into Mexico to search for the Chiricahuas, the tribe of GERONIMO, who were raiding from their sanctuaries in the Sierra Madre. After one skirmish, Crook negotiated the Chiricahuas' peaceful return to the Arizona reservations. A fearsome Indian fighter, he also struggled repeatedly with the U.S. government to uphold its promises to the conquered tribes and urged civil rights and the franchise for Native Americans.

Gen. WILLIAM T. SHERMAN called Crook the greatest American Indian fighter, and the Oglala chief RED CLOUD said of Crook: "His words gave the people hope. He died. Their hope died again. Despair came again."

Crosby, John Schuyler (1839–1914) • military officer and government official, born in Albany County, New York. Crosby was an artillery officer in the CIVIL WAR, and a courier behind enemy lines, for which duty he was thanked by President ABRAHAM LINCOLN. Near the end of the war he joined PHILIP H. SHERIDAN's staff, as assistant inspector general of the Military Division.

After the war, Crosby was the U.S. consul at Florence, Italy (1876–82). As the territorial governor of Montana (1883–84), he worked to protect wildlife in Yellowstone National Park.

---

cross • *n.* a cross-shaped decoration awarded for personal valor: *the Military Cross.*

cross-beach attack • see AMPHIBIOUS ASSAULT.

crossfire • *n.* gunfire from two or more directions passing through the same area, often killing or wounding noncombatants: *a photographer was killed in the crossfire.*

cross guard • a guard on a sword or dagger consisting of a short transverse bar.

crosshairs • *plural n.* a pair of fine wires or lines crossing at right angles at the focus of a gun sight, for use in positioning, aiming, or measuring.

crossing the T • a maneuver in naval tactics in which, with both opposing fleets in column, one fleet succeeds in passing in front of the enemy column and perpendicular to it. In the age of sail and naval gunnery, "crossing the T" gave a decided advantage to the fleet achieving that maneuver in that it was thus able to bring to bear all its guns on the side toward the enemy whereas the enemy ships, being in column, could bring to bear few of their guns, the majority being masked by the friendly ships sailing before them in the column.

Cross Keys, Battle of • a minor CIVIL WAR battle on June 8, 1862, at Cross Keys, Virginia, in ANDREW JACKSON'S SHENANDOAH VALLEY CAMPAIGN. The Confederates were victorious.

crossover point • the range in the air warfare area at which a target ceases to be an air intercept target and becomes a surface-to-air missile target.

cross-posting |kraws; kräs 'pōstiNG| • *n.* the transfer of an officer to a different regiment.

crosstrees |'krôs,trēz| • *plural n.* a pair of horizontal struts attached to a sailing ship's mast to spread the rigging, especially at the head of a topmast.

Crowder, Enoch Herbert (1859–1932) • soldier, diplomat, and jurist, born in Grundy County, Missouri. As a cavalry officer during the SPANISH-AMERICAN WAR (1898), Crowder went to the Philippines as a judge advocate and helped to draw up the terms for Manila's surrender. In 1900 he became secretary to the military governor of the Philippines. He was the legal adviser to provisional government of Cuba (1906–08), and judge advocate general of the army (1911–23), with a rank of brigadier general. As judge advocate general, he streamlined the AMERICAN ARTICLES OF WAR and retooled the court-martial and penal system. Crowder was the first U.S. ambassador to Cuba (1923–27). As provost marshal general in WORLD WAR I, Crowder created and administered the SELECTIVE SERVICE SYSTEM, including 4,000 local draft boards. He drafted almost 3 million men, providing over 70 percent of the army's servicemen during the war.

Crowe, William J., Jr. (1925–) • admiral, chairman of the JOINT CHIEFS OF STAFF, and ambassador, born in Oklahoma City, Oklahoma. Crowe was the deputy director of the Office of the CHIEF OF NAVAL OPERATIONS, and the commander in chief of the U.S. Pacific Command (1983). Appointed chairman of JOINT CHIEFS OF STAFF by President RONALD REAGAN (1985–89), Crowe was the first JCS chairman to operate under the 1986 GOLDWATER-NICHOLS ACT, which mandated greater cooperation among the services and made the JCS chairman the principal military adviser to the United States. As JCS chairman, Crowe aided in decreasing U.S. Soviet rivalry toward the end of the COLD WAR. He developed military-to-military agreements and exchanges with his Soviet counterpart, and oversaw U.S. military operations in the Persian Gulf and Mediterranean.

Crown Point • a town on Lake Champlain, New York, that was the site the French fort Fort Frederic. It fell to British forces under Maj. Gen. JEFFREY AMHERST in 1759 in the FRENCH AND INDIAN WAR (1754–63). The British began a new fort, Fort Amherst (later named CROWN POINT). The fort was captured in May 1775 by the GREEN MOUNTAIN BOYS. It was finally abandoned in 1777 to Gen. JOHN BURGOYNE.

crow's-foot • *n.* (pl. **-feet**) a caltrop.

crow's-nest • *n.* a shelter or platform fixed near the top of the mast of a vessel as a place for a lookout to stand.

C.R.P. (or **CRP**) • *abbr.* crisis relocation planning.

cruise missile • a jet- and rocket-propelled guided missile with wings to take advantage of lift. It flies at low altitudes to avoid radar detection, is guided to its target by an onboard computer, and carries conventional or nuclear warheads.

cruiser |'kro͞ozər| • *n.* a relatively fast warship larger than a destroyer and less heavily armed than a battleship.

cruising level • a level maintained during a significant portion of a flight.

cruising range • the maximum distance a ship or aircraft can travel at a given speed without refueling.

crump |'krəmp| • *n.* a loud thudding sound, especially one made by an exploding bomb or shell. • *v.* make such a sound.

Crusader • (**F-8**) a powerful heavy supersonic fighter capable of operating from carrier decks because it had a variable incidence wing. Originally a fast day fighter, this aircraft enjoyed a long, successful career, performing effectively in the VIETNAM WAR. Later models had all-weather capability.

cryptanalysis • *n.* the steps and operations performed in converting encrypted messages into plain text without initial knowledge of the key employed in the encryption.
DERIVATIVES: **cryptanalytic** *adj.*

cryptography • *n.* the art of writing or solving codes.
DERIVATIVES: **cryptographer** *n.* **cryptographic** *adj.* **cryptographically** *adv.*

cryptology • *n.* the science which deals with hidden, disguised, or encrypted communications. Cryptology includes communications security and communications intelligence.

cryptomaterial • *n.* all material, including documents, devices, equipment, and apparatus, essential to the encryption, decryption, or authentication of telecommunications. When classified, cryptomaterial is designated CRYPTO and subject to special safeguards.

cryptonym |'kriptə,nim| • *n.* a code name.
DERIVATIVES: **cryptonymous** |krip 'tänəməs| *adj.*

cryptosecurity • *n.* the measures undertaken to create secure codes and ciphers and to protect encryption methods and systems from enemy discovery, interception, decryption, or tampering.

cryptosystem • *n.* the associated items of cryptomaterial (documents, devices, equipment, apparatus, etc., essential to the encryption, decryption, or authentication of telecommunications) that are used as a unit and provide a single means of encryption and decryption.

CSC • *abbr.* Civil Service Commission.

CSM • *abbr.* Brit. Company Sergeant Major.

CTR • *abbr.* Cooperative Threat Reduction.

Cuban Missile Crisis • a COLD WAR confrontation between the United States and the Soviet Union over the installation of ballistic missiles in Cuba. President JOHN F. KENNEDY, on learning of the installation of the missiles in 1962, considered an invasion, air strikes, or a naval blockade of Cuba. The blockade was implemented and diplomatic negotiations began between Kennedy and NIKITA KHRUSHCHEV. The Soviet leader agreed to remove the missiles, and the crisis was diffused. Many consider that it was the world's closest approach to nuclear war.

Cullum, George Washington (1809–92) • Union army officer and author, born in New York City. As chief of staff to HENRY W. HALLECK, the commanding general of the army, Cullum helped to handle his chief's correspondence and supported efforts to coordinate overall Union strategy during the CIVIL WAR. As the commandant of the U.S. MILITARY ACADEMY (1864–66), he compiled a monumental biographical register of its officers and graduates.

Culp's Hill • an important strategic position at GETTYSBURG (1863). Gen. RICHARD S. EWELL sent troops to capture part of the hill for the Confederates but was repulsed by GEORGE SEARS GREENE's troops. It was never taken and its successful defense was a factor in the Union victory.

culture • *n.* man-made features of the terrain, such as roads, buildings, and canals, as well as boundary lines and, in a broad sense, all names and legends on a map.

culverin • *n.* **1** a 16th- or 17th- century cannon with a relatively long barrel for its bore, typically about 10 to 13 feet long. **2** a kind of handgun of the 15th and 16th centuries.

***Cumberland*, CSS** • a Union steam sloop-of-war that was rammed and destroyed by the CSS *Virginia* after the USS *Congress* had fired on the *Virginia* during a CIVIL WAR naval battle at HAMPTON ROADS, Virginia on March 8, 1862. The *Cumberland* sank.

Cunningham, Alfred Austell (1882–1939) • U.S. Marine Corps officer and aviator, born in Atlanta, Georgia. Cunningham organized and commanded the 1st Marine Aviation Force, which flew forty-three missions in support of Allied ground troops (1918), and led bombing raids on German submarines. At the end of WORLD WAR I he became the main lobbyist for marine aviation; in 1920 Congress designated 1,020 marine personnel for aviation service.

Cunningham was the first marine corps officer assigned to aviation duty, and the date he reported to ANNAPOLIS (May 22, 1912) is considered the birthdate of marine aviation. By firmly attaching an aircraft component to the organization of the corps, Cunningham earned the title "Father of Marine Aviation."

cupola |ˈkyo͞opələ| • *n.* a gun turret; a small domed hatch above a gun turret on some tanks.

Current Force • the force that exists today. The Current Force represents actual force structure and/or manning available to meet present contingencies. It is the basis for operations and contingency plans and orders.

current intelligence • intelligence of all types and forms of immediate interest which is usually disseminated without the delays necessary to complete evaluation or interpretation.

curtain fire • (also **curtain of fire**) a wall of fire, a barrage of artillery falling vertically in massed concentration, intended to cut off the enemy's escape or reinforcement.

Curtis, Samuel Ryan (1805–66) • Union army officer and engineer, born near Champlain, New York. Curtis was adjutant general of Ohio's state militia during the the MEXICAN WAR (1846–48). Elected to Congress in 1856, he served on the COMMITTEE ON MILITARY AFFAIRS and promoted a transcontinental railroad. In the CIVIL WAR, Curtis was elected colonel of the 2nd Iowa Infantry and rose to the rank of major general of volunteers.

curve of pursuit • the curved path described by a fighter plane making an attack on a moving target while holding the proper aiming allowance.

Cushing, William Barker (1842–74) • Union naval officer, born in Delafield, Wisconsin. After being dismissed from the U.S. NAVAL ACADEMY, Cushing volunteered for blockade duty and rose from acting master's mate to flagship commander. On blockade duty off the Carolinas, he led daring and successful night raids behind enemy lines. He used a small boat and an improvised spar torpedo to destroy the powerful Confederate ironclad *Albemarle* at Plymouth, North Carolina, (October 27, 1864), and received the thanks of Congress at President ABRAHAM LINCOLN's request. At FORT FISHER, commanding the *Monticello*, Cushing led a charge over the parapet (January 15, 1865). Commanding the *Wyoming*, he landed at Santiago, Cuba, intervening to stop executions of crew of American steamer *Virginius* (1873).

Only weeks before his class was to graduate, Cushing's examination included the evaluation: "General conduct: bad. Aptitude for Naval Service: not good. Not recommended for continuance at the Academy."

Custer, George Armstrong (1839–76) • CIVIL WAR general and Indian fighter, born in New Rumley, Ohio. Custer established his fame during the CIVIL WAR as the youngest general in the Union army, famous for his cavalry charges, heedless bravery, flamboyance, and tactical brilliance. Made brigadier general at twenty-three, he fought with distinction at GETTYSBURG (1863) and his 1864 campaign to rid the SHENANDOAH VALLEY of Confederate forces catapulted him to military stardom. Among Union cavalry officers he was second only to Gen. PHILIP H. SHERIDAN. After the war "General" Custer served in the rank of lieutenant colonel of the 7th Cavalry (1866–76). After WINFIELD SCOTT HANCOCK's 1867 CHEYENNE campaign, Custer was court-martialed for misconduct in the field. He defeated BLACK KETTLE's Cheyennes at the Washita (November 1868), killing women and children. He explored the Black Hills (1874), setting off a gold rush. Custer's final campaign, during the GREAT SIOUX WAR of 1876, ended in the battle of the LITTLE BIGHORN on June 25, 1876 (known as "Custer's Last Stand"), where five companies under his immediate command—more than 200 officers and troopers—were wiped out by nearly 2,000 warriors.

custody • *n.* the responsibility for the control of, transfer and movement of, and access to, weapons and components. Custody also includes the maintenance of accountability for weapons and components.

cut • *n.* the point of intersection of two direction-finding lines of bearing.

cutlass • *n.* a short sword with a slightly curved blade, formerly used by sailors.

cutoff • *n.* the deliberate shutting off of a reaction engine.

cutoff attack • an attack that provides a direct vector from the interceptor's position to an intercept point with the target track.

cutoff velocity • the velocity attained by a missile at the point of cutoff.

cutter |ˈkət̬ər| • *n.* **1** a light, fast coastal patrol boat. **2** a ship's boat used for carrying light stores or passengers. **3** a small fore-and-aft-rigged sailing ship with one mast, more than one headsail, and a running bowsprit, used as a fast auxiliary.

cutwater |ˈkətˌwôt̬ər; -ˌwät̬ər| • *n.* **1** the forward edge of a ship's prow. **2** a wedge-shaped projection on the pier of a bridge, which divides the flow of water and prevents debris from becoming trapped against the pier.

CV • *abbr.* attack aircraft carrier.

CV-5 • see *Yorktown*, USS.

CV-14 • see *Ticonderoga*, USS.

CV-31 • see *Bon Homme Richard*, USS.

CV-33 • see *Kearsarge*, USS.

CV-45 • see *Valley Forge*, USS.

CVL-27 • see *Langley*, USS.

CVN • *abbr.* attack aircraft carrier, nuclear powered.

CWO • *abbr.* Chief Warrant Officer.

Dd

Dachau |ˈdäkow| • NAZI concentration camp in Germany, operating from March 10, 1933 to 1945. Of the at least 160,000 prisoners that were held in the main camp, at least 32,000 died there from disease, malnutrition, mistreatment, and Nazi medical experiments.

During WORLD WAR II the main camp, 12 miles north of Munich outside of the town of Dachau, was supplemented by 150 other camps throughout Austria and Germany. This system of camps was also called Dachau.

Dahlgren gun • any of various weapons developed by JOHN A.B. DAHLGREN of the U.S. Navy and used from the mid 19th century onwards, particularly in the CIVIL WAR. They are usually divided into three groups: boat howitzers and rifles, iron smoothbores, and iron rifles, and all were designed primarily for use against boats on inland waterways.

Dahlgren, John Adolphus Bernard (1809–70) • Union naval officer and ordnance manufacturer born in Philadelphia, Pennsylvania, noted for the successful siege of CHARLESTON (1861) during the CIVIL WAR and for the design of the DAHLGREN GUN, as well as other significant advances in ordnance.

daisy-cutter bomb • a large bomb that explodes above ground with a shock wave that forms a wide-area impact crater, typically used for clearing dense vegetation or against hard targets.

Dakota • (**C-47**) a transport aircraft used to carry troops and cargo, but capable of carrying out a variety of tasks. It has, for example, been used for navigation training, search-and-rescue, and counter-insurgency. Also called SKYTRAIN.

Most of the Dakotas still active today are in THIRD WORLD air forces.

Dakota II • see SKYTROOPER.

Dak To, Battle of • a battle in the Central Highlands of Vietnam in November 1967, one of the bloodiest of the war. It was an American victory, with more than a thousand fatalities on the North Vietnamese Army side, and casualties in the hundreds for the Americans.

Dale, Sir Thomas (?–1619) • English-born soldier who twice served as governor of the Virginia colony. Dale is credited with helping to bring order to the disease-plagued settlement and ensuring its continued existence.

Dale was instrumental in bringing about the marriage between Pocahontas and the Englishman John Rolfe that established a peace between settlers and Indians.

damage assessment • **1** the determination of the effect of attacks on targets. **2** a determination of the effect of a compromise of classified information on national security.

damage control • in naval usage, the measures necessary aboard ship to: **a** preserve and reestablish the ship's watertight integrity, stability, maneuverability, and offensive power. **b** control the ship's list and trim. **c** effect rapid repairs of materiel. **d** limit the spread of, and provide adequate protection from, fire. **e** limit the spread of, remove the contamination by, and provide adequate protection from, toxic agents. **f** provide for the care of wounded personnel.

damage estimation • a preliminary appraisal of the potential effects of an attack.

damage threat • the probability that a target ship passing once through a minefield will explode one or more mines and sustain a specified amount of damage.

Da Nang (or **Danang**) • the second-largest city in South Vietnam, and headquarters of the Republic of Vietnam I Corps Tactical Zone, a military zone. As a major port city with an airport capable of handling jets, it became an important logistical base for South Vietnamese and U.S. forces. The first U.S. combat units in Vietnam landed near Da Nang on March 8, 1965. During the war, refugees increased the city's population to about 500,000. Communist forces seized the city without a fight on March 29, 1975.

dan buoy |dæn bo͞o-ē; boi| • a temporary marker buoy used during minesweeping operations to indicate boundaries of swept paths, swept areas, known hazards, and other locations or reference points.

Danforth anchor • a type of stockless lightweight anchor with flat flukes.

danger area • **1** a specified area above, below, or within which there may be potential danger. **2** in air traffic control, an airspace of defined dimensions within which activities dangerous to the flight of aircraft may exist at specified times.

danger close • in artillery and naval gunfire support, the information given in a call for fire to indicate that friendly forces are within 600 meters of the target.

dangerous cargo • cargo that, because of its dangerous properties, is subject to special regulations for its transport.

Daniel, John Warwick (1842–1910) • Confederate army officer, U.S. senator, and legal scholar born in Lynchburg, Virginia. Daniel fought in several battles, including GETTYSBURG (1863). An accomplished orator, he was a champion of secession and white supremacy who came to be identified with the romantic version of the Old South.

Daniel was called the "Lame Lion of Lynchburg" because a wound received at the BATTLE OF THE WILDERNESS in 1864 put him on crutches for the rest of his life.

Daniels, Josephus (1862–1948) • born in Washington, North Carolina. A journalist and publisher committed to democratic principles and social reform, who, as naval secretary in President WOODROW WILSON's administration (1913–21), instituted important reforms in the U.S. Navy including the requirement of sea service for promotion, compulsory education for poorly educated seamen, and improvements in the quality of the U.S. NAVAL ACADEMY. FRANKLIN D. ROOSEVELT was Daniels's Assistant Secretary and, when Roosevelt became president, he appointed Daniels as his ambassador to Mexico. Daniels wrote a five-volume autobiography chronicling his experiences as a journalist and statesman.

dan runner • a ship running a line of dan buoys.

D'Aquino, Iva Toguri Ikoku • see TOKYO ROSE.

DAR • *abbr.* Daughters of the American Revolution.

Dariac • a province in the central highlands of Vietnam. Its capital, Ban Me Thuot, was attacked by VIETCONG forces on January 31, 1968, as part of the TET OFFENSIVE, and fighting swept across the province often. It was the scene of one of the final tests of the military will of the South Vietnamese government, when VIETCONG forces attacked the capital again and succeeded in capturing it. This convinced President NGUYEN VAN THIEU that the highlands could no longer be held and triggered a military and civilian withdrawal from the area, which soon turned into a frantic melee as the Vietcong followed up on their success.

DARPA • *abbr.* Defense Advanced Research Projects Agency.

dart • *n.* a target towed by a jet aircraft and fired at by fighter aircraft. Darts are used for training purposes only.

data link • the means of connecting one location to another for the purpose of transmitting and receiving data.

date line • short for international date line.

Daughters of the American Revolution • (**DAR**) a patriotic society in the United States, founded in 1890 with headquarters in Washington, D.C. It is active in the preservation and marking of historic places, and membership is open to women with one or more ancestors who were active in the REVOLUTIONARY WAR.

Daughters of the Confederacy • (**United Daughters of the Confederacy** or **UDC**) an organization composed of the descendants of those who served or supported the CONFEDERACY during the CIVIL WAR. Founded in Nashville, Tennessee, in 1894, it continued to be involved in public and educational causes long after the UNITED CONFEDERATE VETERANS organization, which excluded women, was defunct.

DAV • *abbr.* Disabled American Veterans.

Davidson, William Lee (c. 1746–81) • Revolutionary army officer born in Pennsylvania but reared in North Carolina. Davidson led militiamen in defending Charlotte against CHARLES CORNWALLIS.

Davidson County and Davidson College, both in North Carolina, as well as Davidson County in Tennessee, were named in his honor.

Davies, Henry Eugene, Jr. (1836–94) • Union army officer, captain in DURYÉE'S ZOUAVES, a prominent New York regiment, and later major in the 2nd New York Cavalry, which saw action during the SECOND BATTLE OF BULL RUN (1862) in the Army of Virginia. Davies served with distinction in post-GETTYSBURG engagements along the Rappahannock and Rapidan Rivers.

Davies was one of only a few nonprofessional soldiers to attain star rank in the cavalry in the East.

Davie, William Richardson (1756–1820) • English-born Revolutionary army officer who served as a captain of cavalry in the Carolinas, attaining the rank of colonel. Davie subsequently served in the North Carolina House of Commons and as governor of the state.

Davie was instrumental in the founding of the University of North Carolina and in recognition was awarded the first doctorate of laws granted by that institution.

Davis, Benjamin Oliver, Jr. (1912–) • U.S. army officer and aviator. Benjamin O. Davis, Jr. was born in Washington, D.C., the son of the first African-American general. He graduated from WEST POINT in 1936 as an infantryman, but he was among the first group of blacks admitted to pilot training in 1941, and became the first to make a solo flight. He organized and commanded the all-black 99th Fighter Squadron and 332rd Fighter Group, both which he led with distinction in European combat. After the war he served as chief of the fighter branch for the new U.S. Air Force, and in 1953 he took over the crack 51st Fighter-Interceptor Wing in Korea. He became the first black major general in 1959, and the first to get a third star in 1965. When he retired in 1970 he was deputy commander of the U.S. Strike Command. After retirement he served in a number of important government posts, including assistant secretary of transportation. In 1998 President BILL CLINTON promoted Davis to full general on the retired list.

Davis, Benjamin Oliver, Sr. (1877–1970) • U.S. army officer. Benjamin O. Davis Sr. was born in Washington, D.C., and saw his first military service as a first lieutenant in the 8th Infantry Volunteers in the SPANISH-AMERICAN WAR (1898). After mustering out, he immediately reenlisted as a private in the 9th Cavalry and began working his way through the ranks. He regained his commission in the Philippines in 1901. He spent most of his army career teaching at Wilberforce or Tuskegee, until he took command of the 369th New York NATIONAL GUARD infantry regiment in 1938. Two years later his promotion as the first African-American brigadier general caused some controversy, since many saw it as a political maneuver by President FRANKLIN D. ROOSEVELT a month before the election. Davis was commanding a brigade of the 2nd Cavalry Division when he retired in June 1941, but he was soon recalled to active duty to serve with the inspector general's office. During WORLD WAR II he served in Europe as an adviser on race relations. He retired again in 1948 after fifty years of service.

Davis, Charles Henry (1807–77) • naval officer and hydrographer born in Boston, Massachusetts. Davis directed the compilation of the *American Ephemeris and Nautical Almanac* (first volume, 1852) and authored important articles of scientific scholarship on the laws of tidal action. Through his hydrographic knowledge he made a significant contribution to the capture of PORT ROYAL, South Carolina (1861). After the war Davis became superintendent of the NAVAL OBSERVATORY, leaving that position temporarily to serve as commander of the Norfolk Navy Yard (1870-73).

Davis's translation of, and additional notes on, Charles Marie Philippes de Kerhallet's *General Examination of the Pacific Ocean* (1851), first published in 1861, became the standard book on navigating the Pacific.

Davis, Jefferson (1808?–89) • president of the CONFEDERATE STATES OF AMERICA and U.S. senator, born in Christian (later Todd) County, Kentucky but reared largely in Mississippi. Davis studied at WEST POINT (1824–28), where he was noted more for his escapades than for his academic achievements and barely escaped dismissal. Davis saw little or no action during his first years in the infantry. Dissatisfied with the verdict in a court-martial for insubordination, Davis resigned from the army (1835). After several years farming on his brother's Mississippi plantation, he entered politics and was elected to Congress (1845), where he became a strict states' rightist. His exploits during the MEXICAN WAR (1846–48), in which he played a prominent role in the capture of MONTERREY (1846) and in repelling an attack by ANTONIO LÓPEZ DE SANTA ANNA at the BATTLE OF BUENA VISTA (1847) (in which he was wounded), made him a military hero in Mississippi. Appointed to the U.S. Senate in 1847, he spoke out strongly in favor of expansionism and in defense of slavery, fiercely opposing the COMPROMISE OF 1850. After resigning from the Senate and unsuccessfully running for governor, Davis became secretary of war in the administration of President FRANKLIN PIERCE, where he was considered competent and hard-working and acted as an influential pro-Southern voice. He reentered the Senate in 1857, where he was a voice of moderation in working for State's rights within the union and he did not favor immediate secession when President ABRAHAM LINCOLN was elected in 1860. His moderation during the secession crisis helped make him an attractive choice for president of the Confederate States once the dissolution of the UNION became reality. In pursuing his goal of independence for the South, Davis built a powerful central government, insisting that state troops be merged into one military body. He obtained extensive power over railroads and shipping, encouraged industries, and procured materials through impressment. As president of the Confederate States, Davis obtained a power then unprecedented in American history: the power to conscript men to fight. Though he labored over the details of military planning and support, he did not meddle excessively with commanders in the field. His style of leadership, however, and neglect of the common people's suffering, hampered his ability to counter problems of morale. More committed to independence than to the maintenance of slavery, late in the war he proposed arming and freeing the South's slaves. After the war Davis was imprisoned for two years. Though defeated, he remained an unrepentant Confederate throughout his life.

Davis was briefly married to Sarah Knox Taylor, the daughter of President ZACHARY TAYLOR. She died within three months of their marriage in 1835.

Davis, Jefferson Columbus (1828–79) • Union army officer and member of the garrison of FORT SUMTER when its bombardment initiated the CIVIL WAR (1861). Davis left the regular army when he was appointed colonel of an Indiana volunteer regiment. He played a key role in securing the Union victory at PEA RIDGE (1862). He was a division commander in the battles of STONES RIVER (1862–63), CHICKAMAUGA, and CHATTANOOGA (both 1863).

Davis's military successes were severely clouded by two unfortunate incidents: his mortal wounding of Maj. Gen WILLIAM NELSON, by whom he believed he had been insulted while under his command—an offense for which he was never court-martialed (1862); and his destruction of a pontoon bridge during SHERMAN'S MARCH TO THE SEA (1864–65), stranding black refugees who, fearful of the pursuing Confederate cavalry, drowned in their attempt to swim across the creek.

davit |ˈdævit; ˈdā-| • *n.* a small crane on board a ship, especially one of a pair for suspending or lowering a lifeboat.

Davy Jones's locker • informal the bottom of the sea, especially regarded as the grave of those drowned at sea.
ORIGIN: extension of early 18th-century nautical slang *Davy Jones*, denoting the evil spirit of the sea.

day fighter • a fighter aircraft designed for air interception purposes, primarily in visual meteorological conditions. It may or may not carry electronic devices to assist in interception and in aiming its weapons.

Dayton Accords • peace agreements initialed at WRIGHT-PATTERSON AFB in Dayton, Ohio, on November 21, 1995, by the three Balkan presidents. They were signed in Paris on December 14, 1995. Negotiated with the assistance of President BILL CLINTON and other members of the UNITED NATIONS, they established an international peacekeeping force in BOSNIA-HERZEGOVINA to end fighting in the region. They also sought to protect the return of refugees and the conduct of free local elections to establish a new republic in that region.

Dayton, Jonathan (1760–1824) • REVOLUTIONARY WAR officer, born in Elizabethtown (now Elizabeth), New Jersey. Dayton saw action at BRANDYWINE and GERMANTOWN (1777), at MONMOUTH (1778), and at the siege of YORKTOWN (1781). On the 1779 expedition against the IROQUOIS in New York, he served as aide-de-camp to Gen. JOHN SULLIVAN. After leaving the army in 1783, Dayton served several terms in the New Jersey state legislature, as well as in both the U.S. House (1791–99), including two terms as speaker, and Senate (1799–1805). Dayton was not yet sixteen when he was commissioned in the Continental army; during the war he served in two New Jersey regiments, both of which were commanded by his father.

Dayton, Ohio, settled in 1796, was named for Jonathan Dayton, who received a land grant along the Ohio River.

dazzle • *n.* temporary loss of vision or a temporary reduction in visual acuity. See also FLASH BLINDNESS.

DC-3 • see SKYTROOPER.

DC-4 • see SKYMASTER.

DCI • *abbr.* Director of Central Intelligence; the senior executive officer of the CENTRAL INTELLIGENCE AGENCY, responsible by law for coordinating U.S. intelligence activities.

DCM • *abbr.* Distinguished Conduct Medal.

DD-731 • see *Maddox*, USS.

D-Day • **1** see D-DAY LANDING. **2** the day on which an important operation is to begin or a change to take effect.
ORIGIN: from *D* for 'day' + *day*.

D-Day Landing • (June 6, 1944) the day the Allied Forces staged the largest amphibious attack in history, landing on the beaches of NORMANDY. Nearly 175,000 American, Canadian, and British troops landed, supported by 6,000 aircraft and 6,000 naval vessels. The object of the attack was to win a beachhead in France in order to open a second front against ADOLF HITLER'S armies and to use the beachhead as a springboard for the liberation of France and Belgium, and the eventual conquest of NAZI Germany. There were nearly 5,000 Allied casualties, nearly half of them at OMAHA BEACH.

DDG • *abbr.* guided missile destroyer.

DEA • *abbr.* Drug Enforcement Administration.

deactivate • *v.* make (something, typically technical equipment of a virus) inactive by disconnecting or destroying it: *the switch deactivates the alarm.*
DERIVATIVES: **deactivation** *n.* **deactivator** *n.*

deadeye • *n.* **1** a circular wooden block with a groove around the circumference to take a lanyard, used singly or in pairs to tighten a shroud. **2** informal an expert marksman.

dead letter • a law or treaty that has not been repealed but is ineffectual or defunct in practice.

deadlight |'ded,lit| • *n.* a protective cover or shutter fitted over a porthole or window on a ship.

dead reckoning |'ded 'rek(ə)niNG| • the process of calculating one's position, especially at sea, by estimating the direction and distance traveled rather than by using landmarks, astronomical observations, or electronic navigation methods.

dead space • **1** an area within the maximum range of a weapon, radar, or observer, that cannot be covered by fire or observation from a particular position because of intervening obstacles, the nature of the ground, the characteristics of the trajectory, or the limitations of the pointing capabilities of the weapons. **2** an area or zone that is within range of a radio transmitter, but in which a signal is not received. **3** the volume of space above and around a gun or guided missile system into which it cannot fire because of mechanical or electronic limitations.

dead weight (also **deadweight**) • the total weight of cargo, stores, etc., that a ship carries or can carry at a particular draft.

Dearborn, Henry (1751–1829) • REVOLUTIONARY WAR army officer and politician, born in Hampton, New Hampshire. Dearborn took an active role in some of the major engagements of the Revolution, including the battles of LEXINGTON (1775), CONCORD (1775), BUNKER HILL (1776), SARATOGA (1777), and YORKTOWN (1781), rising in rank to lieutenant colonel. Dearborn was appointed secretary of war by President THOMAS JEFFERSON in 1801, and senior major general of the U.S. Army by President JAMES MADISON in 1812, but he lacked knowledge of military strategy and his leadership during the WAR OF 1812 was ineffective and largely unsuccessful.

death camp • a prison camp, especially one for political prisoners or prisoners of war, in which many die from poor conditions and treatment or from mass execution.

death march • any forced march under conditions likely to result in the death of some of the participants, especially a march of prisoners of war, and most particularly the 65-mile forced march from Mariveles to San Fernando made by the some 78,000 U.S. and Filipino troops who surrendered to the Japanese on Bataan Peninsula in April 1942 (the BATAAN DEATH MARCH).

death squad • an armed paramilitary group formed to kill particular people, especially political opponents.

De Brahm, William Gerard (1718–99?) • surveyor, cartographer, and military engineer, born in Koblenz, Germany. De Brahm settled in Georgia but remained a LOYALIST all his life. De Brahm was responsible for design and construction of fortifications for Charleston, South Carolina, and Savannah. He surveyed and mapped the eastern coast of Florida, including detailed descriptions of its flora and fauna; these maps and reports have proved accurate and valuable to the present day. His observations on the Gulf Stream current helped accelerate voyages from the Colonies to Europe, and his maps played an important role in the REVOLUTIONARY WAR.

De Brahm embraced Quakerism later in life and abandoned all scientific and geographic pursuits. Afterwards his writings were exclusively of a religio-philosophical bent, dealing with biblical themes and revelations.

---

decapitate • *v.* to damage an enemy's chain of command by killing its leaders.

decapitating attack • a deep assault behind the lines against the enemy commanders that bypasses the forces between the front and enemy headquarters.

Decatur, Stephen (1752–1808) • merchant ship captain, naval officer, and privateer born in Newport, Rhode Island, but primarily associated with Philadelphia, where he spent most of his life. As a privateer Decatur made a number of valuable captures during the REVOLUTIONARY WAR. Later, as a captain in the U.S. Navy, Decatur made the first capture of the QUASI-WAR WITH FRANCE (1798). After the war he was engaged in the manufacture of gunpowder, which he supplied to the navy.

Decatur, Stephen (1779–1820) • U.S. naval officer, born in Sinepuxent, Maryland. Decatur attended the University of Pennsylvania before joining a merchant shipping firm as a clerk. In 1798, he obtained a midshipman's warrant and sailed for the West Indies with Captain JOHN BARRY aboard the USS *United States* to hunt for French shipping. He was promoted to lieutenant in 1799 and distinguished himself during the BARBARY WAR (1801–05), notably in sailing the captured Tripolitan ketch *Mastico*, renamed the USS *Intrepid*, into Tripoli harbor on February 16, 1804, in order to set fire to the USS *Philadelphia* which had run aground there. For this daring twenty-minute action Decatur was promoted to Captain, the youngest person to hold that rank up to that time. He subsequently commanded in turn the USS *Constitution*, the USS *Congress*, a gunboat flotilla in the Chesapeake Bay, the frigate USS *Chesapeake*, and the USS *United States*. His greatest naval victory came as commander of the USS *United States* during the WAR OF 1812. On station between the Azores and the Canary Islands on October 25, 1812, Decatur engaged the thirty-eight-gun British frigate HMS *Macedonian*. The superior guns of the

United States and Decatur's seamanship led to the surrender of the *Macedonian*. Forced to keep to harbor during 1813–1814, Decatur put to sea on January 14, 1815, in command of the USS *President*, but after an extended battle with four British warships, the *President* was captured and its captain and crew were interned in Bermuda. Decatur was later absolved of responsibility and served with distinction in operations in the Mediterranean against the dey of Algiers. From 1815 to his death, Stephen Decatur served on the BOARD OF NAVY COMMISSIONERS and was a prominent member of Washington society. In 1820 he was killed near Bladensburg, Maryland, in a duel with James Barron, a former naval officer on whose court-martial Decatur had served in 1808.

deception • *n.* those measures designed to mislead the enemy by manipulation, distortion, or falsification of evidence.

deck • *n.* a structure of planks or plates, approximately horizontal, extending across a ship or boat at any of various levels, especially one of those at the highest level and open to the weather: *he stood on the deck of his flagship.*
PHRASES: **on deck** on or onto a ship's main deck: *she stood on deck for hours.*
DERIVATIVES: **decked** *adj.*: *a three-decked vessel.*

deck beam • a horizontal beam supporting a ship's deck.

deckhand • *n.* a member of a ship's crew whose duties include maintenance of hull, decks, and superstructure; mooring, and cargo handling.

deckhead • *n.* the underside of the deck of a ship.

deckhouse • *n.* a superstructure on the deck of a ship or boat, used primarily to house equipment or for storage, or (formerly) for accomodations.

deckie (also **decky**) • *n.* informal short for DECKHAND.

Declaration of Independence • a U.S. document adopted by the Continental Congress on July 4, 1776, during the REVOLUTIONARY WAR, to announce the separation of the American colonies from Britain. It included charges against the crown and Parliament for violations against the colonists, and it was the first formal document affirming a people's right to a government of their own choice. Written predominately by THOMAS JEFFERSON, it asserted "that all men are created equal, that they are endowed by their Creator with certain unalienable Rights, that among these are Life, Liberty and the pursuit of Happiness."

On only twelve of the thirteen colonies voted unanimously to approve the declaration. New York's delegation lacked permission to act and had to abstain until July 15.

Declaration of Moscow • a conference in October 1943 where U.S. President FRANKLIN D. ROOSEVELT, British Prime Minister WINSTON CHURCHILL, and Soviet premier JOSEF STALIN signed the Declaration Concerning Atrocities. It asserted that those responsible for atrocities committed during WORLD WAR II would be "judged and punished according to the laws" of the countries in which the acts were committed.

declaration of war • an announcement stating that a state of war exists between two countries.

declassification • *n.* the determination that in the interests of national security, classified information no longer requires any degree of protection against unauthorized disclosure, coupled with removal or cancellation of the classification designation.

declassify • *v.* to cancel the security classification of an item of classified matter. See also DOWNGRADE.

decompression |ˌdēkəmˈpreSHən| • *n.* a release of compressing forces, in particular: **a** reduction in air pressure: *decompression of the aircraft cabin.* **b** a gradual reduction of air pressure on a person who has been experiencing high pressure while diving in order to prevent decompression sickness.

decompression chamber • a small room in which the air pressure can be varied, used chiefly to allow deep-sea divers to adjust gradually to normal air pressure.

decoy • *n.* an imitation in any sense of a person, object, or phenomenon, the intention of which is to deceive enemy surveillance devices or mislead enemy evaluation. Also called DUMMY.

decoy ship • a ship disguised as a noncombatant vessel, with its armament and fighting equipment hidden, but capable of unmasking and using its weapons quickly. Also called Q-SHIP.

decrypt • *v.* convert encrypted text into its equivalent plain text by means of a cryptosystem.
DERIVATIVES: **decryption** *n.*

deep |dēp| • *adj.* in a specified number of ranks one behind another: *they were standing three-deep.* • *n.* (usually **deeps**) a deep part of the sea: *the* dark and *menacing deeps.*

DEF • *abbr.* Disarmed Enemy Forces.

defaulter • *n.* chiefly Brit. a member of the armed forces guilty of a military offense.

DEFCON |ˈdefkän| • *abbr.* defense readiness conditions. A uniform system of progressive alert postures for use between the chairman of the JOINT CHIEFS OF STAFF and the commanders of unified and specified commands and for use by the Services. Defense readiness conditions are graduated to match situations of varying military severity: DEFCON V is normal, peacetime readiness. DEFCON IV is normal, with increased intelligence and strengthened security measures. DEFCON III is an increase in force readiness above normal readiness. DEFCON II is a further increase in force readiness, but less than maximum readiness. DEFCON I is maximum force readiness.

defense |dəˈfens; dēˈfens; ˈd;ēˌfens;| (Brit. **defence**) • *n.* **1** the action of defending from or resisting attack: *methods of defense against this kind of attack they relied on missiles for the* *country's defense.* **2** military measures or resources for protecting a country: *the minister of defense.* **3 a** a means of protecting something from attack: *the base is one of the main defenses of Moscow.* **4** (**defenses**) fortifications or barriers against attack: *German defenses were sited in depth all along the ridge.*

Defense Advanced Research Projects Agency • (**DARPA**) Also called **Advanced Research Projects Agency** (ARPA) an agency of the DEPARTMENT OF DEFENSE established on February 7, 1958, as the first U.S. response to the Soviet Union's launch of SPUTNIK, and charged with maintaining the United States's lead in developing and applying state-of-the-art technologies to military capabilities. Originally called the ADVANCED RESEARCH PROJECTS AGENCY (ARPA), the name was changed on March 23, 1972, to the Defense Advanced Research Projects Agency (DARPA) and it became a separate defense agency under the secretary of defense. President BILL CLINTON renamed the agency as the Advanced Research Projects Agency on February 22, 1993, in his strategy paper, "Technology for America's Economic Growth, A New Direction to Build Economic Strength." On February 10, 1996, Public Law 104–106, under Title IX of the Fiscal Year 1996 DEFENSE AUTHORIZATION ACT, the agency's name was changed back to Defense Advanced Research Projects Agency. Although the Agency reports directly to the secretary of defense, it is independent of the military research and development establishment and was intended to provide a challenge to conventional military thinking and approaches. The DoD, understanding the value of an independent R&D group that investigates ideas and approaches considered too risky by the traditional R&D establishment, has protected the organization from outside influences, and the freedom to act quickly has paid well in terms of revolutionary military abilities.

defense area • for any particular command, the area extending from the forward edge of the battle area to its rear boundary. It is here that the decisive defensive battle is fought.

Defense, Department of • a central military organization created by Congress in 1947, and given its present name in 1949. At the end of WORLD WAR II, the U.S. government decided that a central military organization was needed at the national and major command levels. In 1947, Congress created a civilian position with cabinet rank, secretary of defense; a new department, the NATIONAL MILITARY ESTABLISHMENT, the Air Force and its own department; and it made the WAR DEPARTMENT the DEPARTMENT OF THE ARMY, and put all three armed services under the new secretary's control. In 1949, a further effort to centralize authority resulted in an amendment to the original act that made the new agency an executive department, renamed it the Department of Defense, and withdrew the cabinet-level status of the three military secretaries.

Defense Distinguished Service Medal • U.S. military decoration awarded for "exceptionally meritorious service to the Government in a duty of great responsibility" while serving in a joint service activity. The Defense Distinguished Service Medal may be awarded to persons serving with any branch of the DEPARTMENT OF DEFENSE.

defense-in-depth • the siting of mutually supporting defense positions designed to absorb and progressively weaken attack, prevent initial observations of the whole position by the enemy, and to allow the commander to maneuver his reserve.

Defense Intelligence Agency • (**DIA**) established in October 1961 by President JOHN F. KENNEDY's secretary of defense, ROBERT S. MCNAMARA, on the basis of the report by the Joint Study Group, which sought more effective ways of organizing U.S. intelligence activities. After WORLD WAR II, each of the three military departments collected, produced, and dispersed intelligence, a system characterized by needlessly duplicated effort, and ineffective and expensive as well. Since its establishment, the DIA has filled a critical need for a central intelligence organization for the military and other policymakers.

Defense Language Institute Foreign Language Center • (DLIFLC) a school for foreign language instruction and testing for DEPARTMENT OF DEFENSE personnel. Established in 1847, at the Presidio in Monterey, California, 125 miles south of San Francisco. Some 3,000 military and 1,300 civilian personnel are assigned to the DLIFLC and its supporting activities.

Defense Meteorological Satellite Program • a joint satellite system managed by the U.S. Air Force that provides weather and meteorological data for military use to the Air Force, Navy, and other military users.

Defense Monitor, The • periodical publication since 1972 of the CENTER FOR DEFENSE INFORMATION, Washington, D.C., dealing with defense and security matters; published ten to twelve times per year.

Defense Production Act of 1950 • a law passed on September 8, 1950, during the KOREAN WAR, to expand production and secure economic stability in the United States. It included provisions on inflation and stabilization, rent control, agricultural prices, defense mobilization, and taxes and appropriations for defense use. It established the Joint Committee on Defense Production to supervise the act's implementation.

defense readiness conditions • see DEFCON.

Defense Reorganization Acts • a series of acts passed by Congress to amend the NATIONAL SECURITY ACT of 1947, which attempted to unify the armed forces in the DEPARTMENT OF DEFENSE. The Acts included the ARMY REORGANIZATION ACT OF 1950 and the Defense Reorganization Acts of 1953 and 1958. The GOLDWATER-NICHOLS ACT was passed in 1986 as the most comprehensive revision since the 1947 act.

Defense Support Program • U.S. DEPARTMENT OF DEFENSE ultra-sensitive satellite early-warning system designed to detect the launch of ICBMs or SLBMs and to relay warning data to the North American Air Defense (NORAD) command center and to the STRATEGIC AIR COMMAND.

Defense Transportation System • U.S. DEPARTMENT OF DEFENSE system for coordinating routine requirements for military sealift, airlift, and ground transportation. When an overseas deployment is ordered, the air, ground, and ocean shipping is coordinated by the Department of Defense Transportation Command.

defensive fire • fire delivered by supporting units to assist and protect a unit engaged in a defensive action.

defensive mine countermeasures • countermeasures intended to reduce the effect of enemy minelaying.

defensive minefield • **1** in naval-mine warfare, a minefield laid in international water or international straits with the declared intention of controlling shipping in defense of sea communications. **2** in land-mine warfare, a minefield laid in accordance with an established plan to prevent a penetration between positions and to strengthen the defense of the positions themselves.

defensive sea area • a sea area (usually including the approaches to and the waters of important ports, harbors, bays, or sounds) for the control and protection of shipping, for the safeguarding of defense installations bordering on waters of the areas, and for the provision of other security measures required within the specified areas. It does not extend seaward beyond territorial waters.

defensive zone • a belt of terrain, generally parallel to the front, that includes two or more organized, or partially organized, battle positions.

defilade |ˌdefə'lād; 'defəˌlād| • *n.* the protection of a position, vehicle, or troops against enemy observation or gunfire. • *v.* protect (a position, vehicle, or troops) against enemy observation or gunfire.

defoliant |dē'fōlēənt| • *n.* a chemical that removes the leaves from trees and plants and is often used in warfare.

defoliant operation • the employment of defoliating agents on vegetated areas in support of military operations.

defoliate • *v.* remove leaves from (a tree, plant, or area of land) as a military tactic: *the area was defoliated and napalmed many times.*
DERIVATIVES: **defoliation** *n.*

de Gaulle, Charles (1890–1970) • French general and statesman who organized the Free French movement while exiled in London during the German occupation of France in WORLD WAR II. He was the head of government from 1944 to 1946 and again rose to power with the civil war in Algeria in 1958 and became first president of the Fifth Republic (1959–69). During his tenure France withdrew from NATO (1966).

degauss |dē'gows| • *v.* (**degaussing**) neutralize the magnetic field of (a ship) by encircling it with a conductor carrying electric currents.
DERIVATIVES: **degausser** |dē'gowsər| *n.*

degrade • *v.* **1** reduce (someone) to a lower rank, especially as a punishment. **2** break down or deteriorate chemically: *when exposed to light, the materials will degrade.*
DERIVATIVES: **degradability** *n.* **degradable** *adj.* **degradative** *adj.* **degrader** *n.*

degree of nuclear risk • (also **degree of risk**) as specified by the commander, the risk to which friendly forces may be subjected from the effects of the detonation of a nuclear weapon used in the attack of a close-in enemy target. Acceptable degrees of risk under differing tactical conditions are *emergency*, *moderate*, and *negligible*.

Delafield, Richard (1798–1873) • army officer, born in New York City. Delafield worked on fortification projects for the defense of HAMPTON ROADS, Virginia, supervised fortifications below New Orleans, and oversaw navigational improvements on the Mississippi and Ohio Rivers. Delafield was twice superintendent of the U.S. MILITARY ACADEMY (1838–1845; 1856–1861), and was known for tightening discipline and for architectural and program improvements. Too old for active field duty during the CIVIL WAR, Delafield first served as an advisor to the New York state government on the mobilization of its volunteers and later as supervisor of coast defenses in New York Harbor.

delaying action • action taken to gain time, especially a military engagement that delays the advance of an enemy.

deliberate attack • a type of offensive action characterized by the preplanned coordinated employment of firepower and the maneuver to close with and destroy or capture the enemy.

deliberate breaching • the creation of a lane through a minefield or a clear route through a barrier or fortification, which is systematically planned and carried out.

deliberate defense • a defense normally organized when out of contact with the enemy, or when contact with the enemy is not imminent and time for organization is available. It normally includes an extensive fortified zone incorporating pillboxes, forts, and communications systems. Compare with HASTY DEFENSE.

Delta Force • an elite military force whose main responsibilities are rescue operations and special forces work.

delta wing • the triangular swept-back wing that is frequently a feature of military aircraft. It was first developed in the 1930s by the German Dr. Alexander Lippisch and was test-flown with Convair's experimental XF-92A in 1948.

Demarcation Line of 1954 • a provisional military line dividing Vietnam at the 17TH PARALLEL and extending a demilitarized zone for 3 miles along each side. Established as a temporary line of demarcation by the GENEVA AGREEMENT ON INDOCHINA, it became the permanent political boundary between North and South Vietnam.

demilitarize • *v.* **1** (**demilitarized**) remove all military forces from (an area): *a demilitarized zone.* **2** remove the militaristic culture or character from: *we have to demilitarize both our economy and our mentality.*
DERIVATIVES: **demilitarization** *n.*

demilitarized zone • a defined area in which the stationing, or concentrating of military forces, or the retention or establishment of military installations of any description, is prohibited.

demob • *v.* see DEMOBILIZE.

demobilize |dēˈmōbəˌlīz| • *v.* **1** (usually **be demobilized**) take (troops) out of active service, typically at the end of a war: *he was demobilized in February 1946.* **2** cease military operations: *Germany demanded that they demobilize within twelve hours.*
DERIVATIVES: **demobilization** *n.*

Democratic party • one of the two main political parties in the United States, the other being the Republican party, which follows a broadly liberal program, tending to support social reform and minority rights.

demolition • *n.* the destruction of structures, facilities, or material by use of fire, water, explosives, or mechanical or other means.

demolition belt • a selected land area sown with explosive charges, mines, and other available obstacles to deny use of the land to enemy operations, and as a protection to friendly troops. A (**primary demolition belt**) is a continuous series of obstacles across the whole front, selected by the division or higher commander. The preparation of such a belt is normally a priority engineer task. A (**subsidiary demolition belt**) is a supplement to the primary belt. Its function is to give depth in front or behind or to protect the flanks.

demolition guard • a local force positioned to ensure that a target is not captured by an enemy before orders are given for its demolition and before the demolition has been successfully fired.

denial • *n.* the act of hindering or denying the enemy the use of space, personnel, or facilities. Denial measures may include destruction, removal, contamination, or erection of obstructions.

denuclearize |dēˈn(y)o͝okliəˌrīz| • *v.* remove nuclear weapons from: *the United States said it would denuclearize most of its naval vessels.*
DERIVATIVES: **denuclearization** *n.*

Denver, James William (1817–92) • territorial governor of Kans as and Union army officer. Denver served a brief stint as captain of a volunteer regiment during the MEXICAN WAR (1846–48). He served in the state senate and in 1854 was elected to the U.S. House of Representatives, where he sat on the MILITARY AFFAIRS COMMITTEE. During the CIVIL WAR he saw duty in Kansas and with the ARMY OF THE TENNESSEE, where he commanded a brigade in the march on CORINTH (1862).

When gold was discovered in a section of Kansas that is now Colorado (1858), Denver sent a party to the site. The town they named for him is now the capital of Colorado.

Denys de la Ronde, Louis |ˈdenis də lä ˈränd| (1675–1741) • French military officer, spy, and explorer, born in Québec City, Canada. He was a member of expeditions that established the colony of Louisiana. Denys de la Ronde served on several voyages along the coast of New England, and his familiarity with the area and command of English led to his role as a French spy during the WAR OF THE SPANISH SUCCESSION (1701–13). He sailed into Boston to gather information on the British, but was found out and condemned to death, escaping through the intervention of the governor.

Department of Defense Reorganization Act of 1986 • see GOLDWATER-NICHOLS ACT.

Department of Defense • see DEFENSE, DEPARTMENT OF.

Department of Energy • see ENERGY, DEPARTMENT OF.

Department of the Army • see ARMY, DEPARTMENT OF THE.

Department of the Navy • see NAVY, DEPARTMENT OF THE.

Department of Veterans Affairs • see VETERANS AFFAIRS, DEPARTMENT OF.

departure |diˈpärCHər| • *n.* the amount of a ship's change of longitude.

Dependent Pension Act of 1890 • an act passed by Congress on June 27, 1890, to provide a pension for any CIVIL WAR veteran of the Union Army. Created in response to political pressure from Union veterans, many of whom were members of the GRAND ARMY OF THE REPUBLIC, it also provided a pension to a soldier's widow under certain conditions.

depleted uranium ordnance • (**DU**) weapons, antitank missiles, shells, and bullets whose tips are made of depleted uranium, a byproduct of enriched uranium that is an especially hard and dense metal, to increase their ability to penetrate armor. On impact, DU shells can be pulverized into a toxic radioactive dust, and the munitions have been linked with deaths from leukemia and with other illnesses.

During OPERATION ALLIED FORCE in the spring of 1999, American attack jets fired some 31,000 rounds of DU shells at Serbian targets in Kosovo, Serbia, and Montenegro. About 10,000 rounds were fired in Bosnia from 1994 to 1995.

---

deploy • *v.* **1** move (troops) into position for military action: *forces were deployed at strategic locations.* **2** (of troops) move into position for such action: *the air force began to deploy forward.*
DERIVATIVES: **deployment** *n.*

depot |ˈdeˌpō ˈdēˌpō| • *n.* **1** a place for the storage of large quantities of equipment, food, or some other commodity: *an arms depot.* **2** the headquarters of a regiment; a place where recruits or other troops are assembled: *only conscripts who lived near a training depot had permission to commute to it.*

depower • *v.* adjust or alter (a sail) so that the wind no longer fills it.

depth charge (also **depth bomb**) • an explosive charge designed to be dropped from a ship or aircraft and to explode under water at a preset depth, used for attacking submarines.

depth finder • an echo sounder or other device for measuring water depth, especially for navigation and fishing.

depth sounder • another term for echo sounder.

Derby, George Horatio (1823–61) • military engineer, born in Dedham, Massachusetts. Derby spent most of his career on the Pacific Coast, where he mapped the mining country and the lower Colorado River, oversaw construction of a dam in San Diego, and led road-building expeditions to Fort Vancouver and the Oregon Territory.

During his lifetime Derby was a well-known literary figure and frontier humorist. Collections of his sketches, published as *Phoenixiana* and *The Squibob Papers*, remained popular throughout the 19th century.

de-rig |dē'rig| • *v.* dismantle the rigging of (a ship, boat, or light aircraft).

desert |də'zərt dē'zərt| • *v.* (of a soldier) illegally run away from military service. *his life in the army had been such a hell that he decided to desert.*

DERIVATIVES: **desertion** *n.*

deserter |də'zərdər dē'zərdər| • *n.* a member of the armed forces who deserts: *deserters from the army.*

Desert Fox, Operation • an operation begun late in 1998 against military and security targets in Iraq. Carried out jointly by the United States and Britain, its goals were to degrade Iraq's ability to make and to use weapons of mass destruction and to punish Saddam Hussein for violating international obligations.

Desert One • the site of a failed mission in April 1980 to rescue American hostages held in the U.S. Embassy in Teheran. The mission, to have been carried out by the elite DELTA FORCE, went disastrously wrong when three of its aircraft failed and two others were destroyed by colliding in flight near the staging post for the mission in the Iranian desert south of Teheran.

desert rat • **1** a soldier serving in a desert campaign such as the PERSIAN GULF WAR. **2** informal a soldier of the 7th British armored division (with the jerboa as a badge) in the North African desert campaign of 1941–2.

Desert Rock • a set of training exercises for nuclear battle conducted in the Nevada dessert between 1951 and 1957. Military personnel participating in the exercises received doses of radiation, some of them excessive.

Desert Shield, Operation • the multinational buildup of forces in the PERSIAN GULF that began in August 1990, immediately after Iraq's invasion of KUWAIT. Its immediate purpose was to protect Saudi Arabia against attack, with a longer-range goal of preparedness for war with Iraq. About 500,000 troops participated.

Desert Storm, Operation • the multinational bombing campaign against Iraq, beginning in January 1991, after Iraq had failed to meet the demands of a U.N. resolution that it withdraw from KUWAIT. The operation was under the general command of NORMAN SCHWARZKOPF and sought to disable Iraq's war-making ability by systematically destroying its military and support infrastructure.

desert warfare • warfare conducted on desert terrain and usually characterized by difficulties in navigation, cross-country mobility, resupply, water supply, and maintenance occasioned by the hot, dry, sandy, windy, and featureless terrain of the desert.

desired ground zero • (**DGZ**) the point on the surface of the earth at, or vertically below or above, the center of a planned nuclear detonation.

desk job • a job based at a desk, especially as opposed to one in active military service.

desk pilot • slang an officer, usually a pilot, assigned to staff or other duties not involving aerial flight.

de Soto, Hernando (also **Fernando**) (1496–1542) • a Spanish conquistador who, with Francisco Pizarro, conquered Central America and Peru. He was the first European to see the Mississippi River. At eighteen, de Soto's eagerness and skill as a horseman earned him a place on the 1514 expedition to the West Indies. In Panama he profited trading slaves in Nicaragua, and, after defeating his rival Gil González de Ávila, gained control of Nicaragua and expanded his trade in Native American slaves (1524–1527). After providing two ships to Pizarro's search for gold on the Pacific Coast of South America (1530), de Soto joined Pizarro, who made him his chief lieutenant in exchange for the use of his ships. When the conquest of Peru began in 1532, de Soto, as Pizarro's captain of horse, was instrumental in the defeat of the Incas and the first European to meet the Inca emperor Atahualpa. Made wealthy by the sack of Peru, de Soto returned to Spain (1536), where he hoped to be made a governor in the Americas. In 1537 he asked for special permission from the Spanish crown to conquer Ecuador, but instead was commissioned to conquer what is now Florida and made governor of Cuba. He embarked from Spain in April 1538 and landed, after a brief stop in Cuba, on the western coast of Florida in May 1539. He wintered at the Native American village of Apalachee (now Tallahassee), then headed north and west through what would become Georgia, the Carolinas, and Tennessee with the help of Native American guides he abducted along the way. In southeastern Tennessee, near Lookout Mountain, he turned south into Alabama with his expedition (1540), and was met at Mauvila (now Mobile) by a confederation of Native Americans. The Spaniards thoroughly defeated the native warriors, but de Soto's army lost most of its equipment. De Soto allowed his men to rest for a month before turning back north to seek treasure inland. As his expedition traveled northwest through Alabama and west through Mississippi, Native Americans attacked repeatedly, but the Spaniards pushed on, until they reached the Mississippi River in May 1541, south of present-day Memphis. They crossed the river and went south again, through Arkansas and Louisiana. Early in 1542, they turned back to the Mississippi River. De Soto died of a fever in Louisiana and his men buried him in the Mississippi. His successor, Luis de Moscoso, led the remaining half of de Soto's expedition down the Mississippi River on rafts, and they reached the coast of Mexico in 1543.

destroyer |di'stroiər| • *n.* a small, fast warship, especially one equipped for a defensive role against submarines and aircraft. Destroyers can carry a wide variety of weapons, including guns, torpedoes, depth charges, and guided missiles.

Destroyers-for-Bases Agreement • an agreement negotiated between U.S. President FRANKLIN D. ROOSEVELT and British Prime Minister WINSTON CHURCHILL to replenish British losses in WORLD WAR II. Announced by Roosevelt on September 3, 1940, it transferred fifty U.S. destroyers of WORLD WAR I vintage to England, in exchange for ninety-nine-year leases to seven British air and naval bases in the Western Hemisphere. It established the Anglo-American alliance of World War II.

detach • *v.* (usually **be detached**) send (a group of soldiers or ships) on a separate mission: *we were detached to Tabuk for the exercise.*
DERIVATIVES: **detachability** *n.* **detachable** *adj.*

detachment • *n.* **1** a group of troops, aircraft, or ships sent away on a separate mission: *a detachment of Marines.* **2** a temporary military or naval unit formed from other units or parts of units.

detail |də'tāl 'dē,tāl| • *n.* **1** a small detachment of troops or police officers given a special duty: *the governor's security detail.* **2** a special duty assigned to such a detachment: *I didn't often get the toilet detail.* **3** the distribution of orders for the day. • *v.* assign (someone) to undertake a particular task: *the ships were detailed to keep watch.*
DERIVATIVES: **detailer** *n.*

detainee • *n.* any person captured or otherwise detained by an armed force.

detarget • *v.* remove a planned target from an approved target list or from the programmed memory of a missile.

détente |dā'tänt| (also **detente**) • *n.* the easing of hostility or strained relations, especially between countries: *a serious effort at détente with the eastern bloc.*
ORIGIN: early 20th cent.: French, literally 'loosening, relaxation.'

deterrence • *n.* the prevention from action by fear of the consequences. Deterrence is a state of mind brought about by the existence of a credible threat of unacceptable counteraction.

deterrent • *n.* a nuclear weapon or weapons system regarded as deterring an enemy from attack.

detonate |'detn,āt| • *v.* explode or cause to explode: *two other bombs failed to detonate | a trigger that can detonate nuclear weapons.*
DERIVATIVES: **detonative** *adj.*

Deuce and a Half (also **Deuce**) • slang any of several 2 ½ ton trucks used by the U.S. Army in from the 1930s on, including the CCKW, the M-135, the M-211, and the M-35. They were built by GMC, Reo Motors, and Studebaker, among others, and had 6x6 drive.

Deutch, John Mark (1938–) • director of the CENTRAL INTELLIGENCE AGENCY (1995–), born in Brussels, Belgium. Deutch was appointed by President BILL CLINTON and began his tenure by replacing many agency veterans with outside candidates, a move that was well-received by politicians but resented by longtime agency officials.

Development of Space Systems • see DIRECTIVE 5160.

Devens, Charles, Jr. (1820-91) • Union army officer born in Charlestown, Massachusetts. Devens participated in the PENINSULAR CAMPAIGN (1862) and in the battles of FAIR OAKS, FREDERICKSBURG (both 1862, where his command covered the army's retreat across the Rappahannock River), CHANCELLORSVILLE (1863), and COLD HARBOR (1864).

deviation • *n.* the deflection of a vessel's compass needle caused by iron in the vessel, which varies with the vessel's heading.

Devil's Den • a labyrinth of rock on the battlefield of GETTYSBURG (1863) that became a nest for Confederate sharpshooters who took aim at the Union soldiers on LITTLE ROUND TOP.

Devin, Thomas Casimir (1822–78) • Union army officer, born in New York City. As a volunteer officer in the 6th New York Cavalry, Devin participated with the ARMY OF THE POTOMAC in the battles of SOUTH MOUNTAIN and ANTIETAM (both 1862). As commander of the 2nd Cavalry Brigade under division commander Maj. Gen. JOHN BUFORD, he helped delay the advance of the Confederate troops into GETTYSBURG (1863) sufficiently to ensure a Union victory.

An outstanding disciplinarian and field tactician, Devin was known as "Buford's Hard Hitter" and "Buford's Old War Horse."

DEW |'d(y)o͞o| • *abbr.* distant early warning, a radar system in North America for the early detection of a missile attack.

Dewey, George (1837–1917) • naval officer who saw extensive service in the CIVIL WAR but is remembered primarily for his success in the BATTLE OF MANILA BAY during the SPANISH-AMERICAN WAR (1898), when as commander of the Asiatic Squadron, then-commodore Dewey totally destroyed the Spanish squadron. He returned to tremendous public adulation, including a parade down 5th Avenue. In 1899 Congress created for him the rank of Admiral of the Navy. Dewey was appointed president of the GENERAL BOARD OF THE NAVY (1900), the highest advisory body to the secretary of the Navy. In 1915 he accepted the newly created position of CHIEF OF NAVAL OPERATIONS.

De Witt, John L. (1880–1962) • army chief of the Western Defense Command who directed the removal of Japanese Americans from their homes on the West Coast to internment camps, as called for by presidential executive order. De Witt was awarded the DISTINGUISHED SERVICE MEDAL (1918) for exceptional service in WORLD WAR I. He served as QUARTERMASTER GENERAL from 1930 to 1934. He was commandant of the ARMY AND NAVY STAFF COLLEGE in Washington (1943). De Witt was promoted to rank of full general by Congress in 1954.

DF • *abbr.* direction finder.

DFC • *abbr.* (in the UK) Distinguished Flying Cross, a decoration for distinguished active service awarded to members of the RAF, instituted in 1918.

DFM • *abbr.* (in the UK) Distinguished Flying Medal, a decoration awarded to RAF personnel for acts of courage or devotion to duty when not in action against an enemy, instituted in 1918.

DGZ • *abbr.* desired ground zero.

DI • *abbr.* (in the UK) Defence Intelligence.

DIA • *abbr.* DEFENSE INTELLIGENCE AGENCY.

diaphone |ˈdīəˌfōn| • *n.* a low-pitched fog signal operated by compressed air, characterized by the "grunt" that ends each note.

Dickinson, Philemon (1739–1809) • Revolutionary army officer, brigadier general of the New Jersey militia, born in Talbot County, Maryland. Dickinson participated in the battle of TRENTON (1777), and he was acclaimed by GEORGE WASHINGTON for successfully deploying his militia against a foraging party of CHARLES CORNWALLIS near the Somerset County courthouse. Washington also attributed much of the American success at MONMOUTH (1778) to Dickinson and his men.

died of wounds received in action • (**DWRIA**) a casualty category applicable to a hostile casualty (other than the victim of a terrorist activity) who dies of wounds or other injuries received in action after having reached a medical treatment facility.

Diego Garcia • the largest island of the Chagos Archipelago in the middle of the Indian Ocean, site of a strategic Anglo-American naval base established in 1973.

Diem, Ngo No Dingh (1901–63) • South Vietnamese president (1955–63), born into the Catholic social elite and minister of the interior under the emperor Bao Dai (1933). When the French were unwilling to approve of Diem's legislative reforms, he resigned in frustration, gave up his titles and decortations, and spent the next twelve years living quietly in Hue. In 1945 Communist forces captured him, and Ho CHI MINH, hoping to gain support among Catholics, asked Diem to join his government in the North. Diem declined the offer and, instead, lived abroad in self-imposed exile for most of the next ten years. He returned in 1954 at the request of Bao Dai to serve as the prime minister of a U.S.-backed government in South Vietnam. Diem accepted, then ousted the emperor and declared himself president of the newly created Republic of Vietnam. Refusing to carry out the GENEVA AGREEMENT ON INDOCHINA, which required that free elections be held throughout Vietnam in 1956, Diem set up an autocratic government, supported by U.S. money and military advisers, and with his family members installed at the highest levels. The NATIONAL LIBERATION FRONT (VIETCONG) carried on an intense guerrilla war against Diem's dictatorship, and his inept militarism, heavy-handed as it was, only increased his government's isolation and lack of support among the South Vietnamese. When Diem claimed that Buddhists were helping the Vietcong and used that claim as a pretext for imprisoning and murdering hundreds of them, the United States withdrew its support from Diem's government. His generals assassinated him in 1963, during a coup d'état.

Dien Bien Phu • the site of a French-fortified base in Vietnam that fell to communist VIETMINH forces in 1954. This prompted the French to agree to talks (the GENEVA AGREEMENT ON INDOCHINA) that ended the war and led to the partition of Vietnam. The talks also provided for elections that could have led to reunification, but these were never held.

digger • *n.* Austral./NZ informal a man, especially a private soldier (often used as a friendly form of address): *how are you, Digger?*
ORIGIN: early 20th cent.: from *digger* 'miner,' reinforced by association with the digging of trenches on the battlefields.

Digges, Thomas Attwood (1742–1821) • revolutionary and spy, born in Warburton, Maryland. Digges spent much of his life abroad, passing on from London to American leaders political gossip, lists of American prisoners of war, and reports on activities in Parliament. He smuggled war supplies to America via Spain, and after the war smuggled artisans and machinery from Britain to America.

Digges was disowned by his family, imprisoned for debt in Dublin, arrested for shoplifting in Scotland, active in Irish nationalist struggles, yet a personal friend of GEORGE WASHINGTON—one of the few invited to his funeral. Also a writer, his *Adventures of Alonso* (1775) is sometimes described as the first novel by an American.

---

dinghy • *n.* (pl. **-ies**) a small, inflatable rubber boat.

Dinwiddie, Robert (1692–1727) • royal customs official and lieutenant governor of Virginia (1751–58), born in Glasgow, Scotland. His demand (sent via then-Major GEORGE WASHINGTON) that the French commanders leave the lands south of the Great Lakes claimed by the British crown and the colony of Virginia precipitated the FRENCH AND INDIAN WAR (1754–1763).

Dinwiddie gave Washington his first field commands with the 1st Virginia Regiment, and though they later clashed over military policies, Dinwiddie's patronage was significant in advancing Washington's military career.

---

dioxin • *n.* a highly toxic compound produced as a by-product in some manufacturing processes, notably herbicide production (especially AGENT ORANGE) and paper bleaching. It is a serious and persistent environmental pollutant.

diplomacy • *n.* the profession, activity, or skill of managing international relations, typically by a country's representatives abroad: *an extensive round of diplomacy in the Middle East.*

direct action • short-duration strikes and other small-scale offensive actions by special operations forces to seize, destroy, capture, recover, or inflict damage on designated personnel or materiel. In the conduct of these operations, special operations forces may do the following: employ raid, ambush, or direct assault tactics; emplace mines and other munitions; conduct standoff attacks by fire from air, ground, or maritime platforms; provide terminal guidance for precision-guided munitions; and conduct independent sabotage.

direct action mission • in special operations, a specified act involving operations of an overt, covert, clandestine, or low-visibility nature conducted primarily by a sponsoring power's special operations forces in hostile or denied areas.

direct fire • gunfire delivered on a target, using the target itself as a point of aim for either the gun or the director of the gunfire.

direct-fire artillery • artillery employed to deliver its fires on a target using the target itself as a point of aim for either the gun or the director.

directional mine • a mine that sprays out its explosive charge in a wide, directional arc.

direction finder • a special radio receiver with a system of antennas for locating the source of radio signals, used as an aid to navigation.

directive • *n.* an official or authoritative instruction: *moral and ethical directives.* • *adj.* involving the management or guidance of operations: *he is seeking a directive role in defense policy.*

Directive 5160 • a 1961 directive by Secretary of Defense ROBERT S. MCNAMARA that sought to coordinate the research and development of space defense systems. Its official name was Development of Space Systems, and it assigned responsibility for space defense largely to the Air Force.

Directorate of Intelligence • in the post-WORLD WAR II period, that element of the U.S. Army GENERAL STAFF responsible for intelligence and counter-intelligence matters; formerly entitled the Office of the Assistant Chief of Staff G–2 and later renamed the Assistant Chief of Staff for Intelligence.

direct supporting fire • fire delivered in support of part of a force (as opposed to general supporting fire, which is delivered in support of the force as a whole).

dirigible • *n.* see AIRSHIP.

Disabled American Veterans • (**DAV**) a nonprofit organization of more than 1 million disabled U.S. veterans. As a result of inadequate services for disabled veterans, WORLD WAR I veterans formed local groups that merged into the Disabled American Veterans organization in 1920. This group was chartered by Congress in 1932. It pushed for legislation to create a centralized government agency, the Veterans Bureau, which is now the DEPARTMENT OF VETERANS AFFAIRS. The veterans' group provides assistance to members in obtaining benefits and lobbies on behalf of members at the federal, state, and local level.

disaffected person • a person who is alienated or estranged from those in authority or lacks loyalty to the government.

disarm • *v.* **1** take a weapon or weapons away from (a person, force, or country): *Germany had been defeated and disarmed.* **2** (of a country or force) give up or reduce its armed forces or weapons: *the other militias had disarmed by the agreed deadline.* **3** remove the fuse from (a bomb), making it safe: *police yesterday disarmed a parcel bomb.* **4** deprive (a ship, etc.) of its means of defense. • *n.* an act of taking a weapon away from someone.
DERIVATIVES: **disarmer** *n.*

disarmament • *n.* the reduction or withdrawal of military forces and weapons: *the public wanted peace and disarmament.*

Disarmed Enemy Forces • (**DEF**) official designation of German soldiers who surrendered to the ALLIES at the end of WORLD WAR II in Europe and were subsequently held under abominable conditions in camps in the Rhine valley. By 1947 most DEF, except for members of the SS and GESTAPO and those held for war crimes trials, were released by U.S. occupation authorities.

discharge • *v.* **1** (often **be discharged**) tell (someone) officially that they can or must leave, in particular: **a** send (a patient) out of the hospital after being judged fit to go home. **b** dismiss or release (someone) from a job, especially from service in the armed forces or police. **c** release (someone) from the custody or restraint of the law. **2** (of a person) fire (a gun or missile): *when you shoot you can discharge as many barrels as you wish.* **3** (of a firearm) be fired: *there was a dull thud as the gun discharged.* **4** unload (cargo or passengers) from a ship: *ninety ships were waiting to discharge.* • *n.* |ˈdisˌCHärj| **1** the action of discharging someone from a hospital or from a job: *his discharge from the hospital* | *a dishonorable discharge.* **2** an act of releasing someone from the custody or restraint of the law: *thirty days in jail and one year probation.* **3** the action of firing a gun or missile: *a police permit for discharge of an air gun* | *sounds like discharges of artillery.* **4** the action of unloading a ship of its cargo or passengers. *freight for discharge.* **5** a written certificate of a release, etc.
DERIVATIVES: **dischargeable** *adj.*

discharger • *n.* a device that releases nerve gas, smoke, or other substances for military purposes.

Disciplinary Barracks • established by the U.S. Congress in 1874 and originally called the United Military Prison, it is the only maximum containment facility for military offenders and is an organization of the DEPARTMENT OF DEFENSE. It is located in FORT LEAVENWORTH, Kansas.

discipline • *n.* **1** the practice of training people to obey rules or a code of behavior, using punishment to correct disobedience: *a lack of proper parental and school discipline.* **2** the controlled behavior resulting from such training: *he was able to maintain discipline among his men.* **3** activity or experience that provides mental or physical training: *Kung fu is a discipline open to old and young.* **4** a system of rules of conduct: *he doesn't have to submit to normal disciplines.* • *v.* **1** train (someone) to obey rules or a code of behavior, using punishment to correct disobedience: *he was afraid to discipline his men.* **2** (often **be disciplined**) punish or rebuke (someone) formally for an offense: *a member of the staff was to be disciplined by the general.*

DERIVATIVES: **disciplinable** *adj.* **disciplinal** *adj.*

dishonorable discharge • the dismissal of someone from the armed forces as a result of criminal or morally unacceptable actions.

disinformation • *n.* false information that is intended to mislead, especially propaganda issued by a government organization to a rival power or the media.

ORIGIN: 1950s: formed on the pattern of Russian *dezinformatsiya.*

dismantle • *v.* **1** (often **be dismantled**) take to pieces: *the engines were dismantled and the bits piled into a heap.* **2** deprive of defenses or equipment.

DERIVATIVES: **dismantlement** *n.* **dismantler** *n.*

dismast • *v.* break or force down the mast or masts of (a ship): (**dismasted**) *a dismasted ship wallowing in stormy seas.*

dismiss • *v.* **1** order or allow to leave; send away: *she dismissed the taxi at the corner of the road.* **2** discharge from employment or office, typically on the grounds of unsatisfactory performance or dishonorable behavior: *he was dismissed for insubordination.* **3** (of a group assembled under someone's authority) *disperse: he told his company to dismiss.*

DERIVATIVES: **dismissal** *n.* **dismissible** *adj.*

dispatch |dis'pæCH| (also **despatch**) • *v.* **1** send off to a destination or for a purpose: *he dispatched messages back to base.* **2** deal with (a task, problem, or opponent) quickly and efficiently: *they dispatched the opposition.* **3** kill: *he dispatched the animal with one blow.* • *n.* **1** the sending of someone or something to a destination or for a purpose: *a resolution authorizing the dispatch of a peacekeeping force.* **2** speed in action: *the situation might change, so he should proceed* ***with dispatch.*** **3** an official report on state or military affairs: *in his battle dispatch he described the gunner's bravery.* **4** a report sent in by a newspaper's correspondent from a faraway place: *he conducted meetings for the correspondents and censored their dispatches.* **5** the killing of someone or something: *the legendary dispatch of villains by a hero.*

DERIVATIVES: **dispatcher** *n.*

dispatch box • (also **dispatch case**) a container for dispatches, especially official state or military documents.

dispatches, mention in • see MENTION IN DISPATCHES.

dispatch rider • a messenger who delivers military dispatches by motorcycle or (formerly) on horseback.

dispersion • *n.* **1** a scattered pattern of hits around the mean point of impact of bombs and projectiles dropped or fired under identical conditions. **2** in antiaircraft gunnery, the scattering of shots in range and deflection about the mean point of explosion. **3** the spreading or separating of troops, materiel, establishment, or activities which are usually concentrated in limited areas to reduce vulnerability. **4** in chemical and biological operations, the dissemination of agents in liquid or aerosol form. **5** in airdrop operations, the scatter of personnel and/or cargo in the drop zone. **6** in naval control of shipping, the reberthing of a ship in the periphery of the port area or in the vicinity of the port for its own protection in order to minimize the risk of damage from attack.

displaced person • a civilian who is involuntarily outside the national boundaries of their country.

displacement ton • see TON.

disposition • *n.* (**dispositions**) military preparations, in particular the stationing of troops ready for attack or defense: *the new strategic dispositions of our forces.*

disrate • *v.* (usually **be disrated**) reduce (a sailor) to a lower rank.

Distant Early Warning Line • (**DEW Line**) a line of radar stations close to the 70th Parallel jointly operated by the United States and Canada and designed to detect hostile bombers or missiles en route to targets in North America.

Distinguished Conduct Medal • British military decoration for valor awarded to enlisted personnel. The Distinguished Conduct Medal is the equivalent for enlisted personnel of the MILITARY CROSS awarded to junior officers and warrant officers.

Distinguished Flying Cross • U.S. military decoration awarded for "heroism or extraordinary achievement while participating in aerial flight." Established by Congress on July 2, 1926, the Distinguished Flying Cross may be awarded to members of any branch of service and to members of the armed forces of friendly nations.

Distinguished Service Cross • U.S. military decoration for "extraordinary heroism in connection with military operations against an armed enemy." Established by Congress on July 9, 1918, the Distinguished Service Cross is awarded to personnel serving with the U.S. Army.

Distinguished Service Medal • **1** (Army) U.S. military decoration for "exceptionally meritorious service to the Government in a duty of great responsibility." Established by Congress on July 9, 1918 and awarded to persons serving in any capacity with the U.S.

Army. **2** (Navy) U.S. military decoration for "exceptionally meritorious service to the Government in a duty of great responsibility." The Navy DSM was established on February 4, 1919 and may be awarded to persons serving with the U.S. Navy or Marine Corps.

Distinguished Service Order • see DSO.

disunionism • *n.* the doctrine, advocated before and during the CIVIL WAR, that the UNION between the states should be dissolved.

dive-bombing • *n.* an aerial bombing technique in which the bombing aircraft dives steeply downward toward the target.

diversion • *n.* **1** the act of drawing the attention and forces of an enemy from the point of the principal operation; an attack, alarm, or feint that diverts attention. **2** a change made in a prescribed route for operational or tactical reasons. A diversion order will not constitute a change of destination. **3** a rerouting of cargo or passengers to a new transshipment point or destination or on a different mode of transportation prior to arrival at ultimate destination. **4** in naval-mine warfare, a route or channel bypassing a dangerous area. A diversion may connect one channel to another, or it may branch from a channel and rejoin it on the other side of the danger.

diversionary attack • an attack wherein a force attacks, or threatens to attack, a target other than the main target for the purpose of drawing enemy defenses away from the main effort.

diversionary landing • an operation in which troops are actually landed for the purpose of diverting enemy reaction away from the main landing.

diving bell • an open-bottomed chamber supplied with compressed air, in which a person can be let down under water.

division • *n.* a group of army brigades or regiments: *an infantry division.*

Dix, Dorothea Lynde (1802–87) • superintendent of U.S. Army nurses during the CIVIL WAR, born in Hampden, Maine. Dix was responsible for training young women for medical duty, but was known primarily for her advocacy, both before and after the war, of humane treatment of prisoners and the mentally ill, for which she traveled throughout the United States, Canada, Great Britain, Europe, and Japan.

Dixie • a CIVIL WAR-era song usually attributed to northerner Daniel D. Emmett, who is believed to have written it in 1859 as a minstrel song. It was first performed in New York City. It was the most popular song of the war both in the North, where President ABRAHAM LINCOLN had the WHITE HOUSE Band perform it, and the South, where it became identified as a Confederate marching song and unofficial anthem. The word *Dixie* became a popular nickname for the South because of the region's association with the song.

Dix, John Adams (1798–1879) • Union army officer, born in Boscawen, New Hampshire. Dix joined the army at the age of fourteen to fight in the WAR OF 1812, serving in the battles of Chrysler's Field and LUNDY'S LANE (1814). During the CIVIL WAR he was first president of New York City's Union Defense Committee, which was responsible for raising money, supplies, and volunteers, and later a major general in the army serving in various politically sensitive administrative posts.

DMSP • *abbr.* Defense Meteorological Satellite Program.

DMZ • *abbr.* demilitarized zone.

dock |däk| • *n.* **1** a structure extending alongshore or out from the shore into a body of water, to which boats may be moored: *the gangplank was lowered to the dock.* **2** an enclosed area of water in a port for the loading, unloading, and repair of ships. **3** (**docks**) a group of such enclosed areas of water along with the wharves and buildings near them. **4** short for DRY DOCK. **5** (also **loading dock**) a platform for loading or unloading trucks or freight trains. • *v.* **1** (of a ship) tie up at a dock, especially in order to load or unload passengers or cargo: *the ship docked at San Francisco.* **2** bring (a ship or boat) into such a place: *the riverbank where the fur traders docked their boats.* **3** (of a spacecraft) join with a space station or another spacecraft in space.

dockage |ˈdäkij| • *n.* **1** accommodation or berthing of ships at docks. **2** the charge made for using docks.

dockyard |ˈdäkˌyärd| • *n.* an area or establishment with docks and equipment for repairing and maintaining ships.

doctrine • *n.* fundamental principles by which the military forces or elements thereof guide their actions in support of national objectives. Doctrine is authoritative but requires judgment in application.

DoD or **DOD** • *abbr.* Department of Defense.

Dodge Commission • a body appointed by President WILLIAM MCKINLEY in 1898 to investigate charges of neglect that led to appalling conditions in U.S. military camps during the SPANISH-AMERICAN WAR (1898). It was headed by Maj. Gen. GRENVILLE DODGE, and its main conclusions were that lack of preparedness and bureaucratic inefficiency were to blame for supply shortages and failure to contain the outbreak of disease.

Dodge, Grenville Mellen (1831–1916) • Union army officer and civil engineer, born in Danvers, Massachusetts. Dodge distinguished himself as brigade commander of the 4th Iowa Volunteer Regiment at the BATTLE OF PEA RIDGE (1862). In the VICKSBURG CAMPAIGN (1862–63) Dodge not only commanded fighting troops but used his engineering skills to reconstruct bridges and railroads essential to the Union victory.

Dodge is best known as a railroad builder whose miles of track opened up the West to settlement. He was nicknamed "Long Eye" by Indians because of his habit of carrying a telescope while overseeing construction of the Union Pacific Railroad.

---

dodger • *n.* a canvas screen on a ship giving protection from spray.

Dodge, Theodore Ayrault (1842–1909) • Union army officer born in Pittsfield, Massachusetts. Dodge participated in the BULL RUN (1861–62) and PENINSULAR (1862) campaigns, at CHANCELLORSVILLE (1863), and at GETTYSBURG (1863), where his regiment was virtually wiped out. He later he devoted himself to writing military history, to which he brought the experience of a soldier and the objectivity of a scholar, achieving a distinguished place among 19th-century American military writers.

dogface • *n.* informal, dated a soldier, especially an infantryman.

dogfight • *n.* a close combat between military aircraft: *Sergeant Smith and a colleague were* ***in a dogfight with*** *an enemy aircraft.* • *v.* engage in a dogfight.
DERIVATIVES: **dogfighter** *n.*

dog-robber • *n.* informal an army or navy officer's orderly: *Sergeant Major sent me to be the lieutenant's dog-robber.*

dogshore |ˈdôgˌSHôr| • *n.* a temporary support for a ship just before launching.

Dog Soldiers • see CHEYENNE DOG SOLDIERS.

dog tag • informal a soldier's metal identity tag.

dog tag on file • WWI slang dead and buried.

dogwatch • *n.* either of two short watches on a ship (4–6 or 6–8 P.M.).

dolphin • *n.* **1** a bollard, pile, or buoy for mooring. **2** a structure for protecting the pier of a bridge or other structure from collision with ships.

domestic • *adj.* existing or occurring inside a particular country; not foreign or international: *Korea's domestic affairs.*
DERIVATIVES: **domestically** *adv.*
ORIGIN: late Middle English: from French *domestique*, from Latin *domesticus*, from *domus* 'house.'

domestic emergencies • emergencies affecting the public welfare and occurring within the fifty United States states, the District of Columbia, the Commonwealth of Puerto Rico, U.S. possessions and territories, or any political subdivision thereof, as a result of enemy attack, insurrection, civil disturbance, earthquake, fire, flood, or other public disasters or equivalent emergencies that endanger life and property or disrupt the usual process of government. Domestic emergencies are categorized as: **a** (**civil defense emergency**) a disaster situation resulting from devastation created by an enemy attack and requiring emergency operations during and following that attack. **b** (**civil disturbance**) a riot, act of violence, insurrection, unlawful obstruction or assemblage, or other disorder prejudicial to public law and order. **c** (**major disaster**) any flood, fire, hurricane, tornado, earthquake, or other catastrophe that, in the determination of the president, is or threatens to be of sufficient severity and magnitude to warrant disaster assistance by the federal government. Such assistance supplements the efforts and available resources of state and local governments in alleviating the damage, hardship, or suffering caused thereby. **d** (**natural disaster**) any domestic emergency not created as a result of enemy attack or civil disturbance.

Dominion of New England • a territory comprised of northeastern American colonies, formed in 1686 by King James II. It included Connecticut, Massachusetts, New Hampshire, East Jersey, West Jersey, New York, Plymouth, and Rhode Island. A lack of control over New England and the fear that the colonies would not be able to defend themselves against France if disconnected prompted England to consolidate them. But colonists had no voice in government, and most opposed the dominion. The breakup of the dominion in 1689 was aided by the revolution a year before in England that overthrew James II.

domino theory • a geopolitical theory popular in the United States during the 1950s and 1960s which posited that South Vietnam was the linchpin of Southeast Asia and that if South Vietnam fell to the Communists, the other free states of Southeast Asia (Laos, Cambodia, Thailand) and perhaps South Korea, Taiwan, Burma, and even India would also fall and be added to the Communist camp in quick succession.

Dong Ha |ˈdôNG ˈhä| • capital of the Quang Tri province in Vietnam, a combat base and supply center for the U.S. Marines and the site of a U.S. Marine Corps battle from April 29 to May 15, 1968. The Marines turned it over to the South Vietnamese Army in November 1969.

Doniphan, Alexander (1808–87) • army officer during the MEXICAN WAR (1846–48), born near Maysville, Kentucky. Doniphan, while in command of the conquered New Mexican region, drafted a code of laws and secured peace with the Navajo. He then before proceeded south and twice defeated superior Mexican forces, eventually entering Chihuahua unopposed.

Donovan, William J. (1883–1959) • born in Buffalo, New York, U.S. intelligence official. "Wild Bill," as he was known, was the WORLD WAR II director of the American intelligence effort. He hoped to make the OFFICE OF STRATEGIC SERVICES a permanent agency, but President HARRY S. TRUMAN abolished the agency in October 1945. His plan for the OSS was eventually adapted as the blueprint for the CENTRAL INTELLIGENCE AGENCY.

Donovan, who saw considerable action in WORLD WAR I, was awarded the DISTINGUISHED SERVICE CROSS, the DISTINGUISHED SERVICE MEDAL, and the MEDAL OF HONOR. In 1957, he was awarded the National Security Medal, making him the first person to receive the four highest U.S. decorations.

"Don't Ask, Don't Tell, Don't Pursue" policy • a compromise policy regarding the service of gays and lesbians in the U.S. armed forces developed following President BILL CLINTON's attempt in 1993 to overturn the then-existing policy which called for the immediate discharge of armed forces personnel found to be homosexual. Despite significant support by gay rights advocates, President Clinton's move was strongly opposed by many military, political, and religious leaders. As a result, a compromise policy was worked out which permits homosexuals to serve so long as they do not openly declare their sexual preferences and do not engage in homosexual activities (which remain illegal in some states). At the same time, military authorities are prohibited from actively seeking out gay and lesbian service members.

doodlebug • *n.* Brit. informal term for V-1.

Doolittle, James Harold (1896–1993) • aviation pioneer and air force officer, born in Alameda, California. Doolittle played a pivotal part in establishing the role of aviation in modern warfare. Doolittle was a flight leader and gunnery instructor in the Army Reserve Corps during WORLD WAR I. He was awarded the DISTINGUISHED FLYING CROSS for the first transcontinental flight across North America within twenty-four hours in 1922. He helped develop the gyroscope, which makes instrument flying possible. Doolittle resigned from active duty in 1930. He returned to active duty in the ARMY AIR CORPS in WORLD WAR II. He planned and led the first aerial raid on Japan (1942), after which he was awarded the CONGRESSIONAL MEDAL OF HONOR. He directed the forces in support of the invasion of French North Africa (1942) and strategic air operations against German forces in the Mediterranean (1943). He transferred to the Pacific theater after the German surrender, but saw little action, and returned to reserve status in 1946. He was made a four-star general in 1985 and was awarded the Presidential Medal of Freedom in 1989.

Doolittle Raid • a daring raid of aircraft-carrier launched American bombers on Tokyo in April 1942. Plans for a precision-targeted campaign had to be abandoned at the last minute owing to unexpected obstacles, but the sixteen planes that took part succeeded in destroying military and industrial targets all over the city. [The incident is named for Lt. Col. JAMES H. DOOLITTLE, leader of the squadron.]

doomsday clock • a clock representing the time remaining until civilization is destroyed in a nuclear war. It became a famous symbol of nuclear destruction when it first appeared on the cover of the June 1947 issue of the *Bulletin of the Atomic Scientists*. The cover depicted a large clock face, called "The Clock of Doom," that was set at seven minutes to midnight, and an editorial stated that the clock "represents the state of mind of those whose closeness to the development of atomic energy does not permit them to forget ... the survival of civilization ... hangs in the balance." The hands on the clock have been moved sixteen times to reflect global tensions and cooperation. It has been set as close as two minutes to midnight and as far back as seventeen minutes in 1991 with the signing of the START I TREATY. In 1998 it was reset to nine minutes when India and Pakistan tested nuclear weapons, world diplomacy failed on nuclear issues, and earlier agreements were not fully implemented.

Doomsday device • a hypothetical weapon that could kill everyone on earth. It would require a radioactive isotope that could be dispersed worldwide before it decays, for which the only candidate is cobalt-60.

doppler effect • the phenomenon evidenced by the change in the observed frequency of a sound or radio wave caused by a time rate of change in the effective length of the path of travel between the source and the point of observation.

doppler radar • a radar system that differentiates between fixed and moving targets by detecting the apparent change in frequency of the reflected wave due to motion of the target or the observer.

Dorchester Heights • an elevated area south of (and today part of) Boston, Massachusetts, that was stealthily fortified by troops under Gen. GEORGE WASHINGTON in early March 1776, with a view to taking Boston back from the British. The fortification made Boston Harbor unsafe for any British ship, and Gen. WILLIAM HOWE, thinking that a battle would not prove wise, evacuated his troops, taking about 1,000 loyalists with him to New York on March 17

dossier |'dôsē,ā; 'däs-| • *n.* a collection of documents about a particular person, event, or subject: *we have a* ***dossier on*** *him.*

double • *v.* Nautical sail around (a headland): *we struck out seaward to double the headland of the cape.*

PHRASES: **on the double 1** at running speed; very fast: *he disappeared on the double.* **2** without hesitation; immediately *he summoned his officers on the double.*

double-action • *adj.* (of a gun) needing to be cocked and fired as two separate actions.

double agent • agent in contact with two opposing intelligence services, only one of which is aware of the double contact or quasi-intelligence services.

Doubleday, Abner (1819–93) • Union army officer and graduate of WEST POINT, born in Ballston Spa, New York. Doubleday served at MONTERREY (1846) and BUENA VISTA (1847) during the MEXICAN WAR (1846–48) and also participated in military campaigns against the Apaches in the Southwest and the Seminoles in Florida. Doubleday claimed to have aimed and ordered the first retaliatory shot from FORT SUMTER at the time of its bombardment (1861). His brigade saw action at the SECOND BATTLE OF BULL RUN and he led his division in the battles of ANTIETAM and FREDERICKSBURG (all 1862). A brigade under his command at GETTYSBURG (1863), his last major battle, played a key role in repelling the final Confederate assault. He held administrative duties in Washington for the remainder of the war, and retired from the military in 1873.

Although Doubleday is popularly recognized as the inventor of baseball, scholars of the game have largely discredited the claim.

double-quick • *v.* to march or cause to march at double-time, quick time being the normal marching pace. Also known as DOUBLE-TIME.

double-time • *n.* a regulation running pace: *the sergeants march a shaven-headed squad in double-time. v. to run or cause to run at this pace.*

Double Ugly • nickname for the F-4G.

Double-V Campaign • the WORLD WAR II-era effort of black Americans to gain "a Victory over racism at home as well as Victory abroad."

doughboy • *n.* WWI slang an American infantryman.

doughface • *n.* WWII slang infantryman.

ORIGIN: a play on the WORLD WAR I term "doughboy."

Douglas, H. Ford (1831–65) • a former slave and abolitionist, born in Virginia. His father was a white man named William Douglas, and his mother, Mary, was a slave. Douglas was one of fewer than thirty black commissioned officers in the Union army and probably the only black combat captain during the CIVIL WAR. Douglas had passed for white and joined an Illinois volunteer regiment in 1862 but requested a transfer to a black unit once the Union army officially enlisted blacks. Ford chose to abbreviate his first name, Hezekiah.

As an abolitionist, Ford advocated that African Americans emigrate rather than wait for conditions to improve in the United States.

Douhet, Giulio (1869–1930) • an Italian army general of WORLD WAR I. Although trained as an artillery officer, he commanded Italy's first aviation unit, the Aeronautical Battalion, from 1912 to 1915. His harsh criticism of how the war was being managed led to his court-martial, imprisonment, and retirement. After a 1917 investigation of an Italian loss at Caporetto, demonstrated that Douhet's criticisms had been justified, and his conviction was reversed and he was appointed to head the aviation service. He is remembered primarily for his book, *Il dominio dell'aria* (1921; *The Command of the Air* [1942])—the first formal treatise on air strategy—in which he challenged the hostile resistance aroused by the military potential of flight until that potential was accepted and realized. Although some of his ideas have become obsolete, many of them were adopted by all of the major powers before and during WORLD WAR II. His idea that strategic bombing could disorganize and destroy an enemy's war effort was well demonstrated throughout that war.

douse |dows| (also **dowse**) • *v.* **1** extinguish (a fire or light): *stewards appeared and the fire was doused.* **2** Sailing lower (a sail) quickly.

dove |dəv| • *n.* a person who advocates peaceful or conciliatory policies, especially in foreign affairs. Compare with HAWK.

DERIVATIVES: **dovelike** *adj.* **dovish** *adj.* (in sense 2).

Dowding, Hugh (1882–1970) • a squadron commander in the ROYAL FLYING CORPS during WORLD WAR I, and commander of the newly organized Fighter Command in 1936. During WORLD WAR II, he was a significant element in the eventual defeat of the German Luftwaffe in the BATTLE OF BRITAIN (1940); his energetic support for the uses of radar and the superiority of new fighter aircraft, such as the SPITFIRE and HURRICANE, had the British military prepared when ADOLF HITLER's attention turned toward Britain.

down |down| • *adv.* **1** (of sailing) with the current or the wind. **2** (of a ship's helm) moved around to leeward so that the rudder is to windward and the vessel swings toward the wind. • *v.* informal knock or bring to the ground: *175 enemy aircraft had been downed.*

downgrade • *v.* determine that classified information requires, in the interests of national security, a lower degree of protection against unauthorized disclosure than currently provided, coupled with a changing of the classification designation to reflect such lower degree.

downhaul |ˈdownˌhôl| • *n.* a rope used for hauling down a sail, spar, etc., especially in order to control a sail's shape.

downwinder • slang (**downwind message**) a message used in nuclear, chemical, and biological weapons operations to provide friendly forces with information on wind speed and direction so that possible fallout and spread of chemical or biological agents can be predicted.

Dow Shalt Not Kill • during the VIETNAM WAR, a slogan of antiwar protesters, directed at the Dow Chemical Company, manufacturer of napalm and an estimated three-fourths of the defoliant Agent Orange used in Vietnam. See also AGENT ORANGE. This slogan was sometimes printed on orange T-shirts.

draft board • a group of civilian citizens responsible for the local administration of the SELECTIVE SERVICE SYSTEM or other compulsory military service laws.

draft deferment • the temporary postponement of, or permanent exemption from, induction into military service by virtue of one's health, the number of one's dependents, one's work in an essential war industry, or other some reason deemed sufficient by the draft authorities.

draft dodger • derogatory a person who has avoided compulsory military service.

DERIVATIVES: **draft dodging** *n.*

draft registration, compulsory • the requirement that all military-age male citizens enroll with government authorities so as to be in the pool from which conscripts are selected.

draft resistance and evasion • civil disobedience directed at government authorities responsible for administering a system of compulsory military service (draft resistance) and the measures taken to avoid draft registration and induction for military service (draft evasion).

Draft Riots • violent demonstrations in New York City in July 1863 against a newly enacted conscription law. The law was seen to unfairly discriminate against the poor since anyone able to pay a fee of $300 could be exempted from the draft. Rioters converged on and destroyed the office of the Provost Marshal responsible for conscription, then turned their violence upon others including many free blacks who lived in the city. More than 100 were killed and property damage was about $1 million.

drag |dræg| • *v.* **1** (of a ship) trail (an anchor) along the seabed, causing the ship to drift. **2** (of an anchor) fail to hold, causing a ship or boat to drift. **3** search the bottom of (a river, lake, or the sea) with grapnels or nets.

drag-anchor • *n.* another term for sea anchor.

Dragon • (**M-47**) a portable antitank weapon, consisting of a round (missile and launcher) and a tracker that provides antitank or assault fire for targets such as emplaced weapons or fortifications.

dragon's teeth • Brit. informal concrete obstacles pointing upward from the ground in rows, used against tanks in WORLD WAR II.

dragoon • *n.* **1** a member of any of several cavalry regiments in the household troops of the British army: *the Royal Scots Dragoon Guards.* **2** historical a mounted infantryman armed with a short rifle or musket. • *v.* persecute, especially with troops.

ORIGIN: early 17th cent. (denoting a kind of carbine or musket, thought of as breathing fire): from French *dragon* 'dragon.'

Drake, Francis Marion (1830–1903) • Union army officer, born in Rushville, Illinois. Drake raised a company of volunteers for an Iowa infantry unit; he was severely wounded and captured by Confederate forces. Drake was governor of Iowa (1896–98) but was primarily known for his role in railroad building in the Midwest.

draw • *v.* (past **drew**; past part. **drawn**) **1** (of a ship) require (a specified depth of water) to float in: *boats that draw only a few inches of water.* **2** (of a sail) be filled with wind: *as the sail drew, he put the helm over to circle back.* • *n.* **1** an act of removing a gun from its holster in order to shoot: *he went for the quick draw and leveled a long-barrelled pistol at all of us.*

PHRASES: **draw a bead on** see BEAD. **draw blood** cause someone to bleed, especially in the course of a fight: *the blow drew blood from the corner of his mouth.* **draw fire** attract hostile criticism, usually away from a more important target: *the vaccination campaign continued to draw fire.* **quick on the draw** very fast in taking one's gun from its holster. **draw back 1** choose not to do something that one was expected to do, often through a lack of nerve: *the government has **drawn back from** attempting reform.* **2** withdraw (troops). **3** lead out, detach, or array (troops).

drawdown • *n.* a reduction in the size or presence of a military force: *the unit is the first to leave Germany as part of the drawdown.*

Drayton, Percival (1812–65) • naval officer, born in Charleston, South Carolina. Drayton was recognized for his expertise in ordnance. Drayton served as chief of staff to DAVID FARRAGUT and as captain of the *Hartford,* Farragut's flagship, during the attack on MOBILE BAY (1864). Earlier he had commanded the gunboat *Pocahontas* during the attack on PORT ROYAL (1861) and the ironclad *Passaic* in attacks against Fort McAllister (1863). During the war Drayton also served as superintendent of ordnance for the New York Navy Yard (1863).

At the time of the attack on Port Royal, its Confederate fortifications were commanded by Drayton's brother Thomas.

---

dreadnought • *n.* historical a type of battleship introduced in the early 20th century, larger and faster than its predecessors and equipped entirely with large-caliber guns.

ORIGIN: Named after Britain's HMS *Dreadnought,* which was the first to be completed (1906).

***Dreadnought*, HMS** • a ship of advanced design, produced first by the British, and completed in 1906, marking the beginning of rapid development in big-gun firepower. It displaced about 18,000 tons, had steam turbines (instead of reciprocating engines), could attain a speed of 21 knots, and gave its name to a new class of advanced battleships.

Britain and the United States both built twenty-two dreadnoughts, and Germany nineteen, while Japan and Italy each built six. Russia and France both built seven of these ships.

---

dredger |ˈdrejər| • *n.* a barge or other vessel designed for dredging harbors or other bodies of water.

Dred Scott v. Sanford • a decision of the U.S. Supreme Court on March 6, 1857, ruling against Dred Scott to make slavery legal in all territories, the MISSOURI COMPROMISE unconstitutional, and Congress powerless to prohibit slavery. Antislavery lawyers helped Scott sue for his freedom in 1846 in Missouri, a slave state he, his family, and his owner returned to after living temporarily in free areas. They asserted that he was a free man for having lived in free territory. Scott initially won his case, but the Missouri Supreme Court overturned the ruling, and the case was taken to the U.S. Supreme Court. The court concluded that since Scott was a slave and not a citizen, he could not sue in a federal court.

dress • *v.* **1** draw up (troops) in the proper alignment. **2** (of troops) come into such an alignment. • *n.* denoting military uniform or other clothing used on formal or ceremonial occasions: *a dress suit.*

▸**dress ship** decorate a ship with flags, for a special occasion.

dressing station • a place for giving emergency treatment to troops injured in battle. *the family received a letter from Joe written in a field dressing station.*

dress parade • a military parade in full dress uniform.

drift |drift| • *n.* the deviation of a vessel, aircraft, or projectile from its intended or expected course as the result of currents or winds: *the pilot had not noticed any appreciable drift.*

drifting mine • a floating mine that drifts under the influence of waves, wind, current, or tide.

drill • *n.* **1** dismounted drill, the standardized precision movement of military personnel in formation for the purpose of developing discipline and coordination of effort. **2** a training session for Reserve components.

drill sergeant • a noncommissioned officer who trains soldiers in military parade exercises.

drogue |drōg| • *n.* **1** a device, typically conical or funnel-shaped with open ends, towed behind a boat, aircraft, or other moving object to reduce speed or improve stability. **2** a similar object used as an aerial target for gunnery practice or as a windsock. **3** (in tanker aircraft) a funnel-shaped part on the end of the hose into which a probe is inserted by an aircraft being refueled in flight.

drone • *n.* a vehicle designed to be remotely controlled during operations on land or sea or in the air. See also REMOTELY PILOTED VEHICLE; UNMANNED AERIAL VEHICLE.

drop zone • a specific area upon which airborne troops, equipment, or supplies are airdropped.

Drug Enforcement Administration • a U.S. federal agency under the aegis of the Department of Justice whose primary goal is the enforcement of U.S. drug laws. The agency, which dates from 1973, works with other federal bodies such as the U.S. Customs Service, other countries, and international organizations such as the UNITED NATIONS and Interpol.

drum • *n.* historical a military drummer. ▸**drum someone out** expel or dismiss someone with ignominy from a place or institution: *he was* ***drummed out of*** *the air force.*
ORIGIN: with allusion to the formal military drumbeat accompanying dismissal from a regiment.

drumfire • *n.* heavy continuous rapid artillery fire.

drumhead • *n.* **1** chiefly historical the circular top of a ship's capstan, with holes into which bars are placed to turn it. • *adj.* carried out by or as if by an army in the field; improvised or summary: *a drumhead court-martial.*

drum major • a noncommissioned officer commanding the drummers of a regimental band.

dry dock • a dock that can be drained of water to allow the inspection and repair of a ship's hull. • (**dry-dock**) place (a ship) in a dry dock.

dry run • another term for dummy run.

DSC • *abbr.* (in the UK) Distinguished Service Cross, a decoration for distinguished active service at sea, instituted in 1914.

DSCS • *abbr.* Defense Satellite Communications System, a satellite-based communications system that provides super-high frequency communications among the DEPARTMENT OF DEFENSE, commanders at multiple locations, and troops in the field.

DSM • *abbr.* (in the UK) Distinguished Service Medal, a medal for distinguished service at sea, instituted in 1914.

DSO • *abbr.* (in the UK) Distinguished Service Order, a decoration for distinguished service awarded to officers of the army and navy, instituted in 1886.

DSP • *abbr.* Defense Support Program.

DU • *abbr.* depleted uranium.

dual agent • one who is simultaneously and independently employed by two or more intelligence agencies covering targets for both.

dual-purpose weapon • a weapon that can be used effectively against air or surface targets.

Duchambon, Louis Du Pont (Chevalier) (1680–1775) • born in France. Duchambon's military career took him to New France, and he was at PORT ROYAL when it fell to the English in 1710. When the French had to build a new capital in 1713, he was in the founding party when it stepped ashore at what would become Louisbourg. Duchambon was promoted to second in command at LOUISBURG in April 1744, early in KING GEORGE'S WAR (1744–48), but the sudden death of Governor Duquesnel the following October unexpectedly made Duchambon first in command. On July 15, 1745, Duchambon and his companions were put aboard a British ship and taken to France, where Duchambon lived on his pension for the next thirty years.

duck • *n.* another term for DUKW.

Duck and Cover! • catchphrase popular in the 1950s to describe the immediate actions necessary for individuals to take to protect themselves in the event of a nuclear detonation. Elementary schoolchild in the United States in the early 1950s learned by heart the phrase and the actions it invoked.

dud • *n.* explosive munition that has not been armed as intended or that has failed to explode after being armed.

Duffy, Francis Patrick (1871–1932) • Roman Catholic military chaplain, born in Cobourg, Ontario, Canada. He was later U.S. naturalized. During WORLD WAR I Duffy served in France as part of the AMERICAN EXPEDITIONARY FORCES. He was called the "warrior priest," and known for his bravery, compassion, and warmth toward all soldiers. Duffy was awarded the DISTINGUISHED SERVICE CROSS and the DISTINGUISHED SERVICE MEDAL. His funeral was a national event, attended by tens of thousands.

As an editor and writer, Duffy's theological views were considered modernist and consequently frowned upon by the church hierarchy.

---

dugout • *n.* a shelter that is dug in the ground and roofed over, especially one used by troops in warfare: *the German gun crews kept in their dugouts.*

Dugway Proving Grounds • located some 85 miles southwest of Salt Lake City, Utah, and established in 1942, it serves as the principal test and evaluation area for Department of Defense defensive equipment and countermeasures against chemical and biological agents as well as for battlefield smoke and obscurants, production qualification testing of mortar and artillery munitions, and environmental testing technology. Some sixteen military and 435 civilian personnel work on the 798,855-acre installation.

Duke, Basil Wilson (1838-1916) • Confederate army officer, born in Kentucky. Duke saw action at SHILOH (1862), where he was wounded, and later at a number of engagements in Tennessee. After the war Duke was active in law and civic affairs, and he wrote articles and books about the CIVIL WAR.

DUKW • **(duck)** *n.* an amphibious transport vehicle, especially as used by the Allies during WORLD WAR II.

ORIGIN: an official designation, being a combination of factory-applied letters referring to features of the vehicle.

Dulles, Allen Welsh (1893–1969) • director of the CENTRAL INTELLIGENCE AGENCY (1953-61), an organization which he helped establish. Dulles, born in Watertown, New York, was generally well-regarded despite such significant failures during his tenure as the Soviet downing of a U-2 spy plane over Russian territory and the BAY OF PIGS fiasco (1961), which ended his career. Dulles was active in the State Department's Foreign Service during WORLD WAR I and in the OFFICE OF STRATEGIC SERVICES during WORLD WAR II. Dulles practiced law with his older brother, JOHN FOSTER DULLES.

Dulles, John Foster (1888–1959) • secretary of state (1953-59), born in Washington, D.C. Dulles advocated the threat of nuclear retaliation as the chief deterrent to Soviet aggression during the COLD WAR. He served on the War Trade Board during WORLD WAR I and acted as delegate to the PARIS PEACE CONFERENCE (1919), where he sought to limit German reparations. Between the wars he actively advocated Wilsonian principles. Postwar planning became his primary interest once war again seemed inevitable. He chaired the Commission to Study the Bases of a Just and Durable Peace (1941) and personally presented its plan to President FRANKLIN D. ROOSEVELT (1943). He represented President HARRY S. TRUMAN at most major international meetings (1945) and negotiated the treaty ending the occupation of Japan (1951).

dumb bomb • a bomb that is neither powered nor guided and depends on accurate dropping on the target for its effectiveness.

dumdum (also **dumdum bullet**) • *n.* a kind of soft-nosed bullet that expands on impact and inflicts laceration.

ORIGIN: late 19th cent.: from *Dum Dum*, name of a town and arsenal near Calcutta, India, where such bullets were first produced.

Dummer's War • (1721–1725) a series of skirmishes and raids in New England between British and French colonial forces. These engagements came to be called Dummer's War in reference to William Dummer, the acting colonial governor of Massachusetts, who built Fort Dummer near present-day Brattleboro, Vermont, in 1724. In 1721, the British raided Norridgewock, an Abenaki Indian village and French stronghold in Maine, and drove off the French Jesuit missionary, Father Sebastien Rasle, and seized the dictionary of the Abenaki language which he had been compiling. In 1724 the British again raided Norridgewock, took the village, and killed Father Rasle. These colonial raids and skirmishes are also known as LOVEWELL'S WAR, so named after JOHN LOVEWELL.

dummy • *n.* (pl. **-ies**) **1** a figure used as a target in shooting or bayonet practice or in safety tests for vehicles: *crash-test dummies.* **2** an object designed to resemble and serve as a substitute for the real or usual one. **3** a blank round of ammunition.

dummy run • any simulated firing practice, particularly a dive-bombing approach made without release of a bomb. Also called DRY RUN.

Dunbar, Moses (1746–77) • loyalist and traitor during the REVOLUTIONARY WAR, born in Wallingford, Connecticut. Dunbar was condemned for illegal recruitment for England. His loyalist views came from his membership in the local Church of England.

Dunbar was the first civilian executed for treason in the state of Connecticut.

Dunker • a member or the German Baptist Brethren, a sect of Baptist Christians founded in 1708 but living in the United States since the 1720s. The Dunkers maintain a strictly disciplined church life of nonresistance, simplicity, and separation from the world. They and other German-speaking pacifists were attracted to William Penn's colony of Pennsylvania, whose pacifist-oriented social ideals and institutions worked a lasting influence upon American life.

ORIGIN: early 18th century: from Pennsylvanian German, from dunke 'dip,' from German *tunken* 'dip or plunge,' because they baptize by immersing the candidate three times, once for each person of the Trinity.

Dunkirk • (French **Dunkerque**) the northernmost seaport of France which was the site of a massive week-long evacuation of Allied European troops to England after France fell to the Germans in May–June 1940. The effort, involving dozens of military and voluntary private boats, succeeded in rescuing more than 330,000 troops amid heavy shelling and bombardment while British and French forces held back the Germans from land attack.

Dunmore's War • see LORD DUNMORE'S WAR.

dunnage • *n.* **1** pieces of wood, matting, or similar material used to keep a cargo in position in a ship's hold. **2** a person's belongings, especially those brought on board ship.

dunnage bag • a kitbag.

du Pont, Henry Algernon (1838–1926) • Union army officer and WEST POINT graduate, born at the Eleutherian Mills, near Wilmington, Delaware. Du Pont was first engaged in the defense of Washington (1861). and Lynchburg. He was awarded the

CONGRESSIONAL MEDAL OF HONOR for gallantry at CEDAR CREEK (1864). He was involved in the family business, E.I. Du Pont de Nemours & Co. and in railroading before pursuing a political career. As U.S. senator from Delaware (1906–1916), he was a member and chairman of the MILITARY AFFAIRS COMMITTEE. His postwar literary pursuits included works on the war.

Du Pont, Samuel Francis (1803–65) • Union naval officer and noted tactitian, born in Bergen Point (now Bayonne), New York. His capture of the forts at PORT ROYAL (1861) was the first major Federal victory of the CIVIL WAR. He also led the failed invasion of CHARLESTON HARBOR (1863), the worst Federal naval defeat of the war. That attack, ordered by the Navy Department, was considered doomed by naval hydrographers.

Du Pont Circle in Washington, D.C., and several U.S. Navy vessels were named for him.

Duryée's Zouaves • the CIVIL WAR-era 5th New York Volunteer Infantry Regiment organized in April 1861 and first commanded by Abram Duryée. The regiment entered Federal service on May 9, 1861, and was assigned to the ARMY OF THE POTOMAC. The regiment distinguished itself in the battles of GAINES' MILL and at SECOND BULL RUN in 1862 before being mustered out in May 1863. Called one of the best volunteer regiments of the war, Duryée's Zouaves were equipped on the pattern of the 19th century French Army zouaves with a fancy uniform consisting of white leggings, billowy red trousers, a sash, a short embroidered jacket, and a tasseled fez. The zouave uniform was impractical in the field but was attractive for recruiting purposes. The 165th New York Volunteer Infantry, organized in late 1862, is sometimes referred to as the 2nd Duryée's Zouaves.

Duster • (**M-42**) a self-propelled twin 40-mm rocket-launcher used as an antiaircraft weapon for use against low-flying aircraft.

dust shot • the smallest size of gunshot.

DUSTWUN • *abbr.* duty status-whereabouts unknown.

Dutch-Indian Wars • a series of conflicts between Native Americans and Dutch settlers on Long Island, in the area that is now New York City, and in the Hudson Valley between 1643 and 1660. The fighting arose over divergent views about what ownership of land entailed, and the two sides' inability to find peaceable mutual coexistence.

duty status-whereabouts unknown • (**DUSTWUN**) a transitory casualty status, applicable only to military personnel, that is used when the responsible commander suspects that the member may be a casualty whose absence is voluntary, but does not feel sufficient evidence currently exists to make a definite determination of "missing" or "deceased."

Dwight, William (1831-88) • Union army officer, born in Springfield, Massachusetts. His controversial career included charges of misconduct for remaining in the rear while his men were engaged in battle. Dwight was also accused of drunkenness and of literally using black soldiers as cannon fodder. He was active in the battles of WILLIAMSBURG (1862) and CEDAR CREEK (1864) and the siege of PORT HUDSON (1863).

DWRIA • *abbr.* died of wounds received in action.

Ee

E-2 • see HAWKEYE.

E-2C • see HAWKEYE.

E-3 • see SENTRY.

E-8A J-STARS • see JSTARS.

EA-6A • see INTRUDER.

EA-6B • see PROWLER.

eagle • *n.* a figure of an eagle, especially as a symbol of the United States, or formerly as a Roman or French ensign.

eagle, the • slang **1** the federal government of the United States. **2** money, especially U.S. currency. **3** in the CIVIL WAR, a certificate of discharge from the Union Army. See also EAGLE DAY.

Eagle • (**F-15**) an air-superiority fighter also capable of playing a strike/attack role. Its first version, the F-15A, was a single-seat, twin-turbofan aircraft with fixed-geometry swept wings of low aspect. Production continued until 1979, with a total of 385 built. The F-15B, developed simultaneously, had a two-seat cockpit. The F-15C variant (and its companion derivative, the two-seat F-15D), a single-engine mixed power fighter with a radial engine in the nose and a jet engine behind the wing, was the last U.S. Navy fighter built by Curtiss. It remains in operation in the United States with Air Force tactical fighter wings and fighter interceptor squadrons, and is credited with nearly all the "kills" in the (second) PERSIAN GULF WAR.

Eagle Claw, Operation • a disastrous mission, on April 24, 1980, to rescue fifty-two Americans held hostage by Iranian militants.

Eight helicopters flew 600 miles to a site called DESERT ONE to rendezvous with C-130 transport planes. Bad weather and mechanical failure aborted the mission, leaving eight marines dead. The failed mission followed the CARTER DOCTRINE, announced by President JIMMY CARTER on January 23, 1980, which asserted that the United States would use military force if necessary to defend its "vital interests" in the Persian Gulf region.

eagle day • slang (in WORLD WAR II and the VIETNAM WAR) payday. See also EAGLE.

Payday was also referred to as "the day (or when) the eagle (flies, screams, shits, squawks, etc.)."

Eaker, Ira Clarence (1896–1987) • air force officer and noted pilot, born in Field Creek, Texas. Eaker participated in historic firsts in midair refueling and instrument flying. He was awarded the DISTINGUISHED FLYING CROSS for his role in a goodwill tour of Latin America (1926). During WORLD WAR II he was commander of the 8th Air Force in its combined bomber offensive with the ROYAL AIR FORCE, and he later commanded the allied air forces in the Mediterranean. Eaker also served as deputy commander in chief of the U.S. Army Air Forces (1945–47). He was made a four-star general (1985) by special act of Congress.

Eaker was active in postwar defense work at both Hughes Aircraft and Douglas Aircraft.

Early, Jubal Anderson (1816–94) • Confederate army officer in the ARMY OF NORTHERN VIRGINIA, born near Rocky Mount, Franklin County, Virginia. Early played important roles at the Battles of BULL RUN (1861) and ANTIETAM (1862), earning praise from ROBERT E. LEE. Later Early suffered decisive defeats in the SHENANDOAH VALLEY, (1864).

Early's postwar writings greatly influenced 19th-century views of the war, arguing for the South's greatness, the valor of its fighting troops, and the superiority of its generals. In the South he was considered the preeminent authority on Confederate military affairs.

Early Spring • an antireconnaissance satellite weapon system.

early warning • early notification of the launch or approach of unknown weapons or weapon carriers.

earthquake bomb • (also **Grand Slam**) a 22,000 pound. deep-penetration bomb equipped with a 9,135 pound. warhead of Torpex explosive, used in WORLD WAR II to destroy bridges, viaducts, and other infrastructure. It was designed by British engineer Barnes Wallis and introduced in March 1945.

At 26½ feet in length, the Grand Slam was the heaviest bomb used in the war, streamlined and equipped with angled fins that caused the bomb to spin rapidly as it fell at speed-of-sound velocity. The bomb penetrated the ground and, when it exploded, set off shock waves powerful enough to topple nearby buildings; the blast could create a crater 30 feet deep and 125 feet wide.

earthwork • *n.* **1** a large artificial bank of soil, especially one made as a defense in ancient times. **2** the process of excavating soil in civil engineering work.

ease • *v.* **1** (**ease something away/down/off**) slacken a rope or sail slowly or gently. **2** (**at ease**) in a relaxed attitude with the feet apart and the hands behind the back (often as a command): *all right, **stand at ease!***

Eastern bloc • the countries of eastern and central Europe that were under Soviet domination from the end of WORLD WAR II until the collapse of the Soviet communist system in 1989–91.

Easter Offensive • an assault on South Vietnam by the NORTH VIETNAMESE ARMY (NVA) in the early months of 1972, the aim of which appeared to be winning the war outright. The offensive made initial territorial gains and brought the NVA periously close to the doors of Saigon. American and South Vietnamese resistance was then better organized to repel the advances, and a heavy American-led bombing campaign, the first since 1968, began. The NVA suffered an estimated 100,000 casualties.

easting • *n.* **1** distance traveled or measured eastward, especially at sea. **2** a figure or line representing eastward distance on a map (expressed by convention as the first part of a grid reference, before northing).

Eastman, William Reed (1835–1925) • soldier and chaplain with the Union army (1859–64), born in New York City. After the CIVIL WAR he played a pivotal role in library development, a career he undertook after more than twenty years as a clergyman.

easy • *adj.* (**easier** |ˈēzēər|, **easiest** |ˈēzēist|) (of an object of attack or criticism) having no defense; vulnerable: *he was vulnerable and an easy target.*

PHRASES: **stand easy!** used to instruct soldiers standing at ease that they may relax their attitude further.

Eberle, Edward Walter |ˈebərlē| (1864–1929) • chief of naval operations (1923–27), born in Denton, Texas. During his tenure he was involved in such major strategic concerns as the defense of the Philippines and Guam. As a commander, Eberle developed and implemented the use of smokescreen tactics. He also served as superintendent of the U.S. NAVAL ACADEMY (1915–19).

Eberstadt Report • a study commissioned by Navy Secretary JAMES V. FORRESTAL in 1945 and conducted by private businessman Ferdinand Eberstadt. It examined the possibility of and made recommendations concerning the merging the U.S. Army, including its subordinate air force, and the U.S. Navy. It also recommended coordination and improved support for the intelligence program.

E-boat • a German torpedo boat used in WORLD WAR II.

ORIGIN: from *E-* for *enemy* + BOAT.

echelon |ˈesHəˌlän| • *n.* **1** a part of a military force differentiated by position in battle or by function: *the rear echelon.* **2** a formation of troops, ships, aircraft, or vehicles in parallel rows with the end of each row projecting further than the one in front. • *v.* arrange in an echelon formation: (**echeloning**) *the echeloning of fire teams.*

echo sounder • a device for determining the depth of the seabed or detecting objects in water by measuring the time taken for sound echoes to return to the listener.

Eckert, William Dole (1909–71) • air force officer and fighter pilot, born in Freeport, Illinois. Eckert saw active duty only briefly during World War II. After the war he held a series of increasingly responsible administrative appointments, including vice commander of the Tactical Air Command (1956–61) and comptroller of the air force (1961), from which he retired the same year because of illness. Eckert received a number of honors during his career, including the Distinguished Flying Cross and two Distinguished Service Medals.

As commissioner of major league baseball (1965–68), Eckert, a surprise appointment, was weak and ineffective. He was ultimately forced to resign.

ECM • *abbr.* electronic countermeasures.

ecological terrorism • the deliberate destruction or pollution of an area of the environment as an act of warfare or terrorism. See ecoterrorism.

Economic Cooperation Act • an act signed by President Harry S. Truman on April 3, 1948, after World War II, to establish the Economic Cooperation Administration to administer the Marshall Plan. It authorized U.S. financial aid to certain European countries to restore agricultural and industrial productivity, stabilize currency, and expand foreign trade.

economic retention stock • that portion of the quantity of an item excess of the approved force retention level that has been determined will be more economical to retain for future peacetime issue in lieu of replacement of future issues by procurement. To warrant economic retention, items must have a reasonably predictable demand rate.

ecoterrorism • *n.* **1** violence carried out to further environmentalist ends. **2** the action of causing deliberate environmental damage in order to further political ends. Another term for ecological terrorism.

E-day • the day on which a NATO exercise commences.

Eddy, Jonathan (1727–1804) • army officer, born in Norton, Massachusetts. Eddy emigrated to Nova Scotia where he led the siege of Fort Cumberland (1776) in an unsuccessful attempt to oust the British from that colony and win it for the American cause. After fleeing back to America, he eventually settled in Maine, where he played a key role in preserving the northeastern area of the state for America.

Edmonds, Sara Emma Evelyn (1841–98) • soldier, nurse, and spy for the Union army, born in New Brunswick, Canada. Edmonds joined the army under the name of Franklin Thompson, successfully hiding her true sex from most of her comrades. Edmonds/Thompson participated in the battle of First Bull Run (1861) and the Peninsular Campaign (1862). She made several information-gathering trips behind Confederate lines, posing variously as a slave woman, a young Confederate boy, and an Irish peddler woman. Edmonds deserted in 1863 (but eventually had Thompson's name cleared) and lived again as a woman. In the last year of the war, she nursed the wounded at Harpers Ferry.

Emma Edmonds Seeyle (her married name) is the only woman ever acknowledged as a member of the Grand Army of the Republic. She also received a pension for her war service.

Edson's Ridge, Battle of • see Bloody Ridge, Battle of.

education, military • the systematic instruction of individuals in subjects which will enhance their knowledge of the science and art of war.

EF-111A • see Raven.

effective • *n.* a soldier fit and available for service.

egress |ˈēˌgres| • *n.* **1** the action of going out of or leaving a place: *direct means of access and egress for passengers.* **2** a way out: *a narrow egress.* • *v.* go out of or leave (a place): *they'd egress the area by heading southwest.*

Einstein, Albert (1879–1955) • theoretical physicist, born in Ulm, Germany. Einstein's 1939 letter to President Franklin D. Roosevelt urging that the United States develop an atomic bomb gave rise to the Manhattan Project. Einstein himself however, played no role in that undertaking. He received the Nobel Prize in physics (1921) for his elaboration of the quantum theory.

Eisenhower Doctrine • a foreign-policy program presented by President Dwight D. Eisenhower and approved by Congress on March 9, 1957, during the Cold War. Often characterized as an extension of the Truman Doctrine, it authorized the use of military and economic aid to prevent the spread of communism in nations in the Middle East.

Eisenhower, Dwight David (1890–1969) • U.S. Army general and 34th president of the United States (1953–61), born in Denison, Texas and raised in Abilene, Kansas. He graduated from West Point in 1915, but saw no action in World War I, in which he was in charge of training camps. Eisenhower held various staff assignments in the interwar years, but his military career began to rise when he was named to head the War Plans Division (later Operations Division) of the War Department in 1941, responsible for planning the strategy of the war. He took command of American forces in Great Britain in 1942 and was soon named supreme commander of the ALLIED EXPEDITIONARY FORCE, leading the invasion of French North Africa, Sicily, and Italy. He was promoted to four-star general (1943) and made supreme commander for OPERATION OVERLORD (1944), the invasion of France. Eisenhower was recognized as an outstanding strategist, adept at handling complex joint operations. In 1944 he was promoted to five-star General of the Army. He led the BATTLE OF THE BULGE (1944–45), the greatest single battle ever fought by the U.S. Army, before moving into Germany. After receiving the unconditional German surrender (May 1945), Eisenhower served as head of the occupation in the American zone for several months until he was named CHIEF OF STAFF of the U.S. Army (1945), a post which he held until his retirement in 1948. After two years as president of Columbia University, in 1951 he was sent to Paris by President HARRY S. TRUMAN as the first supreme commander of the Allied forces in Europe, where he organized the beginning of a NATO armed force and advocated the creation of a united Europe. In 1952 Eisenhower successfully ran for president on the Republican ticket, with RICHARD M. NIXON as his running mate. During his two terms (1953–61), he negotiated a truce to end the KOREAN WAR (1953); launched the interstate highway system (1956); reduced spending on conventional weapons while building more bombs and bombers; and constantly searched for peace with the Soviets. At the Geneva Conference in 1954, together with secretary of state JOHN FOSTER DULLES, he agreed to the division of Vietnam and the creation of the SOUTHEAST ASIA TREATY ORGANIZATION (SEATO), which formed the basis for later U.S. involvement in Vietnam. When the governor of Arkansas defied court-ordered school desegregation, Eisenhower sent federal troops to Little Rock to enforce the decree (1957). In 1958 he sent U.S. troops into Lebanon in accordance with his earlier proclaimed EISENHOWER DOCTRINE. The last year of his presidency was devoted to the pursuit of peace, but a planned summit conference in May 1960 was thwarted by the U-2 INCIDENT. His farewell address (1961) warned of "unwarranted influence" on government "by the military-industrial complex."

ejection • *n.* **1** escape from an aircraft by means of an independently propelled seat or capsule. **2** in air armament, the process of forcefully separating an aircraft store from an aircraft to achieve satisfactory separation.

ejection system • **a** (**command ejection system**) a system in which the pilot of an aircraft or the occupant of the other ejection seat(s) initiates ejection, resulting in the automatic ejection of all occupants. **b** (**command select ejection system**) a system permitting the optional transfer, from one crew station to another, of the control of a command ejection system for automatic ejection of all occupants. **c** (**independent ejection system**) an ejection system that operates independently of other ejection systems installed in one aircraft. **d** (**sequenced ejection system**) a system that ejects the aircraft crew in sequence to ensure a safe minimum total time of escape without collision.

El Alamein, Battle of • a WORLD WAR II battle in the Egyptian desert in late October, 1942, between Allied forces under the British command of Field Marshall BERNARD LAW MONTGOMERY, and German and Italian Axis forces under the command of ERWIN ROMMEL. The fighting extended into early November and was eventually won by the Allied forces to become the first British land victory over the German army in the war.

Elbert, Samuel (1740–88) • Revolutionary army officer in command of the Continental forces in Georgia, born in either Savannah, Georgia, or Prince William Country, South Carolina. Elbert, though he saw no major victories, was well-regarded for the gallant fighting of his troops and for his courage and patriotism. As governor of Georgia (1785) Elbert worked toward improved relations with Indians and oversaw the chartering of the state university.

Electric Boat • a Groton, Connecticut-based company that in 1900 built the first U.S. Navy submarine, the USS *Holland.* It has achieved many other firsts in submarine technology since then, including the USS *Nautilus*, the world's first nuclear powered vessel. Electric Boat grew into GENERAL DYNAMICS and is today a division of it.

Electric Jet • slang F-16. See FIGHTING FALCON.

electric torpedo • a torpedo that is powered by an electric motor. It was first developed by Germany in WORLD WAR II and then widely copied. It travels quietly and without a wake and represented a significant advance in torpedo technology.

electrode sweep • in naval-mine warfare, a magnetic cable sweep in which the water forms part of the electric circuit.

electromagnetic interference • (**EMI**) any electromagnetic disturbance that interrupts, obstructs, or otherwise degrades or limits the effective performance of electronics or electrical equipment. It can be induced intentionally, as in some forms of electronic warfare, or unintentionally, as a result of spurious emissions and responses, intermodulation products, and the like.

electromagnetic pulse • (**EMP**) the electromagnetic radiation from a nuclear explosion. The resulting electric and magnetic fields may couple with electrical or electronic systems to produce damaging current and voltage systems. Electromagnetic pulses may also be caused by nonnuclear means.

electromagnetic radiation • radiation made up of oscillating electric and magnetic fields and propagated with the speed of light. Electromagnetic radiation includes gamma radiation, X rays, ultraviolet radiation, visible radiation, infrared radiation, radar, and radio waves.

electronic countermeasures • actions taken to deny or degrade the enemy's ability to effectively use the electromagnetic spectrum against friendly forces.

electronic deception • deliberate activity designed to mislead an enemy in the interpretation or use of information received by the enemy's electronic systems.

electronic jamming • the deliberate radiation, reradiation, or reflection of electromagnetic energy for the purpose of disrupting enemy use of electronic devices, equipment, or systems.

electronic reconnaissance • the detection, identification, evaluation, and location of foreign electromagnetic radiations emanating from other than nuclear detonations or radioactive sources.

electronics intelligence • (**ELINT**) technical and geolocation intelligence derived from foreign non-communications electromagnetic radiations emanating from other than nuclear detonations or radioactive sources.

electronic warfare • any military action involving the use of electromagnetic and directed energy to control the electromagnetic spectrum or to attack the enemy.

electro-optical intelligence • (**ELECTRO-OPTINT**) intelligence, other than signals intelligence, derived from the optical monitoring of the electromagnetic spectrum from ultraviolet (0.01 micrometers) through far infrared (1,000 micrometers).

electro-optic guided bomb • (**EOGB**) an aerial bomb equipped with electro-optical guidance systems designed to ensure highly accurate target lock-on and terminal homing.

electro-optics • *n.* the technology associated with those components, devices, and systems that are designed to interact between the electromagnetic (optical) and the electric (electronic) state.

ELECTRO-OPTINT • *abbr.* electro-optical intelligence.

elevate • *v.* to raise the axis of a piece of artillery to increase its range.

elevation • *n.* **1** the vertical distance of a point or level on or affixed to the surface of the Earth measured from mean sea level **2** the setting on the sight of a mortar, artillery piece, or other gun or missile launcher used to regulate the arc of the projectile or missile and thus its distance and striking point.

elicitation • *n.* acquisition of information from a person or group in a manner that does not disclose the intent of the interview or conversation. A technique of human source intelligence collection, generally overt, unless the collector is other than he purports to be.

ELINT |'elint| • covert intelligence-gathering by electronic means.

ORIGIN: 1960s: blend of *electronic* and *intelligence*.

Elkhorn Tavern, Battle of • see PEA RIDGE, BATTLE OF.

Ellis, "Pete" Earl Hancock (1880–1923) • Marine officer and amphibious warfare specialist noted for his descriptions of assault operations for seizing islands in the Pacific (1920). Ellis died while on a covert mission to Micronesia.

Ellsberg, Daniel (1931?–) • military analyst and nonviolent activist, born in Chicago. Ellsberg spent two years in South Vietnam as a STATE DEPARTMENT advisor (1965–67) and contributed to the PENTAGON's internal classified history of the war. Rebuffed by his failed attempts to release this information to Congress, he provided these so-called PENTAGON PAPERS, which revealed presidential failures and deceptions, to the *New York Times* and *Washington Post,* where they were published in 1971, helping to mobilize public opposition to the war. Ellsberg was tried for espionage but the charges were dismissed because of government tampering.

Ellsworth, Elmer Ephraim (1837–61) • the first prominent Union soldier to die in the CIVIL WAR, though not, strictly speaking, in battle. Ellsworth, born in Malta, New York, first gained prominence as commander of a championship drill outfit (based on the ZOUAVE model) that toured the country in 1860. He entered the Springfield, Illinois, law office of ABRAHAM LINCOLN later that year, and soon accompanied him to Washington. When war broke out, Ellsworth raised a voluntary infantry in New York, and while leading a detachment in Alexandria, Virginia, impetuously cut down a Confederate flag from the roof of a hotel. As he was carrying it off, he was shot and killed by the proprietor. Ellsworth's funeral was held in the East Room of the WHITE HOUSE, and his body later lay in state at city hall in New York and the state house in Albany.

Ellsworth was viewed as a martyr to the cause, and his death galvanized the Northern war effort.

Elmira • a city in southern New York that was the site of the worst UNION prison during the CIVIL WAR. Confederate prisoners of war were held at the prison, which had a death rate of 25 percent.

El Salvador • Central American country that experienced a civil war in the 1980s, in which the United States was involved, mostly in the provision of arms, intelligence, and tactical advice for right-wing civilian and military groups who opposed the FMLN. The protracted struggle, lasting for most of the 1980s, never involved U.S. troops but claimed many lives on both sides. With the end of the COLD WAR and the depoliticization of the conflict in U.S. perception, the fighting wound down and peace talks were held in the early 1990s, leading to free elections in 1994.

Elzey, Arnold (1816–71) • Confederate army officer, born in Somerset City, Maryland. Elzey was instrumental in the victory at FIRST BULL RUN (1861), but nevertheless ranks as one of the least famous major generals in that army. After being wounded at GAINES' MILL (1862), he was made commander of the DEPARTMENT OF RICHMOND, responsible for organizing and mobilizing local defense troops.

He was born Arnold Elzey Jones, but dropped the surname when commissioned as a lieutenant following his graduation from WEST POINT.

emancipation • *n.* **1** the action or process of setting free, especially from legal, social, or political restrictions. **2** the action or process of delivering from slavery.

Emancipation Proclamation, Preliminary • on September 22, 1862, five days after the Battle of ANTIETAM, President ABRAHAM LINCOLN declared Union support for the freedom of slaves in states still in rebellion at the start of the following year. The announcement marked a shift in the North's military policy and made the CIVIL WAR a war between slavery and freedom. He issued the **Emancipation Proclamation** on January 1, 1863.

embankment • *n.* **1** a wall or bank of earth or stone built to prevent a river flooding an area. **2** a bank of earth or stone built to carry a road or railroad over an area of low ground.

embargo • *n.* (pl. **-oes**) **1** an official ban on trade or other commercial activity with a particular country: *an* ***embargo on*** *grain sales | the oil embargo of 1973.* **2** an official prohibition on any activity. **3** an order of a state forbidding foreign ships to enter, or any ships to leave, its ports. • *v.* (**-oes, -oed**) **1** (usually **be embargoed**) impose an official ban on (trade or a country or commodity): *the country has been virtually embargoed by most of the noncommunist world.* **2** officially ban the publication of: *documents of national security importance are routinely embargoed.* **3** archaic seize (a ship or goods) for state service.

embarkation • *n.* the process of putting personnel and/or vehicles and their associated stores and equipment into ships and/or aircraft.

embarkation area • an area ashore, including a group of embarkation points, in which final preparations for embarkation are completed and through which assigned personnel and loads for craft and ships are called forward to embark.

embattled • *adj.* (of a place or people) involved in or prepared for war, especially because surrounded by enemy forces: *the embattled Yugoslavian republics.*

embay • *v.* (usually **be embayed**) (chiefly of the wind) confine (a sailing vessel) to a bay: *ships were embayed between two headlands.*

emergency anchorage • a place to anchor for naval vessels, support units, auxiliaries, or merchant ships. It may have only limited means of defense. See also ADVANCED FLEET ANCHORAGE; ASSEMBLY ANCHORAGE; HOLDING ANCHORAGE; WORKING ANCHORAGE.

emergency in war • an operational contingency in a limited area caused by a critical aggravation of combat operations and requiring special and immediate action by national and allied commanders. The existence of such an emergency shall be determined by the allied commander responsible for the limited area involved, in consultation with the national commander concerned.

emergency nuclear risk • a degree of nuclear risk where anticipated effects may cause some temporary shock, casualties, or both and may significantly reduce the unit's combat efficiency.

Emergency Plan White • a detailed outline prepared in the early 1920s by the Army GENERAL STAFF'S MILITARY INTELLIGENCE DIVISION in response to alleged Communist threats to U.S. internal security. It included instructions for army intervention to suppress potential civil disturbances and armed insurrections within the United States.

It also included a fill-in-the-blank presidential proclamation to commit troops if state authorities were unable to handle a disturbance.

emergency scramble • in air intercept, a code meaning, "Carrier(s) addressed immediately launch all available fighter aircraft as combat air patrol." If all available aircraft are not required, numerals and/or type may be added to the code.

EMI • *abbr.* electromagnetic interference.

emissary |ˈeməˌserē| • *n.* (pl. **-ies**) a person sent on a special mission, usually as a diplomatic representative.

Emory, William Hemsley (1811–87) • army officer, born in Queen Annes County, Maryland. Emory was better known as a surveyor and cartographer who mapped the border between the United States and Mexico (completed 1857). The U.S. Senate published his maps of the upper Mississippi basin (1843) and Texas (1844). Emory also worked on the survey to determine the boundary between the United States and the British provinces of Canada. During the MEXICAN WAR (1846–48) he was chief engineer officer and acting assistant adjutant general of the Army of the West. During the CIVIL WAR he saw action at WILLIAMSBURG, Hanover Courthouse, and SECOND BULL RUN (all 1862).

A western oak, *Quercus emoryi*, was named in his honor, as was Emory Peak, a 2,370-meter mountain in the Big Bend country of Texas.

EMP • *abbr.* electromagnetic pulse.

emplacement • *n.* **1** a structure on or in which something is firmly placed. **2** a platform or defended position where a gun is placed for firing.

encamp • *v.* settle in or establish a camp, especially a military one: *100,000 soldiers are still encamped around the city.*

encipher • *v.* convert plain text into unintelligible form by means of a cipher system.

encrypt • *v.* convert plain text into unintelligible forms by means of a cryptosystem.
DERIVATIVES: **encryption** *n.*

Endecott, John (c. 1588–1665) • a founder of the MASSACHUSETTS BAY COLONY who served several years, intermittently, as its governor or deputy governor between 1629 and 1664. He led an ineffectual expedition against the PEQUOT (1636), who had been attacking isolated settlements. Their attacks resumed, and they were wiped out the following year in the PEQUOT WAR (1637).

endurance • *n.* the time an aircraft can continue flying, or a ground vehicle or ship can continue operating, under specified conditions (for example, without refueling).

enemy • *n.* (pl. **-ies**) **1** a person who is actively opposed or hostile to someone or something. **2** (**the enemy**) a hostile nation or its armed forces or citizens, especially in time of war: *the enemy shot down four helicopters | enemy aircraft.*

Energy, Department of • an agency of the U.S. government created in October 1977 responsible for long-range, high-risk research and development of energy technology, power marketing at the federal level, the promotion of energy conservation, oversight of the nuclear weapons program, regulatory programs, and the collection and analysis of energy data. The need for energy research, development, and regulation began with the creation of the MANHATTAN PROJECT in 1942. At the end of WORLD WAR II, after vigorously debating whether control of the atom should lie with a civilian or military organization, Congress passed the Atomic Energy Act of 1946 and created the ATOMIC ENERGY COMMISSION (AEC), a civilian agency. In 1974, Congress decided to split the AEC's oversight responsibilities, and created the Nuclear Regulatory Commission, responsible for regulating the private nuclear power industry, and the Energy Research and Development Administration, responsible for managing nuclear weapons, naval reactors, and related energy programs. During the 1970s' energy crisis, the need for centralization and planning resulted in the creation of the Department of Energy in 1977, and it took over the responsibilities of the Federal Energy Administration, the Energy Research and Development Administration, the Federal Power Commission, and related concerns from other agencies.

Enfield rifle • a bolt-action rifle developed in the late 19th century, now largely obsolescent but still found in large numbers in African countries.

enfilade |ˈenfəˌlād; -ˌläd| • *n.* a volley of gunfire directed along a line from end to end. • *v.* direct a volley of gunfire along the length of (a target).

Enforcement Acts • a series of acts passed between 1870–71 to protect the voting rights of blacks and to suppress the KU KLUX KLAN. The act of May 31, 1870, outlawed actions intended to deprive blacks of the right to vote. The act of February 28, 1871, an amendment to the first act, was designed to eliminate fraudulent registration practices and to establish a system of federal machinery to supervise state elections. The act of April 20, 1871, known as the Ku Klux Klan Act, attempted to prevent the intimidation of blacks by any illegal action. It also gave the president the right to employ the militia and to suspend the right of HABEAS CORPUS when public safety was threatened.

engage • *v.* enter into conflict or combat with (an adversary).

engagement • *n.* a fight or battle between armed forces.

engine • *n.* a mechanical device or instrument, especially one used in warfare: *a siege engine.*

Engineer School • see U.S. ARMY ENGINEER SCHOOL.

engine room • the room containing the engines, especially in a ship.

Enhanced Nuclear Detonation System • formal name for the so-called "neutron bomb," a nuclear weapon capable of destroying living things while leaving material objects and infrastructure relatively undamaged.

ENIAC |ˈenēˌæk| • (Also called **Electronic Numerical Integrator and Computer.**) an early digital computer developed at University of Pennsylvania in the 1940s. Its first achievement was in connection with calculations for the hydrogen bomb, and it was later used to chart ballistic trajectories for artillery shells.

ENIGMA • a machine used by the Germans before and during World War II to encode strategic messages. The code was broken by a British intelligence project known as ULTRA.

Eniwetok (or **Eniwetok atoll**) |ˌenəˈwēˌtäk| • a group of forty small islands in the west Pacific Ocean, belonging to the Marshall Islands. U.S. forces captured the atoll from the Japanese in February 1944, during WORLD WAR II, and established a naval base. Along with BIKINI ATOLL, Eniwetok was evacuated and became a nuclear testing ground from 1948 to 1958. It was the site of the first thermonuclear test, November 1, 1952. With explosive force 1000 times greater than the HIROSHIMA bomb, the explosion left a gigantic crater that obliterated the island of Elugelab. Two new elements, einsteinium (atomic number 99) and fermium (100) were discovered in the fallout.

enlist • *v.* enroll or be enrolled in the armed services: *he **enlisted in** the army yesterday | hundreds of thousands new of recruits had been enlisted.*

DERIVATIVES: **enlister** *n.* **enlistment** *n.*

enlisted man • a member of the armed forces below the rank of NCO.

enlisted personnel • soldiers, sailors, airmen, and Marines in pay grades of E-1 through E-9 whose terms of service are governed by a contract; military personnel not holding a commission.

Enlisted Reserve Corps • an organization of the Aviation section of the U.S. ARMY SIGNAL CORPS created in 1916 as one element of a congressional "deficiency act" that allocated increased funds for airfields and personnel. Both the Signal Enlisted Reserve Corps (2,000 enlisted men) and the Signal Officers Reserve Corps (297 officers) were established by this act.

enlistment bounty • a cash payment made as an incentive to enlist or reenlist for military service.

Enola Gay • the B-29 "superfortress" bomber that carried and dropped the atomic bomb that destroyed HIROSHIMA. The B-29 was designed for high-altitude high-speed flight over long distances. Fifteen of these superfortresses were modified specifically to carry out the atomic bomb missions.

Paul Tibbets (1915–), who piloted the aircraft on its mission, named the plane to honor his mother, Enola Gay, and had the name painted on the bomber's side just before taking off. The Smithsonian's National Air and Space Museum held an Enola Gay exhibition from June 28, 1995 until May 18, 1998. Although the size of the Enola Gay makes it impossible to display in the museum, Smithsonian aircraft restoration specialists have spent nearly a decade (44,000 staff hours) restoring it.

enroll • *v.* (**enrolled**, **enrolling**) recruit (someone) to perform a service: *a campaign to enroll more nurses.*
DERIVATIVES: **enrollee** *n.*

Enrollment Act • a Union draft order passed on March 3, 1863, during the CIVIL WAR, to replace the MILITIA ACT OF 1862. It allowed able-bodied men twenty to thirty-five years of age to evade the draft by hiring a substitute or paying a $300 commutation fee. It provoked riots and complaints for enabling wealthier conscripts to buy their way out of the draft.

ensign • *n.* **1** |'ensən| a commissioned officer of the lowest rank in the U.S. Navy and Coast Guard, ranking above chief warrant officer and below lieutenant. **2** |'ensən; 'en,sīn| a flag or standard, especially a military or naval one indicating nationality.

entanglement • *n.* an extensive barrier, typically made of interlaced barbed wire and stakes, erected to impede enemy soldiers or vehicles: *the attackers were caught up on wire entanglements.*

entrench • *v.* establish (a military force, camp, etc.) in trenches or other fortified positions: *we were entrenched by Christmas.*

entrepôt • *n.* a port, city, or other center to which goods are brought for import or export or for collection or distribution.

entry • *n.* the forward part of a ship's hull below the waterline, considered in terms of breadth or narrowness.

envelop |en'veləp| • *v.* (**enveloped** |ən'veləpt; en'veləpt|, **enveloping** |ən'veləpiNG; en'veləpiNG|) (of troops) surround (an enemy force).

envelopment • *n.* an offensive maneuver in which the main attacking force passes around or over the enemy's principal defensive positions to secure objectives to the enemy's rear.

EOGB • *abbr.* electro-optic guided bomb.

EPG • *abbr.* electronic proving ground.

EPIRB • *abbr.* emergency position-indicating radio beacon.

EPW (or **E.P.W.**) • slang (in the PERSIAN GULF WAR) enemy (Iraqi) prisoner of war.

EPW replaced POW in PENTAGON terminology after the VIETNAM WAR to distinguish between American prisoners of war still listed as missing in action in Southeast Asia and enemy forces captured in more recent conflicts, especially the Persian Gulf War.

Erben, Henry (1832–1909) • (or **Erban**) Union naval officer, born in New York City. Erben mostly served blockade duty on the Gulf and Atlantic coasts and the Mississippi River. His most significant postwar service was operational command of the European Station or Squadron (1893–94) with the steel cruiser *Chicago* as his flagship. During the SPANISH-AMERICAN WAR (1898), Erben commanded the Patrol Fleet responsible for the Atlantic coastline, which never saw combat.

Erben coined the phrase "the man behind the gun," crediting the men, not the ships, of the navy with being its backbone and strength.

Ericsson, John (1803–89) • inventor and engineer, born in Wermland, Sweden. Ericsson introduced the use of the screw propeller as a means of marine propulsion. Ericsson designed vessels for the U.S. Navy, among them the armored USS *Monitor* (launched 1862), which revolutionized naval warfare. He also anticipated the submarine and torpedo ordnance.

Erlanger loan • an arrangement made in 1863 during the CIVIL WAR for the CONFEDERACY to receive $15 million worth of Confederate bonds, which were backed by cotton, from the French banking house of Emile Erlanger & Company. By the end of the war, the South had received more than $6 million, which they used to fund the war.

escalade |,eskə'lād| • *n.* the scaling of fortified walls using ladders, as a form of military attack.

escalation • *noun* **1** the use of successively more powerful types of weapons in war. **2** the development of conventional warfare into nuclear warfare. **3** the process of increasing armaments, prices, wages, etc.
ORIGIN: From *escalate,* which originally meant 'ride on an escalator,' a back-formation from *escalator,* originally a trade name.

escapee • *n.* any person who has been physically captured by the enemy and succeeds in getting free.

escape hatch • a hatch for use as an emergency exit, especially from a submarine, ship, or aircraft.

escort • *n.* **1** an armed military group assigned to accompany and protect another force or convoy. **2** aircraft that accompany and protect other aircraft during a mission. **3** an armed guard who accompanies a convoy, a train, prisoners, or another group. **4** an armed guard who accompanies important people. • *v.* to accompany, especially in order to provide protection. • *adj.* a member of the U.S. military who accompanies, assists, or guides an individual or group: *an escort officer.*

Esopus War |ə'sōpəs wôr| • (1660–64) a war between the MOHAWK (aided by Dutch settlers) and Munsee tribes, over dominance in the region of present day Ulster County, New York. The Mohawk were victorious.

espionage • *n.* the act of obtaining, delivering, transmitting, communicating, or receiving information about the national defense with an intent, or reason to believe, that the information may be used to the injury of the nation or to the advantage of any foreign nation.

Espionage Act • a law enacted on June 5, 1917, after American entry to WORLD WAR I, to suppress public opposition to the war. Provisions included $10,000 fines and imprisonment for up to twenty years for persons who interfered with military operations, and it authorized the Postmaster General to remove from the mail materials obstructing the war effort. It led to the SEDITION ACT of 1918 and was re-enacted in the post-WORLD WAR II era.

espionage against the United States • overt, covert, or clandestine activity designed to obtain information relating to the national defense with intent or reason to believe that it will be used to the injury of the United States or to the advantage of a foreign nation.

esplanade |ˈesplə͵näd; -͵nād| • *n.* an open, level space separating a fortress from a town.

esprit de corps |e͵sprē də ˈkôr| • a feeling of pride, fellowship, and common loyalty shared by the members of a particular group.
ORIGIN: late 18th century:French, literally 'spirit of the body.'

essential industry • any industry necessary to the needs of a civilian or war economy. The term includes the basic industries as well as the necessary portions of those other industries that transform the crude basic raw materials into useful intermediate or end products (for example, the iron and steel industry, the food industry, and the chemical industry).

estimate of the situation • a logical process of reasoning by which a commander considers all the circumstances affecting the military situation and arrives at a decision as to the course of action to be taken in order to accomplish the mission. Also called APPRECIATION OF THE SITUATION..

ethnic cleansing • the mass expulsion or killing of members of an unwanted ethnic or religious group in a society.

ethnic conflict • war, civil war, or other conflict between or among two or more racial, language, or religious groups.

ethno-nationalist • *adj.* fighting to establish a new political order or state based on ethnic dominance or homogeneity. Another term for NATIONALIST-SEPARATIST.

EUCOM • *abbr.* the unified command of U.S. forces deployed in Europe that was organized in 1947. It was reorganized more inclusively as USEUCOM in 1952.

Euromissile (also **euromissile**) • *n.* a medium-range nuclear weapon deployed in Europe.

European Command • see U.S. EUROPEAN COMMAND.

European Recovery Program • see MARSHALL PLAN.

Europe-first strategy • the primary strategy of the United States in WORLD WAR II which prescribed that the priority of effort should be given to the defeat of the AXIS powers (principally Germany and Italy) in North Africa and Europe before mounting an all-out effort to defeat the Japanese in the Pacific and Asia.

Eutaw Springs, Battle of • a REVOLUTIONARY WAR battle near Charleston, South Carolina, that occurred on September 8, 1781. British troops were led by Col. ALEXANDER STEWART against American attacks under Gen. NATHANAEL GREENE. Greene wanted to prevent Stewart from joining CHARLES CORNWALLIS and thus put an end to the British threat to the south. Although 2,000 American troops were poorly clothed, barefoot, and slightly outnumbered, they won, and Stewart withdrew his forces to Charleston, where they stayed until the end of the war.

evacuate • *v.* **1** remove (someone) from a place of danger to a safe place: *several families were evacuated from their homes.* **2** (of troops) withdraw from (a place): *the last British troops evacuated the Canal Zone.*

evacuation • *n.* the action of evacuating a person or a place: *there were waves of evacuation during the blitz* | *a full-scale evacuation of the city center.*

evacuee • *n.* a civilian removed from a place of residence by military direction for reasons of personal security or the requirements of the military situation.

Evans, Nathan George (1824–68) • Confederate army officer, born in Marion, South Carolina. His brigade played a pivotal role at FIRST BULL RUN (1861) and fought gallantly at SECOND BULL RUN and ANTIETAM (both 1862) as well, despite heavy losses, which came to be considered Evans's trademark—though whether for vigorous fighting or poor preparation is disputed. He was twice court-martialed and twice acquitted for intoxication and disobedience of orders.

Evans, Robley Dunglison (1846–1912) • Union naval officer, born in Floyd County, Virginia. Evans participated in the assault on FORT FISHER (1865), where he was wounded and consequently saw no further action. In the SPANISH-AMERICAN WAR, he commanded the USS *Iowa*, which played a central role in the BATTLE OF SANTIAGO (1898). Evans rose to the rank of rear admiral (1901) and served as commander in chief, Asiatic Station (1902), and later of the Atlantic Fleet (1904–08), presiding over its rapid growth.

evasion and escape • the procedures and operations whereby military personnel and other selected individuals are enabled to emerge from an enemy-held or hostile area to areas under friendly control.

even |ˈēvən| • *adj.*
PHRASES: **on an even keel** (of a ship or aircraft) having the same draft forward and aft.

evil empire • derogatory the Soviet Union.

The term was popular in the United States during the administration of President RONALD REAGAN.

Ewell, Richard Stoddert |ˈyo͞owəl| (1817–72) • Confederate general, born in Georgetown, D.C. Ewell served in the U.S. Army in the MEXICAN WAR (1846–48) and at frontier posts in New Mexico and Arizona, where he gained a reputation as one of the country's premier officers. Ewell was instrumental in several Confederate victories but is remembered mainly for his decision at GETTYSBURG (1863) not to attack CEMETERY HILL, despite the urging of ROBERT E. LEE. He was wounded at SECOND BULL RUN (1862,) resulting in amputation of a leg.

Ewing, Hugh Boyle (1826–1905) • Union general, born in Lancaster, Ohio. Ewing led his regiment at SOUTH MOUNTAIN and ANTIETAM (both 1862), where his action allowed the safe withdrawal of Gen. AMBROSE BURNSIDE's command. His regiments fought valiantly at the siege of VICKSBURG (1862–63) before being driven back, and his division led the assault against Tunnel Hill at MISSIONARY RIDGE (1863). Ewing was awarded rank of major general.

Ewing was both a foster brother and brother-in-law to WILLIAM T. SHERMAN, who was married to Ewing's sister Ellen.

Ewing, James (1736–1806) • REVOLUTIONARY WAR general, born in Lancaster County, Pennsylvania. Ewing was in the Pennsylvania militia with GEORGE WASHINGTON's army in late 1776. Because of weather conditions, he decided against crossing the Delaware below Trenton as called for in Washington's battle plan. Ewing saw no important military campaigning afterwards.

Ewing, Thomas, Jr. (1829–96) • Union army officer, born in Lancaster, Ohio. Ewing achieved an outstanding military record in the turbulent border area of Kansas and Missouri. When in command of the St. Louis District, Ewing resisted the advance of STERLING PRICE at Fort Davidson (1864). He was promoted to major general and resigned in 1865. After the war he served two terms in Congress (elected 1876) as a Democratic representative from Ohio.

executing commander • a commander to whom nuclear weapons are released for delivery against specific targets or in accordance with approved plans.

executive officer • **1** an officer with executive power. **2** (in naval vessels and some other military contexts) the officer who is second in command to the captain or commanding officer.

Executive Order 9066 • an order signed by President FRANKLIN D. ROOSEVELT on February 19, 1942, after the attack on PEARL HARBOR, to authorize military areas "from which any or all persons may be excluded." It led to the internment and relocation to the interior of the United States of nearly 120,000 Japanese Americans and Japanese nationals living on the West Coast. The government justified the order on the grounds that racial ties could cause disloyalty and pose a threat to American security during the war. The camps were closed in late 1945.

Executive Order 9981 • an order signed by President HARRY S. TRUMAN on July 26, 1948, after WORLD WAR II, to establish "equality of treatment and opportunity for all persons in the armed services without regard to race, color, religion, or national origin."

exercise • *n.* **1** (often **exercises**) a military drill or training maneuver. **2** (**exercises**) ceremonies: *graduation exercises.*

exfiltrate • *v.* withdraw (troops or spies) surreptitiously, especially from a dangerous position.

DERIVATIVES: **exfiltration** *n.*

existence load • items, other than those in the fighting load and not normally carried by the individual, that are required to sustain and protect the combat soldier.

exit strategy • a plan for terminating a war, campaign, or other military operation. A good exit strategy defines the objectives of the operation, states how the achievement of objectives is to be measured, and outlines exactly when and how the forces employed will be disengaged.

Exocet |ˈeksō,set| • trademark a French-made guided anti-ship missile.

ORIGIN: 1970s: from French, literally 'flying fish.'

expanding bullet • a soft-nosed bullet that expands on impact to inflict extensive injury. Their use was banned at the first HAGUE PEACE CONFERENCE. Also called DUMDUM BULLET.

expansionism, Soviet • a policy of military, strategic, economic, and ideological expansion in the Soviet Union after WORLD WAR II. In this era, the Soviet Union constructed a formidable nuclear arsenal and enormous conventional forces, and tested a nuclear weapon (September 1949). It supported Communist insurgencies in Greece and Italy and put pressure on Turkey to allow Soviet military access to the straits connecting the Black Sea to the Mediterranean. The Soviet Union also invaded Hungary (1956), sponsored and led nationalist movements in the THIRD WORLD, and invaded Afghanistan in 1979. The postwar era of Soviet expansionism ended with MIKHAIL GORBACHEV's policy of GLASNOST, which was designed to save and strengthen the Soviet system but which instead contributed to its collapse.

expeditionary • *adj.* of or forming an expedition, especially a military expedition.

expeditionary force • an armed force organized to accomplish a specific objective in a foreign country.

explosive ordnance • any munition that contains explosives, including bombs and warheads; guided and ballistic missiles; artillery, mortar, rocket, and small arms ammunition; mines, torpedoes, and depth and demolition charges.

explosive ordnance disposal unit • specially trained and equipped personnel who render explosive ordnance (bombs, mines, projectiles, booby traps, etc.) safe, make intelligence reports on such ordnance, and supervise the safe removal thereof.

explosive ordnance reconnaissance • reconnaissance (by specially trained agents) involving the investigation, detection, location, marking, initial identification, and reporting of suspected unexploded explosive ordnance, in order to determine further action.

explosive train • a succession of initiating

and igniting elements arranged to cause a charge to function.

Export Control Act of 1949 • a trade measure passed by Congress on February 26, 1949, to restrict the export of strategic materials and equipment to Soviet bloc nations. It was a result of the anticommunist sentiment of the post-WORLD WAR II period.

exposure dose • a measurement of radiation, at a given point, in relation to its ability to produce ionization. The unit of measurement of the exposure dose is the roentgen.

express • *adj.* operating at high speed. • *n.* an express rifle.

express rifle • a rifle that discharges a bullet at high speed and is used in big-game hunting.

ex-service • *adj.* chiefly Brit. denoting or relating to former members of the armed forces: *ex-service personnel.*

ex-serviceman • *n.* (pl. **-men**) a man who was formerly a member of the armed forces.

ex-servicewoman • *n.* (pl. **-women**) chiefly Brit. a woman who was formerly a member of the armed forces.

extralegal • *adj.* (of an action or situation) beyond the authority of the law; not regulated by the law.

extremist • *n.* chiefly derogatory a person who holds extreme or fanatical political or religious views, especially one who resorts to or advocates extreme action: *political extremists | an extremist conspiracy.*

eye • *n.* **1** a loop at the end of a rope, especially one at the top end of a shroud or stay. **2** (**eyes**) the extreme forward part of a ship: *it was hanging in **the eyes of** the ship.*

PHRASES: **eyes front** (or **left** or **right**) a military command to turn the head in the particular direction stated.

eye splice • a splice made by turning the end of a rope back on itself and interlacing the strands, thereby forming a loop.

Ff

F.1 • see SOPWITH CAMEL.

F-4 • see PHANTOM II.

F4F • see WILDCAT.

F-4G • see WILD WEASEL.

F4U • see CORSAIR.

F6F • see HELLCAT.

F-8 • see CRUSADER.

F9F-5 • see PANTHER.

F9F-6 • see COUGAR.

F-14 • see TOMCAT.

F-15 • see EAGLE.

F-15C • see EAGLE.

F-15E • see STRIKE EAGLE.

F-16 • see FIGHTING FALCON.

F-18 • see HORNET.

F-22 • see RAPTOR.

F-80 • see SHOOTING STAR.

F-86 • see SABRE.

F-100 • see SUPER SABRE.

F-104 • see STARFIGHTER.

F-105 • see THUNDERCHIEF.

F-111 • see AARDVARK.

F-117 • see NIGHTHAWK.

F-117A • a stealth fighter aircraft, the first warplane to be specifically designed for low radar observability. Preliminary planning began in the 1950s but a prototype was not completed until 1977. Its outer skin is covered by radar absorption material and it incorporates many other features to evade radar detection. It was used extensively in the PERSIAN GULF WAR. A great deal of information concerning this aircraft is still classified.

F/A-18 • see HORNET.

FAA • *abbr.* **1** Federal Aviation Administration. **2** (in the UK) Fleet Air Arm.

face • *v.* (of a soldier) turn in a particular direction: *the men had faced about to the front.*

factor • *n.* a circumstance, fact, or influence that contributes to a result or outcome: *she worked fast, conscious of the time factor.*

Fagen, David (1875–1901?) • African-American captain in the Filipino nationalist army, born in Tampa, Florida. Fagen defected from the U.S. Army to participate in a guerrilla war against the American troops enforcing concessions granted by the treaty that ended the SPANISH-AMERICAN WAR (1898). Many African-American soldiers sympathized with the Filipino cause, and Fagen's rebellion came to represent their resistance to American imperialism. Fagen's uncanny ability to evade capture by the U.S. Army was embarrassing to his American opposition.

Fagot • the NATO designation for the MIG-15.

Fairchild, Lucius (1831–96) • Union army officer, born in Portage County, Ohio. Fairchild distinguished himself at SECOND BULL RUN, SOUTH MOUNTAIN, and FREDERICKSBURG (all 1862), and played a conspicuous role in the Union success at GETTYSBURG (1863), where he sustained a wound resulting in the loss of an arm and ending his military career. He subsequently began a political career, serving three terms as Republican governor of Wisconsin and later in diplomatic posts in England, France, and Spain. He also served as commander in chief of the GRAND ARMY OF THE REPUBLIC (1886–87).

fairlead • *n.* a ring mounted on a boat or ship to guide a rope, keeping it clear of obstructions and preventing it from cutting or chafing.

Fair Oaks, Battle of • see SEVEN PINES, BATTLE OF.

fairwater • *n.* a structure that improves the streamlining of a ship to assist its smooth passage through water.

fairway • *n.* **1** a navigable channel in a river or harbor. **2** a regular course or track followed by ships.

fake • *n.* & *v.* variant spelling of FLAKE.

Falaise-Argentan gap • the hole in Allied lines between the two French towns of Falaise and Argentan in August 1944, through which many Germans escaped. In the controversial strategy of the Allied reconquest of France in August 1944, Allied forces failed to close the gap between the two French towns, thus allowing German troops to escape Allied encirclement. OMAR N. BRADLEY's plan involved the Canadians pressing southward from Falaise and the Americans, under Gen. GEORGE S. PATTON's leadership, moving north from Argentan, in order to narrow and close the gap. However, the plan was halted amid Allied concerns that an unexpected encounter between U.S. and Canadian troops might result in a considerable number of friendly casualties. Thus German troops were provided with an escape route through the Falaise-Argentan gap. Even so, 10,000 enemy soldiers were killed and 50,000 captured in the Falaise-Argentan pocket. The gap was finally closed on August 21, 1944.

Falaise Gap, Battle of • a fierce WORLD WAR II battle (August 13–25), 1944 near Falaise and Argentan, in France, in which U.S., Canadian, and Polish forces attempted to cut off the escape route of the German army during the final hours of the liberation of France. The possibility of friendly-fire casualties prevented the plan from succeeding as quickly as it might have. At the end of the battle the remaining German troops surrendered.

fall • *v.* (past **fell**; past part. **fallen**) **1** (of a building or place) be captured or defeated: *their mountain strongholds* ***fell to*** *enemy attack.* **2** die in battle: *an English leader who had fallen at the hands of the Danes.* • *n.* the loss of a city or fortified place during battle: ***the fall of*** *Jerusalem.*

PHRASES: **fall short (of)** (of a missile) fail to reach its target. **fall back** move or turn back; retreat. **fall in** take one's place in a military formation: *the soldiers fell in by the side of the road.* **fall out** leave one's place in a military formation, or on parade: *the two policemen at the rear fell out of the formation.*

fallback • *n.* **1** an alternative plan that may be used in an emergency: *teaching was a last resort, a fallback.* **2** a reduction or retreat: *the offering will hit the market after a fallback from record highs.*

Fallen Timbers, Battle of • a battle on August 20, 1794, between U.S. forces lead by Gen. ANTHONY WAYNE and Shawnee at FALLEN TIMBERS, south of present day Toledo, Ohio. Wayne routed the Native Americans in a matter of hours. The victory speeded the end of native resistance in the northwest frontier and in underlined the power of the new FEDERAL government. It also, ended permanently the power of the British on American soil, when British forces at a nearby fort refused sanctuary to the defeated Shawnee, fearing war with the United States.

fallout • *n.* **1** the precipitation to earth of radioactive particulate matter from a nuclear cloud. **2** the particulate matter itself.

Fannin, James Walker (1809–36) • army colonel from Georgia who fought in the TEXAS WAR OF INDEPENDENCE (1836) and whose surrender to Mexican forces led to his execution and that of more than 340 Texans in what came to be known as the GOLIAD MASSACRE.

fantail • *n.* the overhanging part of the stern of a boat, especially a warship.

farb • *n.* derogatory a military reenactor who behaves in a 20th-century manner during reenactments.

Far East Air Force • (**FEAF**) a named air force created by rapid expansion of the AIR CORPS and the need for an independent structure for the air forces within the U.S. Army. During this period of growth and reorganization, the Air Corps established a new subdivision that would soon become the numbered air forces. On October 28, 1941, the Philippine Department Air Force (activated on September 20, 1941) was redesignated the Far East Air Force.

Fargo • see *Langley*, USS.

FARM GATE, Operation • the first U.S. military detachment of AIR COMMANDOS sent to VIETNAM, in 1961. They flew combat missions with South Vietnamese pilots, and trained them in counterinsurgency warfare.

farm gate type operations • operational assistance and specialized tactical training provided a friendly foreign air force by the U.S. armed forces to include, under certain specified conditions, the flying of operational missions in combat by combined U.S./foreign aircrews as a part of the training being given when such missions are beyond the capability of the foreign air force.

Farnsworth, Elon John (1837–63) • Union army officer, born in Green Oak, Michigan. He served with the 8th Illinois Cavalry in the PENINSULAR and MARYLAND CAMPAIGNS (1862). A brigade under his command in the cavalry corps of the ARMY OF THE POTOMAC successfully repulsed J.E.B. STUART's cavalry at Hanover, Pennsylvania (1862). Farnsworth was killed while leading a failed cavalry attack against the Confederate infantry at GETTYSBURG (1863).

Farragut, David Glasgow (1801–70) • first U.S. Navy admiral, born at Campbell's Station, Tennessee. His military career at sea began in his childhood during the WAR OF 1812 but came into prominence only with the CIVIL WAR, when he first distinguished himself at NEW ORLEANS (1862), after which he was made rear admiral by Congress. Later achievements included the blockade of the Gulf Coast (1862) and the victory at MOBILE BAY (1865), the first significant Union success in nearly a year. The offices of vice admiral (1864) and admiral (1866) were created especially for Farragut.

Farragut is best known in the popular mind for his cry of "Damn the torpedoes!" at Mobile Bay. Farragut was born James David but changed his name in 1814 in honor of his guardian, David Porter, Jr.

fascine |fə'sēn| • *n.* a bundle of rods, sticks, or plastic pipes bound together, used in construction or military operations for filling in marshy ground or other obstacles and for strengthening the sides of embankments, ditches, or trenches.

fascism • *n.* an **1** authoritarian and nationalistic right-wing system of government and social organization. **2** (in general use) extreme right-wing, authoritarian, or intolerant views or practice. The term fascism was first used of the totalitarian right-wing nationalist regime of BENITO MUSSOLINI in Italy (1922–43), and the regime of the NAZIS in Germany were also Fascist. Fascism tends to include a belief in the supremacy of one national or ethnic group, a contempt for democracy, an insistence on obedience to a powerful leader, and a strong demagogic approach.
DERIVATIVES: **fascist** *n.* **fascistic** *adj.*
ORIGIN: from Italian *fascismo*, from *fascio* 'bundle, political group,' from Latin *fascis* 'bundle.'

Fast Carrier Attack Force • (**Task Force 58**) a WORLD WAR II force organized in late 1943 under Adm. MARC MITSCHER. It participated in the attacks on GUAM, the MARIANAS ISLANDS, SAIPAN, and Tinian.

fast carrier task force • a naval task force composed of one or more aircraft carriers and their supporting vessels.

fatherland • *n.* **1** (often **the Fatherland**) a person's native country, especially when referred to in patriotic terms. **2** Germany, especially during the period of ADOLF HITLER's control.

fathom • *n.* a unit of length equal to six feet (1.8 meters), chiefly used in reference to the depth of water: *sonar says that we're **in 18 fathoms**.*
ORIGIN: Old English *fæthm*, of Germanic origin; related to Dutch *vadem*, *vaam* and German *Faden* 'six feet.' The original sense was 'something which embraces,' (plural) 'the outstretched arms;' hence, a unit of measurement based on the span of the outstretched arms, later standardized to 6 feet.

Fathometer • trademark a type of echo sounder.

fatigue • *n.* **1** (**fatigues**) loose-fitting clothing, typically khaki, olive drab, or camouflaged, of a sort worn by soldiers when performing such menial tasks or on active duty: *battle fatigues.* **2** (**fatigues**) a menial task of a nonmilitary nature performed by a soldier, sometimes as a punishment: *we're **on** cookhouse **fatigues**, sir.* **3** (**fatigue party**) a group of soldiers ordered to do such a duty. **4** weakness in materials, especially metal, caused by repeated variations of stress: *metal fatigue.* • *v.* weaken (a material, especially metal) by repeated variations of stress.

Fat Man • the nickname of the atomic bomb dropped on NAGASAKI in WORLD WAR II, so called because of the bomb's bloated appearance. See also LITTLE BOY.

FB-111 • a twin-engine strategic bomber aircraft developed from the F-111. The FB-111 is longer and can carry more fuel than the F-111, but it lacks true intercontinental range, a deficiency that its missile armament makes up for.

FEAF • *abbr.* Far East Air Force(s).

Febiger, Christian (1746–96) • Revolutionary army officer, born in Fâborg, Denmark. Febiger was cited for valuable service at BUNKER HILL (1775), and also saw action at BRANDYWINE and GERMANTOWN (both 1777). His skills as a provisioner helped get GEORGE WASHINGTON's army through their winter encampment at VALLEY FORGE (1777–78). Chosen by Washington in 1779 to command a regiment for the storming of Stony Point, Febiger captured the British commander and was commended to the Continental Congress. He introduced marching music into the Continental army to improve morale.

federal • *adj.* **1** (**Federal**) historical of the Northern States in the CIVIL WAR. **2** of, relating to, or denoting the central government of the United States. **3** (also **Federal**) favoring centralized government: *the federal party.* **4** having or relating to a system of government in which several states form a unity but remain independent in internal affairs: *a federal Europe.* **5** of, relating to, or denoting the central government as distinguished from the separate units constituting a federation: *the federal agency that provides legal services to the poor.*

Federal Civil Defense Administration • founded January 12, 1951, as part of the U.S. COLD WAR defenses, this administration received a small budget for bomb-shelter construction and publicity. Spending increased, and the administration was renamed the Office of Civil and Defense Mobilization under President JOHN F. KENNEDY, who made civil defense a priority in his administration. After the Kennedy administration, less emphasis was placed on civil defense.

In 1962, a DEPARTMENT OF DEFENSE report stated that there were more than 112,000 fallout shelters in the United States, with possible protection for about 60 million civilians.

Federal Emergency Management Administration • (**FEMA**) a U.S. federal agency responsible for planning for and responding to disaster. In 1979 President JIMMY CARTER ordered the merger of the many separate disaster-related agencies into one body. Since then, the scope of the agency has expanded, and it now responds to hazards associated with nuclear power plants and the transportation of hazardous substances. It also responds to large-scale devastation caused by acts of terrorism, in addition to addressing issues of civil defense.

federalist • *n.* (**Federalist**) **1** a member or supporter of the Federalist Party, an early political party in the United States that emphasized strong central government. **2** one who advocates a political system in which two or more states constitute a political unity while remaining more or less independent with regard to their internal affairs.

The *Federalist Papers* are eighty-five essays written in 1787–88 in support of ratification of the U.S. Constitution by the states. Authored by the statesmen ALEXANDER HAMILTON and JAMES MADISON and the jurist John Jay, the essays played a significant role in the adoption of the Constitution and are considered to be outstanding works of political philosophy.

Federal Stock Number • (**FSN**) a number assigned to each item of supply in the U.S. Federal supply system, consisting of a four-digit class code from the Federal Supply Classification plus a sequentially assigned seven-digit Federal Item Identification Number. The FSN replaced NATIONAL STOCK NUMBERS on September 30, 1974.

feet dry • in air operations, a code meaning, "I am, or contact designated is, over land."

feet wet • in air operations, a code meaning, "I am, or contact designated is, over water."

feint |fānt| • *n.* **1** a deceptive or pretended blow, thrust, or other movement. **2** a mock attack or movement in warfare, made in order to distract or deceive an enemy. • *v.* make a deceptive or distracting movement, typically during a fight: *he feinted left, drawing a punch and slipping it.*

FEMA • *abbr.* Federal Emergency Management Administration.

Fenner, Charles Erasmus (1834–1911) • Confederate army officer, born in Jackson, Tennessee. Fenner was active in the defense of PORT HUDSON (1863), in the ATLANTA campaign (1864), and at the BATTLE OF NASHVILLE (1864), where he commanded all the artillery of the battalion. Fenner refused promotion beyond captain to remain with his battery. After the war, he was active in Democratic party politics in Louisiana, serving in the state legislature and later on the state supreme court, where he became noted as an interpreter of the state constitution.

Ferguson, Patrick (1744–80) • born in Scotland, British army officer sent to North America in 1777 as captain commandant of his own rifle company. Ferguson fought in New Jersey, at Philadelphia, and at BRANDYWINE (1777) before being charged with the recruitment and training of Southern loyalists. He was killed at KINGS MOUNTAIN (1780), which marked a turning point in the war, ending Britain's hope of using loyalists to suppress rebellion in the Southern countryside.

Ferguson, who had a reputation as a brilliant marksman, had a chance to shoot a senior-looking Rebel officer at Brandywine but decided against doing so. The officer was later said to be GEORGE WASHINGTON, though some accounts claim it was CASIMIR PULASKI.

Fermi, Enrico (1901–54) • physicist, born in Rome, Italy. Fermi emigrated to the United States (1938) and became one of the architects of the MANHATTAN PROJECT as chief designer of the atomic pile that produced the first sustained chain reaction. Fermi was involved in the project throughout WORLD WAR II, concentrating on perfecting nuclear reactors and producing suitable fissionable material for a bomb. He became a naturalized citizen in 1944 and received the Presidential Medal for Merit in 1946. Fermi was a member of the National Academy of Sciences (elected 1945), the General Advisory Committee of the U.S. ATOMIC ENERGY COMMISSION (1947–50), and numerous international organizations. He opposed construction of the hydrogen bomb (1949). Fermi was awarded the Nobel Prize in physics in 1938.

The Institute for Nuclear Studies at the University of Chicago (site of the Manhattan Project) was renamed the Enrico Fermi Institute in 1954.

ferret • *n.* an aircraft, ship, or other vehicle that has been equipped in order to detect, locate, record, and analyze electromagnetic radiation.

ferry • *n.* (pl. **-ies**) (also **ferryboat**) **1** a boat or ship for conveying passengers and goods, especially over a relatively short distance and as a regular service. **2** a service for conveying passengers or goods in this way. **3** the place where such a service operates from. **4** a similar service using another mode of transportation, especially aircraft. • *v.* (**-ies, -ied**) **1** convey in a boat, especially across a short stretch of water: *riverboats ferried weekend picnickers to the park.* **2** transport (someone or something) from one place to another: *helicopters ferried 4,000 men into the desert.*

DERIVATIVES: **ferryman** (pl. **-men**) *n.*

feu de joie |ˌfœ də ˈZHwä| • *n.* (pl. **feux de joie** |ˌfœ(z)| pronunc. same) a rifle salute fired by soldiers on a ceremonial occasion, each soldier firing in succession along the ranks to make a continuous sound.

ORIGIN: early 18th century: French, literally 'fire of joy.'

Few, the • the U.S. MARINE CORPS. The name is part of a recruiting phrase used by the Corps: "The few, the proud, the Marines."

FF • *abbr.* frigate.

FFG • *abbr.* guided missile frigate.

Fg. Off. • see flying officer.

fiddle • *n.* a contrivance, such as a raised rim, that prevents things from rolling or sliding off a table in bad weather.

field • *n.* an area on which a battle is fought: *a field of battle.* • *v.* deploy (an army): *the small gulf sheikdoms fielded 11,500 troops with the Saudis.* • *adj.* (of equipment) light and mobile for use on campaign: *field artillery.*

PHRASES: **in the field** on campaign; (while) engaged in combat or maneuvers: *troops in the* *field.* **keep the field** archaic continue a military campaign. **take the field** start a military campaign.

field army • administrative and tactical organization composed of a headquarters, certain organic army troops, service support troops, a variable number of corps, and a variable number of divisions.

field artillery • artillery consisting of cannon, rocket, or surface-to-surface missile launchers that are sufficiently mobile to accompany fielded troops. Field artillery is divided into three groups based on the bore of ammunition. Light field artillery uses ammunition of 120 millimeters or less; medium uses 121-160 millimeters, and heavy artillery uses ammunition of 161-210 millimeters or greater.

field boot • a close-fitting, knee-length military boot.

fieldcraft • *n.* the techniques involved in living, traveling, or making military or scientific observations in the field, especially while remaining undetected.

field day • a review or an exercise, especially in maneuvering.

field exercise • an exercise conducted in the field under simulated war conditions in which troops and armament of one side are actually present, while those of the other side may be imaginary or in outline.

field fortifications • an emplacement or shelter of a temporary nature that can be constructed with reasonable facility by units requiring no more than minor engineer supervisory and equipment participation.

field glasses • binoculars for outdoor use.

field gray • a dark shade of gray, the regulation color of the uniform of a German infantryman.

field hospital • a temporary hospital set up near a combat zone to provide emergency care for the wounded.

field jacket • a light- or medium-weight waterproof cotton coat in olive drab or camouflage pattern worn by soldiers in the field.

field marshal • an officer of the highest rank in the British and other armies.

field officer • a major, lieutenant colonel, or colonel.

field of fire • the area that a weapon or a group of weapons may cover effectively with fire from a given position.

field rank • the rank attained by a military field officer.

field telegraph • historical a movable telegraph for use on campaign.

fieldwork • *n.* a temporary fortification.

fifth column • a group within a country at war who are sympathetic to or working for its enemies.

DERIVATIVES: **fifth columnist**.

ORIGIN: the term dates from the Spanish Civil War, when Gen. Mola, leading four columns of troops toward Madrid, declared that he had a fifth column inside the city.

fight • *v.* (past and past part. **fought**) **1** take part in a violent struggle involving the exchange of physical blows or the use of weapons: *the men were fighting.* **2** engage in (a war or battle): *there was another war to fight | we fought and died for this country.* • *n.* **1** a violent confrontation or struggle. **2** a battle or war: *the country was not eager for a fight with the United States.*

fighter • *n.* **1** a fast military aircraft designed for attacking other aircraft: *designers employ stealth to render a fighter invisible to radar | fighter pilots.* **2** a person or animal that fights, especially as a soldier or a boxer.

fighter aircraft • an aircraft designed for the purpose of gaining and maintaining control of airspace thought to be strategically essential by destroying enemy defenders, whether comparable fighters or bombers with protective armament. In order to successfully accomplish this purpose, fighters must be able to outfly and outmaneuver their opponents, and, at the same time, must carry weapons capable of destroying enemy aircraft.

fighter-bomber • *n.* an aircraft serving as both a fighter and bomber.

Fighting Falcon • (**F-16**) a single-seat single-engine fighter, the most successful of its generation (mid 1970s) and one of the best dogfighting aircraft ever produced because of its maneuverability and large size.

fighting load • collectively, the items of individual clothing, equipment, weapons, and ammunition that are carried by the combat soldier and that are essential to the effectiveness of the soldier and the accomplishment of the immediate mission of the unit when the soldier is on foot.

figurehead • *n.* **1** a nominal leader or head without real power. **2** a carving, typically a bust or a full-length figure, set at the prow of an old-fashioned sailing ship.

file • *n.* **1** a line of people or things one behind another: *Plains Cree warriors riding* ***in file*** *down the slopes.* **2** a small detachment of men: *a file of English soldiers had ridden out from Perth.* • *v.* (of a group of people) walk one behind the other, typically in an orderly and solemn manner.

filibuster • *n.* **1** a person engaged in unauthorized warfare against a foreign state Democrats. **2** an action such as prolonged speaking that obstructs progress in a legislative assembly in a way that does not technically contravene the required procedures. • *v.* **1** act in an obstructive manner in a legislative assembly, especially by speaking at inordinate length: *several measures were killed by Republican filibustering.* **2** obstruct (a measure) in such a way.

ORIGIN: late 18th century: from French *flibuster*, first applied to pirates who pillaged the Spanish colonies in the West Indies. In the mid 19th century (via Spanish *filibustero*), the term denoted American adventurers who incited revolution in several Latin American states, whence sense 1. The verb was used to describe tactics intended to sabotage U.S. congressional proceedings, whence sense 2.

fill • *v.* **1** (of a sail) curve out tautly as the wind blows into it. **2** (of the wind) blow into (a sail), causing it to curve outward.

Fillmore, Millard (1800–74) • 13th president of the United States (1850–53), born in

Cayuga County, New York. Fillmore spent three terms in the state legislature and four terms (three consecutive) in Congress before being elected (1848) vice president on the WHIG ticket that had ZACHARY TAYLOR at its head. He became president when Taylor died suddenly in 1850. As president, Fillmore won Congressional approval for the COMPROMISE OF 1850, which Taylor had opposed, and sent Commodore MATTHEW C. PERRY to open diplomatic relations with Japan. Fillmore failed to win the Whig presidential nomination in 1852, but in 1856 he ran as the candidate of the AMERICAN PARTY (also called the KNOW NOTHING PARTY). His disastrous defeat destroyed the party and ended his political career.

film badge • a photographic film packet to be carried by personnel, in the form of a badge, for measuring and permanently recording (typically) gamma-ray dosage.

FIM-43 • see REDEYE.

FIM-92A • see STINGER.

Final Solution • (in German, **Endlösung**) the term used to designate the policies and methods employed by ADOLF HITLER and the NAZI regime in Germany to effect the complete extermination of European Jewry between 1933 and 1945. The "Final Solution" was adopted after programs of severe political, economic, and social discrimination; the expropriation of property owned by Jews; and forced emigration failed to satisfy the urges of Hitler and the Nazi Party for racial purity. In the end, the "Final Solution" was never achieved, but some 6 million Jews and large numbers of other "undesirable" minorities (Slavs, Gypsies, homosexuals, Seventh Day Adventists, political dissidents, and others) from all over Europe were systematically murdered by the Nazis.

Finance School • see U.S. ARMY FINANCE SCHOOL.

finite deterrence • a strategy which calls for maintaining the capability, with a limited number of strategic weapons, of inflicting a high level of damage (presumably unacceptable) on an enemy's population and industry thereby deterring the enemy from initiating aggression.

fire • *n.* the shooting of projectiles from weapons, especially bullets from guns: *a burst of machine-gun fire.* • *v.* **1** discharge a gun or other weapon in order to explosively propel (a bullet or projectile): *he fired a shot at the retreating prisoners* | *they* ***fired off*** *a few rounds.* **2** discharge (a gun or other weapon): *another gang fired a pistol* | *troops* ***fired on*** *crowds.* **3** (of a gun) be discharged.

PHRASES: **under fire** being shot at: *observers sent to look for the men came under heavy fire.*

fire-and-forget • *adj.* (of a missile) able to guide itself to its target once fired.

firearm • *n.* a rifle, pistol, or other portable gun.

fireball • *n.* a ball of flame or fire. **2** an extremely hot, luminous ball of gas generated by a nuclear explosion. **3** a ball filled with combustibles or explosives, fired at an enemy or enemy fortifications.

Firebee • (**BQM-34**) a remotely controlled target drone powered by a turbojet engine. It achieves high subsonic speeds and is designed to be ground launched or air launched. It is used to test, train, and evaluate weapon systems employing surface-to-air and air-to-air missiles.

firebomb • *n.* a bomb designed to cause a fire. • *v.* attack or destroy (something) with such a bomb: *he suspects that someone firebombed his business.*

fire control • **1** the process of targeting and firing heavy weapons. **2** the containment and extinguishing of fires in buildings, ships, etc.

firefight • *n.* a battle using guns rather than bombs or other weapons.

fire for effect • **1** fire that is delivered after the mean point of impact or burst is within the desired distance of the target or adjusting/ranging point. **2** in a call for fire, a term used to indicate that the adjustment/ranging is satisfactory and that fire for effect is desired.

firelock • *n.* a musket in which the priming is ignited by sparks.

fireman • *n.* (pl. **-men**) **1** an enlisted man in the U.S. Navy who operates engineering machinery. **2** a person who tends a furnace or the fire of a steam engine or steamship.

firepower • *n.* the destructive capacity of guns, missiles, or a military force (used with reference to the number and size of guns available): *the enormous disparity in firepower between the two sides.*

fireship • *n.* a military vessel loaded with explosives and allowed to drift among enemy ships or fortifications in order to destroy them.

fire-step • *n.* a step or ledge on which soldiers in a trench stand to fire.

firestorm • *n.* an intense and destructive fire (typically one caused by bombing) in which strong currents of air are drawn into the blaze from the surrounding area, making it burn more fiercely: *within the firestorm every building was burned to a shell.*

firing • *n.* **1** the action of setting fire to something: *the deliberate firing of 600 oil wells.* **2** the discharging of a gun or other weapon: *the prolonged firing caused heavy losses* | *no missile firings were planned.*

firing chart • a map, photo map, or grid sheet showing the relative horizontal and vertical positions of batteries, base points, base point lines, checkpoints, targets, and other details needed in preparing firing data.

firing line • the front line of troops in a battle.

firing party • **1** a group of soldiers detailed to fire the salute at a military funeral. **2** another term for FIRING SQUAD.

firing squad • **1** a group of soldiers detailed to shoot a condemned person. **2** a group of soldiers detailed to fire the salute at a military funeral.

firing step • another term for FIRE-STEP.

first lieutenant • **1** a commissioned officer in the U.S. Army, Air Force, or Marine Corps ranking above second lieutenant and below captain. **2** a naval officer responsible for the maintenance of a ship or shore station.

first light • the beginning of morning nautical twilight (that is, when the center of the morning sun is 12° below the horizon).

first mate • the deck officer second in command to the master of a merchant ship.

first officer • **1** the first mate on a merchant ship. **2** the second in command to the captain on an aircraft.

first sergeant • (in the U.S. Army or Marine Corps) the highest-ranking noncommissioned officer in a company or equivalent unit.

first strike • an attack with nuclear weapons designed to destroy the enemy's nuclear weapons before their use.

first use • the initial employment of specific military measures, such as nuclear or chemical weapons, during the conduct of a war.

First World War • see WORLD WAR I.

fish • *n.* informal a torpedo.

Fish, Nicholas (1758–1833) • Revolutionary army officer, born in New York City. He commanded a troop of infantry at the BATTLE OF MONMOUTH (1778). A friend of ALEXANDER HAMILTON, Fish served as his second in command at YORKTOWN (1781). He remained with the Continental army until the close of the war. After the war Fish married into a prominent New York family (the Stuyvesants) and served in many civic positions.

Fiske, John (1744–97) • naval officer and merchant seaman, born in Salem, Massachusetts. Fiske led numerous successful expeditions against enemy shipping as part of a small provincial (later state) navy established by the Massachusetts General Court (1776) to resist English encroachments on colonial liberties.

fission • *n.* the process whereby the nucleus of a heavy element splits into (typically) two nuclei of lighter elements, with the release of substantial amounts of energy.

Fithian, Philip Vickers |ˈfiTHēən| (1747–76) • chaplain in the New Jersey militia for the few months before his death from dysentery, during which he visited field hospitals. Fithian, born in Greenwich, New Jersey, is better known for his journal and letters, written when he was acting as a tutor in a Virginia home (1773–74) and which present an insightful picture of the Virginia aristocracy on the eve of the REVOLUTIONARY WAR.

fitted mine • a submersible mine containing an explosive charge, a primer, a detonator, and firing system.

Five Civilized Tribes • the Cherokee, Choctaw, Creek, Chickasaw, and Seminole Indian tribes of the southeastern United States, all of which were involuntarily removed to the Oklahoma Territory in accordance with the INDIAN REMOVAL ACT of 1830.

Five Forks, Battle of • the last major battle of the CIVIL WAR, fought on April 1, 1865, in Dinwiddie County, Virginia, between Union forces under Gen. PHILIP H. SHERIDAN and Confederates under Gen. GEORGE E. PICKETT. The gains of the Union victory were instrumental in forcing ROBERT E. LEE to abandon the defense of RICHMOND.

Five O'Clock Follies • slang or derogatory the daily press briefing sponsored by the Joint United States Public Affairs Office in Saigon during the VIETNAM WAR.

five-star • *adj.* having or denoting the highest military rank (awarded only in wartime), distinguished by five stars on the uniform: *a five-star general.*

fixed ammunition • ammunition in which the cartridge case is permanently attached to the projectile.

fixed artillery • artillery that is designed for permanent emplacement, such as that mounted in harbor defenses or in fixed antiaircraft establishments.

flag |flæg| • *n.* **1** a piece of cloth or similar material, typically oblong or square, attachable by one edge to a pole or rope and used as the symbol or emblem of a country or institution or as a decoration during public festivities: *the American flag.* **2** used in reference to the country to which a person has allegiance: *the private's heroism served as an example for every soldier under the flag.* **3** the ensign carried by a flagship as an emblem of an admiral's rank. • *v.* **1** provide or decorate with a flag or flags. **2** register (a vessel) in a specific country, under whose flag it then sails: *the **flagging out** of much of the fleet to flags of convenience.*

PHRASES: **fly the flag** (of a ship) be registered in a particular country and sail under its flag. **keep the flag flying** represent one's country or organization, especially when abroad. **show the flag** (of a naval vessel) make an official visit to a foreign port, especially as a show of strength. **wrap yourself in the flag** make an excessive show of one's patriotism, especially for political ends.

flag captain • the captain of a flagship.

Flagg, James Montgomery (1877–1960) • artist and illustrator, born in Pelham Manor, New York. His depiction of Uncle Sam in a 1917 poster has become an American icon. Flagg used his own face as a model for the familiar picture of the red-white-and-blue clad, white-haired, finger-pointing, intensely staring, sharply featured figure above the words "I Want You for U.S. Army." The poster was created through an organization of artists called the Division of Pictorial Publicity, which produced posters for various federal agencies. It was reprinted and widely displayed during WORLD WAR II, when Flagg also designed recruitment and RED CROSS posters. Flagg, whose illustrations were found on the covers of and inside all the leading magazines of the day, was also known for his pictures and portraits of celebrities, as well as for numerous short stories.

Flagg, Josiah (1737–94) • Revolutionary army officer, born in Woburn, Massachusetts. Flagg was a friend of PAUL REVERE, with whom he was a member of a society of bell ringers as well as of the SONS OF LIBERTY. During the REVOLUTIONARY WAR he served in the Rhode Island armed forces, attaining the rank of lieutenant colonel.

Flagg compiled and published collections of psalms and anthems, for some of which Revere did the engraving. He also performed in public concerts in Boston, some of which were accompanied by a band of the 64th Regiment that Flagg claimed to have organized and trained.

---

flag lieutenant • a lieutenant acting as an admiral's aide-de-camp.

flag officer • an admiral, vice admiral, or rear admiral.

ORIGIN: mid 17th century: *flag*, because the officer had the privilege of carrying a flag that denoted his rank.

flag of truce • a white flag indicating a desire for a truce.

flagship • *n.* the ship in a fleet that carries the commanding admiral.

flak • antiaircraft fire.

ORIGIN: a contraction of the German *fliegerabwehrkanone*.

flake (also **fake** |fāk|) • *n.* a single turn of a coiled rope or hawser. • *v.* **1** lay (a rope) in loose coils in order to prevent it tangling: *a cable had to be **flaked out**.* **2** lay (a sail) down in folds on either side of the boom.

flak jacket (also **flak vest**) • a sleeveless jacket made of heavy fabric reinforced with metal or kevlar, worn as protection against bullets and shrapnel.

flame gun • a device for producing a jet of flame, used especially for destroying weeds.

flamethrower • *n.* a mounted or portable weapon that projects burning incendiary fuel.

flame weapon • a weapon that projects ignited incendiary fuel with the aim or burning the target. hardly seems worthwhile in light of the forgoing

Flaming Dart, Operation • a program of retaliatory air raids against targets in North Vietnam ordered by President LYNDON B. JOHNSON in early 1965.

flank • *n.* the right or left side of a body such as an army or a naval force: *the left flank of the Russian 3rd Army.* • *v.* **1** (often **be flanked**) be situated on each side of or on one side of (someone or something). **2** (**flanking**) guard or strengthen (a military force or position) from the side: *massive walls, defended by four flanking towers.* **3** (**flanking**) attack down or from the sides, or rake with gunfire from the sides: *a flanking attack from the northeast.*

flanker • *n.* a fortification guarding or menacing the side of a force or position.

flank guard • a security element operating to the flank of a moving or stationary force to protect it from enemy ground observation, direct fire, and surprise attack.

flanking attack • an offensive maneuver directed at the flank of an enemy.

flare • *n.* **1** a device producing a bright flame, used especially as a signal or marker: *a helicopter spotted a flare set off by the crew | a flare gun.* **2** an upward and outward curve of a vessel's bow, designed to throw the water outward when under way.

flash • *v.* shine or show a light to send (a signal): *red lights started to flash a warning.*

flash blindness • the temporary or permanent impairment of vision resulting from an intense flash of light. It may be associated with retinal burns.

flash burn • a burn caused by excessive exposure (of bare skin) to thermal radiation.

flash point (also **flashpoint**) • **1** a place, event, or time at which trouble, such as violence or anger, flares up: *the flash point of the conflagration is just blocks away.* **2** the temperature at which a particular organic compound gives off sufficient vapor to ignite in air.

flash suit • a set of heatproof protective clothing.

flash-to-bang time • the time from light being first observed until the sound of the nuclear detonation is heard. Also used in regard to conventional artillery detonations, missile impacts, and bomb explosions.

flatboat • *n.* a cargo boat with a flat bottom for use in shallow water.

flat hat • slang the flat-crowned service hat worn as part of the general duty (Class A) uniform of the Army, Air Force, Navy, and Marine Corps.

flattop • *n.* informal an aircraft carrier.

flechette |flā'sHet; flesH'et| • **1** a missile resembling a dart that is dropped from an aircraft. Also called AERIAL DART. **2** a pointed projectile that is used as shrapnel in exploding antipersonnel weapons.

ORIGIN: early 20th cent.: from French *fléchette*, diminutive of *flèche* 'arrow.'

fleet • *n.* **1** a group of ships sailing together, engaged in the same activity, or under the same ownership: *the small port supports a fishing fleet | **a fleet of** battleships.* **2** (**the fleet**) a country's navy: *the U.S. fleet.* **3** a number of vehicles or aircraft operating together: ***a fleet of** ambulances took the injured to the hospital.*

fleet admiral • an admiral of the highest rank in the U.S. Navy (awarded only in wartime).

fleet ballistic missile submarine • (**SSBN**) a nuclear-powered submarine capable of delivering ballistic missile attacks to designated targets either from a submerged position or from the surface.

fleet in being • a fleet that avoids decisive action, but, because of its strength and location, causes opposing forces to locate nearby, and so reduces the number of opposing units available for operations elsewhere.

Fleet Marine Force(s) • a balanced armed force of the U.S. Marine Corps that includes land, air, and service components. Such a force is an integral part of a U.S. Fleet and has the status of a command.

Fleet Reserve Association • (**FRA**) a nonprofit organization for active duty, reserve, and retired men and women of the Navy, Marine, and Coast Guard. It was formed in 1924 as a forum to address pay and benefits needs and provide fellowship for enlisted sailors. The association was chartered by Congress and remains the leading organization for Sea Service personnel with over 150,000 members and 300 branches. It has worked on behalf of its members for legislation and is a founding member of The Military Coalition (TMC), a powerful lobby group of 30 military associations. In addition, the association sponsors programs for members and their families, upholds traditions of the Navy, Marines, and Coast Guard, and is involved in recruiting military personnel.

Fletcher class • a large class of destroyers and one of the outstanding destroyer classes of all time. These ships performed every kind of duty in every theater of WORLD WAR II, and some, equipped to control fighter aircraft, were used for that purpose in the Philippines and off OKINAWA in the Pacific theater. After the war, Fletcher-class destroyers continued to serve the United States and other nations.

Fletcher, Frank Jack (1885–1973) • naval officer, born in Marshalltown, Iowa. Fletcher received the CONGRESSIONAL MEDAL OF HONOR for his bravery in the MEXICAN WAR (1846–48), the NAVY CROSS for service in submarine-infested waters in WORLD WAR I, and the DISTINGUISHED SERVICE MEDAL for his role in the BATTLE OF MIDWAY (1942) in WORLD WAR II. Fletcher commanded naval forces in the North Pacific (1943–45) and oversaw the occupation of northern Honshu and Hokkaido after the surrender of Japan. He was promoted to full admiral and retired in 1947.

flexible response • a strategy developed in the United States in the early 1960s which was predicated on meeting aggression at an appropriate level or place with the capability of escalating the level of conflict if required or desired.

FLFO • *abbr.* Fort Lewis Field Office.

flight • *n.* **1** the movement or trajectory of a projectile through the air. **2** a group of aircraft operating together, especially an air force unit of about six aircraft: *a refueling mission in which his crew topped off three flights of four F-16A jets.* **3** the action of fleeing or attempting to escape: *refugees on the latest stage of their flight from turmoil.*

PHRASES: **in full flight** escaping as fast as possible. **put someone/something to flight** cause someone or something to flee: *a soldier who held off, and eventually put to flight, waves of attackers.*

flight deck • **1** the cockpit of a large aircraft from which the pilot and crew fly it. **2** the deck of an aircraft carrier, used for takeoff and landing.

flight lieutenant • a rank of officer in the RAF, above flying officer and below squadron leader.

flight line • in air photographic reconnaissance, the prescribed ground path over which an air vehicle moved during the execution of its photo mission.

flight officer • a special rank in the U.S. ARMY AIR FORCES in WORLD WAR II corresponding to a warrant officer in grade and privileges.

flight path • the line connecting the successive positions occupied, or to be occupied, by an aircraft, missile, or space vehicle as it moves through air or space.

flight plan • the specified information provided to air traffic services units relative to an intended flight or portion of a flight of an aircraft.

flight profile • the flight path of an aircraft expressed in terms of altitude, speed, range, and maneuver.

flight sergeant • a rank of noncommissioned officer in the RAF, above sergeant and below warrant officer.

flight surgeon • a physician specially trained in aviator medical practice whose primary duty is the medical examination and medical care of aircrew.

flight test • the test of an aircraft, rocket, missile, or other vehicle by actual flight or launching. Flight tests are planned to achieve specific test objectives and gain operational information.

flight visibility • the average forward horizontal distance from the cockpit of an aircraft in flight at which prominent unlighted objects may be seen and identified by day and prominent lighted objects may be seen and identified by night.

flint • *n.* a piece of flint used with steel to produce an igniting spark, e.g., in a flintlock gun.

flintlock musket • a smooth-bore gun that ignited its charge by a spark produced with flint, thus obviating the need for a match and reducing the risk of powder explosions. It was introduced in the late 18th century.

float • *n.* a thing that is buoyant in water, especially a hollow structure fixed underneath an aircraft enabling it to take off and land on water.

floatage (or **flotage**) • **1** things floating in the water, such as debris. **2** the part of a ship's hull above the water line.

floating dock • a submersible floating structure used as a dry dock.

floating light • a lightship.

floating mine • a contact mine that floats on the surface of the water.

floatplane • *n.* an aircraft with one or more attached floats that enable it to land on or take off from a body of water.

flog • *v.* (**flogged**, **flogging**) beat (someone) with a whip or stick to punish or torture them: *the stolen horses will be returned and the thieves flogged* | (**flogging**) *public floggings.*

DERIVATIVES: **flogger** *n.*

flooder • *n.* in naval-mine warfare, a device fitted to a buoyant mine that, on operation after a present time, floods the mine case and causes it to sink to the bottom.

Flora, William (fl. 1775–1818) • REVOLUTIONARY WAR hero and patriot, born at Portsmouth, Virginia. One of the few free blacks in Virginia at the time, his bravery in combat was recognized in the early Battle of Great Bridge (1775). Flora also fought at YORKTOWN (1781). After the war he acquired considerable wealth from a variety of business enterprises.

flotilla |flō'tilə| • *n.* a fleet of ships or boats: ***a flotilla of*** *cargo boats.*

flotsam |'flätsəm| • *n.* the wreckage of a ship or its cargo found floating on or washed up by the sea. Compare with JETSAM.

Floyd, John Buchanan (1806–63) • Confederate army officer, born in Montgomery City, Virginia. Floyd engaged primarily in attempts to secure western Virginia for the Confederacy but his performance was generally considered inept and his actions foolhardy. Earlier, as governor of Virginia (elected 1848), Floyd had been an ardent supporter of slavery, and as secretary of war during the administration of JAMES BUCHANAN, he became infamous for his weak administration and his favoritism toward relatives and friends.

Flt Lt • Brit. *abbr.* Flight Lieutenant.

Flt. Off. • *abbr.* flight officer.

Flt Sgt • Brit. *abbr.* Flight Sergeant.

fluke • *n.* a broad triangular plate on the arm of an anchor.

flybridge (also **flying bridge**) • *n.* an open deck above the main bridge of a vessel such as a yacht or cabin cruiser, typically equipped with duplicate controls.

flyby • *n.* (in the PERSIAN GULF WAR) a missile that misses its target.

fly by • to fly past a reviewing stand or other area, for inspection or ceremony.

flying bomb • a small pilotless aircraft with an explosive warhead, especially a V-1.

Flying Boxcar • (**C-119**) a transport aircraft, a more powerful version of the C-82, used by the United States and France in the VIETNAM WAR. The rear loading doors were frequently taken off for airdrops.

Flying Circus • a mobile group of German aerial aces who fought in tightly disciplined formations to gain air superiority over the WORLD WAR I battlefields. Although usually associated in the popular mind with BARON MANFRED VON RICHTHOFEN ("The Red Baron"), the first flying circus was actually led by the German ace OSWALD BOELCKE in 1916.

Flying Fortress • see FORTRESS.

flying officer • a rank of commissioned officer in the RAF, above pilot officer and below flight lieutenant.

Flying Tigers • the nickname of U.S. fighter pilots of the AMERICAN VOLUNTEER GROUP.

fm. • *abbr.* fathom(s).

FM. • *abbr.* **1** Brit Field Marshal. **2** frequency modulation: *an FM radio station.*

FMLN • (Also called **Farabundo Martí para la Liberación Nacional.**) a Salvadoran political organization formed in 1980 from various splinter groups and with Cuban backing that carried out acts of terrorism in El Salvador.

FMP • *abbr.* force module package.

FO • *abbr.* **1** field officer. **2** Flying Officer. **3** Foreign Office.

foam path • a path of fire-extinguisher foam laid on a runway to assist aircraft in an emergency landing.

fo'c'sle |ˈfōksəl| (also **fo'c's'le**) • *n.* variant spelling of FORECASTLE.

fog bank • a dense mass of fog, especially at sea.

foghorn • *n.* a device making a loud, deep sound as a warning to ships in fog.

foil • *n.* each of the structures fitted to a hydrofoil's hull to lift it clear of the water at speed.

following • *adj.* (of a wind or sea) blowing or moving in the same direction as the course of a vehicle or vessel.

follow-on procurement • the purchase of replacements, spare parts, and auxiliary equipment for a major end item of military equipment, such as an airplane, a vehicle, or the like. Follow-on procurement is intended to support a type system over its service life cycle and to replace losses due to combat, accident, or normal wear.

foot • *n.* **1** Brit. formal infantry; foot soldiers: *a captain of foot.* **2** the lower edge of a sail.

foot artillery • artillery other than mechanized or horse-artillery. In point of fact, foot artillery pieces were drawn by horses and the crews often rode the team horses or caissons.

Foote, Andrew Hull (1806–63) • naval officer, born in New Haven, Connecticut. During the CIVIL WAR Foote commanded operations in the capture of FORT HENRY (1862) but his gunboats were forced to withdraw at FORT DONELSON (1862). Foote saw no further action in the conflict because of ill health. He died en route to an appointment as commander of the South Atlantic Blockading Squadron. Foote is remembered primarily because of his reform efforts in applying his religious and moral principles to his commands. As a first lieutenant (1843–45) aboard the *Cumberland,* flagship of the Mediterranean squadron, he conducted shipboard prayer meetings and organized a temperance society, launching the movement that culminated in the elimination of the grog ration in 1862. As executive officer of the Brooklyn Navy Yard (1858–61), Foote instituted regular religious instruction for the yard's workers.

foot guards • (**Foot Guards**) (in the British army) the regiments of the Brigade of Guards: the Grenadier, Coldstream, Scots, Irish, and Welsh Guards.

footprint • *n.* **1** the area in which a broadcast signal from a particular source can be received. **2** the area beneath an aircraft or a land vehicle that is affected by its noise or weight.

foot rope • **1** a rope to which the lower edge of a sail is sewn. **2** a rope below a yard on which a sailor can stand while furling or reefing a sail.

footslog • *v.* (**-slogged, -slogging**) (especially of a soldier) walk or march for a long distance, typically wearily or with effort: *they footslogged around the two villages.* • *n.* a long and exhausting walk or march.

DERIVATIVES: **footslogger** *n.*

foot soldier • a soldier who fights on foot; an infantryman.

forage • *v.* obtain food or provisions from (a place).

DERIVATIVES: **forager** *n.*

forage cap • Brit a billed cap forming part of a soldier's uniform.

for'ard |ˈfôrərd; ˈfär-| • *adj.* & *adv.* nonstandard spelling of FORWARD, used to represent a nautical pronunciation.

foray • *n.* a sudden attack or incursion into enemy territory, especially to obtain something; a raid: *the garrison made a foray against the guerrilla camp.* • *v.* make or go on a foray: *the place into which they were forbidden to foray.*

DERIVATIVES: **forayer** *n.*

Forbes, John (1707–59) • British army officer, born in Fifeshire, England. During the FRENCH AND INDIAN WAR (1754–63) he led the expedition to FORT DUQUESNE (1758) by constructing a road across the Pennsylvania mountains. His planned assault proved unnecessary because the French, who had been deserted by the Indians, abandoned and destroyed the site before his arrival.

force • *n.* **1** an aggregation of military personnel, weapons systems, vehicles, and necessary support, or combination thereof. **2** a major subdivision of a fleet.

forced labor • any compulsory labor service, particularly that demanded by a dominant military force of prisoners of war, detainees, or a conquered civilian population. Under some circumstances a government may compel uncompensated labor services from its own population, either in accordance with existing national laws or on an ad hoc basis.

force in readiness • military forces maintained in a state of preparation for immediate employment without additional reinforcement, training, or provisioning.

force list • a total list of forces required by an operation plan, including assigned forces, augmentation forces, and other forces to be employed in support of the plan.

Force, Manning Ferguson (1824–99) • Union army officer, born in Washington, D.C., who saw early action at FORT DONELSON and SHILOH (both 1862), in the VICKSBURG (1862–63) and ATLANTA (1864) campaigns; and who led his brigade in SHERMAN'S MARCH TO THE SEA (1864–65). He was awarded the MEDAL OF HONOR in 1892. Force was also a noted author of books and articles on history and archaeology.

force module package • (**FMP**) a group of combat, combat support, and combat service support forces with a specific function (for example, air superiority, close air support, or reconnaissance).

force multiplier effect • the effect produced by a capability that, when added to and employed by a combat force, significantly increases the combat potential of that force and thus enhances the probability of successful mission accomplishment.

force-on-force maneuvers • two-sided training exercises in which one force plays the role of the enemy.

force package • (in the PERSIAN GULF WAR) an aircraft armed with a high-powered array of missiles and bombs.

Force package was a winner, along with "service the target," of the 1991 Doublespeak Award from the National Conference of Teachers of English.

---

force rendezvous • a checkpoint at which formations of the same type (aircraft or ships) join and become part of the main force before proceeding. Also called GROUP RENDEZVOUS.

force structure • the numbers, size, and composition of the units that comprise U.S. armed forces. Force structure includes personnel, weapons systems, and support systems. See also MILITARY CAPABILITY.

ford • *n.* a shallow place in a river or stream allowing one to walk or drive across. • *v.* (of a person or vehicle) cross (a river or stream) at a shallow place.

DERIVATIVES: **fordable** *adj.* **fordless** *adj.*

Ford, Gerald Rudolph (1913?–) • 38th president of the United States (1974–77) and decorated navy veteran of WORLD WAR II. Born Leslie Lynch King, Jr., in Omaha, Nebraska, Ford was raised in Michigan and given the name of his adoptive father. Ford served in the South Pacific, attaining the rank of lieutenant commander. In 1948 he was elected to Congress as a Republican representative from Michigan; he served for twenty-five years, becoming minority leader of the House of Representatives in 1965. In 1973, following the forced resignation of Spiro T. Agnew, Ford was named vice president by RICHARD M. NIXON, and in 1974, following Nixon's resignation in the face of probable impeachment, Ford became president. His first official act was to pardon Nixon for his role in the WATERGATE affair. He also granted conditional amnesty to draft evaders and deserters of the VIETNAM WAR. As president, Ford largely continued Nixon's policies. His attempts to battle inflation resulted in severe recession (1974–75), and he proved ineffective in working with the Democratic-controlled Congress. In 1975 he sent the U.S. Marines to retaliate for an attack on an American merchant vessel, the *Mayaguez*, by Cambodia. Ford received his party's nomination in 1976, but lost the election to JIMMY CARTER, making him the first incumbent not reelected since HERBERT HOOVER in 1932. He retired from public life after leaving the WHITE HOUSE.

Ford was the nation's only unelected chief executive.

---

fore |fôr| • *n.* the front part of something, especially a ship.

fore and aft • **1** (of a hat, especially one worn as part of a uniform) having three corners and a bill at the front and back: *we were in full dress, with fore-and-aft hats and swords.* **2** (of a sail or rigging) set lengthwise, not on the yards: *a fore-and-aft-rigged yacht.* **3** at the front and rear (often used with reference to a ship or plane): *we're moored fore and aft.*

forecabin • *n.* a cabin in the forward part of a vessel.

forecastle |ˈfōksəl; ˈfawrˌkæsəl| (also **fo'c's'le**) • *n.* **1** the forward part of a ship below the deck, traditionally used as the crew's living quarters. **2** a raised deck at the front of a ship.

foredeck • *n.* the deck at the forward part of a ship.

forefoot • *n.* (pl. **forefeet**) **1** each of the front feet of a four-footed animal. **2** the very front section of a ship's keel.

Foreign Assistance Act of 1961 • an act passed by Congress on September 4, 1961, to reorganize existing U.S. foreign assistance programs. It focused on the development in foreign nations of economic growth and democratic, political stability, and it separated military and non-military foreign aid. It authorized the creation of the U.S. Agency for International Development, which executed foreign assistance programs.

Foreign Legion • a military formation of the French army established in 1831 to fight France's colonial wars. Composed, except for the higher ranks, of non-Frenchmen, the Legion was famed for its audacity and endurance. Its most famous campaigns were in French North Africa in the late 19th and early 20th centuries. The Foreign Legion is an elite fighting force and has been used traditionally by France in her overseas territories, notably Algeria, Tunisia, French Morocco, and Indochina.

foremast • *n.* the mast of a ship nearest the bow.

forenoon • *n.* the morning.

forepeak • *n.* the forwardmost division of a vessel's hull, often used in ships as a ballast tank.

foresail | 'fôr,sāl; -səl | • *n.* the principal sail on a foremast.

foresheet • *n.* **1** a rope by which the lee corner of a foresail is kept in place. **2** (**foresheets**) the inner part of the bows of a boat.

forestay • *n.* a stay leading forward and down to support a ship's foremast.

foretop • *n.* a platform around the head of the lower section of a sailing ship's foremast.

fore-topgallant mast • the third section of a sailing ship's foremast, above the fore-topmast.

fore-topgallant sail • the sail above a sailing ship's fore-topsail.

fore-topmast • *n.* the second section of a sailing ship's foremast.

fore-topsail • *n.* the sail above a sailing ship's foresail.

foretriangle • *n.* **1** the triangular space between the deck, foremast, and forestay of a sailing vessel. **2** the area of sail within this area.

foreyard • *n.* the lowest yard on a sailing ship's foremast.

form • *v.* (**form people/things into**) organize people or things into (a group or body): *peasants and miners were formed into a militia.*
▸**form people/things up** (or **form up**) bring or be brought into a certain arrangement or formation: *Mortimer formed up his troops for the march.*

Forman, David (1745–97) • Revolutionary army officer born near Englishtown, New Jersey. Forman was active in the BATTLE OF GERMANTOWN (1777) and present during the winter encampment at VALLEY FORGE (1777–78) but his primary role for much of the war was providing intelligence about movements of the British and French fleets in the vicinity of New York. Forman was known for his vindictive zeal against dissenters and for self-aggrandizing schemes that took advantage of his public positions.

formation • *n.* a formal arrangement of aircraft in flight or troops: *a battle formation | the helicopters hovered overhead* ***in formation.***

Formosa Resolution • an act of Congress passed in 1955 that authorized the use of force if China invaded Taiwan. It arose in response to sporadic fighting between the People's Republic of China (PRC) and the Republic of China (ROC) forces that threatened to escalate.

forrard | 'fôrərd; 'fär- | • *adj.* & *adv.* nonstandard spelling of FORWARD, used to represent a nautical or dialect pronunciation.

Forrestal, James Vincent (1892–1949) • U.S. public official and financier. Born in Matteawan, New York, he graduated from Princeton in 1915 and soon established himself as a bond salesman on Wall Street. After serving as a naval aviator in WORLD WAR I, he continued to build his reputation in the securities market, and attracted the notice of President FRANKLIN D. ROOSEVELT, who appointed Forrestal to a number of government positions. In August 1940 he became undersecretary of the Navy, and performed a vital role building up the service for war. He became secretary in 1944, and though he initially opposed unification of the armed services, in 1947 he was confirmed as the first secretary of defense to head the NATIONAL MILITARY ESTABLISHMENT created by the NATIONAL SECURITY ACT OF 1947. Despite his diligent work to merge the services, Forrestal was especially criticized for failing to control the air force, and he had many policy disagreements with President HARRY S. TRUMAN. He resigned in March 1949 at Truman's request, suffering from nervous exhaustion and depression. While undergoing treatment at the naval hospital in Bethesda, Maryland, he jumped from a window to his death.

Forrest, Nathan Bedford (1821–77) • Confederate general, born in Marshall County, Texas. Forrest was considered the most brilliant cavalry officer of the war but was known for being bloodthirsty and ruthless. Forrest had extensive battle experience, mainly in Tennessee, including FORT DONELSON and SHILOH (both 1862); STONES RIVER (1862–63), at which he captured an entire garrison of infantry and cavalry as well as four cannon; and FORT PILLOW (1864), where he was seen as responsible for the massacre of many African-American defenders, giving rise to his being a symbol of the violence and racism of the war. He took Memphis (1863) and successfully eluded Federal capture, specifically ordered by WILLIAM T. SHERMAN. Forrest had no military training but was considered a natural military genius. Before the war, he had earned a fortune as a plantation owner and dealer in slaves and real estate. Following it, he was active in politics and was one of the organizers and early leaders of the KU KLUX KLAN.

Forrest Sherman class • a class of destroyers designed during the late 1940s and built in the 1950s. These were the last standard destroyers built by the U.S. Navy after WORLD WAR II, with the most modern weapons and crew conveniences, including air conditioning throughout the ship and more living space for the crew than earlier destroyers. This destroyer class continued to be modified during the 1960s and 1970s. The last ship of this class was decommissioned in the early 1980s.

FORSCOM |'fôr,skäm| • *abbr.* U.S. Army Forces Command.

fort • *n.* **1** a fortified building or strategic position, that serves as an encampment and base for military forces. A fort may be as simple as a primitive log stockade or as complex as a large, sprawling collection of barracks, armories, training areas, and supporting facilities. **2** a permanent army post.

Fort Albany • see FORT ORANGE.

Fort Amsterdam • a fortification that was first built by the Dutch in 1625, in what is now lower Manhattan. Settlers had been instructed to build in an area favorable to long-term settlement and cultivation. The original design called for a pentagonal building, surrounded by a moat 54 feet (16 meters) wide and 8 feet (2.4 meters) deep, with a circumference of over 1,000 feet (305 meters). The site of the original fort is roughly that of the area between present-day Pearl, Broad, Beaver, and Whitehall Streets in lower Manhattan. The site proved difficult to defend, particularly after the English became determined to make the Dutch colony their own. When PETER STUYVESANT surrendered to the English in 1664, the fort was renamed FORT JAMES, in honor of the proprietor, James, Duke of York.

Fort Beausèjour • a star-shaped fort in modern-day New Brunswick, Canada. It was built by the French in 1751. The fort was captured by British and colonial forces after a two-week siege in June 1755. The fort was renamed Fort Cumberland and repelled American attacks in 1776. It was reinforced during the WAR OF 1812 and abandoned in 1835. It became a Canadian historic site in 1926.

Fort Benning • a U.S. Army installation south of Columbus, Georgia, and home of the U.S. Army Infantry School. Named after HENRY LEWIS BENNING, the facility was founded in 1918 as Camp Benning and became Fort Benning in 1922. Originally covering about 97,000 acres, Fort Benning grew to about 187,000 acres by the 1950s. It is considered a leader in developing infantry tactics and weapons.

Fort Belvoir • named for the manor house of Col. William Fairfax built nearby (1736–41) and located 11 miles southwest of Alexandria, Virginia Fort Belvoir was established in 1912 and today serves as the home of some 100 tenant and satellite organizations. Some 4,500 military and 15,700 civilian personnel work on the 8,656 acre installation.

Fort Bliss • a U.S. Army fort near El Paso, Texas. The present fort was occupied for the first time in 1893, by the 18th Infantry, and is one of the nation's major military installations. From 1848 to 1893, predecessors in five different locations stood near El Paso. The fort was named in 1854 for William Wallace Smith Bliss, a veteran of the MEXICAN WAR (1846–48)who served as a private secretary to President ZACHARY TAYLOR.

Fort Bragg • a U.S. Army fort 50 miles (80 kilometers) south of Raleigh, North Carolina. It is a major training site for airborne units. It covers about 200 square miles (518 square kilometers) and serves roughly 158,000 people, including about 40,000 assigned active-duty soldiers. Established in 1918, the fort was named for Gen. BRAXTON BRAGG, a Confederate artillery officer from North Carolina.

Fort Donelson • a fort on the Cumberland River near Dover, Tennessee. Fort Donelson was the site of a CIVIL WAR battle on February 14, 1862, between Union Gen. ULYSSES S. GRANT 15,000 troops and 13,000 Confederates under SIMON BOLIVAR BUCKNER. NATHAN BEDFORD FORREST managed to escape the fort before it was surrendered, along with supplies and 500 men. The Union lost nearly 2,500 men, while Confederate losses were estimated at over 1,400.

Fort Duquesne • a fort built at the junction of the Allegheny and Monongahela rivers, on the site of Pittsburgh, Pennsylvania. The fort was begun in 1754 by colonists from Virginia. The French drove the Virginians away and completed the fort, naming it after the governor-general of New France. The French abandoned and burned the fort in 1758. The English rebuilt it and named it FORT PITT.

Fort Eustis • a fort named for WAR OF 1812 veteran Brevet Brig. Gen. Abraham Eustis, located between Williamsburg and Newport News, Virginia, established in 1918. Some 9,300 military and 4,200 civilian personnel work on the 8,228-acre installation.

Fort Fayette • a fort built in 1791–92, in Pittsburgh, Pennsylvania, for protection of the town's inhabitants against Native American attacks after the dismantling of FORT PITT (erected in 1759 by the British). The fort was called Fort Franklin during its construction, and was later officially designated Fort La Fayette. From 1792 to 1794, Fort Fayette served as the main supply base for Gen. ANTHONY WAYNE's army. During the WAR OF 1812, it functioned as Commodore MATTHEW C. PERRY's headquarters for supplies and military training. In 1815, Fort Fayette was abandoned and the property put up for public sale. The site is now occupied by the Edison Hotel.

Fort Fisher • a Confederate fort at the mouth of the Cape Fear River in North Carolina that was the subject of a Union attack toward the end of the CIVIL WAR in January 1865. The Union victory enabled an advance upriver and the capture ofWilmington, and the CONFEDERACY lost its last open seaport.

Fort Fumble • derogatory slang the Pentagon.

Fort Gordon • a fort named for Confederate Lt. Gen. JOHN B. GORDON and located 12 miles southwest of Augusta, Georgia. It was established in 1941 and today serves as the home of the U.S. Army SIGNAL CENTER and SCHOOL and several tenant units. Some

11,000 military and 4,700 civilian personnel work on the 55,597 -acre installation.

Fort Hatteras • the site of a CIVIL WAR battle off the North Carolina coast on August 28–29, 1861. The attack was part of a campaign to enforce a Union blockade along the coast. Maj. Gen. BENJAMIN BUTLER and Flag Officer SILAS STRINGHAM led Union forces from FORT MONROE to Hatteras Inlet, an important opening in the blockade through which Confederate soldiers slipped supplies. The Union offensive used naval and military forces. While the navy fired on Forts Clark and Hatteras, Union troops rushed the beach and attacked Confederate units. On August 29, Col. William F. Martin surrendered the Confederate forts, one of the first portions of the Confederacy to fall during the Civil War.

Fort Henry • a Confederate fort on the Tennessee river separating Tennessee and Kentucky that was attacked during the CIVIL WAR by U.S. forces under Gen. ULYSSES S. GRANT in February 1862. Gen. Lloyd Tilghman, knowing that a Union victory was a certainty, arranged for the removal of his men from the fort, to which he later returned and surrendered. The victory opened a major part of the Tennessee River to Union gunboats and shipping.

Fort Holabird • a fort in Baltimore City, Maryland, closed in 1995. It was the headquarters of U.S. ARMY INTELLIGENCE.

Fort Hood Field Office • an Electronic Proving Ground at Fort Hood, Texas, under the command of the U.S. ARMY ELECTRONIC PROVING GROUND at FORT HUACHUCA, Arizona.

Fort Huachuca • a fort located in Cochise County, some 70 miles southwest of Tucson, Arizona, established in 1877. Some 5,900 military and 2,400 civilian personnel work on the 73,242 -acre installation.

fortification • *n.* **1** (often **fortifications**) a defensive wall or other reinforcement built to strengthen a place against attack. **2** the action of fortifying or process of being fortified: *the fortification of the frontiers.*

fortify • *v.* (**-ies**, **-ied**) strengthen (a place) with defensive works so as to protect it against attack: *the whole town was heavily fortified* | (**fortified**) *a fortified outpost.*

DERIVATIVES: **fortifiable** *adj.* **fortifier** *n.*

Fortitude, Operation • the elaborate and highly successful deception plan that kept the German attention centered on Calais rather than NORMANDY, where, on June 5–6, 1944, the Allied forces launched OPERATION OVERLORD (D-DAY). The Allies' deception plan, which included a phantom army near Dover, complete with false radio messages and inflatable rubber tanks, had convinced ADOLF HITLER that they would land at Pas de Calais, the most direct route to Germany. The Germans even thought the invasion in Normandy was itself a diversion, and thus important reinforcements remained idle in the north until long after the D-DAY LANDING.

Fort Jackson • a U.S. Army Training Center in South Carolina that was established in June 1917, soon after the entry of the United States into WORLD WAR I. It became the biggest and most active U.S. training center, setting the standards for other U.S. Army bases. Initially known as the 6th National Cantonment, the base was renamed Camp Jackson in honor of Maj. Gen. ANDREW JACKSON, (later President), a South Carolina native. Fort Jackson was incorporated into the city of Columbia in 1968 and designated a U.S. ARMY TRAINING CENTER in 1973.

Fort James • see FORT AMSTERDAM.

Fort Jay • a star-shaped U.S. military facility on Governors Island, a half mile (three quarters of a kilometer) from Manhattan in Upper New York Bay. The fortification was built in from 1794 to 1800 in preparation for war with France, and was named for the jurist John Jay. After it was rebuilt in from 1806 to 1808, it was renamed Fort Columbus, probably because of the unpopularity of a treaty with England (1795) that Jay had negotiated. However, the name Fort Jay was restored in 1904. During WORLD WAR II, in 1942, Governors Island was designated Eastern Defense Command. The U.S. Army left Governors Island in 1966; from then until 1997 the island was East Coast headquarters and a training center for the U.S. Coast Guard.

Fort Knox • a major U.S. Fort in northern Kentucky, 30 miles southwest of Louisville. Established as Camp Knox in 1918, it was made a permanent fort in 1932. It is the U.S. Army Armor Headquarters. It is also the home of the bulk of the U.S. gold reserve.

In WORLD WAR II, the gold vault at Fort Knox was used to keep the original copies of the Constitution, the DECLARATION OF INDEPENDENCE, the Magna Carta, and the original draft of the GETTYSBURG ADDRESS safe.

Fort Laramie • a fort in eastern Wyoming that was a private fur-trading post from 1834 to 1849 and a U.S. military post from 1849 to 1890. Two fur traders, William Sublette and Robert Campbell, established the post because of its useful setting in prime beaver-trapping country. Many settlers and migrants to the West Coast used the post in the 1830s and 1840s. In 1849 the U.S. Army bought the fort in order to protect settlers and migrants from attack by Native Americans. In 1890 the fort was abandoned and partly dismantled, but in 1938 it was named a historic site under control of the National Park Service.

Fort Laramie Treaty • a treaty made between the U.S. government and the SIOUX in 1868, after Sioux tribes led by Oglala Chief RED CLOUD stopped U.S. construction of the BOZEMAN TRAIL between FORT LARAMIE and western Montana. It guaranteed the Sioux the territory in South Dakota west of the Missouri River, but the government failed to honor the treaty when gold was discovered in the Black Hills in the 1870s.

Fort Leavenworth • the oldest continuously active army post west of the Mississippi River, located about 20 miles (32 kilometers) from Kansas City, Kansas. Dating from 1827, Fort

Leavenworth functioned as a major outpost in the early Indian wars and during the CIVIL WAR, and has gained prominence as a training ground for international military officers. The first federal military prison, the U.S. Military Prison, was built at Fort Leavenworth in 1875. This facility, now called the U.S. DISCIPLINARY BARRACKS, is still operated by the army, and is the only existing long-term maximum security facility operated by the DEPARTMENT OF DEFENSE.

Fort Le Boeuf • the second French fort in Pennsylvania, built in July and August of 1753 at the site of present-day Waterford, Pennsylvania.

Fort Lee • the first WOMEN'S ARMY CORPS Training Center, established in Virginia in 1948. The establishment of Fort Lee closely followed the uniting of the women's armed services with the regular forces of the United States after their successful performance during WORLD WAR II. The Center was run entirely by women. Training sessions included basic training similar to that required of male counterparts, except that it did not include combat instruction. From 1948 to 1950, Fort Lee was the only source of WOMEN'S ARMY CORPS (WAC) officers. It was also the home of the only all-WAC band, the 14th Army Band. Activities ended at Fort Lee in 1954 with the opening of a new center in Fort McClellan, Alabama.

Fort Leonard Wood • a fort named for Maj. Gen. Leonard Wood (Army Chief of Staff, 1910–14) and located near Waynesville, Missouri. It was established in 1941 and today serves as the home of the U.S. ARMY MANEUVER SUPPORT CENTER and School, responsible for training chemical, engineer, and military police specialists for all of the armed services. Some 13,500 military and 3,400 civilian personnel work on the 64,735-acre installation.

Fort Lewis Field Office • (**FLFO**) a testing site at Fort Lewis, Washington, for electronic systems for command, control, communications, computer, intelligence, and electronic warfare equipment. Originally known as the Army Experimentation Site, it became an Electronic Proving Ground in 1995, under the command of the U.S. ARMY ELECTRONIC PROVING GROUND at FORT HUACHUCA, Arizona.

Fort Loyal • a fort on the present-day site of Portland, Maine, that was destroyed by the French and their Native American allies in KING WILLIAM'S WAR (1689–97).

Fort Meade • a fort in Maryland, midway between Baltimore and Washington, D.C. It is the home of the National Security Agency, the Defense Information School, and the U.S. Army Field Band. Founded in 1917, Fort Meade was named for Gen. GEORGE C. MEADE.

Fort Monmouth • a fort located in New Jersey that is a leading center of research, development, and training for military electronics. The work is conducted by SIGNAL CORPS units. Established in 1917, the site was originally known as the Signal Corps Camp, and was the only Signal Corps post in the country. In 1925 it was renamed in reference to the BATTLE OF MONMOUTH in the REVOLUTIONARY WAR, a battle that took place on June 28, 1778, near the future location of the fort.

Fort Monroe • a fort built in 1819 on the Chesapeake Bay, near Hampton, Virginia. From 1861 to 1865, during the CIVIL WAR, Fort Monroe was the only Union outpost in the CONFEDERACY. In 1861, Maj. BENJAMIN BUTLER used Fort Monroe as a place of refuge for escaping slaves. In 1862, Gen. GEORGE B. MCCLELLAN used the fort as a base from which to launch the PENINSULAR CAMPAIGN. The 1st and 2nd Regiments of U.S. Colored Cavalry and the Second U.S. Colored Light Artillery were raised in Monroe. In 1865, the Bureau of Freedmen and Refugees ("FREEDMEN'S BUREAU") established its headquarters there. The former Confederate president JEFFERSON DAVIS was imprisoned at Fort Monroe in October 1865 and held there until released on bail in May 1867. It is currently the only active moat-encircled fort in the United States.

Fort Moultrie • the name of three forts on the same site on Sullivan's Island, South Carolina. The first fort, built in 1776, was destroyed by a hurricane in 1783, and it was cannibalized for building materials. The second fort, built in 1798, was also destroyed by a hurricane, in 1804. The third fort, completed in 1809, is still standing.

The fort is named for Col. WILLIAM MOULTRIE, who commanded the fort at the June 28, 1776 REVOLUTIONARY WAR battle of Sullivan's Island. Seminole chief OSCEOLA is buried at Fort Moultrie, except for his head, which was removed before burial and taken to the New York University Medical School, where it was allegedly lost in a fire.

Fort Necessity • an entrenched camp built by GEORGE WASHINGTON in July 1754, near what is now Uniontown, Pennsylvania. A large French force, attacking in reprisal for a the defeat of a French patrol near Great Meadows, forced Washington to surrender on July 4. Washington was able to return to Virginia with all of his remaining men and supplies.

Fort Niagara • a fort on the southern shore of Lake Ontario, in New York. The fort was built in 1729 on the site of a blockhouse that had been built in 1679 by the French explorer Robert LaSalle. The British captured the fort in 1759 during the FRENCH AND INDIAN WAR (1754–63). They held the fort until 1796, when they turned it over to the United States. They recaptured the fort during the WAR OF 1812, but returned it in 1815. The fort was a U.S. military post until 1846.

Fort Orange • a fortification that was the first Dutch foothold in America. It was first built in 1613 on Castle Island on the Hudson River, near what is now Albany. It began as a small redoubt called Fort Nassau, probably built on a French foundation dating to 1540, and was rebuilt in 1616 after a flood. By 1624, the building was deserted and neglected, and Dutch colonists under the aegis of the Dutch East India Company rebuilt and settled it, this time calling it Fort Orange. It was reduced to a trading post after the settlement of Manhattan in 1626. In 1664, at the fall of New Netherland to the English, the fort was occupied by the English and renamed Fort Albany.

Fort Pillow, Battle of • a CIVIL WAR battle in April 1864 at Fort Pillow on the Mississippi in Tennessee. A vastly superior Confederate force under Gen. NATHAN BEDFORD FORREST attacked the fort and, in the view of many, needlessly carried out the slaughter of 200 of the black troops stationed there.

Fort Pitt • one of the western forts besieged by Indians during PONTIAC'S REBELLION (1763–66) that followed the FRENCH AND INDIAN WAR (1754–63). At one point, during the siege, Capt. Simeon Ecuyer tried to weaken the besiegers by distributing smallpox-contaminated blankets during a parley, which may have caused an epidemic.

Fort Pulaski • a fort near the mouth of the Savannah River, on Cockspur Island, Georgia. Constructed from 1829 to 1847, the fort was seized by Confederate troops in January 1861, but was retaken in April 1862 by Union forces. Rifled cannon were used for the first time in the CIVIL WAR at that battle; they proved more than able to defeat masonry forts.

Fortress • (**B-17, Flying Fortress**) originally designed to meet specifications for a bomber issued by the (then) U.S. ARMY AIR CORPS in 1934, the prototype first flew on July 28, 1935, and the first B-17B was delivered to the Army in June 1939. In the spring of 1944, twelve B-17Cs were ferried across the Atlantic for service with the British ROYAL AIR FORCE, the first Fortresses to go into combat.

Fortress Europe • a propaganda phrase devised in the fall of 1942 to assure the German population, and to warn the ALLIES, that an invasion of NAZI-occupied Europe was doomed to fail because of the formidable defenses erected and manned by the German armed forces.

ORIGIN: English translation of the German term *Festung Europa*.

Fort Rucker • a military post in southeast Alabama that is known as the "home of army aviation." All army aviation flight training has been consolidated at Fort Rucker since 1973. Air Force helicopter pilots and foreign students are also trained there. In July 1941 the WAR DEPARTMENT selected lands for construction of an infantry training camp, originally named Ozark Triangular Division Camp. But before the camp was officially opened on May 1, 1942, the War Department named it Camp Rucker in honor of Col. Edmund W. Rucker, a CIVIL WAR Confederate officer.

Fort Sill • a fort near Lawton, Oklahoma, staked out in 1869 to stop Native American tribes from attacking settlers along the borders with Texas and Kansas and to keep order in the area. Campaigns involved frontier scouts such as "Buffalo Bill" Cody and "Wild Bill" Hickok and included the RED RIVER CAMPAIGN, which was launched in response to tribal warfare in 1874. GERONIMO and 341 other Apache prisoners were brought to the fort in 1894; Geronimo died and was buried there in 1909. Troops camping at Fort Sill included the BUFFALO SOLDIERS, black regiments that built many of the stone structures still standing on the site, and Troop L of the Seventh Cavalry, a Native American unit considered one of the best troops in the west. In 1901, 29,000 homesteaders registered at Fort Sill for the land lottery. The fort continues today as the U.S. ARMY FIELD ARTILLERY SCHOOL. It is the only army fort built on the South Plains during the Indian Wars that is still active.

Fort Stanwix • a fort in the Mohawk Valley of New York that was the site of a twenty-day siege by British forces during the SARATOGA campaign in August 1777. The siege ended with the arrival of forces under the command of BENEDICT ARNOLD.

Fort Stedman • the site of a CIVIL WAR battle on March 25, 1865, between Union Maj. Gen. JOHN G. PARKE and Confederate Gen. ROBERT E. LEE and Maj. Gen. JOHN B. GORDON. Lee gathered more than half of his forces to attempt to break through ULYSSES S. GRANT'S PETERSBURG defenses and threaten a supply depot. A pre-dawn assault overpowered the fort's garrison, but Union forces contained the breakthrough and captured more than 1900 Confederates, seriously weakening Lee's army.

Fort St. Frederic (or **Frédéric**) • a fort built in 1736 by the French on the shores of Lake Champlain in what is now New York State. It was successively reinforced until 1742, when it was the strongest French installation in North America except for Quebec. The FRENCH AND INDIAN WAR (1754–63), and the French retreated to this stronghold in 1759 after Gen. JEFFREY AMHERST took Fort Carillon (later FORT TICONDEROGA). Amherst soon advanced on Fort St. Frederic, and discovered that the French had destroyed and abandoned the site; he then erected Fort Crown Point, one of North America's largest colonial forts, on the site.

Fort Sumter • a fort in the harbor of Charleston, South Carolina, that was the scene of a bombardment from April 12 to 14, 1861, the opening engagement of the CIVIL WAR. There was a Union garrison at the Fort under Maj. ROBERT ANDERSON, who refused to surrender the fort and was subsequently attacked by Confederates under Brig. Gen. P.G.T. BEAUREGARD, whose attack forced an evacuation and surrender.

Fort Ticonderoga • a stronghold during the REVOLUTIONARY WAR in New York on Lake Champlain. It was built by the French in 1755, during the FRENCH AND INDIAN WAR (1754–63), on a vital inland water route to Canada. The French first named it Fort Vaudreuil, but soon changed the name to Fort Carillon. The fort was captured in 1759 by the British and renamed Fort Ticonderoga. In 1775, during the REVOLUTIONARY WAR, it was seized from the British by ETHAN ALLEN and the GREEN MOUNTAIN BOYS (Vermont troops) in a surprise attack. The British recaptured Fort Ticonderoga in 1777 but abandoned it in 1780. The fort was rebuilt in 1908, and a museum was opened there.

Fort Wagner • a fort on the harbor of Charleston, South Carolina, that was the subject of a fifty-seven-day siege in the summer of 1863 by Union forces, after repeated lesser attacks had failed. The fort was finally won, but only after Confederate troops had secretly abandoned it. It is remembered for the bravery of the black regiments who fought for the Union there.

Fort William Henry • a fort in southern New York on Lake George. Built by the British in 1755, the fort was captured and destroyed by the French in 1757, during the FRENCH AND INDIAN WAR (1754–63). The fort was rebuilt in 1953 and is now a museum.

forward • *adv.* (also **forwards**) **1** positioned near the enemy lines: *troops moved to the forward areas.* **2** in, near, or toward the bow or nose of a ship or aircraft. • *v.* hand over or send (an official document): *their final report was forwarded to the Commanding Officer.*

forward area • an area in proximity to combat.

forward defense • a U.S. strategic concept which calls for containing or repulsing military aggression as close to the original line of contact as possible so as to defend the entire territory of a nation or alliance. The forward defense concept provides the rationale for the stationing of U.S. armed forces in Europe, Korea, and other overseas locations.

forward observer • an observer operating with front-line troops and trained to adjust ground or naval gunfire and pass back battlefield information. In the absence of a forward air controller, the observer may control close air support strikes.

Forwood, William Henry (1838–1915) • Union army medical officer, born in Brandywine Hundred, Delaware. Forwood served both in hospitals and in the field with the ARMY OF THE POTOMAC, and was recognized for his courage and devotion to duty. After the war he served as attending surgeon for the Soldiers' Home; on the staff of the Army Medical School, becoming president of its faculty; and briefly as head of the ARMY MEDICAL DEPARTMENT, during which time he effectively stopped work on the yellow fever vaccine through restrictions he placed on the project.

Foster, John Gray (1823–74) • Union army officer and military engineer, born in Whitefield Coos County, New Hampshire. Foster was in charge of the fortifications in Charleston harbor and second in command at FORT SUMTER when it was shelled (1861). Foster conducted several important expeditions disrupting Confederate supplies and diverting Confederate troops. He concluded the war as major of engineers and brevet major general in the regular army. After the war Foster was superintending engineer of various river and harbor improvements, including submarine blasting operations in Boston harbor. Foster also saw extensive action in the Mexican War (1846–48), serving with Gen. WINFIELD SCOTT at VERACRUZ (1847).

Foster, Robert Sanford (1834–1903) • Union army officer, born in Vernon, Indiana. He was with an Indiana regiment that served conspicuously in the SHENANDOAH VALLEY (1864) and in Lt. Gen. ULYSSES S. GRANT's operations against RICHMOND in 1864, where he executed a maneuver giving the ARMY OF THE JAMES a foothold it never relinquished. His troops were instrumental in halting ROBERT E. LEE's retreat near APPOMATTOX COURT HOUSE (1865) and in persuading him to surrender to Grant. Foster helped found the GRAND ARMY OF THE REPUBLIC (1866).

foul • *adj.* **1** (of wind or tide) opposed to one's desired course. **2** (of a rope or anchor) entangled. **3** (of a ship's bottom) overgrown with weed, barnacles, or similar matter. • *adv.* **1** (of a ship) collide with or interfere with the passage of (another). **2** cause (a cable, anchor, or other object) to become entangled or jammed: *watch out for driftwood which might **foul up** the engine.* **3** become entangled in this way.

Foulois, Benjamin Delahauf |fo͞ol'wä| (1879–1967) • army officer and aviation pioneer, born in Washington, Connecticut. Foulois first saw service as an underage volunteer during the SPANISH-AMERICAN WAR (1898). One of the first to recognize the potential of aircraft in warfare, he organized the U.S. Army's first aircraft tactical unit (1914). During WORLD WAR I Foulois drafted the aviation program to support the AMERICAN EXPEDITIONARY FORCES in France, and was made commander of the AIR SERVICE, American Expeditionary Forces (1917). Following the war Foulois served as air attaché in Berlin (1920–24). Later, as chief of the AIR CORPS (1931–35), he pushed for the development of strategic bombers despite small Depression-era appropriations, resulting in the Boeing B-17 FLYING FORTRESS, and for greater autonomy for the Air Corps. These efforts contributed to the successful mobilization of U.S. air power for WORLD WAR II.

found • *adj.* (of a ship) equipped; supplied: *the ship was two years old, well found and seaworthy.*

founder • *v.* (of a ship) fill with water and sink: *six drowned when the ship foundered.*

Four Freedoms • freedom of speech and expression, freedom of religion, freedom from want, and freedom from fear, as presented by President FRANKLIN D. ROOSEVELT in his State of the Union Address to Congress on January 6, 1941, during WORLD WAR II.

Four Policemen • slang the United States, the United Kingdom, the Soviet Union, and the Republic of China. [stemming from their supposed role in controlling international conflicts in the post-WORLD WAR II period.]

four-star • *adj.* having or denoting the second-highest military rank, distinguished by four stars on the uniform.

Fourteen Points • fourteen proposals given by President WOODROW WILSON to Congress on January 8, 1918. The Fourteen Points outlined the post-WORLD WAR I peace treaty later negotiated at the PARIS PEACE CONFERENCE and were partially fulfilled in the conference's resulting TREATY OF VERSAILLES. Seven of the points proposed territory adjustments, and the fourteenth point was the basis for the LEAGUE OF NATIONS, which the United States never joined.

Fourteenth Amendment • an amendment to the U.S. Constitution, adopted in 1868. Its five sections established the citizenship of African Americans. It also excluded from political office those who aided the CONFEDERACY, and it declared that the U.S. government was not responsible for the debts of the Confederacy or liable for claims arising from the loss of slaves.

Fox, Gustavus Vasa (1821–83) • Union naval officer, born in Saugus, Maryland. Fox, as assistant to Secretary of the Navy GIDEON WELLES, was de facto chief of naval operations during the CIVIL WAR. He advocated the construction of armored vessels, and ignored the seniority system for promotion in order to secure able commanders. Fox is largely credited with the successes at PORT ROYAL (1861), NEW ORLEANS (1862), and MOBILE BAY (1864), but is also blamed for squandering resources in the attempt to capture CHARLESTON (1861).

foxhole • *n.* a hole in the ground used by troops as a shelter against enemy fire or as a firing point. (Also called **fighting hole, hasty pit, slit trench** (especially in WORLD WAR II), **titty-deep**, and **Individual Fighting Position.**)

This term originated in the trench warfare of World War I; before 1917 such a pit would have been called a skirmisher's trench.

FRA • *abbr.* Fleet Reserve Association.

frag slang • *n.* a hand grenade. • *v.* (**fragged, fragging**) deliberately kill (an unpopular senior officer), typically with a hand grenade. ORIGIN: late 20th cent.: from *fragmentation grenade*.

fragmentation bomb • a bomb designed to break into small fragments as it explodes.

fragmentation hand grenade • a hand-thrown grenade that explodes on impact.

fraise • *n.* a defense made of pointed stakes projecting from ramparts horizontally or angled slightly upward; they were used frequently in CIVIL WAR fortifications.

France, Liberation of • (June–September 1944) one of the Allies' primary strategic goals in WORLD WAR II. After the success of the D-DAY LANDING in Normandy, Allied generals sought to surround and defeat German armies in France, in hopes that such moves would not only return the country to French control but also bring about German surrender. Between June 6 and September 14, in the liberation effort, the Allies landed 2.1 million soldiers on French soil and suffered losses of 40,000 killed, 165,000 wounded and 20,000 missing. A new French government was installed in Paris by August 25, and by the end of September France was almost completely secured. Nevertheless, despite taking over 700,000 casualties, the German military managed to retreat with strong enough forces to necessitate a further BATTLE FOR GERMANY. Almost two months after D-Day, German armies counterattacked at Mortain in an attempt to push the Allies back across the English Channel. Alerted by ULTRA intelligence, the allies thwarted the effort in only two days. The U.S. First Army commander, OMAR N. BRADLEY, ordered Gen. GEORGE S. PATTON to circle the German left and seize Argentan, while the Canadian First Army under Henry Crerar was to take Falaise on the German right. Had it worked according to plan the pincer move should have trapped the German army and prevented it from escaping across the Seine. Stiff German resistance, which slowed the Canadians, and Allied commands ordering Patton and Crerar to halt, given for fear of accidental friendly fire between the Americans and Canadians, kept the FALAISE-ARGENTAN GAP open—a fact that has spurred one of the enduring historical controversies pertaining to the European theater. The allies killed 10,000 German soldiers and captured 50,000 more, but the bulk of the German armies escaped. On August 15, U.S. Gen. Jacob Dever's Sixth Army Group, consisting of a combined U.S. and French troops, conducted Operation Dragoon, invading the port city Marseille and marching up the Rhône River valley. Before Dever's forces met the other Allies, the Germans managed to remove more than half their forces from southern France. Still, on August 19, Supreme Allied Commander DWIGHT D. EISENHOWER changed his original plan of stopping at the Seine, and decided to push on toward Germany. Spurred by the advancing Allies, Free French forces rose up in active resistance. By August 25, the U.S.V Corps entered Paris behind the French 2nd Armored Division, and Gen. CHARLES DE GAULLE established his government that day. As the main Allied force began a broad frontal attack beyond the Seine, other Allied troops struggled with varying degrees of success to dislodge German armies from the port cities of Brittany. The lack of access to French ports caused logistical problems for the liberating forces, some of which were as far as 300 miles from the sea. Although Allied support forces utilized air drops and a continuing truck convoy called "The Red Ball Express," severe fuel shortages slowed the front line's advance. At one point, Patton's armored group was forced to stop because it ran out of gas. Responding to the Allied advance, ADOLF HITLER put Field Marshal Gerd von Rundstedt in charge of the western German Army. Rundstedt established a dense line of mutually supporting pillboxes stretching the length of the German border called the West Wall. In an attempt to skirt the West Wall, Field Marshal MONTGOMERY attempted to gain access to the Rhine River at the Dutch town of Arnhem in an unsuccessful and costly attempt. As a result, Allied momentum was temporarily slowed, and strategists had to redesign. Although France had been liberated by the end of 1944, the Allies had failed to bring the German Army to surrender, and were forced to engage further with Germany.

France, Undeclared Naval War with • (1798–1800) a series of incidents between France and the United States where French ships or French privateers seized neutral American ships carrying British goods. (France and Britain were at war at the time.) France declined to receive the American representatives and demanded $6 million in loans and $250,000 in presents to stop the depredations. It was during this conflict that "Millions for defense, but not one cent for tribute" became a Federalist slogan. In ten important naval engagements in 1799, the Americans only lost once. After Napoleon's return to power in 1799, a convention was signed that restored amity between the two nations.

During the conflict, President JOHN ADAMS remarked that France was more likely to invade heaven than the United States.

Franck Report • a top-secret report released on June 11, 1945, by seven scientists at the University of Chicago recommending that the atom bomb be tested "before the eyes of representatives of all UNITED NATIONS, on the desert or a barren island." They recommended that the United States not use the bomb against Japan.

Franco-American Alliance • an agreement signed by Benjamin Franklin and the comte de Vergennes, the French foreign minister, on February 6, 1778, during the REVOLUTIONARY WAR. Consisting of the TREATY OF AMITY AND COMMERCE and the Treaty of Alliance, it provided the Americans with French trading privileges and military and financial aid, which helped them defeat the British, and recognized America's independence, thereby undermining British control.

frankie • slang **1** (in WORLD WAR I) the French people. **2** the French unit of currency, the franc.

Franklin and Nashville Campaign • a Confederate plan pursued by Confederate Gen. JOHN B. HOOD during the CIVIL WAR that attempted to cut communication lines between Union Gen. WILLIAM T. SHERMAN, who had just captured ATLANTA, and Union forces to the north. Hood's forces tried to destroy the railroad between Murfreesborough and Nashville in Tennessee. Hood's attempt led to the BATTLE OF FRANKLIN on November 30, 1864, and the BATTLE OF NASHVILLE on December 15, 1864. Both were Union victories; they marked the last major battles west of the Appalachians.

Franklin, Battle of • a CIVIL WAR battle in November 1864 between Union forces under Maj. Gen. JOHN M. SCHOFIELD and Confederates under Gen. JOHN B. HOOD in Franklin, Tennessee. It was a major Union victory, with casualties in the thousands on the Confederate side.

Franklin, William Buel (1823–1903) • Union Army officer and military engineer, born in York, Pennsylvania. Franklin saw creditable action at FIRST BULL RUN (1861), in the PENINSULAR CAMPAIGN (1862), and at ANTIETAM (1862), but is remembered mainly for his part in the failure at FREDERICKSBURG (1862). Earlier in his military career, while in the Corps of Topographical Engineers, Franklin had participated in expeditions to survey the Great Lakes and to analyze routes to California. After service in the MEXICAN WAR (1846–48), he oversaw several engineering projects in Washington, including construction of the dome of the Capitol.

frap • *v.* (**frapped, frapping**) bind (something) tightly.

fratricide • *n.* the accidental killing of one's own forces in war.

Frayser's Farm • a CIVIL WAR battle that occurred on June 30, 1862, during the SEVEN DAYS' BATTLE. It was fought as part of the PENINSULAR CAMPAIGN up the Virginia peninsula between the York and James Rivers. Union Gen. GEORGE B. MCCLELLAN moved north to capture RICHMOND and encountered Gen. ROBERT E. LEE's forces on June 26, with fighting continuing until July 1. McClellan's troops crossed White Oak Swamp near Frayser's Farm on June 30. Gen. "STONEWALL" JACKSON's army met them there, while other skirmishes between Confederate and Union troops took place nearby. Although the Confederates kept Union troops from advancing, retreating Union artillery caused many casualties. In fact both sides suffered heavy casualties 6,500 at Frayser's Farm alone and over 20,000 men combined during the seven days of battle. McClellan failed to reach Richmond, marking the end of the Peninsular Campaign.

freak • *n.* in air intercept usage, frequency in megacycles.

freddie • *n.* in air intercept usage, a controlling unit.

Fredericksburg, Battle of • a major CIVIL WAR battle near Fredericksburg, Virginia, on December 13, 1862, between Union forces under Gen. AMBROSE BURNSIDE and Confederates under Gen. ROBERT E. LEE. The Confederate's entrenched position made Union attacks futile but fighting continued for weeks, leading to casualties of more than 13,000 on the Union side. The Confederate victory was instrumental in the later removal of Burnside as a commanding officer.

free • *adj.* (**freer, freest**) **1** (of a state or its citizens or institutions) subject neither to foreign domination nor to despotic government: *a free press.* **2** (often **Free**) denoting an ethnic or political group actively opposing an occupying or invading force, in particular the groups that continued resisting the Germans in WORLD WAR II after the fall of their countries: *the Free French.* **3** (of the wind) blowing from a favorable direction to the side or stern of a vessel. • *adv.* with the sheets eased.

PHRASES: **the free world** the noncommunist countries of the world, as formerly opposed to the Soviet bloc.

freeboard • *n.* the height of a ship's side between the waterline and the deck.

freebooter • *n.* a pirate or lawless adventurer.

DERIVATIVES: **freeboot** *v.*

Freedmen's Bureau Act • an act passed by Congress on March 3, 1865, to establish a bureau for blacks and whites left destitute by the CIVIL WAR. The bureau supervised all affairs relating to refugees and freedmen, such as employment and the allotment of rations, clothing, and medicine, and it controlled abandoned or confiscated lands and property. The agency received military aid and operated primarily in the former Confederate and Border states and the District of Columbia. The bureau was officially abolished on June 10, 1872.

free drop • the dropping of equipment or supplies from an aircraft without the use of parachutes.

free fall • a parachute maneuver in which the parachute is manually activated at the discretion of the jumper, or automatically activated at a preset altitude.

free flight • the flight of a spacecraft, rocket, or missile when the engine is not producing thrust.

Freeman's Farm • (also called the First Battle of SARATOGA) a REVOLUTIONARY WAR battle that took place in Saratoga, New York, on September 19, 1777. British troops advanced south from Canada to capture Albany and the Hudson River, thus dividing New England colonies from all other colonies. Maj. Gen. JOHN BURGOYNE found the city well-fortified under Maj. Gen. HORATIO GATES. The British attacked on September 19 near Freeman's Farm, which belonged to Loyalist John Freeman. While the Patriots were reinforced there by Maj. Gen. BENEDICT ARNOLD, they could not hold off the British and retreated.

free mine • a naval mine that has been cut or otherwise parted from its mooring.

free port • **1** a port open to all traders. **2** a port area where goods in transit are exempt from customs duty.

free rocket • a rocket not subject to guidance or control in flight.

Free-Soil party • an American political party organized in 1848 on a platform that opposed the admission of any new slave states into the UNION. It was organized primarily by the abolitionist Liberty Party, the Whigs, and the Barnburners, a faction of the New York Democrats. Free-Soil candidates were MARTIN VAN BUREN for president and Charles Francis Adams for vice-president. In addition to opposing the extension of slavery, the platform backed a homestead law and a tariff for revenue. The party slogan was "free soil, free speech, free labor, and free men." Though carrying no states, the party did elect two U.S. senators and fourteen representatives. It was absorbed into the newly formed REPUBLICAN PARTY in 1854.

FREEZE • see PEACE ACTION.

freight • *n.* **1** goods transported by truck, train, ship, or aircraft. **2** the transport of goods by truck, train, ship, or aircraft. **3** a charge for such transport. **4** (in full **freight train**) a train of freight cars: *sugar and molasses moving by freight.* • *v.* transport (goods) in bulk by truck, train, ship, or aircraft: *the metals had been freighted from the city | ships freighting to Dublin.*

freighter • *n.* **1** a vehicle, aircraft, or ship used to move cargo. **2** someone who ships cargo.

Frémont, John C. |ˈfrēmänt| (1813–90) • born in Savannah, Georgia, Frémont was a member of the U.S. Army's Corps of Topographical Engineers and wilderness explorer in the region of Oregon and California. His reports of his expeditions, written with his wife (who accompanied him on his explorations), captured the public imagination and contributed to the westward movement. In 1849 Frémont was elected California's first senator, and in 1856 he became the first presidential candidate of the newly formed REPUBLICAN PARTY but lost the election to JAMES BUCHANAN. During the CIVIL WAR Frémont was for a time in charge of the Department of the West and in command of Union troops in western Virginia, but he proved ineffective in an administrative capacity.

Frémont's guide on one of his first expeditions was the then little-known Christopher "Kit" Carson. In 1841 Frémont eloped with the seventeen-year-old daughter of Missouri senator Thomas Hart Benton, whose influence proved instrumental in his career.

French and Indian War (1754–1763) • (known in Europe as the Seven Years War) was the culmination of the struggle between Great Britain and France for supremacy in North America. Each side was augmented by colonial militia forces and Indian allies. The first phase of the war (1754–57) was fought largely in the frontier areas of Virginia, Pennsylvania, New York, and New England and was marked by several defeats for the British forces, including GEORGE WASHINGTON's surrender of FORT NECESSITY (July 3, 1754), the annihilation of Gen. EDWARD BRADDOCK's column on the Monongahela River near FORT DUQUESNE (July 9, 1755), and the taking of Forts Oswego (1756) and WILLIAM HENRY (1757) in New York. In 1757, WILLIAM PITT the Elder became Prime Minister, and in 1758, the British took the initiative and seized the French fortress at Louisbourg in July and the French outposts at Forts Frontenac and DUQUESNE later in the year. However, Maj. Gen. JEFFREY AMHERST's attempt to take Fort Carillon (TICONDEROGA) on Lake Champlain failed miserably. The British renewed their offensive in 1759, and Fort Carillon (Ticonderoga), Crown Point, and FORT NIAGARA fell to the British. On September 13, 1759, Maj. Gen. JAMES WOLFE gained a major victory by taking the city of QUEBEC, a victory marred by the death of both Wolfe and his opponent, the Marquis de Montcalm. The precarious British hold on the St. Lawrence River, and thus on New France, was reinforced by the surrender of French forces at Montreal on September 8, 1760. The French and Indian War was ended by the TREATY OF PARIS (February 10, 1763) which confirmed the British conquest of New France and its incorporation into the British empire. The war gave the British unchallenged control of North America, but it also provided the American colonists with military experience and aroused their resistance to dominance and economic exploitation by the mother country which led to the REVOLUTIONARY WAR less than a decade later.

French Resistance, The • the forces and actions taken by French citizens to oppose the occupation of France and its overseas territories by the AXIS powers in WORLD WAR II. The French Resistance movement included both the MAQUIS (those resisters operating from bases in the forests and mountains) and those resisters operating covertly in the cities and villages. Among the most active and effective resistance forces in metropolitan France were those resistance groups led by the Communists. Participation in the resistance movement came to be a virtual requirement for successful participation in French public life after World War II.

French Riviera • the section of France's southern coastline that borders the Mediterranean Sea. During WORLD WAR II, it came under AXIS control in 1940. In 1944, the ALLIES began planning to attack France from two directions: from the northwest, across the English Channel, and from the south, either from Italy or the Mediterranean. The plans for the invasion of the Riviera were known as OPERATION ANVIL, changed to OPERATION DRAGOON on July 27, 1944, when Allied military leaders thought that the German forces had cracked their code. The invasion was originally scheduled to coincide with the D-DAY invasions of NORMANDY, but was postponed because of a lack of landing craft. The invasion of the Riviera took place on August 15, 1944, between the cities of Toulon and Cannes, and was notable for its lack of casualties. American troops from the 7th Army and the 6th Corps soon made their way north to rendezvous with Gen. GEORGE S. PATTON's men in Dijon.

French, William Henry (1815–81) • Union army officer, born in Baltimore, Maryland. French proved to be a competent brigade and division commander at FREDERICKSBURG (1862) and CHANCELLORSVILLE (1863), and he received favorable recognition for initiative taken in the GETTYSBURG campaign (1863). But as a corps commander in the ARMY OF THE POTOMAC he proved inept; his tardiness and confusion in executing troop movements forced GEORGE G. MEADE to abandon his MINE RUN campaign (1863).

Frenchyville • slang (in WORLD WAR I) Paris.

fresh target • a request or command sent by the observer or spotter to the firing ship to indicate that fire will be shifted from the original target to a new target by spots (corrections) applied to the computer solution being generated.

friction • *n.* **1** the resistance that one surface or object encounters when moving over another: *a lubrication system that reduces friction.* **2** the action of one surface or object rubbing against another: *the friction of braking.* **3** conflict or animosity caused by a clash of wills, temperaments, or opinions: *a considerable amount of* ***friction between*** *the commanders.* DERIVATIVES: **frictionless** | *adj.*

friendly • *adj.* (**friendlier**, **friendliest**) (of troops or equipment) of, belonging to, or in alliance with one's own forces.

friendly fire • weapon fire coming from one's own side, especially fire that causes accidental injury or death to one's own forces.

frigate |ˈfrigit| • *n.* **1** (**FF**) a warship that can respond alone or in combination with strike, antisubmarine, or amphibious forces to threats from air, surface, and submarine enemy craft. See also GUIDED MISSILE FRIGATE. **2** a warship with a mixed armament, generally heavier than a destroyer (in the U.S. Navy, heavier) and of a kind originally introduced for convoy escort work. **3** a sailing warship of a size and armament just below that of a ship of the line.

Fritz • slang (in WORLD WARS I and II) a German, the German people collectively, or things German.

frock coat • a man's double-breasted, long-skirted coat, now worn chiefly on formal occasions.

frog • *n.* an attachment to a belt for holding a sword, bayonet, or similar weapon.

From the Halls of Montezuma (**Marine Hymn** or **Marines' Hymn**) • a marine service song whose words and music were first printed together in 1918. The author is unknown but is believed to have written the lyrics after marine involvement in the occupation of CHAPULTEPEC, in Mexico City, in 1847 during the MEXICAN WAR (1846–48). The hymn's music was composed in 1868 by Jacques Offenbach for "Couplet des Deux Hommes d'Armes," a song from his opera bouffe, "Genviéve de Brabant." The U.S. Marine Corps copyrighted the song in 1919.

front • *n.* **1** the foremost line or part of an armed force; the furthest position that an army has reached and where the enemy is or may be engaged: *his regiment was immediately sent to the front.* **2** the direction toward which a line of troops faces when formed. **3** a particular formation of troops for battle. **4** a particular situation or sphere of operation: *there was some good news on the western front.* **5** [often in names] an organized political group: *the Palestinian Liberation Front.* **6** a person or organization serving as a cover for subversive or illegal activities: *the CIA identified the company as* ***a front for*** *a terrorist group.* **7** a well-known or prestigious person who acts as a representative, rather than an active member, of an organization. • *exclam.* used to summon someone to the front or to command them to assume a forward-facing posi-

tion, as in giving orders to troops on parade: *soldiers, **front and center**!*
DERIVATIVES: **frontward** *adj.* & *adv.* **frontwards** *adv.*

frontal assault • a rapid, violent offensive maneuver in which the main action is directed against the front of the enemy forces.

frontal attack • an offensive maneuver in which the main action is directed against the front of the enemy forces.

front line • (also **frontline**) (usually **the front line**) the military line or part of an army that is closest to the enemy.

fruit salad • slang a display of medals and other decorations.

frustrated cargo • any shipment of supplies and/or equipment that, while en route to destination, is stopped prior to receipt and for which further disposition instructions must be obtained.

Fry, Birkett Davenport (1822–91) • Confederate army officer with an Alabama infantry unit noted for his gallantry, born in Kanawha County, Virginia (now West Virginia). Fry sustained wounds in several battles: SEVEN PINES (1862), ANTIETAM (1862), CHANCELLORSVILLE (1863), and GETTYSBURG (1863). After the BATTLE OF COLD HARBOR (1864), he was made commander of the military district of Augusta, Georgia, where he remained until the end of the war.

Fry, James Barnet (1827–94) • Union army officer, born in Carrollton, Illinois. Fry briefly saw combat before being assigned to administrative posts, most notably as provost marshal general (1863–66). In this position he successfully oversaw the implementation of the North's first national conscription system.

FSN • *abbr.* Federal Stock Number.

fubar • *abbr.* slang acronym for "fouled (or fucked) up beyond all recognition."

Fuchs, Klaus Emil Julius |fo͝oks| (1911–88) • physicist and Soviet spy, born in Russelheim, near Frankfurt, Germany. Fuchs was a spy first in England and later in the United States, where he worked at LOS ALAMOS on the design of the atomic bomb. In 1950 Fuchs was convicted in Britain and sentenced to fourteen years in prison, but in 1959 he was repatriated to the German Democratic Republic, a Soviet satellite, where he lived until his death.

fuel-air-explosive bomb • an antimateriel and antimine bomb that produces a cloud of volatile gas which it then ignites, producing a huge fireball and concussion wave.

Fugitive Slave Law • a law enacted by Congress in 1793 to enable the return of runaway slaves to their owners. It allowed slave owners to retrieve a runaway in any state or territory and to apply to a judge for a custody certificate. Some Northerners opposed it as a violation of civil liberties, and slaveholders argued that its provisions were too ambiguous.

A second Fugitive Slave Law was passed as a measure of the COMPROMISE OF 1850.

fugleman |ˈfyo͞ogəlmən| • *n.* (pl. **-men**) a soldier placed in front of a regiment or company while drilling to demonstrate the motions and time.

full and by • close-hauled but with sails filling.

full command • the military authority and responsibility of a superior officer to issue orders to subordinates. It covers every aspect of military operations and administration and exists only within national services. The term *command*, as used internationally, implies a lesser degree of authority than when it is used in a purely national sense. It follows that no NATO commander has full command over the forces that are assigned to him. This is because nations, in assigning forces to NATO, assign only operational command or operational control.

full dress uniform • a military uniform worn on ceremonial occasions.

full-rigged • *adj.* (of a sailing ship) having three or more masts that all carry square sails.

full steam (or **speed**) **ahead** • used to indicate that one should proceed with as much speed or energy as possible.

Fulton, Robert (1765–1815) • engineer and entrepreneur, born in Little Britain Township (later Fulton), Pennsylvania. Fulton's improvements over earlier designs led to the successful commercial development of the steamboat (1807), resulting in his being popularly perceived as the vehicle's inventor. In 1813–15 Fulton adapted the steam ferry, a catamaran, into the first steam warship or "steam battery," but the WAR OF 1812 concluded before it was put into service.

Fulton spent much of his early career in England and France working on underwater naval weapons, but conceptually he was too far ahead of the technology of his time.

functions • *n. pl.* the appropriate or assigned duties, responsibilities, missions, or tasks of an individual, office, or organization.

fundamentalism • *n.* **1** a form of Protestant Christianity that upholds belief in the strict and literal interpretation of the Bible, including its narratives, doctrines, prophecies, and moral laws. **2** strict maintenance of ancient or fundamental doctrines of any religion or ideology, notably Islam.
DERIVATIVES: **fundamentalist** *n. & adj.*

Modern Christian fundamentalism arose from American millenarian sects of the 19th century, and has become associated with reaction against social and political liberalism and rejection of the theory of evolution. Islamic fundamentalism appeared in the 18th and 19th centuries as a reaction to the disintegration of Islamic political and economic power, asserting that Islam is central to both state and society and advocating strict adherence to the Koran (Qur'an) and to Islamic law (sharia), supported if need be by jihad or holy war.

Funston, Frederick (1865–1917) • army officer, born in New Carlisle, Ohio. Funston received the CONGRESSIONAL MEDAL OF HONOR during the SPANISH-AMERICAN WAR (1898) for his fighting against Filipino insurgents after the armistice. He later (1901) personally captured the leader of the Filipino nationalists and returned home a hero. Though Funston was recognized as a daring and imaginative military leader, his unorthodox and war-mongering tendencies hindered his career advancement. He achieved lieutenant general for his performance during the Mexican Revolution, just before his sudden death prior to the outbreak of WORLD WAR I.

furling • *n.* equipment for rolling up sails securely and neatly around their yards or booms.

furlough |ˈfərlō| • *n.* leave of absence, especially that granted to a member of the armed services: *a civil servant home on furlough* | *a six-week furlough in Australia.* • *v.* grant such leave of absence to.

furniture • *n.* the mountings of a rifle.

furrow • *n.* a rut, groove, or trail in the ground or another surface: *truck wheels had dug furrows in the sand.* • *v.* make a rut, groove, or trail in (the ground or the surface of something): *gorges furrowing the deep-sea floor.*

fuse (also **fuze**) • *n.* **1** a length of material along which a small flame moves to explode a bomb or firework, meanwhile allowing time for those who light it to move to a safe distance. **2** a device in a bomb, shell, or mine that makes it explode on impact, after an interval, at set distance from the target, or when subjected to magnetic or vibratory stimulation. • *v.* fit a fuse to (a bomb, shell, or mine): *the bomb was fused to go off at dawn.*
DERIVATIVES: **fuseless** *adj.*

fuselage • *n.* the main body of an aircraft.

fusil |ˈfyo͞ozəl| • *n.* a light flintlock musket.

fusilier |ˌfyo͞ozəˈlir| (also **fusileer**) • *n.* **1** (usually **Fusiliers**) a member of any of several British regiments formerly armed with fusils: *the Royal Scots Fusiliers.* **2** a soldier armed with a fusil.

fusillade |ˈfyo͞osəˌläd; -ˌlād| • *n.* a series of shots fired or missiles thrown all at the same time or in quick succession: *marchers had to dodge a fusillade of missiles.* • *v.* archaic attack (a place) or shoot down (someone) by a series of shots fired at the same time or in quick succession.

fusion • *n.* **1** the process whereby the nuclei of light elements combine to form the nucleus of a heavier element, with the release of tremendous amounts of energy. **2** in intelligence usage, the process of examining all sources of intelligence and information to derive a complete assessment of activity.

fusion bomb • a bomb deriving its energy from nuclear fusion, especially a hydrogen bomb.

fuze • *n.* (also **fuse**) a mechanical or electronic device that initiates an explosive train.

fuze cavity • a recess in a charge for receiving a fuze.

Gg

G-1 • in a U.S. Army or U.S. Marine Corps division, brigade, or similar unit, the general staff officer responsible for assisting the commander with personnel responsibilities. See GENERAL STAFF.

G-2 • in a U.S. Army or U.S. Marine Corps division, brigade, or similar unit, the general staff officer responsible for assisting the commander with intelligence activities. See GENERAL STAFF.

G-2 Air • U.S. Army officers assigned at the division, corps, and headquarters level to help plan and coordinate joint operations involving ground and air units.

G-3 • in a U.S. Army or U.S. Marine Corps division, brigade, or similar unit, the general staff officer responsible for assisting the commander with operations and training responsibilities. See GENERAL STAFF.

G-3 Air • U.S. Army officers assigned at the division, corps, and headquarters level to help plan and coordinate joint operations involving ground and air units.

G-4 • in a U.S. Army or U.S. Marine Corps division, brigade, or similar unit, the general staff officer responsible for assisting the commander with logistics responsibilities. See GENERAL STAFF.

G-5 • in a U.S. Army division, brigade, or similar unit, the general staff officer responsible for assisting the commander with civil affairs or military governments. See GENERAL STAFF.

Gaddafi, Muammar (1942?–) • Arab nationalist leader of Libya (1970–) who removed U.S. and British military bases from the country shortly after leading a coup that overthrew the monarchy of King Idris I (1969). In 1973 he nationalized all foreign-owned petroleum assets in the country. His government's financing of revolutionary and terrorist groups worldwide brought him into conflict with the United States, and in 1986 U.S. warplanes bombed several sites in Libya.

gaff • *n.* a spar to which the head of a fore-and-aft sail is bent.

Gage, Thomas (1719 or 1720–87) • commander in chief of British forces in North

America (1764–75) and the last royal governor of Massachusetts (1774–75), born in Firle, Sussex, England. Gage was charged with enforcing the INTOLERABLE ACTS in the face of a well-organized and angry populace. When he sent troops to seize military stores at CONCORD and to apprehend John Hancock and SAMUEL ADAMS (April 19, 1775), the fighting that broke out marked the start of the AMERICAN REVOLUTION. At the BATTLE OF BUNKER HILL (1775), Gage's only other significant engagement of the war, the British casualty rate was nearly 40 percent. As an outnumbered wartime commander in a hostile region, Gage was unable to meet the unrealistic expectations of his home government and was recalled to England in October 1775.

Gaillard, David Du Bose |gil'yärd; 'gä,lärd| (1859–1913) • army officer and military engineer, born in Fulton, South Carolina. Gaillard's most notable achievement was as supervisory engineer during the construction of the PANAMA CANAL. His responsibilities included the digging of the most difficult section (called the Culebra Cut), much of which was solid rock. After his death, its name was changed by presidential executive order to the Gaillard Cut. During the SPANISH-AMERICAN WAR (1898) Gaillard served in the volunteer service in both the United States and Cuba before returning to the regular army after the war.

Gaines' Mill, Battle of • the third of the SEVEN DAYS' Battles, on May 27, 1862, between forces under ROBERT E. LEE and Gen. FITZ JOHN PORTER. The Confederate victory and subsequent retreat of Porter saved RICHMOND for the Confederacy.

Galaxy • (**C-5**) an aircraft designed for assault and heavy logistics transport, it was the world's largest military aircraft for many years. Its twenty-eight-wheel landing gear gave it the capability of using partially prepared runways in combat areas, and its size enabled it to airlift 345 combat-ready troops.

gale |gāl| • *n.* **1** a wind of force 7 to 10 on the Beaufort scale (28-55 knots or 32-63 mph). **2** a storm at sea.

galleon |'gælēən; 'gælyən| • *n.* a sailing ship in use (especially by Spain) from the 15th through 17th centuries, originally as a warship, later for trade. Galleons were mainly square-rigged and usually had three or more decks and masts.

galley • *n.* (pl. **-eys**) **1** a low, flat ship with one or more sails and up to three banks of oars, chiefly used for warfare, trade, and piracy. **2** a long rowboat used as a ship's boat. **3** the kitchen in a ship or aircraft.

game theory (also **games theory**) • the branch of mathematics concerned with the analysis of strategies for dealing with competitive situations where the outcome of a participant's choice of action depends critically on the actions of other participants. Game theory has been applied to contexts in war, business, and biology.

Game Warden, Operation • a naval operation in the VIETNAM WAR that used swift boats on rivers of the Mekong Delta system to disrupt Communist supply traffic.

gamma rays • high-energy electromagnetic radiation emitted from atomic nuclei during a nuclear reaction. Gamma rays and very-high-energy X rays differ only in origin (X rays do not originate from atomic nuclei).

gangboard • *n.* another term for GANGPLANK.

gangplank • *n.* a movable plank used as a ramp to board or disembark from a ship or boat.

gangway • *n.* **1** a raised platform or walkway providing a passage. **2** a movable bridge linking a ship to the shore. **3** an opening in the bulwarks by which a ship is entered or left. • *exclam.* |'gæNG'wā| make way!; get out of the way!

Gansevoort, Peter |'gænzvôrt| (1749–1812) • REVOLUTIONARY WAR army officer, born in Albany, New York. He was noted for his stalwart defense of FORT STANWIX, for which he was subsequently named colonel commandant (1777). After the war Gansevoort was a prominent New York businessman whose portrait was painted by Gilbert Stuart. He was appointed brigadier general by President JAMES MADISON (1809).

Gansevoort was the grandfather of novelist Herman Melville, who named his second son Stanwix after the fort Gansevoort commanded.

garble • *n.* an error in transmission, reception, encryption, or decryption that changes the text of a message or any portion thereof in such a manner that it is incorrect or undecryptable.

Garden, Alexander (1757–1829) • Revolutionary army officer, born in Charleston, South Carolina. Garden was a member of Lee's Legion (a noted cavalry force commanded by HENRY "LIGHT-HORSE HARRY" LEE), and later an aide-de-camp to Gen. NATHANAEL GREENE, but known primarily for his postwar role in celebrating and romanticizing the REVOLUTIONARY WAR in a published collection of anecdotes and character portraits (1822). Garden was active in the South Carolina SOCIETY OF THE CINCINNATI (1808–29) and became famous for his eulogies of dead patriots.

Gardiner, Lion (1599–1663) • born on England, military engineer and colonist responsible for building the fort and developing the settlement at Saybrook, Connecticut. The garrison was attacked by the PEQUOT, and Gardiner sent his men as part of the Puritan expedition that carried out the massacre of the native tribe at Fort Mystic in the PEQUOT WAR (1637). In 1639 Gardiner moved to an island off the eastern end of Long Island, called Montauk, which he purchased from the Indians and where his family lived independently of the nearby mainland colonies.

Montauk Island is now called Gardiner's Island and is part of New York state. It is still privately held by his descendants.

Garfield, James Abram (1831–81) • 20th president of the United States (1881), born in

Orange Township (now Moreland Hills), Ohio. Garfield was active in politics (Republican representative in the state legislature, 1859) before the CIVIL WAR, during which he achieved a modest triumph by gaining control of eastern Kentucky and was then given a brigade command at SHILOH (1862). In 1862 he was elected to Congress, the first of nine consecutive victories, but before assuming his legislative duties Garfield planned the TULLAHOMA CAMPAIGN and earned his major general's stars at the stand at CHICKAMAUGA (1863). He resigned his commission to take his seat in the House of Representatives, where he became a part of the inner leadership circle through his eloquence, amiability, and judiciousness. In 1880 he was elected to the Senate by the Ohio legislature, but that same year a deadlocked Republican National Convention made him its surprise presidential candidate, though he had not even been nominated. He defeated the Democratic candidate and GETTYSBURG hero Gen. WINFIELD SCOTT HANCOCK and was inaugurated in March 1881. His brief tenure focused primarily on attempts to bring harmony to the many factions of the Republican party. In July 1881, Garfield was shot by an assassin (Charles J. Guiteau). He died two months later.

Garnett, Robert Selden (1819–61) • first general officer of either army to be killed in action in the CIVIL WAR. Garnett, born in Essex County, Virginia, had earlier seen significant combat in the MEXICAN WAR (1846–48) and in the Indian wars in Florida (1850). After the secession of his native Virginia, he resigned his commission and served as ROBERT E. LEE's de facto chief of staff (1861). He later aided in the defense of the SHENANDOAH VALLEY (1864), where he was killed at Carrick's Ford in July.

Garrard, Kenner (1827–79) • Union army officer, born in Fairfield, Kentucky. Garrad was commander of a New York volunteer infantry regiment in the ARMY OF THE POTOMAC who participated in the campaigns of FREDERICKSBURG (1862) and CHANCELLORSVILLE (1863). Garrard distinguished himself as a brigade commander at GETTYSBURG (1863) and NASHVILLE (1864), but was less successful in an intervening assignment as a cavalry commander in the ARMY OF THE CUMBERLAND at CHATTANOOGA (1863).

garrison • *n.* **1** the troops stationed in a fortress or town to defend it. **2** the building occupied by such troops. • *v.* **1** provide (a place) with a body of troops: *troops are garrisoned in the various territories.* **2** station (troops) in a particular place: *Soviet forces were garrisoned in Lithuania.*

garrison cap • a cap without a bill, especially one worn as part of a military uniform.

garrison force • all units assigned to a base or area for defense, development, operation, and maintenance of facilities.

Gartrell, Lucius Jeremiah (1821–91) • Confederate army officer, born in Wilkes County, Georgia. Gartrell alternated political and military service during the CIVIL WAR, prior to which he had been a member of the Georgia state legislature (1857–61) and an advocate of secession. After seeing action at FIRST BULL RUN (1861), Gartrell returned to civilian life and was elected to the Confederate House of Representatives (1862–64). He then returned to battle, where forces under his command acquitted themselves admirably in slowing Sherman's MARCH TO THE SEA (1864).

Gary, Martin Witherspoon (1831–81) • Confederate army officer, born in Cokesbury, South Carolina. His company within HAMPTON'S LEGION emerged as heroes after FIRST BULL RUN (1861). Gary was considered a brilliant, if sometimes unorthodox, soldier and eventually took command of the Hampton Legion infantry, fighting at RICHMOND, SECOND BULL RUN, ANTIETAM, FREDERICKSBURG (all 1862), and CHICKAMAUGA (1863), as well as in many lesser battles. He commanded the last Confederate troops to leave Richmond and never surrendered or requested a pardon. After the war he was the main force behind the overthrow of South Carolina's RECONSTRUCTION, but his political career was hampered by his outspoken racism and contempt for African Americans.

Under Gary's orders, his company took no black Union soldiers as prisoners, but summarily executed them instead.

---

gas • *n.* (pl. **gases** or **gasses**) **1** gas or vapor used as a poisonous agent to kill or disable an enemy in warfare. **2** informal short for gasoline. • *v.* (**gases, gassed, gassing**) **1** attack with or expose to poisonous gas. **2** kill by exposure to poisonous gas.

gas mask • a protective mask used to cover a person's face as a defense against poisonous gas.

Gates, Horatio (1727/8–1806) • REVOLUTIONARY WAR general, born in Maldon, England. Gates had seen service in North America with the British before moving to Virginia (1772) and taking up the patriot cause. He joined the Continental army in 1775 and his military experience proved invaluable throughout the war, one of his greatest successes being against JOHN BURGOYNE at SARATOGA (1777). Though his reputation was tarnished for a time after the BATTLE OF CAMDEN (1780), he later served as second in command to GEORGE WASHINGTON at Newburgh (1782–83), retiring from service shortly thereafter.

Gates, Robert Michael (1943?–) • director of the CENTRAL INTELLIGENCE AGENCY (1991–93), born in Wichita, Kansas. He was deputy director from 1982 to1991. Gates was among directors who presided over the agency after the breakup of the Soviet Union and who were engaged with trying to find a postCOLD WAR role for the CIA, such as monitoring drug traffic and terrorist threats. Most of Gates's earlier Washington career was on the NATIONAL SECURITY COUNCIL staff in the WHITE HOUSE.

Gates, Thomas (1906–83) • secretary of defense (1959–61) during President DWIGHT D. EISENHOWER's administration, born in Germantown, Pennsylvania. Gates improved relations with the JOINT CHIEFS OF STAFF and created the JOINT STRATEGIC TARGET PLANNING STAFF to coordinate targeting plans between the STRATEGIC AIR COMMAND and the navy, resulting in the first SIOP, or SINGLE INTEGRATED OPERATIONAL PLAN. Gates also served as SECRETARY OF THE NAVY (1957–59). As a navy officer in WORLD WAR II, he participated in campaigns in the Pacific and Mediterranean, attaining the rank of lieutenant commander.

Gatling gun • (also **Gatling**) a rapid-fire, crank-driven gun with a cylindrical cluster of several barrels. The first practical machine gun, it was officially adopted by the U.S. Army in 1866.

ORIGIN: named after Richard J. *Gatling* (1818–1903), its American inventor.

gauge |gāj| • (also **gage**) *n.* **1** a measure of the diameter of a gun barrel, or of its ammunition, expressed as the number of spherical pieces of shot of the same diameter as the barrel that can be made from 1 lb (454 grams) of lead: *a twelve-gauge shotgun.* **2** the thickness of sheet metal or plastic: *500-gauge polyethylene.* **3** the distance between the rails of a line of railroad track: *the line was laid to a gauge of 2 feet 9 inches* **4** (usually **the gage**) the position of a sailing vessel to windward (**weather gage**) or leeward (**lee gage**) of another.

G-day • in NATO terminology, a day on which an order is given to deploy a unit.

gear |gir| • *n.* **1** (often **gears**) one of a set of toothed wheels that work together to alter the relation between the speed of a driving mechanism (such as the engine of a vehicle or the crank of a bicycle) and the speed of the driven parts (the wheels). **2** informal equipment that is used for a particular purpose. **3** a person's personal possessions and clothes. **4** clothing, especially of a specified kind: *combat gear.*

Gearing class • a class of destroyer that succeeded the SUMNER CLASS, differing only in a 14-foot extension inserted in the middle of the hull, a modification that enabled it to carry more fuel and antiaircraft armament. It was the best destroyer to come out of WORLD WAR II and continued to serve usefully in the U.S. fleet for more than three decades.

Geary, John White (1819–73) • army officer, born near Mount Pleasant, Pennsylvania. Geary gained a glowing reputation in the MEXICAN WAR (1846–48), leading the assault on CHAPULTEPEC (1847). Geary also compiled a distinguished record as a Union officer in the CIVIL WAR, with notable service at CEDAR MOUNTAIN (1862), CHANCELLORSVILLE (1863), and GETTYSBURG (1863). He drove the defenders from LOOKOUT MOUNTAIN (1863), and his division was the first to enter Savannah on Sherman's MARCH TO THE SEA (1864–65). Between those wars Geary served successfully as the first mayor of San Francisco and as territorial governor of Kansas, where he restored order but lost legislative support because of his antislavery stance. After the war he was elected Republican governor of Pennsylvania (1866).

Geiger counter |ˈgīgər| • (also **Geiger-Müller counter** |ˈmələr; ˈmyo͝olər|) a device for measuring radioactivity by detecting and counting ionizing particles.

Geiger, Roy Stanley |ˈgīgər| (1885–1947) • U.S. Marine Corps officer, born in Middleburg, Florida. Geiger was one of the first marines to be designated a naval aviator. He received the NAVY CROSS for his actions in WORLD WAR I. Following further study and several assignments of increasing responsibility, he held a variety of major combat commands in WORLD WAR II as American forces moved across the Pacific toward Japan, including establishing air control over GUADALCANAL in the SOLOMON ISLANDS (fall 1942) and leading the 10th Army at OKINAWA (1945). As commander of the FLEET MARINE FORCE, Pacific, he oversaw the transition from war to peace (1945–46).

Gen. • *abbr.* General: *Gen. Eisenhower.*

gendarme |ˈZHändärm| • *n.* an armed police officer in France and other French-speaking countries.

gendarmerie |ZHänˈdärmərē| • *n. pl.* **1** an elite national police force organized and equipped along military lines. Normally, in time of war a gendarmerie will be mobilized and assigned to perform military police functions. **2** a force of gendarmes. **3** the headquarters of such a force.

Perhaps the best known gendarmerie is that of France. Elsewhere the gendarmerie may be known by some other name, such as *Carbinieri* (Italy) or *Guardia Civil* (Spain).

---

general • *n.* **1** a commander of an army, or an army officer of very high rank. **2** an officer in the U.S. Army, Air Force, or Marine Corps ranking above lieutenant general and below field marshal, general of the army, or general of the air force.

An army general may be of five ranks: brigadier general, major general, lieutenant general, general, or general of the army. General is the highest rank in the U.S. Air Force and U.S. Marine Corps.

General Agreement on Tariffs and Trade • an agreement to implement a postWORLD WAR II global trade organization and treaty, which was signed by twenty-three nations on October 30, 1947, and enacted in January 1948. It was established during the COLD WAR to facilitate international and preferential trade agreements between countries, thereby strengthening the economies and political stability of participant nations. In 1995 it became the WORLD TRADE ORGANIZATION.

It originated as a charter for the International Trade Organization, a proposed specialized agency of the UNITED NATIONS that never came into being.

---

general and complete disarmament • reductions of armed forces and armaments by all states to levels required for internal security and for an international peace force.

General Board of the Navy • established on March 13, 1900, as the successor to the Naval War Board, a temporary organization created during the SPANISH-AMERICAN WAR (1898) to advise the SECRETARY OF THE NAVY on naval strategy and to assist him in coordinating intelligence and strategic planning as well as the conduct of naval operations. The General Board consisted of nine officers, including the chief of the BUREAU OF NAVIGATION, the chief naval intelligence officer, the president of the NAVAL WAR COLLEGE, and the Admiral of the Navy, and was charged with making plans for the effective preparation of the U.S. fleet for wartime service and coordination of various Navy activities. In effect a naval general staff, the General Board lost most of its *raison d'être* with the establishment of the position of CHIEF OF NAVAL OPERATIONS in August 1916.

General Dynamics Corporation • a leading producer of defense systems for the United States and its allies. Headquartered in Falls Church, Virginia, General Dynamics Corporation has its roots in a company founded in 1899 that built the first submarine in 1900. The company went on to produce more submarines and ships. In 1954 it launched the USS *Nautilus*, the first nuclear-powered submarine, and became an important manufacturer of military aircraft in the 1950s. Following the end of the COLD WAR era, the company refocused on marine and combat systems and surveillance technology. The F-16 combat fighter, F-111 fighter-bomber, the ABRAMS main battle tank, and sea- and ground-launched cruise missiles are some of its designs, and the company has been a contractor for the U.S. Navy TRIDENT Nuclear Submarine Program.

general headquarters • the headquarters of a military commander.

General Intelligence Division • an element of the U.S. Department of Justice's Bureau of Investigation set up by J. Edgar Hoover during WORLD WAR I to investigate radicalism and subversion. The General Intelligence Division was closed following the RED SCARE of 1919.

generalissimo |ˌjenərə'lisəˌmō| • *n.* (pl. **-os**) the commander of a combined military force consisting of army, navy, and air force units.

general of the air force • an officer of the highest rank in the U.S. Air Force, ranking above general (awarded only in wartime).

general of the army • an officer of the hightest rank in the U.S. Army, above general (awarded only in wartime).

General Order 100 • see LIEBER CODE.

General-Purpose Vehicle • see JEEP.

general quarters • (**GQ**) a shipboard command used in drills and emergencies to ensure that movement around the ship is minimal and orderly. All personnel have an assigned station and task when a GQ is sounded.

generalship • *n.* the skill or practice of exercising military command.

General Staff • a group of officers in the headquarters of U.S. Army or U.S. Marine divisions, Marine brigades and aircraft wings, or similar units, responsible for assisting their commanders in planning, coordinating, and overseeing operations, and may include four or more functional sections: personnel (G-1), military intelligence (G-2), operations and training (G-3), logistics (G-4), and, in Army organizations, civil affairs/military governments (G-5). In Army and Marine brigades and smaller units (unit staff), or a Marine unit smaller than an aircraft wing (executive staff), staff sections are designated S-1, S-2, and so on. The parallel staff in the U.S. Air Force lies in the wing and units larger, and has units designated personnel, operations, and so forth. G-2 and G-3 Air are Army officers assigned at division, corps, and headquarters level to help plan and coordinate joint operations involving ground and air units. Naval staffs are rarely organized in a way comparable to these, but are designated N-1, N-2, and so on when they are. Similarly, a joint staff would be designated J-1, J-2, and so on.

General Staff Act • an act adopted by Congress in 1903 and initiated by U.S. Secretary of War ELIHU ROOT as part of a series of army reforms after inefficient mobilization for the SPANISH-AMERICAN WAR (1898). It established an army GENERAL STAFF Corps, which consisted of forty-four officers assigned to the WAR DEPARTMENT to plan military defense and mobilization. It also created the position of chief of staff, who was in charge of all army forces and the staff departments and who reported to the secretary of war. It sanctioned the ARMY WAR COLLEGE, created by Root in 1900.

general support • the support that is given to the supported force as a whole and not to any particular subdivision thereof.

general war • armed conflict between major powers in which the total resources of the belligerents are employed, and the national survival of a major belligerent is in jeopardy.

Geneva Agreement on Indochina • an agreement negotiated following the fall of the French fortress at DIEN BIEN PHU, Vietnam. Signed on July 21, 1954, it included a cease-fire, a military demarcation line along the 17th parallel to divide the country of Vietnam, and a call for free elections in July 1956 to reunify Vietnam. The United States and southern Vietnam refused to sign the agreement. The United States subsequently led the formation of the SOUTHEAST ASIA TREATY ORGANIZATION (SEATO).

Geneva Agreement on Laos • a conference to establish a truce within Laos between warring factions, which were Pathet Lao Communists, Souvanna Phouma's neutralist Laotian government, which received some U.S. support, and a revolutionary committee led by Gen. Phoumi Nosavan, which received covert support from the U.S. CENTRAL INTELLIGENCE AGENCY. It led to the July 23, 1962 Declaration and Protocol on the Neutrality of Laos to establish neutrality and a tripartite government and to remove foreign military units.

Geneva Conventions • the first multilateral humanitarian treaty, established in Geneva August 22, 1864. It included provisions to protect all establishments and personnel that treated wounded soldiers, incorporate volunteers into the medical corps, and establish the RED CROSS symbol as a sign of neutrality. Subsequent Geneva conventions were established in 1906 and 1929 to extend the provisions and concepts of the first. Another Geneva convention was approved on August 12, 1949, after WORLD WAR II in response to the need to codify the nature of war crimes. They included torture and other inhumane treatment as violations of the laws of war and extended provisions from previous conventions. On June 8, 1977, two protocols to the 1949 conventions were approved to protect civilians from becoming objects of attack, extend protection to guerrilla combatants, and establish commissions to investigate violations of international law. Over 150 nations have approved the 1949 conventions, and approximately half that number have approved those of 1977. The United States has not approved the latter. The HAGUE CONVENTIONS also established similar treaties.

Geneva Protocol on Chemical Warfare • an agreement signed on June 17, 1925, by most major world powers in response to the use of poison gas in WORLD WAR I. It restated prohibitions of the TREATY OF VERSAILLES of 1919 and restricted the use of chemical warfare but not its development, production, or possession. Japan and the United States rejected the agreement, and several signatories reserved the right to use the weapons against non-signatories or if attacked with such warfare.

genocide • *n.* the deliberate killing of a large group of people, especially those of a particular ethnic group or nation.

DERIVATIVES: **genocidal** *adj.*

ORIGIN: 1940s: from Greek *genos* 'race' + -cide.

geographic coordinates • the latitude and longitude that define the position of a point on the earth.

georef • *n.* a worldwide position reference system that may be applied to any map or chart graduated in latitude and longitude regardless of projection. It is a method of expressing latitude and longitude in a form suitable for rapid reporting and plotting.

ORIGIN: *georef* is derived from "World *Geo*graphic *Ref*erence System."

George, David Lloyd • see LLOYD GEORGE, DAVID.

George III (1738–1820) • king of Great Britain (1760–1820) at the time of the REVOLUTIONARY WAR and usually held responsible, through policies carried out by his prime minister Lord North, for the loss of the American Colonies. During the last years of his life (from 1811) he was intermittently mad, and his son, the future George IV, acted as regent.

***George Washington*, USS** • an active multipurpose aircraft carrier with nuclear propulsion. It was first launched in July 1990, commissioned in July 1992, and is part of the U.S. Atlantic Fleet.

geosynchronous orbit • a satellite orbit at approximately 35,800 kilometers above the Equator in which objects travel at the same speed as the Earth and thus remain in a stationary position with reference to the Earth.

German High Command • the highest command headquarters of the German armed forces. In WORLD WAR II, the WEHRMACHT High Command (in German, the **Oberkommando der Wehrmacht** or **OKW**) was headed by Field Marshal Wilhelm Keitel and, under ADOLF HITLER's direct supervision, directed the conduct of the war.

German-Soviet Treaty of Non-Aggression • see NAZI-SOVIET PACT OF 1939.

Germantown, Battle of • a REVOLUTIONARY WAR battle at Germantown, Pennsylvania on October 4, 1777. Forces under the command of Gen. GEORGE WASHINGTON marched by night with the aim of a surprise attack on the British stronghold. Initial advances were successful but thick fog and smoke prevented the coordinated attack that Washington had planned, and he retreated in the end.

Germany, Battle for • (1945) the final European campaign of WORLD WAR II, won by the 4-million-strong Allied army, under the leadership of Supreme Allied Commander DWIGHT D. EISENHOWER. Despite disagreement over tactics, particularly from British Field Marshal BERNARD LAW MONTGOMERY, Eisenhower successfully rallied recalcitrant generals and straightened the forces for a decisive broad-front attack that began in early March. Between March 7 and 25, all seven Allied armies had successfully crossed the Rhine after deliberate attacks and the construction of sixty-two bridges by the U.S. ARMY'S CORPS OF ENGINEERS. With air, naval, and artillery support, the forces advanced quickly through early April, forcing the surrender of 400,000 German troops. Along the way, they liberated several concentration camps, including BUCHENWALD and DACHAU, revealing to the world the ghastly extent of NAZI atrocities. By April 21, U.S. forces were within 63 miles of Berlin, but after fulfilling the prearranged meeting with the RED ARMY on the Elbe River, advanced no further. At the same time, British and Canadian forces moved through northern Germany, French forces through the south, and Gen. GEORGE S. PATTON's 3rd Army raced through Czechoslovakia, Bavaria, and Austria. By early May, American forces linked with troops from the Italian theater. The superior power and tactical preparation forced the surrender of the Germans, signed by Field Marshal Alfred Jodl on May 7, a week after ADOLF HITLER committed suicide in his Berlin bunker. The Soviets, who had seized Berlin, eastern Germany, and more territory in Central Europe, demanded a second surrender in Berlin on May 8, which, as V-E DAY (Victory in Europe Day), marked the official end of the European war. On June 5, the Allied Control Council divided Germany into four occupation zones.

germ warfare • another term for BIOLOGICAL WARFARE.

Geronimo (1823?–1909) • Apache war leader in the American Southwest involved in the general warfare between the Apaches and the United States in the 1860s and who for many years repeatedly resisted efforts to remain on a reservation, crossing and recrossing the Mexican border as he fled U.S. troops. He attained a fearsome reputation, perhaps due to the attacks of his associates more than to his own. Geronimo finally surrendered in 1886 and spent the remainder of his life in confinement in Florida and Oklahoma.

Gestapo • the German secret police under NAZI rule. It ruthlessly suppressed opposition to the Nazis in Germany and occupied Europe and sent Jews and others to concentration camps.

ORIGIN: from German *Geheime Staatspolizei*, 'secret state police.'

Getty, George Washington (1819–1901) • Union army officer, born in Georgetown, D.C. Getty commanded a brigade in the siege of Yorktown; played a part in the success at SOUTH MOUNTAIN and ANTIETAM (both 1862) as a chief of artillery; led an infantry division at FREDERICKSBURG (1862); and delayed a Confederate assault during the BATTLE OF THE WILDERNESS (1864). Getty had earlier seen service during the MEXICAN WAR (1846–48) and the SEMINOLE WARS.

Gettysburg Address • a speech delivered by President ABRAHAM LINCOLN at a dedication ceremony on November 19, 1863, four months after the BATTLE OF GETTYSBURG, for the Soldiers' National Cemetery at the GETTYSBURG NATIONAL MILITARY PARK in Pennsylvania. He defined American democracy, sanctified the war for the Union, and described America as "a new nation, conceived in Liberty, and dedicated to the proposition that all men are created equal."

Gettysburg, Battle of • (July 1–3, 1863) a CIVIL WAR battle in and around Gettysburg, Pennsylvania, that was the bloodiest and most decisive of the war. Combined casualties, with slightly more on the Confederate side, were more than 50,000. Numerous forces took part, principally under the command of Gen. GEORGE G. MEADE on the Union side and Gen. ROBERT E. LEE for the South. It was a Union victory through slow attrition; Lee's army began retreating on July 4, 1863. The South made no further invasions and could never make up the losses in men and equipment it suffered here.

Gettysburg National Military Park • a national military park established in 1895 in Gettysburg, Pennsylvania, to preserve the site of the BATTLE OF GETTYSBURG (July 1863). Statues of Confederate general ROBERT E. LEE and Union general GEORGE G. MEADE are among the more than 1,300 monuments there.

Ghent, Treaty of • an agreement negotiated in Ghent, Belgium, and signed on December 24, 1814, by Great Britain and the United States to end the WAR OF 1812. Peace was established on the status quo ante bellum. It included the concession to the United States of all British territory in the American Northwest, which enabled American expansion.

Gholson, Samuel Jameson |'gōlsən| (1808–83) • CIVIL WAR army officer, born in Madison County, Kentucky. Gholson served with a Mississippi militia unit that became part of the Confederate army in 1864. He saw constant action and suffered repeated injuries throughout the war. After the war he twice served as speaker of the state house and also became chief of the county KU KLUX KLAN.

Ghost Dance • a messianic religious frenzy among the Columbia River tribes in the 1870s, the White Mountain Apaches in 1881, and the tribes of the northern Great Plains ca. 1889–90. The Ghost Dance movement can be traced to the Paiute shaman Wovoka who preached a blissful afterlife in which believers would be reunited with dead friends and relatives, game (particularly the bison) would be plentiful, and there would be no "white man." Among the LAKOTA SIOUX the movement took on an aggressive cast and led to active attempts to expel the white intruders from Indian lands which ended in the battle of WOUNDED KNEE in December 1890, marking the end of the PLAINS INDIANS WARS.

GHQ • *abbr.* General Headquarters.

GI • *n.* (pl. **GIs**) a private soldier in the U.S. Army.

ORIGIN: 1930s (originally denoting equipment supplied to U.S. forces): abbreviation of *galvanized iron*; later misinterpreted as an abbreviation of *government* (or *general*) *issue*.

Giap, Vo Nguyen (1910?–) • general in the Vietnamese army, born in Quang binh, Vietnam. Giap is credited with the victory over the French at DIEN BIEN PHU (1954) and later, as both political and military leader of North Vietnam after its partition, for the victory over South Vietnam and the United States in the VIETNAM WAR. Giap had been active in the Vietnamese independence movement and the Communist party since his youth. He was considered a brilliant military strategist and tactician, and an authority on guerrilla warfare. Giap held several high government positions after the reunification of Vietnam.

Gibbon, John (1827–96) • Union army officer, born in Holmesburg, Pennsylvania. Gibbon gained fame at GETTYSBURG (1863) when his division repulsed Gen. GEORGE E. PICKETT's charge and then successfully defended CEMETERY HILL. As a commander he was known as a firm disciplinarian (his unit was called the "Iron Brigade").

As a youth Gibbon moved with his family to North Carolina, where his parents remained when war broke out. His three brothers fought for the CONFEDERACY.

G.I. Bill of Rights • (also **G.I. Bill**) the series of benefits granted by the U.S. Congress under the SERVICEMEN'S READJUSTMENT ACT OF 1944 and extended by later legislation to the present day. Initially for WORLD WAR II veterans, it included grants for higher education or vocational training, mortgage loan guarantees for home buying, and cash payments for those unemployed after discharge. By providing help for more than 3.5 million home mortgages, the bill was instrumental in encouraging the rapid growth of suburbia after 1945; at the peak, in 1947, about 40 percent of all housing starts in the nation were funded by the guarantee. In addition, over half of the nearly 16 million eligible veterans used the bill's educational benefits from 1945 to 1956. College enrollments increased by 70 percent over prewar levels. In 1947 almost half of all college students had served in the military.

Gihon, Albert Leary |ˈgīˌhän; ˈgēˌhōn| (1833–1901) • enlisted naval officer, born in Philadelphia, Pennsylvania. Gihon devoted his entire medical career to the U.S. Navy as a surgeon and medical administrator (1855–95). He spent most of the CIVIL WAR aboard the *St. Louis*, which cruised the Atlantic islands searching for Confederate privateers. From 1879 until his retirement (with the rank of commodore) in 1895 he was medical director in charge of four naval hospitals, including those in Norfolk, Virginia, and Brooklyn, New York.

Gihon was the author of several books on sanitation and public health and is considered a pioneer for his work in the control of syphilis.

Gilbert Islands • a group of atolls in the western Pacific Ocean that were of strategic importance during WORLD WAR II. The Gilbert Islands, now part of Kiribati, Micronesia, were the first targets of the U.S. approach toward the Philippines from the east. U.S. troops drove the Japanese occupation forces out on November 20–23, 1943, through amphibious, naval, and air assault. Once the Gilbert Islands were captured, U.S. forces headed west toward the MARSHALL ISLANDS.

Gillars, Mildred Elizabeth (1900–88) • WORLD WAR II radio propagandist known as "AXIS SALLY," the first woman in American history to be convicted of treason. Gillars, born in Portland, Maine, moved to Europe seeking to fulfill her frustrated theatrical ambitions and eventually settled in Berlin (1934), where she became a star of German radio. Her shows, which were beamed to American GIs in North Africa and Europe, featured nostalgic music and sought to persuade the soldiers that they faced certain defeat. Convicted (1949) of giving aid and comfort to the enemy and sentenced to thirty years in prison, Gillars was paroled in 1961. She later taught in a convent school and completed her college education.

Unlike others involved in similar subversive activities, Gillars was seen to have drifted into treason as a matter of career convenience, rather than for reasons of ideology.

Gillem, Alvan Cullem (1830–75) • Union army officer, born in Jackson County, Tennessee. Gillem participated in the SHILOH and CORINTH campaigns (both 1862) and later oversaw construction of the rail line between Nashville and the Tennessee River needed to furnish supplies to the ARMY OF THE CUMBERLAND. His wartime record was modest but it made him a prominent figure in Tennessee politics. After the war he was placed in charge of the 4th Military District in the South, where he pursued conservative policies committed to home rule.

Gillmore, Quincy Adams (1825–88) • Union army officer, born in Black River, Lorain County, Ohio. Gilmore, regarded as the preeminent military engineer of his day, was the first to demonstrate the power of rifled cannon against masonry works (at FORT PULASKI, 1862). Gillmore was also successful in directing the artillery placements on Morris Island that led to the demolition of FORT SUMTER, but the success was mixed because his efforts failed to dislodge the Confederates. Gillmore had a distinguished postwar career, mainly as superintending engineer of fortifications and of river and harbor improvements along the Atlantic coast.

gimbal |ˈgimbəl; ˈjim-| • *n.* (often **gimbals**) a contrivance, typically consisting of rings pivoted at right angles, for keeping an instrument such as a compass or chronometer horizontal in a moving vessel or aircraft.

DERIVATIVES: **gimbaled** (or **gimballed**) *adj.*

GIUK gap • the area of the Atlantic ocean bounded by Greenland, Iceland, and the United Kingdom.

glacis |ˈglāsis; ˈglæs-| • *n.* (pl. same) a gently sloping bank, in particular one that slopes down from a fort, exposing attackers to the defenders' missiles.

glareshield • *n.* a screen attached to the cockpit canopy of an aircraft designed to reduce the effects of glare.

glasnost |ˈglæzˌnōst ; ˈglæs-; ˈgläz-; ˈgläs- | • (in the former Soviet Union) the policy or practice of more open consultative government and wider dissemination of information, initiated by leader MIKHAIL GORBACHEV in 1985.

ORIGIN: from Russian *glasnost'*, literally 'the fact of being public', from *glasnyy* 'public, open' + *-nost'*

glide bomb • a bomb fitted with airfoils to provide lift. It is carried and released in the direction of a target by an aircraft.

glide mode • in a flight control system, a control mode in which an aircraft is automatically positioned to the center of the glide slope course.

glider • *n.* **1** a light aircraft that is designed to fly for long periods without using an engine. **2** the pilot of such an aircraft.

Global Positioning System • (**GPS**) See GLOBAL SATELLITE POSITIONING SYSTEMS.

Global Protection Against Limited Strikes • see GPALS.

global satellite positioning system(s) • any one of several systems for finding an exact location on the Earth's surface through the use of radio/radar signals and satellites in the Earth's orbit. Such systems came into general use in the 1970s, are now extremely accurate, and have significant military applications (for targeting, tracking, and position reporting and the like).

Globemaster III • (**C-17**) a long-range transport aircraft designed to carry more than twice its own weight and capable of taking off and landing on short airfields.

Glover, John (1732–97) • Massachusetts fishing merchant and Revolutionary army officer, born in Salem, Massachusetts. Glover was active in the local militia as early as 1759. His schooner *Hannah* was chartered by GEORGE WASHINGTON, armed, and sent to sea to intercept British supply vessels. Glover's unit later joined Washington in New York, where they ferried his troops, which were nearly surrounded by the British, across the East River to safety. It was also Glover's troops who manned the boats that carried Washington and his army across the Delaware River to attack the HESSIANS at TRENTON(1776). Glover's regiment was disbanded at the end of 1776, but he later returned to service at Washington's request, serving in the SARATOGA campaign (1777) and in the Hudson River highlands.

Gnr. • *abbr.* General.

go 911 • slang (in the PERSIAN GULF WAR) to panic.

go about • change to an opposite tack.

go around • (of an aircraft) abort an approach to landing and prepare to make a fresh approach.

go-around mode • in an automatic flight control system, a control mode that terminates an aircraft approach and programs a climb.

gob • *n.* informal, dated an American sailor.

go down • (of a ship or aircraft) sink or crash: *he saw eleven B-17s go down.*

go downtown • slang (in the VIETNAM WAR) to bomb Hanoi.

Goebbels, Paul Joseph |ˈgəbəlz| (1897–1945) • minister of propaganda for the THIRD REICH under ADOLF HITLER. Goebbels, born in Rheydt, Germany, was largely responsible for creating the mythic Führer hailed by the German people. A gifted orator and formidable journalist, Goebbels also used his considerable powers to control the press, radio, theater, and films. He killed himself and his family after the German defeat.

Goering, Hermann |ˈgəriNG| • (or **Göring**) (1893–1946) a leading figure of NAZI Germany, born in Rosenheim, Bavaria. Goering was one of the earliest and most loyal supporters of ADOLF HITLER. He served as president of the REICHSTAG (1932), established the GESTAPO (1933), and acted as head of the LUFTWAFFE. After the Luftwaffe's failure in the BATTLE OF BRITAIN (1940), Goering largely retired into private life. He surrendered to the Americans after Hitler's suicide. Goering was condemned as a war criminal by the INTERNATIONAL MILITARY TRIBUNAL at NÜRNBERG and sentenced to hanging but took poison before his execution was carried out.

After being severely wounded during the abortive Munich Putsch (1923), Goering became addicted to morphine. He had to undergo treatments for drug addiction periodically for the remainder of his life.

Goethals, George Washington |ˈgōTHəlz| (1858–1928) • military officer and chief engineer of the PANAMA CANAL, born in Brooklyn, New York. Goethals's responsibilities included housing and provisioning the work force on the Canal, for which he became a hero. Following the successful completion of the canal (1914), ahead of time and under budget, Goethals remained as governor of the Panama Canal Zone (1914–17). After a series of mediocre results in positions in which he did not have absolute authority, he was given control of, and totally reorganized, the Quartermaster Department, for which he was awarded the DISTINGUISHED SERVICE MEDAL (1918).

Gold Beach • one of the five beaches targeted for the D-DAY LANDING at NORMANDY, and one of the two under British control. It is east of OMAHA BEACH, near Arromanches. See also SWORD BEACH.

Golden Fleece, Operation • defensive operations in the VIETNAM WAR carried out by the Marines in 1965 and 1966, intended to protect the rice harvest in the Mo Duc District from VIETCONG battalions who were expected to sabotage it. Marines also participated in the transportation of the harvest.

goldie lock • a signal used only by air support radar team operators to indicate that the ground controller has electronic control of an aircraft.

Goldsborough, Louis Malesherbes (1805–77) • naval officer, born in Washington, D.C. He served in both the MEXICAN WAR (1846–48) and the CIVIL WAR. In the latter he lost favor early (1862) with SECRETARY OF THE NAVY GIDEON WELLES for his performance as a commander of the North Atlantic Blockading Squadron, and he held routine administrative posts afterwards. A brief return to military duty late in the war did not redeem his reputation. Before the war he had served as head of U.S. NAVAL ACADEMY (1853–57).

Goldwater-Nichols Act • (Also known as the **Department of Defense Reorganization Act of 1986**) a law presented by Senator Barry Goldwater and Representative William Nichols in 1986 to propose the most extensive reforms to the DEPARTMENT OF DEFENSE since the organization's creation under the NATIONAL SECURITY ACT OF 1947. It strengthened the authority of the chairman of the JOINT CHIEFS OF STAFF and created the position of vice chairman, increased the influence of the unified combatant commands, and created a specialization within each service to prepare officers assigned to the Joint Staff. The goal of the act was to encourage unity among the services to improve national defense planning.

Goliad • a town in southern Texas, 85 miles (137 kilometers) southeast of San Antonio, that was the site of two crucial battles of the TEXAS WAR OF INDEPENDENCE (1836). The war began with the battle of Gonzales near the presidio at Goliad. Texans formed a volunteer army and seized the Mexican constabulary under the command of JAMES W. FANNIN, and JAMES BOWIE. In March 1836 Mexican Gen. JOSÉ DE URREA defeated Fannin's men shortly after the fall of the ALAMO. Fannin surrendered, and his men were imprisoned at Goliad. Mexican leader ANTONIO LÓPEZ DE SANTA ANNA ordered Fannin and his men executed on March 27, which became known as the **Goliad Massacre**. The final battle of the war, in which the Texans defeated Santa Anna, was fought to cries of "Remember the Alamo!" and "Remember Goliad!"

gondola • *n.* **1** a light flat-bottomed boat used on Venetian canals, having a high point at each end and worked by one oar at the stern. **2** (also **gondola car**) an open railroad freight car. **3** an enclosed compartment suspended from an airship or balloon.

gone Elvis • slang to have died or disappeared, or be lost, missing in action.

go no-go • the condition or state of operability of a component or system: "go" means functioning properly; "no go" means not functioning properly.

Gooch, Sir William (1681–1751) • colonial governor of Virginia (1727–49), born in Yarmouth, England. His tenure was marked by prosperity and the absence of conflict with the mother country. Gooch involved the burgesses in formulating legislation, promoted settlement of western lands, and instituted measures that improved the quality and prices of tobacco. He also established personal ties with the colony through land and business investments, as well as through the marriage of his son to a Maryland woman.

Good Neighbor Policy • the policy of President FRANKLIN D. ROOSEVELT toward Latin America. The term was taken from Roosevelt's first inaugural address on March 4, 1933. The policy reversed a previous attitude of interventionism in the internal affairs of Latin American nations. Specific acts included the repeal of the PLATT AMENDMENT authorizing U.S. intervention in Cuba in 1933, and the withdrawal of U.S. Marines from Haiti in 1934.

go off • (of a gun, bomb, or similar device) explode or fire.

gooseneck • *n.* a metal fitting at the end of a boom, connecting it to a pivot or ring near the base of the mast.

goose step • a military marching step in which the legs are not bent at the knee. • *v.* (**goose-step**) march with such a step: *German soldiers goose-stepped outside the monument.*

Gorbachev, Mikhail (1931–) • Soviet statesman, and General Secretary of the Communist Party of the Soviet Union (1985–91) and President (1988–91). His foreign policy brought about an end to the COLD WAR, while within the USSR he introduced major reforms known as GLASNOST and PERESTROIKA. He resigned following an attempted coup. He won the Nobel Peace Prize in 1990.

Gordon, John Brown (1832–1904) • Confederate soldier with an Alabama regiment, born in Upson County, Georgia. Gordon fought at SOUTH MOUNTAIN and ANTIETAM (both 1862), where he was wounded five times. Later as brigade commander, he fought in the CHANCELLORSVILLE, GETTYSBURG, and MINE RUN campaigns (all 1863), and particularly distinguished himself at the BATTLE OF THE WILDERNESS and SPOTSYLVANIA (both 1864).

Gorgas, Josiah (1818–83) • Confederate army officer, born in Running Pumps, Pennsylvania. As chief of ordnance, Gorgas enacted policies of importation, industrial expansion, and blockade running that turned the South from an area virtually devoid of manufacturing facilities and centralized supplies to one capable of meeting the demands of the many large Confederate armies. Earlier in his career Gorgas played a significant role at the siege of VERACRUZ (1847) during the MEXICAN WAR (1846–48).

Josiah was the father of WILLIAM CRAWFORD GORGAS.

Gorgas, William Crawford (1854–1920) • army surgeon and sanitarian, born near Mobile, Alabama. Gorgas is credited with eliminating mosquito breeding places in Havana, Cuba, thereby effecting a dramatic decline in the incidence of yellow fever and malaria. He subsequently carried out similar disease control policies that made possible the construction of the PANAMA CANAL. In 1914 he was appointed surgeon general of the U.S. Army.

Gorgas became involved in treating yellow fever epidemics because he was immune to the disease, having contracted it early in his army career.

Gorrell, Edgar Staley (1891–1945) • U.S. aviator and industrialist. Born in Baltimore, Maryland, Gorrell graduated from WEST POINT in 1912 with a commission in the infantry. He became a pilot with the SIGNAL CORPS in 1915. He was on the Army staff when America entered WORLD WAR I in April 1917, and helped create a budget for the Army AIR SERVICE JOHN J. PERSHING appointed Gorrell to the AMERICAN EXPEDITIONARY FORCES staff, and as chief of the Technical Section of the Air Service, he developed a strategic bombing plan based on British concepts that, though not adopted, was the first extensive American vision of the potential for the new air arm. After the war Gorrell compiled documents on the AEF air service that is known simply as "Gorrell's History" and is the main source of information on American air operations in World War I. He resigned from the Army in 1920, and continued to advocate a strong air force. At President FRANKLIN D. ROOSEVELT's request Gorrell served in 1934 as a member of the Army Air Service Investigating Commission (or "Baker Board") that looked at the future of the ARMY

Air Corps. Before World War II he campaigned to build up American airpower. He died in Washington, D.C., and by his request, had his ashes scattered over West Point by a military aircraft.

Gosport Navy Yard • the original name for the Norfolk Naval Shipyard, a major building and repair facility for the U.S. Navy in Portsmouth, Virginia. Established in 1767 by the Scottish merchant Andrew Sprowle, the shipyard was confiscated by Virginia during the Revolutionary War and, in 1798, became the Gosport Navy Yard with the establishment of the U.S. Navy. On June 17, 1833, the first dry dock in the western hemisphere opened at Gosport. Early in the Civil War, with the yard under Confederate control, the partly burned frigate USS *Merrimack* was converted into the ironclad CSS *Virginia*, which fought the ironclad USS *Monitor* at Hampton Roads on March 9, 1862. The ships' new features included use of steam power, screw propellers, and ironclad hulls, and the durability of both ships in the battle spurred changes in naval technology throughout the world. Later in 1862 Union forces took the shipyard and the surrounding cities, and Gosport was renamed Norfolk Navy Yard after the area's largest city. In 1945 the name became Norfolk Naval Shipyard.

Gothic Line • the last line of defense of the Germans in Italy in World War II, running north of Florence, that they held until May 1945.

government-owned, Military Sealift Command-operated ships • ships owned by the U.S. government and operated by the Military Sealift Command with civil service employees. Such ships are designated U.S. Naval Ships, with the prefix "USNS" before the ship's name and the letter "T" prefixed to the ship's classification (for example, T-AKR). See also Military Sealift Command.

GPALS • *abbr.* Global Protection Against Limited Strikes; a missile defense system announced by President George H. Bush on January 29, 1991, to reorient the Strategic Defense Initiative begun by President Ronald Reagan in 1983. It included ground-based national and theater missile defenses, in addition to a space-based global defense.

GPS • *abbr.* Global Positioning System.

GQ • *abbr.* general quarters.

Graham, James Duncan (1799–1865) • army officer and military engineer, born in Prince William County, Virginia. Graham's career was spent on a variety of topographical projects, many involving border determinations. His maps were valued by military planners because of their precision and detail. During the Civil War he was in charge of maintaining harbor works along the East Coast from Maine to the Chesapeake Bay.

Mt. Graham in Arizona was named for Graham, who was responsible for surveying the eastern portion of the U.S.-Mexican border.

Graham, Joseph (1759–1836) • Revolutionary War army officer and political leader, born in Chester County, Pennsylvania. Graham, as a volunteer, fought in fifteen minor engagements of the war (1778–81). He later served as a North Carolina state senator (1788–93) and was active in public affairs throughout his life.

Grand Alliance • **1** an alliance between the Holy Roman Emperor Leopold I, William III of England, the Netherlands, and the Austrian Hapsburgs against Louis XIV of France in 1689. This coalition began the War of the Grand Alliance in 1689 to prevent the Bourbon family of France from gaining power in Europe. The war ended in 1697 with the Treaty of Rijswijk, but the union re-formed in 1701 when a grandson of Louis XIV became king of Spain, which led to the War of the Spanish Succession (1701–13). (Also called the **League of Augsburg**.) **2** the alliance between the United States and Great Britain that specified goals for the outcome of World War II and afterwards, as set out in the Atlantic Charter of 1941.

Grand Army of the Republic • the largest association of Union army and navy veterans, formed by former army surgeon Benjamin F. Stephenson in 1866 in Decatur, Illinois. It grew slowly but eventually reached a peak membership of 409,489 in 1890, accounting for about 40 percent of eligible Union veterans. Organized into local branches, the group was open to any honorably discharged Union veteran. The organization wielded significant political power as a result of its strong lobbying for benefits for veterans and their dependents. Its influence ebbed after 1900, and its last member died in 1956.

Grand Fleet • the main British naval fleet based at Scapa Flow in World War I.

grand slam • term used to indicate that all enemy aircraft originally sighted have been shot down.

Granger, Gordon (1822–76) • army officer, born in Joy, New York. Granger was twice cited for gallantry in the Mexican War (1846–48) and similarly cited after his role at Wilson's Creek (1861) in the Civil War. His most noteworthy accomplishment in the latter conflict was at Chickamauga (1863), where his actions helped prevent the complete rout of Union forces. Despite his successes, his advance in the Union army was hindered by a reputation for insubordination and by Ulysses S. Grant's belief that he lacked the qualities needed to command a large mission. After the war Granger was briefly in charge of the District of Texas, but his politics resulted in his removal.

Grant tank • a tank used in World War II, which entered the service in 1942. The Grant tank had a 75-mm main gun and a 37-mm secondary gun, could carry a crew of six, had 57 mm armor, and could travel at 42 km per hour. The Grant tank weighed more than 27 tons, and was 18 feet, 6 inches long and 8 feet, 9 inches tall.

Grant, Ulysses Simpson (1822–85) • Union army general and 18th president of the United States (1869–77), born in Point

Pleasant, Ohio. Grant first exhibited the coolness under fire and successful control of men for which he later became famous during the MEXICAN WAR (1846–48), when he twice rode into action, even though his role as regimental quartermaster did not require him to do so. Grant resigned from the army in 1854 but returned with the outbreak of the CIVIL WAR. Under his leadership, the Union experienced its first significant victories–at FORT HENRY and FORT DONELSON (both 1862)—after which Grant had the attention of President ABRAHAM LINCOLN, who ignored to charges of drunkenness and excessive casualties. (Though Grant had recurrent bouts of heavy drinking throughout his adult life, with intermittent periods of abstinence, there is scant, if any, reliable evidence of drunkenness during the war.) His reputation as a brilliant leader was cemented with the capture of VICKSBURG (1863), which split the CONFEDERACY and gave the Union control of the Mississippi River. Later victories included MISSIONARY RIDGE (1863), after which Lincoln promoted him to lieutenant general, naming him general in chief of all Union armies. As such he devised a plan for coordinating the offensives of the various armies, which had been acting independently. This ultimately led to the Union victory. ROBERT E. LEE surrendered to Grant at APPOMATTOX COURT HOUSE (1865). Grant was promoted to four-star general by President ANDREW JOHNSON (1866) and twice elected president of the United States (1868, 1872) on the Republican ticket. Though Grant's administrations were marked by scandal and corruption, they did achieve gains in civil service reform, civil rights, and monetary policy. Nevertheless, historians generally rank him among the worst presidents. Grant's memoirs, which he completed just days before his death, are considered by many to be among the finest military memoirs ever written. They were published by Samuel Clemens (Mark Twain).

Though always called Ulysses, Grant was baptized Hiram Ulysses. When registering at WEST POINT, he transposed the two given names to avoid having the initials H.U.G. But the congressman who had obtained his appointment had misstated his name as Ulysses Simpson, and, since the academy refused to correct it, so it remained. Classmates called him Sam, because the new initials, U.S., were seen to stand for Uncle Sam. Later in his career they came to stand for "Unconditional Surrender."

---

grape • *n.* short for grapeshot.

grapeshot • *n.* ammunition consisting of a number of small iron balls fired together from a cannon.

grapnel |'græpnəl| • *n.* **1** a grappling hook. **2** a small anchor with several flukes.

grasshopper • *n.* slang any small military observation or liaison light aircraft.

Grattan Massacre • a confrontation in 1854 between settlers at FORT LARAMIE, Wyoming and indigenous Sioux. The Sioux killed and ate a cow that had escaped from a wagon train and wandered into their village. A Lt. Grattan left the Fort with 28 men, intent on punishing the Sioux. The Sioux offered a horse to replace the cow but were repulsed, and Lt. Grattan killed the Sioux chief point-blank. Further killing and hostilities ensued.

grave • *v.* clean (a ship's bottom) by burning off the accretions and then tarring it.

graving dock • another term for DRY DOCK.

gray propaganda • propaganda that does not specifically identify any source.

Grayson, William (1736–90) • Virginia statesman and Revolutionary army officer, born in Prince William County, Virginia. A friend of GEORGE WASHINGTON, Grayson was with him at VALLEY FORGE (1777–78) and in the Battles of NEW YORK and WHITE PLAINS (both 1776). As a regimental commander he later fought at BRANDYWINE, GERMANTOWN (both 1777), and MONMOUTH (1778). After the war he was Virginia's leading antifederalist and the state's first U.S. senator.

greaser • *n.* **1** a motor mechanic or unskilled engineer on a ship. **2** informal a gentle landing of an aircraft.

Great Power • a nation whose actions have substantial global significance. The traditional "Great Powers" include the United Kingdom, France, Germany, Russia/the Soviet Union, and the United States, to which list were added on occasion Italy, Japan, and China.

Great Sioux War • (1876) one of the PLAINS INDIANS WARS between the United States and the SIOUX. It grew out of a dispute about rights to gold in the Black Hills of South Dakota; the gold was on Sioux reservation land and the United States wished to buy it back, but native leaders who were not party to the treaty establishing the reservation refused to negotiate. The first incident in the war was CUSTER'S LAST STAND, which galvanized opinion against the indigenous population.

Great Spring Victory • the liberation of South Vietnam in 1975, as seen by the Communist North.

Great Swamp Fight • a 1675 battle in KING PHILIP'S WAR (1675–77) between New England militiamen under Gov. JOSIAH WINSLOW and the NARRAGANSETT near present-day Kingston, Rhode Island. The Narragansett lost heavily and were no longer able to defend themselves.

Great War, the • see WORLD WAR I.

Great White Fleet • a fleet consisting of sixteen battleships and 14,000 sailors of the U.S. Navy set out on on December 16, 1907 (sent by President THEODORE ROOSEVELT), on a journey around the world, a feat that had never before been attempted. Traveling down the eastern coasts of North and South America, then up the Pacific coast of South America (the PANAMA CANAL was not open yet), the fleet eventually visited New Zealand, Australia, Manila, Yokohama, Ceylon, Suez, and several Mediterranean ports before returning to Virginia on February 22, 1909.

Greek fire • a combustible compound emitted by a flame-throwing weapon and used in ancient times to set light to enemy ships. It was first used by the Greeks besieged in Constantinople (673–78). It ignited on contact with water, and was probably based on naphtha and quicklime.

Greely, Adolphus Washington (1844–1935) • army officer and Arctic explorer, born in Newburyport, Massachusetts. Greely fought briefly in the CIVIL WAR but spent most of his army career with the U.S. SIGNAL CORPS, which he joined in 1869. In 1881 he led an ill-fated expedition to Greenland; resupply ships never arrived, and most of the party died before a naval rescue operation found the survivors (1884). Greely's leadership and judgment were subsequently called into question. During his tenure as chief officer (1887–1906), the Signal Corps expanded its weather forecasting service, laid undersea cables during the SPANISH-AMERICAN WAR (1898), and established the Alaskan telegraph, cable, and wireless system. Greely was a founding member of the National Geographic Society and a recipient of the CONGRESSIONAL MEDAL OF HONOR (1935).

Green Beret • informal a member of the U.S. ARMY SPECIAL FORCES.

Greene, George Sears (1801–99) • Union army officer who fought in several major battles but achieved his greatest distinction at GETTYSBURG (1863), where his troops held off the Confederates at CULP'S HILL. Greene is better known for his pre- and postwar accomplishments as a civil engineer, particularly on projects related to the expansion of New York City's water supply.

Greene, Nathanael (1742–86) • REVOLUTIONARY WAR general and adviser to GEORGE WASHINGTON, who assisted him in planning and executing the American retreat across New Jersey and the attack on TRENTON (1776). Considered by many the outstanding military strategist of the period, Greene played a pivotal role at BRANDYWINE (1777) and as commander of the Southern Department (1780–82).

Greene, Samuel Dana (1840–84) • Union naval officer, born in Apponang, Rhode Island. Greene was executive officer of the *Ironclad Monitor* from its launching until its sinking during a gale. During its battle with the Confederate ironclad *Virginia* (1862), Greene, who had been in the turret directing the ship's guns, assumed command when the captain was wounded. When the damaged *Virginia* turned away, rather than pursue her, Greene reverted to his first charge, protecting a grounded Union ship. The criticism heaped on him for this decision affected him for the rest of his life, much of which he spent in attempts to justify it. Eventually he committed suicide. Most of Greene's postwar career was spent at the U.S. NAVAL ACADEMY.

Greenhow, Rose O'Neal (1815?–64) • Confederate spy, born in Montgomery County, Maryland. Greenhow's prominence in Washington, D.C. social and political circles, combined with her strongly held states' rights position, led to her being recruited to head an espionage ring during the Civil War. Greenhow supplied the information that led to the Confederate victory at FIRST BULL RUN (1861). Her punishment, by a military commission, was exile to the CONFEDERACY, where she was received as a heroine. She continued to promote the Confederate cause at home and abroad, and died in an accident at sea on a return trip from Europe.

Green Mountain Boys • an army organized in Vermont by ETHAN ALLEN in 1770, originally to oppose territorial expansion from New York and subsequently influential in the REVOLUTIONARY WAR, especially in taking FORT TICONDEROGA.

Green, Nathan (c. 1784–1825) • privateer captain out of Salem, Massachusetts. He was noted for his extraordinary success in finding and capturing British merchant vessels during the WAR OF 1812.

Greenville, Treaty of • a peace treaty signed in August 1775 by the Indians and the Americans after the BATTLE OF FALLEN TIMBERS, which was led by Maj. Gen. ANTHONY WAYNE to end the struggle over the Ohio Valley. It allowed the Americans to settle the southern two-thirds of the Ohio Territory and temporarily secured American control over the Northwest Territory.

Greenwich Mean Time • former term for UNIVERSAL TIME.

Gregg, David McMurtrie (1833–1916) • U.S. Army officer, born in Huntingdon, Pennsylvania. Gregg participated in both the 1862 PENINSULAR and MARYLAND CAMPAIGNS under Gen. GEORGE B. MCCLELLAN and was later praised for his leadership role as part of the cavalry of the ARMY OF THE POTOMAC in its battles against the forces of J.E.B. STUART, particularly at GETTYSBURG (1863). After the war Gregg served briefly as a foreign consul and for three years as a Pennsylvania state official.

Gregg, John (1828–64) • Confederate army officer with a Texas infantry unit, born in Lawrence County, Alabama. Gregg fought and was captured at FORT DONELSON (1862), served with distinction during the VICKSBURG CAMPAIGN (1862–63), was wounded in the BATTLE OF CHICKAMAUGA (1863), and led his command with distinction through battles of the WILDERNESS TO PETERSBURG CAMPAIGN (1863) before being killed in action outside RICHMOND. Prior to the war Gregg had been active in state legal and political circles as a proponent of secession, and he was a member of the Texas delegation to the Provisional Confederate Congress.

Gregg, Maxcy (1814–62) • Confederate army officer and leader of South Carolina's first infantry regiment, born in Columbia, South Carolina. Gregg later commanded a brigade that acquitted itself admirably at the battles of GAINES' MILL, SECOND BULL RUN, and FREDERICKSBURG (all 1862), where he was mortally wounded.

Grenada • a Caribbean island nation that was the target of a surprise invasion by U.S. forces under the order of President RONALD REAGAN, to put down a left-wing coup in 1983. U.S. intervention was requested by the Organization of Eastern Caribbean States (OECS), who had been contacted by Grenada's governor general. The three-day siege brought the country under the control of U.S. and OECS forces.

grenade • *n.* a small bomb thrown by hand or launched mechanically.

grenade launcher • a device that is fitted to the muzzle of a gun to launch rifle grenades.

grenadier |ˌgrenəˈdir| • *n.* **1** a soldier armed with grenades or a grenade launcher. **2** (**Grenadiers** or **Grenadier Guards**) (in the UK) the first regiment of the royal household infantry.

grenadier company • from the 17th through the 19th centuries, a company in each infantry regiment or battalion composed of usually tall, hand-picked men armed with grenades and hatchets and employed as assault troops; in more recent times, a company of elite infantry assault troops.

grey propaganda • see GRAY PROPAGANDA.

grid coordinate system • a plane-rectangular coordinate system usually based on, and mathematically adjusted to, a map projection in order that geographic positions (latitudes and longitudes) may be readily transformed into plane coordinates and the computations relating to them may be made by the ordinary method of plane surveying.

gridiron • *n.* a frame of parallel metal bars used for grilling meat or fish over an open fire.

Gridley, Charles Vernon (1844–98) • naval officer, born in Logansport, Indiana. His career was unremarkable but for his role in the BATTLE OF MANILA BAY during the SPANISH-AMERICAN WAR (1898), when as commander of the USS *Olympia,* flagship of the American squadron approaching the Spanish fleet, he was told by Commodore GEORGE DEWEY, "You may fire when you are ready, Gridley," which he did.

Gridley, Richard (1711–96) • military engineer, born in Boston, Massachusetts. Gridley served as chief engineer and commander of the artillery in the Continental army during the REVOLUTIONARY WAR. He built a number of fortifications in the area of Boston harbor, one of which was the cause of the British withdrawal by sea in March 1776. He also supervised the digging of entrenchments before the BATTLE OF BUNKER HILL (1775).

Grierson, Benjamin Henry |ˈgrirsən| (1826–1911) • Union army officer, born in Pittsburg, Pennsylvania. His diversionary sixteen-day raid into Mississippi (April–May 1863) significantly aided ULYSSES S. GRANT's seizure of VICKSBURG (1862–63); it was considered a military masterpiece and brought him national acclaim. He conducted another devastating raid into Mississippi in the winter of 1864–65. Most of the remainder of his military career was spent on the western frontier as colonel of an all-black cavalry unit commanded by white officers. His regiment fought with distinction in various Indian encounters. He was an outspoken supporter of his troops, who met with considerable prejudice and discrimination. Grierson devoted much of his time to surveying, mapping, and locating sources of water in the areas under his care, particularly in INDIAN TERRITORY and West Texas. In 1890 he was made brigadier general; he retired a few months later.

Griffin, Charles (1825–67) • Union army officer, born in Granville, Ohio. Griffin was considered one of the outstanding soldiers of the ARMY OF THE POTOMAC, despite an unpleasant personality and actions that kept him from rising to corps command until late in the war. He commanded a division at FREDERICKSBURG (1862), CHANCELLORSVILLE (1863), and the WILDERNESS (1864) and throughout the RICHMOND and PETERSBURG campaigns (1864). Before the CIVIL WAR Griffin served during the MEXICAN WAR (1846–48) and on the frontier. He died during a yellow fever epidemic in Galveston, where he was in temporary command of the 5th Military District.

Grimes, Absalom Carlisle (1834–1911) • steamboat pilot and Confederate mail runner, born in Anchorage, Kentucky. Grimes carried letters from Missouri through Union lines into Tennessee and Mississippi, succeeding in penetrating the federal blockade of VICKSBURG (1863). Grimes was frequently captured and sentenced to death, but just as frequently escaped, until his sixth and last attempt, when he was wounded. He was released after a brief prison confinement (1864) and returned to piloting.

gripe • *v.* **1** secure (a boat) with gripes. **2** (of a ship) turn to face the wind in spite of the helm. • *n.* (**gripes**) lashings securing a boat in its place on deck or in davits.

grog • *n.* spirits (originally rum) mixed with water.

ORIGIN: mid 18th century: said to be from *Old Grog,* the reputed nickname (because of his grogram cloak) of Admiral Vernon (1684–1757), who in 1740 first ordered diluted (instead of neat) rum to be served out to sailors.

grommet • *n.* an eyelet placed in a hole in a sheet or panel to protect or insulate a rope or cable passed through it or to prevent the sheet or panel from being torn.

gross error • a nuclear weapon detonation at such a distance from the desired ground zero as to cause no nuclear damage to the target.

Grotius, Hugo (or **Huigh** or **Hugeianus de Groot**) (1583–1645) • a Dutch scholar and jurist who wrote *De Jure Belli ac Pacis* (1625; *On the Law of War and Peace*), among the earliest works devoted to international law.

Groton • a Connecticut coastal city that is the home of a major U.S. Navy submarine base. It is also the headquarters of the ELECTRIC BOAT division of GENERAL DYNAMICS and the home of the *Nautilus* museum.

groundage • *n.* **1** the bottom, as suitable or otherwise for anchoring a vessel. **2** a duty levied on vessels lying upon a shore or beach or entering a port. **3** running aground; stranding.

ground alert • the status in which aircraft on the ground or deck are fully serviced and armed, with combat crews in readiness to take off within a specified short period of time (usually fifteen minutes) after receipt of a mission order.

ground control • a system of accurate measurements used to determine the distances and directions, or differences in elevation, between points on the earth.

ground crew • a group of workers responsible for the servicing and maintenance of aircraft on the ground.

ground effect machine • see AIR-CUSHION VEHICLE.

ground fire • the ground-to-air fire of small arms directed against aircraft.

ground readiness • the status wherein aircraft can be armed and serviced and personnel alerted to take off within a specified length of time after receiving orders.

ground reconnaissance • reconnaissance carried out by troops on the ground rather than by satellites, aircraft, or electronic means.

ground speed • an aircraft's speed relative to the ground. Compare with AIRSPEED.

ground-surveillance-radar team • the crew of a military radar, usually portable, designed to detect and track the movement of enemy ground forces including troops and vehicles.

groundswell • *n.* a large or extensive swell in the sea.

ground tackle • the equipment used to anchor or moor a boat or ship.

ground war • war conducted on land by infantry, artillery, armor, and supporting forces.

ground zero • the point on the surface of the earth at, or vertically below or above, the center of a planned or actual nuclear detonation.

group • *n.* **1** a unit of the U.S. Air Force, consisting of two or more squadrons. **2** a unit of the U.S. Army, consisting of two or more battalions.

group burial • a burial in a common grave of two or more individually unidentified remains.

group captain • Brit. an officer in the RAF ranking above wing commander and below air commodore.

group rendezvous • another term for FORCE RENDEZVOUS.

Grover, Cuvier (1828–85) • Union army officer, born in Bethel, Maine. Grover was repeatedly recognized for gallantry in leading his troops, from his first experience at WILLIAMSBURG (1862) through the SHENANDOAH VALLEY CAMPAIGN and the BATTLE OF CEDAR CREEK (1864). Grover, a career soldier, served in a variety of peacetime posts both before and after the CIVIL WAR.

Groves, Leslie Richard, Jr. (1896–1970) • army officer and engineer, born in Albany, New York. His reputation as a results-focused manager and problem solver led to his being tapped to head up the MANHATTAN PROJECT (officially, commanding officer of the Manhattan Engineer District). Insisting on total security, Groves worked effectively with top scientists, developing a particularly fruitful relationship with J. ROBERT OPPENHEIMER. Groves was also involved in the planning and policy making related to the deployment of the weapons produced, and was instrumental in persuading President HARRY S. TRUMAN to proceed with the strike against Japan. Earlier service included occupation duty in France immediately following WORLD WAR I and a number of routine engineering assignments in which he distinguished himself. Subsequent to that was his appointment as chief of the Operations Branch, CORPS OF ENGINEERS in the WAR DEPARTMENT (1940), a position that saw him directing construction of barracks, training camps, and munitions plants throughout the country. After the war Groves was chief of the Armed Forces Special Weapons Project. He was awarded the DISTINGUISHED SERVICE MEDAL for his work on the Manhattan Project (1948), shortly after which he retired and returned to civilian life.

grt • *abbr.* gross registered tonnage, a measure of a ship's size found by dividing the volume of the space enclosed by its hull (measured in cubic feet) by one hundred.

Grumman • an aviation company started by Leroy Grumman during the stock boom of 1927–29. It helped sustain a competitive industry during the early Depression years. Since WORLD WAR II it has developed the Grumman A-6 INTRUDER bomber, a tactical aircraft with multirole capabilities, and in the 1960s the Grumman F-14 TOMCAT fighter, part of a category of "superfighters" that still define the modern standards of fighter excellence. In 1994 the company was acquired by Northrop.

grunt • *n.* **1** informal a low-ranking or unskilled soldier or other worker: *he went from grunt to major in less than five years.*
ORIGIN: alteration of *ground*, from *ground man* (with reference to unskilled railway work before progressing to lineman). **2** a common soldier.

GSR team • see GROUND-SURVEILLANCE-RADAR TEAM.

G-suit • a garment with pressurized pouches that are inflatable with air or fluid, worn by fighter pilots and astronauts to enable them to withstand high gravitational forces.
ORIGIN: 1940s: from *g* (symbol of gravity) + *suit*.

Guadalcanal, Battle of • a long-running air, sea, and land battle on the island of Guadalcanal in the SOLOMON ISLANDS in WORLD WAR II. The Japanese had initially targeted the island as a strategic staging area for the planned isolation of Australia. U.S. Marines invaded in August 1942 and captured a nearly completed Japanese airfield. Opposing forces fought for control of the island during the next six months. There were heavy losses of men and materiel on both sides, but particularly for the Japanese, who finally fled in February 1943. This U.S. victory destroyed the myth of Japanese invincibility and boosted U.S. morale.

Guadalupe-Hidalgo, Treaty of • a treaty signed in Guadalupe-Hidalgo on February 2, 1848, to end the MEXICAN WAR (1846–48). The United States agreed to pay Mexico $15 million and assume $3 million in adjusted claims of U.S. citizens. It established a boundary for Texas at the Rio Grande, and the United States annexed Mexico's northern provinces. It included provisions ensuring the civil and property rights of Mexicans in the transferred territories, but the United States subsequently failed to honor them.

Guam • an island in the western Pacific that was awarded to the United States after the SPANISH-AMERICAN WAR in 1898 and has had military significance since that time. It was governed by the Navy until 1950 and is still the home of a large U.S. naval station. The Japanese invaded and occupied Guam for thirty months starting in December 1941. It was liberated in July 1944. Restitution to the native Chamorros was made in an act of Congress in 1995 for the atrocities they had endured during the Japanese occupation.

Guan, Heights of • a series of ridges running from east to west along Long Island, New York, near the area of Brooklyn Heights, in what is now the Greenwood Cemetery. In the summer of 1776, GEORGE WASHINGTON placed American troops along the hills, giving them a strong, fortified position of great strategic importance. Once in place, the Americans were vulnerable to attack only from the southern shore road or through the four passes through the Heights. But the northernmost pass, Jamaica Pass, was guarded only by five militia officers, who were to signal if the British troops came. On August 26–27, 1776, British troops under Sir WILLIAM HOWE's command split so that half the men massed along the three defended routes while the other half executed a night march through the Jamaica Pass, capturing the militia officers before they could signal. The Americans awoke on August 27 to realize that they were surrounded. Howe failed to act on his advantage and laid siege to the Americans, allowing Washington and his men to beat a strategic retreat off Long Island on August 29—30.

Guantánamo Bay |gwän'tänəmō 'bä| • a bay on the southeast coast of Cuba. It is the site of a U.S. naval base established in 1903.

guard • *v.* **1** watch over to keep safe: *they were sent to* ***guard*** *villagers* ***from*** *attack by bandits.* **2** watch over in order to control entry and exit: *the gates were guarded by uniformed soldiers.* **3** watch over (someone) to prevent them from escaping. • *n.* **1** a soldier formally assigned to protect a person or to control access to a place: *a security guard | he distracted the soldier on guard duty.* **2** [treated as sing. or pl.] a body of soldiers serving to protect a place or person: *the dog belonged to a member of the compound's guard.*

PHRASES: **guard of honor** a group of soldiers ceremonially welcoming an important visitor or escorting a casket in a funeral. See also HONOR GUARD. **keep** (or **stand**) **guard** act as a guard. **on guard** on duty to protect or defend something. **under guard** being guarded: *he was held in an empty stable under guard.*

guardhouse • *n.* **1** a building used to accommodate a military guard or to detain military prisoners. **2** a building accommodating a guard who controls entrance to the grounds of a house, housing development, school, or other facility.

guardroom • *n.* a room in a military base used to accommodate a guard or detain prisoners.

guardsman • *n.* (pl. **-men**) **1** (in the U.S.) a member of the NATIONAL GUARD. **2** (in the UK) a soldier of a regiment of Guards.

gudgeon • *n.* **1** a pivot or spindle on which a bell or other object swings or rotates. **2** a socket at the stern of a vessel, into which a rudder is fitted.

guerre de course • see COMMERCE RAIDING.

guerrilla |gə'rilə| (also **guerilla**) • *n.* a member of a small independent group taking part in irregular fighting, typically against larger regular forces: *this small town fell to the guerrillas | guerrilla warfare.*

ORIGIN: early 19th century (introduced during the Peninsular War (1808–14): from Spanish, diminutive of *guerra* 'war.'

guerrilla warfare |gə'rilə 'wôr,fer| • military and paramilitary operations conducted in enemy-held or hostile territory by irregular, predominantly indigenous forces.

guest rope • **1** a second rope fastened to a boat in tow to keep it steady. **2** a rope slung outside a ship to give a hold for boats coming alongside.

guidance • *n.* **1** policy, direction, decision, or instruction having the effect of an order when promulgated by a higher echelon. **2** the entire process by which target intelligence information received by the guided missile is used to effect proper flight control to cause timely direction changes for effective target interception.

guided missile • a missile, typically carrying a warhead, whose trajectory or flight path is capable of being altered by an external or internal mechanism.

guided missile cruiser • (**CG**) a warship designed to counter air, surface, and subsurface threats in combination with strike and amphibious forces, usually equipped with 5-inch guns, antisubmarine weapons, and an advanced area-defense antiair-missile.

guided missile destroyer • (**DDG**) a kind of destroyer armed with standard guided missiles, naval guns, long-range sonar, and antisubmarine weapons.

guided missile equipment carrier • an unarmored carrier used to transport guided missile systems and related equipment. These carriers are self-propelled, amphibious, full-tracked, and able to be moved by air transport.

guided missile frigate • (**FFG**) a warship that carries standard missile launchers, a battery of 5 54 or 76-mm guns, torpedoes, and helicopters as well as a towed array sonar.

guided missile submarine • (**SSG, SSGN**) a submarine capable of launching guided missile attacks. The SSGN is nuclear-powered.

guidon |ˈgīdn| • *n.* a pennant that narrows to a point or fork at the free end, especially one used as the standard of a light cavalry regiment.

guidon bearer • the individual designated to carry the guidon authorized to identify companies, detachments, and separate platoons of thirty or more personnel. The guidon bearer plays a key role in dismounted drill by signaling visually the commander's oral instructions and by acting as a reference point for alignment of the unit.

Guilford Court House, Battle of • a pivotal battle in the REVOLUTIONARY WAR in North Carolina in March 1781. It was a costly British victory under Gen. CHARLES CORNWALLIS, but it strategically altered the course of the war and marked the beginning of NATHANAEL GREENE's liberation of the South for the Americans.

guinea pig • in naval-mine warfare, a ship used to determine whether an area can be considered safe from influence mines under certain conditions, or, specifically, to detonate pressure mines.

Gulf of Tonkin Incidents • sporadic attacks during the VIETNAM WAR against U.S. naval destroyers in August 1964, that were in the Gulf of Tonkin for intelligence-gathering. Retaliatory hostilities that followed these led to the adoption of the GULF OF TONKIN RESOLUTION.

Gulf of Tonkin Resolution • a resolution passed by Congress on August 7, 1964, to approve President LYNDON B. JOHNSON's decision to use military force to prevent further Communist aggression in South Vietnam. It was a functional, not actual, declaration of war. It was repealed by Congress in January 1971, but American involvement in the VIETNAM WAR continued through the early 1970s.

Gulf War syndrome • a medical condition affecting many veterans of the 1991 PERSIAN GULF WAR, causing fatigue, chronic headaches, and skin and respiratory disorders. Its origin is uncertain, though it has been attributed to exposure to a combination of pesticides, vaccines, and other chemicals.

gull • *n.* in electronic warfare, a floating radar reflector used to simulate a surface target at sea for deceptive purposes.

gun • *n.* **1** a weapon incorporating a metal tube from which bullets, shells, or other missiles are propelled by explosive force, typically making a characteristic loud, sharp noise. **2** a gunman: *a hired gun.* **3** (**guns**) slang, dated used as a nickname for a ship's gunnery officer. **4** the firing of a piece of artillery as a salute or signal: *the boom of the one o'clock gun echoed across the river.* • *v.* (**gunned, gunning**) (**gun someone down**) shoot someone with a gun: *they were gunned down by masked snipers.*

Gunbelt • the parts of the United States where military production facilities are clustered, such as the Northeast corridor from New Hampshire to Virginia; the Sunbelt states of Florida, Georgia, Texas, Arizona, and California; some areas in Colorado, Missouri, and Utah; Silicon Valley; and Seattle, Washington.

gunboat • *n.* a small, fast ship mounting guns, for use in shallow coastal waters and rivers.

gun carriage • a wheeled support for a piece of artillery.

gun crew • the personnel assigned to service an artillery piece.

gun deck • **1** a deck on a vessel on which guns are placed. **2** the lowest such deck on a ship of the line.

gun direction • the distribution and direction of the gunfire of a ship.

gunkhole • informal *n.* a shallow inlet or cove that is difficult or dangerous to navigate. • *v.* cruise in and out of such inlets or coves: *they were gunkholing through the coral archipelago.*

gun laying • the process of applying to an artillery piece the range, azimuth, and elevation settings required to aim the piece at the intended target.

gunlock • *n.* a mechanism by which the charge of a gun is exploded.

gunman • *n.* (pl. **-men**) a man who uses a gun to commit a crime or terrorist act.

gunnel • *n.* variant spelling of GUNWALE.

gunner • *n.* a serviceman who operates or specializes in guns, in particular: **a** a naval warrant officer in charge of a ship's guns, gun crews, and ordnance stores. **b** a member of an aircraft crew who operates a gun, especially (formerly) in a gun turret on a bomber.

gunnery sergeant • a noncommissioned officer in the U.S. Marine Corps ranking above staff sergeant and below master sergeant.

Gunnison, John Williams (1812–53) • army officer and topographical engineer, born in Goshen, New York. Gunnison surveyed the Great Salt Lake (one of the islands is named in his honor), worked on harbor improvements on Lake Michigan, and surveyed the Pacific Road for a railroad route from the Mississippi River to the Pacific Ocean. He helped the Mormons with an Indian uprising (1850) and later wrote a book about the sect. While in Utah on a later expedition (1853), Gunnison was killed by Pahvant Indians, as were others of his party. The incident aroused animosity against the Mormons, whom some accused of being responsible for the massacre, which was part of a struggle among the Mormons, Indians, and U.S. government for control over the Utah Territory.

Many of the geographic areas Gunnison explored were later named in his honor, including the Grand River (Gunnison River); Poncha Pass (Gunnison Pass); Gunnison County, Colorado; and two towns named Gunnison, one in Utah and one in Colorado. In addition there is Gunnison National Forest; Mount Gunnison; and the Gunnison Valley in Grand County, Utah.

---

gunpowder • *n.* a low-explosive powder that consists of a mixture of potassium nitrate, ground charcoal, and sulfur that is used for fuzes, fireworks, blasting, and in muzzle-loading weapons.

gunpower • *n.* a measure of the total weight of the projectiles thrown by the main batteries of a battleship in one broadside.

gunroom • Brit. *n.* a set of quarters for midshipmen or other junior officers in a warship.

guns free (or **weapons free**) • in air defense, a weapon control order imposing a status whereby weapons systems may be fired at any target not positively recognized as friendly.

gunship • *n.* an airplane or a helicopter heavily armed with machine guns or with machines guns and cannon, providing air support for ground troops in combat.

gunsight • *n.* a device on a gun that enables it to be aimed accurately.

gun-site • *n.* a site designated for the emplacement of artillery.

guns tight (or **weapons tight**) • in air defense, a weapon control order imposing a status whereby weapons systems may be fired only at targets recognized as hostile.

gunstock • *n.* the wooden stock or support to which the barrel of a gun is attached.

gun-target line • an imaginary straight line from gun to target.

gunwale |ˈgənl| (also **gunnel**) • *n.* (often **gunwales**) the upper edge of the side of a boat or ship.

Gustav Line • a line of German defense during WORLD WAR II that crossed the Italian peninsula from the Garigliano in the west through Cassino and then to the Sangro in the east. German forces held the line against the invading ALLIES from autumn 1943 until May 11–18, 1944, when the line was breached and the Germans retreated into northern Italy.

gyro • *n.* (pl. **-os**) short for GYROSCOPE or GYROCOMPASS.

gyrocompass • *n.* a nonmagnetic compass in which the direction of true north is maintained by a continuously driven gyroscope whose axis is parallel to the earth's axis of rotation.

gyromagnetic • *adj.* (of a compass) combining a gyroscope and a normal magnetic compass.

gyropilot • *n.* a gyrocompass used to provide automatic steering for a ship or aircraft.

gyroscope • *n.* a device consisting of a wheel or disc mounted so that it can spin rapidly about an axis that is itself free to alter in direction. The orientation of the axis is not affected by tilting of the mounting; so gyroscopes can be used to provide stability or maintain a reference direction in navigation systems, automatic pilots, and stabilizers.
DERIVATIVES: **gyroscopic** *adj.* **gyroscopically** *adv.*

gyrostabilizer • *n.* a gyroscopic device for maintaining the equilibrium of something such as a ship, aircraft, or platform.

Gy Sgt • *abbr.* Gunnery Sergeant.

Hh

H-2 • **1** see LANDGRAF TWIN-ROTOR HELICOPTER. **2** see SEASPRITE.

H-3 • see SEA KING.

H-13 • see BELL 47.

H-46 • see SEA KNIGHT.

habeas corpus • a common-law writ ordering a person who detains another to present that person before a court or judge in order to determine the legality of the detention. Protected by Article I, Section 9 of the U.S. Constitution, the right to habeas corpus is a protection of individual liberty.

Habeas Corpus Act • a measure enacted by Congress in March 1863 to legitimize the suspension of the writ of habeas corpus proclaimed by President ABRAHAM LINCOLN in 1861 at the outbreak of the CIVIL WAR. It authorized suspensions throughout the war and enabled the government to detain persons suspected of disloyalty to the Union.

Chief Justice Roger Taney challenged the act when he ordered a writ for John Merryman, a Confederate sympathizer detained in May 1861. Taney argued that only Congress had the authority to suspend the writ, but Lincoln overruled him, asserting that the president as well as Congress had the authority.

Hagood, Johnson (1829–98) • Confederate army officer, born in Barnwell County, South Carolina. Hagood took part in the attack on FORT SUMTER (1861) and also saw action at FIRST BULL RUN (1861). At the siege of PETERSBURG (1864), he commanded a section of trenches that saw heavy losses. After the war he was elected to the state legislature and served a single term as governor.

Hagood was a graduate of the CITADEL, South Carolina's military college, and as governor was instrumental in its reopening after the war.

Hague Conventions • a series of international treaties resulting from the HAGUE PEACE CONFERENCES held at The Hague, Netherlands in 1899 and 1907. The 1899 conference resulted in three conventions, the most prominent one establishing the Permanent Court of Arbitration. The 1907 conference resulted in thirteen conventions addressing many of the issues presented in the earlier conference.

Hague Peace Conferences • two international conferences held at The Hague, Netherlands. The first was initiated by Czar Nicholas II of Russia to discuss arms limitations for the first time in history at an international assembly. It was held on May 18–July 29, 1899, and was attended by representatives from twenty-six countries. It revised codes of warfare and established the Permanent Court of Arbitration to preside over arbitration of issues between nations. The second, attended by forty-four governments, was proposed by U.S. President THEODORE ROOSEVELT in 1904, initiated by the czar in 1907, and held on June 15–October 18, 1907. It dealt with issues similar to the first and focused on principals and laws of war at sea and on land. The United States secured an international arbitration agreement. Neither conference successfully established arms limitations.

After 1919 and until the establishment of the UNITED NATIONS in 1945, the LEAGUE OF NATIONS fulfilled many of the conference's roles in international issues.

Haig, Alexander Meigs (1924?–) • army general and public official, born near Philadelphia, Pennsylvania. Haig served in both the KOREAN and VIETNAM wars and as Supreme Allied Commander Europe of NATO forces (1974–79). He held several important government posts during the administration of President RICHARD M. NIXON, including assistant to the president and White House chief of staff. During that same period he served as military adviser to national security adviser HENRY KISSINGER (1969–73). Haig was considered knowledgeable about the political-diplomatic aspects of military affairs and played an important role in the PARIS PEACE AGREEMENTS (1973). He retired from the army in 1979 to become president and CEO of United Technologies, a major defense contractor. In 1981 he was appointed secretary of state by President RONALD REAGAN, but served only slightly more than a year before resigning in 1982, reportedly over disputes with defense secretary CASPAR WEINBERGER.

Haig, Douglas (1861–1928) • field marshal and commander in chief of the British forces in France during WORLD WAR I, born in Edinburgh, Scotland. His strategy of attrition resulted in staggering numbers of British casualties, particularly at the SOMME (1916) and the THIRD BATTLE OF YPRES (1917), bringing him considerable criticism. Haig led the victorious Allied assault that began in August 1918. He was created an earl in 1919 (1st Earl Haig of Bemersyde).

Haiphong • a port in northern Vietnam, on the delta of the Red River in the Gulf of Tonkin pop. 783,100 (est. 1992). In 1970, during the VIETNAM WAR, President RICHARD M. NIXON ordered the mining of Haiphong Harbor to cut off Soviet aid. The strategy, originally conceived by the JOINT CHIEFS OF STAFF, apparently helped the North Vietnamese to accept a negotiated settlement to the Vietnam War.

Halderman, John Adams (1833–1908) • Union army officer, born in Fayette County, Kentucky. Halderman fought at Wilson's Creek (1861) and later organized the northern division of the Kansas State Militia. He left the service in 1864. He was appointed the first U.S. consul and later U.S. minister to Siam, now Thailand (1880–85).

Hale, Nathan (1755–76) • Revolutionary soldier, patriot, and spy, born in Coventry, Connecticut. Hale joined the Continental army in 1775 and volunteered for a spy mission shortly thereafter (1776). He was apprehended by the British and condemned to be hanged. His final words, "I only regret that I have but one life to lose for my country," made him a hero of the revolution and a symbol of the patriot cause.

half cock • the partly raised position of the cock of a gun.

half deck • a deck reaching half the length of a ship or boat, fore or aft.

DERIVATIVES: **half decked.**

half hitch • a knot formed by passing the end of a rope around its standing part and then through the loop.

half-life • *n.* the time required for the activity of a given radioactive species to decrease to half of its initial value due to radioactive decay. The half-life is a characteristic property of each radioactive species and is independent of its amount or condition. The effective half-life of a given isotope is the time in which the quantity in the body will decrease to half as a result of both radioactive decay and biological elimination.

Halleck, Henry Wager (1815–1872) • U.S. army officer and military intellectual; Commanding General of the Army, 1862–64. Born in Westernville, New York, Halleck attended Union College before leaving to attend WEST POINT from which he was graduated and commissioned in the CORPS OF ENGINEERS in 1839. After a short assignment on the West Point faculty, he became assistant to the Board of Engineers for Atlantic Coast Defenses in New York City and worked on the city's harbor defenses (1840–46). In 1845, he toured fortifications in France, and upon his return gave a series of lectures at the Lowell Institute in Boston. His lectures on military policy, strategy, and tactics were subsequently published in 1846 as *Elements of Military Art and Science*, the first comprehensive study of the military art by an American, and, confirmed Halleck's reputation as a leading Army intellectual as well as his Army sobriquet of "Old Brains." Ordered to the West coast in 1846, Halleck served in California during the MEXICAN WAR (1846–48), acted as secretary of state for the military government of California, and worked on coastal fortifications. In the summer of 1861, Halleck was appointed major general in the REGULAR ARMY by President ABRAHAM LINCOLN, and in November

1861 he replaced JOHN C. FRÉMONT as commander of the Department of the Missouri with headquarters in St. Louis, Missouri. After the battle of SHILOH (1862), he took personal command of the Union forces around CORINTH, Mississippi, which fell in June 1862. The success of Union forces in the Western theater led to his appointment as Commanding General of the Army on July 11, 1862. In that position, he ably administered the Army and acted as military advisor to the President and the SECRETARY OF WAR until March 1864, when he was replaced by ULYSSES S. GRANT. Halleck remained in Washington as Grant's chief of staff until the end of the CIVIL WAR. For a short time after APPOMATTOX (1865), he served as commander of the Division of the James before being transferred to command the Division of the Pacific (1865–69) and later the Division of the South (1869–72).

Halpine, Charles Graham (1829–68) • Union army officer, born near Oldcastle, County Meath, Ireland. Halpine accepted the surrender of FORT PULASKI (1862) and took part in the 1864 expedition up the SHENANDOAH VALLEY. Halpine achieved his fame mainly as a war propagandist. Already a well-known journalist and satirist, he was given the staff assignment (in the Department of the East) of building support for the war among the Irish. His stories and poems about a fictional "Miles O'Reilly" succeeded in doing so, and also changed the image of the Irish in the North. After the war Halpine continued his journalistic endeavors, calling on Miles O'Reilly once again, this time in the cause of good government.

Halsey, John (1670–1716) • seaman, born in Boston, Massachusetts. Halsey was commissioned as a privateer by the governor of Rhode Island during the WAR OF THE SPANISH SUCCESSION (1701–13). He captured several Spanish vessels and sizable booty. When his commission expired, Halsey turned to piracy on the Red Sea and Indian Ocean, which proved extremely profitable.

Halsey, William Frederick, Jr. (1882–1959) • naval officer, born in Elizabeth, New Jersey. His early interest in naval aviation led to his playing a prominent role in the South Pacific during WORLD WAR II, particularly in the capture of the SOLOMON ISLANDS, as commander, South Pacific Force and South Pacific Area (1942). He also led raids against Japanese positions in the MARSHALL and GILBERT ISLANDS and on WAKE ISLAND (1942). He was later criticized for his actions at LEYTE GULF (1944) and elsewhere; heavy losses sometimes resulted from his dogged determination (he was nicknamed "Bull"). Halsey was aboard the *Missouri,* the flagship of his fleet, when the Japanese surrender was formalized (1945). His WORLD WAR I service was aboard destroyers; escorting convoys and patrolling for German submarines; his ships never saw combat. Early in his career Halsey was briefly naval attaché in Germany and Scandinavia (1922–24).

During the BATTLE OF MIDWAY (1942), Halsey was hospitalized with a severe skin inflammation, so he missed this decisive turning point in the Pacific. He called his absence from Midway "the most grievous disappointment of my career."

halyard |ˈhælyərd| • *n.* a rope used for raising and lowering a sail, spar, flag, or yard on a sailing ship.

Hambleton, Thomas Edward (1829–1906) • blockade runner during the CIVIL WAR, born in New Windsor, Maryland. His firm, based in Richmond, Virginia, ran cotton to Bermuda and returned with supplies for the CONFEDERACY, breaking the Federal blockade each time, a risky but lucrative undertaking. Prior to this, Hambleton had carried messages from JEFFERSON DAVIS across the Potomac, an even riskier venture.

Hamburger Hill, Battle of (May 1969) • a ten-day VIETNAM WAR battle between U.S., South Vietnamese, and North Vietnamese forces in the A SHAU VALLEY. North Vietnamese troops had dug into Dong Ap Bia mountain, and after all sides suffered heavy losses and abandoned the conflict, the mountain was renamed Hamburger Hill. The battle led to strong criticism of President RICHARD M. NIXON'S VIETNAMIZATION policy and confirmed his determination to withdraw U.S. forces as quickly as possible.

Hamilton, Alexander (1755–1804) • Revolutionary army officer, statesman, and first secretary of the Treasury, born in Nevis, British West Indies. Hamilton exerted a profound influence on the nascent nation. During the REVOLUTIONARY WAR, Hamilton acted as GEORGE WASHINGTON's aide-de-camp (1777–81); he then obtained a field command and led a victorious regiment at YORKTOWN (1781). One of the authors of *The Federalist Papers* and an ardent nationalist, he believed in a strong federal government, and believed too that this required independent sources of revenue for Congress. As the first secretary of the treasury (1789–95), Hamilton moved to establish national credit and a national bank. He also advocated a military establishment, and it was largely through his influence and active involvement that the WHISKEY REBELLION (1794) was quelled by an aggregate of state militias that came to constitute a Federalist force. Hamilton continued to play a vital role even after leaving federal government (1795), as an adviser and speechwriter (composing most of Washington's Farewell Address). Hamilton was mortally wounded in a duel with AARON BURR (1804), who attributed his losing bid for the governorship of New York to remarks Hamilton had made.

Hamilton's son Philip was killed in a duel three years before his father, on the same dueling ground in Weehauken, New Jersey.

Hamlin, Charles (1837–1911) • Union army officer, born in Hampden, Maine. Hamlin saw action in a number of engagements; he was officially commended for his conduct at

LITTLE ROUND TOP at GETTYSBURG (1863). After the assassination of President ABRAHAM LINCOLN, Hamlin called out his troops to secure the streets against possible unrest.

Hamlin was the son of Hannibal Hamlin, vice president of the United States during the first administration of Abraham Lincoln.

Hammarskjöld, Dag Hjalmar Agne Carl (1905–61) • statesman and diplomat, born in Jonkoping, Sweden. Hammarskjöld served as secretary general of the UNITED NATIONS (1953–61), enhancing the prestige and power of that body during his tenure. He was influential in the resolution of the Suez Canal crisis (1956) and initiated peace moves in the Middle East (1957–58). Hammarskjöld was killed in a plane crash while on a peace mission to central Africa; he was posthumously awarded the Nobel Peace Prize (1961).

hamper • *n.* necessary but cumbersome equipment on a ship.

Hampton Roads, Battle of • (March 9, 1862) the world's first combat between armored warships, the CSS *Virginia* and the USS *Monitor*, near Norfolk, Virginia, during the CIVIL WAR. Following four hours of battle, the *Virginia* withdrew and the UNION proclaimed victory, leaving in place the Union blockade.

Hampton Roads Conference • unsuccessful peace talks at Hampton Roads, Virginia, on February 3, 1865, during the CIVIL WAR, between Union and Confederate representatives. It was the first meeting with the South that President ABRAHAM LINCOLN agreed to since the start of the war. Northern demands included a reunion of the nation and the emancipation of slaves, but the South would accept independence only.

Hampton's Legion • an elite Confederate unit raised by, and equipped largely at the expense of, WADE HAMPTON. It enlisted the sons of the South Carolina aristocracy and consisted of companies of infantry, cavalry, and artillery.

Hampton, Wade (1754?–1835) • Revolutionary army officer and supplier, through his extensive South Carolina business enterprises, of corn and corn meal to the Continental army. His most significant military success was at EUTAW SPRINGS (1781). During the WAR OF 1812 Hampton took part in a disastrous invasion of Canada (1813), tarnishing his reputation. He was twice elected to Congress (1795, 1803). His prominence lay largely in his accumulation of wealth from his business successes.

Hampton is often known as Wade Hampton I to distinguish him from two noted descendants of the same name.

Hampton, Wade (1818–1902) • Confederate general, born in Charleston, South Carolina. Hampton was the creator of HAMPTON'S LEGION who fought with J.E.B. STUART's cavalry corps at ANTIETAM (1862), led a series of successful raids the following winter (1862–63), and was wounded at GETTYSBURG (1863). After Stuart's death (1864), he replaced him as corps commander. After the war, Hampton, one of the wealthiest men in the South, was elected governor in 1876 and again in 1878, but that same year was named to the U.S. Senate, where he remained until 1891.

Hampton was the son of Wade Hampton II, a wealthy South Carolina planter.

Hancock, Winfield Scott (1824–86) • Union army officer in the ARMY OF THE POTOMAC, born in Mongomery Square, Pennsylvania. Hancock fought with distinction at ANTIETAM (1862), CHANCELLORSVILLE (1863), and GETTYSBURG (1863), where his troops repulsed Gen. GEORGE E. PICKETT's charge. Hancock remained in the postwar army, mainly with commands in the West. He received the Democratic nomination for president in 1880, but was defeated by JAMES A. GARFIELD.

Hancock was named Winfield Scott in honor of the military hero of the WAR OF 1812, but was not related to him.

hand • *n.* a person who engages in manual labor, especially on board a ship: *the ship was lost with all hands.* • *v.* take in or furl (a sail): ***hand in the main!***

Hand, Edward (1744–1802) • Revolutionary army officer, born in Leinster, Ireland. Hand took part in the siege of Boston (1775) and fought in the battles of NEW YORK and TRENTON (both 1776). Hand was a close friend of GEORGE WASHINGTON. He was with him during the surrender at YORKTOWN (1781), and after the war served him as adjutant general of a militia during the WHISKEY REBELLION (1794). Washington appointed him a district inspector of customs in Pennsylvania (1791), an office he held for eleven years. Hand was active in the formation of the SOCIETY OF THE CINCINNATI, which he served as president (1789).

hand grenade • a hand-thrown grenade.

handgun • *n.* a gun designed for use by one hand, chiefly either a pistol or a revolver.

handspike • *n.* a wooden rod with an iron tip, used as a lever on board ship and by artillery soldiers.

hand-to-hand • *adj.* (of fighting) at close quarters: *training in* ***hand-to-hand combat.***

hangar • *n.* a large building with extensive floor area, typically for housing aircraft. • *v.* place or store in a hangar: *the army choppers that were hangared out at Springs.*

DERIVATIVES: **hangarage** *n.*

hangar lice • slang (in WORLD WAR II) airplane mechanics.

hang fire • an undesired delay in the functioning of a firing system.

Hanging Rock, Battle of • (Aug. 6, 1780) a battle at Hanging Rock in South Carolina. Hanging Rock was the British forces' primary defense of their base at Camden, and was normally strong enough to turn back American advances. Hanging Rock's defenses were weakened when forces were taken from it to defend its sister post at Rocky Mount.

THOMAS SUMTER then planned an assault, and though the frontal attack went off course, the troops were fortunate to end up striking the vulnerable British flank. Battle ensued between the two forces, but upon the return of the British troops dispatched to Rocky Mount, the Americans retreated. Both sides suffered heavy losses, and the post was evacuated shortly after the battle due to the advance of HORATIO GATES's army.

Hanoi |hæ'noi; hə-| • the capital of Vietnam, situated on the Red River in the north of the country. It was the capital of French Indochina from 1887 to 1946 and of North Vietnam before the reunification of North and South Vietnam. In December 1972, during the VIETNAM WAR, Hanoi was bombed heavily by the United States.

Hanoi Hilton • a nickname for the Hoa Loa Prison in Hanoi which was used for prisoners of war.

Hans • slang (WORLD WAR I) an individual German soldier or the German army collectively.

harass • *v.* make repeated small-scale attacks on (an enemy): *the squadron's task was to harass the retreating enemy forces.*
DERIVATIVES: **harasser** *n.* **harassingly** *adv.* **harassment** *n.*

harassing fire • fire designed to disturb the resting of the enemy troops, to curtail movement, and, by threat of losses, to lower the enemy's morale.

harassment • *n.* an incident in which the primary objective is to disrupt the activities of an enemy unit, installation, or ship, rather than to inflict serious casualties or damage.

harbor • (Brit. **harbour**) *n.* a place on the coast where vessels may find shelter, especially one protected from rough water by piers, jetties, and other artificial structures.

harborage • *n.* a harbor or other place of shelter.

harbor defense • the defense of a harbor or anchorage and its water approaches against external threats such as submarine, submarine-borne, or small surface craft attack, as well as enemy minelaying operations or sabotage.

The defense of a harbor from guided or dropped missiles while such missiles are airborne is considered to be a part of AIR DEFENSE.

---

harbormaster (also **harbor master**) • *n.* an official in charge of a harbor.

hard beach • a portion of a beach specially prepared with a hard surface extending into the water, employed for the purpose of loading or unloading directly into or from landing ships or landing craft.

Hardee's Tactics • a military tactical handbook used by Confederate officers in the CIVIL WAR. While JEFFERSON DAVIS tended to favor WEST POINT-educated professionals for his high command, *Hardee's Tactics* attempted to enable for untrained officers at company or field grade to overcome their deficiencies and ascend through the ranks.

Hardee, William Joseph (1815–73) • Confederate army officer with the ARMY OF TENNESSEE, born in Camden County, Georgia. Hardee commanded the first wave of the assault at SHILOH (1862) and briefly commanded the army after MISSIONARY RIDGE (1863). Prior to resigning his army commission to join the Confederate cause, he had fought in the SEMINOLE WARS (1835–42), and with distinction at VERACRUZ (1847) during the MEXICAN WAR (1846–48).

hardened • *adj.* **1** having become or been made hard or harder: *hardened steel.* **2** strengthened or made secure against attack, especially by nuclear weapons: *the silos are* ***hardened against*** *air attack.* **3** experienced in a particular job or activity and therefore not easily upset by its more unpleasant aspects: *a battle-hardened veteran.*

hardened site • a site, normally constructed under rock or concrete cover, designed to provide protection against the effects of conventional weapons. It may also be equipped to provide protection against the side effects of a nuclear attack and against a chemical or biological attack.

Hardie, James Allen (1823–76) • Union army officer, born in New York City. Hardie served as an aide to GEORGE B. MCCLELLAN during the PENINSULAR and ANTIETAM campaigns (1862). While on special duty with the WAR DEPARTMENT (1863), Hardie personally carried out the delicate mission of the change of command from Gen. JOSEPH HOOKER to Gen. GEORGE G. MEADE, before GETTYSBURG.

Harding, Warren Gamaliel (1865–1923) • 29th president of the United States (1921–23), born near Blooming Grove, Ohio. A prominent newspaperman and leading citizen of Marion, Ohio, Harding served two terms in the state senate (1900–04) and one term as lieutenant governor (1904–06) before being elected to the U.S. Senate. As a Republican senator (1915–21), he supported most of President WOODROW WILSON's war measures, but became highly critical of them after WORLD WAR I. In 1920 he received his party's presidential nomination and was swept to victory on a platform that called for a return to "normalcy," opposition to the LEAGUE OF NATIONS, protective tariffs, and stricter immigration standards. But once in office, Harding proved ill-suited for the challenges of the position. His administration was marked by highly publicized scandals (many of which came to light only after his death) involving officials in several departments. The most notorious of these was the Teapot Dome affair, concerning the transfer of naval oil reserves at Teapot Dome, Wyoming, to the Department of the Interior, whose secretary subsequently leased them to private interests. The administration's greatest diplomatic achievement was the complex of treaties negotiated and signed at the Washington Conference on the Limitation of Armaments and on Far Eastern and Pacific Questions (1921–22), resulting in the slowing of a naval arms race and international recognition for the U.S. OPEN DOOR POLICY in regard to China.

Albert B. Fall, Harding's secretary of the interior, was the first U.S. cabinet member to be convicted of a felony committed while in office.

Hardin, John (1753–92) • Revolutionary army officer, born in Fauquier County, Virginia. Hardin, who had learned Indian tracking and woodland skills and was a proficient marksman, fought at SARATOGA (1777), where he won the praise of Gen. HORATIO GATES. He foraged against British supply lines during the winter of 1777–78 at VALLEY FORGE. Hardin left the Continental army in 1779, but returned to service in 1786 to take part in an expedition against the Indians in Indiana, and for the remainder of his life continued to be active in Indian raids. He was murdered by ostensibly friendly Indians while on a mission to negotiate a peace treaty.

hard missile base • a launching base that is protected against a nuclear explosion.

hardtack • *n.* hard dry bread or biscuit, especially as rations for sailors.

hard target • **1** any militarily significant structure that has been fortified with layers of concrete, steel, earth, etc., for protection against the blast effects of conventional and nuclear weapons. **2** (in the PERSIAN GULF WAR) a tank, building, military installation, etc., as distinct from a human being. See also SOFT TARGET.

hardware • *n.* tools, machinery, and other durable equipment: *tanks and other military hardware.*

Harkins, Paul D. (1904?–84) • army general who commanded MACV (MILITARY ASSISTANCE COMMAND VIETNAM) from 1962 to 1964. Harkins had a generally optimistic view about the possibility of putting an early end to the war, but after the military coup that overthrew the government of NGO DINH DIEM (1963), the VIETCONG's strength only increased in the south. Harkins was replaced with Gen. WILLIAM C. WESTMORELAND, who immediately set about a massive boost in troop numbers. Harkins was also Gen. GEORGE S. PATTON's deputy chief of staff.

HARM • *abbr.* high-speed antiradiation missile; a high-technology, aircraft-launched guided missile that is directed against surface-to-air missile and early warning radar installations, and radar-directed air defense artillery systems. It is typically fired before locking onto threat radar and utilizes sophisticated on-board sensors to home in on the target.

Harmar, Josiah (1753–1813) • REVOLUTIONARY WAR soldier, born in Philadelphia, Pennsylvania. Harmar participated in several battles, including BRANDYWINE (1777) and MONMOUTH (1778). Most of his postwar duties were on the frontier; in 1790 he was ordered to lead an offensive against Indian villages on the Maumee River but was forced to retreat.

Harmar's Defeat • in the fall of 1790, the Washington administration sent Brig. Gen. JOSIAH HARMAR with 1,500 men north from Cincinnati against Indian villages on the Maumee River. Harmar and his troops successfully destroyed fields and homes, but some were later attacked by Indians near present-day Fort Wayne. Harmar's troops were startled by the attack and Harmar was forced to retreat.

Harpers Ferry, Virginia • town (in present-day West Virginia) at the confluence of the Shenandoah and Potomac Rivers, and site of a federal arsenal. Because of the arsenal and the town's significance as a transportation hub for western Virginia, Maryland, and Pennsylvania, abolitionist JOHN BROWN targeted it in a raid that took place October 16–18, 1859. He hoped that the action would lead to an invasion of the South and a liberation or rebellion of slaves. The raid failed, with most of Brown's twenty or so followers either killed or, like Brown, captured and hanged afterward. The raid drew national attention to the issue of slavery and increased passions on both sides of the debate. Harpers Ferry also was an important objective for the Union and Confederate armies during the CIVIL WAR, and control of the town switched several times.

Harpoon • (**AGM-84, RGM-84, UGM-84**) an antiship cruise missile that is fired from surface ships (RGM-84), aircraft (AGM-84A), or submarines (UGM-84). The radar-guided missile is jet-powered and typically carries a 500-pound conventional warhead.

harquebus (also **arquebus**) • *n.* historical an early type of portable gun supported on a tripod or a forked rest.

Harrier • (**AV-8**) a single-engine, vectored thrust, turbojet, light attack aircraft capable of vertical or short takeoffs and landings. It is designed to operate from land bases and naval bases in a close air support role. It can carry a variety of conventional and/or nuclear weapons.

Harrier II • (**AV-8B**) the successor to the AV-8, designed to provide quick response to U.S. Marine ground troops from a variety of assault ships or other bases. It can be used as a fighter plane, a strategic bomber, an assault transport, or for reconnaissance. It has nuclear capability and can carry both air-to-air and air-to-surface missiles.

Harriman, W.(illiam) Averell (1891–1986) • businessman and public official, born in New York City. Harriman held a variety of positions during Democratic administrations from FRANKLIN D. ROOSEVELT to LYNDON B. JOHNSON. Harriman was Roosevelt's special representative ("defense expediter") to Britain for the government program that provided material support to U.S. allies (1941–43). As the number-two man in the Economic Cooperation Administration, he was largely responsible for division of MARSHALL PLAN aid among the nations of western Europe (1948–50). In 1950, early in the KOREAN WAR, he served briefly as a special assistant to President HARRY S. TRUMAN. As director of the Mutual Security Administration (1951–53), Harriman supervised the rearmament of America's allies in Europe, dispensing billions in military assistance. In 1961 he joined President JOHN F. KENNEDY's administration as assistant secretary of state for Far Eastern affairs and undersecretary of state for political affairs; in 1963 he negotiated and signed the LIMITED TEST BAN TREATY. In the role of ambassador-at-large during the Johnson administration (1965–68), Harriman began negotiations for peace in VIETNAM. Between his early and later Washington assignments, Harriman served a single term as governor of New York (1955–59).

Harrison, Benjamin (1833–1901) • 23rd president of the United States (1889–93), born in North Bend, Ohio. During the CIVIL WAR he fought in the campaign to capture ATLANTA (1864), leading the forces that beat back the Confederate troops at Peach Tree Creek. After the war he settled in Indiana, where he resumed his law practice and political career. In 1881 the state legislature sent him to the U.S. Senate, and in 1888 he received the Republican nomination for president, campaigning on a platform that defended the protective tariff. His achievements were in the realm of foreign policy, where he advocated construction of a modern navy, control of a Central American canal, and acquisition of naval bases in the Caribbean and the Pacific. During his administration Congress approved construction of the first three American coastal battleships and the first seagoing battleship. Midway through his term the party lost control of the House to the Democrats, who then swept to victory in 1892. Following his defeat, Harrison returned to the practice of law in Indiana.

Harrison was the grandson of President WILLIAM HENRY HARRISON and the great-grandson of BENJAMIN HARRISON, a prominent Virginian who had signed the DECLARATION OF INDEPENDENCE.

Harrison, William Henry (1773–1841) • 9th president of the United States (1841), born at "Berkeley," his family's plantation on the James River in Virginia. As a member of the U.S. Infantry, Harrison fought Indian skirmishes in the OLD NORTHWEST from 1791 to 1798. In 1800 he was appointed governor of the Indiana Territory by President JOHN ADAMS, a position which he held for twelve years, during which time he showed a tolerance for slaveholding and acquired as much Indian land as possible. An outcome of the latter was the noted BATTLE OF TIPPECANOE (1810). The Americans barely won, enduring greater casualties than the Indians, and no peace resulted. Nevertheless, the dubious victory gave him his nickname, "Old Tippecanoe," and the slogan for his eventual presidential campaign, "Tippecanoe and Tyler, Too." As an officer in the regular army during the WAR OF 1812, Harrison, after some early failures, succeeded in retaking Detroit and shortly thereafter also won a decided victory over the British at the THAMES River (1813). In 1818 Congress awarded him a gold medal for his wartime service. From 1816 to 1828 Harrison served first in the Ohio state senate and then in the U.S. Senate (1826–28). He was elected president in 1840, but served only thirty-one days, dying from pneumonia shortly after his inauguration.

***Hartford*, USS** • an attack submarine equipped with the TOMAHAWK CRUISE MISSILE system and capable of land attack and strike, and an improved version of the LOS ANGELES class with a hardened sail and retractable bow planes for surfacing through ice during missions in the Arctic Ocean.

Hart, Nancy (c. 1735–c. 1830) • REVOLUTIONARY WAR hero (born Ann Morgan in Pennsylvania or North Carolina) reputedly responsible for the capture and hanging of several Tories in Georgia in 1780, one or more of whom she murdered. Accounts of her exploits depend on oral tradition; the first written version did not appear until 1848, making it virtually impossible to distinguish the historical from the legendary Nancy Hart.

Hartranft, John Frederick |'härtrænft| (1830–89) • Union army officer, born near Pottstown, Pennsylvania. Hartranft was recognized for his heroism at SPOTSYLVANIA and PETERSBURG (both 1864). After the war he was active in Republican politics in Pennsylvania, serving two terms as governor (elected 1872).

Hascall, Milo Smith (1829–1904) • Union army officer, born in Le Roy, New York. Hascall commanded a brigade during the capture of NASHVILLE (1862) and took over the division command during the battle at STONES RIVER (1862–63), successfully holding out against Confederate assaults. Throughout the next two years he performed solidly as a division commander; he resigned in 1864 when he failed to be promoted to major general.

Haskell, Franklin Aretas (1828–64) • Union army officer, born in Tunbridge, Vermont. Haskell participated in several major battles, including SECOND BULL RUN (1862), ANTIETAM (1862), FREDERICKSBURG (1862), CHANCELLORSVILLE (1863), and GETTYSBURG (1863). At Gettysburg, Haskell provided crucial leadership after the division commander and other key officers were wounded. He was killed while leading the assault at COLD HARBOR (1864). Haskell is widely known for the essay he wrote about Gettysburg; it was privately published and has often been reprinted.

hasty attack • in land operations, an attack in which preparation time is traded for speed in order to exploit an opportunity.

hasty breaching • in land-mine warfare, the creation of lanes through enemy minefields by expedient methods such as blasting with demolitions, pushing rollers or disabled vehicles through the minefields when the time factor does not permit detailed reconnaissance, deliberate breaching, or bypassing the obstacle.

hasty defense • a defense normally organized while in contact with the enemy, or when contact is imminent and time available for the organization is limited. It is characterized by improvement of the natural defensive strength of the terrain by utilization of foxholes, emplacements, and obstacles. Compare with DELIBERATE DEFENSE.

hatch • *n.* an opening of restricted size allowing for passage from one area to another, in particular: **a** a door in an aircraft, spacecraft, or submarine. **b** an opening in the deck of a boat or ship leading to the cabin or a lower level, especially a hold: *a cargo hatch.*

Hatch, Edward (1832–89) • Union army officer, born in Bangor, Maine. Hatch was noted for his significant part in the successful diversionary raid through Mississippi led by Col. BENJAMIN GRIERSON (1863) and for outstanding leadership of his cavalry division at FRANKLIN and NASHVILLE (both 1864). After the war Hatch held a series of assignments on the western frontier, fighting in the APACHE WARS (1877–81) and other Indian skirmishes, endeavors in which he proved less successful than he had during the CIVIL WAR.

hatchway • *n.* an opening or hatch, especially in a ship's deck.

haul • *v.* **1** (of a vehicle) pull (an attached trailer or load) behind it: *the train was hauling a cargo of liquid chemicals.* **2** (especially of a sailing ship) make an abrupt change of course.

Haupt, Herman |howpt| (1817–1905) • civilian railway engineer, born in Philadelphia, Pennsylvania. Haupt designed, built, and repaired critically important lines and bridges during the CIVIL WAR. His role during the battle of GETTYSBURG (1863) was particularly crucial, anticipating and meeting the army's demanding logistical requirements. He also developed a torpedo for destroying railroads and bridges. When pressed to accept a commission, he refused, and his army responsibilities were terminated.

haven • *n.* an inlet providing shelter for ships or boats; a harbor or small port.

haversack |'hævər,sæk| • *n.* a small, sturdy bag carried on the back or over the shoulder, used especially by soldiers.

ORIGIN: mid 18th century: from obsolete German *Habersack*, denoting a bag used by soldiers to carry oats as horse feed.

Havoc • see BOSTON II.

hawk |hawk| • *n.* a person who advocates an aggressive or warlike policy, especially in foreign affairs: *severe limits were put on the peace plan by party hawks.* Compare with DOVE.

DERIVATIVES: **hawkish** *adj.* **hawkishly** *adv.* **hawkishness** *n.* **hawklike** *adj.*

HAWK • (**MIM-23**) a surface-to-air missile system that provides air defense coverage for ground forces. It was first deployed in the 1960s and is still in use today.

ORIGIN: HAWK is an acronym for Homing All the Way Killer.

Hawker Hurricane • a versatile bomber aircraft that was the backbone of ROYAL AIR FORCE defense in WORLD WAR II. It carried two 40-mm guns and two Browning machine guns. Compare SPITFIRE.

Hawkeye • (**E-2**) a carrierborne and land-based airborne early warning and control aircraft initially flown on October 21, 1961. There are currently three versions, the E-2A, which entered service with the U.S. Navy in 1964 (being highly successful at controlling strike packages in VIETNAM), the E-2B, some of which remained in use until the late 1980s, and the E-2C, equipped with a turboprop powerplant that provides great fuel economy and superb patrol endurance.

Hawley, Joseph Roswell (1826–1905) • Union army officer, born in Stewartsville, North Carolina. He was praised for his leadership of Connecticut volunteers at FIRST BULL RUN (1861) and his troops helped force the surrender of FORT PULASKI (1862). He continued to serve with distinction throughout the war, after which he returned to Connecticut and served a single term as governor (1867). He later served in both the U.S. House (1872–75) and Senate (1881–1905), where, as a member of the MILITARY AFFAIRS COMMITTEE, he sought to reorganize the army, provide the navy with more modern warships, and upgrade the nation's coastal defenses.

hawse |hawz| • *n.* **1** the part of a ship's bows through which the anchor cables pass. **2** the space between the head of an anchored vessel and the anchors.

hawsehole |'hôz,hōl| • *n.* a hole in the deck of a ship through which an anchor cable passes.

hawsepipe |'hôz,pīp| • *n.* an inclined pipe leading from a hawsehole to the side of a ship, containing the shank of the anchor when the anchor is raised.

hawser |'hawzər| • *n.* a thick rope or cable for mooring or towing a ship.

Hay-Bunau-Varilla Treaty • an agreement of November 1903 to allow the United States to build a canal through a 10-mile-wide perpetually leased section of central Panama, to use more land if needed, and to intervene militarily in Panama. Negotiated by Phillipe Bunau-Varilla, a French citizen and official of the French canal company, it required the United States to guarantee Panama's independence and pay $10 million, plus $250,000 annually. No Panamanian ever signed the treaty.

Hayes, Ira Hamilton (1922–1955) • U.S. marine. Born on a Pima Indian reservation in Arizona, Hayes enlisted in the marines at the beginning of WORLD WAR II. He was immortalized in Joe Rosenthal's famous photograph of the six marines raising the flag atop Mount Suribachi on IWO JIMA on February 23, 1945, that eventually was turned into the famous monument by Felix de Welden unveiled in Arlington, Virginia, in 1954. Hayes did not handle his fame well, and became an alcoholic and eventually was found dead from alcohol and exposure on the Sacaton Indian Reservation in Arizona. His body lay in state in Phoenix before being interred at ARLINGTON NATIONAL CEMETERY.

Hayes, Rutherford Birchard (1822–93) • 19th president of the United States (1877–81); born in Delaware, Ohio. An early defender of runaway slaves (1853) and opponent of the spread of slavery, Hayes fought with an Ohio volunteer unit during the CIVIL

WAR and was seen as an inspirational leader. He was wounded five times and was brevetted major general. Following the war he became active in politics, serving as a U.S. congressman (1865–67) and then as governor of Ohio (1868–72). In 1876 Hayes was elected president over Democrat Samuel J. Tilden in a bitterly disputed contest that was not resolved for four months. Despite assuming office under suspicions of fraud, Hayes proved a surprisingly effective president, ending military occupation of southern states; reforming the civil service, putting the country back on the gold standard, and suppressing railroad strikes. Hayes refused to run for a second term, but after leaving office continued to actively work for the causes he believed in—education of blacks and of the poor, federal regulation of industry, and a humane penal system.

Hays, Alexander (1819–64) • Union army officer, born in Franklin, Pennsylvania. Hays was often cited for his courage in battle, particularly during the PENINSULAR CAMPAIGN (1862) and at SECOND BULL RUN (1862), where he was severely wounded. A division under his command played a significant role in repulsing PICKETT'S CHARGE at GETTYSBURG (1863). Hays was killed when leading his brigade into the BATTLE OF THE WILDERNESS (1864).

haze • *v.* force (a new or potential recruit to the military to perform strenuous, humiliating, or dangerous tasks: *rookies were mercilessly hazed.*

Hazen, Moses (1733–1803) • army officer, born in Haverhill, Massachusetts. Hazen served in a British colonial unit during the FRENCH AND INDIAN WAR (1754–63) and remained in Canada afterwards. After the outbreak of the REVOLUTIONARY WAR Hazen recruited a Canadian force that earned a high reputation for its fighting at BRANDYWINE (1777), GERMANTOWN (1777), and YORKTOWN (1781), but the Canadian unit, which received few of the benefits granted to state units, was disbanded in 1783.

Hazen, William Babcock (1830–87) • Union army officer, born in West Hartford, Vermont. Hazen served in several major CIVIL WAR battles, among them SHILOH (1862), STONES RIVER (1862–63), and MISSIONARY RIDGE (1863), and in the MARCH TO THE SEA (1864–65). Despite his commendable performance in battle, he often became embroiled in controversies with superiors and cohorts. Later in his career, was belatedly charged with desertion and cowardice, but was exonerated.

hazing • *n.* **1** the imposition of strenuous, often humiliating, tasks as part of a rigorous physical training program: *army cadets were hospitalized for injuries caused by hazing.* **2** humiliating and sometimes dangerous initiation rituals: *seven upperclassmen at the academy were charged with hazing.*

H-bomb • another term for HYDROGEN BOMB.
ORIGIN: 1950s: from *H* (denoting hydrogen) + BOMB.

HC-130 • see HERCULES.

head • *n.* **1** the source of a river or stream. **2** the end of a lake or inlet at which a river enters. **3** a promontory: *Beachy Head.* **4** the top of a ship's mast. **5** the bows of a ship. **6** slang a toilet, especially on a boat or ship.
▸**head up** steer toward the wind.

headboard • *n.* an upright panel forming or placed behind the head of a bed.

headmost • *adj.* archaic (chiefly of a ship) holding a position in advance of others; foremost.

headquarters • *n.* the premises occupied by a military commander and the commander's staff.

headsail • *n.* a sail on a ship's foremast or bowsprit.

head sea • waves coming from directly in front of a vessel: *we tried out the boat in a steep head sea.*

headstay • *n.* a forestay, especially in a small vessel.

head-up display • a display of flight, navigation, attack, or other information superimposed upon the pilot's forward field of view.

headway • *n.* **1** forward movement or progress: *they appear to be **making headway** in bringing the rebels under control | the ship was making very little headway against heavy seas.* **2** the average interval of time between vehicles moving in the same direction on the same route.

HEAT • *abbr.* high explosive antitank (denoting a class of warheads).

Heath, William (1737–1814) • Revolutionary patriot and officer in the Continental army, born in Roxbury, Massachusetts. Heath was responsible for the defense of the Hudson Highlands in New York state. Early in the war (1777) he failed to successfully carry out GEORGE WASHINGTON'S command to attack the British at Fort Independence, having his army retreat because of an expected snowstorm. Following this debacle Heath was placed in positions not likely to be involved in battle, though he continued in his Highlands command, headquartered at WEST POINT.

Heath resigned his membership in the SOCIETY OF THE CINCINNATI because he considered the organization, with its emphasis on heredity, too aristocratic.

heat-seeking • *adj.* (of a missile) able to detect and home in on infrared radiation emitted by a target, such as the exhaust vent of a jet aircraft.

heat-seeking missile • a missile with a guidance system that detects and homes in on infrared radiation emitted by a target.

heave • *v.* (past and past part. **heaved** |hēvd| or **hove** |hōv|) pull, raise, or move (a boat or ship) by hauling on a rope or ropes.
▸**heave to** (of a boat or ship) come to a stop, especially by turning across the wind leaving the headsail backed.

heaving line • a lightweight line with a weight at the end, made to be thrown between a ship and the shore, or from one ship to another, and used to pull a heavier line across.

heavy • *adj.* (**heavier, heaviest**) **1** of or containing atoms of an isotope of greater than the usual mass. **2** (of ground or soil) hard to travel over because muddy or full of clay. **3** slang (of a large aircraft) leaving a large amount of turbulence behind in its flight.

heavy antitank weapon • a weapon that is operated from the ground or a vehicle and used against armor and other material targets.

heavy drop • a system of delivery of heavy supplies and equipment by parachute.

heavy-lift cargo • **1** any single cargo lift, weighing more than 5 long tons, and to be handled aboard ship. **2** in Marine Corps usage, individual units of cargo that exceed 800 pounds in weight or 100 cubic feet in volume.

heavy metal • **1** a metal of relatively high density, or of high relative atomic weight. **2** slang (in the PERSIAN GULF WAR) heavy artillery, tanks, gunships, etc.

Hébert, Paul Octave |ˌāˈber| (1818–80) • Confederate army officer, born in Iberville Parish, Louisiana. Hébert participated in only one major battle, at Milliken's Bend, Louisiana (1863). He spent the entirety of the war west of the Mississippi River, the last year in various minor roles in Texas.

Hecker, Friedrich Karl Franz |ˈhekər| (1811–81) • German revolutionary and Union army officer, born in Eichtersheim, Grand Duchy of Baden. Hecker arrived in the United States in 1848, fleeing arrest for treason, and settled in Illinois. He was wounded at CHANCELLORSVILLE (1863), and later participated in the battle of MISSIONARY RIDGE (1863) and in the capture of CHATTANOOGA (1863). He commanded a brigade at LOOKOUT MOUNTAIN (1863) but resigned his commission in 1864, believing he had been unfairly passed over for promotion.

hedgehog • *n.* **1** an obstacle made of barbed wire strung on frames. **2** an anti-submarine weapon developed in 1943 which consists of multiple mortar tubes which throw contact-fused anti-submarine depth charges in a pattern from the deck of a sub-hunting surface vessel.

heel • *v.* **1** (of a boat or ship) be tilted temporarily by the pressure of wind or by an uneven distribution of weight on board. Compare with LIST. **2** cause (a boat or ship) to lean over in such a way. • *n.* **1** an instance of a ship leaning over in such a way. **2** the degree of incline of a ship's leaning measured from the vertical.

hegemony |həˈjemənē; ˈhejəˌmōnē| • *n.* leadership or dominance, especially by one country or social group over others: *Germany was united under Prussian hegemony after 1871.*

Heintzelman, Samuel Peter |ˈhīntsəlmən| (1805–80) • Union army officer, born in Manheim, Pennsylvania. Heintzelman showed personal courage in a number of losing battles against numerically inferior but better led forces. At FIRST BULL RUN (1861) his division was driven from the field. He was a corps commander in the failed effort to capture RICHMOND during the PENINSULAR CAMPAIGN (1862). At SECOND BULL RUN (1862) he was again forced to retreat and saw little battle action thereafter.

helicopter • *n.* an aircraft that becomes airborne and travels using one or more blades that rotate on a vertical shaft. • *v.* to travel or transport by means of a helicopter.

helicopter assault force • a task organization in which helicopters, their support units, and troop units are combined for helicopter-borne assault missions.

heliport • *n.* a facility designated for operating, basing, servicing, and maintaining helicopters.

Hellcat • (**F6F**) a single-seat single-engine ship-based fighter aircraft that accounted for 76 percent of all the enemy aircraft destroyed by U.S. Navy carriers during WORLD WAR II.

Some F6Fs were made into unmanned flying bombs and used in the KOREAN WAR.

Hellfire • (**AGM-114**) a helicopter-launched air-to-ground missile that is primarily an antitank weapon. It homes in on its target by means of a laser detector that finds a signal trained on the target by the firing aircraft or a ground-based unit.

helm • *n.* (**the helm**) **1** a tiller or wheel and any associated equipment for steering a ship or boat: *she stayed at the helm, alert for tankers.* **2** a helmsman. • *v.* steer (a boat or ship).

helmet • *n.* **1** a hard or padded protective hat, various types of which are worn by soldiers, police officers, motorcyclists, athletes, and others.

DERIVATIVES: **helmeted** *adj.*

helmsman • *n.* (pl. **-men**) a person who steers a ship or boat.

Helms, Richard McGarrah (1913?–) • director of the CENTRAL INTELLIGENCE AGENCY (1966–73), born in St. David's, Pennsylvania. His tenure came under increased scrutiny and criticism for its role in fomenting coups and assassinations in foreign countries, as well as for WATERGATE-related intrigue. Helms was indicted for perjury before the Senate Foreign Relations Committee for testimony denying CIA involvement in Chile; he pleaded no contest, was fined $2,000 and given a two-year suspended prison sentence. He was the first career intelligence officer to head the agency, and was also instrumental in its creation (1947).

Helsinki Accords • see CONFERENCE ON SECURITY AND COOPERATION IN EUROPE.

Helsinki Watch • a division of HUMAN RIGHTS WATCH that was founded in 1978 to monitor and promote the human rights provisions of the 1975 HELSINKI ACCORDS. The Helsinki Accords codified diplomatic guidelines for the remainder of the COLD WAR, making economic and security cooperation between participating countries dependent on respect for human rights. Activists in EASTERN BLOC countries began to press their governments to comply with the human rights provisions of the Accords. Helsinki Watch was created in response to the arrest of human rights monitors by Soviet authorities in 1977, and it campaigned internationally for the release of those prisoners as well as other imprisoned dissidents. Through the 1980s the group worked closely with the U.S. government to promote greater vigilance regarding human rights and civil and political freedoms in the Soviet Union and Eastern Europe. Recently, the group has concentrated on human rights concerns in Chechnya and Bosnia.

hemispheric hegemony • the situation in which one nation or allied group of nations dominates all or almost all of the nations in a given hemisphere of the world, particularly the dominance of the United States in North and South America.

Henderson, Archibald (1783–1859) • commandant of the U.S. Marine Corps, born in Colchester, Virginia. Henderson was commandant from 1820 until his death. During his long tenure he sought to preserve the corps's existence by giving it a legitimate operational mission and by integrating its headquarters within the Washington community. The first he achieved by having its role and mission codified in legislation; the second he achieved through the institution of free, public parades, reviews, and band concerts, which continue to this day. Henderson did not support an amphibious role for the marines, stressing instead their role aboard ship. Before becoming commandant, Henderson had distinguished himself in battle during the WAR OF 1812, for which he received a Silver Medal from Congress.

Henderson served under eleven presidents and eighteen secretaries of the navy, and had to justify the role and mission of the marines to each new administration.

Henningsen, Charles Frederick (1815–77) • mercenary, filibuster, and munitions expert. Henningsen, who had come to the United States in 1851 after fighting as a mercenary in various European nationalist movements, was among those filibusters who favored the expansion of slavery into Central America, invading countries there that were at peace with the United States. Henningsen served under WILLIAM WALKER in Nicaragua, where he burned the capital, the focus of Walker's opposition, in 1856. The following year Henningsen surrendered, along with Walker, to the U.S. Navy. He pursued filibuster schemes for a few years, fought a year for the CONFEDERACY (1861–62) during the CIVIL WAR, and then fell out of the public eye.

Henry, Guy Vernon (1839–99) • Union army officer, born at Fort Smith in INDIAN TERRITORY. Henry fought at FIRST BULL RUN (1861) and was awarded a MEDAL OF HONOR for his actions at COLD HARBOR and the siege of PETERSBURG (both 1864). During the SPANISH-AMERICAN WAR (1898), he commanded a brigade in the invasion of Puerto Rico, where he remained as military governor until shortly before his death.

Herbert, Hilary Abner (1834–1919) • Confederate army officer and secretary of the navy (1893–97), born in Laurensville, South Carolina. Herbert was cited for gallantry in the PENINSULAR CAMPAIGN (1862); fought admirably at SECOND BULL RUN (1862), FREDERICKSBURG (1862), ANTIETAM (1862), and GETTYSBURG (1863); and was wounded at the BATTLE OF THE WILDERNESS (1864). He served several terms in Congress as a representative from Alabama (elected 1876), and in 1885 was appointed to the Naval Affairs Committee, where he strongly pushed for the building of more and larger ships. During his subsequent tenure as secretary of the navy, authorizations for warships increased dramatically.

herbicide |ˈ(h)ərbəˌsīd| • *n.* a chemical compound that will kill or damage plants.

Hercules • **1** (**C-130**) a medium-range troop and cargo transport aircraft. It is designed for air-drop or air-land delivery into a combat zone as well as for conventional airlift. It has four turboprop engines and an integral ramp and cargo door. The D model is equipped with skis. The E model has an increased fuel capacity for extended range. The inflight tankers are designated as **KC-130** and **HC-130** (also used for aerial rescue missions). The gunship version is designated as **AC-130**. **2** (**M-88A1**) a full-tracked armored medium recovery vehicle used to undertake rescue and recovery missions, including towing, hoisting, and winching, on the battlefield. Also called MRV. See also COMBAT TALON; RECOVERY VEHICLE, MEDIUM.

Herkimer, Nicholas (1728–77) • Revolutionary army officer, born near what is now Herkimer, New York. He was wounded while on a mission to rescue Fort Schuyler, which was besieged by British forces, and died of complications from the resulting leg amputation. Although his troops had been forced to retreat, they had successfully slowed the advance of additional British forces and allowed American relief troops to reach Fort Schuyler in timely fashion.

Herron, Francis Jay (1837–1902) • Union army officer, born in Pittsburg, Pennsylvania. Herron distinguished himself in battle at PEA RIDGE (1862), for which he received the CONGRESSIONAL MEDAL OF HONOR thirty-one years later. His timely arrival at PRAIRIE GROVE (1862) saved outnumbered Federal forces and turned an apparent disaster into a decisive Union victory. His division aided Gen. ULYSSES S. GRANT at the siege of VICKSBURG (1863) and he was one of the three generals appointed to take possession of the city.

Hershey, Lewis Blaine (1893–1977) • general of the army and director of the selective service system, born in Steuben County, Indiana. Hershey was director of the selective service system from WORLD WAR II, when more than 10 million men were drafted, until the VIETNAM WAR, when he became the target of those who opposed the war and was removed from office by President RICHARD M. NIXON in 1969. He refused to retire on his own and was involuntarily retired from the army in 1973, having served for more than sixty-two years.

Hershey was the only four-star general to reach that rank without ever having served in a combat role.

HESH • *abbr.* high explosive squash-head.

Hessians • German mercenaries who fought with the British forces in North America during the REVOLUTIONARY WAR. The 29,000 German mercenaries represented about one-third of all British forces in America. Only some 17,000 were actually subjects of the Landgrave of Hesse-Cassel (i.e., genuine Hessians), the remainder came from other German principalities. They served in almost all the campaigns of the Revolutionary War suffering notable defeats at TRENTON (1776) and during the SARATOGA campaign (1777). A large number of Hessians remained in North America after the Revolutionary War.

Heth, Henry (1825–99) • army officer born at Blackheath, Chesterfield County, Virginia. Heth had commendably filled several posts before resigning his commission to fight for the CONFEDERACY. At CHANCELLORSVILLE (1863) he successfully assumed leadership of the division when the commander was wounded, but a series of repeated blunders at GETTYSBURG (1863), where Heth commanded his own division, tarnished his reputation.

hetman | 'hetmən | • *n.* (pl. **-men**) a Polish or Cossack military commander.

ORIGIN: Polish, probably from German *Hauptmann* 'captain.'

Heywood, Charles (1839–1915) • Marine Corps commandant (1891–1903), born in Waterville, Maine. Heywood pushed a reform agenda, including increasing the size of the corps, raising officer standards, and redefining the marine mission. While continuing to fight for the traditional marine roles on board ship, Heywood oversaw the establishment of and transition to a new mission: the marines as a landing force to establish advanced bases for the fleet. This mission was first accomplished at the capture of GUÁNTANAMO during the SPANISH-AMERICAN WAR (1898).

HH-3 • see JOLLY GREEN GIANT.

HH-60G • see BLACK HAWK.

HH-60H • see SEAHAWK.

H-hour • the time of day at which an attack, landing, or other military operation is scheduled to begin.

ORIGIN: WORLD WAR I: from *H* (for *hour*) + hour.

hidey-hole • *n.* slang (in the VIETNAM WAR) a hastily dug pit, usually not as deep as a foxhole, where a soldier takes cover. See also FOXHOLE.

hierarchy | 'hī(ə),rärkē | • *n.* (pl. **-ies**) **1** a system or organization in which people or groups are ranked one above the other according to status or authority. **2** (**the hierarchy**) the upper echelons of a hierarchical system; those in authority.

DERIVATIVES: **hierarchic** | ,hī(ə)'rärkik | *adj.* **hierarchization** | ,hī(ə),rärki'zāshən | *n.*

Higgins boat • a 78-foot motor torpedo boat produced by Higgins Industries of New Orleans, Louisiana, and the standard motor torpedo boat used during WORLD WAR II.

Higginson, Thomas Wentworth (1823–1911) • minister, reformer, and abolitionist, born in Cambridge, Massachusetts. As a Union officer, Higginson commanded the first federally authorized African-American regiment, the 1st South Carolina Volunteers, made up of slaves freed by Union forces. Wentworth led his troops on skirmishing and raiding expeditions in Georgia and Florida, freeing, enlisting, and training former slaves. Though never engaged in a major battle, his regiment played a secondary role in the attack on FORT WAGNER, South Carolina (1863). A battle wound and malaria caused him to leave the army in the spring of 1864.

Higginson was a correspondent of the poet Emily Dickinson (1830–86).

High Admiral • an admiral of the most exalted rank (British or German; not used in U.S. Navy).

high altitude bombing • horizontal bombing with the height of release at over 15,000 feet.

high command • the commander in chief and associated senior staff of an army, navy, or air force.

high explosive • a chemical explosive that is rapid and destructive, used in shells and bombs.

high explosive antitank • (**HEAT**) the usual warhead filled with high explosives for antitank missiles and gun projectiles which relies on the size of the explosive charge rather than high velocity to achieve its destructive effect.

high explosive squash-head • (**HESH**) a type of antitank missile or gun projectile which relies on the size and shape of the explosive charge rather than high velocity to achieve its destructive effect. The ammunition incorporates plastic explosives in a ballistically capped round. The round strikes a hard surface and the cap flattens the round evenly onto the surface. A piezoelectric crystal in the base shatters on striking the armor surface, detonating the plastic explosive.

high-mobility vehicle • (**HMV**) a mulitpurpose all-terrain vehicle first designed in the 1970s. In 1983, the U.S. Army ordered 55,000 from AM General. It performed so well that 70,000 were actually produced over a five-year period. Also called HUMMER, HUMVEE.

high-powered (also **high-power**) • *adj.* (of a machine or device) having greater than normal strength or capabilities: *a high-powered rifle.*

high seas • (**the high seas**) the open ocean, especially that not within any country's jurisdiction.

high tide • **1** the state of the tide when at its highest level: ***at high tide*** *you have to go inland.* **2** the highest point of something: ***the high tide of*** *nationalism.*

high water • **1** another term for HIGH TIDE. **2** the highest level reached by any body of water, especially a river: *high water from early January flooding has receded.*

high-water mark • **1** the level reached by the sea at high tide, or by a lake or river at its highest stand. **2** a maximum recorded level or value: *crime stood at a high-water mark.*

hijack • *v.* **1** illegally seize (an aircraft, ship, or vehicle) in transit and force it to go to a different destination or use it for one's own purposes: *three armed men hijacked a white van.* **2** steal (goods) by seizing them in transit: *the U.N. convoys have been tamely allowing gunmen to hijack relief supplies.* **3** take over (something) and use it for a different purpose: *the organization had been hijacked by extremists.* • *n.* an incident or act of hijacking.

DERIVATIVES: **hijacker** *n.*

Hill 64, Battle of • (February 8, 1968) a battle during the VIETNAM WAR for the outpost of that number, which U.S. forces were successful in defending. This was one battle in the siege of KHE SANH, a village that had been a U.S. military post since 1962. North Vietnamese forces laid siege to KHE SANH for seventy-eight days, prompting U.S. OPERATION PEGASUS on April 7, 1968, which ultimately ended the siege.

Hill 861A, Battle of • (February 5, 1968) a battle during the VIETNAM WAR for the outpost of that number, which U.S. forces were successful in defending. This was one battle in the siege of Khe Sanh, a village that had been a U.S. military post since 1962. North Vietnamese forces laid siege to Khe Sanh for 78 days, prompting U.S. OPERATION PEGASUS on April 7, 1968 which ended the siege.

Hill, A.(mbrose) P.(owell) (1825–65) • Confederate army officer, born near Culpeper, Virginia. His success in leading a brigade into battle at WILLIAMSBURG (1862) led to his being given command of the largest division of the ARMY OF NORTHERN VIRGINIA. Later successes at CEDAR MOUNTAIN (1862) and SECOND BULL RUN (1862) further cemented his reputation, but he proved less successful as a corps commander at GETTYSBURG (1863). Though seriously ill due to complications from gonorrhea contracted in his youth, Hill continued to fight at the BATTLE OF THE WILDERNESS (1864) and brilliantly commanded a small corps at PETERSBURG (1864–65), where he was killed.

Hill, Daniel Harvey (1821–89) • educator; U.S. and Confederate army officer. Born in York District, South Carolina. Hill was graduated from WEST POINT in 1842. He subsequently served in the MEXICAN WAR, (1846–48). In 1849, Hill resigned his U.S. Army commission to teach mathematics at Washington College (1849–54) and later at Davidson College (1854–59). He was also Superintendent of the North Carolina Military Institute (1859–61). With the coming of the CIVIL WAR, Hill led the 1st North Carolina Infantry Regiment at the Battle of Big Bethel Church on June 10, 1861, being promoted to brigadier general the same day. He was subsequently promoted to major general in early 1862 and to lieutenant general in 1863. Hill served for the first two years of the war in the eastern theater and participated in the PENINSULAR CAMPAIGN (1861–62) and the battles of SECOND BULL RUN, SOUTH MOUNTAIN, and ANTIETAM in 1862. In 1863, he was transferred to the Confederate ARMY OF TENNESSEE and contributed to the defeat of Union forces at CHICKAMAUGA. Shortly after Chickamauga, Hill was relieved of his command and subsequently commanded troops only twice, at PETERSBURG and at Bentonville, in 1865. Certainly the smartest, and perhaps the best all-around, general officer in the Confederate Army, Hill did not forebear to criticize his commanders, particularly ROBERT E. LEE and then BRAXTON BRAGG, a fault which led to his exclusion from greater responsibilities after 1863.

Hillenkoetter, Roscoe Henry (1897–1982) • naval officer and first director of the CENTRAL INTELLIGENCE AGENCY (1947–50), born in St. Louis, Missouri. As director, Hillenkoetter pursued a moderate course, concentrating on the development of the agency's research and informational needs rather than on covert operations, particularly avoiding schemes with a paramilitary dimension. A graduate of the U.S. NAVAL ACADEMY, Hillenkoetter served with the navy both before and after his time with the CIA. He served with the Atlantic Fleet during WORLD WAR I; worked with the French underground in France (1940–41); and after PEARL HARBOR (1941), at which he was wounded, he organized naval intelligence in the Pacific. He again saw active duty during the KOREAN WAR, and afterwards served as inspector general of the navy, retiring in 1957 with the rank of vice admiral.

hilt • *n.* the handle of a weapon or tool, especially a sword, dagger, or knife.

Hindenburg Line • in WORLD WAR I, a German fortified line of defense on the WESTERN FRONT to which Field Marshal PAUL VON HINDENBURG directed retreat. The triple-lined entrenched position, which extended from Arras to Soissons, had barbed wire and concrete pillboxes with machine guns. The line was breached during the Battle of Cambrai on November 20, 1917; at Arras at the end of August 1918; and finally near Cambrai in mid October. Also called SIEGFRIED LINE.

Hindenburg, Paul von (1847–1934) • German field marshal during WORLD WAR I and president of the WEIMAR REPUBLIC (1925–34), born in Posen, Germany. His tenure was marked by the rise to power of ADOLF HITLER, whom he appointed chancellor in 1933.

Hindman, Thomas Carmichael (1828–68) • Confederate army general, born in Knoxville, Tennessee. Hindman experienced frequent changes of command because of his practice of TOTAL WAR and tendency to become embroiled in conflicts with his superiors. He fought with the Army of Mississippi at PRAIRIE GROVE (1862) and with the ARMY OF TENNESSEE at CHATTANOOGA (1863) before returning to the Trans-Mississippi, where he spent the remainder of the war. Hindman had been active in politics before the war, serving in the Mississippi state legislature (1854) and in Congress as a representative from Arkansas (first elected 1858).

Hindman was assassinated, but his murderer was never found and the motivation for the deed remains murky.

Hines, John Leonard (1868–1968) • army general and chief of staff (1924–26), born in Greenbrier, West Virginia. He commanded a brigade at the second battle of the MARNE (1918), receiving the DISTINGUISHED SERVICE CROSS for his actions at SOISSONS. Later that same year he commanded a division in the MEUSE-ARGONNE offensive that remained on attack for a record twenty-five consecutive days. As army chief of staff, his primary challenge was maintaining a standing peacetime army; he also sought to upgrade the various army schools. Earlier in his career Hines had fought in the SPANISH-AMERICAN WAR (1898), receiving a SILVER STAR and citation for gallantry.

Hines was the only American officer during WORLD WAR I to command in battle a regiment, brigade, division, and corps. When Hines died, at the age of 100, he was then the oldest living graduate of WEST POINT.

Hirohito (1901–89) • emperor of Japan (1926–89) during WORLD WAR II, though the military controlled the government and conducted the war in his name. It was Hirohito, however, who eventually brought about the peace by intervention in a government deadlock and a broadcast to the nation (1945) announcing Japan's surrender. After the war he was retained on the throne in a purely ceremonial capacity.

Hirohito was the longest reigning monarch in Japan's history, and the first Japanese crown prince and the first reigning Japanese monarch to travel abroad.

Hiroshima, bombing of • (August 6, 1945) after Japan failed to surrender to Allied Forces, on July 30 President HARRY S. TRUMAN approved the use of the atomic bomb developed by the MANHATTAN PROJECT scientists. Orders for the bombing were issued on August 3, and three days later the ENOLA GAY dropped one bomb, nicknamed "LITTLE BOY," on the industrial city of Hiroshima, with the blast, fire and radiation killing 60,000 civilians, several thousand military personnel, and 60,000 additional casualties from radiation poisoning and injuries. Eighty-one percent of the city's structures were also destroyed. The bombings of Hiroshima and NAGASAKI ultimately led to Japan's unconditional surrender in September 1945.

Hiss, Alger (1904–96) • STATE DEPARTMENT official and accused spy. In 1950, Hiss was convicted of perjury, stemming from his testimony before a grand jury that he had never given a Communist courier, Whittaker Chambers, documents. He was given a five-year prison sentence. In 1996, the U.S. government released secret Soviet cables that had been intercepted during WORLD WAR II that provided compelling evidence of Hiss's guilt.

Future president RICHARD M. NIXON was prominent in the investigation that led to Hiss's indictment.

Historic Naval Ships Association • a nonprofit organization established in 1966 to assist with the preservation of historically significant naval ships. The association's membership includes museum ships from around the world, spanning in time from the REVOLUTIONARY WAR to the COLD WAR.

hitch • *n.* a period of service: *his twelve-year hitch in the navy.*

Hitchcock, Ethan Allen (1798–1870) • Union army officer, born in Mobile, Alabama. Hitchcock directed the exchange and return of captives during the CIVIL WAR. Hitchcock had earlier seen service in the SECOND SEMINOLE WAR (1835–42) and other Indian encounters and during the occupation of Texas (1845), experiences which cemented his nonconformist views of the United States as an arrogant and presumptuous aggressor. He nevertheless continued in his military career and fought with distinction during the MEXICAN WAR (1846–48) on the campaign from Veracruz to Mexico City (1847).

Hitler, Adolf (1889–1945) • leader *(der Führer)* of the NAZI party (from 1921) and dictator of Germany (1933–45) whose expansionist policies and racist views led to WORLD WAR II. His early *Mein Kampf* (1924) outlined his vision of a racially pure Reich whose master Aryan, or Germanic, race would rule inferior races, of which the Jews were the most insidious—extermination was to be the "FINAL SOLUTION" to the "Jewish problem." Early victories over Poland (1939) and Western Europe (1940) were soon followed by reversals (STALINGRAD, 1942; the invasions of Italy, 1943, and NORMANDY, 1944), but Hitler and his generals persisted. Hitler isolated himself from the realities and preserved a fantasy world of eventual victory, refusing to allow his armies to surrender. He survived an assassination attempt in 1944 but committed suicide in Berlin a few days before Germany surrendered.

hit-to-kill • *n.* a type of interceptor missile which tracks the target at high speed, homes in on it, and finally smashes into it, destroying it on impact.

***H. L. Hunley*, CSS** • a submarine of the Confederate Navy and the first submersible craft to engage and sink a warship. Privately built in 1963 in Mobile, Alabama, the *Hunley* was made from a cylindrical iron steam boiler, made deeper and lengthened by the addition of tapered ends, and hand-powered by a crew of nine: eight to turn the propeller by hand, and one to steer the craft. On the night of February 16, 1864, the *Hunley* attacked the 1,800-ton sloop-of-war the USS *Housatonic* with a spar torpedo packed with explosive powder. The explosion not only sent the *Housatonic* to the bottom of Charleston Harbor (off the coast of South Carolina) but the *Hunley* as well.

The wreck of the vessel was finally found by the writer Clive Cussler in 1995, and the *Hunley* was raised in August 2000.

HMS • *abbr.* Her or His Majesty's Ship, used in

the names of ships in the British navy: *HMS Ark Royal.*

HMV • *abbr.* high-mobility vehicle.

ho • *exclam.* used to draw attention to something seen: *land ho!*

Hobby hat • a WORLD WAR II-era WAAC service hat. [named for Oveta Culp Hobby, the first Director of the WAAC.]

Hobby, Oveta Culp (1905–95) • lawyer, journalist, and politician, born in Killeen, Texas. Hobby was the first director of the Women's Auxiliary Army Corps (WAAC) (later WAC), initially with the rank of major, but was quickly promoted to colonel. She dropped the word "Auxiliary" from the name of the service and worked to give the WAC status equal to that of the all-male army. By the end of the war in 1945 there were 100,000 WACs on active duty in noncombat posts.

Hobkirk's Hill, Battle of • a fight between British and American troops on April 25, 1781, during the REVOLUTIONARY WAR, at Hobkirk's Hill, South Carolina. American Gen. NATHANAEL GREENE's army was defeated by British soldiers and loyalists. The victory came at a high cost for the British, who had to retreat because of Revolutionary partisans in the surrounding area.

Hobson, Richmond Pearson (1870–1937) • naval officer, born in Greensboro, Alabama. Hobson became a national hero for his exploits during the SPANISH-AMERICAN WAR (1898) when he was captured (then exchanged) in a failed attempt to take the *Merrimac* into the entrance of Santiago harbor and sink it, effectively bottling up the Spanish squadron. He was later awarded the CONGRESSIONAL MEDAL OF HONOR (1933) for his deed. Before the war, Hobson, who was in the Construction Corps, designed and ran the postgraduate course in naval construction at the U.S. NAVAL ACADEMY. Hobson had difficulty getting along with others, and was often ostracized by classmates and fellow officers.

Ho Chi Minh (1890?–1969) • international Communist and president of the Democratic Republic of Vietnam until his death. Ho spent many years in Europe and Russia where he was active in communist circles. He returned to Vietnam in 1941 and led the VIETMINH (Vietnamese Independence League) to power in the 1945 revolution, remaining at the helm during the ensuing decades of fighting for independence against French rule and American intervention. Despite the more repressive and totalitarian quality of his rule in the North following the partition established by the GENEVA AGREEMENT ON INDOCHINA (1954), Ho remained immensely popular with the Vietnamese people.

Ho Chi Minh Trail • a network of trails through eastern Laos and Cambodia into South Vietnam, encompassing over 12,500 miles (20,000 kilometers). It was named by the U.S. media after HO CHI MINH. The trails were used by NATIONAL LIBERATION FRONT (NLF) and Communist troops of North Vietnam during the VIETNAM WAR to supply North Vietnamese troops and local NLF guerrillas throughout South Vietnam. Much of the Ho Chi Minh Trail is now incorporated into the road systems of Laos and Cambodia.

Hodge, John Reed (1893–1963) • army general, born in Golconda, Illinois. Hodge was considered one of the best combat commanders in the Pacific during WORLD WAR II, with successful operations at GUADALCANAL (1942), BOUGAINVILLE (1943–44), LEYTE (1944), and OKINAWA (1945). During WORLD WAR I he had taken part in the ST. MIHIEL and MEUSE-ARGONNE offensives (1918). After World War II, Hodge was military administrator and commander of U.S. forces in the south of Korea (1945–48), where he sought to promote stability by suppressing Communism and fostering a moderate pro-American coalition, a position that made him enemies on both the left and the right. Hodge retired in 1953 with the rank of full general.

Hodge was called "the PATTON of the Pacific" because of his hard-driving style.

---

hog • *v.* (usually **be hogged**) distort (a ship) by supporting it in the center and allowing the bow and stern to droop.

Hog-60 • slang (in VIETNAM) the M-60 light machine gun, particularly the helicopter door gunner's M-60.

A "pig" is any firearm that can be operated by one man, especially the M-60. "Hog" was also a nickname for the helicopter gunship itself, especially the "Huey Hog" UH-1B and UH-1C.

Hogun, James (?-1781) • born in Ireland, REVOLUTIONARY WAR general who enlisted and trained a North Carolina regiment that participated in the battles of BRANDYWINE and GERMANTOWN (both 1777). He later returned to North Carolina to raise reinforcements for the Continental army in New York (1778). Hogun died as a result of the conditions aboard the fever-ridden prison ships on which he was held after being captured in the fall of CHARLESTON (1780).

hoist • *n.* **1** the part of a flag nearest the staff. **2** a group of flags raised as a signal.
PHRASES: **hoist one's flag** (of an admiral) take up command.

Hoke, Robert Frederick (1837–1912) • Confederate army officer, born in Lincolnton, North Carolina. Hoke was considered one of the most consistent field commanders in the East for the first three years of the war, especially at SECOND BULL RUN, ANTIETAM, FREDERICKSBURG (all 1862), and CHANCELLORSVILLE (1863) but who suffered a succession of inadequate performances in 1864 at COLD HARBOR, PETERSBURG, and RICHMOND. On the one occasion that he was given a free hand, he performed brilliantly: against the garrison at Plymouth, North Carolina, he forced the surrender of the Confederate general and his 2,800 men (1864).

Holcomb, Thomas (1879–1965) • general and commandant of the U.S. Marine Corps (1936–44), born in New Castle, Delaware. Holcomb presided over the continuing refinement of the corps' amphibious mission, experimented with new kinds of landing craft, and established clear lines of authority in the field between navy and marine personnel. Holcomb received the NAVY CROSS and the SILVER STAR with three oak leaf clusters for his service in WORLD WAR I, during which he saw action in several battles, among them BELLEAU WOOD, CHÂTEAU-THIERRY, SOISSONS, and the ARGONNE FOREST (all 1918). In 1944 Holcomb was made a full general and awarded the DISTINGUISHED SERVICE MEDAL.

Holcomb was the first marine to hold the rank of full general.

hold • *n.* a large space in the lower part of a ship or aircraft in which cargo is stowed.

holding action • an action designed to hold the enemy in position, to deceive him as to where the main attack is being made, to prevent him from reinforcing the elements opposing the main attack, and/or to cause him to commit his reserves prematurely at an indecisive location.

holding anchorage • a temporary place where ships can anchor in case: **a** the assembly or working anchorage to which they are assigned is full. **b** they have been delayed by enemy threats or other factors from proceeding on their next voyage. **c** they have been dispersed from a port to avoid the results of a nuclear attack.

holding ground • an area of seabed where an anchor will hold.

hole • *v.* **1** make a hole or holes in: *a fuel tank was holed by the attack and a fire started.* **2** pierce the hull of (a ship), allowing water to run in.

holiday • *n.* an unintentional omission in imagery coverage of an area.

Hollandia, Battle of • a battle in eastern New Guinea during WORLD WAR II. On April 22, 1944, Allied forces in the Pacific made two landings at Hollandia, in Western New Guinea, as part of their push northward toward the Philippines. Japan's airfields in Hollandia were captured in four days, and thereafter Hollandia became an important base for Allied forces in the Southwest Pacific.

hollow square • a body of infantry drawn up in a square with a space in the middle.

Holmes, Theophilus Hunter (1804–80) • Confederate army officer and ranking general from North Carolina, born in Sampson City. Holmes was a former classmate of JEFFERSON DAVIS, who acted as his patron. Through his actions at MALVERN HILL (1862), Holmes, who had been initially successful and popular with his men, garnered a reputation for lethargic action and lack of initiative. Prior to the CIVIL WAR Holmes had been cited for gallantry in both the MEXICAN WAR (1846–48) and the Second SEMINOLE WAR (1835–42).

Holmes was one of just fifteen field grade U.S. Army officers who resigned their commissions to join the CONFEDERACY.

holocaust • *n.* **1** destruction or slaughter on a mass scale, especially caused by fire or nuclear war: *a nuclear holocaust | the threat of imminent holocaust.* **2** (**the Holocaust**) the mass murder of Jews under the German NAZI regime during the period from 1941 to 1945. More than 6 million European Jews, as well as members of other persecuted groups, such as gypsies and homosexuals, were murdered at concentration camps such as AUSCHWITZ.

holystone |ˈhōlēˌstōn| • *n.* chiefly historical a piece of soft sandstone used for scouring the decks of ships. • *v.* scour (a deck) with a holystone.

ORIGIN: early 19th century: probably from holy + stone. Sailors called the stones "bibles" or "prayer books," perhaps because they scrubbed the decks on their knees.

home front • civilian population, activity, and life during a war that is being waged overseas.

home guard • **1** a local defense militia. **2** (**Home Guard**) British militia created in July 1940 from the Local Defence Volunteers and intended to augment Britain's defenses against invasion by German forces.

home port • the port from which a ship originates or in which it is registered.

homing • *adj.* (of a weapon or piece of equipment) fitted with an electronic device that enables it to find and hit a target.

homing guidance • a system by which a missile steers itself toward a target by means of a mechanism that is activated by some distinguishing characteristics of the target.

homing torpedo • any torpedo with a device that enables it to home in on its target after it has been fired.

Homma, Masaharu (1887–46) • Japanese army general who led the Japanese invasion of the Philippine Islands (1941) following the attack on PEARL HARBOR. Homma surrendered to U.S. forces in 1945 and was subsequently brought to trial. Convicted of ordering the BATAAN DEATH MARCH (1942) and condoning other atrocities, he was executed by a firing squad.

honorable discharge • a discharge from active military service which acknowledges that the individual's service has been honest and faithful, with conduct ratings of at least "good" and efficiency ratings of at least "fair," and with no convictions by general court-martial and no more than one conviction by a special court-martial.

honor guard • a body of troops detailed to greet or accompany important visitors or to accompany the casket of the deceased at a military funeral. The term is sometimes used improperly to refer to a COLOR GUARD.

honors of war • privileges granted to a capitulating force, for example that of marching out with colors flying.

honor system • a system of payment or examination that relies solely on the honesty of those concerned. In some military academies, the honor system requires not only that students not break any rules, but also report any student who does.

hooch • *n.* slang **1** a small, roughly constructed building, particularly one used as a billet. **2** liquor.

Hood, John Bell (1831–79) • Confederate army officer, born in Owingsville, Kentucky. His heroic leadership was noted at GAINES' MILL (1862) and SECOND BULL RUN (1862). Hood was wounded at GETTYSBURG (1863) and again at CHICKAMAUGA (1863). As commander of the ARMY OF TENNESSEE, his attempts to prevent the capture of ATLANTA failed, and the army was nearly wiped out near NASHVILLE in late 1864, after which he was relieved of command.

hooker • *n.* informal an old boat.

Hooker, Joseph (1814–79) • Union army officer, born in Hadley, Massachusetts. Hooker performed admirably during the SEVEN DAYS' battles, SECOND BULL RUN, and ANTIETAM (all 1862). As commander of the ARMY OF THE POTOMAC, his retreat at CHANCELLORSVILLE (1863) impaired his further effectiveness in that position, from which he resigned. Despite later successes as a corps commander at LOOKOUT MOUNTAIN and on MISSIONARY RIDGE (both 1863), Hooker failed to achieve the advancement he sought, largely because of a bitter enmity between him and Gen. WILLIAM T. SHERMAN.

Hooker was known as "Fighting Joe" because of his rashness and aggressiveness.

Hoover, Herbert Clark (1874–1964) • 31st president of the United States (1929–33), born in West Branch, Iowa. As a mining engineer with multiple foreign investments, Hoover became a millionaire by the age of forty. He came to public attention through his active leadership role in various relief efforts during and following WORLD WAR I, primarily in the area of food distribution. He was sought as a presidential nominee by both parties in 1920, but refused to run. As secretary of commerce in the administrations of WARREN G. HARDING and CALVIN COOLIDGE, Hoover made that department one of the most important and well publicized by developing advanced economic theories about business cycles, promoting government regulation of radio and aviation, and supporting federal supervision of foreign loans. By 1928 he was viewed as a postwar economic superman and he easily defeated Democrat Alfred E. Smith for the presidency. But implementation of his progressive principles, which included cooperative economic organization, self-regulation by business, and voluntary activity through American society, was almost immediately thwarted by the stock market crash in October 1929. Remedial legislation failed to deal with the growing problem of the unemployed, but Hoover remained adamantly opposed to direct federal relief. Though he signed the Emergency and Relief Construction Act (1932), he placed many restrictions on its implementation. Perhaps Hoover's greatest blunder was accepting responsibility for DOUGLAS MACARTHUR's burning of the veterans' camps that had been set up outside Washington, D.C., to protest the government's refusal to redeem veteran certificates, which Hoover considered equivalent to the dole. He left office in disgrace, blamed for the Depression and the routing of the veterans, which had been done in violation of his orders. His conservative fiscal policies, aversion to direct federal relief, and failure of relief initiatives (such as the Reconstruction Finance Corporation and the earlier Federal Farm Board) left millions unemployed at the end of his term. In foreign relations Hoover met with better success. Drawing on his early Quaker training, he relied on negotiation rather than the use of force, and supported arms limitation as well as international arbitration, positions which he continued to advocate after leaving office. Throughout the 1920s, WORLD WAR II, and into the 1940s and 1950s, he supported various ways to avoid military conflict. His belief in the superiority of American capitalism made him fear neither fascism nor communism. Both HARRY S. TRUMAN and DWIGHT D. EISENHOWER called upon Hoover's administrative skills to head up the reorganization of the executive branch of government, resulting in two Hoover Commission reports (1949 and 1955), many of whose recommendations were adopted.

Hopkins, Esek (1718–1802) • Revolutionary naval officer, born in Providence (now Scituate), Rhode Island. Hopkins was commander in chief of the Continental fleet, with the title of commodore. His refusal to follow congressional orders (to sail into the Chesapeake Bay for an encounter with the British there) and a subsequent embarrassing engagement with the British frigate *Glasgow* led to his censure (1776). He was removed in early 1778, following a formal complaint from all the officers aboard his flagship.

Hopkins, Samuel (1753–1819) • Revolutionary army officer from Albemarle County, Virginia, whose ardor for fighting and devotion to duty impressed GEORGE WASHINGTON early in the conflict. Hopkins participated in the battles of TRENTON (1776), PRINCETON (1777), BRANDYWINE (1777), GERMANTOWN (1777), and MONMOUTH (1778). During the WAR OF 1812, as commander in chief of the western frontier, he led a failed expedition against hostile Indian villages in Illinois, shortly after which he retired from military service. Hopkins, who had settled in western Kentucky after the Revolution, also had an active political career. Between the wars, he served extended terms in both the state house and senate, and in 1813 he was elected to the U.S. Congress.

hop-over • *n.* slang (in WORLD WAR I) leaving the foxhole and going into combat in no-man's-land. See also OVER THE TOP.

HOP TAC, Operation • a U.S.-South Vietnamese operation launched in the summer of 1964 to pacify the six heavily-populated provinces surrounding the South Vietnamese capital of SAIGON. In Vietnamese, *hop tac* means 'cooperation,' but the operation failed due to a lack of cooperation among the many South Vietnamese and U. S. military and civilian agencies involved.

Hornet • (**F-18**) a twin-engine medium-size

shipboard fighter/attack aircraft, its official designation is F/A-18. It is heavier than the F-16, but lighter than either the F-14 or the F-15. The F-18E "Super Hornet" made its first carrier landing in 1997, and, like the F-18F, is easily recognizable by the rectangular engine intakes, which reduce radar reflection and supply more mass flow for its powerful engines. It was expected to enter service in 2000.

Hornets' Nest • a site along a sunken wagon road at SHILOH which became a magnet for Confederate assaults. The Confederates surprised Union troops and were able to drive back the divisions under Brig. Gen. Benjamin M. Prentiss, Brig. Gen. WILLIAM T. SHERMAN, and Maj. Gen. JOHN A. MCCLERNAND. Prentiss rallied his troops at this site. Eleven attacks were made on the Hornets' Nest before it was finally blasted away by a Confederate sixty-two-gun attack. Prentiss and his troops surrendered at 5:30 P.M. on April 3, 1862.

horse • *n.* **1** cavalry: *forty horse and sixty foot.* **2** a horizontal bar, rail, or rope in the rigging of a sailing ship for supporting something. • *v.* (usually **be horsed**) provide (a person or vehicle) with a horse or horses.

DERIVATIVES: **horseless** *adj.*

horse collar • another term for RESCUE STROP.

Horse Guards • a complex of buildings in central London originally used as a barracks for the elite mounted regiments of the British Army. By extension, the general headquarters of the British Army in the late 18th and the 19th century came to be called Horse Guards.

horse latitudes • a belt of calm air and sea occurring in both the northern and southern hemispheres between the trade winds and the westerlies.

horse pistol • a large pistol carried at the pommel of the saddle by a rider.

Horseshoe Bend, Battle of • (March 27–28, 1814) a battle in the CREEK WAR (1811–14) between U.S. forces and the Creek in present-day Alabama. In response to U.S. intervention in Creek government, the Red Stick Creek attacked Creek villages allied with the United States as well as Fort Mims, where several U.S. citizens were killed. Following the Fort Mims incident, the United States entered the Creek civil war under Gen. ANDREW JACKSON. Five thousand American troops attacked the Red Stick at Tohopeka, near the Horseshoe Bend on the Tallapoosa River. The Creek suffered more than 800 losses, and in the wake of the battle the Creek Nation accepted the Treaty of FORT JACKSON, which ceded 22 million acres of Creek land to the U.S. government.

horse-soldier • *n.* a cavalryman.

hospital ship • a ship that functions as a hospital, especially to receive or take home sick or wounded military personnel.

hospital train • a train car that functions as a hospital, especially to receive or take home sick or wounded military personnel.

hostage • *n.* a person seized and held as a pledge that certain terms or agreements will be kept.

According to the rules of the GENEVA CONVENTIONS, the taking of hostages is a forbidden act.

hostile acts • basic rules established by higher authority for defining and recognizing hostile acts by aircraft, submarines, surface units, and ground forces will be promulgated by the commanders of unified or specified commands, and by other appropriate commanders when so authorized.

hostiles • *n.* slang **1** (in the 19th and early 20th century in the U.S. Army) members of Indian tribes engaged in active raids or warfare against whites and/or friendly Indians; later, the INSURRECTOS or ordinary bandits in the Philippine Islands. **2** enemy aircraft.

hostilities • *n. pl.* acts of warfare: *he called for an immediate cessation of hostilities.*

hot launch • the launching of a missile with the missile motor running, as opposed to a COLD LAUNCH.

hotline (also **hot line**) • *n.* a direct telephone line set up for a specific purpose, especially for use in emergencies or for communication between heads of government.

Hot-Line Agreement • an agreement between Soviet Premier NIKITA KHRUSHCHEV and U.S. President JOHN F. KENNEDY to install a direct communications link between Moscow and Washington "for use in time of emergency." Signed at Geneva on June 20, 1963, during the COLD WAR, it was created to reduce the risk of nuclear war between the two countries.

Measures to add two satellite circuits to the line were signed on September 30, 1971, and an accord signed on July 17, 1984, added a facsimile line.

hot shot • (also called **heated shot**) an older naval and land gunnery practice in which a solid round shot for a cannon was heated to a glow before firing so as to have an incendiary effect on the target.

hot spot • region in a contaminated area in which the level of radioactive contamination is considerably greater than in neighboring regions in the area.

hot war • a war with active military hostilities.

Hound Dog • (**AGM-28A** or **AGM-28B**) an air-to-surface nuclear missile designed to be carried outside on the B-52 and propelled by turbojet. It can be used either for high- or low-altitude attacks. It was developed in the 1950s to replace the NAVAHO missile. It was removed from active service in the 1970s.

***Housatonic*, USS** • a screw sloop-of-war built during the CIVIL WAR and commissioned in August 1862, it played an active role in the U.S. Navy's blockade of CHARLESTON, South Carolina. Anchored off Charleston on February 17, 1864, the *Housatonic* became the first warship sunk by a submarine when the CSS *H. L. Hunley* attacked it.

House Armed Services Committee • a committee of the U.S. House of Representatives organized under the Legislative Reorganization Act of 1946, uniting the House

Military Affairs Committee and the Naval Affairs Committee. The House Armed Services Committee is responsible for the common defense generally, for any activity undertaken by the Department of Defense or by departments of the Army, Navy, or Air Force, and for the Selective Service system. Committee membership, averaging between thirty-three and fifty-four members, reflects party membership in the House as a whole. Subcommittees deal with hearings, investigations, and drafting legislation concerning military installations, personnel, procurement, readiness, research and development, sea power, and strategic materials.

house flag • a flag indicating the company that a ship belongs to.

household troops • Brit. troops employed to guard a sovereign.

housing • *n.* the part of a mast below the deck.

Houston, Sam (1793–1863) • president of the Republic of Texas (1836–38; 1841–44) and U.S. senator, born Samuel Houston in Rockbridge County, Virginia. Houston's early life and career were varied: two extended periods living with the Cherokees; several years in the U.S. army; additional time in the Tennessee militia; reading and practicing law in Nashville; representative to the U.S. Congress; and governor of Tennessee. But it is with Texas that his name is linked, from its early days as a province of Mexico through its annexation to the United States. As commander in chief of the Texas army, Houston led the fight for independence from Mexico, becoming first president of the new Republic of Texas in 1836. He then served in the Texas congress before being returned to the presidency (1841). While in office he repeatedly worked for annexation, but it was not achieved until after his term expired (1844). Elected to the U.S. Senate (1846), Houston took what became an unfavorable stance against sectionalism and in support of the Union, for which the Texas legislature failed to return him when his final term ended in 1859. That same year he became governor of Texas but was removed from office in March 1861 when he refused to take an oath of loyalty to the Confederacy. However, he eventually sided with the Confederate cause.

Houstoun, John (1750?–1796) • Revolutionary army officer, born in St. George's Parish, Louisiana. As governor of Georgia, Houstoun led the state militia on an ill-fated expedition against St. Augustine in 1778. When, later that year, the British took Savannah and then Augusta, he fled to South Carolina, where he served on the staff of Gen. Lachlan McIntosh in Charleston. He returned to Georgia when the British evacuated, was again elected governor (1784), served in the state legislature (1785), and became the first mayor of Savannah (1790).

hovercraft • *n.* see air-cushion vehicle.

Howard, John Eager (1752–1827) • Revolutionary army officer, born in Baltimore County, Maryland. Howard was in Maryland's militia throughout the war, seeing action at the battles of White Plains (1776), Germantown (1777), Monmouth (1778), Guilford Court House (1781), and Eutaw Springs (1781), where he was severely wounded and forced to resign his commission. During the War of 1812 he raised a regiment of veterans, but they were not called into service.

It was during Howard's tenure as governor (elected 1788) that Maryland granted the section of land that became part of the District of Columbia.

Howard, Oliver Otis (1830–1909) • Union officer, born Leeds, Maine. Howard fought at First Bull Run (1861) and commanded troops at Antietam (1862) and Fredericksburg (1862) before being routed at Chancellorsville (1863) by Thomas "Stonewall" Jackson. They later performed well at Chattanooga (1863), and in 1864 Howard was given command of the Army of the Tennessee. His men played a key role in forcing the abandonment of Atlanta to William T. Sherman and took part in the March to the Sea (1864–65). After the war, Howard was put in charge of the Freedmen's Bureau, which managed southern lands abandoned during wartime and arranged for their distribution to emancipated slaves. Despite the bureau's failures in the area of land management, under Howard it met with considerable success in its educational endeavors and its support for black veterans.

Howard cofounded Howard University in Washington, D.C., in 1867 and served as its president from 1869 to 1874.

Howe, John Homer (1822–73) • U.S. soldier and jurist, born in New York. Howe practiced law in Ohio and Illinois. He commanded the 124th Illinois Volunteer Regiment at Vicksburg (1863), where a detachment he led earned the nickname "the Mad Moles" for tunneling under Confederate works. After the Union victory he administered the occupied area, and left the army in 1865 as a brevet brigadier general. Later President Ulysses S. Grant appointed Howe chief justice of the Wyoming Territory, where he impaneled the first women on a jury in the United States.

Howell, Evan Park (1839–1905) • Confederate army officer, born in Warsaw, Georgia. His Georgia unit (called "Howell's Battery") played a prominent role at Chickamauga (1863) and in and around Atlanta during Sherman's March to the Sea (1864–65). Howell is better known for his role after the war, as a widely respected and influential newspaper editor *(Atlanta Constitution)* and progressive politician who advocated reconciliation between the North and South.

Howell, John Adams (1840–1918) • career naval officer, born in Bath, New York. Howell participated in several Civil War battles with the Union fleet and commanded a squadron blockading Cuba during the Spanish-American War (1898). Howell is remembered less for his wartime achievements than for his innovations in ordnance. He invented the self-steering torpedo and also patented torpedo launchers, gyroscopes for the guidance of torpedoes, explosive shells, a disappearing gun carriage for shore defense emplacement, and an amphibious lifeboat.

Howell, Richard (1754–1802) • Revolutionary army officer, born in Newark, Delaware. Howell's New Jersey company was involved in several engagements, including TICONDEROGA (1776), BRANDYWINE (1777), and GERMANTOWN (1777), although it did not play a prominent role. He later served several terms as governor of New Jersey (1793–1801), during which time he helped raise four companies of infantry and personally commanded New Jersey troops during the WHISKEY REBELLION (1794).

Howe, Richard (1726–99) • British admiral, commander of the North American squadron early in the REVOLUTIONARY WAR, during which the British failed to exploit their naval strength. After France became a party to the conflict, Howe had one significant success in preventing the French squadron from capturing Newport, Rhode Island. He was sympathetic with the colonists and influenced his brother WILLIAM HOWE in pursuing a course of conciliation.

Howe, who twice served as first lord of the ADMIRALTY, is best known in British history as commander of the Channel fleet at the Battle of the First of June (1794) during the French Revolutionary Wars, a brilliant victory unsurpassed even by the later exploits of HORATIO NELSON.

Howe, William (1729–1814) • commander in chief of the British army (1775–78) during the early years of the REVOLUTIONARY WAR. His conciliatory strategy of cautious maneuvers and small victories, intended to lead to a negotiated settlement, collapsed with major American victories at TRENTON (1776) and PRINCETON (1777). He then sought to end the war with a climactic battle, but his defeat of the Continental army at BRANDYWINE (1777) was not sufficiently decisive. Faced with criticism from home for his continued failure, Howe resigned his commission.

howitzer |ˈhowətsər| • *n.* a short gun for firing shells on high trajectories at low velocities.

hoy • *n.* **1** a small single-masted sailing ship used to travel close to shorelines. **2** a large barge for hauling freight.

HTK interceptor • a high-technology weapon designed to identify the specific nature of and destroy inbound ballistic missiles in the exoatmosphere.

ORIGIN: HTK is an acronym for hit-to-kill.

HTL • see BELL 47.

HUD • *abbr.* a head-up display.

Hué, Vietnam • a Central Vietnamese city that once served as the capital of Vietnam, the seat of the Imperial family and the Roman Catholic Church, and the site of the Imperial Citadel. Its importance, in addition its geostrategic value, made it a target for VIETCONG and North Vietnamese attacks during the VIETNAM WAR. On January 31, 1968, during the TET OFFENSIVE, North Vietnamese forces blocked the major highway in and out of the city, and a combined North Vietnamese and Vietcong force invaded and took the city. The following day the U.S. launched a counterattack that required more than three weeks to retake the city. The city was devastated by combat, with more than half the buildings and houses destroyed and more than 6,000 noncombatants killed, in addition to the thousands of residents executed by the Vietcong in the first days of the occupation. The Vietcong and North Vietnamese armies suffered more than 5,000 losses, while the Americans lost 216 and the South Vietnamese 384.

Huey • see IROQUOIS.

HueyCobra • (**AH-1**) a U.S. Army helicopter with both all-weather and rough field capabilities, and designed to function in various capacities, including as a fighter, strategic bomber, and transport.

Designed by Bell, the HueyCobra was first delivered to the Army in June 1967 and was quickly put to use in VIETNAM.

Hughes-Ryan Act • an act passed by Congress in 1974 to prohibit CIA expenditures for non-intelligence operations in foreign countries unless authorized by the president, who must first report the operation to the relevant congressional committees for review. It was an amendment to the Foreign Assistance Act of 1974.

hulk • *n.* an old ship stripped of fittings and permanently moored, especially for use as storage or (formerly) as a prison.

hull • *n.* the main body of a ship or other vessel, including the bottom, sides, and deck but not the masts, superstructure, rigging, engines, and other fittings. • *v.* (usually **be hulled**) hit and pierce the hull of (a ship) with a shell or other missile.

DERIVATIVES: **hulled** *adj.: a wooden-hulled narrowboat.*

Hull, Agrippa (1759–1848) • African-American REVOLUTIONARY WAR soldier, born in Northhampton, Massachusetts. Hull served as personal orderly to Gen. JOHN PATERSON and later to Gen. TADEUSZ KOSCIUSZKO. As such he performed a variety of personal and military duties, including serving as a surgeon's assistant, and witnessed some of the most important fighting of the Revolution. He was with Kosciuszko during battles from SARATOGA (1777) through the campaign in the South, and on until the end of the war (1783). Hull's discharge was personally signed by GEORGE WASHINGTON and he received a veteran's pension from Congress. Hull settled in Stockbridge, Massachusetts, after the war.

Hull, Cordell (1871–1955) • secretary of state (1933–44) during the administrations of FRANKLIN D. ROOSEVELT, born near Byrdstown, Tennessee. His continued push for freer trade resulted in the RECIPROCAL TRADE AGREEMENTS ACT (1934). The legislation, which established the "most-favored nation" status with trading partners that still exists today, remains the foundation for modern American foreign trade policy. Hull constantly sought to lower trade barriers, believing that economic intercourse fostered peaceful relations. Prior to the outbreak of WORLD WAR II, he negotiated with the Japanese in hopes of halting their expansionist plans and lobbied for solutions to Sino-Japanese problems. He strongly advocated a postwar global peace organization, but, though he had the honorary title of senior delegate to the UNITED NATIONS conference in 1945, he was too ill to play a role in the founding of that organization. That same year he was awarded the Nobel Peace Prize.

Hull, William (1753–1825) • Revolutionary army officer, born in Derby Connecticut. Hull served throughout the entire war, fighting in most of the important battles of the northern theater, including WHITE PLAINS (1776), TRENTON (1776), SARATOGA (1777), and MONMOUTH (1778). After the war he settled in Newton, Massachusetts, where he held a number of state and local offices until 1805, when THOMAS JEFFERSON appointed him governor of the Michigan Territory. During the WAR OF 1812 he commanded a force of Ohio militia that eventually surrendered Detroit, bringing him into disgrace. Convicted of cowardice and neglect of duty, he was sentenced to be shot, but because of his services during the Revolution the president commuted his sentence.

human remains pouch • a plastic bag used for return to the United States of bodies of soldiers killed in action. See also BODY BAG.

The term was derided as being an exceptionally sanitized euphemism, even by PENTAGON standards.

---

human resources intelligence • the intelligence information derived from the intelligence collection discipline that uses human beings as both sources and collectors, and where the human being is the primary collection instrument.

human rights • rights that are believed to belong justifiably to every person.

Human Rights Watch • an organization based in New York City whose aim is to protect human rights around the world. The group was founded in 1978 as HELSINKI WATCH; other organizations, such as Americas Watch (1981), followed, and these were combined in 1988 under the name Human Rights Watch. The group investigates and publicizes abuses of human rights, observes court proceedings and election preparations, monitors prison conditions, and works with other organizations, including the UNITED NATIONS and the ORGANIZATION OF AMERICAN STATES. Since 1990 it has issued an annual survey of worldwide human rights practices.

Humbert, Jean Joseph Amable |ˌəm'ber| (1767–1823) • French general and military adventurer, born in Saint-Nabord, Vosges, France. Humbert emigrated to the United States in 1812. When the British invaded Louisiana in 1814, he offered his service to the country and was assigned to the staff of Gen. ANDREW JACKSON, playing minor roles in the battle of NEW ORLEANS (1815).

humint • *n.* covert intelligence-gathering by agents or others.

ORIGIN: late 20th century: from *human intelligence*.

Hummer • **1** see HIGH-MOBILITY VEHICLE. **2** slang the E-2 long-range early warning radar carrier aircraft.

Humphreys, Andrew Atkinson (1810–83) • Union army officer and military engineer, born in Philadelphia, Pennsylvania. Humphreys served as chief topographic engineer for the ARMY OF THE POTOMAC, supervising all map-making for the PENINSULA CAMPAIGN. (1862) He later served as aide-de-camp to Gen. GEORGE B. MCCLELLAN, seeing action in several battles of the WILDERNESS TO PETERSBURG CAMPAIGN (1864). Late in 1864 he was given command of a corps which he led through to the final surrender at APPOMATTOX (1865). Humphreys was chief of the U.S. ARMY CORPS OF ENGINEERS from 1866 until 1879, when he retired.

Humphreys' report on the hydraulics of the Mississippi River (1861), resulting from a long-range survey of the delta, was the most significant contribution made by U.S. Army engineers to hydraulic engineering in the 19th century. Humphreys was the grandson of JOSHUA HUMPHREYS.

Humphreys, Benjamin Grubb (1808–82) • Confederate army officer, born in Claiborne County, Mississippi Territory. Humphreys, with ROBERT E. LEE's army, participated in most of the major battles in the eastern theater, winning distinction at FREDERICKSBURG (1862) and assuming a brigade command at GETTYSBURG (1863) when the commander was killed.

Humphreys, Joshua (1751–1838) • shipbuilder and naval architect, born in Haverford, Pennsylvania. Humphreys designed the first warships for the U.S. Navy, including the frigate *Constitution* ("Old Ironsides"), which was launched in 1797. Humphreys had designed ships during the REVOLUTIONARY WAR, and in 1794 he was commissioned to design six frigates for the navy. The efficiency of his designs, known for their speed and maneuverability, influenced naval architecture for decades, well beyond the advent of steam.

Humvee |'həm'vē| • trademark a modern military vehicle. See HIGH-MOBILITY VEHICLE.

ORIGIN: late 20th century: alteration, from the initials of *high-mobility multipurpose vehicle*.

Hun, The • slang, derogatory the individual German combatant and the German armed forces collectively, particularly during WORLD WAR I.

ORIGIN: derived from the name of an historical tribe which invaded Europe in the early Middle Ages and the supposed barbaric behavior of the German troops which invaded Belgium and France in 1914.

hungry Liz • slang (also **hungry Lizzie**) (in WORLD WAR I) an ambulance standing by at airfields in case of emergency.

Hunter, David (1802–86) • Union army officer, born in Washington, D.C. Hunter, of mediocre abilities, received his commission through his political influence with ABRAHAM LINCOLN. While in the SHENANDOAH VALLEY (1864), controversial burnings and pillaging by his forces prompted a retaliatory raid by Gen. JUBAL EARLY, from which Hunter retreated. Gen. ULYSSES S. GRANT then asked him to step aside.

hunter-killer • *adj.* (of a naval vessel, especially a submarine) equipped to locate and destroy enemy vessels, especially other submarines.

Hunt, Henry Jackson (1819–89) • Union army officer and recognized artillery expert, born in Detroit, Michigan Territory. As commander of the Artillery Reserve of the ARMY OF THE POTOMAC, Hunt served with particular distinction during the PENINSULAR CAMPAIGN (1862). He was subsequently appointed chief of artillery, and performed admirably at ANTIETAM (1862) and GETTYSBURG (1863). After the war he held a series of RECONSTRUCTION commands in the occupied South. From 1885 until his death he served as governor of the SOLDIERS' HOME in Washington, D.C.

Huntington, Jabez (1719–86) • early leader of the Revolutionary cause, born in Norwich, Connecticut. Huntington was commander of the Connecticut militia, and an influential member of that state's COUNCIL OF SAFETY, which provided the executive leadership in revolutionary matters. As militia commander, Huntington did not participate in battle but coordinated military plans and political decisions. A prosperous merchant, Huntington also procured provisions for the troops with his own credit, for which he was never repaid. It is generally believed that he sacrificed both his fortune and his health to the cause, retiring due to illness in 1779.

Four of Huntington's sons played significant roles in the Revolution, JEDIDIAH HUNTINGTON being the most prominent. Ebenezer served in the Continental army, and Andrew Huntington financed privateers and ran a commissary for military supplies. Joshua Huntington supervised the construction of the thirty-six-gun frigate, the *Confederacy,* the largest naval ship commissioned by the Continental Congress.

Huntington, Jedediah (1743–1818) • Revolutionary army officer, born in Norwich, Connecticut. Huntington was the son of patriot and Revolutionary leader JABEZ HUNTINGTON. In 1775 he led a Connecticut regiment to join the rebels besieging the British in Boston. When the British evacuated in 1776, he accompanied Gen. GEORGE WASHINGTON to New York and was given command of a regiment in the Continental army, whose performance in the battle of NEW YORK (1776) merited praise from the commander in chief. Huntington was also with the commander in chief during the winter at VALLEY FORGE (1777–78). He was among the officers that tried and condemned Maj. JOHN ANDRÉ for spying.

Hunton, Eppa (1822–1908) • Confederate army officer, born in Fauquiet Country, Virginia. Hunton made significant contributions to several Confederate victories. At FIRST BULL RUN (1861), his regiment's timely maneuver helped thwart an enemy penetration. When Gen. GEORGE E. PICKETT was wounded at GAINES' MILL (1861), Hunton assumed brigade command, which he maintained through the remainder of the PENINSULAR CAMPAIGN and again at SECOND BULL RUN (both 1862). Hunton served admirably at COLD HARBOR and PETERSBURG (both 1864). He was captured on the way to APPOMATTOX COURT HOUSE (1865).

Hurlbut, Stephen Augustus (1815–82) • Union army officer, born in Charleston, South Carolina. Hurlbut was division commander in the ARMY OF THE TENNESSEE, and his significant leadership was noted at SHILOH (1862) and during the CORINTH CAMPAIGN (1862). As commander of the occupation troops in West Tennessee, Hurlbut was responsible for the protection of Memphis during the VICKSBURG CAMPAIGN (1862–63). Removed from that command by Gen. WILLIAM T. SHERMAN, he was later assigned to the Department of the Gulf (1864). Accused of corruption and public drunkenness, he was spared an imminent court-martial and allowed to resign in 1865. He nevertheless had an active political career afterwards, serving in the Illinois legislature and twice being elected to Congress. Hurlbut was also the first commander in chief of the GRAND ARMY OF THE REPUBLIC.

Hurricane • see HAWKER HURRICANE.

hurricane deck • a covered deck at or near the top of a ship's superstructure.

hurtin' • *adj.* slang injured, dead.

Huse, Caleb (1831–1905) • Confederate army officer and arms procurement agent in Europe throughout the CIVIL WAR, born in Newburyport, Massachusetts. Huse purchased, primarily in England but also in Austria, rifles, cannon, and other military supplies that were to be paid for with shipments of southern cotton smuggled through the Federal naval blockade of Confederate ports. By the end of the war Huse had sent the Confederate War Department munitions whose value exceeded $10 million. He was left nearly destitute by the collapse of the CONFEDERACY and returned to the United States in 1868.

Huse was born in Massachusetts but had close associations with many Southerners. He had served at WEST POINT under ROBERT E. LEE and been commandant of cadets at the University of Alabama. In addition, his wife was from a Southern family. Early in 1861 he chose to resign his U.S. Army commission rather than accept a transfer to Washington, D.C.

Husky, Operation • see SICILY CAMPAIGN.

hussar |həˈzär| • *n.* a soldier in a light cavalry regiment that had adopted a dress uniform modeled on that of the Hungarian hussars.

Hussein, Saddam (1937?–) • president of Iraq (1979?–) whose rule has been marked by dictatorial control and attempts to take over neighboring Persian Gulf countries. The IRAN-IRAQ WAR (1980–88) ended in a stalemate, but his 1990 invasion of KUWAIT brought opposition from the West as well as from much of the Arab world. In early 1991, a U.S.-led coalition army liberated Kuwait in the six-week PERSIAN GULF WAR. Hussein suppressed internal uprisings that followed, but the country suffers from U.N.-imposed sanctions that have caused severe shortages of food and medicine.

Hustler • (**B-58**) a delta-wing supersonic jet bomber, the first U.S. bomber capable of supersonic flight. It made its initial flight on November 11, 1956, and flew supersonically on December 30, 1956. The Hustler was operational in the STRATEGIC AIR COMMAND from 1960 to 1970, set nineteen speed and altitude records, and won five different aviation trophies.

hut • *n.* a small single-story building of simple or crude construction, serving as a poor, rough, or temporary house or shelter. • *v.* (**hutted, hutting**) provide with huts: (**hutted**) *a hutted encampment.*

DERIVATIVES: **hutlike** *adj.*

HVAP • *abbr.* hypervelocity armor-piercing.

HY-4 • (**Hai-Ying 4**) a Chinese antiship cruise missile with a turbojet engine, modeled on the U.S. FIREBEE and found widely in countries that are developing their defense capability. It is the last in the series of SILKWORM missiles.

hydrofoil • *n.* **1** a boat whose hull is fitted underneath with shaped vanes (foils) that lift the hull clear of the water to increase the boat's speed. **2** another term for FOIL.

hydrofoil patrol craft • (**PHM**) a patrol craft that can react quickly to and engage offensively with major enemy surface combat units.

hydrogen bomb • (**H-bomb**) an immensely powerful bomb in which hydrogen nuclei combine to form helium nuclei and release energy in an uncontrolled self-sustaining fusion reaction.

hydrographic reconnaissance • reconnaissance of an area of water to determine depths, beach gradients, the nature of the bottom, and the location of coral reefs, rocks, shoals, and man-made obstacles.

hydrography • *n.* the science that deals with the measurements and description of the physical features of the oceans, seas, lakes, rivers, and their adjoining coastal areas, with reference to their use for navigational purposes.

hydrophone • *n.* a microphone that detects sound waves under water.

hydroplane • *n.* **1** a light, fast motorboat designed to skim over the surface of water. **2** a finlike attachment that enables a moving submarine to rise or fall in the water. **3** a seaplane. • *v.* (of a boat) skim over the surface of water with its hull lifted.

hygiene • *n.* conditions or practices conducive to maintaining health and preventing disease, especially through cleanliness: *poor standards of food hygiene | personal hygiene.*

hyperbaric chamber • a chamber used to induce an increase in ambient pressure as would occur in descending below sea level, in a water or air environment. It is the only type of chamber suitable for use in the treatment of decompression sickness in flying or diving.

hypersonic • *adj.* of or pertaining to speeds equal to, or in excess of, five times the speed of sound.

hypervelocity armor-piercing • an armor-piercing tank or anti-tank gun projectile with a muzzle velocity of at least 3,350 feet per second.

hypobaric chamber • a chamber used to induce a decrease in ambient pressure as would occur in ascending to altitude. This type of chamber is primarily used for training and experimental purposes.

Ii

Ia Drang Valley, Battle of the • (November 14–16, 1965) a significant battle of the VIETNAM WAR, it marked strategic changes on the part of both North Vietnam and the United States. For the NVA, it signaled the shift from VIETCONG guerrilla tactics toward the use of conventional military forces, while for the United States it marked the beginning of direct massive involvement in ground combat opertations and a test of helicopter air mobility tactics.

i/c • *abbr.* Brit. **1** (especially in military contexts) in charge of: *the Quartermaster General is i/c rations.* **2** in command: *2 i/c = second in command.*

ICBM • *abbr.* intercontinental ballistic missile.

iceboat • *n.* **1** a light, wind-driven vehicle with sails and runners, used for traveling on ice. **2** a boat used for breaking ice on a waterway.

icebreaker • *n.* a ship designed for breaking a channel through ice.

ICEX • (**intelligence coordination and exploitation**) a program begun in 1967 to systematically destroy VIETCONG infrastructure; it later became the PHOENIX program.

icing • *n.* the formation of ice on an aircraft, ship, or other vehicle, or in an engine.

identification • *n.* **1** the process of determining the friendly or hostile character of an unknown detected contact. **2** in arms control, the process of determining which nation is responsible for the detected violations of any arms control measure. **3** in ground combat operations, discrimination between recognizable objects as being friendly or enemy, or the name that belongs to the object as a member of a class.

identification, friend or foe • (**IFF**) a system using electromagnetic transmissions to which equipment carried by friendly forces automatically responds, for example, by emitting pulses, thereby distinguishing themselves from enemy forces.

IFOR • (**I-For**) the multinational military implementation force set up in Bosnia under NATO supervision as a peacekeeping force with fairly wide discretionary powers.

IFV • *abbr.* infantry fighting vehicle.

igloo space • an area in an earth-covered structure of concrete and/or steel designed for the storage of ammunition and explosives.

Igloo White • (in the VIETNAM WAR) the code name for a system of electronic sensing devices planted along the HO CHI MINH TRAIL and the border of South Vietnam. Some of the motion-detecting sensors were linked to cluster bombs and antipersonnel mines, and others fed data into Air Force computers and generated targets for air strikes.

imagery • *n.* collectively, the representations of objects reproduced electronically or by optical means on film, electronic display devices, or other media.

imagery intelligence • (**IMINT**) intelligence derived from the exploitation of collection by visual photography, infrared sensors, lasers, electro-optics, and radar sensors such as synthetic aperture radar wherein images of objects are reproduced optically or electronically on film, electronic display devices, or other media.

Imboden, John Daniel (1823–95) • Confederate army officer, born in Augusta County, Virginia. Imboden's infantry rangers made guerrilla raids behind enemy lines. The most significant of their exploits was an 1863 raid into West Virginia during which they fought several skirmishes, cut off the Baltimore & Ohio Railroad, and brought back thousands of much-needed horses and cattle to the ARMY OF NORTHERN VIRGINIA. Later that same year Imboden captured the Union garrison of CHARLESTON, West Virginia, meriting commendation from Gen. ROBERT E. LEE.

IMINT |ˈimint| • *abbr.* imagery intelligence.

immediate air support • air support that cannot be planned in advance because it is requested in the midst of a battle.

immediate operational readiness • those operations directly related to the assumption of an alert or quick-reaction posture. Typical operations include strip alert, airborne alert/indoctrination, no-notice launch of an alert force, and the maintenance of missiles in an alert configuration.

Immelmann, Max (1890–1916) • German fighter pilot during WORLD WAR I who developed the 180° climbing turn that bears his name. This so-called **Immelmann turn**, or **Immelmann**, is an aerobatic maneuver consisting of a half loop followed by a half roll, resulting in reversal of direction and increased height. The maneuver is seen as the genesis of aerial tactical development.

immobilize • *v.* prevent (something or someone) from moving or operating as normal: *I want you to immobilize their vehicle.*

IMO • *abbr.* International Maritime Organization.

impact area • an area having designated boundaries within the limits of which all ordnance will detonate on impact.

impeller • *n.* **1** the rotating part of a centrifugal pump, compressor, or other machine designed to move a fluid by rotation. **2** a similar device turned by the flow of water past a ship's hull, used to measure speed or distance traveled.

Imperial Fleet • the entirety of the naval vessels of the Imperial Japanese Navy in the WORLD WAR II period. The Imperial Fleet included all naval units including combatant, transport, and auxiliary vessels, naval aviation units, and marines. The Imperial Fleet was divided administratively into a number of fleets, task forces, and special units which were controlled for the most part by the commander of the COMBINED JAPANESE FLEET.

imperialism • *n.* a policy of extending a country's power and influence through diplomacy or military force: *the struggle against Western imperialism.*

DERIVATIVES: **imperialistic** *adj.* **imperialistically** *adv.*

Imperial Japanese Navy • (**IJN**) a formidable well-trained, well-disciplined, and well-equipped naval force with a large number of capital ships, including a number of aircraft carriers and naval aircraft. The IJN struck the devastating blow against United States naval forces at PEARL HARBOR (1941) and supported the military expansion of the Japanese Empire in Asia and the Pacific during WORLD WAR II. Following the battle of the CORAL SEA in May 1942 and the U.S. victory the following month at MIDWAY, the Imperial Japanese Navy, hampered by a lack of oil reserves and other raw materials, was gradually reduced in size and effectiveness and by early 1945 was no longer a potent fighting force.

imperial overstretch • (of the Great Powers) phrase used by historian Paul Kennedy in his 1987 book *The Rise and Fall of the Great Pow-*

ers to describe the situation in which the leading nations of the world have found that their political, economic, and military capacity is inadequate to protect and fulfill their global interests and obligations.

implementation planning • operational planning (including the assignment of tasks to specific forces and planning for logistical support) for the conduct of a continuing operation, campaign, or war already decided upon.

implosion weapon • a weapon in which a small quantity of fissionable material has its volume suddenly reduced by compression so that it achieves supercritical mass and produces a nuclear explosion.

impregnable • *adj.* **1** (of a fortified position) unable to be captured or broken into: *an impregnable wall of solid sandstone.* **2** unable to be defeated or destroyed; unassailable: *the guerrillas found the citadel impregnable.*

DERIVATIVES: **impregnability** *n.* **impregnably** *adv.*

impress • *v.* **1** force (someone) to serve in an army or navy: *a number of Poles, impressed into the German army.* **2** commandeer (goods or equipment) for public service.

DERIVATIVES: **impressment** *n.*

Impressment Act • an 1863 act of the CONFEDERACY allowing its agents to seize food and property for the war effort, compensating the suppliers with below-market prices. It was subject to widespread abuse and fraud and contributed to divisions within the South.

inactive • *adj.* not immediately available for active service; not mobilized.

inactive aircraft inventory • aircraft placed in storage or bailment or on loan or lease outside the defense establishment and so unavailable to the military services.

Inactive National Guard • (**ING**) U.S. Army NATIONAL GUARD personnel in an inactive status, not in the SELECTED RESERVE, who are attached to a specific National Guard unit but do not participate in training activities.

In order for these personnel to remain members of the Inactive National Guard, they must muster once a year with their assigned unit. Like the INDIVIDUAL READY RESERVE, all members of the Inactive National Guard have legal, contractual obligations. Members of the Inactive National Guard may not train for retirement credit or pay and are not eligible for promotion.

inactive status • status of reserve members on an inactive status list of a reserve component or assigned to the INACTIVE NATIONAL GUARD.

inboard • *adv.* & *adj.* **1** within a ship, aircraft, or vehicle: *the spray was coming inboard now* | *the uncovered inboard engine.* **2** toward the center of a ship, aircraft, or vehicle: *move the clew inboard along the boom* | *the inboard ailerons on the wings were dead.* • *n.* **1** a boat's engine housed inside its hull. **2** a boat with such an engine.

incapacitating agent • an agent that produces temporary physiological or mental effects, or both, that will render individuals incapable of concerted effort in the performance of their assigned duties.

incendiary bomb • a bomb filled with a flammable substance, designed to shatter on impact and start a fire.

incendiary raid • an attack, usually by bomber aircraft, involving the delivery of incendiary bombs or devices with the intention of damaging enemy military installations or civilian areas by causing widespread fires.

incendiary shell • a canon or mortar projectile filled with a flammable substance, designed to shatter in the air or on impact and start a fire.

Inchon landing • (September 15, 1950) an amphibious operation during the KOREAN WAR led by Gen. DOUGLAS MACARTHUR which led to the securing of Seoul on September 28. Despite logistical challenges and hastily organized troops, a Marine battalion landed on nearby Wolmi-do Island and was followed by two Marine regiment landings against Inchon itself. With a five-to-one strength disadvantage, the 2,200 North Korean troops at Inchon were easily defeated. The march to SEOUL began the following day.

incident control point • a designated point close to a terrorist incident where crisis management forces will rendezvous and establish control capability before initiating a tactical reaction.

incidents • *n.* brief clashes or other military disturbances generally of a transitory nature and not involving protracted hostilities.

Incidents-at-Sea Treaty • see AGREEMENT ON THE PREVENTION OF INCIDENTS AT SEA.

inclination angle • see PITCH ANGLE.

inclinometer • *n.* a device for measuring the angle of inclination of something, especially from the horizontal.

in-country • *adj.* slang assigned to duty in a country outside the United States, especially Vietnam.

incursion • *n.* an invasion or attack, especially a sudden or brief one: *incursions into enemy territory.*

DERIVATIVES: **incursive** *adj.*

Independence Day • **1** (also called **Fourth of July**) a U.S. holiday observed every July 4 to commemorate the adoption by the Continental Congress of the DECLARATION OF INDEPENDENCE on July 4, 1776. Although observance of the holiday began in Philadelphia on July 8, 1776, the day was not made a legal holiday until 1941. Traditionally it is celebrated with parades, fireworks, patriotic speeches, and picnics. **2** a day celebrating the anniversary of national independence.

Indian Country • during the VIETNAM WAR, territory held by the VIETCONG. [The term alluded to the phrase used by 19th-century American cavalry soldiers to denote land occupied by Native Americans. Many Native American soldiers found the term offensive.]

Indian Removal Act • a law passed on May 28, 1830, to relocate eastern Indian tribes to land west of the Mississippi. Promoted by President ANDREW JACKSON in order to acquire land within state borders for white settlement, it guaranteed Indian rights to western land in the INDIAN TERRITORY, created by Congress in 1834. Many tribes resisted the army-enforced relocation, which resulted in incidents such as the SEMINOLE WARS and the TRAIL OF TEARS.

Indian Territory • the land west of the Mississippi River that was set aside by the Indian Intercourse Act of 1834 for relocated Native American tribes. The land, which included the area in present-day Oklahoma north and east of the Red River, Kansas, and Nebraska, came to be known as Indian Territory, though it was never an organized territory as others were. The term is also used more specifically to denote the area to which the FIVE CIVILIZED TRIBES (Choctaw, Creek, Seminole, Cherokee, and Chickasaw) were forced to move by treaties between 1820 and 1845. Other tribes moved there also, but each remained self-governing. The size of Indian Territory was reduced by the creation of Kansas and Nebraska territories in 1854, and its western half was ceded to the United States in 1866, eventually becoming the Territory of Oklahoma. Under the Dawes Act of 1887, individual landholdings were granted to Native Americans who renounced their tribal holdings, and the Dawes Commission, appointed in 1893, sought to reorganize Indian Territory by abolishing tribal land titles in favor of individual allotments. This effort succeeded in 1906. The next year Indian Territory and the Territory of Oklahoma were merged to create the state of Oklahoma.

indications • *n.* in intelligence usage, information in various degrees of evaluation, all of which bears on the intention of a potential enemy to adopt or reject a course of action.

indicator • *n.* in intelligence usage, an item of information that reflects the intention or capability of a potential enemy to adopt or reject a course of action.

indirect air support • all air support provided that does not immediately assist the land or naval forces in the tactical battle.

indirect fire • fire delivered on a target that is not itself used as a point of aim for the weapons or the director of the fire.

indirect-fire artillery • artillery capable of inflicting damage on a target that is not itself used as a point of aim for the weapon.

indirect illumination • battlefield illumination provided by employing searchlight or pyrotechnic illuminants using diffusion or reflection: **a** (**illumination by diffusion**) illumination of an area beneath and to the flanks of a slightly elevated searchlight or of pyrotechnic illuminants, by the light scattered from atmospheric particles. **b** (**illumination by reflection**) illumination of an area by reflecting light from low clouds.

Individual Ready Reserve • (**IRR**) a manpower pool consisting of individuals who have had some training and who have served previously in the Active Component or in the SELECTED RESERVE and have some period of their military service obligation remaining. Members may voluntarily participate in training for retirement points and promotion with or without pay.

Indochina • the peninsula of southeast Asia containing Burna (Myanamar), Thailand, Malaya, Laos, Cambodia, and Vietnam; especially, the part of this area consisting of Laos, Cambodia, and Vietnam, which was a French dependency from 1862 to 1954.

indoctrinate • *v.* teach (a person or group) to accept a set of beliefs uncritically.
DERIVATIVES: **indoctrination** *n.* **indoctrinator** *n.*

induced radiation • radiation produced as a result of exposure to radioactive materials, particularly the capture of neutrons.

induction • *n.* enlistment into military service.

Industrial College of the Armed Forces • a postgraduate joint senior service school at Fort McNair, Washington, D.C. It has been a school of the NATIONAL DEFENSE UNIVERSITY since 1976. It grants the degree of Master of Science in National Resource Strategy.

industrial espionage • actions directed toward the acquisition of information on industrial production facilities, techniques, or capabilities through clandestine operations.

industrial preparedness • the state of preparedness of industry to produce essential materiel to support the national military objectives.

in extremis |ˌin ek'strāmēs; ik'strēmis| • term used to describe a situation of such exceptional urgency that immediate action must be taken to minimize imminent loss of life or catastrophic degradation of the political or military situation.

INF • *abbr.* Intermediate-range Nuclear Forces.

infanteer • *n.* slang an infantryman.

infantry • *n.* soldiers marching or fighting on foot; foot soldiers collectively.

Infantry and Cavalry School • an army service school at FORT LEAVENWORTH, Kansas. Established in 1904 as the first year course of study offered by the General Service and Staff College, it traces its history back to 1882 when the SCHOOL OF APPLICATION FOR INFANTRY AND CAVALRY was established at Fort Leavenworth. It coexisted with the ARMY STAFF COLLEGE, the second year course of the General Service and Staff College, which Infantry and Cavalry School students competed to attend. In 1907 it was renamed the Army School of the Line and, after additional name changes, it became the U.S. ARMY COMMAND AND GENERAL STAFF COLLEGE in 1946.

infantry fighting vehicle • a tank.

infantryman • *n.* (pl. **-men**) a soldier belonging to an infantry regiment.

infiltration • *n.* **1** the movement through or into an area or territory occupied by either friendly or enemy troops or organizations. The movement is made, either by small groups or by individuals, at extended or irregular intervals. When used in connection with the enemy, it infers that contact is avoided. **2** in intelligence usage, the placing of an agent or other person in a target area in hostile territory. It usually involves crossing a frontier or other guarded line. Methods of infiltration are **black** (clandestine), **gray** (through a legal crossing point but under false documentation), and **white** (legal).

influence mine • a mine actuated by the effect of a target on some physical condition in the vicinity of the mine or on radiations emanating from the mine.

informant • *n.* **1** a person who, wittingly or unwittingly, provides information to an agent, a clandestine service, or the police. **2** in reporting, a person who has provided specific information and is cited as a source.

information superiority • having greater access to information of all types than an enemy and/or the ability to process and use such information faster than an enemy.

information system • the organized collection, processing, transmission, and dissemination of information, in accordance with defined procedures, whether automated or manual. This includes the entire infrastructure, organization, and components that collect, process, store, transmit, display, disseminate, and act on information.

information warfare • a form of conflict in which the objective is to capture, degrade, or destroy the enemy's means of gathering, analyzing, and distributing data, particularly data regarding the enemy's armed forces. Information warfare is normally conducted using computers and other electronic means.

Information Warfare Squadron • activated in 1995 by the U.S. Air Force, the 609th Information Warfare Squadron, located at Shaw AFB in South Carolina, is responsible for protecting important computer networks. The protection was to take the form of passwords and firewalls, as well as responding to intrusions into the network once they are detected. In the event of war, this squadron will deploy to protect any future air operations centers from informational attacks.

infowar • *n.* see INFORMATION WARFARE.

infrared • *adj.* **1** (of electromagnetic radiation) having a wavelength just greater than that of the red end of the visible light spectrum but less than that of microwaves. Infrared radiation has a wavelength from about 800 nm to 1 mm, and is emitted particularly by heated objects. **2** (of equipment or techniques) using or concerned with this radiation: *infrared cameras.* • *n.* the infrared region of the spectrum; infrared radiation.

infrared film • film carrying an emulsion especially sensitive to "near-infrared." Infrared film is used to photograph through haze, because of the penetrating power of infrared light; and in camouflage detection to distinguish between living vegetation and dead vegetation or artificial green pigment.

infrared imagery • the imagery produced as a result of sensing electromagnetic radiations emitted or reflected from a given target surface in the infrared position of the electromagnetic spectrum (approximately 0.72 to 1,000 microns).

infrared photography • photography employing an optical system and direct image recording on infrared film

infrastructure • *n.* the basic physical and organizational structures and facilities (e.g., buildings, roads, and power supplies) needed for the operation of a society or enterprise. DERIVATIVES: **infrastructural** *adj.*

ING • *abbr.* Inactive National Guard.

Ingersoll, Royal Eason (1883–1976) • career naval officer, born in Washington, D.C. As commander of the Atlantic Fleet during WORLD WAR II, Ingersoll effectively neutralized the German submarine menace, thereby making the NORMANDY landings (1944) possible. During WORLD WAR I he superintended the Navy Department's Communications Office and afterwards established the communications office at the Versailles peace conference (1918–19). Ingersoll, a full admiral, retired in 1946.

Ingersoll was the son of Rear Adm. ROYAL RODNEY INGERSOLL and the father of Lt. Royal Rodney Ingersoll II, who was killed on board the aircraft carrier *Hornet* at the BATTLE OF MIDWAY (1942).

Ingersoll, Royal Rodney (1847–1931) • career naval officer, born in Niles, Michigan. Ingersoll served as chief of staff of the GREAT WHITE FLEET, frequently acting as proxy for the ill commander in chief. During the voyage Ingersoll became a rear admiral. Ingersoll was an ordnance specialist who wrote several books on the subject and twice served as head of the ordnance department at the U.S. NAVAL ACADEMY. During WORLD WAR I he was called out of retirement to head a special naval ordnance board that advised the Navy Department on new gunnery inventions.

Ingraham, Prentiss (1843–1904) • adventurer, born in Adams County, Mississippi. Ingraham fought briefly for the CONFEDERACY during the CIVIL WAR but is known mainly as a soldier of fortune and writer. As a prolific writer of dime novel westerns, Ingraham helped shape the image of the cowboy in American popular culture and promoted the popular phenomenon of Buffalo Bill, about whom he began writing in 1876.

inhaul • *n.* a rope used to haul in the clew of a sail.

initial path sweeping • in naval mine warfare, initial sweeping to clear a path through a mined area dangerous to the minesweepers that will be following.

Initial Photo Interpretation Report • a first-phase interpretation report, subsequent to the JOINT TACTICAL AIR RECONNAISSANCE/SURVEILLANCE MISSION REPORT, presenting the results of the initial readout of new imagery to answer the specific requirements for which the mission was requested.

initial radiation • the radiation (essentially neutrons and gamma rays) resulting from a nuclear burst and emitted from the fireball within one minute after burst.

injury • *n.* a condition of bodily damage. Injuries include fractures, wounds, sprains, strains, dislocations, concussions, and compressions. Conditions resulting from extremes of temperature or prolonged exposure, as well as acute poisonings (except those due to contaminated food) resulting from exposure to a toxic or poisonous substance are also classed as injuries.

inland navigation • transportation by canals, rivers, and lakes.

In Min Gun • see NORTH KOREAN PEOPLE'S ARMY (NKPA).

Innes, James (1754–98) • Revolutionary army officer, born in Caroline County, Virginia. Innes fought in numerous actions, including the battle of GERMANTOWN (1777), and led militia forces against the invasion of Virginia by the British in 1781. Although Innes was in ill health by the mid 1790s, GEORGE WASHINGTON continued to call upon him to carry out special duties of national importance.

inshore • *adj.* **1** at sea but close to the shore: *both mackerel and bluefish have returned to inshore waters by now.* **2** used at sea but close to the shore: *an inshore lifeboat.* • *adv.* toward or closer to the shore.

PHRASES: **inshore of** nearer to shore than.

inshore patrol • a naval defense patrol operating generally within a naval defense coastal area and comprising all elements of harbor defenses, the coastal lookout system, patrol craft supporting bases, aircraft, and Coast Guard stations.

insignia • *n.* (pl. same or **insignias**) a badge or distinguishing mark of military rank, office, or membership of an organization; an official emblem: *a colonel's insignia.*

USAGE: **Insignia** is, in origin, a plural noun; its singular form is **insigne** but this is rarely used. In modern use, **insignia** takes the plural **insignia** or, occasionally, **insignias**; both are acceptable.

inspection • *n.* in arms control, the physical process of determining compliance with arms control measures.

inspector • *n.* **1** an official employed to ensure that official regulations are obeyed, especially in public services: *a prison inspector.* **2** a police officer ranking below a superintendent or police chief: [as title] *Inspector Simmons.*

inspector general • a staff officer responsible for conducting inspections and investigations.

installation • *n.* a grouping of facilities, located in the same vicinity, that support particular functions. Installations may be elements of a base.

Institute for Advanced Study • a private, academic, non-degree granting institution founded in 1930 in Princeton, New Jersey. Students are postdoctorate or senior scholars who conduct independent, intensive research through any of the institute's four schools.

It is not affiliated with any other academic institution but has an informal relationship with Princeton University.

instruction • *n.* **1** (often **instructions**) a direction or order: *he issued instructions to the sheriff | he was acting on my instructions.* **2** teaching; education: *the school offers personalized instruction in a variety of skills.*

DERIVATIVES: **instructional** *adj.*

instrument flight • a flight in which the path and attitude of the aircraft are controlled solely by reference to instruments.

insubordinate • *adj.* defiant of authority; disobedient to orders: *an insubordinate attitude.*

DERIVATIVES: **insubordinately** *adv.* **insubordination** *n.*

insurgency • *n.* an organized movement aimed at the overthrow of a constituted government through use of subversion and armed conflict.

insurgent • *adj.* **1** rising in active revolt: *alleged links with insurgent groups.* **2** of or relating to rebels. • *n.* a rebel or revolutionary.

insurrection • *n.* a violent uprising against an authority or government: *the insurrection was savagely put down.*

DERIVATIVES: **insurrectionary** *adj.* **insurrectionist** *n.* & *adj.*

Insurrectos (or **insurrectos**) • Filipino nationalists who fought against the Spanish and then against the United States in the Philippine Insurrection of 1899–1902.

Integrated Operational Nuclear Detection System • (**IONDS**) former name of the NUCLEAR DETONATION DETECTION SYSTEM (NDDS).

integrated warfare • the conduct of military operations in any combat environment wherein opposing forces employ nonconventional weapons in combination with conventional weapons.

intelligence • *n.* **1** the product resulting from the collection, processing, integration, analysis, evaluation, and interpretation of available information concerning foreign countries or areas. **2** information and knowledge about an adversary obtained through observation, investigation, analysis, or understanding.

Intelligence Authorization Acts • two acts passed in 1991 and 1992 to tighten legislative oversight over the CIA and to require prior notice for all covert intelligence actions. The act of December 4, 1992, amended the NATIONAL SECURITY ACT OF 1947 to authorize the CIA to collect foreign intelligence from human sources. Both were passed after the IRAN-CONTRA AFFAIR (1985–86), which revealed CIA violations of congressional restraints.

intelligence contingency funds • appropriated funds to be used for intelligence activities when the use of other funds is not applicable or would either jeopardize or impede the mission of the intelligence unit.

intelligence cycle • the steps by which information is converted into intelligence and made available to users. The five steps of the intelligence cycle are: planning and direction, collection, processing, production, and dissemination.

intelligence discipline • adherence to sound principles of intelligence production and dissemination as well as of security.

Intelligence Oversight Act • an act passed in 1980 under President JIMMY CARTER's administration to expand the role of Congress in monitoring covert operations. It required the heads of intelligence agencies to keep the congressional intelligence oversight committees informed of their activities. It also established detailed procedures for reporting covert actions to Congress.

Intelligence Reform Act • an act passed by Congress in 1980 to allow the CIA to receive presidential approval for covert operations before congressional oversight committee approval. Earlier restraints in the HUGHES-RYAN ACT of 1974 had prohibited presidential approval before congressional committee approval.

intelligence report • (**INTREP**) a specific report of information, usually on a single item, made at any level of command in tactical operations and disseminated as rapidly as possible in keeping with the timeliness of the information.

interallied • *adj.* of or relating to two or more states formally cooperating for military purposes.

Inter-American Treaty of Reciprocal Assistance • an agreement signed by the United States and twenty Latin American nations in September 1947, during the COLD WAR, to establish regional collective defense against Communist aggression. A pact permitted under Article 51 of the UNITED NATIONS Charter, it included the principle that an attack against one was considered an attack against all. Also known as the RIO TREATY.

intercept • *v.* obstruct (someone or something) so as to prevent them from continuing to a destination: *intelligence agencies intercepted a series of telephone calls.* • *n.* an act or instance of intercepting something: *he read the file of radio intercepts.*
DERIVATIVES: **interception** *n.* **interceptive** *adj.*

intercepting search • a type of search designed to intercept an enemy whose previous position is known and the limits of whose subsequent course and speed can be assumed.

interceptor • *n.* a fast aircraft for stopping or repelling hostile aircraft.

intercept point • the point to which an airborne vehicle is vectored or guided to complete an interception.

intercept receiver • a receiver designed to detect and provide visual and/or aural indication of electromagnetic emissions occurring within the particular portion of the electromagnetic spectrum to which it is tuned.

intercom • *n.* a telephone apparatus by means of which personnel can talk to each other within an aircraft, tank, ship, or activity.

intercommand exercise • an exercise involving two or more major NATO commanders and/or their subordinates.

intercontinental ballistic missile • (**ICBM**) a ballistic missile with a range capability from about 3,000 to 8,000 nautical miles.

interdict • *v.* **1** impede (an enemy force), especially by aerial bombing of lines of communication or supply. **2** intercept and prevent the movement of (a prohibited commodity or person): *the police established roadblocks throughout the country for interdicting drugs.*
DERIVATIVES: **interdiction** *n.*

interdiction fire • fire placed on an area or point to prevent the enemy from using the area or point.

interdiction mission • a military mission assigned to air, land, or sea forces, the purpose of which is to divert, disrupt, delay, or destroy the enemy's surface military potential before it can be used effectively against friendly forces.

interdictor |ˌintərˈdiktər| • *n.* an aircraft designed to interrupt enemy supply operations by aerial bombing.

Intermediate Force Planning Level • the force level established during Planning Force development to depict the buildup from the CURRENT FORCE to the Planning Force.

intermediate-range ballistic missile • a ballistic missile with a range capability from about 1,500 to 3,000 nautical miles.

Intermediate-range Nuclear Forces Treaty • (**INF Treaty**) an agreement signed on December 8, 1987, by President RONALD REAGAN and Soviet general secretary MIKHAIL GORBACHEV. Enacted on June 1, 1988, it called for the elimination of intermediate- and shorter-range missiles within three years of the treaty's entry into force and was the first arms control agreement to eliminate, not simply restrict, nuclear missile systems. Its provisions for on-site inspections led to the creation of the ON-SITE INSPECTION AGENCY, and its verification provisions have served as the model for subsequent agreements.

intern • *v.* |inˈtərn| confine (someone) as a prisoner, especially for political or military reasons: *the family was interned for the duration of the war as enemy aliens.*
DERIVATIVES: **internment** *n.*

internal radiation • nuclear radiation resulting from radioactive substances in the body.

international actual strength • the total number of military and civilian personnel currently filling international posts.

international atomic time • (**TAI**) the time reference scale established on the basis of atomic clock readings from various laboratories around the world.

international date line • an imaginary north-south line through the Pacific Ocean, adopted in 1884, to the east of which the date is a day earlier than it is to the west. It lies chiefly along longitude 180°, with diversions to pass around some island groups.

internationalism • *n.* the advocacy of cooperation and understanding between nations.
DERIVATIVES: **internationalist** *n.*

international logistics • the negotiating, planning, and implementation of supporting logistics arrangements between nations, their forces, and agencies. It includes the furnishing of logistic support (major end items, materiel, and/or services) to, or receiving logistic support from, one or more friendly foreign governments, international organizations, or military forces, with or without reimbursement. It also includes the planning and actions related to the intermeshing of a significant element, activity, or component of the military logistics systems or procedures of the United States with those of one or more foreign governments, international organizations, or military forces on a temporary or permanent basis. It includes planning and actions related to the utilization of U.S. logistics policies, systems, and/or procedures to meet requirements of one or more foreign governments, international organizations, or forces.

International Military Education and Training Program • a U.S. military training program for foreign military personnel and a limited number of civilians. Created in 1976, it is funded by foreign aid appropriations. Foreign governments receive grants for students to take courses in the United States at military training facilities, or, less frequently, for hosting U.S. instructors.

international military personnel • military persons assigned or appointed to authorized international military posts.

international military post • an international post authorized to be filled by a military person whose pay and allowances remain the responsibility of the parent nation.

International Military Tribunal • the organization authorized by the London Agreement (August 8, 1945) among Great Britain, the provisional government of France, the Soviet Union, and the United States to conduct the trials of those major Axis war criminals of WORLD WAR II whose offenses were not contained by a specific geographic location. It consisted of one member, plus an alternate, selected by each of the four nations, and its first session occurred on October 18, 1945.

International Military Tribunal for the Far East • the tribunal created to try the important Japanese leaders for WORLD WAR II war crimes. The nations that began sitting for the trials in May 1946 were the United States, Great Britain, Australia, the Netherlands, France, the Philippines, and China. There were eleven judges and no alternates, and the trials were held in two languages.

international post • a post, position, job, or billet that is authorized in a peacetime establishment or emergency establishment and that carries a specific international job description, whose incumbent is responsible to international authority.

International Stabilization Force • a group formed by the NORTH ATLANTIC TREATY ORGANIZATION (NATO), under the authority of the UNITED NATIONS, in December 1995, to remain in BOSNIA-HERZEGOVINA for one year as an implementation force. In December 1996, the U.N. SECURITY COUNCIL created the Stabilization Force when it became clear that a continuing international military presence was necessary. Made up of about 35,000 troops, the Force has rules of engagement to ensure that all warring factions comply with the DAYTON ACCORDS.

interoperability • *n.* **1** the ability of systems, units, or forces to provide services to and accept services from other systems, units, or forces and to use the services so exchanged to enable them to operate effectively together. **2** the condition achieved among communications-electronics systems or items of communications-electronics equipment when information or services can be exchanged directly and satisfactorily between them and/or their users.

interpretability • *n.* the suitability of imagery for interpretation with respect to answering adequately requirements on a given type of target in terms of quality and scale. Interpretability is rated as *poor* (imagery is unsuitable for interpretation to answer adequately requirements on a given type of target), *fair* (imagery is suitable for interpretation to answer requirements on a given type of target but with only average detail), *good* (imagery is suitable for interpretation to answer requirements on a given type of target in considerable detail), and *excellent* (imagery is suitable for interpretation to answer requirements on a given type of target in complete detail).

interrogation • *n.* systematic effort to procure information by direct questioning of a person under the control of the questioner.

interservice rivalry • the competition between military services (Army, Navy, Air Force, and Marines) for prestige, funding, and influence, particularly in the Congress.

Interstate Highway System • a federally funded American highway system resulting from the Highway Revenue Act of 1956. By the 1940s, heightened use of automobiles and success of smaller highways made it clear that the road system needed to be improved and expanded by a network of national roads. The interstate highway system was first approved by Congress in 1944, but because of WORLD WAR II it was delayed until 1956. A large-scale construction project, the highway system has had a profound impact on the economy, national defense, and lifestyle of Americans. The Act's expiration date of 1972 has been extended many times by Congress.

intervention • *n.* interference by a country in another's affairs: *the administration was reported to be considering military intervention.*

interview • *v.* to gather information from a person who is aware that information is being given although there is ignorance of the true connection and purposes of the interviewer. Generally overt unless the collector is other than what they purport to be.

interwar • *adj.* existing in the period between two wars, especially the two world wars (i.e., between 1918 and 1939).

Intolerable Acts • measures passed by the British Parliament in 1774 as a reprisal for American colonial resistance to the TEA ACT of 1773. The Protestant Colonists named the acts, which consisted of the COERCIVE ACTS and the QUEBEC ACT, and convened in the First Continental Congress in 1774 to oppose them.

INTREP • *abbr.* intelligence report.

Intruder • (**A-6**, **EA-6A**) a long-range, all-weather, turbojet, twin-engine, carrier-based aircraft designed for low-altitude attacks. It is equipped with an integrated attack-navigation and central computer system so that it can locate, track, and destroy small moving targets and large fixed targets. It carries both nuclear and non-nuclear weapons, SIDEWINDER, HARPOON, napalm, and all standard Navy rockets, and it can refuel in the air.

intruder operation • an offensive operation by day or night over enemy territory with the primary object of destroying enemy aircraft in the vicinity of their bases.

Invader • (**A-26**) a three-seat attack bomber first flown on July 10, 1942, and that went into action in Europe on November 19, 1944. It carried nearly twice the bomb load, exceeded every performance guarantee, and weighed 700 pounds less than required in the original specifications.

invest • *v.* archaic surround (a place) in order to besiege or blockade it: *Fort Pulaski was invested and captured.*

investigation • *n.* a duly authorized, systematized, detailed examination or inquiry to uncover facts and determine the truth of a matter. This may include collecting, processing, reporting, storing, recording, analyzing, evaluating, producing, and disseminating the authorized information.

inwale • *n.* a longitudinal structural piece on the inside of a boat; an internal gunwale.

IONDS • *abbr.* Integrated Operational Nuclear Detection System.

Iran-Contra Affair • an American political scandal of 1985–86, in which high-ranking members in the administration of President RONALD REAGAN arranged for the covert sale of arms to Iran and diverted the profits to fund the anti-Communist contras in NICARAGUA. The weapons were sold to the Iranian government in order to obtain the release of American hostages held in Lebanon by pro-Iranian terrorists. The actions of the administration first became publicly known in November 1986. Investigations by a presidentially appointed panel and a joint committee of Congress focused on whether or not Reagan knew about or had authorized the diversion, and whether Congress's constitutional foreign policy and budget prerogatives as well as U.S. laws had been violated. An independent counsel investigated the legality of third-country fund-raising for projects banned by Congress, as well as the obstruction of justice by administration officials. Congress ultimately found that there had been "secrecy, deception, and disdain for the law," but that President Reagan had not broken the law. Nearly a dozen senior administration officials and private citizens were convicted of crimes, but all convicted U.S. officials and those awaiting trial were pardoned in December 1992 by President GEORGE H. BUSH.

Iran-Iraq War • (1980–88) a major conflict between the two most potent military powers of the Middle East, the long and bloody Iran-Iraq War began on September 22, 1980, with the Iraqi invasion of Iran, then in revolutionary ferment following the overthrow of the Shah. Iraqi leader SADDAM HUSSEIN's forces met little resistance but soon outran their supply lines. Meanwhile, Iran mobilized to meet the threat, and by May 1982 Saddam Hussein had lost most of his initial gains and ordered a unilateral cease-fire and the withdrawal of Iraqi troops. Iran rejected the cease-fire and launched Operation RAMADAN, the first of several attempts to take the Iraqi port city of BASRA, on July 13, 1982. Thereafter the conflict settled into a vicious protracted battle for small territorial gains reminiscent of the trench warfare of WORLD WAR I. The struggle was notable for indiscriminate ballistic missile attacks on cities by both sides and the large-scale use of chemical weapons (primarily by the Iraqis). Both sides also attacked third-country oil tankers in the Persian Gulf. Ironically, Iraq was supported by KUWAIT and Saudi Arabia, both of which would be the target of Saddam Hussein's aggression only a few years later. Revolutionary Iran, having seized the U.S. embassy in Teheran, was estranged from its major supplier of weapons, parts, and ammunition and thus had to rely on mass infantry attacks rather than its once formidable armor and air forces. The end of the war came following a large-scale offensive by Iraq in April 1988. On July 18, 1988, Iran accepted U.N. Resolution 598 which called for an immediate cease-fire, and the war ended two days later when the Iraqi forces ceased operations. The war, which cost perhaps one million dead, half a million maimed, $228 billion in direct expenditures, and over $400 billion in damage to oil facilities and urban areas, produced little gain for either side. The Iraqis did gain control over the key Shatt-al-Arab waterway, but later surrendered it to Iran to ensure Iran's neutrality in the 1990–91 PERSIAN GULF WAR.

IRBM • *abbr.* intermediate-range ballistic missile.

iron | ˈīərn | • *n.* **1** (**irons**) fetters or handcuffs. **2** informal a handgun.

PHRASES: **in irons 1** having the feet or hands fettered. **2** (of a sailing vessel) stalled head to wind and unable to come about or tack either way.

iron Betsy • slang (also, **Brown Betsy, Brown Betty**) (WORLD WAR II) a rifle.

ORIGIN: The nickname may be a variant on Brown Bess, a musket.

ironclad • *n.* a 19th-century warship with armor plating.

Ironclad Oath • part of the 1865 Constitution of Missouri, it required that every teacher, voter, officeholder, attorney, clergyman, or juror take an oath that he had never, directly or indirectly, committed any of a long list of disloyal acts. It was designed to keep anti-slavery Republicans in control of the state government. The U.S. Supreme Court found the oath unconstitutional in 1867, but it remained a qualification for suffrage until 1870.

Iron Cross • German military decoration awarded for valor or exceptionally meritorious service. Awarded in several degrees (Grand Cross, Knight's Cross, Knight's Cross with Diamonds, etc.), the Iron Cross was established by the King Frederick William III of Prussia in 1813 but was discontinued after WORLD WAR II.

iron curtain • (usually **the Iron Curtain**) the notional barrier separating the former Soviet bloc and the West prior to the decline of communism that followed the political events in eastern Europe in 1989.

"Iron Curtain" speech • an address given by former British Prime Minister WINSTON CHURCHILL on March 5, 1946, at Westminster College in Fulton, Missouri. He named his speech "The Sinews of Peace" and called for an alliance against the spread of Soviet communism, which he believed had spread an "iron curtain" across Eastern Europe.

iron rations • a small emergency supply of food.

Ironsides • *n.* (**ironsides**) an ironclad.

Iron Triangle • **1** the nickname for a Communist stronghold near SAIGON during the VIETNAM WAR. The area was generally defined by the Saigon River on the southwest, the Thi Tinh River on the east, and a line extending from Ben Cat to Ben Suc on the Saigon River on the north. Saigon was only 12 miles (20 kilometers) away. **2** the nickname for an area in North Korea extending from Pyongyang in the north at the apex, to the bases at Chorwon on the west and Kumwha on the east. This area, a central staging point for North Korean troops, was strategic terrain that was hotly contested.

Iroquois |ˈirə,kwoi| • **1** a member of any of the powerful tribes of the Five Nations (the Mohawks, Oneidas, Onondagas, Cayugas, and Senecas) or a member of any of the other Iroquoian-speaking tribes (for example, the Cherokees, the Conestogas, the Eries, and the Wyandots). **2** (**UH-1**) a light helicopter with one rotor used to transport troops and cargo and also to support attack helicopters. Some versions of the Iroquois carry machine guns and light air-to-ground rockets. Also called HUEY.

Iroquois Confederacy |ˈirə,kwoi kənˈfedərəsē| • an alliance of the five most powerful Iroquois-speaking Indian tribes (the Mohawks, Oneidas, Onondagas, Cayugas, and Senecas, known as the Five Nations) formed before 1600 in what is now upstate New York. The Tuscaroras were added as the sixth nation of the Iroquois Confederacy in the 18th century. Although members of the Iroquois Confederacy fought on both sides in the FRENCH AND INDIAN WAR (1754–63), they generally favored the British.

IRR • *abbr.* Individual Ready Reserve.

irregular • *adj.* (of troops) not belonging to regular or established army units. • *n.* (usually **irregulars**) a member of an irregular military force.

irregular forces • armed individuals or groups who are not members of the regular armed forces, police, or other internal security forces.

Irvine, James (1735–1819) • Revolutionary army officer,born in Philadelphia, Pennsylvania. Innes was an officer in both the Pennsylvania militia and Continental army. Irvine commanded a brigade at the battle of GERMANTOWN (1777), and it was on his advice that Gen. GEORGE WASHINGTON took up winter quarters at VALLEY FORGE (1777–78). He was wounded and captured during a skirmish against British forces in 1777 and not released until 1781.

Irvine, William (1741–1804) • REVOLUTIONARY WAR officer in the Continental army, born near Enniskillem, Fermanagh County, Northern Ireland. Irvine was captured during the Canadian expedition (1776) and later fought at the battle of MONMOUTH (1778). Irvine was commander of the western military department from 1781 to 1783, resigning that same year. After the war he served as a representative from Pennsylvania in the U.S. House (1793–95) and led state troops during the WHISKEY REBELLION (1794) and the QUASI-WAR WITH FRANCE (1798).

Isherwood, Benjamin Franklin (1822–1915) • chief engineer in the Engineer Corps of the U.S. Navy (1849), engineer in chief of the U.S. Navy (1861), and first chief of the Bureau of Steam Engineering (1863–69), born in New York City. Isherwood's main achievement was the rapid design and construction of a steam-powered fleet for the CIVIL WAR. He had to provide a sufficient number of ships to blockade Confederate supply routes, a daunting task given the state of the navy in 1861. During the war Isherwood designed machinery for forty-six paddlewheel vessels and seventy-nine screw steamers. In 1862 he advocated building large, fast, heavily armed and armored ships, which were in construction from 1863 until after the war. He also conducted numerous experiments on marine engines to study the practical use of steam for power. Although his *Wampanoag* (1868) was the fastest ship in the world, Isherwood came under increasing criticism from civilian engineers, Congress, and naval officers who believed steam-powered vessels had too many drawbacks, and he was removed from office. He retired in 1884, after which he was made rear admiral.

isolationism • *n.* a policy of remaining apart from the political affairs of other countries. DERIVATIVES: **isolationist** *n.*

Italy, invasion of • (1943–45) the longest campaign by the Western ALLIES in WORLD WAR II. Following Italy's surrender in July 1943, JOSEF STALIN demanded opening a second front in the west. Because a cross-Channel invasion of France was not possible, Italy was an attractive alternative for the British, who wanted to stall the movement of German troops from Italy to France or the eastern front. The campaign was long stalemated after the initial invasion of SALERNO on September 9, 1943, before Rome was finally occupied on June 4, 1944. The final Allied offensive in Italy resulted in the surrender of all German forces on May 2, 1945. Allied casualties were 312,000 in this 602-day campaign, while German losses have been estimated at 434,646

Ivan • slang term for the individual Russian soldier and the military forces of Russia/the Soviet Union collectively.

Ives, Joseph Christmas (1828–68) • army officer in the corps of topographical engineers, born Christmas Day in New York City. Returning from an expedition up the Colorado River (1857–58), Ives and his fellow explorers passed through the Grand Canyon. (They are believed to be the first white men to set foot on its floor.) Ives was the engineer and architect of the Washington Monument (1859–60). When the CIVIL WAR broke out, he chose to serve as a captain of engineers with the Confederate forces—his wife was from the South, ROBERT E. LEE had been his commandant at WEST POINT, and JEFFERSON DAVIS, to whom he became aide-de-camp, was a personal friend.

Iwabuchi, Sanji (?-1945) • Japanese rear admiral during WORLD WAR II, in command of the naval forces in Manila in 1945. Iwabuchi sought to defend the city, which was surrounded by American forces, in the face of insuperable odds. He engaged the Americans in street-by-street fighting, with devastating consequences: the loss of 17,000 Japanese defenders (including Iwabuchi himself), 100,000 civilians, and more than 1,000 Americans.

Iwo Jima, Battle of • (February 1945) a battle during the western Pacific campaign in WORLD WAR II. When the Allied Forces PACIFIC FLEET commander was directed to occupy an island, Iwo Jima was the only significant one available. Working against a Japanese force of 21,000 men and 1,000 guns, the Allied advance was slow, and the island was only secured on March 26, 1945. By that time, 71,245 Marines had been put ashore, with 5,931 killed and 17,372 wounded. The costs to Japan have not been determined. The island then became an important emergency landing site for heavy bombers, with 2,251 of them landing on Iwo Jima.

Jj

J-1 • see GENERAL STAFF.

J-2 • see GENERAL STAFF.

J-3 • see GENERAL STAFF.

J-4 • see GENERAL STAFF.

J-5 • see GENERAL STAFF.

jack • *n.* a small version of a national flag flown at the bow of a vessel in harbor to indicate its nationality.

jackboot • *n.* **1** a large leather military boot reaching to the knee. **2** this used as a symbol of cruel or authoritarian behavior or rule: *a country **under the jackboot** of colonialism.* DERIVATIVES: **jackbooted** *adj.*

jacket • *n.* a metal casing for a bullet.

Jackson, Andrew (1767–1845) • U.S. Army major general and 7th president of the United States (1829–37), born in the Waxhaw Settlement, South Carolina. At the age of thirteen Jackson participated in the REVOLUTIONARY WAR, probably as a courier, and was captured by the British. He later settled in Tennessee, where he practiced law and eventually entered politics. In 1796 he was elected to represent the new state of Tennessee in the U.S. Congress. His legislative record there, and during a brief term in the Senate the following year, was undistinguished. He returned to Tennessee, where he engaged in land speculation and commercial trade. During the WAR OF 1812, Jackson, who had been elected major general of the Tennessee militia, proved himself an excellent general and military leader, earning the sobriquet "Old Hickory" from his soldiers. He crushed the Creek Indians, stripping them of their lands in present-day Alabama and Georgia. His subsequent checking of a British invasion of NEW ORLEANS (1815) made him a national hero. Jackson went on to defeat the Seminoles in Florida, a move that led to its acquisition from Spain. Elected to the Senate for the second time in 1823, he lost his first bid for the presidency in 1824, when the election was thrown into the House of Representatives, and JOHN QUINCY ADAMS emerged the victor. (Jackson had received both a popular and electoral plurality, but not the required electoral majority.) Preparatory to a second bid in 1828, Jackson and his friends formed an organization that became the DEMOCRATIC PARTY. Jackson's brand of democracy advocated equality of opportunity and belief in the sovereignty of the people. He was swept to victory. One blotch on Jackson's record was the INDIAN REMOVAL ACT, which called for the removal of the Cherokees to territory beyond the Mississippi, to an area that is now Oklahoma. The implementation of this measure in 1838—known as the TRAIL OF TEARS—is one of the greatest tragedies the United States has inflicted on a minority population.

Jackson was the first president to veto legislation for other than constitutional reasons, thereby expanding presidential power. He was known as a man with a mean and vicious temper whose outbursts frequently led him into duels and gunfights.

Jackson, Thomas Jonathan (1824–63) • Confederate general (known as "Stonewall"), born in Clarksburg, Virginia (now West Virginia). Jackson first gained notice with the victory at FIRST BULL RUN (1861). During the SHENANDOAH VALLEY CAMPAIGN (1862), he completely disrupted Federal operations throughout Virginia, bringing hope to the CONFEDERACY. His actions at SECOND BULL RUN (1862) made possible ROBERT E. LEE's victory and led to his being given corps command, which he performed admirably at FREDERICKSBURG (1862). At CHANCELLORSVILLE (1863) Jackson, who was pressing the attack after dark, was accidentally shot by his own men and died a few days later from complications of a resulting amputation. Prior to the CIVIL WAR, Jackson, a career soldier in the U.S. Army, had been promoted for gallant conduct during the MEXICAN WAR (1846–48).

Jackson was a devoted Presbyterian and Calvinist who believed that the more devout side would win the war. Jackson's sobriquet was reputedly given him at FIRST BULL RUN by Gen. Barnard E. Bee, who exhorted his faltering troops by shouting: "Look, men! There stands Jackson like a stone wall. Rally behind the Virginians!"

Jackson, William (1759–1828) • REVOLUTIONARY WAR officer with a South Carolina regiment, born in Cumberland County, England. He participated in the 1778 expedition into Florida and led a sortie during the British siege of CHARLESTON (1780). He later served as secretary of the Constitutional Convention (1787) and delivered the Constitution to Congress. From 1799 until his death Jackson served as secretary general of the SOCIETY OF THE CINCINNATI.

Jackson, William Hicks (1835–1903) • Confederate army officer and cavalry commander, born in Paris, Tennessee. Jackson gained a reputation as a bold and aggressive leader of mounted troops. He took part in the raid that destroyed ULYSSES S. GRANT's supply base in Mississippi (1862); in the peripheral combat of the VICKSBURG CAMPAIGN (1863); and in the ATLANTA CAMPAIGN (1864).

jackstaff • *n.* a short flagpole at a ship's bow, on which a jack is flown.

jackstay • *n.* a rope, bar, or batten placed along a ship's yard to bend the head of a square sail to.

Jack tar • Brit. informal, dated a sailor.

Jacob's ladder • a rope ladder with wooden rungs, especially for access to a ship up the side.

Jadwin, Edgar (1865–1931) • army officer and chief of engineers (1926–29), born in Honesdale, Pennsylvania. His Jadwin Plan formed the basis of flood control work on the lower Mississippi River. The result of an investigation he ordered following the disastrous floods of 1927, the plan called for complementing levees with dredging, controlled outlets, and revetment work. During WORLD WAR I Jadwin organized railway troop regiments, one of which he commanded. During the SPANISH-AMERICAN WAR (1898) he oversaw many municipal projects in Cuba, where he greatly improved sanitary conditions. Jadwin was made lieutenant general on his retirement in 1929.

Jagdpanzer • WORLD WAR II-era German tank destroyer. The Jagdpanzer IV (Sd. Kfz. 162) was mounted on the PANZER IV chassis, weighed just over 23 tons, and had a speed of 24 mph, a range of 124 miles, a 75 mm gun, and a crew of four. The Jagdpanzer VI ("Jagdtiger") was the most powerful armored vehicle to enter service in WORLD WAR II. It was mounted on a TIGER II chassis, weighed 70.5 tons, and had a speed of 23 mph, a cruising range of 105 miles, a 128 mm gun plus a machine gun, and a crew of six.

Jagdstaffeln • squadron-size units of German fighter aircraft which were employed to gain and maintain air superiority over the German lines in WORLD WAR I. The term was also used for LUFTWAFFE fighter elements in WORLD WAR II. [from the German meaning "hunting packs."]

Jahrah (**Al-Jahrah**) • an oasis town and governorate in central KUWAIT. Located about 30 miles (50 kilometers) west of KUWAIT CITY, Jahrah is the capital of the governorate and the agricultural center of the country. Jahrah covers about two-thirds of Kuwait, but except for the principal agricultural region it is sparsely populated desert.

jam • *v.* (**jammed, jamming**) make (a radio transmission) unintelligible by causing interference.

James, Army of the • see ARMY OF THE JAMES.

James, Daniel, Jr. (1920–78) • air force officer, born in Pensacola, Florida. James was the first black four-star general (1975), and served from the time of his promotion to that rank until shortly before his death as commander of the North American Air Defense Command (1975–78). As commander of the U.S. base in Libya when MUAMMAR GADDAFI revoked agreements on base rights (1969), he headed the delicate negotiations with the Libyans. James flew combat missions as a fighter pilot in the VIETNAM WAR (1966–67) and in the KOREAN WAR. During WORLD WAR II he was an instructor pilot for black pilot trainees in the U.S. ARMY AIR CORPS (1943–45).

janfu • *abbr.* slang joint Army-Navy foulup.

janissary |ˈjæniˌserē| (also **janizary** |ˌzerē|) • *n.* (pl. **-ies**) a devoted follower or supporter.

Japanese American Internment • the forced relocation of Japanese nationals and Japanese Americans in the United States to camps during WORLD WAR II. On February

19, 1942, the U.S. Army, acting under an order signed by President FRANKLIN D. ROOSEVELT (and ratified by Congress a month later), ordered nearly 120,000 Japanese nationals and Japanese Americans into internment camps located in the central regions of the United States. Lawsuits were subsequently filed by Japanese Americans who claimed that their civil rights as U.S. citizens had been violated. However, the U.S. Supreme Court steadfastly upheld the legality of the evacuations. In 1983, a team of attorneys reopened cases resulting from the internment policy because of findings that the government's lawyers had suppressed evidence and made false statements in their original presentation to the Supreme Court. Lower courts overturned two wartime convictions. In 1988, Congress provided for partial restitution payments of $20,000 to each of the 60,000 survivors of the internment camps.

Japanese Mobile Fleet • see COMBINED JAPANESE FLEET.

Japan, peace treaties with • three agreements negotiated by JOHN FOSTER DULLES, who was President HARRY S. TRUMAN's envoy, and Japanese Prime Minister Yoshida Shigeru. The agreements addressed the U.S. military presence in Japan and U.S. assistance and protection to Japan to contain the communist threat in Asia. The first was a multinational peace treaty signed in San Francisco on September 8, 1951, to end the U.S. occupation of Japan. On the same day, the United States and Japan signed a bilateral agreement to allow U.S. troops to remain indefinitely. On February 8, 1952 both parties signed another treaty to authorize U.S. military bases in Japan and OKINAWA. Tensions between the two countries led to the negotiation in 1960 of a new security agreement.

Japan, surrender of • on August 10, 1945, after the bombings of HIROSHIMA and NAGASAKI and the Soviet declaration of war against Japan, Japanese emperor HIROHITO issued a statement of surrender. President HARRY S. TRUMAN accepted Japan's surrender on August 15, 1945. The Japanese signed formal surrender documents at a ceremony on September 2, 1945, aboard the battleship USS *Missouri* in Tokyo Bay. It signified the ending of WORLD WAR II.

Japan, U.S. occupation of • U.S. occupation of Japan began in August 1945, at the end of WORLD WAR II, under the supervision of Gen. DOUGLAS MACARTHUR. Occupation was intended to demilitarize and to democratize. It included the implementation of a new constitution and the stabilization of Japan's economy and society. In September 1950, after the outbreak of the KOREAN WAR, the administration of President HARRY S. TRUMAN began negotiations to end the occupation. A peace treaty signed in September 1951 formally ended the occupation, effective April 1952.

JATO • *abbr.* jet-assisted take off; a disposable solid-fuel rocket that is used to give heavy military transport planes the impetus required for taking off from short airfields.

Jay, Fort • see FORT JAY.

jayhawker • *n.* **1** a guerrilla raider in Kansas during the CIVIL WAR. **2** any freebooting guerrilla.

Jay's Treaty • a treaty between the United States and Great Britain to regulate commerce and navigation. It corrected problems arising from violations of the TREATY OF PARIS of 1793.

JCS • *abbr.* Joint Chiefs of Staff, the chief military advisory body to the president of the United States.

Jedburgh Teams • the code name used by Britain and the United States for three-man special operations teams that worked with resistance units behind enemy lines during WORLD WAR II.

Jeep (jeep) • trademark a small sturdy all-purpose vehicle first mass-produced for use in the U.S. military in 1940. Made with the ruggedness of a truck and the speed and maneuverability of a light automobile, standard Jeeps could haul more than half a ton and travel easily over mud or rough terrain. In the 1980s, the larger HUMVEE replaced the Jeep for military use.

ORIGIN: WORLD WAR II: from the initials *GP*, standing for *general purpose*, influenced by 'Eugene the Jeep,' a creature of great resourcefulness and power in the *Popeye* comic strip.

Jefferson Barracks • a site in Missouri, 10 miles (16 km) south of St. Louis, that for a time was the largest military base in the United States. A U.S. Army infantry school was first established there in 1826. Among the soldiers stationed at the post were the future Confederate general ROBERT E. LEE and the future Union general and U.S. president ULYSSES S. GRANT. It served as a hospital center during the CIVIL WAR, and in 1898 it was a training center for volunteers for the SPANISH-AMERICAN WAR (1898). During WORLD WARS I and II, troops were inducted and mustered out there. The base was closed in 1946, but a national cemetery and a large military hospital still operate at the site.

Jefferson Proving Ground • (JPG) a proving ground in Indiana, constructed by the U.S. Army between 1940 and 1941 and closed in 1995. The grounds tested mainly conventional weapons and ammunition.

Jefferson, Thomas (1743–1826) • philosopher, author of the DECLARATION OF INDEPENDENCE, and 3rd president of the United States (1801–09), born in Albemarle County, Virginia. His political career began in 1769 when he was elected, Virginia's House of Burgesses, and he never resumed his earlier law practice. An early leader in the movement for American independence, Jefferson believed that Americans possessed the natural right to govern themselves. Jefferson was a classical scholar, author, and architect, who built his home, Monticello, and later designed the Virginia state capitol and the campus of the University of Virginia. His writing talents were already recognized at the Second Continental Congress (1775), and he was given the task of writing the document that would declare America's independence from Britain. Although the delegates later made many changes to the body of the work, it remains essentially Jefferson's. As a lawmaker in Virginia, Jefferson was responsible for the Statute of Religious Freedom, which greatly influenced the infant nation's church-state relationship. As governor of Virginia (1779–81), Jefferson was relatively ineffective, but his service in Congress (1783–84) was highly productive: he proposed legislation dealing with the decimal system of currency and wrote the legislation establishing the principle of creating new states as Americans moved west. As minister to France (1785–89) he sought to expand markets for America's agricultural surpluses. During his tenure as secretary of state (1790–93) under President GEORGE WASHINGTON, Jefferson worked toward settlement of Anglo-American issues left over from the war; expansion of American commerce; a strengthened alliance with France; freeing the West from European colonialism; and pacification of the Indians. He also sought to advance national interests by manipulating American neutrality in European conflicts. In 1796, after a brief retirement during which he pursued his intellectual and agrarian interests, Jefferson ran unsuccessfully for president, becoming JOHN ADAMS's vice president. In the next presidential election, Jefferson was victorious over Adams in a bitter contest that was decided by the House of Representatives (Jefferson and AARON BURR had tied). As president Jefferson sought to restore harmony to the nation and the government, which had been rent by strife between Federalists and Republicans. Jefferson's greatest presidential achievement, though of doubtful constitutionality, was the LOUISIANA PURCHASE (1803), which doubled the size of the country. He also planned the LEWIS AND CLARK EXPEDITION (1804-06). Jefferson's second term was less successful, marred by continued conflicts with Chief Justice John Marshall and with the question of American neutrality in the war between Britain and France. Eventually, his plan for a state university in Virginia was approved, and the University of Virginia was chartered in 1819. Jefferson was not only its architectural designer—he selected its faculty, determined its curriculum, and acquired its library.

Jefferson's library of about 6,000 volumes, which he sold to Congress in 1815, became the nucleus of the Library of Congress.

Jeffers, William Nicholson (1824–83) • career naval officer, born in Swedesboro, New Jersey. As chief of ordnance (1873–81), Jeffers was responsible for modernizing U.S.'s naval firepower prior to its use in the SPANISH-AMERICAN WAR (1898). Jeffers first joined the navy as a midshipman at the age of fifteen and later completed his training at the new U.S. NAVAL ACADEMY. After a decade of survey activities in Latin America, he saw duty in the CIVIL WAR, initially as skipper of several ships involved in blockade duties. Later he was assigned to shore duty, charged with improving ordnance.

Jeffreys, Herbert (?–1678) • royal governor of Virginia (1677), replacing WILLIAM BERKELEY after BACON'S REBELLION (1676).

Jellicoe, John R. (1859–1935) • admiral of the British Navy. He served in the First Peking Relief Expedition and the BOXER REBELLION (1900), and was the commander-in-Chief of the GRAND FLEET during the early part of WORLD WAR I. In that capacity he oversaw the blockade against Germany and commanded the fleet in the battle of JUTLAND.

Jenkins, Albert Gallatin (1830–64) • Confederate army officer, born in Cabell County, Virginia (now West Virginia). Jenkins was the leader of a cavalry unit that initially engaged in raids in western Virginia and across the Ohio River (1861–63). Later, when the brigade was attached to the ARMY OF NORTHERN VIRGINIA, the raids continued in Pennsylvania (1863) until the unit reached GETTYSBURG, where Jenkins was severely wounded. He died the following year from complications of a later wound, received in 1864.

Jenkins, Micah (1835–64) • Confederate army officer, born on Edisto Island, South Carolina. Jenkins saw action in several major battles of the CIVIL WAR, from FIRST BULL RUN (1861), through the SEVEN DAYS' CAMPAIGN (1862), SECOND BULL RUN (1862), FREDERICKSBURG (1862), CHICKAMAUGA (1863), and on up to the BATTLE OF THE WILDERNESS, during which he was struck by FRIENDLY FIRE and died a few hours later.

Jenkins's Ear, War of • see WAR OF JENKINS'S EAR.

Jenkins, Thornton Alexander (1811–93) • career naval officer, born in Orange County, Virginia. Jenkins served as chief of the BUREAU OF NAVIGATION (1865–69). He achieved a distinguished record during the CIVIL WAR as skipper of a number of ships engaged in action or blockade duty. He was Adm. DAVID FARRAGUT's flag captain on the USS *Mississippi* (1863) and skipper of the *Hartford* when it ran the guns of the Confederate bastions of PORT HUDSON (1863). At the battle of MOBILE BAY (1864) he commanded the 2nd Division under Farragut. Prior to the Civil War, Jenkins had participated in coastal surveys, seen service in the MEXICAN WAR (1846–48), and made a study of lighthouses (he drafted the law creating the U.S. Lighthouse Service).

Jennison, Charles R. (1834–84) • leader of the 7th Kansas Cavalry, born in Jefferson County, New York. The 7th Kansas Cavalry was formed at FORT LEAVENWORTH, Kansas, on October 28, 1861, during the CIVIL WAR. The unit was known as Jennison's JAYHAWKERS (see JAYHAWKERS) because its members committed looting, arson, and murder, terrorizing communities in Missouri. The regiment also took part in many severe military engagements during late 1861 and early 1862 in western Missouri. It moved to Humboldt, Kansas, on January 31, 1862. On March 26, 1862, the regiment was ordered to Lawrence,

Kansas, where Col. Jennison resigned. Later he took command of Fort Leavenworth.

Jerry • slang term for the individual German combatant and the German armed forces collectively in both World Wars. Used particularly by British troops, the nickname Jerry did not carry the derogatory connotation of other nicknames for the Germans such as "KRAUT" or "THE HUN."

jet • *n.* an aircraft powered by one or more jet engines.

jetfoil • *n.* a type of passenger-carrying hydrofoil.

jet lag • extreme tiredness and other physical effects felt by a person after a long flight across different time zones.

DERIVATIVES: **jet-lagged** *adj.*

jet pipe • the exhaust duct of a jet engine.

jet-propelled • *adj.* moved by jet propulsion.

jet propulsion • reaction propulsion in which the propulsion unit obtains oxygen from the air, as distinguished from rocket propulsion, in which the unit carries its own oxygen-producing material. In connection with aircraft propulsion, the term refers to a gasoline (or other fuel) turbine jet unit that discharges hot gas through a tail pipe and a nozzle that provides a thrust that propels the aircraft.

jetsam |ˈjetsəm| • *n.* unwanted material or goods that have been thrown overboard from a ship and washed ashore, especially material that has been discarded to lighten the vessel. Compare with FLOTSAM.

ORIGIN: late 16th century (as *jetson*): contraction of JETTISON.

jet stream • a narrow band of high-velocity wind in the upper troposphere or in the stratosphere.

jettison • *n.* the selective release of stores from an aircraft other than during a normal attack.

jetty • *n.* (pl. **-ies**) **1** a landing stage or small pier at which boats can dock or be moored. **2** a bridge or staircase used by passengers boarding an aircraft.

Jiang Jie Shi • see CHIANG KAI-SHEK.

jib • *n.* a triangular staysail set forward of the forwardmost mast.

jib boom • a spar run out forward as an extension of the bowsprit.

jibe • *v.* **1** change course by swinging a fore-and-aft sail across a following wind: *they jibed, and the boat turned over.* **2** swing (a sail or boom) across the wind in such a way. **3** (of a sail or boom) swing or be swung across the wind: (**jibing**) *the skipper was hit by a jibing boom.* • *n.* an act or instance of jibing.

jib sheet • a rope by which a jib is trimmed.

jock • *n.* informal a pilot or astronaut.

Joe One • code name for the explosion of the first Soviet atomic bomb (August 1949).

ORIGIN: from JOSEPH STALIN.

Joffre, Joseph Jacques Césaire (1852–1931) • French marshal, commander in chief of the French army on the WESTERN FRONT during WORLD WAR I , born in Rivesaltes. Joffre was known as "the Victor of the MARNE" for repulsing the German advance that threatened to capture Paris early in the conflict (1914), but his subsequent failure to break through the German lines, coupled with the German attack on VERDUN (1916), led to his being stripped of command and his consequent resignation (1916).

Johnny, Get Your Gun • a song written in 1886 by F. Belasco, a pseudonym used by Monroe H. Rosenfeld, who was a newspaper reporter, composer, and lyricist. It was adapted in 1917 by George M. Cohan as the popular WORLD WAR I song "OVER THERE."

Johnny Reb • slang term for the individual Confederate soldier and inhabitants of the CONFEDERACY collectively. Johnny Reb's Union counterpart was BILLY YANK.

Johns Hopkins University School of Advanced International Studies • see PAUL H. NITZE SCHOOL OF ADVANCED INTERNATIONAL STUDIES.

Johnson, Andrew (1808–75) • 17th president of the United States (1865–69) and the first president to be impeached, born in Raleigh, North Carolina. He later settled in Tennessee, where he twice served in the state house (elected 1835, 1839) and later in the senate (1841), establishing a reputation as a Jacksonian Democrat with a firm commitment to fiscal economy. He served in the U.S. House of Representatives for ten years (first elected 1843) and was twice elected governor of Tennessee (1853, 1855) before being sent to the U.S. Senate in 1857. Johnson was a firm defender of slavery who nonetheless opposed secession and remained loyal to the UNION, making him a traitor in the South and a hero in the North. Although he came to recognize the need for, and consequently support, emancipation, he never abandoned his racist prejudices. Johnson, a so-called war Democrat, was nominated for vice president on the Union ticket in 1864, sworn in in March 1865, and inaugurated as president six weeks later, following the assassination of ABRAHAM LINCOLN. His RECONSTRUCTION policies for dealing with the South after the war allowed for a resurgence of conservative power there, bringing him into conflict with the Republicans in Congress. Eventually the split became so great that Congress was able to override all his vetoes of more stringent Reconstruction legisla n. His dismissal of SECRETARY OF WAR EDWIN . ⌈. STANTON led to his impeachment by the House, on the grounds that he had violated the tenure of office act, as well as other tenuous charges (1868). The Senate failed to convict him, by one vote. During the remainder of his term in office, he had little power. The most significant achievement of his tenure was the purchase of Alaska (1867). After leaving office, Johnson returned to Tennessee, eventually again winning election to the Senate (1875) after two unsuccessful attempts.

Johnson was the only member of the U.S. Senate from a seceding state who remained loyal to the Union.

Johnson, Bushrod Rust (1817–80) • Confederate army officer, born near Morristown, Ohio. Johnson fought in several early battles of the CIVIL WAR, including FORT DONELSON,

SHILOH, and STONES RIVER (all 1862). At CHICKAMAUGA (1863) he led the breakthrough of the Union center. In the defense of RICHMOND (1864) his brigade repulsed a Union attack and protected a vital railroad from damage.

Johnson, Edward (1816–73) • Confederate army officer, born in Chesterfield County, Virginia. Johnson earned his nickname, "Old Alleghany," and his reputation early, winning a tough fight on a ridge of the Alleghany (Allegheny) Mountains in 1861. He commanded his division in the bitter fighting on CULP'S HILL at GETTYSBURG (1863). His career effectively ended when he was captured at SPOTSYLVANIA (1864), for though he was eventually exchanged, he was again captured soon thereafter and paroled only after the war's end.

Johnson was a colorful figure, known for his creative swearing and eccentric appearance.

Johnson, Harold Keith (1912–83) • U.S. Army general, born in Bowesmont, North Dakota. Johnson was chief of staff (1964–68) during a critical period in the VIETNAM WAR. His belief in the need for the rapid deployment of a large force brought him into conflict with President LYNDON B. JOHNSON and other civilian leaders, who favored a more gradual buildup. He also opposed the strategy of Gen. WILLIAM C. WESTMORELAND, commander of the U.S. forces in Vietnam. Johnson retired at the expiration of his term as chief of staff. During WORLD WAR II Johnson served as a battalion commander in the defense of the Bataan Peninsula and participated in the BATAAN DEATH MARCH (1942), following which he was imprisoned for the remainder of the war.

Johnson, Hugh Samuel (1882–1942) • army officer and legal specialist, born in Fort Scott, Kansas. Johnson developed and implemented the SELECTIVE SERVICE SYSTEM in 1917 during WORLD WAR I, for which he received the DISTINGUISHED SERVICE MEDAL. Johnson resigned from the military in 1919 and held several civilian positions before becoming one of the New Deal's top administrators under President FRANKLIN D. ROOSEVELT.

Johnson wrote two boys' adventure books and several short stories about military life that appeared in major magazines of the day.

Johnson, Louis Arthur (1891–1966) • secretary of defense (1949–50), born in Roanoke, Virginia. Johnson's tenure was marked by controversy and friction among the services, particularly the newly established (1947) U.S. Air Force and the Navy, as they competed for scarce funds during a period of budgetary retrenchment. He also differed with Secretary of State DEAN ACHESON on foreign policy, although they agreed on and recommended development of the hydrogen bomb. When the KOREAN WAR broke out in 1950, Johnson's budget cuts were seen as the cause of the nation's lack of military preparedness. Following further friction with President HARRY S. TRUMAN on matters relating to Gen. DOUGLAS MACARTHUR, Johnson resigned at the president's request. During WORLD WAR I, Johnson fought in France, attaining the rank of major; from 1932 to 1933, he served as national commander of the AMERICAN LEGION, which he had helped organize; and as assistant secretary of war (1937–40), he strongly pushed for preparedness.

Johnson, Lyndon Baines (1908–73) • 36th president of the United States (1963–69), born near Stonewall, Texas. Johnson's long political career began in 1932, when, after a brief stint as a secondary school teacher, he joined the Washington staff of a Texas congressman. In 1938 he was elected to the House of Representatives, where the political skills honed earlier were quickly recognized. He remained in the House until 1949, except for a brief tour of active duty in the navy during WORLD WAR II . During his single combat experience (1942), the mission came under heavy fire and he was awarded a SILVER STAR. In 1948 Johnson was elected to the Senate, becoming minority leader in 1953 and majority leader in 1955. His greatest achievement was getting the support of Southern Democrats for passage of the 1957 Civil Rights Act. After SPUTNIK brought concerns about national security and military readiness to the fore, Johnson chaired a special Senate Preparedness Subcommittee whose hearings gave him further national exposure. Chosen JOHN F. KENNEDY's running mate in 1960, Johnson found himself excluded from policy deliberations and decision-making during his years as vice president (1961–63). Assuming office after Kennedy's assassination (1963), Johnson returned to his role as master mover and doer. Declaring a war on poverty and outlining his vision of a Great Society, he backed an unprecedented series of bills extending the federal government's assistance to the poor. He won the 1964 election with more than 61 percent of the popular vote. He created the Office of Economic Opportunity to coordinate the many federal assistance programs, which varied in their success. Among the most successful were the Headstart programs for preschool children and the Medicare and Medicaid programs for the elderly. Johnson oversaw passage of civil rights legislation that had been stalled in the Congress during the Kennedy administration, but the VIETNAM WAR was to be his downfall. The bombing campaign and massive buildup or troops in 1965 that followed the GULF OF TONKIN incident (1964) marked a major escalation of the conflict and a change in the nature of the war. The TET OFFENSIVE early in 1968, an election year, further aggravated the protracted conflict. Two months later Johnson announced, in the same address, cessation of the bombing and his decision not to seek another term. Despite his achievements on the domestic front, he left office in disrepute, defeated by what had come to be called "Mr. Johnson's War."

Johnson, Opha Mae • the first female Marine. Johnson enlisted August 12, 1918, in order to "free a man to fight" in WORLD WAR I.

Johnson, Richard W. (1827–97) • Union army officer born near Smithland, Kentucky. Johnson failed to achieve distinction in any of his many encounters during the CIVIL WAR. His division was routed by Confederates at STONES RIVER (1862–63) and was responsible for turning a potential victory into a defeat at Pickett's Mill (1864) during the ATLANTA campaign. His troops performed adequately at CHICKAMAUGA (1863) and at CHATTANOOGA (1863); his command of a cavalry division during the defeat of Gen. JOHN B. HOOD in Tennessee (1864) was seen as little more than satisfactory.

Johnson, William (c. 1715–74) • born in Ireland, British colonial leader in America whose long experience with the IROQUOIS led to his becoming superintendent of Indian affairs north of the Ohio in 1756, during the FRENCH AND INDIAN WAR (1754–63).

Johnston, Albert Sidney (1803–62) • Confederate general, born in Washington, Kentucky. Johnston was in command of the vast lands stretching from the Appalachian Mountains to the INDIAN TERRITORY and was killed at SHILOH (1862). Before joining the Confederate forces, Johnston had a distinguished military career with the U.S. Army. A graduate of the U.S. MILITARY ACADEMY, he fought in the BLACK HAWK WAR (1832) before becoming active in the TEXAS WAR OF INDEPENDENCE (1836). He served as senior brigadier general of the Texas army. As Texas's secretary of war, he conducted the successful Cherokee campaigns of 1839. After a decade in civilian life, he returned to the military during the MEXICAN WAR (1846–48) and served with distinction at the battle of MONTERREY (1846). In 1857–58 he commanded an expedition against the Mormons in Utah, marching unopposed into Salt Lake City. Johnston resigned from the U.S. Army when Texas seceded.

Johnston was the father of WILLIAM PRESTON JOHNSTON, who wrote his biography.

Johnston, Joseph Eggleston (1807–91) • Confederate general, born near Farmville, Kentucky. Johnston commanded forces at HARPERS FERRY (1861), participated in action at FIRST BULL RUN (1861), and oversaw the defense of VICKSBURG (1863). He merited the disfavor of JEFFERSON DAVIS, who held him responsible for the fall of Vicksburg and the loss of excessive territory in his engagements with the forces of WILLIAM T. SHERMAN. Davis, with whom he had had a long-running feud, removed him from command, but six months later he was reappointed and placed in charge of Confederate forces in the Carolinas (1865). Forced to retreat in the face of advancing federal troops, Johnston eventually surrendered his army to Gen. William T. Sherman on April 26, 1865. After the war he served a single term as congressman from Virginia. Johnston was on the staff of Gen. WINFIELD SCOTT during both the Second SEMINOLE WAR (1836–37) and the MEXICAN WAR (1846–48). He also served as quartermaster general (1860–61) until resigning his commission to join the Confederate forces.

Johnston died from pneumonia contracted while serving as a pallbearer at the funeral of William T. Sherman.

Johnston, Peter (1763–1831) • Revolutionary war officer, born at Osborne's Landing on the James River, Virginia. Johnston was recognized for great courage in battle while serving with the cavalry legion of HENRY "LIGHT-HORSE HARRY" LEE, distinguishing himself at several battles, including that at GUILFORD COURT HOUSE (1781). He later served as captain of the Light Corps established by Gen. NATHANAEL GREENE.

He was the father of JOSEPH EGGLESTON JOHNSTON, a leading general in the Confederate army.

Johnston, William Preston (1831–99) • Confederate army officer with a Kentucky regiment, born in Louisville, Kentucky. Johnston became aide-de-camp to JEFFERSON DAVIS and saw action at the battles of SEVEN PINES (1862), COLD HARBOR (1864), and PETERSBURG (1864). After the war Johnston had a notable career in academia, as a department chairman at Washington College (later Washington and Lee University), as president of Louisiana State University, and as one of the founders of Tulane University.

joint • *adj.* a term used to describe activities, operations, etc., in which elements of two or more military departments participate.

Joint Army and Navy Munitions Board • a board established by letter of the Joint Board in June 1922, and approved by the Secretaries of War and the Navy, responsible for coordinating army and navy munitions procurement, stockpiling critical materials, making foreign purchases, and allocating machine tools during WORLD WAR II, and directly controlled by the president by military order in July 1939. Thereafter, it was made accountable to the Chairman of the War Board in 1942, then supervised by the JOINT CHIEFS OF STAFF in 1943. The Board was reconstituted by presidential order in 1945, and terminated by the NATIONAL SECURITY ACT of 1947, which established the Munitions Board.

Joint Chiefs of Staff • (**JCS** or **J.C.S.**) the primary military advisory group to the president of the United States, comprised of the chiefs of each of the armed forces—the Air Force, Army, Navy—and the commandant of the Marine Corps.

Joint Deployment Agency • an organization established in 1979 at MacDill Air Force Base, Florida, to coordinate mobilization and deployment plans, after a command post exercise revealed that military and civilian participants weren't communicating effectively.

joint doctrine • fundamental principles that guide the employment of forces of two or more Services in coordinated action toward a common objective. In the United States joint doctrine is developed and promulgated by the JOINT CHIEFS OF STAFF in coordination the various Services and the combatant (unified and specified) commands.

Joint Expeditionary Force • a combat force composed of all four of the U.S. armed forces: the Air Force, Army, Marine Corps, and Navy.

joint force • a general term applied to a force composed of significant elements, assigned or attached, of two or more military departments, operating under a single commander.

Joint Forces Command • see U.S. JOINT FORCES COMMAND.

joint intelligence • intelligence produced by elements of more than one Service of the same nation.

joint littoral warfare • combat operations conducted by integrated ground, sea, and air forces in coastal areas.

joint operations • integrated military operations involving forces drawn from two or more Services.

Joint Strategic Capabilities Plan • (**JSCP**) part of the United States joint strategic planning process developed in the 1950s, the JSCP was prepared each year by the JOINT CHIEFS OF STAFF and translated the strategic planning guidance issued by the NATIONAL SECURITY COUNCIL into a strategic global war plan for the following year.

Joint Strategic Objectives Plan • (**JSOP**) part of the United States joint strategic planning process developed in the 1950s, the JSOP was prepared each year by the JOINT CHIEFS OF STAFF and translated the strategic planning guidance issued by the NATIONAL SECURITY COUNCIL into a specific, integrated, strategic nuclear war plan for the coming four to six-year-time frame.

Joint Strategic Target Planning Staff • the joint U.S. Army-Navy-Air Force staff is located at Offutt Air Force Base, near Omaha, Nebraska, and is responsible for determining the targets for U.S. strategic (nuclear) weapons and the priority in which they should be engaged in the event of a general nuclear war. Established in August 1960, the Joint Strategic Target Planning Staff prepares the SINGLE INTEGRATED OPERATIONAL PLAN.

Joint Surveillance and Target Attack Radar System • (**JSTARS**) U.S. airborne radar system for surveying the situation deep in enemy territory in order to provide early warning of enemy concentrations and possible attacks and to target enemy forces for attack by deep-strike systems. JSTARS consists of a combination of synthetic aperture radar technology with advanced computer processing and is mounted on the EC-18C, a variant of the Boeing 707 aircraft.

Joint Tactical Air Reconnaissance/Surveillance Mission Report • (**MISREP**) a preliminary report of information from tactical reconnaissance aircrews rendered by designated debriefing personnel immediately after landing and dispatched prior to compilation of the INITIAL PHOTO INTERPRETATION REPORT. It provides a summary of the route conditions, observations, and aircrew actions and identifies sensor products.

joint tactics, techniques, and procedures • (**JTTP**) the actions and methods that implement joint doctrine and describe how forces will be employed in joint operations. They are promulgated by the chairman of the JOINT CHIEFS OF STAFF (JCS), in coordination with the combatant commands, the services, and the JCS.

joint task force • (**JTF**) a joint force that is constituted and so designated by the secretary of defense, a combatant commander, a subunified commander, or an existing joint task force commander.

joint training exercises • (**also joint training maneuvers**) maneuvers, command post exercises, or other training activities involving two or more services.

joint use agreement • a formal agreement for the sharing of a base, facility, or system by two or more military services.

Joint War Planning Committee • established in 1919 to assist the Joint Board, comprised of eight officers from the War Plans Division of the U.S. Army and the Navy. It was responsible for detailed study and investigation for policy decisions, the preparation of war plans, and all other matters involving joint actions of the Army and Navy. It made its reports and recommendations directly to the Joint Board.

Joint War Plans Committee • (**JWPC**) a WORLD WAR II committee of all the U.S. JOINT CHIEFS OF STAFF along with the British chiefs of staff.

jolly (also **jolly boat**) • *n.* (pl. **-ies**) a lapstraked ship's boat that is smaller than a cutter, typically hoisted at the stern of the ship.

Jolly Green Giant • (**CH/HH-3**) the U.S. Air Force version of the S-61 amphibious transport helicopter originally developed for the U.S. Navy. The Air Force initially used six of the Navy versions in 1962, which they designated CH-3A/Bs. In 1963, the first Ch-3C, with a rear fuselage ramp, flew, and, in 1966, when forty-one CH-3Cs were provided with more powerful engines, they were redesignated as CH-3Es. Still later, fifty CH-3Es were provided with armor, defensive armament, self-sealing fuel tanks, a rescue hoist, and the capability for inflight refueling so that they could engage in combat rescue missions. These fifty helicopters were then redesignated HH-3Es and used in VIETNAM, where they were nicknamed "Jolly Green Giant."

Jolly Roger • a pirate's flag with a white skull and crossbones on a black background.

Jomini, Antoine-Henri (1779–1869) • Swiss authority on the art of war who wrote histories of the campaigns of Frederick the Great and of Napoleon, in whose service he fought. In his writings he concentrated on the offensive strategy of NAPOLEONIC WARFARE. He has been mistakenly credited with influencing the generals of the CIVIL WAR, who were influenced by Napoleon.

Jonesboro, Battle of • a CIVIL WAR battle

fought on August 31 and September 1, 1864, in Jonesboro, Georgia, a rail hub whose control was essential for the CONFEDERACY to defend ATLANTA. Massive Union forces under Gen. WILLIAM T. SHERMAN overcame Confederate forces under Gens. PATRICK CLEBURN and WILLIAM HARDEE. The Union victory precipitated the evacuation of Atlanta.

Jones, Catesby ap Roger (1821–77) • Confederate naval officer and ordnance specialist, born in Fairfield, Virginia. Jones was in charge of the Confederate Foundry and Ordnance Works (1863–65). Jones personally supervised the manufacture of 200 heavy cannon and initialed each. When capture of the foundry appeared imminent, Jones had its machinery dismantled and transferred to steamboats and railroad cars. Before his assignment to the foundry, Jones had seen significant battle service. He was in command of the ironclad *Virginia*—the rebuilt USS *Merrimac,* on which he had been ordnance officer (1856) before resigning his commission to join the Confederate forces—during its battle with the *Monitor* (1862).

Jones, David (1921–) • air force chief of staff (1974–78) and chairman of the JOINT CHIEFS OF STAFF (1978–82), born in Aberdeen, South Carolina. As air force chief of staff, he reduced the size of the headquarters staff and reorganized the air force hierarchy. As chairman of the JCS, he proposed changes that increased the authority of the chairman and streamlined the chain of command, but these were enacted only well after his tenure, with the passage of the GOLDWATER-NICHOLS ACT in 1986. During his term of office he encountered congressional hostility because of his support of the SALT II agreement (1979) and the failed Iranian hostage rescue (1980).

Jones, John Paul (1747–92) • Naval officer and REVOLUTIONARY WAR hero; "Father of the American Navy." Born John Paul in Kirkbean Parish, Scotland, on July 6, 1747, Jones (a pseudonym he adopted in 1774) was apprenticed to an English shipbuilder at age thirteen and soon thereafter went to sea, making several voyages to the West Indies and the North American colonies. He obtained his first command in 1768 and soon gained a reputation as a formidable seaman and demanding leader. Living in Virginia at the beginning of the Revolution, he obtained a commission as a senior lieutenant in the Continental Navy in December 1775. Promoted to captain in October 1776, Jones was given command of the new eighteen-gun sloop *Ranger* in June 1777, and was ordered to sail it to France where he would assume command of a new frigate being built in Holland for the American navy. When delivery of the frigate was delayed, Jones retained command of the *Ranger* and raided British shipping off the European coast and coastal towns in England. Despite his success in *Ranger*, he was not offered a suitable ship to command, and was forced to accept an old, rotting East Indiaman, the forty-two-gun *Duc de Duras,* which he refitted and renamed the *Bonhomme Richard.* Jones sailed from the French port of L'Orient in *Bonhomme Richard* on August 14, 1779, to raid the English coasts, but had only limited success until, on September 23, 1779, he encountered a forty-one-ship British convoy escorted by the forty-four-gun HMS *Serapis* and HMS *Countess of Scarborough.* After a bloody battle, the *Serapis* and *Countess of Scarborough* were forced to surrender, although the *Bonhomme Richard* was heavily damaged and sank. After a forced delay in the Dutch port of Texel, during which he was forced to give up his prizes to the French, Jones returned to L'Orient in February 1780. He returned to the United States in February 1781 in command of the captured British sloop *Ariel.* Although Congress denied his promotion to rear admiral, he was given command of the first American ship of the line, the seventy-four-gun *America,* which was, however, soon turned over to France. After the REVOLUTIONARY WAR he returned to Europe to obtain the prize money owed him and his crew by the governments of France and Denmark. He eventually obtained satisfaction in France but not in Denmark. In 1787, he was again refused promotion to rear admiral by the U.S. Congress, although Congress ordered a gold medal struck in his honor, the only such honor granted an officer of the Continental Navy. In April 1788, Jones accepted a commission in the Russian imperial navy and subsequently commanded Russian naval forces against the Ottoman Empire in the Black Sea. In September 1790, he returned to Paris.

Joseph, Chief (1840–1904) • NEZ PERCÉ Indian chief, leader of a band in eastern Oregon who became embroiled in conflicts with U.S. armies. He is remembered for leading several hundred Nez Percé on a 1,000-mile trek toward refuge in Canada. The desperate bid ended in a battle at Bear Paw Mountain, where he surrendered in 1877 with the famous lines: "From where the sun now stands, I will fight no more forever." He spent the rest of his life on reservations in Oklahoma and Washington.

Jouett, James Edward (1826–1902) • career naval officer, born in Lexington, Kentucky. His reputation for battle prowess was assured during the CIVIL WAR when, at the blockade of Galveston (1861), he captured a Southern armed schooner, took the crew, and set fire to the ship. He later was given command of the fastest gunboat in the squadron, the *Metacomet,* which was charged with protecting Adm. DAVID FARRAGUT and his flagship during the battle of MOBILE BAY (1864). He performed brilliantly, capturing one Confederate gunboat and badly damaging another. Jouett was made rear admiral in 1880. In 1885 he led an expedition to Panama, where his actions resulted in the resumption of trans-isthmus rail traffic, which had been curtailed due to an insurrection in Colombia. Jones retired in 1890.

JPG • *abbr.* Jefferson Proving Ground.

JS-3 • the third in a series of WORLD WAR II

tanks named for JOSEPH STALIN, the JS-3 had all the advantages of the tanks that had preceded it, and it came to be regarded as the "mother" of modern tank designs. It was nicknamed "Pike" because of its narrow frontal aspect, which made it difficult to knock out. In Russia, these tanks were designated "-IS-1, -2," etc.

JSCP • *abbr.* Joint Strategic Capabilities Plan.

JSOP • *abbr.* Joint Strategic Objectives Plan.

JSTARS • *abbr.* Joint Surveillance and Target Attack Radar System.

JTF • *abbr.* joint task force.

JTTP • *abbr.* joint tactics, techniques, and procedures.

judge advocate • a lawyer who advises a court-martial on points of law and sums up the case.

judge advocate general • an officer in supreme control of the courts-martial in the armed forces.

jump • *v.* informal attack (someone) suddenly and unexpectedly. • *n.* an act of descending from an aircraft by parachute.

PHRASES: **jump ship** (of a sailor) leave the ship on which one is serving without having obtained permission to do so: *he jumped ship in Cape Town.*

▸**jump off** (of a military campaign) begin: *the air-attack phase will begin before the ground attack jumps off.*

jumper • *n.* **1** a loose outer jacket worn by sailors. **2** a rope made fast to keep a yard or mast from jumping.

jump jet • a jet that can take off and land vertically, or on a very short runway. Prototypes were developed in the early 1960s. The model most widely in use is the HARRIER AW-8.

jumpmaster • *n.* the assigned airborne-qualified individual who controls parachutists from when they enter the aircraft until they exit.

jump speed • the airspeed at which parachute troops can jump from an aircraft with comparative safety.

Junction City, Operation • (February–April 1967) a big push by Gen. WILLIAM C. WESTMORELAND to win the VIETNAM WAR. Since South Vietnamese forces were assigned primarily to occupation, pacification, and security duties, U.S. troops were able to conduct massive combat sweeps in order to locate and destroy the enemy.

Juneteenth • a festival that commemorates June 19, 1865, when slaves in Galveston, Texas, learned of the EMANCIPATION PROCLAMATION. The announcement that the war had ended and that the slaves were free was made by Maj. Gen. GORDON GRANGER, who had landed at Galveston with his regiment of Union soldiers. President ABRAHAM LINCOLN's proclamation was issued on January 1, 1863, but millions of slaves became aware of it only gradually, as Union forces moved through the South. The announcement in Galveston is considered the final execution of the proclamation. The word 'Juneteenth' is a blend of 'June' and 'nineteenth.' For decades Juneteenth existed predominantly as a local festival, but recently it has spread throughout the country as an expression of African-American culture. The day is associated traditionally with barbecuing and with themes of education and self-improvement. June 19 became an official Texas holiday in 1979.

Jungle Jim • nickname for the Air Force 4400th Combat Crew Training Squadron. They performed counterinsurgency and combat operations beginning in April 1961, in areas including Vietnam, Mali, and the PANAMA CANAL Zone.

jungle rot • slang trench foot.

jungle warfare • warfare conducted in a jungle environment and usually characterized by forbidding climate and terrain, the prevalence of tropical diseases, limited visibility and mobility, and difficult resupply and medical evacuation operations.

junior birdman • slang (in the VIETNAM WAR) a young pilot without combat experience.

junior technician • a rank in the RAF, above senior aircraftman or senior aircraftwoman and below corporal.

Junkers • a class of Prussian aristocratic landholders of the early 18th century who were the main sources of the officer corps of the Prussian military. In return for their service they were allowed to enserf peasants. They contributed substantially to ADOLF HITLER's rise to power.

Juno Beach • one of the five beaches along the NORMANDY coast of France that were invaded as part of the D-DAY assault of WORLD WAR II on June 6, 1944. Allied Forces, under U.S. Gen. DWIGHT D. EISENHOWER, assembled the largest invasion fleet in history in order to attack the northern coast of France and begin a push eastward toward NAZI Germany. Of the five code-named beaches (UTAH, OMAHA, GOLD, JUNO, and SWORD), all were taken easily except "Bloody Omaha."

junta |ˈhoontə; ˈjəntə| • *n.* a military or political group that rules a country after taking power by force: *the ruling military junta.*

Jupiter • an intermediate range ballistic missile originally put on an accelerated development schedule after the Soviet Union completed ICBM tests in 1957. It was later scrapped because of problems finding sites for the missiles in other countries.

jurisdiction • *n.* **1** the official power to make legal decisions and judgments: *federal courts had no* ***jurisdiction over*** *the case* | *the District of Columbia was placed under the* ***jurisdiction of*** *Congress.* **2** the extent of this power: *the claim will be* ***within the jurisdiction*** *of the industrial tribunal.* **3** the territory or sphere of activity over which the legal authority of a court or other institution extends.

DERIVATIVES: **jurisdictional** *adj.*

jury • *adj.* (of a mast or other fitting) improvised or temporary: *get that jury rudder fixed.*

jury-rigged • *adj.* (of a ship) having temporary makeshift rigging.

DERIVATIVES: **jury-rig** *v.*

jus ad bellum • the aspect of the international law of war which addresses the circumstances under which war may be resorted to in order to solve a dispute among nations.

jus in bello • the aspect of the international law of war which addresses the practices forbidden to belligerents during a war.

Just Cause, Operation • an operation launched by U.S. President GEORGE H. BUSH in December 1989 to capture PANAMANIAN DEFENSE FORCES chief Gen. MANUEL NORIEGA, who was accused of electoral fraud and drug trafficking. The invasion resulted in hundreds of U.S. casualties and possibly more than 1,000 Panamanian deaths; it also made clear that the United States would not easily sacrifice its historic prerogatives over Panama and the canal.

just war • an armed conflict in which one side enjoys the sanction of moral, religious, and legal tradition with respect to the initiation of the conflict, its conduct, and the objectives sought.

Jutland, Battle of • the largest naval battle in history, a confrontation between Germany's High Seas Fleet and Great Britain's GRAND FLEET in the summer of 1916. German Admiral Reinhard Scheer had planned an open sea encounter between his fleet and a squadron of British battle cruisers at Rosyth, in order to take advantage of their numerical advantage. The Germans laid their trap, but the signal for it to begin was intercepted and partially decoded by the British. The British Grand Fleet was on its way to the southwest Norwegian coast that same evening (May 30). On May 31, battle broke out between the British cruisers and the German fleet, with the British suffering greater initial losses. Once the British fleet arrived, though, British forces were able to perform a tactical maneuver (CROSSING THE T) to gain the advantage in firepower. Scheer was able to guide his fleet out, but in the process ended with the British fleet between his fleet and the German ports. Without further options, Scheer ordered his cruisers and destroyers to charge the British ships while the remaining battleships retreated. The British lost fourteen ships and 6,274 officers and men, while the Germans lost eleven ships and 2,545 officers and men. The battle was claimed by both sides as a victory.

JWPC • *abbr.* Joint War Plans Committee.

Kk

K-9 Corps • (WORLD WAR II) an American corps of dogs trained for military uses. See also M-DOGS.

The K-9 Corps was originally called D4D, Dogs for Defense.

Kai-shek, Chiang • see CHIANG KAI-SHEK.

Kalashnikov |kəˈläsнnə,kôf; -,kôv| • a type of rifle or submachine gun made in Russia, especially the AK-47 assault rifle.

ORIGIN: 1970s: named after Mikhail T. *Kalashnikov* (born 1919), the Russian designer of the weapons.

Kalb, Johann (1721–80) • Revolutionary war officer and mercenary, born in Hüttendorf, Bavaria. He was with GEORGE WASHINGTON during the winter encampment at VALLEY FORGE (1777–78), was second in command to the MARQUIS DE LAFAYETTE in the aborted invasion of Canada (1778), and was mortally wounded at the battle of CAMDEN (1780) when he persisted in assaults against superior British forces. Kalb had previously undertaken a secret mission to America on behalf of a French government minister hoping to enlist colonists in a war against the British (1767). Kalb had determined that despite their antipathy toward the British, colonists were too independent-minded to ally themselves with a foreign power. This independent-mindedness attracted him, and a decade later he returned to participate in their struggle.

kamikaze |,kämiˈkäzē| • (WORLD WAR II) (a crewman of) a Japanese aircraft, usually loaded with explosives, making a deliberate suicidal crash on an enemy target, such as an aircraft carrier; a suicide pilot or plane. Japan officially formed a kamikaze force in late 1944. During the American invasion of OKINAWA (April 1945), Japanese suicide sorties called *kikusui* ("floating chrysanthemums") sank thirty-six ships and damaged 368. An estimated 5,000 kamikaze pilots died in action.

In Japanese tradition, the kamikaze, or "divine wind," was a gale that destroyed the fleet of the invading Mongols in 1281.

Kanagawa, Treaty of • a treaty signed in Japan at Kanagawa, now part of Yokohama, on March 31, 1854, by Japan and the United States to allow U.S. ships into the ports of Hakodate and Shimoda, where a U.S. consul was also accepted. It was proposed by U.S. Commdore MATTHEW C. PERRY after he arrived in Tokyo Bay in July 1853 with a fleet of warships and demanded supplies. The Japanese accepted it when he returned in February 1854, and it was the first treaty Japan signed with a Western country.

Kane, Thomas Leiper (1822–83) • Union army officer, born in Philadelphia, Pennsylvania. Kane organized a volunteer Pennsylvania regiment and fought at CHANCELLORSVILLE (1863) and GETTYSBURG (1863) before resigning later that year because of poor health. Leiper is mainly known as, defender of the Mormons, though he himself never joined the Church of Jesus Christ of Latter-day Saints. Before the CIVIL WAR he had been involved in recruiting the Mormon Battalion for service in the MEXICAN WAR (1846–48) in return for government assistance.

Kansas-Nebraska Act • a bill creating the states of Kansas and Nebraska and allowing popular sovereignty in the territory. Passed on May 30, 1854, it was proposed by Illinois Democratic senator Stephen A. Douglas in an attempt to gain support from southern senators for his organization of the territory. It annulled the prohibition against slavery north of 36°30′ that was passed in the MISSOURI COMPROMISE.

Kasserine Pass, Battle of • a mountain pass where, on February 20, 1943, American forces attempted to force their way past Gen. ERWIN ROMMEL's German and Italian armored units as part of the Allied effort to expel the AXIS from North Africa. Rommel turned back the inexperienced American troops, but it proved to be his last major desert victory. Well-supplied Allied forces won back the pass despite heavy losses on February 25.

Kautz, August Valentine |kowts| (1828–95) • Union army cavalry officer, born in Ispringen, Baden (now Germany). Kautz saw action in the PENINSULAR CAMPAIGN (1862) and attained notoriety when, after the battle at Monticello, Kentucky (1863), his unit assisted in the capture of Confederate cavalry raider JOHN HUNT MORGAN. He was later involved in the Federal siege of Knoxville (1864).

Kautz was a member of the military court that tried and convicted those connected with the assassination of ABRAHAM LINCOLN.

KBE • *abbr.* (in the UK) Knight Commander of the Order of the British Empire.

KC-135 • see STRATOTANKER.

K-day • **1** In the PERSIAN GULF WAR, January 16, 1991, the day the ALLIED COALITION began the offensive. See OPERATION DESERT STORM. **2** the basic date for the introduction of a convoy system on any particular convoy lane.

Kearny, Philip (1814–62) • Union army officer, born in New York City. His division first saw combat during the 1862 PENINSULAR CAMPAIGN, helping to prevent disaster at the battle of WILLIAMSBURG. At SECOND BULL RUN (1862) he led the most successful Union attack of the battle but was killed during a subsequent encounter while retreating. He was considered one of the best division commanders in the Union army. Kearny had previously served on the staff of Gen. WINFIELD SCOTT, and during the MEXICAN WAR (1846–48) he lost an arm in the unsuccessful attack on MEXICO CITY (1847).

Kearny, Stephen Watts (1794–1848) • army officer, born in Newark, New Jersey. Kearny fought in the WAR OF 1812 and the MEXICAN WAR (1846–48), during which he was commander of the Army of the West. He easily subdued Santa Fe but encountered more difficulty with the subjugation of California, where he became entangled in squabbles with Cmd. ROBERT F. STOCKTON and JOHN C. FRÉMONT. Kearny is mainly remembered, however, for his intervening thirty-year career on the frontier. He participated in Yellowstone expeditions in 1819 and 1824 and conducted a major expedition along the OREGON TRAIL in 1845.

***Kearsarge*, USS** • (**CV-33**) an aircraft carrier, and the third U.S. ship to bear the name *Kearsarge*, this ship was commissioned in 1946 and engaged in training operations and maneuvers before joining the 6th Fleet in the Mediterranean. The *Kearsarge* operated along the Atlantic Coast and in the Caribbean until January 1950, when it left for the West Coast, where it was decommissioned in June 1950 for modernization that would enable it to handle new jet aircraft. Recommissioned in February 1952, the *Kearsarge* engaged in combat missions during the KOREAN WAR. While serving in KOREA the ship's classification was changed to CVA-33. In 1958, it was fitted out as an antisubmarine warfare support carrier and reclassified CVS-33.

The ship was recognized for the help it provided to the victims of a typhoon in Japan in 1959, and for rescuing four Russians 1,200 miles off WAKE ISLAND. In 1964 and 1965, the *Kearsarge* provided antisubmarine protection for the 7th Fleet during the VIETNAM WAR.

---

kedge • *v.* **1** move (a ship or boat) by hauling in a hawser attached to a small anchor dropped at some distance. **2** (of a ship or boat) move in such a way. • *n.* (also **kedge anchor**) a small anchor used for such a purpose.

keel • *n.* the longitudinal structure along the centerline at the bottom of a vessel's hull, on which the rest of the hull is built, in some vessels extended downward as a blade or ridge to increase stability. • *v.* (**keel over**) (of a boat or ship) turn over on its side; capsize.

DERIVATIVES: **keeled** *adj.* **keelless** *adj. a deep-keeled yacht.*

keelboat |ˈkēlˌbōt| • *n.* **1** a yacht built with a permanent keel rather than a centerboard. **2** a large, flat freight boat used on rivers.

keelson |ˈkēlsən| (also **kelson**) • *n.* a centerline structure running the length of a ship and fastening the timbers or plates of the floor to its keel.

Keifer, Joseph Warren (1836–1932) • |ˈkīfər| Union army officer, born near Spring, Ohio. Keifer enlisted in April 1861 and remained in the service throughout the war, though he was wounded four times. After the battles of PETERSBURG and RICHMOND (1864–65), he was promoted to major general. He returned to service during the

SPANISH-AMERICAN WAR (1898), commanding the forces that marched into Havana in 1899.

Keitt, Laurence Massillon |kĭt| (1824–64) • Confederate army officer with a South Carolina infantry regiment, born in Orangeburg District, South Carolina. He saw little fighting until 1864 at the battle of COLD HARBOR, where his inexperience and foolhardiness led to his death. As a politician in South Carolina, Keitt advocated secession as early as 1850.

Kell, John McIntosh (1823–1900) • Confederate naval officer, born near Darien, Georgia. Kell was executive officer of the *Alabama,* the South's most famous commerce raider, which not only took more than sixty prizes but also fought and sank a Union warship. It was itself eventually sunk in 1864 in an encounter with the USS *Kearsarge* off the coast of France, but both Kell and the commander were rescued.

Kell and three other passed midshipmen were courtmartialed, found guilty, and dismissed the service in 1848 when they refused an order they considered demeaning: lighting a candle to summon the relief attendant (usually done by ordinary midshipmen, not passed midshipmen). They were readmitted to the service in 1850.

Kellogg-Briand Treaty • an agreement signed in Paris on August 27, 1928, by fifteen nations to renounce war except for self-defense. Negotiated by U.S. Secretary of State Frank Kellogg and French foreign minister Aristide Briand in the aftermath of WORLD WAR I, it was politically ineffective although cited as grounds for the NUREMBERG TRIALS.

Kelly, Colin Purdie (1915–41) • bomber pilot in the U.S. ARMY AIR CORPS during WORLD WAR II, born in Madison, Florida. Kelly became that conflict's first American hero shortly after PEARL HARBOR (1941) when his plane, a B-17C FLYING FORTRESS, was shot down while on a mission to attack a Japanese convoy. Much of the myth surrounding Kelly has been shown to be based on erroneous information widely circulated at the time regarding the ship he supposedly hit. Nevertheless, his bravery in commanding his crew to bail out of the crippled craft while he attempted to regain control is unquestioned. His death served to crystallize the country's purpose in the early days of the war, as did the focus on his wife, the first official widow of the war. Kelly was posthumously awarded the DISTINGUISHED SERVICE MEDAL.

kelson • *n.* variant spelling of KEELSON.

Kemper, James Lawson (1823–95) • Confederate army officer, born in Madison County, Virginia. Kemper fought at FIRST BULL RUN (1861) and GETTYSBURG (1863). Wounds resulting from the latter battle prevented further combat duty, and he worked behind the lines in administrative posts for the remainder of the war. Following the war he became a leader in Virginia's Conservative party, advocating white supremacy. But as governor of the state (1874–78), he pursued surprisingly moderate policies. As a volunteer during the MEXICAN WAR (1846–48) Kemper had spent more than a year with the American occupation forces under the command of Gen. ZACHARY TAYLOR.

Kempff, Louis |kempf| (1841–1920) • career naval officer, born in Belleville, Illinois. Kempff first saw service early in the CIVIL WAR when he took part in the blockade of CHARLESTON, South Carolina, and the battle of PORT ROYAL (1861). He subsequently rose in rank and responsibility, and as a commanding officer took part in the bombardment of Servell's Point and the reoccupation of the former U.S. Navy yard at NORFOLK, VIRGINIA (1863). He was executive officer aboard the USS *Connecticut* on blockade duty off the coast of North Carolina (1863–64). Most significant was his role during the CHINA RELIEF EXPEDITION (1900), when he commanded the flotilla supporting U.S. ground operations. He distinguished himself during the fighting and by his refusal to join with allied forces in firing on fortresses at Ta-ku, a decision which some criticized but for which he was commended by the navy. Kempff, a rear admiral, retired in 1903 after forty-six years of continuous naval service.

Kennan, George F. (1904–) • diplomat, historian, and foreign policy critic, born in Milwaukee, Wisconsin. Kennan was the chief architect of America's COLD WAR strategy of CONTAINMENT. As director of the policy planning staff in the STATE DEPARTMENT (1947–50), Kennan advocated limiting the spread of Communism through political and economic measures, such as the MARSHALL PLAN, rather than by military means such as NATO and the HYDROGEN BOMB. He supported U.S. entry in the KOREAN WAR, but opposed crossing the 38th parallel. Although Kennan left the State Department in 1950 because of dissent with the policies of secretary of state DEAN ACHESON, he continued to have a strong, if less direct, influence on U.S. foreign policy through a career as a distinguished historian and commentator with a recognized expertise on the Soviet Union.

Kennedy, John Fitzgerald (1917–63) • 35th president of the United States (1961–63), born in Brookline, Massachusetts. During WORLD WAR II he served with the navy in the Pacific and was hailed as a hero when he helped rescue crew members after a Japanese destroyer sunk their PT BOAT (1943). In Kennedy's three terms in the U.S. House of Representatives (first elected 1946), his record was undistinguished. But his political career took off with his election to the Senate in 1952, in which the young Irish-Catholic candidate defeated the Yankee incumbent HENRY CABOT LODGE, scion of an old New England family. His 1956 book *Profiles in Courage* (reputedly ghostwritten) won a Pulitzer Prize. In 1958 he was reelected by a lopsided margin and, in preparation for a run for the presidency in 1960, began speaking out on issues related to national defense and an alleged MISSILE GAP with the Soviet Union. With LYNDON

B. JOHNSON as his running mate, Kennedy won a razor-thin popular plurality of about 100,000, although he had a comfortable margin in the electoral college (303 to 219), over his opponent RICHARD M. NIXON, becoming the first Roman Catholic president of the United States. The staff and cabinet he brought to Washington were known for their youth and vigor, particularly in contrast with the departing administration of DWIGHT D. EISENHOWER. His main concern was the Soviet Union and its increasing sphere of influence, which led to his involvement in South Vietnam and Cuba. He approved the ill-conceived BAY OF PIGS INVASION (1961). Tensions with the Soviets came to a head with the CUBAN MISSILE CRISIS (1962), when NIKITA KHRUSHCHEV backed down and removed Soviet missiles from the island, marking a key turning point in the COLD WAR. In 1963 the LIMITED TEST BAN TREATY was signed by the United States, Great Britain, and the Soviet Union. The situation in VIETNAM was heightened when Kennedy sent combat troops, under the guise of "advisers;" their number was doubled by November 1963. One success in his attempts to keep THIRD WORLD countries out of the Communist bloc was the creation of the Peace Corps, an organization of volunteers who worked at the grass-roots level in remote areas. His Alliance for Progress was less successful in its aim of establishing democratic policies in Latin America. Kennedy was assassinated in November 1963 while on a routine political trip to Texas to raise money for the upcoming campaign. His murder made him a martyr, and his image and that of his administration were romanticized by his friends and family. Despite later revelations that his personal life was less than impeccable, Kennedy remains a figure of reverence in the eyes of many Americans.

Kennesaw Mountain • site of a confrontation between Confederate Gen. JOSEPH E. JOHNSTON and Union Gen. WILLIAM T. SHERMAN during the CIVIL WAR. The battle occurred at Kennesaw Mountain, Cobb County, Georgia, 20 miles (32 kilometers) from Atlanta, on June 27, 1864. Johnston and his 18,000 troops set up fortifications near the mountain to defend against the attack of Sherman and his 16,000 troops. Union troops withdrew after suffering casualties of approximately 2,500, the greatest Union loss during the Georgia Campaign.

Kenney, George Churchill (1889–1977) • military aviator and commander, born in Yarmouth, Nova Scotia (his family was from Brookline, Massachusetts). His career spanned the evolution of U.S. air power from the Aviation Section of the Army SIGNAL CORPS, to the ARMY AIR CORPS (1925), to the independent U.S. Air Force (1947). As a fighter pilot during WORLD WAR I, Kenney flew seventy-five missions, shot down two German planes, and received a DISTINGUISHED SERVICE CROSS and a SILVER STAR. From 1942 until the end of WORLD WAR II (1945) Kenney held various commands in the Pacific, where he became known for his bold and innovative tactics, as well as his administrative skills. His command seized control of the skies from the Japanese and provided air support for numerous amphibious invasions of the ground forces led by Gen. DOUGLAS MACARTHUR. Kenney's most notable achievements included the destruction of the enemy armada in the battle of the BISMARCK SEA (1943), and daring airborne assaults in Northeast New Guinea (1943) and in the Philippines (1945).

Kentucky long rifle • a version of the PENNSYLVANIA LONG RIFLE that was built in Kentucky in the early 19th century.

kepi |'kāpē; 'kepē| • *n.* (pl. **kepis**) a French military cap with a horizontal bill.

Kernstown • site of a battle for the Union garrison at Winchester, near Kernstown, Virginia, that occurred on March 23, 1862, during the CIVIL WAR. This first battle at Kernstown was part of Maj. Gen. "STONEWALL" JACKSON's SHENANDOAH VALLEY CAMPAIGN. Jackson took the offensive, believing the Union forces to be approximately 3,000 in number, which would have been an even match for his 3,400 men. Instead, Union forces numbering 8,500 defeated Jackson. Despite the Confederate loss, Jackson's attack at Kernstown resulted in the diversion of Union forces to protect the approach to Washington, leaving RICHMOND, Virginia, vulnerable to capture.

Kershaw, Joseph Brevard (1822–94) • Confederate army officer, born in Camden, South Carolina. Kershaw saw the first shot of the CIVIL WAR and fought in increasingly important army leadership positions until the last days of the conflict. His volunteer regiment defended Morris Island in Charleston Harbor during the bombardment of FORT SUMTER (1861) and fought at FIRST BULL RUN (1861), in the PENINSULAR CAMPAIGN (1862), and at SECOND BULL RUN (1862). Kershaw led his brigade at ANTIETAM (1862) and FREDERICKSBURG (1862). He attained particular eminence for his actions at CHANCELLORSVILLE, GETTYSBURG, and CHICKAMAUGA (all 1863) and commanded a division at the BATTLE OF THE WILDERNESS, SPOTSYLVANIA, COLD HARBOR, and PETERSBURG (all 1864).

ketch • *n.* a two-masted, fore-and-aft-rigged sailboat with a mizzenmast stepped forward of the rudder and smaller than the foremast.

Kettle Hill, Battle of • the actual site of the charge by THEODORE ROOSEVELT's ROUGH RIDERS during the BATTLE OF SAN JUAN HILL (July 1, 1898). U.S. army regulars and dismounted cavalry advanced against heavy fire to dislodge Spanish soldiers entrenched at the top of Kettle Hill in Santiago, Cuba. Although only a small part of the advance, the press and public focused on the Rough Riders.

kevel • *n.* a large cleat fitted to the gunwale of a ship and used in belaying ropes.

Kevlar • trademark a synthetic fiber of high tensile strength used as a reinforcing agent for helmets and body armor.

Kevlar helmet • (in the PERSIAN GULF WAR) a standard issue high-tech helmet made of Kevlar. Also called **K-pot, bone dome.**

key • *n.* **1** an explanatory list of symbols used in a map, table, etc. **2** a word or system for solving a cipher or code.
DERIVATIVES: **keyed** *adj.* **keyer** *n.* **keyless** *adj.*

Keyes, Erasmus Darwin (1810–95) • Union army officer, born in Brimfield, Massachusetts. Keyes commanded a brigade at FIRST BULL RUN (1861) and was later a corps commander in the ARMY OF THE POTOMAC. Later accused of lack of aggressiveness, Keyes was transferred to administrative duties in 1863 and resigned his commission the following year. Before the CIVIL WAR Keyes had served as aide-de-camp to Gen. WINFIELD SCOTT (1837–41). During the 1850s he was stationed in the Pacific Northwest and involved in combat with the NATIVE AMERICANS of the area.

Keyhole • unmanned U.S. satellites operated by the CENTRAL INTELLIGENCE AGENCY from 1960 onward. The first satellite, KH-1 (-Keyhole-1), was used for surveillance of the Soviet Union from space. The early KH satellites used film, which was returned to Earth in capsules. KH-11s, developed in 1976, use an electro-optical system similar to television, which can transmit signals to a relay satellite, which are then received by a station at FORT BELVOIR, Virginia. Advanced KH-11s have infrared capability for night imaging. Today satellites are used to view areas of the world for signs of ballistic missiles, development of chemical or nuclear weapons, and drug production, among other things. The newest satellites can resolve details as small as a few yards.

key point • a concentrated site or installation, the destruction or capture of which would seriously affect the war effort or the success of operations.

Key West Agreement • a 1948 provision that allowed members of the JOINT CHIEFS OF STAFF to serve as direct executive agents for unified commands. This authority was abolished by Congress in a 1953 amendment to the NATIONAL SECURITY ACT.

KGB • the state security police (1954–91) of the former USSR with responsibility for external espionage, internal counterintelligence, and internal "crimes against the state."
ORIGIN: Russian, abbreviation of *Komitet gosudarstvennoĭ bezopasnosti* 'Committee of State Security.'

KH-11 spy satellite • (**Kennan**) an older U.S. digital readout and imaging photographic reconnaissance satellite used to produce real-time images of enemy civilian and military installations.

Khafji, Battle of, |ˈkäfjē| • (January 29–31, 1991) the only major offensive during the PERSIAN GULF WAR. Iraqi troops attacked the Saudi gulf city, Ra's Al Khafji, located 8 miles south of the KUWAITI border. Iraqis held the city for shortly more than a day, but American air attacks and ground offensives led by combined Arab forces retook the city by January 31.

khaki • *n.* (pl. **khakis**) **1** a textile fabric of a dull brownish-yellow color, in particular a strong cotton fabric used in military clothing. **2** (**khakis**) clothing, especially pants, of this fabric and color.
ORIGIN: mid 19th century: from an Urdu word meaning 'dust-colored.'

Khe Sanh, Siege of • a siege of a remote hilltop outpost in the NW corner of South Vietnam from January 20–April 7, 1968. 30–40,000 North Vietnamese Army forces surrounded 6,000 U.S. Marines and South Vietnamese regulars in one of the VIETNAM WAR's largest setpiece battles. Although U.S. and ARVN forces were relieved in April by OPERATION PEGASUS, the North Vietnamese declared it a victory because the defenders evacuated on July 6.

Khmer Rouge • a communist guerrilla organization which opposed the Cambodian government in the 1960s and waged a civil war from 1970, taking power in 1975. Under POL POT the Khmer Rouge undertook a forced reconstruction of Cambodian society, involving mass deportations from the towns to the countryside and mass executions. More than 2 million died before the regime was overthrown by the Vietnamese in 1979. Khmer Rouge forces have continued a program of guerrilla warfare from bases in Thailand.

Khrushchev, Nikita Sergeyevich (1894–1971) • first secretary of the Communist Party of the Soviet Union (1953–64) and premier of the Soviet Union (1958–64) during a crucial period of the COLD WAR. Despite his strong attacks on capitalism, Khrushchev pursued a policy of peaceful coexistence with the West. A 1959 visit to the United States and meeting with President DWIGHT D. EISENHOWER improved U.S.-USSR relations considerably. But his attempts in 1962 to build missile bases in Cuba brought the two nations to the brink of nuclear war (CUBAN MISSILE CRISIS).

KIA • *abbr.* killed in action.

kicking strap • a rope lanyard fixed to a boom to prevent it from rising.

Kieft's War • (also known as **Wappinger War**) (1643–45) fighting led by Director-General of New Netherlands WILLIAM KIEFT in which Dutch colonists killed over 100 Indians in Pavonia (now Jersey City) in February 1643. This touched off two years of fighting between Indians and colonists resulting in over 1,500 casualties, and a further two years of sporadic fighting until PETER STUYVESANT replaced Kieft in 1647.

Kieft, Willem (1597–1647) • born in Amsterdam, director of New Netherland (1638–47), an American colony of the Dutch West India Company. His dictatorial policies, particularly in relation to the local Indian tribes, led to the Dutch-Indian War (1640–45) and a brutal massacre of Weckquaskee Indians (1643). He ruled by decree and effectively thwarted colonists' attempts to establish a more representative government. Because of numerous complaints, the West India Company recalled him in 1647. He was lost at sea when the ship returning him sank en route.

kill • *v.* **1** cause the death of (a person, animal, or other living thing): *the casualty report listed three killed, thirteen wounded.* **2** put an end to or cause the failure or defeat of (something): *the committee voted to kill the project.* • *n.* informal an act of destroying or disabling an enemy aircraft, submarine, tank, etc.

PHRASES: **go** (or **move in** or **close in**) **for the kill** take decisive action, often ruthlessly, to turn a situation to one's advantage.

killed in action • (**KIA**) a casualty category applicable to a hostile casualty (other than the victim of a terrorist activity) who is killed outright or who dies as a result of wounds or other injuries before reaching a medical treatment facility.

Killer Bee • slang F-16, especially when used as a bomber. See FIGHTING FALCON.

Killer, Operation • the third of five offensives launched by U.N. forces in early 1951 during the KOREAN WAR. The success of these offensives led President HARRY S. TRUMAN to invite the Communists to negotiate a cease fire. Gen. DOUGLAS MACARTHUR, however, broadcast an ultimatum to the enemy commander that undermined the president's plan. After Congressman Joseph Martin released a letter from MacArthur in which the general repeated his criticism of the administration, Truman began the process which was to end with MacArthur being relieved from command on April 11, 1951.

kill-fire • *n.* slang (in the VIETNAM WAR) an assault of (usually automatic) gunfire that leaves no enemy alive to shoot back.

killick • *n.* **1** a heavy stone used by small craft as an anchor. **2** any anchor, especially a small one.

killing zone • an area in which a commander plans to force the enemy to concentrate so as to destroy the enemy with conventional weapons or the tactical employment of nuclear weapons.

kill probability • a measure of the probability of destroying a target.

kill ratio • the proportion of casualties on each side in a military action.

kill zone (also **killing zone**) • **1** the area of a military engagement with a high concentration of fatalities. **2** the area of the human body where entry of a projectile would kill, especially as indicated on a target for shooting practice.

kiloton • *n.* a measurement of the yield of a nuclear weapon equivalent to the explosion of 1,000 tons of trinitrotoluene (TNT).

kiloton weapon • a nuclear weapon, the yield of which is measured in terms of thousands of tons of trinitrotoluene (TNT) explosive equivalents, producing yields from 1 to 999 kilotons.

Kilpatrick, Hugh Judson (1836–81) • Union army officer, born in Deckertown (now Sussex), New Jersey. Kilpatrick was a cavalry leader in several engagements of the CIVIL WAR. As a division commander his encounter with Gen. J.E.B. STUART contributed to the Confederate cavalry's late arrival at GETTYSBURG (1863). Until early 1864 he took part in all major cavalry actions of the ARMY OF THE POTOMAC, and later that year he commanded a division of the ARMY OF THE CUMBERLAND in the invasion of Georgia.

Kilpatrick was called "Kil-Cavalry" because he wore out his horses and his men.

Kilroy • a mythical person, popularized by American servicemen in WORLD WAR II, who left such inscriptions as "Kilroy was here" on walls all over the world.

ORIGIN: of the many unverifiable accounts of the source of the term, one claims that James J. *Kilroy* of Halifax, Massachusetts, a shipyard employee, wrote "Kilroy was here" on sections of warships after inspection; the phrase is said to have been reproduced by shipyard workers who entered the armed services.

Kimball, Nathan (1823?–98) • Union army officer, born in Fredericksburg, Indiana. Kimball assumed division command in an 1862 battle with Gen. STONEWALL JACKSON, checking his advance, driving him from the field, and inflicting hundreds of casualties on the Confederates. He again distinguished himself at FREDERICKSBURG (1862), where he was badly wounded. His skill in directing his men at the battle of PEACHTREE CREEK (1864) led to his being given a division; he subsequently participated in the battles of FRANKLIN and NASHVILLE (1864). After the war Kimball was active in civil and political service and in veterans' affairs, helping to organize the GRAND ARMY OF THE REPUBLIC in Indiana. He served two terms as state treasurer and in 1872 was elected to the state legislature. In 1873 President ULYSSES S. GRANT appointed him surveyor general of Utah.

Kimmel, Husband Edward (1882–1958) • U.S. Navy rear admiral, born in Henderson, Kentucky. Kimmel was commander in chief of the U.S. PACIFIC FLEET on Oahu at the time of the attack on PEARL HARBOR (1941). In 1942 a presidential commission headed by the chief justice of the Supreme Court found Kimmel guilty of dereliction of duty on the grounds that he had been given advance warnings of a possible attack and imminent war, yet failed to institute adequate defense measures, thus making possible the effectiveness of the Japanese attack. Kimmel, who had been relieved of his command following the attack, was then forced into retirement. A later Congressional inquiry considered him guilty of errors in judgment rather than dereliction of duty. He was never court-martialed.

King, Ernest J. (1878–1956) • U.S. Navy admiral, born in Lorain, Ohio. King was commander in chief of the U.S. Fleet (1941–45) and chief of naval operations (1942–45). In these two capacities, King had authority over all aspects of the navy and its operations during WORLD WAR II. As a member of the JOINT CHIEFS OF STAFF, he worked with the British chiefs of staff on the ANGLO-AMERICAN COMBINED CHIEFS OF STAFF to plan the global strategy of the war. Before U.S. entry into the war with the attack on PEARL HARBOR (1941), King had been commander in chief of the Atlantic Fleet, responsible for protecting vital supplies being sent to the ALLIES. King was made fleet admiral, a five-star rank, in 1944.

King George's War • (1744–48) a precursor to the FRENCH AND INDIAN WAR (1754–63), and an outgrowth of British and French antagonisms in the WAR OF THE AUSTRIAN SUCCESSION (1740–48). British colonists named the sporadic conflicts with their French counterparts in Canada after the English sovereign. Its most notable event, the New Englanders' capture of Fort LOUISBOURG on Cape Breton Island on June 17, 1745, was negated when the PEACE OF AIX-LA-CHAPELLE returned the fort to French control. See also KING WILLIAM'S WAR.

King Philip • see METACOM.

King Philip's War • (1675–77) first large-scale military action in the American colonies that began in Plymouth Colony and spread throughout New England. It pitted various Indian tribes against New England colonists and their Indian allies. Marked by heavy slaughter on both sides (including women and children), the war cost thousands of lives, including 500 colonial soldiers.

King, Rufus (1814–76) • Union army officer, born in New York City. King was a brigade then division commander whose reputation was scarred by his actions at SECOND BULL RUN (1862). Rather than hold his position when attacked by the forces of Gen. THOMAS "STONEWALL" JACKSON while proceeding, as ordered, toward Centreville, Virginia, King retreated toward Manassas Junction. Although he had never received the orders to hold his position, he made a handy scapegoat after the Union defeat. A court of inquiry reprimanded him for disobedience of orders and dereliction of duty. King never held another combat post, and resigned his commission in 1863. King's participation in the CIVIL WAR interrupted his post as minister to the Papal States (1861–68).

King's brigade, which consisted of four Wisconsin regiments and one from Indiana, was the only unit of its size to serve in the eastern theater composed entirely of troops from west of the Appalachians. It was called the "Iron Brigade."

Kings Mountain, Battle of • (October 7, 1780) site in northwestern South Carolina where a coalition of frontiersmen directed by WILLIAM CAMPBELL of Virginia defeated English Maj. PATRICK FERGUSON's loyalist forces. It marked the turning point in revolutionary military fortunes by convincing loyalists to remove themselves from the conflict and setting the stage for ultimate British surrender at YORKTOWN (1781). See also COWPENS, BATTLE OF.

King William's War • (1689–97) the first in what can be thought of as the FRENCH AND INDIAN WARS (1754–63). Remotely tied to the War of the GRAND ALLIANCE (1689–97), it pitted French Canadians and their Indian allies against New England colonists and their Indian allies in long-term warfare throughout lower Canada and New England. The British took PORT ROYAL in Nova Scotia and the French carried out successful attacks in New York, New Hampshire, and Maine. The TREATY OF RIJSWIJK ended the war, although hostilities broke out soon after. See also KING GEORGE'S WAR.

Kinkaid, Thomas C. (1888–1972) • career naval officer and commander during WORLD WAR II, born in Hanover, New Hampshire. Kinkaid landed Gen. DOUGLAS MACARTHUR's troops at LEYTE GULF (1944) and, following that great naval victory, on LUZON (1945), after which he became a full admiral. In 1942 Kinkaid commanded cruiser divisions in the battle of the CORAL SEA and at MIDWAY, then carrier task forces around GUADALCANAL. Late that year he took command of the North Pacific Force, a joint navy, army, and ARMY AIR FORCE command in Alaska, ejecting the Japanese from Attu and Kiska islands, for which he received his third DISTINGUISHED SERVICE MEDAL.

Kiowa Warrior • (**OH-58D**) a lightly armed scout helicopter used by the U.S. Army for reconnaissance since the VIETNAM WAR, and intended to be capable of working with the APACHE (AH-64).

Kissinger, Henry (1923–) • U.S. statesman, born in Fürth, Germany. Kissinger served as national security advisor (1969–75) and secretary of state (1973–77). During his tenure (the administrations of Presidents RICHARD M. NIXON and GERALD R. FORD), he helped to craft the policy of DÉTENTE with the Soviet Union and to end U.S. involvement in VIETNAM. Kissinger was awarded the Nobel Peace Prize for bringing about the 1973 ceasefire in Vietnam, though the cessation was short-lived. Before assuming roles of national prominence, Kissinger had become a noted academic specialist in international relations and nuclear strategy while a professor of government at Harvard University. During WORLD WAR II (1939–45) he served with the army and remained in Germany with the occupation forces.

kit • *n.* **1** a set of articles or equipment needed for a specific purpose: *a first-aid kit.* **2** Brit. the clothing and other items belonging to a soldier.

kit bag (also **kitbag**) • a rectangular canvas bag, used especially for carrying a soldier's clothes and personal possessions.

kitchen police (**KP**) • **1** slang enlisted personnel detailed to help the cook by washing dishes, peeling vegetables, and other kitchen duties. **2** the assigned duty of these personnel: *we were put **on KP** for four days.*

kite • *n.* informal a spinnaker or other high, light sail.

kite balloon • a captive balloon fitted with a tail to keep it headed into the wind.

KMT • *abbr.* Kuomintang.

kn • *abbr.* knot(s).

knapsack • *n.* a bag with shoulder straps,

carried on the back, and typically made of canvas or other weatherproof material.

knee • *n.* an angled piece of wood or metal frame used to connect and support the beams and timbers of a wooden ship.

knot |nät| • *n.* **1** a unit of speed equivalent to one nautical mile per hour, used especially of ships, aircraft, and winds. **2** a length marked by knots on a log line, as a measure of speed: *some days the vessel* ***logged 12 knots.***

Know Nothing party (**Know-Nothing**) • a secretive movement established in New York City in 1849. Members were told to answer "I know nothing" when asked about their society's activities. In 1852, under James W. Barker, the Know-Nothings organized nationally. The party, which was officially called the AMERICAN PARTY, believed in preserving and defending fundamental American traditions. It was against foreign immigration, and particularly against Catholics, whose allegiance to the Pope was feared. Strongest in the northeast, the Know-Nothings elected many candidates to federal and state offices in 1854. Initially neutral on the slavery issue, in 1855 the Know-Nothings adopted a proslavery stand, driving out most antislavery members. By 1857 most northern members had joined the REPUBLICAN PARTY.

Knox, Henry (1750–1806) • REVOLUTIONARY WAR general and chief of artillery for the Continental army, born in Boston, Massachusetts. In 1775 Knox brought the captured arsenal at FORT TICONDEROGA to GEORGE WASHINGTON'S camp at Cambridge, Massachusetts. The resultant heavy firepower on Dorchester Heights, overlooking Boston Harbor, led the British to evacuate Boston. Knox's artillery continued to be important to Washington's army throughout the war, right up to the battle of YORKTOWN (1781). In 1783 he was designated by Washington to succeed him as commander in chief, and in 1785 the Confederation Congress named him secretary at war. During his tenure as secretary of war (1789–94) under the new government, most of the WAR DEPARTMENT'S work focused on Indian affairs.

In 1782 Knox became the youngest major general in the Continental army.

---

knuckle knife • slang (in WORLD WAR I) a long, sharp-pointed, double-edged blade dagger or trench knife with spiked brass knuckles arrayed over the grip, designed for hand-to-hand combat, especially in trench raids.

Komer, Robert William (1922–2000) • U.S. Army lieutenant colonel and foreign service officer, born in Chicago. Komer was in charge of the pacification program in the VIETNAM WAR (1967–68). While in Vietnam he was officially Gen. WILLIAM C. WESTMORELAND'S deputy for civil operations and revolutionary development support (CORDS), the agency coordinating pacification efforts. Komer had previously been a senior intelligence analyst with the CENTRAL INTELLIGENCE AGENCY, which he joined shortly after WORLD WAR II; in 1961 he became a member of the NATIONAL SECURITY COUNCIL. During WORLD WAR II Komer served as a first lieutenant in army intelligence and was awarded the BRONZE STAR. Komer was a recipient of the National Medal of Freedom.

The brash and abrasive Komer was known as "Blowtorch Bob." The name was reputedly given him by HENRY CABOT LODGE, who had once said, more or less, that arguing with Komer was like having a flamethrower aimed at the seat of your pants.

Kontum (**Kon Tum**) • the capital of Kontum Province in Vietnam, located deep in the central highlands, 24 miles (39 kilometers) north of Pleiku. It was the site of a major battle between NORTH VIETNAMESE ARMY (NVA) forces and Republic of Vietnam Army units during the EASTER OFFENSIVE of 1972. The NVA crossed the demilitarized zone on March 30, 1972, while other units from that army approached Kontum from Cambodia on April 6 and surrounded the city on April 22. The Republic of Vietnam Army held its ground and forced the attacking NVA divisions to retreat back to Laos. President RICHARD M. NIXON responded by ordering aggressive air attacks on North Vietnam until October 1972. The losses of men from the NVA caused Russia to put secret peace talks in motion and to pressure Vietnam to negotiate with the United States.

Korean War • (1950–53) a conflict between North Korean and Chinese armies fought to a stalemate against South Korean and UNITED NATIONS forces led by the United States. After back and forth fighting, including the dramatic INCHON LANDING, U.N. armies came close to Korea's northern border, drawing China into the war. After being pushed back again and suffering 459,360 casualties, the United Nations, led by newly elected President DWIGHT D. EISENHOWER, offered peace talks. Both sides agreed to an armistice that kept Korea divided and is still in effect.

Kosciuszko, Tadeusz Andrzej Bonawentura |käs'cHōōskō; ˌkäsē'əskō| (1746–1817) • Polish patriot and REVOLUTIONARY WAR general, born near Kosów, Poland. As engineer to the northern army under Gen. HORATIO GATES, Kosciuszko selected the battlefield and supervised fortifications that contributed to the American victory at SARATOGA (1777) and was responsible for building the defenses at WEST POINT (1778–80). Later, as chief of engineers for the SOUTHERN DEPARTMENT, Kosciuszko served with Gen. NATHANAEL GREENE, supervising transportation of his army over the Dan River (1780–81). One of Kosciuszko's feats was the building of wagons, with detachable wheels, that could also serve as boats. After the war Kosciuszko returned to Poland where he led the failed cause of Polish independence. *Maneuvers of Horse Artillery,* a manual written (in French) by Kosciuszko in 1800 and published in English in 1808, was widely used by the American army. As a result, Kosciuszko is regarded as the father of American artillery tactics.

While at WEST POINT Kosciuszko cultivated a garden that is still maintained at the U.S. Military Academy as "Kosciuszko's Garden."

Kosovo Crisis • (1999) the largest military assault in Europe since WORLD WAR II, and NATO's first combat experience. Prompted by mistreatment of Albanians in the Yugoslavian province of Kosovo, NATO air assaults on Serbia begin March 24, 1999. After a ten-week air war comprising 35,000 missions that delivered 23,000 bombs, President SLOBODAN MILOSEVIC accepted a Finnish- and Russian-brokered peace plan on June 3. Yugoslavia granted partial autonomy to Kosovo, but Milosevic retained his position.

KP • *abbr.* kitchen police.

Krag-Jorgensen rifle • a longarm developed at the Königsberg Arms Factory in Norway and used by the U.S. military forces beginning in SPANISH-AMERICAN WAR (1898). It was the first magazine rifle used by the military.

K-rations • (WORLD WAR II) a food package that came in three sealed, waxed cardboard boxes—breakfast, lunch, and dinner—and provided 3,000 calories and the daily requirement of vitamins. Originally developed for paratroopers but soon given much wider use, the rations contained (various combinations of) meat, egg, cheese, biscuit, fruit bar, candy bar, sugar and salt tablets, chewing gum, cigarettes, matches, water purification tablets, and toilet paper. See also MRE.

K-rations were named after nutritionist Dr. Ancel Keys (author of *Eat Well and Stay Well*).

kraut |krowt| • *n.* slang, derogatory the individual German combatant and the German armed forces collectively, particularly during WORLD WAR II.

ORIGIN: supposedly derived from the frequency and gusto with which the German soldier consumed sauerkraut.

kraut fish |krowt fish| • slang (in WORLD WAR I) a German submarine.

Krueger, Walter (1881–1967) • U.S. Army general, born in Flatow, West Prussia (now Zlotow, Poland). Krueger supervised the training of the 6th Army in Australia and led it through twenty-one major engagements against the Japanese, from New Guinea to the Philippines (1943–45), including the largest American land campaign (LUZON, 1945) in the Pacific. After the surrender of Japan, he commanded the 6th Army during the OCCUPATION OF JAPAN. Krueger joined the army during the SPANISH-AMERICAN WAR (1898) and saw duty in the Philippines during the subsequent insurrection (1901). During WORLD WAR I he served in France and Germany. During the 1920s and 1930s, he held several staff positions and commands, including commander of the 3rd Army and Southern Defense Command (1941–43) until being given overseas duty, despite his relatively advanced age. He retired in 1946. His many distinctions included the DISTINGUISHED SERVICE CROSS, DISTINGUISHED SERVICE MEDAL (army and navy), and the LEGION OF MERIT.

Krueger held every army rank from private to full general.

KT • *abbr.* (in the UK) Knight of the Order of the Thistle.

kt. • *abbr.* **1** kiloton(s). **2** knot(s): *a cruising speed of 240 kt.*

Ku Klux Klan • (**KKK**) an extremist right-wing secret society in the United States. The Ku Klux Klan was originally founded in the southern states after the CIVIL WAR to oppose social change and black emancipation by violence and terrorism. Although disbanded twice, it reemerged in the 1950s and 1960s and continues at a local level. Members disguise themselves in white robes and hoods, and often use a burning cross as a symbol of their organization.

DERIVATIVES: **Ku Kluxer; Ku Klux Klansman** (**pl. -men**)

Kuomintang (**KMT**) • the Nationalist Party of China. A highly centralized, hierarchical, and authoritarian party/government, the Kuomintang, led by Generalissimo CHIANG KAI-SHEK, ruled China from the 1930s through WORLD WAR II. Defeated by the Chinese Communists led by MAO ZEDONG in the civil war which ended in 1949, the vestiges of the Kuomintang withdrew to the island of Taiwan and there reestablished the government of the Republic of Korea.

Kurita, Takeo (1889–1977) • Japanese vice admiral who was one of the most actively employed flag officers during WORLD WAR II. He commanded a cruiser division at the BATTLE OF MIDWAY (1942), led a battleship division in the GUADALCANAL campaign (1942–43), and commanded major naval forces during the battles of the PHILIPPINE SEA (1944) and LEYTE GULF (1944). During the latter, one of the giant battleships in Kurita's central force was sunk, forcing him to reverse course—which led the Americans to think he was retreating. But Kurita doubled back and proceeded to enter the strait as planned. After losing three heavy cruisers, he ordered a withdrawal, without having touched the American transports and landing craft at Leyte.

Kuwait |kə'wāt| • a country on the northwest coast of the Persian Gulf; pop. 1,200,000 (est. 1991); official language, Arabic; capital, KUWAIT CITY. Kuwait has been an autonomous Arab sheikhdom, under the rule of an amir, from the 18th century, although the British established a protectorate from 1897 until 1961. One of the world's leading oil-producing countries, Kuwait was invaded by Iraq in August 1990, the occupying forces being expelled in the PERSIAN GULF WAR of 1991.

Kuwait City • a port on the Persian Gulf, the capital city of KUWAIT.

Kwajalein, Battle of • (February 1944) the first prewar capture of a Japanese territory by American troops. Noted for intensive preinvasion bombardment directed by Adm. CHESTER W. NIMITZ, Kwajalein cost less than 500 American lives compared to over 7,000 by the Japanese.

Ll

laager |'lägər| • *n.* a camp or encampment formed by a circle of wagons. • *v.* **1** form (vehicles) into a laager. **2** make camp.

labor • *v.* (of a ship) roll or pitch heavily.

LAC • *abbr.* leading aircraftman.

LACW • *abbr.* leading aircraftwoman.

LADAR • *abbr.* (**Light Amplification for Detection and Ranging**) an imaging system that provides near-photographic quality images of potential targets by measuring elapsed time from a laser transmission to the reflected return of the pulse. (Also called **Laser Radar**) .

lade • *v.* (past part. **laden**) **1** archaic load (a ship or other vessel). **2** ship (goods) as cargo. **3** (of a ship) take on cargo.

lading • *n.* **1** archaic the action or process of loading a ship or other vessel with cargo. **2** a cargo.

Lafayette Escadrille • the Escadrille Américaine (Escadrille No. 124), a WORLD WAR I French army aviation unit composed of American volunteers led by French officers. Activated on March 21, 1916, the Escadrille Américaine was commanded by French Captain Georges Thenault. Some 267 Americans served in the unit which was credited with destroying 199 German aircraft. Its most famous American pilot was RAOUL LUFBERY, who downed seventeen German planes before his death in 1918. On December 25, 1917, ninety-three members of the Lafayette Escadrille transferred to the American Air Service and another twenty-six to the U.S. Navy's air arm, and on February 13, 1918, the Lafayette Escadrille became officially the 103rd Aero Squadron of the American Air Service.

Lafayette, James (c. 1748–1830) • patriot spy also known as James Armistead, a slave who volunteered, with his owner's permission, to spy for the MARQUIS DE LAFAYETTE in the hope that it would win him his freedom. He soon earned the trust of the British and served as a double agent, feeding Gen. CHARLES CORNWALLIS insignificant or misleading information from Lafayette and keeping Lafayette informed of Cornwallis' movements along the Virginia coast. It was James who informed Lafayette that Cornwallis was fortifying a position at YORKTOWN (1781). After the war, James returned to the household of his owner, William Armistead, who in 1786 arranged for his manumission through the Virginia legislature, for which he was compensated well above the norm. When James was freed in 1787, he took Lafayette's surname.

Lafayette, Marquis de (1757–1834) • soldier and statesman, born in Chavaniac, France. Lafayette was a major general in the Continental army and fought at BRANDYWINE (1777); led an abortive expedition to invade Canada; and served in actions at MONMOUTH and in Rhode Island (1778). He led the Continental forces that bottled Gen. CHARLES CORNWALLIS at YORKTOWN (1781), causing his eventual defeat. He twice returned to America (1784, 1824–25), where he was received as a hero. Lafayette also worked on behalf of American commerce with the French ministries (1785–89). After the REVOLUTIONARY WAR Lafayette was active in the cause of liberty in France, citing American political principles and the American experience as a model.

Scores of counties, cities, and public places in the United States were named for Lafayette or for La Grange, his estate in France.

Lafitte, Jean (or **John**) (c.1780-c.1825) • a French privateer who commanded a fleet of pirate ships in the Gulf of Mexico. Their principal target was Spanish slave ships, which they captured in order to sell the slaves in the thriving Louisiana market. He also fought under Gen. ANDREW JACKSON in the WAR OF 1812 and contributed to the victory in the BATTLE OF NEW ORLEANS (1815).

lagan • *n.* archaic (in legal contexts) goods or wreckage lying on the bed of the sea.

Laird, Melvin R. (1922–) • secretary of defense (1969–73), born in Omaha, Nebraska. His tenure brought cuts in military spending, the closing of military installations, and the withdrawal of forces in the VIETNAM WAR. Nevertheless, he maintained good relations with the services by restoring to the military departments authority and responsibility that had been taken away during the highly centralized decision-making style of his predecessor, ROBERT S. MCNAMARA. Laird also helped the move toward an ALL-VOLUNTEER FORCE by 1972.

Laird was the first member of Congress to be secretary of defense.

Lake Erie, Battle of • a U.S. naval victory on Lake Erie on September 10, 1813, during the WAR OF 1812. After British warships under Capt. Robert Heriot Barclay destroyed the U.S. flagship *Lawrence*, Master Commandant OLIVER HAZARD PERRY transferred to the *Niagara* and forced a British surrender. The victory forced the British to abandon Detroit.

Lake Okeechobee, Battle of • a battle fought on Christmas Day, 1837, during the second SEMINOLE WAR (1835–42), near Lake Okeechobee in Florida, north of which a reservation for Seminoles had been established. Brig. Gen. ZACHARY TAYLOR directed some 800 American men against a position prepared by three bands of Seminole Indians, who numbered less than 500. Taylor finally dislodged them but sustained some 138 casualties.

Lakota Sioux • North American Indian tribe occupying the northern Great Plains from

Minnesota westward into the Dakotas and southward into Nebraska. Under chief SITTING BULL and other excellent leaders the Lakota Sioux dominated the other northern Plains tribes and after 1860 strongly resisted the invasion of their sacred sites and hunting areas by the white man, fighting a series of often successful battles with the U.S. Army, including the battle of the LITTLE BIGHORN in June 1876, before being finally crushed in 1890 at WOUNDED KNEE, Dakota Territory.

Lamb, John (1735–1800) • REVOLUTIONARY WAR officer, born in New York City. Lamb participated in the Canadian invasion of 1775 and the defense of an army depot in Connecticut; served as commander of artillery at WEST POINT (1779–80) and as surveyor of ordnance (1779–80); and commanded the heaviest bombardment at the siege of YORKTOWN (1781). He was an early leader in the New York SONS OF LIBERTY and led mobs that unloaded provisions destined for the British troops in Boston, closed New York Harbor, and seized weapons and other military stores.

Lam Son 719 • the code name for the ill-fated South Vietnamese (ARVN) assault, under U.S. tactical air support, on Laos in March 1971, during the VIETNAM WAR. As part of the U.S. policy of VIETNAMIZATION, it was an attempt to destroy strategic zones of the HO CHI MINH TRAIL, which was a Communist supply line. It included 659 U.S. and ARVN helicopters, 444 of which were shot down by March 21, 1971. It ended in a confused retreat by the ARVN.

lance • *n.* a long weapon for thrusting, having a wooden shaft and a pointed steel head, used by a horseman in charging.

Lance • a surface-to-surface, short-range guided missile with nuclear and nonnuclear capability, used widely by NATO countries.

lance bombardier • a rank of noncommissioned officer in an artillery regiment of the British army, corresponding to that of a lance corporal in the infantry.

lance corporal • an enlisted person in the U.S. Marine Corps ranking above private first class and below corporal.

lancer • *n.* a soldier of a cavalry regiment armed with lances.

Lancer • (**B-1B**) a long-range bomber designed for stealth and low-altitude attacks. It can fly intercontinental missions, then penetrate sophisticated enemy defenses, without refueling, as well as serve as a conventional weapons carrier for theater operations.

lance sergeant |læns 'särjənt| • a rank in the FOOT GUARDS equivalent to corporal.

land • *n.* the space between the rifling grooves in a gun. • *v.* **1** put ashore: *the lifeboat landed the survivors safely ashore.* **2** go ashore; disembark: *the marines landed at a small fishing jetty.* **3** come down through the air and alight on the ground: *planes landing at the rate of two a minute.* **4** bring (an aircraft or spacecraft) to the ground or the surface of water, especially in a controlled way: *the copilot landed the plane.*

Lander, Frederick West (1821–62) • military engineer, born in Salem, Massachusetts. Lander was recognized for his exploration and improvement of the central wagon route connecting the country. As chief engineer (1857) and later superintendent (1858–1860) for the Fort Kearney, South Pass, and Honey Lake Wagon Road, Lander led explorations to find the best locations for the route, supervised its construction, and worked toward pacifying Indians in the area. Lander died early in the CIVIL WAR, of pneumonia contracted from remaining in the field during the winter despite a lingering leg wound received while commanding a brigade at Edward's Ferry (1861).

landfall • *n.* an arrival at land on a sea or air journey.

land force • the component of a nation's armed forces organized, trained, and equipped primarily for land combat.

Landgraf twin-rotor helicopter • (**H-2**) a single-seat twin-rotor experimental helicopter developed by The Landgraf Helicopter Co. for the U.S. Army and first flown in 1944.

landing • *n.* **1** an instance of coming or bringing something to land, either from the air or from water: *we made a perfect landing at the airstrip.* **2** the action or process of doing this: *the landing of men on the moon.* **3** (also **landing place**) a place where people and goods can be landed from a boat or ship: *the ferry landing.*

landing area • **1** the part of the objective area within which are conducted the landing operations of an amphibious force. It includes the beach, the approaches to the beach, the transport areas, the fire support areas, the air occupied by close supporting aircraft, and the land included in the advance inland to the initial objective. **2** the general area used for landing troops and materiel either by airdrop or air landing. This area includes one or more drop zones or landing strips. **3** any specially prepared or selected surface of land, water, or deck designated or used for takeoff and landing of aircraft.

landing attack • an attack against enemy defenses by troops landed from ships, aircraft, boats, or amphibious vehicles.

landing craft • a boat specially designed for putting troops and military equipment ashore on a beach.

landing force • a task organization of troop units (aviation and ground) assigned to an amphibious assault. It is the highest troop echelon in the amphibious operation.

landing mat • a prefabricated, portable mat so designed that any number of planks (sections) may be rapidly fastened together to form surfacing for emergency runways, landing beaches, etc.

landing roll • the movement of an aircraft from touchdown through deceleration to taxi speed or full stop.

landing schedule • in an amphibious operation, a schedule that shows the beach, hour, and priorities of landing of assault units, and that coordinates the movements of landing craft from the transports to the beach in order to execute the scheme of maneuver ashore.

landing ship • an assault ship designed for long voyages and rapid unloading on a beach.

Landing Ship, Dock • see AMPHIBIOUS LANDING SHIPS.

Landing Ship, Medium • see AMPHIBIOUS LANDING SHIPS.

Landing Ship, Medium (Rocket) • see AMPHIBIOUS LANDING SHIPS.

landing ship tank • (**LVTE-1**) an amphibious tracked vehicle designed to clear mines and other obstacles during an amphibious assault.

Landing Ship, Vehicle • see AMPHIBIOUS LANDING SHIPS.

landing stage • a platform, typically a floating one, onto which passengers from a boat or ship disembark or cargo is unloaded.

landing zone • any specified zone used for the landing of aircraft.

landlubber • *n.* informal a person unfamiliar with the sea or sailing.

land mine • an explosive mine laid on or just under the surface of the ground.

land, sea, or aerospace projection operations • the employment of land, sea, or air forces, or appropriate combinations thereof, to protect U.S. military power into areas controlled or threatened by enemy forces. Operations may include penetration of such areas by amphibious, airborne, or land-transported means, as well as air combat operations by land-based and/or carrier air.

landsknecht |ˈlänts,kneKHt| • *n.* a member of a class of mercenary soldiers in the German and other continental armies in the 16th and 17th centuries.

landsman • *n.* (pl. **-men**) a person unfamiliar with the sea or sailing.

land warfare • warfare conducted primarily on land.

lane • *n.* a path or course prescribed for or regularly followed by ships or aircraft.

Lane, James Henry (1833–1907) • Confederate army officer, born in Mathews Court House, North Carolina. He led a brigade at the battles of FREDERICKSBURG (1862) and CHANCELLORSVILLE (1863), and in the WILDERNESS TO PETERSBURG CAMPAIGN (1864). He also took part in the siege of RICHMOND (1864) and was present with ROBERT E. LEE's army at its surrender at APPOMATTOX (1865). Early in the war he had led his North Carolina regiment at the battle of MALVERN HILL and in the SEVEN DAYS' battles (both 1862). After participating in the capture of HARPERS FERRY and the battles of SECOND BULL RUN and ANTIETAM (all 1862), his regiment formed the rear guard of the retreating Confederate Army.

Langley • a town in Virginia that is the headquarters of the CIA.

Langley Aeronautical Laboratory • the first civilian aeronautics laboratory in the United States. Established in 1917 at Langley Field in Hampton, Virginia, it operated under the NATIONAL ADVISORY COMMITTEE FOR AERONAUTICS until 1958, when it was renamed the NASA Langley Research Center.

The first pressurized wind tunnel in the world, the Variable Density Tunnel, was built and first used at Langley in 1922.

***Langley*, USS** • (**CVL-27**) an aircraft carrier, originally named *Fargo* (CL-85) and renamed *Langley* in 1942, that provided invaluable service in the Pacific Theater during WORLD WAR II. In January 1944, the *Langley*'s aircraft raided Wotje and Taora to support Allied landings and repeated the performance in February at ENIWETOK, in March at Palau, Yap, and Woleai in the Caroline Islands, and then proceeded to New Guinea to take part in the capture of HOLLANDIA on April 25. Only days later, the *Langley*'s aircraft accounted for thirty-five enemy planes destroyed or damaged in the two-day strike against Truk, making the important naval base virtually useless to Japan. In all, the *Langley* received nine battle stars for service in World War II. In 1963, the ship was sold for scrap.

Lang Vei, Battle of • a battle on February 7, 1968, during the VIETNAM WAR, at the Lang Vei Special Forces camp in South Vietnam. Located near the U.S. Marine combat base at KHE SANH, which had been under siege by the NORTH VIETNAMESE ARMY (NVA) since January 20, the camp, occupied by Special Forces Detachment A101, was overrun by an NVA combined infantry-tank assault which forced the defenders to evacuate.

Lansdale, Edward Geary (1908–87) • U.S. intelligence officer, general, and COLD WAR COUNTERINSURGENCY specialist, born in Detroit, Michigan. His dual career began in WORLD WAR II when he worked simultaneously for the civilian OFFICE OF STRATEGIC SERVICES and U.S. Army intelligence. After the war, the air force (to which he had transferred) loaned him to the OFFICE OF POLICY COORDINATION, a highly secret interagency espionage group that became part of the CENTRAL INTELLIGENCE AGENCY in 1952. Although he was never an employee of the CIA, Lansdale often worked on its behalf using the cover of an air force officer. During the early decades of the Cold War, he became legendary for identifying and funding effective noncommunist alternative leaders. He engineered PSYCHOLOGICAL WARFARE operations in North Vietnam (1954–55) and channeled U.S. support to the new Republic of South Vietnam and its president. Under President JOHN F. KENNEDY, Lansdale was put in charge of OPERATION MONGOOSE, which involved attempts to eliminate FIDEL CASTRO and disrupt the economy of Communist Cuba. Lansdale was retired from active duty, a major general, in 1963.

Lansdale became so mythologized as a secret warrior that he formed the prototype for two fictional characters: Alden Pyle in Graham Greene's *The Quiet American* (1955) and Col. Edwin B. Hillandale in William J. Lederer and Eugene Burdick's *The Ugly American* (1958).

LANTCOM • the Unified Combatant Command for the Atlantic region.

lanyard • *n.* **1** a rope threaded through a pair of deadeyes, used to adjust the tension in the rigging of a sailing vessel. **2** a cord attached to a breech mechanism for firing a gun.

Laos, raid into • an Army of the Republic of Vietnam (ARVN) invasion of Laos beginning on February 8, 1971, to destroy the Communist supply line along the Ho Chi Minh Trail and to test the new ARVN. In an attempt approved by President Richard M. Nixon, who was advised by Gen. Creighton Abrams, some 21,000 ARVN troops, supported by American B-52 bombers, invaded Laos and were met by some 36,000 North Vietnamese troops. The ARVN suffered over 9,000 casualties, and the North Vietnamese suffered 14,000. After six weeks of the war's heaviest fighting, the South Vietnamese troops retreated into Vietnam.

lapstrake • *adj.* (also **lapstraked**) (of a boat) having external planks that overlap downward and are secured with clinched nails. • *n.* a boat built in such a way.

La Rocque, Gene • (1918–) naval officer and founder of the Center for Defense Information. La Rocque served thirty-one years of active duty, participating in 113 major battles in the Pacific during World War II. His postwar career included a variety of ship commands and seven years in the Strategic Plans Directorate of the Joint Chiefs of Staff. La Rocque retired in 1972, disillusioned over the Vietnam War, and established the Center for Defense Information as a source of critical information on military spending and policies. He retired from the center in 1993.

laser • *n.* a device that generates an intense beam of coherent monochromatic light (or other electromagnetic radiation) by stimulated emission of photons from excited atoms or molecules. Lasers are used in drilling and cutting, alignment and guidance, and in surgery; the optical properties are exploited in holography, reading bar codes, and in recording and playing compact discs.

ORIGIN: 1960s: acronym from *light amplification by stimulated emission of radiation.*

laser-guided weapon • (**LGW**) a weapon that homes in on its target by detecting and following laser energy reflected from it, the laser being trained on the target by the firer of the weapon or by another coordinated source.

laser intelligence • (**LASINT**) technical and geo-location intelligence derived from laser systems; a subcategory of electro-optical intelligence.

Laser Radar • see LADAR.

laser target designating system • a system that is used to direct (aim or point) laser energy at a target. The system consists of the laser designator or laser target marker with its display and control components necessary to acquire the target and direct the beam of laser energy thereon.

lashing • *n.* (usually **lashings**) a cord used to fasten something securely.

LASINT • *abbr.* laser intelligence.

last post • (in the British armed forces) the second of two bugle calls giving notice of the hour of retiring at night, played also at military funerals and acts of remembrance.

lat. • *abbr.* latitude: *between approximately 40° and 50° S. lat.*

latrine • *n.* a toilet, especially a communal one in a camp or barracks.

launch • *n.* **1** a large motorboat, used especially for short trips. **2** the largest boat carried on a man-of-war.

launcher • *n.* **1** a structure that holds a rocket or missile during launching. **2** a rocket that is used to convey a satellite or spacecraft into orbit. **3** a catapult for aircraft. **4** an attachment to the muzzle of a rifle permitting the firing of grenades.

launch on warning • (**LOW**) the U.S. policy of launching a retaliatory strategic nuclear strike once confirmation of an enemy attack in preparation or in progress is received but before the incoming warheads arrive.

launch pad • a concrete or other hard surface area on which a missile launcher is positioned.

launch under attack • (**LUA**) execution by National Command Authorities of Single Integrated Operational Plan forces subsequent to tactical warning of strategic nuclear attack against the United States and prior to first impact.

Laurens, John (1754–82) • Revolutionary War officer, born outside Charleston, South Carolina. Laurens was aide-de-camp to George Washington, whom he served as secretary and translator to French allies. He fought at Brandywine and Germantown (both 1777), Monmouth (1778), and later, when the British invaded the South, in Georgia and his native South Carolina (1779). In 1781 Laurens, who was fluent in French, traveled to France and successfully negotiated for money for military supplies by avoiding the diplomatic route and going directly to Louis XVI. Later that same year he took part in the siege of Yorktown, leading a difficult bayonet attack on British fortifications and afterwards taking part in negotiating the British surrender.

Lawn Dart • slang F-16. See Fighting Falcon.

Lawrence Livermore National Laboratory • (**LNLL**) established in July 1952 when, on the advice of Edward Teller, the Atomic Energy Commission made Livermore a branch of the University of California Radiation Laboratory and located it at a former naval air station in Livermore, California. The Laboratory is responsible to the Department of Energy and is still operated by the University of California. Among its responsibilities are finding ways to apply science and technology in the national interest (while focusing on global security) and providing research on global ecology and bioscience.

laws of war • international rules and conventions that limit belligerents' action.

lay • *v.* follow (a specified course).

laydown bombing • a very-low-level bombing technique wherein delay fuzes and/or devices are used to allow the attacker to escape the effects of the bomb.

Lay, John Louis (1832–99) • Union naval engineer, born in Buffalo, New York. Lay worked on various torpedo designs as well as serving active duty in various blockade expeditions during the CIVIL WAR. A torpedo of his design was used in the sinking of the Confederate ironclad *Albemarle* (1864). He resigned from the navy in 1865. Lay later completed work on several inventions, including a steam engine and locomotive for which he received patents in 1867. He sold the rights to his electrically propelled movable torpedo submarine (the U.S. Navy had purchased two) to the Russian and Turkish governments for a sizable sum.

lazarette |ˌlæzəˈret| (also **lazaret**) • *n.* a small compartment below the deck in the after end of a vessel, used for stores.

LBDR • *abbr.* Lance Bombardier.

LCAC • *abbr.* landing craft, air cushion

LCC • *abbr.* landing craft, control. See AMPHIBIOUS COMMAND SHIP.

LCM • *abbr.* landing craft, mechanized.

LCP(L) • *abbr.* landing craft, personnel (large).

LCpl • *abbr.* Lance Corporal.

LCP(R) • *abbr.* landing craft, personnel (ramp).

LCR(L) • *abbr.* landing craft, rubber (large).

LCR(S) • *abbr.* landing craft, rubber (small).

LCS(S) • *abbr.* landing craft, support (small).

LCT • *abbr.* landing craft, tank.

LCV • *abbr.* landing craft, vehicle.

LCVP • *abbr.* landing craft, vehicle, personnel.

Ldg • *abbr.* Leading (in navy ranks).

lead[1] |lēd| • *v.* be in charge or command of.

lead[2] |led| • *n.* **1** a lead casting suspended on a line to determine the depth of water. **2** bullets.

lead aircraft • **1** the airborne aircraft designated to exercise command of other aircraft within the flight. **2** an aircraft in the van of two or more aircraft.

leadership • *n.* **1** the action of leading a group of people or an organization: *different styles of leadership.* **2** the state or position of being a leader: *the leadership of the party.* **3** the leaders of an organization, country, etc.: *a change of leadership had become desirable.* **4** the ability to lead skillfully.

leading aircraftman • a male rank in the RAF, above aircraftman and below senior aircraftman.

leading aircraftwoman • a female rank in the RAF, above aircraftwoman and below senior aircraftwoman.

leading seaman • a rank in the ROYAL NAVY, above able seaman and below petty officer.

lead shot |led| • another term for SHOT (sense 6).

League of Nations • an association of countries established in 1919 by the TREATY OF VERSAILLES to promote international cooperation and achieve international peace and security. It was powerless to stop Italian, German, and Japanese expansionism leading to WORLD WAR II, and was replaced by the UNITED NATIONS in 1945. It included provisions for arbitrating international disputes, reducing armaments, and imposing collective military and economic sanctions against any nation that violated the political independence and territorial integrity of another. However, the United States never joined the League of Nations because irreconcilable disputes developed between progressives and conservatives in the American internationalist movement over whether the United States should be able to expand its army and navy and exert force independently.

Leahy, William Daniel (1875–1959) • U.S. Navy admiral, born in Hampton, Iowa. Leahy was chief of staff to the commander in chief (the president) during WORLD WAR II. Leahy presided over meetings of the JOINT CHIEFS OF STAFF, but the leadership role usually associated with that position was held by Gen. GEORGE C. MARSHALL. Leahy remained on the JCS through the duration of the war, and as a member of the combined chiefs of staff, helped plan its global strategy. In his earlier navy career Leahy had held a variety of sea and shore positions, including chief of the NAVY BUREAU OF ORDNANCE (1927–31), chief of the BUREAU OF NAVIGATION (1933–36), and CHIEF OF NAVAL OPERATIONS (1937–39). During the SPANISH-AMERICAN WAR (1898) he participated in the battle of SANTIAGO, and during WORLD WAR I he commanded a troop transport. A recipient of the DISTINGUISHED SERVICE MEDAL (with two gold stars), Leahy was made a fleet admiral, a five-star rank, in 1944.

leapfrogging • *n.* a form of movement in which like supporting elements are moved successively through or by one another along the axis of movement of supported forces.

leatherneck • *n.* informal a U.S. marine.

ORIGIN: The term appears to have originated with navy men, possibly in reference to the leather neckband inside the collar of the Marine Corps dress uniform around the mid to late 1800s.

leave • *n.* (also **leave of absence**) time when one has permission to be absent form work or from duty in the armed force.

Leavenworth, Fort • see FORT LEAVENWORTH.

Lebanon Crisis • (1958) the protests against and potential overthrow of the pro-Western Lebanese government of President Camille Chamoun, a Christian, after the creation of a pro-Soviet United Arab Republic by Egypt and Syria in February 1958 and after the Arab nationalist coup in Iraq on July 14, 1958. Using the EISENHOWER DOCTRINE, Chamoun requested U.S. troops, who, at President DWIGHT D. EISENHOWER's orders, first arrived in Lebanon on July 15 and had completely withdrawn by October 15. It was the United States's first intervention in the Middle East, and it was the first time NATO-committed troops were withdrawn for out-of-area operations.

Ledo Road • (**Stilwell Road**) a highway constructed by U.S. Army engineers during WORLD WAR II, from Ledo, Assam, India, across the Naga Hills, joining the eastern,

Chinese-held sector of the BURMA SUPPLY ROAD near Wanting, Burma. The highway was built as a replacement for the Burma Road, the 717-mile (1,154-km) supply route between Burma and Kunming, China, which was destroyed by the Japanese conquest of Burma in 1942. Ledo Road was built at the request of Gen. JOSEPH STILWELL and was completed in January 1945.

lee • *n.* **1** shelter from wind or weather given by a neighboring object, especially nearby land: *we pitch our tents in the lee of a rock.* **2** (also **lee side**) the sheltered side; the side away from the wind: *ducks were taking shelter on the lee of the island.* Compare with WEATHER.

Lee, Charles (1731–82) • REVOLUTIONARY WAR general, born in Chester, England. His ineffective leadership early in the battle of MONMOUTH (1778) led to his being reprimanded by GEORGE WASHINGTON. He was later court-martialed, and after repeated open and public attacks on the commander in chief, dismissed from the army. Lee had previously commanded patriot forces that repelled a British assault on FORT MOULTRIE in South Carolina (1776), and a year earlier he had been in Boston with Washington, engaged in constructing entrenchments and training troops. During the FRENCH AND INDIAN WAR (1754–63), he had seen service in America with a British regiment.

Lee–Enfield (also **Lee–Enfield rifle**) • a bolt-action rifle of a type formerly used by the British army.

Lee, Fitzhugh (1835–1905) • Confederate army officer, born in Fairfax County, Virginia. Lee served ably in a number of early battles— SOUTH MOUNTAIN (1862), ANTIETAM (1862), CHANCELLORSVILLE (1863), GETTYSBURG (1863)—and was often praised for his resourcefulness and skillful tactics. Lee was made chief of cavalry for the ARMY OF NORTHERN VIRGINIA in 1865; he and his cavalry surrendered two days after APPOMATTOX, at Farmville, Virginia (1865). After the war Lee served a single term as governor of Virginia. He returned to active service during the SPANISH-AMERICAN WAR (1898), but his troops saw only occupation duty.

Fitzhugh Lee was the grandson of HENRY "LIGHT-HORSE HARRY" LEE and the nephew of ROBERT E. LEE.

Lee, George Washington Custis (1832–1913) • Confederate army officer, born in Fort Monroe, Virginia. Lee was a military engineer and aide-de-camp to JEFFERSON DAVIS who performed such duties as inspecting and organizing the defenses at crucial sites and carrying messages of great importance to generals in the field. Though he requested a transfer to combat command, Davis considered him indispensable. Late in the war, however, as Lee led a division in the retreat from RICHMOND (1865). Early in the conflict Lee designed and directed the construction of the fortifications at RICHMOND. Before resigning his U.S. Army commission, Lee was assistant to the chief engineer of the army in Washington. After the war Lee succeeded his father, ROBERT E. LEE, as president of Washington College (later Washington and Lee University).

Lee, Henry (1756–1818) • cavalry officer in the Continental army during the REVOLUTIONARY WAR, born in Leesylvania, Virginia. He was known as "Light-Horse Harry" Lee. An exceptional horseman whose skill and bravery became legendary, he led an independent partisan corps (three troops of horse and a small body of infantry) that came to be called "Lee's Legion." For his brilliant performance in capturing a British force at Paulus Hook, New Jersey (1779), he was presented a gold medal by Congress. Lee continued to perform with distinction during the 1780–81 southern campaign, proving himself a remarkable strategist and battlefield leader. He resigned his commission in 1782. After the Revolution he served as governor of Virginia (1791–94) and led the army militia that suppressed the WHISKEY REBELLION (1794).

Lee's two marriages resulted in nine children, the youngest of whom was ROBERT E. LEE. It was Lee who eulogized GEORGE WASHINGTON as "first in war, first in peace, and first in the hearts of his countrymen."

---

lee ho • a command or warning given by a helmsman to indicate the moment of going about.

Lee, Robert E. (1807–70) • Confederate general, commander of the ARMY OF NORTHERN VIRGINIA, and general in chief of the CONFEDERATE STATES Army during the CIVIL WAR, born Robert Edward Lee in Westmoreland County, Virginia. In 1862 and 1863 Lee won a series of brilliant victories—SECOND BULL RUN, CHANCELLORSVILLE, and FREDERICKSBURG—as well as a standoff with Gen. GEORGE B. MCCLELLAN at ANTIETAM. But his strategy of taking the offensive in battle and confronting the enemy on their own territory led to a costly defeat at GETTYSBURG (1863). This was followed by a skillful but ultimately failed defense against Gen. ULYSSES S. GRANT's OVERLAND CAMPAIGN in Virginia (1864–65), ending with Lee's surrender of his army at APPOMATTOX (1865). Though some have questioned his leadership as a general, he remains a hero much revered not only in the South but throughout the country. After the war Lee served as president of Washington College (now Washington and Lee University), where he proved an excellent administrator. He is buried on its grounds. Before the Civil War Lee's performance in the MEXICAN WAR (1846–48) and on the frontier had established his reputation as a proven combat leader. He had also served as superintendent of WEST POINT (1852–55).

Lee's three sons—GEORGE WASHINGTON CUSTIS LEE, WILLIAM HENRY FITZHUGH LEE, and Robert E. Lee, Jr.—all served as officers in the Civil War. Lee opposed secession and disliked slavery (he emancipated the few slaves he owned before the Civil War), but felt he could not take up arms against his native Virginia.

Lee, Samuel Phillips (1812–97) • naval officer, born in Fairfax County, Virginia. During the CIVIL WAR, Lee commanded the North Atlantic Blockade along the coastlines of Virginia and North Carolina (1862–64), capturing or destroying more than a hundred ships, thereby contributing significantly to the Union victory. Lee also participated in the blockade of CHARLESTON (1861); served under Adm. DAVID FARRAGUT in the campaign that captured NEW ORLEANS, Baton Rouge, and Natchez (1862); and commanded the Mississippi Squadron patrolling the Mississippi River (1864–65), where his actions contributed to the defeat of the Confederate army of Gen. JOHN B. HOOD in Tennessee.

Lee was a cousin of ROBERT E. LEE.

lee shore • a shore lying on the leeward side of a ship (and onto which a ship could be blown in foul weather).

Lee, Stephen Dill (1833–1908) • Confederate army officer, born in Charleston, South Carolina. Lee was commander of all cavalry in Mississippi (1863–64), and successfully opposed a series of Union raids into that state before suffering heavy losses at Tupelo (1864). Lee then commanded a corps in the defense of ATLANTA (1864–65), twice incurring heavy losses because of precipitate attacks. Previously Lee's artillery battalion had played major roles at SECOND BULL RUN (1862) and ANTIETAM (1862), and his brigade had performed admirably during the defense of VICKSBURG (1862). From 1904 until his death, Lee was commander in chief of the UNITED CONFEDERATE VETERANS.

When Lee was promoted to lieutenant general at the age of thirty, he was the youngest person to hold that rank up to that point in U.S. history.

leeward • *adj.* & *adv.* on or toward the side sheltered from the wind or toward which the wind is blowing; downwind: *the leeward side of the house* | *we pitched our tents* ***leeward of*** *a hill.* Compare with WINDWARD. • *n.* the side sheltered or away from the wind: *the ship was drifting* ***to leeward.***

leeway • *n.* the sideways drift of a ship or an aircraft to leeward of the desired course: *the leeway is only about 2°.*

Lee, William Henry Fitzhugh (1837–91) • Confederate army officer, born in Arlington, Virginia. He commanded brigades at FREDERICKSBURG (1862) and CHANCELLORSVILLE (1863), and led a cavalry division through the OVERLAND and PETERSBURG campaigns (1864). He was with his father, ROBERT E. LEE, in the APPOMATTOX campaign and surrendered with him in 1865.

left • *adj.* of or relating to a person or group favoring liberal, socialist, or radical views: *Left politics.*
ORIGIN: see LEFT WING. • *n.* **1** the left wing of an army: *a token attack on the Russian left.* **2** (often **the Left**) a group or party favoring liberal, socialist, or radical views: *the Left is preparing to fight presidential elections.* **3** the section of a party or group holding such views more strongly: *he is on the left of the party.*

left hook • the popular name given to the massive, highly mobile thrust by United States, British, and French armored and airmobile forces initiated on February 24, 1991, which drove around and through the Iraqi forces west of KUWAIT in an effort to cut the lines of communications from Basra to Kuwait and thus envelop the elite Iraqi REPUBLICAN GUARD forces then occupying Kuwait.

left wing • (**the left wing**) **1** the left side of an army: *the Allied left wing.* **2** the liberal, socialist, or radical section of a political party or system.
ORIGIN: with reference to the National Assembly in France (1789–91), where the nobles sat to the president's right and the commons to the left. • *adj.* liberal, socialist, or radical: *left-wing activists.*
DERIVATIVES: **left-winger** *n.*

legend • *n.* an explanation of symbols used on a map, chart, sketch, etc., commonly printed in tabular form at the side of the map, etc.

Leggett, Mortimer Dormer (1821–96) • volunteer Union army officer, born near Ithaca, New York. Leggett was renowned for his division's contribution to the fall of ATLANTA (1864). The command had seized an elevation outside the city, called Bald Hill (since called Leggett's Hill), and held its strategic position against counterattacks from two directions, fighting alternately on the east and west sides. Leggett also accompanied Gen. WILLIAM T. SHERMAN on his MARCH TO THE SEA (1864–65). Earlier in the conflict, he had served with distinction at FORT DONELSON (1862), SHILOH (1862), and in the VICKSBURG campaign (1863). After the war Leggett, who left the army a major general, served as commissioner of patents (1871–74), reorganizing and expanding the Patent Office.

legion • *n.* **1** (**the Legion**) any of the national associations of former servicemen and servicewomen instituted after WORLD WAR I, such as the AMERICAN LEGION. **2** (**the Legion**) the FOREIGN LEGION.

legionnaire • *n.* a member of a legion, in particular the AMERICAN LEGION, the French FOREIGN LEGION, or an ancient Roman legion.

Legion of Honor • (**Légion d'Honneur**) the highest French decoration for military or civilian service, established by the Emperor Napoleon I on May 19, 1802. The Légion d'Honneur is awarded only for gallantry in action or for 20 years of distinguished service in peacetime.

Legion of Merit • U.S. military decoration for "exceptionally meritorious conduct in the performance of outstanding services." Established by Congress on July 20, 1942, the Legion of Merit without reference to degree may be awarded to members of any branch of service. The Legion of Merit, in four degrees, also may be awarded to personnel of the armed forces of friendly nations. The degrees of Chief Commander and Commander are equivalent to the DISTINGUISHED SERVICE MEDAL, and the degrees of Officer and Legionnaire are equivalent to the Legion of Merit awarded to U.S. military personnel.

Legion of the United States • established in 1792 when GEORGE WASHINGTON commissioned ANTHONY WAYNE a major-general and Commander in Chief of the newly legislated organization. In time, the Legion became the U.S. Army.

Leisler, Jacob |'līslər| (1640?–91) • officer of the Dutch East India Company, born in Frankfurt-am-Main, Germany. Leisler was a prosperous merchant and prominent leader of New Amsterdam, and de facto lieutenant governor of New York (1689–91). Leisler held several government positions under both Dutch and English administrations, including militia captain. When the militia revolted in 1689, the lieutenant governor fled and Leisler later assumed the title. When the newly commissioned governor arrived, Leisler was arrested, found guilty of treason, hanged, and then beheaded. In 1695 Parliament reversed the New York court's sentences and legitimized his administration.

Leisler's Rebellion • the seizure of British colonial government in New York by Capt. JACOB LEISLER in May 1689. Following the abdication of James II in England, Leisler led a revolt against Lieut. Gov. FRANCIS NICHOLSON, who was the crown's agent in New York, and seized FORT JAMES on Manhattan Island on May 31. He assumed the title of Lieutenant Governor in December, and he effectively controlled the area for more than eighteen months.

Lejeune, John Archer |lə'jo͞on| (1867–1942) • Marine Corps commandant (1920–29), born in Pointe Coupee Parish, Louisiana. Lejeune was responsible for the codification of the corps's primary wartime mission as the seizure of enemy-held bastions by amphibious assault. Following his tenure as commandant, Lejeune served as superintendent of the VIRGINIA MILITARY INSTITUTE (1929–37). During WORLD WAR I Lejeune had commanded a division at the offensives of ST. MIHIEL, MONT BLANC, and MEUSE-ARGONNE (1918).

LeMay, Curtis Emerson (1906–90) • air corps and air force officer and noted aviation strategist, born in Columbus, Ohio. LeMay served as Air Force chief of staff (1961–65) and as head of the STRATEGIC AIR COMMAND (1948–57). One of the first qualified pilot/navigators of the B-17 heavy bomber (1937), in 1941 LeMay flew several experimental missions to England and North Africa, for which he received the DISTINGUISHED FLYING CROSS. During WORLD WAR II LeMay commanded divisions in the European and the CHINA-BURMA-INDIA THEATERS. In China he overcame problems with the B--29 and initiated nighttime bombing of the Japanese mainland with devastating results there. LeMay also helped orchestrate the atomic bombings of HIROSHIMA and NAGASAKI (1945). When the air force became a separate entity (1947), LeMay was given command of all air forces in Europe. In this role he organized the BERLIN AIRLIFT (1948–49). LeMay is credited with turning the STRATEGIC AIR COMMAND into the world's finest strategic bomber force through his skill at procuring modern, complicated weapons systems as well as top-rate flight and ground crews. LeMay also espoused a more confrontational policy toward the Soviet Union than did the chairman of the JOINT CHIEFS OF STAFF, and a more aggressive policy in VIETNAM than did the commander in chief, President LYNDON B. JOHNSON. LeMay resigned as chief of staff and from the Air Force in 1965, after thirty-seven years of military service.

LeMay was harshly criticized for his call to bomb North Vietnam "back into the Stone Age," made while campaigning as vice president on the ticket with segregationist governor George C. Wallace in 1968.

Lemnitzer, Lyman Louis (1899–1988) • U.S. Army general, born in Honesdale, Pennsylvania. Lemnitzer served as NATO's supreme Allied commander, Europe (1963–69), chairman of the JOINT CHIEFS OF STAFF (1960–62), and as army chief of staff (1959–60). Lemnitzer gained renown through his skills as an administrator and planner, rather than as a field general or strategist. Though he did see limited combat in WORLD WAR II, he is known more for his involvement in the planning of the NORTH AFRICA CAMPAIGN (1942–43) and the invasion of SICILY (1943). Lemnitzer was also an Allied negotiator for the German surrender (1945) and involved in the diplomatic negotiations leading to the NORTH ATLANTIC TREATY ORGANIZATION. After commanding a division in KOREA, he remained in Asia in various roles, culminating with commander in chief of the Far Eastern Command (1955–57). His tenure as chairman of the Joint Chiefs of Staff was marred by the BAY OF PIGS INVASION (1961). As supreme Allied commander, Europe, Lemnitzer dealt with the French withdrawal from NATO (1966) and the relocation of headquarters from Paris to Brussels. He retired at the rank of four-star general in 1969 after fifty-one years of service.

Lend-Lease Act • a law passed by Congress on March 11, 1941, during WORLD WAR II, allowing the president to "sell, transfer title to, exchange, lease, lend, or otherwise dispose of" weapons and materials to help defend nations vital to U.S. security. Suggested by President FRANKLIN D. ROOSEVELT in December 1940 to help countries fighting the AXIS, it provided $31.6 billion to Britain and $11 billion to the USSR.

L'Enfant, Pierre Charles |ˌlän'fän(t)| (1754–1825) • military engineer, architect, and urban designer, born in Paris. L'Enfant laid out the basic plan for Washington, D.C. L'Enfant, who came to America in 1777 to participate in the REVOLUTIONARY WAR, was a captain in the corps of engineers who was wounded at the battle of Savannah (1779), taken prisoner at CHARLESTON (1780), and later exchanged. He was discharged in 1784. L'Enfant had several design commissions after the war, both domestic and military, most notably the conversion of New York city hall into Federal Hall. His designs were seen as lavish and too grand in scale, often leading to his dismissal before their completion. His inability to cooperate with the city commissioners led to his being dismissed as planner of Washington as well, but the essence of his design was ultimately carried out.

Leopard • post-WORLD WAR II German main battle tank. The Leopard I was introduced in 1965. The Leopard 1A3 tank has a combat weight of 21 tons and is armed with a 105 mm main gun.

let daylight into • slang (WORLD WAR II) to shoot or stab.

letter of marque |märk| • (usually **letters of marque**) (in full **letter of mark and reprisal**) **1** a license to fit out an armed vessel and use it in the capture of enemy merchant shipping and to commit acts which would otherwise have constituted piracy. **2** a ship carrying such a license.

levee • *n.* **1** an embankment built to prevent the overflow of a river. **2** a landing place; a quay.

levée en masse • universal military conscription; the call-up for military service of all or most of a nation's male population of military age. The first levée en masse in modern times was the announcement by the French revolutionary government in August 1793 of the conscription of the entire male population (of military age) to resist counter-revolutionary forces.

levy • *v.* (**-ies, -ied**) **1** archaic enlist (someone) for military service: *he sought to levy one man from each parish for service.* **2** begin to wage (war). • *n.* (pl. **-ies**) **1** an act of enlisting troops. **2** (usually **levies**) a body of troops that have been enlisted: *lightly armed local levies.*

Lewis and Clark Expedition • U.S. military expedition, from 1804 to 1806, commissioned by President THOMAS JEFFERSON and led by Captain Meriwether Lewis and Lt. William Clark, the purpose of which was to explore the northern portion of the recently acquired LOUISIANA PURCHASE. The party of some thirty men departed St. Louis in May 1804; ascended the Missouri River; wintered over near the site of the present Bismarck, North Dakota; acquired the assistance of the Shoshone woman Sacagawea; crossed the Continental Divide; and descended the Salmon, Snake, and Columbia rivers to the Pacific coast; and returned by essentially the same route to St. Louis in 1806.

Lewis, Andrew (1720–81) • military and political leader in southwestern Virginia during the FRENCH AND INDIAN (1754–63) and REVOLUTIONARY WARS. Lewis, born in County Donegal, Ireland, gained his greatest prominence as a frontier military leader of the local militia in expeditions against the French on the Upper Ohio River. In 1774 he commanded forces that won an important victory over the Shawnee Indians that resulted in their ceding all territory south of the Ohio to Virginia. During the Revolutionary War, Lewis commanded troops against Loyalist forces in Chesapeake Bay (1776), successfully forcing them from the colony. Disappointed at not being made major general, he resigned from the Continental army in 1777.

Lewis gun • a light, air-cooled machine gun with a magazine operated by gas from its own firing, used mainly in WORLD WAR I.

ORIGIN: early 20th century: named after its inventor, Isaac N. *Lewis* (1858–1931), a colonel in the U.S. Army.

lewisite |'lo͞oəˌsīt| • *n.* a dark, oily liquid producing an irritant gas that causes blisters, developed for use in chemical warfare.

ORIGIN: 1920s: named after Winford L. *Lewis* (1878–1943), American chemist.

Lewis, Morgan (1754–1844) • REVOLUTIONARY WAR officer, born in New York City. Lewis served as chief of staff to Gen. HORATIO GATES and received the surrender of the British army at SARATOGA (1777). He later participated in expeditions to the Mohawk Valley (1778) and against CROWN POINT (1780), following which he served as assistant quartermaster general until the end of the war. During the WAR OF 1812 he served as quartermaster general. Between the wars Lewis had an active political life in his native New York, serving in the state assembly, as state attorney general, as chief justice of the state supreme court, and as governor.

Lexington, Battle of • a conflict marking the beginning of the REVOLUTIONARY WAR in Lexington, Massachusetts, on April 19, 1775. An American force of about seventy MINUTEMEN under Capt. John Parker assembled on Lexington green after receiving word from dispatch riders, including PAUL REVERE, that a British force of about 250 men, under Maj. John Pitcairn, was advancing to Concord to confiscate provincial military supplies. British soldiers fired on Parker's force after hearing a gunshot, although which side the shot came from is uncertain, and it may have been accidental. When the British force arrived at Concord, the supplies had already been removed. A firefight ensued at the North Bridge over the Concord River (BATTLE OF CONCORD), and the Americans demonstrated that they were capable of using armed force to resist the British regulars. As the British retreated to Boston, colonists fired at them, mostly from behind stone walls. The two battles led to the siege of Boston.

***Lexington*, USS** • an aircraft carrier, originally named Cabot 15 and renamed *Lexington* in 1942, the *Lexington* participated in numerous actions in the Pacific Theater of WORLD WAR II, including raids on TARAWA (September 1943) and WAKE ISLAND (October 1943), and provided air cover for the landings in the GILBERT ISLANDS that November, downing twenty-nine enemy aircraft. For outstanding service in WORLD WAR II, the carrier received the Presidential Unit

Citation and eleven battle stars. In 1947, *Lexington* decommissioned at Bremerton, Washington, and entered the Reserve Fleet there. In 1952, the ship was redesignated attack carrier CVA-16 and began conversion and modernization, being provided with the new angled flight deck. Recommissioned on October 1, 1955, the *Lexington* served several peacekeeping missions, then, in 1962, was redesignated CVS-16, although it resumed duty as an attack carrier during the CUBAN MISSILE CRISIS. Into 1963, *Lexington* served in the training of active and reserve naval aviators, and, on October 17, 1967, marked its 200,000th arrested landing. On January 1, 1969, the *Lexington* was redesignated CVT-16.

Leyte Gulf, Battle for • a WORLD WAR II battle between U.S. and Japanese naval forces on October 23–25, 1944, that resulted in the overwhelming defeat of the Japanese IMPERIAL NAVY. Following the U.S. invasion of the PHILIPPINES, U.S. amphibious ships of the 7th Fleet commanded by Vice Adm. THOMAS C. KINKAID carried out the landings at LEYTE, and the 3rd Fleet under Adm. WILLIAM F. HALSEY provided cover. The Japanese plan, OPERATION SHO-I, involved the coordination of four separate forces. The Americans engaged 216 warships; the Japanese, sixty-four; and the Australians, two. It is both the largest naval battle in history and the last clash between battleships.

LGM-118 • see PEACEKEEPER.

LGM-30 • see MINUTEMAN.

LGW • *abbr.* laser-guided weapon.

LHA • *abbr.* amphibious assault ship.

LI • *abbr.* Brit. light infantry.

Libby Prison • a notorious prison of the CIVIL WAR in RICHMOND, Virginia. It was in three relatively new buildings, formerly a chandlery, that were commandeered for prison use following the FIRST BATTLE OF BULL RUN (1861), owing to the stream of prisoners entering Richmond. More than 50,000 men passed through this prison while it was used by the CONFEDERACY; it was briefly used in mid 1865 by the Union for the same purpose after the fall of Richmond.

Liberator • (**B-24**) a long-range heavy bomber, first flown in 1939, that virtually replaced the B-17 during WORLD WAR II. It was used by both the United States and Britain, and saw service in Europe, North Africa, and the Pacific theaters.

liberty • *n.* shore leave granted to a sailor.

liberty boat • Brit. a boat carrying sailors who have leave to go ashore.

liberty cabbage • slang (WORLD WAR I) sauerkraut.

Liberty Loan campaigns • a series of propaganda campaigns begun in 1917 by U.S. Secretary of the Treasury William G. McAdoo to finance U.S. participation in WORLD WAR I by shifting private savings of Americans into bonds. To encourage the American public to purchase Liberty bonds, McAdoo used speaking tours, posters, celebrity endorsements, "Four Minute Men" in front of audiences, and the selling services of the Boy Scouts.

liberty man • Brit. a sailor with leave to go ashore.

Liberty ship • a prefabricated U.S.-built freighter of WORLD WAR II.

LIC • *abbr.* low intensity conflict.

Liddell Hart, Basil H. (1895–1970) • English military writer and theorist, born in Paris. Liddell Hart was known for his advocacy of mechanized tank warfare. He emphasized the importance of air support to tanks and the need for a mechanized infantry. His innovative ideas were resisted by professional officers of the time, and his influence was greater in Germany than in Britain or the United States. (The German BLITZKREIG was based on theories he had propounded.) During WORLD WAR II he opposed sending British troops to Europe, as well as the war policies of WINSTON CHURCHILL. After the war he was among the first to argue that nuclear weapons could deter all-out conflict but not prevent conventional warfare; he advocated restraint and avoidance of showdowns. Liddell Hart had served as an infantry officer during WORLD WAR I but had retired from the army in 1924 for health reasons.

Lieber Code, the • an order prepared for the Union Army in 1863, during the CIVIL WAR, by Professor Francis Lieber of Columbia College as the first codification of standards of the laws of war, or what is now called international humanitarian law. Also known as General Order 100, "Instructions for the Government of Armies of the United States in the Field," it became known as "Hague law" after the international standard setting in 1899 of the Hague Regulations.

lie off • (of a ship) stand some distance from shore or from another ship.

lie to • (of a ship) come almost to a stop with its head toward the wind.

lie up • **1** (of a ship) go into dock or be out of commission. **2** (**lie something up**) put a boat in dock or out of commission.

lieutenant |lo͞oˈtenənt| • *n.* **1** see FIRST LIEUTENANT, SECOND LIEUTENANT. **2** a naval officer of a high rank, in particular a commissioned officer in the U.S. Navy or Coast Guard ranking above lieutenant junior grade and below lieutenant commander. **3** a deputy or substitute acting for a superior: *two of Lenin's leading lieutenants.*

DERIVATIVES: **lieutenancy** |-ˈtenənsē| *n.* (pl. **-ies**).

lieutenant colonel • a commissioned officer in the U.S. Army, Air Force, or Marine Corps ranking above major and below colonel.

lieutenant commander • a commissioned officer in the U.S. Navy or Coast Guard ranking above lieutenant and below commander.

lieutenant general • a commissioned officer in the U.S. Army, Air Force, or Marine Corps ranking above major general and below general.

Lieutenant Junior Grade • an officer grade in the U.S. Navy and U.S. Coast Guard corresponding to 1st Lieutenant in the U.S.

Army, Air Force, and Marine Corps; pay grade O-2.

lifebelt • *n.* a life preserver in the shape of a belt.

lifeboat • *n.* **1** a specially constructed boat launched from land to rescue people in distress at sea. **2** a small boat kept on a ship for use in emergency, typically one of a number on deck or suspended from davits.

DERIVATIVES: **lifeboatman** *n.* (pl. **-men**).

lifebuoy • *n.* a life preserver, especially one in the shape of a ring.

life jacket • a sleeveless buoyant or inflatable jacket for keeping a person afloat in water.

lifeline • *n.* **1** a rope or line used for life-saving, typically one thrown to rescue someone in difficulties in water or one used by sailors to secure themselves to a boat. **2** a line used by a diver for sending signals to the surface.

life raft • a raft, typically inflatable, for use in an emergency at sea.

life ring • another term for LIFEBELT.

Lifesaving Service, U.S. • (**USLSS**) founded in 1878 to save rescue shipwreck victims and help ships in distress. In 1915 the service became the U.S. Coast Guard.

Liggett, Hunter (1857–1937) • commander of the first American army corps in WORLD WAR I, born in Reading, Pennsylvania. Liggett fought at CANTIGNY and the MARNE (1918). He was awarded the DISTINGUISHED SERVICE MEDAL.

light • *adj.* **1** carrying only light armaments: *light infantry.* **2** (of a vehicle, ship, or aircraft) traveling unladen or with less than a full load.

light artillery • field artillery pieces of a caliber of 120 mm or less.

light at the end of the tunnel • part of a phrase uttered by U.S. National Security Adviser WALT W. ROSTOW in December 1967, in regard to the VIETNAM WAR. The entire phrase was "I see light at the end of the tunnel," which was an attempt to reassure the American public that victory was at hand, despite years of fighting and heavy casualties.

lighter • *n.* a flat-bottomed barge or other unpowered boat used to transfer cargo to and from ships in harbor. • *v.* transport (goods) in a lighter: *they lightered their cargo ashore.*

lighterage • *n.* the transfer of cargo by means of a lighter; the charge levied for such transfer.

lighthouse • *n.* a tower or other structure containing a beacon light to warn or guide ships at sea.

Lightning • (**P-38**) a heavily armed fighter-interceptor aircraft used in WORLD WAR II by the U.S. Army Air Force. The P-38 was the primary fighter escort for medium U.S. bombers in Europe, and was also used in the Pacific theater.

lightship • *n.* (also **light vessel**)a moored or anchored vessel with a beacon light to warn or guide ships at sea.

Lilienthal, David Eli |ˈlilēən,THôl| (1899–1981) • government official, born in Morton, Illinois. Lilienthal was the chair of the Tennessee Valley Authority (1941–46) and head of the ATOMIC ENERGY COMMISSION (1947–50). As chair of the TVA, a federal electric power and flood-control program of which he had been a director since 1933, Lilienthal expanded its program during the war years to serve the needs of private and government plants producing ammunition and other war-related materials, making it the nation's leading producer of electric power by 1944. As chair of the AEC, he expanded the production of atomic bombs and encouraged the use of atomic power in private industry.

limber • *n.* the detachable front part of a gun carriage, consisting of two wheels and an axle, a pole, and a frame holding one or more ammunition boxes.

Limited Test Ban Treaty • an agreement signed in Moscow on August 5, 1963, by representatives of the USSR, United Kingdom, and United States, after U.S. President JOHN F. KENNEDY and Soviet premier NIKITA KHRUSHCHEV reached a compromise. Entered into force on October 10, 1963, it prohibits "any nuclear weapon test explosion, or any other nuclear explosion" in the atmosphere, in outer space, or under water. It failed to ban underground tests, as the United States and the USSR could not agree on procedures for on-site inspections.

limited war • a war in which the weapons used, the nations or territory involved, or the objectives pursued are restricted in some way, in particular one in which the use of nuclear weapons is avoided.

limit of fire • **1** the boundary marking off the area on which gunfire can be delivered. **2** safe angular limits for firing at aerial targets.

limpet mine • a mine designed to be attached magnetically to a ship's hull and set to explode after a certain time.

Lincoln, Abraham (1809–65) • 16th president of the United States (1861–65), born in Hardin County, Kentucky. In Illinois, where he later settled, Lincoln pursued law and politics (as a Whig), serving in the state legislature (1834–41) and in the U.S. House of Representatives (1847–49), where he spoke out against the MEXICAN WAR (1846–48). Prompted by the controversy over the expansion of slavery into the territories, he returned to public life in 1854. In 1858, though he lost the election, he gained national prominence when he challenged Stephen A. Douglas for the U.S. Senate and engaged him in a series of debates that brought the issue to a head. Nominated in 1860 for president on the Republican ticket, Lincoln carried the electoral vote despite winning slightly under 40 percent of the popular vote. Before his inauguration, in March 1861, seven of the ten states that would form the CONFEDERACY had already seceded. One month later, with the Southern capture of FORT SUMTER, the CIVIL WAR had begun. Lincoln's intention, he said, was to preserve the Union and to stop the spread of slavery, not to attack it where it existed. Lincoln devoted most of his time to his duties as commander in chief, studying military history and strategy and frequently visiting troops at the front. He grew impatient with the failures of Union generals to act with the aggressiveness he believed necessary. Though Confederate successes (First and Second BULL RUN, 1861–62) in the first two years of the war gave way to Union victories at GETTYSBURG and VICKSBURG (both 1863), the conflict dragged on. Lincoln came to see that his hoped-for decisive victory that would end the war was not to be; the bloody and remorseless struggle would end only when the will of the South was broken. Weary of war and its costly human sacrifice, Northerners appeared ready in early 1864 to turn Lincoln out of office. But the victory at ATLANTA that year, followed by successes in the SHENANDOAH VALLEY, restored their faith in the commander in chief and ensured his reelection on the Union ticket. The changes in fortune had come about with Lincoln's appointment of ULYSSES S. GRANT as general in chief of all Union armies. Grant's strategy of attacking on several fronts at once was to be the key to the Union victory, which was effectively sealed with the surrender of ROBERT E. LEE and his ARMY OF NORTHERN VIRGINIA at APPOMATTOX in April 1865. Five days later Lincoln was shot, the first president to be assassinated. He died the following morning (April 15). Though Lincoln has been criticized for exceeding his powers in curtailing civil liberties during the war, he remains a figure revered as the preserver of the republic and the destroyer of slavery. Though the EMANCIPATION PROCLAMATION (1863) did not itself end that institution, it set the wheels in motion; and Lincoln himself proposed, but did not live to see enacted, a constitutional amendment to abolish slavery.

Lincoln, Benjamin (1733–1810) • Revolutionary war officer, born in Hingham, Massachusetts. Lincoln led the march of patriot forces from New York to YORKTOWN, commanded the right wing during the siege, and was appointed by GEORGE WASHINGTON to receive the sword of British Gen. CHARLES CORNWALLIS at the surrender (1781). Previously Lincoln had participated in several significant battles, among them WHITE PLAINS (1776) and CHARLESTON, where he had been compelled to surrender the city and his army (1780). After the revolution he served for two years as secretary of war under the new national government. Lincoln later played a major role in quelling SHAYS'S REBELLION (1786–87), leading an expeditionary force of volunteers that overwhelmed the rebels.

Lindbergh, Charles Augustus (1902–74) • the most acclaimed aviator in American history, born in Detroit, Michigan. Lindbergh was glorified as a national hero and awarded the CONGRESSIONAL MEDAL OF HONOR after being the first person to fly solo nonstop from New York to Paris (1927). Lindbergh actively opposed U.S. involvement in WORLD WAR II, becoming the leading spokesman for the noninterventionist AMERICA FIRST COMMITTEE. Once the United States did enter the war, he ceased these activities and supported the war effort as a civilian by testing and developing military aircraft and by flying combat missions in the South Pacific (1944). But his reputation never recovered from allegations that he was pro-NAZI and anti-Semitic. After the war Lindbergh performed a variety of services for the U.S. Air Force and the Defense Department. In 1954 President DWIGHT D. EISENHOWER restored his commission in the Air Force Reserve.

line • *n.* **1** a length of cord, rope, wire, or other material serving a particular purpose: *wring the clothes and hang them on the line | a telephone line.* **2** a telephone connection: *we've got headquarters* ***on the line***. **3** a direction, course, or channel: *lines of communication | he opened another line of attack.* **4** a connected series of military fieldworks or defenses facing an enemy force: *raids behind enemy lines.* **5** an arrangement of soldiers or ships in a column or line formation; a line of battle. **6** (**the line**) regular army regiments (as opposed to auxiliary forces or household troops).

PHRASES: **in the line of duty** while one is working (used mainly of police officers, firefighters, or soldiers). **line of fire** the expected path of gunfire or a missile: *residents within line of fire were evacuated from their homes.* **line of flight** the route taken through the air. **line of march** the route taken in marching. **line of sight** a straight line along which an observer has unobstructed vision: *a building that obstructs our line of sight.*

▸**line up 1** arrange a number of people or things in a straight row. **2** (of a number of people or things) be arranged in this way: *we would line up across the parade ground.*

Linebacker I • a series of air attacks launched by President RICHARD M. NIXON in May 1972 against North Vietnam and in response to the EASTER OFFENSIVE. The raids were designed to hinder the North Vietnamese invasion of the South by destroying its petroleum storage facilities, power-generating plants, and major bridges. It was the first campaign to rely heavily on precision-guided munitions. By the end of June, the air force and navy had destroyed or damaged 400 bridges in North Vietnam, including ones that had been bombed previously to no effect.

Linebacker II • an eleven-day campaign, also known as the "Christmas bombings," launched by President RICHARD M. NIXON in late December 1972. The second series of Linebacker attacks, it was the most intense air assault of the VIETNAM WAR. Tactical aircraft flew more than 1,000 sorties and B--52s, about 740 against targets in the heart of HANOI and HAIPHONG. The North Vietnamese destroyed twenty-seven American aircraft, including eighteen B-52s. By the end of the campaign, Hanoi had used its entire supply of antiaircraft missiles, and B-52s could fly over the North Vietnamese cities with impunity.

line of battle • **1** a disposition of troops for action in battle. **2** a battle formation of warships in line ahead (one behind another).

line of departure • **1** in land-mine warfare, a line designated to coordinate the departure of attack elements. **2** in amphibious warfare, a suitably marked offshore coordinating line to assist assault craft to land on designated beaches at scheduled times.

line of duty • **1** within one's range of authorized responsibilities. **2** a medical determination that an injury or disability did not result from any fault or neglect on the part of the individual concerned.

line officer • in the U.S. Army, a combat arms officer serving in a line unit; in the U.S. Navy, an officer other than an officer of the Supply, Medical, Judge Advocate, or other specialist corps.

liner • *n.* **1** (also **ocean liner**) a large luxurious passenger ship of a type formerly used on a regular line. **2** a large commercial ship or aircraft outfitted to carry passengers, especially one that follows a regular route and schedule.

lines of communication • (**LOC**) all the routes (land, water, and air) that connect an operating military force with a base of operations and along which supplies and military forces move.

linkspan • *n.* a hinged bridge on the quay at a port or ferry terminal which can be connected with a ramp on a vessel to allow loading or unloading.

liquid explosive • an explosive that is fluid at normal temperatures.

liquid propellant • any liquid combustible fed to the combustion chamber of a rocket engine.

Lisbon Agreement on NATO Force Levels • the Lisbon force goals were adopted by the NORTH ATLANTIC COUNCIL in February 1952 in an attempt to augment the conventional forces defending Western Europe after the outbreak of the KOREAN WAR. The goals adopted were twenty-five ready divisions and twenty-eight and two-thirds reserve divisions mobilizable within thirty days. Actual forces at the end of 1952 were twenty-five ready divisions and twenty reserve divisions.

list • *v.* (of a ship) lean to one side, typically because of a leak or unbalanced cargo. Compare with HEEL.

listening post • **1** a station for intercepting electronic communications. **2** a position from which to listen or gather information. **3** a point near an enemy's lines for detecting movements by sound.

Little Bighorn, Battle of • a clash on June 25, 1876, during the GREAT SIOUX WAR OF 1876, between U.S. cavalry and SIOUX and CHEYENNE Indians, who had gathered under SITTING BULL and CRAZY HORSE. Lt. Col. GEORGE ARMSTRONG CUSTER, leader of the 7th Cavalry, which was part of Brig. Gen. ALFRED H. TERRY's column, led his battalion in an attack on the Indian village on the Little Bighorn. Maj. Marcus A. Reno and his three companies charged the upper end of the village and soon retreated, allowing the Indians to focus on Custer at the other end of the village. The Indians completely destroyed Custer and the five companies under his immediate command, some 210 men. Reno's men were joined by the three companies under Capt. Frederick W. Benteen and held hilltop positions 4 miles to the south through the next day. As Terry approached from the north, the Indians pulled off to the south. The defeat so outraged Americans that the army launched a counteroffensive that ended warfare on the northern plains. Also known as CUSTER'S LAST STAND.

"Little Boy" • the nickname given to the Uranium 235 atomic bomb that struck HIROSHIMA, Japan, on August 3, 1945. The USAAF B-29 bomber *Enola Gay* dropped it from 31,600 feet, at 8:15 A.M. local time, and fifty seconds later it detonated in the center of the city. It produced a 20,000-foot mushroom cloud of smoke and debris; resulted in over 120,000 immediate and subsequent fatalities; and destroyed 81 percent of the city's structures.

Little Boy • the nickname for the atomic bomb dropped on HIROSHIMA in WORLD WAR II. See also FAT MAN.

Little, George (1754–1809) • U.S. naval officer. Born in Massachusetts, Little entered the navy early in the REVOLUTIONARY WAR. He was imprisoned twice by the British, and the second time escaped to France where Benjamin Franklin helped him return to America. Little took command of the sloop *Winthrop* in 1782 and captured nearly the entire British garrison at Penobscot. He returned to his farm in 1783, but was called back to duty for the QUASI-WAR WITH FRANCE in 1799. As captain of the frigate Boston he was held liable for taking a Danish brig, but he also captured a French privateer and the naval corvette *Berceau*.

little people • slang (in the VIETNAM WAR) the enemy, the Vietnamese people generally.

In WORLD WAR II, "little men" referred to the Japanese.

Little Round Top • a hill of strategic importance at GETTYSBURG (1863), during the CIVIL WAR. Success during this pivotal battle 35 miles (56 km) southwest of Harrisburg, Pennsylvania, depended on which forces could hold high ground. Little Round Top, though slightly smaller than the nearby Big ROUND TOP, was abandoned by Union Brig. Gen. DANIEL SICKLES on the first day of fighting. Brig. Gen. GEORGE G. MEADE's chief engineer, Maj. Gen. GOUVERNEUR K. WARREN, noticed that the empty hill left the Union's left flank vulnerable and ordered troops to cover it. During the second day of the battle, Gen. JOSHUA LAWRENCE CHAMBERLAIN defended Little Round Top from fierce attacks, which earned him the CONGRESSIONAL MEDAL OF HONOR. The Confederates retreated from Gettysburg on July 3 after heavy losses on both sides.

littoral |ˈlit̬ərəl| • *adj.* of, relating to, or situated on the shore of the sea or a lake: *the littoral states of the Indian Ocean.* • *n.* a region lying along a shore: *irrigated regions of the Mediterranean littoral.*

littoral warfare • warfare conducted by naval, air, and ground (landing) forces in coastal areas.

live |līv| • *adj.* of, containing, or using undetonated explosive: *live ammunition.*

live fire mission • an artillery, mortar, or direct fire mission involving the use of live ammunition, either in training or in combat.

living-room war • a war in which scenes of actual combat operations are recorded by commercial television crews and replayed on network news programs, thus "bringing the war into the viewer's living room." The VIETNAM WAR was the first such war, and the PERSIAN GULF WAR (1990–91) had almost real time coverage of the key events of the conflict.

Livingston, James (1747–1832) • Continental army officer whose Canadian forces took part in the assault on QUÉBEC (1775) and in the SARATOGA campaign (1777) before being assigned to garrison duty along the Hudson River (1780). During the last mentioned, Livingston unwittingly contributed to the capture of JOHN ANDRÉ by firing on the British ship that was, unbeknownst to Livingston, awaiting the informer. The ship departed, André traveled by land, and was captured. When the Continental army was reorganized in 1780, Livingston's Canadian unit was eliminated.

LKA • *abbr.* attack cargo ship.

Lloyd George, David (1863–1945) • British statesman and prime minister (1916–22), and one of the three main negotiators at the TREATY OF VERSAILLES (1919). Lloyd George played a moderating role between the draconian demands of GEORGES CLEMENCEAU and the progressive peace policies of WOODROW WILSON.

Lloyd's • an incorporated society of insurance underwriters in London, made up of private syndicates. Founded in 1871, Lloyd's originally dealt only in marine insurance.

ORIGIN: named after the coffeehouse of Edward *Lloyd* (*fl.* 1688–1726), in which underwriters and merchants congregated and where *Lloyd's List* was started in 1734.

LNLL • *abbr.* Lawrence Livermore National Laboratory.

load displacement • the displacement of a ship loaded to full capacity.

load line • another term for PLIMSOLL LINE.

lobscouse |'läbˌskows| • *n.* a stew formerly eaten by sailors, consisting of meat, vegetables, and ship's biscuit.

LOC • *abbr.* lines of communication.

lock • *n.* **1** a short confined section of a canal or other waterway in which the water level can be changed by the use of gates and sluices, used for raising and lowering vessels between two gates. **2** an airlock. **3** the mechanism that explodes the powder charge of a gun.

▸**lock onto** locate (a target) by radar or similar means and then track.

lockage • *n.* **1** the construction or use of locks on waterways. **2** the amount of rise and fall of water levels resulting from the use of locks. **3** money paid as a toll for the use of a lock.

locker • *n.* a chest or compartment on a ship or boat for clothes, stores, equipment, or ammunition.

Lockheed Martin Corporation • a U.S. company that produces military aircraft and technology, space satellites and systems, and electronic products. Founded as the Lockheed Aircraft Company in 1916 by Allan and Malcolm Loughhead (pronounced "Lockheed") in California, the company produced important military products, including the P-38 LIGHTNING fighter-bomber in WORLD WAR II. In 1995 Lockheed merged with MARTIN MARIETTA Corporation to become the largest U.S. defense contractor.

lock-keeper • *n.* a person who is employed to attend and maintain a lock on a river or canal.

locksman • *n.* **1** a turnkey; jailer. **2** a lock-keeper.

lockstep • *n.* a way of marching with each person as close as possible to the one in front: *the trio marched **in lockstep**.*

Lodge, Henry Cabot (1850–1924) • U.S. senator (1893–1924), born in Boston, Massachusetts. As chairman of the Foreign Relations Committee, Lodge successfully led the opposition to ratification of the TREATY OF VERSAILLES following WORLD WAR I. A conservative Republican and longtime foe of WOODROW WILSON, Lodge objected not to the main terms of the peace treaty itself, but to the covenant of the LEAGUE OF NATIONS that it contained, which he believed infringed on national sovereignty. He led the Republicans in drawing up fourteen reservations as conditions for ratification of the League, but the necessary two-thirds was never mustered in the Senate, either for unconditional ratification or with the Lodge reservations.

Lodge, Henry Cabot (1902–85) • U.S. senator (1937–44; 1947–53) and diplomat, born in Nahart, Massachusetts. Lodge served as ambassador to the UNITED NATIONS (1953–60) and ambassador to South Vietnam (1963–64; 1965–67). During his tenure at the United Nations he was called upon to deal with a number of crises, including the revolutions in Hungary (1956) and Cuba (1957–58) and the U-2 INCIDENT (1960). During these episodes, Lodge adhered to an aggressive line against the Soviets. His first tour of duty in Vietnam included the U.S.-sanctioned removal, if not murder, of President NGO DINH DIEM, which failed to stop Communist expansion. As ambassador under President LYNDON B. JOHNSON, Lodge helped plan and carry out the escalation of U.S. troop involvement and the air war against North Vietnam. In 1969 he headed the U.S. delegation to the unsuccessful Paris peace talks with North Vietnam. Lodge earned a BRONZE STAR and six battle stars in World War II. In 1960 Lodge ran as vice president on the losing Republican ticket headed by RICHARD M. NIXON.

Lodge, also known as Henry Cabot Lodge Jr., was the grandson and namesake of HENRY CABOT LODGE (1850–1924).

loft bombing • a method of bombing in which the delivery plane approaches the target at a very low altitude, makes a definite pullup at a given point, releases the bomb at a predetermined point during the pullup, and tosses the bomb onto the target.

loftsman • *n.* (pl. **-men**) a person who draws up full-size outlines from the drawing or plans for parts of a ship or aircraft.

log • *n.* **1** (also **logbook**) an official record of events during the voyage of a ship or aircraft: *a ship's log.* **2** a regular or systematic record of incidents or observations: *keep a detailed log of your activities.* **3** an apparatus for determining the speed of a ship, originally consisting of a float attached to a knotted line wound on a reel, the distance run out in a certain time being used as an estimate of the vessel's speed. • *v.* (**logged, logging**) **1** enter (an incident or fact) in the log of a ship or aircraft or in another systematic record: *the incident has to be logged | the red book where we log our calls.* **2** (of a ship or aircraft) achieve (a certain distance or speed): *it had logged more than 12,000 miles since it had been launched.* **3** (of an aircraft pilot) attain (a certain amount of flying time).

Logan, Benjamin (c. 1742–1802) • frontier civil and military officer, born in Augusta County, Virginia. Logan played a major role in the settling and securing of Kentucky. Before the REVOLUTIONARY WAR, Logan twice fought with local militias in campaigns against the Indians in southwestern Virginia and Kentucky (then part of Virginia). During the Revolutionary War, as a captain and later colonel in the militia, he led a number of retaliatory expeditions across the Ohio River that destroyed Ohio Indian villages and cornfields. In 1786 he led a raid that devastated seven Ohio Indian villages.

Logan, James (1776?–1812) • Shawnee warrior (Spemica Lawba) who became an American hero during the WAR OF 1812 when he was fatally wounded in an encounter with a British party. As a boy Logan had been captured by Kentuckians who attacked his town (1786); he apparently acquired the name by which he was known to whites from their leader, BENJAMIN LOGAN, who befriended him. From 1789 to 1795 Logan, who had been released in exchange, fought with the Shawnees against the United States, but once hostilities were concluded, he became friendly with Americans and advocated peace. His reliability and knowledge of English made him useful as an intermediary. During the WAR OF 1812, Logan served with American forces, helping guide the army of Gen. WILLIAM HULL through Ohio to Detroit, and later serving under the commander in chief WILLIAM HENRY HARRISON.

Logan, John Alexander (1826–86) • Union army officer, born in Jackson County, Illinois. Logan fought at FORT DONELSON (1862), during the VICKSBURG (1862–63) and ATLANTA (1864) campaigns, and in WILLIAM T. SHERMAN's campaign through the Carolinas (1865). After the conflict, Logan played a major role in organizing the GRAND ARMY OF THE REPUBLIC. He also had an active political career, serving in both the House and Senate and running unsuccessfully for vice president on the Republican ticket in 1884. In Congress Logan, a radical Republican, frequently denounced former Confederates and attacked President ANDREW JOHNSON. Logan had also served in Congress before the war, as a Democrat, when he was outspoken in his pro-slavery and anti-abolitionist views. His eventual siding with the UNION surprised many. He remained a War Democrat during the conflict, but campaigned for ABRAHAM LINCOLN's reelection in 1864.

As commander of the Grand Army of the Republic, Logan proclaimed the first formal MEMORIAL DAY in 1868.

Logan, Thomas Muldrup (1840–1914) • Confederate army officer, born in Charleston, South Carolina. Logan was a member of HAMPTON'S LEGION who fought at FIRST BULL RUN (1861), was wounded at GAINES' MILL (1862), commanded a company at SECOND BULL RUN (1862), and was commended for bravery at ANTIETAM (1862). He subsequently fought at CHICKAMAUGA (1863) and led the last Confederate cavalry charge of the war at the battle of Bentonville, North Carolina (1865).

logistics • *n.* the organization of moving, housing, and supplying troops and equipment.

logistics, principles of • a series of fundamental interrelated concepts, based on experience, which purport to encapsulate those factors leading to success in military logistical operations. The U.S. Army subscribes to nine such principles which can be grouped under five general headings: Concentration, Austerity, Visibility, Mobility, and Flexibility.

logistic support • the support that encompasses the logistic services, materiel, and transportation required to support the continental U.S.-based and worldwide deployed forces.

log line • a line to which a ship's log is attached.

Logstown Treaty • a treaty of June 13, 1752, to open land west of the Alleghany mountains to white settlement. It was negotiated at the village of Logstown on the upper Ohio River by Indian tribes including the Delaware, IROQUOIS, and Shawnee, and by commissioners from Virginia and representatives of the Ohio Company. It authorized settlements south of the Ohio River and two trading houses on the river.

lone eagle • an aerial tactic in which a single aircraft patrols alone; a sortie by a single aircraft.

Long Gray Line, the • the tradition of all the cadets who have graduated from West Point. ORIGIN: the name comes from the uniforms worn by the cadets, which are gray.

Long Island, Battle of • see NEW YORK, BATTLE OF.

Long, James (1792 or 1793–1822) • leader of two filibustering expeditions from the United States into Spanish Texas. The first of these (1819) captured Nacogdoches and resulted in Long's being chosen president of the newly created REPUBLIC OF TEXAS, but the venture ended the same year when a Spanish expedition attacked the Anglo-American invaders. The following year Long took command of Anglo-American filibusterers on Bolivar Peninsula, but their situation became complicated by the struggle for Mexican independence from Spain, with the result that Long was arrested and sent to Mexico City, where he was killed, perhaps intentionally, by a sentry.

long-range bomber aircraft • a bomber designed to have a tactical operating radius of 2,500 nautical miles at design gross weight and design bomb load.

longrifle • *n.* a long-barreled, muzzle-loading flintlock rifle that was used extensively in the 18th century.

Long, Stephen Harriman (1784–1864) • army explorer and topographical engineer, born in Hopkinton, New Hampshire. Long's career as an explorer was relatively short-lived; three major assignments failed to achieve significant results: an expedition up the Missouri River by steamboat to the Rocky Mountains (1819); an expedition to explore the central plains (1820); and an attempt to explore the headwaters of the Mississippi River and the border between the United States and Canada (1823). Long then turned his attention to transportation and went on detached duty for several years as a consulting engineer with various railroads. When he returned to active duty, he supervised dredging of the navigation channels in the Ohio, Arkansas, Red, and Mississippi Rivers. He was briefly called to Washington when the CIVIL WAR broke out, but soon retired (1863).

Longstreet, James (1821–1904) • U.S. and Confederate army officer. Born in Edgefield District, South Carolina, Longstreet grew up in Gainesville and Augusta, Georgia. He was graduated from WEST POINT in 1842 and joined the 4th Infantry at JEFFERSON BARRACKS near St. Louis, Missouri. He served under both ZACHARY TAYLOR and WINFIELD SCOTT during the MEXICAN WAR (1846–1848), participating in almost all of the major battles before being seriously wounded at CHAPULTEPEC (1847). With the outbreak of the CIVIL WAR he resigned his U.S. commission on June 1, 1861, and on June 17, 1861, he was commissioned as a brigadier general in the Confederate Army. He was promoted to major general after the battle of FIRST BULL RUN (1861), and commanded a division during operations on the Peninsula and at the battles of SECOND BULL RUN and ANTIETAM in 1862. He was promoted to lieutenant general and given command of the I Corps of the ARMY OF NORTHERN VIRGINIA under ROBERT E. LEE on October 11, 1862. Longstreet proved to be the best of Lee's corps commanders and participated in all the major battles in the East in 1862–63, except for CHANCELLORSVILLE. PICKETT's famous charge at GETTYSBURG (1863) was carried out under Longstreet's command. In the fall of 1863, Longstreet led his corps west to participate in the battle of CHICKAMAUGA (1863) and operations in eastern Tennessee, but returned to the east for the BATTLE OF THE WILDERNESS (1864) and the subsequent defense of RICHMOND. He surrendered his corps with Lee at APPOMATTOX in April 1865. After the war, Longstreet ran an insurance agency and was a cotton merchant in New Orleans. He joined the REPUBLICAN PARTY and held a number of political offices. He was a Customs official in New Orleans; postmaster of Gainesville, Georgia, U.S. minister to Turkey (1880–81), U.S. marshal for Georgia, and U.S. railroad commissioner (1881–84).

Long Telegram • a telegram sent from Moscow to Washington and written by U.S. diplomat GEORGE F. KENNAN on February 22, 1946, at the start of the COLD WAR. It discussed Soviet foreign policy and post-war Soviet ideology on international relations, as well as the potential effects of U.S. foreign policy. Kennan concluded that a policy of opposition and the containment of Soviet power was necessary.

looey (also **looie**) • *n.* (pl. **-eys** or **-ies**) slang short for LIEUTENANT.

look lively • (or **look alive**) informal move more quickly and energetically: *"Look lively, men!" Charlie shouted.*

Lookout Mountain, Battle of • a CIVIL WAR battle on November 24, 1863, that, along with the battle of MISSIONARY RIDGE (November 25), ended the Confederate siege of Union troops at CHATTANOOGA (1863). Gen. JOSEPH HOOKER, commanding the right wing of ULYSSES S. GRANT's Union army, drove Gen. BRAXTON BRAGG's Confederate forces off the mountain, which they had held since the battle of CHICKAMAUGA (1863).

It is also called the **Battle above the Clouds** because low-hanging clouds hid contending forces from observers in the valley of the Tennessee.

loose order • in tactics, the deployment of troops and/or combat vehicles with more than the normal space between individuals/vehicles so as to minimize the effect of enemy fires.

loran (also **Loran**) • *n.* a system of long-distance navigation in which position is determined from the intervals between signal pulses received from widely spaced radio transmitters.

ORIGIN: 1940s: from *lo(ng-)ra(nge) n(avigation)*.

Lord Dunmore's War • (**Dunmore's War, Gov. Dunmore's War**) the seizure of FORT PITT early in 1774 by the Virginia militia in an attempt to conquer the area of what is now Pittsburgh and to remove Indian opposition to white settlement there. The fort was renamed Fort Dunmore for JOHN MURRAY, the fourth earl of Dunmore and royal governor of New York and Virginia, and who led the attack along with Col. ANDREW LEWIS. The Delaware, influenced by Moravian missionaries, remained peaceful; but the Shawnee, under Chief Cornstalk, defended their homeland and were defeated on October 10 at the Battle of Point Pleasant. The Shawnee subsequently signed the Treaty of Camp Charlotte to relinquish their land and to secure protection from further attacks.

Lord Dunmore's War is sometimes called the first battle of the REVOLUTIONARY WAR, since Dunmore was accused of starting the battle to divert Virginians from conflicts with the governing of the colony.

Lord High Admiral • a title of the British monarch, originally the title of an officer who governed the ROYAL NAVY and had jurisdiction over maritime causes.

Loring, Charles Harding (1828–1907) • naval officer and engineer, born in Boston, Massachusetts. Loring oversaw the conversion from sail to steam-powered, and from wooden-hulled to ironclad, vessels during the CIVIL WAR. Loring was general inspector of such craft constructed west of the Alleghenies and chief technician for the monitors employed in the campaign to secure the Mississippi River for the UNION. After the war he served on several planning and decision-making boards considering the future course of the navy and its vessels. For a short period he was the navy's engineer in chief (1884–85). Loring retired in 1890 but returned to active duty as inspector of naval construction in New York during the SPANISH-AMERICAN WAR (1898).

Loring, William Wing (1818–86) • Confederate army officer, born in Wilmington, North Carolina. Loring held several assignments and commands during the course of the CIVIL WAR, but these repeated changes failed to bring any notable victory or particular distinction. Among them: defense of the SHENANDOAH VALLEY (1861); the Romney expedition (1861–62); an encounter at Fort Pemberton, Mississippi (1862), where he turned back a formidable Union force; a skirmish with troops of Gen. WILLIAM T. SHERMAN in northwestern Georgia (1864); the advance to NASHVILLE and retreat to Tupelo (1864); and battles with troops of Sherman in the Carolinas (1865). After the war Loring spent ten years as a mercenary in Egypt (1869–79). A career soldier prior to offering his services to the CONFEDERACY, Loring had participated in the MEXICAN WAR (1846–48), losing an arm at CHAPULTEPEC (1847).

Los Alamos National Laboratory • established in 1943, one of the national laboratories under the DEPARTMENT OF ENERGY (DOE) and operated by the University of California; it is a multiprogram facility located in New Mexico. It provides technical assistance to the DOE weapons complex, performs basic research for DOE programs, and supports energy and environmental technologies.

Los Angeles-class submarine • a class of nuclear-powered submarine of which the USS *Los Angeles*, built in 1976, was the first example. They are armed with HARPOON and TOMAHAWK missiles and MK-48 torpedoes.

Lost Cause, the • the idea, popular after the CIVIL WAR and in some areas of the South today, that the CONFEDERACY was doomed from the start because of the superior military might of the UNION, but that they fought heroically against all odds for the cause of states' rights. Gen. JUBAL EARLY was one of the first proponents of this idea.

Louisbourg Siege |ˈlo͞oisˌbərg ˈsēj| • (also **Louisburg**) the besieging of Louisbourg fortress at Cape Breton Island in 1745. It was a response to the renewed ANGLO-FRENCH WAR in 1744 and included 4,000 New England volunteers, led by William Pepperell and supported by Peter Warren's British naval squadron. On April 30, Pepperell landed his men at Gabrus Bay, and on May 3, the colonials captured the French Royal Battery of thirty cannon. On June 15, the colonials forced Louisbourg to surrender and intercepted the vessels of the French fleet as they arrived. Won primarily through the efforts of the colonials, it was the first important English victory in America. The colonists felt betrayed when England returned Louisbourg to France at the PEACE OF AIX-LA-CHAPELLE (1748).

Louisiana Purchase • the acquisition, for $15 million, of the vast territory (approximately 900,000 square miles, or 2.3 million square km) by the United States from France in 1803, during THOMAS JEFFERSON's first administration. The territory extended from the Mississippi River west to the Rocky Mountains, and from the Gulf of Mexico north to the Canadian border. Eventually, all or part of fifteen states were formed within that region.

Lovell, Mansfield (1822–84) • Confederate army officer and civil engineer, born in Washington, D.C. Lovell was charged with defending the inadequately fortified city and port of NEW ORLEANS, which was surrendered to Adm. DAVID FARRAGUT early in the conflict (1862). During his next assignment, retaking the strategic railroad junction of CORINTH, Mississippi, (1862), his failure to obey orders resulted in his being relieved of command. He remained without any assignment virtually for the remainder of the war. (Another came in March 1865, but the end of the war rendered it meaningless.) After the war Lovell worked as a civil engineer and surveyor in New York, as he had done in the years just prior to the war. Before the CIVIL WAR, Lovell had been a career soldier who saw combat during the MEXICAN WAR (1846–48) and was wounded at the BATTLE OF MONTERREY (1846) and the storming of MEXICO CITY (1847).

Lovell, Solomon (1732–1801) • REVOLUTIONARY WAR officer, born in Abington, Massachusetts. Lovell is remembered primarily for his participation in the Penobscot expedition (1779), the largest amphibious operation of the Revolution. Lovell was in command of the land forces in this disastrous attempt to expel the British from what is now Penobscot Bay, Maine; (then Massachusetts). Lovell and the naval commander (DUDLEY SALTONSTALL) could not agree on strategy. Lovell had previously led a militia unit in the battle of Rhode

Island (1778) and was with the rebel force that seized DORCHESTER HEIGHTS (1776).

Lovett, Robert A. (1895–1986) • secretary of defense (1951–53), born in Huntsville, Texas. His contributions included completing the KOREAN WAR mobilization; planning and implementing a long-range rearmament program; and submitting proposals to restructure the DEPARTMENT OF DEFENSE (which were largely implemented by the next administration). These involved giving the secretary of defense more explicit authority over the services, a military staff of his own to augment the joint chiefs, and greater flexibility to deal with problems of supply and logistics. During WORLD WAR II Lovett had been assistant secretary of war for air, overseeing the expansion of the army air forces and the procurement of aircraft, for which he was awarded the DISTINGUISHED SERVICE MEDAL (1945). During WORLD WAR I Lovett flew patrol and combat missions with the British Naval Air Service and later commanded a U.S. naval air squadron.

Lovewell, John (1691–1725) • frontier soldier born in what is now Nashua, New Hampshire (then Massachusetts). Lovewell led a company of rangers on retaliatory expeditions into Indian villages following a series of frontier disturbances that initiated a conflict known as DUMMER'S WAR (1722–26). Lovewell and his men killed and captured several Indians, and gained considerable fame when they paraded their scalps and weapons around Boston. Lovewell was killed early on in one such foray when his group was ambushed by the Pequawkets, but the battle lasted for several more hours, resulting in numerous casualties on both sides.

Lovewell's War • see DUMMER'S WAR.

LOW • *abbr.* launch on warning.

lower deck • the deck of a ship situated immediately above the hold.

low intensity conflict • political-military confrontation, ranging from propaganda and subversion to the actual use of armed forces, between contending states or groups below the level of conventional war and above the level of routine, peaceful competition among states. Low intensity conflicts are often localized, generally in the THIRD WORLD, but contain regional and global security implications.

low-level flight • see TERRAIN FLIGHT.

Lownds, David E. (1920–) • U.S. Marine officer, born in Holyoke, Massachusetts. Lownds was in command of the combat base at the siege of KHE SANH (1968) during the VIETNAM WAR. As a result of his leadership during that encounter, Lownds received the NAVY CROSS and accepted on behalf of the defenders of Khe Sanh a Presidential Unit Citation from LYNDON B. JOHNSON. During WORLD WAR II Lownds led a Marine platoon at the invasions of SAIPAN (1944) and IWO JIMA (1945). He was recalled to active status during the KOREAN WAR. He held various staff positions in the 1960s before being assigned to Vietnam in 1967 as regimental commander of the 26th Marines.

low tide • the state of the tide when at its lowest level: *islets visible **at low tide**.*

low-visibility operations • sensitive operations wherein the political-military restrictions inherent in covert and clandestine operations are either not necessary or not feasible; actions are taken as required to limit exposure of those involved and/or their activities. Execution of these operations is undertaken with the knowledge that the action and/or sponsorship of the operation may preclude plausible denial by the initiating power.

low water • **1** another term for LOW TIDE. **2** water in a stream or river at its lowest point.

low-water mark • the level reached by the sea at low tide, or by a lake or river during a drought or dry season.

loxodrome |ˈläksəˌdrōm| • *n.* another term for RHUMB (sense 1).

loxodromic |ˌläksəˈdrämik| • *adj.* of or relating to motion or alignment at a constant angle to the meridians, especially sailing by the rhumb (on a constant compass bearing). • *n.* (**loxodromics**) [treated as sing.] the art or practice of sailing to a constant compass bearing.

loyalist • *n.* **1** one who supports and defends his monarch or government, especially in times of crisis or war. **2** (**Loyalist**) a colonist who remained loyal to the British crown during the REVOLUTIONARY WAR.

loyalty • *n.* (pl. **-ies**) **1** the quality of being loyal to someone or something: *her **loyalty to** her husband of thirty-four years.* **2** (often **loyalties**) a strong feeling of support or allegiance: *fights with in-laws are distressing because they cause **divided loyalties**.*

loyalty oath • an oath of allegiance and faithfulness to the state required by a government of its citizens, particularly those in military service or government employment.

lozenge • *n.* a diamond shape that, when placed within the chevrons of an insignia, indicates the rank of first sergeant. It is a figure borrowed from heraldry and was first used in 1920.

LSD • *abbr.* Landing Ship, Dock. See AMPHIBIOUS LANDING SHIPS.

LSM • *abbr.* Landing Ship, Medium. See AMPHIBIOUS LANDING SHIPS.

LSM(R) • *abbr.* Landing Ship, Medium (Rocket). See AMPHIBIOUS LANDING SHIPS.

LST • *abbr.* Landing Ship, Tank. See AMPHIBIOUS LANDING SHIPS.

LSV • *abbr.* Landing Ship, Vehicle. See AMPHIBIOUS LANDING SHIPS.

Lt • *abbr.* **1** Lieutenant. **2** (also **lt**) light.

LUA • *abbr.* launch under attack.

lubber's line (also **lubber line**) • a line marked on the compass in a ship or aircraft, showing the direction straight ahead.

Luce, Stephen Bleeker (1827–1917) • career naval officer, born in Albany, New York. Luce was a leader and catalyst for the development of professional education and training in the U.S. Navy, and responsible for the establishment of the NAVAL WAR COLLEGE (1884). He lobbied for its existence, recruited its faculty, and served as its first president

(1885–86). Luce was recalled to active duty in 1901, returning to the staff of the Naval War College, where he remained until 1910.

Lucky Dragon • a Japanese fishing boat which was exposed in 1954 to a cloud of radioactive fall-out from a U.S. HYDROGEN BOMB test at the BIKINI ATOLL in the Pacific. This focused world public attention on the dangers of nuclear testing. The remote Bikini atoll was a much used site for U.S. nuclear bomb tests in the early 1950s.

Ludendorff, Erich (1865–1937) • German general (1914–18) born near Posen, Prussia (now Poznan, Poland). Ludendorff is identified with German imperialism and TOTAL WAR during WORLD WAR I. He was chief of staff to PAUL VON HINDENBURG and later, when Hindenburg became supreme military commander, his deputy. Ludendorff was architect of the victory over the Russians at Tannenberg (1914), but his offensives in the west (1918) lacked strategic objective and exhausted Germany's fighting power, leading to the armistice. During the WEIMAR REPUBLIC, Ludendorff took part in two unsuccessful putsches, including that by ADOLF HITLER in 1923, and became an outspoken Aryan racist.

Lufbery, Raoul |'ləfberē| (1885–1918) • WORLD WAR I aviator in the LAFAYETTE ESCADRILLE, born Gervais Raoul Victor Lufbery in Clermont, France. Lufbery was the first American ace with five confirmed aerial victories (1916). When the United States joined the war (1917), Lufbery, an American citizen, was transferred to the U.S. Air Service where he trained fighter pilots and led the first combat patrol (1918). He was killed in action when his aircraft was struck by enemy fire. Lufbery won the LEGION D'HONNEUR, the Medaille Militaire, the Croix de Guerre with ten palms, and the British Military Medal.

Luftwaffe |'lo͝oft,wäfə; -,väfə| • the German air force in WORLD WAR II. The Luftwaffe, headed by Reichsmarschall HERMANN GOERING, was created surreptitiously by the NAZIS in the 1930s in defiance of the TREATY OF VERSAILLES. Hampered by shortages of raw materials, production deficiencies, and the lack of a heavy strategic bomber, the Luftwaffe proved no match for the combined Allied air forces, even though the Luftwaffe introduced jet fighter aircraft toward the end of the war.
ORIGIN: German, from *Luft* 'air' + *Waffe* 'weapon.'

Luger |'lo͞ogər| • trademark a type of German automatic pistol.
ORIGIN: early 20th century: named after George *Luger* (1849–1923), German firearms expert.

lullaby in lead • slang (WORLD WAR II) a machine gun attack.

lunar distance • the angular distance of the moon from the sun, a planet, or a star, used in finding longitude at sea.

lunar observation • a measurement of the position of the moon in order to calculate longitude from lunar distance.

Lundy's Lane, Battle of • a battle between British and American troops at Lundy's Lane in Canada, one mile west of Niagara Falls, on July 25, 1814, during the WAR OF 1812. Although neither side won a decisive victory, it ended a U.S. invasion of Canada. Losses on both sides were the heaviest of the war; the British suffered 878 casualties, eighty-four of whom were killed; the Americans, 853 casualties, 171 of whom were killed.

American brigadier general WINFIELD SCOTT was severely wounded during the battle, after which he became a national hero.

---

lunette |lo͞o'net| • *n.* a fortification with two faces forming a projecting angle, and two flanks.

Lusitania, Sinking of the • the sinking, without warning, of the British liner *Lusitania* in its approach to the Irish Sea by the German submarine *U-20* on May 7, 1915, during WORLD WAR I. The giant Cunard Vessel, carrying 4,200 cases of contraband ammunition, sank in twenty minutes, and 1,128 out of 1,959 passengers and crew perished–128 of them American. On May 13, U.S. President WOODROW WILSON asked Germany to disavow its action but avoided a diplomatic break. Germany eventually suspended unrestricted attacks, and in February 1916 it apologized and offered indemnity without acknowledging illegality.

Luzon • the largest and most populated of the Philippine Islands, and the site of many battles in which the U.S. was involved, including the battle of MANILA BAY during the SPANISH-AMERICAN WAR (1898), and the battles at BATAAN and CORREGIDOR in WORLD WAR II.

LVT • *abbr.* landing vehicle, tracked.

LVT(A) • *abbr.* landing vehicle, tracked (armored).

LVTE-1 • see LANDING SHIP TANK.

LWM • *abbr.* low-water mark.

Lyon, Matthew (1749–1822) • Continental army officer, born in Wicklow County, Ireland. Lyon was court-martialed and dishonorably discharged after acquiescing to the demands of his mutinous troops that they abandon their posts because of the threat of Indian attack along the boundary they were guarding. Lyon was later taken on as a scout and guide, however, and was eventually made captain and paymaster of a regiment. He also served as a volunteer during the battle of SARATOGA (1778). Lyon, who had come to America as an indentured servant, earlier fought with the GREEN MOUNTAIN BOYS in their struggle to prevent New York from taking over the land between it and New Hampshire, and played an important role in the capture of FORT TICONDEROGA (1775). He served two terms in Congress as a representative from Vermont (1797–1801) and several more terms later as a representative from Kentucky (1803–11). In the presidential election of 1800 that resulted in a tie between THOMAS JEFFERSON and AARON BURR, throwing the vote into the House, Lyon cast the deciding ballot for Jefferson.

Lyon was elected to his second term in the House (1798) while serving time in jail. He had been found guilty under the SEDITION ACT of 1798 of maligning the government for charging that the FEDERALISTS were pro-British. He was fined $1,000 and jailed for four months. In 1840 Congress voted to remit Lyon's fine to his heirs on the grounds that the SEDITION ACT was unconstitutional.

LZ • *abbr.* landing zone.

Mm

M-1 • see ABRAMS.

M-1A1 • see ABRAMS.

M-1 Garand rifle • a gas-operated .30-06 rifle developed by the Army in the1920s that uses an eight-round en bloc clip.

M-2 • a light (60 mm caliber) mortar of U.S. Army origin but extensively imitated and used for firing high explosives, illuminating bombs, and smoke bombs.

M2A3 • see BRADLEY FIGHTING VEHICLE.

M 3 • **1** (**light**) see STUART II TANK. **2** (**medium**) see GRANT TANK.

M3A3 • see BRADLEY FIGHTING VEHICLE.

M-4 • see COMMAND AND CONTROL VEHICLE.

M-14 Garand rifle • a gas-operated .30-06 rifle developed by the Army in the 1950s that uses a twenty-round detachable box-type magazine.

M-16 • a gas-operated rifle developed by the Army in the 1950s and used extensively since then by the United States and its allies. The M-16 uses a twenty or thirty-round box-type magazine.

M 24 • see CHAFFEE TANK.

M 26 • see PERSHING TANK.

M36 • see TANK DESTROYER.

M-42 • see DUSTER.

M-47 • see DRAGON.

M-48 • a series of U.S. main battle tanks, first produced in 1952 and armed with a 90-mm main gun, a 7.62-mm coaxial machine gun, and a 12.7-mm antiaircraft machine gun on top of the commander's observation dome. Early versions had a top speed of 26 mph and a range of 113 km.

M-48A3 • a fully tracked combat tank that served as the main battle tank during the VIETNAM WAR. It carried a 90mm gun-cannon, weighed 52 tons combat-loaded, and was capable of doing 40 mph on a road.

M-60 • **1** see PATTON SERIES. **2** a general-purpose machine gun of the U.S. Army, which entered service in the 1950s. It is operated by two soldiers: one gunner and one assistant, and stands on two legs. The gun makes a grunting sound when firing and was nick-named "pig."

M-88A1 • see HERCULES, def. 2

M-202 Flash • a rocket launcher that fires white phosphorus rockets.

M-548 • see M-548A3.

M-548A3 • the upgraded version of the M-548, an unarmored full-tracked vehicle that carries troops, ammunition, and other cargo to forward areas in support of field units. The M-548A3 can be delivered by C-130 and C-141 aircraft, can cross water up to 40 inches deep, and travels easily over highways and rough terrain as well. In 1994 a powerpack, including a 275 hp turbocharged diesel engine and a four-speed hydrostatic steer transmission, improved its fuel economy, acceleration, and braking capability.

M-551 • see SHERIDAN.

ma'am • *n.* a term of address for a ranking female officer in the police or armed forces.

MAC • *abbr.* Military Airlift Command.

MacArthur, Arthur (1845–1912) • army general, born in Springfield, Massachusetts. MacArthur first came to prominence as a member of a volunteer regiment during the CIVIL WAR, during which he was frequently promoted and cited for gallantry. At MISSIONARY RIDGE (1863) he led a daring charge that routed the Confederates and for which he eventually was awarded the CONGRESSIONAL MEDAL OF HONOR. En route from Tennessee to ATLANTA (1864), he led his regiment in thirty battles. At the battle of FRANKLIN (1864), the actions of his regiment turned the tide in favor of the UNION, but MacArthur was wounded and did not again see combat. In 1866 he joined the regular army, serving mainly at frontier posts in the West until the outbreak of the SPANISH-AMERICAN WAR (1898), when he commanded a brigade in the capture of MANILA. He subsequently headed operations against the Filipino insurgents and in 1900 was made overall commander of American forces in the Philippines as well as military governor.

The youngest of his three sons was DOUGLAS MACARTHUR.

MacArthur, Douglas (1880–1964) • army general, born in Little Rock, Arkansas. MacArthur was five-star General of the Army (1944), commander of the SOUTHWEST PACIFIC AREA Theater (1942–45) during WORLD WAR II, supreme allied commander in occupied Japan (1945–50), and commander of U.S. and UNITED NATIONS forces (1950–51) early in the KOREAN WAR. MacArthur was awarded the CONGRESSIONAL MEDAL OF HONOR for his defense of the Philippines prior to the Japanese takeover in 1942 (when he made his famous pledge—"I shall return"). Ordered to evacuate to Australia, from there MacArthur launched an offensive against Japanese forces on New Guinea, while the U.S. Navy pushed through the Central Pacific. His invasion of the Philippines in 1944 did not bring the anticipated quick ending to the Japanese occupation. While MacArthur undoubtedly had genuine achievements in the PACIFIC WAR, many Americans mistakenly credit him with Pacific victories won by the navy and marines under separate command. As supreme allied commander in occupied Japan, however, his achievements are unquestioned. He successfully presided over a complex process of demilitarizing and democratizing an authoritarian state, implementing generally liberal economic, social, and political reforms and imposing a written constitution that abolished Japan's right to maintain armed forces or conduct war (1947). As commander of forces in Korea, MacArthur was initially successful in liberating South Korea, but he repeatedly clashed with President HARRY S. TRUMAN and the joint chiefs over expanding the war to China. His public criticism of the commander in chief led to his being removed from all his commands (1951). He was received as a hero on his return to the United States, and his flair for the apt statement and dramatic gesture culminated in an address to Congress which he ended by quoting from an army song: "Old soldiers never die, they just fade away." MacArthur was an unsuccessful contender for the Republican presidential nomination in 1952 (as he had been in 1948). Before WORLD WAR II, MacArthur had earned several decorations while fighting in France during WORLD WAR I; served a term as superintendent at WEST POINT; and spent two tours of duty in the Philippines. His tenure as army chief of staff (1930–35) was tarnished when he used military force to rout demonstrating veterans from the nation's capital (1932).

MacDill Air Force Base • a U.S. Air Force Base in Tampa Bay, Florida, established in 1941. First named Southeast Air Base, it was renamed for Col. Leslie MacDill. The base was a major training center and staging area for Air Force personnel and the WOMEN'S ARMY CORPS during WORLD WAR II, housing up to 15,000 troops at one time. In addition, German prisoners of war were interned there. Almost closed in 1960, MacDill was kept open due to the CUBAN MISSILE CRISIS (1962–63). It became TACTICAL AIR COMMAND in 1963. Today it also runs the 6th Air Refueling Wing, U.S. CENTRAL COMMAND, and U.S. SPECIAL OPERATIONS COMMAND.

Mace • (**MGM-13**) a tactical surface-launched missile designed to destroy ground targets. It is launched from a mobile trailer or from a bomb-proof shelter and powered during flight by a jet engine. It is an improved version of the MATADOR missile.

MACG • *abbr.* Marine Air Control Group.

Machias • a coastal town in Maine that was the site of the first naval battle of the REVOLUTIONARY WAR on June 12, 1775. Local people fought from the land and on sea against the British ship *Margaretta*. To their surprise, the rebels won and towed the vanquished gunboat up the Middle River into the town.

machine gun • an automatic gun that fires bullets in rapid succession for as long as the trigger is pressed. • *v.* (**machine-gun**) shoot with a machine gun.

DERIVATIVES: **machine-gunner** *n.*

Machin, Thomas (1744–1816) • REVOLUTIONARY WAR engineer and artillery officer, born near Wolverhampton, Staffordshire, England. Machin was best known for the design and installation of a large chain floated across the Hudson River from West Point to Constitution Island (1778). As captain of artillery (1780–83), Machin sighted the first cannon to be fired in the siege of YORKTOWN (1781). Before joining the Continental army in 1775, Machin had been active early in the Revolutionary cause, belonging to the SONS OF LIBERTY, participating in the BOSTON TEA PARTY, and laying out the fortification lines on BUNKER HILL.

mach number |ˈmäk ˈnəmbər| • the ratio of the velocity of a body to that of sound in the surrounding medium.

Machtpolitik • *n.* another term for POWER POLITICS.

Mackellar, Patrick (1717–78) • military engineer who came to America (in 1754) with a British unit at the time of the FRENCH AND INDIAN WAR (1754–63). Mackellar built roads and bridges in the wilderness (1755), but his flawed maps contributed to Gen. EDWARD BRADDOCK'S loss at MONONGAHELA (1755). He was also present at the capitulation of Fort Oswego (1756) and the capture of the fortress at LOUISBOURG (1758). Mackellar was chief engineer in the expedition against Quebec (1759) and later at the Halifax citadel (1760) before taking part in the expedition against Martinique (1762) and conducting siege operations against Havana (1762).

Mackenzie, Alexander Slidell (1803–48) • naval officer and author, born in New York City. Mackenzie was at the center of a mid-19th-century incident resulting from his actions while in command of a training vessel. Apprised of a possible mutiny among the crew, Mackenzie hanged at the yardarm and buried at sea the three alleged ringleaders, one of whom, only eighteen years old, was the son of the secretary of war. The ensuing furor attracted a number of leading notables of the day, with Richard Henry Dana coming to Mackenzie's defense, and James Fenimore Cooper and Thomas Hart Benton coming down on the opposite side. Though a court-martial returned a verdict of not proven (1843), Mackenzie's navy career was effectively at an end.

Mackenzie, Ranald Slidell (1840–89) • Union army officer in the corps of engineers, born in New York City. Mackenzie saw action at FIRST BULL RUN (1861), FREDERICKSBURG (1862), CHANCELLORSVILLE (1863), and GETTYSBURG (1863). As a brigade commander he distinguished himself at CEDAR CREEK (1864) before taking part in the final siege and capture of PETERSBURG (1865). After the war Mackenzie held a series of frontier commands, becoming recognized as one of the Indian-fighting army's most capable officers. His behavior, however, became increasingly erratic. He was found insane and in 1884 was retired from military service.

Mackenzie was the son of ALEXANDER SLIDELL MACKENZIE.

MACV • *abbr.* Military Assistance Command Vietnam.

MAD • *abbr.* mutual assured destruction.

***Maddox*, USS** • (**DD-731**) a SUMNER-class destroyer launched in March 1944 and commissioned in June that year. The ship was decommissioned in 1972 and sent to Taiwan, where it was renamed *Po Yang*. In 1985 the ship was broken up and sold for scrap.

Madison, James (1751–1836) • 4th president of the United States (1809–17), and a major framer of the Constitution, born in King George County, Virginia. An outspoken proponent of civil and religious liberties, Madison was involved in the Revolution from its earliest days. As a Confederation congressman (1780–83; 1878–89) and member of the Virginia state legislature, he acquired a reputation for mastery of legislative business and defender of individual liberties against the tyranny of the majority. Madison believed firmly in the need for a strong central government. As a delegate to the Constitutional Convention (1787), he made many crucial contributions to the writing of the Constitution and is generally acknowledged as the most important of its framers. To help achieve its ratification, he wrote, with ALEXANDER HAMILTON, *The Federalist Papers*, arguing in his most famous essay that the conflicting factions of large republics would lessen the likelihood of majority tyranny. During the First Federal Congress (1789), Madison drafted the Bill of Rights. In the 1790s Madison aligned himself with THOMAS JEFFERSON in opposing the Federalist financial policies of Alexander Hamilton, advocating that the new nation establish itself as an agrarian society friendly to France, not Britain. In 1798, during the QUASI-WAR WITH FRANCE, he authored the Virginia Resolutions, which called for repeal of the ALIEN AND SEDITION ACTS. As Jefferson's secretary of state (1801–09), Madison sought to pursue a policy of neutrality between Great Britain and France, but the trade embargo he adopted failed to achieve this desired end and was repealed. Once he became president, Madison was forced to obtain a declaration of war. The resulting WAR OF 1812, for which the still-fledgling nation was ill-prepared and which failed to resolve the issues that gave it rise, has since been called "Mr. Madison's War." Its disasters—among them, the botched invasion of Canada and the burning of Washington, D.C.—forever tarnished his presidency. When his tenure of office ended, Madison retired to his home at Montpelier, Virginia.

Mae West • informal, dated an inflatable life jacket, originally as issued to pilots during WORLD WAR II.

ORIGIN: 1940s: from the name of the U.S. movie actress *Mae West*, noted for her large bust.

MAF • *abbr.* Marine Amphibious Force.

Maffitt, John Newland (1819–86) • Confederate naval officer, was born at sea while his mother was traveling from Ireland to America to join her husband. Maffitt was one of the most successful blockade runners of the CIVIL WAR. While in command of the *Florida*, Maffitt captured or destroyed more than twenty Union vessels in a period of six months (1863). His last command was of the blockade runner *Owl*, which made several successful runs, the last at Galveston.

magazine • *n.* **1** a chamber for holding a supply of cartridges to be fed automatically to the breech of a gun. **2** a store for arms, ammunition, explosives, and provisions for use in military operations.

Maggie's drawers • slang a red flag used to indicate a miss in target practice.

ORIGIN: 1940s: said to be in reference to a song entitled *Those Old Red Flannel Drawers That Maggie Wore*.

Maginot Line |ˈmæzHəˌnō; ˈmæj-| • a system of fortifications constructed by the French along their eastern border between 1929 and 1934, outflanked by German forces in 1940.

ORIGIN: named after André *Maginot* (1877–1932), a French minister of war.

magnetic compass • an instrument containing a freely suspended magnetic element that displays the direction of the horizontal component of the earth's magnetic field at the point of observation.

magnetic exploder • a device used in detonating a mine or torpedo underneath a ship, thus directing most of the power of the explosion upwards. It works either by detecting the permanent magnetization of a ship's hull or the perturbation of the earth's magnetic field caused by the presence of a ship.

magnetic mine • a mine detonated by the proximity of a magnetized body such as a ship or tank.entry was mine, magnetic

magnetic north • the direction indicated by the north-seeking pole of a freely suspended magnetic needle, influenced only by the earth's magnetic field.

magnetic tape • a tape or ribbon of any material impregnated or coated with magnetic or other material on which information may be placed in the form of magnetically polarized spots.

magnum • *n.* (pl. **magnums**) (often **Magnum**) trademark a gun designed to fire cartridges that are more powerful than its caliber would suggest: *his .357 Magnum pistol.*

Magruder, John Bankhead (1807–71) • Confederate army officer, born in Port Royal, Virginia. His performance during the SEVEN DAYS' BATTLE (1862) was initially impressive (at MECHANICSVILLE and GAINES' MILL) but was later tarnished by inadequate assaults and disastrous attacks (at Savage Station and MALVERN HILL). Although charges that he had been inebriated at Malvern Hill were dismissed, Magruder nevertheless was given a lesser subsequent command than the one anticipated. For the remainder of the conflict, he served in the western CONFEDERACY, and competently orchestrated the recapture of Galveston (1863).

MAGTF • *abbr.* Marine Air-Ground Task Force.

Mahan, Alfred Thayer |mə'hæn| (1840–1914) • naval officer, author, and world-renowned theorist on history and strategy, born at West Point, New York. His *The Influence of Sea Power upon History, 1660–1783* (1890), as well as a two-volume sequel that dealt with the years 1793 to 1812, became a primer on international relations, the use of force, and the role of diplomacy, which Mahan believed should follow, not precede, battle. International relations, he argued, hinged on power projection, which was best exercised by gaining control of the seas. Though his theories and arguments have since been seen as flawed, there is little question about his significance as a naval historian and theoretician in the latter part of the 19th century. Mahan's early career was undistinguished. He saw only a few hours of combat during the CIVIL WAR and rose slowly through the ranks afterward. The change began with his appointment to the NAVAL WAR COLLEGE (1885) to teach naval history and the subsequent publication of the first *Influence* book, a collection of his lecture notes. He resigned from the navy in 1895 to pursue his writing career full time. In all, Mahan published twenty-one books, as well as numerous magazine articles and letters to the editor.

Mahan, Dennis Hart |mə'hæn| (1802–71) • military engineer and theorist, born in New York City. Mahan reformed the teaching of engineering at the U.S. MILITARY ACADEMY, where he spent nearly all of his career (1824–71), but for an early four-year leave of absence. Mahan published several texts, some of which were used extensively in the CIVIL and MEXICAN (1846–48) WARS. He dominated the academy during his long tenure, influencing all curriculum decisions. Shortly after the academy's board recommended his retirement, Mahan committed suicide.

Mahan was the father of noted historian and strategist ALFRED THAYER MAHAN.

Mahone, William |mə'hōn| (1826–95) • Confederate army officer, born in Monroe, Virginia. Mahone achieved his greatest fame in the fighting around PETERSBURG (1864), when, at the BATTLE OF THE CRATER, he led the counterattack that restored a badly broken Confederate line, earning the praise of Gen. ROBERT E. LEE. Previously Mahone had taken part in the battle of SEVEN PINES and the SEVEN DAYS' battles (1862), as well as FIRST BULL RUN (1861) (at which he was wounded), FREDERICKSBURG (1862), and CHANCELLORSVILLE (1863).

main • *n.* **1** (**the main**) archaic or poetic/literary the open ocean. **2** short for MAINSAIL OR MAINMAST.

main attack • the principal attack or effort into which the commander throws the full weight of the offensive power at his disposal; an attack directed against the chief objective of the campaign or battle.

main battle area • the portion of the battlefield in which the decisive battle is fought to defeat the enemy. For any particular command, the main battle area extends rearward from the forward edge of the battle area to the rear boundary of the command's subordinate units.

main battle tank • see TANK, MAIN BATTLE.

main deck • the principal deck of a vessel, often the deck on which the superstructure is mounted.

***Maine*, Sinking of the USS** • a U.S. battleship sent to protect American lives and property exploded and sank in Havana on February 15, 1898, killing 260 men. Encouraged by the sensationalist press, the American public largely believed that Spanish forces mined the ship. In March, the U.S. Naval Court of Inquiry found that an external explosion caused the sinking, rejecting viable alternative explanations. The true cause remains unknown, despite further official inquiries in 1911 and 1975. While many see the sinking as the final step to the SPANISH-AMERICAN WAR (1898), this argument ignores President WILLIAM MCKINLEY's attempts to avoid war for a month after the initial court's finding.

mainmast • *n.* the principal mast of a ship, typically the second mast in a sailing ship of three or more masts.

mainsail |'mānsəl; -ˌsāl| • *n.* **1** the principal sail of a ship, especially the lowest sail on the mainmast in a square-rigged vessel. **2** the sail set on the after side of the mainmast in a fore-and-aft-rigged vessel.

mainsheet • *n.* a sheet used for controlling the mainsail of a sailing vessel.

mainstay • *n.* a stay that extends from the maintop to the foot of the foremast of a sailing ship.

maintain • *v.* **1** hold (a position) in the face of attack or competition: *the objective to maintain the position until reinforcements arrive.* **2** keep (a military unit) supplied with equipment and other requirements.

DERIVATIVES: **maintainability** *n.* **maintainable** *adj.*

maintenance • *n.* **1** all action taken to retain materiel in a serviceable condition or to restore it to serviceability, to include inspection, testing, servicing, classification as to serviceability, repair, rebuilding, and reclamation. **2** all supply and repair action taken to keep a force in condition to carry out its mission. **3** the routine recurring work required to keep a facility (plant, building, structure, ground facility, utility system, or other real property) in such condition that it may be continuously used, at its original or designed capacity and efficiency for its intended purpose.

maintop • *n.* a platform around the head of the lower section of a sailing ship's mainmast.

main-topmast • *n.* the second section of a sailing ship's mainmast.

main yard • the lower yard on the mainmast of a sailing vessel.

Maj. • *abbr.* Major.

major • *n.* an army officer of high rank, in particular (in the U.S. Army, Air Force, and Marine Corps) an officer ranking above captain and below lieutenant colonel.

ORIGIN: shortening of SERGEANT MAJOR, formerly a high rank.

major fleet • a principal, permanent subdivision of the operating forces of the navy with certain supporting shore activities. Presently there are two such fleets in the U.S. Navy: the **Pacific Fleet** and the **Atlantic Fleet**.

major general • an officer in the U.S. Army, Air force, and Marine Corps ranking above brigadier general and below lieutenant general.

ORIGIN: mid 17th century: shortening of *sergeant major general.*

major installation • in the air force, a self-supporting center of operations for actions of importance to air force combat, combat support, or training. It is operated by an active, reserve, or guard unit of group size or larger with all land, facilities, and organic support needed to accomplish the unit mission. It must have real property accountability through ownership, lease, permit, or other written agreement for all real estate and facilities. Agreements with foreign governments that give the U.S. Air Force jurisdiction over real property meet this requirement. Major installations include air force bases, air bases, air reserve bases, and air guard bases. Shared-use agreements (as opposed to joint-use agreements where the air force owns the runway) do not meet the criteria to be major installations.

make • *v.* (past and past part. **made**) appoint or designate (someone) to a position: *he was made a colonel in the Mexican army.*

PHRASES: **make sail 1** spread a sail or sails. **2** start a voyage. **make way** make progress; travel.

malaria • *n.* an intermittent and remittent fever caused by a protozoan parasite that invades the red blood cells. The parasite is transmitted by mosquitoes in many tropical and subtropical regions.

DERIVATIVES: **malarial** *adj.*

ORIGIN: mid 18th cent.: from Italian, from *mal'aria*, contracted form of *mala aria* 'bad air.' The term originally denoted the unwholesome atmosphere caused by the exhalations of marshes, to which the disease was formerly attributed.

malinger |mə'liNGgər| • *v.* exaggerate or feign illness in order to escape duty or work.

DERIVATIVES: **malingerer** *n.*

Mallery, Garrick (1831–94) • army officer and ethnologist, born in Wilkes-Barre, Pennsylvania. His studies of American-Indian sign language and pictographs began while he was stationed in Dakota Territory (1876). Mallery had been commissioned an officer in the regular army after the CIVIL WAR, during which he had served with volunteer Pennsylvania infantry and cavalry units. In 1877 Mallery was assigned to the U.S. Geographical and Geological Survey to study Indian drawings. He retired from the army in 1879 to work as a civilian on the staff of the Bureau of Ethnology.

Mallory, Stephen Russell (1813–73) • secretary of the navy of the CONFEDERATE STATES OF AMERICA, born in Trinidad. At the outbreak of the CIVIL WAR , Mallory was faced with the challenge of constructing a navy virtually from scratch. Among his successes was the use of commerce raiders to harass and destroy Union shipping. Most notably, Mallory believed in the ability of ironclads to break the Union blockade. He ordered the conversion of the USS *Merrimack* into the ironclad CSS *Virginia.* Its subsequent encounter with the USS *Monitor* at the battle of HAMPTON ROADS (1862), though inconclusive in terms of the immediate conflict, transformed the face of naval warfare.

Malta Conference • an Allied meeting in Malta during WORLD WAR II where the Americans and British disagreed over strategy for defeating Germany. The conference lasted from January 30 to February 2, 1945, and was the first phase of what was code-named "Argonaut," conferences that began in Malta and were followed by the YALTA CONFERENCE. The British argued for a single push across northern Germany to Berlin and wanted most of the Allied supplies to go into that effort; American armies would be placed on the defensive. Supreme Allied Commander DWIGHT D. EISENHOWER's approach was to give that plan first priority but also to keep American armies on the move.

Malvern Hill, Battle of • the last of the SEVEN DAYS' Battles in Virginia during the CIVIL WAR, ending the PENINSULAR CAMPAIGN. On July 1, 1862, Union forces, under Gen. GEORGE B. MCCLELLAN, successfully defended their upper position against Gen. ROBERT E. LEE's poorly coordinated and ultimately costly frontal attack. McClellan withdrew to James River. With Richmond no longer threatened, Gen. THOMAS "STONEWALL" JACKSON was sent to begin the Northern Virginia campaign.

man • *n.* (pl. **men**) (**men**) ordinary members of the armed forces as distinct from the officers: *he had a platoon of forty men to prepare for battle.* • *v.* (**manned, manning**) (often be **manned**) provide (something, especially a place or machine) with the personnel to run, operate, or defend it: *the firemen manned the pumps and fought the blaze.*

Manassas, First Battle of • see BULL RUN, FIRST BATTLE OF.

Manassas, Second Battle of • see BULL RUN, SECOND BATTLE OF.

man-at-arms • *n.* (pl. **men-at-arms**) archaic a soldier, especially one heavily armed and mounted on horseback.

Manchuria Crisis • instigated by Japan's invasion of Chinese Manchuria in September 1931, by which it thus repudiated its pledge in the Five-Power and Nine-Power Pacts. President HERBERT HOOVER declined to issue economic sanctions against Japan for fear this would lead to war. In early 1932, the U.S. refused to recognize Japan's puppet government in Manchuria, and threatened to rescind its involvement in the Five-Power Pact. The Japanese seemed undeterred, signing an armistice with China in May and then preparing for further war.

maneuver • *n.* **1** a movement to place ships or aircraft in a position of advantage over the enemy. **2** a tactical exercise carried out at sea, in the air, on the ground, or on a map in imitation of war. **3** the operation of a ship, aircraft, or vehicle, to cause it to perform desired movements. **4** employment of forces on the battlefield through movement in combination with fire, or fire potential, to achieve a position of advantage in respect to the enemy in order to accomplish the mission.

maneuverable reentry vehicle • part of a space vehicle that can reenter the earth's atmosphere in the final part of its trajectory and perform planned flight maneuvers during its reentry.

Maney, George Earl (1826–1901) • Confederate officer with a Tennessee regiment, born in Franklin, Tennessee. Maney fought ably at SHILOH (1862), was wounded at CHATTANOOGA (1863), and commanded a division during the ATLANTA campaign until his capture in August 1864, after which he saw no further action.

Mangin, Joseph François • (1764–after 1818) military engineer, born in Chalons-sur-Marne, France. Mangin became a U.S. citizen in 1796 and worked for several years as a city surveyor in New York. He also worked on harbor fortifications in 1801 and in 1813, during the WAR OF 1812. Mangin is primarily known as an architect. Among his most noted achievements are New York City Hall (1802, with John McComb, Jr.), and the old St. Patrick's Cathedral (1809–15, at Prince and Mott Streets).

Manhattan Project • the code name for the American project set up in 1942 to develop an atom bomb. The project culminated in 1945 with the detonation of the first nuclear weapon, at White Sands in New Mexico.

manhunt • *n.* an organized search for a person, especially a criminal.

manifest • *n.* **1** a document giving comprehensive details of a ship and its cargo and other contents, passengers, and crew for the use of customs officers. **2** a list of passengers or cargo in an aircraft. **3** a list of the cars forming a freight train. • *v.* record in such a manifest: *every passenger is manifested at the point of departure.*

manifest destiny • a doctrine used to rationalize U.S. territorial expansion in the 1840s and 1850s. It asserted that expansion of the United States throughout the American continents was both justified and inevitable. The phrase was coined by the U.S. journalist John L. O'Sullivan, and was initially used in regard to Mexican and Indian land in Texas and the Southwest. The concept was invoked later in a dispute with Great Britain over Oregon and in relation to territory controlled by the United States as a result of the SPANISH-AMERICAN WAR (1898).

Manigault, Arthur Middleton (1824–86) • Confederate army officer, born in Charleston, South Carolina. His brigade fought well and suffered heavy casualties at CHICKAMAUGA (1863), MISSIONARY RIDGE (1863), and during the ATLANTA campaign (1864). Earlier Manigault had taken part in the defense and evacuation of CORINTH (1862), BRAXTON BRAGG's invasion of Kentucky (1862), and the battle of STONES RIVER (1862–63), often as acting brigade commander. A wound received at the battle of FRANKLIN (1864), kept him from combat for the remainder of the war. His memoirs, written shortly after the war but not published until 1983, are considered a classic of CIVIL WAR military literature.

Manila Bay, Battle of • a one-sided battle in the Philippines on May 1, 1898. The U.S. Navy's ASIATIC SQUADRON, led by Commodore GEORGE DEWEY and armed with modern warships, easily destroyed the weak and meager Spanish squadron, and blockaded Manila. This decisive triumph made Dewey a popular figure, and more importantly, paved the way to the American annexation of the Philippines, thus helping to secure victory in the SPANISH-AMERICAN WAR.

Manley, John (1732?–93) • English-born Revolutionary naval officer who captured the first legitimate prize taken by a Continental warship (1775). Numerous others followed, and Manley was made captain in the new Continental navy and given command of a thirty-two-gun frigate, the *Hancock*, which he subsequently lost to the British (1777) through failure to cooperate with another Continental captain (HECTOR MCNEILL), with whom he had a long-running feud. Though acquitted when court-martialed, Manley was not immediately given another command, so he undertook a successful career as a privateer.

Since Manley's death, three ships of the U.S. Navy have been named after him.

---

manned bomber • a bombing aircraft actually manned by a human crew. The perfection of intercontinental ballistic missiles in the 1950s provoked debate over the relative merits of manned bombers and missiles, particularly in a general nuclear war. The manned bomber advocates argued that the judgment and flexibility of a human pilot/crew was indispensable.

Manned Orbital Laboratory • a manned military space station proposed by President JOHN F. KENNEDY's administration in December 1963, the purpose of which was to test the military usefulness of human beings in Earth orbit. The project was canceled by President RICHARD M. NIXON in 1969.

man-of-war (also **man-o'-war**) • *n.* (pl. **men-of-war** or **men-o'-war**) an armed sailing ship.

man-portable • *adj.* capable of being carried by one person over long distance without serious degradation of the performance of his normal duties. Man-portable equipment has an upper weight limit of about 31 pounds (14 kg).

manrope • *n.* a safety rope on a ship's deck.

Mansfield, Joseph King Fenno (1803–62) • career army officer and military engineer, born in New Haven, Connecticut. Mansfield was recognized for his fortification work, MEXICAN WAR (1846–48) exploits, and successful management of the Department of Washington, D.C., during the early months of the CIVIL WAR. In 1862 Mansfield was given a corps command in the ARMY OF THE POTOMAC and was fatally wounded at ANTIETAM. Early in his military career Mansfield worked on construction of coastal fortifications, most notably FORT PULASKI (Georgia), and civil works, including harbor improvements along the south Atlantic coast.

mantelet |ˈmæntlət; ˈmæntl-ət| (also **mantlet**) • *n.* a bulletproof screen for a soldier.

mantlet |ˈmæntlet| • *n.* variant spelling of MANTELET.

manual • *adj.* **1** of or done with the hands: *manual hauling of boats along the towpath.* **2** (of a machine or device) worked by hand, not automatically or electronically: *a manual typewriter.* • *n.* **1** a book of instructions, especially for operating a machine or learning a subject; a handbook: *a training manual.* **2** a thing operated or done by hand rather than automatically or electronically.

DERIVATIVES: **manually** *adv.*

Manual for Courts-Martial • the official compilation of laws governing the conduct of U.S. military personnel and the methods for handling offenses, applying non-judicial punishments, and conducting trials by courts-martial.

manumission • *n.* formal release from slavery or servitude.

Mao Zedong (1893–1976) • (also **Mao Tse-tung**) Chinese statesman, leader of the Chinese Communist Party (1931–76) and chairman of the People's Republic of China (1949–59). As the architect of China's communist revolution, Mao developed the modern form of revolutionary INSURGENCY. He defeated both the occupying Japanese and the KUOMINTANG nationalist forces to create the People's Republic in 1949. In 1950 Mao sent Chinese forces to aid North Koreans when U.S. and U.N. troops crossed the 38th parallel. Initially Mao followed the Russian communist model, but later gave the Chinese brand his own stamp and came to see himself in competition with the Soviets. In 1972 he and ZHOU ENLAI met with RICHARD M. NIXON in Beijing in an attempt to improve relations with Americans in order to gain advantage over Soviet Communists.

Maquis • Frenchmen who took to the mountains and forests to avoid compulsory labor service for the Germans in WORLD WAR II. Armed and trained by the British Special Operations Executive and the U.S. OFFICE OF STRATEGIC SERVICES, the maquis became an important part of the overall French resistance movement. Following the allied invasion of NORMANDY in June 1944 and southern France in August of that year, many of the men of the MAQUIS joined Gen. de Lattre de Tassigny's First French Army for the subsequent Rhine River crossings and battle for Germany.

ORIGIN: from the word for the local brushwood found on the island of Corsica.

Marauder • (**B-26**) a twin-engine medium bomber, first flown on November 25, 1940, and put into production on February 25, 1941, and into action in the Australian theater in April 1942. By the end of 1944, more than 5,000 had been produced.

march • *v.* **1** walk in a military manner with a regular measured tread: *they marched past the cemetery.* **2** walk or proceed quickly and with determination: *without a word she marched from the room.* **3** force (someone) to walk somewhere quickly: *she gripped Rachel's arm and marched her out through the doors.* • *n.* **1** an act or instance of marching: *the relieving force was more than a day's march away.* **2** a piece of music composed to accompany marching or with a rhythmic character suggestive of marching. **3** a procession as a protest or demonstration: *a protest march.*

PHRASES: **on the march** marching: *the army was on the march at last.*

Marchbanks, Vance Hunter, Jr. (1905–88) • aerospace surgeon and pioneer in aerospace medicine research, born at Fort Washikie, Washington. Marchbanks was the first African-American physician to be commissioned in the U.S. Army (1946). Over his long career Marchbanks collected medical data and published articles for military manuals and research publications, focusing on human reactions to speed, noise, and altitude during jet flight. Stress tests and rating systems he developed to evaluate air crews in combat were later adapted for astronaut training. In 1960 Marchbanks served as aeromedical monitor and support physician for Project Mercury and two years later he was one of eleven specialists who monitored astronaut John Glenn's vital signs during his orbital flight. During WORLD WAR II Marchbanks had served as a flight surgeon with the Tuskegee Airmen during campaigns in Italy, earning a BRONZE STAR; and he flew three combat missions early in the KOREAN WAR.

marching order • equipment for marching: *they were dressed in full marching order.*

marching orders • instructions from a superior officer for troops to depart.

march past • chiefly Brit. a formal march by troops past a saluting point at a review.

March, Peyton Conway (1864–1955) • army chief of staff (1918–21), born in Easton, Pennsylvania. March was responsible for the accelerated shipment of American troops to France toward the close of WORLD WAR I, a massive reinforcement to the Allied cause that helped put an end to that conflict. The remainder of his tenure was devoted to overseeing the demobilization of the wartime force and the development of the postwar military establishment. Earlier in that conflict, as the top artillerist in the AMERICAN EXPEDITIONARY FORCES, March trained the artillery in France (1917–18). He had previously achieved distinction during combat in the SPANISH-AMERICAN WAR (1898) and the ensuing Filipino insurrection, for which he eventually received a DISTINGUISHED SERVICE CROSS (1920).

March to the Sea, Sherman's • a five-week, 285-mile raid from Atlanta to Savannah in late 1864 that ultimately devastated the Confederate morale. Displaying a rare grasp of psychological warfare, Gen. WILLIAM T. SHERMAN, with somewhat reluctant support from President ABRAHAM LINCOLN and Gen. ULYSSES S. GRANT, instructed his troops to destroy crops and property, especially that of the planter class, but to leave citizens physically unharmed. Despite Sherman's characteristic bravado and occasionally undisciplined troops—and notwithstanding what his superiors labeled the treasonous peace terms he negotiated with Confederate leaders—the march probably saved lives and shortened the war, and certainly punctured Southern hopes for victory.

Marianas Islands • a group of islands in the western Pacific, comprising Guam and the Northern Marianas. In June 1944, during WORLD WAR II, the BATTLE OF THE PHILIPPINE SEA between the United States and Japan took place off the Marianas. It was the largest carrier duel of World War II, and the JAPANESE MOBILE FLEET and its aviation arm were left grievously hurt. (Also called **Mariana Islands**.)

Marianas Turkey Shoot • see PHILIPPINE SEA, BATTLE OF THE.

marina • *n.* a specially designed harbor with moorings for pleasure craft and small boats.

marine • *adj.* **1** of or relating to shipping or naval matters: *marine insurance.* • *n.* a member of a body of troops trained to serve on land or at sea, in particular a member of the U.S. Marine Corps.

PHRASES: **tell that** (or **it**) **to the marines** a scornful expression of disbelief.

ORIGIN: from the saying *that will do for the marines but the sailors won't believe it,* referring to the *horse marines,* an imaginary corps of cavalrymen employed to serve as marines (thus out of their element).

Marine Air Control Group • (**MACG**) the part of the Marine air control group responsible for providing, operating, and maintaining ground facilities to detect and intercept hostile aircraft and for directing friendly aircraft as they carry out support missions.

Marine Air-Ground Task Force • (**MAGTF**) an organization of Marine forces, including division, aircraft wing, and service support groups, under a single command and set up to accomplish a specific mission. Its various components usually include command, aviation combat, ground combat, and combat service support groups. There are two kinds of Marine air-ground forces that can be task-organized: the Marine expeditionary unit and the Marine expeditionary force. Since the end of the COLD WAR, the Marines are responsible for providing security for U.S. diplomats and various overseas installations.

Marine Amphibious Force • (**MAF**) a division-size force that includes integral air support.

Marine Amphibious Unit • (**MAU**) former name of MARINE EXPEDITIONARY UNIT.

Marine Corps Association • a professional organization for U.S. Marines, founded in 1913 at Guantanamo Bay, Cuba, by Marines of the 2nd Provisional Brigade. It was formed to disseminate military knowledge to its members, provide for professional advancement, and promote Marine Corps traditions. It publishes the *Leatherneck* and *Marine Corps Gazette* magazines. Membership is open to all active duty, reserve, retired, and honorably discharged Marine veterans, members of other military services who are serving with or have served with Marine Corps units, children of association members over fifteen years of age, and unmarried former spouses or widows of association members.

Marine Corps Aviation • initiated in May 1912 when Lt. ALFRED A. CUNNINGHAM reported to the Naval Aviation Camp, Annapolis, Maryland. Marine aviators have been responsible for many "firsts" in military flight, including bombing from a naval plane, dive-bombing, being catapulted from a moving battleship, and transporting troops and supplies by air. Since the mid 1970s, the U.S. Marines have maintained and operated their own aircraft.

Marine Corps Communication-Electronics School • one of the largest formal schools in the Marine Corps for training Marines to use advanced communications and electronics systems. Training can include operating and repairing communications equipment and operating equipment for anti-air warfare. The program started in 1932 as the Pigeon and Flag Handler Platoon. In 1942 the school was established in QUANTICO, VIRGINIA, as a signal school, and in 1943 it moved to Camp Lejeune in North Carolina. During WORLD WAR II it began offering communications courses. After several more moves and name changes, the school moved again to its present location of Twentynine Palms, California, in 1967, and in 1971 took its current name.

Marine Corps Hymn • see FROM THE HALLS OF MONTEZUMA.

Marine Corps Reserve • established by Congress in August 1916 to provide a force of combat-ready reserve units to fight alongside and supplement the active duty Marines whenever needed. On June 6, 1992, with the establishment of the Marine Reserve Force, Marine Corps Reserve Support Command (MCRSC) accepted an expanded nationwide responsibility, but maintains its traditional focus on the provision of administrative support and training for INDIVIDUAL READY RESERVE, Fleet MARINE CORPS RESERVE, and STANDBY RESERVE Marines.

Marine Corps University • a postgraduate service school at QUANTICO, VIRGINIA. It consists of several component schools, including the AMPHIBIOUS WARFARE SCHOOL, and grants the degree of Master of Military Studies.

Marine Corps, U.S. • (**USMC**) a separate military service that is part of the U.S. Navy, responsible for providing marine troops to seize and defend advanced bases, operations on land and in the air in conjunction with naval campaigns, and, especially, amphibious landings. The Marine Corps also provides troops for duty aboard certain Navy ships, as well as guards for U.S. diplomatic missions in foreign countries.

The Marines have fought in every major naval action since 1775.

Marine Corps Women's Reserve • (**MCWR**) initiated in August 1918 when 305 "Reservists (Female)" were brought into the Marine Corps as clerks, and formally organized in July 1942 as part of the MARINE CORPS RESERVE. By June 1944, Women's Reserves accounted for 85 percent of the enlisted personnel on duty at the Marine Corps headquarters. President LYNDON B. JOHNSON signed the law that repealed the standing limit on the number of women in the armed services in 1967, and by 1994 the only positions in which women could not serve in the Marines were in direct combat ground units.

Marine Expeditionary Brigade • (**MEB**) a brigade comprised of 16,500 Marines and sustainment for them for thirty days. It consists of four elements: a Command element at headquarters, a regimental landing team, one or two Marine air groups, and a brigade service support group.

Marine Expeditionary Force • (**MEF**) the largest of the Marine air-ground task forces and usually organized around a division/wing team. It can include several divisions and aircraft wings as well, combined with a combat service support organization. It can carry out a wide range of amphibious assault operations and, in addition, sustained operations on land. It can accomplish a variety of combat missions in any geographic environment.

Marine Expeditionary Unit • (**MEU**) an organization intended to meet routine forward afloat deployment requirements, react immediately to crisis situations, and function to a limited extent in combat operations. Such a unit is usually comprised of a battalion landing team, a reinforced helicopter squadron, and a logistic support group.

Marine Hymn (or **Marine's Hymn**) • see FROM THE HALLS OF MONTEZUMA.

mariner • *n.* a sailor.

marine stores • see NAVAL STORES.

Marine TACC • see TACTICAL AIR COMMAND CENTER.

Marion, Francis (1732–95) • REVOLUTIONARY WAR soldier, born in St. John's Parish, Berkeley County, South Carolina. Marion was known as the "Swamp Fox" for his campaign of harassment against British detachments in South Carolina (1780)—he would strike swiftly and then seemingly melt back into the swamps. He subsequently commanded militia forces on the field at the battle of EUTAW SPRINGS (1781). Earlier Marion had played an important role in repulsing a British assault against CHARLESTON (1776) and in the patriot assault on Savannah (1779).

maritime • *adj.* connected with the sea, especially in relation to seafaring commercial or military activity: *a maritime museum.*

maritime area • a portion of a maritime theater, designated for the purposes of decentralization of command of operations.

maritime control area • an area generally similar to a defensive sea area in purpose, except that it may be established any place on the high seas. Maritime control areas are normally established only in time of war.

Maritime Prepositioned Force • (**MPF**) U.S. strategic program developed in the 1980s in response to the lack of sufficient amphibious shipping to move large U.S. forces to overseas crisis areas quickly. Three groups of cargo ships, each loaded with most of the combat equipment required by a MARINE EXPEDITIONARY BRIGADE (MEB) and about thirty days of supply for an MEB, were positioned at strategic locations around the world at relatively short sailing distance from potential trouble spots.

maritime prepositioning ships • (**MPS**) ships crewed by civilians that have been chartered by the MILITARY SEALIFT COMMAND. They are organized into three squadrons and are usually used near the front line. In order to support three Marine military units, they carry equipment and thirty days of supplies prepared in advance.

mark • *n.* **1** a piece of material or a knot used to indicate a depth on a sounding line. **2** a target: *few bullets could have missed their mark.*
PHRASES: **mark time** (of troops) march on the spot without moving forward.

Mark 24 Mine • a wire-guided acoustic torpedo armed with a high explosive warhead that is detonated by a magnetic proximity fuse and an impact.

Mark 45 ASTOR torpedo • a wire-guided, submarine-launched antisubmarine torpedo with nuclear capability, used in the 1960s. It used a seawater-activated battery to power a 160 hp electric motor.

Market-Garden, Operation • the largest airborne and glider operation of WORLD WAR II, led by British field marshal BERNARD LAW MONTGOMERY, who, along with U.S. Gen. OMAR N. BRADLEY, favored a single, direct strike to end the war, while Supreme Allied Commander DWIGHT D. EISENHOWER preferred a broad-front attack. On September 17, 1944, U.S. and British Airborne Divisions dropped near Arnheim, a Dutch town near the German border, in an attempt to gain a bridgehead on the Lower Rhine. Without the help of supporting British armored divisions slowed by enemy fire and bad weather, the paratroopers suffered almost 10,000 casualties at the hands of two PANZER divisions. Montgomery's plans thus failed and the operation's diversion of troops also delayed Allied triumph in other battles in Holland.

Mark I • see RIVER PATROL BOAT.

marksman • *n.* (pl. **-men**) a person skilled in shooting, especially with a pistol or rifle: *a police marksman.*

DERIVATIVES: **marksmanship** *n.*

marline • *n.* light two-stranded rope.

marlinspike (also **marlinespike**) • *n.* a pointed metal tool used by sailors to separate strands of rope or wire, especially in splicing.

Marne, Second Battle of the • a three-day WORLD WAR I battle in 1918 in France between German and Allied Forces that ended in Allied victory. The German offensive had begun successfully in mid June, defeating French and Italian divisions, but its point was eventually stymied by the French Army and the U.S. 3rd Division. Surrounded on three sides, the 3rd received help on July 16–17 from British and French divisions, as well as from Allied artillery and aircraft, which bombed the Marne bridges, cutting off German supplies and reinforcements. On July 18, the GERMAN HIGH COMMAND halted the offensive, the last westward incursion by Germany in World War I. Though recent joiners to the war, American forces proved themselves in this bloody battle under intense summer heat, and the 3rd Division became known as "The Rock of the Marne."

maroon • *v.* (often **be marooned**) leave (someone) trapped and isolated in an inaccessible place, especially an island.

marque • *n.* see LETTER OF MARQUE.

marry • *v.* (**-ies, -ied**) splice (ropes) end to end without increasing their girth.

marshal • *n.* **1** an officer of the highest rank in the armed forces of some countries, including France. **2** an official responsible for supervising public events, especially sports events or parades. • *v.* (**marshaled, marshaling**) **1** arrange or assemble (a group of people, especially soldiers) in order: *the general marshaled his troops.* **2** guide or usher (someone) ceremoniously: *guests were marshaled into position.* **3** correctly position or arrange (rolling stock). **4** guide or direct the movement of (an aircraft) on the ground at an airport.

DERIVATIVES: **marshaler** *n.* **marshalship** *n.*

marshaling • *n.* **1** the process by which units participating in an amphibious or airborne operation assemble or group together when feasible or move to temporary camps in the vicinity of embarkation points, complete preparations for combat, or prepare for loading. **2** the process of assembling, holding, and organizing supplies and/or equipment, especially vehicles of transportation, for onward movement.

Marshall, George Catlett, Jr. (1880–1959) • General of the Army and statesman, army chief of staff (1939–45), secretary of state (1947–49), and secretary of defense (1950–51). Marshall was born in Uniontown, Pennsylvania. He is generally recognized as the architect and organizer of the Allied victory during WORLD WAR II, during which he was unofficial leader of the joint chiefs, first among equals within the combined chiefs, and key military advisor to the commander in chief, FRANKLIN D. ROOSEVELT. He played a major role in such crucial strategic decisions as the invasion of NORMANDY and the unity of command for all British and American forces. As secretary of state in the early years of the COLD WAR, Marshall helped to define the U.S. role in international affairs and to restructure the state department accordingly. The EUROPEAN RECOVERY PROGRAM, commonly known as the MARSHALL PLAN and for which he was awarded the Nobel Prize (1953), provided more than $13 billion in aid to the war-torn nations of Western Europe. In his brief tenure as secretary of defense Marshall was involved in the decision to recall Gen. DOUGLAS MACARTHUR from Korea. Earlier in his career Marshall had played a major role in planning the offensives of ST. MIHIEL and MEUSE-ARGONNE(1918) during WORLD WAR I while on the operations staff of Gen. JOHN J. PERSHING's headquarters.

Marshall Islands • an archipelago of thirty-four islands in the North Pacific Ocean. A republic, its capital is Majuro, which in 1944 became the first Japanese possession taken by U.S. forces in WORLD WAR II. Other islands were later occupied, and the Marshall Islands remained under U.S. control until the end of the war. In 1946, BIKINI ATOLL, part of the archipelago, was used by the U.S. as a nuclear testing ground. The Marshalls became self-governing in 1979.

Marshall Plan • a four-year program proposed by U.S. Secretary of state GEORGE C. MARSHALL on June 5, 1947, and instituted at the Paris Economic Conference in July 1947 to provide foreign assistance to seventeen western and southern European nations during WORLD WAR II reconstruction. Implemented by the Economic Cooperation Administration, it was created to restore economic stability in Europe and to facilitate foreign trade, and it dispensed over $13 billion between 1948 and 1951. It was also designed to contain Soviet and communist expansionism. It was a predecessor of NATO and the Atlantic alliance.

The USSR declined to participate in the program and subsequently established the Cominform to oppose the Marshall Plan.

---

martial law • military government involving the suspension of ordinary law.

Martin, Alexander • (c. 1740–1807) REVOLUTIONARY WAR officer, born in Hunterdon County, New Jersey. Martin led his North

Carolina regiment in the defense of CHARLESTON (1776) but was accused of cowardice for his performance in the battle of GERMANTOWN (1777) and, though acquitted, resigned his commission shortly thereafter.

martinet • *n.* a strict disciplinarian, especially in the armed forces.

DERIVATIVES: **martinetish** (also **martinettish**) *adj.*

ORIGIN: late 17th century (denoting the drill system invented by Martinet): named after Jean *Martinet*, 17th-century French drillmaster.

Martin, John Alexander (1839–89) • Union army officer with a Kansas volunteer regiment, born in Brownsville, Pennsylvania. Martin took part in the principal engagements of the ARMY OF THE CUMBERLAND, including CHICKAMAUGA (1863), MISSIONARY RIDGE (1863), and the campaign in East Tennessee the following winter (1863–64). Martin was mustered out of the service in November 1864.

Martin Marietta • a corporation founded in 1961 for the production of aerospace and defense systems for the U.S. government. Martin Marietta Corporation resulted from the merger of the Martin Company and the American-Marietta Company. During the 1980s Martin Marietta Corporation was the main contractor for the space shuttle program, the MX MISSILE program, as well as PATRIOT and PERSHING missile production. Martin Marietta merged with the LOCKHEED Corporation in 1995 to become the largest defense contractor in the United States.

Martin NBS-1 • a two-engine night bomber developed from the Martin MB-1 (GMB) in 1920 and capable of speeds up to 99 mph. The excellent performance of the MB-1 was sacrificed so that the NBS-1 (MB-2) could carry a larger load of bombs.

Maryland Campaign • (also called the **Antietam Campaign**) Confederate Gen. ROBERT E. LEE's attempted invasion of Virginia in September 1862, in which his forces captured the Union garrison at HARPERS FERRY, clearing communications in the SHENANDOAH VALLEY, but were defeated at SOUTH MOUNTAIN and ANTIETAM.

MASH • *abbr.* Mobile Army Surgical Hospital.

mask • *n.* a respirator used to filter inhaled air or to supply gas for inhalation. • *v.* conceal (something) from view: *the trees masked a depot.*

DERIVATIVES: **masked** *adj.*

masking • *n.* **1** screening or covering for concealing any military installation or operation. **2** in artillery fire, the interposition between the guns and the target of friendly troops or some terrain feature which poses the risk of hitting friendly troops or prevents observation or striking of the target.

Mason-Dixon Line • the boundary between Maryland and Pennsylvania, named after the British astronomers, Charles Mason and Jeremiah Dixon, who conducted the boundary survey in 1763-67. In the 1820 congressional debates over the MISSOURI COMPROMISE, which determined the area where slavery would be allowed as the United States expanded, the term was first used to denote the line separating the slave states in the South from the free states in the North. Henceforth the name referred not only to the Maryland-Pennsylvania boundary but also to a line along the Ohio River from Pennsylvania to the Mississippi River, then along the east, north, and west boundaries of Missouri, and then west along the 36°30′ parallel.

Mason, John (c. 1600–72) • ENGLISH-BORN commander of the Connecticut forces in the PEQUOT WAR (1636–37), a series of clashes between colonial settlers and local Indians. In an 1637 retaliatory attack, Mason's combined force of Connecticut and Massachusetts militia and other Indian tribes set upon a Pequot village, taking it by surprise and burning it and its inhabitants to the ground, killing any that managed to escape the flames. Mason himself wrote the history of the encounter on the basis of which later historians condemn his cruelty.

Mason, Richard Barnes (1797–1850) • U.S. army officer and military governor, born in Fairfax County, Virginia. He received a U.S. Army commission as a second lieutenant of infantry in 1817. He served in the BLACK HAWK WAR and participated in expeditions to intimidate the Plains tribes and map new areas. At the beginning of the MEXICAN WAR (1846–48), he was appointed colonel and commander of the 1st Dragoon Regiment. Sent to California in February 1847 to take command of conquering American forces there, Mason carried WAR DEPARTMENT instructions that established STEPHEN W. KEARNY as military governor. In May, Mason began a two year period where he held the combined military command and governorship of California. He faced and handled a host of problems most significantly the beginnings of the Gold Rush and the transition after the signing of the TREATY OF GUADALUPE-HIDALGO (1848). He then took command of JEFFERSON BARRACKS, outside Saint Louis, where he died of cholera.

mass • *v.* assemble or cause to assemble into a mass or as one body: *both countries began massing troops in the region*

Massachusetts Bay Colony • a Puritan settlement in Massachusetts, founded in 1630 by approximately 1,000 English refugees. The Puritans of the Massachusetts Bay Colony developed a theocracy based on their Protestant beliefs.

Massachusetts Militia Act of 1647 • a series of laws passed on November 11, 1647, by the General Court of Massachusetts to amend provisions of a 1645 law. It allowed each regiment in the colony to set its own dates for training, which must occur eight days a year but not during the agricultural months of July and August. It also clarified legal standards for weapons and defined who was required to own a weapon but exempt from training. Additionally, it stated company officer election procedures.

mass casualty • any large number of casualties produced in a relatively short period of time, usually as the result of a single incident such as a military aircraft accident, hurricane, flood, earthquake, or armed attack that exceeds local logistical support capabilities.

massed fire • **1** the fire of the batteries of two or more ships directed against a single target. **2** fire from a number of weapons directed at a single point or small area.

Massing, Hede Tune (1899–1981) • European-born Communist spy who became disillusioned during the STALINist purges and later became an informant for the Federal Bureau of Investigation. In the 1930s Massing, who had acquired U.S. citizenship, worked as a Soviet agent in the United States, obtaining data from government contacts that was relayed to Moscow. In 1947 she was approached by the FBI and chose to cooperate, becoming an expert witness against her first husband. In 1950 she testified against ALGER HISS, corroborating Whittaker Chambers's testimony that Hiss was a Communist spy. Massing later provided her services to the CENTRAL INTELLIGENCE AGENCY.

massive retaliation • a strategic doctrine, championed by U.S. Secretary of State JOHN FOSTER DULLES and others in the mid-1950s, calling for the countering of aggression of any type with tremendous destructive power, particularly a crushing nuclear response to any provocation deemed serious enough to warrant military action.

mast • *n.* **1** a tall upright post, spar, or other structure on a ship or boat, in sailing vessels generally carrying a sail or sails. **2** a similar structure on land, especially a flagpole or a television or radio transmitter. **3** (in full **captain's mast**) (in the U.S. Navy) a session of court presided over by the captain of a ship, especially to hear cases of minor offenses.
PHRASES: **before the mast** serving as an ordinary seaman in a sailing ship (quartered in the forecastle).
DERIVATIVES: **masted** *adj. a single-masted fishing boat.*

master[1] • *n.* the captain of a merchant ship.

master[2] • *n.* a ship or boat with a specified number of masts: *a three-master.*

Master Aircrew • a generic RAF rank equivalent to warrant officer, only applied to members of an aircrew.

master-at-arms • *n.* (pl. **masters-at-arms**) a naval petty officer appointed to carry out or supervise police duties on board a ship.

master chief petty officer • a noncommissioned officer in the U.S. Navy or Coast Guard ranking above senior chief petty officer and below warrant officer.

Master Chief Petty Officer of the Navy • the highest ranking noncommissioned officer in the U.S. Navy and the principal enlisted advisor to the CHIEF OF NAVAL OPERATIONS.

master corporal • a rank in the Canadian army and air force, above corporal and below sergeant.

master force list • (**MFL**) a file that contains the current status of each requirement for a given operation plan.

master gunnery sergeant • a noncommissioned officer in the U.S. Marine Corps ranking above master sergeant and below sergeant major.

master mariner • a seaman qualified to be a captain, especially of a merchant ship.

master seaman • a rank in the Canadian navy, above leading seaman and below petty officer.

master sergeant • a noncommissioned officer in the U.S. armed forces of high rank, in particular (in the Army) an NCO above sergeant first class and below sergeant major, (in the Air Force) an NCO above technical sergeant and below senior master sergeant, or (in the Marine Corps) an NCO above gunnery sergeant and below master gunnery sergeant.

master warrant officer • a rank in the Canadian army and air force, above warrant officer and below chief warrant officer.

masthead • *n.* the highest part of a ship's mast or of the lower section of a mast. • *v.* **1** send (a sailor) to the masthead, especially as a punishment. **2** raise (a flag or sail) to the masthead.

Matador • (**MGM-1C**) a surface-to-surface cruise missile developed in the 1940s that carried a nuclear or conventional warhead. It was rocket-launched from a mobile trailer and was controlled electronically from the ground during flight.

Matamoros • a northeastern Mexican city occupied by Gen. ZACHARY TAYLOR on May 17, 1846, at the outset of the MEXICAN WAR (1846–48), before he moved deeper into Mexico.

matchlock • *n.* **1** a type of gun with a lock in which a piece of wick or cord is placed for igniting the powder. **2** a lock of this kind.

mate • *n.* a deck officer on a merchant ship subordinate to the master. See also FIRST MATE.

matelot |ˌmætl'ō; mæt'lō| • *n.* Brit. & informal a sailor.

materiel |məˌtirē'el| (also **matériel**) • *n.* military materials and equipment.

Mathews, George (1739–1812) • soldier, born in Augusta County, Virginia. Mathews saw limited action in the REVOLUTIONARY WAR, being captured at GERMANTOWN (1777) and released four years later, serving out the remainder of the conflict under Gen. NATHANAEL GREENE in the southern campaign.

Matsu • see TAIWAN STRAIT CRISES.

MAU • *abbr.* Marine Amphibious Unit.

Mauldin, Bill • (1921–) cartoonist, born William Henry Mauldin in Mount Park, New Mexico. Mauldin gained fame during WORLD WAR II for his sardonic depictions of the enlisted man's life in the military. Mauldin joined the army as a private in 1940 and in 1943 was assigned to the *Stars and Stripes*, for which he covered the fighting in Italy, France, and Germany. His most famous characters were Willie and Joe, two riflemen. Mauldin was twice awarded the Pulitzer Prize, in 1945 and again in 1959, for his work as an editorial cartoonist with the St. Louis *Post-Dispatch*.

Maury, Dabney Herndon (1822–1900) • Confederate army officer, born in Fredericksburg, Virginia. Maury was commander of the District of the Gulf (1863–65) who supervised the construction of Mobile's defenses but was forced to order the city's evacuation (1865). Earlier in the conflict he had performed admirably at the battle of PEA RIDGE (1862) and commanded a division at CORINTH (1862) and at VICKSBURG (1863). After the war Maury served as U.S. minister to Colombia (1885–89). Before resigning his U.S. Army commission to join the Confederate forces, Maury had been recognized for meritorious conduct during the MEXICAN WAR (1846–48).

Maury, Matthew Fontaine (1806–73) • naval officer and oceanographer, born near Fredricksburg, Virginia. During the CIVIL WAR Maury joined the Confederate navy, working on harbor defenses and traveling to England to obtain ships for the Confederacy. He is known primarily, however, for his earlier work as an author on scientific and technological subjects and as head of the U.S. NAVAL OBSERVATORY and Hydrographic Office (1854). His research on winds and currents resulted in great savings in sailing time between ports, and his *The Physical Geography of the Sea* (1855) laid the foundations of the modern science of oceanography.

Maury was the uncle of DABNEY MAURY.

Maus • see TANKS, GERMAN, WORLD WAR II–ERA.

Mauser |ˈmowzər| • trademark a make of firearm, especially a repeating rifle: *a Mauser rifle.*

ORIGIN: late 19th century: named after Paul von *Mauser* (1838–1914), German inventor.

Maverick • (**AGM-65**) an air-to-surface missile that is designed for use against stationary or moving small, hard targets such as tanks, armored vehicles, and field fortifications. Its precision onboard guidance system has contributed to its popularity as a "fire-and-forget" weapon.

Maxim gun • *n.* the first fully automatic water-cooled machine gun, designed in Britain in 1884 and used especially in WORLD WAR I.

ORIGIN: named after SIR HIRAM S. *MAXIM*.

Maxim, Sir Hiram S. (1840–1916) • self-taught engineer and inventor of the first automatic machine gun. Maxim, born Hiram Stevens Maxim near Sangersville, Maine, became a British subject. He had first focused his inventive efforts on the incandescent light bulb, experimenting with machine guns only on the side. His MAXIM GUN was not the first machine gun, but it was vastly superior to its predecessors. In 1889 it was adopted by the British army, which used it extensively in suppressing colonial insurrections. Its revolutionary impact on warfare was not immediately recognized.

Growing eccentric and anticlerical in his later years, he was arrested in 1913 for harassing Salvation Army workers with a pea-shooter.

maximum operating depth • the depth that a submarine is not to exceed during operations. This depth is determined by the submarine's national naval authority.

maximum takeoff weight • the maximum gross weight, due to design or operational limitations, at which an aircraft is permitted to take off.

May Act • a 1941 law that made it a federal offense to practice prostitution in areas designated by the secretaries of the army and the navy. It was an attempt to control prostitution near military bases and to check the spread of sexually transmitted disease.

***Mayaguez* Incident** (1975) • a publicly popular though perhaps excessively dangerous and costly attempt to rescue the crew of the U.S. merchant ship *Mayaguez*. On May 12, Cambodian gunboats had seized the ship and imprisoned its forty crew members on charges of spying. Declining U.S. credibility in the wake of the VIETNAM WAR led President GERALD R. FORD and Secretary of State HENRY KISSINGER to authorize the Marines to attack Koh Tang Island where the *Mayaguez* crew was believed to be detained. The Khmer Rouge government had been holding the ship's crew on the mainland, and had released them on its own as soon as the attack had begun. The Marines, however, suffered heavy casualties. Although some members of Congress accused Ford of abusing the law by ordering the operation, polls showed that the public largely approved of the forceful response to what the president had labeled "piracy."

Mayday (also **mayday**) • *exclam.* an international radio distress signal used by ships and aircraft. • *n.* a distress signal using the word "Mayday": *we sent out a Mayday.*

ORIGIN: 1920s: representing a pronunciation of French *m'aider*, from *venez m'aider* 'come and help me.'

MB-2 • see MARTIN NBS-1.

MC-130 • see COMBAT TALON.

McArthur, John (1826–1906) • Union army officer, born in Renfrewshire, Scotland. McArthur was commended for his performance at FORT DONELSON (1862) and at CORINTH (1862). Following the surrender of VICKSBURG (1863), he guarded supply lines as Gen. WILLIAM T. SHERMAN advanced towards Jackson, and later his division was responsible for construction of the defenses guarding the approaches to that city. McArthur and his division were in the forefront in the decisive battle of NASHVILLE (1864).

McCabe, Charles Cardwell (1836–1906) • military chaplain of an Ohio infantry unit during the CIVIL WAR. McCabe, born in Athens, Ohio, was captured and imprisoned for several months after the battle of Winchester (1863), an experience he later detailed in a popular lecture. McCabe resigned his chaplaincy for health reasons early in 1864 but continued to help the war effort through the U.S. Christian Commission, an organization that assisted chaplains and medical personnel. He was made a bishop in 1896, and in 1902 he became chancellor of American University in Washington, D.C.

McCabe became closely associated with "Battle Hymn of the Republic," which he sang at public gatherings, taught to his soldiers and fellow inmates, and sang in connection with the funeral and burial of ABRAHAM LINCOLN, who was said to be particularly fond of McCabe's rendition.

McCarran Internal Security Act • a law enacted by Congress on September 23, 1950, during the COLD WAR and after U.S. intervention in the KOREAN WAR, to require the registration of alleged communist organizations and to monitor individuals who potentially threatened U.S. security. President HARRY S. TRUMAN rejected it as a violation of civil liberties, and several of its provisions were repealed by 1971.

McCausland, John (1836–1927) • Confederate army officer, born in St. Louis, Missouri. McCausland, while under the command of JUBAL EARLY, led his brigade in a retaliatory raid on Chambersburg, Pennsylvania, burning the town to the ground, destroying more than 500 structures, and causing nearly $1 million in property damage, all the while engaging in drunkenness and looting (1864). He later led his command in the final operations in the SHENANDOAH VALLEY (1864), and participated in the APPOMATTOX campaign (1865). After the war he went into exile because of an indictment against him in Pennsylvania and a War Department order for his arrest, but he returned to the United States in 1868 when assured he would not be prosecuted. Prior to the raid that led to his being called "the Hun of Chambersburg," McCausland, a member of a Virginia infantry unit, had seen most of his action under various commanders in the western portions of that state (now West Virginia).

McClellan, George B. (1826–85) • CIVIL WAR general, general in chief of the Union forces (1861–62) and commander of the ARMY OF THE POTOMAC (1861–62), born George Brinton McClellan in Philadelphia. After his troops successfully drove Confederate forces from western Virginia (1861), McClellan was called to the capital by ABRAHAM LINCOLN to restore and command the Army of the Potomac, which had been demoralized by the defeat at FIRST BULL RUN (1861). Although McClellan successfully rebuilt the army, his late and ultimately indecisive PENINSULAR CAMPAIGN culminating in the SEVEN DAYS' battles (1862) led Lincoln to replace him. Later recalled, he was once again relieved when despite the opportunity to do so, he failed to totally destroy the rebel forces at ANTIETAM (1862). The general once dubbed the "Young Napoleon" never received another army assignment. Though recognized as an able organizer and motivator of troops, McClellan proved incapable of decisive and timely action. Further, his tendency toward delay and exaggeration of the opposition's strength fueled a suspicion that the pro-slavery Democrat was not fully committed to winning the war. In 1864 McClellan ran for president but was trounced by Abraham Lincoln. That same year he resigned from the army. After the war he obtained considerable wealth as a consulting engineer, and also served a single term as governor of New Jersey.

McClernand, John Alexander (1812–1900) • Union general, born near Hardinsburg, Kentucky. McClernand commanded a brigade under the command of Gen. ULYSSES S. GRANT. Promoted to major general after the victory at FORT DONELSON (1862), McClernand widely boasted of his success, claiming more for his own brigade than was warranted. More self-aggrandizing claims and congratulatory kudos to his own corps followed SHILOH (1862) and VICKSBURG (1863), the latter angering Grant sufficiently to have him dismiss McClernand. Though restored to command the following winter, McClernand destroyed what little of his reputation remained during the botched and ill-fated RED RIVER CAMPAIGN. He resigned later that year (1864).

McCloy, John Jay, Jr. (1895–1989) • diplomat, born in Philadelphia. McCloy was assistant secretary of war (1941–45) and U.S. high commissioner for occupied Germany (1949–52). As assistant secretary during wartime, McCloy had broad duties and played a central role in many controversial decisions of the period, such as those to intern Japanese Americans and not to bomb the NAZI extermination camp at AUSCHWITZ. McCloy, who considered espionage a fact of international relations, participated in the creation of the OFFICE OF STRATEGIC SERVICES. His willingness to countenance a significant increase in the power and secrecy of the national government makes him one of the founders of the NATIONAL SECURITY STATE. In Germany, together with Konrad Adenauer he laid the foundation for West Germany's integration into the economies and military forces of Western Europe. McCloy later pursued a career in banking but continued to be an advisor to presidents, including JOHN F. KENNEDY, LYNDON B. JOHNSON, and JIMMY CARTER. During WORLD WAR I McCloy had served in France but saw little action; he remained with the army of occupation until fall 1919.

McCloy, a prominent Wall Street lawyer, gained fame through his successful pursuit of the so-called Black Tom case, in which Bethlehem Steel sought compensation for a 1916 explosion at a munitions depot on Black Tom Island in New York Harbor. Despite two losing efforts before the World Court, McCloy eventually won the case in 1939, demonstrating that the explosion was sabotage ordered by the German government.

McCone, John A. (1902–91) • chairman of the ATOMIC ENERGY COMMISSION (1958–61) and director of central intelligence (1961-65), born John Alex McCone in San Francisco. As chairman of the AEC, McCone successfully promoted civilian uses of nuclear power and concluded agreements with the Soviet Union for shared nuclear research, though, despite repeated attempts, not for an end to nuclear weapons testing. McCone took over the CIA when it had been demoralized by the BAY OF PIGS (1961) fiasco and revived morale within the agency. As director he instituted management reforms and emphasized the gathering and analysis of information over covert operations. The most significant event of his tenure was the CUBAN MISSILE CRISIS (1962), during which he was on the committee of those who decided U.S. policy. Disagreement with LYNDON B. JOHNSON'S VIETNAM WAR policies led to McCone's increasing alienation from the president, and he resigned in April 1965. In 1987 McCone was awarded the Presidential Medal of Freedom.

McCook, Alexander McDowell (1831–1903) • Union army officer, born in Columbiana County, Ohio. His corps was trounced at PERRYVILLE (1862), his divisions were savaged at STONES RIVER (1862–63) and when routed at CHICKAMAUGA (1863), he retreated into Chattanooga, for which he was relieved of his command. He never again led large numbers of troops in the field. Before these three unsuccessful outings, McCook had been commended for his actions at SHILOH (1862).

Alexander McDowell McCook was the highest ranking of the fourteen "Fighting McCooks" that fought for the Union during the CIVIL WAR. They included his father, his seven brothers, and five cousins. Two of his brothers, Daniel Jr. and Robert Latimer, and his first cousin, EDWARD MOODY MCCOOK, also became generals.

McCook, Edward Moody (1833–1909) • Union army officer, born in Steubenville, Ohio. McCook was in command of the cavalry of the ARMY OF THE CUMBERLAND. His most distinguished exploit occurred when his cavalry prevented Confederate reinforcements from reaching Gen. JOHN B. HOOD at ATLANTA, paving the way for the fall of that city and for Sherman's MARCH TO THE SEA (1864–65). After the war McCook served briefly as military governor of Florida; as U.S. minister to Hawaii (1866–69); and as governor of Colorado territory (1869–73).

At one time McCook's investments in mining and other ventures made him the largest taxpayer and real estate owner in Colorado. He was a cousin of ALEXANDER MCDOWELL MCCOOK.

McCulloch, Ben (1811–62) • Confederate general, born in Rutherford County, Tennessee. His brigade figured in two major battles in the western theater of the CIVIL WAR. The Confederates' loss at PEA RIDGE (1862) cost them Missouri and McCulloch his life. Before the war McCulloch had fought in the TEXAS WAR OF INDEPENDENCE (1836) and been elected to the Congress of the Republic of Texas (1839). He was also one of the first TEXAS RANGERS, achieving fame as an Indian fighter. As a ranger he also fought with Gen. ZACHARY TAYLOR during the MEXICAN WAR (1846–48).

McCulloch was a natural woodsman who hunted with the legendary frontiersman DAVY CROCKETT.

McCutcheon, Keith Barr (1915–71) • U.S. Marine Corps officer, born in East Liverpool, Ohio. He played a prominent role in exploring and promoting the combat capabilities of helicopters during the 1950s, developing new tactics and techniques for their use. He later helped plan the initial deployment of marines to VIETNAM, where from 1965 to 1966 he supervised the marines aerial involvement in the war. McCutcheon also made important contributions to the doctrine and practice of close air support during WORLD WAR II, developing the concept of air liaison parties. In addition, in 1945 McCutcheon flew behind enemy lines to gather information on Japanese defense positions in the Philippines and subsequently directed the air strikes that led to the success of landings on Mindanao, for which he received a SILVER STAR. He was placed on the retired list with the grade of general shortly before he died.

McDonald, Donald (?–1788) • born in Scotland, British army officer during the REVOLUTIONARY WAR who was sent to North Carolina to organize Scots settlers as loyalists in a campaign against the local revolutionaries. Although various inducements brought significant numbers to his camp, his forces were eventually routed by the patriots at Moore's Creek Bridge (1776), effectively putting an end to British hopes of enlisting Southern loyalists against the revolutionaries.

McDonnell • an aircraft manufacturer, now merged with Boeing in 1997, that began as the McDonnell Aircraft Company in Lambert Field, Missouri, in 1939. The company has developed into a major manufacturer of aircraft and aircraft parts for the U.S. military. In the 1950s McDonnell manufactured smaller U.S. Air Force fighter (F) jets that were fitted with bomb-carrying pylons under the wings, such as the McDonnell-Douglas F-4 PHANTOM II, which saw action in the VIETNAM WAR with a variety of conventional ordnance and is capable of nuclear weapon delivery. In the 1970s the Air Force began taking delivery of the McDonnell-Douglas F-15, which is capable of multirole operations and demonstrated the new generation of "smart weapons" (guided bombs, stand-off missiles, etc.) in the PERSIAN GULF WAR.

McDowell, Battle of • (also called **Sitlington's Hill**) a battle that took place on May 8, 1862, at the town of McDowell in Highland County, Virginia, between Union Brig. Gen. ROBERT MILROY'S forces and those of Confederate Maj. Gen. THOMAS "STONEWALL" JACKSON during the CIVIL WAR. Milroy attacked the

Confederates on Sitlington's Hill, attempting to prevent Jackson's troops from pushing further north. Jackson prevailed, continuing his SHENANDOAH VALLEY CAMPAIGN, and Union troops retreated west.

McDowell, Irvin (1818–85) • Union general, born in Columbus, Ohio. He commanded forces at 1st (1861) and 2nd (1862) BULL RUN but who held no important commands after his performance at those two disastrous defeats, which proved him ineffective in the field.

McElroy, Neil (1904–72) • secretary of defense (1957–59), born in Berea, Ohio. His brief tenure focused on concerns about the so-called MISSILE GAP and reorganization of the DEPARTMENT OF DEFENSE. Though McElroy did not believe the recent successful Soviet launching of SPUTNIK significantly affected the world's military balance, he recognized its powerful impact on public opinion and concentrated on speeding up the U.S. effort in missile development. He ordered production of intermediate-range missiles and accelerated the development of intercontinental missiles and submarine-launched missiles. He also presided over a comprehensive reorganization of the DoD in 1958, which enhanced the position of the secretary of defense.

McIntosh, John Baillie (1829–88) • Union army officer, born at Fort Brooke, (now Tampa) Florida. His cavalry was considered one of the most effective regiments of volunteer horsemen in the ARMY OF THE POTOMAC. He led his command brilliantly on the third day at GETTYSBURG (1863), when he built and maintained a formidable barrier against the advance of J.E.B. STUART. He later won praise for his performance at Third Winchester (1864), where he was severely wounded. After the war McIntosh served as governor of the SOLDIERS' HOME in Washington, D.C. (1867–68) and as superintendent of Indian Affairs in California (1869–70).

McIntosh's older brother James was a Confederate general. McIntosh was born in Florida and had ties to the South, but had settled in New Jersey and cast his lot with the union.

McIntosh, Lachlan (1725–1806) • REVOLUTIONARY WAR officer. Born in Scotland, emigrated to Georgia with his family. In January 1776 he was appointed a colonel in the Georgia militia, and in September he became a brigadier general in the Continental Army. He was reassigned from Georgia after killing the state president in a duel, but after stints at VALLEY FORGE (1777–78) and in command of the Western Department headquartered at FORT PITT, he rejoined the army in the South. He commanded two regiments in the failed attack on Savannah in 1779, and was taken prisoner when the British took Charleston in 1780. He did not return to Georgia until 1783.

McKinley, William (1843–1901) • 25th president of the United States (1897–1901), born in Niles, Ohio. During the CIVIL WAR McKinley fought with an Ohio infantry unit and displayed bravery in combat at Antietam (1862). As a U.S. representative (1877–91), he was identified with the protective tariff and economic nationalism. He became chairman of the Ways and Means Committee in 1889. The McKinley Tariff of 1890, which raised customs duties but authorized trade reciprocity, cost him his seat in the next election. After two terms as governor of Ohio (elected 1891, 1893), McKinley obtained the Republican nomination for president in 1896 and conducted his famous "front-porch" campaign against WILLIAM JENNINGS BRYAN on a platform endorsing the gold standard as well as the protective tariff. Remaining at his Ohio home while the oratorically flamboyant Bryan toured the country, McKinley, aided by an intense and expensive promotional print campaign, won both the popular and electoral vote. McKinley proved a forceful executive who traveled widely and cultivated the press, setting aside space in the WHITE HOUSE for daily news briefings from the administration. Domestically his tenure was marked by increased tariffs and consolidation of the gold standard. In foreign policy, the key event of his tenure was the SPANISH-AMERICAN WAR (1898), brought about by the rebellion against Spanish rule in Cuba and precipitated by the sinking of the battleship *Maine* in Havana harbor (February 1898). Throughout the short conflict and later protracted Philippine insurrection, McKinley played a key role as commander in chief, giving the attack order that sent GEORGE DEWEY to MANILA BAY and then governing the islands through the war powers. McKinley shaped the strategy of the peace talks that resulted in U.S. acquisition of the Philippines, Guam, and Puerto Rico. His administration also initiated the OPEN DOOR POLICY with China and oversaw the treaty that cleared the way for the building of the PANAMA CANAL. His foreign policy record coupled with prosperity and complemented by THEODORE ROOSEVELT as a running mate led to a decisive victory in the 1900 presidential election, in which his opponent was again Bryan. A few months after his inauguration, McKinley was shot by an anarchist while visiting the Pan-American Exposition in Buffalo, New York. He died eight days later.

Throughout his political career McKinley was known as "Major" McKinley—a holdover from the brevet rank of major he had attained in the Civil War.

McLane, Allen (1746–1829) • army officer, born in Philadelphia. During the REVOLUTIONARY WAR McLane, together with his Delaware company, gained fame for actions around British-occupied Philadelphia (1777–78), interrupting trade and engaging in a series of irritants against the enemy. His men were the first to enter Philadelphia when the British withdrew. McLane's later raids, though successful and significant, received scant attention because his company was then attached to Lee's Legion and was overshadowed by the exploits of LIGHT-HORSE HARRY LEE. Early in the conflict McLane had fought with GEORGE WASHINGTON's army at the battles of NEW YORK and PRINCETON (1776–77).

McLane's exploits were popularized in such novels as S. Weir Mitchell's *Hugh Wynne* (1897) and Howard Fast's *Conceived in Liberty* (1939). An account of his escape from British dragoons became the subject of a painting by James Peale.

McLaws, Lafayette (1821–97) • Confederate army officer, born in Augusta, Georgia. He achieved his greatest success at FREDERICKSBURG (1862) when his division repulsed multiple frontal assaults by the ARMY OF THE POTOMAC. The division served in most of the major campaigns of the ARMY OF NORTHERN VIRGINIA from 1862 to 1863, achieving a solid combat record, but McLaws was relieved of command and charged with neglect of duty when the division attack at Knoxville was repulsed (1863). He was transferred out of the eastern theater and spent the remainder of the war in the south, participating in the Savannah and Carolinas campaigns (1864–65).

McNair, Frederick Vallette (1839–1900) • naval officer, born in Jenkintown, Pennsylvania. As commander of the ASIATIC SQUADRON (1895–98), McNair played an important part in its successful buildup before the SPANISH-AMERICAN WAR (1898). Cmdr. GEORGE DEWEY, under whom he served during that conflict, considered the squadron's level of proficiency a significant factor in the victory at Manila. He later served as commandant of the U.S. NAVAL ACADEMY (1898–1900) and was appointed first president of the Government Lighthouse Board, a position he never actively assumed because of declining health. During the CIVIL WAR McNair had served on the *Iroquois* under DAVID FARRAGUT in the Mississippi River campaign, and as executive officer on the *Juanita,* he was involved in attacks on FORT FISHER (1864–65). He attained the rank of rear admiral.

McNair, Lesley James (1883–1944) • U.S. army officer. Born in Minnesota, McNair graduated from WEST POINT in 1904 with a commission in the artillery. He took part in the occupation of VERACRUZ in 1914 and the Mexican PUNITIVE EXPEDITION (1916). He finished WORLD WAR I as a temporary brigadier general on the staff of General Headquarters, AMERICAN EXPEDITIONARY FORCES. After a tour as commandant of the COMMAND AND GENERAL STAFF SCHOOL at FORT LEAVENWORTH, he took a position on the army staff responsible for the training, organization, and mobilization of the expanding force. When the army command structure was reorganized in March 1942 Lt. Gen. McNair became commander of Army Ground Forces, where he was responsible for many key training and organizational innovations that shaped the American Army that fought in WORLD WAR II. In June 1944 he went to England as commander of an imaginary army group as part of the deception plan for the NORMANDY invasion. He was killed by a short American bomb while observing the air attack that launched OPERATION COBRA and the breakout from Normandy, the highest ranking American officer ever killed in action. He was promoted posthumously to full general in 1945.

McNamara, Robert S. (1916–) • secretary of defense (1961–68), born in San Francisco. McNamara brought civilian management practices to the DEPARTMENT OF DEFENSE. Such reforms as centralized decision making and the application of quantitative cost analysis to procurement decisions kept McNamara at odds with the military brass. His tenure, which coincided with a period of heightened COLD WAR tensions and VIETNAM WAR escalation, also saw a military buildup that included improved strategic nuclear forces and increases in intercontinental and submarine-launched missiles, as well as an expansion of conventional forces. His support of the Vietnam policies of JOHN F. KENNEDY and LYNDON B. JOHNSON made him a prime target of attack as opposition to the war grew. McNamara resigned to become president of the World Bank, where he remained until 1981.

McNeill, Daniel (1748–1833) • privateer during the REVOLUTIONARY WAR and later a naval officer, born in Charlestown, Massachusetts. Commissioned by the Massachusetts Provincial Congress in 1775, McNeill commanded six privateers, the last and most successful of which was *General Mifflin* (1778–79), which took thirteen prizes. McNeill joined the new navy during the QUASI-WAR WITH FRANCE (1798–1800) and successfully performed several commands, but his career ended negatively, when he set sail precipitously from a Mediterranean port, leaving several crew members behind. He was called home in disgrace and, though no charges were brought against him, dismissed from the service in 1802.

McNeill, Hector (1728–85) • Revolutionary naval officer, born in County Antrim, Ireland. McNeill commanded the Continental frigate *Boston* and his rivalry with JOHN MANLEY resulted in the American squadron being routed in an encounter with the British (1777). Although the *Boston* escaped (the *Hancock,* Manley's ship, was lost), McNeill, in fear of the British fleet, went into hiding for a month before returning home. Both captains were court-martialed, but only McNeill was found guilty and dismissed from the service (1778).

McNeill, John Hanson (1815–64) • farmer and Confederate soldier. Born in Hardy County, Virginia, McNeill eventually became a well-known stockbreeder in Missouri. When the CIVIL WAR began, he raised a cavalry company that fought with STERLING PRICE in his campaign to conquer Missouri for the CONFEDERACY. McNeill was captured by a Union patrol, but he escaped in June 1862, and after the failure of Price's campaign McNeill and his son returned to Virginia. McNeill recruited a company under the terms of the

Confederate Congress's Partisan Ranger Act and mounted effective guerrilla raids, initially under the command of Col. JOHN IMBODEN, and later independently with a unit known as McNeill's Partisan Rangers. When the Confederate Congress repealed the Partisan Ranger Act, only McNeill's and John Mosby's units were retained. McNeill was killed leading a raid to slow PHILIP H. SHERIDAN's devastating invasion of the SHENANDOAH VALLEY.

McPherson, James B. (1828–64) • Union army officer and military engineer, born James Birdseye McPherson in Green Creek Township, Ohio. His corps played a prominent role in the operations against VICKSBURG (1862–63). Later given command of the ARMY OF THE TENNESSEE, McPherson took part in WILLIAM T. SHERMAN's campaign against ATLANTA, the battle in which he was killed. Earlier in the conflict McPherson had supervised the fortifications of Boston harbor, acted as chief engineer in the campaign against FORTS HENRY and DONELSON (1862), served as superintendent of railroads in ULYSSES S. GRANT's department, and commanded troops for the first time after the battle of CORINTH (1862). Before the CIVIL WAR McPherson had worked on harbor fortifications in New York City and supervised the fortification of Alcatraz Island.

MCpl • *abbr.* Master Corporal.

MCPO • *abbr.* Master Chief Petty Officer.

MCWR • *abbr.* Marine Corps Women's Reserve.

M-day • the unnamed day on which full mobilization commences or is due to commence. An M-day is assumed to be 24 hours long and ends at 2400 hours (UNIVERSAL TIME).

M-Dogs • slang (WORLD WAR II) the elite of the K-9 Corps; bomb-sniffing dogs trained by the army to detect antipersonnel mines and booby traps.

Me 109 • see MESSERSCHMITT 109.

Meade, George Gordon (1815–72) • Union general, born in Cadiz, Spain. He was commander of the ARMY OF THE POTOMAC (1863–65). Meade first came to prominence during the 1862 PENINSULAR CAMPAIGN and further distinguished himself later that year at SECOND BULL RUN, ANTIETAM, and FREDERICKSBURG. Despite his victory at GETTYSBURG (1863), Meade was criticized for its execution and his failure to aggressively pursue the losing forces. He continued to command the Army of the Potomac with competence and dedication for the remainder of the war, though he was never accorded the stature of other military leaders of the conflict. His postwar career consisted of a series of administrative posts. Before the CIVIL WAR Meade had seen action in the MEXICAN WAR (1846–48) and supervised the Great Lakes geodetic survey.

Meade, Richard Worsam, III (1837–97) • career naval officer, born in New York City. His numerous contributions to the navy included administrative innovations, reforms in naval education, and advocacy of a multifaceted global fleet. During the CIVIL WAR, he held several commands and was cited for gallant conduct. He later worked on coastal surveys; published textbooks and articles; advocated for reform of naval administrative structure and navy yard management; commanded one of the nation's first steel warships (1885–86) and the North Atlantic Squadron (1894–95); and wrote reports and recommendations on topics ranging from ordnance to methods of inventory. Meade retired in 1895, a rear admiral.

Meagher, Thomas Francis |ˈmähər| (1823–67) • Union army officer, born in Waterford, Ireland. He raised the famed Irish Brigade, which he commanded during the PENINSULAR CAMPAIGN and at SECOND BULL RUN, ANTIETAM, and FREDERICKSBURG (all 1862). When denied replacements for casualties suffered in the last encounter, Meagher resigned his commission (1863) but later accepted an appointment as a military administrator. During the last year of the conflict he assisted with the military occupation of Savannah, Georgia. After the war he served as acting territorial governor of Montana until his death by drowning.

As an Irish nationalist who advocated violent overthrow of the British, Meagher was convicted of high treason and condemned to death in 1848. The following year his sentence was commuted and he was banished for life to Tasmania. He escaped in 1852 and made his way to New York City.

---

meal ticket • **1** slang (in WORLD WAR I) an identification tag worn on the wrist. Also called a **dog tag**. **2** a ticket entitling a person to a meal, especially at a specified place for a reduced cost.

mean sea level • the sea level halfway between the mean levels of high and low water.

Means, Gaston Bullock (1879–1938) • spy, born in Blackwelder's Spring, North Carolina. Means relayed information about armaments and ship movements to the Germans before the 1917 U.S. entry into WORLD WAR I. Such information was intended to show that the United States was violating neutrality laws. Means was later a swindler who obtained large sums of money through a variety of hoaxes and confidence games. Despite his reputation, he had brief careers as an FBI agent and as a customs agent for the treasury department, during which he shook down criminal suspects and solicited bribes, respectively. He was convicted of Prohibition violations and of extortion, for which he served time in federal prison.

MEB • *abbr.* Marine Expeditionary Brigade.

Mechanicsville, Battle of • the second of the SEVEN DAYS' battles in Virginia during the CIVIL WAR. On June 26, 1862, Union forces, under Gen. GEORGE B. MCCLELLAN and Brig. Gen. FITZ JOHN PORTER, rebuffed a series of assaults by Gen. ROBERT E. LEE's army, which suffered heavy casualties. Approaching Confederate reinforcements, however, forced Porter and McClellan south of the James River, at GAINES' MILL.

mechanize • *v.* equip (a military force) with modern weapons and vehicles: (**mechanized**) *the units comprised tanks and mechanized infantry.*

DERIVATIVES: **mechanization** *n.* **mechanizer** *n.*

mechanized warfare • warfare conducted with the use of armored and motorized vehicles and weapons and usually involving rapid movement over long distances.

Médaille Militaire • a French military honor instituted in 1852 that has been awarded to soldiers of foreign armies for their services to France.

Medal of Honor • the highest U.S. military decoration awarded for "conspicuous gallantry and intrepidity at the risk of life and above and beyond the call of duty in action" during actual armed conflict with an enemy of the United States. Established by act of Congress in December 1861, the Medal of Honor may be awarded to members of any branch of service. Each service (Army, Navy/Marine Corps, and Air Force) has a slightly different pattern for the medal itself, but all share the distinctive light blue ribbon sprinkled with white stars.

medevac |ˈmediˌvæk| • *n.* **1** in the VIETNAM WAR, a medical evacuation, usually by helicopter, during or after a battle, to a field hospital. There were three levels of medical evacuation: emergency of soldiers near death; priority, of soldiers seriously wounded and unable to walk; and routine, of soldiers able to walk, or killed in action. **2** the helicopters used in such missions.

medic • *n.* a medical corpsman who dispenses first aid at combat sites.

medical intelligence • the category of intelligence resulting from collection, evaluation, analysis, and interpretation of foreign medical, bio-scientific, and environmental information which is of interest to strategic planning and to military medical planning and operations for conservation of the fighting strength of friendly forces and the formation of assessments of foreign medical capabilities in both military and civilian sectors.

medical officer • a doctor serving in the armed forces, in a prison, or in a public health service.

Medicine Lodge, Treaty of • a peace treaty signed in October 1867 by KIOWA, Comanche, Kiowa-Apache, CHEYENNE, and ARAPAHO tribes and the United States near Medicine Lodge, Kansas. The Indians agreed to live on reservations in exchange for protection, supplies, and services of the federal government, but the government subsequently failed to honor these provisions. It also opened the area to white settlement and railroads.

medium-range ballistic missile • a ballistic missile with a range capability from about 600 to 1,500 nautical miles.

medium-range bomber aircraft • a bomber capable of tactical performance within a radius of 1,000 nautical miles at design maximum weight and bomb load.

medium-range transport aircraft • see TRANSPORT AIRCRAFT.

MEF • *abbr.* Marine Expeditionary Force.

megaton • *n.* a measurement of the yield of a nuclear weapon equivalent to the explosion of 1 million tons of TNT.

megaton weapon • a nuclear weapon, the yield of which is measured in terms of millions of tons of TNT explosive equivalents.

Megee, Vernon Edgar (1900–92) • Marine Corps officer, born in Tulsa, Oklahoma Territory. Megee was a proponent and developer of CLOSE AIR SUPPORT. Megee's strategy of placing control in marine detachments ashore with troops rather than in naval commanders offshore, as had previously been practiced, was proved effective at the invasion of IWO JIMA (1945) and during the battle for OKINAWA (1945). During the KOREAN WAR Megee regained operational control of marine aircraft, which had been taken over by the air force. From 1956 to 1957 he served as assistant commandant/chief of staff of the Marine Corps, the first aviator to hold the position. When Megee retired in 1959, he received a promotion to four-star general.

Meigs, Montgomery Cunningham |megz| (1816–92) • quartermaster general of the army, born in Augusta, Georgia. Meigs is considered one of the most effective administrators in U.S. Army history. During the CIVIL WAR, he transformed a small, disorganized department into a smoothly functioning bureau that supplied the needs of nearly 1 million soldiers. In the process he overhauled transportation regulations and orchestrated a complicated seatrain of supply ships that provided victuals to the army of Gen. WILLIAM T. SHERMAN. He frequently went to the field himself—in 1864 he personally commanded Gen. ULYSSES S. GRANT's supply bases in Virginia. After the war Meigs remained with the quartermaster department in Washington until his retirement in 1882, after forty-six years of service.

Meigs's eldest son, John Rodgers Meigs, also a Union officer, was allegedly murdered by Confederate partisans while scouting the SHENANDOAH VALLEY in 1864.

Meigs, Return Jonathan |megz| (1740–1823) • officer in the Continental army, born in Middletown, Connecticut. Meigs won a reputation as a daring and enterprising soldier for his raid at Sag Harbor (1777), when he took the enemy by surprise and burned twelve vessels, destroyed military stores, killed six of the enemy, and took ninety prisoners—without any loss to his 160-man force. He subsequently served in the Hudson highlands, commanding a light infantry regiment in the assault on Stony Point (1779). He retired from the army in 1781. In 1801 he was appointed agent for Indian affairs in the Cherokee Nation, a position he held until his death.

Mekong River • a river of Southeast Asia, which rises in Tibet and flows southeast and south for 2,600 miles (4,180 km) through southern China, Laos, Cambodia, and Vietnam to its extensive delta on the South China Sea. It forms the boundary between Laos and its western neighbors Burma and Thailand.

melee |ˈmāˌlā; māˈlā| (also **mêlée**) • *n.* a confused fight, skirmish, or scuffle: *several people were hurt in the melee.*

Melville, George Wallace (1841–1912) • naval engineer and administrator, and Arctic explorer, born in New York City. As chief of the Bureau of Steam Engineering (1887–1903), Melville introduced innovations that made the U.S. Navy competitive with the great European navies. He was also responsible for building the three fastest warships then afloat. Earlier, as chief engineer aboard a vessel on an Arctic expedition, Melville landed on and claimed Henrietta Island for the United States (1881), but the trip and his reputation were marred by his delay in searching for other members of the party once their ship sank. He also served as chief engineer aboard the *Thetis,* which went in search of the members of the ADOLPHUS GREELY expedition, who were lost north of Greenland. During the CIVIL WAR, Melville saw considerable hazardous duty, much of it volunteer. He went aboard the Confederate ship *Florida* as a spy, for example, and he made the suggestion to ram and capture it as it lay in a neutral harbor (1864). He retired from the navy in 1903.

Memorial Day • in the United States, a day on which those who died on active service are remembered, usually the last Monday in May.

Mention in Dispatches • the custom of naming in a commander's official report of a battle or campaign those military personnel who distinguished themselves by exceptional heroism, service, or achievement. In the British and some other armies, a "Mention in Dispatches" is considered a decoration and entitles the individual so mentioned to wear a small metallic device, usually a star, on the campaign ribbon for that battle or campaign. The custom is not maintained in the United States armed forces, although individuals may be cited by name for outstanding service in a commander's report.

Menu Bombings • a fourteen-month campaign (1969–70) of secret U.S. bombings aimed ostensibly at VIETCONG bases in Laos and Cambodia. Beginning in March 1969, the campaign ended in April 1970, after Lon Nol, a conservative, pro-U.S. general, orchestrated a successful coup and then granted the U.S. permission to eradicate remaining enemy bases.

mercantile • *adj.* of or relating to trade or commerce; commercial.

mercantilism • *n.* belief in the benefits of profitable trading; commercialism.

DERIVATIVES: **mercantilist** *n.* & *adj.* **mercantilistic** *adj.*

mercenary • *n.* a professional soldier hired to serve in a foreign army.

ORIGIN: late Middle English (as a noun): from Latin *mercenaruis* 'hireling,' from *merces, merced-* 'reward.'

merchantman • *n.* (pl. **-men**) a ship used in commerce; a vessel of the merchant marine.

merchant marine • (often **the merchant marine**) a country's shipping that is involved in commerce and trade, as opposed to military activity.

merchant navy • all of a nation's ships engaged in commerce, including personnel.

merchant ship • any vessel engaged in mercantile trade, with the exception of river craft, estuarial craft, or craft that operate solely within harbor limits.

Merriam, Henry Clay (1837–1912) • Union army officer, born in Houlton, Maine. Merriam led the assault on Fort Blakely (1865), where his courage and gallantry contributed to the capture of 6,000 Confederates and for which he was awarded the CONGRESSIONAL MEDAL OF HONOR. Merriam had previously demonstrated bravery at the battles of ANTIETAM and FREDERICKSBURG (both 1862) and been cited for gallantry in the attack on PORT HUDSON, Louisiana (1863).

Merrill's Marauders • a U.S. ground unit, organized during WORLD WAR II following the QUEBEC CONFERENCE of 1943, used to spearhead the Chinese Army's mission to destroy Japanese communications and supply lines. The unit was named for its leader, Brig. Gen. Frank Merrill.

***Merrimack*, USS** • a conventional steam frigate built by the United States, salvaged from the Norfolk navy yard by the CONFEDERACY, converted into an ironclad vessel, and rechristened the CSS *Virginia.* See also CSS *Virginia.*

Meserve, Nathaniel (c. 1705–58) • provincial military leader and shipbuilder, born in Newington, New Hampshire. His engineering contributions were significant to British successes in the colonial wars of the 18th century. During KING GEORGE'S WAR (1744–48) Melville, a member of a New Hampshire regiment, placed artillery, furnished transport, and constructed fortifications on the New England expedition against the French fortress of LOUISBOURG (1745). During the FRENCH AND INDIAN WAR (1754–63) he took part in expeditions against CROWN POINT (1756–57) and was commended for his skill in building fortifications and commanding the defense of Fort Edward (1756). He died of smallpox while on a later expedition to Louisbourg as head of a company of carpenters.

messenger • *n.* **1** (also **messenger line**) an endless rope, cable, or chain used with a capstan to haul an anchor cable or to drive a powered winch. **2** a light line used to haul or support a larger cable.

Messerschmitt 109 • (**Me 109**) a single-seat single-engine low-wing monoplane fighter aircraft built by Bayerische Flugzeugwerke (BFW; Bavarian Airplane Co.) for NAZI Germany. Originally designated Bf 109, its designer, Willy Messerschmitt, founded a firm to produce the Me 109 after BFW went out of business. With a high speed of 350 miles (570 km) per hour and a ceiling of 36,000 feet (11,000 m), it was Germany's best fighter plane and was used widely in the BATTLE OF BRITAIN (1940). At least 35,000 of these aircraft were produced.

mess hall • a room or building where groups of people, especially soldiers, eat together.

Messina, Battle of • the final battle in the WORLD WAR II invasion of SICILY, won by the ALLIES on August 17, 1943. It was a noted triumph for the U.S. 7th Army under Gen. GEORGE S. PATTON, which reached Messina while British Gen. BERNARD LAW MONTGOMERY's troops were bogged down outside of it. One month later, however, Montgomery would lead the Allied invasion of the Italian mainland from there.

mess jacket • a short jacket worn by a military officer on formal occasions.

mess kit • a set of cooking and eating utensils, as used especially by soldiers, scouts, or campers.

messmate • *n.* a person with whom one takes meals, especially in the armed forces.

mess tin • Brit. a rectangular metal dish with a folding handle, used by soldiers for cooking and for eating or drinking out of.

Metacom • (c. 1640–76) leader, or sachem, of the Wampanoag tribe of New England (1662–76), also known as PHILIP. Despite his many attempts to maintain an uneasy peace, tensions between settlers and local Indians erupted KING PHILIP'S WAR (1675–77). He was killed when the forces of BENJAMIN CHURCH attacked his encampment. His body was drawn, quartered, and beheaded, and his head placed up a pole at Plymouth to serve as a reminder and a warning.

meteorology, military • the study of the atmosphere, including climate and weather, with special attention to the impact of climate, weather, and atmospheric conditions on military operations.

metrology • *n.* the science of measurement, including the development of measurement standards and systems for absolute and relative measurements.

Metz, Battle of • a long fight of WORLD WAR II eventually won by the U.S. troops under Gen. GEORGE S. PATTON in late November 1944, liberating the northeastern French city from four years of German occupation.

Meuse-Argonne Offensive (1918) • a forty-seven-day campaign in 1918 that was the last, decisive, and costliest one for Gen. JOHN J. PERSHING's army. As part of the massive Allied offensive that ended WORLD WAR I, 600,000 American troops with French support began advancing north across the Argonne Forest, east of the Meuse River, on September 26. Strong German defenses depleted and delayed the advancing column, but more experienced U.S. reinforcements arrived in early October to clear the forest of German soldiers. Ever-mounting casualties, many of them from influenza, forced a defensive posture, until the creation of a 2nd Army, led by Pershing, forced the Germans north of the Meuse. The November 11 armistice, which Berlin was forced to accept as a result of the offensive, halted further fighting. Of the 1.2 million Americans involved in the battle, 117,000 were killed or wounded—roughly half of the U.S.'s total war casualties.

Mexican Cession • lands relinquished to the United States from Mexico in 1848. The TREATY OF GUADALUPE-HIDALGO ceded territory to the United States after the MEXICAN WAR (1846–48). California, Arizona, New Mexico, Nevada, Utah, Texas, and parts of Colorado were exchanged for 15 million dollars. The United States also assumed citizens' claims against Mexico as part of the terms of the treaty.

Mexican War • (1846–48) a war that vastly increased U.S. territory and contributed to the sectional crisis. Elected in 1844 on a platform of expansionism, JAMES K. POLK moved quickly to fulfill his promises, obtaining Oregon from Britain and negotiating to buy California and other Mexican territories. Mexican President Mariano Paredes predictably rejected American offers. Already seething from the U.S. annexation of Texas in 1845 and the attempts to stretch the border to the Rio Grande, he declared a state of "defensive" war on April 23, 1846. When word of a Texas skirmish eventually reached Washington, Polk asked Congress to acknowledge war, which it did on May 13. Although Mexico's regular army owned superior numbers, the U.S. army possessed better training, leadership, and weaponry; and over 73,000 volunteers more than evened out the size differential. The U.S. mounted several nearly simultaneous offensive actions. The fighting began on May 8, and Gen. ZACHARY TAYLOR's troops won the Battle of PALO ALTO (near Brownsville, Texas). As they moved steadily southward, capturing MONTERREY by late September and Saltillo in November, Col. Stephen Watts's troops easily occupied Santa Fe, from which they began an overland march to California. Aided by the navy, the army captured California by early January. Around the same time, ALEXANDER DONIPHAN's forces occupied Chihuahua, and the United States won every battle in the first phase of the war. While Polk and WINFIELD SCOTT drew up plans to capture Mexico City and thus force surrender, the new Mexican president, Gen. ANTONIO LÓPEZ DE SANTA ANNA, rebuilt his army and prepared to attack Taylor's forces at Saltillo. Helped by an intercepted letter containing Santa Anna's plans and by Col. JEFFERSON DAVIS's Mississippi volunteers, Taylor withstood the attack. As Santa Anna retreated to the capital, Scott captured VERACRUZ, from where the march to Mexico City began. Scott's troops eventually reached the outskirts of the city by mid August, and, after a series of battles, U.S. forces entered MEXICO CITY on September 14. The TREATY OF GUADALUPE-HIDALGO was signed on February 2, and confirmed by both sides on May 30, 1848, officially ended the war. The United States gained the territories that would become California, New Mexico, Arizona, Nevada, Colorado, and Utah, and stretched the Texas border to the Rio Grande. On a federal level, Polk had greatly expanded the powers of the commander in chief. On the strength of his war record, Taylor won the 1848 election. Scott, in turn, was the Whigs' presidential nominee in 1852, but lost to his former subordinate, Democrat FRANKLIN PIERCE. Most importantly, the war heightened tensions over slavery, as a series of postwar measures granted slavery in California, abolished it in Washington, D.C., and created the new Fugitive Slave Law, thus bringing the country closer to the CIVIL WAR.

Mexico City, Battle of • the final campaign of the MEXICAN WAR, won by the United States on September 14, 1848. In early 1847, President JAMES K. POLK and Gen. WINFIELD SCOTT planned to occupy Mexico City in order to force Mexico to concede in the war. Slowed by Mexican troops, as well as disease, Scott's army reached the outskirts of Mexico City in mid August, and after a series of major battles, finally outflanked Gen. ANTONIO LOPEZ DE SANTA ANNA's men. On February 2, 1848, diplomats signed the TREATY OF GUADALUPE-HIDALGO, which granted the U.S. roughly half of what had hitherto been Mexican territory.

MFL • *abbr.* master force list.

MGM-1C • see MATADOR.

MGM-13 • see MACE.

MGM-21 • see NORD SS-10 MISSILE.

MGM-29A • see SERGEANT.

MGM-31A • see PERSHING.

MGM-51 • see SHILLELAGH.

MH-53E • see SEA DRAGON.

MH-60G • see BLACK HAWK.

MI6 (in the UK) the governmental agency responsible for dealing with matters of internal security and counter-intelligence overseas. Formed in 1912, the agency was officially named the SECRET INTELLIGENCE SERVICE in 1964, but the name MI6 remains in popular use.

MI8 • the codebreaking group of the MILITARY INTELLIGENCE DIVISION.

MIA • *abbr.* **1** missing in action. **2** a member of the armed forces who is missing in action.

Miami • an Algonquian-speaking Indian tribe located in what is now the states of Wisconsin, Indiana, and Ohio. The Miami joined PONTIAC'S REBELLION against the British in 1763–65 and together with the Shawnees opposed the westward expansion of American settlers into the Ohio Valley in the 1790s. After several victories over ill-led U.S. troops, the Miami were decisively defeated by Gen. ANTHONY WAYNE at the battle of FALLEN TIMBERS (1794), and subsequently signed the TREATY OF GREENVILLE in 1795 ending the conflict in the Old Northwest.

Michael, Operation • an attempt by the GERMAN HIGH COMMAND to destroy the French Army and drive the British from the Continent through a series of offensives. With Russia removed from the war in the winter of 1917–18, Commander in chief of the AMERICAN EXPEDITIONARY FORCES JOHN J. PERSHING resisted the inclusion of American units in British and French divisions. In September 1918, however, in an independent operation Pershing launched a successful offensive on the German salient into Allied positions at ST. MIHIEL, south of Verdun, in northern France.

MIDAS • *abbr.* Missile Detection and Alarm System.

middle watch • the period from midnight to 4 A.M. on board a ship.

midship • *n.* the middle part of a ship or boat: *its powerful midship section.*

midshipman • *n.* (pl. **-men**) a naval cadet in the U.S. Navy.

Midshipmen's School • see U.S. MIDSHIPMEN'S SCHOOL.

midships • *adv.* & *adj.* another term for AMIDSHIPS.

Midway, Battle of • a WORLD WAR II battle of June 4–6, 1942, the turning point in Pacific naval warfare. American cryptanalysts had decoded Japanese plans to destroy the U.S. PACIFIC FLEET at MIDWAY, an atoll 1,100 miles northwest of PEARL HARBOR. Ignoring a feint attack on two barren Aleutian islands, Adm. CHESTER W. NIMITZ concentrated his three carriers at Midway, where, between June 4 and 6, they destroyed four Japanese carriers, a cruiser, and numerous aircraft. The United States lost one carrier, the *Yorktown*, and many planes, but it was now even with Japan's hitherto superior Combined Fleet. See also GUADALCANAL.

Midway Islands • two small islands in the central Pacific that were the site of the BATTLE OF MIDWAY (1942). The islands, which are surrounded by a coral atoll, are located in the western part of the Hawaiian chain.

Mifflin, Thomas (1744–1800) • American army officer and politician; Governor of Pennsylvania. Born in Philadelphia, he was one of the youngest and most radical members of the First and Second Continental Congresses (1774–76). Although nominally a Quaker, he was active in recruiting and training troops after LEXINGTON and accepted a commission as major in the Continental army in May 1775. He became aide-de-camp to Gen. GEORGE WASHINGTON, who appointed him the first quartermaster general of the Continental Army on August 14, 1775. Relieved as quartermaster general in May 1776, he amply demonstrated his personal bravery in command of the covering party during the withdrawal from NEW YORK and at TRENTON (both 1776) and PRINCETON (1777), rising to the rank of major general in February 1777. Mifflin served a second, less successful tour as quartermaster general from September 1776 to March 1778. He neglected his duties and was in large part responsible for the difficulties of the army at VALLEY FORGE in the winter of 1777–78. From November 1777 to April 1778, Mifflin served on the BOARD OF WAR AND ORDNANCE, and he was involved in the infamous Conway Cabal which sought to replace George Washington with HORATIO GATES. He resigned his commission as major general in February 1779 under accusations of financial malfeasance as quartermaster general. Mifflin was elected to Congress in 1782 and served as its president (December

1783–June 1784) and as a member of the Constitutional Convention in 1787. He served three terms as Governor of Pennsylvania (1790–99) and played a prominent role in the suppression of the WHISKEY REBELLION (1794).

MiG (also **Mig** or **MIG**) • *n.* a type of Russian fighter aircraft.

ORIGIN: 1940s: from the initial letters of the surnames of A.I. *M*ikoyan and M.I. *G*urevich, linked by Russian *i* 'and.'

MiG-15 • a single-seat single-engine Soviet fighter aircraft. Powered by a copy of a Rolls-Royce engine, the MiG-15. was used extensively in the KOREAN WAR and was among the best of the early jet fighters.

MiG-29 • a single-seat twin-engine air-to-air fighter aircraft, first used in 1985.

Miles, Nelson Appleton (1839–1925) • army officer, born in Westminster, Massachusetts. Miles was one of the most aggressive and effective fighters in the ARMY OF THE POTOMAC during the CIVIL WAR and was later recognized as one of the most effective fighters in the West against Indians. Appleton received the MEDAL OF HONOR (1892) for his actions at CHANCELLORSVILLE (1863), where he was severely wounded. He first gained fame for his fighting against Indians during the RED RIVER WAR (1874–75), while stationed in Kansas. Transferred to Montana, he drove many tribes into Canada (1876) and won a victory against CRAZY HORSE (1877). His 1877 campaigns against the NEZ PERCÉ cut off their flight into Canada and forced the surrender of CHIEF JOSEPH. While he was in charge of the Department of Arizona, Miles's campaign against the Apaches led GERONIMO to surrender to him (1886). While in command of the Division of the Missouri, he directed the GHOST DANCE campaign, which led to the slaughter at WOUNDED KNEE (1890). Although Miles was at the time the commanding general (1895–1903), President WILLIAM MCKINLEY in effect directed the SPANISH-AMERICAN WAR (1898). Miles did, however, lead the successful strike against Puerto Rico.

militarism • *n.* chiefly derogatory the belief or desire of a government or people that a country should maintain a strong military capability and be prepared to use it aggressively to defend or promote national interests.

DERIVATIVES: **militarist** *n.* & *adj.* **militaristic** *adj.*

militarize • *v.* **1** (**militarized**) give (something, especially an organization) a military character or style: *militarized police forces.* **2** equip or supply (a place) with soldiers and other military resources.

DERIVATIVES: **militarization** *n.*

military • *adj.* of, relating to, or characteristic of soldiers or armed forces: *both leaders condemned the buildup of military activity.* • *n.* (**the military**) the armed forces of a country.

DERIVATIVES: **militarily** *adv.*

military academy • a public or private school that educates and trains professional officers for the armed forces. The four major military SERVICE ACADEMIES in the United States, one for each branch of the armed forces, are the U.S. Air Force Academy, U.S. Coast Guard Academy, U.S. Military Academy, and U.S. Naval Academy. Graduates of these schools must serve five years of active duty in exchange for the government-provided education they receive. Private, state-supported military academies include THE CITADEL and the VIRGINIA MILITARY INSTITUTE.

Military Affairs Committee • see COMMITTEE ON MILITARY AFFAIRS.

military age • the age range within which a person is eligible for military service.

Military Airlift Command • (**MAC**) the U.S. Air Force's Military Airlift Command, a component of the unified U.S. TRANSPORTATION COMMAND (USTRANSCOM) since its creation in 1987. USTRANSCOM is located at Scott Air Force Base in Illinois.

Military Assistance Command, Vietnam • (**MACV**) the U.S. military advisers in Vietnam responsible for training and equipping the South Vietnamese armed forces.

Military Assistance Program • a foreign assistance program implemented in 1950, during the COLD WAR, by the United States to provide allies with direct military assistance. Between 1950 and 1967, $33.4 billion in arms and services and $3.3 billion worth of surplus weaponry were provided under the program.

military attaché • an army officer serving with an embassy or attached as an observer to a foreign army.

military capability • the ability to achieve a specified wartime objective. It includes four major components: **a** (**force structure**) the numbers, size, and composition of the units that comprise the U.S. defense forces (e.g., divisions, ships, air wings. **b** (**modernization**) the technical sophistication of forces, units, weapon systems, and equipments. **c** (**unit readiness**) the ability to provide capabilities required by the combatant commanders to execute their assigned missions. This is derived from the ability of each unit to deliver the outputs for which it was designed. **d** (**sustainability**) the ability to maintain the necessary level and duration of operational activity to achieve military objectives. Sustainability is a function of providing for and maintaining those levels of ready forces, materiel, and consumables necessary to support military effort.

military censorship • all types of censorship conducted by personnel of the U.S. Armed Forces, to include armed forces censorship, civil censorship, prisoner of war censorship, and field press censorship.

Military Cross • British military decoration for valor. Established on December 31, 1941, the Military Cross may be awarded to junior officers and warrant officers of the British Army or to junior officers and warrant officers of the ROYAL AIR FORCE for ground actions.

Military Department • **1** one of the departments within the DEPARTMENT OF DEFENSE created by the NATIONAL SECURITY ACT of

1947, as amended, specifically the Department of the Army, the Department of the Navy, and the Department of the Air Force. **2** in the 19th and early 20th centuries in the United States and its territories, a geographical area under the administrative and operational control of a designated military commander.

military education • the professional development of officers and personnel for activity in the armed forces. Students learn various subjects and skills through a combination of theory and practice. Each branch of the armed forces maintains its own professional education program, beginning at the undergraduate level and progressing through service, staff, and senior service level colleges.

military engineering • the branch of civil engineering encompassing the construction and maintenance of field fortifications and of buildings, roads, airfields, railroads, ports, and other facilities for military use. Military engineering also includes the installation, maintenance, and removal of minefields and the provision of water to troops in the field. In the United States military engineers also construct and maintain dams, locks, levees, harbors, and inland waterways.

military geography • the aspects of physical and cultural geography dealing with natural and manmade physical features that may affect the planning and conduct of military operations. Such aspects might include the climate, weather, terrain, availability of potable water, trafficability, existing transport infrastructure, ethnic composition of the population, etc.

military grid • two sets of parallel lines intersecting at right angles and forming squares; the grid is superimposed on maps, charts, and other similar representations of the surface of the Earth in an accurate and consistent manner to permit identification of ground locations with respect to other locations and the computation of direction and distance to other points.

military grid reference system • a system that uses a standard-scaled grid square, based on a point of origin on a map projection of the surface of the earth in an accurate and consistent manner to permit either position referencing or the computation of direction and distance between grid positions.

military honors • ceremonies performed by troops as a mark of respect at the burial of a member of the armed forces: *he was buried with full military honors.*

military hospital • a hospital for sick or wounded military personnel, usually operated by military medical personnel.

military-industrial complex • a country's military establishment and those industries producing arms or other military materials, regarded as a powerful vested interest.

military intelligence • intelligence on any foreign military or military-related situation or activity which is significant to military policy-making or the planning and conduct of military operations and activities.

Military Intelligence Corps • the combat support branch of the U.S. Army responsible for the collection, processing, and dissemination of militarily significant information and the defense against enemy intelligence activities.

Military Intelligence Division • in the U.S. Army, that section of the Army GENERAL STAFF established August 26, 1918, and charged with overseeing matters of intelligence production and counterintelligence activities. The title was subsequently changed to the office of the Assistant Chief of Staff, G-2, and then to office of the Assistant Chief of Staff for Intelligence.

military intervention • the deliberate act of a nation or a group of nations to introduce its military forces into the course of an existing controversy.

military Keynesianism • a version of the macroeconomic theories of the economist John Maynard Keynes which holds that military spending by the so-called military-industrial complex is one means of using fiscal policy to manage the national economy.

military occupation • a condition in which territory is under the effective control of a foreign armed force.

Military Order of the Loyal Legion of the United States • a veterans organization established on April 15, 1865, and composed of former officers of the Union army, navy, and marine corps who had served honorably in the CIVIL WAR. Pledged to fidelity to the Federal government and ensuring that the rebellion did not reignite, it subsequently became a fraternal organization of Union officer veterans dedicated to the relief of war widows and orphans, and compiling histories of the Civil War campaigns.

military planning • the devising of plans for military operations and other actions by military forces, to include the thorough coordination of such plans and activities with all concerned agencies.

military police • the corps responsible for police and disciplinary duties in an army.
DERIVATIVES: **military policeman** *n.* **military policewoman** *n.*

Military Policy of the United States • a book written by Col. EMORY UPTON in response to the inefficiencies of the army in the CIVIL WAR. Published in 1904 by Secretary of War ELIHU ROOT, it criticized reliance on state militia and volunteers and advocated a professional army headed by a GENERAL STAFF. It was unfinished when Upton committed suicide in 1881.

military posture • the military disposition, strength, and condition of readiness as it affects capabilities.

military robotics • the application of the science of robotics to military uses, such as remotely piloted vehicles, automated ammunition and supply handling, and the like.

Military Sealift Command • (**MSC**) the component command of the U.S. TRANSPORTATION COMMAND that provides authorized sealift services.

Military Sea Transportation Service • (**MSTS**) a single agency, organized in August 1949, responsible for controlling, operating, maintaining, and managing ocean transportation for all components of the U.S. military forces and departments.

Military Service Institution of the United States • a professional association for members of the U.S. Army, founded after the CIVIL WAR. It maintained a museum and offices at Governors Island, New York, and published a journal of military history, which became defunct after WORLD WAR I.

military strategy • the art and science of employing the armed forces of a nation to secure the objectives of national policy by the application of force, or the threat of force.

Military Traffic Management Command • (**MTMC**) the component command of USTRANSCOM responsible for military traffic, air and land transportation duties within the continental United States, and global surface transportation for all the armed forces. Its headquarters is in Alexandria, Virginia and it was established in 1965.

military training • **1** the instruction of personnel to enhance their capacity to perform specific military functions and tasks. **2** the exercise of one or more military units conducted to enhance their combat readiness.

militia • *n.* **1** a military force that is raised from the civil population to supplement a regular army in an emergency. **2** a military force that engages in rebel or terrorist activities, typically in opposition to a regular army. **3** all able-bodied civilians eligible by law for military service.

Militia Act • **1** (1792) an order passed after the REVOLUTIONARY WAR to obligate all able-bodied white male citizens, eighteen to forty-five years of age, to serve under state control in the militia. It standardized organization and training procedures for the militias, but the system was short-lived, and the U.S. Volunteers provided most army support until the CIVIL WAR. **2** (1862) a Union draft order passed on July 17, 1862, during the CIVIL WAR, to raise 300,000 militia men for nine months of service. It subjected a state that failed to meet its troop quota through volunteers to a militia draft. After increased volunteering and opposition to the act as an infringement on individual liberty, it was replaced by the ENROLLMENT ACT of 1863. **3** (1903) an act passed by Congress to designate the NATIONAL GUARD, or Organized Militia, as the nation's primary military reserve, which was a recognition never before granted to a state soldiery. It placed the Guard, which agreed to tighter army supervision in exchange for increased financial assistance, under dual federal-state control.

militiaman • *n.* (pl. **-men**) a member of a militia.

Miller, Dorie (1919–43) • sailor, African-American hero of WORLD WAR II, recipient of the NAVY CROSS (1942), born Doris Miller in Waco, Texas. A mess attendant aboard the *West Virginia* during the attack on PEARL HARBOR (1941), Miller, despite strafing and enemy fire, carried the ship's mortally wounded captain to a safer place and then, though untrained, manned one of the guns until ordered to abandon the burning bridge. In the segregated services of that era, his actions went without official public recognition until demands from the black community reached President FRANKLIN D. ROOSEVELT, who personally ordered the awarding of the NAVY CROSS. Miller, who had joined the navy in 1939, was lost when the escort carrier *Liscome Bay* sank during the battle for Makin. Repeated efforts to award him the MEDAL OF HONOR have been unsuccessful.

The Service School Command barracks at Great Lakes Naval Station, Illinois, were named in Miller's honor, and in 1973 his mother christened the USS *Miller,* a destroyer escort.

Milligan, Robert Wiley (1843–1909) • U.S. naval engineer and officer. Milligan was born in Philadelphia, Pennsylvania, and began his naval career as a third assistant engineer on the Mackinaw during the later CIVIL WAR campaigns off the east coast. When the SPANISH-AMERICAN WAR opened in 1898, his ship, the *Oregon,* was based in San Francisco, and it steamed to Florida in only sixty-eight days, averaging over 11 knots in the 14,000 mile voyage. He achieved much acclaim for that feat, as well as for the *Oregon*'s superior performance in battles with the Spanish fleet in Cuba. Milligan was promoted to captain, and later to rear admiral, and was instrumental in bringing attention to the importance of engineers in a steam navy.

Milliken's Bend, Battle of • a CIVIL WAR battle fought in Madison Parish, Louisiana, on June 7, 1863. Fierce hand-to-hand combat lead to many casualties, especially on the Union side, but the battle was ultimately a Union victory owing to the timely appearance of the Union gunboats *Choctaw* and *Lexington,* which fired mercilessly on the Confederates and eventually forced them to retreat.

Mills bomb • a fragmentation grenade that was the standard British hand grenade from WORLD WAR I until its withdrawal in the 1960s. It consisted of a cast-iron body filled with high explosive.

Milosevic, Slobodan • (1941–) president of the Federal Republic of Yugoslavia (1997–2000) who initiated a terrorist campaign to drive the ethnic Muslim majority out of the province of Kosovo, leading to the KOSOVO CRISIS. As president of Serbia (1989–97) Milosevic dominated the Yugoslav federation; his nationalist policies and resistance to reform contributed to its breakup and led to repeated conflicts with the resulting Balkan states. See also BOSNIAN CRISIS.

Milroy, Robert Huston (1816–90) • Union army officer, born in Washington City, Indiana. Milroy gained recognition early in the CIVIL WAR when he waged a relentless campaign that suppressed Confederate guerrillas in western Virginia (1861), an effort that contributed to the creation of the state of West Virginia (1863). Later, however, Milroy was blamed for the loss at Winchester (1863), where his positions were overrun and his forces retreated, allowing for the advance of the Confederates into Pennsylvania. Though exonerated by a military court of inquiry, Milroy did not receive another significant command for the remainder of the war.

MILVAN |ˈmilˌvæn| • a military-owned demountable container, conforming to U.S. and international standards, operated in a centrally controlled fleet for movement of military cargo.

MIM-23 • see HAWK.

MIM-72 • see CHAPARRAL.

MIM-104 • see PATRIOT.

mine • *n.* **1** a type of bomb placed on or just below the surface of the ground or in the water that detonates when disturbed by a person, vehicle, or ship. **2** a subterranean passage under the wall of a besieged fortress, especially one in which explosives are put to blow up fortifications. • *v.* **1** lay explosive mines on or just below the surface of (the ground or water): *the area was heavily mined.* **2** destroy by means of an explosive mine.
DERIVATIVES: **mineable** (also **minable**) *adj.*

mine clearance • the process of removing all mines from a route or area.

mine defense • the defense of a position, area, etc., by land or underwater mines. A mine defense system includes the personnel and equipment needed to plant, operate, maintain, and protect the minefields that are laid.

mine detector • an instrument used for detecting explosive mines.

mine disposal • the operation, by suitably qualified personnel, designed to render safe, neutralize, recover, remove, or destroy mines.

minefield (also **mine field**) • *n.* an area planted with explosive mines.

minefield breaching • in land-mine warfare, the process of clearing a lane through a minefield under tactical conditions.

minefield density • in land-mine warfare, the average number of mines per meter of minefield front, or the average number of mines per square meter of minefield.

minehunting • *n.* the employment of sensor and neutralization systems, whether air, surface, or subsurface, to locate and dispose of individual mines. Minehunting is conducted to eliminate mines in a known minefield when sweeping is not feasible or desirable, or to verify the presence or absence of mines in an area.

minelayer • *n.* a warship, aircraft, or land vehicle from which explosive mines are laid.
DERIVATIVES: **minelaying** *n.*

miner • *n.* a person who digs tunnels in order to destroy an enemy position with explosives.

mine row • a single row of mines or clusters.

Mine Run Campaign • a series of CIVIL WAR engagements from November 27 to December 2, 1863, between the ARMY OF THE POTOMAC, commanded by Union Maj. Gen. GEORGE G. MEADE, and the ARMY OF NORTHERN VIRGINIA, led by Confederate Gen. ROBERT E. LEE, in the Mine Run area of Virginia. Meade launched an offensive against Lee's army near the Rapidan River. After the Battle of Payne's Farm, the Battle of New Hope Church, and the Battle of Mine Run, Meade concluded that the Confederates could not be routed from the WILDERNESS, and retreated for the winter.

mine strip • in land-mine warfare, two parallel mine rows laid simultaneously 6 meters (or six paces) apart.

minesweeper • *n.* a warship equipped for detecting and removing or destroying tethered explosive mines.

minesweeping • *n.* the technique of clearing mines using mechanical, explosive, or influence sweep equipment: **mechanical minesweeping** removes, disturbs, or otherwise neutralizes the mine; **explosive minesweeping** causes sympathetic detonations in, damages, or displaces the mine; and **influence minesweeping** produces the acoustic and/or magnetic influence required to detonate the mine.

mine warfare chart • a special naval chart, at a scale of 1:50,000 or larger (preferably 1:25,000 or larger) designed for planning and executing mine warfare operations, either based on an existing standard nautical chart, or produced to special specifications.

mine warfare forces • naval forces charged with the strategic, operational, and tactical use of naval mines and their countermeasures. Such forces are capable of offensive and defensive measures in connection with laying and clearing mines.

mine warfare, land • the strategic, operational, and tactical use of land mines and mine countermeasures.

minié ball • a conical bullet with a hollow base that expanded when fired. It was used extensively in the CIVIL WAR.

minimum-altitude bombing • horizontal or glide bombing with the height of release under 900 feet.

Minimum Risk Force • the minimum acceptable size of the U.S. armed forces that can be maintained in readiness without incurring serious military risks in any future threat environment.

mining • *n.* the process of placing land or naval mines in order to destroy or damage ground vehicles, boats, or aircraft, or to kill or wound enemy forces.

Ministry of Defence • (**MOD**) the bureau of the British government that oversees the military. The U.S. equivalent is the DEPARTMENT OF DEFENSE or PENTAGON.

minuteman • *n.* **1** (pl. **-men**) (in the period preceding and during the REVOLUTIONARY WAR) a member of a class of American militiamen who volunteered to be ready for service at a minute's notice. **2** slang (WORLD WAR II) a person selling bonds and stamps in support of the war effort. The bonds' promotional posters depicted a heroic REVOLUTIONARY WAR minuteman. **2** (**Minuteman**) (**LGM-30**) an intercontinental ballistic missile that is guided to its target by an all-inertial guidance and control system. It is equipped with nuclear warheads and designed for deployment in underground silos.

Mirage 2000 • a delta-wing multipurpose fighter aircraft, produced by Dassault-Breguet, a French aeronautics firm, that replaced the Mirage F-1 in the French air force.

Mirage F-1 • a multipurpose fighter aircraft that entered the French air force in 1973.

MIRV |ˈmərv| • a type of intercontinental nuclear missile carrying several independent warheads.

ORIGIN: 1960s: acronym from *Multiple Independently targeted Re-entry Vehicle*.

misfire • *n.* **1** the failure to fire or explode properly. **2** the failure of a primer or the propelling charge of a round or projectile to function wholly or in part.

MISREP • see JOINT TACTICAL AIR RECONNAISSANCE/SURVEILLANCE MISSION REPORT.

missile • *n.* **1** an object that is forcibly propelled at a target, either by hand or from a mechanical weapon. **2** a weapon that is self-propelled or directed by remote control, carrying a conventional or nuclear explosive.

missile control system • a system that serves to maintain a missile's attitude stability and to correct deflections.

Missile Detection and Alarm System • (**MIDAS**) a U.S. reconnaissance satellite system developed by the LOCKHEED Corporation beginning in the 1950s. Its infrared sensors and a telescope were designed to detect the hot exhaust of enemy missiles being launched and to radio a warning to Earth stations allowing the U.S. Air Force to scramble its bombers before the enemy warheads struck. The system was renamed the DEFENSE SUPPORT PROGRAM in the 1960s.

missile gap • an assumed inferiority in the number of intercontinental ballistic missiles with nuclear warheads available to the United States as compared to the number available to the Soviet Union at the end of the 1950s. The issue of a "missile gap" was raised by President JOHN F. KENNEDY as a political ploy during the presidential election of 1960, but was subsequently shown never to have existed.

missile guidance system • a system that evaluates flight information, correlates it with target data, determines the desired flight path of a missile, and communicates the necessary commands to the missile flight control system.

missile intercept zone • the geographical division of the destruction area where surface-to-air missiles have primary responsibility for destruction of airborne objects.

missilery • *n.* **1** the study of the use and characteristics of missiles. **2** missiles collectively.

missing in action • (**MIA**) a casualty of hostile action, other than the victim of a terrorist activity, who is not present at his or her duty location due to apparent involuntary reasons and whose location is unknown.

mission • *n.* **1** the task, together with the purpose, that clearly indicates the action to be taken and the reason for it. **2** in common usage, especially when applied to lower military units, a duty assigned to an individual or unit; a task. **3** the dispatching of one or more aircraft to accomplish one particular task.

Missionary Ridge, Battle of • an Union victory near CHATTANOOGA on November 24–25, 1863, that prepared the ground for Gen. WILLIAM T. SHERMAN's march on ATLANTA several months later. Under Gen. ULYSSES S. GRANT's command, Sherman, Gen. JOSEPH HOOKER, and Gen. GEORGE H. THOMAS led a three-pronged attack to lift the two-month-long Confederate siege. Thomas led the improbable charge on Missionary Ridge, which was won because of natural cover, ill-sited defenses, and Confederate backbiting. The aggressive FEDERALS had redeemed their September defeat at CHICKAMAUGA, and Confederate Gen. BRAXTON BRAGG was cashiered.

Missouri Compromise • an agreement between the North and the South and passed by Congress in 1820 that allowed Missouri to be admitted as the 24th state in 1821. The North's attempt to force emancipation upon Missouri when it applied for admission as a slave state in 1819 rankled white southerners, and they threatened secession during the debates over the conditions under which Missouri should be granted statehood. The debates resulted in a compromise that involved the drawing of a line through the LOUISIANA PURCHASE territory prohibiting slavery north of the latitude 36°30′ and allowing it in the south.

Mitchell • (B-25) the most-utilized medium bomber during WORLD WAR II. It was made famous by the DOOLITTLE RAID on Tokyo.

Mitchell, Billy (1879–1936) • army air service officer, born William Lendrum Mitchell in Nice, France. Mitchell was one of the outstanding combat air officers of WORLD WAR I, commanding the largest concentration of allied air power of the war at ST. MIHIEL (1918). In recognition of his wartime service, he received the DISTINGUISHED SERVICE CROSS and the DISTINGUISHED SERVICE MEDAL, as well as various foreign honors. Appointed assistant chief of the ARMY AIR SERVICE after the war, a position which he held until 1925, Mitchell began speaking out about the eventual prominence of air power, arousing the ire of the army and navy hierarchy, which itself became a target of his increasingly open and vitriolic criticism. After he was court-martialed, found guilty of insubordination, and demoted from general to colonel, Mitchell resigned from the service (1926). He was posthumously awarded the CONGRESSIONAL MEDAL OF HONOR in recognition of his work toward the establishment of a separate air force (1946).

Mitchell, Robert Byington (1823–82) • Union army officer, born in Mansfield, Ohio. Mitchell was cited for bravery at Wilson's Creek (1861), participated in the Union offense in Tennessee (1863), and led a cavalry corps in the battle of CHICKAMAUGA (1863). He was later assigned to territorial districts where he took part in campaigns against the Plains Indians (1864–65). In a postwar appointment as governor of the territory of New Mexico (1865–69), Mitchell encountered difficulty in adapting to civilian methods of governance.

Mitscher, Marc Andrew (1887–1947) • naval officer and leading exponent and practitioner of naval aviation, born in Hillsboro, Wisconsin. During WORLD WAR II Mitscher was active throughout the Pacific theater: He was captain of the *Hornet* when it served as the base for the bombing of Tokyo (1942); helped sink four Japanese carriers at the battle of MIDWAY (1942); controlled Allied air power during the closing phases of the GUADALCANAL campaign (1943); led a mixed force that covered Allied advances through the SOLOMON ISLANDS (1943); conducted operations against the MARSHALL ISLANDS (1944); and led the task force that bombarded IWO JIMA and OKINAWA (1945). At the time of his death, Mitscher, a four-star admiral, was commander in chief of the Atlantic Fleet. During WORLD WAR I Mitscher had commanded naval air stations in the United States. In 1918 he piloted a giant seaplane in an unsuccessful attempt at the first transatlantic flight, for which he received the NAVY CROSS.

The most celebrated event of Mitscher's career occurred during the battle of the PHILIPPINE SEA (1944) when he disregarded submarine threats and turned on all ship lights to enable weary pilots to land safely.

mixed minefield • a minefield containing both antitank and antipersonnel mines.

mizzen |ˈmizən| (also **mizen**) • *n.* **1** (also **mizzenmast**) the mast aft of a ship's mainmast. **2** (also **mizzensail**) the lowest sail on a mizzenmast.

MLF • *abbr.* multilateral nuclear force.

MLRS • *abbr.* a multiple launch rocket system, capable of firing up to twelve surface-to-surface rockets in a single load and typically deployed from an armored vehicle.

MM • *abbr.* Military Medal, a British decoration issued in WORLD WAR I.

MN • *abbr.* (in the UK) Merchant Navy.

moat • *n.* a deep, wide ditch surrounding a castle, fort, or town, typically filled with water and intended as a defense against attack. • *v.* (**moated**) surround (a place) with a moat: *a moated castle.*

mobile artillery • artillery mounted on wheels or wheeled vehicles, including rail vehicles.

Mobile Bay, Battle of • an eighteen-boat attack on the well-fortified and heavily-mined bay, led by Union Adm. DAVID FARRAGUT on August 5, 1864. Along with three wooden gunboats, the ironclad *Tennessee* had managed to defend what since 1862 had been the major Confederate port, but the squadron, now outclassed and outnumbered, succumbed in five hours.

mobile defense • the defense of an area or position in which maneuver is used with organization of fire and utilization of terrain to seize the initiative from the enemy.

mobile mine • a naval mine that is propelled to its proposed laying position by a torpedo.

Mobile Riverine Force • see BROWN WATER NAVY.

mobility • *n.* a quality or capability of military forces that permits them to move from place to place while retaining the ability to fulfill their primary mission.

mobilization • *n.* **1** the act of assembling and organizing national resources to support national objectives in time of war or other emergencies. **2** the process by which the armed forces or part of them are brought to a state of readiness for war or other national emergency. This includes activating all or part of the Reserve components as well as assembling and organizing personnel, supplies, and materiel. Mobilization of the armed forces includes, but is not limited to, the following categories: **a** (**selective mobilization**) expansion of the active armed forces resulting from action by Congress and/or the president to mobilize Reserve component units, Individual Ready Reservists, and the resources needed for their support to meet the requirements of a domestic emergency that is not the result of an enemy attack. **b** (**partial mobilization**) expansion of the active armed forces resulting from action by Congress (up to full mobilization) or by the president (not more than 1,000,000 for not more than twenty-four consecutive months) to mobilize READY RESERVE component units, individual reservists, and the resources needed for their support to meet the requirements of a war or other national emergency involving an external threat to the national security. **c** (**full mobilization**) expansion of the active armed forces resulting from action by Congress and the president to mobilize all Reserve component units in the existing approved force structure, all individual reservists, retired military personnel, and the resources needed for their support to meet the requirements of a war or other national emergency involving an external threat to the national security. Reserve personnel can be placed on active duty for the duration of the emergency plus six months. **d** (**total mobilization**) expansion of the active armed forces resulting from action by Congress and the president to organize and/or generate additional units or personnel, beyond the existing force structure, and the resources needed for their support, to meet the total requirements of a war or other national emergency involving an external threat to the national security.

mobilize • *v.* (of a country or its government) prepare and organize (troops) for active service: *the government mobilized regular forces, reservists, and militia.*

DERIVATIVES: **mobilizable** *adj.* **mobilizer** *n.*

MOD • *abbr.* (in the UK) MINISTRY OF DEFENCE.

Model Treaty of 1776 • an agreement between the United States and France that codified reciprocal commercial practices and strictly defined contraband, while rejecting any formal political or military alliance. It was drafted by John Adams and is regarded as the first expression of American foreign policy.

moderate nuclear risk • a degree of nuclear risk where anticipated effects are tolerable, or at worst a minor nuisance.

modernization • see military capability.

modus vivendi |ˈmōdəs vəˈvendē; -ˌdī| • (pl. **modi vivendi** |ˈmōˌdē; ˈmōˌdī|) an arrangement or agreement allowing conflicting parties to coexist peacefully, either indefinitely or until a final settlement is reached.
ORIGIN: Latin, literally 'way of living.'

Moffett, William Adger (1869–1933) • U.S. Navy rear admiral, born in Charleston, South Carolina. Moffett was chief of the Navy Bureau of Aeronautics (1921–33) who laid the foundations for the aviation-dominated navy that emerged in World War II. During his tenure he advocated the development of the aircraft carrier, as well as a program to equip battleships and cruisers with catapults and aircraft. Moffett's belief in the uses of the dirigible was his only serious mistake, but it proved a fatal one: He was killed when the navy airship *Akron* crashed during a storm. Moffett had first seen action during the Spanish-American War (1898), and for his actions while in command of the cruiser *Chester* during the American invasion of Veracruz (1914), he was awarded the Congressional Medal of Honor.

Mogadishu |ˌmôgəˈdisHōō; ˌmägə-; ˈdēsHōō| • (also called **Muqdisho**; Italian name **Mogadiscio**) the capital of Somalia, a port on the Indian Ocean pop. 377,000 (1982).

Mohawk • an Iroquois-speaking Indian tribe, one of the member of the Five Nations, located along the Mohawk River in upstate New York. Expelled by the French and their Indian allies from the St. Lawrence Valley in the early 17th century, the Mohawks subsequently allied themselves with the British colonists in King Philip's War (1675-76) and in the Anglo-French conflicts of the 18th century.

Mohican |mōˈhēkən| • (also **Mohegan** or **Mahican**) an Algonquian-speaking Indian tribe located along the Hudson River north to Lake Champlain.

MOL • *abbr.* Manned Orbital Laboratory.

mole • *n.* **1** a large solid structure on a shore serving as a pier, breakwater, or causeway. **2** a harbor formed or protected by such a structure.

Molino del Rey, Battle of • one of the final battles of the Mexican War (1846–48), won by Gen. Winfield Scott's American forces on September 8, 1847. After a late-August armistice had not yet yielded peace terms, Scott attacked Molino del Rey, one of several fortifications on the outskirts of Mexico City. Both sides suffered heavy casualties in this and a simultaneous battle at Casa de Malta.

Molotov breadbasket |ˈmäləˌtôf ˈbred ˈbæskit; ˈmôlə-; -ˌtôv| • (also **Molotoff breadbasket**) a cluster of incendiary bombs or a large container filled with bombs, usually incendiary, dropped from an aircraft and scattered over an area.

Molotov cocktail |ˈmäləˌtôf ˈkäkˌtāl; ˈmôlə-; -ˌtôv| • a crude incendiary device typically consisting of a bottle filled with flammable liquid such as gasoline and stuffed with a rag, lighted, and thrown, often in street fighting.

Possibly first used by Loyalists in the Spanish Civil War, the production of similar grenades was organized by Soviet foreign minister Vyacheslav Molotov during World War II. Molotov cocktails were used against tanks; the burning gasoline would heat the tank and drive out the crew for killing or capture.

Mongoose, Operation • (1961–62) a campaign authorized on November 3, 1961, by President John F. Kennedy to undermine Fidel Castro's Cuba. Led by Edward Lansdale, the operation included plans to assassinate Castro and to foment an overthrow of the Communist government. Emerging from a reassessment of Cuba policy after the Bay of Pigs, the plans of Operation Mongoose were ultimately superseded by the Cuban Missile Crisis.

monitor • *n.* a person who listens to and reports on foreign radio broadcasts and signals. • *v.* **1** maintain regular surveillance over: *it was easy for the enemy to monitor his movements.* **2** listen to and report on (a foreign radio broadcast or a telephone conversation).

***Monitor*, USS** • an ironclad Union ship, with an armored revolving gun turret, that engaged in the famous naval battle of ironclads during the Civil War. Early on March 9, 1862, the CSS *Virginia* opened fire on the *Minnesota*, which it had run aground the day before, and the *Monitor* appeared. Both ships were hard to maneuver and the crews were untrained, so much of the firing, as the ships passed back and forth on opposite courses, was ineffective. Finally, the *Virginia* hit the pilothouse of the *Monitor*, and John Worden, the commander of the *Monitor*, was blinded by iron splinters driven into his eyes. As the disabled *Monitor* wandered into shallow water, the *Virginia* again opened fire on the *Minnesota*, but, because of a leak and low ammunition, eventually headed for its navy yard about 12:30 P.M.

monkey jacket • **1** (**monkey suit**) in the early 1800s, a seaman's short, close-fitting jacket, or pea jacket. **2** (in World Wars I and II) a fur suit or airman's coveralls for high-altitude flying. **3** a formal, full-dress military uniform.

monkey meat • slang **1** canned beef, or corned beef, of cheap quality, often from South America, often served with carrots, during World Wars I and II. See also bully beef. **2** (World War II) a dead Japanese.

Monmouth, Battle of • the lengthiest uninterrupted battle of the Revolutionary War which showcased the increasing skills of the Continental army more than it did anything to settle the outcome of the war. As British Gen. Henry Clinton marched his troops from Philadelphia to New York City in late June, his rear guard was attacked by Gen. Charles Lee's troops on June 28, 1778, in northern New Jersey, just 20 miles from Sandy Hook, whence the Royal Navy would ferry its army cohorts to New York City. Scorching summer heat and poor field generalship weakened the Revolutionaries' attack, until GEORGE WASHINGTON arrived with the main army and fortified the position. Under night's cover, however, the British absconded and reached Sandy Hook two days later.

monohull • *n.* a boat with only one hull, as opposed to a catamaran or multihull.

Monongahela, Battle of the • a confrontation between British troops and a French force together with Indians and Canadian irregulars on July 9, 1755, during the FRENCH AND INDIAN WAR (1754–63). British Maj. Gen. EDWARD BRADDOCK led 1,450 men toward the Monongahela River in western Pennsylvania to repel French "encroachments." Unprepared for an attack by 783 French, Indians, and Canadians, the British suffered 977 casualties, including Braddock, who died four days after the battle. The phrase "BRADDOCK'S DEFEAT" came to be used to refer to the superiority of frontiersmen over European regulars.

Monroe Doctrine • a principle of U.S. policy, originated by President JAMES MONROE during his time in office (1817–25), that any intervention by external powers in the politics of the Americas is a potentially hostile act against the United States. The principle arose partly from a conflict with Russia over the northwest coast of North America, and partly from the fear that reactionary European states would attempt to take over the Latin American countries that had become independent from Spain.

Monroe, James (1758–1831) • 5th president of the United States (1817–25), born in Westmoreland County, Virginia. Monroe fought in the REVOLUTIONARY WAR and was wounded at the battle of TRENTON (1776). He later studied law with THOMAS JEFFERSON and served in the Virginia legislature (1782). As a delegate to the Continental Congress (1783–86), Monroe opposed ratification of the Constitution, believing it granted too much power to the central government. While serving in the Senate (1790–94), Monroe became a staunch anti-Federalist, allying himself with the Jeffersonians. As governor of Virginia (1799–1802; 1811) Monroe proved a solid administrator. In 1803 he helped negotiate the LOUISIANA PURCHASE; giving him national prominence. As minister to Great Britain (1803–07), Monroe failed to effect a treaty acceptable to Jefferson. In 1811 JAMES MADISON appointed Monroe secretary of state, and for a time during the WAR OF 1812 he was secretary of war as well (1814–15), reorganizing that department. In the presidential election of 1816 Monroe handily defeated his Federalist opposition, and four years later was easily reelected. His inauguration ushered in what came to be called the "Era of Good Feeling." Monroe toured the country, put together a strong cabinet, acquired Florida (1819), and approved the MISSOURI COMPROMISE (1820). His most significant achievement came in the realm of foreign affairs with the declaration, later known as the MONROE DOCTRINE, that the United States considered the Americas closed to further colonization and would regard as an unfriendly act any interference in their affairs. The principle was formulated with the assistance of secretary of state JOHN QUINCY ADAMS and issued in Monroe's annual message of 1823.

Monroe was the last of the revolutionary generation to hold the presidency.

Mons, Battle of • (August 22–23, 1914) the first engagement between the Germans and British in WORLD WAR I, ending with a famous British retreat. On its way to Paris, the German Army had torn through Belgium, decimating the French Army. British forces tried to defend Mons, but were outnumbered and outgunned by the Germans on August 22. The Germans continued to attack the retreating British, inflicting heavy casualties until a Belgian Army diversion distracted them long enough to delay their advance.

Mont Blanc, Battle of • part of the CHÂTEAU-THIERRY campaign in 1918, in which the U.S. 2nd Division helped the French Army drive back the Germans after a lengthy stalemate.

Montcalm, Louis-Joseph de Montcalm-Grozon |ˌmänt'kä(l)m gə'zōn| • (1712–59) commander in chief of French forces in Canada during the FRENCH AND INDIAN WAR (1754–63). Montcalm, born near Nîmes, conquered Forts Oswego (1756) and WILLIAM HENRY (1757) and successfully defended TICONDEROGA against a powerful British assault (1758), but he was mortally wounded at QUEBEC.

Monterrey, Battle of • an American victory in the MEXICAN WAR (1846–48), led by Gen. ZACHARY TAYLOR and Gen. William J. Worth, on September 21–22, 1846. While Worth seized Federation and Independence Hills, Taylor led his troops into the heart of the city, eventually forcing the surrender of Gen. Pedro de Ampudia's forces after an engagement that claimed more American than Mexican casualties.

Montgomery, Bernard Law (1887–1976) • British field marshal and Allied commander during WORLD WAR II, known as Monty. Montgomery first gained fame in 1942 with his defeat of the forces of ERWIN ROMMEL at the battle of EL ALAMEIN, following which he pursued the German armies across North Africa to their surrender in Tunisia (1943). He led the Allied invasion of NORMANDY (1944) under the command of Gen. DWIGHT D. EISENHOWER, with whom he had a contentious relationship throughout the war. In Britain he was hailed as another Wellington and made viscount of Alamein in 1946.

Montgomery, Richard (1738–75) • officer in the Continental army, born at Swords, County Dublin, Ireland. Montgomery captured Montreal but was killed in the subsequent attack on Quebec. Montgomery had been in America with the British army during the FRENCH AND INDIAN WAR (1754–63), when he took part in the siege of LOUISBOURG (1758) and in the expedition against Forts

TICONDEROGA and CROWN POINT (1759). In 1772 he sold his commission in the British army and moved to New York.

Montojo, Patricio • (1839–1917) Spanish admiral whose fleet was annihilated by the American squadron under Cmdr. GEORGE DEWEY at MANILA BAY (1898). Dewey's six modern warships completely outclassed the Spanish squadron, which consisted of seven antiquated cruisers and gunboats.

Montrésor, James Gabriel |ˈmäntrəˌsôr| (1702–76) • British military engineer, born in Fort William, Scotland. Montrésor was chief engineer in North America (1754–60) during the FRENCH AND INDIAN WAR (1754–63) who achieved a solid record as designer and constructor of military works.

Montrésor, John |ˈmäntrəˌsôr| (1736–99) • British military engineer, born in Gibraltar. Montrésor was chief engineer in America (1775–78) during the early years of the REVOLUTIONARY WAR. In addition to working on a variety of engineering projects, Montrésor saw action as an aide-de-camp to Gen. WILLIAM HOWE at the battle of NEW YORK (1776) and the subsequent fighting on Manhattan and in New Jersey. In 1777 he directed the position and attack of most of the artillery at BRANDYWINE and later constructed the lines of defense around Philadelphia. After fighting at the battle of MONMOUTH (1778), Montrésor, who had lost his superior's confidence, left America for England. He resigned his commission in 1779. Montrésor, who had accompanied his father, JAMES GABRIEL MONTRÉSOR, to North America at the time of the FRENCH AND INDIAN WAR (1754–63), also served ably in that conflict and remained to compile an impressive record of engineering achievements between it and the Revolution. He was with Gen. EDWARD BRADDOCK on an expedition against FORT DUQUESNE (1755), commanded detachments from Fort Edward (1756), took part in the capture of LOUISBOURG (1758), and commanded a light infantry regiment at QUEBEC (1759). From 1760 to 1764 Montrésor conducted an engineering survey of the St. Lawrence River, and in 1764 he constructed a chain of redoubts on the shore of Lake Erie.

Moody, James (1744–1809) • British spy during the REVOLUTIONARY WAR, born in Little Egg Harbor, New Jersey. After being repeatedly harassed for taking no side in the struggle for independence, Moody joined a loyalist militia in 1777 and by the next year was being sent behind enemy lines to gain information on GEORGE WASHINGTON's army and to rescue prisoners from rebel jails. Frequently captured, he just as frequently escaped. In 1781 Moody and his brother were betrayed when they broke into the Philadelphia state house to steal congressional papers and plans; he escaped again, but his brother was executed. The following year he went to England, where he was awarded an annual pension.

moor • *v.* **1** (often **be moored**) make fast (a vessel) to the shore or to an anchor: *twenty or so fishing boats were* ***moored to*** *the pier.* **2** (of a boat) be made fast somewhere in this way: *we moored alongside a jetty.*

moored mine • a contact or influence-operated buoyant mine that is held below the surface of water by a sinker or anchor on the bottom.

Moore, James (1737–77) • REVOLUTIONARY WAR general, born in New Hanover County, North Carolina. Moore crushed the loyalist forces at Moore's Creek Bridge (1776) through skillful maneuvering of inexperienced militia. Considered the ablest military leader of North Carolina, Moore was given command of the SOUTHERN DEPARTMENT, but died suddenly shortly thereafter. Before the Revolution Moore had been a militia captain during the FRENCH AND INDIAN WAR (1754–63), twice served in the North Carolina legislature, and been active in the SONS OF LIBERTY.

Moore, James • (c. 1650–1706) soldier and governor of South Carolina (1700–03) who led campaigns against Spanish and French settlements in the area, including an assault on Saint Augustine (1702). In 1704 he led a military campaign against Spanish missions among the Apalachee Indians southwest of Carolina.

Moore, James, Jr. (1675?–1724) • militia commander of South Carolina prominent in Indian affairs in the Southeast. Moore, an Indian trader and trader in Indian slaves, led a force that included friendly Indians in numerous campaigns against other native tribes in the area. In 1713 the combined forces crushed the Tuscarora, who moved to New York and were incorporated into the IROQUOIS CONFEDERACY. In 1715 Moore successfully commanded a force against the Yamassee. Moore also served as agent in negotiations with the Cherokee that secured South Carolina's trade with that powerful tribe and effectively doomed the league of Indian peoples that had formed against the Carolinians. From 1719 until 1721, Moore served as provisional governor of the state. In 1724 he was made commissioner for Indian affairs, with the sole authority for regulating the activities of South Carolina's Indian traders, but he died before accomplishing anything significant in the position.

mooring • *n.* **1** (often **moorings**) a place where a boat or ship is moored. **2** the ropes, chains, or anchors by or to which a boat, ship, or buoy is moored.

mopping up • the liquidation of remnants of enemy resistance in an area that has been surrounded or isolated, or through which other units have passed without eliminating all active resistance.

morale • *n.* the confidence, enthusiasm, and discipline of a person or group at a particular time: *their morale was high.*

moratorium • *n.* (pl. **moratoriums** or **moratoria**) **1** a temporary prohibition of an activity: *an indefinite* ***moratorium on*** *the use of drift nets.* **2** (**Moratorium**) a large, peaceful, nationwide anti-VIETNAM WAR protest on October 15, 1969.

Morgan, Daniel • (c. 1735–1802) REVOLUTIONARY WAR general whose tactical genius contributed significantly to the victory at COWPENS (1781), for which he was eventually awarded a medal by Congress (1790). He left the army in 1781 because of physical infirmities. Earlier in the conflict he had commanded the only rifle unit in the armies, which had exacted heavy tolls at the battles of SARATOGA (1777). Dissatisfied with his role thereafter, Morgan took an honorable furlough in 1779, but after HORATIO GATES's defeat at CAMDEN, South Carolina (1780), he joined the Southern army.

Morgan, John Hunt (1825–64) • Confederate army cavalry officer, born in Huntsville, Alabama. Morgan achieved fame as a master of guerrilla warfare, going behind enemy lines to gather intelligence, disrupt communications, and capture supplies. His most noted raids took place in Kentucky during 1862, though the following year he moved further north, into Indiana, Ohio, and West Virginia. He was captured and imprisoned in Ohio, but escaped. He later carried out further raids in Kentucky and Tennessee, during one of which he was killed. Much admired for his daring and panache, Morgan received a commendation of gratitude from the Confederate Congress in 1863. Moore's only full-scale military engagement was at SHILOH (1862).

Morgan's Rangers • a group of guerilla fighters commanded by DANIEL MORGAN during the REVOLUTIONARY WAR. In an effort to slow Lord CHARLES CORNWALLIS's progress in the South, Morgan's rangers moved slowly north and then suddenly turned and confronted British troops, under the command of Col. BANASTRE TARLETON, at COWPENS (1781), winning an unexpected victory.

Morgenthau, Henry, Jr. (1891–1967) • secretary of the treasury (1934–45), born in New York City. Morgenthau was responsible for the financing of WORLD WAR II. Morgenthau's plan to increase income taxes as a means of retarding inflation did not obtain Congressional approval, but he did organize several highly publicized and successful bond drives. Morgenthau, a gentleman farmer and member of a prominent New York German family, made the Treasury Department one of the few federal agencies that pressed for the United States to take action against the HOLOCAUST. He prevailed upon President FRANKLIN D. ROOSEVELT, a close personal friend, who established the WAR REFUGEE BOARD by executive order. In 1944 Morgenthau advocated a harsh peace settlement, which was rejected by Roosevelt and his successor, HARRY S. TRUMAN. That same year, however, he had a significant impact on the postwar international monetary system through his organization of the BRETTON WOODS CONFERENCE, which established the International Monetary Fund and the International Bank for Reconstruction and Development (later the World Bank). Morgenthau resigned shortly after Truman assumed the presidency. He devoted the remainder of his life to Jewish philanthropic causes and was an ardent supporter of the state of Israel.

Mormon War • a bloodless but significant conflict between the Mormons and the federal government in 1857–58. In July 1857, President JAMES BUCHANAN sent a 2,500-member expeditionary to secure the Utah Territory for its new governor, Alfred Cumming, a non-Mormon from Georgia. Buchanan had earlier appointed Cumming to replace Mormon Governor Brigham Young in order to quell complaints that the Mormons were traitors. As the U.S. troops slowly advanced, Young organized the UTAH MILITIA to prepare for a guerrilla war and its presence successfully held the army at bay through the winter. In June 1858, peace was reached as Young resigned, the government pardoned the Mormons for rebellious acts, and U.S. troops set up Camp Floyd near Salt Lake City.

morning watch • the period from 4 to 8 A.M. on board a ship.

Morrill Land Grant Act • an act of 1863 that extended military-style education to land-grant colleges. It required the schools to provide male students with basic military instruction, but the schools could remain essentially civilian institutions.

Morris, Robert (1734–1806) • preeminent Philadelphia merchant and revolutionary financier, born in Liverpool, England. His administrative and financial skills are considered to have been indispensable to military success in the REVOLUTIONARY WAR. Called the "financier of the Revolution," Morris, who was a signer of the DECLARATION OF INDEPENDENCE, was a shrewd entrepreneur who often disguised public ventures as private ones to facilitate secrecy and economy. From 1775 to 1778 he served in the Second Continental Congress, where he chaired the SECRET COMMITTEE OF TRADE (Congress's war department) and managed international procurement and naval affairs. As superintendent of finance (1781–84) Morris raised money and supplies for the YORKTOWN (1781) campaign and then worked to reestablish public credit through such measures as founding the nation's first bank and settling the public debt.

mortal • *adj.* **1** (of a battle) fought to the death: *from the outbuildings came the screams of men in* ***mortal combat.*** **2** (of an enemy or a state of hostility) admitting or allowing no reconciliation until death.

mortar • *n.* **1** a short smoothbore gun for firing shells (technically called bombs) at high angles. **2** a similar device used for firing a lifeline or firework. • *v.* attack or bombard with shells fired from a mortar.

mosaic • *n.* an assembly of overlapping photographs that have been matched to form a continuous photographic representation of a portion of the surface of the earth.

Mosby, John Singleton (1833–1916) • Confederate partisan officer, born in Powhatan County, Virginia. Mosby led a cavalry unit in guerrilla operations behind Union lines in northern Virginia. Mosby and his rangers provided ROBERT E. LEE with valuable intelligence information, seized hundreds of thousands of dollars worth of federal material, and captured thousands of enemy troops. Unlike many partisans, however, Mosby did not engage in ruthless attacks on civilians. Mosby never surrendered; he disbanded his battalion twelve days after Lee's surrender at APPOMATTOX (1865). After the war Mosby became friends with ULYSSES S. GRANT, joined the REPUBLICAN PARTY (for which he was much criticized in the South), and served in a variety of government posts.

Mosby's Raiders • a Confederate unit of rangers that operated behind Union lines south of the Potomac River during the CIVIL WAR. The unit was under the command of Col. JOHN S. MOSBY.

Mose, Edward Warren |mô'ēz| (1832–1903) • Confederate officer with a Georgia regiment, born in Charleston, South Carolina. Mose saw action at GETTYSBURG (1863) and PETERSBURG, as well as in other significant engagements of the CIVIL WAR (1861–65), achieving the rank of major.

mosquito boat • see PT BOAT.

mothball storage • semi-permanent protective storage of ships or military equipment usually involving a coating of protective material.

mother of all battles • Iraqi term for the PERSIAN GULF WAR (1991). SADDAM HUSSEIN claimed the fight for KUWAIT would be the "mother of all battles" (in Arabic, *Um al-Mar'rik*) and the phrase received considerable media currency.

mother ship • a large spacecraft or ship from which smaller craft are launched or maintained.

motorboat • *n.* see POWERBOAT.

motorize • *v.* (**motorized**) equip (troops) with motor transportation.

DERIVATIVES: **motorization** *n.*

motorsailer • *n.* a boat equipped with both sails and an engine.

motor torpedo boat • see PT BOAT.

Motor Transport Corps • a U.S. Army organization responsible for transporting troops and equipment during WORLD WAR I.

Mott, Gershom (1822–84) • Union army officer with a New Jersey regiment, born in Lamberton (now part of Trenton), New Jersey. He first distinguished himself at WILLIAMSBURG during the PENINSULAR CAMPAIGN (1862) and subsequently led a regiment through the battle of SEVEN PINES (1862). He was seriously wounded at SECOND BULL RUN (1862) and again at CHANCELLORSVILLE (1863). At the battle of the WILDERNESS (1864) he commanded a division, but it broke and ran for the rear, as it did again at SPOTSYLVANIA (1864). Briefly demoted to brigade command, Mott gained recognition for his performance in again leading a division at the battle of the CRATER (1864); he continued in command of the division throughout the PETERSBURG siege (1864–65). Mott resigned from the army in 1866.

Moultrie, William (1730–1805) • REVOLUTIONARY WAR general, born in Charleston, South Carolina. His lackluster record as a field commander in the Continental army never equaled the promise of his first major success as commander of a South Carolina regiment on Sullivan's Island at the mouth of Charleston harbor. Advised by the general in charge of Charleston's defenses to evacuate the fort because it was certain to fall in the face of a probable British attack, Moultrie declined to do so. A large British expeditionary force launched an assault which Moultrie's troops successfully repelled. For his achievement he received the official thanks of Congress.

mount • *v.* **1** (often **be mounted**) set (someone) on horseback; provide with a horse: *she was mounted on a white horse.* **2** establish; set up: *security forces mounted checkpoints at every key road.* **3** grow larger or more numerous: *casualties mounted as the siege wore one.* **4** place (a gun) on a fixed mounting. • *n.* **1** a support for a gun, camera, or similar piece of equipment. **2** a horse being ridden or that is available for riding: *he hung on to his mount's bridle.*

PHRASES: **mount guard** keep watch, especially for protection or to prevent escape.

DERIVATIVES: **mountable** *adj.* **mounter** *n.*

Mountbatten, Louis (1900–79) • (1st Earl Mountbatten of Burma) British statesman and admiral, born Louis Francis Albert Victor Nicholas Mountbatten in Windsor, England. As supreme Allied commander for Southeast Asia (1943–45) during WORLD WAR II, Mountbatten conducted operations against Japanese-occupied Burma. Mountbatten was also the last viceroy (1947) and first governor general of India (1947–48), overseeing its transition to independence. Mountbatten was assassinated when Irish Republican Army terrorists planted a bomb on his yacht.

Mountbatten was the great-grandson of Queen Victoria.

---

movement • *n.* (**movements**) the activities and whereabouts of someone, especially during a particular period of time: *your movements and telephone conversations are recorded.*

moving mine • any mine that is not fixed to a particular position between the time that it is set and the time it is activated.

Mower, Joseph Anthony (1827–70) • army officer; born in Woodstock, Virginia. Mower was one of the few CIVIL WAR commanders to achieve distinction in regimental, brigade, division, and corps command. Mower distinguished himself during the VICKSBURG (1862–63) and RED RIVER (1864) campaigns, but his most significant success was his defeat of Gen. NATHAN BEDFORD FORREST (1864), the Confederacy's most successful cavalry commander. For this he was made major general. After the war Mower commanded a series of occupation areas in the South. Before the Civil War, Mower had served two years as a private in the MEXICAN WAR (1846–48). He received a commission into the regular army in 1855.

MP • *abbr.* **1** military police. **2** military policeman.

MPF • *abbr.* Maritime Prepositioned Force.

MPS • *abbr.* maritime prepositioning ships.

Mr. • (often as **Mister**) used in the armed forces to address a senior warrant officer, officer cadet, or junior naval officer.

MRBM • *abbr.* medium-range ballistic missile.

MRE • *abbr.* meal ready to eat, the standard field ration that replaced the C- and E-rations of WORLD WAR II. The MRE's aluminum foil pouch may contain precooked spaghetti, beef stew, sliced ham, chicken à la king, Swiss steak, etc. See also K-RATIONS.

MRV • *abbr.* medium recovery vehicle. See HERCULES, def. 2.

MS • *abbr.* motor ship.

MSC • *abbr.* Military Sealift Command.

MSgt • *abbr.* (also **MSGT**) Master Sergeant.

MSTS • *abbr.* Military Sea Transportation Service.

MTB • *abbr.* Brit. motor torpedo boat.

MTBF • *abbr.* mean time between failures; a measure of how reliable a system or system component is, determined by intensive testing or experience, or predicted by analyzing known factors. It may be expressed as a quantity of time or of successful usages or cycles between failures.

MTMC • *abbr.* Military Traffic Management Command.

mufti • *n.* plain clothes worn by a person who wears a uniform for their job, such as a soldier or police officer: *I was a flying officer* ***in mufti.***

Muhlenberg, John Peter Gabriel |ˈmyo͞oˌlənˌbərg| (1746–1807) • (also known as Peter Muhlenberg) REVOLUTIONARY WAR officer, born in Trappe, Pennsylvania. Muhlenberg fought with distinction at the battles of BRANDYWINE and GERMANTOWN (both 1777), commanded two brigades at MONMOUTH (1778), and played a major role in the siege of YORKTOWN (1781). After retiring from the service (1783), he returned to his native Pennsylvania, where he began an active political life, serving three terms in Congress.

Mulberry • code name for the two artificial harbors built for the NORMANDY invasion of June 1944. Each Mulberry harbor consisted of concrete breakwaters and pontoon jetties floated across the Channel from England and sunk in place and protected by old ships which were sunk as breakwaters. The Mulberry at OMAHA BEACH in the American sector was destroyed by bad weather soon after it was installed, but the one at Arromanches in the British sector was used for several months.

Muleshoe salient • a horseshoe-shaped strategic position developed by the Confederate army in the CIVIL WAR battle of SPOTSYLVANIA (1864) and broken by Union troops.

Mullan, John (1830–1909) • military engineer, born in Norfolk, Virginia. Mullan lobbied for and eventually oversaw construction of a 600-mile military road from Fort Benton (Montana) to the Walla Walla Valley (Washington) which, though useful in some circumstances, never achieved the popularity of the supply routes from the south and west. Mullan resigned from the army in 1863. He never took part in the CIVIL WAR.

Mullany, James Robert Madison |məˈlānē| (1818–87) • naval officer, born in New York City. He commanded the side-wheel steamer *Bienville* (1862–65) during the CIVIL WAR, capturing a total of eleven blockade runners. He served under SAMUEL F. DU PONT in the South Atlantic Blockading Squadron and under DAVID FARRAGUT in the West Gulf Blockading Squadron. Farragut commended him for gallant conduct during the battle of MOBILE BAY (1864), at which Mullany was severely wounded, resulting in the loss of an arm. (He temporarily commanded the steam sloop *Oneida* during that battle.) He retired in 1879, a rear admiral. During the MEXICAN WAR (1846–48) Mullany participated in the naval expedition to TABASCO.

multihull • *n.* a boat with two or more hulls, especially three.

multilateral • *adj.* **1** agreed upon or participated in by three or more parties, especially the governments of different countries: *multilateral negotiations.* **2** having members or contributors from several groups, especially several different countries: *multilateral aid agencies.*

DERIVATIVES: **multilateralism** *n.* **multilateralist** *adj.* & *n.* **multilaterally** *adv.*

multiple independently targetable reentry vehicle • a reentry vehicle carried by a system that can deliver one or more such vehicles separately to each of several different targets.

multiple reentry vehicle • the reentry mechanism of a ballistic missile that places more than one reentry vehicle over an individual target.

Munich agreement • a peace settlement reached in Munich on September 30, 1938, by leaders of France, Germany, Great Britain, and Italy to allow German annexation of the Sudetenland in Czechoslovakia. It was accepted by all parties to prevent an attack planned by ADOLF HITLER on Czechoslovakia, which had alliances with France and Great Britain, who both felt unprepared to defend the country.

The agreement was introduced by BENITO MUSSOLINI, but it was later discovered to have been prepared in the German Foreign Office.

---

munition • *plural n.* (**munitions**) military weapons, ammunition, equipment, and stores: *reserves of nuclear, chemical, and conventional munitions* | (**munition**) *munition factories.* • *v.* supply with munitions.

Munitions Investigation Committee • see NYE COMMITTEE.

Murfreesboro, Battle of • see STONES RIVER, BATTLE OF.

Murphy, Audie (1924–71) • the most highly decorated American soldier of WORLD WAR II, born in Hunt County, Texas. His prowess and initiative in combat earned Murphy, an enlisted infantryman, a battlefield commission. He won the Distinguished Service Cross for destroying several enemy machine guns in a matter of minutes in southern France (1944) and the Congressional Medal of Honor for his standoff (firing a machine gun atop a burning tank destroyer) against a German counterattack in Alsace (1945). Accounts of his heroism in the popular press made him a national celebrity and resulted in a brief career as a film actor. He played mainly in Westerns, capitalizing on his origins as a poor farm boy from Texas. Murphy was killed in a plane crash.

Murphy's autobiographical bestseller *To Hell and Back* was made into a successful but much sanitized war movie (1955).

Murray, Alexander (1755–1821) • naval officer, born in Chestertown, Maryland. He saw action during the Revolutionary War and the Quasi-War with France (1798–1800). Unable to obtain the desired navy commission, Murray fought for a time with the Continental army, taking part in the Battle of White Plains (1776), and then sailed as a privateer, with only modest success, being twice captured. Finally obtaining a commission (1781), Murray was again captured and released, and returned to privateering until his appointment as a lieutenant aboard a warship, where he remained until it was decommissioned (1785). During his first command of the Quasi-War, Murray lost a ship of his squadron and captured one prize. His next command (1799) resulted in not a single capture in more than two months before he took two modest prizes.

Murray, John • (1730 or 1732–1809) (4th earl of Dunmore) royal governor of Virginia (1771–76), born probably in Perthshire, Scotland. His expedition against the Shawnee of Kentucky, known as Lord Dunmore's War (1774), forced their withdrawal north of the Ohio River and removed the last obstacle to colonial conquest of that area. Murray was much disliked by the colonialists, who believed he threatened their liberties. Forced to flee from the capital (1775), he gathered a small loyalist force that raided plantations and captured rebel munitions in the vicinity of Norfolk while awaiting reinforcements that never came. He later became governor of the Bahamas (1786–96), where many loyalists had emigrated.

Murray fell from favor at court when his daughter married a son of George III in violation of the Royal Marriage Act, and the king dismissed him from office (1796).

music • *n. informal* in air intercept, electromagnetic jamming.

musket • *n.* an infantryman's light gun with a long barrel, typically smooth-bored, muzzle-loading, and fired from the shoulder.

musketeer • *n.* a soldier armed with a musket.

musketry • *n.* **1** musket fire: *a terrible explosion of musketry.* **2** soldiers armed with muskets: *the Prussian musketry.* **3** the art or technique of handling a musket.

musket shot • **1** a shot fired from a musket. **2** the ball or other projectile fired from a musket. **3** the distance (approximately 300 yards) traveled by a ball fired from a musket.

Mussolini, Benito (1883–1945) • Italian Fascist statesman, Prime Minister 1922–43; known as Il Duce ('the leader'). He founded the Italian Fascist Party in 1919. He annexed Abyssinia in 1936 and entered World War II on Germany's side in 1940. Forced to resign after the Allied invasion of Sicily, he was rescued from imprisonment by German paratroopers, but was captured and executed by Italian communist partisans.

Mustang • (**P-51**) an escort fighter originally built to British specifications in 1940 by North American Aviation; delivery to the Royal Air Force began in November 1941. Because the aircraft performed poorly at high altitudes, the P-51 was remustered as a low-altitude reconnaissance fighter and refitted with an oblique camera for tactical photographic reconnaissance. Later versions of the P-51, provided with more powerful engines, served well as fighter escorts for bombers during World War II, enabling the bombers to travel deep into enemy territory.

mustard gas • a colorless oily liquid that is a powerful poison and vesicant, acting directly on the skin, and often causing blindness and death. It was introduced by the Germans in World War I as a chemical weapon.

muster • *v.* **1** assemble (troops), especially for inspection or in preparation for battle. **2** (of troops) come together in this way. • *n.* **1** a formal gathering of troops, especially for inspection, display, or exercise. **2** short for muster roll.

PHRASES: **pass muster** be accepted as adequate or satisfactory: *a treaty that might pass muster with the voters.*

▸**muster someone in** (or **out**) enroll someone into (or discharge someone from) military service.

muster book • a book in which military personnel were registered.

muster roll • an official list of officers and men in a military unit or ship's company.

mutineer • *n.* a soldier or sailor who rebels or refuses to obey the orders of a person in authority.

mutinous • *adj.* (of a soldier or sailor) refusing to obey the orders of a person in authority.

DERIVATIVES: **mutinously** *adv.*

mutiny • *n.* (pl. **-ies**) an open rebellion against the proper authorities, especially by soldiers or sailors against their officers: *a mutiny by those manning the weapons could trigger a global war* | *mutiny at sea.* • *v.* (**-ies, -ied**) refuse to obey the orders of a person in authority.

Mutiny Cases • in August 1917, violence erupted in Houston, Texas, between black soldiers of the U.S. 24th Infantry Regiment and local white civilians. Over 100 black soldiers were court-martialed, and thirteen were executed, without benefit of an appeal to the War Department. The summary justice meted out to the black soldiers shocked black citizens throughout the United States, and the incident aroused southern protests against the quartering of black troops in the South.

Mutual and Balanced Force Reduction talks • an attempt by NATO and WARSAW PACT forces in 1973 to negotiate conventional arms control in central Europe. The talks ended inconclusively in 1987 and were followed by the CFE.

mutual assured destruction • (**MAD**) a strategic situation in which both sides possess the ability to inflict unacceptable damage upon the opponent at any time during the course of a strategic nuclear exchange, even after absorbing a surprise first strike.

Mutual Defense Assistance Act • a law signed by President HARRY S. TRUMAN on October 6, 1949. The first global U.S. military assistance legislation of the COLD WAR, it anticipated the need for arms aid, among signatories of a pending North Atlantic defense treaty, to resist Communist aggression.

mutual deterrence • a stable situation in which two or more countries or coalitions of countries are inhibited from attacking each other because the casualties and/or damage resulting from certain retaliation would be unacceptable.

Mutual Security Act • a law passed on October 10, 1951 to create the Mutual Security Administration to supervise all foreign aid programs and to unite military and economic programs with technical assistance. Congress disproved of the foreign aid bill and reduced its request for funds to ensure the predominance of military over economic assistance. It succeeded the MARSHALL PLAN and the MUTUAL DEFENSE ASSISTANCE ACT.

muzzle • *n.* the open end of the barrel of a firearm.

muzzleloader (also **muzzle-loader**) • *n.* a gun that is loaded through its muzzle.
DERIVATIVES: **muzzleloading** (also **muzzle-loading**) *adj.*

muzzle velocity • the velocity with which a bullet or shell leaves the muzzle of a gun.

MV • *abbr.* **1** motor vessel: *on board the MV Alcinous.* **2** muzzle velocity.

MX missile • a ten-warhead intercontinental ballistic missile that was developed in the 1980s.

MY • *abbr.* motor yacht: *MY Fleury.*

Myer, Albert James (1828–80) • army officer, born in Newburgh, New York. Myer was first chief signal officer (1866), and first head of the National Weather Service (1870). During the CIVIL WAR Myer established a signal system for the Union army and trained officers and enlisted men in its use. The U.S. military academies later adopted his system, using a manual he had written for its instruction. Myer's suggestion that the SIGNAL CORPS use telegraphy to monitor and predict the movement of destructive storms eventually led to the establishment of a national weather service as part of the WAR DEPARTMENT and under the direction of the chief signal officer. His staff served both as meteorological observers and intelligence agents, reporting on such occurrences as strikes and Indian uprisings, as well as droughts and frosts, picked up through their information network.

Fort Myer, Virginia, still an important Signal Corps post, was named in his honor in 1881.

Myers, Abraham Charles (1811–89) • quartermaster general of the Confederate army, born in Georgetown, South Carolina. Myers served from the start of the war until removed by JEFFERSON DAVIS in 1863. Myers proved inadequate for the major logistical problems faced by the department and failed to exercise administrative leadership as well. Refusing to remain in the department in a subordinate position, he was dismissed from the army.

My Lai Massacre • (1968) the most notorious incident of U.S. brutality in the VIETNAM WAR. On March 16, U.S. soldiers, with orders to burn and destroy, entered My Lai, which was wrongly thought to be a VIETCONG stronghold. Finding no enemy soldiers, they brutally raped several women and killed everyone (between 175–400 civilians), mostly old men, women, and children. The incident was covered up until mid 1969, when word unofficially reached PENTAGON officials. The subsequent commission of inquiry implicated thirty soldiers, charged sixteen, court-martialed five, and found only one guilty, sentencing Lt. WILLIAM L. CALLEY to life at hard labor for killing no fewer than twenty-two Vietnamese civilians. Many Americans thought Calley had acted understandably in the heat of battle; and left-wingers also insisted that My Lai was nothing out of the ordinary (for obviously different reasons). My Lai resulted in new procedures and instruction regarding the laws of war, perhaps making it easier for other U.S. soldiers to stop further atrocities from escaping the attention of both military officials and the press.

My Tho • a city in the Mekong Delta, south Vietnam, where U.S. troops created a base for the Mobile Riverine Force during the VIETNAM WAR. The base was located at the intersection of the sole highway (Route 4) crossing the delta, and the My Tho River. The Mobile Riverine Force base at My Tho was operational between 1966 and 1969, lending support to the U.S. Army 9th Infantry Division, U.S. Navy River Patrol Boats (PBRs) and River Assault Squadrons, and the Vietnamese Marine Corps. The base was relinquished to the Vietnamese navy in November 1969.

Nn

N-1 • see GENERAL STAFF.
N-2 • see GENERAL STAFF.
N-3 • see GENERAL STAFF.
N-4 • see GENERAL STAFF.
N-5 • see GENERAL STAFF.
N-69 • see SNARK.

NAC • *abbr.* North Atlantic Council; the principal forum for consultation among NATO member governments on issues affecting their common security. It meets at least twice a year under the chairmanship of the NATO General Secretary.

NACA • *abbr.* National Advisory Committee for Aeronautics.

NACC • *abbr.* North Atlantic Cooperation Council.

NAF • *abbr.* numbered air force.

Nagasaki, Bombing of • the second nuclear blast on Japan, somewhat less destructive of human life than in HIROSHIMA, but nonetheless the last step in forcing Japanese surrender. Nicknamed "Fat Man," the bomb was dropped by Maj. Charles W. Sweeney at 10:58 A.M., August 9, 1945. Originally a secondary target, Nagasaki lay among hills that prevented higher fatalities than the still terrifying numbers of 35,000 initial dead and 40,000 more fatalities from radiation and injuries. In light of Hiroshima, Nagasaki, and the concurrent Soviet triumph in Manchuria, Emperor HIROHITO surrendered on August 14.

Nagumo, Chuichi (1886–1944) • vice admiral in the Japanese navy during WORLD WAR II. Nagumo commanded the aircraft carrier strike force that launched the attack on PEARL HARBOR (1941). His decision not to carry out a planned third wave that would have destroyed U.S. storage tanks and repair facilities enabled the United States to keep the remainder of the fleet operational and to return most of the damaged ships to active duty. His force was decisively defeated in the battle of MIDWAY (1942), losing all four carriers present. He committed suicide during the final stages of the defense of Saipan.

Nanjing (**Nanking**) |ˈnänˈjiNG| • a city in eastern China, on the Yangtze River, capital of Jiangsu province. It was the capital of various ruling dynasties and of China from 1368 until replaced by Beijing in 1421. Nanjing became the provisional capital of the new Republic of China in 1912, falling to Communist control in 1927 and being retaken by Nationalists under CHIANG KAI-SHEK in 1928. Seized and held by Japanese forces from 1937 to 1945, Nanjing experienced such atrocities that this period was called 'the rape of Nanjing.' In 1949 Beijing became the capital of the new People's Republic of China, and Nanjing was developed as a center for heavy industry, becoming a provincial capital in 1952.

napalm • *n.* a highly flammable sticky jelly used in incendiary bombs and flamethrowers, consisting of gasoline thickened with special soaps. • *v.* attack with bombs containing napalm.

ORIGIN: 1940s: from *na(phthenic)* and *palm(itic acid)*.

napoleonic warfare • the methods of warfare which became common in Europe in the early 19th century as a result of the campaigns of Napoleon Bonaparte between 1799 and 1815. Not all of the changes in the art of war during the Napoleonic era can be attributed to Bonaparte, but he instituted many organizational and tactical innovations. Chief among these were the introduction of the permanent army corps structure of several divisions with supporting artillery, cavalry, and logistical troops under one commander. Tactically, napoleonic warfare emphasized the offensive; the flank attack; highly mobile artillery and the integration of infantry, cavalry, and artillery forces; and the use of the infantry column as well as the line formation. His principles of were codified by the Swiss Baron ANTOINE-HENRI JOMINI, whose writings were highly honored at WEST POINT and thus indirectly provided the basis for American strategy and tactics through the CIVIL WAR.

Narraganset • an Algonquian-speaking Indian tribe located in what is now the state of Rhode Island. Led by the sachem Canonicus, the Narragansets maintained good relations with the English colonists until 1643 when the colonists turned over Canonicus' brother to the MOHICAN enemies of the Narragansets who subsequently joined with the Wampanoags against the colonists in KING PHILIP'S WAR (1675–76).

NASA • *abbr.* National Aeronautics and Space Administration.

Nashville, Battle of • a devastating 1864 defeat of Gen. JOHN B. HOOD's troops at the hands of Gen. GEORGE H. THOMAS's Union forces. In November, Hood surrounded JOHN M. SCHOFIELD's forces near Spring Hill, Tennessee, but Schofield managed to escape. Hood, furious, began an ill-advised chase to the outskirts of Nashville, where he positioned his ill-fated troops, outnumbered as they were almost two to one by Thomas's men. Thomas finally attacked on December 15 and 16, routing the Confederates and taking 4,500 prisoners. This was the last major clash west of the Appalachians.

National Academy of Sciences • a private, nonprofit organization of scientists charged with advising the U.S. government and promoting science and technology to the public. Chartered by Congress in 1863, new members are selected based on their distinguished advances in research. It has nearly 2,000 members and 300 foreign associates, including 170 members who have won the Nobel Prize.

National Advisory Committee for Aeronautics • (**NACA**) a federal civilian committee for administration of research on aviation technology. Founded in 1915 by President Woodrow Wilson, the committee promoted research that resulted in significant advances in aircraft design, including drag-reduction, engine-cooling, and airfoil technique. In the 1920s, aircraft evolved from using wooden structures to employing a light metal frame. Notable members of the committee included Orville Wright and Charles Lindbergh. The committee was replaced in 1958 by the National Aeronautics and Space Administration under President Dwight D. Eisenhower.

National Air and Space Museum • a museum of aviation and space exploration history on the National Mall in Washington, D.C. The museum contains the largest collection of historic air- and spacecraft in the world, and is the most frequently visited museum of the Smithsonian Institution complex.

National Association for Uniformed Services • an organization providing legislative representation for all branches of the military and veteran community. The nonprofit, nonpartisan organization supports members' interests in areas such as Medicare, Social Security, and other earned federal entitlements.

national censorship • the examination and control, under civil authority, of communications entering, leaving, or transiting the borders of the United States, its territories, or its possessions.

national command • a command that is organized by, and functions under the authority of, a specific nation. It may or may not be placed under a NATO commander.

National Command Authorities • (**NCA**) the president and the secretary of defense or their duly deputized alternates or successors.

National Committee for a Sane Nuclear Policy • see Peace Action.

National Communications System • (**NCS**) the telecommunications system that results from the integration of the separate telecommunications systems of several executive branch departments.

National Defense Act • **1** (1916) a law enacted by Congress on May 13, 1916, prior to U.S. entry into World War I, to reorganize the U.S. Army and to designate the National Guard the primary trained reserve, increase its funding and regulation, and make Guardsmen available for overseas service. It authorized expanding the size of the Guard and the regular army, and established a campus-based ROTC for officer preparation. **2** (1920) a law signed by President Woodrow Wilson on June 4, 1920 to systematize the regular army, National Guard, and Army Reserve after World War I. Based on the National Defense Act of 1916, it relied on voluntarism and established the size of each component of the army, expanded programs for commissioning reserve officers, and made the General Staff responsible for overall military planning.

national defense area • (**NDA**) an area established on nonfederal lands located within the United States or its possessions or territories for the purpose of safeguarding classified defense information or protecting Department of Defense equipment and/or material.

Establishment of a national defense area temporarily places such nonfederal lands under the effective control of the DoD and results only from an emergency event. The senior DoD representative at the scene will define the boundary, mark it with a physical barrier, and post warning signs. The landowner's consent and cooperation will be obtained whenever possible; however, military necessity will dictate the final decision regarding location, shape, and size of the national defense area.

National Defense Authorization Act • an act approved on October 23, 1992, that included a provision to make the vice chairman of the Joint Chiefs of Staff a full voting member of the organization. The position of vice chairman was created under the Goldwater-Nichols Act of 1986.

National Defense Education Act • an act of 1958 signed by President Dwight D. Eisenhower to provide American students with government support for graduate study in science and technology. It was created to improve American education programs in response to the Soviet Union's orbiting of the first artificial satellite on October 4, 1957.

National Defense Research Committee • a quasi-governmental organization formed by President Franklin D. Roosevelt in 1940 and headed by Dr. Vannevar Bush, the purpose of which was to mobilize American civilian scientists for military research and to enhance the adaptation of science and technology to the war effort during World War II.

National Defense University • a postgraduate joint service school at Fort Lesley J. McNair, Washington, D.C. Established in 1976 as a parent of the National War College and the Industrial College of the Armed Forces, it traces its history back to 1903, when the U.S. Army War College was founded at Fort McNair. In 1981 the Armed Forces Staff College joined the university.

national emergency • a state of emergency declared either by the Congress or the President under which a partial, full, or total mobilization of the U.S. armed forces may be called for.

National Guard • **1** (in the U.S.) the primary reserve military force, partly maintained by the states but also available for federal use. **2** the primary military force of some other countries. **3** an armed force existing in France at various times between 1789 and 1871, first commanded by the Marquis de Lafayette. **4** a member of this force.

DERIVATIVES: **National Guardsman** *n.*

National Guard Association of the United States • an association of U.S. Army National Guard and Air National Guard commissioned and warrant officers. It was founded in 1878 with the goal of providing

National Guard representation before Congress. The objectives of its first meeting after RECONSTRUCTION (1865–77) were to improve the equipment and training of the National Guard to create a more combat-ready force; the objectives remain the same today.

nationalism • *n.* **1** patriotic feeling, principles, or efforts. **2** an extreme form of this, especially marked by a feeling of superiority over other countries. **3** advocacy of political independence for a particular country: *Palestinian nationalism.*

nationalist-separatist • *adj.* fighting to establish a new political order or state based on ethnic dominance or homogeneity. Another term for ETHNO-NATIONALIST.

National Liberation Front • the Communist-dominated nationalist organization formally established in December 1960 and also known as the National Front for the Liberation of South Vietnam (Mat Tran Dan Toc Giai Phong). It sought to overthrow the pro-Western government of the Republic of (South) Vietnam and unite North and South Vietnam under Communist rule. Nominally led by non-Communist southerners, the National Liberation Front was for all practical purposes an arm of the Communist Lao Dong Party and the government of the Democratic Republic of (North) Vietnam. The National Liberation Front was disbanded following the Communist take-over of South Vietnam in 1975.

National Memorial Cemetery of the Pacific • a national cemetery in Honolulu, Hawaii, containing the graves of more than 24,000 WORLD WAR II, KOREAN WAR, and VIETNAM WAR dead. The first internment at the cemetery was an unknown soldier killed in the attack on PEARL HARBOR (1941).

The cemetery is in the 2,000-foot-wide Punchbowl crater, which is also known as *Puowaina*, literally "Hill of Sacrifice."

National Military Establishment • an organization created by the NATIONAL SECURITY ACT of 1947, comprised of the heads of the armed forces departments, and responsible for coordinating and responding to defense issues after WORLD WAR II. The CIA and the NATIONAL SECURITY COUNCIL were created by the same Act.

national missile defense • the measures and weapons systems designed to protect the United States against an enemy intercontinental ballistic missile strike. Among the elements of the U.S. national missile defense system deployed or contemplated since the early 1960s were the NIKE ZEUS missile, the SENTINEL and SAFEGUARD systems, the STRATEGIC DEFENSE INITIATIVE (SDI; the so-called "Star Wars" program), and the Global Protection Against Limited Strikes (GPALS) system.

National Research Council • organized in 1916 by the NATIONAL ACADEMY OF SCIENCES and responsible for coordinating research within the community of science and technology and advising the federal government on related issues.

National Science Foundation • (**NSF**) established by the U.S. Congress by the National Science Foundation Act of 1950, it is an independent agency of the U.S. government responsible for supporting basic research and education in the sciences, mathematics, and engineering. It grants funding for research and provides support for educational programs in mathematics and sciences.

national security • a collective term encompassing both the national defense and foreign relations of the United States. Specifically, national security is the condition provided by: **a** a military or defense advantage over any foreign nation or group of nations, **b** a favorable foreign relations position, or **c** a defense posture capable of successfully resisting hostile or destructive action from within or without, overt or covert.

National Security Act • a law signed on July 26, 1947 to reorganize and centralize the military after WORLD WAR II. It established a NATIONAL SECURITY COUNCIL, which included the newly created Office of the Secretary of Defense to coordinate policy, and the CENTRAL INTELLIGENCE AGENCY to evaluate intelligence relating to national security. It also gave the newly named U.S. Air Force co-equal status with the army and the navy. As amended in 1949, it created the DEPARTMENT OF DEFENSE and institutionalized the JOINT CHIEFS OF STAFF.

National Security Action Memoranda • a system of documents that was institutionalized by President JOHN F. KENNEDY to replace the NATIONAL SECURITY COUNCIL paper policy. President LYNDON B. JOHNSON also used this system. The memoranda included instructions to government departments, communication of policy decision, and requests for specific information or for studies on a range of issues. It was replaced by the NATIONAL SECURITY STUDY MEMORANDA and the NATIONAL SECURITY DECISION MEMORANDA.

National Security Action Memorandum No. 328 • a memorandum issued on April 6, 1965, by President LYNDON B. JOHNSON that authorized the use of American combat troops in the VIETNAM WAR. It included an approval for an 18–20,000 man increase in U.S. military support forces and a general framework of continuing action against North Vietnam and Laos.

National Security Council • (**NSC**) a group of cabinet-level advisers who advise the president, coordinate different aspects of policy, formulate and ratify policy decisions, and manage important initiatives. The entity dates from 1947. Presidential use of the council is discretionary. As it was originally conceived during the presidency of HARRY S. TRUMAN, the Council was supposed to ensure prompt and decisive action during times of crisis, avoid the organizational confusion of WORLD WAR II, and check the authority of the president.

National Security Decision Memoranda • a system of documents established under President RICHARD M. NIXON's administration. The memoranda announced a presidential policy decision made after a study and review process initiated in the NATIONAL SECURITY STUDY MEMORANDA. A more formal system than the NATIONAL SECURITY ACTION MEMORANDA, it has been a model for all subsequent presidencies.

National Security Intelligence Directive • documents issued by the NATIONAL SECURITY COUNCIL specifying tasks to be performed by the various U.S. intelligence agencies.

National Security Resource Board • created by the NATIONAL SECURITY ACT of 1947, the board focuses the connection of industrial readiness to military preparedness.

national security state • a post-WORLD WAR II state in which nearly all aspects of political, economic, intellectual, and social life are dominated by considerations of national defense and the drive to maintain a defense establishment capable of protecting the state against all comers.

National Security Study Memoranda • a system of documents established under President RICHARD M. NIXON's administration. The memoranda were requests for studies on a particular issue by a government or NATIONAL SECURITY COUNCIL agency, and they were used in conjunction with the NATIONAL SECURITY DECISION MEMORANDA. It was a more formal system than the NATIONAL SECURITY ACTION MEMORANDA.

national service • a period of compulsory service in the armed forces of some countries during peacetime.

National Socialist German Workers' Party • (**NSDAP**) a nationalist, racist, and authoritarian German political party formed by ADOLF HITLER in the 1920s. Hitler and the NSDAP came to power in 1933 and proceeded to plan and initiate an aggressive war of conquest in Europe and the systematic destruction of Jews and other "undesirables." Also known as the NAZI Party.

National Stock Number • the thirteen-digit stock number replacing the eleven-digit FEDERAL STOCK NUMBER. It consists of the four-digit Federal Supply Classification code and the nine-digit National Item Identification Number. The National Item Identification Number consists of a two-digit National Codification Bureau number designating the central cataloging office of the NATO or other friendly country which assigned the number and a seven-digit (xxxxxxx) nonsignificant number.

National War College • a postgraduate joint senior service school at Fort McNair, Washington, D.C. Established in 1946 to replace the Army-Navy Staff College, it is a school of the NATIONAL DEFENSE UNIVERSITY, which it joined in 1976. It has granted a master of arts degree in national security and strategic studies since 1991.

nation-state • *n.* a sovereign state whose citizens or subjects are relatively homogeneous in factors such as language or common descent.

Native American Wars • wars among Native Americans; and wars between Native Americans and Europeans and Euro-Americans. East of the Mississippi, the first type of war often took the form of "mourning wars," fought to take captives to avenge and replace the loss of a group member, rather than to acquire land or goods. European contact, however, brought disease and trade, intensifying these rivalries. Both factors led to a long series of "BEAVER WARS" which broke out from the 1640s to 1680s between Iroquian and Algonquian groups. In the Eastern Woodlands, Indian groups fought against each other in larger European wars, such as KING WILLIAM'S WAR (1698–97), QUEEN ANNE'S WAR (1702–13), KING GEORGE'S WAR (1744–48), and the FRENCH AND INDIAN WAR (1754–63). In the Plains and the Southwest, on the other hand, wars tended to pit nomadic groups against horticulturist ones, rivalries that were also exacerbated by European contact. The horse played a critical role, shifting the balance of military power to nomadic groups, who drove agricultural groups, such as the Plains Apache and the Navajo from their lands. By the 1840s, the dominance of the nomadic LAKOTA SIOUX led many Plains horticulturists to favor a military alliance with the United States to ensure their own survival. Wars between Native Americans and Europeans and Americans almost always arose as a result of European settlers claiming territory already inhabited by Indians. Thus, in 1622 and 1644, the Powhatan Confederacy tried to eradicate the Virginia Colony; in 1636–37, the Pequots were virtually wiped out in New England; in 1675–76, Algonquians tried to repossess land in KING PHILIP'S WAR; and in 1680, Pueblo Indians drove the Spanish out of New Mexico, though only for thirteen years. And while in these and other wars, groups considered a pan-Indian alliance, this became difficult to accomplish as Indian survival usually depended on continued competition between two European powers. The REVOLUTIONARY WAR and subsequent encouragement for Euro-Americans to settle the land engendered a number of conflicts in which Indians continued to lose their lands in the Old Northwest. These groups tried to capitalize on the WAR OF 1812 to regain their lands, but only succeeded in delaying American dominion, finalized by their defeat in the BLACK HAWK WAR in 1832. In the South, unified Creek resistance was put down in the CREEK WAR (1811–14), while the Cherokees were driven west on the famous TRAIL OF TEARS; and Florida Indians were likewise conquered and driven west after the SEMINOLE WARS in 1818, 1835–42, and 1855–58. The staunchest resistance was mounted in the Pacific Northwest by the Modocs and NEZ PERCÉS,' but that, too, was eventually quashed in the 1870s. Americans' westward migration kept tensions high through the 19th century. Treaties, such as the 1851 TREATY OF FORT LARAMIE, tended to last for fewer years than the wars they settled. In the PLAINS INDIANS

WARS that were fought between 1854 and 1890, Plains Indians resisted the expansion of the railroad and American settlement, but U.S. soldiers, with the help of Shoshone and Crow fighters, destroyed buffalo and attacked villages to subdue them. It was in these wars that GEORGE ARMSTRONG CUSTER was defeated by CRAZY HORSE at the BATTLE OF LITTLE BIGHORN (1876) and that the tragic BATTLE OF WOUNDED KNEE (1890) took place. The southwest was the final area of warfare, and while prominent Apache leaders, including COCHISE, Victorio, and GERONIMO, mounted determined resistance, the Apaches were eventually subdued by the U.S. Army.

NATO |ˈnātō| • *abbr.* North Atlantic Treaty Organization.

NATO airspace • the airspace above any NATO nation and its territorial waters.

NATO commander • a military commander in the NATO chain of command. Also called ALLIED COMMANDER.

NATO Defense College • an advanced international school for military and civilian personnel of NATO and NATO Partner for Peace countries, in Rome, Italy. Proposed by Gen. DWIGHT D. EISENHOWER and approved by the NORTH ATLANTIC COUNCIL, it was established in 1951 in Paris, France, and has been in Rome since 1966. Students receive instruction in global and regional security issues. The school's six month Senior Course prepares students for NATO and NATO-related appointments.

Nat Turner's Rebellion • see TURNER, NAT.

nautical almanac • a yearbook containing astronomical and sometimes also tidal and other information for navigators.

nautical mile • a measure of distance equal to one minute of arc on the earth's surface. The United States has adopted the international nautical mile equal to 1,852 meters.

***Nautilus*, USS** • (**SSN-571**) the first nuclear submarine ever built. The keel was laid on June 14, 1952, at Groton, Connecticut, the *Nautilus* was launched on January 21, 1954, and, on September 30, 1954, the submarine was commissioned into the U.S. Navy.

Probably the most famous submarine in history, the *Nautilus* was also the first submarine to cross under the North Pole, on August 3, 1958; and it set many endurance records for submerged operations. On March 30, 1980, the *Nautilus* was decommissioned, and, on May 20, 1982, declared a National Historic Landmark.

Navaho • (**SM-64A**) an early intercontinental ballistic missile, developed after WORLD WAR II and capable of carrying a nuclear warhead. None were ever used defensively but extensive testing in the 1950s led to the development of better ICBMs.

navaid |ˈnævˌād| • *n.* a navigational device in an aircraft, ship, or other vehicle.
ORIGIN: 1950s: from *navigational aid.*

Navajo Code Talkers • U.S. military personnel of the Navajo tribe used in WORLD WAR II, principally in the Pacific theater, to make and receive voice radio transmissions in the Navajo language during combat. The difficult Navajo tongue could not be understood by Japanese radio intercept personnel and thus provided a secure means of communicating information on the battlefield.

Naval Academy • (also known as **Annapolis**) an undergraduate navy and marine corps service school at Annapolis, Maryland. Established by GEORGE BANCROFT in 1845 when the Philadelphia Naval Asylum School was moved to Annapolis, it received its current name in 1850. The intensive four-year curriculum includes academic course work, professional training, and a practice cruise. Candidates are appointed by political nomination. Female cadets were first admitted in 1976.

Naval Advanced Logistics Support Base • an overseas site responsible for handling the transfer of troops and equipment from one conveyance to another in a theater of operations. Such a site has ample storage, consolidation, and transfer capacities, as well as responsibility for supporting forward-deployed units during major contingency and wartime periods.

Naval Affairs Committee • a committee created in 1822 to address all matters related to the naval establishment and its maintenance. In 1885 the committee's jurisdiction was expanded to cover all legislation relating to the naval establishment, including naval appropriations bills, but this responsibility was returned to the Appropriations Committee in 1920. Under the Legislative Reorganization Act of 1946, it was merged with the committee on MILITARY AFFAIRS to create the ARMED SERVICES COMMITTEE.

Naval Air Systems Command • an agency of the DEPARTMENT OF DEFENSE that trains U.S. Navy reservists to fill the reserve element of the Naval Aviation Systems Team's "total force" structure during a national emergency or other crisis. One of its tasks is to assist private industry in shifting from peacetime to wartime production.

Naval Amphibious Base Little Creek • first developed during WORLD WAR II, and located near Norfolk, Virginia, this base was established under its current name on August 10, 1945, and was designated a permanent installation in 1946. It is the focal point for U.S. Navy/Marine Corps amphibious training and operations on the East Coast of the United States. Actually encompassing some 12,000 acres at four locations in three states, Little Creek is the major operating base for the amphibious forces of the U. S. Atlantic Fleet. It provides support services for over 15,000 personnel of the twenty-seven ships home-ported at Little Creek and some seventy-eight resident and/or supported activities. It is the largest base of its kind in the world.

naval architecture • the designing of ships.

naval auxiliaries • **1** naval support vessels, such as oilers, coalers, hospital ships, and tugs. **2** personnel or units—such as the Sea Scouts, private yachting associations, and the like—intended to augment standing naval forces.

naval base • a base primarily for the support of the forces afloat, contiguous to a port or anchorage, consisting of activities or facilities for which the navy has operating responsibilities, together with interior lines of communication and the minimum surrounding area necessary for local security. Typically, this is not greater than an area of 40 square miles.

naval campaign • an operation or a connected series of operations conducted essentially by naval forces, including all surface, subsurface, air, and amphibious troops, for the purpose of gaining, extending, or maintaining control of the sea.

Naval Consulting Board • WORLD WAR I–era U.S. Navy board comprised of civilian scientists and industrialist, chaired by Thomas A. Edison, the purpose of which was to assist the Navy in the application of new science and technology. It was generally a failure, having focused much of its effort on a dispute over the creation of a naval research laboratory.

Naval Expansion Act • an act of Congress in 1940 that increased the Navy's fleet by more than 1.3 million tons with provision for construction of new capital ships, aircraft carriers, cruisers, destroyers, and submarines, as well as the modernization of existing ships.

Naval Forces Europe • see U.S. NAVAL FORCES EUROPE.

Naval Forward Logistics Site • a naval support base, usually located ashore, that provides logistic support such as cargo and repair and maintenance services to naval expeditionary forces. It is built and dismantled as required by the movement and needs of the operation it assists. It is a local extension of an advanced logistic support site, which is also temporary but located farther from the operation.

Naval Gun Factory • see WASHINGTON NAVY YARD.

Naval Institute • a nonprofit membership society in Annapolis, Maryland. Established in 1873 by a group of naval officers at the U.S. NAVAL ACADEMY, it promotes knowledge of naval and military affairs through educational programs and publications by the Naval Institute Press.

Naval Lyceum • an officers' school established by MATTHEW C. PERRY in 1833 at the BROOKLYN NAVY YARD. It was a place for self-directed study and included a library, reading room, and lecture hall. Midshipmen typically received instruction at sea or on receiving ships at navy yards, and the Lyceum, opposed by many, provided an academic setting for instruction.

naval mine • a mine that is deployed in the water.

Naval Observatory • (**USNO**) one of the oldest scientific agencies in the United States, established in 1830 as the U.S. Navy Depot of Charts and Instruments, responsible for the Navy's chronometers, charts, and other navigational equipment. Over the years its mission expanded to include a full range of scientific astronomical research. Today the USNO is the preeminent authority on timekeeping and celestial observation and is responsible for supporting all U.S. Government agencies and the general public with astronomical and time data essential to navigation, communications, and other purposes. The official residence of the Vice President of the United States is located on the Observatory grounds.

naval operation • **1** a naval action, or the performance of a naval mission, which may be strategic, operational, tactical, logistic, or training. **2** the process of carrying on or training for naval combat to gain the objectives of any battle or campaign.

Naval Overseas Transportation Service • established in 1918 and responsible for transporting troops, supplies, and equipment during WORLD WAR I.

Naval Postgraduate School • a postgraduate technical service school in Monterey, California. Tracing its history back to 1909, when it was established as a school of marine engineering at the U.S. NAVAL ACADEMY at Annapolis, it became the Postgraduate Department of the NAVAL ACADEMY in 1912. It gained full accreditation in 1945 and relocated to Monterey in 1951.

Naval Research Laboratory • (**NRL**) commissioned by the U.S. Congress in 1923 and responsible for a program of scientific research and advanced technological development, including maritime applications for new and improved materials, techniques, equipment, system, and ocean, atmospheric, and space sciences.

Naval Research Vessel • (**NR-1**) a compact nuclear-powered undersea research and ocean engineering submarine capable of finding and identifying ships or other objects lost at sea and recording topographic and geological features of the ocean floor.

Naval Reserve • an organization of the U.S. Navy responsible for preparing and training a reserve naval force to augment the active duty forces in times of war or crisis.

Naval Reserve Cargo Handling Battalion • see NAVY CARGO HANDLING BATTALION.

Naval Reserve Cargo Handling Training Battalion • see NAVY CARGO HANDLING BATTALION.

Naval Sea Systems Command • (**NAVSEA**) the largest of the Navy's five systems commands, its engineers build and support U.S. ships and combat systems, and serve in four shipyards, in undersea and surface warfare centers, and at major shipbuilding sites. Its headquarters is at Crystal City, Arlington, Virginia.

Naval Space Command • (**NAVSPACECOM**) an organization for coordinating U.S. Navy space-related systems, established in 1983 at the Naval Surface Warfare Center in Dahlgren, Virginia. Naval Space Command develops and operates space technology such as satellites for use in shipboard communications, meteorology, and reconnaissance.

Naval Special Warfare Command • commissioned in April 1987, the Navy's component of the U.S. SPECIAL OPERATIONS COMMAND. It is responsible for preparing naval special warfare forces to successfully execute assigned missions and to develop special operations tactics, strategy, and doctrine.

naval stores • any articles or commodities used by a naval ship or station, such as equipment, consumable supplies, clothing, petroleum, oils, and lubricants, medical supplies, and ammunition.

Naval Submarine Base New London • see ADVANCE BASE SCHOOL.

naval tactics • doctrine and methods for the combat employment of naval vessels at sea.

Naval Transportation Service • one of the four U.S. armed forces responsible for transporting troops, supplies, and equipment during WORLD WAR II. In 1949, it was subsumed by the MILITARY SEA TRANSPORTATION SERVICE, which put sealift operations under a single manager, the SECRETARY OF THE NAVY.

Naval War College • the senior professional school of the U.S. Navy. It was founded in 1884 and is located on Coaster's Harbor Island, off Newport, Rhode Island. It is renowned for pioneering techniques of war gaming as a pedagogic and strategic tool.

NAVCHAPGRU • *abbr.* Navy Cargo Handling and Port Group.

navigable • *adj.* (of a waterway or sea) able to be sailed on by ships or boats.
DERIVATIVES: **navigability** *n.*

navigation • *n.* **1** the process or activity of accurately ascertaining one's position and planning and following a route. **2** the passage of ships.
DERIVATIVES: **navigational** *adj.*

navigation head • a transshipment point on a waterway where loads are transferred between water carriers and land carriers.

navigation lights • a set of lights shown by a ship or aircraft at night to indicate its position and orientation.

Navigation Satellite Tracking and Ranging/Global Positioning System • (**NAVSTAR/GPS**) a space-based radio navigation system operated jointly by the U.S. Army, Navy, and Air Force to provide U.S. and allied military forces with concise, continuous, all-weather, common-grid, three-dimensional, world-positioning and navigation, and time reference information on land, sea, and in the air. The NAVSTAR/GPS is accurate to within about 50 feet as to position and to within one second every 300,000 years as to time.

navigator • *n.* **1** a person who directs the route or course of a ship, aircraft, or other form of transportation, especially by using instruments and maps. **2** an instrument or device that assists in directing the course of a vessel or aircraft.

NAVSEA • *abbr.* Naval Sea Systems Command

NAVSPACECOM • *abbr.* Naval Space Command.

NAVSTAR/GPS • *abbr.* Navigation Satellite Tracking and Ranging/Global Positioning System.

navy • *n.* (pl. **-ies**) **1** (often **the navy** or **the Navy**) the branch of a nation's armed services that conducts military operations at sea. **2** the ships of a navy: *a 600-ship navy.*

Navy and Marine Corps Medal • U.S. military decoration awarded for "heroism not involving actual conflict with an armed enemy." Established in August 1942, the Navy and Marine Corps Medal may be awarded to any person serving with the U.S. Navy or the U.S. Marine Corps and is the equivalent of the Army's Soldier's Medal.

Navy Bureau of Aeronautics • established in 1921 and staffed by officers of the Construction Corps, engineering duty officers, and line officers. It was the predecessor of the NAVAL AIR SYSTEMS COMMAND.

Navy Bureau of Ordnance • the U.S. Navy agency responsible for procuring, maintaining, and issuing weapons, ammunition, and combat vehicles until it was merged with the NAVY BUREAU OF AERONAUTICS to form the NAVY BUREAU OF WEAPONS in 1959.

Navy Bureau of Weapons • an agency of the U.S. Navy formed by the merger of the NAVY BUREAU OF AERONAUTICS and the NAVY BUREAU OF ORDNANCE in 1959, and responsible for procuring, maintaining, and issuing weapons, ammunition, and combat vehicles until 1966, when the four material bureaus split into six functional systems commands.

Navy Cargo Handling and Port Group • see NAVY CARGO HANDLING BATTALION.

Navy Cargo Handling Battalion • (**CHB**) a mobile support unit that handles the acquisition, distribution, maintenance, and replacement of materiel and personnel that can be deployed worldwide in its entirety or in specialized units. This battalion is organized, trained, and equipped to load and unload Navy and Marine Corps cargo from maritime prepositioning ships, merchant ships, and from aircraft controlled by the military in all environments and to operate a temporary ocean or air cargo terminal in connection with such cargo. Navy Cargo Handling Battalions can come from three sources: (1) the Navy Cargo Handling and Port Group, a battalion-sized unit of active duty personnel (also called NAVCHAPGRU); (2) the Naval Reserve Cargo Handling Training Battalion, a cargo handling training battalion containing both active and reserve personnel (also called NRCHTB); (3) the Naval Reserve Cargo Handling Battalion, a cargo handling battalion made up solely of selected reserve personnel (also called NRCHB). See also MARITIME PREPOSITIONING SHIPS.

Navy Cross • U.S. military decoration awarded for valor in combat against an armed enemy of the United States. Established on February 4, 1919, the Navy Cross may be awarded to personnel serving with the U.S. Navy or U.S. Marine Corps. The Navy Cross is the equivalent of the DISTINGUISHED SERVICE CROSS.

Navy, Department of the • the executive component of the U.S. Navy, having, under its command, the U.S. Marine Corps; all the active and reserve forces of the Navy, including aviation, and the Marine Corps; all field activities, headquarters, bases, installations, and functions controlled by the secretary of the Navy, and, as well, the U.S. Coast Guard when it functions as part of the Navy.

Navy League • a civilian organization founded in 1902 to support the members of the sea services and to educate the general public about the U.S. Navy, Marine Corps, Coast Guard, and Merchant Marines. Its motto is "Only with power at sea can America survive."

Navy List • **1** a list of officers in the U.S. or British Navy, arranged by rank and date of rank. **2** a list of ships in the U.S. Navy

Navy Nurse Corps • see NURSING CORPS.

Navy SEALs • see SEALS.

Navy Supply Corps School • a school for logistical training in supply, transportation, and maintenance for the DEPARTMENT OF DEFENSE. It was established in 1921 in Washington, D.C., and has been located in Athens, Georgia, since 1954.

Navy, U.S. • the part of the U.S. armed forces with primary responsibility for defending the nation at sea. Since WORLD WAR II, the Navy has been the most powerful in the world. A part of the DEPARTMENT OF DEFENSE, the Navy is headed by a secretary of the navy. It includes the U.S. Marine Corps, and, in wartime, the U.S. Coast Guard.

The **Continental Navy** was established in 1775, lasting until 1784. The permanent Navy was reconstituted in 1798 to fight the BARBARY WARS.

---

navy yard • a shipyard for the construction, repair, and equipping of naval vessels.

Nazi • a member of the NATIONAL SOCIALIST GERMAN WORKERS' PARTY (NSDAP), ADOLF HITLER's political party. • *adj.* of or about the National Socialist German Workers' Party (NSDAP).

ORIGIN: a contraction of the first word of the *Nationalsozialistische Deutsche Arbeiterpartei.*

Nazi-Soviet Pact of 1939 • (**German-Soviet Treaty of Non-Aggression**) a treaty of August 23, 1939, in which ADOLF HITLER's Germany and JOSEF STALIN's Soviet Union pledged friendship and cooperation as well as to refrain from aggression against each other. The secret protocols of the treaty provided for spheres of influence in Eastern Europe and a pledge by each signatory not to interfere should the other choose to invade and conquer one or more of the states assigned to its influence. The Nazi-Soviet Pact appears to have had two major outcomes: it effectively neutralized the Soviet Union long enough for Germany to attack and defeat Poland, Czechoslovakia, Norway, France, and the Low Countries, and it lulled Stalin into complacency and led to his failure to prepare the Soviet Union for the war with NAZI Germany which began in 1941.

NBC defense • nuclear defense, biological defense, and chemical defense collectively.

NBS-1 • see Martin NBS-1.

NCA • *abbr.* National Command Authorities.

NCO • *abbr.* noncommissioned officer.

NCOA • *abbr.* Non Commissioned Officers Association.

NCS • *abbr.* National Communications System.

NDA • *abbr.* national defense area.

NDDS • *abbr.* Nuclear Detonation Detection System.

neap |nēp| • *n.* (usually **neap tide**) a tide just after the first or third quarters of the moon when there is the least difference between high and low water. • *v.* (**be neaped**) (of a boat) be kept aground or in harbor by a neap tide.

near miss • any circumstance in flight where the degree of separation between two aircraft is considered by either pilot to have constituted a hazardous situation involving potential risk of collision.

near real time • a designation that pertains to the timeliness of data or information that has been delayed by the time required for electronic communication and automatic data processing. This implies that there are no significant delays.

needle |ˈnēdl| • *n.* a steel pin that explodes the cartridge of a breech-loading gun.

negative peace • the condition characterized by the absence of war and "direct" violence.

ORIGIN: coined by Norwegian peace scholar Johan Galtung.

negligible nuclear risk • a degree of nuclear risk where personnel are reasonably safe, with the exceptions of dazzle or temporary loss of night vision.

negotiate • *v.* **1** try to reach an agreement or compromise by discussion with others: *his government's willingness to negotiate.* **2** obtain or bring about by negotiating.

DERIVATIVES: **negotiator** *n.*

Nelson, Viscount Horatio • (1758–1805) foremost British admiral throughout the French Revolutionary War and in the early stages of the Napoleonic War. Among many illustrious victories, he commanded the battle that virtually annihilated the combined French and Spanish fleet off Cape Trafalgar in a single day's fighting in 1805. He lost his right arm and vision of his right eye in the line of duty. He is buried in St. Paul's cathedral and a statue of him sits atop Nelson's Column in Trafalgar Square, London.

Nelson, William (1824–62) • career naval officer, born in Maysville, Kentucky. He fought with the Union army in the CIVIL WAR. At the request of President ABRAHAM LINCOLN, Nelson raised a Kentucky volunteer regiment. He later commanded a division at SHILOH (1862) and CORINTH, Mississippi (1862), before his forces were nearly annihilated at RICHMOND, Kentucky (1862). Following the last battle, Nelson repaired to a Louisville hotel where he became engaged in an altercation with Union Gen. JEFFERSON DAVIS. Insults and challenges were exchanged, with the result that Davis shot Nelson, mortally wounding him. Davis was never brought to trial. During the MEXICAN WAR (1846–48) Nelson was with the fleet that supported Gen. WINFIELD SCOTT's landing at VERACRUZ (1847).

Neptune aspirin • slang a depth bomb; a steel container loaded with a high explosive charge and dropped from a ship, helicopter, or aircraft on an underwater target, such as a submarine, in WORLD WAR II.

nerve agent • a potentially lethal chemical agent that interferes with the transmission of nerve impulses.

nerve gas • a chemical weapon that interferes with the transmission of nerve impulses and particularly impairs respiration. Most types of nerve gas are derivatives of phosphoric acid.

net sweep • in naval mine warfare, a two-ship sweep, using a netlike device, designed to collect drifting mines or scoop them up from the sea bottom.

Neumann, John Louis von (1903–57) • American mathematician, computer pioneer, and founder of GAME THEORY, born in Budapest, Hungary. As WORLD WAR II approached, von Neumann, then at Princeton, began focusing his study on ballistics, explosives, and shock wave dynamics. He was one of the scientists on the MANHATTAN PROJECT who perfected the implosion trigger for an atomic bomb. At the same time he began promoting the use of computers, which were then primitive, for military and scientific research. After the war von Neumann served on the ATOMIC ENERGY COMMISSION and advocated the development of the hydrogen bomb and the first U.S. intercontinental missiles. Von Neumann was the recipient of the U.S. Navy Distinguished Civilian Service Award (1947) and two presidential awards, the Medal of Merit (1947) and the Medal of Freedom (1956). He was a member of numerous academies and learned societies both in the United States and abroad.

neutral • *adj.* **1** not helping or supporting either of two opposing sides, especially countries at war; impartial: *during the World War II Portugal was neutral.* **2** belonging to an impartial party, country, or group: *on neutral ground.* **3** unbiased; disinterested: *neutral, expert scientific advice.* • *n.* **1** an impartial and uninvolved country or person: *Sweden and its fellow neutrals.* **2** an unbiased person. **3** a disengaged position of gears in which the engine is disconnected from the driven parts: *she slipped the gear into neutral.*

DERIVATIVES: **neutrally** *adv.*

neutrality • *n.* in international law, the attitude of impartiality, during periods of war, adopted by third states toward a belligerent and recognized by the belligerent, which creates rights and duties between the impartial states and the belligerent. In a U.N. enforcement action, the rules of neutrality apply to impartial members of the United Nations, except so far as they are excluded by the obligation of such members under the UNITED NATIONS CHARTER.

Neutrality Acts • a series of acts passed in 1935, 1936, 1937, and 1939 to limit U.S. involvement in possible future wars and that was created in response to the belief that U.S. involvement in WORLD WAR I resulted from loans and trade with the ALLIES. The 1935 act banned the shipment of war materials to belligerents and forbade U.S. citizens to travel on belligerent vessels. The 1936 act banned loans to belligerents. The 1937 act extended these provisions to civil wars and allowed the president to restrict nonmunitions sales to a "cash-and-carry" basis. The 1939 act banned U.S. ships from carrying goods or passengers to belligerent ports but allowed U.S. sales of munitions on a "cash-and carry" basis. The LEND-LEASE ACT OF 1941 diminished the laws, and they were repealed on November 13, 1941.

neutron bomb • a nuclear weapon that produces large numbers of neutrons rather than heat or blast like conventional nuclear weapons.

Neville, Wendell Cushing (1870–1930) • Marine Corps commandant (1929–30), born in Portsmouth, Virginia. Neville achieved a reputation for forceful and decisive leadership on the western front during WORLD WAR I. He led his brigade in the ST. MIHIEL and MEUSE-ARGONNE offensives (1918), receiving multiple citations, among them both the army and navy DISTINGUISHED SERVICE MEDALS. He had previously seen action early in the SPANISH-AMERICAN WAR (1998), during the CHINA RELIEF EXPEDITION (1900), and during the Cuban rebellion (1906). He received the MEDAL OF HONOR for his actions at VERACRUZ during the 1913–14 conflict with Mexico.

newbuilding • *n.* **1** (also **newbuild**) a newly constructed ship. **2** the construction of ships.

Newburgh Conspiracy • a still somewhat murky affair in 1783 that illustrated GEORGE WASHINGTON's leadership and a civil-military rift. During almost sixteen months of relative military inactivity since YORKTOWN (1781), soldiers groused about poor pay and miserable conditions, while Congress grew increasingly, and probably exaggeratedly, fearful of a standing army. On March 15, Washington called a meeting in Newburgh, New York, in which he reasserted to his troops the principle of civilian control over the military. What degree of conspiracy there may have hitherto been promptly collapsed.

New Guinea Campaign • (1942–44) an attack on Port Moresby by the Japanese in an attempt to isolate Australia. The attack began in the summer of 1942, when the Japanese were secure on the island's northern coast, in Buna. The Australians rebuffed that attack, and by January 1943, American forces defeated the Japanese at Buna. Gen. DOUGLAS MACARTHUR, head of the SOUTHWEST PACIFIC AREA, subsequently created the 6th U.S. Army, under the efficient command of Lt. Gen. WALTER KRUEGER, which captured the northern coast by the fall of 1944.

New London • a city and port on Long Island Sound at the mouth of the Thames River in southeastern Connecticut. Incorporated in

1784, it has one of the deepest harbors on the Atlantic Coast. It is a U.S. naval station and submarine base and the location of the U.S. Coast Guard Academy and the U.S. Submarine Officers' School.

In 1781, during the Revolutionary War, it was burned by the British under the direction of Benedict Arnold.

New Look • a policy of President Dwight D. Eisenhower, consisting of four parts: reliance on the threat of massive nuclear retaliation to fight communism; liberation from communism for Eastern Europe; use of covert operations by the CIA in Third World countries; and the creation of non-communist alliances such as SEATO and NATO to surround the Soviet Union and China.
origin: from the name of a new post–World War II Paris fashion by Christian Dior.

New Market, Battle of • a successful attack on May 15, 1864, by an outnumbered, makeshift Confederate army, under Maj. Gen. John C. Breckinridge, on Maj. Gen. Franz Sigel's troops on their way to blow up the railroad and canal at Lynchburg. Sigel's forces retreated down the Shenandoah Valley to Strasburg, where Maj. Gen. David Hunter took over.

New Netherland • a Dutch colony stretching from New Amsterdam (New York City) to Fort Orange (Albany, New York). Founded in 1624 at Fort Orange by the Dutch West India Company, the colony was part of Dutch plans for further expansion in America. The English captured the colony in 1664, and it was renamed New York after James, Duke of York, brother of Charles II, and placed under the Duke's governance. The Dutch recaptured New York in 1673 and held it for over a year before losing it again to the English.

New Orleans, Battle of • (January 8, 1815) a largely symbolic but still significant engagement which ended the War of 1812. On December 23, one day before the signing of the Treaty of Ghent, Gen. Andrew Jackson, commanding a force made up of army regulars, New Orleans's free blacks, three state militias, and the pirates of Barataria, tried to fend off the British. The British, who were trying to relieve military pressure on Canada and improve their status during peace negotiations, attacked on January 8. American artillery shelled the British, who suffered 2,400 casualties, while the Americans lost only seventy men.

New Orleans Greys • two companies of volunteers from New Orleans that fought in the Texas War of Independence. Organized in 1835 and led by Adolphus Sterne, the Greys fought in the siege of Béxar (1835), and many died at the Alamo (1836).

New Orleans, Siege of • on April 18, 1862, a Union fleet, under the command of Capt. David Farragut, along with soldiers led by Maj. Gen. Benjamin Butler, launched an attack on the enemy's undersized fleet and depleted garrisons. Farragut captured the city on April 25, and three days later, civilian authorities surrendered and Confederate forces evacuated. Butler occupied the city on May 1, thus giving the Union control of the Lower Mississippi. A Confederate court of inquiry blamed Jefferson Davis's administration for having critically misread signs of the impending Union assault in early April.

Newport, Battle of • a bungled attempt in 1778 to drive out the British, who had occupied Newport since December 1776. French Admiral Comte d'Estaing and American Gen. John Sullivan were supposed to coordinate an attack, but the distrust between the two, the unanticipated size and power of the British fleet, and heavy seas combined to stifle the campaign. Sullivan attacked on August 14, but he settled for a defensive siege, and when Estaing's help did not arrive, he retreated, just before British reinforcements arrived. The British remained in Newport until October 1779.

Newport, Christopher (1561–1617) • English privateer and sea captain who commanded the Virginia Company's first fleet (1606) and was a member of the first council that chose Jamestown for the settlement. Newport made numerous voyages back and forth from Jamestown to England, on one of which he brought Thomas Gates. After his final return to England (1612), Newport sailed for the East India Company.

Though its precise origin is obscure, it is generally believed that Newport News, Virginia, owes its name to the English sea captain (and to Sir William Newce, who arrived from Ireland in 1621).

Newton, John (1822–95) • army officer and military engineer, born in Norfolk, Virginia. Newton was chief of engineers from 1884 to 1886. Although Newton saw active service during the Civil War, his record as a leader of troops was uneven and he gained his greatest distinction as an engineer. He resigned from the army in 1886 to become commissioner of public works for New York City. During the Civil War Newton had participated in the Peninsular and Maryland campaigns (1862) and the Chancellorsville campaign (1863) before commanding a corps at Gettysburg (1863) and leading a division through the Atlanta campaign (1864). Early in the war he worked as assistant engineer in the construction of the defenses of Washington, D.C. (1861). His only field service prior to the Civil War was as chief engineer of the Mormon Expedition (1858).

New York, Battle of • a critical British victory in 1776, which, had it been fully realized, might have seriously crippled the rebels. As it was, the Americans, under George Washington's command, committed mistakes and suffered significant losses. The British sent their largest force yet—40,000 soldiers and sailors under brothers Gen. William Howe and Adm. Richard Howe—to reestablish Royal authority and regain a harbor, of which both they had neither between New Hampshire and Georgia. After landing on fortless

Staten Island on July 2, Gen. Howe, using the same strategy he had unsuccessfully employed at BUNKER HILL, routed the Americans out of their Long Island earthworks, forcing them to retreat to Manhattan by late August and then to Westchester County on November 16, as the last American position on the island, Fort Washington, fell.

Nez Percé • a North American Indian tribe of Shahaptian located in Idaho, Oregon, and Washington. In 1877, the Nez Percé, led by the great CHIEF JOSEPH, engaged the U.S. Army in a series of running battles as they sought refuge in Canada. At last forced to surrender at Bear Paw Mountain, the Nez Percé were confined in the INDIAN TERRITORY (Oklahoma) until 1885 when they were allowed to go to a reservation in Washington.

Nguyen Van Thieu (1923–) • president of the Republic of Vietnam (South Vietnam) (1967–75). Thieu played a significant part in the 1963 coup against NGO DINH DIEM and held various government offices before being elected president in 1967 and again in 1971. Throughout the period of escalation of the VIETNAM WAR, the United States supported his authoritarian regime. Thieu, who had participated only reluctantly in the 1973 peace agreements, held onto power and resigned only when communist troops from North Vietnam surrounded the southern capital. He left the country shortly afterward and eventually settled in England.

Nha Trang • a city in southeastern Vietnam on the South China Sea coast that was the site of a U.S. military base during the VIETNAM WAR.

Niagara, Operation • launched on February 21, 1968, during the seventy-eight-day siege of KHE SANH, a bombing campaign that supported the South Vietnamese Rangers at the main base. It is still unclear whether Gen. WILLIAM C. WESTMORELAND's operation thwarted the anticipated North Vietnamese attack or if the attack was ever even planned. On the whole, the high concentration of U.S. divisions at Khe Sanh helped Hanoi concentrate its own forces for the TET OFFENSIVE.

Nicaragua |nikəˈrägwə| • the largest country in Central America, with a coastline on both the Atlantic and the Pacific Ocean; capital, Managua. Colonized by the Spaniards, Nicaragua broke away from Spain in 1821 and, after brief membership of the United Provinces of Central America, became an independent republic in 1838. In 1979 the dictator Anastasio Somoza was overthrown by a popular revolution; the new left-wing Sandinista regime then faced a counterrevolutionary guerilla campaign by the U.S.-backed CONTRAS. (See IRAN-CONTRA AFFAIR.) In the 1990 election the Sandinistas lost power to an opposition coalition.

DERIVATIVES: **Nicaraguan** *adj. & n.*

Nicholson, Francis (1655–1728) • first royal governor of South Carolina (1720–25), born in Yorkshire, England. Nicholson had previously served in a variety of capacities as both an administrative and military representative of royal authority, among them lieutenant governor of New York (1688–89), lieutenant governor of Virginia (1690–92), governor of Maryland (1694–98), and captain general and governor in chief of Virginia (1698–1705). In nearly all of these positions he alienated the colonists, whom he considered provincial and incapable of ruling themselves. Nicholson also served as governor of Nova Scotia (1712–14), which he had reconquered for Britain (1710). Early in his military career he had served in America with SIR EDMUND ANDROS (1686–87).

Nicholson, James (c. 1736–1804) • captain in the Continental navy, born in Chestertown, Maryland. Nicholson failed to capture or defeat a single enemy ship throughout the REVOLUTIONARY WAR. The *Trumbull* fought a fierce battle with the HMS *Watt,* but neither emerged victorious. Nicholson was later forced to surrender the *Trumbull* (1781).

Nicholson, James William Augustus (1821–87) • career naval officer, born in Dedham, Massachusetts. During the CIVIL WAR, Nicholson commanded the steamer *Isaac Smith* in the South Atlantic Blockading Squadron, participating in the capture of Port Royal Sound (1861) and the seizure of Jacksonville and ST. AUGUSTINE (1862). While in command of the monitor *Manhattan,* Nicholson participated in the assault on MOBILE BAY (1864) under DAVID FARRAGUT, engaging in a duel with the Confederate ironclad ram *Tennessee* and successfully penetrating its armor plating.

Nicolls, Richard (1624–72) • first English governor of the province of New York (1664–68), born at Ampthill, Bedfordshire, England. When Charles II laid claim to the Dutch colony of New Netherland, he gave it to his brother, the duke of York, who sent Nicolls to be its governor. Nicolls gradually introduced English laws and institutions. His administration was seen as efficient and fair by Dutch as well as English settlers.

Nicolls renamed both the colony (New Netherland) and its chief city (New Amsterdam) in honor of his patron, the duke of York.

---

night fighter • a fighter aircraft guided by ground personnel (during WORLD WAR I), assisted by ground radar (during WORLD WAR II), but neither practical nor entirely effective until equipped with a radar compact enough to be borne aloft by the fighter.

Nighthawk • (**F-117**) a stealth attack jet aircraft with a triangular shape, a flat angled fuselage, and wing panels that direct radar reflections in a few specific directions. Because of the computer controls, it is an easy aircraft to pilot. It can carry out precision attacks on point targets, but carries only limited weapons. During the PERSIAN GULF WAR, F-117s flew hundreds of missions in the bombing of Iraqi installations.

Its out-of-series designation has never been explained.

---

night ops • night operations or maneuvers.

night owl • slang a night bombing mission.

night vision • the faculty of seeing in very low light, especially after the eyes have become adapted. • (**night-vision**) denoting devices that enhance nighttime vision: *night-vision goggles.*

Nike missile • a class of missiles developed in the 1940s and 1950s for defense against ICBMs and deployed to fixed sights around the United States and abroad in NATO countries. Models included the Nike HERCULES, Nike Ajax, and NIKE ZEUS. They became largely obsolete by the 1970s as ICBMs became more sophisticated. The Nike missile program was terminated in 1974.

Nike Zeus missile • a surface-to-air missile designed to intercept and destroy ICBMs. It was first developed in the 1950s, and later versions were capable of intercepting targets outside the atmosphere. It was a predecessor of the SENTINEL and the SPARTAN missiles.

Nimitz, Chester William (1885–1966) • five-star Fleet Admiral (1944), commander in chief of the Pacific Fleet (1941–45) Pacific Ocean Area (1942–45) during WORLD WAR II, born in Fredricksburg, Texas. As commander of all American and Allied sea, land, and air forces in the north, central, and south Pacific, Nimitz directed the American forces in the battles of the CORAL SEA and MIDWAY (1942) and in the reconquest of GUADALCANAL (1942–43), victories that turned the tide of the war. He also directed the battles of the PHILIPPINE SEA and LEYTE GULF (1944), which virtually eliminated the Japanese fleet. Nimitz then directed the invasions of IWO JIMA and OKINAWA (1945) and ordered the bombings and bombardments of Japan that preceded the Japanese capitulation. After the war Nimitz served two years as chief of naval operations (1945–47) before reaching the mandatory retirement age. During WORLD WAR I Nimitz, a diesel engine specialist, served as engineering aide and chief of staff to the commander of the U.S. Atlantic submarine flotilla.

niter (Brit. **nitre**) • *n.* another term for POTASSIUM NITRATE.

Nitze, Paul Henry (1907–) • government official and policymaker, born in Amherst, Massachusetts. His public career spanned fifty years. As director of the STATE DEPARTMENT's policy and planning staff (1950–53), Nitze was the principal writer of a NATIONAL SECURITY COUNCIL document that became the basic blueprint for the ensuing COLD WAR military buildup. As assistant secretary of defense for international security during the JOHN F. KENNEDY administration, he played a key role during the BERLIN WALL (1961) and CUBAN MISSILE (1962) crises. In the seventies and eighties Nitze focused on arms control and disarmament. He was a delegate to the first SALT talks (1969–73) but opposed SALT II (1979) because of concessions it granted the Russians. He helped negotiate the 1987 ban on U.S. and Soviet intermediate-range nuclear missiles.

Nixon, Richard Milhous (1913–94) • 37th president of the United States (1969-74), born in Yorba Linda, California. After serving in the navy in the South Pacific (1942–46), Nixon began his political career in the U.S. House of Representatives (1947–51), where he gained prominence as a member of the House Un-American Activities Committee during the investigation of ALGER HISS. He was elected to the Senate in 1950, but in 1952 he was tapped to be DWIGHT D. EISENHOWER's running mate on the Republican ticket. Nixon performed effectively during periods of Eisenhower's extended illnesses. Nominated to be his party's standard bearer in 1960, he lost an extremely close election to JOHN F. KENNEDY, after which he briefly retired to private life. In 1962 he ran unsuccessfully for governor of California. After this defeat he moved to New York where he practiced law, all the while working to shore up his reputation as a party healer and foreign policy specialist. Again nominated for president in 1968, he won in another close contest. As president, Nixon worked toward a policy of détente with the Soviet Union. He initiated arms control talks (1969), which led to the signing of SALT I (1972). He also made a historic visit to the People's Republic of China (1972), opening relations with that communist power. Many consider these his greatest achievements. He was less successful with concluding the VIETNAM WAR, as he had pledged to do during his campaign. He did authorize withdrawal of troops and undertake settlement negotiations that eventually led to a cease-fire, but only after he had ordered the bombing of CAMBODIA (1970) and LAOS (1971), fueling the already enflamed passions of the ever-increasing antiwar population. Before the WATERGATE scandal, Nixon's second administration was marked by worsening relations with the Arab states, leading to an oil embargo that adversely affected the American public. He did, however, end conscription in 1973, making the U.S. military an ALL-VOLUNTEER FORCE. Most of the focus of his truncated second term was on Watergate. After prolonged hearings, the House Judiciary Committee recommended impeachment (July 1974) on the grounds of obstruction of justice, abuse of power, and failure to comply with Congressional subpoenas. Faced with the certainty that the House would impeach, in August Nixon resigned, the first president to do so. He was granted an unconditional pardon by his successor GERALD R. FORD, who had been named vice president when Nixon's running mate Spiro T. Agnew had been forced to resign (1973) because of earlier scandals in his home state. After leaving the presidency Nixon slowly undertook his rehabilitation. He wrote several books and traveled extensively. At his death he was eulogized as an elder statesman esteemed for his expertise in foreign affairs, but in the public mind his stature remained sullied by the stigma of Watergate.

NKPA • *abbr.* North Korean People's Army.

NLF • *abbr.* National Liberation Front.

NMD • *abbr.* national missile defense.

Noemfoor, Battle of • a WORLD WAR II amphibious assault on an island off the northern coast of New Guinea on July 2, 1944. Along with several similar attacks in June and July, it paved the way for the U.S. invasion of the Philippines by that fall.

no-fire line • a line short of which artillery or ships do not fire except on request or approval of the supported commander, but beyond which they may fire at any time without danger to friendly troops.

Nolan, Philip (c. 1771–1801) • contraband trader, born in Belfast, Ireland. His exploits contributed toward opening Texas to Anglo-Americans. Nolan was not a politically motivated filibuster, however, but a monetarily motivated horse thief who captured wild mustangs and delivered them, at princely sums, to his stateside connections. On his first trips across the border, Nolan had a legitimate passport authorizing him to obtain horses for the Louisiana militia regiment, but Spanish authorities in Texas later revoked his permission to trade goods. Without a passport but determined to continue his pursuits, Nolan was intercepted on his next trip into Texas and killed by troops from Nacogdoches.

no-man's-land • (in WORLD WAR I) the area between the Allied and German front lines; any land between two opposing armies or fortified frontiers.

ORIGIN: Middle English: originally the name of a plot of ground lying outside the north wall of the city of London, the site of place of execution.

nom de guerre |ˌnäm də ˈger| • (pl. **noms de guerre** pronunc. same) an assumed name under which a person engages in combat or some other activity or enterprise.

ORIGIN: French, literally 'war name.'

nominal weapon • a nuclear weapon that produces a yield of approximately 20 kilotons.

non-aggression • *n.* the absence of the desire or intention to be aggressive, especially on the part of nations or governments; frequently used to characterize treaties, as in the NAZI-SOVIET PACT OF 1939.

nonbattle casualty • a person who is not a battle casualty, but who is lost to their organization by reason of disease or injury, including persons dying from disease or injury, or by reason of being missing where the absence does not appear to be voluntary or due to enemy action or to being interned.

nonbelligerent • *adj.* not aggressive or engaged in a war or conflict. • *n.* a nation or person that is not engaged in a war or conflict.

DERIVATIVES: **nonbelligerence** *n.*

nonclassified • *adj.* (of information or documents) not designated as officially secret; freely available (tending to be less forceful in meaning than **unclassified**).

noncom |ˈnänˌkäm| • *n.* informal a noncommissioned officer.

noncombatant • *n.* a person who is not engaged in fighting during a war, especially a civilian, chaplain, or medical practitioner.

noncommissioned • *adj.* (of an officer in the armed forces) ranking below warrant officer, as sergeant or petty officer.

Noncommissioned Officers Academy • an army training school at the U.S. Army ARMOR CENTER in FORT KNOX, Kentucky. Established provisionally in 1959 and permanently in 1966, it currently has a program of leadership and technical training that resulted from the 1975 redevelopment of the NCO Education System, which was originally implemented in 1971. It established the Drill Sergeant School in 1964.

Non Commissioned Officers Association • (**NCOA**) a nonprofit organization founded in 1960 to provide support and lobbying for enlisted service members of the U.S. Army, Marines, Navy, Air Force, Coast Guard, NATIONAL GUARD, and Reserves, as well as for their families. Programs include veterans' services, scholarships, and emergency assistance. The group's motto is "Strength in Unity."

Non-Importation Act of 1806 • an act passed by Congress on March 25, 1806, before the WAR OF 1812, to ban certain imports from Britain. It was an attempt to counter British violations of neutrality and to compel Britain to accept American demands. Upon approval, use of the act was suspended until November 15 to allow for a British response to the threat of losing its American market.

In 1807 THOMAS JEFFERSON implemented the act along with an embargo when Britain attacked the USS *Chesapeake.*

Non-Intercourse Act • a restriction passed by Congress on March 1, 1809, before the WAR OF 1812, to forbid direct American trade with European belligerents and in response to British control of American trade. It was used as a coercive measure to deprive France and England of the American commercial market until they resolved their economic warfare and returned to neutral trade policies.

nonnuclear • *adj.* **1** not involving or relating to nuclear energy or nuclear weapons. **2** (of a country) not possessing nuclear weapons.

nonprogram aircraft • aircraft, excluding those in the active or reserve categories, in the total aircraft inventory, including X-models, that are no longer used either in the active or reserve category, and those that are in the process of being dropped from the total aircraft inventory.

nonproliferation • *n.* the prevention of an increase or spread of something, especially the number of countries possessing nuclear weapons: *a nuclear nonproliferation treaty.*

nonviolence • *n.* the use of peaceful means, not force, to bring about political or social change.

NORAD • *abbr.* North American Aerospace Defense Command.

Nordenfelt gun • an early machine gun that was developed in the late 19th century. It had from one to five breech-loaded, horizontally aligned barrels that fired in succession.

Nord SS-10 missile • a French-made antitank guided missile that was developed in the

1950s. It was also used by U.S. forces and designated MGM-21 in 1962.

Norfolk • a city in southeastern Virginia on the Elizabeth River. Together with Portsmouth and Newport it makes up the Port of Hampton Roads, a superb natural harbor. The headquarters of the 5th Naval District, the Atlantic Fleet, the Second Fleet, and the Supreme Allied Command are here, as the naval complex extending from Norfolk to Portsmouth has the largest operating base in the United States.

Norfolk Navy Yard • see GOSPORT NAVY YARD.

Norfolk suit • WORLD WAR I era woman's uniform.

Noriega, Manuel (1936–) • Panamanian general and de facto head of state (1983–89). Although he was a dictatorial ruler and suspected of collusion with drug lords, the United States supported Noriega, a one-time operative for the CENTRAL INTELLIGENCE AGENCY, in return for his help against the counterrevolutionary CONTRAS in Nicaragua. When his was no longer needed and Noriega's involvement in drug trafficking became apparent, U.S. officials urged him to step down but he refused. When a U.S. marine was murdered in Panama City, President GEORGE H. BUSH ordered troops to Panama (1989). Noriega was brought to the United States, where he was tried, convicted on charges related to drug trafficking (1992), and sentenced to forty years in prison.

normalize • *v.* bring or return to a normal condition or state: *Vietnam and China agreed to normalize diplomatic relations in 1991.*
DERIVATIVES: **normalization** *n.* **normalizer** *n.*

Normandy, Invasion of • nearly three years in the making, on June 6, 1944, this decisive campaign opened the long-awaited second front in World War II. Codenamed OPERATION OVERLORD, the invasion was led by Supreme Allied Commander DWIGHT D. EISENHOWER, with ground forces led by British Gen. BERNARD LAW MONTGOMERY, and air support led by British Air Chief Marshal Sir Arthur Tedder. Field Marshal ERWIN ROMMEL was convinced—by a wood-figure army and inflatable rubber tanks—that the ALLIES would attack at Calais, the most direct route to Germany. This belief was reinforced by the initial ineffectiveness of the airborne D-DAY attack that began early morning on June 6. The seaborne landing at UTAH BEACH proceeded quickly and with few casualties, while at OMAHA BEACH, Lt. Gen. OMAR N. BRADLEY's army battled heavy seas and nearly aborted. Still, by the end of the day, 130,000 troops had landed safely, and in the next three weeks, they expanded the beachhead and built airfields to allow roughly 900,000 more men and requisite supplies to reach northern France. Though the aim of rebuilding the nearly annihilated port of CHERBOURG was delayed for months, the successful lodgment in Normandy set the stage for the ST. LÔ breakout in late July and greatly hastened German surrender.

Norstad, Lauris |ˈnôrstæd; -städ| (1907–88) • air force officer, born in Minneapolis, Minnesota. Norstad was the supreme allied commander in Europe from 1956 to 1963. Norstad first achieved distinction during WORLD WAR II, when his abilities were recognized and tapped by Gens. HENRY H. "HAP" ARNOLD and DWIGHT D. EISENHOWER. Norstad helped plan the NORTH AFRICAN air campaign and later became director of operations of the Mediterranean Allied Air Forces (1943), helping plan bombing missions against AXIS forces and installations in the Balkans and in Italy. In 1944 he went to Washington where he planned B-29 missions against Japan that preceded the atomic bombing of HIROSHIMA and NAGASAKI. He was named Supreme Allied Commander, Europe (SACEUR) (1952), the only air force officer to achieve that position. As SACEUR Norstad advocated giving NATO increased control over and latitude to use tactical nuclear weapons.

When promoted to brigadier general, Norstad was thirty-six—below the required age at the time, necessitating a congressional exception. When he became a full general at age forty-five, he was the youngest American officer to be promoted to that rank.

North Africa Campaign • codenamed OPERATION TORCH, this was the first major joint Allied offensive of WORLD WAR II and hitherto the largest amphibious military assault (1942–43). While the Soviets and the U.S. WAR DEPARTMENT favored opening a second major front, President FRANKLIN D. ROOSEVELT was reluctant to authorize a potentially costly campaign, and Prime Minister WINSTON CHURCHILL preferred to expose what he called Europe's "soft underbelly" from North Africa rather than risk slaughter on the heavily fortified French beaches. On November 8, over 100,000 Anglo-American troops under Supreme Commander DWIGHT D. EISENHOWER and British Adm. Sir Andrew Cunningham landed in Morocco and Algeria and quickly overwhelmed the VICHY French resistance. ADOLF HITLER quickly ordered his army to occupy Vichy France and rushed troops to Tunisia before it was captured. In early 1943, the United States, led by Maj. Gen. GEORGE S. PATTON and Maj. Gen. OMAR N. BRADLEY, and the British, led by Gen. BERNARD LAW MONTGOMERY, moved into Tunisia and eventually forced the AXIS surrender on May 13, successfully ending the campaign.

North American Aerospace Defense Command • (**NORAD**) a combined U.S.-Canadian command established in 1957 and commanded by a U.S. Air Force four-star general (CINCNORAD) from headquarters at Peterson AFB, Colorado. CINCNORAD also serves as Commander in Chief, U.S. Space Command (CINCUSSPACECOM), and Commander, Air Force Space Command. CINCNORAD is responsible for surveillance and control of North American airspace and warning, assessment, and defense against aerospace attack of North America.

North American Air Defense Agreement • an agreement signed on May 12, 1958, during the COLD WAR, to formalize existing cooperative air defense agreements between Canada and the United States. To integrate air and space defense forces of the two nations, it established the North American Air Defense Command, which was responsible for managing the DEW line and responding to any threat detected. In 1981 "Aerospace" was substituted for "Air" in the title.

North Anna, Battle of • a conflict between troops of Confederate Gen. ROBERT E. LEE and the superior forces of Union Lt. Gen. ULYSSES S. GRANT on May 23–26, 1864, during the CIVIL WAR. Grant attacked Lee's ARMY OF NORTHERN VIRGINIA near the North Anna River, resulting in a total of 4,000 casualties. The battle's outcome was inconclusive, but Grant skirted Lee's forces and pursued his attack on RICHMOND.

North Atlantic Cooperation Council • an organization created in 1991 to establish a partnership and forum for dialogue on political and security-related matters between NATO countries, Central and Eastern European and Baltic states, and the former Soviet Republics. The council's first meeting was held on December 20, 1991, and attended by twenty-five countries. Georgia and Albania joined in April and June 1992, respectively.

North Atlantic Council • a formal decision-making structure established after the signing of the NORTH ATLANTIC TREATY in 1949 to act as the governing body of NATO. The council's first meeting, attended by a foreign minister from each member country, was held on September 17, 1949.

North Atlantic Treaty • a treaty signed on April 4, 1949, in Washington, D.C., by twelve independent nations including the United States, Canada, and several western European states. It was entered into force on August 24, 1949. It established an international military security alliance, known as the NORTH ATLANTIC TREATY ORGANIZATION, or NATO, to oppose Soviet expansionism in Europe after WORLD WAR II.

North Atlantic Treaty Organization (NATO) • an association of European and North American countries, formed in 1949 for the defense of Europe and the North Atlantic against the perceived threat of Soviet aggression. It includes most major Western powers, although France withdrew from the military side of the alliance in 1966.

North Carolina Regulators • a coalition of planters and small farmers organized in 1767. Because the assembly failed to provide the backcountry with courts and the means to establish law and order, the REGULATORS set up courts to resolve legal disputes and brought criminals to justice. The governor and the assembly, recognizing that the Regulators' grievances were justified, did nothing to stop the movement. By 1768, order had been restored, and the Circuit Court Act of 1769, which provided six court districts for the backcountry, led to the dissolution of the Regulators.

northing • *n.* **1** distance traveled or measured northward, especially at sea: *we should have to make 300 miles of northing.* **2** a figure or line representing northward distance on a map (expressed by convention as the second part of a grid reference, after easting).

North Korean People's Army • (**NKPA**) Communist-led army of the Democratic People's Republic of Korea, also known as the IN MIN GUN. Created February 8, 1948, the NKPA was armed, trained, and supported by the Soviet Union and Communist China. The NKPA invaded the Republic of South Korea on June 25, 1950, and, being well-armed and well-trained, was initially successful. The intervention of United States and other United Nations forces, however, led to the virtual destruction of the NKPA in the fall of 1950, and the principal Communist military role was played by CHINESE PEOPLES VOLUNTEERS for the remainder of the KOREAN WAR. The NKPA was reformed after 1953 and has since played a dominant role in North Korean society.

North, Oliver Laurence (1943–) • Marine lieutenant colonel, born in San Antonio, Texas. North received notoriety for his role in the IRAN-CONTRA AFFAIR. North, a NATIONAL SECURITY COUNCIL aide (1981–86), directed a network of former military and intelligence officials and business people in the resupply operation, which had its own pilots, planes, secure communications, and secret Swiss bank accounts. His conviction (1989) on criminal charges for his role in the affair was reversed on the grounds that immunized testimony before Congress had been used at the trial. North has since had a career as a talk-show host and conservative columnist. In 1994 he ran unsuccessfully for the U.S. Senate from Virginia.

Northrop, Lucius Bellinger (1811–94) • Confederate commissary general of subsistence, born in Charleston, South Carolina. Though not up to the daunting task of procuring, storing, and distributing foodstuffs for the Confederate army, Northrop remained in the position for nearly four years because of his close friendship with JEFFERSON DAVIS. Eventually the clamor of dissatisfied generals demanding his replacement led to his being made subordinate to an officer of superior rank, effectively removing him from authority without officially removing him from office.

North Vietnamese Army • the People's Army of Vietnam (PAVN), the successor to the VIETMINH as the national army of the Democratic Republic of (North) VIETNAM. The PAVN bore the brunt of the fighting against South Vietnamese and U.S.-led Free World Military Forces during the VIETNAM WAR, particularly after the disastrous TET OFFENSIVE of 1968. In the spring of 1975, the PAVN invaded and quickly conquered South Vietnam.

North, William (1755–1836) • officer in the Continental army, born at Fort Frederic

Pemaquid, Maine. North was aide-de-camp (1779–83) to Baron FRIEDRICH VON STEUBEN, the army's inspector general, whom he was with at the siege of YORKTOWN (1781), and the capture of Lord CHARLES CORNWALLIS's army (1783). North had previously seen action in the battle of MONMOUTH (1778). After serving several terms in the New York state assembly, in 1798 he was appointed to the U.S. Senate, where he played a significant role in supporting the administration's military program for the QUASI-WAR WITH FRANCE (1798). Later that year he was appointed adjutant general of the army and then assistant inspector general; as such he served as ALEXANDER HAMILTON's chief of staff until both their offices were abolished by Congress in 1800.

Norwood, Henry (1614–89) • royalist soldier, treasurer and auditor of Virginia (1650–82), born in Gloucester, England. Norwood spent only a few months in Virginia, in 1650. Arriving after a nightmare passage undertaken following the beheading of Charles I, he was made treasurer and quitrent receiver by his cousin Sir WILLIAM BERKELEY, the royal governor. Later that same year he returned to England, where he worked surreptitiously for the restoration of the monarchy.

nosedive • *n.* **1** (since WORLD WAR I) a steep downward plunge by an aircraft. **2** a tailspin. **3** slang intoxication.

NOTS • *abbr.* Naval Overseas Transportation Service.

NR-1 • see Naval Research Vessel.

NRCHB • *abbr.* Navy Cargo Handling Battalion.

NRCHTB • *abbr.* Navy Cargo Handling Training Battalion.

NRL • *abbr.* Naval Research Laboratory.

NSC • *abbr.* National Security Council.

NSDAP • *abbr.* National Socialist German Workers' Party.

NSF • *abbr.* National Science Foundation.

NUCINT • *abbr.* nuclear intelligence.

nuclear • *adj.* **1** denoting, relating to, or powered by the energy released in nuclear fission or fusion: *nuclear submarines.* **2** denoting, possessing, or involving weapons using this energy: *a nuclear bomb | nuclear nations.*

> USAGE: The standard pronunciation of the word **nuclear** rhymes with **clear**. A variant pronunciation exists, famously used by Presidents EISENHOWER and CARTER, which pronounces the second part of the word like **-ular** in **circular** or **particular**. This pronunciation is not acceptable in standard English although it is still widely heard.

nuclear blackmail • the threat of the use of nuclear weapons as a means of inducing an opponent to accede to the will of the nation issuing the threat.

nuclear cloud • an all-inclusive term for the volume of hot gases, smoke, dust, and other particulate matter from the nuclear bomb itself and from its environment, which is carried aloft in conjunction with the rise of the fireball produced by the detonation of the nuclear weapon.

nuclear club • the nations possessing nuclear weapons.

Nuclear Detonation Detection System • (**NDDS**) a U.S. system of satellite sensors for detecting nuclear detonations anywhere on Earth and for assessing U.S. nuclear strikes, targeting follow-on strikes, and reconstituting military forces and communications facilities during and after a nuclear war.

nuclear energy • all forms of energy released in the course of nuclear fission or nuclear transformation.

nuclear-free • *adj.* (of a country or region) not having or allowing any nuclear weapons, materials, or power: *a nuclear-free zone.*

nuclear freeze • a halt in the construction and/or testing of nuclear weapons.

nuclear fusion • a nuclear reaction in which atomic nuclei of low atomic number fuse to form a heavier nucleus with the release of energy.

nuclear incident • an unexpected event involving a nuclear weapon, facility, or component, resulting in any of the following, but not constituting a nuclear weapon(s) accident: **a** an increase in the possibility of explosion or radioactive contamination. **b** errors committed in the assembly, testing, loading, or transportation of equipment, and/or the malfunctioning of equipment and materiel that could lead to an unintentional operation of all or part of the weapon arming and/or firing sequence, or that could lead to a substantial change in yield, or increased dud probability **c** any act of God. unfavorable environment, or condition resulting in damage to the weapon, facility, or component.

nuclear intelligence • (**NUCINT**) intelligence derived from the collection and analysis of radiation and other effects resulting from radioactive sources.

nuclear pacifism • the belief that a war involving nuclear weapons is not a winnable or "just" war, and is unjustifiable because of its uniquely devastating consequences.

nuclear parity • the situation in which two or more nations possessing nuclear weapons have equal or near equal numbers and quality of launch vehicles, warheads, etc., so that no one nation possesses a decisive (or apparently decisive) advantage.

nuclear power • **1** a country that has nuclear weapons. **2** electric or motive power generated by a nuclear reactor.

DERIVATIVES: **nuclear-powered** *adj.*

nuclear proliferation • the process by which one nation after another comes into possession of, or into the right to determine the use of, nuclear weapons, with each nation potentially able to launch a nuclear attack upon another nation.

nuclear radiation • particulate and electromagnetic radiation emitted from atomic nuclei in various nuclear processes. The important nuclear radiations, from the weapons standpoint, are alpha and beta particles, gamma rays, and neutrons.

All nuclear radiations are ionizing radiations, but the reverse is not true; X-rays, for example, are included among ionizing radiations, but they are not nuclear radiations since they do not originate from atomic nuclei.

nuclear rainfall • the water that is precipitated from the base surge clouds after an underwater burst of a nuclear weapon. This rain is radioactive and presents an important secondary effect of such a burst.

nuclear reactor • a facility in which fissile material is used in a self-supporting chain reaction (nuclear fission) to produce heat and/or radiation for both practical application and research and development.

nuclear stalemate • a concept that postulates a situation wherein the relative strength of opposing nuclear forces results in mutual deterrence against employment of nuclear forces.

nuclear stockpile • the total number of nuclear warheads held by a given country.

nuclear strike warning • a warning of impending friendly or suspected enemy nuclear attack.

nuclear threshold • a point in a conflict at which nuclear weapons are or would be brought into use.

nuclear umbrella • the supposed protection gained from an alliance with a country possessing nuclear weapons.

nuclear warfare • warfare involving the employment of nuclear weapons.

nuclear weapon • a complete assembly (that is, implosion type, gun type, or thermonuclear type) in its intended ultimate configuration that, upon completion of the prescribed arming, fusing, and firing sequence, is capable of producing the intended nuclear reaction and release of energy.

nuclear weapon(s) accident • an unexpected event involving nuclear weapons or radiological nuclear weapon components that results in any of the following: **a** accidental or unauthorized launching, firing, or use by U.S. forces or U.S.-supported allied forces, of a nuclear-capable weapon system that could create the risk of an outbreak of war. **b** nuclear detonation. **c** the nonnuclear detonation or burning of a nuclear weapon or radiological nuclear weapon component. **d** radioactive contamination. **e** the seizure, theft, loss, or destruction of a nuclear weapon or radiological nuclear weapon component. **f** public hazard, actual or implied.

Nuclear Weapons Freeze Campaign • see PEACE ACTION.

nuclear winter • a period of abnormal cold and darkness predicted to follow a nuclear war, caused by a layer of smoke and dust in the atmosphere blocking the sun's rays.

nuclear yield • the energy released in the detonation of a nuclear weapon, measured in terms of the kilotons or megatons of trinitrotoluene (TNT) required to produce the same energy release.

Nuclear yields are categorized as **very low yield** (less than 1 kiloton), **low yield** (1 kiloton to 10 kilotons), **medium yield** (more than 10 kilotons to 50 kilotons), **high yield** (more than 50 kilotons to 500 kilotons) and **very high yield** (more than 500 kilotons).

nuisance minefield • a minefield laid to delay and disorganize the enemy and to hinder the use of an area or route.

Nullification Crisis • an unsuccessful but premonitory attempt (1832–33) by South Carolina's ruling planters, led by JOHN C. CALHOUN, to nullify federal legislation which violated state interests. Prompted by a receding cotton economy, high tariffs, the rise of abolitionism, and NAT TURNER's uprising, the upper-class Nullifiers flamed fears of a humiliating conspiracy. Civil war loomed in early 1833 after Congress gave President ANDREW JACKSON authorization to forcefully subdue the Nullifiers, who pledged armed resistance. A compromise tariff agreement, however, was shortly reached, thus meeting South Carolina's request for economic relief while bolstering Jackson's status as a staunch unionist.

numbered air force • (**NAF**) the senior warfighting echelon of the U.S. Air Force, composed of two or more wings with auxiliary units.

number one informal • a lieutenant junior grade in the navy or the coast guard.

nun buoy • a buoy that is circular in the middle and tapering to each end.

ORIGIN: early 18th century: from obsolete *nun* 'child's top' and BUOY.

Nunn, Sam (1938–) • U.S. senator (1973–96), member (1973–96) and chairman (1987–94) of the SENATE ARMED SERVICES COMMITTEE, born in Perry, Georgia. In the late 1970s he urged major increases in NATO's conventional firepower while also advocating the neutron bomb and the adoption of NATIONAL SERVICE. Nunn was an outspoken critic of SALT II. Before being elected to the Senate, Nunn had been legal counsel to the HOUSE ARMED SERVICES COMMITTEE (1963).

Nuremberg Trials • a series of trials held in Nuremberg, Germany, from November 1945 to October 1946. They were held by the INTERNATIONAL MILITARY TRIBUNAL to indict and try twenty-four former NAZI leaders for committing and conspiring to commit war crimes and crimes against humanity during WORLD WAR II. Six organizations also were indicted for aiding the Nazis. All of the officers pleaded not guilty. On October 1, 1946, the tribunal declared verdicts, which included three acquittals and the sentencing of four officers to imprisonment ranging from ten to twenty years, three to life imprisonment, and twelve to death by hanging. The tribunal rejected arguments from the defendants that the trials were ex post facto and that only the state, not individuals, were accountable for violations of international law.

Nursing Corps • the U.S. Army Nurse Corps, which traces its history to the second Continental Congress in 1775. At the end of the REVOLUTIONARY WAR, nurses disappeared from military rolls until the CIVIL WAR when the SECRETARY OF WAR appointed DOROTHEA LYNDE DIX as Superintendent of Women Nurses in the Union Army in 1861. In 1887, Congress authorized the establishment of the Hospital Corps, comprised of enlisted men, but the Hospital Corps proved inadequate during the SPANISH-AMERICAN WAR (1898) when epidemics of typhoid and other tropical diseases swept through the armed forces. The Surgeon General then appointed Dr. Anita Newcomb McGee as Assistant Attorney General and charged her with establishing criteria for choosing nurses for the U.S. Army. In 1901, the Army Recognition Act established a permanent Nurses Corps. At the beginning of WORLD WAR I there were 403 nurses on active duty; by the end of the war, approximately 22,000 nurses had served. Following the end of WORLD WAR II, in 1947, the Army Nurse Corps was established as a component of the Department of the U.S. Army. The Navy Nurse Corps was established in 1908 by the U.S. Congress.

NUSC • *abbr.* Naval Underwater Systems Center, which consolidated with the Naval Undersea Warfare Engineering Station in 1992 to become the NUWC.

NUWC • *abbr.* the Naval Underwater Warfare Center, a research and development facility of the U.S. Navy that tests and evaluates submarines and other autonomous underwater systems, as well as offensive and defensive weapons systems associated with undersea warfare. Its two main divisions are in Newport, Rhode Island, and Keyport, Washington.

NUWEP • *abbr.* Nuclear Weapons Employment Policy; a declaration of a nuclear-capable nation's policy on the employment, deployment, and acquisition of nuclear weapons. Current NUWEPs and those of the recent past are typically classified.

NVA • *abbr.* North Vietnamese Army.

Nye Committee • a committee established on April 12, 1934, under the leadership of Senator GERALD NYE of North Dakota, to investigate the structure, activities, and profits of the munitions industry and its role in U.S. entry into WORLD WAR I. It held ninety-three hearings from September 1934 until February 1936. It failed to prove that arms manufacturers had conspired to begin the war or to force the United States into it.

Nye, Gerald Prentice (1892–1971) • U.S. senator (1925–45), born in Hortonville, Wisconsin. Nye gained prominence through his chairmanship of a special Senate committee, usually referred to as the NYE COMMITTEE, formed to look into allegations that the munitions industry was responsible for provoking international conflict (1934–36). Nye became not only a strong proponent of neutrality legislation, but also, as war began to come closer, an outspoken advocate for nonintervention. A powerful orator who took to the airwaves to disseminate his views, Nye was one of the leading speakers at rallies of the AMERICA FIRST COMMITTEE. Like most noninterventionists, he supported the war following the attack on PEARL HARBOR (1941). Nye was defeated for reelection in 1944.

Oo

oak leaf cluster • a small bronze (or silver) metal device in the shape of a twig of four oak leaves with three acorns on the stem to be attached to the ribbon of U.S. military decorations and representing a second or succeeding award of that decoration. A silver oak leaf cluster may be worn in lieu of five bronze oak leaf clusters.

Oak Ridge National Laboratory • originally known as Clinton Laboratories, established in 1943 for the purpose of producing and separating plutonium for the MANHATTAN PROJECT, Oak Ridge is now a multipurpose science and technology laboratory in Tennessee managed by the University of Tennessee for the DEPARTMENT OF ENERGY.

oar • *n.* **1** a pole with a flat blade, pivoting in an oar lock, used to row or steer a boat through the water. **2** an oarsman; a rower. • *v.* row; propel with or as with oars.

oared • *adj.* (of a boat) having an oar or oars: *four-oared sculls.*

oarlock • *n.* a fitting on the gunwale of a boat that serves as a fulcrum for an oar and keeps it in place.

oarsman • *n.* (pl. **-men**) a rower, especially as a member of a racing team.

DERIVATIVES: **oarsmanship** *n.*

OAS • *abbr.* Organization of American States.

Oates, William Calvin (1833–1910) • Confederate army officer, born in Pike County, Alabama. His regiment saw action in several of the early (1862) battles in the eastern theater of the CIVIL WAR, including SECOND BULL RUN, ANTIETAM, and FREDERICKSBURG. Oates first commanded his regiment at GETTYSBURG (1863), but it was swept from the field and had to retreat. Oates and his men were later in the thick of the fighting in much of the WILDERNESS TO PETERSBURG CAMPAIGN (1864), including SPOTSYLVANIA and COLD HARBOR. Oates was wounded six times during the war, twice severely. At Fussell's Mills (Virginia) he lost his right arm and never returned to battle (1864). During the SPANISH-AMERICAN WAR (1898) Oates commanded three different brigades but did not see combat.

In the retreat from Gettysburg, Oates had to leave behind his brother John, who had been mortally wounded in the fighting.

oath of allegiance • an oath required of military personnel and other citizens pledging fealty and support to the state (or occasionally, to an individual leader, cause, or nongovernmental organization).

OBE • *abbr.* Officer of the Order of the British Empire.

objective • *n.* the physical object of the action taken (for example, a definite tactical feature), the seizure and/or holding of which is essential to the commander's plan.

oblique • *adj.* neither parallel nor at a right angle to a specified or implied line; slanting.

O'Brien, Jeremiah (1744–1818) • naval officer and privateer during the REVOLUTIONARY WAR, born in Kittery, Maine. O'Brien led a group of fellow townsman in the capture off the Maine coast of the *Margaretta,* the first vessel of the ROYAL NAVY to surrender to an American force (1775). He later took part in the capture of two vessels in the Bay of Fundy, where he continued to harass British trade. After losing his command because of squabbles with the Massachusetts provincial congress, O'Brien undertook the role of privateer (1777). He was captured in 1780 and imprisoned in England. He escaped, but never returned to sea.

observables, low • the characteristics of aircraft, ships, and other military vehicles and equipment which present minimal possibilities of detection by enemy electromagnetic, visual, sound, or heat detection systems. Also called STEALTH.

observation • *n.* **1** the action or process of observing something or someone carefully or in order to gain information: *she was brought into the hospital for observation | detailed observations were carried out.* **2** the taking of the altitude of the sun or another celestial body for navigational purposes.

observation post • a post for watching the movement of enemy forces or the effect of artillery fire.

observe • *v.* **1** notice or perceive (something) and register it as being significant. **2** watch (someone or something) carefully and attentively.
DERIVATIVES: **observable** *adj.* **observably** *adv.*

observed fire • fire for which the point of impact or burst can be seen by an observer. The fire can be controlled and adjusted on the basis of observation.

observer • *n.* a person posted to an area in an official capacity to monitor political or military events: *elections scrutinized by international observers.*

OC • *abbr.* Officer Commanding.

OCAS • *abbr.* the Organization of Central American States; a union of political cooperation among the countries of Central America formed in 1951. It is more commonly known as **Odeca**, an acronym of the Spanish name *Organización de Estados Centroamericanos.*

occulting light • a light in a lighthouse or buoy that is cut off briefly at regular intervals.

occupation • *n.* the action, state, or period of occupying or being occupied by military force: *crimes committed during the Nazi occupation.*

occupied territory • territory under the authority and effective control of a belligerent armed force. The term is not applicable to territory being administered pursuant to peace terms, treaty, or other agreement, express or implied, with the civil authority of the territory.

occupy • *v.* (**-ies, -ied**) **1** take control of (a place, especially a country) by military conquest or settlement: *Syria was occupied by France under a League of Nations mandate.* **2** enter, take control of, and stay in (a building) illegally and often forcibly, especially as a form of protest: *the workers occupied the factory.*
DERIVATIVES: **occupier** *n.*

oceangoing (also **ocean-going**) • *adj.* (of a ship) designed to cross oceans.

Oceania • the islands of the Pacific Ocean and adjacent seas.
DERIVATIVES: **Oceanian** *adj. & n.*

ocean manifest • a detailed listing of the entire cargo loaded into any one ship, showing all pertinent data that will readily identify such cargo and where and how the cargo is stowed.

oceanography • *n.* the study of the sea, embracing and integrating all knowledge pertaining to the sea and its physical boundaries, the chemistry and physics of seawater, and marine biology.

oceanology • *n.* **1** another term for OCEANOGRAPHY. **2** the branch of technology and economics dealing with human use of the sea.
DERIVATIVES: **oceanological** *adj.* **oceanologist** *n.*

ocean tramp • a merchant vessel which is available to haul cargo of all types to all parts of the world.

Octagon • see QUEBEC CONFERENCE.

octant • *n.* an obsolete instrument in the form of a graduated eighth of a circle, used in astronomy and navigation.

Oerlikon • any of various Swiss-developed 20 mm automatic aircraft or antiaircraft machine guns manufactured by the Oerlikon company in Switzerland, especially one used in WORLD WAR II by the British.

offense |əˈfens| • *n.* **1** a breach of a law or rule; an illegal act: *neither offense violates any federal law.* **2** the action of attacking: *reductions in strategic offense arsenals.*

"offense-defense" theory • a politico-military theory developed by the political scientist Robert Jervis in 1978 which holds that the risk of war increases as a nations offensive force grows stronger and conquest of an enemy grows easier. At the same time, nations favoring the status quo grow more aggressive as they seek more defensible borders.

offensive • *adj.* **1** actively aggressive; attacking: *offensive operations against the insurgents.* **2** (of a weapon) meant for use in attack. • *n.* an attacking military campaign: *an impending military offensive against the guerrillas.*

PHRASES: **go on** (or **take**) **the offensive** take the initiative by beginning to attack or act aggressively: *security forces took the offensive.*

offensive minefield • in naval mine warfare, a minefield laid in enemy territorial water or other enemy-controlled waters.

Office Hours • see CAPTAIN'S MAST.

Office of Civil and Defense Mobilization • see FEDERAL CIVIL DEFENSE ADMINISTRATION.

Office of International Security Affairs • see CENTER FOR INTERNATIONAL SECURITY AFFAIRS.

Office of Naval Intelligence • (**ONI**) a U.S. Department of the Navy organization that provides joint operational commanders with a worldwide network and an integrated workforce of active duty, reserve, officer and enlisted, and civilian professionals. Among its missions are responsibility for monitoring merchant ship activity, counternarcotics operations, and enforcing environmental treaties that govern marine resources.

Office of Policy Coordination • (**OPC**) established in June 1948 by the NATIONAL SECURITY COUNCIL, to perform covert missions, especially spreading unrest in Communist countries. The OPC was unsuccessful, and was criticized by CIA agents who were attempting the same kinds of missions. The OPC was disbanded in 1952.

Office of Scientific Research and Development • (**OSRD**) established in 1941 under the directorship of VANNEVAR BUSH, and responsible for coordinating the scientific effort that produced radar and the atomic bomb. It was comprised of a number of divisions, each committed to a specific research area, and nearly every engineer and scientist in the United States worked for the OSRD. Within each division, the armed forces researchers, industry, and the academic laboratories worked together.

Office of Strategic Services • (**OSS**) an agency created during WORLD WAR II when WILLIAM J. DONOVAN, its first head, convinced President FRANKLIN D. ROOSEVELT in 1941 to form the office of the Coordinator of Information (COI) for collecting and analyzing data as well as other activities, special operations, in particular. In 1942, it was officially designated the Office of Strategic Services. It is generally acknowledged that the CENTRAL INTELLIGENCE AGENCY originated with the OSS.

Office of War Information • (**OWI**) established in 1942 and responsible for creating and disseminating pro-Allied Powers propaganda. Among its wide-ranging operations were film productions and the review and design of government posters. It was made up of two photographic units, one headed by Roy E. Stryker, the other the News Bureau. (The two units were merged in 1943.) Stryker's OWI section was transferred from the Department of Agriculture's Farm Security Administration (FSA) in late 1942, and a world-famous collection of documentary photographs (numbering 108,000), mostly black-and-white, is at the Library of Congress. The advertising specialists in OWI came to dominate the group in 1943 and, from that time until the end of WORLD WAR II, government posters looked like magazine illustrations, and the idea of "war art" quietly died.

Office of War Mobilization and Reconversion • created as an independent agency by the War Mobilization and Reconversion Act of 1944, the agency was responsible for coordinating wartime and postwar economic planning, combining the functions of the Office of War Mobilization and the Office of Contract Settlement. In 1945, it acquired the functions of the Office of Economic Stabilization as well.

officer • *n.* a person holding a position of command or authority in the armed services, in the merchant marine, or on a passenger ship. • *v.* **1** provide with military officers: *the aristocracy continued to wield considerable political power, officering the army.* **2** act as the commander of (a unit): *foreign mercenaries were hired to officer new regiments.*

Officer Personnel Act • an act passed by Congress in 1947 to provide non-disability retirement to officers of all services. It specified the length of an officer's career and that an officer serving for twenty years or more would receive a minimum of 50 percent and a maximum of 75 percent of their base pay for life upon retirement. It was the first legislation in which non-disability retirement was combined for all services.

Officers' Reserve Corps • forerunner of the contemporary Army Reserve, active in WORLD WAR I, WORLD WAR II, and the KOREAN WAR. The Corps was created in 1916 by the National Defense Act. Between 1952 and 1955, new legislation renamed the Organized Reserve Corps as the Army Reserve, and divided it into the READY RESERVE, STANDBY RESERVE, and Retired Reserve, and authorized the president to call up to 1 million Reservists of all services.

officialese • *n.* derogatory the formal and typically verbose style of writing considered to be characteristic of official documents, especially when it is difficult to understand.

official information • information that is owned by, produced for or by, or subject to the control of the government of the United States.

offing • *n.* the more distant part of the sea in view.

off-route mine • a mine that is aimed at a point where a target will pass and is activated by the target passing over a fiber-optic sensor cable or activating its infrared sensor. A microchip inside calculates the moment of detonation, based on the detected speed of the target.

offset bombing • any bombing procedure that employs a reference or aiming point other than the actual target.

offshore patrol • a naval defense patrol operating in the outer areas of navigable coastal waters. It is a part of the naval local defense forces consisting of naval ships and aircraft and operates outside those areas assigned to the inshore patrol.

off the wind |wind| • with the wind on the quarter.

oflag |ˈôfˌläg; ˈäf-| • *n.* a German prison camp for captured enemy officers. Compare STALAG.
ORIGIN: German, contraction of *Offizier(s)lager* 'officers' camp.'

Ogden, Aaron (1756–1839) • army officer, born in Elizabethtown, New Jersey. His career spanned the entire REVOLUTIONARY WAR, from militia service in 1776, to the battle of BRANDYWINE in 1777, through the YORKTOWN campaign of 1781, during which he led an assault on British positions. Before being commissioned in the regular army in 1776, Ogden had helped seize a British ship and served in the state militia. After the Revolution, Ogden served as governor of New Jersey (1812).

Oglesby, Richard James |ˈōgəlzbē| (1824–99) • Union army officer, born in Oldham County, Kentucky. Oglesby led a brigade at FORT DONELSON (1862) and was wounded at CORINTH (1862). He resigned his commission in 1864 to run for governor of Illinois (1865–69). He later served a single term as U.S. senator before returning to the gubernatorial post (1885–89). Oglesby was in Washington at the time of the assassination of ABRAHAM LINCOLN and was among those present at his deathbed. In his pre-CIVIL WAR career Oglesby had seen action at VERACRUZ during the MEXICAN WAR (1846–48) and had served in the Illinois senate (1860).

Oglesby is credited with devising the sobriquet "rail-splitter" for Abraham Lincoln at the Illinois state convention in 1860.

Oglethorpe, James Edward |ˈōgəlˌTHôrp| (1696–1785) • British legislator, colonial governor, and army officer. Born in London, he became a member of Parliament in 1722 and supported plans for the establishment of a debtors' colony in North America. Oglethorpe and his associates succeeded in establishing the Georgia colony in February 1733, and Oglethorpe was appointed Governor. He gained the trust of local Creek Indians by ensuring fair trade practices, and during the war with Spain he led British forces into Florida (1740) and defeated a Spanish invasion of Georgia (1742). He subsequently returned to England to defend himself against various charges and was eventually appointed major general. Following the abortive Jacobite uprising in 1745, Oglethorpe was tried and acquitted for failing to pursue Prince Charles Stuart's army aggressively.

OH-6A • see CAYUSE.

OH-58 • see KIOWA WARRIOR.

O'Hara, James (1752?–1819) • army officer during the REVOLUTIONARY WAR and quartermaster general of the U.S. Army (1792–96). O'Hara, born in County Mayo, Ireland, was a leader in western Pennsylvania whose initial efforts focused on defending the American position against the Indians and preventing them from helping British forces. O'Hara appears to have been present at the battles of COWPENS, GUILFORD COURT HOUSE, and EUTAW SPRINGS (all 1781). From 1781 until 1783 he was assistant quartermaster under Gen. NATHANAEL GREENE. Before the Revolutionary War, O'Hara, who had immigrated to America in 1772 and settled in Pittsburgh, had been appointed an Indian government agent. Afterwards O'Hara again became involved in the commercial, military, and political activities on the western Pennsylvania frontier. As quartermaster general he traveled widely, inspecting forts and purchasing supplies.

Ohio, Army of the • see ARMY OF THE OHIO.

***Ohio*, USS** • (**SSBN 726**) the first nuclear submarine of the Ohio Class, ordered in July 1974, it made its first operational patrol in October 1982. This class is the largest and the most expensive class of submarines built in the West (costing more than $1.75 billion in 1985), and these submarines serve as ballistic missile platforms, carrying twenty-four TRIDENT C-4 or D-5 multiple warhead nuclear missiles.

oil • *n.* **1** a viscous liquid derived from petroleum, especially for use as a fuel or lubricant. **2** petroleum. • *v.* **1** lubricate or coat (something) with oil. **2** supply with oil as fuel: *do not oil individual tanks too rapidly.*
DERIVATIVES: **oilless** *adj.*

oiler • *n.* a thing that holds or supplies oil, especially: **a** an oil tanker. **b** an oilcan. **c** a person who oils machinery.

oil tanker • a ship designed to carry oil in bulk.

Okinawa, Battle of • the final land battle of the Pacific War, on Easter Sunday, April 1, 1945, on the island of Okinawa. Led by Lt. Gen. SIMON BOLIVAR BUCKNER, the landing force crossed the island almost without enemy contact. Japanese Lt. Gen. MITSURU USHIJIMA's plan was to delay his counterattack until much of the supporting U.S. invasion fleet of some 1,200 ships was crippled by combined sea and air action, including kamikaze tactics. Though the battle was a victory for the Americans, Buckner, who was killed by a Japanese shell while watching the action, was criticized for his unimaginative and costly frontal assaults which resulted in 7,613 killed or missing in action and 31,800 wounded. Estimates of Japanese casualties ran over 142,000, including many Okinawan citizens.

Old Dominion • a nickname for Virginia. King Charles II gave Virginia this name because of its loyalty to England during the English Civil War (1642–49).

Old Northwest Territory • the first territorial government set up by the United States. It was created in 1787 and was officially called "the Territory Northwest of the River Ohio."

Hostile Indians limited settlement initially, but Gen. ANTHONY WAYNE's victory over their forces at FALLEN TIMBERS on August 20, 1794, opened up all the territory to settlement, and growth exploded. In 1800, the Indiana Territory was created out of land west of Kentucky, and in 1802 the Michigan Territory was established to break the region into more manageable areas of governance. The original territory became the state of Ohio in 1803.

Olive Branch Petition • a document of American colonial grievances addressed to King GEORGE III and signed by members of the Continental Congress in July 1775. It was delivered by Richard Penn to the King in London in August 1775. The King refused to see him or the document. It was an effort by the Americans to resolve differences with Britain and to avert the REVOLUTIONARY WAR.

olive drab • a dull olive-green color, used in some military uniforms.

Olmsted, Gideon (1749–1845) • ship captain and privateer during the REVOLUTIONARY WAR, born in East Hartford, Connecticut. Olmsted enjoyed considerable success in taking numerous prizes but is mainly remembered for his long-running battle to obtain the proceeds from one of them, the British sloop *Active*. Olmsted had been captured and put aboard the *Active*, but he led other captives in overthrowing their guards and taking over the sloop. He was leading it to port when it was taken by other American vessels out of Philadelphia, who claimed it as their prize. Despite several denials of his claim on the proceeds, Olmsted carried his appeal to the Supreme Court, which found in his favor, setting important precedents in maritime law (1790). He did not receive the ordered compensation from Pennsylvania, however, until President JAMES MADISON intervened in 1809.

Omaha Beach • one of five Allied landings that comprised OPERATION OVERLORD (D-DAY), the greatest amphibious attack in history, which penetrated ADOLF HITLER's ATLANTIC WALL. The air and sea bombardment in the early morning on June 6, 1944, before the first-wave attack was highly effective at all the beaches except Omaha, where most of the shells landed far in land. But thanks to heroic action by individual soldiers the crisis was overcome. Over half of the 4,900 Allied inland casualties came at Omaha.

on a wind |wind| • against a wind on either bow.

on-board • *adj.* available or situated on a ship, aircraft, or other vehicle.

one-star • *adj.* having or denoting the rank of brigadier general, distinguished by one star on the uniform: *a one-star general.*

on hand • the quantity of an item that is physically available in a storage location and contained in the accountable property books records of an issuing activity.

ONI • *abbr.* Office of Naval Intelligence.

on-site inspection *n.* • a method of control used to verify compliance with a nuclear test ban treaty or nuclear arms control and disarmament agreement, and used especially with underground test bans.

On-Site Inspection Agency • a U.S. agency established by the DEPARTMENT OF DEFENSE on January 15, 1988, to implement the inspection provisions of the INTERMEDIATE-RANGE NUCLEAR FORCES TREATY. The agency expanded as subsequent nuclear weapons elimination and reduction treaties began to include compliance verification through on-site inspections.

on station • **1** in air intercept usage, a code meaning, "I have reached my assigned station." **2** in close air support and air interdiction, a term used to indicate that airborne aircraft are in position to attack targets or to perform the mission designated by the control agency.

OP • *abbr.* observation post.

op • *n.* informal a military operation.

OPC • *abbr.* Office of Policy Coordination.

OPCON • *abbr.* operational control.

OPDOC • *abbr.* operational documentation.

Opechancanough |ō,pecHən'känō| • (c.1545–1644) an Algonquian leader who was the first chief to recognize the encroachment of English colonization on native lands and resist it as a serious threat to Indian life. He was responsible for the uprising of 1622 against the English colonists in Virginia and was killed by one of them in 1644 while a prisoner. He was believed by English contemporaries to be the brother of POWHATAN and an uncle to Pochohantas.

open • *adj.* **1** free from obstructions. **2** (of an area of land) not covered with buildings or trees. **3** (of an object of attack) unprotected; vulnerable. **4** (of a boat) without a deck. **5** (of a town or city) officially declared to be undefended, and so immune under international law from bombardment. **6** (of a hand) not clenched into a fist. **7** (of conflict) fully developed and unconcealed. • *v.* **1** improve or make possible access to or passage through: *the government opened the border.* **2** achieve a clear view of (a place) by sailing past a headland or other obstruction.

PHRASES: **in** (or **into**) **the open 1** out of doors; not under cover. **2** not subject to concealment or obfuscation; made public: *we have never let our dislike for him come into the open.* **open fire** begin to shoot a weapon.

▸**open up** begin shooting: *the enemy artillery had opened up.*

Open Arms Program • (**Chieu Hoi**) part of the U.S. pacification policy during the VIETNAM WAR. Though many U.S. pacification efforts failed, the *Chieu Hoi* programs, which offered clemency to insurgents, produced positive results throughout the war.

"open door" policy • U.S. policy with respect to China in the late 19th century intended to ensure that China would not be divided among the various European nations and Japan and to ensure free access to China for U.S. political and business interests.

open ice • ice-covered water through which navigation is possible.

open sea • (usually **the open sea**) an expanse of sea away from land.

Open Skies Treaty • an agreement signed on March 24, 1992, by member states of NATO and the then WARSAW PACT, "to encourage reciprocal openness on the part of the participating states and to allow the observation of military activities" through unarmed observation flights. It included provisions for on-site inspections to verify compliance with current and future arms control agreements.

U.S. President DWIGHT D. EISENHOWER originally proposed the idea in 1955, but the first meeting to initiate the program was not held until February 12, 1990.

open source information • information of potential intelligence value (i.e., intelligence information) which is available to the general public.

open-source intelligence • (**OSINT**) information of potential intelligence value that is available to the general public.

operate • *v.* **1** (of an armed force) conduct military activities in a specified area or from a specified base: *the mountain bases from which the guerrillas were operating.* **2** (of a person) control the functioning of (a machine, process, or system): *a shortage of workers to operate new machines.* **3** (of a machine, process, or system) function in a specified manner: *market forces were allowed to operate freely.*

operation • *n.* **1** a piece of organized and concerted activity involving a number of people, especially members of the armed forces or the police: *a rescue operation | military operations.* **2** (**Operation**) preceding a code name for such an activity: *Operation Desert Storm.* For entries beginning with Operation, please see the second part of the name.

operational • *adj.* **1** in or ready for use: *the new laboratory is fully operational.* **2** of or relating to the routine functioning and activities of a business or organization: *the deputy mayor in operational charge of the city.* **3** engaged in or relating to active operations of the armed forces, police, or emergency services: *an operational fighter squadron.*
DERIVATIVES: **operationally** *adv.*

operational art • the conception and execution, by military forces, of operations to attain strategic objectives, through such actions as apportioning resources to tactical units, or coordinating the logistics requirements of an operation. Operational art forms a bridge between strategy, with which the political aims of a war are defined, and tactics, with which the battles of a war are fought.

operational chain of command • the chain of command established for a particular operation or series or continuing operations.

operational characteristics • those military characteristics that pertain primarily to the functions to be performed by equipment, either alone or in conjunction with other equipment.

operational command • the authority to assign missions, deploy units, and retain or delegate operational control of forces.

operational control • (**OPCON**) transferable command authority that may be exercised by commanders at any echelon at or below the level of combatant command. Operational control is inherent in COMBATANT COMMAND (COMMAND AUTHORITY). Operational control may be delegated and is the authority to perform those functions of command over subordinate forces involving organizing and employing commands and forces, assigning tasks, designating objectives, and giving authoritative direction necessary to accomplish the missions. Operational control includes authoritative direction over all aspects of military operations and joint training necessary to accomplish missions assigned to the command. Operational control should be exercised through the commanders of subordinate organizations. Normally this authority is exercised through subordinate joint force commanders and service and/or functional component commanders. Operational control normally provides full authority to organize commands and forces and to employ those forces as the commander in operational control considers necessary to accomplish assigned missions. Operational control does not, in and of itself, include authoritative direction for logistics or matters of administration, discipline, internal organization, or unit training.

operational control authority • the naval commander responsible within a specified geographical area for the naval control of all merchant shipping under allied naval control.

operational documentation • (**OPDOC**) visual information documentation of activities to convey information about people, places, and things. It is general documentation normally accomplished in peacetime.

operational intelligence • intelligence that is required for planning and conducting campaigns and major operations to accomplish strategic objectives within theaters or areas of operations.

operational procedures • the detailed methods by which headquarters and units carry out their operational tasks.

operational readiness • the capability of a unit/formation, ship, weapon system, or equipment to perform the missions or functions for which it is organized or designed. The term may be used in a general sense or to express a level or degree of readiness.
DERIVATIVES: **operationally ready**

operation order • (**OPORD**) a directive issued by a commander to subordinate commanders for the purpose of effecting the coordinated execution of an operation.

operation plan • a plan for a single or series of connected operations to be carried out simultaneously or in succession. It is usually based upon stated assumptions and is the form of directive employed by higher authority to permit subordinate commanders to prepare supporting plans and orders. The designation "plan" is usually used instead of "order" in preparing for operations well in advance. An operation plan may be put into effect at a prescribed time, or on signal, and then becomes the operation order.

operations research • (also **operational research** or **operations analysis**) the analytical study of military problems undertaken to provide responsible commanders and staff agencies with a scientific basis for decision on action to improve military operations.

operations room • a room from which military or police operations are directed.

operations security • (**OPSEC**) a process of identifying critical information and subsequently analyzing friendly actions attendant to military operations and other activities in order to: **a** identify those actions that can be observed by adversary intelligence systems, **b** determine indicators hostile intelligence systems might obtain that could be interpreted or pieced together to derive critical information useful to adversaries, **c** select and execute measures that eliminate or reduce to an acceptable level the vulnerabilities of friendly actions to adversary exploitation.

OPORD • *abbr.* operation order.

Oppenheimer, J. Robert (1904–67) • theoretical physicist and director of the Los Alamos National Laboratory (1942–45), born Julius Robert Oppenheimer in New York City. As director of the bomb design unit of the Manhattan Project, Oppenheimer recommended the site, recruited the scientists, and supervised more than 1,500 people, successfully mediating the egos and demands of the military with those of the scientists. In addition, he solved innumerable theoretical and practical scientific problems. Deeply affected by the devastation wrought by the bomb, Oppenheimer resigned from the laboratory and later opposed development of the hydrogen bomb. From 1946 until 1952 Oppenheimer chaired the general advisory committee of the Atomic Energy Commission, but in 1953 his security clearance was revoked because of leftist associations dating from the prewar period. He also directed the Institute for Advanced Study at Princeton (1947–52).

OPSEC • *abbr.* operations security.

optical minehunting • the use of an optical system (for example, television or towed diver) to detect and classify mines or minelike objects on or protruding from the seabed.

OR • *abbr.* Brit. other ranks (as opposed to commissioned officers).

oranges • **1 (sour)** in air intercept, a code meaning, "Weather is unsuitable for aircraft mission." **2 (sweet)** in air intercept, a code meaning, "Weather is suitable for aircraft mission."

orbat • *abbr.* order of battle.

Ord, Edward Otho Cresap (1818–83) • Union army officer, born in Cumberland, Maryland. Ord gained national attention when he defeated J.E.B. Stuart in a major skirmish in Virginia (1861). Ord was often used by Ulysses S. Grant to replace problematic commanders. In 1864 he led an expedition into the Shenandoah Valley, assaulting and capturing Fort Harrison, Virginia. He later commanded the Army of the James in the final battles around Petersburg (1865). Before the war Ord had fought against the Seminoles in Florida (1839–42) and participated in several American Indian expeditions in the Northwest while in command of a company in California (1855). He had also assisted in suppressing John Brown's raid on Harpers Ferry (1859) when stationed in Virginia.

ORDEN • a government-sponsored paramilitary group created in El Salvador in the 1960s to counter a surge of political activity among peasants and urban workers. It is considered to be the precursor of El Salvador's death squads.

order • *n.* **1** an authoritative command, direction, or instruction written, oral, or by signal, which conveys instructions from a superior to a subordinate. In broad terms, an "order" and a "command" are synonymous, but an order implies discretion as to the details of execution whereas a command does not: *the skipper gave the order to abandon ship.* **2** equipment or uniform for a specified purpose or of a specified type: *drill order.* **3** (**the order**) the position in which a rifle is held after ordering arms. See order arms. • *v.* **1** give an authoritative direction or instruction to do something: *she ordered me to leave.* **2** command (something) to be done or (someone) to be treated in a particular way: *he ordered the anchor dropped.*

order arms • **1** in dismounted drill, the two-part command directing personnel to return to the position of attention after rendering a salute. **2** hold a rifle with its butt on the ground close to one's right side.

orderly • *n.* a soldier who carries out orders or performs minor tasks for an officer.

orderly room • the room used for regimental or company business.

order of battle • the identification, strength, command structure, and disposition of the personnel, units, and equipment of any military force.

Order of the British Empire • (**OBE**) (in the UK) an honorary order of knighthood instituted in 1917 and divided into five classes, each with military and civilian divisions.

Order of the Garter • the highest order of English knighthood, founded by Edward III *c.* 1344. According to tradition the garter was that of the Countess of Salisbury, which the king placed on his own leg after it fell off while she was dancing with him. The king's comment to those present, "Honi soit qui mal y pense" (shame be to him who thinks evil of it), was adopted as the motto of the order.

ordinance • *n.* a law, regulation, or mandatory instruction.

ordinary seaman • the lowest rank of merchant seaman, below able-bodied seaman.

ordnance |ˈôrdnəns| • *n.* **1** mounted guns; artillery. **2** military weapons, ammunition, and equipment used in connection with them. **3** a branch of the armed forces dealing with the supply and storage of weapons, ammunition, and related equipment.

Ordnance Corps • the combat service support branch of the U.S. Army responsible for the development, production, acquisition, storage, and maintenance of ammunition, vehicles, and weapons.

Ordnance Department • established by an act of Congress in 1812 and charged with providing military supplies (weapons, ammunition, and so on) for the army and militia. In 1812, and, again, in 1815, the Ordnance Department was reorganized, including the addition of a body of officers.

Ordnance Survey • a national mapping agency of the United Kingdom, established in 1791, and managed by the military for close to one hundred years. Widely regarded as the best in the field of cartography, it produces, maintains, and markets a wide range of maps, computer data, and other geographical information for business, leisure, educational, and administrative use.

Ordway, John (c.1775–c.1817) • soldier and member of the LEWIS AND CLARK EXPEDITION, born in Dumbarton, New Hampshire. After the diaries of the two captains, Ordway's notebooks were considered the most valuable resource for information on the expedition. Lewis and Clark themselves purchased his three-volume expedition journal for $300. It was first published in 1916.

Oregon Trail • (also **Oregon-California Trail**) a route across the central United States, from Missouri to Oregon, some 2,000 miles (3,000 km) in length. It was used chiefly in the 1840s by settlers moving west.

organic • *adj.* assigned to and forming an essential part of a military organization. Organic parts of a unit are those listed in its table of organization for the U.S. Army, Air Force, and Marine Corps, and are assigned to the administrative organizations of the operating forces for the U.S. Navy.

Organization for Security and Cooperation in Europe • see CONFERENCE ON SECURITY AND COOPERATION IN EUROPE.

Organization of American States • (**OAS**) an association including most of North and South America, originally founded in 1890 for largely commercial purposes. From 1948 it has aimed to work for peace and prosperity in the region and to uphold the sovereignty of member nations. Its headquarters are in Washington, D.C.

Orion • (**P-3**) an aircraft used by the U.S. Navy for sea reconnaissance and antisubmarine warfare, it is powered by four turboprop engines.

Oriskany, Battle of • a battle between British and American forces near Oriskany, New York, on August 6, 1777, during the REVOLUTIONARY WAR. On August 3, British Lt. Col. Barry St. Leger and his army of approximately 1,200 men, mostly Tories under Col. John Butler and Sir John Johnson and Indians under MOHAWK chief JOSEPH BRANT, demanded the surrender of FORT STANWIX (also called Fort Schuyler, and now Rome, New York) during their march across New York to join with British forces at Albany. Two miles west of Oriskany Creek, the British force ambushed a colonial force of some 800 men under Gen. NICHOLAS HERKIMER, who were en route to help defend the fort. Both sides suffered heavy casualties, and Herkimer was mortally wounded. On August 22, St. Leger, unable to force the surrender of the fort, retreated to Oswego.

OS • *abbr.* Ordinary Seaman.

Osceola (c. 1804–38) • Native American war leader, born in Alabama. Osceola became a symbol of Indian resistance to forced removal. A member of a Tallassee tribe, he was outspoken in his denouncement of the treaties by which the United States sought to remove Florida Indians from their lands and confine them to reservations. Along with tribal leaders, he planned the opening gambits of the Second SEMINOLE WAR (1835–42) and led warriors in its first major engagements (1836–37). Captured while under a white flag of truce (1837), Osceola was imprisoned in South Carolina, where he died a few months later.

Osceola was much romanticized as a noble, tragic figure because of his defiance and treacherous capture. Noted Indian artist George Catlin painted his portrait, further contributing to the mythical aura surrounding him.

OSINT • *abbr.* open-source intelligence.

Osprey • (**V-22**) an assault transport helicopter being developed for the U.S. Marine Corps. Intended to replace the Boeing Vertol CH-46 and the SIKORSKY CH-53, the Osprey is a tilt-rotor hybrid rotary/fixed-wing transport. The most significant difference between the Osprey and other transport helicopters is its propulsion/vertical lift system, with a single large proprotor and its engine positioned at each wing tip. These proprotors, along with their engines and nacelles, can be operated in the vertical position, in which they provide direct lift, and the horizontal position, in which they provide direct thrust.

OSRD • *abbr.* Office of Scientific Research and Development.

OSS • *abbr.* Office of Strategic Services.

Osterhaus, Peter Joseph |'ästər,hows| (1823–1917) • Union army officer, born in Koblenz, Germany. Osterhaus was best known for leading successful assaults on LOOKOUT MOUNTAIN and MISSIONARY RIDGE, when his forces crushed the Confederate left flank and captured thousands of prisoners (1864). Osterhaus continued division command in the battle for ATLANTA and throughout Sherman's MARCH TO THE SEA (1864). He had previously commanded a division at PEA RIDGE (1862) and in the campaign to take VICKSBURG (1863). After retiring in 1900, Osterhaus, who had fled to America following the revolutions of 1848, returned to Germany.

Ostpolitik |'ôst,päli'tēk| • *n.* the foreign policy of détente of western European countries with reference to the former communist bloc, especially the opening of relations with the

EASTERN BLOC by the Federal Republic of Germany (West Germany) in the 1960s.
ORIGIN: German, from *Ost* 'east' + *Politik* 'politics.'

OTC • *abbr.* (in the UK) Officers' Training Corps.

other ranks • Brit. (in the armed forces) all those who are not commissioned officers.

Otis, Elwell Stephen (1838–1909) • army officer, born in Frederick, Maryland. His career began during the CIVIL WAR (1861–65) and extended through the SPANISH-AMERICAN WAR (1898) and the subsequent insurrection in the Philippines, where he was military governor (1898–1900). During the Civil War Otis commanded a New York infantry regiment but a wound received late in 1864 prevented his return to combat. Following the war Otis served on the frontier, where he engaged in several actions against American Indians. In 1880 he founded a school for army officers at FORT LEAVENWORTH, Kansas, and remained as commandant until 1885. With the outbreak of the Spanish-American War, Otis was sent to the Philippines, where he was put in charge of all U.S. combat forces and named military governor. He directed forces in suppressing the rebellion until relieved of his duties by Gen. ARTHUR MACARTHUR.

Otis, George Alexander (1830–81) • U.S. Army medical officer, born in Boston, Massachusetts. After serving in campaigns in Maryland, Virginia, and North Carolina, Otis was assigned to the Army Medical Museum (1864–81), where he became noted for his collections relating to surgery and photography, particularly his collection of skulls. Otis also conducted research on how best to transport the wounded, published numerous monographs, and edited the three-part surgical volume of the *Medical and Surgical History of the War of the Rebellion*.

outboard • *adj.* & *adv.* **1** on, toward, or near the outside, especially of a ship or other vehicle: *the outboard rear seats.* **2** (of a motor) portable and usually mounted on the outside of the stern of a boat. • *n.* **1** an outboard motor. **2** a boat with such a motor.

outbreak • *n.* the sudden or violent start of something unwelcome, such as war, disease, etc.: *the outbreak of World War II.*

outdrive • *n.* the portion of an inboard-outboard engine that is outside the hull, providing steering and propulsion.

outfight • *v.* (past and past part. **-fought** |-fôt|) fight better than and beat (an opponent).

outflank • *v.* move around the side of (an enemy) so as to outmaneuver them: *the Germans had sought to outflank them from the northeast.*

outgun • *v.* (**-gunned, -gunning**) (**outgunned**) **1** have better or more weaponry than: *offensives that overwhelmed the outgunned and outmanned armies* **2** shoot better than: *the correspondents proudly outgunned the army sharpshooters.*

outhaul • *n.* a rope used to haul out the clew of a boom sail or the tack of a jib.

out-of-area • *adj.* (of a military operation) conducted away from the place of origin or expected place of action of the force concerned.

outpoint • *v.* sail closer to the wind than (another ship).

outpost • *n.* **1** a small military camp or position at some distance from the main force, used especially as a guard against surprise attack. **2** a remote part of a country or empire.

outride • *v.* (past **-rode**; past part. **-ridden**) archaic (of a ship) come safely through (a storm).

outrigger • *n.* **1** a beam, spar, or framework projecting from or over the side of a ship or boat. **2** a float or secondary hull fixed parallel to a canoe or other boat to stabilize it. **3** a boat fitted with such a structure.

outside cabin • a ship's cabin with an outside window or porthole.

outwork • *n.* a section of a fortification or system of defense that is in front of the main part.

OV-10 • see BRONCO.

overkill • *n.* the amount by which destruction or the capacity for destruction exceeds what is necessary: *the existing nuclear overkill.*

Overland Campaign • see WILDERNESS TO PETERSBURG CAMPAIGN.

Overlord, Operation • (**D-Day**) the greatest amphibious attack in history. Nearly 175,000 American, Canadian, and British troops landed in NORMANDY on June 6, 1944, supported by 6,000 aircraft and 6,000 naval vessels. At dawn, there was a tremendous air and sea bombardment, which, for the most part, was highly effective. By nightfall, the Allies were ashore on a beachhead that stretched 55 miles. ADOLF HITLER's ATLANTIC WALL, built at enormous expense, had not held up to the Allied landings for even one day.

overseer |'ōvər,siər| • *n.* a person who supervises others, especially workers.

overshoot • a phase of flight wherein a landing approach of an aircraft is not continued to touchdown.

overside • *adv.* over the side of a ship: *he was dumped overside by the guards.*

overslaugh |,ōvər'slô| • *n.* Brit. a passing over of one's ordinary turn of duty in consideration of another duty that takes precedence. • *v.* dated **1** pass over (someone) in favor of another: *during the war officers were often overslaughed.* **2** Brit. pass over (one's ordinary turn of duty) in consideration of another duty that takes precedence.

over-the-horizon radar • a radar system that makes use of the atmospheric reflection and refraction phenomena to extend its range of detection beyond line of sight. Over-the-horizon radars may be either forward-scatter or back-scatter systems.

over there • **1** France, and Europe generally, from the American perspective, where WORLD WAR I was being fought for nearly three years before the United States joined the Allies (April 6, 1917). **2** (**Over There**) a popular song ("The Yanks are coming . . .") written by George M. Cohan as a patriotic tribute when the United States entered WORLD WAR I. Published in 1917, it was first professionally sung by Nora Bayes in the same year. Cohan, an actor, singer, and songwriter, adapted the verse of the song from "Johnny, Get Your Gun," written in 1886 by Monroe H. Rosenfeld under the name F. Belasco. In 1940 President FRANKLIN D. ROOSEVELT awarded Cohan a CONGRESSIONAL MEDAL OF HONOR for the song.

over-the-shoulder bombing • a special case of loft bombing where the bomb is released past the vertical in order that the bomb may be thrown back to the target.

over the top • in WORLD WAR I, an order, usually by the British, directing the infantry to leave the trenches and attack the German lines. The order was often given as, "Over the top! With the best of luck and give 'em hell." American troops were usually ordered, "Jump off." See also HOP-OVER.

overt operation • an operation conducted openly, without concealment.

OWI • *abbr.* Office of War Information.

Ox Hill, Battle of • see CHANTILLY, BATTLE OF.

Ozawa, Jisaburo (1886–1966) • Japanese vice admiral during WORLD WAR II (1939–45), commander of Japan's carrier forces (1942–45). Ozawa led the JAPANESE MOBILE FLEET in the battle of the PHILIPPINE SEA (1944), the largest carrier duel of the war. The fleet was grievously damaged and its aviation arm never recovered from the losses it sustained.

Pp

P-3 • see ORION.

P-38 • see LIGHTNING.

P-47 • see THUNDERBOLT.

P-51 • see MUSTANG.

P-61 • see BLACK WIDOW.

P-80 • see SHOOTING STAR.

pacesetter • *n.* an individual, selected by the column commander, who travels in the lead vehicle or element to regulate the column speed and establish the pace necessary to meet the required movement order.

Pacific Command • see U.S. PACIFIC COMMAND.

Pacific Fleet • see MAJOR FLEET.

Pacific War Memorial Commission • established by the then–Territory of Hawaii in 1949 and responsible for constructing the USS *Arizona* Memorial, which was completed in 1961 and dedicated in 1962.

pacifism • *n.* the belief that war and violence are unjustifiable and that all disputes should be settled by peaceful means.
DERIVATIVES: **pacifist** *n. & adj.*

pacifist • *n.* a proponent of pacifism • *adj.* of or relating to pacifism.

pacify • *v.* (**-ies, -ied**) bring peace to (a country or warring factions), especially by the use or threatened use of military force: *the general pacified northern Italy.*
DERIVATIVES: **pacification** *n.* **pacificatory** *adj.*

pack drill • Brit. a military punishment of marching back and forth carrying full equipment.

packet • *n.* (also **packet boat**) dated a ship traveling at regular intervals between two ports, originally for the conveyance of mail.

Packet • (**C-82**) a twin-engine cargo and troop transport aircraft begun by Fairchild Aircraft in 1941 and approved by the U.S. Army in 1942. In all, the development, engineering, and construction of the prototype took less than twenty-one months. Only 224 were built. Most were canceled at the end of the war because the C-119 was considered superior in capabilities.

pack ice • an expanse of large pieces of floating ice driven together into a nearly continuous mass, as occurs in polar seas.

pacta sunt servanda • the principle in international law and diplomacy which holds that international treaties, once entered into, should be upheld by all the signatories.

paddle • *n.* **1** a short pole with a broad blade at one or both ends, used without an oarlock to move a small boat or canoe through the water. **2** an act of using a paddle in a boat: *a gentle paddle on sluggish water.* • *v.* **1** move through the water in a boat using a paddle or paddles: *he paddled along the coast.* **2** propel (a small boat or canoe) with a paddle or paddles: *he was teaching trainees to paddle canoes.*

paddle steamer • a boat powered by steam and propelled by paddle wheels.

paddle wheel • a large steam-driven wheel with boards around its circumference, situated at the stern or side of a ship so as to propel the ship through the water by its rotation.

paddy foot • slang (in the VIETNAM WAR) trench foot.

padre |ˈpädrā| • *n.* informal a chaplain (typically a Roman Catholic chaplain) in any of the armed services.

Page, Thomas Jefferson (1808–99) • Confederate naval officer and explorer, born in Gloucester County, Virginia. In 1853 he began a commercial and scientific expedition to South America and commanded the first foreign ship ever to sail up the Paraguay and the Paraná rivers. He served as a military commander and diplomat during the CIVIL WAR.

During his years in South America, Page commanded the *Water Witch*, the only side-wheel steamer man-of-war ever owned by the U.S. Navy.

Paine, Thomas (1737–1809) • REVOLUTIONARY WAR patriot and pamphleteer, born in Thetford, England. Paine emigrated in 1774 to Pennsylvania, where he gravitated toward those who supported colonial independence. Paine's pamphlet *COMMON SENSE* appeared in January 1776 and caused an immediate sensation, selling approximately 150,000 copies. In it, Paine both supported American independence and attacked the corruption of the British hereditary monarchy. He fought in the Revolutionary War and continued to publish; his 1776 essay *The American Crisis* opens with the famous line, "These are the times that try men's souls."

paint • *v.* display a mark representing (an aircraft or vehicle) on a radar screen.

painter • *n.* a rope attached to the bow of a boat for making it fast.

PAL • *abbr.* Permissive Action Link.

Palermo, capture of • an action in July 1943, led by Gen. GEORGE S. PATTON. Media coverage of the Allied invasion of SICILY emphasized the contrast between British Marshal MONTGOMERY's caution and Patton's aggressiveness.

palisade |ˌpæləˈsād| • *n.* **1** a fence of wooden stakes or iron railings fixed in the ground, forming an enclosure or defense. **2** a strong pointed wooden stake fixed deeply in the ground with others in a close row, used as a defense. • *v.* (**palisaded**) enclose or provide (a building or place) with a palisade.

pallet • *n.* a flat base for combining stores or carrying a single item to form a unit load for handling, transportation, and storage by materials-handling equipment.

Palmer, James Shedden (1810–67) • Union naval officer, born in New Jersey. During the battle of VICKSBURG (1863), his effort to draw fire away from Admiral DAVID FARRAGUT's ship won him Farragut's respect and support.

Palmer earned the nickname "Piecrust Palmer" by his habit of donning formal dress before entering battle.

Palo Alto, Battle of • the first major battle of the MEXICAN WAR (1846–48), which occurred on May 8, 1846, at Palo Alto, near Brownsville in southern Texas. American Gen. ZACHARY TAYLOR, who would become president of the United States in 1849, defeated Mexican Gen. MARIANO ARISTA. Taylor pursued the retreating Mexican forces and launched the BATTLE OF THE RESACA DE LA PALMA the next day.

pan • *n.* a part of the lock that held the priming in old types of guns.

Panama Canal • a canal about 50 miles (80 km) long, across the isthmus of Panama, connecting the Atlantic and Pacific Oceans. Its construction, begun by Ferdinand de Lesseps in 1881 but abandoned in 1889, was completed by the United States between 1904 and 1914. The United States ceded control of the canal to Panama on December 31, 1999.

Panamanian Defense Forces • the most recent name for what was once the National Guard (armed forces) of the Republic of Panama. The Panamanian National Guard was organized, trained, and armed with United States assistance. The Panamanian Defense Forces loyal to their chief, Gen. MANUEL NORIEGA, resisted the U.S. invasion of Panama in OPERATION JUST CAUSE in December 1989.

Panamax |ˈpænəˌmæks| • denoting a ship with a dead-weight tonnage of not more than 69,000, the maximum size for a ship transiting the Panama canal.
ORIGIN: 1980s: blend of PANAMA and the adjective *maximum*.

Panay Incident • on December 12, 1937, Japanese warplanes, during the SECOND SINO-JAPANESE WAR, sank the U.S. Navy's gunboat *Panay* on the Yangtze, killing three Americans and wounding nearly thirty. President FRANKLIN D. ROOSEVELT considered an embargo and possible naval action; congressional and press opinion, on the other hand, concluded that no vital American interests were involved. The crisis subsided after Tokyo offered a formal apology and agreed to pay a $2 million indemnity. Anti-Japanese sentiment in the United States increased as a result of the incident.

Panmunjom • a village in the demilitarized zone of central Korea that was established in the aftermath of the KOREAN WAR. It was the site of the two-year-long truce conference (1951–53) held between representatives of the U.N. forces and the opposing North Korean and Chinese armies. After the armistice was signed there on July 27, 1953, Panmunjom also hosted liaison officials and guards of Sweden, Poland, Switzerland, and Czechoslovakia, the four countries that formed the Neutral Nations Supervisory Commission. In 1968, the United States and North Korea used Panmunjom as the site from which to negotiate the release of prisoners taken from a U.S. intelligence ship seized by the North Koreans. The village has since served as the location for various conferences between North and South Korea.

pan-pan • *n.* an international radio distress signal, of less urgency than a mayday signal.
ORIGIN: 1920s: *pan* from French *panne* 'breakdown.'

Panther • **1** (**F9F-5**) a straight-wing jet fighter aircraft, a conventional aircraft except for the refinement of its details and ease of maintenance. Although its performance and handling were inferior to that of good fighter aircraft, it made an excellent fighter-bomber and was used in combat during the KOREAN WAR. It had only limited commonality with the COUGAR, and the two fighter aircraft have the same designation only for political reasons. **2** WORLD WAR II-era German tank. See TANKS, GERMAN, WORLD WAR II-ERA.

panzer (or **Panzer**) |ˈpænzər| • *n.* a German armored vehicle, especially a tank used in

World War II: *panzer divisions.* See TANKS, GERMAN, WORLD WAR II-ERA.
ORIGIN: from German *Panzer,* literally 'coat of mail.'

Panzerfaust • any of a family of German manportable, single shot, antitank projectile launchers that were used during WORLD WAR II.

Panzerkampfwagen • (**PzKpfw**) see TANKS, GERMAN, WORLD WAR II-ERA.

paper blockade • a blockade on land, at sea, or in the air which has been formally declared but for which enforcement forces have not been deployed, making it ineffective.

Papua New Guinea • a country in the western Pacific comprising the eastern half of the island of New Guinea together with some neighboring islands; capital, Port Moresby. Starting with the Portugese landing on New Guinea in 1527 and continuing through the 19th century, the island (all or parts of it) have been claimed or colonized by the Spanish, Dutch, British, and Germans. In 1906 British New Guinea was passed to Australia, and its name changed to the Territory of Papua. With the advent of WORLD WAR I in 1914, Australian armed forces occupied German New Guinea, the northeastern quadrant of the island taken over by the German New Guinea Company in 1884, and remained there for seven years. Between World War I and World War II, the Australians and the Japanese struggled for control over the Territory. In 1921 the LEAGUE OF NATIONS granted Australia a mandate to govern German New Guinea (except for Nauru and Micronesia). In 1942 the Japanese invaded New Guinea and part of Papua, but by 1945 Australia recovered the occupied land. The administration of Papua and the New Guinea mandate was then combined into the Territory of Papua and New Guinea. In 1969 Indonesia annexed Dutch New Guinea as the province of Irian Jaya. In 1975 Papua New Guinea achieved complete independence from Britain.

para *n.* informal • a paratrooper.

Parabellum |ˌpærə'beləm| • trademark a make of automatic pistol or machine gun.
ORIGIN: early 20th century: from Latin *para bellum,* from *para!* 'prepare!' + *bellum* 'war.'

parachute • *n.* a cloth canopy which fills with air and allows a person or heavy object attached to it to descend slowly when dropped from an aircraft, or which is released from the rear of an aircraft on landing to act as a brake. • *v.* drop or cause to drop from an aircraft by parachute: *airborne units parachuted in to secure the airport.*
ORIGIN: late 18th century: from French *para-* 'protection against' + *chute* 'fall.'

parachute flare • a pyrotechnic signal flare that is carried up into the air by a rocket and floats suspended from a small parachute.

parachutist • *n.* a person who uses a parachute.

parade • *n.* **1** a formal march or gathering of troops for inspection or display. **2** a parade ground. • *v.* (of troops) assemble for a formal inspection or ceremonial occasion: *the recruits were due to parade that day.*
PHRASES: **on parade** taking part in a parade.

parade ground • a place where troops gather for parade.

parados |'pærəˌdäs| • *n.* an elevation of earth behind a fortified place as a protection against attack from the rear, especially a mound along the back of a trench.

paradrop • *n.* the delivery by parachute of personnel or cargo from an aircraft in flight.

Paramarines • a group of U.S. Marines trained to parachute from aircraft behind enemy lines in order to disrupt and destroy troops and supply lines during WORLD WAR II; organized at Lakehurst, NewJersey on October 26, 1940.

paramilitary • *adj.* (of an unofficial force) organized similarly to a military force: *soldiers and police have been killed in conflicts with the drug cartels and their paramilitary allies.* • *n.* (pl. **-ies**) a member of an unofficial paramilitary organization.

paramilitary forces • forces or groups that are distinct from the regular armed forces of any country, but resembling them in organization, equipment, training, or mission.

parapet • *n.* a protective wall or earth defense along the top of a trench or other place of concealment for troops.
DERIVATIVES: **parapeted** *adj.*

pararescue team • specially trained personnel qualified to penetrate to the site of an incident by land or parachute, render medical aid, accomplish survival methods, and rescue survivors.

paratrooper • *n.* a member of a paratroop regiment or airborne unit.

paratroops • *plural n.* troops equipped to be dropped by parachute from aircraft: (usually **paratroop**) *a paratroop regiment.*
ORIGIN: 1940s: from an abbreviation of PARACHUTE + *troops* (plural of TROOP).

paravane • *n.* a device towed behind a boat at a depth regulated by its vanes or planes, so that the cable to which it is attached can cut the moorings of submerged mines.

parbuckle • *n.* a loop of rope arranged like a sling, used for raising or lowering casks and other cylindrical objects along an inclined plane. • *v.* raise or lower with such a device.

Paris Declaration of 1856 • an agreement signed on April 16, 1856, at the Congress of Paris to codify international maritime law. The first attempt to establish such a law, it prohibited privateering, allowed a neutral flag to protect an enemy's goods except for war contraband, prohibited the capture of neutral goods when under an enemy's flag, and specified conditions for the use of blockades.

Paris, liberation of • a WORLD WAR II Allied victory, on August 25, 1944. After OPERATION OVERLORD gained a foothold in NORMANDY, Allied forces made slow progress east. The German counterattack at Avranches, however, enabled the ALLIES to pick up a head of steam, sweeping through France rapidly, liberating Paris on August 25 and moving into the Low Countries.

Paris Peace Agreements • an "Agreement on Ending the War and Restoring Peace to Vietnam," signed on January 27, 1973, in Paris by the Republic of Vietnam, the Democratic Republic of Vietnam, the Provisional Revolutionary Government of Vietnam, and the United States. It was followed by three detailed protocols derived from it and signed by the same signatories. It called for a cease-fire throughout North and South Vietnam and the ending of direct U.S. participation in the VIETNAM WAR by a withdrawal of all U.S. forces in South Vietnam, the dismantlement of U.S. bases, and a Four-Power Joint Military Commission to oversee the agreement's implementation. It also called for the release of all prisoners of war, limitations on arms replacement in both regions, and negotiations between North and South Vietnam to establish peaceful relations and reunification. Despite the agreements, violations of the cease-fire and other provisions had resumed by the fall of 1973.

HENRY KISSINGER, President RICHARD M. NIXON's national security adviser, and LE DUC THO, the special adviser to the North Vietnamese Politburo, had held "backchannel" negotiations in 1970–71 in an attempt to reach an agreement. After the 1973 agreement was signed, Kissinger and Le Duc Tho were jointly awarded the Nobel Peace Prize for 1973, but the latter declined to accept it.

Paris Peace Conference • a meeting begun on January 18, 1919, to address post-WORLD WAR I peace issues. Among the controversial issues addressed at the conference were territory disputes, governance of colonies captured during the war, and reparations. It resulted in the TREATY OF VERSAILLES and ended with the formal establishment of the LEAGUE OF NATIONS on January 16, 1920.

Paris, Treaty of • **1** (1783) a treaty signed on September 3, 1783, to end the REVOLUTIONARY WAR. Negotiated by British representatives and the U.S. delegates JOHN ADAMS, John Jay, and Benjamin Franklin, it recognized U.S. independence and a western boundary to the Mississippi River, and gave the United States rights to Newfoundland fisheries. It recommended fair treatment of loyalists and the restoration of their property. **2** (1898) a treaty signed by Spain and the United States on December 20, 1898, to end the SPANISH-AMERICAN WAR. The United States gained temporary control of Cuba and actual control over Guam and Puerto Rico. Spain ceded the Philippines on the condition that the United States pay the Islands $20 million for public works.

Parke, John (1754–89) • Revolutionary army officer, born in Dover, Delaware. Parke served under Gen. GEORGE WASHINGTON at the Battle of MONMOUTH (1778); Parke's troops were part of a disorganized retreat that drew Washington's wrath. Later, Parke became a published poet.

Parke, John Grubb (1827–1900) • Union army officer, born in Chester County, Pennsylvania. Parke served as major general of volunteers and chief of staff under Gen. AMBROSE BURNSIDE during the CIVIL WAR. He commanded the 9th Corps at VICKSBURG (1863). He ended his career as superintendent of WEST POINT from 1887 to 1989.

Parker, Ely S. (1828–95) • U.S. commissioner of Indian affairs (1869–71). Son of a SENECA chief and born on a reservation in New York, he worked as a civil engineer on federal projects and befriended ULYSSES S. GRANT. During the CIVIL WAR he served as Grant's military secretary.

Parker was the first Native American to serve as commissioner of Indian affairs.

Parker, Foxhall Alexander, Jr. (1821–79) • Union naval officer, born in New York City to a military family. Parker was an adroit military tactician whose books were used as texts at WEST POINT. Parker's flotilla tried and failed to apprehend JOHN WILKES BOOTH as he fled after assassinating President ABRAHAM LINCOLN in April 1865.

Parker's brother, WILLIAM HARWAR PARKER, aligned with the family's Virginia roots and fought for the CONFEDERACY.

Parker, William Harwar (1826–96) • Confederate naval officer, born in New York City. Parker's ship, the *Beaufort*, served as tender to the iron-clad *Virginia* (formerly the *Merrimack*) during fighting off HAMPTON ROADS in 1862. His was thanked for his service by the Confederate Congress. During the CONFEDERACY's evacuation of RICHMOND in 1865, Parker was in charge of the government's archives and treasury and escorted the wife of President JEFFERSON DAVIS to safety.

parley |ˈpärlē| • *n.* (pl. **-eys**) a conference between opposing sides in a dispute, especially a discussion of terms for an armistice. • *v.* (**-eys, -eyed**) hold a conference with the opposing side to discuss terms: *they disagreed over whether to* ***parley with*** *the enemy.*

parole |pəˈrōl| • *n.* **1** historical a promise or undertaking given by a prisoner of war not to escape or, if released, to return to custody under stated conditions: *I took their* ***paroles of honor*** | *a good many French officers had been living on parole in Melrose.* **2** the release of a prisoner temporarily (for a special purpose) or permanently before the completion of a sentence, on the promise of good behavior: *he committed a burglary while* ***on parole.*** • *v.* (usually **be paroled**) release (a prisoner) on parole.

DERIVATIVES: **parolee** |-ˌrōˈlē| *n.*

ORIGIN: late 15th century: from Old French, literally 'word,' also 'formal promise.'

Parrott, Enoch Greenleafe (1815–79) • Union naval officer. A native of Portsmouth, New Hampshire, Parrott participated in a number of naval operations during the CIVIL WAR. He rose to the command of the double-turreted ironclad *Monadnock*, participating in the attack on Wilmington, North Carolina, the last Confederate port of any strategic value to remain operational. The Union attack succeeded in shutting down the city.

Parrott, Robert Parker (1804–77) • Union army officer and ordnance manufacturer. As owner of the West Point Foundry in Cold Spring, New York, and later the Greenwood Furnace, Parrott developed a cast-iron rifled cannon strengthened by a wrought-iron band on the breech. Parrott's rifles were used in the CIVIL WAR, first by the Confederacy and later by the UNION as well, despite complaints that the guns were inaccurate and that there were problems with the ammunition.

partisan |ˈpärt̬əzən| • *n.* a member of an armed group formed to fight secretly against an occupying force, in particular one operating in enemy-occupied Yugoslavia, Italy, and parts of eastern Europe in WORLD WAR II.

Partnership for Peace • an arm of NATO formed in 1994. It arranges exercises, exchanges, and other military contacts to encourage military reform, and it also provides for peacekeeping, humanitarian, and rescue operations. The organization has a membership of twenty-five nations, including Hungary, Romania, and Russia. Russia joined the group in June 1994.

pass • *v.* **1** move in a specified direction: *the shells from the Allied guns were passing very low overhead.* **2** (of a candidate) be successful in (an examination, test, or course): *she passed her driving test.* **3** judge the performance or standard of (someone or something) to be satisfactory: *he was passed fit by army doctors.* **4** be accepted as adequate; go uncensured: *she couldn't agree, but **let it pass**.*
PHRASES: **pass muster** see MUSTER.

Passchendaele, Battle of • see YPRES, BATTLES OF.

Passendale • see YPRES.

passive homing guidance • a system of homing guidance wherein the receiver in the missile utilizes radiation from the target.

patch • *n.* **1** a piece of cloth sewn onto clothing as a badge or distinguishing mark. **2** Brit. & informal an area for which someone is responsible or in which they operate: *we didn't want any secret organizations on our patch.* **3** a temporary electrical or telephone connection. • *v.* **1** connect by a temporary electrical, radio, or telephonic connection: *Ralph had **patched** her **through** to the meeting by walkie-talkie.* **2** become connected in this way: *stay on the open line and we'll patch in on you.*

patent log • a mechanical device used to measure the speed and distance traveled through the water of a ship or boat.

Paterson, John (1744–1808) • REVOLUTIONARY WAR army officer and U.S. representative (1803–05), born in Farmington, Connecticut. Paterson was an early supporter of American independence and was a regimental commander and later a brigadier general and a major general in the war.

pathfinder • *n.* an aircraft or its pilot sent ahead to locate and mark the target area for bombing.

pathfinder aircraft • **1** an aircraft that leads a formation to a drop zone, release point, or target. **2** an aircraft that carries military teams that are dropped or air-landed in order to set up and operate navigational equipment that will guide other aircraft to drop and landing zones. **3** an aircraft equipped with a radar device used for navigating or finding a target when bad visibility would otherwise make it impossible to navigate visually. **4** an aircraft that delivers military teams into enemy territory so that they can identify the best approach and withdrawal lanes, landing zones, and places where helicopter-borne forces can be successfully dropped.

patria |ˈpātrēə; ˈpæ-; ˈpä-| • *n.* one's native country or homeland: *they remained faithful to their patria, Spain.*

Patrick, Marsena Rudolph (1811–88) • Union army officer, born in upstate New York. Patrick was a successful farmer and his innovative methods led to his appointment as the first president of the new State Agricultural College. His successful term as military governor of the occupied city of Fredericksburg, Virginia, led to his appointment as provost marshal general of the ARMY OF THE POTOMAC and later of all Union armies.

patriot • *n.* **1** a person who vigorously supports their country and is prepared to defend it against enemies or detractors. **2** (**Patriot**) (**MIM-104**) trademark a modern surface-to-air missile, first developed in the 1970s as an antiaircraft weapon and adapted in the 1980s to defend against ballistic missiles as well. It was used extensively in the PERSIAN GULF WAR (1991). **3** a missile deployed in this system.
DERIVATIVES: **patriotism** *n.*

patrol • *n.* **1** a person or group of people sent to keep watch over an area, especially a detachment of guards or police: *a police patrol stopped the man and searched him.* **2** the action of keeping watch over an area by walking or driving around it at regular intervals: *the policemen were **on patrol** when they were ordered to investigate the incident.* **3** an expedition to carry out reconnaissance: *we were ordered to investigate on a night patrol.* **4** a detachment of troops sent out to reconnoiter: *you couldn't go through the country without meeting an enemy patrol.* **5** a routine operational voyage of a ship or aircraft: *a submarine patrol.* • *v.* (**patrolled, patrolling**) keep watch over (an area) by regularly walking or traveling around or through it: *the garrison had to patrol the streets to maintain order.*
DERIVATIVES: **patroller** *n.*

patrol boat • a boat or ship assigned to protect a particular area or to gather useful military information about the area. See also PATROL CRAFT.

patrol craft • an airplane or watercraft that protects a specific area or gathers needed military information about the area. See also PATROL BOAT.

pattern bombing • the bombing of a target from a number of aircraft according to a prescribed pattern intended to produce the maximum effect.

pattern laying • in land-mine warfare, the laying of mines in a fixed relationship to each other.

DERIVATIVES: **pattern-laid** *adj.*

Pattison, Thomas (1822–91) • Union naval officer, born in Troy, New York. Pattison was a successful commander in the early years of the CIVIL WAR and for its duration he either held responsible positions on shore or commanded warships. He was commander of the U.S. Navy Station, Memphis, Tennessee, from 1863 to 1865.

Patton, George S. (1885–1945) • military officer, born in San Gabriel, California. Patton was an aide to Gen. JOHN J. PERSHING during the army's attempt to capture the Mexican revolutionary PANCHO VILLA (1916–17). Patton accompanied Pershing to France in 1917 and became an expert in tank warfare. He commanded the Western Task Forces whose invasion of NORTH AFRICA in 1942 led to the French surrender there in only three days. Patton led the Allied invasion of SICILY (1943), another quick victory. He trained the U.S. 3rd Army to follow the ALLIES into France after D-DAY (1944) and won praise for his boldness and surefootedness. Patton's quick action in the BATTLE OF THE BULGE (1944–45) was instrumental in stopping the NAZI offensive and led to his becoming a four-star general. However, his concerns about future Soviet aggression led him to oppose rapid denazification of postwar Germany, a controversial position that cost him his command. He died from a broken neck suffered in an automobile accident.

Patton Series • (**M-60**) a main battle tank first produced in 1960 and used for twenty years before the M-1 was introduced. With a four-person crew, it carried a 105-mm main gun into battle. Production ended in 1983, and M-60s are now found mostly in U.S. Reserve and NATIONAL GUARD units.

Paulding, Hiram (1797–1878) • Union naval officer, born in Westchester County, New York. In 1824 Paulding couriered messages between naval officials and Simon Bolívar, the South American revolutionary, and he demonstrated extraordinary bravery during service in the South Pacific. He headed the New York Navy Yard for the final four years of the CIVIL WAR, supervising the construction of ironclads and repairing and supplying ships involved in the blockade of the South.

Paul H. Nitze School of Advanced International Studies • a postgraduate school at The Johns Hopkins University in Washington, D.C. It instructs students in international relations through an emphasis on language and economics. Established in 1944 by PAUL H. NITZE and Christian Herter, it became part ofThe Johns Hopkins University in 1950 and was named in Nitze's honor in 1986.

Pave Hawk • see BLACK HAWK.

Paveway • (**I, II, III**) a group of modern laser guided bombs that are fired from aircraft and guided to their targets by detection of a laser trained on the target. The Paveway III overcame some limitations of the earlier versions and can be delivered at lower altitudes and at longer range.

PAVN • *abbr.* People's Army of Vietnam. See NORTH VIETNAMESE ARMY.

Pax Americana • the impact of U.S. military, economic, and political power since 1945 which has restrained the outbreak of either a nuclear war or a general global war.

pay • *v.* (past and past part. **payed**) seal (the deck or hull seams of a wooden ship) with pitch or tar to prevent leakage.

payload • *n.* **1** the part of a vehicle's load, especially an aircraft's, from which revenue is derived; passengers and cargo. **2** an explosive warhead carried by a missile. **3** equipment, personnel, or satellites carried by a spacecraft.

paymaster • *n.* an official who pays troops or workers.

PBR • *abbr.* river patrol boat.

PCF • *abbr.* personnel control facilities.

PDF • *abbr.* Panamanian Defense Forces.

peace |pēs| • *n.* **1** freedom from or the cessation of war or violence: *the Straits were to be open to warships in time of peace.* **2** a treaty agreeing to the cessation of war between warring states: *support for a negotiated peace.* **3** freedom from civil disorder: *police action to restore peace.*

PHRASES: **keep the peace** refrain or prevent others from disturbing civil order: *the police must play a crucial role in keeping the peace.*

Peace Action • the largest and most influential nuclear disarmament organization in the United States. Originally known as the NATIONAL COMMITTEE FOR A SANE NUCLEAR POLICY (SANE), it was founded in 1957 by prominent citizens concerned about the hazards associated with nuclear testing and the proliferation of nuclear weapons. The LIMITED TEST BAN TREATY of 1963, which halted atmospheric nuclear tests, is considered the organization's greatest achievement. SANE merged in 1987 with the Nuclear Weapons Freeze Campaign (FREEZE), which originated in response to President RONALD REAGAN's nuclear weapons policies. In 1993 the group's name was changed to Peace Action.

Peace Chief • a chief who illegally cedes lands to whites, a term used disparagingly by the Shawnee chief TECUMSEH at the signing of the TREATY OF GREENVILLE (Ohio) in August 1795. Tecumseh believed that all Native American land was the common property of all the Native American tribes and that any one tribe should not cede or sell land on its own. He accused the chiefs of giving away territory that was not theirs.

peace establishment • the authorized size, composition, and organization of a nation's armed forces in peacetime.

peace implementation • the use of neutral military forces to assist in the implementation of a peace treaty between former belligerents.

Peacekeeper • (**LGM-118**) a strategic intercontinental ballistic missile capable of delivering ten independently targeted warheads. It was tested during the 1980s and is due to be phased out by 2003 as a result of SALT II.

peacekeeping • *n.* the active maintenance of

a truce between nations or communities, especially by an international military force: *the 2,300-strong U.N. peacekeeping force.*
DERIVATIVES: **peacekeeper** *n.*

peacekeeping mission • the deployment of military forces, usually under U.N. or other international control, to prevent or deter further military action by the military or paramilitary forces of two opposing nations or groups.

peace observation • the deployment of military and civilian observers to observe and report upon the implementation of an armistice or other peace agreement between nations.

peacetime • *n.* a period when a country is not at war.

"Peace Without Victory" speech • an address given by President WOODROW WILSON on January 22, 1917. He proposed peace terms for ending the war and defined the traditional use of victory as being anathema to the establishment of peace among nations. After U.S. entry into WORLD WAR I on April 16, 1917, he proposed peace terms in the FOURTEEN POINTS address, which was based on this speech.

Peach Orchard • an area of fighting that, together with the Wheatfield and DEVIL'S DEN, comprised the Union left flank at GETTYSBURG (1863), during the CIVIL WAR. During the second day of the battle, Confederate Lt. Gen. JAMES LONGSTREET managed to capture the Peach Orchard from Union Maj. Gen. DANIEL SICKLES, who retreated to CEMETERY RIDGE. Union troops won victory at Gettysburg the following day.

Peachtree Creek, Battle of • a CIVIL WAR battle fought on July 20, 1864, in Fulton County, Georgia, between Confederate forces under Gen. JOHN B. HOOD and Union forces under Gen. GEORGE THOMAS. It was a Union victory mainly through attrition, and cost the Confederates nearly 5,000 casualties while they were trying to delay the inevitable attack on ATLANTA.

pea jacket (also **peacoat, pea coat**) • a short, double-breasted overcoat of coarse woolen cloth, formerly worn by sailors.

peak • *n.* **1** chiefly Brit. a stiff brim at the front of a cap. **2** the narrow part of a ship's hold at the bow or stern. **3** the upper, outer corner of a sail extended by a gaff.

Pea Ridge, Battle of • (also known as the Battle of Elkhorn Tavern) this battle, fought from March 6–8, 1862, pitted the Confederate Army of the West under the command of Maj. Gen. EARL VAN DORN against Brig. Gen. SAMUEL R. CURTIS's Army of the Southwest. After several days of fierce fighting, the Union forces drove off the Confederates, allowing them to march across Arkansas, and thus take an important step towards controlling the Trans-Mississippi region. The Confederate casualties were 2,000; the Union losses, 1,384.

Pearl Harbor • a surprise Japanese attack on the U.S. Navy's base at Pearl Harbor and on Oahu in the Hawaiian Islands on December 7, 1941. It destroyed much of the American PACIFIC FLEET and brought the United States into WORLD WAR II. The attack followed the decision of the Japanese government that the FRANKLIN D. ROOSEVELT's administration would not abandon China and Southeast Asia to the Japanese military nor continue to supply Tokyo with vital materials. Early Sunday morning, December 7, Japanese aircraft launched an assault that destroyed or disabled nineteen ships and 292 planes. American deaths totaled 2,335 and 1,178 were wounded. Ultimately, though the attack was a tactical success, the Japanese failure to destroy American repair yards, fuel reserves, and submarine base prevented them from achieving their goal of destroying the U.S. Navy in the Pacific.

Pearl Harbor National Historic Landmark • a landmark located on the island of Maui in the state of Hawaii. It contains the remains of the USS *Utah* and the aircraft lost when Japan bombed PEARL HARBOR on December 7, 1941.

peep sight • a rear sight for rifles with a circular hole through which the front sight is brought into line with the object aimed at.

Peers Commission • a commission of inquiry established in November 1969 and headed by Lt. Gen. W. R. PEERS to investigate the MY LAI MASSACRE, also known as the Son My incident (March 16–19, 1968). Of the thirty individuals implicated by the commission's findings, sixteen were criminally charged, five were tried by court-martial, and only one, First Lt. WILLIAM L. CALLEY, was found guilty. He was convicted on March 29, 1971 and paroled November 19, 1974.

PEFTOK • *abbr.* PHILIPPINE EXPEDITIONARY FORCE TO KOREA.

Pegasus, Operation • was the overland attack, involving some 30,000 troops, that relieved the besieged U.S. Marine base at KHE SANH on April 7, 1968. The siege, which had lasted for seventy-eight days, resulted in 730 battle deaths, 2,598 wounded, and 7 missing. The relationship between Khe Sanh and the TET OFFENSIVE of 1968 continues to be the most controversial aspect of the siege as many believe Hanoi deceived Gen. WILLIAM C. WESTMORELAND into excessively focusing on Khe Sanh. The United States withdrew from Khe Sanh on July 6.

Pelham, John (1838–63) • Confederate army officer, born in Alabama. Pelham was a capable officer who became a favorite of Col. J.E.B. STUART, whose patronage aided his move up through the ranks. Pelham assisted THOMAS "STONEWALL" JACKSON's brigade at the FIRST BATTLE OF BULL RUN (1861) and saw almost continuous action during the PENINSULAR CAMPAIGN (1862). He also fought at the SECOND BATTLE OF BULL RUN, at ANTIETAM, and, notably, at FREDERICKSBURG (all 1862).

pellet • *n.* a piece of small shot or other lightweight bullet.

pelorus |pə'lawrəs| • *n.* a sighting device on a ship for taking the relative bearings of a distant object.
ORIGIN: mid 19th cent.: perhaps from

Pelorus, said to be the name of Hannibal's pilot.

Pemberton, John Clifford (1814–81) • Confederate army officer, born in Philadelphia. In the early years of his military career, he participated in the second SEMINOLE WAR (1835–42) and in the MEXICAN WAR (1846–48). When the CIVIL WAR broke out, he was promoted quickly up the ranks of the Confederate army, despite considerable personal unpopularity, stemming partly from his Northern roots. Pemberton, placed in charge of defending Mississippi and East Louisiana, was bested by Gen. ULYSSES S. GRANT in the drive through the South that culminated at VICKSBURG (1863). The defeat cemented his unpopularity.

pen • *n.* a covered dock for a submarine or other warship.

pencil beam • a searchlight beam reduced to, or set at, its minimum width.

Pender, William Dorsey (1834–63) • Confederate army officer, born in North Carolina. Pender was an ardent defender of STATES' RIGHTS who joined the Confederate army at the outbreak of the CIVIL WAR. He was a brave and resourceful commander who fought at many major engagements, including HARPERS FERRY (1861) and MECHANICSVILLE (1862). He was wounded in battle in 1863 and died from his injury.

penetration • *n.* **1** in intelligence, the recruitment of agents within, or the infiltration of agents or technical monitoring devices in, an organization or group for the purpose of acquiring information or of influencing its activities. **2** in land operations, a form of offensive that seeks to break through the enemy's defense and disrupt the defensive system.

penetrator • *n.* **1** a person or thing that penetrates something. **2** a missile containing a hard alloy rod, designed to penetrate the armor of tanks or fortifications.

Peninsular Campaign • a big offensive planned and led by Union Gen. GEORGE B. MCCLELLAN, that took place from March to July 1862. McClellan, commander of the ARMY OF THE POTOMAC, hoped to seize Richmond, Virginia, a goal which he came within five miles of achieving. In the SEVEN DAYS' BATTLE, however, Confederate Gen. ROBERT E. LEE repelled McClellan's forces. Disillusioned by McClellan's apparent lack of progress and demands for additional manpower, President ABRAHAM LINCOLN withdrew McClellan and his army from the peninsula, and placed JOHN POPE in charge of Union forces in northern Virginia.

pennant • *n.* **1** a tapering flag on a ship, especially one flown at the masthead of a vessel in commission. **2** a long triangular or swallow-tailed flag, especially as the military ensign of lancer regiments. **3** a short rope or pendant hanging from the head of a ship's mast.

pennon |ˈpenən| • *n.* PENNANT.
DERIVATIVES: **pennoned** *adj.*

Pennsylvania long rifle • a longrifle developed in Pennsylvania by German craftsmen in the early 18th century. A typical rifle was .50 caliber, with a 42 to 46 inch barrel.

pentagon • *n.* **1** (**the Pentagon**) the pentagonal building serving as the headquarters of the U.S. DEPARTMENT OF DEFENSE, near Washington, D.C. **2** the U.S. Department of Defense: *the Pentagon said 19 soldiers had been killed.*

Pentagonese • *n.* informal the euphemistic or cryptic language supposedly used among high-ranking U.S. military personnel.

Pentagon Papers • a collection of confidential DEPARTMENT OF DEFENSE documents commissioned by Defense secretary ROBERT S. MCNAMARA in 1967 and that detailed post-WORLD WAR II U.S. actions concerning the VIETNAM WAR. They were turned over to the press by Defense Department analyst Daniel Ellsburg, and *The New York Times* began publishing the history on June 13, 1971, followed by publication in the *Washington Post.* President RICHARD M. NIXON's lawyers sued in the to suspend publication in the interest of national security but lost.

pentomic division • U.S. Army infantry division structure developed during the 1950s to complement the Eisenhower administration's "New Look" policy of reliance on nuclear weapons. Designed to operate on a nuclear battlefield, the "pentomic division," so-called because it was organized with five infantry "battle groups" rather than the traditional four regiments or three brigades, emphasized organic nuclear-capable rocket and tube artillery, high mobility, and effective communications.

People's Liberation Army • (**PLA**) the armed forces of the Communist-led People's Republic of China. Created on August 1, 1927, the PLA, led by MAO ZEDONG and ZHOU ENLAI, used both guerrilla and conventional methods to defeat the Nationalist Chinese forces of CHIANG KAI-SHEK in the Chinese civil war of 1945-1949. The PLA provided the leadership, matefriel, and manpower for the CHINESE PEOPLE'S VOLUNTEERS (CPV) in the KOREAN WAR.

pepperbox • *n.* a gun or piece of artillery with a revolving set of barrels.

Pepperrell, William (1696–1759) • soldier and merchant. Born in Maine to a prosperous and socially prominent family, Pepperrell entered the family business and also became active in the local militia. His most noted exploit was the 1745 expedition he led against the French fort at LOUISBOURG, Cape Breton Island, which had been used as a base to interfere with Massachusetts shipping; after a month-long siege, the fort surrendered. Pepperrell commanded the Eastern Frontier during the SEVEN YEARS WAR (1756-63) and in 1759 was named a brigadier general in the British army, although poor health kept him from field service.

Pequot (or **Pequod**) • an Algonquian-speaking Indian tribe located in coastal southern New England. In the 1630s, the Pequots antagonized the other tribes in the area as well as the Dutch by trying to monopolize Indian-

Dutch trade. Having failed to form an alliance with the English settlers in the Massachusetts Bay Colony, In 1637, the Pequot sachem Sassacus and his followers were attacked by the English and some Narragansetts and Mohegans and fled to the Mohawks who subsequently betrayed them. The defeat of the Pequots opened Connecticut to English settlement.

Pequot War • a short, sharp, and decisive conflict between English colonists in Massachusetts and the Pequots in 1636–37. Punishing the Pequots for the death of an English trader, Massachusetts militia attacked men, women, and children at the stockaded Mystic village, setting it ablaze and shooting escapees.

perception management • actions to convey and/or deny selected information and indicators to foreign audiences (in order to influence their emotions, motives, and objective reasoning) and to intelligence systems and leaders at all levels (in order to influence official estimates), ultimately resulting in foreign behaviors and official actions favorable to the originator's objectives.

percussion • *n.* the striking of one solid object with or against another with some degree of force.

DERIVATIVES: **percussive** *adj.* **percussively** *adv.*

percussion cap • a small metallic container filled with fulminating powder. It was a component of firing small arms before the development of the bullet. Striking it with the hammer of a gun caused the ignition of gunpowder, whose explosive power activated the projectile ball.

perestroika |ˌperəˈstroikə| • *n.* (in the former Soviet Union) the policy or practice of restructuring or reforming the economic and political system. First proposed by LEONID BREZHNEV in 1979 and actively promoted by MIKHAIL GORBACHEV, perestroika originally referred to increased automation and labor efficiency, but came to entail greater awareness of economic markets and the ending of central planning. See also GLASNOST.

ORIGIN: Russian, literally 'restructuring'.

perimeter • *n.* a defended boundary of a military position or base.

perimeter defense • a defense without an exposed flank, consisting of forces deployed along the perimeter of the defended area.

periscope • *n.* an apparatus consisting of a tube attached to a set of mirrors or prisms, by which an observer (typically in a submerged submarine or behind a high obstacle) can see things that are otherwise out of sight.

Permanent Constitution • the constitution of the CONFEDERATE STATES OF AMERICA, adopted March 11, 1861 in Montgomery, Alabama. It drew heavily on the constitution of the United States, establishing a bicameral legislature and other institutions modeled on those of the Union, and also made many specific provisions for perpetuating and administering the institution of slavery.

Permissive Action Link • a device included in or attached to a nuclear weapon system to preclude arming and/or launching until the insertion of a prescribed discrete code or combination. It may include equipment and cabling external to the weapon or weapon system to activate components with the weapon or weapon system.

Perry, Edward Aylesworth (1831–89) • governor of Florida and Confederate army officer. Despite his Massachusetts birth, after his family moved to the South Perry became a southerner in outlook and a believer in secession. He led the 2nd Florida at ANTIETAM (1862) but offered his most outstanding service at CHANCELLORSVILLE (1863), where he drove a Union force into disorganized retreat, enabling Gen. ROBERT E. LEE to unite his own army and rout the Northern forces. Health problems kept him from further significant service, and he returned to Florida, where he served as governor from 1884 to 1888.

Perry, Matthew Calbraith (1794–1858) • naval officer and diplomat, born in Newport, Rhode Island. In 1833 he became second officer at the New York Navy Yard and an exponent of educational reform and technological innovation; in 1841 he became commandant of the Yard. The high point of his military career was the MEXICAN WAR (1846–48), when with Gen. WINFIELD SCOTT he succeeded in capturing the city of VERACRUZ (1847). In 1852 he began negotiations with Japan and opened that formerly closed nation to the West, making Japanese ports accessible to U.S. ships for provisioning, establishing a U.S. consulate, and eventually seeing the beginning of trade relations between the two countries.

Perry, Oliver Hazard (1785–1819) • naval officer. Born into a naval family in Rhode Island, Perry first served on his father's frigate. He served ably in the BARBARY WARS (1801–05) and in protecting U.S. shipping interests from privateers; in 1813 he assumed command of a naval force on Lake Erie. His defeat of a British squadron under Gen. Robert H. Barclay, despite personal illness, was a major victory, considered by some the most important engagement of the WAR OF 1812; it also helped Gen. WILLIAM H. HARRISON's troops to defeat British troops in the area. For years after, however, controversy raged about the failure of one of Perry's officers to engage the enemy during the battle.

Having defeated the British fleet in Lake Erie on September 10, 1813, Perry famously cabled his superior, "We have met the enemy and they are ours."

Perryville, Battle of • the largest CIVIL WAR battle in Kentucky, fought near Perryville on Oct. 8, 1862. Confederate commander BRAXTON BRAGG mistakenly believed that he faced one Union corps at Perryville, but there were actually 58,000 Federal troops in the area. Despite early success in the battle, Bragg withdrew after belatedly learning that he confronted the bulk of Union Gen. DON CARLOS BUELL's army. Bragg's army took over 3,000 casualties; Union army totals exceeded 4,000.

Soon after, the Confederates retreated into Tennessee, abandoning Bragg's boldly conceived Kentucky invasion.

Perry, William James (1927–) • secretary of defense (1993–97), born in Pennsylvania. Perry served as undersecretary of defense for research and engineering in the CARTER administration and worked on missile development, including the Stealth missile. He was named deputy secretary of defense by President BILL CLINTON in 1993 and became secretary, with some reluctance, after LES ASPIN, who held the position, was forced to resign in the face of criticism of his performance. Perry was considered an expert on military hardware and an able administrator.

Pershing (also **Pershing missile**) • *n.* (**MGM-31A**) a U.S. short-range surface-to-surface ballistic missile, capable of carrying a nuclear or conventional warhead.

ORIGIN: 1950s: named after John J. *Pershing* (1860–1948), American general.

Pershing, John J. (1860–1948) • commander of the AMERICAN EXPEDITIONARY FORCES, World War I. After service in the SPANISH-AMERICAN WAR (1898), he went to Washington, D.C., where his broad background won him appointment as head of the Bureau of Insular Affairs within the War Department. He served ably in the Philippines, combining his military, diplomatic, and administrative skills to pacify rival chieftains. President WOODROW WILSON named him to head the American Expeditionary Force when the nation entered WORLD WAR I in 1917; he built a strong U.S. force and cooperated with the Allies in stopping German offensives while protecting U.S. positions, an accomplishment that won him high praise. The offensive he launched in the MEUSE-ARGONNE region in 1918 was instrumental in convincing Germany to sue for peace. For his accomplishments, Pershing was named general of the army, an honor previously accorded only to GEORGE WASHINGTON. From 1921 to 1924 he served as army chief of staff, and he was mentioned as a possible presidential candidate in 1924.

Pershing was nicknamed "Black Joe" because of his service with the Buffalo Soldiers.

Pershing tank • U.S. WORLD WAR II and KOREAN WAR-era M–26 heavy tank. Introduced late in World War II, the Pershing tank weighed 46 tons and had a maximum speed of 20 MPH, a cruising range of 75 miles, and a crew of five. It was armed with a 90–mm main gun with a coaxial .30 caliber machine gun, a flexible .30 caliber machine gun mounted in the bow, and a .50 caliber machine gun mounted on the turret.

Persian Gulf War • this war in 1991, caused by Iraq's invasion of Kuwait on August 2, 1990, had two major phases: OPERATIONS DESERT SHIELD and DESERT STORM. The former was a defensive operation in which the U.S. and Saudi Arabia rushed to bolster defensive forces in case of further Iraqi aggression. At the same time, the U.N. tried to force Iraq out of Kuwait by employing economic sanctions and organizing an international military coalition that could force Iraq to leave Kuwait if Iraqi leader SADDAM HUSSEIN refused to do so voluntarily before the U.N. January 15, 1991 deadline. The second phase of the war, Operation Desert Storm, was the battle to liberate Kuwait that took place after Iraq refused to abide by the U.N. deadline. Ultimately, the Persian Gulf War left Iraqi leader Saddam Hussein in power, though it destroyed almost all of Iraq's conventional forces and allowed the U.N. to destroy most of Iraq's long-range missiles, chemical weapons, and nuclear weapon capabilities. Hussein's reasons for invading Kuwait were both political and economic. At once, he could greatly increase Iraq's share of world oil reserves (adding at least 2 million barrels a day to Iraq's exports) and demonstrate the military capacity of his army. Iraq's invasion of Kuwait met very little resistance from the unprepared Kuwaitis. Hussein's troops gained control of the country in two days and announced that it would annex Kuwait as its nineteenth province within a week. Shortly thereafter, Hussein placed five Iraqi divisions on the Kuwait-Saudi Arabia border, threatening Saudi Arabia's oil-rich Eastern Province. Middle East states were divided over the invasion; while Algeria, Egypt, Syria and Saudi Arabia supported Kuwait, Jordan, Libya, the Sudan, and the Palestine Liberation Organization (PLO) backed Iraq. Most European nations as well as the U.S., Canada, and Japan condemned the invasion, and on the day of the invasion the U.N. Security Council voted 14–0 to demand Iraq's immediate and unconditional withdrawal. Gen. NORMAN SCHWARZKOPF led the U.N. coalition in Operation Desert Shield which was to enforce U.N. sanctions and defend Saudi Arabia. After obtaining U.N. authorization "to use all necessary means" if Iraq did not withdraw by January 15, the U.S. deployed a total of 527,000 personnel, 2,000 tanks, 1,800 fixed-wing aircraft, and 1,700 helicopters. Britain, France, Saudi Arabia, Egypt, and Syria too deployed significant forces. Iraq responded by building up its military forces in the Kuwait theater of operation to a total of 336,000 troops, 3,475 battle tanks, 3,080 other armored vehicles, and 2,475 major artillery weapons. This build-up, in turn, sparked many political debates about the need for war, culminating in close votes in the House of Representatives (250 to 183) and in the Senate (52–47) in favor of authorizing the use of force. The second phase of the war began early Jan. 17, 1991 when the U.S. launched a devastating series of air attacks on Iraqi command and control facilities, communication systems, air bases, and land-based air defenses. Within three days, U.N. Coalition fighter aircraft had established near air superiority. Victory in the air was achieved by Jan. 24, when Iraq ceased to attempt active air combat. This created a safe zone for U.N. aircraft and allowed them to shift most of their assets to attack on Iraqi ground forces. For the following thirty days, U.N. Coalition aircraft attacked Iraqi armor and artillery in the Kuwait theater of operations, as well as bombing Iraq's forward defenses, elite REPUBLICAN GUARD units, air bases, and biological, chemical, and nuclear warfare facilities in Iraq itself. Iraq's only ability to retaliate consisted of launching modified surface-to-surface SCUD missiles against targets in Saudi Arabia and Israel. The Scud attacks, however, did not alter the course of the war. The U.N.'s airpower attacks, according to U.S. estimates, led to the desertion or capture of 84,000 Iraqi soldiers and destroyed 1,385 Iraqi tanks, 930 other armored vehicles, and 1,155 artillery pieces. On February 24, U.S. land forces attacked along a broad front from the Persian Gulf to Rafha on the Iraqi-Saudi border. This attack had two principle thrusts: an enormous yet mobile "left hook" around and through Iraqi positions to the west of Kuwait; and a thrust straight through Iraq's defenses along the Kuwaiti border. Though some Iraqi Republican Guard units fought well, the bulk of Iraq's army consisted of poorly trained conscripts with low morale and little motivation. As a result, U.N. forces reached their major objective in Kuwait in half the time originally planned. By February 26, Coalition land forces were in Kuwait City, and U.S. forces had advanced to positions in Iraq to the south of Nasiriya. These advances, and concurrent air attacks that cut off Iraqi land forces from the roads along the Tigris River north of Basra, effectively ended the war. Baghdad radio announced on February 26 that all Iraqi forces would withdraw from Kuwait. A day later, President GEORGE H. BUSH declared that the U.S. would cease military operations on February 28. Iraq agreed to abide by all U.N. resolutions in the cease-fire that was signed on April 6. Iraqi military casualties totaled 25,000 to 65,000; U.N. forces suffered just 200 combat losses. The war reshaped the face of modern warfare by demonstrating the importance of joint operations, high-paced air and armored operations, precision strike systems, night and all-weather warfare capabilities, and the ability to target and strike deep behind the front line. It did not, however, bring stability to the gulf or drive Saddam Hussein and the Ba'ath Party elite from power. Indeed, he suppressed Kurdish and Shi'ite rebellions in 1991, retained biological and nuclear weapons technology, and by 1998 had the largest army in the gulf region.

personnel • *n.* the individuals required in either a military or civilian capacity to accomplish the assigned mission.

personnel carrier • an armored vehicle for transporting troops.

Personnel Reliability Program • U.S. DEPARTMENT OF DEFENSE program to insure that all personnel who control, handle, have access to, or control access to nuclear weapons are mentally and emotionally stable, reliable, and not subject to blackmail. The program covers the selection, screening, and continuous evaluation of all personnel assigned to duties involving nuclear weapons.

personnel security investigation • an inquiry into the activities of an individual that is designed to develop pertinent information pertaining to trustworthiness and suitability for a position of trust as related to loyalty, character, emotional stability, and reliability.

Petersburg, Siege of • a siege begun in June 1864 when the Union ARMY OF THE POTOMAC crossed the James River after failing to destroy Confederate Gen. ROBERT E. LEE's ARMY OF NORTHERN VIRGINIA. From June 15–18, Union forces made repeated efforts to seize Petersburg, an important railroad center twenty miles south of Richmond. When these failed, Lt. Gen. ULYSSES S. GRANT initiated siege operations, which continued until April 2, 1865. By early 1865, Lee's lines had been stretched near the breaking point and fearing the approach of Maj. Gen. WILLIAM T. SHERMAN's forces, Lee evacuated Petersburg, leading the fall of RICHMOND. Lee surrendered a week later at APPOMATTOX. Casualties for the siege totaled about 42,000 Union troops and 28,000 Confederates.

Petersburg to Richmond Campaign • the culminating campaign in the CIVIL WAR, beginning with the two battles in PETERSBURG in 1864 and ending with the fall of RICHMOND in April, 1865. It comprised sixteen battles, mainly under the leadership of Gens. ROBERT E. LEE and ULYSSES S. GRANT.

Pettigrew, James Johnston (1828–63) • Confederate army officer, born in North Carolina. Pettigrew trained as a lawyer and became an ardent secessionist as the CIVIL WAR drew near. After FORT SUMTER (1861), he enlisted in HAMPTON'S LEGION. His brigade attacked Union forces on McPherson's Hill at GETTYSBURG (1863); he was slightly wounded as he led his troops up CEMETERY RIDGE during PICKETT'S CHARGE. During the Confederate retreat after the battle, Pettigrew was severely wounded in a rearguard action and died from his injuries.

petty officer • a noncommissioned officer in a navy, in particular an NCO in the U.S. Navy or Coast Guard ranking above seaman and below chief petty officer.

Petty Officer Second Class • a noncommissioned officer rank in the U.S. Navy and Coast Guard corresponding to the rank of Sergeant in the U.S. Army or Marine Corps or Staff Sergeant in the U.S. Air Force; pay grade E-5.

Petty Officer Third Class • the lowest noncommissioned officer rank in the U.S. Navy and Coast Guard corresponding to the rank of Corporal in the U.S. Army and Marine Corps and Airman First Class in the U.S. Air Force; pay grade E-4.

PFC (also **Pfc.**) • *abbr.* Private First Class.

PFD • *abbr.* personal flotation device, a life jacket or similar buoyancy aid.

PGM • *abbr.* precision-guided munitions.

PGM-11A • see REDSTONE.

phalanx |ˈfālæNGks; ˈfæl-| • *n.* **1** (pl. **phalanxes** |ˈfā,læNGksəz|) a body of troops or police officers, standing or moving in close formation: *six hundred marchers set off, led by a phalanx of police.* 2 (**Phalanx**) a close-range weapons system that includes self-contained search and track radars and guns for firing sub-caliber penetrators. It is used to engage antiship cruise missiles and fixed-wing aircraft at short range.

Phalanx point-defense gun • an electric 20 mm gatling gun used in the PHALANX defense system, delivering 3000-4500 rounds per minute of APSD ammunition.

Phantom II • (**F-4**) a two-seat, twin-engine multipurpose all-weather turbojet fighter and bomber built by McDonnell Aircraft Corp. for the U.S. Navy and Air Force. With a wingspan of more than 38 ft. (11 m), the wings of the Navy version folded for stowage on carriers. The first F-4s were equipped with air-to-air missiles, but, after serious losses to Soviet MiG fighters over North Vietnam, later versions were equipped with 20 mm cannon to make them more effective during close-range dogfighting. During the Arab-Israeli War of 1973, F-4s led Israeli assaults on Egyptian and Syrian targets. RF-4 is the designation of the photo-reconnaissance version.

***Philadelphia*, USS** • (**CL-41**) a light cruiser, launched in 1936 and commissioned in 1937, that saw extensive service during WORLD WAR II, especially in the Atlantic and the Mediterranean, and provided shore bombardment during troop landings at Casablanca and Sicily as well as escorting convoys across the Atlantic. Decommissioned in Philadelphia in 1947, the *Philadelphia* was sold to the Brazilian Navy and serves under the name *Barroso*.

Philip • see METACOM.

Philippine Expeditionary Force to Korea • (**PEFTOK**) a force of more than 7000 Filipino soldiers that fought in the KOREAN WAR under the UNITED NATIONS command. More than 400 Filipinos were killed in the conflict.

Philippine Sea, Battle of the • the largest carrier battle of WORLD WAR II, fought off the Mariana Islands between the Japanese Mobile Fleet and the U.S. Fifth Fleet on June 19, 1944. The Japanese lost well over 300 carrier aircraft, three carriers, two oilers, and thousands of men while the U.S. lost 58 men and only 22 planes to enemy fire. The next day, the U.S. lost 49 more men and 120 aircraft, most of which crashed or were ditched after running out of fuel on a partially successful evening sortie against the rest of the Mobile Fleet.

Philippines, independence of • the U.S. granted Philippine independence on July 4, 1946, less than a year after the end of WORLD WAR II. A U.S. colony since 1900, the Philippines, according to the 1934 Tydings-McDuffie Act, was to be granted independence after a ten-year transition phase under a commonwealth government. The Japanese, however, invaded and drove out commonwealth president Manuel Quezon in 1941, controlling the islands for the next three years. After Gen. DOUGLAS MACARTHUR obtained President FRANKLIN D. ROOSEVELT's permission to liberate the archipelago, he and his troops waded ashore in October 1944, starting the year and a half reconquest that would eventually result in the independence of the Philippines.

Philippines, Invasion of • the invasion began with an assault on the island of Leyte on October 20, 1944. Gen. DOUGLAS MACARTHUR and Philippine commonwealth president Manuel Quezon had left the island three years earlier after the Japanese invaded. Fulfilling his pledge, "I shall return," MacArthur moved slowly across the islands, suffering heavy casualties to the fierce Japanese resistance. When the Japanese surrendered at the end of the war on August 15, 1945, the liberation of the Philippines had cost the U.S. Army 13,884 killed and 48,541 wounded. Japanese military and civilian dead numbered over 250,000, and 114,010 others surrendered.

Philippine War (1899–1902) • a conflict directly resulting from the SPANISH-AMERICAN WAR (1898). After a U.S. Army expedition captured Manila on August 13, 1898, Spain ceded the Philippine archipelago to the U.S. in the TREATY OF PARIS. President WILLIAM MCKINLEY hoped to convince Filipinos to allow American rule under the policy of "benevolent assimilation," but Filipino nationalists instead proclaimed the Philippine Republic on January 21, 1899, with EMILO AGUINALDO as president. For most of 1899, the Republican Army, comprised of volunteers, conscripts and former Spanish soldiers, battled American forces. Though Filipino troops often fought with great personal courage, they were poorly armed and abysmally led. The U.S. Army made significant inroads into Republican-held territory by the end of March, but undermanned and ravaged by sickness they could not hold territory or sustain an offensive. Only after a five-month hiatus could Maj. Gen ELWELL S. OTIS lead a three-pronged attack into north-central Luzon. As a result, virtually every important town in the archipelago lay under the U.S. flag by February 1900. From December 1889 until its official termination of July 4, 1902, the war continued as a series of localized campaigns of counterinsurgency and pacification. Aguinaldo proclaimed a policy of continued resistance through guerrilla warfare, hoping that faced with a long and brutal war the American public would reject McKinley for antiannexationist WILLIAM JENNINGS BRYAN in the upcoming presidential election. The U.S. High Command, however, was slow to recognize the depth of the resistance. Otis supported McKinley's policy of benevolent assimilation, ordering his officers to establish local governments, restore trade, build schools, and otherwise demonstrate America's good intentions. As the guerillas became adept at harassment, garrison and provincial commanders began to develop their own pacification policies. The war, in short, became a series of regional struggles, differing greatly from island to island and even village to village. In December 1900, bolstered by reinforcements and McKinley's reelection, Maj. Gen. ARTHUR MACARTHUR, Otis's successor, instituted a comprehensive pacification campaign aimed at disrupting the connections between the guerrillas and their civilian supporters. By July, when WILLIAM H. TAFT became governor, only a few provinces remained under military control and the war appeared all but over. The massacre of an American infantry company at BALANGIGA, Samar on September 28, 1901, however, proved that significant resistance remained, provoking severe countermeasures. By July 4, 1902, after a brutal campaign that inflicted terrible hardships on the population, President THEODORE ROOSEVELT declared the "insurrection" over. Among the least costly wars the U.S. ever fought, the Army saw 1,037 soldiers killed in action, 2,818 wounded, and a total of 4,374 died of all causes. Still, postwar disorder in the Philippines took years to suppress. Thee conquest, moreover, had been highly controversial. Though the government claimed it was necessary for economic and humanitarian reasons and the public supported the annexation, anti-imperialists condemned the war as immoral and unconstitutional.

Phips, Sir William (1651–95) • colonial governor, born in Woolwich, Maine. Phips discovered a sunken treasure in the Bahamas; in gratitude for the boost to its treasury, the Crown awarded him a knighthood and named him provost marshal for the Dominion of New England, a peacekeeping post. In 1687, Phips was named to lead an expedition against the French settlement at PORT ROYAL, Nova Scotia; this successful venture and the continuing political strife ended with his being named the first royal governor of Massachusetts, in 1692.

PHM • *abbr.* hydrofoil patrol craft.

Phnom Penh |(pə)ˌnäm 'pen| • the capital of Cambodia, a port at the junction of the Mekong and Tonlé Sap Rivers. It became the capital of a Khmer kingdom in the mid-15th century. Between 1975 and 1979 the Khmer Rouge forced a great many of its population (then 2.5 million) to leave the city and resettle in the country.

Phoenix • (**AIM-54A**) a long-range air-to-air missile with electronic guidance and homing. It was designed during the Soviet era for attacking Soviet bombers at long range and remains the longest-range air-to-air missile system in use today.

Phoenix program • part of the American efforts starts in 1969 to coordinate their many pacification efforts in Vietnam, called CORDS (Civil Operations and Revolutionary Development Support). CORDS sought to destroy the VIETCONG infrastructure (VCI) by identifying and arresting clandestine cadres in southern villages. The Phoenix program was formed to coordinate American and South Vietnamese military, intelligence, and police operations against the VCI. Although Phoenix was criticized as a thinly veiled terror and assassination program, its operations emphasized intelligence collection and many commentators agree that it was effective.

phosgene |'fäsjēn| • *n.* a colorless poisonous gas made by the reaction of chlorine and carbon dioxide. It was used as a poison gas, notably in WORLD WAR I.

ORIGIN: early 19th cent.: from Greek *phōs* 'light' + -gen, with reference to its original production by the action of sunlight on chlorine and carbon monoxide.

photogrammetry • *n.* the science or art of obtaining reliable measurements from photographic images.

photographic intelligence • (also **photoimage intelligence**) the collected products of photographic interpretation, classified and evaluated for intelligence use.

photomap • *n.* a reproduction of a photograph or photomosaic upon which the grid lines, marginal data, contours, place names, boundaries, and other data may be added.

physical exemption • an exemption from compulsory military service by virtue of some inherent physical defect, such as a missing limb, a chronic debilitating disease, or lack of sufficient teeth to chew military rations.

Physical Fitness School • an army physical training school at Fort Benning, Georgia. The program was established in 1982 by Army Secretary John D. Marsh, Jr. in an attempt to improve the declining physical fitness of combat soldiers. It was moved in 1993 from Fort Benjamin Harrison to Fort Benning.

pickelhaube |'pikl,howbə| • *n.* a spiked helmet worn by German soldiers.

Pickens, Andrew (1739–1817) • REVOLUTIONARY WAR army officer. Pickens was born in Pennsylvania, but his family moved to Virginia in the 1740s. Marriage into a prominent local family of independence-minded gentry established him in the area and helped form him into an ardent patriot. As an important militia leader, he helped defeat area Tories and thus thwarted the British plan to solidify their position in the South.

Pickering, Timothy (1745–1829) • REVOLUTIONARY WAR army officer, U.S. representative, U.S. senator, and secretary of state, born in Massachusetts. Pickering became a member of that colony's Committee of Correspondence and supported the cause of independence, although he opposed the creation of a colonial army. In 1777, when it was clear that there was to be no compromise between the Crown and the colonists, he accepted a commission in the Continental army. As quartermaster, he found it increasingly difficult to supply the troops and resigned, disillusioned. In 1790, he was appointed by President GEORGE WASHINGTON to negotiate with the Seneca Indians, and did so patiently and effectively, attempting to protect them and other tribes from land speculators and retroceding to them thousands of acres of land. In 1795 Washington named him secretary of war. He supported JAY'S TREATY and was rewarded later that year with the position of secretary of state. He conspired to undermine

President JOHN ADAMS's attempts to cement peace with France and as a result was dismissed from his post. In 1803 he was appointed to fill out the terms of a retiring U.S. senator and during his time in the Senate remained rigidly pro-British and anti-Republican. Denied a second term in the Senate, he won election to the House of Representatives, where he opposed the WAR OF 1812; having antagonized the political powers, in 1816 he was denied renomination and retired from politics.

picket • *n.* **1** a small body of troops or a single soldier sent out to watch for the enemy. **2** a soldier or party of soldiers performing a particular duty: *a* ***picket of*** *soldiers fired a volley over the coffin.* **3** a pointed wooden stake driven into the ground, typically to form a fence or palisade or to tether a horse.

Pickett, George Edward (1825–75) • Confederate army officer, born in Virginia. Pickett fought in the MEXICAN WAR (1846–48), where he won praise and promotion. Pickett's name is linked forever with his action at GETTYSBURG, on July 3, 1863, when Gen. ROBERT E. LEE had Pickett's divison spearhead a charge against the Union center (known as PICKETT'S CHARGE). The attack was a disaster, as Union forces mowed down the advancing Confederates. Lee took the brunt of the blame, but Pickett was severely criticized for being at the rear of his troops instead of in front. Neither he nor his reputation ever recovered from the debacle, although he continued to serve in the Confederate army.

Pickett's Charge • the final engagement at GETTYSBURG, July 3, 1863, following Confederate Gen. ROBERT E. LEE's invasion of Pennsylvania. After two days of battle with very heavy casualties on both sides, Lee ordered a frontal attack on Union forces. Led by Maj. Gen. GEORGE E. PICKETT, 12,000 to 15,000 Southerners charged towards the Union center, but the plan proved disastrous. Only 5,000 Southerners survived the charge and shortly afterwards Lee retreated to Virginia. After the battle, Union Gen. GEORGE G. MEAD was roundly criticized by President ABRAHAM LINCOLN for not counterattacking and thus allowing Lee to escape.

Pick, Lewis Andrew (1890–1956) • military engineer and army officer, born in Virginia. Trained as a civil engineer, Pick worked on the relief commission headed by Secretary of Commerce HERBERT HOOVER after the Mississippi River flooded in 1927 and in the wake of the Missouri River flood of 1943. Reassigned to the Far East as head of Army Service Forces, Pick oversaw construction of the LEDO ROAD, nicknamed Pick's Pike, a supply line for the Chinese in their war against Japan that is considered one of the greatest engineering achievements in army history.

pickoff • *n.* a device in the control or guidance system of an aircraft or boat that emits or alters an electrical, optical, or pneumatic output in response to a change in motion.

pick off • *v.* kill or disable a single enemy soldier, weapon, or vehicle.

pictomap • *n.* a topographic map in which the photographic imagery of a standard mosaic has been converted into interpretable colors and symbols.

piecemeal • *adj.* & *adv.* characterized by unsystematic partial measures taken over a period of time: *the village is slowly being killed off by piecemeal development.*

Pierce, Franklin (1804–69) • 14th president of the United States. Born in New Hampshire, he trained as a lawyer and entered politics as a Democrat, reaching the House of Representatives in 1833 and the U.S. Senate in 1836. Resigning from the Senate, he joined the army and served in the MEXICAN WAR (1846–48). He returned to New Hampshire and supported the FUGITIVE SLAVE LAW that formed part of the COMPROMISE OF 1850. The Democratic nominating convention of 1854, deadlocked, finally nominated a reluctant Pierce on the forty-eighth ballot to run again the Whig nominee, WINFIELD SCOTT. Pierce won by 242 electoral votes to Scott's 42 (the popular vote was closer), promising limited federal government and recognition of states' rights. Pierce ran a conservative administration, attempting few internal improvements and vetoing bipartisan legislation that would have funded institutions for the indigent mentally ill, arguing that it violated states' rights. His foreign policy was expansionist; he concluded the Gadsden Purchase (1853), acquiring a strip of land from Mexico, and signed the Clayton-Bulwer Treaty (1853), aimed at ensuring U.S.-British cooperation in building a Central American canal. Plans to acquire Cuba by purchase if possible and by force if necessary caused a domestic uproar. Controversy over the KANSAS-NEBRASKA ACT (1854) reopened the slavery issue and further inflamed tensions between Free Soilers and proslavery southerners, paving the way for the CIVIL WAR. Pierce was extremely unpopular and his policies were perceived as favoring the South. He was denied renomination in 1856. After leaving office, he continued to speak out in favor of states' rights and opposed ABRAHAM LINCOLN's election and, eventually, the EMANCIPATION PROCLAMATION.

Pierce remains the only elected president to be denied renomination by his party.

Pierce, William Leigh (1740?–89) • REVOLUTIONARY WAR army officer and member of the U.S. Constitutional Convention (1787). Pierce participated in many of the major campaigns of the Revolution as an aide to Gen. NATHANAEL GREENE and distinguished himself at EUTAW SPRINGS (1781); he received a sword from the Continental Congress in recognition of his gallantry.

pigeon • *n.* slang an aircraft from one's own side.

pig nose • slang (World War I) the gas mask issued by the French government, preferred by American and British soldiers.

pig-sticker • slang (World War I) a bayonet, or, less commonly, a sword; a long-bladed pocketknife. See also TOAD STABBER.

Pike • see JS-3.

Pike, Albert (1809–91) • Confederate army officer. Pike left his native Massachusetts and headed for the southwest, where he held a variety of jobs and entered the law and politics, becoming famous and wealthy in the process. Personal problems led him to relocate to New Orleans in 1853. There, at the outbreak of the CIVIL WAR, he became commissioner of Indian affairs for the Confederacy and organized several Indian regiments to fight for the South. Mutilation of Union dead by Pike's Indian regiment and Pike's accusation of treason against the Confederacy for treaty violations brought him widespread opprobrium, and he fled as the Confederacy collapsed, living out the rest of his life in the wilds of the Ozarks amid widespread rumors of moral turpitude and becoming a leading Freemason.

pillbox • *n.* a small, low-built defensive fortification with thick walls and a roof, often of concrete, steel, or sandbags, that houses machine guns, antitank weapons, etc., with room for the soldiers firing them.

pillenwerfer • *n.* a sonar-clouding device used by German U-BOATS in WORLD WAR II. The device, when released into the ocean behind the submarine, created a chemical reaction with the salt water and produced masses of noisy bubbles, confusing sonar.

Pillow, Gideon Johnson (1806–78) • Confederate army officer. Having befriended JAMES K. POLK, a native of the same Tennessee region, he received a commission as brigadier general of volunteers from Polk after Polk's election as president, and he served under Gen. ZACHARY TAYLOR during the MEXICAN WAR (1846–48). Despite mishandling his first battle command, Pillow was promoted and participated in other campaigns of the war. He incurred the wrath of Gen. WINFIELD SCOTT when he corresponded directly with President Polk, which damaged his prospects and his reputation, and after the war he returned to private life, becoming a prosperous planter. He was named commander of the Provisional Army of Tennessee but lost his post when Tennessee officially seceded and joined the Confederacy. His loss of FORT DONELSON, in Tennessee, to Gen. ULYSSES S. GRANT in 1862 temporarily cost him his command. A second command that same year, under Col. JOHN C. BRECKINRIDGE at STONES RIVER, was no more successful, and he was placed in an administrative position. One last attempt at command, protecting the mineral-rich areas of Alabama from Union attack, was similarly unsuccessful, and he finished his career in ruin.

pill roller • slang (also **pill pusher**) (especially in World Wars I and II) the hospital corps, or enlisted men in the Medical Corps.

In the 19th century, "pills" was a nickname for the medical officer or surgeon.

---

pilot • *n.* **1** a person who operates the flying controls of an aircraft. **2** a person with expert local knowledge qualified to take charge of a ship entering or leaving confined waters; a helmsman. • *v.* (**piloted, piloting**) act as a pilot of (an aircraft or ship).

pilot biscuit • another term for HARDTACK.

pilot officer • the lowest rank of officer in the RAF, above warrant officer and below flying officer.

pin • *n.* a metal peg that holds down the activating lever of a hand grenade, preventing its explosion.

pincer movement • an offensive maneuver at the tactical or operational level in which the attacking force is divided into two elements, each of which is directed against one of the enemy's flanks or around the enemy's flanks to meet in the enemy's rear and thus surround the enemy force (in which case the maneuver may be called a **double envelopment**).

pinch • *v.* sail (a boat) so close to the wind that the sails begin to lose power.

Pinckney, Thomas (1750–1828) • REVOLUTIONARY WAR army officer. Raised primarily in England, the South Carolina-born Pinckney established a successful law practice in Charleston and openly opposed the INTOLERABLE ACTS (1775). He entered the state legislature in 1778 and served as an aide to Gen. HORATIO GATES; Pinckney fought at YORKTOWN (1781). After the war, he served two consecutive terms as governor of South Carolina (1777, 1778) and supported the adoption of a strong federal constitution, aligning himself with ALEXANDER HAMILTON and the new FEDERALIST party. GEORGE WASHINGTON named him ambassador to Great Britain in 1791, in which position he attempted to negotiate, without much success, issues involving freedom of the seas, fishing rights, and compensation for damage inflicted by the British during the war. Pinckney ran for vice president in 1800, as JOHN ADAMS's running mate; the ticket lost to THOMAS JEFFERSON and AARON BURR. After four years in the House of Representatives, Pinckney returned to South Carolina, where he lived out the rest of his life.

Pinkerton, Allan (1819–84) • detective, born in Scotland. In 1842 Pinkerton emigrated to the United States and eventually settled in Chicago, where he did detective work for local and federal police, investigating mail theft and counterfeiting operations. In 1855 he organized his own agency, the North West Police Agency, specializing in employee malfeasance. During the CIVIL WAR, Pinkerton was asked by his friend Gen. GEORGE B. MCCLELLAN to gather information on the enemy for the Union. Pinkerton became the controversial head of an army spy system in Virginia that was dubbed the "Secret Service." He was dismissed in 1862. He returned to run his private agency and was instrumental in the capture of some notorious criminals, including railroad robbers such as the Dalton gang. His work continued to be controversial; organized labor saw him as working in support of the oppressive capitalist class against the working class.

Pinkerton agents botched an attempt to capture the notorious James brothers, Frank and

Jesse; breaking the arm of the brothers' mother and killing their younger brother.

Pinkerton National Detective Agency • a detective agency founded by ALLAN PINKERTON in 1852.

Its logo, the "All-Seeing Eye," gave rise to the phrase *private eye*.

Pinkerton's Secret Service • a federal agency organized and run by ALLAN PINKERTON, at the request of President ABRAHAM LINCOLN, after Pinkerton exposed a plot to assassinate Lincoln in 1861. It was the predecessor of the U.S. Secret Service, responsible for protecting government leaders and their families.

pinpoint • *n.* **1 a** a precisely identified point, especially on the ground, that locates a very small target, serving as a reference point for rendezvous or for other purposes. **b** the coordinates that define this point. **2** the ground position of aircraft determined by direct observation of the ground.

pioneer • *n.* a member of an infantry group preparing roads or terrain for the main body of troops. • *v.* open up (a road or terrain) as a pioneer.

Pioneer UAV • (**SR**) a small propeller-driven unmanned aircraft designed to provide imagery intelligence (IMINT) for spotters for naval gunfire support from U.S. Navy battleships. Pioneer never met objective requirements and began to have unexpected problems almost as soon as it was put into operation. Nevertheless, Pioneer has served in every major U.S. military operation and, as of November 1999, has logged more than 20,000 flight hours.

pip • *n.* Brit. a star (1–3 according to rank) on the shoulder of an army officer's uniform.

pipe • *n.* a boatswain's whistle. • *v.* use a boatswain's whistle to summon (the crew) to work or a meal: *the hands were piped to breakfast.*

pipe band • a band, especially a military one, consisting of bagpipe players, drummers, and a pipe major.

pipe berth (Brit. also **pipe cot**) • a collapsible bed with a frame of metal pipes, used on a boat.

pipeline • *n.* in logistics, the channel of support, or a specific portion thereof, by means of which materiel or personnel flow from sources of procurement to their point of use.

pipe major • an NCO commanding regimental pipes and drums.

piracy • *n.* **1** the practice of attacking and robbing ships at sea. **2** a similar practice in other contexts, especially hijacking: *air piracy.*

pirate • *n.* a person who attacks and robs ships at sea. • *v.* rob or plunder (a ship).

DERIVATIVES: **piratical** *adj.* **piratically** *adv.*

pistol • *n.* a small firearm designed to be held in one hand. • *v.* (**pistoled, pistoling**) dated shoot (someone) with a pistol.

pistoleer • *n.* archaic a soldier armed with a pistol.

pitch • *n.* a swaying or oscillation of a ship, aircraft, or vehicle around a horizontal axis perpendicular to the direction of motion. • *v.* **1** (of a moving ship, aircraft, or vehicle) rock or oscillate around a lateral axis, so that the front and back move up and down: *the little steamer pressed on, pitching gently.* **2** (of a vehicle) move with a vigorous jogging motion: *a jeep came pitching down the hill.*

▸**pitch in** join in a fight or dispute.

pitch into forcefully assault.

pitch angle • the angle between the aircraft's longitudinal axis and the horizontal plane. Also called INCLINATION ANGLE.

pitch control • **1** control of the pitch of a helicopter's rotors or an aircraft's propellers. **2** control of the pitching motion of an aircraft.

pitched battle • a planned military encounter on a prearranged battleground.

Pitcher, Molly (1744? or 1754?–1832) • REVOLUTIONARY WAR hero and patriot. The facts of Pitcher's early life are uncertain, including the identity of her first husband, who may have been John Hays of Carlisle, Pennsylvania. She became famous because of her actions during MONMOUTH, in June 1778, when, on a blazingly hot day, she carried pitchers of water to her husband and his fellow soldiers (hence her nickname); when he fell, wounded, she took his place, helping to load his cannon. After the war, the Hayses returned to Carlisle, where Molly Pitcher was twice widowed and remarried once. In recognition of her services, in 1822 Congress awarded her a $40 grant and a $40 annuity.

pitchpole • *v.* (of a boat) be overturned so that its stern pitches forward over its bow.

Pittsburgh Landing • see SHILOH, BATTLE OF.

Pitt, William (1708–78) • prime minister of Great Britain (1756–61, 1766–68). Born into a prominent family, Pitt entered Parliament in 1735. As prime minister, he attempted to extend Britain's empire around the world, largely by taking on Britain's ancient rival, France. During the SEVEN YEARS WAR (1756–63) he attacked French possessions and succeeded in driving France out of Canada, as well as West Africa and India. The part of the FRENCH AND INDIAN WAR (1754–63) that took place in the North American colonies broke out after the French began fortifying the territory between Lake Erie and the forks of the Ohio River, where they constructed FORT DUQUESNE. GEORGE WASHINGTON led an unsuccessful expedition (1754) to take the fort, marking the beginning of hostilities. Pitt, however, determined to oust the French, allied himself with the colonists and appointed a series of capable commanders; the result was total French defeat after the British took Montreal (1760). Under the main provisions of the TREATY OF PARIS (1763), the French ceded Canada and all French territories east of the Mississippi to Britain, thus ensuring British cultural hegemony over the colonies.

pivot • *n.* the person or people about whom a body of troops wheels.

pivot gun • a gun mounted on a pivot that can rotate 360 degrees, allowing targeting in all directions.

pl. • *abbr.* platoon.

PLA • *abbr.* People's Liberation Army.

Plains Indians Wars • the wars between the Great Plains Indian tribes and the U.S. Army (1854–90) which grew out of the westward movement of Americans. Typically, the major wars with the Plains tribes followed treaties negotiated by government commissioners that bound the Indians to settle on a designated reservation. The Plains tribes that fought the U.S. most intensively were the Lakota Sioux, Cheyenne, and Arapaho on the northern plains and the Cheyenne, Arapaho, Kiowa, and Comanche on the southern plains. The U.S. Army maintained a system of forts and fielded heavy offensive columns; the Indians fought with hit-and-run tactics that exploited environmental factors and avoided open engagement. Though most fighting on the Great Plains ended by the 1880s, the end of the Plains Indians War was not finally signaled until the BATTLE OF WOUNDED KNEE, in South Dakota in 1890.

plane • *v.* (of a bird or an airborne object) soar without moving the wings; glide. **2** (of a boat, surfboard, etc.) skim over the surface of water as a result of lift produced hydrodynamically.

plane chart • a chart on which the meridians and parallels of latitude are represented by equidistant straight lines.

planesman • *n.* (pl. **-men**) a person who operates the hydroplanes on a submarine.

plane table • a surveying instrument used for direct plotting in the field, with a circular drawing board and pivoted alidade.

Planning Force • the force level required to provide reasonable assurance of successful execution of the national strategy. It is sized for a specific scenario and is key to the projected threat in the last year of the planning period. The Planning Force is developed by prioritizing missions, sequencing force employment, and accepting a higher level of risk. It is not constrained by fiscal, manpower, logistics, mobility, basing, or similar limitations.

Plan Orange • the plan formulated by the U.S. Joint Army and Navy Board in the early 1900s to defend a naval base in the Philippines against the Japanese. The failure of the two services to agree on the plan undermined the board's influence.

plantation • *n.* **1** an estate on which crops such as coffee, sugar, and tobacco are cultivated by resident laborers, which in former times were slaves. **2** a colony.

plastic explosive • a puttylike explosive capable of being molded by hand.

plastique |plæ'stēk| • *n.* plastic explosive.
ORIGIN: mid 20th cent.: French, literally 'plastic.'

plate armor • protective armor of metal plates, especially as worn in medieval times by mounted knights.

platoon • *n.* a subdivision of a company of soldiers, usually forming a tactical unit that is commanded by a lieutenant and divided into several sections.

Platt Amendment • an amendment signed by President WILLIAM MCKINLEY on March 2, 1901 to specify conditions for the removal of U.S. troops from Cuba. Proposed by Secretary of War ELIHU ROOT and presented to the Senate by Sen. Orville H. Platt, it required that Cuba cede land for U.S. military and naval bases, allow U.S. intervention to preserve Cuban independence, and agree not to transfer land to any other power. Cuba incorporated the provisions into its constitution, and the amendment regulated Cuban-American relations until it was abrogated in 1934.

plausible deniability • with respect to clandestine operations, the state of being capable of being denied by those in authority.

Pleasonton, Alfred 1824–1897 • Union cavalry officer, born in Washington, D.C. Pleasonton attended WEST POINT and graduated seventh in his class. He saw service in the MEXICAN WAR (1846–48) where he won a brevet for gallant and meritorious service. During the CIVIL WAR, he fought well, especially at CHANCELLORSVILLE, but he exaggerated his own accomplishments and infuriated other officers in the calvary. He led a cavalry command at BRANDY STATION, the largest cavalry action of the war, where his troops nearly surprised and overwhelmed J.E.B. STUART's command, but were eventually forced to leave the field. After the war he worked for the Internal Revenue Service.

plebe |plēb| • *n.* informal a newly entered cadet or freshman, especially at a military academy.

plebiscite • *noun* the direct vote of all the members of an electorate on an important public question such as a change in the constitution.

pledge • *n.* a solemn promise or undertaking: *the conference ended with a joint pledge to limit nuclear testing.* • *v.* **1** commit (a person or organization) by a solemn promise: *the government pledged itself to deal with environmental problems.* **2** formally declare or promise that something is or will be the case: *the president pledged that 20,000 troops would be sent.* **3** solemnly undertake to do something: *they pledged to continue the campaign for funding.* **4** undertake formally to give: *Japan pledged $100 million in humanitarian aid.*

Pledge of Allegiance • an oath of loyalty to the U.S. flag and the nation it represents. The pledge is believed to have been the idea of an editor of "The Youth's Companion," a children's magazine. By proclamation of President BENJAMIN HARRISON, the pledge was first recited on October 12, 1892, and after some rewording was officially adopted on Flag Day, June 14, 1924. The words "under God" were added in 1954. The pledge now reads: "I pledge allegiance to the flag of the United States of America and to the republic for which it stands: one nation under God, indivisible, with liberty and justice for all." While reciting the pledge of allegiance, citizens stand at attention or place the right hand over the heart. Men should remove their hats, and military personnel in uniform face the flag and give the military salute.

Pleiku, Battle of • an attack by the VIETCONG on U.S. troops at Pleiku, killing eight Americans on February 7, 1965. In retaliation, President LYNDON B. JOHNSON ordered bombing north of the Demilitarized Zone along the 17th parallel that divided North and South Vietnam. Within a week, the administration began OPERATION ROLLING THUNDER, a gradually intensifying air bombardment of military bases, supply depots, and infiltration routes in North Vietnam.

Plimsoll line |ˈplimsəl; ˈplimsōl| (also **Plimsoll mark**) • a marking on a ship's side showing the limit of submersion legal under various sea conditions.

ORIGIN: named after Samuel *Plimsoll* (1824–98), the English politician whose agitation in the 1870s resulted in the Merchant Shipping Act of 1876, ending the practice of sending to sea overloaded and heavily insured old ships, from which the owners profited if they sank.

plot • *n.* **1** a map, chart, or graph representing data of any sort. **2 a** the representation on a diagram or chart of the position or course of a target in terms of angle and distances from positions. **b** the location of a position on a map or a chart. **3** the visual display of a single location of an airborne object at a particular instant of time. **4** a portion of a map or overlay on which are drawn the outlines of the areas covered by one or more photographs.

Plowshare, Project • an unsuccessful federal program devoted to investigating safe, economic, and peaceful uses for nuclear weapons. Established in 1957 by the ATOMIC ENERGY COMMISSION, Project Plowshare was part of the Atoms for Peace Program. The name came from a passage in the Book of Isaiah: "and they shall beat their swords into plowshares."

plumb • *v.* **1** measure (the depth of a body of water). **2** (of water) be of a specified depth: *at its deepest, the lake scarcely plumbed seven feet.* • *n.* a ball of lead or other heavy object attached to the end of a line for finding the depth of water or determining the vertical on an upright surface.

plumb line • a line with a plumb attached to it, used for finding the depth of water or determining the vertical on an upright surface.

Plummer, Henry Vinton (1844–1906) • former slave and military chaplain. The son of slaves on a Maryland plantation, the young Plummer was sold to a different plantation owner in Maryland. When the CIVIL WAR broke out, Maryland, although a slave state, remained in the Union. Plummer managed to escape and wound up serving on a gunboat on the Potomac River. After the war, he formed the Bladensburg Union to help indigent blacks pay funeral costs; eventually he became a Baptist preacher, being ordained in 1878 after studies at Wayland Seminary. Through the intercession of Frederick Douglass and others, he was named chaplain of the 9th Calvary, making him the first black army chaplain after the CIVIL WAR. Plummer sought, unsuccessfully, government support for an effort to repatriate African Americans to Africa; shortly thereafter, the army charged him with drunkenness and court-martialed him. He returned to preaching.

plummet • *n.* a plumb or plumb line.

plunge • *v.* (of a ship) pitch: *the ship plunged through the 20-foot seas.*

ply • *v.* (**-ies, -ied**) **1** (of a vessel or vehicle) travel regularly over a route, typically for commercial purposes: *ferries ply across a strait to the island.* **2** travel over (a route) in this way.

PM • *abbr.* Provost Marshal.

PO • *abbr.* Petty Officer.

pocket battleship • any of a class of cruisers with large-caliber guns, operated by the German navy in WORLD WAR II.

poilu |pwälˈ(y)o͞o| • informal a French infantryman, especially one at the front lines in WORLD WAR I.

ORIGIN: *Poilu* in French means "hairy," "shaggy," from the unkempt, unshaven appearance of soldiers who have served long at the front; the term may also refer to the thick whiskers traditionally worn by the French infantry.

point • *n.* **1** a narrow piece of land jutting out into a lake or ocean: *the boat came around the point* | [in names] *Sandy Point.* **2** a small leading party of an advanced guard of troops. **3** the position at the head of a column or wedge of troops: *another marine said he would* ***walk point*** *because I had done it on the last patrol.* **4** short for POINT MAN. • *v.* (of a sailing vessel) sail close to the wind.

PHRASES: **point of sailing** a sailboat's heading in relation to the wind.

point-blank • *adj.* & *adv.* **1** (of a shot, bullet, or other missile) fired from very close to its target. **2** (of the range of a shot, bullet, or other missile) so close as to allow no possibility of missing: *the weapon was inaccurate beyond point-blank range.*

ORIGIN: late 16th cent.: probably from POINT + BLANK in the contemporaneous sense 'white spot in the center of a target.'

point man • the soldier at the head of a patrol.

point of no return • a point along an aircraft track beyond which the aircraft's endurance will not permit return to its own base, or some other associated base, on its own fuel supply.

Point Pleasant, Battle of • see LORD DUNMORE'S WAR.

point target • **1** a target of such small dimension that it requires the accurate placement of ordnance in order to neutralize or destroy it. **2** (**nuclear point target**) a target in which the ratio of radius of damage to target radius is equal to or greater than 5.

poison gas • poisonous gas or vapor, used especially to disable an enemy in warfare.

Polaris |pəˈlerəs; -ˈlärəs| • (**UGM-27**) a surface-to-surface solid-propellant ballistic missile that can be launched either from the surface or under water. Like the POSEIDON, it is equipped with inertial guidance and nuclear warheads. The three versions produced have ranges, in nautical miles, from 1,200 to 2,500.

Polaris submarine missile patrol • a detachment of submarine forces responsible for a mission or an operation and configured to deliver POLARIS ballistic missiles.

pole • *v.* propel (a boat) by pushing a pole against the bottom of a river, canal, or lake. PHRASES: **under bare poles** with no sail set.

poleax (also **poleaxe**) • *n.* a short-handled ax with a spike at the back, formerly used in naval warfare for boarding, resisting boarders, and cutting ropes. • *v.* hit, kill, or knock down with or as if with a poleax.

police • *n.* **1** (usually **the police**) the civil force of a federal or local government, responsible for the prevention and detection of crime and the maintenance of public order. **2** members of a police force: *there are fewer women police than men.* • *v.* **1** (**policing**) (of a police force) have the duty of maintaining law and order in or for (an area or event). **2** enforce regulations or an agreement in (a particular area or domain): *a U.N. resolution to use military force to police the no-fly zone.* **3** enforce the provisions of (a law, agreement, or treaty): *the regulations will be policed by inspectors.*

police action • a military action without a formal declaration of war.

political general • especially in the CIVIL WAR, one appointed more on the basis of political affiliations than through military distinction. Slang, 17

political intelligence • intelligence concerning foreign and domestic policies of governments and the activities of political movements.

Polk, James Knox (1795–1849) • 11th president of the United States, born in North Carolinia. Polk, who moved to Tennessee as a child, was admitted to the bar in 1820 and quickly became active in politics, entering the state legislature in 1823. In 1825 he was elected to the U.S. House of Representatives, where he viewed slavery as an evil to be borne. He opposed high tariffs and supported only limited spending for internal improvements. Polk served as House Speaker for two terms (1835–39). To signal his opposition to the new Whig party, headed by HENRY CLAY, Polk ran for governor of Tennessee (1837) as a Democrat and won. Reelected in 1839, he lost his bid for a third term in 1843 and lost again in 1845. At the 1844 Democratic presidential nominating convention, Polk won the nomination on the eighth ballot, after an indiscreet comment on the risks of annexing Texas caused MARTIN VAN BUREN's candidacy to founder. Polk won the election with less than a majority of the popular vote but an Electoral College majority. Polk's goals as president were to reduce the tariff, to free the Treasury of the influence of private banks, and to annex California and Oregon; he achieved all of these. Perhaps the most important action of Polk's administration was his instigation of the MEXICAN WAR (1846–48); his combination of military threats and diplomatic initiatives made almost inevitable the clash that occurred by the Rio Grande River. As a result of the war, the United States annexed the territory that eventually would comprise the states of California, Arizona, Nevada, and Utah, as well as parts of New Mexico, Colorado, and Wyoming.

Polk, Leonidas (1806–64) • Confederate army officer. The North Carolinian was ordained in the Episcopal church and became bishop of the new Diocese of Louisiana in 1841. In the 1850s he devoted himself to organizing and founding the University of the South, which would represent the southern values he accepted, including slavery. At the outbreak of the CIVIL WAR, he was commissioned a major general, thanks to an old friendship with JEFFERSON DAVIS, but his career as a commander was checkered; he tended to go his own way, sometimes in opposition to orders. He clashed repeatedly with Gen. BRAXTON BRAGG and sought to undermine Bragg's career and reputation, eventually succeeding. Polk was killed by artillery fire while observing Union positions near ATLANTA.

Polk, Thomas (c. 1732–94) • REVOLUTIONARY WAR army officer. Born in Pennsylvania, Polk moved to North Carolina and became a prosperous planter. Polk was a supporter of the Revolutionary cause and was active in rousing local support for independence. He also served in the militia and fought in several engagements during the war. Resentful at being passed over for command of the North Carolina brigade, he resigned his commission in 1777. As British troops moved South and threatened to invade North Carolina, Polk accepted appointment as commissary general of the Continental army and as superintendent commissary for the Salisbury district. Efforts to promote him to district head failed, and Polk resigned rather than take a lower title.

Polk, William (1758–1834) • REVOLUTIONARY WAR army officer. The North Carolinian supported at a young age the cause of independence, and after LEXINGTON and CONCORD (both 1775) he joined the 3rd South Carolina Regiment, charged with keeping watch over area Loyalists. In March 1777 he joined Gen. GEORGE WASHINGTON's troops in New Jersey and fought at BRANDYWINE (1777) and GERMANTOWN (1777). After serving with several different units, Polk became a lieutenant colonel in the 4th South Carolina Cavalry Regiment. He fought with distinction at EUTAW SPRINGS (1781) and remained with the South Carolina militia for the rest of the war.

Pollard, Jonathan (1954–) • a civilian U.S. naval intelligence analyst who was accused of passing sensitive military intelligence to Israel in 1985. He sought refuge in the Israeli embassy in Washington, which initially received him and later turned him over to the FBI. In a 1987 plea-bargaining agreement he accepted a life sentence without parole. Israel admitted in 1998 that he was their agent.

Pol Pot (c. 1925–98) • totalitarian leader of Cambodia and mass murderer. Pol Pot spent part of his youth in Paris, studying radio electronics; while there he became involved with the Communist Party and with other leftwing Cambodian youths who with him became the leaders of the KHMER ROUGE. Returning to Cambodia, he spent several years nurturing the growth of the Communist Party there and served as the party's secretary. Pol Pot led the Khmer Rouge forces that overthrew the military dictatorship of Gen. Lon Nol in 1975 and became the country's prime minister, serving from 1975 to 1979, when he was overthrown by invading Vietnamese. During his years in office, he caused the deaths of at least one million people from torture, disease, starvation, and execution as he attempted to put in place a total restructuring of Cambodian society that involved the elimination of any Western influence and a return to a totally agrarian society. After his ouster, Pol Pot hid in the hills of Cambodia as the Khmer Rouge declined in influence and power. In 1998 he was placed under house arrest by his colleagues; during this time he died, apparently of natural causes.

POL raid • a military operation of limited duration conducted for the purpose of destroying enemy petroleum dumps or obtaining petroleum supplies for one's own forces.

Pomeroy, Seth (1706–77) • REVOLUTIONARY WAR officer, born in Massachusetts. Pomeroy became a gunsmith, in the family tradition, and joined the local militia while still young. In 1745 he took part in an invasion of the French fort at LOUISBOURG, on Cape Breton Island, in which his skills as a gunsmith were critical to the colonists' victory. He served in the FRENCH AND INDIAN WAR (1754–63), including the victorious expedition against FORT ST. FREDERIC in 1755. Pomeroy died of pleurisy while riding south to join Gen. GEORGE WASHINGTON's troops in New Jersey.

Pomeroy was the first person to be named a brigadier general of the Continental army, although he never formally served under this commission, which he received in 1775.

pom-pom (also **pompom**) • *n.* an automatic quick-firing two-pounder cannon of WORLD WAR II period, typically mounted on a ship and used against aircraft.

ORIGIN: late 19th cent.: imitative of the sound of the discharge.

pongo • *n.* (pl. **-os**) Brit. & slang a soldier.

ORIGIN: early 20th cent.: originally from Congolese *mpongo*, used as a term in zoology to refer to the gorilla and other apes.

Pontiac (c. 1720–69) • Ottawa Indian chief. After attempting to deal with British settlers on terms of mutual respect, Pontiac, who led a loose confederation of several tribes, realized that the British plan was to exclude the Indians from their homeland. He arranged for every Indian tribe in the area from Lake Superior to the lower Mississippi to attack the nearest British fort (this action, in May 1763, came to be called PONTIAC'S REBELLION). Pontiac himself attempted to capture the fort at Detroit, but his plans were revealed ahead of time to the fort commander, who was able to repel Pontiac's attack with the help of reinforcements. The overall plan was more successful; the Indians captured all but four of the twelve forts they attacked and in general exacted bloody vengeance on the British settlers in the area. After years of fighting between the Indians and the British, Pontiac accepted a peace treaty in 1766. He was assassinated by an Indian from a rival tribe.

Pontiac's Rebellion • a multitribal assault on British western posts after the FRENCH AND INDIAN WAR (1754–63), was the result of several factors, including trade disputes and the encroachment of British settlers. On May 9, 1763, Ottawa war leader PONTIAC initiated the conflict by attacking Fort Detroit. Though Fort Detroit held out, the Indians soon captured six other forts and forced the abandonment of Fort Edward Augustus. Fighting continued for three years, ending with a treaty signed at Oswego, July 1766 in which the British promised to enforce the Royal Proclamation of 1763 that prohibited colonization west of the Appalachian ridge.

pontoon • *n.* **1** a flat-bottomed boat or hollow metal cylinder used with others to support a temporary bridge or floating landing stage. **2** a bridge or landing stage supported by pontoons. **3** a large flat-bottomed barge or lighter equipped with cranes and tackle for careening ships and salvage work. **4** either of two floats fitted to an aircraft to enable it to land on water.

pool reporting • an arrangement for media coverage of military operations or other activities by which a limited number of reporters, cameramen, etc., are selected from the entire media corps and permitted to cover the events in progress and then report their observations to the remaining members of the media.

poop • *n.* (also **poop deck**) the aftermost and highest deck of a ship, especially in a sailing ship where it typically forms the roof of a cabin in the stern. • *v.* (usually **be pooped**) (of a wave) break over the stern of (a ship), sometimes causing it to capsize.

Pope, John (1822–92) • Union army officer, born in Kentucky. Pope was cited for bravery in the MEXICAN WAR (1846–48). A topographical engineer, he helped lay out the Pacific Railway. Pope was commissioned a brigadier general when the CIVIL WAR erupted, and he served under Gen. JOHN C. FRÉMONT, in 1862 heading the army of the Mississippi. President ABRAHAM LINCOLN named Pope to head the new Army of Virginia, a post he accepted reluctantly because he did not trust Gen. GEORGE B. MCCLELLAN to provide adequate backup in battle. His fears were realized during the PENINSULAR CAMPAIGN when McClellan retreated, and Gen. ROBERT E. LEE split his troops and trapped Pope's forces, winning the SECOND BATTLE OF BULL RUN (1862). The defeat cost Pope his field command, although questions still remain about whether he was at fault or whether the inaction of his subordinate FITZ JOHN PORTER was to blame for the debacle.

popular sovereignty • a political condition in which the people are sovereign, that is, the people exercise the definitive decision-making power.

Porkchop Hill • (November 22–25, 1951) one of a series of battles on hilltops in the KOREAN WAR. In the winter of 1951–52, with U.N. allies negotiating with the Chinese and North Koreans, the battlefield in Korea shifted to a static kind of war, reminiscent of WORLD WAR I. Porkchop Hill and a hundred other hilltops, including Sniper's Ridge and Old Baldy, witnessed a seemingly endless succession of violent fire fights waged largely in order to gain leverage in the political battle. The final armistice was not signed until July 27, 1953.

port[1] • *n.* **1** a town or city with a harbor where ships load or unload, especially one where customs officers are stationed. **2** a harbor: *the port has miles of docks | an abundant water supply and port facilities.* **3** (also **inland port**) an inland town or city whose connection to the coast by a river or other body of water enables it to act as a port.

port[2] • *n.* the side of a ship or aircraft that is on the left when one is facing forward: *the ferry was listing to port | the port side of the aircraft.* The opposite of STARBOARD. • *v.* turn (a ship or its helm) to port.

port[3] • *n.* **1** a gunport. **2** a porthole. **3** an opening in the side of a ship for boarding or loading.

port[4] • *v.* carry (a rifle or other weapon) diagonally across and close to the body with the barrel or blade near the left shoulder: *Detail! For inspection—port arms!* • *n.* the position required by an order to port a rifle or other weapon: *Parker had his rifle* ***at the port.***
PHRASES: **at port arms** in the position adopted when given a command to port one's weapon.

portage • *n.* **1** the carrying of a boat or its cargo between two navigable waters: *the return journey was made much simpler by portage.* **2** a place at which this is necessary: *a portage over the dam.* • *v.* **1** carry (a boat or its cargo) between navigable waters: *they are incapable of portaging a canoe | they would only run the rapid if they couldn't portage.* **2** (of a boat) be carried between navigable waters.

Porter, Andrew (1743–1813) • REVOLUTIONARY WAR army officer, born in Pennsylvania. Porter's affinity for books and intellectual interests led him to Philadelphia, where he became a teacher. In June 1776 he accepted a commission as captain of marines; later he switched to the army, becoming captain of the 2nd Continental Artillery. He fought at PRINCETON (1777) and was commended for bravery by Gen. GEORGE WASHINGTON. He continued to serve meritoriously, but in 1780 he was court-martialed for having defamed a fellow officer. Porter was found not guilty, but he filed charges against his accuser, earning Washington's wrath. In 1782 he killed a man in a duel whom he believed had insulted him for being a teacher; Proctor was again acquitted in a court-martial. He declined a commission in the WAR OF 1812 because of failing health.

Porter, David (1780–1843) • U.S. naval officer. Born at Boston, David Porter was a third-generation American naval officer and went to sea in his teens. In January 1798, he received a warrant as midshipman and sailed with Captain Thomas Truxton in the 38-gun frigate USS *Constellation.* He distinguished himself in his first engagement—with the French warship *Insurgente* (February 1798)—and was promoted to Lieutenant in October 1799. He saw active service in BARBARY WARS and was captured when the frigate USS *Philadelphia* ran aground in Tripoli harbor in 1803. Imprisoned until the war was over, Porter was promoted to master commandant in 1806 and to captain on July 2, 1812. During the WAR OF 1812, he successfully commanded the 32-gun frigate USS *Essex* in the Atlantic and in the Pacific until defeated by two British warships off the coast of Chile in February 1814. Porter subsequently served on the BOARD OF NAVY COMMISSIONERS (1815–1823) and commanded the Mosquito Squadron hunting pirates in the West Indies. Following a court-martial in 1825 stemming from an attack on a Spanish fort in Puerto Rico, Porter resigned his U.S. commission in 1826 and took service as commander of the Mexican Navy. He gave up his Mexican commission and returned to the United States in 1829 and held various overseas appointments until his death in Pera, near Constantinople, on March 3, 1843. Porter's son, DAVID DIXON PORTER, and his adoptive son, DAVID FARRAGUT, were noted U.S. naval officers in the CIVIL WAR, and both achieved the highest rank in the U.S. Navy.

Porter, David Dixon (1813–91) • Union naval officer, born in Pennsylvania. The son of DAVID PORTER, Porter went to sea at a young age. His early career included a two-year stint as a commander in the merchant marine. In 1855 he returned to the U.S. Navy. He was contemplating resuming a civilian career when the CIVIL WAR gave him the opportunity to test his mettle. Defying orders, in 1861 he sailed to Pensacola to reinforce Fort Pickens; in 1862 he recommended his adoptive brother, DAVID FARRAGUT, to lead the siege at NEW ORLEANS, at which Porter played a small role. He later commanded the Union gunboat forces on the Mississippi and played a more important role in the victory at VICKSBURG (1863). In the postwar years he served as superintendent of the U.S. NAVAL ACADEMY.

Porter, Fitz John (1822–1901) • Union army officer. Born into a New Hampshire family with a strong military tradition, by 1847 Porter was already serving in the MEXICAN WAR (1846–48), where he was cited for bravery. During the CIVIL WAR, his friendship with Gen. GEORGE B. MCCLELLAN boosted his career, and he was named to command the 5th Corps in 1862. His failure to act in the face of unclear orders won him Gen. JOHN POPE's enmity, left Pope's troops vulnerable to attack by Confederate troops, and contributed to the massive defeat of the Union forces at the SECOND BATTLE OF BULL RUN 91862). In 1863, in a flawed court-martial, Porter was found guilty of disobeying orders during the battle and dismissed from the army; he won a retrial in 1879, at which he was found innocent.

port-fire • *n.* a hand-held fuse used for firing cannons, igniting explosives, etc.

portfolio |pôrt'fōlē,ō| • *n.* (pl. **-os**) the position and duties of a minister of state or a member of a cabinet.

porthole • *n.* **1** a small exterior window in a ship or aircraft. **2** an opening for firing a cannon through.

Port Hudson, battle of • a Union assault against the Confederate stronghold at Port Hudson on the Mississippi River, from May 21 to July 9, 1863, during the CIVIL WAR. As part of Union Maj. Gen. ULYSSES S. GRANT's siege of VICKSBURG (1862-63), Maj. Gen. NATHANIEL P. BANKS initiated a forty-eight-day siege of Port Hudson on May 27, after Confederate forces under Maj. Gen. Franklin Gardner had repelled Banks' frontal assaults. Banks unsuccessfully renewed his assaults on June 14; but on July 9, after the surrender at Vicksburg (July 4), the Confederates at Port Hudson also surrendered. Total Union casualties are estimated at 5,000; and Confederate at 7,208. The surrender gave the Union complete control of the Mississippi and divided the Confederacy in half.

port of call • a place where a ship stops on a voyage.

portolan |'pôrtl-ən; -,æn| (also **portolano** |,pôrtl'änō|) • *n.* (pl. **portolans** |-ənz| or **portolanos** |-'änōz|) a book of sailing directions with charts and descriptions of harbors and coasts.

Port Republic • a Civil War battle between Confederate Gen. "STONEWALL" JACKSON's troops and Union Brig. Gen. Erastus Tyler's forces at the end of Jackson's successful SHENANDOAH VALLEY CAMPAIGN in the CIVIL WAR. Jackson's troops defeated Union forces near the town of Port Republic in northwestern Virginia on June 9, 1862.

Port Royal • a town in southwestern Nova Scotia, Canada. It was the first French colony in North America and is Canada's oldest European settlement. Destroyed by the British in 1613, it was resettled by Scottish colonists, only to be returned to Franch in 1632. The British attacked the new French settlement repeatedly and finally captured it in 1710. The French formally ceded it to the British in the TREATY OF UTRECHT in 1713, and it was renamed Annapolis Royal in honor of Queen Anne.

port security • the safeguarding of vessels, harbors, ports, waterfront facilities, and cargo from internal threats such as destruction, loss, or injury from sabotage or other subversive acts, as well as accidents, thefts, or other causes of similar nature.

port tack • in sailing, to tack or sail to the left (with the wind coming from the right).

Poseidon • (**UGM-73A**) a two-stage solid-propellant ballistic missile equipped with inertial guidance, nuclear warheads, and a maneuverable bus that carries as many as fourteen reentry bodies that can be aimed at fourteen different targets. The Poseidon is launched from a specially configured submarine whether the submarine is surfaced or submerged. It has range of 2000 nautical miles.

Poseidon submarine missile patrol • a detachment of submarine forces responsible for a mission or an operation and configured to deliver POSEIDON ballistic missiles.

Posey, Thomas (1750–1818) • REVOLUTIONARY WAR army officer. A Virginian, as the Revolution approached Posey served on the Botetourt County committee of correspondence, and he became a company commander in the Continental army. He fought at SARATOGA (1777) and was present at YORKTOWN (1781). After the war he resigned his commission but returned to military service in 1793, serving in the Northwest Territory. After an unsuccessful run for the U.S. House of Representatives (1797), he moved to Kentucky, where he won election to several state offices. Unsuccessful in business, he relocated to Baton Rouge, Louisiana, where in 1812 he filled a recess appointment to the U.S. Senate. In 1813 he was named governor of the Indiana Territory; he opposed statehood and, after Indiana joined the Union as a state in 1816, was defeated in the election for the state's first governor.

position • *n.* **1** (often **positions**) a place where part of a military force is posted for strategic purposes: *the guns were shelling the German positions.* **2** a person's particular point of view or attitude toward something: *the official U.S.* ***position on*** *Palestine.*

positive peace • the condition characterized by the existence of peaceful social and cultural beliefs and norms; the presence of justice at all levels (economic, social, and political); the shared democratic use of power; and non-violence.

Posse Comitatus Act • a law enacted in 1878 to prohibit the use of the U.S. army in civilian law enforcement, unless otherwise instructed by the president, thereby excluding the military from the civilian sphere. After President ULYSSES S. GRANT sent a posse comitatus to the polls in the election of 1876, it was presented by Southern Democratic members of the House who resented the use of federal troops during Reconstruction.

post[1] • *n.* publish the name of (a member of the armed forces) as missing or dead: *a whole troop had been posted missing.*

post[2] • *n.* **1** a place where a soldier, guard, or police officer is stationed or which they patrol: *he gave the two armed men orders not to leave their posts | a command post.* **2** a force stationed at a permanent position or camp; a garrison. **3** a local group in an organization of military veterans. • *v.* **1** (usually **be posted**) send (someone) to a particular place to take up an appointment: *he was posted to Washington as military attaché.* **2** station (someone, especially a soldier, guard, or police officer) in a particular place: *a guard was posted at the entrance.*

postbellum |pōst'beləm| • *adj.* occurring or

existing after a war, in particular the American Civil War.
ORIGIN: late 19th cent.: from Latin *post* 'after' + *bellum* 'war.'

post captain • historical a Royal Navy officer holding the full rank of captain, as opposed to a commander with the courtesy title of captain.

post exchange • see PX.

postflight inspection • (also **after-flight inspection**) the inspection of an aircraft at the conclusion of a flight in order to determine whether any damage has occurred and what maintenance actions are required before the aircraft is again flown.

Post, George Browne (1837–1913) • Union army officer, born in New York City. Post trained as a civil engineer and enjoyed a successful career as an architect. During the CIVIL WAR he served as an aide-de-camp to Gen. AMBROSE BURNSIDE and, as a member of the National Guard after the conclusion of the war, reached the rank of colonel.

As an architect, he is best known for his design for the Western Union Telegraph Building (1873–75).

posting • *n.* **1** chiefly Brit. an appointment to a job, especially one abroad or in the armed forces: *he requested a posting to Japan.* **2** the location of such an appointment: *Norway was an attractive posting because of its quality of life.*

poststrike reconnaissance • missions undertaken for the purpose of gathering information used to measure the results of a strike.

post-traumatic stress disorder • (**PTSD**) a condition of persistent mental and emotional stress occurring as a result of injury or severe psychological shock, typically involving disturbance of sleep and constant vivid recall of the experience, with dulled responses to others and to the outside world.

potassium nitrate • a white crystalline salt which occurs naturally in nitre and is used in preserving meat and as a constituent of gunpowder.

pot hat • slang the Army Green service hat formerly issued to female U.S. Army personnel, now replaced by a black beret. Female Military Police continue to wear the pot hat.

Potomac, Army of the • see ARMY OF THE POTOMAC.

Potsdam Conference • a conference held at Potsdam, near Berlin, from July 17 to August 2, 1945, during WORLD WAR II. Attending were President HARRY S. TRUMAN, British Prime Minister WINSTON CHURCHILL (who was replaced on July 28 by Clement Attlee), and Soviet premier JOSEF STALIN. They discussed peace treaties, which were drafted by a Council of Foreign Ministers, to restructure Germany and Eastern Europe and to end the war against Japan. It was the last Allied summit conference.

During the conference, Truman spoke to Stalin about a new weapon to be used against Japan, but failed to identify it as an atomic bomb.

Potsdam Proclamation • a declaration issued to Japan on July 26, 1945, during the Potsdam Conference, by President HARRY S. TRUMAN and British Prime Minister Clement Attlee. It called upon Japan to surrender unconditionally or face destruction.

Potter, Robert Brown (1827–87) • Union army officer, born in Schenectady, New York. Trained as a lawyer, Potter was elected head of the 51st New York Volunteers and sailed with Gen. AMBROSE BURNSIDE for North Carolina's Hatteras Inlet. His brave advance under heavy fire at ANTIETAM (1862) allowed Union forces to inflict heavy damage on the defending Confederate troops. He also commanded a regiment in an ultimately futile attack at FREDERICKSBURG (1862). He also served ably at a number of other important battles, including SPOTSYLVANIA (1864), the BATTLE OF THE WILDERNESS (1864), and PETERSBURG (1865). He was killed while leading a division in the final assault on the Petersburg defenses.

pouch • *n.* a small bag or other flexible receptacle, typically carried in a pocket or attached to a belt: *webbing with pouches for stun grenades.*

pounder • *n.* a gun designed to fire a shell weighing a specified number of pounds.

POW • *abbr.* prisoner of war.

powder • *n.* short for GUNPOWDER.

powder flask • a small container with a nozzle for carrying and dispersing gunpowder.

powder horn • the horn of an ox, cow, or similar animal used to hold gunpowder, with the wide end filled in and a nozzle at the pointed end.

powder monkey • **1** a boy employed on a sailing warship to carry powder to the guns. **2** a person who works with explosives.

Powell, Colin L. (1937?–) • U.S. army officer, chairman of the U.S. Joint Chiefs of Staff, and U.S. Secretary of State, born in New York City to Jamaican immigrant parents. Powell served in the RESERVE OFFICER TRAINING CORPS while a student at the City College of New York. He served in Vietnam (1962–63, 1968–69). After studying at George Washington University, he joined the White House staff, soon becoming an aide to the director of the Office of Management and Budget. Powell held several positions at the PENTAGON and in 1983 became a senior military assistant to Defense Secretary CASPAR WEINBERGER. In 1987 he became assistant to the president for national security affairs, and in 1989 he headed the Army Forces Command. In April 1989 he became a four-star general, and in August of that year President GEORGE H. BUSH nominated him to head the Joint Chiefs of Staff. In that position he helped plan the 1989 invasion of PANAMA and the 1991 PERSIAN GULF WAR. He retired from the military in 1993. In the years since his retirement he was widely mentioned as a possible presidential candidate or secretary of defense. President GEORGE W. BUSH named him as Secretary of State in 2001.

Powell was the first African American to head the U.S. Joint Chiefs of Staff.

Powell doctrine • an approach to the use of military force named for U.S. Army Gen. COLIN L. POWELL, Chairman of the Joint Chiefs of Staff during the PERSIAN GULF WAR (1991), which states that United States forces should be committed to combat only when the political objectives of such use of force are clear and then in sufficient force to overwhelm the enemy quickly and achieve decisive results. The Powell doctrine was a reaction to the uncertain objectives and indecisive piecemeal escalation of force by the United States in the VIETNAM WAR.

powerboat • *n.* a boat driven by an inboard or outboard internal-combustion engine or other type of motor. Also called MOTORBOAT.

power play • **1** the use of physical strength to defeat one's opponent in a sport through sheer force. **2** the concentration of resources and effort toward a particular end, especially in politics and business.

power politics • political action by a person or group that makes use of or is intended to increase their power or influence.

Powers, Gary (1922–77) • spy and aviator, born Francis Gary Powers in Kentucky. Powers enlisted in the air force after graduating from college. Powers received training in resisting brainwashing, survival techniques, and protocol in the event of capture, and he also was trained in the dropping of atomic bombs. He was recruited by the Central Intelligence Agency, which trained him in piloting the U-2, a top-secret high-altitude reconaissance plane used to photograph enemy installations, and he made a number of flights over the Soviet Union and Eastern Europe. In May 1960, as President DWIGHT D. EISENHOWER and Soviet Premier NIKITA KHRUSHCHEV met in Paris to attempt to defuse COLD WAR tensions, a U-2 piloted by Powers was shot down by a surface-to-air missile over Soviet territory. The United States initially denied the plane was on a spy mission, but the wreckage was sufficiently intact for the Soviets to discern the plane's function, and Eisenhower was forced to admit the truth. The summit collapsed amid angry charges from Khrushchev; Powers was tried as a spy, convicted, and sentenced to ten years. He was traded for a Soviet spy in 1962 amid criticism of his conduct while he was in the Soviet Union. In 1963 he went to work for the LOCKHEED Aircraft Corporation. He was killed in 1977 when the helicopter he was piloting while working as a traffic reporter for a Los Angeles television station crashed.

Powhatan (1547–1618) • chief of an Indian confederation, father of Pocahontas. At the peak of his power Powhatan controlled approximately 9,000 Indians in the Virginia Tidewater region. After opposing the British settlement at Jamestown, Powhatan allegedly changed his mind after his daughter, Pocahontas, begged him to show mercy toward the captured English captain JOHN SMITH. Although the British attempted to placate the Indians with gifts, the Indians resented the settlers' relentless encroachment on their territory. After Pocahontas married an Englishman, Captain John Rolfe, in 1614, Powhatan signed a peace treaty with the English, and good relations prevailed between the two groups for the rest of the chief's life.

POW-MIA movement • a U.S. campaign focused on the treatment of prisoners of war (POWs) in Communist captivity and the whereabouts of those classified as missing in action (MIA). It dates to President RICHARD M. NIXON's first years in office, during the VIETNAM WAR. From 1970 to 1972 Nixon encouraged the growth of the movement by contending that during peace talks the North Vietnamese were uncooperative and evasive on the POW-MIA issue. The POW-MIA flag, which was flown over many state capitols during the 1980s, shows a silhouette of a man in front of barbed wire and a guard tower, with the words 'POW-MIA' and 'You are not forgotten.'

Prairie Grove, Battle of • a CIVIL WAR battle fought on December 7, 1862 in Washington County, Arkansas. Casualties of about 2,500 were equally divided between the two sides but it was a strategic victory for the Union under Gen. FRANCIS J. HERRON, giving them control of northwest Arkansas after Confederates under Gen. THOMAS HINDMAN were forced to retreat.

pratique |præ'tēk| • *n.* permission granted to a ship to have dealings with a port, given after quarantine or on showing a clean bill of health.

Pratt, William Veazie (1869–1957) • U.S. CHIEF OF NAVAL OPERATIONS, born in Maine. Pratt's only foray into combat was as part of a landing party in the Philippines in 1899, during the PHILIPPINE WAR. In 1911 he became an instructor at the U.S. NAVAL WAR COLLEGE, in Newport, Rhode Island, which dramatically changed his career, as he sharpened his political and oratorical skills and made important contacts in the navy. In 1917 he was assigned to the naval operations staff; by 1929 he was an admiral and commander in chief of the U.S. fleet. Pratt's support of arms limitations and of international agreements limiting the number of warships each nation could build made him suspect and embroiled him in numerous controversies with those who supported ever-increasing military strength as the best deterrent to war. This controversy followed him to the post of Chief of Naval Operations, to which President HERBERT HOOVER appointed him in 1930.

PRC • *abbr.* the People's Republic of China. Compare ROC.

preassault operation • in amphibious operations, an operation conducted in the amphibious objective area before the assault phase begins.

Preble, George Henry (1816–85) • Union naval officer, born in Maine. Preble served in the MEXICAN WAR (1846–48) and as part of MATTHEW C. PERRY's expedition to Japan (1853–54). His career foundered when, during the blockade of Mobile in 1862, during the CIVIL WAR, he allowed a Confederate ship to get by him and reach Fort Morgan, despite the illness of its commander and most of its crew, who were suffering from yellow fever and who were in no condition to put up a fight. Preble was immediately dismissed from the navy but reinstated five months later. He was more successful as part of a joint naval and army operation that diverted Confederate troops sufficiently to allow Gen. WILLIAM T. SHERMAN's forces to advance through Georgia (1864). However, his failure at Mobile haunted the rest of his career.

precautionary launch • the launching of nuclear-loaded aircraft under imminent nuclear attack so as to preclude the destruction of friendly aircraft and the loss of weapons on the ground (or carrier).

precision bombing • bombing directed at a specific point target.

precision-guided munitions • "smart" bombs, artillery projectiles, and missiles which are terminally guided to their targets with a high degree of accuracy by laser or electro-optical guidance systems.

preemptive attack • an attack initiated on the basis of incontrovertible evidence that an enemy attack is imminent.

preemptive nuclear strike • an attack with nuclear weapons initiated on the basis of incontrovertible evidence that an enemy attack is imminent and designed to destroy or greatly reduce the enemy's ability to launch such an attack.

pre-hostilities reconnaissance • reconnaissance activities, ususally clandestine, conducted prior to the start of hostilities.

preparedness • *n.* a state of readiness, especially for war: *the country maintained a high level of military preparedness.*

preplanned air support • air support that has been planned well in advance of its execution as part of a developed plan.

pre-position • *v.* place military units, equipment, or supplies at or near the point of planned use, or at a designated location, in order to reduce reaction time and to ensure timely support of a specific force during initial phases of an operation.

Prescott, Oliver (1731–1804) • REVOLUTIONARY WAR army officer, born in Massachusetts. Prescott attended Harvard College and began a successful career as a physican while dabbling in politics. He actively opposed the STAMP ACT (1765) and was clerk of the Groton committee of correspondence (1774). Prescott treated the wounded from LEXINGTON and CONCORD and from the BATTLE OF BUNKER HILL (all 1775). He served as brigadier general of the Middlesex County militia and, in 1778, as second major general of the state militia. A well-respected physician, he was a founding member of the American Academy of Arts and Sciences.

Prescott, William (1726–95) • REVOLUTIONARY WAR army officer. Prescott's military career began with a commisson in KING GEORGE'S WAR (1744-48) and continued in the FRENCH AND INDIAN WAR (1754–63). In 1774 he was given command of a militia in the towns of Pepperell and Groton, in his native Massachusetts, and of Hollis, New Hampshire. In 1775, at the start of the Revolution, he was placed in command of the troops gathered in Boston and ordered to fortify BUNKER HILL. On his own initiative, however, he instead moved to defend Breed's Hill. The first assault on Breed's Hill by the British, led by Gen. WILLIAM HOWE, failed. Howe again attacked, but this second British attack also fell short. On the third try, however, a shortage of ammunition hindered Prescott's defense, and the British ran the Americans off the hill. Although the British eventually triumphed at what became known as the BATTLE OF BUNKER HILL, Prescott's successful initial defense against the best-trained troops in the world made him an early hero of the Revolution. After Bunker Hill, Prescott marched with Gen. GEORGE WASHINGTON's army to New York City; after that city fell to the British, he returned to Pepperell, his only other military engagement being the Battle of SARATOGA (1777).

presence • *n.* a group of people, especially soldiers or police, stationed in a particular place: *maintain a presence in the region.*

present |pri'zent| • *v.* hold out or aim (a firearm) at something so as to be ready to fire: *they were to present their rifles, take aim, and fire.* PHRASES: **present arms** hold a rifle vertically in front of the body as a salute.

Presidential Directive • a type of document used during President JIMMY CARTER's administration and that replaced the NATIONAL SECURITY DECISION MEMORANDA. Following a PRESIDENTIAL REVIEW MEMORANDUM and results of the requested study, it was used by the president to declare a decision on a national security issue.

Presidential Review Memorandum • a type of document used during President JIMMY CARTER's administration and that replaced the NATIONAL SECURITY STUDY MEMORANDA. It was used to request a NATIONAL SECURITY COUNCIL committee to research a particular topic or to analyze a problem, and it set a deadline for the completion of the project. The results of the study were followed by a PRESIDENTIAL DIRECTIVE.

presidential selected reserve call-up • the activation by the President under applicable public laws of not more than 200,000 members of the Selected Reserve for up to 90 days to meet the support requirements of any operational mission without a declaration of a national emergency.

Presidential Unit Citation • a three-bar ribbon that is awarded to military units for gallantry in action. It was created in 1942 and has been awarded in all conflicts since then.

President's Foreign Intelligence Advisory Board • an independent board established in 1956 by President DWIGHT D. EISENHOWER to provide the president with information concerning intelligence activity and the effectiveness of intelligence collection. It was originally named the President's

Board of Consultants on Foreign Intelligence Activities and received its current name under the administration of President JOHN F. KENNEDY. It has served all presidents since its establishment except for President JIMMY CARTER. Foreign intelligence activity is reported through the board's Intelligence Oversight Board.

***President*, USS** • a high-speed sailing warship that defeated three British warships (the *Daphne*, *Eliza Swan*, and *Alert*) off the coast of Ireland during the WAR OF 1812. Later blockaded by a British squadron at New York for almost a year, the ship left New York on January 14, 1815, and was captured the next day.

Presidio, the • a Spanish military post in San Francisco (1776–1822), then a Mexican military post (1822–1848), and finally a U.S. Army post (1848–1994) responsible for protecting commerce and trade. Since 1994, the Presidio has been part of the Golden Gate National Recreation Area and is jointly managed by the National Park Service and the Presidio Trust.

press • *v.* force (a man) to enlist in the army or navy. • *n.* a forcible enlistment of men, especially for the navy.

press censorship • the security review of news material subject to the jurisdiction of the U.S. Armed Forces, including all information or material intended for dissemination to the public.

press gang • a body of men employed to enlist men forcibly into service in the army or navy. • *v.* (**press-gang**) forcibly enlist (someone) into service in the army or navy.

pressure hull • the inner hull of a submarine, in which approximately normal pressure is maintained when the vessel is submerged.

pressure mine • **1** a land mine whose fuze responds to the direct pressure of a target. **2** a naval mine whose circuit responds to the hydrodynamic pressure field of a target.

pressure suit • **1** (**partial**) a skin tight suit which does not completely enclose the body but which is capable of exerting pressure on the major portion of the body in order to counteract an increased intrapulmonary oxygen pressure **2** (**full**) a suit which completely encloses the body and which a gas pressure, sufficiently above ambient pressure for maintenance of function, may be sustained.

pressurized cabin • the occupied space of an aircraft in which the air pressure has been increased above that of the ambient atmosphere by compression of the ambient atmosphere into the space.

prestrike reconnaissance • missions undertaken for the purpose of obtaining complete information about known targets, and thereby informing the strike force.

preventive war • a war initiated in the belief that military conflict, while not imminent, is inevitable, and that to delay would involve greater risk.

PRG • *abbr.* Provisional Revolutionary Government.

Price, Sterling (1809–67) • Confederate army officer, born in Virginia. Price moved as a young man to Missouri, where he prospered as a tobacco planter and merchant. He entered politics and held several statewide positions, including Speaker of the General Assembly (1840–44). In 1844 he was elected to the U.S. House of Representatives, a position he promptly resigned to serve in the MEXICAN WAR (1846–48). Returning to Missouri, he served two terms as governor (1853–57). Although he initially opposed secession, he eventually sided with the Confederacy and received a commission in the Confederate army. After participating in a number of military engagements across the South, Price was put in charge of the invasion of Union-occupied Missouri (1864), an invasion that was a military debacle. After the war, he led a failed attempt to establish a camp for Confederate refugees in Mexico.

primary aircraft authorization • the aircraft officially designated to a unit so that it can perform its operational mission. The primary authorization is the basis for the approval of operating funds, which include personnel, support equipment, and flying-hour money.

primary aircraft inventory • the aircraft designated to fulfill the primary aircraft authorization. See also BACKUP AIRCRAFT INVENTORY.

primary censorship • armed forces censorship performed by personnel of a company, battery, squadron, ship, station, base, or similar unit on the personal communications of persons assigned, attached, or otherwise under the jurisdiction of a unit.

prime mover • a vehicle, including heavy construction equipment, possessing military characteristics, designed primarily for towing heavy, wheeled weapons and frequently providing facilities for the transportation of the crew of, and ammunition for, the weapon.

primer • *n.* **1** a cap or cylinder containing a compound that responds to friction or an electrical impulse and ignites the charge in a cartridge or explosive. **2** a small pump for pumping fuel to prime an internal combustion engine, especially in an aircraft.

priming • *n.* **1** another term for PRIMER. **2** gunpowder placed in the pan of a firearm to ignite a charge.

primus inter pares • a Latin phrase meaning "first among equals" used to describe, for example, the Chairman of the United States JOINT CHIEFS OF STAFF with respect to the Chiefs of Staff of the Army and of the Air Force, the Chief of Naval Operations, and the Commandant of the Marine Corps.

Princeton, Battle of • on January 3, 1777, GEORGE WASHINGTON having drawn back across the Delaware after TRENTON) again crossed into New Jersey, this time outflanking British forces in Princeton. The American army, reduced to 1,200 men, attacked disorganized British troops at Princeton with modest success. The victories at Trenton and Princeton helped foil the British conquest of northern New Jersey and marked the turning point of the REVOLUTIONARY WAR.

principles of war • a series of fundamental interrelated concepts, the result of centuries of tradition and experience, which purport to encapsulate those factors leading to victory in war. The U.S. armed forces subscribe to nine such principles: Objective, Offensive, Mass, Economy of Force, Maneuver, Unit of Command, Security, Surprise, and Simplicity.

priority • *n.* with reference to operation plans and the tasks derived therefrom, an indication of relative importance rather than an exclusive and final designation of the order of accomplishment.

prior permission • permission granted by the appropriate authority prior to the commencement of a flight or a series of flights landing in or flying over the territory of the nation concerned.

prisoner • *n.* **1** a person captured and kept confined by an enemy, opponent, or criminal: *American citizens were being **held prisoner** in Iran | 200 rebels were **taken prisoner**.* **2** a person legally committed to prison as a punishment for crimes they have committed or while awaiting trial.

prisoner of war • (**POW**) a person who has been captured and imprisoned by the enemy in war.

prisoner of war camp • an installation established for the internment and administration of prisoners of war.

prisoner of war censorship • the censorship of the communications to and from enemy prisoners of war and civilian internees held by the U.S. Armed Forces.

Prisoner of War Information Center • the U.S. national center that provides information to enemy and U.S. prisoners of war.

private • *n.* an enlisted person in the armed forces of the lowest rank, in particular an enlisted person in the U.S. Army or Marine Corps ranking below private first class. • *adj.* **1** (of a person) having no official or public role or position. **2** not connected with one's work or official position: *the president was visiting China in a private capacity.*

private army • an armed force raised, maintained, and controlled by a private person or group, such as a warlord or a religious sect.

privateer • *n.* **1** an armed ship owned and officered by private individuals holding a government commission and authorized for use in war, especially in the capture of enemy merchant shipping. **2** (also **privateersman**) a commander or crew member of such a ship, often regarded as a pirate. • *v.* engage in the activities of a privateer.

DERIVATIVES: **privateering** *n.*

privateersman • *n.* (pl. **-men**) a commander or crew member of a privateer.

private first class • an enlisted person in the armed forces, in particular (in the U.S. Army) an enlisted person ranking above private and below corporal or (in the U.S. Marine Corps) an enlisted person ranking above private and below lance corporal.

Private Recruit • in some armies, the lowest enlisted rank, usually assigned to newly inducted soldiers.

private soldier • **1** a soldier of the lowest rank. **2** a soldier of this type who is not a recruit.

prize • *n.* an enemy ship captured during the course of naval warfare.

prize court • a naval court that adjudicates on the distribution of ships and property captured in the course of naval warfare.

PRM 10 • U.S. Presidential Review Memorandum 10, formally entitled "Comprehensive Net Assessment and Military Force Posture Review"; an interagency study of national-security policy with a special emphasis on strategic doctrine requested by President Jimmy Carter on his first day in office in 1977. PRM 10 was opposed by the Joint Chiefs of Staff, but it formed the basis of President Carter's nuclear strategy, arms control, and military budgeting policies.

proclamation • *n.* a document, published to the inhabitants of a given area, that sets forth the basis of authority and scope of activities of a commander in the area and that defines the obligations, liabilities, duties, and rights of the population affected.

Proclamation Line of 1763 • the British crown's attempt to separate white settlement from Indian country after the French and Indian War (1754–63). Drawn at the crest of the Appalachians, the Line was a failure as colonial squatters swarmed into the Ohio Valley.

Proclamation of Blockade • see Blockade Proclamation.

procurement • *n.* the action or occupation of acquiring military equipment and supplies: *defense procurement.*

procurement lead time • the interval in months between the initiation of procurement action and receipt into the supply system of the production model (excludes prototypes) purchased as the result of such actions, and is composed of two elements, production lead time and administrative lead time.

production base • the total national industrial production capacity available for the manufacture of items to meet materiel requirements.

profiteer • *v.* to make or seek to make an excessive or unfair profit, especially illegally or in a black market. • *n.* one who profits excessively through wartime production or trade. See also Nye Committee.

program aircraft • every aircraft included in both the active and reserve aircraft.

prohibited area • a specified area of land, or the territorial waters adjacent thereto, over which the flight of aircraft is prohibited or to which access by any means is prohibited.

project equipment • see special equipment.

projectile • *n.* **1** a missile designed to be fired from a rocket or gun. **2** an object propelled through the air, especially one thrown as a weapon: *they tried to shield Johnson from the projectiles that were being thrown.* • *adj.* of or relating to such a missile or object: *a projectile weapon.*

promissory note • a signed document containing a written promise to pay a stated sum to a specified person or the bearer at a specified date or on demand.

prompt radiation • the gamma rays produced in fission and as a result of other neutron reactions and nuclear excitation of the weapon materials appearing within a second or less after a nuclear explosion.

proof • *adj.* able to withstand something damaging; resistant: *the hardened walls were **proof against** most weapons.*

propaganda • *n.* any form of communication in support of national objectives designed to influence the opinions, emotions, attitudes, or behavior of any group in order to benefit the sponsor, either directly or indirectly.

propellant • *n.* **1** the source (specifically, an explosive charge) that provides the energy required for propelling a projectile. **2** a fuel, either solid or liquid, for propelling a rocket or missile.

propeller • *n.* a mechanical device for propelling a boat or aircraft, consisting of a revolving shaft with two or more broad, angled blades attached to it.

prop wash • a current of water or air created by the action of a propeller or rotor.

protected site • a facility that is protected by the use of camouflage or concealment, selective siting, construction of facilities designed to prevent damage from fragments caused by conventional weapons, or a combination of such measures.

protective clothing • clothing especially designed, fabricated, or treated to protect personnel against hazards caused by dangerous working conditions, enemy action, or extreme changes in physical environment.

protective security • the organized system of defensive measures instituted and maintained at all levels of command with the aim of achieving and maintaining security.

prototype • *n.* a model suitable for evaluation of design, performance, and production potential.

Providence • a sloop that was part of the small navy established by the Continental Congress in 1775, and expected to raid commerce ships and transports that were supplying British forces in North America.

proving ground • an area used for testing devices and equipment.

Provisional Constitution • a document of the CONFEDERATE STATES OF AMERICA that was approved by the seceding states on February 4, 1861 in Montgomery, Alabama. It established a provisional government for the Confederacy. It resembled the U.S. Constitution but stressed STATES' RIGHTS, and several of its clauses recognized and protected slavery, although the importation of slaves from any foreign country was prohibited.

Provisional Revolutionary Government • (**PRG**) the government of South Vietnam from 1969 till the end of the VIETNAM WAR in 1975.

proviso |prəˈvīzō| • *n.* (pl. **-os**) a condition attached to an agreement.

provost |ˈprōˌvōst| • *n.* short for PROVOST MARSHAL.

provost guard • a detachment of soldiers acting as military police under the command of a provost marshal.

provost marshal • the head of military police in camp or on active service.

prow |prow| • *n.* the portion of a ship's bow above water.

Prowler • (**EA-6B**) an aircraft developed from the INTRUDER (EA-6A) and designed to provide ELECTRONIC COUNTERMEASURES (ECMs) and an important component of the modern carrier air wing. It carries a crew of four, one pilot and three electronic warfare officers who manage the complicated array of ECM and electronic support measures (ESMs), including the tactical jamming system, which can be operated manually, semi-automatically, or automatically.

proximity fuse • an electronic detonator that causes a projectile to explode when it comes within a preset distance of its target.

proxy war • a war instigated by a major power that does not itself become involved.

Pryor, Roger Atkinson (1828–1919) • Confederate army officer, born in Virginia. Pryor briefly practiced law, then switched to journalism for health reasons. His editorial stance was pro-Southern and staunchly Democratic. In 1859 he was elected to Congress, where he continued his attacks on the North and blamed Unionists for the tension between the North and the South. He resigned his seat in 1861 to protest ABRAHAM LINCOLN's election as president. After Virginia's secession, he was appointed to lead the 3rd Virginia Regiment and fought in the PENINSULAR CAMPAIGN (1862), for which he was cited for gallantry. Dissatisfied with his assigned role, he resigned his commission and joined the 3rd Virginia Cavalry as a private, in which position he served primarily as a courier. In this capacity, he was captured in 1864 and imprisoned. After the war, he worked for the New York *Daily News*, a Democratic organ, while obtaining admission to the New York bar (1865).

psychological consolidation activities • planned psychological activities in peace and war directed at the civilian population located in areas under friendly control in order to achieve a desired behavior that supports the military objectives and the operational freedom of the supported commanders.

psychological media • the media (technical or nontechnical) that establish any kind of communication with a target audience.

psychological operations • (**PSYOP**) planned operations to convey selected information and indicators to foreign audiences in order to influence their emotions, motives, objective reasoning, and ultimately the behavior of foreign governments, organizations, groups, and individuals. Integral to perception management, psychological operations are designed to induce or reinforce foreign attitudes and behavior favorable to the originator's objectives.

psychological situation • the current emotional state, mental disposition, or other behavioral motivation of a target audience, basically founded on its national political, social, economic, and psychological peculiarities but also subject to the influence of circumstances and events.

psychological theme • an idea or topic on which a psychological operation is based.

psychological warfare • (**PSYWAR**) the planned use of propaganda and other psychological actions, having the primary purpose of influencing the opinions, emotions, attitudes, and behavior of hostile foreign groups in such a way as to support the achievement of national objectives.

psychological warfare consolidation • psychological warfare directed toward populations in friendly rear areas or in territory occupied by friendly military forces with the objective of facilitating military operations and promoting maximum cooperation among the civil populace.

PSYOP • *abbr.* psychological operations.

PSYWAR • *abbr.* psychological warfare.

Pt • *abbr.* **1** (**Pt.**) Point (on maps): *Pt. Cloates.* **2** (**pt**) (denoting a side of a ship or aircraft) port.

PT • *abbr.* physical training.

PT-76 • an amphibious tank used by the Russian Army. It carries a crew of three, has a maximum speed of 50km/h, and provides the driver with infrared night vision equipment.

PT-109 • the motor torpedo boat commanded by Lt. Junior Grade JOHN F. KENNEDY. It was rammed and sunk by the Japanese destroyer *Amigiri* off Kolombangara Island in the SOLOMON ISLANDS on August 2, 1943.

PT boat • *n.* a motor torpedo boat (MTB), usually built by one of three ship-builders (Elco, Higgins, or Huckins) between 1942 and 1945, designed originally as antiship weapons and equipped with powerful Packard gasoline engines. These fast, maneuverable boats had wooden hulls and were anywhere from 60 to 100 ft (18 to 30 m) in length. During WORLD WAR II, PT (patrol torpedo) boats operated all over the Pacific, in the Mediterranean, and in the English Channel, and were used primarily to attack surface ships, but they also laid mines, created smoke screens, rescued downed aviators, and performed intelligence or raider missions as well. Also called MOSQUITO BOATS.

ORIGIN: 1940s: from *P(atrol) T(orpedo) boat.*

Pte • *abbr.* Brit., Australian Private (in the army).

PTSD • *abbr.* post-traumatic stress disorder.

public information • information of a military nature, the dissemination of which through public news media is not inconsistent with security, and the release of which is considered desirable or nonobjectionable to the responsible releasing agency.

public opinion • views prevalent among the general public: *shaping public opinion.*

Pueblo Incident • on January 23, 1968 the USS *Pueblo,* while gathering intelligence on the military strength of North Korea, was confronted by North Korean warships in the Sea of Japan, outside the twelve-mile territorial limit of the Communist nation. When the North Koreans opened fire, Commander LLOYD M. BUCHER surrendered, and the 82-man crew was subsequently imprisoned and tortured. Following their release on December 23, 1968, in exchange for an official (though officially declared false) U.S. admission of espionage, a navy court of inquiry recommendation that Bucher be court-martialed was vetoed by Navy Secretary John H. Chafee.

Pueblo Revolt • an organized rebellion of Pueblo Indians against Spanish rule in New Mexico in 1680. Led by Popé, a Tewa medicine man of the San Juan Pueblo who had been imprisoned by the Spaniards, the Pueblo united to attack Spanish settlers on August 10. The Spaniards fled on August 21, many to the El Paso region, with fatalities numbering some 400. In 1692 Gov. Pedro de Vargas reconquered the Pueblos in an expedition to recover New Mexico.

Puff the Magic Dragon • a nickname for the AC-47 gunship.

Pulaski, Casimir |pəˈlæskē| (1748–79) • REVOLUTIONARY WAR army officer. Having failed in attempts to block foreign depredations in his native Poland, Pulaski fled first to Turkey, then to Paris, where Benjamin Franklin provided him with a letter of introduction to GEORGE WASHINGTON and encouraged him to sail for America. Pulaski joined up with Washington and immediately proved his worth; he discovered that British troops were endeavoring to surround Washington's army, allowing Washington to take steps to avert that undesirable occurrence. Washington had him promoted to brigadier general and placed him in charge of cavalry. Because of personal tension between him and his superior, Gen. ANTHONY WAYNE, Pulaski resigned his commission and asked permission to form an independent corps of lancers and light infantrymen. This corps became known as "Pulaski's Legion." For the rest of the war, Pulaski served ably, although he continued to feel that his services were not adequately appreciated by the colonials.

pullback • *n.* an act of withdrawing troops.

pull back • retreat or cause troops to retreat from an area.

Puller, Lewis Burwell (1898–1971) • Marine Corps officer, born in Virginia. Puller's first significant service was as part of a joint Haitian-U.S. peacekeeping force; from 1928 to 1933 he served in Nicaragua and later in China. In 1940 he trained marines at Camp Lejeune, North Carolina, in techniques of jungle fighting and camouflage. Puller's marines fought in the Pacific theater during WORLD WAR II, inflicting heavy casualties on the Japanese while minimizing American losses. After the war, Puller returned to training duty, then fought in Korea, including supporting Gen. DOUGLAS MACARTHUR at the INCHON LANDING (1950). In 1951 he returned to the United States, where he continued to train marines at camps around the nation. He was known as a tough, nononsense marine who was much admired by his men.

pull out • retreat or cause to retreat from an

area: *the army pulled out, leaving the city in ruins* | (**pull someone out**) *the CIA had pulled its operatives out of Tripoli.*

pull up • increase the altitude of an aircraft.

pull-up point • the point at which an aircraft must start to climb from a low-level approach in order to gain sufficient height from which to execute the attack or retirement.

pulsejet • *n.* a jet-propulsion engine that has neither a compressor nor a turbine. This engine has valves in the front that open and shut, taking in air, which creates thrust in rapid bursts rather than continuously. See also RAMJET.

pulse repetition frequency • in radar, the number of pulses that occur each second.

pulsing • *n.* in naval mine warfare, a method of operating magnetic and acoustic sweeps in which the sweep is energized by current that varies or is intermittent in accordance with a predetermined schedule.

pump • *n.* a pump-action shotgun. • *v.* shoot (bullets) into a target.

pump-action • *adj.* denoting a repeating firearm, typically a shotgun, in which a new round is brought from the magazine into the breech by a slide action in line with the barrel.

pump gun • a pump-action rifle with a tubular magazine.

pump room • a room, building, or compartment in which pumps are housed or from which they are controlled.

Punitive Expedition • an attack into northern Mexico in March 1916. On March 9, Gen. PANCHO VILLA, a Mexican revolutionary, attacked Columbus, New Mexico, killing several U.S. soldiers and civilians. On March 15, Brig. Gen. JOHN J. PERSHING and a force consisting of a provisional division, mostly cavalry, crossed the border into Mexico in pursuit of Villa's irregulars. Pershing's men traveled 400 miles into Mexico and, unable to capture Villa but having dispersed the Mexican forces that attacked Columbus, received orders on February 5, 1917, to return to the United States. The expedition was the last true cavalry action mounted by the U.S. Army and the first U.S. military operation to employ mechanized vehicles.

puppet government • a government that is under the control of another power.

pup tent • a small triangular tent, especially one with a pole at either end and room for one or two people.

purchase • *v.* haul up (a rope, cable, or anchor) by means of a pulley or lever.

purple • in air intercept, a code meaning, "The unit indicated is suspected of carrying nuclear weapons." (e.g., "purple VB").

Purple Heart Medal • U.S. military decoration awarded for death or wounds inflicted by forces hostile to the United States. To qualify the wound must have necessitated treatment by a medical officer. The Purple Heart Medal was established on February 22, 1932 as a revival of the Badge of Military Merit originally created by Gen. GEORGE WASHINGTON in 1782.

Before the creation of the Purple Heart, the receipt of wounds in combat was recognized by the award of a small chevron worn on the lower sleeve of the uniform coat.

PURPLE machine • The type of cipher machine (the "J" machine or Type 97 Alphabetical Typewriter) used to encrypt Japanese diplomatic messages shortly before and during WORLD WAR II. U.S. cryptologists were successful in breaking the PURPLE machine-generated ciphers in September 1940 and thus the Allies were privy to Japanese diplomatic message traffic throughout the course of the war.

Pusan • a city in southeast South Korea. At the beginning of the KOREAN WAR, the first U.S. forces were flown to Pusan July 1–4, 1950. U.N. troops were driven south near Pusan in July, but were determined to stand their ground near Pusan as all army units would be forced out of South Korea if pushed any further south. The Pusan Perimeter was established on July 31. On August 17–24 the capital of South Korea was moved to Pusan because of Seoul's capture by North Korea. U.N. air forces protected the city, a main southern port and entry point, from communist air attack. As a result, U.N. forces were able to establish installations there and channel supplies through Pusan that were sent on to the front by rail.

Pusan Perimeter • a defensive line established by Gen. WALTON WALKER on July 31, 1950, during the KOREAN WAR. At the beginning of the Korean War, United Nations troops retreated to the southeastern Pusan perimeter. It was an area in the southeast corner of South Korea bordered by the Naktong River on the west, the Sea of Japan on the east, treacherous mountains on the north, and the Korea Strait on the south. The cities of Pusan and Taegu, where Gen. Walker placed his Eighth Army Headquarters, were enclosed within this perimeter. During August 1950, battles continued at the Pusan Perimeter, and North Koreans attacked on all four fronts. U.N. forces built up strength, equipment, arms, and supplies. U.S. forces attacked August 7-13, 1950. Fighting continued from August 31 to September 7, when North Korean forces retreated. A successful invasion of Inchon created enough diversion September 16-30 so that Walker's troops recrossed the Naktong River and pushed the North Koreans north.

put • *v.* (**putting**; past and past part. **put**) (of a ship) proceed in a particular direction: *she stepped into the boat and* ***put out to sea.***

▸**put about** (of a ship) turn on the opposite tack.

put something down (also **put down**) land an aircraft.

put in a bag • slang (World War I) killed, shrouded.

Putnam, Israel (1718–90) • REVOLUTIONARY WAR army officer. Shortly after his marriage in 1739, Putnam and his bride moved from his native Massachusetts to Connecticut, where they bought a large parcel of land, which they farmed. During his service in the FRENCH AND INDIAN WAR(1754–63), Putnam became known for his resourcefulness and vigor; he was captured in 1758, tortured, and made to endure forced marches. He was finally ransomed a few months later. He also fought in PONTIAC'S REBELLION in 1764 but saw little action. Putnam was elected to the Connecticut General Assembly in 1766; he was also an organizer of the SONS OF LIBERTY in eastern Connecticut and became chairman of its committee of correspondence. After LEXINGTON and CONCORD (both 1775), he was named brigadier general of the Connecticut militia and marched his troops to Boston, where he was named a major general of the Continental army. Putnam was placed in charge of defending BUNKER HILL, the first engagement at which the Continentals, although ultimately ceding the ground to the British, held their own against the much better trained and equipped Redcoats. Putnam was second only to Gen. GEORGE WASHINGTON in planning the BATTLE OF NEW YORK (1776), which in the event was a disaster for the Continentals; Putnam received most of the blame for the debacle. His defense of Philadelphia (1776–77) was more successful.

Putnam is credited with exhorting his men, as they prepared for the Battle of Bunker Hill, "Don't one of you fire until you see the whites of their eyes."

Putnam, Rufus (1738–1824) • American military engineer and frontier administrator. Born in Sutton, Massachusetts, Putnam was self-educated. He served with British forces in the FRENCH AND INDIAN WAR (1755–1763) before settling in Braintree, Massachusetts. A patriot, he constructed defensive works around Boston and New York City and rebuilt the fortifications at WEST POINT, rising to the rank of brigadier general in 1783. After the REVOLUTIONARY WAR, he helped to organize the Ohio Company which promoted settlement on the north bank of the Ohio River. In 1788, Putnam founded Marietta, Ohio, and in 1790, President GEORGE WASHINGTON appointed him a judge of the Supreme Court of the Northwest Territory. He negotiated a treaty with the Indians at Vincennes, and served as Surveyor-General of the United States (1796–1803). He served in the Ohio Constitutional Convention in 1802, arguing successfully against allowing slavery there.

Pvt. (also **PVT**) • *abbr.* (in the U.S. Army) private.

PX • *abbr.* post exchange; a store at a U.S. military base selling food, clothing, and other items.

Pyle, Ernie (1900–45) • journalist, born Ernest Taylor Pyle in Indiana. Pyle studied journalism at Indiana University. His first job was as a reporter for the La Porte *Herald*, in La Porte, Indiana; he then moved on to the Scripps-Howard paper the *Washington Daily News*. He worked for several other papers, including two in New York City, before returning to the *Daily News*, of which he became managing editor in 1932. In 1935 he became a roving reporter for Scripps-Howard, writing amusing columns based on his experiences traveling around the United States. During WORLD WAR II, he reported from London on the effects of the German bombardment on the average citizen, describing vividly the courage of the British amid the amorality of war. In 1942 and 1943, he reported from North Africa, covering the bloody battles there. He followed the troops during the invasion of Italy in 1943 and won the 1944 Pulitzer Prize for journalism for his affecting, colorful, compassionate reporting of that campaign. He landed in Normandy the day after D-DAY (June 6, 1944) and accompanied French troops into Paris. He was covering the invasions of IWO JIMA and OKINAWA when he was killed by Japanese fire.

pyrotechnic • *n.* a mixture of chemicals that, when ignited, is capable of reacting exothermically to produce light, heat, smoke, sound, or gas, and may also be used to introduce a delay into an explosive train because of its known burning time. The term excludes propellants and explosives.

pyrrhic victory |ˈpirik| (also **pyrrhic**) • *adj.* won at too great a cost to have been worthwhile for the victor.

PzKpfw • see TANKS, GERMAN, WORLD WAR II-ERA.

Qq

Qaddafi, Muammar al- • see GADDAFI, MUAMMAR.

QM • *abbr.* Quartermaster.

QMG • *abbr.* Quartermaster General.

QMS • *abbr.* (in the UK) Quartermaster Sergeant.

Q-ship • *n.* a merchant ship with concealed weapons, used by the British in WORLD WAR I and WORLD WAR II in an attempt to destroy submarines.

ORIGIN: World War I: from *Q* as a nonexplicit symbol of the type of vessel + SHIP.

quadrant |ˈkwädrənt| • *n.* **1** an instrument used for taking angular measurements of altitude in astronomy and navigation, typically consisting of a graduated quarter circle and a sighting mechanism. **2** a frame fixed to the head of a ship's rudder, to which the steering mechanism is attached.

Quaker gun • a dummy or decoy gun, as used in the CIVIL WAR and afterward to deceive the enemy. See also OPERATION FORTITUDE.

Quang Tri • a city in northern South Vietnam that was a target for takeover by the NORTH VIETNAMESE ARMY (NVA) in early 1972 at the beginning of their all-out offensive to win the war. The South Vietnamese army abandoned the city in May, 1972. An attempt was begun in June to retake the city, with the aid of U.S. Navy and air bombardment. The South Vietnamese controlled the city again by September, but in March, 1975, it fell to the NVA.

Quantico • a town on the Potomac River in northeast Virginia, United States. It was established as a U.S. naval base during the REVOLUTIONARY WAR. It became the training center of the U.S. Marine Corps in 1917 and has been the location of the Marine Corps University since the school's formal establishment in 1989.

The Federal Bureau of Investigation has its academy in Quantico.

Quantrill, William Clarke (1835–65) • guerrilla leader, born in Ohio. After dabbling in a number of careers, Quantrill became a JAYHAWKER in Kansas; he avoided arrest by misrepresenting his beliefs and betraying other jayhawkers. In 1861 he led a band of guerrillas in attacks on pro-Union Missourians; by 1862 he was notorious for his illegal activities. In 1863 he led 400 guerrillas in an attack on Lawrence, Kansas, that destroyed numerous businesses and resulted in the massacre of 150 men and boys; he also led a group that attacked and killed nearly 100 Union troops. In the years that followed, he was less active, although he continued his attacks; in 1865 he was captured by a troop of "Federal guerrillas" who has been assigned to track him down. He suffered a fatal injury in the assault.

quarantine • *n.* a state, period, or place of isolation in which people or animals that have arrived from elsewhere or been exposed to infectious or contagious disease are placed: *many animals die **in quarantine**.* • *v.* impose such isolation on (a person, animal, or place); put in quarantine.

ORIGIN: mid 17th cent.: from Italian *quarantina* 'forty days,' from *quaranta* 'forty.'

quarter • *n.* **1** either side of a ship aft of the beam: *he trained his glasses over the starboard quarter.* **2** (**quarters**) rooms or lodgings, especially those allocated to servicemen. **3** pity or mercy shown toward an enemy or opponent who is in one's power: *the riot squad **gave no quarter**.* • *v.* **1** cut (the body of an executed person) into four parts: *the plotters were hanged, drawn, and quartered.* **2** (**be quartered**) be stationed or lodged in a specified place: *many were quartered in tents.*

quarterdeck • *n.* **1** the part of a ship's upper deck near the stern, traditionally reserved for officers. **2** the officers of a ship or the navy.

quartering • *n.* the provision of accommodations or lodgings, especially for troops.

quartermaster • *n.* **1** a military officer responsible for providing quarters, rations, clothing, and other supplies. **2** a naval petty officer with particular responsibility for steering and signals.

Quartermaster Corps • established in June 1775 when the Second Continental Congress passed a resolution providing for a Quartermaster General and a deputy, and responsible for procuring, storing, and transporting supplies to troops. In 1912, Congress created the Quartermaster Corps by merging the former Subsistence, Pay, and Quartermaster Departments. The Corps is completely militarized and has its own officers, soldiers, and units that are trained to carry out many supply and service functions on the battlefield.

Quartermaster General • (pl. **Quartermasters General** or **Quartermaster Generals**) the head of the army department in charge of the quartering and equipment of troops.

quartermaster sergeant • Brit. a senior rank of noncommissioned officer in the army, above sergeant, employed on administrative duties.

Quasi-War with France • (1797–1801) an undeclared naval war with France resulting from the taking of U.S. ships by French privateers, and French insistence that the U.S. not trade with Britain. France also refused to negotiate with the U.S. minister when he arrived in Paris, and hinted that a large bribe needed to be paid to restore good relations (the XYZ AFFAIR). The USS *Constitution* won two victories over French men-of-war during the conflict. U.S. ships attacked French privateers until France agreed to settle the conflict.

quatrefoil • *n.* a cross-shaped braid placed atop the barracks covers of Marine officers to allow men in the masts of ships to distinguish their officers from the sailors during a sea battle.

quay |kē; k(w)ā| • *n.* a stone or metal platform lying alongside or projecting into water for loading and unloading ships.

quayside |'kē,sīd; 'k(w)āsīd| • *n.* a quay and the area around it.

Quebec Act • an act passed in 1774 by the British Parliament to establish French civil law and allow the practice of the Roman Catholic religion in the province of Quebec. It extended Quebec's boundaries and gave the province control of the territory and fur trade between the Ohio and Mississippi rivers. Protestants in the American colonies protested the act and named it and the COERCIVE ACTS as the INTOLERABLE ACTS.

Québec, Battle of • a 1759 battle in the FRENCH AND INDIAN WAR (1754–63) that is viewed as the climax in the struggle between Britain and France for North America. British troops under Maj. Gen. JAMES WOLFE attacked the city and surroundings for two months starting in June before making a daring nighttime landing to secure a strategic position. The French general LOUIS-JOSEPH MONTCALM attacked the invaders hastily and without adequate force, resulting in heavy casualties on both sides and control of the city by the English.

Quebec Conference • the second meeting held in the city of Quebec between British Prime Minister WINSTON CHURCHILL and U.S. President FRANKLIN D. ROOSEVELT, on September 11–16, 1944, during WORLD WAR II. Also known as "Octagon," it was used by the two leaders to plan military strategy and to address postwar issues.

Queen Anne's War • (1702–13) the second of four wars between the British and the French for the control of North America, arising initially out of French and Indian raids on British settlements along the New York and New England borders with Canada. The war was contemporaneous with and related to issues in the WAR OF THE SPANISH SUCCESSION. Fought mainly on the eastern seaboard of the United States and the Maritime provinces of Canada, the war was ended by the TREATY OF UTRECHT and resulted in Acadia (renamed Nova Scotia), Newfoundland, and the Hudson Bay territory being ceded to the British.

Queenston Heights, Battle of • a battle in the WAR OF 1812, fought near the Niagara River in what is now western New York in October, 1812. Americans attacking from across the river were unable to secure a position and were heavily defeated by the British. The battle encouraged the idea that a defense of Canada was possible.

Quemoy |ki'moi| • the main island in the Quemoy Islands, a group of islands a few miles off the coast of China's Fuchien Province. Quemoy has been ruled by the Republic of China since Nationalist troops repulsed Communist forces in a pitched battle in 1949. In August 1958 MAO ZEDONG determined to test American resolve to defend Taiwan by shelling Quemoy and Matsu Island from the port of Xiamen. After several days of heavy artillery fire, the United States sent six aircraft carriers, equipped with nuclear weapons, from the Seventh Fleet to help in resupplying the garrison. The Soviet Union promised retaliatory nuclear strikes should the United States use such force on mainland China, creating the first incident of BRINKSMANSHIP, several years before the CUBAN MISSILE CRISIS.

quick march • **1** a brisk military march. **2** a command to begin marching quickly.

quick search procedure • in air-ground or air-sea searches, a method of searching done as quickly as possible by searching the entire area on the outbound leg and by using twice as many aircraft as are normally used.

quick time • marching that is conducted at about 120 paces per minute.

Qui Nhon • a city on the South China Sea coast in central Vietnam that was of strategic importance during the VIETNAM WAR. The U.S. Army upgraded the port in 1965 and created a naval station and military base there.

quinine • *n.* a bitter crystalline compound present in cinchona bark, used as a tonic and formerly as an antimalarial drug.

quinine prophylaxis • the administration of quinine to prevent malaria.

quoin |k(w)oin| • *n.* a wedge for raising the level of a gun barrel or for keeping it from rolling.

Quonset |'kwänsət| (usually **Quonset hut**) • trademark a building made of corrugated metal and having a semicircular cross section. ORIGIN: World War II: named after *Quonset* Point, Rhode Island, where such huts were first made.

Rr

RA • *abbr.* (in the UK) Royal Artillery.

RAAF • *abbr.* Royal Australian Air Force.

Rabaul • the chief town and port of the island of New Britain, Papua New Guinea. Rabaul's harbor, Simpson Harbour, is the finest natural harbor in the southwest Pacific, and its conquest was a central part of Japanese expansion in the region. The Japanese gained control of the port in January 1942, and Rabaul quickly became their primary air and naval base in the region. Neutralizing it became an important goal of the Allied Operation Cartwheel in the Southwest Pacific Theater in early 1943, and this goal was achieved by the end of the year.

RAC • *abbr.* (in the UK) Royal Armoured Corps.

racer • *n.* a circular horizontal rail along which the carriage or traversing platform of a heavy gun moves.

racon | 'rā,kän | • *n.* a radar beacon that can be identified and located by its response to a specific radar signal.
ORIGIN: 1940s: blend of RADAR and BEACON.

rad • *n.* a unit of absorbed dose of ionizing radiation.

radar • *n.* a radio detection device that provides information on range, azimuth, and/or elevation of objects.

radar beacon • a receiver-transmitter combination that sends out a coded signal when triggered by the proper type of pulse, enabling determination of range and bearing information by the interrogating station or aircraft.

radar clutter • unwanted signals, echoes, or images on the face of the display screen, which interfere with the observation of desired signals.

radar cross section • the image produced by radar signals reflected off a given target surface. Radar cross section is an important design characteristic for military air and space vehicles in that a smaller radar cross section improves the chances that an enemy radar will be unable to acquire and track a friendly aircraft, missile, or space vehicle.

radar danning • in naval mine warfare, a method of navigating by using radar to keep the required distance from a line of dan buoys.

radar guardship • a ship assigned to protect a radar system by the officer in command of sustaining the radar watch.

radar intelligence • (**RADINT**) intelligence derived from data collected by radar.

radar netting • the linking of several radars to a single center to provide integrated target information.

radar reconnaissance • reconnaissance by means of radar to obtain information on enemy activity and to determine the nature of terrain.

radar silence • an imposed discipline prohibiting the transmission by radar of electromagnetic signals on some or all frequencies.

Radford, Arthur William (1896–1973) • naval officer and chairman of the JOINT CHIEFS OF STAFF, born in Illinois. Radford served in WORLD WAR I, becoming commander of the Pacific Fleet's Train. After the war he trained as a naval aviator and served as a fighter squadron commander, among other positions. He won praise for his service as a carrier force commander in the Pacific during WORLD WAR II; in 1944 he went to Washington, D.C., to serve as assistant to the deputy chief for naval operations for air and then returned to sea duty as commander of Carrier Division Six, which took part in the invasions of IWO JIMA and OKINAWA (both 1945). After the war, Radford was successively deputy chief for naval operations for air and vice chief of naval operations. In 1949 he became commander of the Pacific Fleet. He argued before Congress for increased funding for naval aviation and naval carriers rather than for air force bombers. In 1953 President DWIGHT D. EISENHOWER named him chairman of the Joint Chiefs of Staff, largely because of his administrative skills and his staunch anti-Communism; Radford also accepted the prevailing idea of using the threat of massive retaliation to reduce the Soviet threat.

Radford, William (1809–90) • Union naval officer. Radford, born in Virginia but raised in Kentucky, spent the first few years of his navy career cruising the Mediterranean and the Caribbean; he was instrumental in the capture of a Mexican warship during the MEXICAN WAR (1846–48). He then spent several years on shore duty, returning to active command of the steam sloop *Dacotah* in 1859. When the CIVIL WAR broke out, Radford's southern roots led to his losing his command of the *Dacotah,* but his command was restored to him and he commanded a warship during the blockade of Virginia.

radiation | ,rādē'āsHən | • *n.* **1** the emission of energy as electromagnetic waves or as moving subatomic particles, especially high-energy particles that cause ionization. **2** the energy transmitted in this way: *background radiation | the radiation dose.*

radiation dose • the total amount of ionizing radiation absorbed by material or tissues, expressed in centigrays. The term "radiation dose" is often used in the sense of the *exposure dose* (expressed in roentgens), which is a measure of the total amount of ionization that the quantity of radiation could produce in air. This could be distinguished from the *absorbed dose* (expressed in rads), which represents the energy absorbed from the radiation per gram of specified body tissue. Further, the *biological dose* (expressed in rems) is a measure of the biological effectiveness of the exposure.

radiation intelligence • intelligence derived

from the collection and analysis of non-information-bearing elements extracted from the electromagnetic energy unintentionally emanated by foreign devices, equipment, and systems, excluding those generated by the detonation of atomic or nuclear weapons.

radiation intensity • (**RI**) the radiation dose rate at a given time and place. It may be used, coupled with a figure, to denote the radiation intensity used at a given number of hours after a nuclear burst (for example, "RI-3" is a radiation intensity 3 hours after the time of burst).

radiation sickness • an illness resulting from excessive exposure to ionizing radiation. The earliest symptoms are nausea, vomiting, and diarrhea, which may be followed by loss of hair, hemorrhage, inflammation of the mouth and throat, and general loss of energy.

RADINT • *abbr.* radar intelligence.

radioactivity • *n.* the spontaneous emission of radiation, generally alpha or beta particles, often accompanied by gamma rays, from the nuclei of an unstable isotope.

radio deception • the employment of radio to deceive the enemy. Methods of radio deception include sending false dispatches, using deceptive headings, and employing enemy call signs.

radio fix • the position of a ship, aircraft, or ground radio transmitter as determined by use of radio signals.

Radio Free Europe • (**RFE**) (Also **Radio Liberty, RL**) a U.S.-sponsored radio station broadcasting to communist Eastern Europe. Radio Free Europe was established as a private, non-profit corporation in 1949 to broadcast to communist Eastern Europe. Radio Liberty was founded two years later to broadcast to nations inside the Soviet Union. The two corporations were merged in 1975. CIA involvement in RFE/RL ended in 1971. Currently, RFE/RL broadcasts in 25 languages and has more than 20 million listeners in 13 time zones.

radiological defense • defensive measures taken against the radiation hazards resulting from the employment of nuclear and radiological weapons.

radiological operation • the employment of radioactive materials or radiation-producing devices in order to cause casualties or restrict the use of terrain. It includes the intentional employment of fallout from nuclear weapons.

Radio Martí • CIA-sponsored radio station broadcasting from Miami, Florida, with the intention of undermining the regime of FIDEL CASTRO in Cuba. Radio Martí began broadcasting in 1985. Television Martí began broadcasting to Cuba in 1990.

radio navigation • radio-location intended for the determination of position or direction or for obstruction warning in navigation.

radio silence • a condition in which all or certain radio equipment and/or specified frequency bands are kept inoperative.

radius of action • the maximum distance a ship, aircraft, or vehicle can travel away from its base along a given course with normal combat load and return without refueling, allowing for all safety and operating factors.

RAF • *abbr.* (in the UK) Royal Air Force.

raft • *n.* **1** a flat buoyant structure of timber or other materials fastened together, used as a boat or floating platform. **2** a small, inflatable rubber or plastic boat, especially one for use in emergencies. • *v.* **1** travel on or as if on a raft: *I have rafted along the Rio Grande.* **2** transport on a raft: *the stores were rafted ashore.* **3** bring or fasten together (a number of boats or other objects) side by side.

rafter • *n.* a person who travels on a raft.

raftsman • *n.* (pl. **-men**) a man who works on a raft.

raid • *n.* a rapid surprise attack on an enemy by troops, aircraft, or other armed forces in warfare: *a bombing raid.* • *v.* conduct a raid on: *officers raided thirty homes yesterday.*

DERIVATIVES: **raider** *n.*

rail • *n.* a steel bar or continuous line of bars laid on the ground as one of a pair forming a railway track.

rail gun • a weapon in which a projectile is accelerated electromagnetically along a pair of rails, used especially as an antimissile weapon.

railhead • *n.* a point on a railway where loads are transferred between trains and other means of transport.

rainfall • *n.* see NUCLEAR RAINFALL.

rainout • *n.* radioactive material in the atmosphere that is brought down by precipitation.

Rains, Gabriel James (1803–81) • Confederate army officer and ordnance manufacturer, born in North Carolina. Rains was commissioned in the infantry after graduating from the U.S. MILITARY ACADEMY and served ably in the SEMINOLE WAR (1839–42) and the MEXICAN WAR (1846–48). At the outbreak of the CIVIL WAR, he was commissioned a brigadier general and was one of the first commanders to use mines, both on land and at sea, as a weapon. In December 1862 he became head of the Conscription Bureau while also continuing research on the use of mines, or torpedoes, which soon became his full-time work; in June 1864 he was appointed superintendent of the Confederate Torpedo Bureau. Rains improved the existing torpedo technology by developing a highly sensitive chemical contact fuse, which was manufactured by his brother, GEORGE WASHINGTON RAINS.

Rains, George Washington (1817–98) • Confederate army officer, born in North Carolina. Early in his career, Rains taught at the U.S. MILITARY ACADEMY and fought with distinction in the MEXICAN WAR (1846–48). When the CIVIL WAR broke out, he was placed in charge of gunpowder production for the Confederacy and commissioned a lieutenant colonel. Rains developed a modern process to prepare niter for gunpowder and oversaw the development of the Confederate Powder Works in Atlanta, Georgia, to manufacture ammunition for the Confederacy. The plant also produced the contact fuses, developed by

Rains's brother GABRIEL JAMES RAINS, that were used in percussion mines.

raise • *v.* **1** bring to the surface (something that has sunk). **2** abandon or force an enemy to abandon (a siege, blockade, or embargo). **3** (of someone at sea) come in sight of (land or another ship): *they raised the low coast by evening.*

DERIVATIVES: **raisable** *adj.* **raiser** *n.*

rake[1] • *v.* sweep (something) from end to end with gunfire, a look, or a beam of light: *McDonald and his company raked the shrubs and undergrowth with their M-16s.*

rake[2] • *v.* **1** (of a ship's mast or funnel) incline from the perpendicular toward the stern. **2** (of a ship's bow or stern) project at its upper part beyond the keel.

ram • *n.* **1** a beak or other projecting part of the bow of a warship, for piercing the hulls of other ships. **2** a warship with such a bow. • *v.* (**rammed, ramming**) **1** (of a vehicle or vessel) be driven violently into (something, typically another vehicle or vessel) in an attempt to stop or damage it: *their boat was rammed by a Japanese warship.* **2** crash violently against something: *the stolen car rammed into the front of the house.*

DERIVATIVES: **rammer** *n.*

Rambo • slang a figure of extreme bravado, "gung ho" personified; an excessively brave and aggressive soldier, with more brawn than brains. 1985).

John Rambo, a character played by Sylvester Stallone in a series of movies in the 1980s, is a former Green Beret who returns to Vietnam in a harrowing, guns-blazing mission to rescue comrades missing in action.

RAMC • *abbr.* the Royal Army Medical Corps; the medical division of the British Royal Army, officially incorporated in 1898.

ramjet • *n.* a jet-propulsion engine that operates on the air compression produced by the forward thrust of the engine. Such an engine contains neither a compressor nor a turbine. See also PULSEJET.

rampart • *n.* (usually **ramparts**) **1** a defensive wall of a castle or walled city, having a broad top with a walkway and typically a stone parapet. **2** a defensive or protective barrier. • *v.* (usually **be ramparted**) rare fortify or surround with or as if with a rampart.

ramrod • *n.* a rod for ramming down the charge of a muzzleloading firearm.

Ramsay, Francis Munroe (1835–1914) • Union naval officer, born in Pennsylvania. Ramsay went to sea at the age of fifteen; by 1862 he was a lieutenant commander. When the CIVIL WAR erupted, he was engaged in a number of battles, including VICKSBURG (1863), where he won the notice of DAVID D. PORTER for his bravery. From 1863 to 1864 he was in command of the Third District of the Mississippi; in 1865 he led an expedition on the James River that neutralized all the torpedoes placed in the river. He also was present at the capture of RICHMOND. In 1881 he was named superintendent of the U.S. NAVAL ACADEMY, the first alumnus to serve in that post. His severe attempts to increase discipline lowered morale at the academy, and his resignation in 1886 was welcomed by faculty and students alike.

Ramseur, Stephen Dodson (1837–1864) • Confederate army officer, born in North Carolina. Ramseur was an ardent defender of slavery; in 1861 he resigned his commission in the U.S. Army and within a few weeks had received an appointment in the Confederate army, rapidly rising to the position of major of artillery. In 1862 he was commissioned colonel of the 49th North Carolina Infantry; in that position he was seriously wounded at MALVERN HILL in July of that year. Promoted to brigadier general, he earned a reputation as a fearless and daring leader. His performance at CHANCELLORSVILLE (1863) won praise from Gen. ROBERT E. LEE and Gen. THOMAS "STONEWALL" JACKSON. He also served memorably at SPOTSYLVANIA (1864). Named to take over Gen. JUBAL EARLY's division, Ramseur reached the rank of major general in 1864. He was killed in battle at CEDAR CREEK, Virginia.

Appointed one day after his twenty-seventh birthday, Ramseur was the youngest WEST POINT alumnus in the Confederate army to achieve the rank of major general.

RAN • *abbr.* Royal Australian Navy.

Ranch Hand, Operation • the aerial mission to apply herbicide defoliants in the VIETNAM WAR between 1962 and 1971. This operation, under control of the U.S. Air Force, accounted for the vast majority of all herbicide application during the war, about 19 million gallons, of which more than half was AGENT ORANGE.

RAND Corporation • (**Rand Corporation**) an independent think tank created in 1945 at the urging of the U.S. Air Force in Santa Monica, California, to do service research under contract. Initially the body was known as Project RAND and operated under the auspices of the Douglas Aircraft Company. It become independent in 1948. RAND gained its reputation primarily through research on national security. In the 1960s the corporation began to address domestic policy as well. [ORIGIN: 'RAND' is a contraction of 'research and development.']

R&D • *abbr.* research and development.

R&R • *abbr.* rest and recuperation.

range • *n.* **1** the maximum distance at which a radio transmission can be effectively received: *planets within radio range of Earth.* **2** the distance that can be covered by a vehicle or aircraft without refueling: *the vans have a range of 125 miles.* **3** the maximum distance to which a gun will shoot or over which a missile will travel: *enemy troops came within range | these rockets have a range of 30 to 40 miles.* **4** an area of land or sea used as a testing ground for military equipment. **5** an open or enclosed area with targets for shooting practice. • *v.* **1** (of a person or animal) travel or wander over a wide area: *patrols ranged thousands of miles deep into enemy territory* **2** obtain the range of a target by adjustment after firing past it or short of it, or by the use of radar or laser equipment: *radar-type transmissions which appeared to be* ***ranging on*** *our convoys.* **3** (of a projectile) cover a specified distance. **4** (of a gun) send a projectile over a specified distance.

PHRASES: **at a range of** with a specified distance between one person or thing and another: *the improved radar system greatly extended the horizontal and vertical range of aerial surveillance.*

rangefinder • *n.* an instrument for estimating the distance of an object, especially for use with a camera or gun.

ranger • *n.* a member of a body of armed men, in particular: **a** a U.S. Army Ranger. **b** a mounted soldier. **c** a commando.

Rangers, Daniel Morgan's • see MORGAN'S RANGERS.

Rangers, Robert Roger's • nine companies of colonists, organized by Maj. ROBERT ROGERS, who fought for the British in the FRENCH AND INDIAN WAR (1754–1763) in 1756. Rogers is credited with codifying and developing the concept of such a military group. He published a list of twenty-eight common-sense combat rules as well as a set of standing orders that stressed operational preparedness, security, and tactics. Rogers set up a training program for his ranger units, including live-fire exercises.

Rangers, U.S. Army • see ARMY RANGERS.

ranging • *n.* the process of establishing target distance. Types of ranging include echo, intermittent, manual, navigational, explosive echo, optical, and radar.

rank • *n.* **1** a single line of soldiers or police officers drawn up abreast. **2** (**the ranks**) common soldiers as opposed to officers: *he was fined and* ***reduced to the ranks.*** • *v.* **1** take precedence over (someone) in respect to rank; outrank: *the Secretary of State ranks all the other members of the cabinet.* **2** arrange in a rank or ranks: *tents ranked in orderly rows.*

PHRASES: **break rank** (or **ranks**) (of soldiers or police officers) fail to remain in line. **close ranks** (of soldiers or police officers) come closer together in a line. **keep rank** (of soldiers or police officers) remain in line. **pull rank** take unfair advantage of one's seniority or privileged position. **rise through** (or **from**) **the ranks** (of a private or a noncommissioned officer) receive a commission.

ranker • *n.* chiefly Brit. **1** a soldier in the ranks; a private. **2** a commissioned officer who has been in the ranks.

Ransom, Matt Whitaker (1826–1904) • U.S. senator and Confederate army officer, born in North Carolina. Ransom developed a thriving law practice and was appointed state attorney general in 1852. After entering politics as a Whig, he switched his allegiance to the Democrats, although he supported secession only reluctantly. At the outbreak of the CIVIL WAR, he enlisted; in 1862 he headed the 35th North Carolina Regiment, fighting to defend RICHMOND in the PENINSULAR CAMPAIGN and at ANTIETAM. In 1864 he participated in the defense of PETERSBURG. Ransom was present at APPOMATTOX (1865); after the war ended he returned to his plantation to grow tobacco and resume the practice of law. After interceding for supporters of the KU KLUX KLAN, he was a favorite of the state's conservatives, who sent him to the U.S. Senate in 1872. In 1895 he was named minister to Mexico, where he arbitrated a boundary dispute between Mexico and Guatemala.

Ransom, Thomas Edward Greenfield (1835–64) • Union army officer, born in Vermont. Ransom trained as a civil engineer at Norwich University. He then relocated to Illinois, where, at the outbreak of the CIVIL WAR, he formed and headed the 11th Illinois Infantry. He was rapidly promoted to lieutenant colonel. In February 1862 he fought valorously at FORT DONELSON despite being wounded; in recognition of his efforts, he was promoted to colonel. Wounded in the head at SHILOH (1862), he led his troops until he could no longer carry on. Again, he was rewarded with promotion, this time to inspector general on the staff of Gen. JOHN A. MCCLERNAND. By 1863 he had risen to brigadier general of volunteers. After winning praise from Gen. ULYSSES S. GRANT for his service at VICKSBURG, Ransom fought in the RED RIVER campaign in Texas in 1864. He fell ill while returning from Alabama, where he had pursued the retreating Confederates after the fall of ATLANTA, and died.

RAOC • *abbr.* (in the UK) Royal Army Ordnance Corps.

Rapid Deployment Joint Task Force • (**RDJTF**) established by President JIMMY CARTER in 1980 to enforce the CARTER DOCTRINE and activated at MacDill AFB. Originally subordinate to the U.S. Readiness Command (USREDCOM), this task force was succeeded by the U.S. CENTRAL COMMAND (USCENTCOM) in 1983.

Rapido River • a river near the town of Cassino, Italy, that served as the German line of defense in 1944, during WORLD WAR II. The U.S. Thirty-Sixth Infantry Division attempted to cross the frigid, raging river on January 20–21, 1944. The attack was mainly meant to divert German forces from Allied troops landing at ANZIO, and ended in defeat with heavy U.S. casualties.

Rappahannock Station • see MINE RUN CAMPAIGN.

Raptor • (**F-22**) the world's first stealth air-to-air multimission fighter, virtually undetectable by radar, deadly at a distance, superb at close dogfighting, and capable of precision-strike ground attack. It will carry existing air-to-air weapons, including AIM advanced medium-range air-to-air missiles and AIM-9 SIDEWINDER short-range missiles, and others that are being developed. It is scheduled to be operational late in 2005.

Raritan |ˈrærɪtn| • an Algonquian-speaking Indian tribe located in the mid-seventeenth century in the lower Hudson River Valley and in the vicinity of Manhattan, Staten Island, and Long Island. Friction with the Dutch settlers in the area led to a series of bloody skirmishes between the Raritans and the Dutch between 1640 and 1664.

rate • *v.* **1** assign a standard, optimal, or limiting rating to (a piece of equipment): *its fuel economy is* ***rated at*** *25 miles a gallon in the city.* **2** to deserve or earn a privilege: *he rated shore leave.* • *n.* a level of proficiency within a rating: *he is a Radioman, third class.*

rate of fire • the number of rounds fired per weapon per minute.

rating • *n* a grouping of enlisted personnel based on military skills: *his rating was Radioman, third class.*

ration • *n.* **1** a fixed amount of a commodity officially allowed to each person during a time of shortage, as in wartime: *1918 saw the bread ration reduced on two occasions.* **2** (usually **rations**) an amount of food supplied on a regular basis, especially to members of the armed forces during a war. **3** (**rations**) food; provisions: *their emergency rations ran out.* • *v.* (usually **be rationed**) allow each person to have only a fixed amount of (a particular commodity): *shoes were rationed from 1943.*

rationalization • *n.* any action that increases the effectiveness of allied forces through more efficient or effective use of defense resources committed to the alliance.

Rationalization includes consolidation, reassignment of national priorities to higher alliance needs, standardization, specialization, mutual support or improved interoperability, and greater cooperation. It applies to weapons and materiel resources as well as to nonweapons military matters.

---

rations spoiler • slang (World War II) a cook.

ratlines |ˈrætlənz| • *plural n.* a series of small ropes fastened across a sailing ship's shrouds like the rungs of a ladder, used for climbing the rigging.

Raum, Green Berry |rowm| (1829–1909) • Union army officer, born in Illinois. Raum entered the Union army at the outbreak of the CIVIL WAR and fought in a number of major engagements, including VICKSBURG, CHATTANOOGA, and MISSIONARY RIDGE (all 1863). He also took part in Gen. WILLIAM T. SHERMAN's MARCH TO THE SEA (1864–65) after the capture of ATLANTA. In 1889 President BENJAMIN HARRISON appointed him commissioner of pensions, in which post he was responsible for overseeing the claims brought by Union soldiers and their survivors. Raum was embroiled in a scandal in which he was accused of espousing policies that would help his personal business interests; although he was cleared, his reputation for sterling character was irreparably damaged.

Raven • (**EF-111A**) a two-seat specialized tactical jamming aircraft designed to provide electronic countermeasures. It has three operational modes: **a** stand-off, remaining in its own airspace and screening the paths of its attack aircraft; **b** escort, accompanying its attack aircraft when they penetrate enemy defenses; **c** close air support, jamming and neutralizing enemy radars.

Rawlins, John Aaron (1831–69) • secretary of war and Union army officer, born in Illinois. He was a member of the staff of Gen. ULYSSES S. GRANT, whose attention he had drawn while still practicing law in Illinois. Rawlins fought at the Battle of SHILOH (1862) and at VICKSBURG (1862–63), after which he was promoted to brigadier general. As adjutant he headed Grant's staff throughout the war; in March 1865 he was appointed to the new position of chief of staff to the commanding general. After the war Rawlins remained Grant's chief of staff, and in 1868 Grant, then president, named him secretary of war, at his request.

RCT • *abbr.* Regimental Combat Team; any of a small number of infantry units who were deployed in the KOREAN WAR.

RDF • *abbr.* **1** radio direction finder (or finding). **2** rapid deployment force.

RDJTF • *abbr.* Rapid Deployment Joint Task Force.

RE • *abbr.* (in the UK) Royal Engineers.

reach • *v.* sail with the wind blowing from the side, or from slightly behind the side, of the ship. • *n.* a distance traversed in reaching.

readiness • *n.* the ability of forces, units, weapon systems, or equipments to deliver the outputs for which they were designed, including the ability to deploy and employ without unacceptable delays.

Ready Reserve • the SELECTED RESERVE, the INDIVIDUAL READY RESERVE, and the INACTIVE NATIONAL GUARD, liable for active duty as prescribed by law.

Reagan Doctrine • President RONALD REAGAN's COLD WAR policy, which advocated using U.S. intelligence operations to sponsor and support guerrilla warfare overseas with the goal of preventing the spread of communism. The doctrine, which was never fully defined, was successful in Afghanistan, important in Angola, but inconclusive and politically costly in Nicaragua.

Reagan, Ronald Wilson (1911?–) • 40th president of the United States. Reagan was born in and spent his childhood in Illinois. After graduating from college, he entered radio broadcasting. He moved to California with the goal of becoming an actor and secured a contract at Warner Brothers. Commissioned a cavalry officer, Reagan, a supporter of President FRANKLIN D. ROOSEVELT, spent World War II in Los Angeles making training films for the U.S. ARMY AIR FORCE. From 1947 to 1951, and again in 1959, he served as president of the Screen Actors Guild; he cooperated with the House Committee on Un-American Activities and with the blacklist. Becoming more conservative politically, he supported DWIGHT D. EISENHOWER for president in 1952 and 1956 and RICHARD NIXON in 1960. During the 1950s he was a spokesman for the General Electric Company, in which capacity he toured the country giving speeches with conservative and pro-business themes, until the company, concerned about the controversial nature of his lectures, fired him. Reagan won national attention in 1964 with his nominating speech for U.S. Senator

Barry Goldwater, and in 1967 he ran successfully for governor of California; during his term he began welfare reforms and eliminated the state budget deficit; he was re-elected in 1971. In 1980 he won the Republican nomination for president and went on to defeat the incumbent, JIMMY CARTER, by a landslide 483 electoral votes to Carter's 43, promising massive tax cuts, increased defense spending, and a balanced budget. His campaign was aided by Carter's inability to free the staff of the U.S. embassy in Teheran held as hostages by the Iranian government and by Reagan's own affable, ingratiating personality. In his two terms as president, Reagan passed massive tax cuts, pared federal spending for environmental and safety regulations and for social programs, and approved huge increases in defense spending, including beginning the development of a STRATEGIC DEFENSE INITIATIVE intended to block incoming missiles. Reagan suffered a major foreign policy blow when 241 marine peacekeepers died in a terrorist attack on army barracks in Lebanon (1983). More successful was his policy toward the Soviet Union. Reagan negotiated a major intermediate-range nuclear arms reduction treaty with the Soviet Union, and his staunch anti-Communism and his defense buildup are credited with helping to bring down the Soviet government in 1991. A major issue during his second term was U.S. funding of partisans of the ousted Somoza government (called CONTRAS) in Nicaragua in their fight to overthrow that country's leftist SANDINISTA government (1986–87); Reagan denied knowing the United States was selling arms to Iran despite his stated policy of refusing to deal with terrorist governments and using the proceeds to fund the Contras' fight against the country's legitimate government in direct violation of a congressional ban on such aid. Despite the foreign policy problems of his second term, Reagan left office in 1989 still tremendously popular.

realpolitik |rāˈälˌpōliˌtēk| • *n.* a system of politics or principles based on practical rather than moral or ideological considerations.
ORIGIN: early 20th century: from German *Realpolitik* 'practical politics.'

real time • pertaining to the timeliness of data or information that has been delayed only by the time required for electronic communication. This implies that there are no noticeable delays.

ream • *v.* widen a bore or hole in (a gun or other metal object) with a special tool.

Reams Station, Battle of • a CIVIL WAR battle on August 25, 1864, at Reams Station, Virginia. It was a Confederate victory under the command of Gen. FITZHUGH LEE, but the Union side succeeded in tearing up more than 60 miles of track, which temporarily disrupted rail traffic into Petersburg.

rear • *n.* **1** the hindmost part of an army, fleet, or line of people: *two blue policemen at the rear fell out of the formation.* **2** the area occupied by the portion of a military force that is farthest from the front lines.

rear admiral • **1** an officer in the U.S. Navy or Coast Guard ranking above commodore and below vice admiral. **2** (**Rear Admiral, upper half**) a flag officer rank in the U.S. Navy and Coast Guard corresponding to Major General in the U.S. Army, Air Force, and Marine Corps; pay grade O-8.

rear area • for any particular command, the area extending forward from its rear boundary to the rear of the area assigned to the next lower level of command. This area is provided primarily for the performance of support functions.

rear commodore • an officer in a yacht club ranking below vice commodore.

rear echelon • the section of an army concerned with administrative and supply duties.

rearguard • *n.* the soldiers positioned at the rear of a body of troops, especially those protecting an army when it is in retreat.

rearguard action • a defensive action carried out by a retreating army.

rearm • *v.* **1** provide with a new supply of weapons: *his plan to rearm Germany.* **2** acquire or build up a new supply of weapons.
DERIVATIVES: **rearmament** *n.*

re-arming • *n.* **1** an operation that replenishes the prescribed stores of ammunition, bombs, and other armament items for an aircraft, naval ship, tank, or armored vehicle, including replacement of defective ordnance equipment, in order to make it ready for combat service. **2** the resetting of the fuze on a bomb, or on an artillery, mortar, or rocket projectile, so that it will detonate at the desired time.

Reb (also **Johnny Reb**) • *n.* informal a Confederate soldier in the CIVIL WAR.
ORIGIN: abbreviation of *rebel.*

Rebel • *n.* in the CIVIL WAR, an adherent of the Confederate States of America, particularly a Confederate soldier.

rebel yell • a shout or battle cry used by the Confederates during the Civil War.

receiver • *n.* **1** a piece of radio or television apparatus that detects broadcast signals and converts them into visible or audible form: *a satellite receiver.* **2** the part of a firearm that houses the action and to which the barrel and other parts are attached.

reception • *n.* **1** all ground arrangements connected with the delivery and disposition of air or sea drops. These arrangements include selection and preparation of site, signals for warning and approach, facilitation of secure departure of agents, and speedy collection of delivered articles and their prompt removal to storage places having maximum security. When a group is involved, it may be called a **reception committee**. **2** arrangements made to welcome and provide secure quarters or transportation for defectors, escapees, evaders, or incoming agents.

receptivity • *n.* the vulnerability of a target audience to particular psychological operations media.

reciprocal • *adj.* **1** (of an agreement or obligation) bearing on or binding each of two parties equally: *the treaty is a bilateral commitment with reciprocal rights and duties.* **2** (of a course or bearing) differing from a given course or bearing by 180 degrees.

Reciprocal Trade Agreements Act • an act passed by Congress in 1934 to authorize the president to establish tariff-reduction agreements with foreign countries and without Congressional approval. Based on an idea proposed by Secretary of State CORDELL HULL, it encouraged mutually beneficial negotiations and trade with foreign governments, and it led to the GENERAL AGREEMENT ON TARIFFS AND TRADE of 1947.

reciprocity treaty • a trade agreement in which the parties involved make mutual concessions, which may address different issues, to establish a reciprocal trade relationship. The idea of reciprocity is fundamental to the purpose of a treaty and implies that the parties receive comparable foreign trade gains.

recoil |ri'koil| • *v.* (of a gun) move abruptly backward as a reaction on firing a bullet, shell, or other missile. • *n.* |'rē,koil; ri'koil| the action of recoiling: *his body jerked with the recoil of the rifle.*

DERIVATIVES: **recoilless** |rə'koil-lis; 'rē ,koil-| *adj.*

recoilless rifle • a weapon in which the recoil upon firing is considerably reduced by deflection of the combustion gas to the rear.

recon |'rē,kän; ri'kän| informal • *n.* short for RECONNAISSANCE. • *v.* |ri'kän| (**reconned, reconning**) short for RECONNOITER.

reconnaissance |ri'känəzəns; -səns| • *n.* military observation of a region to locate an enemy or ascertain strategic features: *an excellent aircraft for low-level reconnaissance.*

reconnaissance in force • an offensive operation designed to discover and/or test the enemy's strength or to obtain information.

reconnoiter |,rēkə'noitər; ,rek-| (Brit. **reconnoitre**) • *v.* make a military observation of (a region): *they reconnoitered the beach some weeks before the landing* • *n.* informal an act of reconnoitering: *a reconnoiter of the camp.*

Reconstruction • *n.* (**the Reconstruction**) the period (1865–77) following the Civil War, during which the states of the Confederacy were controlled by federal government and social legislation, including the granting of new rights to African Americans, was introduced. There was strong white opposition to the new measures, and when a new Republican administration returned power to white southern leaders a policy of racial segregation was introduced.

record information • all forms (narrative, graphic, data, computer memory, etc.) of information registered in either temporary or permanent form so that it can be retrieved, reproduced, or preserved.

recover • *n.* (**the recover**) a defined position of a firearm forming part of a military drill: *bring the firelock* ***to the recover.***

recovery • *n.* **1** in air operations, the phase of a mission that involves the return of an aircraft to a base. **2** in naval mine warfare, the salvage of a mine as nearly intact as possible to permit further investigation for intelligence or evaluation purposes. **3** in amphibious reconnaissance, the physical extraction of landed forces or their link-up with friendly forces. **4** in evasion and recovery operations, the return of evaders to friendly control, either with or without assistance, as the result of planning, operations, and individual actions on the part of recovery planners, conventional/unconventional recovery forces, and/or the evaders themselves.

recovery and reconstitution • those actions taken by one nation prior to, during, and following an attack by an enemy nation to minimize the effects of the attack, rehabilitate the national economy, provide for the welfare of the populace, and maximize the combat potential of remaining forces and supporting activities.

recovery capability • **1** the ability of a nation or military unit to recover from a nuclear or conventional strike **2** the ability of a military unit, particularly a mechanized or armor unit, to recover damaged vehicles, guns, and other equipment from a battlefield and transport such items to a facility for repair or rebuild.

recovery site • in evasion and escape usage, an area from which an evader or an escapee can be evacuated.

recovery vehicle, medium • (**M88A1**) a full-tracked vehicle designed to rescue troops and recover tanks and other vehicles in the midst of battle conditions. See also HERCULES, sense 2.

recruit |ri'kro͞ot| • *v.* **1** enlist (someone) in the armed forces: *they recruit their toughest soldiers from the desert tribes.* **2** form (an army or other force) by enlisting new people: *a basis for recruiting an army.* **3** enroll (someone) as a member or worker in an organization or as a supporter of a cause: *there are plans to recruit more staff later this year.* • *n.* **1** a person newly enlisted in the armed forces and not yet fully trained: *3,000 army recruits at Ft. Benjamin.* **2** a new member or supporter of an organization or cause.

DERIVATIVES: **recruitable** *adj.* **recruiter** *n.*

recruitment • *n.* **1** the action of enlisting new people in the armed forces. **2** the action of finding new people to join an organization or support a cause: *the recruitment of nurses.*

red • *adj.* (**redder, reddest**) **1** used to denote something forbidden, dangerous, or urgent: *the force went on* ***red alert.*** **2** (**Red**) informal, chiefly derogatory communist or socialist (used espcially during the COLD WAR with reference to the Soviet Union): *the Red Menace.* • *n.* (also **Red**) informal, chiefly derogatory a communist or socialist.

PHRASES: **better dead than red** (or **better red than dead**) a cold-war slogan claiming that the prospect of nuclear war is preferable to that of a communist society (or vice versa).

red alert • an alert condition declared when an attack by enemy aircraft is underway or seems to be imminent. See also WARNING RED.

Red Army • **1** name given to the ground forces of Russia under the Bolshevik and Soviet regimes. **2** the army of China or some other communist countries.

Red Arrows • nickname for personnel assigned to the U.S. 32nd Infantry Division, the shoulder patch of which is a red arrow.

Red Baron, the • see RICHTHOFEN, MANFRED VON.

Red Cloud (1822–1909) • Oglala Lakota Indian chief, born in Kansas. As a young man, Red Cloud led Indian expeditions against rival tribes. He gained attention in 1865 when he warned the U.S. government to abandon its plan for a northern spur off the BOZEMAN TRAIL, which linked the OREGON TRAIL to mining settlements in Montana, because the new road would cross the prime hunting ground of the Lakota. During negotiations between the Native Americans and a government commission, the Indians learned that U.S. infantry were already on the disputed land. Fearing a doublecross, Red Cloud and other chiefs withdrew from the negotiations and led a force of 1,000 Lakota to the site. Another force massacred 80 U.S. soldiers. Chiefs of the southern tribes did conclude a treaty with the government allowing the construction of three forts along the Bozeman Trail, but a series of battles between the northern chiefs and the U.S. Army (1866–68) that came to be called RED CLOUD'S WAR forced the government to abandon its plan. In 1868 Red Cloud and other chiefs accepted the government's proposal of a reservation in South Dakota. The discovery of gold in the Black Hills, on the land ceded by the government, brought waves of settlers who wanted the United States to reclaim that land, and full-scale war erupted (1876). Red Cloud did not participate in that war, but, as a Sioux leader, he absorbed some of the blame, and the government announced that it considered him a traitor. By 1882 the United States had decided that the reservation was larger than was required by the Sioux, and it decided to reclaim some of the land. Red Cloud spent his remaining years resisting the government's claim, ultimately unsuccessfully.

Red Cloud's War • skirmishes between Ogallala Sioux and the Army during 1866 and 1867 for control of the Bozeman Trail. It ended with the FORT LARAMIE TREATY in 1868, in which the United States agreed to abandon forts on the trail.

redcoat • *n.* a British soldier or the British army of the eighteenth and nineteenth century. [ORIGIN: from the scarlet tunics worn by most British infantry regiments.]

Red Crescent • a national branch in Muslim countries of the International Movement of the Red Cross and the Red Crescent. The name was adopted in 1906.

Red Cross, American • the U.S. branch of the 175-member International Red Cross movement. CLARA BARTON, who gave humanitarian aid in the CIVIL WAR, lobbied for the United States to join the movement, and it did in 1881. After the American Red Cross served in the SPANISH-AMERICAN WAR (1898), President WILLIAM H. TAFT in 1911 authorized it as the only volunteer society for aiding the military in wartime, and in 1912 the U.S. Army began to provide transportation and support to Red Cross workers. During WORLD WAR I 8,000 American Red Cross workers served in Europe. The society operated fifty-eight base hospitals and ran forty-seven ambulance companies, receiving support from 8 million volunteers in the United States. In WORLD WAR II the American Red Cross's medical services were limited to the collection of 14 million units of blood, but it also provided 28 million food packages for U.S. and Allied prisoners of war and supported mail services for prisoners. Similar work continued during the KOREAN and VIETNAM WARS, with the military providing its own blood supplies in Vietnam. In recent years, in addition to providing disaster relief and supporting public health and safety campaigns in the United States, the American Red Cross has accompanied U.S. armed forces to combat areas including Somalia, Haiti, the Persian Gulf, and Bosnia.

Red Cross, International • the International Movement of the Red Cross and the Red Crescent, an international humanitarian organization bringing relief to victims of war or natural disaster. The Red Cross was set up in 1864 at the instigation of the Swiss philanthropist Henri Dunant (1828–1910) according to the GENEVA CONVENTION, and its headquarters are in Geneva.

red ensign • a red flag with the Union Jack in the top corner next to the flagstaff, flown by British-registered ships.

redeploy • *v.* assign (troops, employees, or resources) to a new place or task: *units would be redeployed to the provinces.*

DERIVATIVES: **redeployment** *n.*

Redeye • (**FIM-43**) a manportable, shoulder-fired air defense artillery weapon for low altitude air defense of frontline troops.

red flag • **1** a red flag as a warning of danger or a problem: *they had overlooked the red flags that should have alerted them to the county's disastrous investment strategy.* **2** a red flag as the symbol of socialist revolution.

Red Machine • an encryption machine introduced in the early 1930s by the Japanese to encrypt diplomatic messages. By 1935, the U.S. Army's Signal Intelligence Service had successfully cracked the Japanese diplomatic codes encrypted by the Red Machine, but it was replaced by the more sophisticated PURPLE MACHINE in 1939.

redoubt • *n.* **1** a temporary or supplementary fortification, typically square or polygonal and without flanking defenses. **2** an entrenched stronghold or refuge.

Red River Campaign • an unsuccessful CIVIL WAR campaign from March to May of 1864 in which the Union attempted to secure the area along the Red River to Shreveport, the temporary Confederate capital. Confederate forces under the command of Gen. RICHARD TAYLOR forced the Union to retreat and probably delayed the Union victory in the war by several months.

Red River War • one of the PLAINS INDIANS WARS, fought in 1874–75 in the area around the Red River in Texas. Kiowas, Comanches,

Cheyennes, and Arapahoes fought against forces under Col. NELSON A. MILES and Col. RANALD MACKENZIE. All of these tribes accepted life on reservations after the war, bringing peace to the region.

red scare • any spate of fear of communist/socialist infiltration, subversion, espionage, and sabotage; particularly that which occurred in the United States at the end of WORLD WAR I.

Red Stick War • see CREEK WAR.

Redstone • (**PGM-11A**) a short-range, land-mobile ballistic missile that was deployed between 1958 and 1964 and carried a nuclear warhead of either 3.8 megatons or 425 kilotons.

Redstone Arsenal • a U.S. Army Technical Test Center at Huntsville, Alabama. It was established in 1941 to provide ordnance shells for the nearby Huntsville Arsenal Chemical Warfare Service during WORLD WAR II. Initially known as the Redstone Ordnance Plant, it was one of the first munitions plants in the country to employ women. By December 1942, forty percent of the production line employees were women. In the 1950s, Redstone Arsenal became a center for research and development of rockets, guided missiles, and space equipment.

red tape • excessive bureaucracy or adherence to rules and formalities, especially in public business: *this law will just create more red tape.* ORIGIN: early 18th century: so named because of the red or pink tape used to bind and secure official documents.

reduce • *v.* archaic conquer (a place), in particular besiege and capture (a town or fortress). PHRASES: **reduce someone to the ranks** demote a noncommissioned officer to an ordinary soldier.

Reed, Joseph (1741–85) • REVOLUTIONARY WAR army officer and leader. Born in New Jersey, Reed established a flourishing law practice in Philadelphia. He became a member of the Philadelphia Committee of Correspondence in 1774 and was president of Pennsylvania's second Provincial Congress (1775). He also was named secretary to Gen. GEORGE WASHINGTON when Washington assumed command of the Continental army. Although he believed the Declaration of Independence to be premature, he fought ably in a number of battles.

Reed, Walter (1851–1902) • U.S. army medical officer, born in Virginia. Reed was, at seventeen, the youngest person to receive a medical degree from the University of Virginia medical school. In 1875 he joined the U.S. ARMY MEDICAL DEPARTMENT; in 1890 he was assigned to FORT HENRY, in Baltimore, in order to study bacteriology at Johns Hopkins Hospital. In 1898 he was named to head the Typhoid Board to study that disease among troops preparing for the SPANISH-AMERICAN WAR (1898). In 1900 he moved to the study of yellow fever; although he and his colleagues failed to identify the specific virus that causes the disease, they did establish its transmission by mosquito. This discovery enabled the army to virtually eliminate yellow fever as a threat to Americans in the Caribbean and tropical regions.

reef • *n.* each of the several strips across a sail that can be taken in or rolled up to reduce the area exposed to the wind. • *v.* **1** take in one or more reefs of (a sail): *reefing the mainsail in strong winds.* **2** shorten (a topmast or a bowsprit).

reefer • *n.* **1** a person who reefs a sail. **2** slang, archaic a midshipman.

reembark • *v.* go on board ship again. DERIVATIVES: **reembarkation** *n.*

reenactments, military • the replication of historically significant battles and campaigns by actors or civilian enthusiasts dressed and equipped in period clothing, weapons, and accouterments. Military reenactment, especially the reenactment of CIVIL WAR battles, is a popular hobby in the United States and is often carried out with great attention to the historical accuracy of drill and tactics as well as uniforms and equipment.

reenactor • *n.* someone who acts out a past event.

reengineer • *v.* **1** redesign (a device or machine). **2** (**reengineering**) restructure (a company or organization or part of a company or organization's operations), especially by exploiting information technology.

reenlist • *v.* enlist again in the armed forces. DERIVATIVES: **reenlister** *n.*

reentry phase • the portion of the trajectory of a ballistic missile or space vehicle where there is a significant interaction of the vehicle and the earth's atmosphere.

reentry vehicle • **1** the part of a space vehicle that is designed to re-enter the earth's atmosphere in the terminal portion of its trajectory. **2** the part of a ballistic missile that contains warheads and is designed for reentry into the atmosphere and delivery to a target.

refit • *v.* (**refitted, refitting**) replace or repair machinery, equipment, and fittings in (a ship, building, etc.): *a lucrative contract to refit a submarine fleet.* • *n.* |ˈrēˌfit| a restoration or repair of machinery, equipment, or fittings.

reflag • *v.* (**reflagged, reflagging**) change the national registry of (a ship).

reflex force • as applied to Air Force units, that part of the alert force maintained overseas or at zone of interior forward bases by scheduled rotations.

refloat • *v.* set (a grounded ship) afloat again.

refuge |ˈrefˌyo͞oj; -ˌyo͞ozh| • *n.* a condition of being safe or sheltered from pursuit, danger, or trouble: *he was forced to* ***take refuge in*** *the French embassy.*

refuge area • a coastal area considered safe from enemy attack to which merchant ships may be ordered to proceed when the shipping movement policy is implemented. See also SAFE ANCHORAGE.

refugee • *n.* a civilian who, by reason of real or imagined danger, has left home to seek safety elsewhere.

Refugio, Battle of • a battle in the TEXAS WAR OF INDEPENDENCE fought at Refugio, Texas in March, 1836. JOSÉ DE URREA captured the defending Texans and later killed more than a dozen of them, including their leader.

regiment • *n.* **1** a permanent unit of an army typically commanded by a colonel and divided into several companies, squadrons, or batteries and often into two battalions: *on the outbreak of war he promptly rejoined his regiment.* **2** an operational unit of artillery. • *v.* rare form (troops) into a regiment or regiments.

regimental • *adj.* of or relating to a regiment: *a regimental badge | regimental traditions.*
DERIVATIVES: **regimentally** *adv.*

regimental color • (in the UK) a regimental standard in the form of a silk flag, carried by a particular regiment along with its Queen's color.

regimentals • *plural n.* military uniform, especially that of a particular regiment.

regimental sergeant major • the senior non-commissioned officer in a unit of regimental size.

register ton • see TON.

registration • *n.* the adjustment of fire to determine firing data corrections.

registration fire • fire delivered to obtain accurate data for subsequent effective engagement of targets.

registration precision fire • artillery, gun, or mortar fire intended to obtain accurate data for subsequent effective engagement of targets.

registry • *n.* (pl. **-ies**) **1** a place or office where registers or records are kept. **2** an official list or register. **3** registration. **4** the nationality of a merchant ship.

regrade • *v.* determine that certain classified information requires, in the interests of national defense, a higher or a lower degree of protection against unauthorized disclosure than currently provided, coupled with a changing of the classification designation to reflect such higher or lower degree.

Regt • *abbr.* Regiment.

regular • *adj.* **1** of or belonging to the permanent professional armed forces of a country: *a regular soldier.* • *n.* a regular member of the armed forces.

Regular Army • the permanently constituted army that is maintained in peace as well as in war. It is one of the major components of the U.S. Army.

regulated item • any item whose issue to a user is subject to control by an appropriate authority for reasons that may include cost, scarcity, technical or hazardous nature or operational significance.

Regulation, the • a feature of SHAY'S REBELLION starting in 1786, in which Massachusetts militiamen marched on debtors' courts throughout western Massachusetts with the stated aim of postponing the seizure of properties until after the next gubernatorial election. They were largely successful.

Regulator Rebellion • see NORTH CAROLINA REGULATORS.

Regulators • *n.* see NORTH CAROLINA REGULATORS.

Regulus I • a nuclear cruise missile that was launched from a watertight hangar on the deck of a submarine, in use in the early 1960s. It was the Navy's first nuclear-armed cruise missile and an important nuclear deterrent in the early days of the COLD WAR.

rehabilitation • *n.* **1** the processing, usually in a relatively quiet area, of units or individuals recently withdrawn from combat or arduous duty, during which units recondition equipment and are rested, furnished with special facilities, filled up with replacements, issued replacement supplies and equipment, given training, and generally made ready for employment in future operations. **2** the action performed in restoring an installation to authorized design standards.

Reichstag • **1** the German national assembly (parliament) from the formation of the German Empire in 1871 through WORLD WAR II. The Reichstag gradually disappeared as a force in German politics during the Nazi era. **2** the building in Berlin in which the Reichstag met. The burning of the Reichstag building on February 27, 1933, led to emergency measures which facilitated ADOLF HITLER'S full assumption of power in Germany.

Reichswehr • the armed forces of Germany during and shortly after WORLD WAR I.

reinforcements • *n.* extra personnel sent to increase the strength of an army or similar force.

reinforcement training unit • see VOLUNTARY TRAINING UNIT.

reinforcing • *n.* in artillery usage, a tactical mission in which one artillery unit augments the fire of another artillery unit.

relative • *adj.* (of a service rank) corresponding in grade to another in a different service.

relative biological effectiveness • the ratio of the number of rads of gamma (or X) radiation of a certain energy that will produce a specified biological effect to the number of rads of another radiation required to produce the same effect as the relative biological effectiveness of the latter radiation.

release • *n.* in air armament, the intentional separation of a free-fall aircraft store, from its suspension equipment, for purposes of employment of the store.

release altitude • the altitude of an aircraft above the ground at the time of release of bombs, rockets, missiles, tow targets, etc.

reliability • *n.* the ability of an item to perform a required function under stated conditions for a specified period of time.

relief • *n.* **1** the replacement of one unit, commander, or individual by another. **2** inequalities of elevation and the configuration of land features on the surface of the Earth which may be represented on maps or charts by contours, hypsometric tints, shading, or spot elevations.

relief map • a map on which the relative elevation and the configuration of land features are represented graphically by contour lines, hypsometric tints, shading, or spot elevations or physically by the use of molded paper or plastic.

relieve |riˈlēv| • *v.* **1** release (someone) from duty by taking their place: *another signalman* *relieved him at 5:30.* **2** bring military support for (a besieged place): *he dispatched an expedition to relieve the city.*

DERIVATIVES: **reliever** *n.*

reload • *v.* load (something, especially a gun that has been fired) again: *he reloaded the chamber of the shotgun with fresh cartridges.*

rem • *n.* (**roentgen equivalent mammal**) the quantity of ionizing radiation that, when absorbed by a human or other mammal, produces the physiological effect equivalent to that produced by the absorption of one roentgen of X-ray or gamma radiation; it is used in connection with calculating the effects of nuclear fallout.

Remagen • a town on the Rhine in German where, in March 1945, U.S. forces stormed across a bridge that was about to be blown up by the defending Germans. They captured the bridge intact, making it the only Rhine bridge to be captured in the war. This allowed for an Allied bridgehead on the eastern side of the Rhine and was a major blow to the Germans, who expected to make the Rhine their final major line of defense on the western front.

remaining forces • the total surviving forces at any given stage of combat operations.

reman • *v.* (**remanned, remanning**) equip with new personnel.

Remembrance Sunday • (in the UK) the Sunday nearest November 11, when those who were killed in WORLD WARS I AND II and later conflicts are commemorated. November 11 is the anniversary of the signing of the armistice ending World War I. (Also called **Remembrance Day** and **Poppy Day**.)

Remey, George Collier (1841–1928) • Union naval officer. An Iowa native, Remey served on a gunboat during the PENINSULAR CAMPAIGN (1862) of the CIVIL WAR and was captured during an ill-fated attempt to take FORT SUMTER (1863). He was eventually released in a prisoner exchange. After the war, Remey served in Latin America and in the Mediterranean. In 1898, he was responsible for many of the naval operations around Cuba during the SPANISH-AMERICAN WAR, and in 1900 he participated in operations in the Philippines. In 1901 he helped suppress the BOXER REBELLION in China. He retired from the navy in 1903 with the rank of admiral.

Remington • *n.* trademark a make of firearm.

ORIGIN: mid 19th cent.: named after Eliphalet *Remington* (1793–1861) and his son Philo (1816–89), gunsmiths of Ilion, New York, the original manufacturers.

Remington Arms Company • a U.S. firearms and ammunition manufacturer established in 1816 by Eliphalet Remington at Ilion Gulch, New York, and incorporated in 1865. The company supplied a large proportion of the U.S. military forces' small arms in the CIVIL WAR and in WORLD WARS I AND II. In 1933 the E.I. DuPont de Nemours & Co. chemical company acquired sixty percent of Remington, and in 1980 Remington became a wholly owned subsidiary of DuPont. In 1993 DuPont sold the assets of Remington to RACI Acquisitions. In addition to the firearms and ammunitions business, Remington, in 1873, produced the first modern typewriter. In 1886 it sold its typewriter business, which decades later became Sperry Rand, itself a significant military contractor.

remotely piloted vehicle • (**RPV**) a vehicle that has no human operator and is controlled at a distance by using a communication link. It is usually designed so that it can be recovered. See also DRONE.

remote sensing • the scanning of the earth by satellite or high-flying aircraft in order to obtain information about it.

remount • *v.* |rē'mownt; 'rē-| mount (something) again, in particular: **a** get on (something) in order to ride it again: *she remounted and rode through the gates.* **b** organize and embark on (a significant course of action) again: *the raid was remounted in August.* • *n.* |'rē ˌmownt| **1** a fresh horse for a rider. **2** a supply of fresh horses for a regiment.

remuster • *v.* to reassemble troops for inspection or to begin an operation.

rendezvous |'rändiˌvo͞o; 'rändā-| • *n.* **1** a meeting up of troops, ships, or aircraft at an agreed time and place. **2** a prearranged meeting between spacecraft in space. • *v.* (**rendezvouses** |-ˌvo͞oz|, **rendezvoused** |-ˌvo͞od|, **rendezvousing** |-ˌvo͞oiNG|) meet at an agreed time and place: *the special forces paratroopers rendezvoused at a predetermined site behind enemy lines.*

Reno, Jesse Lee (1823–62) • Union army officer, born in Wheeling, Virginia (now West Virginia), Reno first saw combat during the MEXICAN WAR (1846–48). During the next decade, he held a series of routine posts. When the CIVIL WAR broke out, he was named brigadier general of volunteers (1861). He led troops in Gen. AMBROSE BURNSIDE's campaign in North Carolina and helped capture Roanoke Island. In the SECOND BATTLE OF BULL RUN (1862) he calmly and capably covered the retreat of Union forces to Washington. He was killed at the battle of SOUTH MOUNTAIN while trying to stop a Confederate advance into Maryland.

reparations • *plural n.* the compensation for war damage paid by a defeated state.

repatriate • *n.* a person who returns to their country or citizenship, having left their native country, either against their will, or as one of a group who left for political, religious, or other pertinent reasons.

repeat • *n.* in artillery and naval gunfire support, an order or request to fire again the same number of rounds with the same method of fire.

repeater • *n.* a firearm that fires several shots without reloading.

repeater-jammer • *n.* a receiver-transmitter device that amplifies, multiplies, and retransmits the signals received, for purposes of deception or jamming.

repeating • *adj.* capable of firing several shots in succession without reloading.

repeating firearm • a firearm capable of firing a number of shots repeatedly without reloading, by holding ammunition in a clip, magazine, or other device. The first ones were developed in the 19th century.

replacements • *plural n.* personnel required to take the place of others who depart a unit.

replenishment at sea • operations required to make a transfer of personnel and/or supplies when at sea.

reporting time interval • **1** in surveillance, the time interval between the detection of an event and the receipt of a report by the user. **2** in communications, the time for transmission of data or a report from the originating terminal to the end receiver.

Republican Guard • the elite elements of the ground forces of Iraq. Better led, better trained, and better equipped than most of the Iraqi armed forces, the Republican Guard is noted for its loyalty to the Iraqi leader, SADDAM HUSSEIN, who relied on it to suppress dissent in other units of the Iraqi armed forces and among the civilian population of Iraq. The Republican Guard units in Kuwait and southern Iraqi only narrowly escaped annihilation by allied forces in the PERSIAN GULF WAR.

Republican party • one of the two main U.S. political parties (the other being the DEMOCRATIC PARTY), favoring a right-wing stance, limited central government, and tough, interventionist foreign policy. It was formed in 1854 in support of the anti-slavery movement preceding the CIVIL WAR.

Republic of Korea Army • (**ROKA**) the army of the Republic of Korea. Created on December 5, 1948 with the assistance of the United States, the Republic of Korea Army was still ill-equipped and ill-trained when faced by an invasion of South Korea by the North Korean People's Army in June 1950. Heavily battered, the ROKA fell back, surrendering the South Korean capital, Seoul, and much of the country to the NKPA. Reformed with the aid of the United Nations forces, the ROKA steadily improved and bore a substantial share of the fighting against Communist forces during the remainder of the KOREAN WAR. The ROKA subsequently became a relatively small but effective fighting force capable of defending the borders of the Republic of Korea against continued North Korean aggression. ROKA forces participated with the United States and other forces in the defense of the Republic of South Vietnam against Communist-led insurgents and North Vietnamese Army forces in the 1960s and early 1970s.

required military force • the armed forces necessary to carry out a military mission over a specified period of time.

required supply rate • in army usage, the amount of ammunition expressed in terms of rounds per weapon per day for ammunition items fired by weapons, and in terms of other units of measure per day for bulk allotment and other items, estimated to be required to sustain operations of any designated force without restriction for a specified period.

Resaca de la Palma, Battle of the • the battle that followed the BATTLE OF PALO ALTO, on May 9, 1846, near the Rio Grande in Texas, during the MEXICAN WAR. Mexican troops defended a line near an old path along the Rio Grande called the Resaca de la Palma, disputed territory between the United States and Mexico. American Gen. ZACHARY TAYLOR took the offensive and broke through Mexican lines in a decisive victory.

rescue combat air patrol • an aircraft patrol provided over a combat search-and-rescue objective area for the purpose of intercepting and destroying hostile aircraft. Its primary mission is to protect the search-and-rescue task forces during recovery operations.

rescue ship • a ship that is stationed at the end of a convoy column in order to rescue survivors of an attack or other mishap.

rescue strop • a piece of rescue equipment that is placed around a person's chest to secure that person to a rescue line or helicopter hoist cable. Also called HORSE COLLAR.

reseau |rā'zō; ri-| • *n.* a grid system of a standard size in the image plane of a photographic system used for measuring purposes.

reserve • *n.* **1** the portion of a body of troops which is kept to the rear, or withheld from action at the beginning of an engagement, available for a decisive movement. **2** members of the military services who are not in active service but who are subject to call to active duty. **3** the portion of an appropriation or contract authorization held or set aside for future operations or contingencies and in respect to which administrative authorization to incur commitments or obligations has been withheld.

reserve aircraft • aircraft in excess of immediate needs but kept in inventory in case of future needs.

reserve components • the units and individuals of the military services who are not in active service but who are subject to call to active duty under certain pre-established conditions and rules. The Reserve Components of the Armed Forces of the United States include the Army National Guard, the Army Reserve, the Naval Reserve, the Marine Corps Reserve, the Air National Guard, the Air Force Reserve, and the Coast Guard Reserve.

reserved demolition target • a target for demolition, the destruction of which must be controlled at a specific level of command because it plays a vital part in the tactical or strategical plan, or because of the importance of the structure itself, or because the demolition may be executed in the face of the enemy.

reserved route • in road traffic, a specific route allocated exclusively to an authority or a formation.

Reserve Forces Act • an act signed by President DWIGHT D. EISENHOWER on August 5, 1955 to improve the reserve components of the U.S. armed services. It increased the size of the READY RESERVE from 1.5 million to 2.9 million personnel and authorized the president to mobilize one million ready reservists in a declared national emergency without congressional approval. It also altered enlistment, training, and service requirements for members of the armed forces. It amended the Armed Forces Reserve Act of 1952 and the Universal Military Training and Service Act of 1951.

Reserve Officers Association • a private organization composed of officers holding a commission in one or another of the reserve components of the armed forces of the United States. The purpose of the organization is to support a strong military policy for the United States and to serve the interests of reserve officers.

Reserve Officers'Training Corps • (**ROTC**) established as one of three components of the U.S. Army, the Organized Reserves (Enlisted and Officers' Reserve Corps), by the National Defense Act of 1920 (which amended the National Defense Act of 1916). By 1928 there were ROTC units at 325 colleges and universities that offered a four-year course of instruction in military science. When many colleges and universities began to abolish compulsory ROTC, Congress passed the ROTC Vitalization Act of 1964 in order to increase program productivity. The Naval Reserve Officers'Training Corps (NROTC) was established in 1926 in order to provide a broad base of civilians trained in naval warfare. The Marine Corps entered the NROTC program in 1932, offering NROTC graduates commissions in the U.S. Marine Corps. The Air Force Reserve Officers' Training Corps, like Army ROTC, was established by the National Defense Act of 1916, and is responsible for training approximately 75 percent of Air Force line officers. In 1997, a new organization—Air Force Officer Accessions and Training Schools (AFOATS)—was created under Air University, and HC AFROTC became a subordinate unit.

reservist • *n.* a member of the military reserve forces.

residual forces • unexpended portions of the remaining U.S. forces that have an immediate combat potential for continued military operations, and that have been deliberately withheld from utilization.

residual radiation • nuclear radiation caused by fallout, artificial dispersion of radioactive material, or irradiation that results from a nuclear explosion and persists longer than one minute after burst.

Resistance, The • the forces and actions taken to resist the occupation of the various countries of Europe and Asia by the AXIS powers during WORLD WAR II. Resistance covered the full range of passive and active means and methods from avoiding compulsory service and disobeying the regulations imposed by the occupying forces through intelligence gathering and sabotage to active armed opposition.

resistance movement • an organized attempt by a group of citizens of a country to resist the legal government or an occupying power and to undermine civil order.

responsibility • *n.* **1** the obligation to carry forward an assigned task to a successful conclusion. With responsibility goes authority to direct and take the necessary action to ensure success. **2** the obligation for the proper custody, care, and safekeeping of property or funds entrusted to the possession or supervision of an individual. Compare with ACCOUNTABILITY.

rest and recuperation • (**R&R**) the withdrawal of individuals from combat or duty in a combat area for short periods of rest and recuperation.

rest-camp • slang (World War I) a cemetery.

rest in pieces • slang (World War I) a "translation" of the letters R.I.P. over a soldier's grave, particularly if the soldier was killed by an exploding bomb or shell. Slang, 92

R.I.P. is an abbreviation for "rest in peace," or, originally, the Latin *requiescat in pace*, "may he (or she) rest in peace."

restricted area • **1** an area (land, sea, or air) in which there are special restrictive measures employed to prevent or minimize interference between friendly forces. **2** an area under military jurisdiction in which special security measures are employed to prevent unauthorized entry.

restricted data • information concerning: **a** the design, manufacture, or use of atomic weapons; **b** the production of special nuclear material; or **c** the use of special nuclear material in the production of energy.

restricted operations area • airspace of defined dimensions, designated by the airspace control authority, in response to specific operational situations/requirements within which the operation of one or more airspace users is restricted.

resupply • *n.* the act of replenishing stocks in order to maintain required levels of supply.

retaliate • *v.* make an attack or assault in return for a similar attack: *Iran* ***retaliated with*** *air attacks on Baghdad.*

DERIVATIVES: **retaliation** *n.* **retaliative** *adj.* **retaliator** *n.* **retaliatory** *adj.*

retaliatory nuclear strike • an attack with nuclear weapons undertaken in response to a previous enemy attack, insult, or provocation.

retire • *v.* **1** (of a military force) retreat from an enemy or an attacking position: *lack of numbers compelled the cavalry to retire.* **2** order (a military force) to retreat: *the general retired all his troops.*

Retired Officers Association, The • (**TROA**) an organization for American members of the uniformed services, including active-duty, former, retired, National Guard, and Reserve members. It provides services and information to approximately 400,000 members. The association lobbies on behalf of members, assists them with financial benefits and spouse and survivor services, and produces *The Retired Officer Magazine*.

retirement • *n.* an operation in which a force out of contact moves away from the enemy.

retreat • *v.* (of an army) withdraw from enemy forces as a result of their superior power or after a defeat: *the French retreated in disarray.* • *n.* **1** an act of moving back or withdrawing: *a* *speedy retreat* | *the army was* ***in retreat.*** **2** a signal for a military force to withdraw: *the bugle sounded a retreat.* **3** a military musical ceremony carried out at sunset, originating in the playing of drums and bugles to tell soldiers to return to camp for the night.

retrocede |ˌretrəˈsēd| • *v.* rare cede (territory) back again: *the British colony of Hong Kong, retroceded to China.*

DERIVATIVES: **retrocession** *n.*

retrograde movement • any movement of a command to the rear, or away from the enemy. It may be forced by the enemy or may be made voluntarily. Such a movement may be classified as a WITHDRAWAL OPERATION, a RETIREMENT, or a DELAYING ACTION.

retrograde personnel • personnel (including medical patients, noncombatants, and civilians) who are evacuated from a theater of operations.

reveille |ˈrevəlē| • *n.* a signal sounded at daybreak on the drum or bugle, alerting military personnel to rise and prepare for the day's duties.

ORIGIN: mid 17th cent.: from French *réveillez!* 'wake up!'

Revenue Cutter Service • established by a 1790 law that authorized the construction and equipment of cutters to enforce the payment of customs charges and tonnage duties on ships. The responsibilities of the Service in Alaska included: enforcing regulations concerning the killing of fur seals and otters; regulating traffic in firearms, ammunition, and liquor (until 1884); protecting salmon spawning grounds and access rivers; protecting Alaskan fishing grounds from foreign encroachment (with the U.S. Navy); and protecting game in Alaska. In 1915, the Revenue Cutter Service was combined with similar organizations, including the Lifesaving Services of the Treasury Department, to form the U.S. COAST GUARD. See also BERING SEA PATROL.

Revenue Cutter Service School of Instruction • a service academy at Fort Trumball in New London, Connecticut, from 1914–15. It replaced the School of Instruction for the Revenue Marine, which was established in 1876 near New Bedford, Massachusetts. In 1915 it merged with the Life Saving Service and became the U.S. Coast Guard Academy.

Revenue Marine Bureau • an organization established in 1843 responsible for preventing shipwrecks and helping shipwreck victims. By the fall of 1849, eight boathouses had been constructed from Sandy Hook to Little Egg Harbor, New Jersey. In the early 1950s, with additional congressional funds, boathouses were positioned from Rhode Island in the North to Florida and Texas in the South. By 1854, there were boathouses on the Great Lakes. In 1869, the surfmen responsible for these positions became paid employees. The Bureau was one of the five federal agencies merged to become the U.S. COAST GUARD.

Revere, Paul (1734–1818) • Revolutionary leader, silversmith, and printer. The Boston-born Revere ran the family business, silversmithing, after his father died in 1754 and expanded into copperplate engraving. In the 1760s and 1770s he became increasingly politically active and joined the SONS OF LIBERTY. His engraving of the BOSTON MASSACRE (1770), although replete with factual errors, was a powerful propaganda piece, arousing indignation against the British. Revere also played a key role in planning the BOSTON TEA PARTY (1773). He became a courier for the Massachusetts government, carrying messages to other colonies. His most famous ride, that of April 18, 1775, began when he was asked to ride to Lexington to warn SAMUEL ADAMS and John Hancock that the British were marching west from Boston. A second rider was dispatched by a different route. Revere did alert the two men, and then he and the second rider decided to continue on to Concord. En route, with a third rider, they were stopped by the British; the other two escaped, but Revere was detained briefly and then left without his horse. He returned to Lexington, where he witnessed the skirmish on Lexington Green. Revere's later service during the Revolution was unremarkable; he was charged with cowardice and insubordination and forced to resign after participating in a failed effort to oust a British force from a fort in Maine. (This decision was overturned in a later court-martial sought by Revere.) After the war, he resumed his smithing business in Boston and in 1797 opened an iron foundry, which became noted for its cast church bells. He also produced ordnance for the new U.S. government.

reverse • *n.* an adverse change of fortune; a setback or defeat: *the division suffered its heaviest reverse of the campaign.*

reverse slope • any slope that descends away from the enemy.

revet |riˈvet| • *v.* (**revetted** |rəˈvedəd; rē ˈvedəd|, **revetting** |rəˈvediNG; rēˈvediNG|) (**revetted**) face (a rampart, wall, etc.) with masonry, especially in fortification: *sandbagged and revetted trenches.*

revetment |riˈvetmənt| • *n.* **1** (especially in fortification) a retaining wall or facing of masonry or other material, supporting or protecting a rampart, wall, etc. **2** a barricade of earth or sandbags set up to provide protection from blast or to prevent planes from overrunning when landing.

review • *n.* **1** a formal assessment or examination of something with the possibility or intention of instituting change if necessary: *a comprehensive review of defense policy.* **2** a ceremonial display and formal inspection of military or naval forces, typically by a sovereign, commander in chief, or high-ranking visitor. • *v.* **1** examine or assess (something) formally with the possibility or intention of instituting change if necessary: *the unit's safety procedures are being reviewed.* **2** make a retrospective assessment or survey of (past events): *ministers will meet to review progress on conventional arms negotiations in March.* **3** (of a sovereign, commander in chief, or high-ranking visitor) make a ceremonial and formal inspection of (military or naval forces).

DERIVATIVES: **reviewable** *adj.* **reviewal** *n.*

revisionism • *n.* **1** often derogatory a policy of revision or modification, especially of Marxism on evolutionary socialist (rather than revolutionary) or pluralist principles. **2** the theory or practice of revising one's attitude to a previously accepted situation or point of view.

DERIVATIVES: **revisionist** *n.* & *adj.*

Revolt of the Admirals • a controversy over the powers of the secretary of defense, in the summer and fall of 1949. Senior navy officers, unhappy with new austerity measures under secretary of defense Louis Johnson, publicly attacked the new service unification under the Deparment of Defense and the reliance on air-atomic power as the country's first line of defense.

revolution • *n.* **1** a forcible overthrow of a government or social order in favor of a new system. **2** an instance of revolving: *one revolution a second.*

DERIVATIVES: **revolutionism** *n.* **revolutionist** *n.*

revolutionary insurgency • see LOW INTENSITY CONFLICT.

Revolutionary War, American • (1775–1783) Following the end of the FRENCH AND INDIAN WAR in 1763, British restrictions on westward expansion and trade as well as heavy taxation and the arbitrary administration of justice in the American colonies stirred the desire for redress among the American colonists, some of whom even began to think of independence and to organize to achieve that goal. On September 5, 1774, the colonists convened the First Continental Congress and petitioned King GEORGE III for relief to no avail. In Massachusetts, avid "patriots" seized control of provincial armories. An attempt by British forces under Gen. THOMAS GAGE to recover the seized weapons resulted in a clash between British troops and American patriots at LEXINGTON and CONCORD on April 19, 1775, and the rebellion quickly spread throughout New England. The Second Continental Congress convened on May 10, 1775, and attempted to restore relations with the Crown but recognized the need to control the growing rebellion and thus began to raise an army, appointed GEORGE WASHINGTON as commander-in-chief, and sought an alliance with France. Relations with the mother country deteriorated rapidly, an American army was dispatched to invade Canada, and some 20,000 New England militiamen laid siege to the British forces in Boston (June 15, 1775) and demonstrated their commitment and fighting abilities in the Battle of BUNKER (actually Breed's) HILL (June 17, 1775). The British acted swiftly to subdue the rebellion by sending additional land and naval forces to North America, but despite being outnumbered and ill-equipped, the American patriots conducted a spirited if often unsuccessful defense of their homes and liberties. The British forces evacuated Boston on March 17, 1776, but the American invasion of Canada launched in June 1775 failed in the summer of 1776. Even as Gen. Washington struggled to transform the infant Continental Army into a capable force, British Gen. Sir WILLIAM HOWE landed on Staten Island on June 25, 1776. On July 4, 1776, the Continental Congress in Philadelphia declared the independence of the American colonies. Washington's troops were subsequently defeated by Howe's forces in the battles of NEW YORK (August 27–30, 1776) and Brooklyn Heights (October 1776), but the bulk of Washington's forces escaped and retreated across New Jersey into Pennsylvania. Undaunted, Washington successfully launched the ragged remnants of his army against the Hessian mercenaries at TRENTON on Christmas Eve 1776, and then defeated the British at PRINCETON in January 1777. Washington was less successful later in the year, meeting defeat at the hands of Gen. Howe at BRANDYWINE (September 11, 1777). Howe then occupied Philadelphia and withstood an attack by Washington at GERMANTOWN (October 4, 1777). Meanwhile, British forces under Gen. Sir JOHN BURGOYNE invaded the rebellious colonies from Canada by way of Lake Champlain but was soundly defeated by the Americans under Gen. HORATIO GATES at SARATOGA (September 17 and October 5, 1777). The defeat of Burgoyne's invasion force and the inability of Howe to win a truly decisive victory over Washington led to diplomatic recognition of the United States by France on December 17, 1777, and a subsequent flow of aid from the French, including ground and naval forces. Even so, Washington's army barely survived a terrible winter encampment at VALLEY FORGE in the winter of 1777–1778. Fortunately, the focus of the war shifted to the south in 1778, where the British began a campaign to "pacify" the southern colonies using loyalist troops. The campaign began well, and the British took Savannah (December 19, 1778) and Augusta (January 29, 1779) and successfully defeated American attempts to retake the lost cities. Using Georgia as a base, the British commander, Gen. Sir HENRY CLINTON, carried the war into South Carolina in 1780, taking Charleston on May 12, thereby obliterating the presence of the Continental Army in the south. Thereafter, the war in the south consisted largely of a guerrilla campaign by American leaders such as FRANCIS MARION against the superior British forces, now commanded by Gen. Lord CHARLES CORNWALLIS, and their loyalist allies led by the notorious British Lt. Col. BANASTRE TARLETON. On August 16, 1780, Cornwallis' troops routed the American forces under Horatio Gates at Camden, but Gen. NATHANAEL GREENE assumed command of the American forces at Charlotte, North Carolina, on December 2 and immediately took the offensive. On January 17, 1781, a small force of Continentals and militiamen under Greene and Brig. Gen. DANIEL MORGAN defeated the British at COWPENS but were defeated in turn by the British at GUILFORD COURT HOUSE on March 15.

Cornwallis then marched his forces into Virginia hoping to defeat the Continental Army forces there commanded by the MARQUIS DE LAFAYETTE. Instead, Lafayette, reinforced by the main Continental Army under Gen. Washington, succeeded in trapping Cornwallis' army at YORKTOWN on the Virginia peninsula. There, aided by a French fleet under Admiral De Grasse which cut Cornwallis off from support by the Royal Navy, the Americans besieged the British on September 28. On October 20, 1781, Cornwallis surrendered to Washington as the band played "The World Turned Upside Down." Tired of the American war and preoccupied with threats to her interests on the Continent, Britain suspended offensive actions in America, and peace negotiations were opened. The Revolutionary War was subsequently ended formally by the TREATY OF PARIS (September 3, 1783).

revolver • *n.* a pistol with revolving chambers enabling several shots to be fired without reloading.

Reykjavik summit • a meeting held in Reykjavik, Iceland, between U.S. President RONALD REAGAN and Soviet leader MIKHAIL GORBACHEV in October 1986, during the COLD WAR, to discuss nuclear disarmament. It led to negotiations of the INTERMEDIATE-RANGE NUCLEAR FORCES TREATY and the START I TREATY.

Reynolds, Charles Alexander (1842–76) • soldier and scout, born in Illinois. Reynolds, after spending some time in the military and working as a prison guard, headed west in 1864 and made his living as a buffalo hunter. In 1872 he served as an army scout for Gen. DAVID S. STANLEY's Yellowstone Expedition. In 1874, he was the chief scout for Lt. Col. GEORGE ARMSTRONG CUSTER, who sent him to the Black Hills to locate a site for a fort and to investigate rumors of gold; Reynolds returned to Fort Laramie with confirmation of the existence of gold in the South Dakota hills. Reynolds was killed while on an expedition to capture the Northern Sioux tribe led by SITTING BULL.

Reynolds, John Fulton (1820–63) • Union army officer, born in Pennsylvania. When the CIVIL WAR broke out, Gen. GEORGE B. MCCLELLAN asked to have him assigned to the ARMY OF THE POTOMAC. In 1862 he was captured at GAINES' MILL, but he was freed at the request of a citizens' group from Fredericksburg, where he had served as military governor. In the generally disastrous SECOND BATTLE OF BULL RUN (1862), he provided strong and decisive leadership. Later that year he was promoted to major general of volunteers. He turned down the chance to replace Gen. JOSEPH HOOKER as commander of the Army of the Potomac and in 1863 led the Union advance into GETTYSBURG. While attempting to engage Gen. ROBERT E. LEE's troops as a diversion intended to enable the arriving Union forces to move into position, he was killed by Confederate fire.

Reynolds, Joseph Jones (1822–99) • Union army officer, born in Kentucky. Reynolds struck up a lifelong friendship with ULYSSES S. GRANT while the two were students at the U.S. MILITARY ACADEMY. In 1845 he served with Gen. ZACHARY TAYLOR as part of the forces occupying Texas; from 1846 to 1855 he taught at WEST POINT. In 1860, having left the army for civilian life, he returned to the military, where he held a number of commands. As chief of staff of the ARMY OF THE CUMBERLAND (1863), he played important roles in the battles of CHATTANOOGA, LOOKOUT MOUNTAIN, and MISSIONARY RIDGE. His conduct while commanding an expedition against the Cheyenne in 1876 led to his court-martial on charges of incompetence and cowardice; his sentence of a one-year suspension was remitted, but he retired the following year.

RF-4 • see PHANTOM II.

RFA • *abbr.* Royal Fleet Auxiliary.

RFC • *abbr.* (in the UK) Royal Flying Corps.

RFE • *abbr.* Radio Free Europe.

RGM-66D • see STANDARD SSM.

RGM-84 • see HARPOON.

RH-53 • see SEA STALLION.

Rhode Island, Battle of • a REVOLUTIONARY WAR battle fought in Portsmouth, Rhode Island in August, 1778. The battle was inconclusive but it is notable for the action of the Black Regiment of Rhode Island, a company of freed slaves who fought bravely for the American side, and for being the first battle of the war in which American forces were joined by French allies.

rhumb |rəm(b)| • *n.* **1** (also **rhumb line**) an imaginary line on the earth's surface cutting all meridians at the same angle, used as the standard method of plotting a ship's course on a chart. **2** any of the 32 points of the compass.

RI • *abbr.* radiation intensity.

RIB • *n.* a small open boat with a fiberglass hull and inflatable rubber sides.

ORIGIN: acronym from *rigid inflatable boat.*

rib • *n.* any of the curved transverse pieces of metal or timber in a ship, extending up from the keel and forming part of the framework of the hull.

Richardson, Ebenezer (c.1718–?) • informant, born in Massachusetts. Richardson was in Boston by 1850, compiling a criminal record. This did not stop local officials from employing him as an informant in matters related to smuggling operations, apparently because of his knowledge of such operations. In the course of this employment, Richardson solidified his reputation as a scoundrel. Politically a Loyalist, Richardson reported those who imported goods illegally from England in violations of colonial nonimportation agreements. His mortal wounding of a young boy while fighting off a mob attack, coming only two weeks before the BOSTON MASSACRE, led to his trial for murder while the city's emotions were inflamed. He was convicted, although he claimed self-defense. The Superior Court succeeded in having the verdict overturned, and Richardson fled Boston. He joined the customs service in

Philadelphia; after that, nothing is known of his life.

Richmond • the capital city of the Commonwealth ofVirginia. Richmond was particularly important during the CIVIL WAR when it also served as the capital of the Confederate States of America and was the principal geographical objective of the Union armies in the East.

Richthofen, Baron Manfred von (1892–1918) • German WORLD WAR I flying ace, known as the "Red Baron." Born in Breslau, Germany, into a prominent family, von Richthofen, like other members of his family, chose a military career. When World War I broke out, he fought in the cavalry in Russia and then in Belgium and France; when trench warfare replaced the cavalry, he turned to flying. In 1916 he assumed command of Flying Group I, which became known as Richthofen's FLYING CIRCUS for its colorful airplanes. Von Richthofen was shot down over Amiens, France, while piloting one of his bright red Fokker fighter planes. He was personally responsible for the downing of eighty Allied aircraft.

Rickenbacker, Eddie |ˈrikənˌbækər| (1890–1973) • U.S. army air force officer and CONGRESSIONAL MEDAL OF HONOR recipient, born Edward Vernon Rickenbacker in Ohio. Rickenbacker starting working at the age of thirteen to help support his family. He turned to race car driving, at which he proved very successful. Rickenbacker's interest in aviation was supported by Col. BILLY MITCHELL, for whom he served as staff driver during WORLD WAR I; Mitchell helped him enter a flight training program in France, and after twenty-five hours in the air Rickenbacker was commissioned a lieutenant in the Army Air Service. Rickenbacker shot down five enemy planes in the space of a month and was quickly made a squadron commander. At war's end he had shot down more enemy planes and balloons (26) than any other pilot, making him the Ace of Aces. For his service he received the French Croix de Guerre, the DISTINGUISHED SERVICE CROSS, and the CONGRESSIONAL MEDAL OF HONOR. Although he initially opposed intervention in WORLD WAR II, he eventually toured army air force bases for the U.S. government to raise morale and to offer suggestions for improvement.

Ricketts, James Brewerton (1817–87) • Union army officer. A native of New York City, Ricketts served in the MEXICAN WAR (1846–47). He also participated in operations against the Seminoles in Florida in 1852. At the outbreak of the CIVIL WAR, he helped capture the city of Alexandria, Virginia (1861). At the FIRST BATTLE OF BULL RUN (1861), the battery he was commanding was nearly destroyed. He was wounded and captured; his distraught wife broke through Confederate lines and remained with him in prison to nurse him until he was released in a prisoner exchange. Ricketts returned to duty and fought at a number of major engagements, including the SECOND BATTLE OF BULL RUN (1862) and ANTIETAM (1862), at which he was again wounded. Rickett's division was the first sent out to meet Gen. JUBAL EARLY when Confederate troops invaded Maryland; although the Confederates ultimately were victorious, Ricketts managed to delay their advance on Washington.

Rickover, Hyman (1900–86) • naval officer and nuclear engineer. Rickover's family fled Russian Poland in the face of persistent anti-Semitism and settled first in New York, then in Chicago. He attended the U.S. NAVAL ACADEMY and studied electrical engineering in its postgraduate program at the academy and at Columbia University. Ambitious and innovative, he unsuccessfully sought a command and also developed expertise in submarine engineering, in which he became the navy's expert. During WORLD WAR II he led the electrical section of the Bureau of Ships and successfully met the rapidly increasing demand for power. In 1946 he was sent to Oak Ridge, Tennessee, to begin research on the use of nuclear fission to power submarines, and in 1949 he became head of a joint commission of the navy and the U.S. ATOMIC ENERGY COMMISSION on nuclear propulsion; this position gave him enormous power over the direction of research and design for nuclear-powered submarines. The world's first such vessel, the *Nautilus,* was launched on January 21, 1954, revolutionizing naval operations. Rickover remained with the program until 1982. In his later years, Rickover admitted to some financial improprieties, but these did not lessen respect for his leadership and technical expertise.

Ridgway, Matthew Bunker (1895–1993) • U.S. army general, army Chief of Staff. Born at Fort Monroe, Virginia, to an army family, Ridgway spent WORLD WAR I in the United States; in the following years he undertook a variety of assignments, including the command of a company at Tientsin, China, work on resolving a border dispute between Bolivia and Paraguay, and service in the Philippines. With the outbreak of WORLD WAR II, Ridgway became commander of the Eighty-second Airborne Division, with the rank of major general. In 1943 he led his troops in the invasions of SICILY and SALERNO. Ridgway and his troops parachuted onto the Cotentin Peninsula, Normandy, as a leading element of the D-DAY LANDING (June 6, 1944); Ridgway was named commander of the Eighteenth Corps, which he led in the BATTLE OF THE BULGE (1944–45)and into Germany. Ridgway was named commander of the Mediterranean theater of operations, and at war's end, he was one of the most honored U.S. commanders. In December 1950, when fighting broke out in Korea, he was made commander of the Eighth Army there, taking over control of the ground war, stopping the Chinese advance, and restoring the unit's morale. In March 1931, Ridgway retook Seoul and pushed north of the thirty-eighth parallel, which divided North and South Korea. When President HARRY S. TRUMAN relieved Gen. DOUGLAS MACARTHUR of his command in Korea, Ridgway was chosen to replace him. In 1952 Truman named him to head the NORTH ATLANTIC TREATY ORGANIZATION (NATO), headquartered in Brussels, replacing Gen. DWIGHT D. EISENHOWER; in October 1953 Eisenhower named him army Chief of Staff. In this position, Ridgway advocated reliance on conventional forces rather than massive nuclear retaliation, the hallmark of Eisenhower's "New Look" defense strategy. He also opposed U.S. involvement in Vietnam following the French defeat at DIEN BIEN PHU (1954). In 1955 he retired from the army and joined the Mellon Institute, from which he continued to criticize American involvement in Vietnam.

riding light • a light shown by a ship at anchor.

rifle • *n.* **1** a gun, especially one fired from shoulder level, having a long spirally grooved barrel intended to make a bullet spin and thereby have greater accuracy over a long distance. **2** (**rifles**) troops armed with rifles. • *v.* (**rifled**) make spiral grooves in (a gun or its barrel or bore) to make a bullet spin and thereby have greater accuracy over a long distance: *a line of replacement rifled barrels.*

rifleman • *n.* (pl. **-men**) **1** a soldier armed with a rifle, especially a private in a rifle regiment. **2** a person skilled at using a rifle.

rifle-musket • (also **rifled musket**) the earliest true rifle, developed by introducing rifling into the bore of a musket. It was introduced in the early 19th century and adopted widely for military use in the CIVIL WAR.

rifle range • a place for practicing shooting with rifles.

riflescope • *n.* informal a telescopic sight on a rifle.

rifling |ˈrīf(ə)liNG| • *n.* the arrangement of spiral grooves on the inside of a rifle barrel.

rig • *v.* (**rigged, rigging**) **1** make (a sailing ship or boat) ready for sailing by providing it with sails and rigging: *the catamaran will be rigged as a ketch* | (**-rigged**) *a gaff-rigged cutter.* **2** assemble and adjust (the equipment of a sailboat, aircraft, etc.) to make it ready for operation: *most sails are kept ready rigged.* **3** provide (someone) with clothes of a particular style or type: *a cavalry regiment* ***rigged out*** *in green and gold.* • *n.* **1** the particular way in which a sailboat's masts, sails, and rigging are arranged: *the yacht will emerge from the yard with her original rig.* **2** a person's costume, outfit, or style of dress: *the rig of the Army Air Corps.*

rigger • *n.* a person who rigs or attends to the rigging of a sailing ship, aircraft, or parachute.

rigging • *n.* **1** the system of ropes, cables, or chains employed to support a ship's masts (**standing rigging**) and to control or set the yards and sails (**running rigging**). **2** the action of providing a sailing ship with sails, stays, and braces. **3** the ropes and wires supporting the structure of an airship, biplane, hang glider, or parachute. **4** the system of cables and fittings controlling the flight surfaces and engines of an aircraft. **5** the action of assembling and adjusting such rigging.

right • *adj.* of or relating to a person or political party or grouping favoring conservative views: *are you politically right, left, or center?* • *n.* **1** the right wing of an army. **2** (often **the Right**) a grouping or political party favoring conservative views and supporting capitalist economic principles. **3** the section of a group or political party adhering particularly strongly to such views.

ORIGIN: see RIGHT WING.

DERIVATIVES: **rightable** *adj.*

right-about (also **right-about face**) • *n.* a right turn continued through 180° so as to face in the opposite direction: *he did a swift right-about and disappeared.*

right of search • the right of a ship of a belligerent state to stop and search a neutral merchant vessel for prohibited goods.

right of visitation • in international maritime law, the right of a country's naval and merchant ships to visit a specified port of another country.

right wing • *n.* (**the right wing**) **1** the conservative or reactionary section of a political party or system. [with reference to the National Assembly in France (1789–91), where the nobles sat to the president's right and the commons to the left.] **2** the right side of an army. • *adj.* conservative or reactionary: *a right-wing Republican senator.*

Riley, Bennet (1787–1853) • military governor and army officer. Riley fought ably in the WAR OF 1812. Between 1816 and 1817 he served as captain with the Regiment of Riflemen. When that unit was disbanded, he moved to the West, where in 1829 he commanded the first army escort on the Santa Fe Trail. He fought in the BLACK HAWK WAR (1831–32) and the SEMINOLE WAR (1840). Riley's career advanced during the MEXICAN WAR (1846–48); he fought at VERACRUZ (1847) and at CERRO GORDO (1847), where his service earned him promotion to brigadier general. He led an important charge in support of Gen. WINFIELD SCOTT at MEXICO CITY (1847). After the war he served as ex officio civil governor of the newly acquired territory of California until its formal admission to the Union.

RIM-66 • see STANDARD MISSILE.

RIM-67 • see STANDARD MISSILE.

rimfire • *adj.* **1** (of a cartridge) having the primer around the edge of the base. **2** (of a rifle) adapted for such cartridges.

Ringgold, Cadwalader (1802–67) • Union naval officer, born in Maryland. Ringgold served from 1823 to 1825 as part of the "mosquito fleet" that controlled piracy in the West Indies. In 1838 he joined an expedition, led by CHARLES WILKES, to explore Pacific Ocean sailing routes and South Seas whaling grounds. After this trip, Ringgold helped chart the west coast of North America. From 1853 to 1856, he led an expedition, planned in conjunction with that of Captain MATTHEW C. PERRY, to explore eastern routes from California to the Far East. Concerns about Ringgold's mental stability led to his being removed from his post and from the active duty roster, but he won a review of his case that reversed the rulings. During the CIVIL WAR, in 1861, during a furious gale outside Port Royal, South Carolina, he courageously rescued 400 marines from a foundering vessel; this action and the rescue of a second vessel, the *Vermont*, in 1862, earned him congressional recognition.

Riot Act • a law enacted by the British Parliament in 1715 to prevent unlawful assembly and civic disturbances. Part of the proclamation was read by a magistrate when members of a crowd of twelve or more had unlawfully gathered and disturbed the peace. It required those assembled to disperse within one hour of the reading or be charged with felony. Magistrates often had difficulty reading the act during disturbances. It was repealed in 1973.

riot control agent • a substance that produces temporary irritating or disabling physical effects that disappear within minutes of removal from exposure. There is no significant risk of permanent injury, and medical treatment is rarely required.

riot control operations • the employment of riot control agents and/or special tactics, formations, and equipment in the control of violent disorders.

Rio Treaty • see INTER-AMERICAN TREATY OF RECIPROCAL ASSISTANCE

rip • *n.* **1** a stretch of fast-flowing and rough water in the sea or in a river, caused by the meeting of currents. **2** short for RIP CURRENT.

ripcord • *n.* a cord that is pulled to open a parachute.

rip current • an intermittent strong surface current flowing seaward from the shore.

ripe • *adj.* slang in mine warfare, a term once used to mean "armed."

Ripley, James Wolfe (1794–1870) • U.S. army officer. Ripley was born in Connecticut and graduated from WEST POINT in 1814 with a commission as a second lieutenant in artillery. When the CIVIL WAR began he was inspector of arsenals, but he was soon appointed head of the ORDNANCE DEPARTMENT and given the rank of brigadier general. Though he did improve the organization of the department, he is best known for his resistance to breechloading rifles for the infantry and repeating carbines for the cavalry. Eventually his lack of imagination and stubborness brought him into conflict with President ABRAHAM LINCOLN and Secretary of War EDWIN M. STANTON, and they forced him into retirement in 1863.

Ripper, Operation • the fourth of five offensives during the KOREAN WAR launched by U.N. forces, under the command of Lt. Gen. MATTHEW B. RIDGWAY, in early 1951. The success of these offensives—by the last Ridgway's army had once again crossed the 38TH PARALLEL—led President HARRY S. TRUMAN to invite the Communists to negotiate a cease fire. Gen. DOUGLAS MACARTHUR, however, broadcast an ultimatum to the enemy commander that undermined the president's plan, which ultimately resulted in Truman dismissing MacArthur on April 11, 1951.

riptide • *n.* another term for RIP CURRENT.

rising mine • a floating mine that is released from a sinker by influence of a proximate target or by a timing device and fired by contact, hydrostatic pressure, or other means.

riverboat • *n.* a boat with a shallow draft, designed for use on rivers.

riverine area • an inland or coastal area comprising both land and water, characterized by limited land lines of communication, with extensive water surface and/or inland waterways that provide natural routes for surface transportation and communications.

riverine assault • a rapid attack conducted by forces organized to cope with and exploit the unique characteristics of a riverine area.

riverine operations • operations conducted by forces organized to cope with and exploit the unique characteristics of a riverine area, to locate and destroy hostile forces, and/or to achieve or maintain control of the riverine area. Joint riverine operations combine land, naval, and air operations, as appropriate, and are suited to the nature of the specific riverine area in which operations are to be conducted.

river patrol boat • (**PBR**) a very maneuverable boat used to patrol rivers during the VIETNAM WAR. Each craft was armed with three .50 caliber machine guns and one grenade launcher, and carried a crew of five.

Riyadh |rē'yäd| • the capital of Saudi Arabia. It is situated on a high plateau in the center of the country.

RL • *abbr.* Radio Liberty.

RM • *abbr.* (in the UK) Royal Marines.

RMA • *abbr.* Royal Military Academy.

RN • *abbr.* (in the UK) Royal Navy.

RNAS • *abbr.* (in the UK) Royal Naval Air Station.

RNZAF • *abbr.* Royal New Zealand Air Force.

RNZN • *abbr.* Royal New Zealand Navy.

road capacity • the maximum traffic flow obtainable on a given roadway, using all available lanes, usually expressed in vehicles per hour or vehicles per day.

road net • the system of roads available within a particular locality or area.

roadstead • *n.* a partly sheltered stretch of water near the shore in which ships can ride at anchor.

Roberdeau, Daniel |ˌrōbər'dō| (1763–1829) • REVOLUTIONARY WAR army officer, born in the West Indies. Roberdeau moved to Philadelphia with his family upon the death of his father. He established a trading business and entered politics. In 1756 he won election to the state assembly, where he served five terms. As tensions between the colonies and England grew, he supported the nonimportation agreements and served on the Pennsylvania Committee of Safety. He was a brigadier general in the Pennsylvania Associators, a militia group, and fought in New Jersey, but illness limited his participation. He was appointed to the Continental Congress in 1777, where he was a radical patriot.

Roberdeau, Isaac (1763–1829) • military engineer. Son of DANIEL ROBERDEAU, Isaac was born in Philadelphia and studied engineering. He was an assistant (1791–92) to

PIERRE CHARLES L'ENFANT, who laid out the design for Washington, D.C., and was frequently caught up in disputes between the city's commissioners and L'Enfant, one of which resulted in Roberdeau's arrest for refusing to stop digging the foundations for the Capitol building, despite having been dismissed by the commissioners; Roberdeau said he took orders only from L'Enfant. When the WAR OF 1812 erupted he became a major in the Topographical Corps of Engineers. He helped survey part of the boundary between the United States and Canada (1815). In 1818 he became the Corps' chief.

Robert, Henry Martyn (1837–1923) • military engineer, born in South Carolina. Robert joined the ARMY CORPS OF ENGINEERS after graduating from the U.S. MILITARY ACADEMY. During the CIVIL WAR he sided with the North and taught military engineering at the Academy. In 1867 he became chief engineer for the Military Division of the Pacific, in San Francisco, where he helped design harbors and lighthouses. During this and other assignments, he continued an early interest in the rules of parliamentary procedure. In 1876 and prepared and published privately *Robert's Rules of Order*, a manual of rules for the orderly conduct of meetings that he distributed widely. The book was a success, and Robert updated and expanded it several times.

Roberts, Benjamin Stone (1810–75) • Union army officer. After four years of military service, Roberts joined the railroad industry, becoming chief engineer of the Champlain and Ogdensburg. In 1842 he traveled to Russia to help design a line from St. Petersburg to Moscow. In 1847 he rejoined the army and served ably under Gen. WINFIELD SCOTT in the MEXICAN WAR (1846–48), winning promotion to lieutenant colonel. He fought against Native Americans in the Southwest and, in 1861, as head of the Third U.S. Cavalry, opposed Confederate moves into the New Mexico Territory. In July 1862 he joined the Army of Virginia and played a minor role in the SECOND BATTLE OF BULL RUN (1862). Roberts's failure to defend the Baltimore and Ohio Railroad against Confederate attack (1863) temporarily cost him his command, but he returned to fighting in 1864.

Roberts Commission, the • an inquiry into the circumstances surrounding the Japanese attack on PEARL HARBOR created by an executive order of President FRANKLIN D. ROOSEVELT on December 18, 1941. The Roberts Commission panel consisted of a U.S. Supreme Court justice, two retired navy admirals, one retired Maj. Gen. of the Army and a Brig. Gen. of the Army. On January 23, 1942, the Roberts Commission concluded that the navy and army commanders of Hawaii, Rear Adm. HUSBAND E. KIMMEL and Maj. Gen. WALTER C. SHORT, were guilty of dereliction of duty and errors of judgment, forcing their retirement.

Robertson, James (1742–1814) • soldier and pioneer. The son of a Virginia planter, Robertson was an early settler in what became Tennessee. He arrived in 1771 near what is now Johnson City and became a leader in the "Watauga Association," which assumed executive, legislative, and judicial functions for the community. In 1779 he moved 200 miles further east, recruiting others to help him establish a community on the Cumberland River, at "Fort Nashborough," and again establishing a form of frontier government for the settlement. In 1783 North Carolina recognized the community as Davidson County and accepted Robertson into the House of Commons as its representative. Robertson was a member of the army during Tennessee's territorial period, reaching the rank of brigadier general. He served in the Tennessee Constitutional Convention (1796) and in the state senate (1798–99).

Robinson, John Cleveland (1817–97) • Union army officer. A New Yorker, Robinson fought in the MEXICAN WAR (1846–48). At the outbreak of the CIVIL WAR, he saved Fort McHenry from Confederate rioters. In 1862 he commanded a brigade in the ARMY OF THE POTOMAC and participated in the PENINSULAR CAMPAIGN and at ANTIETAM (both 1862) ; he was also present at FREDERICKSBURG (1862), CHANCELLORSVILLE (1863), and GETTYSBURG (1863). After losing a leg in an ill-considered attack at SPOTSYLVANIA (1864), he held administrative posts, including leadership of the Freedmen's Bureau in North Carolina. In 1894 he received the MEDAL OF HONOR for his actions at Spotsylvania.

ROC • the Republic of China, or Taiwan. Compare PRC.

rocker • *n.* **1** any of the curved stripes below the chevron of a noncommissioned officer above the rank of sergeant. **2** the curved strip above the chevron of a chief petty officer.

rocket • *n.* a self-propelled vehicle whose trajectory or course, while in flight, cannot be controlled.

rocket and missile artillery • long-range artillery fired from rocket-launchers and equipped with warheads. Missile artillery usually refers to guided missiles; rocket artillery refers to unguided artillery that depends on the initial trajectory and range for accuracy in hitting the target.entry was reversed

rocket, antiarmor • a hand-held, vehicle-mounted, or aircraft rocket designed to damage or destroy enemy armored vehicles.

rocketeer • *n.* a person who works with space rockets.

rocket platoon • a small military unit assigned to man a rocket-firing weapons system.

rocket propulsion • reaction propulsion wherein both the fuel and the oxidizer, generating the hot gases expended through a nozzle, are carried as part of the rocket engine.

Rocket propulsion differs from jet propulsion in that jet propulsion utilizes atmospheric air as an oxidizer, whereas rocket propulsion utilizes nitric acid or a similar compound as an oxidizer.

---

rocketry • *n.* **1** the branch of science that deals with rockets and rocket propulsion. **2** the use of rockets.

Rockwell International (or **Rockwell International Corporation**) • a high-technology and manufacturing corporation based in Seal Beach, California. Rockwell makes electronic controls for aircraft and communications and produces devices for industrial automation and electronic commerce. In 1967 the merger of North American Aviation, an airline manufacturer, and Rockwell-Standard Corporation, a manufacturer of automotive parts, formed North American Rockwell, and in 1973 the acquisition of Collins Radio Company gave rise to the name Rockwell International. In 1996 Rockwell sold its aerospace and defense businesses to Boeing Company of Seattle, Washington, for $3.2 billion, but military contracts remain a significant part of Rockwell's business. The company employs about 40,000 people and does business in more than eighty countries.

Rocky Flats Environmental Technology Site • established in 1952 and located approximately sixteen miles northwest of Denver, Colorado, the Rocky Flats facility was responsible for fabricating the hollow plutonium sphere—the trigger device for nuclear warheads—during the COLD WAR. Without a weapons production mission, Rocky Flats now manages its nuclear wastes and materials until there are national repositories for their storage.

rode • *n.* a rope, especially one securing an anchor or trawl.

Rodes, Robert Emmett (1829–64) • Confederate army officer. A Virginian, Rodes worked as an engineer and entered military service in 1861. He quickly rose to brigadier general; he and his brigade fought valiantly and sucessfully at SEVEN PINES (1862). The sacrifices made by Rodes's troops near ANTIETAM in 1862 earned the lane where they fought the sobriquet of BLOODY LANE; they helped hold the ground for Gen. ROBERT E. LEE until reinforcements could arrive. Rodes also fought bravely at CHANCELLORSVILLE and at GETTYSBURG, both in 1863, although to little effect. In 1864 he continued to fight effectively in the BATTLE OF THE WILDERNESS and at SPOTSYLVANIA; he was killed while fighting with Gen. JUBAL EARLY in the SHENANDOAH VALLEY.

Rodgers, George Washington (1822–63) • Union naval officer. The Brooklyn-born Rodgers began his naval career at a young age, serving in the West Indies, Africa, in the Mediterranean, and, during the MEXICAN WAR (1846–48), in the Gulf of Mexico. In 1861 he replaced his brother Christopher as commandant of midshipmen at the U.S. NAVAL ACADEMY but sought more active duty and received command of the new ship the *Toga*. After patrolling the James River, he was transferred to the West Indies in search of blockade runners. In 1863 he commanded an ironclad, the *Catskill*, in two unsuccessful attacks on Charleston Harbor. He was killed while commanding the *Catskill* in an attack on FORT WAGNER, in a third assault on the harbor.

Rodgers, John (1812–82) • Union naval officer. A native of Maryland, Rodgers entered the navy at sixteen. He served along the Florida coast in the SECOND SEMINOLE WAR. Rodgers was captured by Confederate troops in 1861, during the evacuation of the NORFOLK NAVY YARD at the outbreak of the CIVIL WAR, but he was quickly released, since Virginia had not yet joined the Confederacy. He helped outfit a squadron of gunboats for service on the Ohio and Mississippi; then, back at sea, he participated in the capture of Port Royal, South Carolina, and the blockade of Savannah. He commanded an ironclad, the *Galena*, a poorly designed ship whose crew took heavy casualties. His next ironclad, *Weehawken*, did better, defeating the Confederate ironclad *Atlanta* in 1863. After the war, Rodgers commanded the BOSTON NAVY YARD, served in Asia, and was superintendent of the NAVAL OBSERVATORY in Washington, D.C.

Rodgers, John (1881–1926) • naval officer and naval aviator, born in Washington, D.C. Son of JOHN RODGERS, a Union admiral. In 1911 he trained with ORVILLE WRIGHT and became the second man to qualify as a naval aviator; in 1912 he took the first aerial photograph for the navy. During WORLD WAR I he served aboard navy submarines, but in 1925, despite his marginal piloting skills, he was selected to pilot the navy's first trans-Pacific flight, from San Francisco to Hawaii. The plane ran out of fuel and was forced to land at sea; after some improvising, Rodgers and his crew were picked up by a submarine, only fifteen miles from Kauai. The 400-mile flight brought Rodgers national acclaim. After only a few weeks as assistant chief of the Bureau of Aeronautics, in Washington, D.C., Rodgers transferred out to take command of an experimental squadron of seaplanes. While he was flying to Philadelphia to take on his new position, his plane crashed, and Rodgers died of his injuries.

Rodman gun • a large cannon developed for use in the CIVIL WAR that overcame limitations in strength and durability of its predecessor, the COLUMBIAD, by use of improved casting methods. Guns were manufactured with bores up to 15 inches and capable of firing shells weighing as much as 330 pounds.

roentgen |ˈrentgən; ˈrənt-; -jən| • *n.* a unit of exposure dose of gamma (or X) radiation. One roentgen is essentially equal to one rad.

Rogers, Robert (1731–95) • guerrilla, trader, and scout. Rogers was born in Massachusetts but raised on the frontier. During the FRENCH AND INDIAN WAR (1754–63), he rose to the rank of rank of a group of 600 irregulars, called Rogers' RANGERS, who carried on guerrilla warfare against the enemy. After the war, he fought against the Cherokee (1761) and in PONTIAC'S REBELLION (1763–64). His play *Ponteach; or, the Savages of America* (1766) drew on these experiences. He sought leadership of an expedition to seek the Northwest Passage but was turned down and became commander of Fort Michilmackinac, in Michigan (1765–68). There he sponsored such an expedition on his own authority, which caused trouble with British authorities. He wound up in London, in debtors' prison, was bailed out, and returned to America in 1775, serving, it is believed, as a Tory spy during the REVOLUTIONARY WAR and leading a regiment that fought against the colonials in New York. In 1780 he returned to England, where he died in obscurity.

Rogue River War • a war between Native Americans and settlers in the Rogue River Valley of southwestern Oregon in 1855–56. It resulted in the Native Americans accepting confinement to reservations.

ROK • *abbr.* the Republic of Korea (South Korea).

ROKA • *abbr.* Republic of Korea Army.

roll • *v.* (of a moving ship, aircraft, or vehicle) rock or oscillate around an axis parallel to the direction of motion: *the ship pitched and rolled.* • *n.* **1** a swaying or oscillation of a ship, aircraft, or vehicle around an axis parallel to the direction of motion: *the jeep corners capably with a minimum of roll.* **2** an official list or register of names. **3** the total numbers on such a list: *a review to determine the reasons for diminishing rolls.*

PHRASES: **roll of honor** a list of those who have died in battle.

▸**roll something up** drive the flank of an enemy line back and around so that the line is shortened or surrounded.

DERIVATIVES: **rollable** *adj.*

rollback • *n.* the process of progressive destruction and/or neutralization of the opposing defenses, starting at the periphery and working inward, to permit deeper penetration of succeeding defense positions.

rolling barrage • an artillery barrage fired in front of advancing friendly troops and periodically moved closer to the enemy on a precisely-timed schedule so as to avoid hitting the advancing forces while remaining between them and the enemy.

rolling stock • **1** locomotives, carriages, wagons, or other vehicles used on a railroad. **2** the road vehicles of a trucking company.

Rolling Thunder, Operation • the longest air campaign in American military history, from March 1965 to November 1968 during the VIETNAM WAR, when combined U.S. forces flew more than two million sorties and dropped over one million tons of bombs on North Vietnam. Its goals were to demoralize the North Vietnamese, take out their logistical support, and to raise the morale of political and military elites of South Vietnam.

roll-in-point • the point at which aircraft enter the final leg of the attack.

roll-on roll-off • denoting a passenger ferry or other method of transportation in which vehicles are driven directly on at the start of the voyage or journey and driven off at the end.

roll-up • *n.* the process for orderly dismantling of facilities no longer required in support of operations and available for transfer to other areas.

Rommel, Erwin (1891–1944) • German field marshal, known as the "Desert Fox." After the annexation of Austria in 1938, Rommel became commandant of an officers' school near Vienna; his opportunity for advancement came in 1940, when he assumed command of the 7th Panzer Division, an armored division, providing leadership in the drive through France to the Channel coast. In February 1941 he was sent to save the floundering Italian army in Libya; his daring raids there won him a vast reputation, his nickname, and the attention of ADOLF HITLER, who promoted him to field marshal. In an attack on Cairo and on the Suez Canal, which Rommel opposed but Hitler ordered, the Germans were finally defeated by the British at EL ALAMEIN in 1942, and Hitler recalled him to Germany and placed him in charge of defending the French channel coast against attack by the Allies. His plan of defense, which accurately predicted that if the Allies reached the shore they would be unstoppable, did not win Hitler's support. His involvement with a plot to overthrow Hitler and take his place was discovered, and he committed suicide.

romper • *n.* a ship that has moved more than 10 nautical miles ahead of its convoy, and is unable to rejoin it.

Roosevelt Corollary • a declaration made by President THEODORE ROOSEVELT in December 1904 and based on the MONROE DOCTRINE. It authorized U.S. intervention in the affairs of neighboring American countries in order to counter threats posed to U.S. security and interests. After WOODROW WILSON used it in an attempt to establish a democratic government in Mexico, it was challenged by Republicans in a memorandum of December 17, 1928, and later by Democrats, in favor of a policy of non-intervention.

Roosevelt, Franklin Delano (1882–1945) • 32nd president of the United States. Born to a wealthy upstate New York family, Roosevelt was raised to a life of privilege. After graduating from Harvard and attending Columbia Law School, he practiced law and ran successfully for the state Senate in 1910. Although he won reelection easily in 1912, he left Albany in 1913 to become assistant secretary of the navy, in which position he advocated preparedness for WORLD WAR I. He left the navy post in 1920 to make an unsuccessful run for the vice presidency, with James M. Cox at the head of the ticket. A crippling attack of polio in 1921 led him to spend the next several years searching in vain for some treatment that would enable him to regain use of his legs. He returned to public life in 1928 with a successful run for the governorship of New York, where he developed modest programs to help combat the devastation of the Depression and began to call for federal efforts to combat the economic ruin facing the country. In 1932, having won a huge reelection victory in 1930, he took the Democratic nomination for president on the fourth ballot, pledging "a New Deal" for the country. He defeated HERBERT HOOVER by a comfortable margin and immediately began a remarkable campaign to rebuild the U.S. economy by creating numerous federal agencies that would offer employment opportunities to those out of work while providing economic support to those who could not work. These and other programs enjoyed varying degrees of success, but they began to change the nation's despairing mood. A second round of legislative initiatives, in 1935, dubbed the "Second New Deal," produced profound and sometimes permanent changes in the government's role in America's social patterns. As WORLD WAR II threatened the world's security, he also gradually moved the nation from its postwar isolationism to more active support of Great Britain, in particular, winning congressional approval for LEND-LEASE in 1940, which allowed him to provide Britain with arms without receiving payment for them; in 1941 he and British Prime Minister WINSTON CHURCHILL signed the ATLANTIC CHARTER, in which they condemned fascism and called for national self-determination. Later that year, he extended Lend-Lease to cover Russia. After Japan bombed PEARL HARBOR, on December 7, 1941, which Roosevelt called "a date which will live in infamy," the United States faced a two-front war; Roosevelt decided to concentrate on the war in Europe first. By 1943, the tide of the war seemed to have finally turned. In a series of summit meetings, Roosevelt, Churchill, and JOSEF STALIN negotiated plans for a long-planned Allied invasion of France's channel coast; the invasion was finally launched on June 6, 1944, D-DAY. Roosevelt easily won reelection to a fourth term in 1944; at a final summit, at YALTA, in the Crimea, in January 1945, he appeared frail and ill but vigorously participated in planning for a postwar Europe, although a real accord was reached only on division of Germany. He died of a cerebral hemorrhage at Warm Springs, Georgia, in April.

Roosevelt, Theodore (1858–1919) • 26th president of the United States. A frail, asthmatic youth, Roosevelt, born in New York City, fought against his infirmities and became an avid sportsman. He had an abiding interest in natural history and published a scholarly paper while still in college. By 1882, this prodigious polymath had also begun work on *The Naval War of 1812*, still recognized as a major work of scholarship. After college, he studied law but dropped out. He entered the New York State Assembly in 1882, where, although nominally a Republican, he quickly won a reputation for independence and supported a bundle of "good government" measures. After the death of his wife in 1884, he moved to his ranch in western Dakota and considered quitting politics and becoming a rancher. Nonetheless, in 1886 he ran for mayor of New York City, coming in third; he also remarried. In 1887 he became chairman of the U.S. Civil Service Commission, where he continued to emphasize merit as the basis for advancement. From 1895 to 1897, he served as New York City's police commissioner, tightening discipline and setting high standards for police officers. He was assistant secretary of the navy (1897–99) but resigned to organize a regiment of volunteer cavalry, called the "Rough Riders," whom he led in a famous assault on San Juan Heights, Cuba, during the SPANISH-AMERICAN WAR. In November 1898 he won election as governor of New York, on the strength of his war record and his ebullient personality. In that position he supported progressive measures such as limits on women and child labor, eliminated separate schools for white and black students, and made efforts to preserve the state's natural beauty. Roosevelt ran for vice president in the election of 1900 and became president in 1901 upon the assassination of President WILLIAM MCKINLEY. Believing that federal regulation was necessary to redress inequalities in the nation's social and economic spheres, he moved to break up the huge trusts that dominated the country's economy, beginning with the Northern Securities Company; he also used his influence, and threats of nationalization, to bring miners and owners back to the negotiating table during the 1902 coal strike and to win de facto recognition of the union. During his second term Roosevelt supported additional progressive legislation, including the Pure Food and Drug bill, the expansion of the civil service, and federal inspection of stockyards and slaughterhouses. He also continued to press for preservation of the nation's natural resources. In foreign policy, he supported a buildup of the navy, the OPEN DOOR POLICY in China, and U.S. hegemony in Latin America; he encouraged the revolution in Panama (1903) that allowed for the construction of the PANAMA CANAL, and believed peace could best be maintained by a balance of power. His mediation of the Russo-Japanese War (1905) earned him the Nobel Peace Prize. Despite Roosevelt's energy, his charisma, and his sprawling intellect, he did not command the loyalties of his fellow Republicans, who resented his domination of the party's politics, and who did not share his views on the role of the federal government. Roosevelt responded by condemning them as lackeys of the wealthy and by claiming that corporations were purchasing favors from politicians. In 1912, having been denied renomination by the Republican party, Roosevelt ran on as a third-party candidate representing the Progressive, or Bull Moose, party but came in second to WOODROW WILSON. From 1912 on, he wrote voluminously, explored Brazil, and advocated military preparedness as WORLD WAR I loomed, criticizing pacifists and advocating universal conscription. He supported Charles Evans Hughes for president in 1916 because he though Hughes would better prepare the nation for the inevitability of war. He eventually supported the LEAGUE OF NATIONS, although he continued to believe that U.S. military leadership was essential to world peace.

Roosevelt was, at forty-two, the youngest man ever to win the presidency.

Roosevelt, Theodore, Jr. (1887–1944) • army officer and CONGRESSIONAL MEDAL OF HONOR recipient, born in New York. The son of THEODORE ROOSEVELT and his second wife, Edith Kermit Carow Roosevelt, Roosevelt Jr. served in France during WORLD WAR I as a captain in the army. He was cited for gallantry and received the CROIX DE GUERRE, the DISTINGUISHED SERVICE CROSS, and the DISTINGUISHED SERVICE MEDAL. He helped found the AMERICAN LEGION to honor veterans and as a way to unite American society across racial and economic divisions. In 1919 he was elected to the New York State Assembly. In 1920, although his distant cousin FRANKLIN D. ROOSEVELT was running for vice president, he campaigned for the Republican presidential nominee, WARREN G. HARDING. After serving as assistant secretary of the navy and making an unsuccessful run in 1924 for the New York state governorship, he spent several years in Africa hunting and in 1929 was appointed governor of Puerto Rico; in 1932 he became governor general of the Philippines. Roosevelt spent the 1930s in business endeavors. He was commissioned a brigadier general in 1941, as the United States entered WORLD WAR II, and fought ably in North Africa and in Europe; at his request, he was in the first wave to land at UTAH BEACH, Normandy, on D-DAY. He died of a heart attack in his camp in Normandy; his courage and leadership on D-Day earned him a posthumous CONGRESSIONAL MEDAL OF HONOR.

Root, Elihu (1845–1937) • secretary of state, secretary of war and Nobel Prize winner, born in New York. Root was a successful trial lawyer who served the financial and social elite of his time. He befriended THEODORE ROOSEVELT in 1886 during Roosevelt's unsuccessful run for the New York mayoralty. In 1899 President WILLIAM MCKINLEY named him secretary of war, largely to support the economic development of America's colonial possessions. He resigned in 1904 but returned to Washington as Roosevelt's secretary of state in 1905. In that post he improved U.S. relations with the nations of Latin America but had more difficulty in stabilizing U.S. relations with Japan. He received the 1912 Nobel Peace Prize for his efforts to improve colonial administration and to achieve world peace. From 1909 to 1915 Root served in the Senate, where he sided with old-guard Republicans against Roosevelt, for which Roosevelt never forgave him, and opposed President WOODROW WILSON's attempts to maintain U.S. neutrality in WORLD WAR I. He supported the concept of a LEAGUE OF NATIONS but advocated preserving America's right to decide when to support the territorial and political independence of other nations.

rope • *n.* an element of chaff consisting of a long roll of metallic foil or wire that is designed for broad, low- frequency responses.

Ropes, Joseph (1770–1850) • ship captain and privateer. The Massachusetts-born Ropes went to sea at a young age and at twenty-four commanded his own ship. Back home, he entered politics and also became a privateer, operating out of Salem. He captured several English brigs during the WAR OF 1812 and was hailed a hero in Massachusetts.

rope yarn • loosely twisted fibers used for making the strands of rope.

Rosecrans, William Starke (1819–98) • Union army officer and U.S. representative, born in Ohio. Rosecrans served as a military engineer after his graduation from the U.S. MILITARY ACADEMY and then resigned his commission to go into business. When the CIVIL WAR broke out, he quickly reenlisted and in 1861 was commissioned colonel of engineers. He also became a brigadier general in the regular army. Feeling that his contributions were underappreciated, he complained to Secretary of War EDWIN M. STANTON; however, he overreached on his first assignment by hatching a plan to capture the Confederate general THOMAS "STONEWALL" JACKSON, which, when brought to light, earned him a reprimand. He continued to have an undistinguished record in field command. When he assumed command of the ARMY OF THE CUMBERLAND in 1862, he rejuvenated the demoralized unit; his victory over Gen. BRAXTON BRAGG in Tennessee in December made him the Union's most celebrated commander. He followed that up with another victory over Bragg in June 1863. Despite this, his failure to defeat Bragg again later that year because of a combination of excessive pride, a tendency to underestimate his opponent, and a propensity for delaying action led to his removal from command.

Rosenberg, Ethel (1915–53) • spy. Raised on the Lower East Side in her native New York, Rosenberg held clerical jobs and was a union organizer before marrying JULIUS ROSENBERG in 1939. In the years that followed, she devoted herself to raising her children. In August 1950 Ethel Rosenberg was arrested and charged with spying for the Soviet Union along with her husband; the two were accused of passing on information related to the atomic bomb. Ethel's brother, David Greenglass, provided damaging testimony against the Rosenbergs, placing them at the center of a spy ring. The Rosenbergs' attorney provided a weak defense, and the two were convicted and sentenced to death on April 5, 1951. Despite pleas from around the world that the sentences be commuted, the anti-Communist fervor of the times, along with latent anti-Semitism, prevailed, and the two were executed on June 19, 1953. In the decades that followed, serious questions about aspects of the government's case and the reliability of its witnesses were raised; evidence provided by the Russians after the fall of the Soviet Union and by the Federal Bureau of Investigation, while tending to confirm Julius Rosenberg's guilt, leave open the question of his wife's involvement. The authenticity of this evidence has been challenged by the Rosenbergs' sons.

Rosenberg, Julius (1918–53) • spy. Rosenberg was raised in an Orthodox Jewish family on New York's Lower East Side. At City College, he studied electrical engineering and was active in leftwing activities. In 1945 Julius was removed from his position with the ARMY SIGNAL CORPS on grounds that he was a Communist, which he denied. He opened his own machine shop in partnership with his wife Ethel's brother, David Greenglass, who during WORLD WAR II had worked on the atomic bomb at the Los Alamos, New Mexico, laboratory. In 1950, the Rosenbergs were arrested and charged with spying for the Soviet Union; the government alleged that they had passed secrets on the design of the atomic bomb to a confederate who then passed them on to the Soviets. The Rosenbergs denied the charges but were convicted on April 5, 1951, and sentenced to death. Efforts across the world to have the sentences commuted failed, given the raging anti-Communism that prevailed and the less open anti-Semitism, and the two were executed on June 19, 1953. In the decades since, information released by the Federal Bureau of Investigation and by the Russian government have tended to confirm Julius's guilt, although there is less certainty about Ethel's; the Rosenbergs' sons have challenged the authenticity of these documents.

Rosendahl, Charles Emery (1892–1977) • naval aviator. The naval career of the Chicago-born Rosendahl was unexpectedly changed when he was appointed flight officer on the U.S.S *Shenandoah*, the navy's first lighter-than-air ship, in 1923. Rosendahl's brave actions when the airship crashed and burned on its second flight won him command of a second airship, which was used for research and observation. In 1929 he flew around the world as an observer on the *Graf Zeppelin*, on a voyage financed by William Randolph Hearst. Rosendahl continued to command both airships and to sail on regular ships over the next several years; the crash of the *Hindenburg* in 1937, at which Rosendahl was present, ended the lighter-than-air ship phase of aviation.

Rosie the Riveter • a fictional character created during WORLD WAR II to symbolize women working in the war industries (for example, as riveters in aircraft factories). Rosie was often depicted wearing overalls and work gloves with her hair tied up in a polka-dot cloth.

Ross, Betsy (1752–1836) • seamstress and war hero. Born Elizabeth Griscom in Philadelphia, Pennsylvania, she married John Ross, an Anglican, in 1773 and as a result was expelled from her native Quaker church. John Ross was killed in a gunpowder explosion in January 1776, leaving his upholstery business to his wife, a skilled seamstress. She later remarried, was widowed, and married a third time. Betsy Ross is the subject of a cherished American legend according to which GEORGE WASHINGTON, representing the Continental Congress, visited her husband's shop in the summer of 1776 and commissioned her to make the first American flag, which is said to be partly of her design. This story was apparently first told by her grandson in 1870 at a meeting of the Historical Society of Pennsylvania. In fact, there is little to support its veracity. Washington was at the front when he is supposed to have visited Ross in her Philadelphia shop, and the design of the flag was not fixed that early in the nation's history. However, Betsy Ross did in fact make flags for the new nation; in 1777 Ross received payment of £15 from the Pennsylvania State Navy Board for making ships' flags.

Rosser, Thomas Lafayette (1836–1910) • Confederate army officer, born in Virginia but raised in Texas, Rosser enlisted in the Confederate army immediately after the bombardment of FORT SUMTER (1861). He rose steadily through the ranks, rising to major general, and fought at a number of major engagements, including GETTYSBURG (1863), and he won the last major cavalry victory of the ARMY OF NORTHERN VIRGINIA (1865). When the SPANISH-AMERICAN WAR (1898) broke out, Rosser was appointed brigadier general of volunteers and trained several regiments.

roster • *n.* a list or plan showing turns of duty or leave for individuals or groups in an organization: *next week's duty roster.*

Rostow thesis • the proposition, developed by WALT W. ROSTOW, which held that an externally supported insurgency could be defeated only by military action against the external source of support. Rostow's thesis led inevitably to the United States military strategy in the VIETNAM WAR which was based on a series of escalating military measures designed to raise the cost of supporting the Communist insurgency in South Vietnam.

Rostow, Walt W. (1916?–) • national security adviser, born in New York City. Rostow, educated at Yale and at Oxford, served with the OFFICE OF STRATEGIC SERVICES during WORLD WAR II and later taught history at the Massachusetts Institute of Technology. From 1961 to 1966 he chaired the State Department's policy planning council; from 1966 to 1969 he was national security adviser to President LYNDON B. JOHNSON and an architect of U.S. policy in the VIETNAM WAR, where he strongly supported U.S. military intervention. He received the Presidential Medal of Freedom in 1969.

rotary • *adj.* **1** revolving around a center or axis; rotational: *a rotary motion.* **2** (of a thing) acting by means of rotation, especially (of a machine) operating through the rotation of some part: *a rotary mower.*

ROTC • *abbr.* Reserve Officers' Training Corps.

rotor • *n.* a rotary part of a machine or vehicle, especially a hub with a number of radiating airfoils that is rotated in an approximately horizontal plane to provide the lift for a rotary-wing aircraft.

Rough Riders Regiment • the First Volunteer Cavalry Regiment, commanded by Col.

THEODORE ROOSEVELT (then Secretary of the Navy) in the SPANISH-AMERICAN WAR (1898–1902), and famous for its advance up SAN JUAN HEIGHTS (near Santiago, Cuba) and destruction of the Spanish blockhouse at its top.

roulement |ro͞ol'mäN| • *n.* movement of troops or equipment, especially for a short period of duty to relieve another force.

round • *n.* the amount of ammunition needed to fire one shot. • *v.* pass and go around (something) so as to move on in a changed direction: *the ship rounded the cape at dawn.*

roundel • *n.* **1** a small disk, especially a decorative medallion. **2** Brit. a circular identifying mark painted on military aircraft, as, for example, the red, white, and blue of the RAF.

roundhouse • *n.* a cabin or set of cabins on the after part of the quarterdeck of a sailing ship.

rounds complete • in artillery and naval gunfire support, the term used to report that the number of rounds specified in fire for effect have been fired.

round shot • ammunition in the form of cast-iron or steel spherical balls for firing from cannon.

Round Top • the name of two prominences on the battlefield of GETTYSBURG (1863). **Big Round Top** is 785 feet above sea level and **Little Round Top** is 650 feet. Both were strategic positions in the battle, particularly Little Round Top, from which Confederate sharpshooters sniped at Union troops.

Roundup, Operation • was the second of five offensives launched by U.N. forces during the KOREAN WAR in early 1951. The success of these offensives led President HARRY S. TRUMAN to invite the Communists to negotiate a cease fire. Gen. DOUGLAS MACARTHUR, however, broadcast an ultimatum to the enemy commander that undermined the president's plan. After Congressman Joseph Martin released a letter from MacArthur in which the general repeated his criticism of the administration, Truman began the process which was to end with MacArthur's being relieved from command on April 11, 1951.

Rousseau, Lovell Harrison |ro͞o'sō| (1818–69) • Union army officer and U.S. representative, born in Kentucky. Rousseau helped to prevent its secession from the Union as the CIVIL WAR approached. When the war started, he became a brigade general and in 1862 assumed command of the Fifth Army of the Cumberland. From 1863 to 1865 he commanded of the districts of Nashville and middle Tennessee. When the war ended, he returned to Kentucky and resumed his political career. He served in the U.S. House of Representatives from 1865 to July 1866, when he resigned after being censured for assaulting another House member; his Kentucky constituency reelected him, and he served from December 1866 to March 1867.

rout • *n.* **1** a disorderly retreat of defeated troops: *the retreat degenerated into a rout.* **2** a decisive defeat: *the party lost more than half their seats in the rout.* • *v.* defeat and cause to retreat in disorder: *in a matter of minutes the attackers were routed.*
PHRASES: **put to rout** put to flight; defeat utterly.

route |ro͞ot; rowt| • *n.* **1** a way or course taken in getting from a starting point to a destination: *our route was via the Jerusalem road.* **2** the line of a road, path, railroad, etc. • *v.* (**routing**) send or direct along a specified course: *all lines of communication were routed through Atlanta.*

route capacity • **1** the maximum traffic flow of vehicles in one direction at the most restricted point on the route. **2** the maximum number of metric tons that can be moved in one direction over a particular route in one hour. It is calculated as the product of the maximum traffic flow and the average payload of the vehicles using the route.

route march • a march for troops over a designated route, typically via roads or tracks.

route reconnaissance • reconnaissance along a specific line of communications (such as road, railway, or waterway), to provide new or updated information on route conditions and activities along the route.

ROV • *abbr.* remotely operated vehicle.

rove • *v.* travel constantly without a fixed destination; wander: *a quarter of a million refugees roved around the country.*

Rowan, Stephen Clegg (1808–90) • Union naval officer, born in Ireland. In the CIVIL WAR, he was part of the unsuccessful effort to relieve FORT SUMTER in 1861 and participated in the evacuation of the NORFOLK NAVY YARD. He commanded the naval force that helped achieve Union victory at and occupation of Alexandria, Virginia, in 1861 and supported the successful action at Roanoke Island in 1862. After the war, he headed the Norfolk Navy Yard and then the New York Navy Yard, among other assignments; he retired in 1889.

rowboat |'rō,bōt| • *n.* a small boat propelled by oars.

rowlock |'rō,läk| • *n.* chiefly Brit. an oarlock.

Royal Air Force • (**RAF**) the air forces of the United Kingdom. The successor to the Royal Flying Corps, the RAF was created in 1918 and played a major role in the defense of Britain and the defeat of the Axis Powers in WORLD WAR II. Perhaps its best known element was Fighter Command, which successfully defended against the German LUFTWAFFE in the BATTLE OF BRITAIN in the summer and fall of 1940.

Royal Americans • a British regiment of four battalions, designated the 62d Regiment of Foot at first, then redesignated the 60th (Royal American) Regiment of Foot, and first recruited in 1755 for service in North America. Its soldiers were approximately one fourth Americans (of various kinds), one half from Ireland, and the rest were a miscellany of Germans, Poles, and Bohemians.

Royal British Legion • British veterans' organization formed in 1921 to aid ex-servicemen and servicewomen and their dependents. Compare AMERICAN LEGION.

Royal Engineers • the sapper corps of the British army responsible for construction of fortifications, camps, airfields, roads, and railways; demolition operations; and mining operations. The Royal Engineers were also responsible in overseas theaters for the supply of water, and, curiously, the operation of the military postal system.

Royal Flying Corps • the British air force in WORLD WAR I. On April 1, 1918, the Royal Flying Corps was merged with the Royal Naval Air Service to form the ROYAL AIR FORCE (RAF).

Royal Marines • an integral part of the British Royal Navy and founded in 1664, the Royal Marines had the traditional role aboard ship of maintaining order, helping man the guns of larger vessels, and sweeping the enemy's decks with rifle fire and grenades. Traditionally, the Royal Marines also participated in naval expeditions ashore (such as the "cutting out" of enemy ships or the attack of coastal fortifications), but it was not until WORLD WAR II that the Royal Marines, like their United States counterparts, were formally vested with responsibility for amphibious and commando operations.

Royal Military Academy • see SANDHURST.

Royal Navy • (**RN**) the navy of the United Kingdom. It was the most powerful navy in the world from the 17th century until WORLD WAR II. It is the "Senior Service" of the British armed forces, its headquarters, the Admiralty, having been founded during the reign of King Henry VIII in the 16th century.

RPG • *abbr.* rocket-propelled grenade.

RPV • *abbr.* remotely piloted vehicle.

RSM • *abbr.* (in the British army) Regimental Sergeant Major.

rubbing strake • a protective strip running along a boat's side below the gunwale to prevent damage when coming alongside something.

rudder • *n.* **1** a flat piece hinged vertically near the stern of a boat or ship for steering. **2** a vertical airfoil pivoted from the tailplane of an aircraft, for controlling movement around the vertical axis. **3** application of a rudder in steering a boat, ship, or aircraft: *bring the aircraft to a stall and apply **full rudder.***

Ruger, Thomas Howard (1833–1907) • Union army officer, born in New York but raised in Wisconsin. Ruger was part of the ARMY CORPS OF ENGINEERS but preferred civilian life, so he resigned and studied law. When the CIVIL WAR erupted, he sought active service and trained the Third Wisconsin, becoming colonel of the regiment. He fought in the SHENANDOAH VALLEY in 1862 and was slightly wounded at ANTIETAM that same year. Promoted to brigadier general of volunteers, he fought bravely at CHANCELLORSVILLE (1863) and at GETTYSBURG (1863). He was also part of Gen. WILLIAM T. SHERMAN's advance on ATLANTA (1864) and, as brevet major general of volunteers, of Sherman's MARCH TO THE SEA. In 1871 he became superintendent of the U.S. MILITARY ACADEMY; in 1876 he returned to the Department of the South.

Rugged, Operation • the last of five offensives during the KOREAN WAR launched by U.N. forces, under the command of Lt. Gen. MATTHEW B. RIDGWAY, in early 1951. The success of these offensives—Ridgway's army had once again crossed the 38TH PARALLEL—led President HARRY S. TRUMAN to invite the Communists to negotiate a cease fire. Gen. DOUGLAS MACARTHUR, however, broadcast an ultimatum to the enemy commander that undermined the president's plan, which ultimately resulted in Truman relieving MacArthur from command on April 11, 1951.

Ruhr Industrial Region |ro͝or| • a region of coal mining and heavy industry in North Rhine-Westphalia, western Germany. The Ruhr was occupied by French troops 1923–24, after Germany defaulted on war reparation payments. The Ruhr area is one of the world's largest industrial regions and Germany's most densely populated region. Because of its resources and industry, the Ruhr played a major role in Germany's preparations for WORLD WAR II. The Allies bombed the region heavily, destroying about seventy-five percent of the area and disabling one third of its coal mines.

rule of the road • a custom or law regulating the direction in which two vehicles (or riders or ships) should move to pass one another on meeting, or which should yield to the other, so as to avoid collision.

rules of engagement • directives issued by competent military authority which delineate the circumstances and limitations under which military forces will initiate and/or continue combat engagement with other forces encountered.

Rules of Land Warfare, The • a manual issued by the Union army in 1863, during the CIVIL WAR, as General Order 100. It detailed regulations for the treatment of POWs and enemy civilians in occupied territory.

Rumaila, Battle of • the last battle of the PERSIAN GULF WAR, on March 2, 1991. It took place on the Rumaila oilfield on the Kuwait-Iraq border. American ground and air units made a devastating and aggressive attack on a REPUBLICAN GUARD tank division in one of the most one-sided battles of the war, the day before it formally ended. Congressional inquiry into the battle did not find any fault.

rummage • *v.* (of a customs officer) make a thorough search of (a vessel): *our brief was to rummage as many of the vessels as possible.* • *n.* a thorough search of a vessel by a customs officer.

DERIVATIVES: **rummager** *n.*

Rumsfeld, Donald (1932–) • secretary of defense, 1975–77; 2001–. Born in Chicago, Illinois, Rumsfeld served four terms in Congress, beginning in 1962. He also served at Ambassador to NATO. In 1975 he was named by President GERALD R. FORD to serve as secretary of defense. He was the youngest person to ever serve in that position. In 2001,

President GEORGE W. BUSH recalled him to that position for his cabinet.

run • *v.* (**running**; past **ran**; past part. **run**) **1** move at a speed faster than a walk, never having both or all the feet on the ground at the same time. **2** run as a sport or for exercise: *I run every morning.* **3** (of a boat) sail directly before the wind, especially in bad weather. **4** navigate (rapids or a waterfall) in a boat. **5** (of the sea, the tide, or a river) rise higher or flow more quickly: *there was still a heavy sea running.* **6** bring (goods) into a country illegally and secretly; smuggle: *they run drugs for the cocaine cartels.* • *n.* **1** the distance covered in a specified period, especially by a ship: *a record run of 398 miles from noon to noon.* **2** a short flight made by an aircraft on a straight and even course at a constant speed before or while dropping bombs. **3** a quantity or amount of something produced at one time: *a production run of only 150 jeeps.* **4** the after part of a ship's bottom where it rises and narrows toward the stern.

PHRASES: **run a blockade** see BLOCKADE. **run afoul** (or **foul**) **of** collide or become entangled with (an obstacle or another vessel): *another ship ran afoul of us.*

▸**run someone/something down** (of a boat) collide with another vessel.

run someone/something through stab a person or animal so as to kill them.

runabout • *n.* **1** a small motorboat used for quick trips. **2** a small light aircraft.

runner • *n.* **1** a messenger in the army. **2** a person who smuggles specified goods into or out of a country or area: *a drug-runner.* **3** a rope run through a block.

running battle • a military engagement that does not occur at a fixed location.

running fire • successive gunshots from a line of troops.

running gear • **1** the moving parts of a machine, especially the wheels, steering, and suspension of a vehicle. **2** the moving rope and tackle used in handling a boat.

running knot • a knot that slips along the rope and changes the size of the loop it forms.

running lights • **1** another term for NAVIGATION LIGHTS. **2** small lights on a motor vehicle that remain illuminated while the vehicle is running.

running rigging • see RIGGING (sense 1).

runway • *n.* a defined rectangular area of an airfield, prepared for the landing and takeoff runs of aircraft along its length.

Rush-Bagot Agreement • an accord between the U.S. and Britain after the WAR OF 1812 to end naval rivalry on the Great Lakes. Negotiations for the accord began in April 1817 in letters between British minister Charles Bagot and Acting U.S. Secretary of State Richard Rush. It was ratified by the Senate in 1818.Each side pledged to maintain only one ship on Lakes Champlain and Ontario, and only two on the remaining Great Lakes. It also established peaceful border relations between the United States and Canada. It was the first qualitative disarmament treaty in history.

Rusk, Dean (1909–1994) • U.S. secretary of state during the administrations of Presidents JOHN F. KENNEDY and LYNDON B. JOHNSON, and a stalwart defender of the United States's involvement in Vietnam amidst growing opposition to the war. After World War II, Rusk held positions in the state and war departments, and, in 1950, he became assistant secretary of state for Far Eastern affairs and was involved in prosecuting the KOREAN WAR, which he supported. From 1952–1960 he served as president of the Rockefeller Foundation. In 1961 President Kennedy chose him as his secretary of state, and, after Kennedy's assassination, Lyndon Johnson kept him on.

Russell, David Allen (1820–64) • Union army officer, born in New York. Russell fought in the MEXICAN WAR (1846–48). At the outbreak of the CIVIL WAR, he obtained a command in Massachusetts; he and his regiment fought with the ARMY OF THE POTOMAC in the PENINSULAR CAMPAIGN of 1862. That year he was promoted to brigadier general of volunteers. His regiment fought at CHANCELLORSVILLE (1863) and was present but saw little action at GETTYSBURG (1863). In November of that year he led a brilliant assault on the forces of Gen. JUBAL EARLY at Rappahannock Station, capturing more than 1,300 men. He took on command of the First Division when the commander of the Sixth Corps was killed at SPOTSYLVANIA (1864). Russell himself was killed in action as Union troops pursued Early into the Shenandoah Valley.

Russki (or **Russky**) • *n.* informal a Russian.

ORIGIN: mid 19th century: from Russian *russkiĭ* 'Russian', or from Russian, on the pattern of Russian surnames ending in -skiĭ.

Russo-Japanese War • a war fought 1904–05 between Russia and Japan over conflicting claims to sovereignty in parts of east Asia. The Russians were decisively defeated and abandoned their expansionist policies. The war shifted the balance of power in the East and also changed the perception of modern warfare, presaging many of the strategies deployed in WORLD WAR I.

Rutherford, Griffith (1721?–1805) • Revolutionary army officer, born in Ireland. Rutherford emigrated to Pennsylvania as a child. He moved to North Carolina, where he became a surveyor and landowner, joined the militia, and served in the North Carolina Assembly (1766–75). He responded to the REGULATOR movement with tact and, when the REVOLUTIONARY WAR broke out, became a local political and military leader, serving on the local committee of safety and becoming a colonel in the militia. He decisively put down a Cherokee uprising in 1776 and entered the North Carolina Senate, serving from 1777 to 1786 (except for two years spent as a British prisoner, from 1780 to 1781). In 1781, returning to North Carolina, he put together a force that effectively purged the region of Loyalists. After the war, he remained in the State Senate.

Ryswick, Peace of • a treaty signed at Ryswick, a Dutch village near The Hague, on September 20, 1697. It ended King William's War, which included raids by French and English colonists, aided by Indians, on each other's settlements. It called for the mutual restoration of all conquests but left the colonial problem unresolved. In 1702 warfare resumed in Queen Anne's War.

Ss

S-1 • **1** a code name for the development project that led to atomic bomb; the predecessor of the Manhattan Project. **2** see General Staff.

S-2 • see General Staff.

S-3 • **1** see Viking. **2** see General Staff.

S-4 • see General Staff.

S-5 • see General Staff.

SA • *abbr.* Sturmabteilung.

SAB • *abbr.* Science Advisory Board.

saber (Brit. **sabre**) • *n.* **1** a heavy cavalry sword with a curved blade and a single cutting edge. **2** a light fencing sword with a tapering blade.

sabot • *n.* a device that ensures the correct positioning of a bullet or shell in the barrel of a gun, attached either to the projectile or inside the barrel and falling away as it leaves the muzzle.

sabotage |ˈsæbəˌtäzʜ| • *n.* an act or acts with intent to injure, interfere with, or obstruct the national defense of a country by willfully injuring or destroying, or attempting to injure or destroy, any national defense or war material, premises, or utilities, to include human and natural resources.

Sabre • (**F-86**) the first U.S. Air Force swept-wing fighter, and the aircraft that opposed the MiG-15 during the Korean War. Although the early models of the F-86 were slower and heavier than the Soviet fighter, more powerful engines and the redesigned wings significantly improved the capabilities of later types.

sabretache |ˈsäbərˌtæsʜ| • *n.* a flat satchel on long straps worn by some cavalry and horse artillery officers from the left of the waist-belt.

SAC |sæk| • *abbr.* **1** Senior Aircraftman. **2** Strategic Air Command.

SACEUR |ˈsækˌyo͝or| • *abbr.* (**Supreme Allied Commander in Europe**) the U.S. military officer who is the chief U.S. and NATO military commander in Europe.

sack-coat fatigue blouse • a loose fitting blue woolen uniform coat worn by soldiers of the U.S. Army from before the Civil War to just before World War I.

SACLANT |ˈsækˌlant| • *abbr.* Supreme Allied Atlantic (NATO).

SACW • *abbr.* senior aircraftwoman.

safe anchorage • an anchorage considered safe from enemy attack, and to which merchant ships may be ordered to proceed when the shipping movement policy is implemented.

safe area • an area not liable to attack, especially one designated as such by the United Nations.

Safeguard missile defense system • U.S. Army ballistic missile defense system employing anti-ballistic missile missiles and various ground radar systems designed to detect and accurately track incoming land-based ICBMs at a range of 1,500-3,000 kilometers. Safeguard was deployed in 1974 at Grand Forks, North Dakota, but was deactivated a year later due to ineffectiveness and high costs.

safe house • an innocent-appearing house or premises established by an organization for the purpose of conducting clandestine or covert activity in relative security.

safety boat • an accompanying boat providing support in case of emergency, especially in water sports or competitive situations.

safety fuse • a fuse that burns at a constant slow rate, used for the controlled firing of a detonator.

safety lane • a specified sea lane designated for use in transit by submarine and surface ships to prevent attack by friendly forces.

safety lock (also **safety catch**) • a device that prevents a gun from being fired or a machine from being operated accidentally.

safing and arming mechanism • a mechanism whose primary purpose is to prevent an unintended functioning of the main charge of the ammunition prior to completion of the arming delay and, in turn, allow the explosive train of the ammunition to function after arming.

Sagger • see AT-3.

Saigon |sīˈgän; ˈsīgän| • a city and port on the south coast of Vietnam. It was the capital of the French colony established in Vietnam in the 19th century, becoming capital of South Vietnam in the partition of 1954. The official name (since 1975) is Ho Chi Minh City.

Saigon, battle for • (April 30, 1975) intense fighting in the Vietnam War in early 1968 following the Tet Offensive, when the Vietcong invaded Saigon. The month-long clash caused political uproar in the United States, especially when the Vietcong briefly infiltrated the U.S. Embassy compound, forcing an evacuation.

sail • *n.* **1** a piece of material extended on a mast to catch the wind and propel a boat, ship, or other vessel: *all the sails were unfurled.* **2** the use of sailing ships as a means of transport: *this led to bigger ships as steam replaced sail.* **3** a voyage or excursion in a ship, especially a sailing ship or boat: *they went for a sail.* **4** archaic a sailing ship: *sail ahoy!* **5** something resembling a sail in shape or function, especially the conning tower of a submarine. • *v.* **1** travel in a ship or boat using sails or engine power: *the ferry caught fire sailing between Caen and Portsmouth.* **2** begin a voyage; leave a harbor: *the catamaran sails at 3:30.* **3** travel by ship on or across (a sea) or on (a route): *plastic ships could be sailing the oceans soon.* **4** navigate or control (a boat or ship): *I stole a small fishing boat and sailed it to the Delta.*

PHRASES: **in** (or **under**) **full sail** with all the sails in position or fully spread: *a galleon in full sail.* **sail close to** (or **near**) **the wind** sail as nearly against the wind as possible. **take in sail** furl the sail or sails of a vessel. **under sail** with the sails hoisted: *at a speed of eight knots under sail.*

DERIVATIVES: **sailable** *adj.* **sailed** *adj. a black-sailed ship.*

sailboat • *n.* a boat propelled by sails.

sail close to the wind (or **sail near the wind**) |wind| • sail as nearly against the wind as possible while still making headway.

sailer • *n.* a sailing ship or boat of specified power or manner of sailing: *the great ships were abominable sailers: sluggish and difficult to maneuver | a four-masted motor sailer.*

sailing • *n.* **1** the action of sailing in a ship or boat: *a sailing club.* **2** an act of beginning a voyage or of leaving a harbor.

sailing master • an officer responsible for the navigation of a ship or yacht.

sailing orders • instructions to the captain of a vessel regarding such matters as time of departure and destination.

sailing ship • a ship driven by sails.

sailmaker • *n.* a person who makes, repairs, or alters sails as a profession.

DERIVATIVES: **sailmaking** *n.*

sailor • *n.* a person whose job it is to work as a member of the crew of a commercial or naval ship or boat, especially one who is below the rank of officer.

DERIVATIVES: **sailorly** *adj.*

Sailor's Creek, Battle of • a late CIVIL WAR battle fought along Sailor's Creek in Virginia that signaled the demise of the Confederate Army. A quarter of the army that was already retreating was cut off by Union forces under Gen. PHILIP H. SHERIDAN on April 6, 1865. Most of them surrendered, including nine Confederate generals.

sail plan • a scale diagram of the masts, spars, rigging, and sails of a sailing vessel.

Saint • a satellite inspector system designed to demonstrate the feasibility of intercepting, inspecting, and reporting on the characteristics of satellites in orbit.

Saipan • an island of the western Pacific, now part of the Northern Marianas Islands, that was captured from the Japanese by U.S. forces in June 1944 and thereafter used as a base from which to launch attacks against the Japanese mainland.

saker • a light cannon with a bore or four inches or less, much used in sieges and on ships in the 16th century.

Salerno landing • a major WORLD WAR II Allied landing of troops and materiel at the Italian port of Salerno in 1943, supported mainly by U.S. and British warships. It was the last major effort in the attempt to attack Europe from the "soft underbelly," rather than from across the Channel.

salient |'sālyənt; -lēənt| • *n.* **1** a piece of land or section of fortification that juts out to form an angle. **2** an outward bulge in a line of military attack or defense.

sally port • a small exit point in a fortification for the passage of troops when making a sally.

saloon pistol • a pistol designed for accuracy mainly at close range, for use in shooting galleries.

salted weapon • a nuclear weapon that contains elements or isotopes for capturing neutrons at the time of the explosion and from them produce radioactive products supplementary to the usual debris.

SALT I Treaty • an agreement signed in 1972 by U.S. President RICHARD M. NIXON and Soviet leader LEONID BREZHNEV after the first round of Strategic Arms Limitations Talks (SALT I), held from 1969–72. It consisted of the ANTI-BALLISTIC MISSILE TREATY and an Interim Agreement on the Limitation of Strategic Offensive Arms.

SALT II Treaty • an agreement signed in 1979 by U.S. President JIMMY CARTER and Soviet leader LEONID BREZHNEV after the second round of Strategic Arms Limitations Talks (SALT II), held from 1972–79. It restricted the number of each side's strategic weapons, and its goal was to replace the Interim Agreement reached in SALT I. The U.S. Senate never ratified the treaty, partly in protest to the 1979 Soviet invasion of Afghanistan, but both countries observed its major limitations until 1986.

Saltonstall, Dudley (1738–96) • REVOLUTIONARY WAR naval officer. Saltonstall was born into a prominent Connecticut family that descended from founders of Massachusetts Bay. He went to sea while still young and was a privateer during the FRENCH AND INDIAN WARS (1754–63). He enlisted in the Revolutionary cause at the outbreak of fighting and, because of family connections, was commissioned a captain in the Continental navy and given a command. In battle with a British ship, he and the others ships in his squadron allowed the British ship to escape, but Saltonstall was cleared of any wrongdoing in the affair. In 1797 he led a disastrous assault on British ships in Penobscot Bay, Maine; delays among the Continentals had allowed British reinforcements to arrive, and the Americans lost every vessel in the squadron. Saltonstall was blamed for the debacle and dismissed from the navy.

saltpeter |sôlt'pētər| (Brit. **saltpetre**) • *n.* another term for POTASSIUM NITRATE.

salute • *n.* **1** a prescribed or specified movement, typically a raising of a hand to the head, made by a member of a military or similar force as a formal sign of respect or recognition. **2** the discharge of a gun or guns as a formal or ceremonial sign of respect or celebration: *a twenty-one-gun salute.* • *v.* make a formal salute to: *don't you usually salute a superior officer?* | *he clicked his heels and saluted.*
PHRASES: **take the salute** (of a senior officer in the armed forces or other person of importance) acknowledge formally a salute given by a body of troops marching past.
DERIVATIVES: **saluter** *n.*

salvage • *v.* rescue (a wrecked or disabled ship or its cargo) from loss at sea: *an emerald and gold cross was salvaged from the wreck.* • *n.* **1** the rescue of a wrecked or disabled ship or its cargo from loss at sea: *a salvage operation was under way.* **2** the cargo saved from a wrecked or sunken ship.
DERIVATIVES: **salvageable** *adj.* **salvager** *n.*

salvage operation • the recovery, evacuation, and reclamation of damaged, discarded, condemned, or abandoned allied or enemy materiel, ships, craft, and floating equipment for reuse, repair, refabrication, or scrapping. Naval salvage operations include harbor and channel clearance, diving, hazardous towing and rescue tug services,and the recovery of the materiel, ships, craft, and floating equipment sunk offshore or elsewhere stranded.

salvo • *n.* (pl. **-os** or **-oes**) **1** a simultaneous discharge of artillery or other guns in a battle. **2** a number of weapons released from one or more aircraft in quick succession.

salvor |'sælvər| • *n.* a person engaged in salvage of a ship or items lost at sea.

SAM • *abbr.* surface-to-air missile.

Sam Browne belt • a leather belt with a supporting strap that passes over the right shoulder, worn by army and police officers.
ORIGIN: early 20th cent.: named after Sir *Sam*uel J. *Brown(e)* (1824–1901), the British military commander who invented it.

Sam-D • the developmental name for a missile system that became the PATRIOT missile.

SAMOS Project • Satellite and Missile Observation System; a U.S. Air Force reconnaissance satellite and missile observation system, October 1960–November 1963, which was part of PROJECT CORONA.

Sampson, Deborah (1760–1827) • REVOLUTIONARY WAR hero, lecturer, and patriot. Born into a distinguished Massachusetts family, Sampson spent a difficult childhood in servitude as the result of family misfortunes. She educated herself well enough to allow her to teach school after her indenture ended. In 1782, inspired by the Revolution, she dressed in men's clothes and joined the Massachusetts militia under an assumed name. She was found out and expelled from the militia. Undaunted, however, she enlisted as a man in the 4th Massachusetts Regiment and marched with her unit toward New York. She spent a year and a half in the Continental army, fighting at Tarrytown against New York Loyalists and in other engagements. Wounded in the thigh, she extracted the bullet herself rather than risk having her sex discovered. After becoming ill on a surveying expedition near the Ohio River, she returned east; ending her days as a Continental soldier. Sampson eventually married. In 1792 she petitioned Congress for a pension and was granted £34 in back pay. In 1802 she began giving lectures about her extraordinary time in the army; her friend PAUL REVERE took up her cause, and, in 1805, Congress granted her a pension retroactive to 1803.

Sampson, William Thomas (1840–1902) • Union naval officer, born in New York. Sampson taught at the U.S. NAVAL ACADEMY after graduation and then, during the CIVIL WAR, joined the South Atlantic Blockading Squadron, off South Carolina, as executive officer of a monitor. After the war, he alternated between time at sea and time teaching physics and chemistry at the Academy, and from 1886 to 1890 he was superintendent of the Academy. From 1893 to 1897 he headed the NAVY BUREAU OF ORDNANCE, in which position he consistently fought for high-quality materials. In 1898 he chaired the commission that investigated the sinking of the *Maine* and soon after received command of the North Atlantic Squadron, the navy's most prestigious command. His orders were to blockade Cuba and prevent a Spanish fleet from reaching port. The Spanish eluded Sampson's blockade, docking at Santiago, but were destroyed in battle by Sampson's fleet, although some observers claimed that the victory was more the result of actions by his senior officer, WINFIELD SCOTT SCHLEY, than Sampson's. A 1901 court of inquiry generally upheld Sampson's view of events.

samurai |'sæmə,rī| • *n.* (pl. same) a member of a powerful military caste in feudal Japan.

San Bernardino Straits • one of the sites of the BATTLE OF LEYTE GULF south of Luzon, during WORLD WAR II. In October 1944, American forces invaded the Japanese-occupied island of Luzon in the Philippines. The Japanese Imperial Navy mounted the largest naval battle ever fought (October 23–26) in an attempt to keep the island. After distracting the U.S. Navy by attacking north of Luzon, the Japanese rounded the island through the San Bernardino Straits unopposed. The Americans fought back by air and sea, defeating the Japanese and clearing the way for U.S. occupation of the Philippines.

sanctuary • *n.* a nation or area near or contiguous to the combat area that, by tacit agreement between the warring powers, is exempt from attack and therefore serves as a refuge for staging, logistic, or other activities of the combatant powers.

sandbag • *n.* a bag filled with sand, typically used for defensive purposes or as ballast in a boat. • *v.* (**-bagged**, **-bagging**) (**sandbagged**) barricade using sandbags.

Sand Creek Massacre • a surprise attack by forces organized under Col. JOHN M. CHIV-

INGTON on peacefully assembled Cheyenne near Sand Creek, Colorado, November 29, 1864. Of the 500 Cheyenne in the village, more than 200 were indiscriminately killed, including many women and children. The attack set off widespread fighting between settlers and Plains Indians.

sand fort • a field fortification constructed in desert environments consisting of excavations and embankments of sand.

Sandhurst • (**Royal Military Academy**) a training college at Camberley, Surrey, southeastern England, for officers of the British army. It was formed in 1946 from an amalgamation of the Royal Military College at Sandhurst in Berkshire, which was established in 1799 and moved to Sandhurst in 1812, and the Royal Military Academy at Woolwich, London, which was founded in 1741.

Sandia National Laboratory • a national laboratory established in Albuquerque, New Mexico in 1945 as part of the LOS ALAMOS NATIONAL LABORATORY, and responsible for designing, testing, and manufacturing ordnance. From 1949 to 1993, the Sandia laboratory was managed by AT&T. In 1993, the DEPARTMENT OF ENERGY awarded management of Sandia to Lockheed Martin. The Sandia laboratory facility provides scientific and engineering solutions for nuclear weaponry and related defense systems, energy security, and is responsible, at the same time, for maintaining environmental integrity.

Sandinistas • adherents of the leftist Sandinista National Liberation Front which overthrew the Somoza regime in Nicaragua in 1979 and which ruled Nicaragua from 1979 to 1989 when they were defeated in free elections by an anti-Sandinista coalition. The Sandinistas took their name from the nationalist hero AUGUSTO SANDINO, who opposed the intervention of U.S. Marines in Nicaragua in the 1920s and 1930s. Sandino ended the fighting when the Marines withdrew in 1933, but he was killed the following year by Nicaraguan National Guard (Guardia Nacional) forces commanded by Anastasio Somoza.

Sandino, Augusto César (1893–1934) • nationalist leader in Nicaragua. He fought the conservative government during the Nicaraguan civil war (1926–27) and resisted U.S. occupation, vowing to fight until U.S. forces were withdrawn from Nicaragua. Sandino had widespread popular support and evaded capture by U.S. Marines and the Nicaraguan National Guard. After the withdrawal of the Marines in January 1933, Sandino became involved in peace negotiations. He was assassinated by Anastasio Somoza's National Guard on February 23, 1934. The members of the revolutionary group formed in Nicaragua in 1979 called themselves SANDINISTAS in his honor.

Sands, Benjamin Franklin (1812–83) • Union naval officer. The Maryland native went to sea at sixteen. From 1844 to 1847 he worked at the Bureau of Charts and Instruments at the NAVAL OBSERVATORY in Washington, D.C.; he saw limited action in the MEXICAN WAR (1846–48). In 1858 he was named to head the Naval Bureau of Construction. When the CIVIL WAR broke out, he participated in the evacuation of Union forces from the Norfolk Navy Yard, in 1861; the next year he was senior officer of the blockade of Cape Fear River and Wilmington, North Carolina. Despite the difficulty of maintaining the blockade against small, fast blockade runners, Sands captured fifty-three enemy ships. After the war, from 1867 until his retirement in 1874, he headed the Naval Observatory in Washington.

sand table • a relief model in sand used to explain military tactics and plan campaigns.

SANE • see NATIONAL COMMITTEE FOR A SANE NUCLEAR POLICY.

sangar |ˈsæNGgər| (also **sanga**) • *n.* a small protected structure that is used for observing or firing from and is built up from the ground.

sanitize • *v.* to revise a report or other document in such a fashion as to prevent identification of sources, or of the actual persons and places with which it is concerned, or of the means by which it was acquired. Sanitizing usually involves the deletion or substitution of names and other key details.

San Jacinto, Battle of • the concluding military event of the TEXAS WAR OF INDEPENDENCE on April 21, 1836, in which forces under SAM HOUSTON made a surprise attack on the greater forces ANTONIO LÓPEZ DE SANTA ANNA on the San Jacinto River near present-day Houston, Texas. After the defeat at the Alamo, Texas troops under the command of Sam Houston kept retreating for over a month, avoiding battle because they were the only armed troops left in the republic. But Houston saw a chance for a decisive victory at a ford over the San Jacinto River, and he and his men waited for Mexican general Santa Anna to cross and then demolished a bridge that was their only means of retreat. The attack caught the Mexicans completely off guard, and they were slaughtered. Santa Anna was taken prisoner, and signed an armistice that removed his troops from Texas. "Remember the Alamo!" is said to have been first used as a rallying cry by Houston's men in this battle.

San Juan Hill, Battle of • the best-known U.S. battle in Cuba during the SPANISH-AMERICAN WAR, because of the media coverage of THEODORE ROOSEVELT. (Also known as the Battle of San Juan Heights.) On July 1, 1898, the U.S. Expeditionary Forces under Maj. Gen. WILLIAM R. SHAFTER assaulted the Spanish defenses of SANTIAGO, where the Spanish squadron lay protected in the harbor. The U.S. attacking forces sustained 205 killed and 1,180 wounded, the Spanish defenders 215 killed and 376 wounded. Because of the casualties Shafter did not assault the next and primary Spanish defensive line, but the Spanish governor general ordered the squadron out of the harbor, where it was destroyed on July 3, 1898 by waiting U.S. naval forces. Santiago surrendered on July 17, 1898.

San Patricio Battalion • a battalion of U.S. Army deserters (many of Irish descent) organized in 1846 by Gen. ANTONIO LÓPEZ DE SANTA ANNA to fight for Mexico in the MEXICAN WAR (1846–1848). Hoping to recruit 3,000 deserters from the U.S. Army, Mexican propaganda advertised that the United States planned to destroy Catholicism in Mexico and, if Catholic soldiers fought for the United States, they would be fighting against their own religion. By July of 1847, Santa Anna had recruited sufficient deserters that he organized two battalions, each with about one hundred men. In courts martial held in August 1847 at San Angel and Tacubaya, Mexico, seventy-two members of the San Patricio Battalions were tried for desertion. Although seventy men received the death sentence, Gen. WINFIELD SCOTT, besieged by protests from many sources, reevaluated the courts martial, finally sentencing fifty of the deserters to death. They were executed in September 1847.

San Patricio, Battle of • a battle in the TEXAS WAR OF INDEPENDENCE early in 1836 in which Mexican forces under Gen. JOSÉ DE URREA defeated and killed dozens of Texans.

Sansapor • an area of the Vogelkop Peninsula in Dutch New Guinea taken over by Gen. DOUGLAS MACARTHUR's troops during WORLD WAR II. Army bases and airstrips were created in New Guinea in August 1944, as launching points for attacks against the Japanese in the Philippines.

Santa Anna, Antonio López de (1794–1876) • president of Mexico. As a young army officer, Santa Anna supported the movement for Mexican independence from Spain; he later turned against the government, helping to depose its president. In 1828 he supported another candidate for president but later helped to depose him as well. Santa Anna became a national hero in Mexico's war to prevent Spain from recapturing its former possession, and in 1833 he was elected president. In 1836 he led troops into Texas to suppress a revolt by American settlers there; during this time Texas declared its independence. Santa Anna led a brutal campaign that included a victory at the ALAMO, in San Antonio, but was himself captured by SAM HOUSTON. President ANDREW JACKSON ordered him returned to Mexico, where he went into retirement. After defying French demands for indemnities to French citizens living in Mexico, Santa Anna became the country's dictator (1839–45), but he was then driven into exile. In the MEXICAN WAR (1846–48), Santa Anna was defeated by Gen. WINFIELD SCOTT. Ten years later, he again tried to return to power, this time by ousting the French puppet emperor Maximilian, but the attempt failed.

Santa Fe Trail • a 780-mile (1255-km) wagon route from western Missouri to Santa Fe, New Mexico, that opened in 1821 and was frequently used, mainly for trade, until being superseded by the Atchison, Topeka, and Santa Fe Railroad in 1880.

Santee Sioux War • an uprising of the Santee Sioux in Minnesota 1862–64 in protest of the cash-strapped U.S. government's failure to pay them their annual grant under terms of a treaty agreed in 1851. The revolt was forcibly put down and the Sioux leader Little Crow fled to Canada.

Santiago, Battle of • a largely naval battle of the SPANISH-AMERICAN WAR in the summer of 1898, in which a fleet of battleships, under the command of Maj. Gen. WILLIAM R. SHAFTER, destroyed the Spanish squadron of ships at Santiago de Cuba. As a result, the city was surrendered along with 28,000 Spanish troops and the eastern half of the island. This victory forced the Spanish government to propose peace negotiations.

sap • *n.* a tunnel or trench to conceal an assailant's approach to a fortified place. • *v.* (**sapped**, **sapping**) **1** dig a sap or saps. **2** archaic make insecure by removing the foundations of: *sapped and undermined, the garrison was in imminent danger of collapse.*

sapper • *n.* a military engineer who lays or detects and disarms mines.

SAR • *abbr.* search and rescue.

Saratoga, Battles of • two battles of the REVOLUTIONARY WAR, in September and October of 1777, in which American forces under Gen. BENEDICT ARNOLD defeated British forces under Gen. JOHN BURGOYNE. The American victories led France to sign the Alliance with the United States and provide the forces that ultimately helped win the war.

sarge • *n.* informal sergeant.

Sargent, Winthrop (1753–1820) • REVOLUTIONARY WAR army officer and territorial governor, born in Massachusetts. Sargent served in Gen. HENRY KNOX's artillery unit during the Revolution, reaching the rank of major. In 1791 he was wounded in the major military defeat suffered by U.S. forces at the hands of a confederation of Native American tribes at Fort Recovery; as acting governor of the territory, in 1791 and 1792, he managed to repel later attacks by Indians against other forts. In 1798 he became the first governor of the newly organized territory of Mississippi. He was unpopular with settlers, who wanted more control over local affairs, and was replaced after THOMAS JEFFERSON became president.

SAS • *abbr.* special ammunition storage.

satchel charge • an explosive on a board fitted with a rope or wire loop for carrying and attaching.

satellite • *n.* **1** (also **artificial satellite**) an artificial body placed in orbit around the earth or another planet in order to collect information or for communication. **2** transmitted by satellite; using or relating to satellite technology: *satellite broadcasting.* **3** something that is separated from or on the periphery of something else but is nevertheless dependent on or controlled by it: *satellite offices in London and New York.* **4** a small country or state politically or economically dependent on another: *the Soviet Union and its satellite states.*

The first artificial satellite, Sputnik I, was launched by the USSR on October 4, 1957. Over 5,000 satellites have since been launched into earth orbit and several hundred are still operational. Many of them provide observation or remote sensing of the earth's surface, for military or meteorological purposes, or for research into mineral resources, land use, etc. Others act as relays for telephone and microwave communications, or for the broadcasting of television and radio, or provide precise coordinates for air, sea, and land navigation. A number of satellites carry instruments for astronomical observation at various electromagnetic wavelengths, unhindered by the earth's atmosphere.

satellite and missile surveillance • the systematic observation of aerospace for the purpose of detecting, tracking, and characterizing objects, events, and phenomena associated with satellites and inflight missiles, friendly and enemy.

satnav • *n.* navigation dependent on information received from satellites.
ORIGIN: 1970s: blend of SATELLITE and NAVIGATION.

saturate • *v.* overwhelm (an enemy target area) by concentrated bombing.

Savage's Station, Battle of • an inconclusive CIVIL WAR battle on the fourth day of the SEVEN DAYS' Battle, fought on June 29, 1862 in Henrico County, Virginia. There were casualties in the thousands on both sides, and 2,500 Union soldiers were captured.

sawed-off • *n.* a sawed-off shotgun.

SBI • *abbr.* space-based interceptor.

SBR • *abbr.* special boat squadron.

scabbard • *n.* **1** a sheath for the blade of a sword or dagger, typically made of leather or metal. **2** a sheath for a gun or other weapon or tool.

Scales, Alfred Moore (1827–92) • Confederate army officer and state governor, born in North Carolina. Scales supported secession and in 1861 became a captain, then a colonel, in the Thirteenth North Carolina Regiment. He fought in the PENINSULAR CAMPAIGN (1862), at ANTIETAM (1862), and at FREDERICKSBURG (1863). By then a brigadier general, he was wounded in the charge up SEMINARY RIDGE at GETTYSBURG (1863). In 1864 he fought at SPOTSYLVANIA, the WILDERNESS, and PETERSBURG. After the war, he was a member of the U.S. House of Representatives. He resigned when he was elected governor of North Carolina, in 1884, in which position he served one term.

scaling ladder • a ladder used for climbing fortress walls in an attempt to break a siege or for firefighting.

Scammell, Alexander (1747–81) • REVOLUTIONARY WAR army officer. In 1774 he became involved in antiroyalist activities in New Hampshire and, when fighting broke out, was commissioned a major by both the Massachusetts and the New Hampshire militias. On GEORGE WASHINGTON's recommendation, he was appointed a brigade major in the Continental army. Scammell fought at TRENTON (1776) and PRINCETON (1777) and participated in the unsuccessful defense of FORT TICONDEROGA; he was wounded at the battle of SARATOGA (1777). In 1780 Washington ordered him to conduct the execution of the convicted British spy JOHN ANDRÉ. After 1781 he again held field commands; he was mortally wounded by shrapnel while on an intelligence-gathering mission prior to the battle at YORKTOWN; his unit was surrounded by British troops, and, while surrendering, Scammell was unexpectedly shot.

scan • *n.* **1** in air intercept, a term meaning: "search sector indicated and report any contacts." **2** the path periodically followed by a radiation beam. **3** in electronics intelligence, the motion of an electronic beam through space looking for a target.

scantling • *n.* (often **scantlings**) a set of standard dimensions for parts of a structure, especially in shipbuilding.

scarp • *n.* **1** a very steep bank or slope; an escarpment. **2** the inner wall of a ditch in a fortification. Compare with COUNTERSCARP. • *v.* provide (a ditch in a fortification) with a steep scarp and counterscarp.

sch. • *abbr.* schooner.

Schlesinger, James R. (1929?–) • secretary of defense, born in New York City. Schlesinger received a Ph.D. in economics from Harvard in 1956 and worked as a consultant to the Federal Reserve Board. In 1960 he published a major work, *The Political Economy of National Security,* and in 1963 he joined the RAND CORPORATION as director of strategic studies. In 1969 he became assistant director of the federal Bureau of the Budget (later the Office of Management and Budget); he later served as chairman of the ATOMIC ENERGY COMMISSION before being named director of the CENTRAL INTELLIGENCE AGENCY in 1973. Later that year he was named secretary of defense by President RICHARD M. NIXON. From 1977 to 1979 he was the first U.S. secretary of energy, under President JIMMY CARTER.

Schley, Winfield Scott |slī| (1839–1911) • Union naval officer, born in Maryland. Schley early chose the navy as a career. He sided with the Union as the CIVIL WAR broke out and participated in the blockade of CHARLESTON (1861), and in numerous other naval engagements. When the war ended, he taught at ANNAPOLIS for three years and then returned to sea, participating in a move to seize a Korean fortress after Koreans fired on a U.S. ship. In 1884 he led an expedition to the Arctic to attempt to rescue a team of polar explorers; returning to the United States with the survivors, he was hailed a hero. President CHESTER ARTHUR named him to head the Bureau of Equipment and Recruiting, as well as the Bureau of Provisions and Clothing. In 1889 he again returned to sea; many members of his crew were killed by resentful Argentines as the ship patrolled during a civil disturbance in that nation, but Schley was cleared of any wrongdoing. In 1898 he was given command of the Flying Squadron, which patrolled the mid-Atlantic coast. When the SPANISH-AMERICAN WAR (1898) broke out, he was sent to Cuba under Admiral WILLIAM T. SAMPSON. A confusion in orders allowed a Spanish fleet to arrive safely in the harbor at SANTIAGO, Cuba; as the fleet attempted to leave the harbor it was attacked and disabled by Schley's ships while Sampson was temporarily away from the harbor, and a dispute erupted over which officer should properly take credit for the victory. A court of inquiry, convened in 1901, generally sided with Sampson.

Schofield, John McAllister (1831–1906) • U.S. military officer. Schofield's family moved from New York to Illinois when he was young. He taught at the U.S. MILITARY ACADEMY after graduation and at Washington University, but returned to military service during the CIVIL WAR, becoming major, 1st Missouri. As brigadier general of volunteers, Schofield had dealt with tensions between radicals who called for outright abolition of slavery and military reprisals and more conservative recruits who favored a gradual course. He took command of the Department and ARMY OF THE OHIO in 1864 and joined in Gen. WILLIAM T. SHERMAN's assault on Atlanta. He returned to Tennessee but then, as a brigadier general, U.S. Army, rejoined Sherman, preparing the surrender statement for Sherman to present to the Confederate general JOSEPH E. JOHNSTON in April 1865. Seen as a centrist, he replaced the more controversial EDWIN M. STANTON as secretary of war in President ANDREW JOHNSON's cabinet, serving from June 1868 to March 1869. Schofield continued to serve in various command posts; he was superintendent of WEST POINT from 1776 to 1881 and, from 1888 until his retirement in 1895, held command of the army, with the rank of lieutenant general.

School of Advanced Military Studies • a postgraduate army service school at FORT LEAVENWORTH, Kansas. Established in 1984, it is one of several schools that make up the ARMY COMMAND AND GENERAL STAFF COLLEGE, and its students are graduates of the Command and General Staff School. It grants the degree of Master of Military Arts and Science.

School of Application • a postgraduate marine corps service school in Washington, D.C. It was established in 1891 by Commandant Charles Haywood as the Marine Corps' first formal postgraduate school for newly commissioned lieutenants.

School of Application for Infantry and Calvary • an army service school at FORT LEAVENWORTH, Kansas. Established in 1882 by Gen. WILLIAM T. SHERMAN, it traces its history back to the ARTILLERY SCHOOL OF PRACTICE, which was established in 1824 at Fortress Monroe, Virginia. From 1890–1910, it significantly upgraded its program, training students in both theory and practice. In 1946 it became the ARMY COMMAND AND GENERAL STAFF COLLEGE.

schooner |ˈsko͞onər| • *n.* a sailing ship with two or more masts, typically with the foremast smaller than the mainmast and gaff-rigged lower masts.

Schroeder, Rudolph William |ˈSHrōdər| (1886–1952) • ARMY SIGNAL CORPS aviator, born in Illinois. Schroeder went to work as an auto mechanic after his father died, and went on to work as the mechanic of a colleague who became an aviator. In 1916 he joined the Army Signal Corps, where he either suggested or himself developed a number of mechanical and instrumental improvements for planes. As chief test pilot of the Engineering Division in 1920 and 1921, he set several altitude records; in 1920, in a flight fraught with dangerous mechanical failures and horrific conditions, including temperatures as low as -67 degrees Fahrenheit, he reached altitudes in excess of 33,000 feet. His efforts earned him the DISTINGUISHED FLYING CROSS.

Schurz, Carl |SHo͝orts; SHərts| (1829–1906) • Union army officer, secretary of the interior, and U.S. senator. Schurz grew up in Germany, where he allied himself with those who sought democratic reforms. Wanted for treason, he rescued an imprisoned comrade by bribing a guard, and the two then fled to England. He came to the United States in 1852 and settled in Wisconsin, becoming active in the Republican party. In 1860 he first supported WILLIAM H. SEWARD, then ABRAHAM LINCOLN; his help in campaigning among German immigrants helped Lincoln achieve victory. When the CIVIL WAR broke out, Schurz raised several troops of German immigrants, then became ambassador to Spain, from which position he supported the issuance of the EMANCIPATION PROCLAMATION. He returned to the United States in 1862 and was commissioned a brigadier general; he fought well at the SECOND BATTLE OF BULL RUN (1862), but his performance at CHANCELLORSVILLE and at GETTYSBURG (both 1863) drew criticism, and the rest of his war service was unremarkable. In 1869 he was elected to the Senate from his new home state, Missouri. Schurz's support for clean government, and for the Republican candidate in 1876, brought him a post as secretary of the interior; in this position he introduced civil service reforms and moved to protect natural resources; he also eventually softened the department's treatment of Native Americans. An anti-imperialist, he opposed the SPANISH-AMERICAN WAR (1898) and annexation of new territories.

Schuyler, Philip John |ˈskīlər| (1733–1804) • REVOLUTIONARY WAR army officer, born into a well-positioned family in upstate New York. During the FRENCH AND INDIAN WAR (1754–63), he commanded a unit that advanced on Lake George. Schuyler was chosen a delegate to the Second Continental Congress and was assigned by GEORGE WASHINGTON to assemble an army to invade Canada. Schuyler did not command the force, because of illness, but he took some of the blame for its failure to achieve its goal. A later court-martial totally exonerated him of any responsibility.

Schwarzkopf, H. Norman (1934–) • U.S. army officer and commander of the Allied forces in the PERSIAN GULF WAR. Schwarzkopf was born in New Jersey into a military family. His own military service included two tours of duty in the VIETNAM WAR (1965–66, 1969–70), where he earned numerous commendations. He rose steadily through the ranks, making major general in 1983, the year in which he led the U.S. invasion of GRENADA. In 1988 he became a four-star general and commander in chief of the U.S. CENTRAL COMMAND, making him responsible for any military operations in the Middle East. When Iraq invaded its neighbor Kuwait in 1990, Schwarzkopf headed the U.S.-led international coalition of forces that intervened beginning in January 1991. After enduring a six-week aerial bombardment and a 100-hour ground war, Iraq had suffered significant losses and withdrew its forces from Kuwait. Schwarzkopf retired from active service later that year. In the years since he has been a military analyst for the media.

SCI • *abbr.* Sensitive Compartmented Information.

Science Advisory Board • (**SAB**) established in 1997 as the only federal agency responsible for advising the under secretary of Commerce for Oceans and Atmosphere regarding long- and short-range strategies for research, education, and the application of science to resource management. Made up of eminent scientists, engineers, resource managers, and educators, the Board is part of the National Oceanic and Atmospheric Administration (NOAA).

scimitar • *n.* a short sword with a curved blade that broadens toward the point, used originally in Eastern countries.

scope • *n.* the length of cable extended when a ship rides at anchor. • *abbr.* abbreviation for periscope, radarscope, telescope, etc.

scorched-earth policy • a military policy calling for the heavy destruction of crops, livestock, buildings, and other infrastructure in an area of operations. A scorched-earth policy may be adopted by an army advancing through enemy territory to punish resistance or reduce the enemy's capacity and will to resist, or by an army retreating from its own territory in order to leave nothing of value to the enemy.

Scott, Charles (c.1739–1813) • REVOLUTIONARY WAR army officer and state governor, born in Virginia. Scott ran away to join the militia while still in his teens. After service in the FRENCH AND INDIAN WAR (1754–63) and the CHEROKEE WAR (1759–61), he returned home to his farm. After the outbreak of the Revolution, he was made commander of Virginia's troops, in 1776 becoming colonel of the Fifth Virginia Regiment in the Continental army. He fought in the major engagements in New Jersey, from TRENTON (1776) to MONMOUTH (1778). He then returned to Virginia; he was captured at CHARLESTON in 1780 but exchanged in 1782. After the war, he moved to Kentucky, where two of his sons were killed and scalped by Indians. Scott participated in several military operations against the Indians into the 1790s. In 1808 he was elected governor of Kentucky, largely for sentimental reasons as anti-British feeling began to grow. He sent the state militia to participate in Gen. WILLIAM HENRY HARRISON's invasion of Canada in 1811.

Scott, Robert Kingston (1826–1900) • Union army officer and state governor. Raised in Pennsylvania, Scott first tried mining and medicine, eventually settling in Ohio, where his practice flourished. At the outbreak of the CIVIL WAR, he was responsible for organizing the 68th Ohio Infantry. He fought at SHILOH (1862) and was with Gen. WILLIAM T. SHERMAN on the MARCH TO THE SEA; he reached the rank of major general in 1865. After the war, he worked with the Freeman's Bureau in South Carolina and was elected the state's governor in 1868; he served until 1872, heading what is considered one of the most corrupt administrations in the state's history, rife with kickbacks and bribery schemes, associated especially with state-funded railroad stocks and bonds. (Scott does not appear to have benefited personally from the corruption.) As governor Scott acted to suppress the KU KLUX KLAN, but the state remained bitterly divided over how to treat freed slaves. Indicted in 1878 for conspiracy to defraud the state, Scott fled to Ohio to avoid prosecution.

Scott, Winfield (1786–1866) • Union army officer, born in Virginia. Scott was known as "Old Fuss and Feathers" because of his love of gaudy uniforms. After serving in a volunteer cavalry unit, Scott in 1808 sought and received a military commission. Sent to New Orleans, he clashed with his superior, resulting in a court-martial and suspension. Reinstated after a year, he fought in the WAR OF 1812 and won a decisive victory over the British at CHIPPEWA in 1814. For this and other actions, he was promoted to brevet major general. In 1832 he was sent to the West to fight the in BLACK HAWK WAR. In 1836 he went to Florida to fight in the SEMINOLE WAR. Scott then undertook several diplomatic assignments with Canada and with Native American tribes. He assumed supreme command of all U.S. troops in the MEXICAN WAR (1846–48), taking VERACRUZ, defeating ANTONIO LÓPEZ DE SANTA ANNA at CERRO GORDO, and finally taking MEXICO CITY in September 1847. He was mentioned by the Whigs as a possible presidential candidate in 1848 but lost the nomination to Gen. ZACHARY TAYLOR. In 1852, however, Scott received the Whig nomination, but his candidacy foundered on his failure to please either the northern or the southern branches of the party on the slavery issue. Scott opposed secession and remained loyal to the Union in the CIVIL WAR. He was a valued military adviser at the start of the war but retired for medical reasons at the end of 1861.

While prosecuting the Black Hawk War, Scott prepared himself to cope with the rampant cholera by issuing a memo that required any drunken soldier to dig his own grave, a result of Scott's belief that drunkenness caused cholera.

---

scout • *n.* **1** a soldier or other person sent out ahead of a main force so as to gather information about the enemy's position, strength, or movements. **2** a ship or aircraft employed for reconnaissance, especially a small fast aircraft. **3** an instance of gathering information, especially by reconnoitering an area: *I returned from a lengthy scout around the area.* • *v.* (especially of a soldier) go ahead of a main force so as to gather information about an enemy's position, strength, or movements.

scout car • a fast armored vehicle used for military reconnaissance and liaison.

scouting • *n.* the action of gathering information about enemy forces or an area.

scow |skow| • *n.* **1** a wide-beamed sailing dinghy. **2** a flat-bottomed boat with sloping ends used as a lighter and in other harbor services.

Scowcroft, Brent (1925) • U.S. Air Force officer and national security adviser, born in Utah. Scowcroft was educated at WEST POINT and Columbia University, where in 1967 he received a Ph.D. in international relations. Scowcroft graduated from pilot training in 1948. From 1953 to 1957 he taught Russian history at the U.S. MILITARY ACADEMY; from 1959 to 1961 he was an assistant air attaché at the U.S. embassy in Belgrade, Yugoslavia. In 1962 he returned to the United States, where he taught at several military schools. From 1964 to 1966 he was in the Office of the Deputy Chief of Staff, Plans, and Operations of Headquarters U.S. Air Force; in 1968 he moved to the Office of the Assistant Secretary of Defense for International Security Affairs; and in 1969 he became deputy assistant for NATIONAL SECURITY COUNCIL matters. In 1972 he was named military assistant to the President, and in 1973 he became deputy assistant to the President for national security affairs; he retained that post after President RICHARD M. NIXON resigned in 1974 and GERALD R. FORD became president. Scowcroft was later promoted and served as Ford's national security adviser. He also held that post (1989–92) in the administration of President GEORGE H. BUSH. In 1974 he was promoted to lieutenant general of the Air Force; he retired in 1975. President Bush awarded him the Presidential Medal of Freedom in 1991.

SCPO • *abbr.* Senior Chief Petty Officer.

scram • in air intercept usage, a code meaning, "Am about to open fire. Friendly units keep clear or get clear of indicated contact, bogey, or area."

The scram code may indicate the direction of withdrawal or the type of fire, as with the code **scram proximity** ("Am about to open fire with proximity-fuzed ammunition") or **scram mushroom** ("Am about to fire a special weapon").

---

scramble • *v.* **1** (often **be scrambled**) order (a fighter aircraft or its pilot) to take off immediately in an emergency or for action. **2** (of a fighter aircraft or its pilot) take off in such a way. **3** make (a broadcast transmission, a telephone message, or electronic data) unintelligible unless received by an appropriate decoding device: (**scrambled**) *scrambled television signals.* • *n.* an emergency takeoff by fighter aircraft.

DERIVATIVES: **scrambling** *n.*

scrambled eggs • informal gold braid on a field-grade military officer's cap.

screen • *n.* **1** a thing providing concealment or protection: *his jeep was discreetly parked behind a screen of trees.* **2** a detachment of troops or ships detailed to cover the movements of the main body. • *v.* **1** conceal, protect, or shelter (someone or something) with a screen or something forming a screen: *a high hedge screened all of the front from passersby.* **2** check on or investigate (someone), typically to ascertain whether they are suitable for or can be trusted in a particular situation or job: *all prospective presidential candidates would have to screened by the committee.* **3** evaluate or analyze (something) for its suitability for a particular purpose or application: *only one percent of rain forest plants have been* ***screened for*** *medical use.* **4** (**screen someone/something out**) exclude someone or something after such evaluation or investigation: *only those refugees who are screened out are sent back to Vietnam.*

screw • *n.* (also **screw propeller**) a ship's or aircraft's propeller (considered as acting like a screw in moving through water or air).

scud • *n.* (also **Scud** or **Scud missile**) a type of long-range surface-to-surface guided missile able to be fired from a mobile launcher.

scupper • *n.* (usually **scuppers**) a hole in a ship's side to carry water overboard from the deck.

scurvy • *n.* a disease caused by a deficiency of vitamin C, characterized by swollen bleeding gums and the opening of previously healed wounds, which particularly affected poorly nourished sailors until the end of the 18th century.

scuttle • *v.* sink (one's own ship) deliberately by holing it or opening its seacocks to let water in. • *n.* an opening with a lid in a ship's deck or side.

scuttlebutt • *n.* informal rumor; gossip: *the* ***scuttlebutt has it*** *that he was a spy.*

S-day • *n.* the day that the president authorizes Selective Reserve callup (not more than 200,000 reservists).

SDB-1 Sea Cobra • (**AH-1J**) a dual-crew light attack helicopter with one rotor. It is armed with machine guns, rockets, launchers, and antitank missiles, and is used to support other attack helicopters.

SDI • *abbr.* Strategic Defense Initiative.

SDS • *abbr.* Students for a Democratic Society.

sea • *n.* (often **the sea**) **1** the expanse of salt water that covers most of the earth's surface and surrounds its land masses: *a ban on dumping radioactive wastes in the sea | rocky bays lapped by vivid blue sea | a sea view.* **2** a roughly definable area of this: *the Black Sea.* **3** a large lake: *the Sea of Galilee.* **4** used to refer to waves as opposed to calm sea: *there was still some sea running.* **5** (**seas**) large waves: *the lifeboat met seas of thirty-five feet head-on.*

PHRASES: **at sea** sailing on the sea. **by sea** by means of a ship or ships: *other army units* *were sent by sea.* **go to sea 1** set out on a voyage. **2** become a sailor in a navy or a merchant navy. **put (out) to sea** leave land on a voyage.

sea-air-land team • (also called **SEAL team**) a marine force organized, trained, and equipped for special missions in marine, coastal, and riverine environments. See also SEAL.

sea anchor • an object dragged in the water from the bow of a boat in order to keep the bow pointing into the waves or to lessen leeway.

Seabee • *n.* a member of one of the construction battalions of the Civil Engineer Corps of the U.S. Navy.
ORIGIN: representing a pronunciation of the letters *CB* (from *construction battalion*).

sea biscuit • another term for HARDTACK.

sea boat • a boat or ship considered in terms of its ability to cope with conditions at sea: *she was a surprisingly good sea boat.*

Seaborg, Glenn T. (1912–1999) • born in Michigan and educated at the University of California at Los Angeles and at Berkeley, he is best known for his work isolating and identifying elements heavier than uranium. He shared the 1951 Nobel Prize for Chemistry with Edwin McMillan. Between 1940 and 1955, with his coworkers at UC–Berkeley, Seaborg added ten new elements (atomic numbers 94–102, 106); Element 106, seaborgium, was named for him. Element 94, plutonium, is the most well-known because it is used for nuclear purposes. Seaborg served as chairman of the ATOMIC ENERGY COMMISSION (1961–1971), and returned to UC–Berkeley in 1971.

seaborne • *adj.* transported or traveling by sea: *seaborne trade.*

sea captain • a person who commands a ship, especially a merchant ship.

SeaCat • trademark a large, high-speed catamaran used as a passenger and car ferry on short sea crossings.

sea chest • a sailor's storage chest.

seacock • *n.* a valve in an opening through a ship's hull below or near to the waterline (e.g., one connecting a ship's engine-cooling system to the sea).

sea control operations • the employment of naval forces, supported by land and air forces, as appropriate, to achieve military objectives in vital sea areas. Such operations include the destruction of enemy naval forces, the suppression of enemy sea commerce, the protection of vital sea lanes, and the establishment of local military superiority in areas of naval operations.

sea dog • informal an old or experienced sailor.

Sea Dragon • (**MH-53E**) the largest helicopter currently operating in the West and can carry up to fifty-five troops or a 16-ton payload fifty nautical miles or a 10-ton payload 500 nautical miles. It is used primarily for Airborne Mine Countermeasures by the U.S. Navy, but can also serve for shipboard delivery, air-to-air refueling, search and rescue, and external cargo transport, all in both land and seaborne environments. A heavier helicopter than its ancestor, the SUPER STALLION (CH-53E), it also has a larger fuel capacity.

seafaring • *adj.* (of a person) traveling by sea, especially regularly. • *n.* the practice of traveling by sea, especially regularly.
DERIVATIVES: **seafarer** *n.*

seagoing • *adj.* **1** (of a ship) suitable or designed for voyages on the sea. **2** characterized by or relating to traveling by sea, especially habitually: *a seagoing life.*

sea gull • slang **1** in WORLD WAR I, a Navy airman, especially one based at the Naval Air Station at Pensacola, Florida. **2** chicken, as served in Army mess halls. **3** a prostitute catering to sailors and marines, and sometimes following the men from port to port.

Seahawk • (**HH-60H**) one of eighty-two combat search-and-rescue helicopters received by the U.S. Air Force after its Night Hawk (HH-60D) was canceled. Also see BLACK HAWK.

seakeeping • *n.* the ability of a vessel to withstand rough conditions at sea.

Sea King • (**H-3**) a medium-lift helicopter with one rotor designed to be used for cargo and troop transport as well as air and sea rescue during aircraft carrier operations. Some versions have been modified for use in antisubmarine operations.

Sea Knight • (**CH-46**) a twin-rotor helicopter originally designed for civilian use but engineered for military use as a troop and cargo transport aircraft. It has rough-field capability and a range of 1,000 miles.

SEAL • originating in 1943 with volunteers from the Navy's Construction Battalions (SEABEES), the first two SEAL (Sea, Air, Land) teams were commissioned in 1962 in the Pacific Fleet (SEAL Team ONE) and in the Atlantic Fleet (SEAL Team TWO) and charged with conducting unconventional warfare, counter-guerilla warfare, and clandestine operations in blue and brown water environments. In 1983, existing UNDERWATER DEMOLITION TEAMS (UDTs; organized in 1947) were redesignated as SEAL teams and/or SEAL Delivery Vehicle Teams, making the redesignated SEALs responsible for hydrographic reconnaissance and underwater demolition missions. At the Naval Amphibious Base in Coronado, California, the NAVAL SPECIAL WARFARE COMMAND (commissioned in 1987) prepares U.S. Navy Special Forces to execute their assigned missions and develops special operations strategy, doctrine, and tactics.

sea lane • a route at sea designated for use or regularly used by shipping.

sea-launched ballistic missile • (**SLBM**) ballistic missile launched from a submarine or surface ship.

sealed orders • orders for procedure that are not to be opened before a specified time: *we went to the landing strip to set up a listening post on a wavelength contained in sealed orders.*

sealift • *n.* a large-scale transportation of troops, supplies, and equipment by sea.

sealift support ship • a ship that transports heavy equipment, ammunition, fuel, and other supplies during the beginning of a military operation or to resupply and maintain an ongoing operation.

Sea Lord • one of two naval officers (**First** and **Second Sea Lords**) who serve on the admiralty board of the MINISTRY OF DEFENCE for the United Kingdom.

SEALORDS strategy • an innovative strategy for the employment of United States and South Vietnamese naval forces in the VIETNAM WAR developed in 1968 by then Vice Admiral ELMO R. ZUMWALT, Jr., the Commander of Naval Forces in Vietnam. The SEALORDS strategy, which sought to put the Communist insurgents on the defensive by using U.S. and South Vietnamese riverine forces to set up a patrol boat barrier along the Cambodian border with South Vietnam and to penetrate deep into the Mekong Delta, was generally successful in limiting Communist offensive action in the Mekong Delta region.

seaman • *n.* (pl. **-men**) **1** a person who works as a sailor, especially one below the rank of officer. **2** a sailor of the lowest rank in the U.S. Navy or Coast Guard, ranking below petty officer. **3** a person regarded in terms of their ability to captain or crew a boat or ship: *he's the best seaman on the coast.*

DERIVATIVES: **seamanlike** *adj.*

Seaman Apprentice • an enlisted rank in the U.S. Navy and Coast Guard corresponding to a Private in the U.S. Army, a Private First Class in the U.S. Marine Corps, and an Airman Third Class in the U.S. Air Force; pay grade E-2.

Seaman Recruit • the lowest enlisted rank in the U.S. Navy and Coast Guard corresponding to a Recruit in the U.S. Army, a Private in the U.S. Marine Corps, and an Airman Basic in the U.S. Air Force; pay grade E-1.

seamanship • *n.* the skill, techniques, or practice of handling a ship or boat at sea.

seamark • *n.* a conspicuous object distinguishable at sea, serving to guide or warn sailors in navigation.

sea mile • a unit of distance equal to a minute of arc of a great circle and varying (because the earth is not a perfect sphere) between approximately 2,014 yards (1,842 meters) at the equator and 2,035 yards (1,861 meters) at the pole. Compare with NAUTICAL MILE.

seaplane • *n.* an aircraft with floats instead of wheels, designed to land on and take off from water.

sea power • a country's naval strength, especially as a weapon of war.

search and destroy operations • in the VIETNAM WAR, U.S. and South Vietnamese multi-battalion tactical operations in South Vietnam designed to find, encircle, and destroy large VIETCONG and North Vietnamese Army units. The search and destroy technique was used mainly against known Communist base areas and was largely discontinued in favor of small unit patrolling after the Communist TET OFFENSIVE in 1968.

search and rescue • (**SAR**) the use of aircraft, surface craft, submarines, specialized rescue teams, and equipment to search for and rescue personnel in distress on land or at sea.

search and seizure • in counterinsurgency operations, the procedure for entering a village or area suspected of harboring insurgents or their supplies, searching the area, and arresting suspected insurgents and confiscating any suspect materiel.

search attack unit • the designation given to one or more ships separately organized or detached from a formation as a tactical unit to search for and destroy submarines.

search mission • in air operations, an air reconnaissance by one or more aircraft dispatched to locate an object or objects known or suspected to be in a specific area.

search party • a group of people organized to look for someone or something that is lost.

search radius • in search and rescue operations, a radius centered on a datum point having a length equal to the total probable error plus an additional safety length to ensure a greater than 50-percent probability that the target is in the search area.

search warrant • a legal document authorizing a police officer or other official to enter and search premises.

sea room • clear space at sea for a ship to maneuver in.

Sea Skimmer • see SEA SKIPPER.

Sea Skipper • a program to convert the Beechcraft AQM-37 from a target drone to make it operational for simulated antishipping attacks.

Seasprite • (**H-2**) a light multipurpose naval helicopter first flown in July 1959. Since then, this utility helicopter, with conventional turbine power, has undergone continuous modification and development and is now considered to be an extremely sophisticated antisubmarine weapon for the U.S. Navy.

Sea Stallion • (**CH-53A, CH-53E**) a ship-based transport helicopter designed to carry assault troops and heavy equipment. The **RH-53** is a version equipped for mine countermeasures. The CH-53E was also known as the **Super Stallion**.

sea state • the degree of turbulence at sea, generally measured on a scale of 0 to 9 according to average wave height.

sea superiority • the degree of dominance in the sea battle of one force over another that permits the conduct of operations by the former and its related land, sea, and air forces at a given time and place without prohibitive interference by the opposing force.

sea supremacy • the degree of sea superiority wherein the opposing force is incapable of effective interference.

sea surveillance • the systematic observation of surface and subsurface sea areas by all available and practicable means primarily for the purpose of locating, identifying and determining the movements of ships, submarines, and other vehicles, friendly and enemy, proceeding on or under the surface of the world's seas and oceans.

SEATO • (**Southeast Asia Treaty Organization**) a treaty for the defense of Southeast

Asia, formed by Britain, France, Australia, New Zealand, Thailand and Pakistan, established by the Southeast Asia Collective Defense Treaty, which was signed in Manila on September 8, 1954. U.S. Secretary of State JOHN FOSTER DULLES initiated the organization to protect Southeast Asia against communist aggression after the GENEVA AGREEMENT ON INDOCHINA in 1954 ended the war there. It relied on the military forces if its member states to provide protection. It existed between 1955–77. A protocol later extended the treaty's protection to South Vietnam, Cambodia and Laos.

seavan • commercial or Government-owned (or leased) shipping containers which are moved via ocean transportation without bogey wheels attached.

seaway • *n.* **1** an inland waterway capable of accommodating seagoing ships. **2** a natural channel connecting two areas of sea. **2** a route across the sea used by ships. **3** a rough sea in which to sail: *with the engine mounted amidship, the boat pitches less* ***in a seaway***.

***Seawolf*, USS** • (**SSN-21**) the most advanced fast attack submarine in the U.S. Navy and the first of its class, it has a large weapons load, including antisubmarine torpedoes, HARPOON missiles, and TOMAHAWK cruise missiles. Its design enables it to carry out different types of missions, for example, surveillance, collection of intelligence, as well as antiship, antisubmarine, and mine warfare.

seaworthy • *adj.* (of a vessel) in a good enough condition to sail on the sea.
DERIVATIVES: **seaworthiness** *n.*

secede • *v.* withdraw formally from membership of a federal union, an alliance, or a political or religious organization: *the kingdom of Belgium seceded from the Netherlands in 1830.*
DERIVATIVES: **seceder** *n.*

secesh (or **sucesh**) • *n.* informal someone in favor of the attempt of the Southern States to withdraw from the Union. [ORIGIN: A shortening of *secession*.]

secession • *n* **1** (**the Secession**)) the withdrawal of eleven Southern states from the U.S. Union in 1860, leading to the CIVIL WAR. **2** the action of withdrawing formally from membership of a federation or body, especially a political state.

secessionism • *n.* the principles of those in favor of secession.

second |'sekənd| • *ordinal number* **1** constituting number two in a sequence; coming after the first in time or order; 2nd. **2** denoting someone or something regarded as comparable to or reminiscent of a better-known predecessor: *a fear that the conflict would turn into a second Vietnam.* **3** an act or instance of seconding. **2** subordinate or inferior in position, rank, or importance: *it was* ***second only to*** *Copenhagen among Baltic ports* **3** an attendant assisting a combatant in a duel. • *v.* formally support or endorse (a nomination or resolution or its proposer) as a necessary preliminary to adoption or further discussion: *he seconded the nomination.*

secondary censorship • armed forces censorship performed on the personal communications of officers, civilian employees, and accompanying civilians of the U.S. Armed Forces, and on those personal communications of enlisted personnel of the armed forces not subject to armed forces primary censorship or those requiring reexamination.

second Cold War • the period from the Soviet invasion of Afghanistan in 1979 to the Reykjavik summit in 1986, during which time President RONALD REAGAN increased military spending and actively sought U.S. dominance of the Soviet Union.

second-in-command • *n.* the officer next in authority to the commanding or chief officer.

second lieutenant • a commissioned officer of the lowest rank in the U.S. Army, Air Force, and Marine Corps ranking above chief warrant officer and below first lieutenant.

second mate • an assistant mate on a merchant ship.

second officer • another term for SECOND MATE.

second strike • a retaliatory attack conducted with weapons designed to withstand an initial nuclear attack (a "first strike").

second-strike capability • the ability to survive a first strike with sufficient resources to deliver an effective counterblow (generally associated with nuclear weapons).

Second World War • see WORLD WAR II.

secret • *adj.* (of information or documents) given the security classification above unclassified and below top secret. • *n.* something that is kept or meant to be kept unknown or unseen by others: *a state secret.*

Secretary of the Navy • the civilian head of the U.S. Department of the Navy responsible to the President for the organization, personnel, maintenance, equipment, and operations of the U.S. Navy. The office of Secretary of the Navy was created on April 30, 1798, concurrent with the establishment of a separate Department of the Navy and the transfer of responsibility for the Navy from the SECRETARY OF WAR.

Secretary of War • the civilian head of the U.S. WAR DEPARTMENT responsible to the President for the organization, maintenance, equipment, and operations of the U.S. Army (and, from 1789 to 1798, of the U.S. Navy and Marine Corps). Established pursuant to the Act of August 7, 1789, the office of Secretary of War was abolished on September 18, 1947, pursuant to the NATIONAL SECURITY ACT OF 1947, which separated the U.S. Air Force from the U.S. Army and created separate Departments and Secretaries for each service. The present Secretary of the Army is the lineal descendant of the Secretary of War.

Secret Committee of Trade • the primary organization to purchase foreign supplies for the REVOLUTIONARY WAR. Supplies were bought from European countries or merchants. It was chaired by ROBERT MORRIS, a controversial figure who was the founder of the Bank of North America. Since the countries giving assistance were neutral countries, the activities of the Secret Committee of Trade, which were conducted through the firm of Willing and Morris, were kept secret, and the Committee had unusual discretionary powers. Though the charges were never proven, Morris was later accused of using government funds to make investments and damaging American credit.

Secret Intelligence Service • (**SIS**) official name for MI6.

secret list • a register of research work or developments on sensitive military projects, the details of which may not be disclosed for reasons of national security.

secret service • **1** a government department concerned with espionage. **2** (**Secret Service**) a branch of the Treasury Department dealing with counterfeiting and providing protection for the President.

section • *n.* **1** a specified military unit: *a camouflage section was added to the army.* **2** a subdivision of an army platoon. **3** a measure of land, equal to one square mile. **4** a particular district of a town.

Section 212 • see SECTION 8.

Section 8 • (also spelled **Section VIII**) **1** through World War II, a psychiatric discharge; an other than honorable discharge for being mentally or emotionally unfit for military service. **2** a soldier who has been so discharged, is in line to be, or should be.

Section 8 (Section 212 after World War II) was the section in Army Regulations detailing the grounds for a psychiatric discharge from military service. Before it was numbered 8, the section was 148½.

---

sectionalism • *n.* restriction of interest to a narrow sphere; undue concern with local interests or petty distinctions at the expense of general well-being: *the rise of democracy, capitalism, and sectionalism.*

DERIVATIVES: **sectionalist** *n.* & *adj.*

sector • *n.* **1** a subdivision of an area for military operations. **2** a distinct part or branch of a nation's economy or society or of a sphere of activity such as education: *the Muslim sector of the village.*

secure • *adj.* protected against attack or other criminal activity: *the official said that no airport could be totally secure.* • *v.* protect against threats; make safe.

PHRASES: **secure arms** hold a rifle with the muzzle downward and the lock in the armpit to guard it from rain.

security • *n.* **1** measures taken by a military unit, an activity, or an installation to protect itself against all acts designed to, or that may, impair its effectiveness. **2** a condition that results from the establishment and maintenance of protective measures that ensure a state of inviolability from hostile acts or influences. **3** with respect to classified matter, the condition that prevents unauthorized persons from having access to official information that is safeguarded in the interests of national security.

security alert team • two or more security force members who form the initial reinforcing element responding to security alarms, emergencies, or irregularities.

security classification • a category to which national security information and material is assigned to denote the degree of damage that unauthorized disclosure would cause to national defense or foreign relations of the United States and to denote the degree of protection required.

security clearance • an administrative determination by competent authority that an individual is eligible, from a security standpoint, for access to classified information.

Security Council, United Nations • see UNITED NATIONS SECURITY COUNCIL

security intelligence • intelligence on the identity, capabilities, and intentions of hostile organizations or individuals who are or may be engaged in espionage, sabotage, subversion, or terrorism.

Sedgwick, John (1813–64) • Union army officer. The Connecticut native fought in MEXICAN WAR (1846–48). In 1855 he left the artillery for the newly organized First Cavalry and fought the Indians in the plains. He considered leaving the military but changed his mind at the outbreak of the CIVIL WAR; he was promoted to lieutenant colonel of the Second Cavalry in 1861 and later returned to command his old unit. He was a protégé of Gen. GEORGE B. MCCLELLAN, whom he repaid with steadfast loyalty. Sedgwick fought with distinction in the PENINSULAR CAMPAIGN of 1862 but led his troops into disaster at Antietam that same year, suffering 2,200 casualties in twenty minutes. He fought to victory in a secondary battle at FREDERICKSBURG (1863) while Gen. JOSEPH HOOKER fought the main engagement at CHANCELLORSVILLE, but Sedgwick's indecisive action afterward allowed the Confederates to achieve victory. In pursuit of Gen. ROBERT E. LEE's troops after GETTYSBURG (1863), Sedgwick again was tentative in his actions. He was killed in action at SPOTSYLVANIA.

Sedgwick was the highest ranking Union officer to be killed in action in the Civil War.

---

sedition • *n.* conduct or speech inciting people to rebel against the authority of a state or monarch.

Sedition Act • a law enacted on May 16, 1918, during WORLD WAR I, to restrict public opinion of the U.S. war effort. An amendment to the ESPIONAGE ACT of 1917, it prohibited spoken and written attacks on the U.S. government or the Constitution and led to numerous arrests. It was repealed in 1921.

Socialist opposition leader Eugene V. Debs was arrested under the law.

Seeger, Alan (1888–1916) • soldier and poet. Seeger was born in New York City but passed much of his youth in Mexico, where his father had a business. Seeger began writing while in Mexico and continued upon his return to New York to attend school. He later attended Harvard. In 1912 he moved to Europe and began writing poetry in earnest. He joined the

Foreign Legion of France and became a war correspondent for the *New Republic* and the *New York Sun*, while continuing to write poetry. In 1916, while hospitalized with bronchitis, he wrote his most famous poem, "I Have a Rendezvous with Death," capturing the futility of war. He was killed in the Battle of the Somme. France awarded him the Croix de Guerre in 1916 and the Medaille Militaire in 1924.

seize • *v.* **1** capture (a place) using force: *army rebels seized an air force base.* **2** assume (power or control) by force: *the current president seized power in a coup.*

seizing • *n.* a length of cord or rope used for fastening or tying.

Selected Reserve • those units and individuals within the Ready Reserve designated by their respective services and approved by the Joint Chiefs of Staff as so essential to initial wartime missions that they have priority over all other reserves. All Selected Reservists are in an active status. The Selected Reserve also includes persons performing initial active duty for training.
DERIVATIVES: **Selected Reservist**

selectee • *n.* a conscript.

selective mobilization • the expansion of the active Armed Forces resulting from action by Congress and/or the President to mobilize Reserve component units, individual ready reservists, and the resources needed for their support to meet the requirements of a domestic emergency that is not the result of an enemy attack.

selective service • service in the armed forces under conscription.

Selective Service Act • **1** (1917) a national conscription bill passed by Congress on April 28, 1917, after U.S. entry into World War I. It expanded the regular army and allowed for the federalization of the National Guard. It prohibited substitutes and bounties, but allowed for certain deferments. It also included moral reforms prohibiting prostitution and liquor sales to soldiers. **2** (1940) a national conscription act passed by Congress on September 16, 1940, prior to U.S. entry into World War II. The nation's first prewar draft act, it initially obligated draftees to serve for one year but was altered in December 1941 to extend the period and scope of service. Deferments were limited and dissent was reflected in antidraft incidents. The Selective Service drafted a total of 10.1 million men under the act. **3** (1948) a draft law passed in June 1948 in response to escalating Cold War tensions. It required all men between 18 and 26 to register for the draft and that established rules for liability to induction and reserve duty. It also proposed student deferment guidelines for the first time. It required twenty-one months of service for individuals selescted by their local draft boards. A high rate of volunteer enlistments prompted a suspension of the act in March 1949. On June 22, 1950 Congress extended the draft act for the Korean War.

Selective Service System • the U.S. federal agency that organizes the mobilization of armed forces. Conscription was first used in the United States during the Civil War by both the North and South. Those who were able to could buy their way out of conscription, and the practice was abandoned once the war was over. Mandatory service was employed during World War I with the Selective Service Act of May 18, 1917. All men between the ages of twenty-one and thirty were required to register. Selective Service was not used during the peacetime following the war until 1940, and it was employed during World War II, the Korean War, and the Vietnam War. Selective Service was ended in 1973 and an all-volunteer military established in its place. Draft registration was reinstituted in 1980 for eighteen-year-old men.

self-loading • *adj.* (especially of a gun) loading automatically: *a self-loading pistol.*
DERIVATIVES: **self-loader** *n.*

self-propelled • *adj.* moving or able to move without external propulsion or agency.
DERIVATIVES: **self-propelling** *adj.*

self-propelled sandbags • slang (in the Persian Gulf War) Marines, especially those dug in at the Kuwait-Iraq border.

Selfridge, Thomas Oliver, Jr. (1836–1924) • Union naval officer. A Massachusetts native, Selfridge spent the early part of his naval career in the South Pacific and in Africa. He participated in the confrontation between the USS *Cumberland* and the Confederate vessel CSS *Virginia* in 1861, at the start of the Civil War; he briefly commanded the *Monitor.* He participated in the campaign against Vicksburg and, in 1864, as commander of the ironclad *Osage*, led a mission to rescue a Union flotilla trapped in the Alexandria rapids. After the war, Selfridge taught at the U.S. Naval Academy and explored and mapped parts of Latin America. Promoted to commander in 1869, he oversaw three surveys in Panama in preparation for the construction of a canal there to link the Atlantic and the Pacific oceans. Selfridge was promoted to captain in 1881, at which time he undertook research on the use of torpedoes and ways to defend against them.

self-righting • *adj.* (of a boat) designed to right itself when capsized.

semaphore • *n.* **1** a system of sending messages by holding the arms or two flags or poles in certain positions according to an alphabetic code. **2** an apparatus for signaling in this way, consisting of an upright with movable parts. **3** a signal sent by semaphore. • *v.* send (a message) by semaphore or by signals resembling semaphore: *Josh stands facing the rear and semaphoring the driver's intentions.*
DERIVATIVES: **semaphoric** *adj.* **semaphorically** *adv.*

semiautomatic • *adj.* **1** partially automatic. **2** (of a firearm) having a mechanism for self-loading but not for continuous firing. • *n.* a semiautomatic firearm.

semifixed ammunition • ammunition in which the cartridge case is not permanently attached to the projectileentry was "ammunition, semifixed"

Seminary Ridge • a prominence of the GETTYSBURG (1863) battleground that is the home of a Lutheran theological seminary. Its multistory buildings provided Union lookout posts and some were used during the battle as hospitals.

Seminole Wars • a series of campaigns in the early nineteenth century mounted by the U.S. Army against various groups of runaway slaves, native Indian marauders, and white bandits, collectively known as the Seminoles, occupying parts of the present state of Florida. The **First Seminole War** (1817–1818) began on November 27, 1817, when Maj. Gen. Edmund P. Gaines led a force of some 4,000 men in an invasion of Spanish Florida to suppress the Seminole border marauders. Gaines was replaced on December 26, 1817, by Maj. Gen. ANDREW JACKSON, who destroyed Seminole power west of the Suwanee River and took the towns of St. Marks and Pensacola thereby ending the war on May 30, 1818. In 1819, pursuant to the ADAMS-ONÍS TREATY, Spain transferred Florida to the United States, and the Seminoles were confined to a reservation. White encroachment on Seminole territory led to the **Second Seminole War** (1835–1842), remembered as the bloodiest Indian campaigns in U.S. history. The Second Seminole War began on December 28, 1835, when a band of Seminoles led by the part-white OSCEOLA, massacred a force of 108 men under Army Maj. Francis L. Dade. Under a series of commanding officers—who included, among others, WINFIELD SCOTT and ZACHARY TAYLOR—some 10,000 U.S. Army troops and 30,000 volunteers gradually wore down the resistance of some 5,000 Seminole guerrillas with aggressive patrolling, the detention of key Seminole leaders, the destruction of Seminole villages and crops, and the removal of Seminoles from Florida to reservations elsewhere. The Second Seminole War ended in August 1842, but white settlers continued to press the Seminoles, and the **Third Seminole War** began on December 20, 1855, with a Seminole attack on an Army outpost. The Third Seminole War was fought largely by volunteers rather than Regular Army troops, and the final battle took place on March 5, 1857. One of the principal Seminole leaders, Billy Bowlegs, surrendered with his band, leaving only about 120 Seminoles active in Florida, and the U.S. Army declared the war over on May 8, 1858.

semirigid • *adj.* **1** (of an airship) having a stiffened keel attached to a flexible gas container. **2** (of an inflatable boat) having a rigid hull and inflatable sponsons.

Semmes, Raphael (1809–77) • Confederate naval officer, born in Maryland. He fought in many of the major engagements of the MEXICAN WAR (1846–48), including VERACRUZ, CERRO GORDO, and MEXICO CITY. When the CIVIL WAR broke out, he enlisted in the Confederate army and took the lead in outfitting a ship to serve as a commerce raider against the Union; Semmes took eighteen prizes. He then took command of the CSS *Alabama*, with which he captured sixty-nine Union vessels; however, the ship sank in an ill-advised confrontation with a Union ship off the coast of Cherbourg, France, where it had sailed for repairs. For his efforts, Semmes received a hero's welcome back in the Confederacy and was commissioned a rear admiral. After the war he was threatened with federal charges of piracy but never tried.

Semper fidelis • 'always faithful', the motto of the U.S. Marine Corps.

Semper paratus • 'always ready', the motto and marching song of the U.S. COAST GUARD, originally written and composed in 1927 by Capt. Francis S. Van Boskerck, USCG. The lyrics of the song have been changed several times.

Senate Armed Services Committee • a committee of the U.S. Senate that was established by the Legislative Reorganization Act of 1946, though it has roots dating back to Revolutionary times. The committee has broad responsibilities for the common defense and the departments of Defense, the Army, Navy, and Air Force, as well as the SELECTIVE SERVICE SYSTEM, naval petroleum reserves (except in Alaska), national security aspects of nuclear energy, and strategic and critical materials related to defense. The committee operates through subcommittees that consider, for example, readiness, staffing, and the defense industry; it also drafts legislation that provides program authority for defense activities performed by the executive branch. Congress may create, alter, or abolish any office or program undertaken by the PENTAGON, subject to presidential veto. Thus, the Armed Services Committee has a role in every activity related to national defense.

Seneca • the largest tribe of the Iroquois-speaking Five Nations. Located in western New York, in the 1760s the Senecas actively urged Indian resistance to the British in the Ohio Valley and Great Lakes region and thus provoked what came to be called PONTIAC'S REBELLION (1763–66).

senior aircraftman • a male rank in the RAF, above leading aircraftman and below junior technician.

senior aircraftwoman • a female rank in the RAF, above leading aircraftwoman and below junior technician.

Senior Airman • U.S. Air Force enlisted rank equivalent to an Army or Marine Corps corporal or Navy/Coast Guard Petty Officer Third Class (pay grade E-4).

senior chief petty officer • a noncommissioned officer in the U.S. Navy or Coast Guard ranking above chief petty officer and below master chief petty officer.

senior master sergeant • a noncommissioned officer in the U.S. Air Force ranking above master sergeant and below chief master sergeant.

Senior Service • Brit. the Royal Navy.
ORIGIN: *Senior* with reference to the fact that

it predated the East India Trading Company, which many naval officers joined after resigning their commissions, attracted by advantageous pay following the granting of a royal charter to the company in 1600.

sensitive • *adj.* requiring special protection from disclosure that could cause embarrassment, compromise, or threat to the security of the sponsoring power. The term may be applied to an agency, installation, person, position, document, material, or activity.

Sensitive Compartmented Information • (**SCI**) information and materials bearing special community controls indicating restricted handling within present and future community intelligence collection programs and their end products for which community systems of compartmentation have been or will be formally established; in short, a designated category of intelligence materials which by virtue of their means of collection or other extraordinary aspect of their nature required special handling and more than routine protection.

sentinel • *n.* **1** a soldier or guard whose job is to stand and keep watch. **2** an electronic device designed to detect danger: *an electronic sea sentinel to provide early warnings of storms.* **3** a military watchtower for defense of a camp or city wall: *sentinel towers of medieval period.* • *v.* (**sentineled**, **sentineling**) station a soldier or guard by (a place) to keep watch.
PHRASES: **stand sentinel** (of a soldier) keep watch: *soldiers stood sentinel with their muskets.*

Sentinel missile defense system • a program initiated by President LYNDON B. JOHNSON to provide defense against presumed Chinese missile attack. Though short-lived and inadequate, it was the beginning of standing ballistic missile defense in the United States.

sentry • *n.* (pl. **-ies**) a soldier stationed to keep guard or to control access to a place.
PHRASES: **stand sentry** keep guard or control access to a place.

Sentry • (**E-3**) a surveillance aircraft used as part of the AIRBORNE WARNING AND CONTROL SYSTEMS.

sentry box • a structure providing shelter for a standing sentry.

sentry-go • the duty of being a sentry.

Seoul |sōl| • the capital of South Korea, situated in the northwest of the country on the Han River. Extensively developed under Japanese rule, it became the capital of South Korea after the partition of 1945. The city was captured and retaken four times during the KOREAN WAR, suffering severe damage as a result. On June 28, 1950, Seoul came under North Korean control, and most of the South Korean army was destroyed; the U.N. forces immediately came to the aid of South Korea. South Korea recaptured Seoul on September 26, 1950. When Chinese soldiers entered Korea to assist North Korean troops, they forced U.N. troops to retreat, and Seoul was evacuated on January 4, 1951. The U.S. Army recaptured Seoul on March 15, 1951.

separate-loading ammunition • ammunition in which the projectile and charge are loaded into a gun separately.

separatist • *n.* a person who supports the separation of a particular group of people from a larger body on the basis of ethnicity, religion, or gender: *religious separatists.* • *adj.* of or relating to such separation or those supporting it: *a separatist rebellion.*

sequester |səˈkwestər| • *v.* isolate or hide away (someone or something): *Tiberius was sequestered on an island.* • *n.* a general cut in government spending: *an across-the-board sequester to reduce spending by 3%.*

sequestration |ˌsēkwiˈstrāsʜən; ˌsek-| • *n.* **1** the action of making a general cut in government spending: *the measure brings the federal budget closer to sequestration.* **2** the action of taking legal possession of assets until a debt has been paid or other claims have been met: *if such court injunctions are ignored, sequestration of their assets will follow.* **3** the action of taking forcible possession of something; confiscation: *they demanded the sequestration of the incriminating correspondence.*

sergeant • *n.* a noncommissioned officer in the armed forces, in particular (in the U.S. Army or Marine Corps) an NCO ranking above corporal and below staff sergeant, or (in the U.S. Air Force) an NCO ranking above airman and below staff sergeant.
DERIVATIVES: **sergeancy** *n.* (pl. **-ies**).

Sergeant • (**MGM-29A**) a mobile surface-to-surface missile with nuclear warhead capability, designed to attack targets up to a range of 75 nautical miles.

Sergeant First Class • a non-commissioned officer rank in the U.S. Army corresponding to Master Sergeant in the U.S. Air Force, Chief Petty Officer in the U.S. Navy and Coast Guard, and Gunnery Sergeant in the U.S. Marine Corps; pay grade E-7.

sergeant major • an noncommissioned officer in the U.S. Army or Marine Corps of the highest rank, above master sergeant and below warrant officer.

Sergeant Major of the Army • the highest ranking non-commissioned officer in the U.S. Army and the principal enlisted advisor to the Army Chief of Staff.

Sergeant Major of the Marine Corps • the highest ranking non-commissioned officer in the U.S. Marine Corps and the principal enlisted advisor to the Commandant of the Marine Corps.

Sergeants Major Academy • an advanced army leadership training school at Fort Bliss, Texas. It offers the U.S. Sergeants Major Course, which is the highest noncommissioned officer training course.

Sergt • *abbr.* Sergeant.

serial • *n.* **1** an element or a group of elements within a series that is given a numerical or alphabetical designation for convenience in planning, scheduling, and control. **2** any number of aircraft under one commander, usually conveying one air-transportable unit or subunit to the same objective.

seriously ill or injured • (**SII**) the casualty status of a person whose illness or injury is classified by medical authority to be of such severity that there is cause for immediate concern, but there is not imminent danger to life.

serjeant • *n.* Brit. (in official lists) a sergeant in the Foot Guards.

serve • *v.* **1** be employed as a member of the armed forces: *a military engineer who served with the army.* **2** operate (a gun): *before long Lodge was the only man in his section able to serve the guns.* **3** bind (a rope) with thin cord to protect or strengthen it. **4** perform duties or services for (another person or an organization): *Malcolm has served the church very faithfully.*

service • *n.* (**the services**) the armed forces: (**service**) *service personnel.*
PHRASES: **see service** serve in the armed forces: *he saw service in both world wars.*

service academy • a military academy serving one of the four branches of the U.S. armed forces. See MILITARY ACADEMY.

service ammunition • ammunition intended for combat, rather than for training purposes.

service dress • Brit. military uniform worn on formal but not ceremonial occasions.

service force • a naval task organization that performs missions for the logistic support of operations.

service group • a major naval administration and/or tactical organization, consisting of the commander and the staff, designed to exercise operational control and administrative command of assigned squadrons and units in executing their tasks of providing logistic support of fleet operations.

serviceman • *n.* (pl. **-men**) a man serving in the armed forces.

Servicemen's Readjustment Act of 1944 • a public law, popularly known as the G.I. BILL, that provided benefits for veterans. Its main provisions were education and training benefits; loan guaranties for a home, farm, or business; unemployment pay; job-finding assistance; and military review of dishonorable discharges.

servicepeople • *pl. noun* men and women in the armed forces.

service squadron • an administrative and/or tactical subdivision of a naval service force or service group, consisting of the commander and the staff, organized to exercise operational control and administrative command of assigned units in providing logistic support of fleet units as directed.

service the target • (in the Persian Gulf War) to destroy the enemy, or target.

"Service the target" was a winner, along with "force package," of 1991 Doublespeak Award from National Conference of Teachers of English.

service troops • those units designed to render supply, maintenance, transportation, evacuation, hospitalization, and other services required by air and ground combat units to carry out effectively their mission in combat.

servicewoman • *n.* (pl. **-women**) a woman serving in the armed forces.

set[1] • *v.* put (a sail) up in position to catch the wind: *a safe distance from shore all sails were set.*
PHRASES: **set sail** hoist the sails of a boat. ▸**set something off** detonate a bomb.

set[2] • *n.* the action of a current or tide of flowing in a particular direction: *the rudder kept the dinghy straight against the set of the tide.*

settle • *v.* (of a ship or boat) sink gradually.

Seven Days' Battle • a weeklong series of CIVIL WAR battles from June 25 to July 1, 1862 that ultimately prevented the Union from capturing RICHMOND, the Confederate capital. Union forces were mainly under the command of Gen. GEORGE B. MCCLELLAN and Confederates were under Gen. ROBERT E. LEE. There were casualties approaching 20,000 on both sides. The battles marked the end of the PENINSULAR CAMPAIGN.

Seven Pines, Battle of • an inconclusive CIVIL WAR battle in the PENINSULAR CAMPAIGN from May 31 to June 1, 1862. Forces from both sides continuously fed reinforcements into the battle area, around the Chickahominy River, with the effect that casualties rose considerably on both sides, each of which claimed victory.

17th Parallel • the military demarcation line established in Vietnam by the GENEVA AGREEMENT ON INDOCHINA of April 26–July 21, 1954.

Seventh Fleet • established in March 1943 when the Southwest Pacific Force was renamed, and the largest forward-deployed U.S. fleet. Its area of responsibility covers the Western Pacific and Indian Oceans. In 1947, the Fleet's name was changed to Naval Forces Western Pacific, then, just before the KOREAN WAR began, it was redesignated as U.S. Seventh Task Fleet. In 1950, it was again redesignated as the U.S. Seventh Fleet. It has participated in every major war in which the United States has fought since WORLD WAR II, including the PERSIAN GULF WAR. In 1994, the Fleet was made responsible for the defense of South Korea (Combined Naval Component Command) and, subsequently, named one of three primary Joint Task Force Commands responsible to the Commander in Chief, U.S. Pacific Command.

Seventh U.S. Army • see U.S. ARMY EUROPE/SEVENTH U.S. ARMY.

Seven Years War • see FRENCH AND INDIAN WAR.

Seversky, Alexander de (1894–1974) • aerospace engineer, born in Georgia, then part of imperial Russia, de Seversky received a military education and served in WORLD WAR I, losing a leg in combat. He became chief of naval fighter aviation in the Baltic Sea and the most famous Russian naval pilot of the war. After the Russian Revolution, the provisional government sent him to Washington, D.C., as an assistant naval attaché for air; when the Bolsheviks took over the government in 1918 he defected and became a consulting engineer and test pilot for the U.S. Department of War. In his work for the government, de Seversky developed several technological innovations, including in-flight refueling and the first fully automatic synchronous bombsight (which led the way to automatic pilot). He became a U.S. citizen in 1927 and was commissioned a major in the Air Corps Specialists Reserve. De Seversky founded his own company, Seversky Aircraft Corporation, in 1931, where he developed the world's fastest amphibious airplane and the first all-metal skin-stressed single-seat fighter, whose design became an industry standard. Rebellion against some of his designs within the company led the board of directors to oust him as president in 1939 and to change the name of the company to Republic Aviation Company. De Seversky went on to lobby Congress and to argue forcefully for the role of aviation in warfare, particularly in his book *Victory through Air Power*; his views had great impact. After the war, he warned against Soviet aggression, supported the concept of deterrence through threat of massive retaliation, and researched ways to defend against nuclear attack.

Seward, William (1801–72) • U.S. secretary of state, state governor, and U.S. senator, born in New York. As governor of New York, Seward advocated humane reform of the prison system and mental health care, and was outspokenly antislavery. In 1849 Seward moved to the U.S. Senate, where he opposed slavery's extension into the Western territories and fought vigorously against the KANSAS-NEBRASKA ACT. Fiercely ambitious, Seward was considered the favorite to win the presidential nomination of the new Republican party in 1860, but in the end he lost to ABRAHAM LINCOLN, who was seen as less polarizing. Seward stayed loyal to the party and was named Lincoln's secretary of state. His goal was to preserve the Union, to which end he favored supporting Virginia Unionists by relinquishing FORT SUMTER, but Lincoln demurred; he moved to reprovision the fort, and hostilities broke out. As secretary of state, Seward worked to keep European powers from recognizing or aiding the Confederacy and to prevent British shipbuilders from selling ships to the South. Seward clashed with President ANDREW JOHNSON, who took office on Lincoln's assassination in April 1865; the two disagreed over RECONSTRUCTION, on which Seward was more moderate; he supported the THIRTEENTH AMENDMENT but adopted a conciliatory tone toward the formerly secessionist states and toward former slaveowners. Seward opposed the FOURTEENTH AMENDMENT because of its limits on participation in government by Confederates. His foreign policy was progressive; his most famous act was the acquisition from Russia of Alaska in 1867, a purchase known at the time as "Seward's Folly." He also supported the construction of the PANAMA CANAL.

Both a moral leader and a hard-nosed pragmatist, Seward is considered, along with JOHN QUINCY ADAMS, the nation's greatest secretary of state.

---

sextant |ˈsekstənt| • *n.* an instrument with a graduated arc of 60° and a sighting mechanism, used for measuring the angular distances between objects and especially for taking altitudes in navigation and surveying.

Seymour, Truman (1824–91) • Union army officer, born in Vermont. Seymour fought in the MEXICAN WAR (1846–48). At the outbreak of the CIVIL WAR, he had a leading role in the defense of FORT SUMTER (1861), earning a brevet to major. In 1862 he was promoted to brigadier general of volunteers and given command of the Pennsylvania Reserve Division; he participated in fierce fighting during the PENINSULAR CAMPAIGN that year. He was also present at the SECOND BATTLE OF BULL RUN (1862) and at ANTIETAM (1862). In 1864 he suffered a major defeat in an expedition to return Florida to the Union. His troops also performed poorly in the BATTLE OF THE WILDERNESS (1864); Seymour himself was captured but later exchanged. He was more successful at PETERSBURG, where he earned brevets to major general in the volunteer and the regular armies.

SF • *abbr.* special forces.

SFG • *abbr.* special forces group.

Sgt. (also **SGT**) • *abbr.* Sergeant.

shadower • a maritime unit observing and (not necessarily continuously) maintaining contact with an object; shadowing may be carried out either overtly or covertly.

SHAEF • *abbr.* Supreme Headquarters, Allied Expeditionary Forces.

Shafter, William Rufus (1835–1906) • Union army officer and CONGRESSIONAL MEDAL OF HONOR recipient, born in Michigan. Shafter was wounded at FAIR OAKS (1862), where his valor earned him the Congressional Medal of Honor. He was taken prisoner at the battle of Thompson's Station (1863) but released three months later. Later that year, he trained the 17th U.S. (Colored) Infantry Regiment, one of the army's first black units, which, as a colonel, he led at NASHVILLE (1864). Despite medical problems, he served with distinction in the SPANISH-AMERICAN WAR (1898), taking control of Cuba in four weeks; he convinced the Cubans to surrender SANTIAGO, despite serious supply problems, shortages of weapons, and other difficulties faced by the Americans, in addition to some poor command decisions on the part of Shafter.

shake and bake • slang **1** (in the Vietnam War) a hastily trained sergeant who earned his rank quickly through noncommissioned officer school, particularly in a 21-week leadership and advanced infantry course at Fort Benning, Georgia. (Also called **instant NCOs**.) **2** (in the Persian Gulf War) an air attack using a combination of weapons.

shakedown • *n.* informal **1** a radical change or restructuring, particularly in a hierarchical organization or group: *after the collapse of the Soviet Union, a shakedown of the Russian press was inevitable.* **2** a thorough search of a person or place: *harassment and shakedowns by persons in police uniforms.* **3** a swindle; a piece of extortion: *he wants to eliminate bribery, shakedowns, and bid-rigging in New York City's construction* *industry.* **4** a test of a new product or model, especially a vehicle or ship: *the high-orbit shakedown of the lunar module had its merits.* **5** a makeshift bed.

shako | 'SHækō; 'SHā- | • *n.* (pl. **-os**) a cylindrical or conical military hat with a bill and a plume or pom-pom.

shallop | 'SHæləp | • *n.* a large heavy boat with one or more masts and carrying fore-and-aft or lug sails and sometimes equipped with guns.

shallow fording • the ability of a self-propelled gun or ground vehicle equipped with built-in waterproofing, with its wheels or tracks in contact with the ground, to negotiate a water obstacle without the use of a special waterproofing kit.

SHAPE • *abbr.* Supreme Headquarters Allied Powers Europe.

shaped charge • an explosive charge with a cavity that causes the blast to be concentrated into a small area.

shared use agreement • a treaty or other formal agreement between nations providing for the military forces of one nation to use facilities or supplies belonging to the other nation, with or without compensation.

Sharp Edge, Operation • a MARINE EXPEDITIONARY UNIT using the USS *Saipan* that evacuated U.S. citizens and others from politically unstable Liberia in late 1990 and early 1991.

Sharpsburg, Battle of • see ANTIETAM, BATTLE OF

sharpshooter • *n.* a person who is very skilled in shooting.

DERIVATIVES: **sharpshooting** *n.* & *adj.*

shavetail • slang, often derogatory **1** a newly commissioned officer, especially a second lieutenant. **2** an officer recently graduated from WEST POINT. **3** (**shavetail general**) a new brigadier general. **4** an unbroken mule.

ORIGIN: Around the early 1800s and later, it was customary for the tails of newly purchased mules to be shaved to indicate that they had not yet been broken and trained.

Shaw, Robert Gould (1837–63) • Union army officer. Born in Massachusetts into one of the nation's wealthiest and most staunchly abolitionist families, Shaw had a privileged early childhood but suffered after the family moved to New York and then to Europe. He began drinking and considered himself a failure. His service in the Union army during the CIVIL WAR changed his life; he was a capable soldier who fought at ANTIETAM (1862) and at CEDAR CREEK (1864) and who loved military life. In 1863, Shaw, himself not an abolitionist, rejected but then under pressure accepted the colonelcy of the North's first "colored" regiment, the Fifty-fourth Regiment of the Massachusetts Volunteer Infantry. After coercive training under Shaw, the unit performed poorly in its first military engagement, at Hilton Head, South Carolina. In July 1863, however, the troop performed ably, holding off Confederate forces at James Island, South Carolina, until leaders could organize a defensive retreat. Shaw then volunteered his troops to attack FORT WAGNER, the first step in the assault on Charleston. Although the assault failed, the Fifty-fourth fought valiantly; 272 were killed, wounded, or captured, including Shaw, who died in the attack. The exemplary performance by the unit helped to dispell the idea that blacks lacked the intelligence or the discipline to perform well as soldiers.

A statue by Augustus Saint-Gauden on the Boston Common honors Shaw, and the history of the Fifty-fourth was the subject of an Academy Award-winning motion picture, *Glory* (1989).

Shaw, Samuel (1754–94) • REVOLUTIONARY WAR army officer and diplomat. A native of Boston, Shaw joined the local militia during the siege of Boston (1775); that December he was commissioned a second lieutenant in the Continental Artillery. In 1780 he became captain of the 3rd Artillery. He commanded at Fort Washington in 1776 but was relieved shortly before the British took the fort. From 1779 to 1783 he was an aide-de-camp to Gen. HENRY KNOX, chief of the Continental Artillery. Primarily a staff officer, he was present at a number of important battles, including TRENTON (1776), MONMOUTH (1777), and YORKTOWN (1781). After the war, he sailed on the ship, the *Empress of China*, that opened up the China trade; from 1786 to 1789 he was consul at Canton. He returned to the United States in 1792 but sailed again for China when he was reappointed by President GEORGE WASHINGTON.

Shays, Daniel (1747?–1825) • REVOLUTIONARY WAR army officer and insurgent. A Massachusetts farmer, Shays rose through the ranks of the Continental army from 1775 to 1780. He was promoted to sergeant in recognition of his bravery at BUNKER HILL in 1775, and in 1779 he was commissioned a captain in the Continental army. In 1777 he received a ceremonial sword from the MARQUIS DE LAFAYETTE in recognition of his valor at SARATOGA. In 1780 Shays left the army and returned to his struggling farm in western Massachusetts. He soon became a leader of the movement among farmers seeking redress of their grievances during economic hard times caused by deflation, hard currency shortages, and lack of credit. In 1786 fighting broke out between Shays's followers and the local militia after the farmers tried to block the local courts from sitting and demanded tax and debt relief. The militia put down the insurgency by the disorganized farmers with ease; many were captured and the others sent to their homes. After the failure of SHAYS'S REBELLION to win any relief for the farmers, Shays hid in Vermont and later moved to New York, where he continued to farm.

Shays's Rebellion • an uprising by Massachusetts farmers and others led by former REVOLUTIONARY WAR leaders, chief among them DANIEL SHAYS, against the harsh treatment of debtors by the courts in 1786–87. It included an attempt by the rebels to take the federal arsenal near Springfield, which failed.

sheaf • *n.* in artillery and naval gunfire support, planned planes (lines) of fire that produce a desired pattern of bursts with rounds fired by two or more weapons.

sheath knife • a short knife similar to a dagger, carried in a sheath.

sheer[1] • *v.* (typically of a boat or ship) swerve or change course quickly: *the boat sheered off to beach further up the coast.* • *n.* a sudden deviation from a course, especially by a boat.

sheer[2] • *n.* the upward slope of a ship's lines toward the bow and stern.

sheerlegs |ˈshir,legz| • *plural n.* a hoisting apparatus made from poles joined at or near the top and separated at the bottom, used for masting ships, installing engines, and lifting other heavy objects.

sheet • *n.* **1** a rope attached to the lower corner of a sail for securing or extending the sail or for altering its direction. **2** (**sheets**) the space at the bow or stern of an open boat. • *v.* **1** (**sheet something in/out**) make a sail more or less taut. **2** (**sheet something home**) extend a sail by tightening the sheets so that the sail is set as flat as possible.

sheet explosive • plastic explosive provided in a sheet form.

Shelby, Evan (1719–94) • REVOLUTIONARY WAR army officer. Shelby was born in Wales, but his family emigrated to the United States in 1735, later settling in Maryland. In 1758 Shelby pioneered a trail from the Potomac River to Fort Cumberland while part of an expedition against FORT DUQUESNE. Shelby moved to Virginia in 1772 and established a trading post in what is now Tennessee; the post became an important defense against Indian attack. Four years later, Shelby participated in expeditions against the Cherokee and became colonel of the militia in Washington County, and in 1779 he led a successful raid on the Chickamauga. In reward, he was promoted to brigadier general of the Virginia militia. In 1779, also, it was discovered that Shelby's post was actually in North Carolina and he was elected to the North Carolina Senate in 1781.

Shelby, Isaac (1750–1826) • REVOLUTIONARY WAR army officer and state governor. Son of EVAN SHELBY, Isaac Shelby was born in Maryland. He served as a first lieutenant in LORD DUNMORE'S WAR (1774). Patrick Henry, governor of Virginia, named him commissary agent of the Continental army to provision the frontier outposts; he also fought against British forces in western North Carolina. Warned by the British to desist, he and others nonetheless planned a series of raids in 1780 and repeatedly defeated the opposing forces. The British learned of a planned attack instigated by Shelby; the Americans met a reinforced British unit at COWPENS in 1781 but by sheer brilliance managed a victory that delayed the British advance in North Carolina. Shelby became a local hero and was elected to the North Carolina legislature and reelected in 1782. After the war Shelby attended the Kentucky statehood convention in 1784 and became Kentucky's first governor (1792). Shelby left the governorship in 1796. He reluctantly ran again for the state house in 1812, as concern about the impending war mounted. Winning a landslide election, he strengthened the militia and organized what became a major victory against the British at the BATTLE OF THE THAMES (1813), in which the Shawnee chief TECUMSEH, fighting with the Americans, was killed.

Shelby, Joseph Orville (1830–97) • Confederate army officer. Pro-slavery and a slave owner, he sided with the Confederacy at the outbreak of the CIVIL WAR, leading what was nicknamed "The Iron Brigade" in battles around the Mississippi and earning promotion to colonel. In 1863 he led a raid into Missouri, in which, although seriously outnumbered, his brigade inflicted major losses on Union troops and property. During a second foray into Missouri in 1864 as a division commander under Maj. Gen. STERLING PRICE, Shelby's quick action avoided a Confederate loss. After the war, he led his men to Mexico and offered to fight in support of Emperor Maximilian, but the offer was declined.

shelf life • the length of time during which an item of supply (subject to deterioration or having a limited life that cannot be renewed) is considered serviceable while stored.

shell • *n.* **1** an explosive artillery projectile or bomb: *the sound of the shell passing over, followed by the explosion | shell holes.* **2** a hollow metal or paper case used as a container for fireworks, explosives, or cartridges. **3** a cartridge. • *v.* bombard with shells: *the guns started shelling their positions.*

shellback • *n.* informal an old or experienced sailor, especially one who has crossed the equator.

shellfire • *n.* bombardment by shells.

shell jacket • an army officer's tight-fitting undress jacket reaching to the waist.

shell shock • psychological disturbance caused by prolonged exposure to active warfare, especially being under bombardment. Also called COMBAT FATIGUE.

DERIVATIVES: **shell-shocked** *adj.*

ORIGIN: World War I: with reference to exposure to shellfire.

shelter-half tent • a small, two-man tent formed by joining two shelter-halves; a pup tent.

Shelton, Henry (1942?–) • chairman of the JOINT CHIEFS OF STAFF. The North Carolinian entered the army in 1963 and served two tours in the VIETNAM WAR. From 1987 to 1989 he was deputy operations chief for the Joint Chiefs of Staff, and during the PERSIAN GULF WAR (1991), with the rank of brigadier general, he helped lead the 101st Airborne's deployment. In 1994, as Joint Task Force Commander, he oversaw the U.S. invasion of Haiti; two years later he became head of U.S. Special Operations, headquartered at MacDill Air Force Base in Florida. In 1997 President BILL CLINTON nominated him to be Chairman of the Joint Chiefs of Staff; he was confirmed on September 16.

***Shenandoah*, CSS** • an iron-framed full-rigged ship with auxiliary steam power and teak planking. The Confederate government bought it from the British in 1864 and converted it to a ship-of-war in the waters off Madeira. The *Shenandoah* was assigned to disrupt commerce in areas not directly affected by the CIVIL WAR, and was very successful, pursuing merchant ships along the Cape of Good Hope—Australia route and the whaling fleet in the Pacific. Learning of the Confederate surrender on June 23, 1865, commanding officer JAMES I. WADDELL chose to continue hostile activities, and went on to capture additional prizes, the last eleven of those taken near the Arctic Circle in a period of only seven hours.

The CSS *Shenandoah* was at sea for an entire year, traveled 58,000 miles, and captured a total of thirty-eight Union ships. Two thirds of that number were captured after the Civil War had ended.

Shenandoah Valley • a section of the Great Appalachian Valley, located primarily in Virginia. Campaigns occurred there in the CIVIL WAR between July 1861 and March 1865 in a struggle to control this important region. The South used the transportation advantages of the valley so well that it often became for the North the "valley of humiliation" until late in the war, when the Union defeated Confederate control. Advances by both sides threatened the other side's capitals in Richmond and Washington.

Shenandoah Valley Campaign • **1** Confederate Lt. Gen. "STONEWALL" JACKSON's strategy in Virginia's SHENANDOAH VALLEY, May–June 1862, during the CIVIL WAR. Jackson used his modest force of 4,200 men in an offensive thrust north, causing Union troops to draw reinforcements from other campaigns to protect the capital of Washington. This innovative and aggressive strategy is considered Jackson's greatest accomplishment. **2** an 1864 Union campaign during the CIVIL WAR to take the Shenandoah Valley of Virginia, thus depriving the Confederacy of its strategic and agricultural benefits. The principal Gens. were JUBAL EARLY on the Confederate side, and PHILIP H. SHERIDAN on the Union side with vastly superior forces. The Union prevailed and gained control of the valley, contributing greatly to President ABRAHAM LINCOLN's reelection the same year.

Shepard, William (1737–1817) • REVOLUTIONARY WAR army officer and U.S. Representative. An active patriot, he enlisted as a lieutenant colonel in the Continental army at the outbreak of the war, fighting during the siege of Boston and in the Continental loss at New York City and retreating north with Gen. GEORGE WASHINGTON's troops. He wintered at VALLEY FORGE in 1778 and returned to Massachusetts as a recruiter. In 1786 he was commissioned major general in the New Hampshire militia, in which role he helped put down SHAYS'S REBELLION (1786). In 1796 Shepard was elected to the U.S. House of Representatives, where he served three terms.

Sheridan • (**M-551**) a U.S. light tank, first used in 1966, designed to be air-transportable for U.S. Air Force airborne divisions and armed with a 152 mm gun/launcher, able to fire both SHILLELAGH missiles or conventional ammunition, a 50-caliber machine gun, and a 7.62 mm machine gun. It had a top speed of 65 mph.

Sheridan, Philip Henry (1831–1888) • Union army officer. Born while his family was en route from Ireland to the United States, Sheridan had his first military experience patrolling an Indian reservation in Oregon after graduating from the U.S. MILITARY ACADEMY. When the CIVIL WAR began, he was appointed chief commissary and quartermaster for the Army of the Southwest Missouri District, although he wished for a command. In 1862 he succeeded in obtaining a colonelcy in the Second Michigan Cavalry; one month later he became its commander. Less than month after that, his 800-troop unit was unexpectedly attacked by 5,000 Confederates; Sheridan beat them decisively. He was promoted to brigadier general. In command of the Eleventh Division of the Army of the Ohio, Sheridan won a number of victories but lost to superior numbers at CHICKAMAUGA (1863). In the counterattack, Sheridan led his troops beyond their objective and inflicted major losses on the Confederates. In 1864 Gen. ULYSSES S. GRANT named him chief of cavalry for the ARMY OF THE POTOMAC. Sheridan asserted he could take Richmond; Grant took him up on the boast and let him try, and Sheridan took 10,000 men, defeated Confederate Gen. J.E.B. STUART, who died in the assault, and reached Richmond. His next assignment was to defeat Gen. JUBAL EARLY, who was occupying the SHENANDOAH VALLEY; Sheridan's massive assault sent the Confederates fleeing. When Early launched a surprise attack on Sheridan's forces at Winchester, Sheridan again drove the Confederates from the field. He was equally effective in the waning days of the war, at PETERSBURG and RICHMOND; he raced Gen. ROBERT E. LEE for APPOMATTOX, where the last cache of Confederate food was stored, and arrived before the Confederate general, who was forced to surrender. In 1883 he was named general in chief of the U.S. Army.

Sherman, Forrest Percival (1896–1951) • U.S. naval officer and CHIEF OF NAVAL OPERATIONS. Sherman, born in New Hampshire, became a naval aviator in 1922 and took on assignments of increasing responsibility. In 1932 he was named commander of Fighting Squadron One aboard the aircraft carrier USS *Saratoga*. As WORLD WAR II approached, in 1940 he joined the War Plans Division, Office of the Chief of Naval Operations, and in 1941 he was a naval aviation adviser at the ATLANTIC CHARTER Conference. He returned to sea duty in 1942, commanding the aircraft carrier *Wasp*, and in 1943 helped plan amphibious operations against Japan. After the war, in 1945 Sherman became Deputy Chief of Naval Operations and supported the unification of the armed forces into the DEPARTMENT OF DEFENSE. He was a trusted military adviser to President HARRY S. TRUMAN; his advice underpinned the TRUMAN DOCTRINE and the provision of aid to Greece and Turkey in 1947. He also supported an ongoing U.S. naval presence in the Mediterranean, and Truman named him commander of U.S. Naval Forces, Mediterranean, later renamed the Sixth Task Fleet. In 1949 Sherman was promoted to admiral and named Chief of Naval Operations. He died while on a diplomatic mission to Europe.

Sherman necktie • slang (in the Civil War) an iron railroad rail heated over a bonfire of railroad ties and twisted around a tree as a means of disrupting Confederate rail traffic. (Also called **Sherman's hairpin**.)

Sherman's March to the Sea • the march of an army of 62,000 men under the command of Maj. Gen. WILLIAM T. SHERMAN from Atlanta toward Savannah, Georgia in the final months 1864. He left in his wake a path of almost total destruction. It is often cited as the first example of TOTAL WAR and an inspiration for the German BLITZKRIEG.

Sherman tank • an American type of medium tank, used in large numbers during WORLD WAR II.

Sherman, William Tecumseh (1820–1891) • Union army officer, born in Ohio. Sherman's first military assignments after graduation from the U.S. MILITARY ACADEMY were in the South. He spent the MEXICAN WAR (1846–48) in California, where he saw no combat. From 1853 to 1857 he worked as a bank manager in San Francisco, fearing that the army did not provide adequate financial security. In 1859 he rejoined the army, heading the new Louisiana Military Seminary. In 1861, at the start of the Civil War, he took a command and led his troops ably at FIRST BULL RUN despite the general Union rout. Pessimistic about the Union's chances to win the war and discouraged by the disorganization around him, Sherman began to speak freely of his doubts about the Union effort, and rumors spread questioning his mental stability. He did in fact became so depressed that he contemplated suicide. Association with Gen. ULYSSES S. GRANT bolstered his spirits, and he fought ably at SHILOH and CORINTH (both 1862). He was briefly military governor of Memphis. He led an unsuccessful campaign in 1862 near VICKSBURG that reopened the old charges against him. Sherman was a major participant in Grant's ultimate victory at Vicksburg and continued to command troops in the South. In 1864 he became commander of the Military Division of the Mississippi and began his drive for Atlanta, pushing relentlessly against the forces of Gen. JOSEPH E. JOHNSTON, later replaced by Gen. JOHN B. HOOD. Sherman took Atlanta in September 1864 and cut a swath to the sea, believing that limited and focused destruction intended to demoralize was more effective and merciful than the unending carnage of war. He favored a hard war, followed by a generous peace. When Grant became president, in 1869, Sherman succeeded him as commanding general. He retired in 1884. He was tremendously popular and was mentioned for the presidency numerous times, once responding with a phrase that became famous: "I will not accept if nominated and will not serve if elected."

Sherman court-martialed a Tennessee journalist for his attacks after Sherman's 1862 defeat near Vicksburg, the only time a reporter has been court-martialed.

Sherwood, Isaac Ruth (1835–1925) • Union army officer and U.S. Representative. When the CIVIL WAR began, he enlisted as a private but was mustered out two months later. He returned home, sold his newspaper, and reenlisted as a first lieutenant. He served until 1865 and retired, having been brevetted brigadier general. After the war, he moved to Ohio and resumed his journalism career. He was elected to the U.S. House of Representatives as a Republican and served from 1873 to 1875; in 1906 he ran again, this time as a Democrat, and won election. Memories of the horrors of war still in his mind, he opposed U.S. entry into WORLD WAR I.

shielding • *n.* **1** material of suitable thickness and physical characteristics used to protect personnel from radiation during the manufacture, handling, and transportation of fissionable and radioactive materials. **2** obstructions that tend to protect personnel or materials from the effects of a nuclear explosion.

Shields, James (1806–79) • Union army officer. Shields grew up in Ireland and emigrated to Illinois in 1827. He raised a regiment to fight in the MEXICAN WAR (1846–48) and was present at a number of important battles, including CERRO GORDO and CHAPULTEPEC. He won election to the U.S. Senate in 1849, although the election was of questionable legality since Shields had not been naturalized long enough to meet Constitutional requirements. His service was undistinguished. Shields was not re-elected and he moved to Minnesota. When his new business partner was elected governor, Shields won election to the Senate from his new adopted state, and he took his seat in 1858. When Republicans swept the state in 1859, Shields moved again, this time to California, where he again was politically active. In the CIVIL WAR, he was a brigadier general; he fought off Gen. THOMAS "STONEWALL" JACKSON in the SHENANDOAH VALLEY in 1862 but was defeated by Jackson two months later at WINCHESTER. He resigned his commission, moved to Missouri, and won election to Congress in 1868, although the election was overturned on grounds of fraud. He again was active in local politics and in January 1879 was appointed to the U.S. Senate to fill an unexpired term. He retired in March 1879.

Shields is the only person to have represented three different states in the U.S. Senate.

shifting fire • fire delivered at constant range at varying deflections. Shifting fire is used to cover the width of a target that is too great to be covered by an open sheaf.

Shillelagh |SHə'lālē; -'lālə| • (**MGM-51**) a surface-to-surface missile mounted on a main battle tank or assault reconnaissance vehicle for engagement of enemy armor, troops, and field fortifications.

Shiloh, Battle of • one of the first major battles of the CIVIL WAR, in April, 1862 near Shiloh, Tennessee. Union forces resting under the command of Gen. ULYSSES S. GRANT were first attacked by Confederates and were forced to retreat, but they later gained the lost ground and forced the Confederate army to retreat to Mississippi. There were more than 10,000 casualties on both sides.

ship • *n.* **1** a vessel larger than a boat for transporting people or goods by sea. **2** a sailing vessel with a bowsprit and three or more square-rigged masts. **3** informal any boat, especially a racing boat. **4** a spaceship. **5** an aircraft. • *v.* (**shipped, shipping**) **1** (often **be shipped**) transport (goods or people) on a ship: *the wounded soldiers were shipped home.* **2** dated embark on a ship: *people wishing to get from London to New York ship at Liverpool.* **3** (of a sailor) serve on a ship: *Jack, you shipped with the Admiral once, didn't you?* **4** (of a boat) take in (water) over the side. **5** fix (something such as a rudder or mast) in its place on a ship.
PHRASES: **ship out** (of a naval force or one of its members) go to sea from a home port: *Bob got sick a week before we shipped out.* **take ship** set off on a voyage by ship; embark.
DERIVATIVES: **shipless** *adj.* **shippable** *adj.*

shipbreaker • *n.* a contractor who breaks up old ships for scrap.

shipbuilder • *n.* a person or company whose job or business is the design and construction of ships.
DERIVATIVES: **shipbuilding** *n.*

ship canal • a canal wide and deep enough for ships to travel along it.

ship chandler • (also **ship's chandler**) see CHANDLER.

ship counter • in naval-mine warfare, a device in a mine that prevents the mine from detonating until a preset number of actuations has taken place.

shipload • *n.* as much cargo or as many people as a ship can carry.

shipmaster • *n.* a ship's captain.

shipmate • *n.* a fellow member of a ship's crew.

shipment • *n.* **1** the action of shipping goods: *shipments begin this month.* **2** a quantity of goods shipped; a consignment: *coal and oil shipments.*

ship money • a tax raised in England in medieval times to provide ships for the navy.

ship of the line • a sailing warship of the largest size, used in the line of battle.

shipowner • *n.* a person or company owning a ship or a share in a ship.

shipping • *n.* ships considered collectively, especially those in a particular area or belonging to a particular country.

shipping agent • a licensed agent in a port who transacts a ship's business, such as insurance or documentation, for the owner.

shipping-articles • see SHIP'S ARTICLES.

shipping lane • a term used to indicate the general flow of merchant shipping between two departure/terminal areas.

shipping master • Brit. an official presiding over the signing-on and discharging of seamen.

shipping office • the office of a shipping agent or shipping master.

ship-rigged • *adj.* (of a sailing ship) square-rigged.

ship's articles • a written set of conditions under which sailors or merchant seamen sign on for a given voyage. A ship's articles set forth the pay and other benefits due to the seaman as well as the treatment he may expect and the penalties for infractions of the various rules and standards set forth in the articles.

ship's biscuit • Brit. HARDTACK.

ship's boat • a small boat carried on board a ship.

ship's chandler • see CHANDLER.

ship's company • the crew of a ship.

ship's husband • an agent who is responsible for providing maintenance and supplies for a ship in port.
DERIVATIVES: **ship's husbandry** *n.*

ship's papers • the documents required by international law to be carried by a ship, such as certificates of ownership and registration, crew lists, and cargo manifests.

ship-to-shore • *adj.* from a ship to land: *ship-to-shore phone calls.* • *n.* a radiotelephone connecting a ship to land, or connecting a train or other vehicle to a control center.

ship-to-shore movement • the portion of the assault phase of an amphibious operation that includes the deployment of the landing force from the assault shipping to designated landing areas.

shipway • *n.* a slope on which a ship is built and down which it slides to be launched.

shipwreck • *n.* **1** the destruction of a ship at sea by sinking or breaking up, for example in a storm or after running aground. **2** a ship so destroyed: *the detritus of a forgotten shipwreck.* • *v.* (**be shipwrecked**) (of a person or ship) suffer a shipwreck: *he was shipwrecked off the coast of Sardinia and nearly drowned.*

shipwright |'SHip,rīt| • *n.* a shipbuilder.

shipyard • *n.* a place where ships are built and repaired.

shirk • *v.* avoid or neglect (a duty or responsibility): *his sole motive is to shirk responsibility and avoid extra work.* • *n.* archaic a person who shirks.
DERIVATIVES: **shirker** *n.*

Shirley, William (1694–1771) • colonial governor of Massachusetts. Shirley was born in England into a well-connected family. He took up the practice of law, but some unsuccessful financial investments and general dissatisfaction led him to seek a post in a colonial government, and he arrived in Boston in 1731. He replaced the unpopular governor of Massachusetts, Jonathan Belcher, and quickly resolved a banking and credit crisis; he remained a popular governor, especially after the successful Massachusetts-led raid on FORT LOUISBOURG at Cape Breton, in 1745. He went to Paris to try to negotiate a boundary that would satisfy both Britain and France but found the experience frustrating and returned to Boston in 1753. Shirley was a colonel of a Massachusetts regiment in the FRENCH AND INDIAN WAR (1754–63) and eventually succeeded Gen. EDWARD BRADDOCK as commander of British forces in North America. When the French succeeded in repulsing the British effort to take Fort Oswego, Shirley was blamed, unfairly, for the defeat and recalled to London. He languished there until he won an appointment as governor of the Bahamas in 1759.

shoal • *n.* **1** an area of shallow water, especially as a navigational hazard. **2** a submerged sandbank visible at low water. • *v.* (of water) become shallower. • *adj.* (of water) shallow.

shock front • the boundary between the pressure disturbance created by an explosion (in air, water, or earth) and the ambient atmosphere, water, or earth.

shock troops • a group of soldiers trained specially for carrying out a sudden assault.

shock wave • the continuously propagated pressure pulse formed by the blast from an explosion in air, under water, or under ground.

shogun |ˈsHōgən| • *n.* a hereditary commander in chief in feudal Japan.

DERIVATIVES: **shogunate** |-gənit; -gəˌnāt| *n.*

Sho-I, Operation • see LEYTE GULF, BATTLE FOR.

shooting iron • informal a firearm.

shooting range • an area provided with targets for the controlled practice of shooting.

Shooting Star • (**P-80**) the first U.S. jet fighter to become operational, it had a conventional aircraft design except for its jet engine and laminar flow wing. Produced in 1945, a few of the P-80 arrived in Europe, but too late to engage in any combat missions in WORLD WAR II. By the time of the KOREAN WAR, it was already out-of-date as a fighter, but it performed well as an attack aircraft. Also called F-80.

shooting war • a war in which there is armed conflict, as opposed to a cold war.

shoot-out • *n.* informal a decisive gun battle.

shoot the sun • ascertain the altitude of the sun with a sextant in order to determine one's latitude.

shoran • *n.* a short-range electronic navigation system for precision bombing and other applications that determines precise locations by noting the differences in time of travel between two or more fixed pulse emitters.

ORIGIN: formed from *short-range navigation.*

shore • *n.* **1** the land along the edge of a sea, lake, or other large body of water: *I took the tiller and made for the shore.* **2** (usually **shores**) a country or other geographic area bounded by a coast: *the ripples of Soviet "new thinking" had reached the distant shores of Africa.*

PHRASES: **on shore** ashore; on land: *are any of the crew left on shore?*

shore leave • leisure time spent ashore by a sailor: *the hall was full of sailors **on shore leave**.*

shore party • (also **beach group**) a task organization of the landing force, formed for the purpose of facilitating the landing and movement off the beaches of troops, equipment, and supplies; for the evacuation from the beaches of casualties and enemy prisoners of war; and for facilitating the beaching, retraction, and salvaging of landing ships and craft. It comprises elements of both the naval and landing forces.

shore-to-shore movement • the assault movement of personnel and materiel directly from a shore staging area to the objective, involving no further transfers between types of craft or ships incident to the assault movement.

shorten • *v.* reduce the amount of (sail) exposed to the wind.

short range attack missile • (**AGM-69**) a nuclear-armed, air-to-surface missile that is launched from the B-52 and the FB-111 aircraft. The missile, developed in the 1970s, can be fired in any direction from the attacking aircraft.

short range ballistic missile • (**SRBM**) a ballistic missile with a range of up to 600 nautical miles.

short round • **1** the unintentional or inadvertent delivery of ordnance on friendly troops, installations, or civilians by a friendly weapon system. **2** a defective cartridge in which the projectile has been seated too deeply.

short takeoff and landing • the ability of an aircraft, in takeoff, to clear a 50-foot (15-meter) obstacle within 1,500 feet (500 meters), or, in landing, to stop within 1,500 feet (500 meters) after passing over a 50-foot (15-meter) obstacle.

short-timer • *n.* slang a person nearing the end of their period of military service.

Short, Walter C. (1880–1949) • U.S. army officer. An Illinoisan, Short received the DISTINGUISHED SERVICE MEDAL for his observation of frontline conditions and for his skill in training troops during World War I. He was a gifted administrator, and for this reason, as a major general, was appointed in 1940 to command the U.S. naval base at PEARL HARBOR. His career was destroyed when, on December 7, 1941, the Japanese attacked the base. Short was blamed for the disaster on several counts: that he had not understood his responsibility to protect the ships at the base; his failure to ensure the development of an early warning system that might have alerted the base to the imminent attack, and his failure to anticipate an air attack, rather than an amphibious one. His defenders assert that none of his superiors ever criticized his plans for defense of the base before the attack, only after.

shortwave radio • a radio operating on a wavelength between about 10 and 100 meters and a frequency of 3 to 30 Mhz.

shot • *n.* **1** the firing of a gun or cannon: *he brought down a caribou with a single shot to the neck.* **2** an attempt to hit a target by shooting.

3 the range of a gun or cannon: *six more desperadoes came galloping up and halted just out of rifle shot.* **4** a person with a specified level of ability in shooting: *he was an excellent shot at short and long distances.* **5** (pl. same) a ball of stone or metal used as a missile fired from a large gun or cannon. **6** (also **lead shot**) tiny lead pellets used in quantity in a single charge or cartridge in a shotgun.

shotgun • *n.* a smoothbore gun for firing small shot at short range.

shot tower • a tower in which shot was made from molten lead poured through sieves at the top and falling into water at the bottom.

shoulder • *v.* put (something heavy) over one's shoulder or shoulders to carry: *we shouldered our crippling backpacks and set off slowly up the hill.*

PHRASES: **shoulder arms** hold a rifle against the side of the body, barrel upward.

shoulder belt • a bandolier or other strap passing over one shoulder and under the opposite arm.

shoulder holster • a gun holster worn under the armpit.

shoulder knots • intertwined knots of gold bullion or gold color synthetic fabric cord worn on the shoulders of the formal (mess or evening) dress uniform of officers of the various U.S. military services.

shoulder mark • any insignia of rank or corps/unit identification worn on the shoulder of the uniform.

shoulder strap • a strip of cloth from shoulder to collar on a military uniform bearing a symbol of rank.

Shoup, David Monroe |sHōōp| (1904–83) • Marine Corps officer and CONGRESSIONAL MEDAL OF HONOR recipient, born in Indiana. Shoup had postings in China before becoming an instructor at the marine base at Quantico, Virginia, in 1940. During WORLD WAR II, he fought at GUADALCANAL and in the SOLOMON ISLANDS (both 1942). In 1943 he led the marine assault at TARAWA, the first step in the navy's plan to island-hop across the Pacific to Japan. The invasion was the first to be supported fully as an amphibious assault. Shoup received the Congressional Medal of Honor for his valor in the bloody attack. His support of cooperation among the country's military services won him the post of marine commandant, in 1959, which gave him a place on the JOINT CHIEFS OF STAFF. He served from 1960 to 1963, during which time he was seen more as an effective implementer than maker of policy. His opposition to an invasion of Cuba during the 1962 missile crisis and to intervention in Vietnam did not win support among President JOHN F. KENNEDY's other military advisers. Shoup retired in 1963 and was an outspoken opponent of President LYNDON B. JOHNSON's escalation of the Vietnam War.

Shoup, Francis Asbury (1834–96) • Confederate army officer. A native of Indiana, when the CIVIL WAR began, he volunteered in Florida and helped defend against an anticipated Union attack. In 1861 he commanded an artillery battalion of the regular Confederate army in Kentucky, with which he fought at SHILOH (1862). Promoted to brigadier general, Shoup rose to a divisional command and helped repulse a Union advance at Prairie Grove, Arkansas. Despite his excellent personal performance, Shoup was captured at VICKSBURG when Gen. ULYSSES S. GRANT took that city (1863), but he was soon exchanged. Shoup was artillery chief in the ARMY OF TENNESSEE under Gen. JOSEPH E. JOHNSON, fighting against Gen. WILLIAM T. SHERMAN's advance toward Atlanta in 1864; when Gen. JOHN B. HOOD replaced Johnston, Shoup became his chief of staff. He resigned two weeks after the fall of Atlanta.

shove off • push away from the shore or another vessel in a boat.

show of force • a demonstration of the forces at one's command and of one's readiness to use them.

shrapnel |'sHræpnəl| • **1** an artillery shell designed to explode in mid-air with a lethal spray of metal projectiles. **2** fragments of a bomb, shell, or other object thrown out by an explosion. (Also called **shrap**.)

During the CIVIL WAR and SPANISH-AMERICAN WAR, shrapnel shells projected up to 350 pieces of metal and were capable of wounding or killing at up to 40 yards from the point of explosion. Shrapnel shells were discontinued by WORLD WAR II. The shrapnel shell was invented by British general HENRY SHRAPNEL.

Shrapnel, Henry (1761–1842) • the English artillery officer who invented the antipersonnel projectile named for him. Small shot or spherical bullets (usually lead) are loaded into a projectile, along with an explosive charge. When the charge explodes, it sends the metal fragments flying into enemy troops at extremely high speeds. It was first used in 1804. In WORLD WAR I, shrapnel caused most of the wounds inflicted by artillery.

Shreve, Henry Miller (1785–1851) • steamboat captain, marine architect, and military engineer. Shreve was born in New Jersey but moved with his family to Pennsylvania when very young. He began working on barges and keelboats on the Monongahela and eventually bought his own barge and became a wealthy trader. He helped design a larger, more powerful vessel, a sternwheeler, to compete with Robert Fulton's steamboat and in from 1814 to 15 he brought supplies to Gen. ANDREW JACKSON for the defense of NEW ORLEANS. Shreve designed his own steamboat, the *Washington*, which, despite early disastrous setbacks, eventually became the industry standard for luxury travel. In 1826 he became superintendent of western river improvement; he devised a ship to clear the Mississippi and the Ohio of floating logs and debris.

Shreve brought the first load of furs ever to reach Philadelphia from St. Louis; he himself brought them by wagon, so he could avoid the ruinous charges imposed by middlemen at Pittsburgh.

Shrike • (**AGM-45**) an air-to-surface antiradiation missile designed to home on and destroy radar emitters. It was introduced in the 1960s and is now largely replaced by HARM.

shroud • *n.* **1** (**shrouds**) a set of ropes forming part of the standing rigging of a sailing vessel and supporting the mast from the sides. **2** (also **shroud line**) each of the lines joining the canopy of a parachute to the harness.

Shufeldt, Robert Wilson |ˈshoofelt| (1822–95) • Union naval officer and diplomat, born in New Jersey. Shufeldt began his service in the navy in routine postings. In 1854 he resigned to become a merchant steamboat captain operating between New York, Havana, and Mobile. When the CIVIL WAR broke out, he was appointed consul general at Havana; he reported on Confederate shipping and on European actions in Mexico. Shufeldt was recalled after holding unauthorized discussions with Mexico about the establishment of a colony there for freed American slaves. He rejoined the navy in 1863 and for the rest of the war held sea commands. After the war, he spent time in Japan and China. Shufeldt made a government-sponsored two-year voyage around the globe (1878–80) to promote U.S. commercial interests, putting in at forty-three ports in European possessions around the globe; as part of this trip he helped open Korea to U.S. commerce through a laboriously negotiated treaty that was ratified by the U.S. Senate in 1883. After that, he briefly served as president of the Second Naval Advisory Board, overseeing the construction of the navy's first steel ships. He retired in 1884 and lived for a period in Nagasaki, Japan, before returning to the United States.

Shultz, George Pratt (1920?–) • secretary of state and educator. A New York City native, Shultz headed the business school at the University of Chicago (1962–68) and then took on a variety of federal positions, including secretary of labor (1969–70), director of the Office of Management and Budget (1970–72), and secretary of the Treasury (1972–74). He then left Washington to head a major defense contractor. In 1982 he returned to the cabinet as secretary of state to President RONALD REAGAN; he served until 1989. Shultz was considered a conciliatory and reliable secretary.

shuriken |ˈshoori,ken| • *n.* a weapon in the form of a star with projecting blades or points, used as a missile in some martial arts.

ORIGIN: Japanese, literally 'dagger in the hand.'

shuttle bombing • the bombing of objectives using two bases. By this method, a bomber formation bombs its target, flies on to its second base, reloads, and returns to its home base, again bombing a target if required.

shuttle diplomacy • negotiations conducted by a mediator who travels between two or more parties that are reluctant to hold direct discussions.

SI • *abbr.* Special Intelligence.

Sibert, William Luther |ˈsībərt| (1860–1935) • military engineer, born in Alabama. Sibert studied engineering after graduating from the U.S. MILITARY ACADEMY and then worked on canal projects for the military and commanded the river and harbor district in Little Rock, Arkansas. In 1899 he went to the Philippines, where he became chief engineer of the Eighth Army Corps and reconstructed the Manila and Dagupan Railway. President THEODORE ROOSEVELT named him to the Isthmian Canal Commission in 1907, where he was in charge of the Atlantic Division of the PANAMA CANAL project. When the United States entered WORLD WAR I, he was promoted to major general and given command of the First Division, but his inexperience showed, and he was soon relieved of his command. He returned to the United States and instead was ordered to create the CHEMICAL WARFARE SERVICE.

Sibley, Henry Hastings (1811–91) • Union army officer and governor, born in Michigan Territory. Sibley was a fur trader, in the process becoming well acquainted with local Indian tribes; he married a Sioux woman, from whom he later separated. In 1848 he became active in Democratic party politics and was elected a delegate to Congress from Wisconsin; he represented Minnesota from 1849 to 1853 and in 1858 became its first governor. In 1862, now a colonel of militia, he led troops to put down an Indian uprising; his victory brought him promotion to brigadier general in 1863. He then served in the Dakota Territory, where he opened up new trails and suppressed Indian unrest.

Sibley, Henry Hopkins (1816–86) • Confederate army officer, born in Louisiana. Sibley fought in the second SEMINOLE WAR and the MEXICAN WAR (1846–48), where he was cited for bravery, and in an unsuccessful war against the Navajo in 1860. After the outbreak of the CIVIL WAR, he convinced Confederate president JEFFERSON DAVIS to try to seize Colorado, New Mexico, and California, which he believed would convince doubting European powers of the Confederacy's viability. Sibley led a force out West and won some early victories against Union troops, but the campaign ended disastrously (partly because of Sibley's heavy drinking), with Sibley losing one-third of his men. As a result, he lost his command. After the war, he was briefly a general in the Egyptian army, charged with construction of coastal fortifications, but he was dismissed for incompetence and drinking and returned to the United States.

Henry Hopkins Sibley is not related to Henry Hastings Sibley.

Sicard, Montgomery (1836–1900) • Union naval officer born in New York City. Sicard was executive officer aboard the USS *Oneida* off New Orleans as the CIVIL WAR broke out. He participated in the VICKSBURG campaign (1862–63) and attained the rank of lieutenant commander. He served aboard of number of warships and commanded the left wing of the Second Naval Division at the landing at FORT FISHER. Sicard was commanding the *Saginaw* in the Pacific in 1870 when the ship was wrecked on Ocean Island. Sicard sent five men to try to reach Hawaii, 1,200 miles away, but only one arrived safely. Sicard and the rest of the crew were rescued after two months. Sicard designed a steel breech-loading gun that became the model for the navy's first such weapon and headed the navy's Ordnance Bureau for ten years (1881–91). Malaria kept him from a much desired command in the SPANISH-AMERICAN WAR, but he did head the Naval War Board of Strategy. He retired in 1898.

Sicily Campaign • the first major WORLD WAR II Allied attempt to gain a stronghold on Axis territory, in July and August of 1943. The armada of 2,500 mostly British and American ships was the largest assembled to that time. Under the overall command of Gen. DWIGHT D. EISENHOWER, the Allies secured several beachheads within 48 hours of the initial landing. Control of the island made possible the invasion and conquest of Italy the following month.

sick • in air intercept, a code meaning, "Equipment indicated is operating at reduced efficiency."

sickbay (also **sick bay**) • *n.* a room or building set aside for the treatment or accommodation of the sick, especially within a military base or on board a ship.

sick call • a summons for those reporting sick to attend for treatment.

sick flag • the yellow quarantine flag flown to show the presence of contagious disease aboard a ship or in a port, fortress, or the like.

Sickles, Daniel Edgar (1819–1914) • Union army officer, diplomat, and CONGRESSIONAL MEDAL OF HONOR recipient. Sickles, born in New York City, practiced law and became associated with Tammany Hall, the Democratic political machine. Early in his career he held political positions in New York and was secretary to the U.S. legation to Great Britain. In 1857 he was elected to the U.S. House of Representatives. During his time in Washington, he became embroiled in a marital scandal that led to his trial and acquittal for murder; he pled temporary insanity, the first time such a defense had been used. Because of the scandal, and his reconciliation with his wife, he became a controversial figure, and his appointment as a brigadier general of volunteers at the outbreak of the CIVIL WAR was equally controversial. Sickles was promoted to major general of volunteers and led his troops ably at FREDERICKSBURG (1862) and at CHANCELLORSVILLE (1863). A dispute over Sickles's decision to disobey an order by Gen. GEORGE G. MEADE at Gettysburg led to a protracted feud between the two men. In 1897 he received the Congressional Medal of Honor for gallantry at GETTYSBURG (1863).

sick list • a list, especially in the army or navy, of people who are ill and unable to work.

Sidearm • (**AGM-122**) a short-range air-to-surface antiradar missile designed to counter air defense weapons, such as SAM sites. It is deployed by the same fixed-wing aircraft and helicopters that fire the SIDEWINDER.

side arms • weapons worn at a person's side such as pistols or other small firearms (or, formerly, swords or bayonets).

sidelight • *n.* (**sidelights**) a ship's port (red) and starboard (green) navigation lights.

side-wheeler • *n.* a steamboat with paddle wheels on either side.

Sidewinder • (**AIM-9**) an air-to-air missile with a nonnuclear warhead and an infrared, heat-seeking homing device. It was introduced in the 1950s and is still in use today. The ground-to-air equivalent is the CHAPARRAL.

The Sidewinder got its name from early prototypes that zigzagged in flight, owing to off-center placement of the homing device that caused the target to appear to be moving as the missile spun in flight, thus influencing its flight path.

---

siege |sēj| • *n.* a military operation in which enemy forces surround a town or building, cutting off essential supplies, with the aim of compelling the surrender of those inside: *Verdun had withstood a siege of ten weeks.*

PHRASES: **lay siege to** conduct a siege of (a place): *government forces laid siege to the building.* **under siege** (of a place) undergoing a siege.

siege gun |sēj gən| • a heavy gun used in attacking a place under siege.

siege train |sēj trān| • a set of artillery and other equipment for a siege, together with troops and transport vehicles.

Siegfried Line |ˈsēgˌfrēd| • (also **Hindenburg Line**) the line of defense constructed by the Germans along the western frontier of Germany before WORLD WAR II. The concrete-and-steel fortifications extended from the Swiss frontier to Luxembourg, while the Belgian and Dutch frontiers had smaller emplacements. The line was named for Siegfried, a legendary Teutonic hero. The minimal progress of the Allies in penetrating the line near Aachen from mid November to mid December 1944 came to an end with the German offensive in the Ardennes; however, between February 8 and March 10, 1945, the line was outflanked in the north and then breached between Roermond and Trier.

Sigel, Franz (1824–1902) • Union army officer. Sigel was born in Baden, where he was active in the move for German unification, and entered military service there. In the CIVIL WAR he became an active Unionist, rallying German-American support in Missouri for the North. Although he was at best a modestly successful leader, and often was simply incompetent, he was lionized in the German-American press, which made him a hero. His reputation began to founder when he made unsubstantiated charges against Maj. Gen. IRVIN McDOWELL and deteriorated further after his defeat at NEW MARKET in 1864.

sight • *n.* (usually **sights**) a device on a gun or optical instrument used for assisting a person's precise aim or observation. • *v.* **1** (**sighting**) take aim by looking through the sights of a gun: *she sighted down the barrel.* **2** take a detailed visual measurement of something with or as with a sight. **3** adjust the sight of (a firearm or optical instrument).

PHRASES: **in** (or **within**) **one's sights** visible, especially through the sights of one's gun.

sighting • *n.* actual visual contact. Sightings do not include other contacts, such as radar and sonar contacts, which must be reported by type.

sighting shot • an experimental shot to guide shooters in adjusting their sights.

SIGINT |'sigint| • *abbr.* signals intelligence.

signal • *n.* **1** as applied to electronics, any transmitted electrical impulse. **2** operationally, a type of message, the text of which consists of one or more letters, words, characters, signal flags, visual displays, or special sounds with prearranged meaning, and which is conveyed or transmitted by visual, acoustical, or electrical means.

signal book • **1** a book containing the signal codes to be used for sending messages to other ships, stations, or military units. **2** a book in which are recorded a copy of all messages sent and received by a military installation or unit, a ship, or an aircraft.

Signal Corps Laboratory • located at Fort Monmouth, New Jersey, where several of the Army's technological innovations in communications were developed, including radio tubes and radio telephones (WORLD WAR I), and radar (1937).

Signal Corps, U.S. Army • see ARMY SIGNAL CORPS.

Signal Intelligence Service • U.S. Army SIGNAL CORPS element created in 1929 to manage all U.S. Army code and cipher work. The Signal Intelligence Service, headed by William F. Friedman, also absorbed the covert code-breaking and intelligence-gathering activities formerly conducted by the so-called BLACK CHAMBER within the MILITARY INTELLIGENCE DIVISION of the WAR DEPARTMENT General Staff.

signalman • *n.* (pl. **-men**) a person responsible for sending and receiving naval or military signals.

signal of distress • a visual, audible, or radio signal indicating that the sender is in distress or otherwise requires assistance.

signals intelligence • **1** the branch of military intelligence concerned with the monitoring, interception, and interpretation of radio signals, radar signals, and telemetry. **2** (**SIGINT**) intelligence derived from communications, electronics, and foreign instrumentation signals.

signature • any unique indicator of the presence of certain materiel or troops; especially the characteristic electronic emissions given off by a certain type of vehicle, radar, radio, or unit.

significant track • in air defense, the track of an aircraft or missile that behaves in an unusual manner, specifically a manner that warrants attention and suggests a possible threat to a defended area.

Sigsbee, Charles Dwight |'sigzbē| (1845–1923) • Union naval officer, born in New York. Sigsbee graduated from the U.S. NAVAL ACADEMY in1863, in the middle of the CIVIL WAR. He was assigned to a series of squadron ships and performed capably in the battle of MOBILE BAY (1864). He taught at ANNAPOLIS from 1869 to 1871 and became an expert in marine science, charting the ocean floor and performing coastal surveys. He discovered the deepest spot in the Gulf of Mexico, which was named the Sigsbee Deep in his honor, and invented technology for naval exploration. In 1897 he was promoted to captain and given command of the USS *Maine*. The ship was anchored at Havana Harbor, as a show of strength as relations between the United States and Spain deteriorated, and on February 15, 1898, it was rocked by an explosion that killed 260 men, although Sigsbee escaped unharmed. The ship sank, and "Remember the MAINE!" became the battle cry of the SPANISH-AMERICAN WAR, which rapidly followed. Sigsbee was transferred to another command and was hailed as a hero, both in the United States and in Europe; he served in a number of important posts in the navy; in 1906 he commanded the Second Squadron, North Atlantic Fleet.

SII • *abbr.* seriously ill or injured.

Sikorsky CH-54 • see SKYCRANE.

Sikorsky, Igor (1889–1972) • aerospace engineer, born in Russia. Sikorsky became interested in aviation after reading about the Wright brothers and studied engineering in Paris. He also began making his own designs for helicopters and airplanes. One of his planes won a design competition in Russia in 1912. Also that year, Sikorsky designed the world's first four-engine plane with an enclosed passenger compartment. He designed the world's first long-range strategic bomber and reconnaissance squadron, which became a mainstay of the Russian air force. Sikorsky emigrated to the United States in 1918 and in 1923 founded Sikorsky Aero Engineering Corporation; his major success was an amphibious plane used for commercial transport. In the 1930s he designed the first practical single-rotor helicopter, which was used widely for rescue and supply missions by the U.S. Army.

silencer • *n.* a device for reducing the noise emitted by a gun or other loud mechanism.

Silent Service • a term coined in the 1930s for the U.S. Navy submarine fleet and its work still in use today.

Silkworm • a family Chinese cruise missiles (designated HY-1 through HY-4) that are widely available in countries developing their defense capability. They were largely inspired by Russian STYX missiles and many parts are interchangeable. See also HY-4.

Silliman, Gold Selleck (1732–90) • REVOLUTIONARY WAR army officer from Connecticut. Silliman began a legal practice, and rose through the ranks in the militia, becoming a colonel in 1775. Silliman and his command joined up with Gen. GEORGE WASHINGTON at the Battle of NEW YORK (1776); Silliman oversaw the evacuation of the regiments at the southern tip of Manhattan. In 1776, as a brigadier general in the state militia, Silliman defended Fairfield County, in the southwestern part of Connecticut, fending off Loyalists and defending, unsuccessfully, a supply depot at Bridgeport against a British invasion.

silo • *n.* (pl. **-os**) an underground chamber in which a guided missile is kept ready for firing.

Silver Star Medal • U.S. military decoration awarded for "gallantry in action not warranting the award of a MEDAL OF HONOR or the DISTINGUISHED SERVICE CROSS" against an armed enemy of the United States. The wearing of a small silver star on the service ribbon for the campaign in which valor was displayed was authorized by Congress on July 9, 1918, but the Silver Star Medal as such was not established until 1932. The Silver Star Medal may be awarded to any person serving with the U. S. Army.

Sims, William S. (1858–1936) • commander of U.S. naval forces in Europe during WORLD WAR I. Sims's Canadian family emigrated to the United States in 1872. Sims began his navy career as an instructor in naval navigation and as an intelligence officer; his expansive reports won the praise of Assistant Navy Secretary THEODORE ROOSEVELT. Sims also reported on ordnance and on naval construction; he became an outspoken critic of the current class of navy battleships and encouraged the development of an alternative. After time spent at sea, in 1917 he became president of the NAVAL WAR COLLEGE; when the United States entered World War I, he was appointed commander of all U.S. naval forces in Europe (1917–19) and made a temporary admiral. He continued to push for naval reforms and favored destroyers over the larger, less mobile battleships, and the use of supply convoys. His innovations drastically reduced Allied shipping losses in the waning days of the war. His 1920 book *Victory at Sea*, written with Burton Hendrick, won the 1921 Pulitzer Prize for history.

simulation, computer • see COMPUTER SIMULATION.

simultaneous engagement • the concurrent engagement of hostile targets by combination of interceptor aircraft and surface-to-air missiles.

sinews of war • logistics; those supplies and services necessary to sustain armed forces in active warfare.

single-action • *adj.* (of a gun) needing to be cocked by hand before it can be fired.

single combat • fighting between two people: *their ammunition gone, the two men fell to single combat.*

single file • **1** a line of people or things arranged one behind another: *we trooped along* ***in single file*** **2** one behind another: *we walked single file.*

single-hander • *n.* a boat or other craft that can be sailed single-handed.

Single Integrated Operational Plan • (**SIOP**) U.S. plan for the employment of strategic nuclear weapons in the event of a general nuclear war. Prepared by the JOINT STRATEGIC TARGET PLANNING STAFF, the SIOP allocates primary and secondary targets for all nuclear weapons in the U. S. arsenal and prescribes the schedule for their employment as well as technical details such as the height of burst of each nuclear warhead. The SIOP was first prepared in December 1960, and is constantly updated.

sinker • *n.* in naval mine warfare, a heavy weight to which a buoyant mine is moored. The sinker generally houses the mooring rope drum and depth-setting mechanism. For mines laid by ships, it also serves as a launching trolley.

Sino-Japanese War • a conflict between China and Japan in 1894–95 over sovereignty in Korea. Japan's unexpected victory marked its emergence as a world power. As a result of the war Korea, formerly a client state of China, was recognized as independent, and China ceded some possessions to Japan.

SIOP • *abbr.* Single Integrated Operational Plan.

Sioux • any one of a group of several Plains Indian tribes located between the Mississippi River to the Rocky Mountains and speaking a Souian language. Perhaps the best known of the Sioux tribes was the LAKOTA SIOUX.

Sioux War of 1876 • see GREAT SIOUX WAR OF 1876.

SIS • *abbr.* Secret Intelligence Service.

Sisson, Jack (1743?–1821) • African-American REVOLUTIONARY WAR soldier. Also known as Tack Sisson, Guy Watson, or Prince, little information is available about Jack Sisson before July 1777, when he gained famed for his role in the abduction of Brig. Gen. Richard Prescott, British commander of Newport, Rhode Island. Recruited as one of forty volunteers by Lt. Col. WILLIAM BARTON, Sisson steered one of the whale boats carrying the detachment from Tiverton, Rhode Island and supposedly broke open a panel on the general's locked door by butting it with his head, thereby allowing the latch to be opened and the quarry to be captured. No shots were fired and no one was killed, and Prescott was later exchanged for CHARLES LEE. Afterwards Sisson enlisted in the Rhode Island First Regiment, a unit that recruited approximately 200 African-American soldiers. He died in Plymouth, Massachusetts, reportedly still unhappy that his role in capturing Prescott had not received more acclaim.

sit • *v.* (**sitting**; past and past part. **sat**) ride or keep one's seat on (a horse).

Sitlington's Hill, Battle of • see McDOWELL.

sitrep |ˈsitˌrep| • *n.* informal a report on the current military situation in a particular area.
ORIGIN: 1940s: from *sit(uation) rep(ort)*.

Sitting Bull (1831?–90) • Sioux Indian chief. Sitting Bull became an Indian warrior at the age of fourteen; he also won renown as a buffalo hunter and as a holy man. In the 1860s, Sitting Bull began to actively resist white incursions into Indian territory, leading his tribe against army forts on the upper Missouri. As some Indian tribes signed treaties with the government, Sitting Bull allied himself with those who refused to yield, and after the Treaty of 1868 he became the leader of the nontreaty Indians, or "hostiles." In 1871 Sitting Bull decreed that the Indians would fight only when attacked or when their territory was being invaded; thus they attacked the military commands accompanying workers who arrived to build the Northern Pacific Railroad, which cut through their hunting lands. When gold was discovered in the Black Hills in 1874, the U.S. government ordered the Sioux onto the Great Reservation; they refused, and the result was the GREAT SIOUX WAR OF 1876. The army sent three columns into Sioux territory and attacked; the Sioux regrouped and, in 1876, wiped out Gen. GEORGE ARMSTRONG CUSTER and five companies of his regiment at LITTLE BIGHORN. In the wake of this defeat for the army, the government sent in masses of troops, and Sitting Bull fled to Canada, where his dwindling group of followers and inadequate food supplies forced him to surrender (1881). After two years in prison, he settled into reservation life and toured with Buffalo Bill's Wild West show for one season. In 1890, he was killed by soldiers sent to arrest him for leading the GHOST DANCE religion, which foretold the expulsion of whites from Indian territory.

situation map • a map showing the tactical or administrative situation at a particular time.

situation report • a report giving the situation in the area of a reporting unit or formation.

Sitzkrieg |ˈsitsˌkrēg| • **1** a derogatory term for the inactivity on the western front in Europe in the winter of 1939–40. **2** a war, or a phase of a war, in which there is little or no active fighting.

ORIGIN: German, "sitting war," suggested by *blitzkrieg* ("lightning war"), from German *sitzen*, "sit."

six-gun • *n.* another term for SIX-SHOOTER.

six-pounder • *n.* a gun that discharges a shot that weighs six pounds.

six-shooter • *n.* a revolver with six chambers.

skeg |skeg| • *n.* a tapering or projecting stern section of a vessel's keel, which protects the propellor and supports the rudder.

skid • *n.* a runner attached to the underside of an aircraft for use when landing on snow or grass.

skimmer • *n.* a hydroplane, hydrofoil, hovercraft, or other vessel that has little or no displacement when traveling.

skip bombing • a method of aerial bombing in which a bomb is released from such a low altitude that it slides or glances along the surface of the water or ground and strikes the target at or above water level or ground level. See also MINIMUM-ALTITUDE BOMBING.

skip it • in air intercept, a code meaning, "Do not attack" or "Cease attack" or "Cease interception."

skipjack • *n.* a sloop-rigged sailboat with vertical sides and a flat v-shaped bottom.

skipper informal • *n.* **1** the captain of a ship or boat, especially a small merchant or fishing vessel. **2** the captain of an aircraft. • *v.* act as captain of.

Skipper II • (**AGM-123**) a laser-guided antiship missile that incorporates the body of an Mk 83 1,000-pound. general purpose bomb, the rocket motor of a SHRIKE missile, and a guidance system from a PAVEWAY bomb. It was first used in the 1980s.

skirmish • *n.* an episode of irregular or unpremeditated fighting, especially between small or outlying parts of armies or fleets: *the unit was caught in several skirmishes and the commanding officer was killed.* • *v.* (**skirmishing**) engage in a skirmish.

DERIVATIVES: **skirmisher** *n.*

skirt • *n.* **1** the curtain that hangs around the base of a hovercraft to contain the air cushion. **2** a surface that conceals or protects the wheels or underside of a vehicle or aircraft.

Skunk Works • the special aircraft research and development department of the Lockheed Corporation; or any experimental laboratory or department of a company or institution, typically smaller than and independent of its main research division. The Lockheed Skunk Works developed the U-2 and SR-71 BLACKBIRD reconnaissance planes and the F--117 STEALTH attack aircraft.

Skycrane • (**CH-54**) a versatile heavy-lift helicopter to be used for internal or external lifts of heavy bulk loads that served with the 1st Cavalry Division in the VIETNAM WAR. A light van (**universal pod**) could be attached to the fuselage and used as a mobile command post, a maintenance and repair shop, or a Mobile Army Surgical Hospital (MASH) equipped with X-ray and other lab equipment so that surgery could be performed anywhere it was needed immediately.

skydiving • *n.* the sport of jumping from an aircraft and performing acrobatic maneuvers in the air under free fall before landing by parachute.

DERIVATIVES: **skydive** *v.* **skydiver** *n.*

Skyhawk • (**A-4**) a single-engine, turbojet attack aircraft that operates from aircraft carriers. It is used for firing missiles, providing troop support, or conducting reconnaissance. It can also act as a tanker, and can itself be airrefueled.

Skymaster • (**C-54**) the original military conversion of the DC-4, capable of carrying up to twenty-six passengers in its main cabin. It had no large cargo door or facilities for handling military cargo.

Skyraider • (**A-1**) a large, single-engine, onepilot, carrier-based attack aircraft designed for dive-bombing and carrying torpedoes. It was too late for use in WORLD WAR II, but in various versions was a valuable weapon in both the KOREAN and VIETNAM wars.

skyrocket • *n.* a rocket designed to explode high in the air as a signal or firework.

skysail • *n.* a light sail above the royal in a square-rigged ship.

Skytrain • see DAKOTA.

Skytrooper • (**C-53**) a military version of the DC-3 used to transport troops and cargo during WORLD WAR II. It had a large loading door, a reinforced floor, and the landing gear had been strengthened. Also called DAKOTA II.

Skywarrior • (**A-3**) a twin-engine swept-wing nuclear-powered jet bomber designed to be launched from aircraft carriers. When it was introduced in 1954, it was the biggest and heaviest aircraft ever used on carriers. It was also used by the U.S. Air Force as the B-66.

skywatch • *v.* informal observe or monitor the sky, especially for heavenly bodies or aircraft. DERIVATIVES: **skywatcher** *n.*

slack water • the state of the tide when it is turning, especially at low tide.

Slaughter's Mountain • see CEDAR MOUNTAIN.

slaver • *n.* a ship used for transporting slaves.

SLBM • *abbr.* **1** sea-launched ballistic missile. **2** submarine-launched ballistic missile.

slip • *n.* **1** a slope built leading into water, used for launching and landing boats and ships or for building and repairing them. **2** a space in which to dock a boat or ship, especially between two wharves or piers.

slip knot • **1** a knot that can be undone by a pull. **2** a running knot.

slippery hitch • a kind of knot made fast by catching part of the rope beneath the loop, released by pulling on the free end.

slipway • *n.* another term for SLIP (sense 1).

slit trench • a narrow trench for a soldier or a small group of soldiers and their equipment.

Slocum, Henry Warner (1826–94) • Union army officer, born in New York. When the CIVIL WAR began, he received a commission as a colonel in the Twenty-seventh New York Infantry. He fought at the FIRST BATTLE OF BULL RUN (1861); in 1862 he commanded a division of the ARMY OF THE POTOMAC during the PENINSULAR CAMPAIGN. He was promoted to major general of volunteers and then to commander and fought at the SECOND BATTLE OF BULL RUN (1862) and at ANTIETAM (1862). He commanded the District of Vicksburg so effectively that Gen. ULYSSES S. GRANT blocked an effort to transfer him out. In 1863 Slocum led the first troops to enter Atlanta with Gen. WILLIAM T. SHERMAN's army, and he commanded the left wing of Sherman's army during Sherman's MARCH TO THE SEA. Slocum briefly commanded the Department of Mississippi after the war but resigned and returned to New York.

sloop • *n.* **1** a one-masted sailboat with a fore-and-aft mainsail and a jib. **2** (also **sloop of war**) a small square-rigged sailing warship with two or three masts. **3** a small antisubmarine warship used for convoy escort in WORLD WAR II.

slop • *n.* archaic **1** (**slops**) wide, baggy pants common in the 16th and early 17th centuries, especially as worn by sailors. **2** clothes and bedding supplied to sailors by the navy.

slope • *n.* informal, derogatory an Asian person, especially a Vietnamese.

slops store • a store (often merely a chest or small compartment) aboard ship from which sailors may purchase clothing, sewing and writing materials, tobacco, soap, and similar personal items.

Slovik, Edward (**Eddy**) (1920–45) • private. Slovik, the son of immigrants who settled in Michigan, spent time as a youth in reform school for petty crimes. Despite his criminal record, Slovik was drafted in 1943 and entered the army. Frightened of battle, Slovik sought a noncombat role, but his request was denied. Sent to France after D-DAY, he deserted twice under heavy fire and was captured both times. U.S. authorities offered to allow him to avoid court-martial if he accepted a combat assignment; he refused. Slovik was court-martialed for desertion, condemned to death, and executed by firing squad, by order of Gen. DWIGHT D. EISENHOWER, on January 31, 1945. He was buried in a U.S. cemetery for criminals in France; in 1987 a private citizen paid to have his body reburied next to his wife's in a Michigan cemetery.

Slovik was the only WORLD WAR II U.S. deserter to be executed. A book and a television move, *The Execution of Private Slovik*, were based on the story of his life.

---

slow march • a military marching pace approximately half the speed of the quick march.

slow match • a slow-burning wick or cord for lighting explosives.

SLR • *abbr.* self-loading rifle.

SM • *abbr.* sergeant major.

SM-62 • see SNARK.

SM-64A • see NAVAHO.

small arms • portable firearms, especially rifles, pistols, and light machine guns.

small arms ammunition • ammunition for small arms; all ammunition up to and including 20 mm (.787 inches).

small craft • small boats or vessels collectively.

small sail • on a sailing vessel, the topgallant sails and royals, topmast, topgallant, and lower studding sails.

small ship • any small boat used by the U.S. Navy, including liberty launches and official transports.

small stores • small items for personal use on a sea voyage.

Small Wars Manual • a manual on guerilla and counterinsurgency warfare developed during the 1920s and 1930s by the U.S. Marine Corps. First published in 1940, it provides valuable insights into small-scale military operations. The Manual was updated and republished in 1987.

Smallwood, William (1732–92) • REVOLUTIONARY WAR army officer. Born into a prominent Maryland family, Smallwood fought in the FRENCH AND INDIAN WAR (1754–63) and then entered state politics. An ardent patriot, he supported the nonimportation agreements that followed the passage of the TOWNSHEND ACTS and by 1774 was working on committees that joined the colonies in efforts to resist British policies. In 1776 Smallwood was commissioned a colonel and raised a troop that became the First Maryland Regiment. The troops joined with Gen. GEORGE WASHINGTON in the fighting in and around New York City (1776). In South Carolina (1780), his troops prevented a disaster caused by the inept leadership of Gen. HORATIO GATES. Smallwood was again promoted, to major general. After the war, he retired to his plantation in Maryland and, although elected, declined to serve in the U.S. Congress. He served three terms as governor of Maryland (1785–88).

smart bomb • a highly accurate bomb, often equipped with laser-seeking guidance unit, computer, and control fins, that can be guided to its target by means of a laser, infrared, or electro-optical guidance system.

Smart bombs were beginning to be used near the end of the VIETNAM WAR, and the term has been in use since at least 1972.

smart weapons • missiles, bombs, artillery projectiles, or other munitions with the built-in ability to identify a target and seek it out.

Smith, Andrew Jackson (1815–97) • Union army officer, born in Pennsylvania. Smith held several routine postings in the U.S. Army and he served in the MEXICAN WAR (1846–48). When the CIVIL WAR broke out, he was in California, where he served briefly before becoming chief of cavalry to Gen. HENRY W. HALLECK, with whom he served in Mississippi. He also fought with Gen. WILLIAM T. SHERMAN in the unsuccessful attack at Chickasaw Bayou and held a command during the VICKSBURG campaign (1863). He accompanied Gen. NATHANIEL P. BANKS on an ill-fated expedition up the Red River,and his steady performance on that mission won him promotion to lieutenant colonel of the 5th Cavalry. He helped clear the way for Sherman's advance on Atlanta and led capably in other engagements as well, and was brevetted major general in the regular army.

Smith & Wesson | ˌsmiTH ænd ˈwesən | • trademark a type of firearm, in particular a type of cartridge revolver.

ORIGIN: mid 19th cent.: named after Horace *Smith* (1808–93) and Daniel B. *Wesson* (1825–1906), founders of an American firm of gunsmiths.

Smith, Charles Ferguson (1807–62) • Union army officer, born in Pennsylvania. Smith spent the early part of his career at the U.S. MILITARY ACADEMY, where he rose to commandant of cadets. When the CIVIL WAR began, he was transferred from the Department of Washington to New York, where he served as a recruiter, and later in 1861 he was made head of the District of Western Kentucky. In 1862 he fought under his former student, ULYSSES S. GRANT, in attacking Confederate defenses on the Tennessee-Kentucky border; his performance brought him promotion to brigadier general of volunteers.

Smith, Daniel (1748–1818) • REVOLUTIONARY WAR soldier, statesman, and surveyor, born in Stafford County, Virginia. During the Revolution, he formed a militia company and fought in many key battles in the South, including KINGS MOUNTAIN (1780) and GUILFORD COURT HOUSE (1781). After the war he and his family moved to Tennessee, where he became a leader in the movement for statehood. He wrote much of the bill of rights for the state constitution, and eventually represented Tennessee in the U.S. Senate.

Smith, E. Kirby (1824–93) • Confederate army officer, born Edmund Kirby Smith in Florida. Smith fought with distinction in the MEXICAN WAR (1846–48); after the war he served as botanist to the Mexican Boundary Commission. In the late 1850s he fought the Comanche near the Red River. When Florida seceded from the Union, he was commissioned a lieutenant colonel in the Confederate army; he served in the SHENANDOAH VALLEY and was instrumental in securing Confederate victory at the FIRST BATTLE OF BULL RUN (1861). In 1862 Smith led an unsuccessful effort to retake the Cumberland Gap from Union forces. The following year he was named to head the TRANS-MISSISSIPPI DEPARTMENT, giving him command of all Confederate troops west of the Mississippi. The Union victory at VICKSBURG in 1863 left him cut off from supply routes and from communication with other Confederate troops, demoralizing his troops. Smith was promoted to full general in 1864; in 1865, as part of the Confederate collapse, he surrendered to Gen. EDWARD R. S. CANBY.

Smith, Giles Alexander (1829–76) • Union army officer, born in New York. When the CIVIL WAR broke out, he was in Missouri, where his brother, Col. MORGAN L. SMITH, was raising a regiment; Smith became captain of a volunteer infantry regiment. In 1862 he was appointed to lead a brigade in Gen. WILLIAM T. SHERMAN's army; his performance in the capture of Arkansas Post won him promotion to brigadier general; he also fought with Gen. ULYSSES S. GRANT at VICKSBURG (1863) and with Sherman at ATLANTA (1864). In 1865 he was appointed to the command of a division in the Twenty-fifth Corps, the only all-black corps in the army, and transferred to Texas, where the troops performed noncombat services; Smith was promoted to full major general of volunteers.

Smith, Gustavus Woodson (1822–96) • Confederate army officer. After graduating from the U.S. MILITARY ACADEMY, the Kentucky-born Smith was assigned to the ARMY CORPS OF ENGINEERS; after some field experience, he taught for two years at the Academy. In 1846 he was chosen second in command for a new corps of engineer soldiers and led the corps ably during the MEXICAN WAR (1846–48); afterward, he returned to West Point. When the CIVIL WAR broke out, he joined the Confederate army as a major general. Smith commanded a corps of the ARMY OF THE POTOMAC during the PENINSULAR CAM-

PAIGN; however, he lost the confidence of Gen. ROBERT E. LEE. Complaining that he had been passed over, he resigned his commission and entered private life in Georgia. There, he served in the militia and helped defend against the advance of Gen. WILLIAM T. SHERMAN.

Smith, Holland McTyeire (1882–1967) • Marine Corps officer, born in Alabama, Smith practiced law for two years and then joined the U.S. Marine Corps in 1905, serving in the Philippines and in the Dominican Republic. In 1917 he sailed for France and became the first Marine selected to attend the Army General Staff College at Langres. He fought with distinction in several major engagements and returned to the United States in 1919 as a major. Having graduated from the NAVAL WAR COLLEGE in Newport, Rhode Island, he joined the staff of the Office of Naval Operations. He also served on the Army-Navy Planning Committee between 1921 and 1921, the first Marine to do so. In 1943 Smith took charge of the V Amphibious Corps, which he led in a series of engagements across the Pacific, taking TARAWA atoll, ENIWETOK, GUAM, and other strategic locations. As lieutenant general and commander of the newly created FLEET MARINE FORCE, he led troops onto IWO JIMA in 1945, which he secured in twenty-six days. Throughout his career, Smith was a staunch advocate of amphibious warfare, and pushed for innovations in strategy and technology.

Smith, Jacob Hurd • U.S. army officer. A brigadier general in the U.S. Army, Smith was court-martialed in 1902 on charges that he had ordered U.S. soldiers fighting insurgents in the Philippines to commit atrocities as a way to lower morale among the rebels. Smith was charged with having issued orders to murder civilians and prisoners alike, to destroy villages, and to torture captives. He was convicted, admonished by President THEODORE ROOSEVELT, and forced to take early retirement. Smith's defense was that such tactics were necessary because of the guerrilla nature of the fighting and because it was difficult to distinguish civilians from insurgents out in the countryside.

Smith, John (1580–1631) • colonial governor, born in England. Smith early felt an urge to see the world. He visited several European nations and fought for Austria against Turkey before being captured. Returning to England in 1604, he was selected by the Virginia Company in London to serve as a member of the governing council in its Virginia colony. Smith and his fellow voyagers arrived in what is now Jamestown in May 1607 and established a settlement; Smith was soon captured by local Indians and adopted by their chief, POWHATAN, perhaps because of intervention by Powhatan's daughter, Pocahontas. Smith continued to explore the region and sent maps and reports on the Virginia Indians to London. In 1608 he was elected president of the council, making him in effect the colony's governor; he was an able and effective leader whose administration brought about significant reductions in the death rate from disease among colonists. In 1609 the Virginia Company replaced him, and Smith returned to England, criticizing the company for putting quick commercial profit above the need to strengthen the colony's footing in America. In 1614 Smith visited the region north of Virginia, which he dubbed New England, but he failed in efforts to obtain funding for a new colony there.

Smith, Joseph (1790–1877) • Union naval officer, born in Massachusetts. In 1861 President ABRAHAM LINCOLN named Smith, then head of the Bureau ofYards and Docks, to the commission that was designing the Union ironclad *Monitor*. The *Monitor* arrived in HAMPTON ROADS the day after Smith's son had been killed in battle when his ship was burned by the Confederate ironclad *Virginia*, formerly the *Merrimack*. In the ensuing battle, the *Virginia* eventually withdrew. Smith was promoted to the rank of admiral in recognition of his contribution to the successful design of the *Monitor*.

Smith, Melancton (1810–1893) • Union naval officer. From New York City, Smith began his naval career in the Pacific and in the Caribbean; he served in the SEMINOLE WAR (1839–40) and in the MEXICAN WAR, during which he was executive officer of the Pensacola Navy Yard. During the CIVIL WAR, Smith fought in a number of engagements, including with Admiral DAVID FARRAGUT at NEW ORLEANS, where he heavily damaged a Confederate ram. His actions won him promotion to captain in 1862. He commanded several ships, including the *Wabash*, in which he participated in the attack on FORT FISHER, North Carolina.

Smith, Morgan Lewis (1821–74) • Union army officer. Smith, a New York native, moved west as a young man and entered the U.S. Army in 1845. When the CIVIL WAR broke out, he recruited a regiment around St. Louis and turned it into a disciplined fighting force. (Among his recruits was his brother, GILES ALEXANDER SMITH.) Smith's unit fought bravely at FORT DONELSON in 1862 and then at SHILOH (1862) and at CORINTH (1862), where he earned the praise of Gen. WILLIAM T. SHERMAN. Smith was promoted to brigadier general of volunteers and given a division command. A wound incurred while on reconnaissance near Chickasaw Bayou kept him out of action until late 1863, when he distinguished himself in fighting in Tennessee, near MISSIONARY RIDGE, and in the advance toward Atlanta. After the war he served briefly as the second assistant postmaster general.

Smith died under unclear circumstances, perhaps by suicide, while under investigation by the U.S. House Ways and Means Committee for possibly having taken bribes from a mail steamship company.

Smith, Samuel (1752–1839) • REVOLUTIONARY WAR army officer, U.S. Representative, U.S. Senator. From Maryland, Smith began a career in commerce but accepted a commission as a captain in a Maryland regiment when the Revolution began. He fought well in several engagements in New Jersey and New York, including WHITE PLAINS (1776) and MONMOUTH (1778). As a lieutenant colonel, in 1777 he led his troops in a valiant resistance against British forces at Fort Mifflin; although in the end he was unsuccessful, he managed to tie up British reinforcements that might otherwise have aided Gen. JOHN BURGOYNE at SARATOGA and caused an American defeat. In the 1780s he enjoyed great success in commerce and began vastly wealthy; his interests turned to politics, and in 1792 he was elected to the U.S. House of Representatives, where he served four terms. Smith brokered the deal that gave the election of 1800 to THOMAS JEFFERSON when the Electoral College deadlocked and the election went to the House; he was acting secretary of the navy in Jefferson's cabinet and in 1803 won election to the Senate, where he served two terms. He did not get along with JAMES MADISON, who succeeded Jefferson in 1809, but served ably in the WAR OF 1812.

Smith, Walter Bedell (1895–1961) • U.S. army officer, diplomat, government official. From Indiana, Smith initially joined the Indiana National Guard. When WORLD WAR I broke out, he was recommended for officer training school and then sent to France; wounded in fighting, he recovered and received assignment to the WAR DEPARTMENT Bureau of Military Intelligence. Smith won promotions and admission to the Command and General Staff School at FORT LEAVENWORTH (1934–35). In 1939 he received appointment as an assistant secretary in the War Department, where he gained the trust of Gen. GEORGE C. MARSHALL; in 1941 he was promoted to colonel, then brigadier general, and made secretary to the GENERAL STAFF and then chief of the secretariat to the JOINT CHIEFS OF STAFF and of the secretariat to the Combined Chiefs of Staff, which included U.S. allies. He served as Gen. DWIGHT D. EISENHOWER's chief of staff, forging a close relationship with the Allied commander and playing a major role in Allied planning and coordination, including plans for D-DAY. At the end of the war, his rank was lieutenant general. He served as ambassador to Moscow from 1946 to 1949; in 1950 he became director of the CENTRAL INTELLIGENCE AGENCY. In 1952 Eisenhower named him undersecretary of state; he was also the chief U.S. delegate to the 1954 GENEVA CONVENTION.

Smith, William (1797–1887) • Confederate army officer and state governor. A Virginian, Smith practiced law sporadically throughout his career. From 1853 to 1861 he served in the U.S. House of Representatives, where he supported the Democratic party and southern rights. Smith opposed secession until President ABRAHAM LINCOLN called for troops to fight the Confederacy; he then promptly enlisted in the southern cause. Appointed colonel of an infantry regiment, Smith sustained severe wounds at ANTIETAM (1862). While a brigadier general in the Confederate army, he also served in the Confederate congress (1861–62). In 1863 he was reelected governor of Virginia, in which position he strongly and effectively supported the Confederate cause, even in the face of the Confederate collapse in 1865. After the war, he opposed measures to assist newly freed slaves.

Smith, William Farrar (1824–1903) • Union army officer. A Vermonter, Smith spent the early part of his military career as a surveyor and a teacher of mathematics at the U.S. MILITARY ACADEMY. At the outbreak of the CIVIL WAR, he was appointed colonel of the Third Vermont Volunteers. He fought at the first BATTLE OF BULL RUN (1861) and in the PENINSULAR CAMPAIGN (1862). He was brevetted colonel in the regular army for his performance at ANTIETAM (1862). An intemperate letter to President ABRAHAM LINCOLN criticizing his superior, Gen. AMBROSE BURNSIDE, backfired and cost him promotion to major general, and he reverted to brigadier general. As chief engineer of the Cumberland (1863), he was assigned the task of moving supplies from Alabama to Tennessee for Gen. WILLIAM S. ROSECRANS's starving army; his success won him the promotion to major general that had been denied. Smith's criticism of other of his superiors continued to hurt his advancement; that, plus his indecisive performance at PETERSBURG, caused Gen. ULYSSES S. GRANT to relieve him of his corps command in 1864. In 1865 he was brevetted brigadier general and major general, U.S. Army.

Smith, William Stephens (1755–1816) • REVOLUTIONARY WAR army officer. A New York native, Smith joined the Continental army as a major and aide-de-camp to Gen. JOHN SULLIVAN and then to Gen. NATHANAEL GREENE; in the battle of New York, Smith and some others blew up a bridge connecting Throgs' Neck with the mainland, stalling the British advance. His performance at TRENTON (1776) brought him promotion to lieutenant colonel. He fought notably at MONMOUTH (1778). In 1781 he acted as aide-de-camp to the MARQUIS DE LAFAYETTE from January to July; that month, he became aide-de-camp to Gen. GEORGE WASHINGTON, remaining in that position until 1783. In that year, he supervised the evacuation by the British of New York City. His participation in a scheme to free Venezuela from Spanish rule cost him his post as surveyor of customs in New York; he stood trial for his actions but was acquitted. He served one term in the U.S. House of Representatives (1812–14) but lost a contested race for reelection in 1814.

smoke ball • a projectile filled with material which emits dense smoke on ignition, used to conceal military operations.

smoke bomb • a bomb that emits dense smoke as it explodes, used to produce a smoke screen.

smokeless powder • gunpowder having or emitting little or no smoke when ignited.

smoke screen (also **smokescreen**) • a cloud of smoke created to conceal military operations.

smoothbore • *n.* a gun with an unrifled barrel.

SMSgt (also **SMSGT**) • *abbr.* Senior Master Sergeant.

snafu |snæ'fo͞o| informal • *n.* a confused or chaotic state; a mess: *an enormous amount of my time was devoted to untangling snafus.* • *adj.* in utter confusion or chaos: *the supply ship was torpedoed and the planned assault was snafu.* • *v.* throw (a situation) into chaos: *you ignored his orders and snafued everything.*

ORIGIN: 1940s: acronym from *situation normal: all fouled* (or *fucked*) *up.*

snagline mine • a contact mine with a buoyant line, attached to one of the horns or switches, that may be caught up and pulled by the hull or propellers of a ship.

snake mode • a control mode in which the pursuing aircraft flies a programmed weaving flight path to allow time to accomplish identification functions.

snap-action • *adj.* denoting a gun whose hinged barrel is secured by a spring catch.

Snapper • see AT-1.

snap roll • a maneuver in which an aircraft makes a single quick revolution about its longitudinal axis while flying horizontally.

Snark • (**SM-62**) a small turbojet-powered pilotless bomber aircraft—the first operational U.S. intercontinental missile—that had an important role in the development of Launch facilities and infrastructure at Cape Canaveral. Plans for the Snark cruise missile began in October 1945, but the military budget postponed testing of the prototype, designated N-69, until 1951.

snatch squad • a group of police officers or soldiers detailed to seize troublemakers in a crowd.

SNCO • *abbr.* staff noncommissioned officer.

snipe • *v.* shoot at someone from a hiding place, especially accurately and at long range: *the soldiers in the trench* ***sniped at*** *us.*

DERIVATIVES: **sniper** *n.*

Sniper's Ridge • an elevated site in the KOREAN WAR on one of the fronts of the IRON TRIANGLE in North Korea. Sniper's Ridge was on the middle of the eastern front near Triangle Hill and Twin Peaks (also known as Jane Russell Hill).

snorkel • an apparatus for the ventilation of a submerged submarine, consisting of a retractable tubes for the intake of fresh air and the exhaust of toxic gases.

snow • in air intercept, a term meaning "sweep jamming."

social war • a war, generally a civil war, the cause of which can be attributed to competing social classes or to the need to adjust some inequality or dispute among citizens or groups of citizens.

SOCOM • *abbr.* Special Operations Command.

SOF • *abbr.* special operations forces.

sofar • *n.* the technique of fixing an explosion at sea by the time difference of arrival of sound energy at several separate geographical locations.

ORIGIN: The term *sofar* is derived from the words "*so*und, *f*ixing *a*nd *r*anging."

soften • *v.* undermine the resistance of (someone): *the blockade appears a better weapon with which to* ***soften*** *them* ***up*** *for eventual surrender.*

soft missile base • a launching base that is not protected against a nuclear explosion.

soft-nosed • *adj.* (of a bullet) expanding on impact.

soft tack • archaic bread or other nourishing food, especially as eaten by sailors or soldiers.

soft target • **1** a person or thing that is relatively unprotected or vulnerable, especially to military or terrorist attack. **2** (in the Persian Gulf War) a human being, as distinguished from a hard target such as a tank, military installation, etc. See also HARD TARGET.

software • *n.* a set of computer programs, procedures, and associated documentation concerned with the operation of a data processing system—for example, compilers, library routines, manuals, and circuit diagrams.

SOG • *abbr.* special operations group.

Soissons, battle of • a fierce WORLD WAR I battle in and around the French town of Soissons, northeast of Paris, in July, 1918.The town was left in ruins after the battle, in which the U.S. Marines played a significant role. U.S. casualties were about 10,000; about 6,500 enemy soldiers were captured.

SOLAS |'sōləs| • *n.* the provisions made during a series of international conventions governing maritime safety.

ORIGIN: 1960s: acronym from *safety of life at sea.*

soldier • *n.* **1** a person who serves in an army. **2** (also **common soldier** or **private soldier**) a private in an army. • *v.* serve as a soldier: (**soldiering**) *soldiering was what the colonel understood.*

DERIVATIVES: **soldierly** *adj.*

soldier of fortune • a person who works as a soldier for any country or group that will pay them; a mercenary: *he had fought with soldiers of fortune in South Africa, Chad, and Lebanon.*

Soldier's Bonus, the • see WORLD WAR VETERANS ADJUSTED COMPENSATION ACT.

Soldiers' Home • a veterans' retirement home and a historic landmark since 1973, located in Washington, D.C. It was purchased by the U.S. Government in 1851 and used by President ABRAHAM LINCOLN and his family as a summer home from 1862 to 1864. Lincoln drafted the EMANCIPATION PROCLAMATION at the home. It has also been known as Anderson Cottage since 1884, when it was named after Brevet Maj. ROBERT ANDERSON, a CIVIL WAR commander who advocated the establishment of a home for soldiers.

Soldier's Medal • U.S. military decoration awarded for "heroism not involving actual conflict with an armed enemy." Established by Congress on July 2, 1926, the Soldier's Medal may be awarded to any person serving with the U.S. Army.

soldiery • *n.* (pl. **-ies**) **1** soldiers collectively: *the town was filled with disbanded soldiery.* **2** military training or knowledge.

sole |sōl| • *n.* the floor of a ship's cabin or cockpit.

Solomon Islands • a group of islands in the western Pacific that were the scene of fierce fighting of combined forces starting in 1942, when the Japanese invaded. Allied forces took control of the islands by early 1943, but naval engagements with the Japanese continued in the area throughout the war, resulting in the loss of many ships. The most prominent battle of this period was the one on GUADALCANAL, the largest island.

Somalia |sə'mälēə; sō'mälyə| • a country in the Horn of Africa; capital, Mogadishu. Civil war broke out in Somalia in 1988 and led to the overthrow of the government in 1991; the United States intervened militarily 1992–94. In 1991 northern Somalia declared itself independent as the Somaliland Republic.

Somewhere in France • (World War I) for reasons of secrecy, the only return address allowed by military postal censors on any correspondence mailed from France.

Somme, Battle of the • a long-running battle in WORLD WAR I near the upper basin of the Somme River in France. In the four months and a half months of fighting (July to mid-November, 1916) little ground was gained by the British and French, attacking entrenched German positions. Casualties were in the hundreds of thousands on both sides, leading to the battle to become a emblem of the destructiveness of war. A smaller battle was fought in the same area in WORLD WAR II.

sonar |'sō,när| • *n.* **1** a system for the detection of objects under water and for measuring the water's depth by emitting sound pulses and detecting or measuring their return after being reflected. **2** an apparatus used in this system.

sonar, active • a method developed in 1918 for locating a submarine or other underwater body by measuring its distance and direction by "bouncing" a sound signal off of it. Also known as ASDIC.

sonar, passive • a method developed early in WORLD WAR I for locating a submarine or other underwater body by determining its distance and direction by listening with hydraphones for the sounds made by the target's engines or other machinery.

sonic • *adj.* of or pertaining to sound or the speed of sound.

sonic boom • a loud explosive noise caused by the shock wave from an aircraft traveling faster than the speed of sound.

sonic mine • see ACOUSTIC MINE.

Son My • see MY LAI MASSACRE.

sonobuoy |'sänə,boōē; -,boi| • *n.* a sonar device used to detect submerged submarines.

Sons of Confederate Veterans • the oldest hereditary organization for male descendants of Confederate soldiers. Formed in Richmond, Virginia, in 1896, the group is the direct heir of the veterans' organization called United States Confederate Veterans. Membership is open to all male descendants of veterans who served honorably in the Confederate armed forces.

Sons of Liberty • a New York militia group created during the tax revolts of the North American colonists to intimidate British tax collectors. By organizing local militia, the colonists hoped to obviate the need for British troops, thereby eliminating the Crown's justification for the odious taxes.

S.O.P. (or **SOP**) • *abbr.* slang (World War II) **1** standard operating procedure, or standing operational procedure. **2** senior officer present.

Sopwith Camel • (**F.1**) a compact single-engine British biplane fighter aircraft built in 1917. It scored more hits than any other fighter (1,294) in WORLD WAR I, but, because of its large engine and the concentration of weight in the front of the fuselage, was very difficult to handle.

sortie • *n.* **1** an attack made by troops coming out from a position of defense. **2** an operational flight by a single military aircraft. • *v.* (**sorties, sortied, sortieing**) come out from a defensive position to make an attack.

Sosaku, Suzuki (?-1944) • Japanese army officer. Suzuki served as chief of staff to Gen. TOMOYUKI YAMASHITA during the battle for Singapore (1942). In 1944, Suzuki, a lieutenant general, directed the Japanese troops in the battle for LEYTE GULF, an island in the central Philippines, after U.S. forces landed there as part of their successful effort to "island-hop" across the South Pacific to Japan; Leyte was the first island in the Philippines to be retaken from the Japanese. Suzuki miscalculated the magnitude of the U.S. effort in Leyte, and his soldiers were seriously outnumbered and forced to withdraw to the northern tip of the island. Although the Japanese then made a tremendous effort to hold the island, sending in heavy reinforcements, in the end they lost to the U.S. forces. In the simultaneous naval battle in Leyte Gulf, the U.S. Navy succeeded in nearly wiping out the Japanese fleet. Later that year, Suzuki led the Thirty-fifth Army against Lt. Gen. Robert Eichelberger in the battle for the southern Philippines, but he was killed as he attempted to sail from Cebu to Mindanao.

sound • *v.* **1** ascertain (the depth of water), typically by means of a line or pole or using sound echoes. **2** find the depth of water in (a ship's hold).

sounding • *n.* **1** the action or process of measuring the depth of the sea or other body of water. **2** a measurement taken by sounding. **3** (**soundings**) archaic the area of sea close to the shore that is shallow enough for the bottom to be reached by means of a sounding line.

sounding lead • the lead or other weight on the end of a sounding line.

sounding line • a weighted line with distances marked off at regular intervals, used to measure the depth of water under a boat.

sounding rod • a rod used to measure the depth of water under a boat or in a ship's hold.

source • *n.* **1** a person, thing, or activity from which intelligence information is obtained. **2** in clandestine activities, a person (agent), normally a foreign national, in the employ of an intelligence activity for intelligence purposes. **3** in interrogation activities, any person who furnishes intelligence information, either with or without the knowledge that the information is being used for intelligence purposes. A **controlled source** is in the employment or under the control of the intelligence activity and knows that the information is to be used for intelligence purposes. An **uncontrolled source** is a voluntary contributor of information and may or may not know that the information is to be used for intelligence purposes.

Sousa, John Philip (1854–1932) • composer and bandleader. From Washington, D.C., Sousa was born into a musical family and began his training early. At the age of thirteen, he was apprenticed to the Marine Corps and played in the Marine Band. His first march was published in 1873. Sousa left the Marines and worked for several years as a theatrical violinist and conductor. In 1880 he was offered and accepted the leadership of the Marine Band. He improved the quality of the band's musicianship and enlarged its repertoire; it became a popular source of pride for the Corps. Especially popular were the marches Sousa composed for the band to play at ceremonial functions. In 1892 he resigned to form his own band, which quickly won popular acclaim for its quality and for its repertoire, a blend of popular, classical, and patriotic works and Sousa's own marches. The group toured almost constantly for nearly forty years, both in the United States and in Europe; Sousa took time out during WORLD WAR I to train army bandsmen. After the war, he returned to touring, and died while on tour in Pennsylvania. In all, he wrote 136 marches, among many other kinds of music, and his "Stars and Stripes Forever" is still a mainstay of patriotic band music.

Southeast Asia Collective Defense Treaty • a security agreement signed in Manila on September 8, 1954 and enacted on February 19, 1955. It created the SOUTHEAST ASIA TREATY ORGANIZATION , whose member states agreed to provide military assistance against an aggression or subversion in the treaty area.

Southeast Asia Treaty Organization • see SEATO.

Southern Command • see U.S. SOUTHERN COMMAND.

Southern Manifesto • a declaration of solidarity of Southern states on December 14, 1860, in response to the election of ABRAHAM LINCOLN, declaring that any hope for relief in the Union was gone and that the independence of the South required the organization of a Southern Confederacy. A week later South Carolina seceded.

southing |'sowTHiNG| • *n.* distance traveled or measured southward, especially at sea.

South Mountain, Battle of • a battle between Confederate Gen. ROBERT E. LEE's forces and Union Maj. Gen. GEORGE B. MCCLELLAN's ARMY OF THE POTOMAC during the CIVIL WAR. McClellan's forces attacked Lee's army on September 14, 1862, at South Mountain, near Burkittsville, Maryland. After suffering heavy casualties, the Confederate army retreated, resulting in a Union victory.

Southwestern Proving Ground • a U.S. Army testing site established near Hope, Arkansas, in June 1941, shortly before the United States entered WORLD WAR II. The 50,000-acre proving ground was used until the end of the war in 1945.

Southwest Pacific Area • (**SWPA**) an area that includes the Philippine Islands, the South China Sea, the Gulf of Siam, the Netherlands East Indies (except Sumatra), the Solomon Islands, Australia, and the waters to the south. The area, particularly Papua New Guinea and the Solomon Islands, was the scene of fierce fighting in WORLD WAR II. The Japanese swept through the area in early 1942 and captured nearly all points of strategic and military importance. Reconquering the region became a specific priority of the Allies after the Pacific Military Conference in Washington in March 1943. Operation Cartwheel was the codename given to the project, which included such bloody campaigns as GUADALCANAL. The operation came to an end in August 1944, when the Australians secured control of the northwestern coast of New Guinea, allowing the Allies to turn most of their attention to other parts of the Pacific Theater.

sovereign |'säv(ə)rən| • *n.* a supreme ruler, especially a monarch. • *adj.* **1** possessing supreme or ultimate power: *in modern democracies the people's will is in theory sovereign.* **2** (of a nation or state) fully independent and determining its own affairs: *a sovereign, democratic republic.* **3** (of affairs) subject to a specified state's control without outside interference.

sovereignty |'säv(ə)rəntē| • *n.* (pl. **-ies**) **1** supreme power or authority. **2** the authority of a state to govern itself or another state: *national sovereignty.* **3** a self-governing state.

SOW • *abbr.* special operations wing.

sow |sō| • *v.* (past **sowed** |sōd|; past part. **sown** |sōn| or **sowed**) lay or plant (an explosive mine) or cover (territory) with mines: *the field had both British and German mines sown in it.* PHRASES: **sow the seeds** (or **seed**) **of** do something that will eventually bring about (a particular result, especially a disastrous one): *the seeds of dissension had been sown.*

Spaatz, Carl Andrew (1891–1974) • Air Force Chief of Staff. A Pennsylvanian, Spaatz was among the first twenty-five officers to qualify for the aviation branch of the ARMY SIGNAL CORPS. In WORLD WAR I he conducted an army flying school in France. After the war, Spaatz continued to advocate for a prominent role for aviation in the military. In 1929 he and others set a record for the longest time in continuous flight—150 hours, forty minutes, and fifteen seconds. During the BATTLE OF BRITAIN, he observed German aerial tactics and British defenses. Spaatz was air commander for both the Allied invasion of North Africa and the D-DAY LANDING. After the German surrender, Spaatz commanded the U.S. strategic air offensive in the Pacific, including the dropping of two atomic bombs on Japan in 1945. In 1946, he was named commanding general of the U.S. Army Air Force. He argued successfully for the establishment of an independent air force and became, in 1947, the first chief of staff of the newly formed U.S. Air Force.

space age • **1** (**the space age** or **the Space Age**) the era starting when the exploration of space became possible: *as the Space Age evolved, massive amounts of data gushed in.* **2** (**space-age**) very modern; technologically advanced: *a space-age control room.* • *adj.*

space-based interceptor • a weapon conceived as part of the STRATEGIC DEFENSE INITIATIVE that, while in orbit, would home in on the hot exhaust plumes of hostile missiles during the first few minutes of their flight and then either destroy them directly or initiate a chain of events that would result in their destruction by other layers of the defense system.

Space Command • see U.S. SPACE COMMAND.

space defense • all defensive measures designed to destroy attacking enemy vehicles (including missiles) while in space, or to nullify or reduce the effectiveness of such attack.

Space Detection and Tracking System • NORAD system of global radar, optical, and radiometric sensors linked to computer analysis of all objects in space, including ICBMs.

space power • the ability of a state or group to make use of the space environment in order to achieve its goals in relation to other states or groups.

space race • (**the space race**) the competition between nations regarding achievements in the field of space exploration.

space support operations • operations required to ensure that space control and support of terrestrial forces are maintained. These operations include activities such as launching and deploying space vehicles, maintaining and sustaining space vehicles while in orbit, and recovering space vehicles if required.

Spacetrack • a global system of radar, optical, and radiometric sensors linked to a computation and analysis center in the North American Air Defense Command combat operations center complex. The Spacetrack mission is the detection, tracking, and cataloging of all man-made objects in orbit of the earth. It is the air force portion of the North American Air Defense Command SPACE DETECTION AND TRACKING system.

Spad • **1** (**S.VII**) built by France in 1916, the Spad was a sturdy biplane fighter, very quick in climbing and diving, and was the most used in fighter units for France, Belgium, Italy, and the United States during WORLD WAR I. Several other versions were produced in 1916—1917, but none equaled the performance of the S.VII. **2** slang (in the Vietnam War) a friendly nickname for the A-1E SKYRAIDER single-engine fighter plane because the model seemed old enough to have flown in World War I.

The French Spad models 12 and 13 were the equal of or superior to most German planes they fought against, and Spad pilots Georges Guynemer and René Fonck were among France's most celebrated air aces.

Spadats • (**space detection and tracking system.**) a monitoring system that detects and tracks space vehicles from earth, reporting their orbital characteristics to a central control facility.

spade • *n.* the part of the trail of a gun carriage that digs into the earth to brace the gun during recoil.

span • *n.* a rope with its ends fastened at different points to a spar or other object in order to provide a purchase.

Spanish-American War • (1898) A conflict between the U.S. and Spain triggered by Cuban patriot José Martí's attempt to achieve Cuban independence from Spain. The Spanish government tried to suppress the insurgent forces (also led by Máximo Gómez and Antonio Maceo), including adopting a reconcentration policy that placed the civilian population in detention camps. The reconcentration policy drew the attention of Presidents GROVER CLEVELAND and WILLIAM MCKINLEY, both of whom encouraged Spain to adopt a policy of home rule in Cuba. When Spain responded by issuing such a policy on January 1, 1898, however, the Cuban insurgents rejected it and continued their struggle. The mysterious sinking of the USS *Maine* in Havana Harbor on February 15, 1898 pushed U.S. leaders and public opinion from an ambivalent position to one supporting armed intervention on behalf of the Cubans. President McKinley first pursued diplomatic channels to achieve Cuban independence, but Spain balked, fearing that a failure to defend the colony would trigger revolution in Spain itself. The U.S. then declared war on Spain on April 25, 1898, retroactive to April 21. Spain had a large army in Cuba and a strong garrison in the Philippine Islands, but its naval presence was weak in the Philippines and nonexistent in Cuba. Spain thus adopted a defensive strategy, using troops in the field to fend off American attacks, with the navy periodically reinforcing and resupplying threatened locations. The U.S. had a small regular army of 28,000 men and a large volunteer army that supported its strong navy. It planned a naval blockade of Cuba that would permit land operations, and a second naval campaign in the Philippines. The naval blockade was established in Havana on April 21 and broadened while Spain awaited the arrival of a squadron under Pascual Cervera. By the time the squadron arrived, it had been reduced to six vessels and was quickly blockaded in port by May 28. McKinley organized a force at Tampa to go to Santiago de Cuba to destroy the squadron. Gen. WILLIAM SHAFTER transferred the Fifth Army Corps, 17,000 men, to Santiago de Cuba on June 20. Shafter approached Santiago de Cuba from the east, landed virtually unopposed, and moved toward San Juan Heights, the principal bulwark around the city. Shafter attacked on July

1, struggling into the Spanish positions. All thought of continuing to Santiago de Cuba was forgotten, given the 1,385 casualties suffered that day. Part of this assault was the BATTLE OF SAN JUAN HILL by the First U.S. Volunteer Cavalry Regiment (or ROUGH RIDERS), which THEODORE ROOSEVELT later used in his campaigns for the governorship of New York and the vice presidency. After the action of July 1, Cervera received orders to leave Santiago de Cuba, complying two days later but encountering assaults from the American blockade vessels as they emerged from the channel. Only one Spanish vessel, the *Cristobal Colón*, escaped the harbor. Shafter then decided to besiege the city, which forced its capitulation on July 17. The victory at Santiago de Cuba forced the Spanish government to inaugurate peace negotiations. During this process, however, U.S. forces undertook a campaign in Puerto Rico and an attack on Manila, where U.S. forces had established a presence on May 1. Spain agreed to a protocol on August 12 that ended hostilities among the nations, specifying independence for Cuba, cession of Puerto Rico to the U.S. in lieu of a monetary indemnity, and the cession of a port in the Ladrones (Marianas). However, the protocol did not address the Philippine Islands. McKinley, riding a domestic annexationist wave and lacking a viable alternative, instructed the American peace commission to obtain the entire Philippine archipelago; Spain accepted a payment of $20,000,000. The treaty was ratified on March 6, 1899 by the Senate and on March 19 by the queen regent of Spain (overriding opposition in the Cortes). Ratifications were then exchanged on April 11, 1899. The acquisition of the Philippines led to a long insurgency that was finally quelled in July 1902. The imperialist impulse proved short-lived, though, since by 1916 Congress had begun preparations for Philippine independence, which was ultimately achieved in 1946.

Spanish Main, the • **1** the former name for the northwest coast of South America between the Orinoco River and Panama. **2** the area of the northwest coast of South America, the Caribbean Sea, and the West Indies, where Spanish merchant ships traveled and were often preyed upon by pirates from the sixteenth to the eighteenth century.

span of control • the area of activity or number of functions, people, or things for which an individual or organization is responsible.

span of detonation • (regarding atomic demolition munition employment) that total period of time, resulting from a timer error, between the earliest and the latest possible detonation time. There are three stages of time involved: **a** (**early time**) the earliest possible time that an atomic demolition munition can detonate. **b** (**fire time**) the time that the atomic demolition munition will detonate should the timers function precisely without error. **c** (**late time**) the latest possible time that an atomic demolition munition can detonate.

spar • *n.* **1** a thick, strong pole such as is used for a mast or yard on a ship. **2** the main longitudinal beam of an airplane wing.

spar buoy |bo͞oē; boi| • a buoy made of a spar with one end moored so that the other stands up.

spar deck • an upper deck of a ship or other vessel.

spark • *n.* (also **Spark** or **Sparks**) informal used in the armed forces as a nickname for a radio operator or an electrician.

Sparrow • (**AIM-7**) an air-to-air radar-guided, medium-range missile that carries a nonnuclear warhead. It was first developed in the late 1950s. It is slowly being phased out because of its sometimes disappointing performance in combat.

SPARS • the women's reserve of the Coast Guard, formed in 1942. The name is inspired by the Coast Guard motto, *semper paratus* (always prepared).

Spartan • a nuclear, surface-to-air guided missile that was part of the SAFEGUARD ballistic missile defense weapon system. It was designed to intercept strategic ballistic reentry vehicles in the exoatmosphere.

Spasur • an operational space surveillance system with the mission to detect and determine the orbital elements of all man- made objects in orbit of the earth. The mission is accomplished by means of a continuous fan of continuous wave energy beamed vertically across the continental United States and an associated computational facility. It is the navy portion of the North American Air Defense Command SPACE DETECTION AND TRACKING SYSTEM.

speak • *v.* (past **spoke** ; past part. **spoken**) archaic hail and hold communication with (a ship) at sea.

spear • *n.* a weapon with a long shaft and a pointed tip, typically of metal, used for thrusting or throwing. • *v.* pierce or strike with a spear or other pointed object: *he emerged from hiding only to be speared in the back.*

spearhead • *n.* **1** the point of a spear. **2** an individual or group chosen to lead an attack. • *v.* lead (an attack).

spearman • *n.* (pl. **-men**) a man, especially a soldier, who uses a spear.

special agent • a person, either U.S. military or civilian, who is a specialist in military security or the collection of intelligence or counterintelligence information.

special air operation • an air operation conducted in support of special operations and other clandestine, covert, and psychological activities.

special atomic demolition munition • a very-low-yield, human-portable, atomic demolition munition that is detonated by a timer device.

special boat squadron • (**SBR**) a permanent U.S. Navy major command assigned two or more special boat units for some military purposes and for all administrative ones. Its task is training and deploying the special boat units, as well as assisting naval special warfare groups and task units.

special cargo • cargo that requires special handling or protection, such as pyrotechnics, detonators, watches, and precision instruments.

special equipment • equipment not authorized in standard equipment publications but determined as essential in connection with a contemplated operation, function, or mission. Also called PROJECT EQUIPMENT .

special-equipment vehicle • a vehicle with a general-purpose chassis but a special-purpose body and/or equipment to perform a specific mission. See also VEHICLE.

special flight • an air transport flight, other than a scheduled service, set up to move a specific load.

special forces • (**SF**) combat personnel of the U.S. Army who have been trained and equipped to carry out special operations, such forces have five major responsibilities: unconventional warfare, foreign internal defense, direct action, special reconnaissance, and counterterrorism.

special forces group • (**SFG**) a combat organization that plans, conducts, and supports special operations at any time anywhere. It usually consists of a group headquarters and headquarters company, a support company, and special forces battalions. Although the group is capable of functioning as a unit, the battalions usually plan and conduct missions from many separate locations.

Special Group (Counterinsurgency) • the U.S. Marine group sent into Vietnam in the early 1960s as advisors to the South Vietnamese and responsible for formulating and overseeing the internal defense plan.

specialist • *n.* **1** an individual with a particular skill. **2** a short-hand term and form of address for individuals holding the rank of Specialist-4 through Specialist-7 (pay grades E-4 through E-7) in the U.S. Army.

special operations • operations conducted by specially organized, trained, and equipped military and paramilitary forces to achieve military, political, economic, or psychological objectives by unconventional military means in hostile, denied, or politically sensitive areas. Special operations are conducted in both peacetime and wartime, are frequently shaped by political considerations and involve a degree of political risk, and may be overt, covert, or clandestine.

Special Operations Command • see U.S. SPECIAL OPERATIONS COMMAND.

Special Operations Command, First • located at Fort Bragg, NC, and the successor to the Special Warfare Center, established in the late 1950s. The command is responsible for planning, coordinating, conducting, and supporting joint special operations.

special operations forces • (**SOF**) active and reserve forces of the armed services selected by the secretary of defense and organized, trained, and equipped to carry out and support special operations.

special operations group • (**SOG**) a number of ships and/or aircraft, usually a subdivision of a force, organized, trained, and equipped to carry out and support special operations.

Special Operations School • an air force training school for special operations forces at Hurlburt Field, Florida. Founded in 1967 as the U.S. Air Force Special Air Warfare School, it received its current name in 1968. Since 1990 it has been a division of the Air Force Special Operations Command.

special operations wing • (**SOW**) a U.S. Air Force unit made up of a primary mission group organized, trained, and equipped to carry out and support special operations, plus the required supporting organizations for the mission.

special-purpose vehicle • a vehicle with a special chassis and designed to fulfill a specific purpose. See also VEHICLE.

Special Senate Committee Investigating the Munitions Industry • see NYE COMMITTEE.

special weapons • a term sometimes used to indicate weapons grouped for special procedures, for security, or for other reasons. Specific terminology (for example, "nuclear weapons" or "guided missiles") is preferable.

Spectre • (**AC-130H**) a heavily-armed aerial gunship with side-firing weapons. These gunships have sophisticated sensor, fire control, and navigation systems to provide close air support, air interdiction, and force protection. The AC-130H was first deployed in 1972.

spectrum of war • a term that encompasses the full range of conflict: cold, limited, and general war.

speed of sound • the speed at which sound travels in a given medium under specified conditions. The speed of sound at sea level in the International Standard Atmosphere is 1,108 feet per second (or 658 knots, or 1,215 kilometers per hour).

Speer, Albert (1905–81) • German architect and NAZI minister of armaments and war production. Speer joined the Nazi party in 1931, after hearing ADOLF HITLER speak, and soon became Hitler's personal architect. He conceived a grandiose project for rebuilding Berlin, which never came to fruition. In 1942 he was named minister of armaments and munitions; a year later the position was extended to cover war production. In this capacity Speer headed a system of slave labor, drawn largely from the concentration camps, that produced war materiel for Germany during WORLD WAR II. Speer confessed his guilt at the postwar NUREMBERG TRIALS and served a twenty-year prison sentence.

Spencer, Joseph (1714–89) • REVOLUTIONARY WAR army officer, born into a wealthy Connecticut family, Spencer studied law and entered state politics, winning election to the colonial assembly in 1750. He also held a commission in the militia, fighting in KING GEORGE'S WAR (1744–48) and in the FRENCH AND INDIAN WAR (1754–63). He was a leading advocate of independence in his colony and, after the first fighting in Massachusetts in 1775, formed a regiment in Connecticut and led his troops to Roxbury to fight with the patriots. He was named a brigadier general and placed in charge of defense for Connecticut; his unit was later incorporated into the Continental army. Unhappy about his rank, he left his unit but was persuaded to return. He was a counselor to Gen. GEORGE WASHINGTON in the battle of NEW YORK (1776); his advice, and that of Washington's other advisers, resulted in a major defeat for the Continentals.

spike • *v.* render (a gun) useless by plugging up the vent with a spike.

spill • *v.* (past and past part. **spilled** or **spilt**) let (wind) out of a sail, typically by slackening the sheets.

spin • *v.* (**spinning**; past and past part. **spun**) **1** turn or cause to turn or whirl around quickly. **2** give (a news story) a favorable emphasis or slant. • *n.* **1** a rapid turning or whirling motion: *he concluded the dance with a double spin.* **2** a favorable bias or slant in a news story: *he tried to put a positive spin on the president's campaign.* **3** a fast revolving motion of an aircraft as it descends rapidly: *he tried to stop the plane from* ***going into a spin.***

PHRASES: **spin one's wheels** informal waste one's time or efforts. **spin a yarn** tell a long, far-fetched story.

spinnaker |ˈspinəkər| • *n.* a large three-cornered sail, typically bulging when full, set forward of the mainsail of a yacht when running before the wind.

ORIGIN: mid 19th cent.: apparently a fanciful formation from *Sphinx*, the name of the yacht first using it.

spin-off (also **spinoff**) • *n.* an incidental benefit arising from industrial or military technology: *the commercial spin-off from defense research.*

Spirit • a multi-role stealth strategic bomber capable of delivering both conventional and nuclear munitions. Because it can penetrate previously impenetrable defenses and deliver massive firepower anywhere in the world, it represents a dramatic leap forward in technology.

spit • *n.* a narrow point of land projecting into the sea: *a narrow spit of land shelters the bay.*

Spitfire • a single-seat low-wing monoplane fighter built in Britain that was among the fastest and most effective fighters used in WORLD WAR II. It was first flown in 1936, and began service with the Royal Air Force in 1938. In various versions, the Spitfire served as a fighter, fighter—bomber, and photoreconnaissance aircraft. The last of the Spitfires was retired in 1954.

spitting • in air antisubmarine warfare operations, a code meaning, "I am about to lay, or am laying, sonobuoys. I may be out of radio contact for a few minutes." If transmitted from the submarine, it indicates that the submarine has launched a sonobuoy.

splashed • in air intercept, a code meaning, "Enemy aircraft shot down."

splice • *v.* join or connect (a rope or ropes) by interweaving the strands. • *n.* a union of two ropes, pieces of timber, or similar materials spliced together at the ends.

PHRASES: **splice the main brace** Brit. & historical (in the navy) serve out an extra tot of rum.

splinter-proof • *adj.* capable of withstanding splinters from bursting shells or bombs: *splinter-proof shutters.*

spoiling attack • a tactical maneuver employed to seriously impair a hostile attack while the enemy is in the process of forming or assembling for an attack. A typical spoiling attack would be carried out by armored units as an attack on enemy assembly positions in front of a main line of resistance or battle position.

Spokane War • an 1858 war in Eastern Washington Territory involving Coeur d'Alenes, Spokanes, Palouses, Yakimas, and Northern Paiutes fighting against U.S. forces and settlers in the expanding mining areas. The native tribes exacted heavy casualties in some battles but ultimately surrendered and confined themselves to reservations. Also called the COEUR D'ALENE WAR.

sponson |ˈspänsən| • *n.* **1** a projection on the side of a boat, ship, or seaplane. **2** a gun platform standing out from a warship's side. **3** a short subsidiary wing that serves to stabilize a seaplane. **4** a buoyancy chamber fitted to a boat's hull, especially on a canoe. **5** a triangular platform supporting the wheel on a paddle steamer.

Spooky • (**AC-130U**) a heavily-armed aerial gunship with side-firing weapons. These gunships have sophisticated sensor, fire control, and navigation systems to provide surgical firepower or area saturation during extended periods in the air, and can attack two targets simultaneously. The AC-130U is the third generation of C-130 gunships, and was first deployed in 1995.

spot • *v.* locate an enemy's position, typically from the air: *they were* ***spotting for*** *enemy aircraft.*

spot jamming • the jamming of a specific channel or frequency.

spot report • a concise narrative report of essential information covering events or conditions that may have an immediate and significant effect on current planning and operations. It is afforded the most expeditious means of transmission consistent with requisite security. In reconnaissance and surveillance usage, the spot report is not to be used.

Spotsylvania, Battle of • (also called the **Battle of Spotsylvania Court House**), a major CIVIL WAR battle in May, 1864, that was part of ULYSSES S. GRANT'S OVERLAND CAMPAIGN. Forces under Gen. Ulysses S. Grant and ROBERT E. LEE fought for two weeks without a conclusive outcome; Grant continued his campaign, and both sides suffered casualties of more than 10,000.

spotter • *n.* an observer stationed for the purpose of observing and reporting results of naval gunfire to those who are firing, and who also may be employed in designating targets.

Spr • *abbr.* (in the UK) Sapper.

sprag • *n.* a projection preventing the movement of platforms or pallets in the side guidance rails in an aircraft cabin.

spray dome • the mound of water spray thrown up into the air when the shock wave from an underwater detonation of a nuclear weapon reaches the surface.

spread-eagle • *v.* (usually **be spread-eagled**) stretch (someone) out with their arms and legs extended: *he lay spread-eagled in the road.* • *n.* (**spread eagle**) an emblematic representation of an eagle with its legs and wings extended. • *adj.* **1** stretched out with one's arms and legs extended: *prisoners are chained to their beds, spread-eagle, for days at a time.* **2** loudly or aggressively patriotic about the United States: *spread-eagle oratory.*

spring • *v.* (past **sprang** or **sprung**; past part. **sprung**) • *n.* **1** short for SPRING TIDE. **2** an upward curvature of a ship's deck planking from the horizontal. **3** a split in a wooden plank or spar under strain. **4** a hawser laid out diagonally aft from a ship's bow or forward from a ship's stern and secured to a fixed point in order to prevent movement or assist maneuvering.

Springfield Armory • established at Springfield, Massachusetts in 1777 to manufacture cartridges and gun carriages for Gen. GEORGE WASHINGTON's Revolutionary army. In 1794 President Washington chose Springfield as the site for one of two federal armories, and the Springfield Armory quickly became known for its inventions and development of improved weaponry. When HARPERS FERRY was destroyed during the CIVIL WAR, Springfield became the only federal manufacturing site for small arms until the twentieth century. The last small arm developed at Springfield was the M-14 (now the M-21). In 1968, the Department of Defense closed the installation.

Springfield rifle • any of various rifles used by U.S. forces that were issued by the SPRINGFIELD ARMORY in Springfield, Massachusetts. The earliest was a muzzle-loading single shot rifle used by the Union Army during the CIVIL WAR; the most widely used was probably the bolt-operated 1903 model that was a standard infantry weapon in WORLD WAR I.

Springfield rifled musket • the principal infantry weapon used by both sides during the CIVIL WAR; there more than two million manufactured. It weighed nearly ten pounds, had an effective range of 500 yards, and could be fired about six times per minute under ideal conditions.

Spring Hill, Battle of • a battle on November 29, 1864, that served as a prelude to the larger BATTLE OF FRANKLIN on November 30, during the CIVIL WAR. Union Maj. Gen. JOHN M. SCHOFIELD's troops managed to escape capture by Confederate Gen. JOHN B. HOOD at Spring Hill, in Maury County, Tennessee. It is still unclear how Schofield's men managed to slip by Confederate troops during this controversial battle of the FRANKLIN AND NASHVILLE CAMPAIGN.

spring tide • a tide just after a new or full moon, when there is the greatest difference between high and low water.

Sprint • a nuclear surface-to-air guided missile that was part of the SAFEGUARD ballistic missile defense weapon system. It was designed to intercept ballistic missile reentry vehicles in the endoatmosphere.

sprit |sprit| • *n.* a small spar reaching diagonally from low on a mast to the upper outer corner of a sail.

spritsail |'sprit,sāl; -səl| • *n.* **1** a sail extended by a sprit. **2** a sail extended by a yard set under a ship's bowsprit.

sprog |spräg| Brit. & informal, or chiefly derogatory • *n.* a military recruit or trainee: *it was so familiar to every sprog who ever put on uniform.*
ORIGIN: 1940s (originally services' slang in the sense 'new recruit'): perhaps from obsolete *sprag* 'lively young man,' of unknown origin.

Spruance class • a class of destroyers equipped with either the Mk-41 Vertical Launch System or TOMAHAWK Armored Box Launchers (ABLs). These ships were the first large U.S. Navy warships powered by gas turbine engines.

spur • *n.* a device with a small spike or a spiked wheel that is worn on a rider's heel and used for urging a horse forward.

Sputnik |'spətnik; 'spo͝ot-| • *n.* each of a series of Soviet artificial satellites, the first of which (launched on October 4, 1957) was the first satellite to be placed in orbit.
ORIGIN: Russian, literally 'fellow-traveler.'

Sqn Ldr • *abbr.* Squadron Leader.

squad • *n.* a small number of soldiers assembled for drill or assigned to some special task, especially an infantry unit forming part of a platoon.

squaddie |'skwädē| (also **squaddy**) • *n.* (pl. **-ies**) Brit. & informal **1** a private soldier. **2** a new recruit in the armed forces.

squadron • *n.* **1** an operational unit in an air force consisting of two or more flights of aircraft and the personnel required to fly them. **2** a principal division of an armored or cavalry regiment, consisting of two or more troops. **3** a group of warships detached on a particular duty or under the command of a flag officer.

squadron commander • **1** the commander of a cavalry or armored cavalry unit of squadron (battalion) size or of an aviation unit of squadron size in any of the U.S. armed forces. **2** the commanding officer of a naval organization consisting of two or more divisions of ships (i.e., the number of ships a single flag officer could command handily).

squadron leader • a rank of officer in the RAF, above flight lieutenant and below wing commander.

Squadron Officer School • a postgraduate air force service school course offered by the Squadron Officer College at Maxwell AFB in Alabama. Established in 1954, it replaced the Squadron Officer Course, which had been part of the Air Command and Staff School (renamed the Air Command and Staff College in 1954), since 1950. It has been a separate component school of the Air University since 1959.

square • *n.* a body of infantry drawn up in

rectangular form. • *v.* **1** (**square oneself**) adopt a posture of defense. **2** set (a yard or other part of a ship) approximately at right angles to the keel or other point of reference.

square-bashing • *n.* Brit. & informal military drill performed repeatedly on a barrack square.

square knot • a type of double knot that is made symmetrically to hold securely and to be easy to untie.

square-rigged • *adj.* (of a sailing ship) having the principal sails at right angles to the length of the ship, supported by horizontal yards attached to the mast or masts.

square-rigger • *n.* a square-rigged sailing ship.

square sail • a four-cornered sail supported by a yard attached to a mast.

SR • see PIONEER UAV.

SR-71 • see BLACKBIRD.

SRBM • *abbr.* short range ballistic missile.

SRIG • (Also called **surveillance-reconnaissance-intelligence group**) a unified intelligence-gathering operation of the Marine Corps, first formed in 1988.

SRIGS • *abbr.* surveillance-reconnaissance-intelligence groups.

SS[1] • see SUBMARINE.

SS[2] • the Nazi special police force. Founded in 1925 by ADOLF HITLER as a personal bodyguard, the SS provided security forces (including the GESTAPO) and adminstered the concentration camps.

ORIGIN: abbreviation of German *Schutzstaffel* 'defense squadron.'

SS[3] • *abbr.* steamship: *the SS Canberra.*

SSBN • see FLEET BALLISTIC MISSILE SUBMARINE.

SSBN 726 • see *Ohio*, USS.

SSG • see GUIDED MISSILE SUBMARINE.

SSGN • see GUIDED MISSILE SUBMARINE.

SSN • see SUBMARINE.

SSN-21 • see SEAWOLF.

SSN-571 • see *Nautilus*, USS.

SSN-688I • see CHEYENNE.

stabilizer • *n.* a thing used to keep something steady or stable, in particular: **a** the horizontal tailplane of an aircraft. **b** a gyroscopically controlled system used to reduce the rolling of a ship.

stack • *n.* a pyramidal group of rifles.

PHRASES: **stack arms** place a number of rifles with their butts on the ground and the muzzles together.

staff • *n.* **1** a group of officers assisting an officer in command of an army formation or administration headquarters. **2** (usually **Staff**) short for STAFF SERGEANT. • *v.* (usually **be staffed**) provide (an organization, business, etc.) with staff: (**staffed**) *all units are fully staffed.*

staff college • a military service school that prepares selected mid-career officers for intermediate-level command and staff positions within the armed forces. They include schools such as the AIR COMMAND AND STAFF COLLEGE, ARMED FORCES STAFF COLLEGE, ARMY COMMAND AND GENERAL STAFF COLLEGE, and the COLLEGE OF NAVAL COMMAND AND STAFF.

staff noncommissioned officer • a senior non-commissioned officer assigned to staff duties.

staff officer • an officer serving on the staff of a military headquarters or government department.

staff sergeant • **1** a noncommissioned officer in the Army ranking above sergeant and below sergeant first class. **2** a noncommissioned officer in the Air Force ranking above sergeant and below technical sergeant. **3** a noncommissioned officer in the Marine Corps ranking above sergeant and below gunnery sergeant.

stage • *n.* **1** an element of the missile or propulsion system that generally separates from the missile at burnout or cut-off. Stages are numbered chronologically in order of burning. **2** (according to NATO) the part of an air route from one air staging unit to the next. • *v.* process, in a specified area, troops that are in transit from one locality to another.

staging area (also **staging point** or **staging post**) • a stopping place or assembly point en route to a destination: *a vast staging area for guerrilla attacks.*

staging base • **1** an advanced naval base for the anchoring, fueling, and refitting of transports and cargo ships, and for replenishing mobile service squadrons. **2** a landing and takeoff area with minimum servicing, supply, and shelter provided for the temporary occupancy of military aircraft during the course of movement from one location to another.

Stahel, Julius (1825–1912) • born in Hungary, Stahel fled to Berlin, London, and, finally, New York after fighting with Kossuth (Hungary's revolutionary leader) for the independence of Hungary from Austria. He worked as a journalist until commissioned a Lt. Col. in the Union Army in 1861, and rose quickly to brigadier general that same year. He was awarded the CONGRESSIONAL MEDAL OF HONOR for being wounded near Piedmont in 1864.

stalag |ˈstäˌläg| • *n.* (in World War II) a German prison camp, especially for noncommissioned officers and privates.

ORIGIN: German, contraction of *Stammlager*, from *Stamm* 'base, main stock' + *Lager* 'camp.'

Stalingrad, Battle of • a long-running WORLD WAR II battle in 1942 and 1943 for control of the Russian city of Stalingrad. In mid-1942 German troops had reached the outskirts of the city, their deepest penetration of their forces into Russia. They met fierce resistance and were unable to prevail, finally being circled and forced to surrender along with 90,000 troops. The Axis forces suffered losses of more than 800,000, but the Russians lost more than a million in trying to defend their city.

Stalin, Josef (1879–1953) • secretary general of the Communist party of the Soviet Union and premier of the Soviet Union, born Josef Vissarionovich Djugashvili in the Soviet republic of Georgia, Stalin in his youth was a Marxist revolutionary, allying himself with the Bolshevik group within the

Social Democratic party. He was imprisoned and exiled several times for revolutionary activities. Lenin, in exile, named him to the Central Committee of the Bolshevik party, which had split from the more moderate wing of the Social Democrats, and in the 1917 revolution Stalin played a major role. In 1922 he was named secretary general of the Communist party, a post he held until his death and that he used to consolidate his power and to outmaneuver his opponents, who usually underestimated his cunning and his intelligence. After Lenin's death in 1924, he ousted his rivals and soon instituted a program of centralized, state-run economic planning for the Soviet Union, herding peasants onto collective farms; those who resisted were arrested, tortured, exiled to brutal concentration camps, or murdered. An estimated 10 million people died in the resulting famine. He also instituted a state-run program of industrialization, which was marginally less brutal and which did succeed in industrializing an agrarian country in record time. In 1934 he launched a bloody purge of the Communist party, creating a parade of show trials; those who opposed him were convicted and later executed. In 1939 he concluded a pact with ADOLF HITLER; in its wake, Stalin annexed several East European countries, including Latvia, Lithuania, and eastern Poland. Then, in 1941, Hitler launched an unprovoked invasion of the Soviet Union; Stalin appointed himself supreme commander in chief and personally led the Soviet resistance, at Stalingrad and at Kursk; despite devastating losses, the Soviets prevailed, and Hitler capitulated in May 1945. Stalin met during the war with the Allied leaders, President FRANKLIN D. ROOSEVELT and British Prime Minister WINSTON CHURCHILL, at TEHRAN (1943) and at YALTA (1945). After the war, Stalin extended Soviet control over Eastern Europe, installing nominally independent puppet regimes in Hungary, Yugoslavia, Poland, Czechoslovakia, and other countries; he cast the United States and Britain at his enemies, setting the stage for the COLD WAR.

stall • *n.* an instance of an engine, vehicle, aircraft, or boat stalling: *speed must be maintained to avoid a stall and loss of control.* • *v.* **1** (of a motor vehicle or its engine) stop running, typically because of an overload on the engine: *her car stalled at the crossroads.* **2** (of an aircraft or its pilot) reach a condition where the speed is too low to allow effective operation of the controls. **3** have insufficient wind power in the sails to give controlled motion. **4** cause (an engine, vehicle, aircraft, or boat) to stall.

Stamp Act • an act passed by the British Parliament on March 22, 1765 to obtain money from the American colonies in order to pay debts incurred during the FRENCH AND INDIAN WAR (1754–63), maintain British naval forces, and support a colonial military force. It required the use of stamps on all legal and commercial papers, pamphlets, newspapers, almanacs, and cards and dice. American colonists protested and rioted against the act. It was annulled in March 1766.

STANAG • an agreement to which all NATO members subscribe, dealing with standardization of doctrine, tactics or procedures.
ORIGIN: from *Standardized Agreement.*

stand • *v.* (past and past part. **stood**) **1** (of a ship) remain on a specified course: *the ship was standing north.* **2** act in a specified capacity as: *he stood watch all night.* **3** (of an object, building, or settlement) be situated in a particular place or position: *the town stood on a hill | the hotel stands in three acres of gardens.* • *n.* **1** a determined effort to resist or fight for something: *this was not the moment to* ***make a stand for*** *independence.* **2** an act of holding one's ground against or halting to resist an opposing force: *Custer's legendary last stand.*
▸**stand by** be ready to deal or assist with something: *two battalions were on their way, and a third was standing by.*
stand down (**stand down** or **stand someone down**) relax or cause to relax after a state of readiness: *if something doesn't happen soon, I reckon they'll stand us down.*
stand in sail closer to the shore.
stand off sail further away from the shore.
stand someone off keep someone away: repel someone.
stand on (of a ship) continue on the same course.
stand to stand ready for an attack, especially one before dawn or after dark.

standard • *n.* a military or ceremonial flag carried on a pole or hoisted on a rope.

Standard ARM • (**AGM-78**) an air-launched antiradiation missile designed to home on and destroy radar emitters. It was used extensively in the VIETNAM WAR.

standard-bearer • *n.* a soldier who is responsible for carrying the distinctive flag of a unit, regiment, or army.

Standard B "Liberty" truck • a truck used extensively in World War I, designed by the Army Quartermaster Corps. Production of the truck began in 1917. More than 7500 of the trucks went overseas. The Liberty had a four-cylinder, 52 horsepower engine and a top speed of about fifteen mph.

Standard Missile • (**RIM-66, RIM-67**) an all-weather, shipboard surface-to-air missile that is widely deployed aboard U.S. and allied naval warships. It is the Navy's primary surface-to-air weapon against hostile aircraft and anti-ship cruise missiles. The medium range (RIM-66) missile replaced the TARTAR and the extended range (RIM-67) replaced the TERRIER.

Standard SSM • (**RGM-66D**) a surface-to-surface antiradiation missile equipped with a conventional warhead. It is the ship-launched version of the STANDARD ARM.

Standby Reserve • those units and members of the Reserve components (other than those in the READY RESERVE or Retired Reserve) who are liable for active duty only.

stand-down • *n.* **1** a period of relaxation after a state of alert. **2** an off-duty period.

stand fast • in artillery, the order at which all action on the position ceases immediately.

standing army • an army prepared at all times for action, especially in peacetime, and consisting of regular forces as well as reserve components.

The term is mildly pejorative, the implication being, at least in the United States, that in peacetime such an army "stands around" and consumes inordinate amounts of national resources.

standing operating procedure (or **standard operating procedure**) • (**SOP**) a set of instructions covering those features of operations that lend themselves to a definite or standardized procedure without loss of effectiveness. The procedure is applicable unless ordered otherwise.

standing order • a promulgated order that remains in force until amended or cancelled.

standing rigging • see RIGGING.

Standish, Miles (or **Myles**) (1584?–1656) • colonial founder, born in England, Standish came to America as the military leader of a group of English Leiden separatists who sailed on the Mayflower in 1620. He chose the site of the Pilgrims' settlement at Plymouth, Massachusetts, and designed its defenses; he also negotiated with the neighboring Indian tribes. He was part of the colony's governing structure, serving almost continuously in the Court of Assistants from 1624 until his death. From the 1630s he asserted Plymouth's ascendancy with regard to other settlements and enforced rules of social order, although eventually he had to give way to the larger Massachusetts Bay Colony. Standish was critical in maintaining the colony's financial solvency; he both obtained loans and financing from English investors and provided support from his own funds in return for land and various privileges. In 1637 he and John Alden established the new town of Duxbury, the first new town to separate from the Plymouth settlement; he lived there for the rest of his life.

There is no historical basis for the legend that Standish acted as a surrogate for another man who wished to court Priscilla Mullins, as asserted in Henry Wadsworth Longfellow's poem "The Courtship of Myles Standish."

Standley, William Harrison (1872–1963) • CHIEF OF NAVAL OPERATIONS and diplomat. A California native, Standley served with the ASIATIC FLEET during the SPANISH-AMERICAN WAR (1898) and the PHILIPPINE WAR. He took command of his first battleship in 1919 and reached the rank of vice admiral in 1932. The following year, a full admiral, President FRANKLIN D. ROOSEVELT named him Chief of Naval Operations, a post he held until his retirement in 1937. He served from 1944 to 1945 in the OFFICE OF STRATEGIC SERVICES and then again retired.

stand of arms • Brit. & archaic a complete set of weapons for one man.

stand of colours • Brit. a battalion's flags.

stand-to • *n.* **1** the state of readiness for action or attack. **2** the formal start to a day of military operations.

Stanley, David Sloane (1828–1902) • Union army officer. An Ohioan, Stanley spent his early military career fighting the Cheyenne. He was offered a commission by the Confederate army at the outbreak of the CIVIL WAR but chose the Union cause. In 1862 he assumed command of an infantry division in the Army of the Mississippi; later that year he became chief of cavalry in the ARMY OF THE CUMBERLAND. In 1864 he participated in Gen. WILLIAM T. SHERMAN's march on Atlanta, winning brevet appointments to colonel and brigadier general in the regular army. He assumed command of IV Corps and was wounded in the neck at the battle of Franklin, for which he received the MEDAL OF HONOR.

Stanton, Edwin M. (1814–69) • attorney general and secretary of war. An Ohioan, he moved to Washington, D.C., where he cultivated some political relationships and took on cases that brought him notice. A Democrat despite his antislavery beliefs, he served as attorney general in the closing months of JAMES BUCHANAN's administration, urging the preservation of the Union at all costs. After ABRAHAM LINCOLN's election, Stanton began to separate himself from the Democratic party over the issue of slavery and served as a legal consultant to Simon Cameron, Lincoln's secretary of war. When Cameron resigned, Lincoln named Stanton to take his place. Stanton eliminated the favoritism and corruption that had plagued the WAR DEPARTMENT under Cameron. With Lincoln, he directed the prosecution of the war when the commanding general of the Union army, GEORGE B. MCCLELLAN, and then his successor, HENRY W. HALLECK, proved reluctant leaders. The appointment of ULYSSES S. GRANT as Union commanding general eased this situation. Most controversial was his suspension of HABEAS CORPUS and his creation of what amounted to a national police force to enforce draft regulations and to maintain the peace after the EMANCIPATION PROCLAMATION. Stanton developed a warm relationship with Lincoln and after the president's assassination led the relentless hunt for the conspirators and personally participated in their prosecution. During RECONSTRUCTION he urged the use of strong measures to protect the rights of newly freed blacks and opposed President ANDREW JOHNSON's efforts to end martial law and leave the South to run its own affairs. In 1867 Johnson demanded his resignation, in violation of the Tenure of Office Act; the action was instrumental in leading to Johnson's impeachment. President Grant named him to the U.S. Supreme Court in 1869, but he died before he could assume office.

starboard | 'stärbôrd | • *n.* the side of a ship or aircraft that is on the right when one is facing forward. The opposite of PORT. • *v.* turn (a ship or its helm) to starboard.

starboard tack • in sailing, to tack or sail to the right (with the wind coming from the left).

Starfighter • (**F-104**) a single-seat turbojet day fighter aircraft built for the U.S. Air Force but also used by fifteen other countries. In 1958—1960, it saw first-line use by the Air Force. It carried a six-barreled 20-millimeter cannon and SIDEWINDER air-to-air missiles as well as various combinations of bombs and missiles on wing pylons and fuselage.

Stark, Harold Raynsford (1888–1972) • CHIEF OF NAVAL OPERATIONS. Born in Pennsylvania to a military family, Stark successfully commanded several cruisers early in his naval career. In WORLD WAR I he led his fleet in antisubmarine and escort duties in the Mediterranean, winning his first DISTINGUISHED SERVICE MEDAL. After the war, he returned to sea. In 1939 he was promoted to admiral and named Chief of Naval Operations by President FRANKLIN D. ROOSEVELT. As the threat of war loomed, Stark successfully sought funding to strengthen the navy and helped shape strategy to defeat Germany and Japan. Stark received part of the blame for the navy's unpreparedness for the attack at PEARL HARBOR (1941) and lost his command of the navy's operational forces, although he kept his job title. In 1942, however, Roosevelt named him to command U.S. naval forces in Europe, largely an administrative post. He received a second Distinguished Service Medal for his work in overseeing logistical preparations for D-DAY. In 1944 a navy court of inquiry blamed him for not alerting the commander at Pearl Harbor of deterioration in U.S.-Japanese relations; after a congressional investigation, the presiding admiral retracted his criticism, and Stark received a third Distinguished Service Medal for his service in Europe.

Stark, John (1728–1822) • REVOLUTIONARY WAR army officer, born in New Hampshire. Stark served in the FRENCH AND INDIAN WAR (1754–63), using guerrilla tactics against France's Indian allies. After the fighting at CONCORD in 1775, Stark became colonel of a New Hampshire regiment that fought at BUNKER HILL and, as a colonel, at NEW YORK (1776). Stark led Gen. GEORGE WASHINGTON's advance force at TRENTON (1776) and fought at PRINCETON (1777). Angry at not receiving a promotion, he resigned his commission but formed a brigade to defend the supply depot at Bennington, Vermont, where he won a major victory that indirectly helped the Continentals defeat the British at SARATOGA two months later. In 1780 he served on the board that presided at the trial for treason of JOHN ANDRÉ.

Starlifter • (**C-141**) a large troop and cargo transport aircraft with design features adopted from the versatile HERCULES (C-131) and a range of more than 3,000 miles. It became operational in 1965 with MILITARY AIRLIFT COMMAND and provided daily service across the Pacific during the VIETNAM WAR.

Stars and Bars • the first national flag of the Confederate States of America, the design of which was proposed by Professor Nicola Marschall and adopted by the Provisional Congress of the Confederate States on March 4, 1861. The Stars and Bars resembled somewhat the national flag of the United States. It had a blue canton with seven white stars, one for each state then part of the Confederacy, and three horizontal stripes, the top and bottom ones red and the middle one white.

Stars and Stripes • unofficial daily newspaper for U.S. military personnel stationed overseas operated under U.S. Army sponsorship. *Stars and Stripes* was published in France from February 1918 to June 1919 and resumed publication in April 1942 continuing to the present. Both a European and a Pacific edition are published.

Star-Spangled Banner, The • a song first written as a poem by Francis Key Scott in 1814, and that has been America's official national anthem since 1931. Key wrote the poem in response to the bombing of Fort McHenry during the WAR OF 1812 and wanted the poem set to the English tune "To Anacreon in Heaven," written by Hohn Stafford Smith around 1775.

START I Treaty • an agreement signed in 1991 by President GEORGE H. BUSH and Soviet president MIKHAIL GORBACHEV to reduce the number of U.S. and Soviet ballistic missiles by about one-third and one-half, respectively. Because of the dissolution of the USSR in 1991, implementation was delayed until 1994 when agreements were reached with former Soviet republics.

START II Treaty • an agreement signed in 1993 by U.S. President GEORGE H. BUSH and Russian president Boris Yeltsin proposing more intense reductions in strategic warheads than START I, but which could be implemented only after START I in 1994. Russia has yet to ratify it, and many systems on both sides have yet to be dismantled.

Star Wars |ˈstär ˌwawrz| • popular name for STRATEGIC DEFENSE INITIATIVE.
ORIGIN: with reference to a popular science-fiction film (1977).

State Department • the main U.S. government institution conducting international relations. Established in 1789, the State Department is headed by the Secretary of State, who is the top advisor to the president on foreign affairs.

state of war • the situation in which a state or coalition of states is at war with another state or coalition of states.

stateside • *adj.* & *adv.* informal of, in, or toward the U.S. (used in reference to the U.S. from elsewhere or from the geographically separate states of Alaska and Hawaii): *they were headed stateside.*

states' rights • the rights and powers held by individual states rather than by the federal government.

static line • in air transport, a line attached to a parachute pack and to a strop or anchor cable in an aircraft so that when the load is dropped the parachute is deployed automatically.

station • *n.* **1** a small military base, especially of a specified kind: *a naval station.* **2** the place where someone or something stands or is placed on military or other duty: *the lookout resumed his station in the bow.* **3** a place or building where a specified activity or service is based: *coastal radar stations.* • *v.* put in or assign to a specified place for a particular purpose, especially a military one: *troops **were stationed in** the town.*

station bill • a list showing the prescribed stations of a ship's crew in specified emergencies.

stationkeeping • *n.* the maintenance of a ship's proper position relative to others in a fleet.

station pointer • a navigational instrument that fixes a ship's position on a chart by determining its place relative to two landmarks or conspicuous objects at sea.

status quo ante bellum • the state of affairs existing before the war.

St. Augustine • the oldest city in the United States, in northeastern Florida, founded in 1565 by the Spanish explorer Pedro Menendez de Aviles. It is located near the place where Ponce de Leon, who discovered Florida, landed in 1513. Between 1672 and 1696 Spain authorized the building of the CASTILLO DE SAN MARCOS, which still stands as the oldest masonry fort in the country, in order to fend off attacks from the north. In 1702–03 St. Augustine turned away the South Carolinians, and in 1740 the city repelled an attack by JAMES OGLETHORPE, the founder of Georgia. In 1742 Fort Matanzas was built. In 1763, at the close of the FRENCH AND INDIAN WAR (1754–63), the English gained possession of the city. During the REVOLUTIONARY WAR it attracted large numbers of Tories from the North, but they left when it was passed to the Spanish in 1783. In 1821 Spain ceded Florida to the United States, and St. Augustine began to thrive as never before. This era of growth came to a halt with the SEMINOLE WAR of the 1830s. In March 1862 Union troops occupied the city and maintained their hold on it until the end of the CIVIL WAR.

staunch |stônCH; stänCH| • *adj.* (also **stanch**) archaic (of a ship) watertight.

Stavka • the senior general headquarters of the Soviet military forces in WORLD WAR II. The Stavka of the Supreme Commander (Marshal JOSEF STALIN) was formed in August 1941 and served as the principal planning and executive agency of the Soviet armed forces. Overshadowed by Stalin's personal decision-making, the Stavka was only intermittently effective and was abolished in 1945 before the Soviet Union entered the war against Japan.

stay • *n.* **1** a large rope, wire, or rod used to support a ship's mast, leading from the masthead to another mast or spar or down to the deck. **2** a guy or rope supporting a flagpole or other upright pole. **3** a supporting wire or cable on an aircraft. • *v.* secure or steady (a mast) by means of stays.

PHRASES: **be in stays** (of a sailing ship) be head to the wind while tacking.

St. Clair, Arthur (1737–1818) • REVOLUTIONARY WAR army officer and territorial governor, born in Scotland. St. Clair gave up his commission in the British army when he married Phoebe Bayard, of Boston, and, thanks to her wealth, assumed the life of a gentleman in Pennsylvania, where he took on several local political offices. At the outbreak of the Revolution, he raised a regiment, which named him colonel, and fought at TRENTON (1776) and PRINCETON (1777). Named to command FORT TICONDEROGA, he withdrew under the assault by Gen. JOHN BURGOYNE (1777), for which he was much criticized. St. Clair led a weak expedition in 1791 against Indians in the Northwest Territory that suffered the highest casualties ever taken by U.S. forces in battle with Native Americans; although not blamed, St. Clair nonetheless resigned his military commission.

St. Clair's Defeat • a defeat of the army of Gen. ARTHUR ST. CLAIR while they were encamped on the Wabash River in Ohio in November, 1791. The Miami chieftain Little Turtle surrounded the army at night and made a surprise attack by day, killing nearly 700 people. It was the single worst defeat of U.S. arms by Native Americans, and an embarrassment to the fledgling U.S. government, which soon took steps for the establishment of a regular army with the MILITIA ACT of 1792.

stealth • *adj.* (chiefly of aircraft) designed in accordance with technology that makes detection by radar or sonar difficult: *a stealth bomber.*

Stealth bomber • (**B-2**) currently the world's most advanced bomber, and the only aircraft capable of low observable flight. Virtually invisible to radar, it can probably get within two or three miles of its target without detection; loaded with stand-off stealthy missiles, it doesn't even need to go near its target.

Stealth fighter • see NIGHTHAWK, RAPTOR.

steamboat • *n.* a boat that is propelled by a steam engine, especially a paddle-wheel craft of a type used widely on rivers in the 19th century.

steamer • *n.* a ship or boat powered by steam.

steamship • *n.* a ship that is propelled by a steam engine.

steel-clad • *adj.* covered or partially covered in steel applied over wood or some other material. For example, a wooden warship, the hull of which was covered with steel plates, would be said to be steel-clad.

Steele, Frederick (1819–68) • Union army officer. From New York, Steele served ably in the MEXICAN WAR (1846–48). In January 1862, as a brigadier general, he assumed command of the Division of Southwest Missouri; that spring, he commanded a division in the Army of the Southwest. Steele fought with Gen. WILLIAM T. SHERMAN at the Battle of Chickasaw Bluffs, winning promotion to major general. He was a commander in Gen. ULYSSES S. GRANT's assault on VICKSBURG and then took command of the Department of Arkansas. In 1865 he commanded a division during the siege of Mobile; after the war he was sent to Texas, where he remained for two years.

steel-hulled • *adj.* having a hull constructed primarily of steel.

steerageway • *n.* (of a vessel) the minimum speed required for proper response to the helm.

steersman • *n.* (pl. **-men**) a person who is steering a boat or ship.

stellar guidance • a system wherein a guided missile may follow a predetermined course with reference primarily to the relative position of the missile and certain preselected celestial bodies.

stem • *n.* the main upright timber or metal piece at the bow of a ship, to which the ship's sides are joined. • *v.* (of a boat) make headway against (the tide or current).
PHRASES: **from stem to stern** from the front to the back, especially of a ship: *surges of water rocked their boats from stem to stern.*

Ste-Mère-Église airdrop • an airdrop of food and supplies in the area around Ste-Mère-Église, Normandy in June 1944 to support the D-DAY LANDING. It included many men in gliders who crashed into hedgerows, and others who landed by parachute within range of waiting enemy soldiers, who promptly shot them.

Ste. Mère-Église-Montebourg highway • the highway in northern France that was pivotal to the success of the Allied attempt to oust the Germans from the Cotentin Peninsula during the NORMANDY INVASION, June 1944. Sainte Mère-Église was the first town captured by the Eighty-Second and 101st Airborne Divisions on June 6. The highway from Sainte Mère-Église north to Montebourg, now part of N13 (National Route 13), was secured only after the Seventieth Battalion tanks reached the road from UTAH BEACH to combine forces with the paratroopers. Once the highway was secure, the Germans retreated north toward Cherbourg, where they were ultimately defeated on June 26.

Sten gun |'sten| • a type of lightweight British submachine gun.
ORIGIN: 1940s: from the initials of the inventors' surnames, *S*hepherd and *T*urpin, suggested by BREN.

step • *n.* a block, typically fixed to the vessel's keel, on which the base of a mast is seated. • *v.* set up (a mast) in its step.
PHRASES: **break step** stop walking or marching in step with others. **fall into step** change the way one is walking so that one is walking in step with another person. **in** (or **out of**) **step** putting (or not putting) one's feet forward alternately in the same rhythm as the people one is walking, marching, or dancing with.

Stephen, Adam (c.1721–91) • REVOLUTIONARY WAR army officer. Stephen was born and educated in Scotland, where he probably became a doctor. He emigrated to Virginia in 1848, establishing a medical practice and becoming a planter. Stephen assumed temporary command of the Virginia militia during the FRENCH AND INDIAN WAR (1754–63) when the regular leader, GEORGE WASHINGTON, was absent, and he was promoted to lieutenant colonel. He competed with Washington also in political life, losing a seat in the Virginia House of Burgesses in 1761 to the general; he did hold several local political posts. He joined the Continental army in 1776, becoming a brigadier general, and was with Washington as the army retreated through New Jersey. Stephen was dismissed from the army after a court-martial growing out of criticisms of his leadership at the battle of GERMANTOWN (1777).

sterilize • *v.* **1** in naval mine warfare, permanently render a mine incapable of firing by means of a device (e.g., sterilizer) within the mine. **2** remove, from material to be used in covert and clandestine operations, marks or devices that can identify it as emanating from the sponsoring nation or organization.

stern • *n.* the rearmost part of a ship or boat: *he stood at the stern of the yacht.*

sternpost • *n.* the central upright structure at the stern of a vessel, typically bearing the rudder.

sternway • *n.* backward movement of a ship: *we begin* ***making sternway*** *toward the shoal.*

sternwheeler • *n.* a steamer propelled by a paddle wheel positioned at the stern.

Steuben, Baron Friedrich Wilhelm von |'st(y)o͞obən| (1730–94) • REVOLUTIONARY WAR army officer and inspector general, born into a German military family. Steuben was trained in the Prussian army, handling both field commands and administrative duties in the SEVEN YEARS WAR. Downsized out of the army and hounded by rumors about homosexuality, he went to Paris in 1777 to seek a military appointment. There he made contact with U.S. envoys, including Benjamin Franklin and Silas Deane, who gave him letters of introduction to Gen. GEORGE WASHINGTON. He came to America to volunteer his services and met Washington at VALLEY FORGE; Washington named him inspector general and set him to drilling the troops wintering there. Steuben was so effective that Congress granted him both pay and the rank of major general. In 1780 he became Continental commander in Virginia with orders to expedite the movement of men and supplies to the Continental forces opposing Lord CHARLES CORNWALLIS in the Carolinas, but his efforts were stymied by the exhaustion of the troops and other problems. In 1781 he was replaced in Virginia by the MARQUIS DE LAFAYETTE. Steuben's mistaken insistence that Cornwallis would return to the Carolinas and his decision to lead his troops there to be ready for him led the Continentals to near mutiny before Steuben backed down. He commanded a division when Cornwallis was trapped at YORKTOWN (1781); after the victory there, he returned to his position as inspector general and, in 1783, began to make plans for a postwar army. After the war, Steuben hoped to live graciously in New York, but his claims for payment were denied by

Congress, and he lived in relative penury for the rest of his life.

stevedore |ˈstēvəˌdôr| • *n.* a person employed, or a contractor engaged, at a dock to load and unload cargo from ships.
ORIGIN: late 18th cent.: from Spanish *estivador*, from *estivar* 'stow a cargo.'

Stevens, Isaac Ingalls (1818–62) • Union army officer. From Massachusetts, Stevens joined the U.S. Army Corps of Engineers after graduation from the U.S. MILITARY ACADEMY in 1839. In 1853 he was appointed governor of the Washington Territory. A territorial delegate to Congress (1857–61), he supported the extension of roads, mail service, and other internal improvements in the northwest. He also negotiated treaties for temporary reservations with area Indian tribes. When war did break out, he imposed martial law and demanded action from the regular army; his dispute with a civil judge ended with his arrest for contempt of court and a reprimand from President FRANKLIN PIERCE. Stevens believed the South had a constitutional right to slavery; nonetheless, he received a (minor) commission with a New York brigade. He fought at the SECOND BATTLE OF BULL RUN (1862) and was killed in battle at Chantilly.

steward • *n.* **1** a person who looks after the passengers on a ship, aircraft, or train and brings them meals. **2** an official appointed to supervise arrangements or keep order at a large public event, for example a sporting event. • *v.* **1** (of an official) supervise arrangements or keep order at (a large public event): *the event was organized and stewarded properly.* **2** manage or look after (another's property).
DERIVATIVES: **stewardship** *n.*

Stewart, Alexander Peter (1821–1908) • Confederate army officer. From Tennessee, Stewart taught at the U.S. MILITARY ACADEMY after his graduation, and he eventually resigned from the army and became a university professor. Although he opposed secession, he was commissioned a major in the Artillery Corps of the Provisional ARMY OF TENNESSEE; in 1861 he was promoted to brigadier general and put in command of an infantry brigade. Stewart fought at SHILOH (1862), CORINTH (1862), and in numerous other engagements. A major general after 1863, he was victorious at CHICKAMAUGA and defeated at MISSIONARY RIDGE. He also participated in the advance on ATLANTA in 1864. Gen. JOHN B. HOOD's aggressive tactics as commander of the Army of Tennessee resulted in several bloody battles for Stewart and his brigade, and in 1865 Hood resigned and was replaced by Stewart. In 1890 he became one of three commissioners named to head the nation's first military park, Chickamauga and Chattanooga National Military Park.

Steyr • any firearm manufactured by the Austrian company Steyr Mannlicher, particularly a .308 caliber magazine or single-shot competition rifle with a range of 300 meters.

stick • *n.* **1** a number of bombs or paratroopers dropped rapidly from an aircraft. **2** a small group of soldiers assigned to a particular duty: ***a stick of*** *heavily armed guards.*

Stilwell, Joseph (1883–1946) • army officer. Born in Florida but raised in New York, Stilwell spent his early years in the army alternately stationed in the Philippines or in California and teaching at the U.S. MILITARY ACADEMY. He served as chief intelligence office of IV Corps in France in 1917 and earned several temporary promotions. After the war, Stilwell learned Chinese, and in the 1920s and 1930s, with some breaks, was stationed in China, where he traveled extensively and became an expert in Chinese affairs; he formed a low opinion of the Chinese leader CHIANG KAI-SHEK and his corrupt and inept KUOMINTANG party. He returned from China in 1929 to head the Infantry School at Fort Benning, Georgia, where his highly critical manner earned him the nickname "Vinegar Joe." When the United States entered WORLD WAR II, Stilwell's outstanding tactical skills won him command of the CHINA-BURMA-INDIA THEATER; Japan soon occupied the British colony of Burma, which Stilwell lacked the forces to defend. He encountered frustrations in his relationship with Gen. Chiang, whose main interest was the civil war between the Chinese Nationalists and the Chinese Communists, and with the British. In 1943 Stilwell's command was broadened when he became deputy commander of the newly created Southeast Asia Command, serving under Lord LOUIS MOUNTBATTEN, with whom he often disagreed. After the retaking of Burma, the Chinese government demanded Stilwell be recalled, and the U.S. government acceded to the demand. In 1945, he returned but took command of the 10th Army in OKINAWA. When the war ended, he returned to San Francisco, where he died shortly before his planned retirement in 1946.

Stilwell Road • see LEDO ROAD.

Stimson Doctrine • a U.S. foreign policy of nonrecognition of conquered countries or changes born of aggression. It was formulated by U.S. Secretary of State HENRY L. STIMSON during the 1931–32 Manchuria crisis.

Stimson, Henry L. (1867–1950) • secretary of war. After graduating from the Harvard Law School, Stimson, a New Yorker, practiced law with the law firm of ELIHU ROOT and became active in local Republican politics. He served for three years as U.S. attorney for the Southern District of New York and, in 1910, ran as President THEODORE ROOSEVELT's choice for the New York governorship, but his stiff manner caused him to lose the race decisively. He served as secretary of war in the cabinet of President WILLIAM H. TAFT, where he supported increased government oversight of business, and, in 1915 returned to his law practice. Despite his age, he volunteered for service in WORLD WAR I and fought in France; he then again returned to his practice. In 1927 he negotiated a truce in the civil war in Nicaragua (which ultimately failed); in 1928 he was governor general of the Philippines. In 1929 President HERBERT HOOVER named him secretary of state. When Japan invaded Manchuria in 1931, he proclaimed what became known as the STIMSON DOCTRINE, which rejected any treaty or agreement brought about by aggression, but the Doctrine had little effect on the course of events. He returned to his law practice in 1932 but returned to government in 1940 when President FRANKLIN D. ROOSEVELT, hoping to silence Republican critics of his war policy, invited him to become secretary of war. Stimson instituted a selective service system and supported U.S. moves to strengthen Britain against Germany; he also recommended the internship of 100,000 Japanese-Americans whom he considered threats to national security. Stimson headed the MANHATTAN PROJECT, the secret plan to develop an atomic bomb, and approved the bomb's use in Japan in 1945. He opposed the deindustrialization of postwar Germany, fearing it would weaken all Europe and breed resentment.

stinger • *n.* (**Stinger**) a heat-seeking ground-to-air missile that is launched from the shoulder.

Stinger • (**FIM-92A**) a lightweight, man-portable, artillery missile for low altitude air defense in combat zones.

stitched • slang (in the Vietnam War) (of a person or an airplane) killed; bullet-riddled (as by a machine gun).

St. John, Isaac Munroe (1827–80) • Confederate army officer, born in Georgia. At the outbreak of the CIVIL WAR, he was named chief engineer to Gen. JOHN B. MAGRUDER's Army of the Peninsula. Early in 1862 he was promoted to captain major in the Corps of Engineers; later that year, he was promoted again, this time to major, and named to head the Confederate Nitre Corps in the Ordnance Department, in which capacity he was responsible for ensuring the Confederacy's supply of gunpowder and metals, a position of enormous importance. The significance of his work was recognized in the Confederacy's decision to make the Corps a separate agency, the Nitre and Mining Bureau, equal to other war departments.

St. Lô, Battle of • an important battle following the D-DAY LANDING and leading up to the liberation of France, on July 25, 1944. Unable to make progress across the German lines, the Allies coordinated a massive bombing campaign to prepare for an all-out attack on the German Panzer Lehr division at St. Lô, Normandy. This succeeded in breaking the German line and opened the way into Brittany for the subsequent progress toward the Seine.

St. Mihiel offensive • the first independent operation of the newly organized U.S. First Army during WORLD WAR I. The objective was a German salient into the Allied position at St. Mihiel, near Verdun, northern France. On September 12th, 1918, forces under Gen. JOHN J. PERSHING began an attack that cut off the salient, though it resulted in the capture of fewer Germans than was expected because they had found a way to retreat to stronger positions.

stock • *n.* **1** the part of a rifle or other firearm to which the barrel and firing mechanism are attached, held against one's shoulder when firing the gun. **2** the crosspiece of an anchor. **3** (**stocks**) a frame used to support a ship or boat out of water, especially when under construction.

stockade • *n.* **1** a barrier formed from upright wooden posts or stakes, especially as a defense against attack or as a means of confining animals. **2** an enclosure bound by such a barrier: *we got ashore and into the stockade.* **3** a military prison. • *v.* (**stockaded**) enclose (an area) by erecting such a barrier.

Stockton, Robert F. (1795–1866) • naval officer. From New Jersey, Stockton fought in the WAR OF 1812, battled Algerian pirates in 1815, and served in the Mediterranean squadron from 1816 to 1820. In 1821 he negotiated the purchase of a tract of land in eastern Africa that became Liberia, intended to be a colony for freed U.S. slaves. In 1841 he turned down the secretaryship of the navy but advocated the construction of technologically sophisticated naval battleships. He served as a naval commodore in the Gulf of Mexico and off the coast of California during the MEXICAN WAR (1846–48) and became commander of the Pacific fleet in 1846. His highhanded manner led to conflict with Californians who were resisting annexation by the United States; with Brig. Gen. STEPHEN W. KEARNY, Stockton captured Los Angeles from the rebels, at the same time that fighting in southern California ended. Stockton retired from the navy in 1850; he served in the military one more time as commander of the New Jersey militia when Gen. ROBERT E. LEE invaded Pennsylvania in 1863.

Stoddert, Benjamin (1751–1813) • secretary of the navy. From Maryland, Stoddert fought in the REVOLUTIONARY WAR and served as secretary to the BOARD OF WAR AND ORDNANCE (1779–81). When Congress created a separate Naval Department, in 1798, President JOHN ADAMS named Stoddert to the post. Stoddert rapidly commissioned the construction of new ships and created a departmental infrastructure. During the QUASI-WAR WITH FRANCE later that year, Stoddert pursued the enemy vigorously and defeated the French decisively.

stokehold |ˈstōkˌhōld| • *n.* a compartment in a steamship from which the boiler fires are stoked.

stoker • *n.* a person who tends the furnace on a steamship or steam locomotive.

Stone, Charles Pomeroy (1824–87) • Union army officer. From Massachusetts, Stone served in the MEXICAN WAR (1846–48); he left the military but returned in 1861 to command the volunteer defense forces in Washington, D.C.; in July he rejoined the regular army. Stone's advancement in the army was hurt by his anti-abolitionist views and his stern mien; in addition, he was not a great success as a field commander. In 1861 one of his brigades was wiped out at BALL'S BLUFF, Virginia; as a result of the congressional investigation that followed, and amid evidence of overly friendly relationships with Confederate officers, Stone was arrested in February 1862 and held in solitary confinement without being allowed to review the charges against him (President ABRAHAM LINCOLN had suspended the right of HABEAS CORPUS as a war measure). Stone was later able to refute the evidence against him. He returned briefly to active duty but resigned his commission in 1864.

Stone, John Marshall (1830–1900) • Confederate army officer and state governor. Born in Tennessee but later moving to Mississippi, Stone helped raise a company of troops when the CIVIL WAR broke out and fought at the FIRST AND SECOND BATTLES OF BULL RUN (1861 and 1862), at ANTIETAM (1862), and at GETTYSBURG (1863). In 1864, as a colonel, he led a brigade in the BATTLE OF THE WILDERNESS, where he and his troops fought heroically. As Gen. ROBERT E. LEE was surrendering at APPOMATTOX, in 1865, Stone was captured and held prisoner; he was released three months later. After the war he entered politics and eventually served as governor of Mississippi, becoming acting governor in 1876 on the resignation of the incumbent and then winning a term in his own right in 1877. As governor he sought to strengthen white control of the state by restoring voting rights to former Confederate officers.

Stoneman, George (1822–94) • Union army officer and state governor, born in western New York. Stoneman fought in the MEXICAN WAR (1846–48). He led the first cavalry troop to reach Washington, D.C., when the CIVIL WAR erupted and served with Gen. GEORGE B. MCCLELLAN in Virginia in the summer of 1861 but transferred to the infantry in 1862. Stoneman received several promotions and, as a major general, commanded an infantry company at FREDERICKSBURG in 1862. He took some of the blame for the Union defeat at CHANCELLORSVILLE (1863) because of his failure to cut the rail lines linking Gen. ROBERT E. LEE and Richmond in advance of the battle. Stoneman sought to restore his tarnished reputation during Gen. WILLIAM T. SHERMAN's Atlanta campaign, but his effort to free Union prisoners at a camp in Georgia was a dismal failure. In 1871 he moved to California, where he became railroad commissioner and, in 1882, governor.

Stone, Roy (1836–1905) • Union army officer. A New Yorker, Stone studied engineering and settled in Pennsylvania. At the outbreak of the CIVIL WAR, he enlisted; he spent most of the war in Virginia, in the ARMY OF THE POTOMAC. He fought in several battles there and became a recruiter, raising an entire regiment in one month. He was a commander in the Union's losing effort at CHANCELLORSVILLE (1863) and was seriously wounded at GETTYSBURG (1863) and again in the BATTLE OF THE WILDERNESS (1864). In 1898 he served as chief of engineers and a brigadier general of volunteers in the SPANISH-AMERICAN WAR.

Stones River, Battle of • (also known as the **Battle of Murfreesboro**) this 1862–63 campaign cost each side a third of its men, as the North emerged with a morale-boosting triumph after a recent string of defeats. Under Gen. BRAXTON BRAGG, the Confederates attacked quickly on December 31, but after initial retreat, the Union army held for two bitterly cold days that exhausted both sides. On January 2, Union Maj. Gen. WILLIAM S. ROSECRANS advanced across Stones River, while his superior artillery parried the counterattack. News of Union reinforcements sent the Confederates retreating several miles south, but Rosencrans stayed, fortifying Murfreesboro. Neither depleted side fought again for almost six months.

Stonewall Brigade • a unit of the Confederate Army comprised mostly of men from Virginia's SHENANDOAH VALLEY and named for its commander, Gen. THOMAS "STONEWALL" JACKSON. Its soldiers fought with distinction at some of the most famous and bloodiest battles of the CIVIL WAR, including FIRST AND SECOND BULL RUN (1861–62), ANTIETAM (1862), CHANCELLORSVILLE (1863), and GETTYSBURG (1863).

stonk slang • *n.* Brit. a concentrated artillery bombardment. • *v.* bombard with concentrated artillery fire.

ORIGIN: 1940s: said to be formed from elements of the artillery term *Standard Regimental Concentration.*

stop • *n.* a short length of cord used to secure something; a stopper.

stopway • *n.* a defined rectangular area on the ground at the end of a runway in the direction of takeoff, designated and prepared by the competent authority as a suitable area in which an aircraft can be stopped in the case of an interrupted takeoff. A stopway must be capable of supporting aircraft of approximately 50,000 pounds (23,000 kg).

storage life • the length of time for which an item of supply, including explosives, given specific storage conditions, may be expected to remain serviceable and, if relevant, safe.

storm • *n.* **1** a heavy discharge of missiles or blows: *two men were taken by* ***a storm of*** *bullets.* **2** a direct assault by troops on a fortified place. • *v.* (of troops) suddenly attack and capture (a building or other place) by means of force: *commandos stormed a hijacked plane early today.*

PHRASES: **take something by storm** (of troops) capture a place by a sudden and violent attack.

stormbound • *adj.* prevented by storms from starting or continuing a journey.

storm jib • a small heavy jib for use in a high wind.

storm troops • **1** another term for SHOCK TROOPS. **2** (**Storm Troops**) the NAZI political militia.

DERIVATIVES: **storm trooper**

stormtroop tactics • infantry techniques used by the German Army during WORLD WAR I. The techniques, which were originally employed by Afrikaner soldiers during the

Boer War (1899–1902), involved small tactical units of no more than a dozen men, and the decentralization of command control as in guerrilla warfare.

stowage |ˈstōij| • *n.* space for stowing something in.

St. Petersburg Declaration • a treaty in 1868 that rejected the use of certain projectile weapons in war, on the principle that the only legitimate object of war is to weaken an enemy's military forces. It is often cited as the first formal humanitarian declaration dealing with arms.

strafe |strāf| • *v.* attack repeatedly with bombs or machine-gun fire from low-flying aircraft: *military aircraft strafed the village.* • *n.* an attack from low-flying aircraft.

ORIGIN: early 20th cent.: humorous adaptation of the German WORLD WAR I catchphrase *Gott strafe England* 'may God punish England.'

strafing • *n.* the delivery of automatic weapons fire by aircraft on ground targets.

straggler • *n.* **1** any personnel, vehicles, ships, or aircraft that, without apparent purpose or assigned mission, become separated from their unit, column, or formation. **2** a ship separated from its convoy by more than 5 nautical miles (through inability to keep up) and unable to rejoin before dark, or separated from its convoy by more than 10 nautical miles whether or not it can rejoin before dark.

strake |strāk| • *n.* **1** a continuous line of planking or plates from the stem to the stern of a ship or boat. **2** a protruding ridge fitted to an aircraft or other structure to improve aerodynamic stability.

strangle • a code meaning, "Switch off equipment indicated."

strategic • *adj.* **1** relating to the gaining of overall or long-term military advantage: *New Orleans was of strategic importance.* **2** (of human or material resources) essential in fighting a war: *the strategic forces on Russian territory.* **3** (of bombing or weapons) done or for use against industrial areas and communication centers of enemy territory as a long-term military objective: *strategic nuclear missiles.* Often contrasted with TACTICAL.

DERIVATIVES: **strategical** *adj.* **strategically** *adv.*

Strategic Air Command • (**SAC**) an offensive command of the U.S. Air Force created in March 1946 and located at Offutt AFB in Nebraska, intended to deter possible aggressors from attacking the United States. SAC had numerous bases around the world by the late 1950s, in order to have bases as close to potential enemies, as well as numerous bases across the United States, to keep its aircraft as widely dispersed as possible. In June 1992, SAC was replaced by the U.S. STRATEGIC COMMAND (STRATCOM).

strategic air warfare • air combat and supporting operations designed to effect, through the systematic application of force to a selected series of vital targets, the progressive destruction and disintegration of the enemy's war- making capacity to a point where the enemy no longer retains the ability or the will to wage war. Vital targets may include key manufacturing systems, sources of raw material, critical material, stockpiles, power systems, transportation systems, communication facilities, concentration of uncommitted elements of enemy armed forces, key agricultural areas, and other such target systems.

Strategic Arms Limitations Talks • (**SALT**) negotiations to address the nuclear weapons competition between the United States and USSR. U.S. President LYNDON B. JOHNSON first suggested the talks in 1967. SALT I, held from 1969–72, resulted in the SALT I Treaty, and SALT II, held from 1972–79, resulted in the unratified SALT II Treaty. The SALT process helped to restrain COLD WAR hostilities and the risk of nuclear war. It preceded the 1982 START procedures.

Strategic Arms Reduction Talks • (**START**) negotiations to reduce the United States' and the USSR's supplies of nuclear warheads. U.S. President RONALD REAGAN proposed the program in 1982 as a successor to the 1969–79 SALT process, but the Soviets suspended the talks from 1983–85 in protest to U.S. missile deployment in Europe. START procedures resulted in the START I Treaty, signed in 1991, and the START II Treaty, signed in 1993.

Strategic Army Forces • a component of the U.S. Army trained, equipped, and maintained for use on a national level and in accordance with current plans. This component is usually located in the continental United States.

strategic bomber • as long-range bomber aircraft used in strategic air operations.

Strategic Bombing Survey • a survey ordered by President FRANKLIN D. ROOSEVELT in 1944 that attempted to assess the components of Allied air strategy over Germany during the war that had led to its success and overall superiority, with a view to planning a strategy against Japan, and for overall future planning and development of the armed forces and national defense. The survey played a role in the decision to use the atomic bomb.

Strategic Command • see U.S. STRATEGIC COMMAND.

Strategic Defense Initiative • (**SDI**) a proposal by President RONALD REAGAN on March 23, 1983, to construct a strategic defense system against attack from intercontinental ballistic missiles (ICBMs), potentially from the Soviet Union. Popularly referred to as "Star Wars" after the science fiction film, the Strategic Defense Initiative was conceived as a way to intercept ICBMs from ground, air, and space using a combination of radar, optical, and infrared detection systems and laser beams. Congress initially approved the program in the 1980s, but political controversy, the fall of the Soviet Union, and problems regarding technological feasibility impeded its progress. The project was renamed the BALLISTIC MISSILE DEFENSE ORGANIZATION in 1993.

strategic hamlet program • a counterinsurgency program attempted in the VIETNAM WAR starting in 1961, before the involvement of U.S. troops, in which villagers were rounded up and placed in hamlets constructed by South Vietnamese soldiers. The idea was to isolate the NLF from villagers, its base of support. It was largely a failure in that it caused resentment among the displaced villagers and turned them against the government, convincing many to join the NLF.

strategic intelligence • intelligence required for the formulation of policy, strategy, and military plans and operations at the national or theater level.

strategic mining • the use of sea mines to deny the enemy the use of specific sea routes, sea areas, or port facilities over the long term.

strategic mission • a military mission directed against one or more enemy targets with the purpose of destroying the enemy's war-making capacity and his will to make war. A strategic mission is usually directed against the enemy's industry, stockpiles, communications systems, transportation systems, and similar targets and is designed to have a long-range, rather than immediate, effect.

strategic operations • military operations intended to have a long-range, rather than immediate, effect on the enemy.

strategic psychological activities • planned psychological activities in peace or war designed to gain the support and cooperation of friendly and neutral countries and to reduce the will and the capacity of hostile or potentially hostile countries to wage war.

strategic reconnaissance • reconnaissance conducted by various means to obtain information on the enemy, terrain, and weather for strategic planning purposes.

strategics • *n.* the art or science of strategy; generalship.

strategic transport aircraft • aircraft designed to transport cargo and personnel over long distances.

strategic vulnerability • the susceptibility of vital political, economic, geographic, sociological, scientific, or military elements of national power to degradation or destruction by an enemy.

strategic warning • warning received prior to the initiation of an enemy attack or other threatening action.

strategic warning lead time • the time between the receipt of strategic warning and the beginning of hostilities or other enemy action.

strategy |ˈstræt̬əjē| • *n.* (pl. **-ies**) **1** a plan of action or policy designed to achieve a major or overall aim: *time to develop a coherent evacuation strategy.* **2** the art of planning and directing overall military operations and movements in a war or battle. Often contrasted with TACTICS. **3** a plan for such military operations and movements: *nonprovocative defense strategies.* **4** the art and science of developing and using political, economic, psychological, and military forces as necessary during peace and war, to afford the maximum support to policies, in order to increase the probabilities and favorable consequences of victory and to lessen the chances of defeat.

Stratemeyer, George Edward |ˈstræt̬ə ˌmīyər| (1890–1969) • air force officer. Born in Ohio but raised in Indiana, Stratemeyer trained as a pilot in California as a member of the aviation section of the U.S. SIGNAL CORPS. Just before the outbreak of WORLD WAR II, he was head of the Training and Operations Section in the Office of the Chief of Air Corps. After the United States entered the war, he was named chief of the Air Staff at the Army Air Forces headquarters in Washington, D.C. He later headed AAF operations in the CHINA-BURMA-INDIA THEATER and advised Gen. JOSEPH STILWELL; in 1943 he took command of the Eastern Air Command, which directed joint U.S.-British air operations. In 1945 he became commanding general of the AAF in China and deputy commander of U.S. Forces China theater, with the rank of lieutenant general. After the war he headed the U.S. Air Defense Command and the TACTICAL AIR COMMAND; he later took over the Far East Air Forces (FEAF). During the KOREAN WAR, FEAF provided strong support to ground forces but was unable to incapacitate the Chinese logistical system. He sided with Gen. DOUGLAS MACARTHUR in his disagreement with President HARRY S. TRUMAN over war strategy, believing that it would be advantageous to carry the war to China, instead of restricting the fighting to Korea.

Stratofortress • (**B-52**) the final version of the B-52 group of strategic heavy bombers, an intercontinental strategic cruise missile carrier and bomber with a Mach 1 airspeed. It can fly up to 50,000 feet in altitude at subsonic speeds, saw combat in the VIETNAM WAR and, more recently, in the PERSIAN GULF WAR. It has also been used by NASA as a launch aircraft. First flown in 1955, it has offered unique bomb-carrying capacity in spite of its vulnerability in modern combat environments. Since the early 1990s, these aircraft have been adapted to carry conventional weapons to support U.S. ground and marine operations.

stratosphere |ˈstræt̬əˌsfir| • *n.* the layer of the atmosphere above the troposphere, in which the change of temperature with height is relatively small.

Stratotanker • (**KC-135**) a four-engine turbojet aerial tanker/transport aircraft capable of engaging in a variety of operations, it is used primarily to refuel bomber and fighter aircraft at high speeds at high altitudes, and is the backbone of the U.S. Air Force tanker fleet. Depending on how much fuel it carries, the Stratotanker can also transport up to 83,000 lbs. (37,350 kgs) of cargo or personnel.

stream takeoff • aircraft taking off in column formation.

stretch • *n.* the distance covered on one tack.

stretcher • *n.* a framework of two poles with a long piece of canvas slung between them, used for carrying sick, injured, or dead people.

strike |strīk| • *v.* (past and past part. **struck** |strək|) **1** hit forcibly and deliberately with one's hand or a weapon or other implement: *he raised his hand, as if to strike me.* **2** inflict (a blow): *he struck her two blows on the leg.* **3** carry out an aggressive or violent action, typically without warning: *it was eight months before the murderer struck again.* **4** (usually **be struck down**) kill or seriously incapacitate (someone): *he was struck down by a mystery virus.* **5** take down (a tent or the tents of an encampment). **6** lower or take down (a flag or sail), especially as a salute or to signify surrender: *the ship struck her German colors.* • *n.* an attack that is intended to inflict damage on, seize, or destroy an objective: *the threat of nuclear strikes.*

▸**strike back** retaliate.

strike cruiser • a warship intended to function offensively in combination with carrier strike forces or surface-action groups against surface, air, and submerged threats.

Strike Eagle • (**F-15E**) a two-seat strike aircraft developed from the F-15 fighter. It retained the air-to-air combat capability of the F-15, but has the equipment for all-weather attacks as well.

strike force • a force composed of appropriate units necessary to conduct strikes, or attack or assault operations.

strike package • the combat aircraft, aerial tankers, electronic warfare aircraft, and other supporting aircraft and equipment required to mount a given air attack.

stringer • *n.* a longitudinal structural piece in a framework, especially that of a ship or aircraft.

Stringham, Silas Horton (1797–1876) • Union naval officer. A New Yorker, Stringham went to sea at the age of twelve. In 1819, he was aboard the ship that carried the first former U.S. slaves to Liberia, on the African coast; he remained in Africa, capturing slave ships and pirateers. Stringham participated in the MEXICAN WAR (1846–48), delivering guns for the siege at VERACRUZ (1847). During the CIVIL WAR, in 1861, Stringham commanded the Atlantic Blockading Squadron, which was to close off Atlantic ports from Virginia to Florida. He successfully attacked Fort Clark and Fort Hatteras in North Carolina, the victory boosting Union morale.

strip • *v.* (**stripped, stripping**) **1** (**strip someone of**) deprive someone of (rank, power, or property): *the lieutenant was stripped of his rank.* **2** (of a bullet) be fired from a rifled gun without spin owing to a loss of surface.

stripe • *n.* a chevron sewn onto a uniform to denote military rank.

strip marker • in land-mine warfare, a marker (natural, artificial, or specially installed) located at the start and finish of a mine strip.

strip search • reconnaissance along a straight line between two given reference points.

stronghold • *n.* a place that has been fortified so as to protect it against attack.

strongpoint • *n.* a specially fortified defensive position.

structured message text • a message composed of paragraphs ordered in a specified sequence, each paragraph characterized by an identifier and containing information in free form. It is designed to facilitate manual handling and processing.

Stuart II tank • U.S. World War II-era M-3A1 light tank. The Stuart II weighed just over 14 tons and had a maximum speed of 36 MPH, a cruising range of 70 miles, and a crew of four. It was armed with a 37 mm main gun with a coaxial .30 caliber machine gun, a .30 caliber machine gun mounted in a ball mount on the bow, and a .30 caliber anti-aircraft machine gun mounted on the turret.

Stuart, J.E.B. (1833–64) • Confederate army officer, born James Ewell Brown Stuart in Virginia. Stuart gained battlefield experience soon after his graduation from the U.S. MILITARY ACADEMY and participated in the capture of JOHN BROWN after the latter's raid on the arsenal at HARPERS FERRY. At the outbreak of the CIVIL WAR, Stuart resigned his army commission and enlisted in the Confederate army, where he served under Gen. THOMAS "STONEWALL" JACKSON, with whom he formed a close friendship. Stuart led a much-noticed charge at the Union flank at the FIRST BATTLE OF BULL RUN (1861) and earned promotion to brigadier general. In 1862, he led a highly successful reconnaissance mission on the Virginia peninsula, during which his raids on Union troops established the Confederate army's dominance there. That July, he was promoted to major general and placed in charge of the Confederate cavalry. Stuart continued to distinguish himself, fighting at the SECOND BATTLE OF BULL RUN and at ANTIETAM (both 1862) and taking over the Second Corps in 1862 when Jackson was killed in battle. He was criticized for failing to support Gen. ROBERT E. LEE at GETTYSBURG (1863), a failure that may have affected the outcome of the battle. Stuart was killed in battle outside Richmond while attempting to block the advance of Gen. PHILIP H. SHERIDAN toward the Confederate capital.

Student Army Training Corps • an organization that briefly replaced the RESERVE OFFICERS' TRAINING CORPS in 1918, and created for the purpose of training enlisted men to carry out special assignments.

student deferment • a temporary exemption from compulsory military service based on attendance at a recognized college, university, or other institution of higher learning.

Students for a Democratic Society • (**SDS**) a left-leaning organization of U.S. university students that formed in 1960. It was active in the Civil Rights movement but is best remembered for its resistance to the VIETNAM WAR.

Stuka |ˈstoōkə; ˈSHtoō-| • *n.* a type of German military aircraft (the Junkers Ju 87) designed for dive-bombing, used in WORLD WAR II. ORIGIN: contraction of German *Sturzkampfflugzeug* 'dive-bomber.'

stun grenade • a grenade that stuns people with its sound and flash, without causing serious injury.

Sturgis, Samuel Davis |ˈstərjis| (1822–89) • Union army officer. Born in Pennsylvania, Sturgis fought in the MEXICAN WAR (1846–48) and rose in the pre-CIVIL WAR U.S. cavalry to the rank of captain; he helped settle disputes between the government and the Cherokee in the Southwest. After distinguishing himself in battle in the early years of the Civil War, Sturgis was promoted to brigadier general and given command of the District of Kansas. He led a division at the first BATTLE OF BULL RUN (1861) and led a charge across the Burnside Bridge at ANTIETAM (1862). After the war, he was promoted to full colonel and commanded the Sixth U.S. Cavalry and then the Seventh, which he headed when his subordinate, Gen. GEORGE ARMSTRONG CUSTER, and his troops were annihilated in 1876 at LITTLE BIGHORN.

Sturmabteilung • (**SA**) a NAZI paramilitary organization created by ADOLF HITLER and destroyed in June 1934 to end the embarrassing conduct and political intrigues of its leaders. Also known as the "Brownshirts," the SA was largely manned by thugs and was used by Hitler and the Nazi Party to control the streets during the struggle for power in Weimar Germany.
ORIGIN: from German, 'Storm Detachment.'

Sturmbannführer • a rank in the WORLD WAR II-era German SS and Waffen-SS comparable to the rank of Major in the German Army.

Stuyvesant, Peter |ˈstīvəsənt| (1610?–72) • colonial founder. Stuyvesant was born in the Netherlands and worked for the Dutch West India Company as director general in Curaçao. He led Dutch troops in attacks on Spanish possessions in the Caribbean and lost his right leg in an attack on the Spanish fort on St. Martin. He returned to the Netherlands to recuperate and then was sent back to the New World, where he added the governorship of New Netherland to his responsibilities. He arrived there in 1647. Stuyvesant provided strong, if authoritarian, leadership for the poorly managed colony, defeated Swedish colonists who attempted to take over Dutch territory in the Delaware region, and negotiated a satisfactory border agreement with New England to the north. He also struggled to maintain peaceful relations with area Indian tribes, although he did not always succeed. In August 1664 he was forced to surrender the poorly defended colony to an English fleet.

Styx SS-N-2 missile • a Soviet radar-guided, surface-to-surface missile that was developed in the 1950s. It was used in 1967 against Israel by Egypt, in 1971 by India against Pakistan, and by Iran during its 1980–88 war with Iraq. Its design has been widely copied and it is more or less equivalent to the Chinese HY-1 SILKWORM.

sub informal • *n.* a submarine.

subaltern |səbˈôltərn| • *n.* an officer in the British army below the rank of captain, especially a second lieutenant.

subgravity • a condition in which the resultant ambient acceleration is between 0 and 1 G.

Subic Bay • site of a U.S. naval base 1901–92. Located 35 miles (55 kilometers) northwest of Manila Bay, near Olongapo, the Subic Bay Naval Station was the largest naval installation in the Philippines. This region of the South China Sea was of strategic importance for both WORLD WAR II and the VIETNAM WAR. The Japanese captured Subic Bay in 1942, but the Allies regained it in 1944. The Subic Bay Naval Station served a supply base during the Vietnam War.

subkiloton weapon • a nuclear weapon producing a yield below one kiloton. See also MEGATON WEAPON.

sublieutenant • *n.* an officer in the British Royal Navy ranking above midshipman and below lieutenant.

Sub-Lt. • *abbr.* Sublieutenant.

submachine gun • a hand-held, lightweight machine gun.

submarine • *n.* (**SS** or **SSN**) a warship with a streamlined hull designed to operate completely submerged in the sea for long periods, equipped with an internal store of air and a periscope and typically armed with torpedoes and/or missiles. It carries out missions of locating and destroying both surface and submerged ships, although it can perform other naval missions should the need arise. See also FLEET BALLISTIC MISSILE SUBMARINE.

submarine havens • specified sea areas for submarine noncombat operations including: **a** submarine sanctuaries announced by the area, fleet, or equivalent commander. **b** areas reserved for submarine operations and training in noncombat zones. **c** Moving areas, established by "Submarine Notices," surrounding submarines in transit, extending 50 nautical miles ahead, 100 nautical miles behind, and 15 nautical miles on each side of the estimated position of the submarine along the stated track.

submarine locator acoustic beacon • an electronic device, used by submarines in distress, for emitting a repetitive sonic pulse underwater.

submarine rocket • (**SUBROC**) a submarine-launched, surface-to-surface rocket with nuclear depth charge or homing torpedo payload that is primarily an antisubmarine weapon.

submarine sanctuaries • restricted areas that are established for the conduct of noncombat submarine or antisubmarine exercises. They may be either stationary or moving and are normally designated only in rear areas.

submarine striking forces • submarines having guided or ballistic missile launching and/or guidance capabilities, formed to launch offensive nuclear strikes.

submersible |səbˈmərsəbəl| • *adj.* designed to be completely submerged and/or to operate while submerged. • *n.* a small boat or other craft of this kind, especially one designed for research and exploration.

submunition |ˌsəbmyo͞oˈnisHən| • *n.* a small weapon or device that is part of a larger warhead and separates from it prior to impact.

subnational • *adj.* at a level below the national level; regional or local.

subordinate command • a command consisting of the commander and all those individuals, units, detachments, organizations, or installations that have been placed under the command by the authority establishing the subordinate command.

SUBROC • *abbr.* submarine rocket.

subsidiary landing • in an amphibious operation, a landing usually made outside the designated landing area, the purpose of which is to support the main landing.

subsonic • *adj.* of or pertaining to speeds less than the speed of sound.

substitution • *n.* the action of replacing someone or something with another person or thing: *a tactical substitution.*

DERIVATIVES: **substitutional** *adj.* **substitutionary** *adj.*

subversion • *n.* action designed to undermine the military, economic, psychological, or political strength or morale of a regime.

subversive activity • the lending of aid, comfort, and moral support to individuals, groups, or organizations that advocate the overthrow of incumbent governments by force and violence. All willful acts that are intended to be detrimental to the best interests of the government and that do not fall into the categories of treason, sedition, sabotage, or espionage are placed in the category of subversive activity.

subversive political action • a planned series of activities designed to accomplish political objectives by influencing, dominating, or displacing individuals or groups who are so placed as to affect the decisions and actions of another government.

Sugar Acts • two acts passed by the British Parliament to impose a tax on the American colonists. The Molasses Act of 1733 placed a duty on foreign molasses imported into any British colony and was an attempt to secure a British monopoly on the American molasses market. To end the foreign molasses smuggling trade which began after the first act, the Sugar Act of 1764 lowered the duties on foreign molasses, raised the duties on foreign refined sugar, and increased the export bounty on British refined sugar imported into the American colonies. They were protested by American colonists.

suicide ditch • slang (World War I) the front-line trench.

suit • *n.* a complete set of sails required for a ship or for a set of spars.

Sullivan, John (1741–95) • REVOLUTIONARY WAR army officer and state governor, born in Maine. Sullivan set up a law practice in New Hampshire and became attracted to the patriot cause through his objections to the INTOLERABLE ACTS. He attended the First Continental Congress and led an abortive and much-criticized charge at BUNKER HILL (1775). In 1776 he led a failed invasion of Canada and contributed to Gen. GEORGE WASHINGTON's defeat in the Battle of New York. Sullivan led units at TRENTON (1776) and at PRINCETON (1777) but performed poorly at BRANDYWINE (1777), all the while complaining that he was being passed over for promotion; Washington's support kept him from losing his command. He wintered at VALLEY FORGE and continued to perform erratically. He participated in a devastating attack on the Iroquois in upstate New York in 1779. Sullivan resigned his commission late in that year. His reputation was further damaged when he accepted payments from the French ostensibly to help him pay the costs of serving again in the Continental Congress (1780–81). He was elected governor of New Hampshire in 1786, 1787, and 1789, and strongly supported the adoption of the U.S. Constitution in 1788.

summary justice • a trial or other judicial action accomplished swiftly and without observance of certain formalities of legal procedure, with the connotation of arbitrary and unfair judgment.

Summerall, Charles Pelot (1867–1955) • ARMY CHIEF OF STAFF and educator. A Florida native, Summerall distinguished himself in the SPANISH-AMERICAN WAR (1898), the PHILIPPINE WAR, and the BOXER REBELLION. In WORLD WAR I he was an artillery expert and won promotion to brigadier general in 1917; his innovations in communications and his rapid deployment of supporting fire were instrumental in the Allied victory at CANTIGNY. His use of overwhelming artillery power in the MEUSE-ARGONNE OFFENSIVE of 1918 destroyed several German battalions before they could counterattack and brought him much praise, as well as numerous decorations, including the DISTINGUISHED SERVICE CROSS. His last years in the army were spent as Army Chief of Staff (1927–31); during this time he decried what he saw as preferential treatment accorded the ARMY AIR CORPS.

summit • *n.* the highest altitude above mean sea level that a projectile reaches in its flight from the gun to the target; the algebraic sum of the maximum ordinate and the altitude of the gun.

Sumner class • a destroyer class developed from the FLETCHER class to meet the need for antiaircraft defense. They had the same power plants, but had twin rudders and were slightly longer and wider in the beam. They are sometimes called "short-hulls" because the GEARING class that followed differed only in a 14-foot extension inserted in the middle of the hull. Of the seventy built, only five were lost in battle during WORLD WAR II, four in the Pacific theater and one on D-DAY.

Sumner, Edwin Vose (1797–1863) • Union army officer. Sumner, from Massachusetts, was one of the first three brigadier generals to be commissioned by President ABRAHAM LINCOLN and soon given command of a division of the ARMY OF THE POTOMAC in 1861. He fought in Virginia under Gen. GEORGE B. MCCLELLAN, and his actions at FAIR OAKS (1862) earned him a brevet to major general. He led his division disastrously at ANTIETAM (1862) and at FREDERICKSBURG (1863).

Peeved at having been passed over for promotion, he resigned his position with the Army of the Potomac in 1863. He died while waiting to assume his next command.

Sumner, Jethro (1733–85) • REVOLUTIONARY WAR army officer. A Virginian, Sumner served in the FRENCH AND INDIAN WAR (1754–63), after which he became a landowner in North Carolina. He was elected to the Third Provincial Congress in 1775 and, after the start of the Revolutionary War, appointed colonel of the Third Continental Regiment. He participated in the battles of GERMANTOWN and BRANDYWINE (both 1777), and wintered at VALLEY FORGE. In 1779, a brigadier general, Sumner led his troops in the Battle of Stono Creek; with the surrender of Charleston, he undertook to recruit troops to defend the rest of the state. He provided outstanding leadership in 1779 at the battle of EUTAW SPRINGS. Sumner remained commander of the Continental's defense of North Carolina throughout the rest of the war.

Sumter, Thomas (1734–1832) • REVOLUTIONARY WAR army officer, U.S. Representative and U.S. senator. A Virginian, Sumter fought the Cherokee early in his career; he later became a planter and merchant in South Carolina. He also participated in colonial politics and served in a colonial Ranger unit that, when the Revolution broke out, fought against the British and became part of the Continental army. Sumter resigned his commission because of illness but returned to active duty in 1780 when his estate was plundered by the British. From then on, using volunteer troops, he fought with a vengeance against British efforts to take South Carolina, winning promotion to brigadier general and command of the South Carolina militia. To spur enlistment, he promised each volunteer a slave, a horse, and the right to keep looted items; this policy was vacated by the state governor. In 1782 Sumter again retired from the army. After the war he served in the state Senate (1781–82) and the state House of Representatives (1784–86, 1788); he voted against the ratification of the U.S. Constitution. As a member of the U.S. House of Representatives (1789–93, 1797–1801), he advocated a limited federal government. In 1801 he was appointed to the Senate to fill an unexpired term, and he won election in his own right in 1805.

Sung, Kim Il- (1912–1994) • born Kim Song Ju to parents who fled to Manchuria in 1925 to escape the Japanese occupation of Korea, when he joined the Korean resistance he adopted the name of a legendary Korean guerilla fighter who had also fought against the Japanese. Trained in the Soviet Union, Kim led a unit of North Koreans as a major in the Soviet Red Army during WORLD WAR II and, when the war ended, returned to Korea and established a provisional communist government with other Soviet-trained Koreans. In 1948, he became the first premier of the Democratic People's Republic of Korea, and tried to unify Korea under his rule by invading South Korea in 1950. He held the position of premier from 1948 to 1972, when he became president of North Korea and head of state.

Sun Tzu (c.500 B.C.) • Chinese military strategist and reputed author of *The Art of War* (*Ping-fa*). Sun Tzu was a general who served the state of Wu during the 5th century B.C. The book is a guide for military strategists; it emphasizes the importance of accurate intelligence about the enemy, the importance of flexibility, and an understanding of the relationship between political goals and military operations.

supercarrier • *n.* an aircraft carrier designed to operate very large nuclear-armed strike aircraft.

The first proposed supercarrier, the USS UNITED STATES, was taken out of development after the REVOLT OF THE ADMIRALS in 1949. It wasn't until 1955 that a supercarrier was finally commissioned (the USS *Forrestal*).

Superfortress • (**B-29**) a large four-engine bomber built to replace the B-17 FORTRESS. After the United States entered WORLD WAR II, a huge B-29 production program was begun involving five principal plants, including Seattle and Wichita. The first report of the B-29 in action came on June 5, 1944 in an attack on railway yards at Bangkok, and its first raid on Japan occurred on June 15.

superpower • *n.* a very powerful and influential nation (used especially with reference to the U.S. and the former USSR when these were perceived as the two most powerful nations in the world).

Super Sabre • (**F-100**) a single-seat low-wing jet fighter aircraft with a maximum speed of 822 mph (1,323 km/h), and the first developed for the U.S. Air Force capable of exceeding the speed of sound in level flight. Operational from 1953 to 1973, it was the principal tactical fighter of the U.S. TACTICAL AIR COMMAND, and was used extensively in the VIETNAM WAR.

supersonic • *adj.* of or pertaining to speed in excess of the speed of sound.

Super Stallion • (**CH-53E**) see SEA STALLION.

superstructure • *n.* the parts of a ship, other than masts and rigging, built above its hull and main deck.

supertanker • *n.* a very large oil tanker, specifically one whose dead-weight capacity exceeds 75,000 tons.

supply • *n.* the procurement, distribution, maintenance (while in storage), and salvage of supplies, including the determination of kind and quantity of supplies.

There are two phases of supply: the **producer phase of supply** extends from the determination of procurement schedules to the acceptance of finished supplies by the military services. The **consumer phase of supply** extends from the receipt of finished supplies by the military services through the issue for use or consumption.

---

supplying ship • a ship that provides personnel and/or supplies to be transferred by a replenishment or maintenance operation.

supply point • any point where supplies are issued in detail.

support • *n.* **1** the action of a force that aids, protects, complements, or sustains another force in accordance with a directive requiring such action. **2** a unit that helps another unit in battle. Aviation, artillery, or naval gunfire may be used as a support for infantry. **3** a part of any unit held back at the beginning of an attack as a reserve. **4** an element of a command that assists, protects, or supplies other forces in combat.

support helicopter • see ASSAULT AIRCRAFT; UTILITY HELICOPTER.

supporting aircraft • all active aircraft, excluding unit aircraft.

supporting attack • an offensive operation carried out in conjunction with a main attack and designed to achieve one or more of the following: **a** deceive the enemy, **b** destroy or pin down enemy forces that could interfere with the main attack, **c** control ground whose occupation by the enemy will hinder the main attack, or **d** force the enemy to commit reserves prematurely or in an indecisive area.

supporting fire • fire delivered by supporting units to assist or protect a unit in combat.

supporting forces • forces stationed in, or to be deployed to, an area of operations to provide support for the execution of an operation order. Combatant command (command authority) of supporting forces is not passed to the supported commander.

supporting operations • in amphibious operations, those operations conducted by forces other than those assigned to the amphibious task force. They are ordered by higher authority at the request of the amphibious task force commander and normally are conducted outside the area for which the amphibious task force commander is responsible at the time of their execution.

support ship • a fast combat support ship designed to replenish U.S. Navy task forces, reducing the vulnerability of serviced ships by shortening alongside time.

support site • in the air force, a facility operated by an active, reserve, or guard unit that provides general support to the air force mission and does not satisfy the criteria for a major or minor installation. Examples of support sites are missile tracking sites, radar bomb scoring sites, contractor-operated plants (owned by the air force), and radio relay sites.

supremacy |sə'preməsē; sōō-| • *n.* the state or condition of being superior to all others in authority, power, or status.

Supreme Allied Commander in Europe • see SACEUR.

surface combatant • any ship designed and armed to perform during combat conditions, and able to operate in many marine roles against air, surface, and submerged threats as well as land targets.

surface striking forces • naval forces that are organized primarily to do battle with enemy forces or to conduct shore bombardment. Units comprising such a force are generally incorporated in and operate as part of another force, but with provisions for their formation into a surface striking force, should such action appear likely and/or desirable.

surface-to-air • *adj.* (of a missile) designed to be fired from the ground or a vessel at an aircraft.

surface-to-air guided missile • a surface-launched guided missile for use against air targets.

surface-to-air missile • (**SAM**) a missile fired from the ground or from ships and directed at aircraft or other missiles.

surface-to-air missile envelope • the air space within the kill capabilities of a specific surface-to-air missile system.

surface-to-surface • *adj.* (of a missile) designed to be fired from one point on the ground or a vessel at another such point or vessel.

Surface Warfare Officer School • a post-graduate naval service school at Newport, Rhode Island. It was established in 1975 in response to the 1970s revival of surface warfare as an effective combat branch, and its subsequent need for reorganization and officer training.

surface warship • see SURFACE COMBATANT.

surge • *v.* (of a rope, chain, or windlass) slip back with a jerk.

surgeon • *n.* a medical practitioner qualified to practice surgery.

surgical • *adj.* **1** of, relating to, or used in surgery: *a surgical dressing* | *a surgical ward.* **2** denoting something done with great precision, especially a swift and highly accurate military attack from the air: *surgical bombing.*
DERIVATIVES: **surgically** *adv.*

surprise • *n.* denoting something made, done, or happening unexpectedly: *a surprise attack.* • *v.* capture, attack, or discover suddenly and unexpectedly; catch unawares: *he surprised a gang stealing scrap metal.*
PHRASES: **take someone/something by surprise** attack or capture someone or something unexpectedly.

surprise dosage attack • a chemical operation that establishes on target a dosage sufficient to produce the desired casualties before the targeted troops can mask or otherwise protect themselves.

surrender • *v.* **1** cease resistance to an enemy or opponent and submit to their authority: *over 140 rebels surrendered to the authorities.* **2** give up or hand over (a person, right, or possession), typically on compulsion or demand: *in 1815 Denmark* ***surrendered*** *Norway* ***to*** *Sweden* | *they refused to surrender their weapons.* • *n.* the action of surrendering: *the final surrender of Germany on May 8, 1945* | *the colonel was anxious to negotiate a surrender.*

surround • *v.* (of troops, police, etc.) encircle (someone or something) so as to cut off communication or escape: *troops surrounded the parliament building.*

surveillance • *n.* the systematic observation of aerospace, surface or subsurface areas, places, persons, or things, by visual, aural, electronic, photographic, or other means.

surveillance-reconnaissance intelligence groups • (**SRIGS**) U.S. Marine Corps special operations units developed after 1985 to conduct, control, and coordinate special operations by Marine Corps forces.

survival kit • a pack of emergency equipment, including food, medical supplies, and tools, especially as carried by members of the armed forces.

susceptibility • *n.* the vulnerability of a target audience to particular forms of psychological operations.

suspension strop • a length of webbing or wire rope between the helicopter and the cargo sling.

Susquehannock |ˌsəskwəˈhænək| • an Algonquian-speaking Indian tribe located generally along the Susquehanna River in what is now the state of Pennsylvania, the Susquehannock were conquered by the Iroquois in 1680 and were subsequently wiped out by European diseases and attacks by white settlers.

sustainability • *n.* see MILITARY CAPABILITY.

sustained rate of fire • the actual rate of fire that a weapon can continue to deliver for an indefinite length of time without seriously overheating.

sutler |ˈsətlər| • *n.* a person who followed an army and sold provisions to the soldiers.

S.VII • see SPAD.

swab • *n.* **1** a piece of absorbent material used for cleaning the bore of a firearm. **2** a mop or other absorbent device for cleaning or mopping up a floor or other surface. **3** another term for SWABBIE. • *v.* (**swabbed, swabbing**) clean (a surface) with a swab: ***swabbing down** the decks.*

swabbie (also **swabby**) • *n.* (pl. **-ies**) slang a member of the navy, typically one who is of low rank.

swagger stick • a short cane carried by a military officer.

swamp • *v.* **1** overwhelm or flood with water: *a huge wave swamped the canoes.* **2** (of a boat) become overwhelmed with water and sink.

Swatter • see AT-2.

sway • *n.* rule; control: *the part of the continent **under** Russia's **sway**.*

sweep • *v.* (past and past part. **swept**) **1** examine (a place or thing) for electronic listening devices: *the line is swept every fifteen minutes.* **2** cover (an entire area) with a gun: *they were trying to get the Lewis gun up behind some trees from where they would sweep the trench.* • *n.* a comprehensive search or survey of a place or area: *they finished their sweep through the woods.*

sweep • *v.* **1** examine (a place or thing) for electronic listening devices: *the line is swept every fifteen minutes.* **2** cover (an entire area) with a gun: *they were trying to get the Lewis gun up behind some trees from where they would sweep the trench.* • *n.* a comprehensive search or survey of a place or area: *the patrol finished their sweep through the woods.*

sweep jamming • a narrow band of jamming that is swept back and forth over a relatively wide operating band of frequencies.

swell • *v.* (past part. **swollen** or **swelled**) • *n.* a slow, regular movement of the sea in rolling waves that do not break: *there was a heavy swell.*

swept path • in naval mine warfare, the width of the lane swept by the mechanical sweep at all depths less than the sweep depth.

swift boat • a PATROL CRAFT.

Swift, Joseph Gardner (1783–1865) • military engineer and army officer, born in Massachusetts. Swift was a member of the first class of cadets at the U.S. MILITARY ACADEMY, which he entered in October 1801 and where he trained as an engineer. After graduation, he taught at the Academy and founded the Military Philosophical Society. He worked on coastal fortifications off North Carolina and won rapid promotion, becoming colonel and chief of engineers by 1812. In 1807 he served as WEST POINT's second superintendent; after that he returned to working on coast surveys and fortifications along the eastern seaboard. Swift served in the WAR OF 1812, serving as chief of engineers for the army and being brevetted brigadier general. He left the army in 1818 in a dispute over the proposed appointment of a French engineer to a position equal in rank to his own but retained ties to West Point. Swift later served as surveyor for the City of New York, as an engineer for several railroad companies, and as engineer on several harbor projects.

Because of his membership in the first class at West Point, Swift is considered the first U.S.-trained engineer in the nation.

Swift, William Henry (1800–79) • military engineer, army officer, born in Massachusetts, William Henry Swift attended the U.S. MILITARY ACADEMY, of which his brother, Gen. JOSEPH GARDNER SWIFT, was superintendent. Swift, like his brother, was a trained engineer; he performed surveys for the Chesapeake and Ohio canal and for a canal across Florida and worked on plans for coastal defenses. In 1833 he was assigned to the Coast and Geodetic Survey, where he worked on harbor and river improvements. He was also an engineer for the Massachusetts Western Railway. In 1838 he was assigned to work with the army's topographical engineers, which he did for five years. He became president of the board of trustees of the Illinois and Michigan Canal in 1845, a position he held for 26 years. After resigning from the army in 1849 to pursue private business interests, becoming in succession president of several railroad lines.

swivel turret • a gun turret capable of moving from side to side.

sword • *n.* a weapon with a long metal blade and a hilt with a handguard, used for thrusting or striking and now typically worn as part of ceremonial dress.

PHRASES: **put to the sword** kill, especially in war.

DERIVATIVES: **swordlike** *adj.*

Sword Beach • the easternmost of the five beaches targeted for the D-DAY landing at NORMANDY, and one of the two under British control. The troops landing there failed to take nearby Caen as soon as expected but succeeded in landing 29,000 men. See also GOLD BEACH.

SWPA • *abbr.* Southwest Pacific Area.

Sykes, George (1822–80) • Union army officer. From Maryland, Sykes fought in the MEXICAN WAR (1846–48); he won commendations for courage but was not promoted to captain until 1855. He spent the years between the Mexican War and the CIVIL WAR in the Southwest with the 3rd Infantry. Promoted to major, he fought in the FIRST BATTLE OF BULL RUN (1861); his performance there earned him a promotion to brigadier general of volunteers and a command of a brigade of army regulars. He continued to lead ably at many major Civil War battles, including GAINES' MILL (1862), MALVERN HILL (1862), and at FREDERICKSBURG (1863), ANTIETAM (1862), and CHANCELLORSVILLE (1863), where his troops were involved only peripherally. He led the Fifth Army Corps at GETTYSBURG (1863), at LITTLE ROUND TOP. After Gettysburg, his health declined, and he was relieved of his command in 1864 and given command of the District of South Kansas. After the war he was brevetted to brigadier and major general.

sympathetic detonation • the detonation of a charge by exploding another charge adjacent to it.

synthesis • *n.* in intelligence usage, the examining and combining of processed information with other information and intelligence for final interpretation.

synthetic rubber • rubber manufactured from petroleum and other chemicals rather than the product of raw rubber extracted from a rubber tree.

systems analysis • the analysis of problems and processes in a logical manner, particularly through the use of mathematical models and formulas and with the aid of computers and other data processing equipment.

systems engineering • the process of applying science and technology to the study and solution of a military problem in its entirety.

Szilard, Leo (1898–1964) • biologist and physicist. The Hungarian-born Szilard initially trained as an engineer but switched to chemistry and physics; from 1921 to 1922 he studied at the University of Berlin with ALBERT EINSTEIN and did research in thermodynamics and in X-ray crystallography. He continued to work with Einstein and others in theoretical physics. In 1933 he moved to Britain to escape the Nazis and began the study of nuclear physics; he came to the United States in 1938 and worked with ENRICO FERMI at Columbia University. In 1942 he became chief physicist at the Metallurgical Laboratory at the University of Chicago; in 1946 he became a half-time professor of biophysics at the Institute of Radiobiology and Biophysics and in 1956 a professor of biophysics at the Fermi Institute for Nuclear Studies at the same university. In the 1960s he worked with Jonas Salk at the Salk Institute for Biological Studies in California. In the three areas in which he worked—theoretical physics, nuclear physics, and theoretical biology—his work was seminal and led to breakthroughs such as the electron microscope. He also understood early the implications of nuclear power for military strategy, and its dangers, and he was an early advocate of arms control.

Tt

T-34 • **1** a standard trainer aircraft for the U.S. Navy since its introduction in 1973. **2** a Russian tank produced in 1941 and used throughout WORLD WAR II. The early version had a 76.2 mm gun, but by 1943 the T-34/85 model carried an 85 mm gun and 90 mm of armor.

T-55 • a Soviet main battle tank produced in the 1950s. It was armed with a 100 mm gun and had a top speed of 30 mph.

T-62 • a Soviet main battle tank armed with a 115 mm smooth-bore gun, a 7.61 mm coaxial machine gun, and a 12.7 mm antiaircraft machine gun. It was the first main battle tank to carry a smooth-bore gun, and had a top speed of 32 mph.

T-72 • a Soviet main battle tank armed with a 125 mm main gun and two machine guns. Produced since 1972, it has a top speed of 40 mph.

tab • *n.* **1** a part of a control surface, typically hinged, that modifies the action or response of the surface. **2** a small flap or strip of material attached to or projecting from something, used to hold or manipulate it, or for identification and information.

PHRASES: **keep tabs** (or **a tab**) **on** informal monitor the activities or development of; keep under observation.

DERIVATIVES: **tabbed** *adj.*

Tabasco • a state in southeastern Mexico that was the target of an expedition by the American Gulf Squadron, commanded by Commodore MATTHEW C. PERRY, in October, 1846. He took the capital Villahermosa without difficulty but further up the Tabasco River his mission had to be abandoned because of guerrilla attacks and outbreaks of yellow fever among his men.

TAC • *abbr.* Tactical Air Command.

tacan • an ultra-high-frequency electronic air navigation system, able to provide continuous bearing and slant range to a selected station.
ORIGIN: an acronym derived from *tac*tical *a*ir *n*avigation.

TACC • *abbr.* tactical air command center.

tack • *n.* **1** an act of changing course by turning a vessel's head into and through the wind, so as to bring the wind on the opposite side. **2** a boat's course relative to the direction of the wind: *the brig bowled past* ***on the opposite tack.*** **3** a distance sailed between such changes of course. **4** a rope for securing the weather clew of a course. **5** the weather clew of a course, or the lower forward corner of a fore-and-aft sail. • *v.* **1** change course by turning a boat's head into and through the wind. Compare with WEAR[2]. [ORIGIN: from the practice of shifting ropes to change direction.] **2** alter the course of (a boat) in such a way. **3** make a series of such changes of course while sailing: *she spent the entire night tacking back and forth.*
PHRASES: **on the port** (or **starboard**) **tack** with the wind coming from the port (or starboard) side of the boat.

tackle • *n.* **1** a mechanism consisting of ropes, pulley blocks, hooks, or other things for lifting heavy objects. **2** the running rigging and gear used to work a boat's sails.

tac-log group |tæk läg grōōp| • representatives designated by troop commanders to assist Navy control officers aboard control ships in the ship-to-shore movement of troops, equipment, and supplies.

TACON • *abbr.* tactical control.

tactic • *n.* **1** an action or strategy carefully planned to achieve a specific end. **2** (**tactics**) the art of disposing armed forces in order of battle and of organizing operations, especially during contact with an enemy. Often contrasted with STRATEGY.
DERIVATIVES: **tactician** *n.*

tactical • *adj.* **1** of, relating to, or constituting actions carefully planned to gain a specific military end: *as a tactical officer in the field he had no equal.* **2** (of bombing or weapons) done or for use in immediate support of military or naval operations. Often contrasted with STRATEGIC.
DERIVATIVES: **tactically** *adv.*

Tactical Air Command • (**TAC**) established in 1946 (like the STRATEGIC AIR COMMAND), it developed a mobile strike capability in 1955. Called the COMPOSITE AIR STRIKE FORCE (CASF), it included fighters, transports, tankers (for mid-air refueling), and reconnaissance planes, and was designed to augment other combat-ready U.S. Air Force units all over the world. By the late 1950s, TAC had three hundred sites in twenty different countries.

tactical air command center • (**TACC**) the principal U.S. Marine Corps air command and control agency from which air operations and air defense warning functions are directed. It is the senior agency of the U.S. Marine air command and control system and serves as the operational command post of the aviation combat element commander. It provides the facility from which the commander and battle staff of the aviation combat element plan, supervise, coordinate, and execute all current and future air operations in support of the marine air-ground task force. The tactical air command center can provide integration, coordination, and direction of joint and combined air operations. Also called MARINE TACC.

tactical air control group • **1** (on land) a flexible administrative and tactical component of a tactical air organization. It provides aircraft control and warning functions ashore for offensive and defensive missions within the tactical air zone of responsibility. **2** (on ship) an administrative and tactical component of an amphibious force. It provides aircraft control and warning facilities afloat for offensive and defensive missions within the tactical air command area of responsibility.

tactical air control system • the organization and equipment necessary to plan, direct, and control tactical air operations and to coordinate air operations with other services. It is composed of control agencies and communications-electronics facilities that provide the means for centralized control and decentralized execution of missions.

tactical air force • an air force charged with carrying out tactical air operations in coordination with ground or naval forces.

tactical air operation • an air operation involving the employment of air power in coordination with ground or naval forces, the principal functions of which are the following: **a** to gain and maintain air superiority. **b** to prevent movement of enemy forces into and within the objective area and to seek out and destroy these forces and their supporting installations. **c** to join with ground or naval forces in operations within the objective area, in order to assist directly in attainment of their immediate objective.

tactical air reconnaissance • the use of air vehicles to obtain information concerning terrain, weather, and the disposition, composition, movement, installations, lines of communications, and electronic and communication emissions of enemy forces. Also included are artillery and naval gunfire adjustment, and systematic and random observation of ground battle areas, targets, and/or sectors of airspace.

tactical air support • air operations that are carried out in coordination with surface forces and that directly assist land or maritime operations.

tactical assault • an attack at the tactical level.

tactical command • the authority delegated to a commander to assign tasks to forces under his or her command for the accomplishment of the mission assigned by higher authority.

tactical command, control, communications, and computer system(s) • the facilities, equipment, communications, procedures, and personnel that are essential to theater-level and below-theater-level commanders for planning, directing, and controlling operations of assigned and attached forces pursuant to the mission assigned, and that provide for the conveyance and/or exchange of data and information from one person or force to another.

tactical control • (**TACON**) command authority over assigned or attached forces or commands, or military capability or forces made available for tasking. Tactical control is limited to the detailed and, usually, local direction and control of movements or maneuvers necessary to accomplish missions or tasks assigned. Tactical control is inherent in operational control. Tactical control may be delegated to, and exercised at any level at or below the level of combatant command.

tactical intelligence • intelligence that is required for planning and conducting tactical operations.

tactical operations • military operations conducted on the battlefield, generally in direct contact with the enemy.

tactical operations area • the area between the fire support coordination line and the rear operations area where maximum flexibility in the use of airspace is needed to assure mission accomplishment. The rear boundary of the tactical operations area should normally be at or near the rear boundary of the front-line divisions.

tactical range • a range in which realistic targets are in use and a certain freedom of maneuver is allowed.

tactical reconnaissance • reconnaissance undertaken to secure information about the enemy, terrain, and weather for immediate use on the battlefield.

tactical reserve • a part of a force, held under the control of the commander as a maneuvering force to influence future action.

tactical transport aircraft • aircraft used primarily to transport cargo and/or passengers over short or medium distances.

tactical troops • combat troops, together with any service troops required for their direct support, who are organized under one commander to operate as a unit and engage the enemy in combat.

tactical unit • an organization of troops, aircraft, or ships that is intended to serve as a single unit in combat. It may include service units required for its direct support.

tactical warning • **1** a warning after initiation of a threatening or hostile act, based on an evaluation of information from all available sources. **2** in satellite and missile surveillance, a notification to operational command centers that a specific threat event is occurring. The component elements that describe threat events are as follows: **a** country of origin (the country or countries that are initiating hostilities). **b** event type and size (the identification of the type of event, and the determination of the size or number of weapons). **c** country under attack (this is determined by observing trajectory of an object and predicting its impact point). **d** event time (the time that the hostile event occurred).

tactics • *pl. n.* **1** the employment of units in combat. **2** the ordered arrangement and maneuver of units in relation to each other and/or to the enemy in order to use their full potentialities.

Taft, William Howard (1857–1930) • 27th president of the United States, born in Cincinnati, Ohio. Taft came from a politically active family; his father was secretary of war under President ULYSSES S. GRANT. Taft studied law and also entered Republican party politics while still young; he was named a judge on the superior court of Ohio in 1887 and elected to the position the following year; he was appointed solicitor general by President BENJAMIN HARRISON in 1890 and named to the Sixth District federal court in 1892. In 1900 President WILLIAM MCKINLEY appointed him to head the Philippine Commission; Taft became civil governor of the Philippines the following year. During his four years in the Philippines Taft proved a gifted administrator; he dealt fairly with the Philippine population and materially improved their standard of living. In 1904 Taft declined offers of a Supreme Court appointment but agreed to become secretary of war to President THEODORE ROOSEVELT. Taft developed a close and trusting relationship with Roosevelt and became his logical successor; he easily won the presidency in 1908, defeating WILLIAM JENNINGS BRYAN by a 2-to-1 margin in the Electoral College. Taft's rejection of Roosevelt's progressive, reform-minded cabinet rapidly cooled their relationship; Taft held a more limited view of presidential power than his predecessor and differed with him on policy areas, including preservation of the protective tariff and conservation. As relations between Taft and Roosevelt deteriorated and the Republicans suffered losses in Congress in 1910, Roosevelt decided to run for president in 1912 and, after losing out at the Republican convention, bolted the party; in a bitterly fought campaign, WOODROW WILSON, the Democrat, emerged victorious, with Roosevelt second, and Taft far behind, carrying only Vermont and Utah, for a total of 8 electoral votes. Taft's presidential record included some notable successes, including initiation of constitutional amendments in favor of an income tax and direct election of senators. After leaving the presidency, Taft taught law at Yale, lobbied for a LEAGUE OF NATIONS, and, in 1920, was appointed to the Supreme Court, where he was an effective chief justice who greatly improved the efficiency and coordination of the court; his votes on the Court were largely but not entirely conservative and anti-labor; he did support increased federal regulation of interstate commerce and a minimum wage for women. He served until 1930, when he retired because of ill health.

Taft's loss in the popular vote in the presidential election was the worst ever suffered by an incumbent president.

TAI • see INTERNATIONAL ATOMIC TIME.

tail • *n.* the rear part of an airplane, with the tailplane and rudder.

tail-end Charlie • informal **1** a person or thing that brings up the rear in a group or formation. **2** a member of the crew of a military aircraft who operates a gun from a compartment at the rear.

tail gunner • the aerial gunner operating the machine gun located in the tail of an aircraft. See also TAIL-END CHARLIE.

tail hook • another term for AIRCRAFT ARRESTING HOOK.

Tailhook scandal • a scandal arising out of the 1991 convention of the Tailhook Association, a private group whose members are associated with the Navy and its officer corps. Eighty-three women attending, including some enlisted women, reported being sexually assaulted or harassed in the Las Vegas, Nevada hotel where the convention took place. As a result, the Navy withdrew its recognition of the organization, some enlisted men were fined or disciplined, and the then secretary of the Navy, Lawrence H. Garrett III, resigned. The chief on Naval operations, Adm. Frank B. Kelso II, was also persuaded into early retirement.

Taiwan • an island country off the southeast coast of China; capital, Taipei. In 1949, toward the end of the war with the Communist regime of mainland China, CHIANG KAI-SHEK withdrew there with 500,000 nationalist KUOMINTANG troops. Taiwan became the headquarters of the Kuomintang, which has held power continuously since then. Since the 1950s Taiwan has undergone steady economic growth. In 1971 it lost its seat in the United Nations to the People's Republic of China, which regards Taiwan as one of its provinces. Its official name is the Republic of China, and its former name was Formosa.

Taiwan Strait Crises • two periods in 1955 and 1958 when tensions arose and artillery fire was exchanged between Taiwan and mainland China across the Taiwan Strait, and on the islands Quemoy and Matsu, which both parties claimed. The U.S., which officially supported CHIANG KAI-SHEK's rights to the Strait islands with the signing of the Formosa Resolutions in 1954, threatened in April, 1955, to use nuclear weapons to protect them in case of a Communist attack. Tensions eventually subsided, only to resurface in August, 1958, when Matsu and Quemoy were shelled by mainland batteries. U.S. carriers arrived, and war loomed until negotiations resumed and Beijing backed away. In both cases, a show of force from the United States brought the immediate tensions to an end, without resolving the larger issues.

take • *v.* (past **took** ; past part. **taken**) **1** capture or gain possession of by force or military means: *twenty of their ships were sunk or taken | the French took Ghent.* **2** occupy (a place or position): *within hours the Marines had taken the hill.* **3** furl a sail.

▸**take off** (of an aircraft or bird) become airborne.

take something over (also **take over**) assume control of something: *British troops had taken over the German trenches.*

takedown • *n.* denoting a firearm with the capacity to have the barrel and magazine detached from the stock.

takeoff (also **take-off**) • *n.* the action of becoming airborne: *the plane accelerated down the runway for takeoff.*

takeover • *n.* an act of assuming control of something, especially the buying out of one company by another.

Talbot, Silas (1751–1813) • REVOLUTIONARY WAR naval officer. Talbot moved from his native Massachusetts and worked as a stonemason in Rhode Island. When the Revolutionary War broke out, he was in the Rhode Island militia; he participated in the battles around Boston, New York, and Philadelphia. Although he was an army officer, Talbot commanded the warship *Hawke*, in which he captured a British schooner in Narragansett Bay; this feat earned him promotion to lieutenant colonel. Talbot was given command of several successive vessels, with which he captured twelve British privateers. Talbot received a navy commission and ended up, in 1780, in command of an American privateer, but the ship was captured by the British on its first cruise. Talbot was held as a prisoner and exchanged in 1781. In the postwar years, he moved to New York and served in both the New York State Assembly and the U.S. House of Representatives, where he was a supporter of a strong federal government. He returned to the navy in 1798 during the QUASI-WAR WITH FRANCE and captured several French privateers.

Taliaferro, William Booth |ˈtäləvər| (1822–1898) • Confederate army officer. A Virginian, Taliaferro practiced law and was an active member of the militia. In 1847 he joined the Eleventh U.S. Infantry and served in the MEXICAN WAR (1846–48). He then served in the Virginia House of Delegates and simultaneously rose in the state militia, becoming a major general. In 1858 he took command of the militia at HARPERS FERRY after JOHN BROWN's failed raid. In the CIVIL WAR, he was a colonel in the Twenty-third Virginia Infantry, fighting with Gen. THOMAS "STONEWALL" JACKSON in the SHENANDOAH VALLEY. He was also at the SECOND BATTLE OF BULL RUN and at FREDERICKSBURG (both 1862). In 1863 he successfully directed the defense of Battery Wagner, South Carolina. Promoted to major general in 1865, he led a division in the war's final battles in North Carolina.

Tallmadge, Benjamin (1754–1835) • spy and U.S. representative. A New Yorker, Tallmadge moved to Connecticut and was a lieutenant in the Connecticut militia at the start of the REVOLUTIONARY WAR. Transferring to an elite regiment, the Second Dragoons, he was promoted to major and fought at BRANDYWINE (1777), GERMANTOWN (1777), and MONMOUTH (1778). In 1778, Gen. GEORGE WASHINGTON appointed Tallmadge to head intelligence operations for the Continentals; relying on childhood friends, Tallmadge created the Culper Spy Ring, the most successful spy operation of the war. The ring observed British troop numbers and movements, fortifications, and supplies in and around New York City and reported back to Washington. Tallmadge informed Washington's aide, Lt. Col. ALEXANDER HAMILTON, that the British were moving a fleet to Newport to await the arrival of the French fleet led by the MARQUIS DE LAFAYETTE; Washington pretended to prepare to attack New York, and the British recalled their fleet, allowing Lafayette's fleet to arrive safely. Tallmadge also suspected BENEDICT ARNOLD of treason. Tallmadge continued to fight with the Second Dragoons. After the war, he returned to Connecticut, where he became a prosperous merchant, banker, and land investor. He was elected to the U.S. House of Representatives in 1801 as a Federalist; he served until 1817. Tallmadge opposed the WAR OF 1812, believing its goals to be vague and the war to be unpopular, and favored the establishment of the Bank of the United States.

tall ship • a sailing ship with high masts.

tallyho • a code meaning, "Target visually sighted" (presumably "the target I have been ordered to intercept"). This should be followed by initial contact report as soon as possible.

Talos • a surface-to-air missile developed for the Navy in the 1950s that could also be used against ship or land targets. It carried a conventional or nuclear warhead and could fly at extremely high altitudes.

Tam Ky • a city in Thua Thien Hue Province, Vietnam, that was the site of U.S. military operations in the VIETNAM WAR such as Operation "Apache Snow," 1969. Known by helicopter pilots of the 101st Airborne Division as "Death Valley," the jungles of the A SHAU VALLEY west of Tam Ky harbored strongholds of the NORTH VIETNAMESE ARMY. The infamous battle of HAMBURGER HILL was fought in this area in June 1969.

tampion |ˈtæmpēən| (also **tompion** |ˈtämpēən|) • *n.* a wooden stopper for the muzzle of a gun.

tank • *n.* a heavy armored fighting vehicle carrying guns and moving on a continuous articulated metal track. [ORIGIN: from the use of *tank* as a secret code word during manufacture in 1915.]

tank, combat • **1** (**M-60**) see PATTON SERIES. **2** see M-48. **3** see SHERIDAN.

tank destroyer • (**M36**) an antitank weapon of WORLD WAR II, featuring a a 90-mm high velocity antiaircraft gun mounted on the Sherman M4A3 tank chassis.

tank killer • an aircraft, vehicle, or missile effective against tanks.

tank, main battle • any tank used as the primary means of delivering a main gun to the battlefield, for example, the M-1, M-60, or M-48A3. Also see ABRAMS.

Tanks, German, World War II-era • by the terms of the 1919 TREATY OF VERSAILLES Germany was prohibited from developing armored forces. Nevertheless, tank development continued in Germany, and after ADOLF HITLER became Chancellor in 1933, the Germans developed a series of armored fighting vehicles (Panzerkampfwagen [PzKpfw], or Panzer) or tanks. Production of the **Panzer I** was started in 1935 and over 1,500 were built before production ceased in 1941. The Panzer I was intended as a training vehicle although it saw combat in the Spanish Civil War and the WORLD WAR II campaigns in Poland, France, and Russia. The **Panzerkampfwagen IA** (Sd. Kfz. 101) weighed 5.3 tons and had 15 mm. of armor, a top speed of 24 MPH, a maximum range of 90 miles, two 7.92 mm machine guns, and a crew of two. The **Panzer II** was introduced in 1939 and some 647 were built by 1945. The **Panzerkampfwagen IIC** (Sd. Kfz. 121) weighed 10 tons and had 15 mm. of armor, a top speed of 30 MPH, a maximum range of 124 miles, a 20 mm main gun and a 7.92 mm machine gun, and a crew of three. The **Panzer III** was introduced in September 1939 and some 5,644 were manufactured by the end of the war. The **Panzer IIIJ** (Sd. Kfz 141/1) weighed 22 tons and had 50 mm. of armor, a top speed of 25 MPH, a maximum range of 124 miles, a 50 mm main gun and two 7.92 mm machine guns, and a crew of five. The **Panzer IV**, introduced in 1936, was the backbone of the German armored forces in World War II, and some 8,281 of all versions of the Panzer IV were built by the end of the war. The **Panzerkampfwagen IVH** (Sd. Kfz. 161/2) weighed 25 tons and had a top speed of 24 MPH, a maximum range of 124 miles, a 75 mm main gun and two 7.92–mm machine guns, and a crew of five. Production of the **Panzer V** "Panther" began in November 1942, and some 5,805 were manufactured by the end of the war. The **Panzerkampfwagen VG** "Panther" (Sd. Kfz. 171) weighed 44.1 tons and had 120 mm. of turret armor, a top speed of 28 MPH, a maximum range of 110 miles, a 75 mm main gun and three 7.92 mm machine guns, and a crew of five. Development of the **Panzer VI**, which appeared in two main versions, the "Tiger I" and the "Tiger II," began in late 1941. Some 1.350 **Panzerkampfwagen VI, "Tiger I"** (Sd. Kfz. 181) were built. It weighed just over 54 tons and had 110 mm. of turret armor, a top speed of 24 MPH, a maximum range of 62 miles, a 88 mm main gun and two 7.92 mm machine guns, and a crew of five. The improved Panzerkampfwagen VI **"Tiger II"** (Sd. Kfz. 182), of which 485 were built, weighed 68.6 tons and had 185 mm. of turret armor, a top speed of 24 MPH, a maximum range of 68 miles, a 88 mm main gun and two

7.92–mm machine guns, and a crew of five. In the spring of 1942, the Germans began development of a super-heavy tank which came to be called the **Maus** ("Mouse"). At 185 tons, the **Panzer VIII** "Maus" (Porsche Type 205) was too heavy for most bridges and was thus designed to ford rivers to a depth of about 24 feet. It had 240 mm of turret armor, a top speed of 12 MPH, a maximum range of 118 miles, a 150 mm or 128 mm main gun as well as a 75 mm second gun with a coaxial 7.92 mm machine gun, and a crew of six. The Maus never reached the production stage, and only about five prototypes were built. The Germans also produced a number of assault guns, tank destroyers, and armored recovery vehicles which used the Panzer chassis.

tanto |'täntō| • *n.* (pl. **-os**) a Japanese short sword or dagger.

taps • **1** a signal sounded at night on the drum, bugle, or trumpet, shortly after the tattoo, alerting military personnel that all lights in quarters are to be put out. [ORIGIN: so named because the signal was originally sounded on a drum.] **2** a signal sounded at military funerals and memorial services. **3** a signal sounded on the drum alerting the front of a marching line to slow down.

ORIGIN: [probably from earlier *taptoo* (tattoo)]

tar • *n.* informal, dated a sailor.

ORIGIN: mid 17th cent.: perhaps an abbreviation of TARPAULIN, also used as a nickname for a sailor at this time.

Tarawa, Battle of • an intense battle on the heavily fortified island of Tarawa in the Gilbert Islands in November, 1943. Marines were mainly involved and made a particularly daring attack on a manned Japanese pillbox by climbing to the top and shooting down inside. There were more than 6,000 casualties in the battle that only covered an area of only 300 acres. Tarawa is today the independent nation of Kiribati.

target • *n.* **1** a geographical area, complex, or installation planned for capture or destruction by military forces. **2** a person, object, or place selected as the aim of an attack. **3** in intelligence usage, a country, area, installation, agency, or person against which intelligence operations are directed. **4** an area designated and numbered for future firing. **5** in gunfire support usage, an impact burst that hits the target. **6** a mark or point at which someone fires or aims, especially a round or rectangular board marked with concentric circles used in archery or shooting. • *v.* (**targeted, targeting**) **1** (usually **be targeted**) select as an object of attention or attack: *two men were targeted by the attackers.* **2** aim or direct (something): *a significant nuclear capability targeted on the U.S.*.

PHRASES: **on target** accurately hitting the thing aimed at.

DERIVATIVES: **targetable** *adj.*

target acquisition • the detection, identification, and location of a target in sufficient detail to permit the effective employment of weapons.

target acquisition equipment • equipment used for the detection, identification, and location of a target in sufficient detail to permit the effective employment of weapons.

target analysis • an examination of potential targets to determine military importance, priority of attack, and weapons required to obtain a desired level of damage or casualties.

target audience • an individual or group selected for influence or attack by means of psychological operations.

target combat air patrol • a patrol of fighters maintained over an enemy target area to destroy enemy aircraft and to cover friendly shipping in the vicinity of the target area in amphibious operations.

target intelligence • intelligence which portrays and locates the components of a target or target complex and indicates its vulnerability and relative importance.

target list • the listing of targets maintained and promulgated by the senior echelon of command. It contains those targets that are to be engaged by supporting arms, as distinguished from a "list of targets" that may be maintained by any echelon as confirmed, suspected, or possible targets for informational and planning purposes.

target noise • sounds emitted by, and characteristic of, a target of some sound-locating system, such as sonar.

target of opportunity • **1** a target visible to a surface or air sensor or observer, which is within range of available weapons and against which fire has not been scheduled or requested. **2** a nuclear target that is observed or detected after an operation begins and that has not been previously considered, analyzed, or planned for a nuclear strike. Generally fleeting in nature, it should be attacked as soon as possible within the time limitations imposed for coordination and warning of friendly troops and aircraft.

Tarleton, Banastre (1754–1833) • British army officer. Tarleton, born in Liverpool, parlayed his military skills and his daring and adventurous nature into a lieutenant colonelcy in the British Legion at the age of 23. His initial efforts during the REVOLUTIONARY WAR, in upstate New York, Pennsylvania, and New Jersey, were successful, and he won much acclaim. He acquired a reputation for brutality after the battle of the WAXHAWS (1780), when his troops were alleged to have continued firing at Continentals who had already laid down their weapons; he also was known for waging total warfare, burning property and destroying crops as he went. Tarleton suffered a major defeat at the hands of the Continentals, brilliantly led by Gen. DANIEL MORGAN, at COWPENS, on the northern border of South Carolina, on January 17, 1781. British casualties numbered 500; the Continentals lost 72. After the defeat, Tarleton continued as a commander, but his relationship with CHARLES CORNWALLIS never recovered. After the war, he returned to England, where he was promoted to general and served in Parliament, but he remained unpopular because of his image as a cruel and ruthless fighter and his self-indulgent lifestyle.

tarpaulin |tär'pôlən; 'tärpə-| • *n.* **1** heavy-duty waterproof cloth, originally of tarred canvas. **2** a sheet or covering of this. **3** a sailor's tarred or oilskin hat. **4** archaic a sailor.

Tarrant, Caesar (c.1740–97) • former slave, war hero, and REVOLUTIONARY WAR patriot. Born into slavery in Virginia, Tarrant somehow acquired the skills of a river pilot. During the Revolution, he won appointment to the Virginia State Navy, where his skills and coolness under attack earned him much admiration. After the war, he returned to slavery, but by 1789, for reasons unknown, he had been granted his freedom by the Virginia General Assembly. He then worked to manumit the members of his family and succeeded in winning the freedom of his wife and one of his children; the other two remained in bondage. Tarrant purchased land and continued to work as a river pilot, although as a freed black he lacked the civil rights accorded to whites. He died with his two older children still enslaved; the daughter eventually bought her freedom, but the fate of his son is unknown.

Tartar • a surface-to-air missile developed for the Navy in the 1960s to be deployed on destroyers. entry was Tarter

Taser |'tāzər| (also **taser**) • *n.* trademark a weapon firing barbs attached by wires to batteries, causing temporary paralysis.

ORIGIN: 1970s: from the initial letters of *Tom Swift's electric rifle* (a fictitious weapon), on the pattern of *laser*.

task component • a subdivision of a fleet, task force, task group, or task unit, organized by the respective commander or by higher authority for the accomplishment of specific tasks.

task fleet • a mobile command consisting of ships and aircraft necessary for the accomplishment of a specific major task or tasks that may be of a continuing nature.

task force • **1** a temporary grouping of units, under one commander, formed for the purpose of carrying out a specific operation or mission. **2** a semipermanent organization of units, under one commander, formed for the purpose of carrying out a continuing specific task. **3** a component of a fleet organized by the commander of a task fleet or higher authority for the accomplishment of a specific task or tasks. **4** an armed force organized for a special operation.

task group • a component of a naval task force organized by the commander of a task force or higher authority.

task unit • a component of a naval task group organized by the commander of a task group or higher authority.

tattoo • *n.* **1 a** a signal sounded in the evening on the drum, bugle, or trumpet, shortly before taps, alerting military personnel to repair to their quarters. **b** an evening entertainment of music and military exercises performed by military personnel, often given by torch or other artificial light. **2** a rapid rhythmic tapping, as in a drumbeat.

taut |tôt| • *adj.* (of a ship) having a disciplined and efficient crew.

tax-in-kind • *n.* a tax collected in the form of agricultural produce or animals, raw materials, labor, or some other non-cash commodity.

taxiway • *n.* a specially prepared or designated path on an airfield for the use of taxiing aircraft.

Taylor, Harry (1862–1930) • military engineer and army officer. From New Hampshire, Taylor served in the ARMY CORPS OF ENGINEERS after graduating from the U.S. MILITARY ACADEMY, working primarily on river and harbor sites along both coasts In 1915 he was promoted to colonel and appointed chief engineer in the New York City and Hudson district. In 1917 he was named chief engineer to the AMERICAN EXPEDITIONARY FORCE, led by Gen. JOHN J. PERSHING, and sailed for France, where he was responsible for planning the debarkation of U.S. troops and supplies, building training camps and hospitals, and arranging transportation and communications for thousands of U.S. personnel. By 1918, he was promoted to brigadier general and had a force of 31,000 engineers and troops reporting to him. After the war he returned to Washington, and in 1924 he was named the U.S. Army's chief of engineers.

Taylor, Maxwell Davenport (1901–1987) • Born in Missouri, Maxwell Taylor graduated from WEST POINT in 1922 with a commission in the engineers. He later transferred to field artillery. In 1942 he became chief of staff of the 82nd Infantry Division and assisted MATTHEW B. RIDGWAY in converting it to an airborne unit. He was promoted to brigadier general and jumped into Sicily and Italy with the division. His dangerous secret mission behind enemy lines to Rome found unexpected German strength and prevented a bloody attempt to take the city by airborne assault. As a major general, he commanded the 101st Airborne Division during OPERATIONS OVERLORD and MARKET-GARDEN, though he was in the United States when the division made its famous stand at BASTOGNE. After WORLD WAR II he served as superintendent of West Point, and commanded the Eighth Army during the last few months of the KOREAN WAR. He eventually became commander of all United Nations forces in the Far East, and retired after serving as chief of staff of the army. He was a critic of President DWIGHT D. EISENHOWER's defense policies, and favored "flexible response" over "massive retaliation." Taylor became very influential within the administration of JOHN F. KENNEDY, even briefly returning to active duty as chairman of the JOINT CHIEFS OF STAFF. He retired again to become ambassador to South Vietnam in 1964, a position he held for a year. He then served as a special adviser to Presidents LYNDON B. JOHNSON and RICHARD M. NIXON, and played an instrumental role in getting the United States involved in the VIETNAM WAR.

Taylor, Richard (1826–1879) • Confederate army officer. Born near Louisville, Kentucky, Richard Taylor was the son of future President ZACHARY TAYLOR. The younger Taylor graduated from Yale in 1845, and accompanied his father at the battles of PALO ALTO and RESACA DE LA PALMA during the early days of the MEXICAN WAR (1846–48). After a prolonged illness he became active in Democratic politics in Louisiana, was a delegate to the state secession convention, and was appointed colonel of the 9th Louisiana Infantry Regiment. Taylor was JEFFERSON DAVIS's brother-in-law, but demonstrated considerable military skill to earn his promotions. He served under STONEWALL JACKSON in the SHENANDOAH VALLEY and with ROBERT E. LEE during the SEVEN DAYS' Battles, before being promoted to major general and taking command of the District of West Louisiana. Though often ill, he kept BENJAMIN BUTLER bottled up in New Orleans and turned back NATHANIEL P. BANKS' advance up the Red River in 1864. He briefly retired after clashing with his superior Gen. E. KIRBY SMITH, but in August 1864 was promoted to lieutenant general and put in charge of the Department of East Louisiana, Mississippi and Alabama. His command was the last Confederate force east of the Mississippi when he surrendered on May 4, 1865.

Taylor, Zachary (1784–1850) • U.S. army officer and 12th President of the United States (1849–1850). Born in Orange County, Virginia, on November 24, 1784, Taylor moved with his family to a farm near Louisville, Kentucky, the following year. He obtained a commission as first lieutenant in the U.S. 7th Infantry in 1808 and served on the Old Northwest frontier through the WAR OF 1812. He was promoted to captain in 1810 and was brevetted major in 1812. He returned to the family farm in 1814 but was recalled to active duty by President JAMES MADISON in 1816 and served as lieutenant colonel and then colonel of the U.S. 1st Infantry for over ten years. He led the 1st Infantry in the BLACK HAWK WAR and commanded U.S. troops fighting the Seminoles, whom he defeated at Lake Okeechobee (December 25, 1837), for which action he was brevetted brigadier general and gained the nickname "Old Rough and Ready." He subsequently commanded U.S. troops in the Southern Division of the Western Department. Following the annexation of Texas in December 1845, Taylor fortified a position across the Rio Grande River from the Mexican town of Matamoros in March 1846. Taylor's position was attacked by the Mexican general MARIANO ARISTA, and Taylor's forces repulsed the Mexicans in the BATTLE OF PALO ALTO (May 8, 1846) and then pursued Arista's retreating forces defeating them again at RESACA DE LA PALMA (May 9, 1846). Taylor's victories at PALO ALTO and RESACA DE LA PALMA led to his promotion to major general. His forces were reinforced and in September 1846 he advanced on MONTERREY which he attacked on September 21. The Mexicans requested a truce and withdrew after a three-day defense of the city. Taylor was then ordered to release most of his troops for Gen. WINFIELD SCOTT's expedition against City of Mexico. Taylor's diminished force was attacked by strong Mexican forces under Gen. ANTONIO LÓPEZ DE SANTA ANNA at BUENA VISTA on February 21–23, 1847. Again, the U.S. forces gained victory through effective artillery work. Taylor's fame as a winning general in the MEXICAN WAR led to his nomination as the Whig Party candidate for President in the election of 1848. He defeated MARTIN VAN BUREN and assumed office as the 12th President of the United States in 1849. The question of extending slavery to the new territories won from Mexico dominated his administration. Taylor died in office on July 9, 1850, after serving only sixteen months and was succeeded by his vice president, MILLARD FILLMORE.

T-bone Hill, Battle of • the U.S. nickname for a hill in Korea that was the site of an attack by Chinese forces in December, 1952. The U.S. sustained heavy casualties in the two day battle but were ultimately successful in defending the position. See also PORKCHOP HILL.

TCC • *abbr.* transportation component command.

T, crossing the • see CROSSING THE T.

Tea Act • an act passed by the British Parliament in 1773 to reduce the tax on tea shipped to the colonies. It allowed the British East India Company to sell tea to the American colonies at a price lower than that of smuggled tea and to create a monopoly of the tea trade in the colonies. Tea and other items were previously taxed under the TOWNSHEND ACTS of 1767, which were repealed in 1770 except for the acts' provision to tax tea. Americans saw the act as a violation of their constitutional rights. Their protests led to the BOSTON TEA PARTY.

tear gas • *n.* gas that causes severe irritation to the eyes, chiefly used in riot control to force crowds to disperse. • *v.* (**tear-gas**) (usually **be tear-gassed**) attack with tear gas.

TECDOC • *abbr.* technical documentation.

TECHINT • *abbr.* technical intelligence.

technical • *n.* **1** a small truck with a machine gun mounted on the back. **2** a gunman who rides in such a truck.

technical analysis • in imagery interpretation, the precise description of details appearing on imagery.

technical documentation • (**TECDOC**) visual information documentation (with or without sound as an integral documentation component) of an actual event made for purposes of evaluation. Typically, technical documentation contributes to the study of human or mechanical factors, procedures, and processes in the fields of medicine, science, logistics, research, development, test and evaluation, intelligence, investigations, and armament delivery.

technical evaluation • the study and investigations by a developing agency to determine the technical suitability of material, equipment, or a system, for use in the military services.

technical intelligence • (**TECHINT**) intelligence derived from the exploitation of foreign materiel, produced for strategic, operational, and tactical-level commanders. Technical intelligence begins when an individual service member finds something new on the battlefield and takes the proper steps to report it. The item is then exploited at succeedingly higher levels until a countermeasure is produced to neutralize the adversary's technological advantage.

technical sergeant • a noncommissioned officer in the U.S. Air Force ranking above staff sergeant and below master sergeant.

technical specification • a detailed description of technical requirements stated in terms suitable to form the basis for the actual design development and production processes of an item having the qualities specified in the operational characteristics.

technical survey • a complete electronic and physical inspection to ascertain that offices, conference rooms, war rooms, and other similar locations where classified information is discussed are free of monitoring systems.

technology push • a situation in which new or emerging technology forces a change in military equipment or doctrine.

Tecumseh (1768–1813) • Shawnee chief and military leader. Probably born at Piqua on the Mad River in Ohio in March 1768, Tecumseh grew up during the long conflict between the Indian tribes and white settlers advancing into the Old Northwest after 1774. He took part in many raids against the settlers in Ohio, Kentucky, and Tennessee as well as in the battle against U.S. troops led by Gen. "MAD ANTHONY" WAYNE at FALLEN TIMBERS (August 20, 1794). Together with his brother, the medicine man Tenskwatawa ("The Prophet"), Tecumseh led the Shawnee and other northwest tribes in resisting white expansion into their territory after Fallen Timbers. He quarreled with Indiana governor WILLIAM HENRY HARRISON over the sale of Indian land to white settlers (1809–1811) and traveled south in 1811 to persuade the southeastern tribes to join his confederacy. While he was away Harrison attacked and gained a victory over the Indians at TIPPECANOE (November 7, 1811). Tecumseh returned to the Northwest in 1812 and allied himself with the British in the WAR OF 1812, raiding American forces and settlements along the Detroit River. He was killed in battle against U.S. troops led by Harrison at the BATTLE OF THE THAMES in Canada (October 5, 1813).

Tehran Conference • the first meeting, held November 28–December 1, 1943, in Tehran, Iran, of the three main Allied leaders during WORLD WAR II, President FRANKLIN D. ROOSEVELT, British Prime Minister WINSTON CHURCHILL, and Soviet Premier JOSEF STALIN. Subjects discussed included the Eastern Front and the planned invasion of Nazi-occupied France. The three leaders also signed a declaration that guaranteed the independence and territorial integrity of Iran after the war. The Tehran Conference was held between the two meetings of the CAIRO CONFERENCE.

telecommunication (often as **telecommunications**) • any transmission, emission, or reception of signs, signals, writings, images, sounds, or information of any nature by wire, radio, visual, or other electromagnetic systems.

teleconference • a conference between persons remote from one another but linked by a telecommunications system.

telegraph • *n.* **1** a system for transmitting messages from a distance along a wire, especially one creating signals by making and breaking an electrical connection: *news came from the outside world* ***by telegraph***. **2** a device for transmitting messages in such a way. • *v.* send (someone) a message by telegraph: *I must go and telegraph Mom.* | *she would rush off to telegraph news to her magazine.*

DERIVATIVES: **telegrapher** *n.*

telemetry • the sensing and measurement of any physical characteristic and the automatic transmission of such measurements elsewhere for interpretation.

telemetry intelligence • (**TELINT**) technical intelligence derived from the intercept, processing, and analysis of foreign telemetry. Telemetry is a category of foreign instrumentation signals intelligence.

teleran system • a navigational system that employs ground-based search radar equipment along an airway to locate aircraft flying near that airway. The system transmits, by television means, information pertaining to these aircraft and other information to the pilots of properly equipped aircraft. It also provides information to the pilots appropriate for use in the landing approach.

ORIGIN: an acronymn of *tele*vision *r*adar *a*ir *n*avigation.

telescopic sight • a small telescope used for sighting, typically mounted on a rifle.

Television Martí • see RADIO MARTÍ.

television war • an armed conflict in which combat actions are routinely recorded by commercial television crews and the resulting tapes replayed on network television broadcasts in the home country. See also LIVING-ROOM WAR.

TELINT • *abbr.* telemetry intelligence.

Teller Amendment • an amendment sponsored by Republican senator Henry M. Teller and adopted by Congress on April 20, 1898. It authorized the use of U.S. military force to establish Cuban independence from Spain. It followed President WILLIAM MCKINLEY's request for force on April 11 and was supported in lieu of a U.S. annexation of Cuba. A U.S. protectorate over the island was established under the PLATT AMENDMENT.

Teller, Edward (1908–) • Hungarian-born nuclear physicist who worked under J. ROBERT OPPENHEIMER on the MANHATTAN PROJECT at Los Alamos, New Mexico after becoming a U.S. citizen in 1941. He earned a Ph.D. in physical chemistry in 1930, then studied under Niels Bohr in Copenhagen, going on to teach at the University of Göttingen from

1931 to 1933. He moved to the United States with his wife, Augusta Harkanyi, in 1935 and, after he became a U.S. citizen, he joined ENRICO FERMI's team, which was trying to produce the first self-sustaining nuclear chain reaction, at the University of Chicago. Teller then accepted an invitation to work at the University of California at Berkeley with J. Robert Oppenheimer on theoretical studies on the atomic bomb. When Oppenheimer agreed to set up and head the project to build a fission bomb at Los Alamos Scientific Laboratory, Teller was among the first men recruited. In 1946, Teller returned to the University of Chicago, working at its Institute for Nuclear Studies and returning frequently to Los Alamos as a consultant. Teller wanted the United States to build a hydrogen bomb, and, in spite of the opposition of Oppenheimer, who now headed the ATOMIC ENERGY COMMISSION, and other atomic scientists, President HARRY S. TRUMAN approved the project after the Soviet Union exploded an atomic bomb in 1949. The hydrogen bomb was tested at ENIWETOK atoll in the Pacific Ocean in November 1952. Teller played an important role in the establishment of the Lawrence Livermore National Laboratory in 1952—the United States's primary thermonuclear weapons manufacturer—and served as its associate director (1954–1958) and director (1958–1960); at the same time he taught physics at the University of California at Berkeley. A prominent advisor to United States government officials on nuclear weapons, and was a major influence in President RONALD REAGAN's proposed STRATEGIC DEFENSE INITIATIVE.

telltale |ˈtelˌtāl| • *n.* (on a sailboat) a piece of string or fabric that shows the direction and force of the wind.

Ten Broeck, Abraham |ten ˈbro͝ok| (1734–1810) • REVOLUTIONARY WAR statesman and soldier. Born in Albany, New York, Abraham Ten Broeck was a large land owner and representative in the New York Provincial Assembly at the outbreak of the Revolution. As one of the leading critics of British authority, he assumed an important role in New York's Patriot government. As a brigadier general from 1775 to 1781 he also commanded the Albany County militia. He and his men contributed significantly to the American victory at the BATTLE OF BEMIS HEIGHTS on October 7, 1777 which sealed the fate of JOHN BURGOYNE's trapped British army and compelled its surrender. After the war Ten Broeck served as a judge, state senator, and mayor of Albany.

tender • *n.* **1** a vehicle used by a fire service for carrying specified supplies or equipment or fulfilling a specified role. **2** a vehicle used in mobile operations by the armed forces. **3** a boat used to ferry people and supplies to and from a ship. **4** a person who looks after someone else or a machine or place: *Alexei signaled to one of the engine tenders.*

Tenet, George J. (1953–) • born in New York City and the son of Greek immigrants, Tenet attended Georgetown University's School of Foreign Affairs (1976), and received a Master's degree in International Affairs from Columbia University (1978). He went on to work in both the executive and legislative branches of the government on intelligence issues, and moved up the Washington career ladder very quickly. From 1993 to 1995 he was Special Assistant to the President and Senior Director for Intelligence Programs at the NATIONAL SECURITY COUNCIL, and in 1995 became the deputy director of the CENTRAL INTELLIGENCE AGENCY. In 1997 he became the Director of that agency.

Tennery, Thomas D. (1819–1891) • U.S. soldier. Born in Greenup County, Kentucky, Thomas D. Tennery moved with his family to Illinois. In July 1846 he enlisted in Company E, Fourth Regiment, Illinois Volunteer Infantry for service in the MEXICAN WAR (1846–48). The diary he kept provides one of the most insightful and revealing accounts of the life of a common soldier during that conflict. Tennery participated in the amphibious landing that led to WINFIELD SCOTT's capture of VERACRUZ and was wounded at the BATTLE OF CERRO GORDO, but most of his writings deal with the training, travel, and daily experiences of Army life. After the war he returned to Illinois and served his community as a teacher, justice of the peace, and county supervisor.

terminal guidance • **1** the guidance applied to a guided missile between midcourse guidance and arrival in the vicinity of the target. **2** electronic, mechanical, visual, or other assistance given an aircraft pilot to facilitate arrival at, operation within or over, landing upon, or departure from an air-landing or airdrop facility.

terminal operations • the reception, processing, and staging of passengers; the receipt, transit storage, and marshaling of cargo; the loading and unloading of ships or aircraft; and the manifesting and forwarding of cargo and passengers to destination.

terminal phase • that portion of the trajectory of a ballistic missile between reentry into the atmosphere or the end of the mid-course phase and impact or arrival in the vicinity of the target.

terminal velocity • **1** the hypothetical maximum speed a body could attain along a specified flight path under given conditions of weight and thrust if diving through an unlimited distance in air of specified uniform density. **2** the remaining speed of a projectile at the point in its downward path where it is level with the muzzle of the weapon.

terrain |təˈrān| • *n.* a stretch of land, especially with regard to its physical features: *they were delayed by rough terrain.*

terrain exercise • an exercise in which a stated military situation is solved on the ground, the troops being imaginary and the solution usually being in writing.

terrain flight • flight close to the earth's surface during which airspeed, height, and/or altitude are adapted to the contours and cover of the ground in order to avoid enemy detection and fire. Also called LOW-LEVEL FLIGHT.

terreplein | ˈterəˌplān | • *n.* a level space where a battery of guns is mounted.

Terrier • *n.* **1** a two-stage, surface-to-air missile developed for the Navy in the 1950s. **2** Brit. & informal a member of the Territorial Army.

territorial • *adj.* of or relating to the ownership of an area of land or sea: *territorial disputes.* • *n.* (**Territorial**) (in the UK) a member of the Territorial Army.

Territorial Army (in the UK) a volunteer force locally organized to provide a reserve of trained and disciplined manpower for use in an emergency.

terror-bombing • **1** the detonation of an explosive device, usually in a public location, by a terrorist. **2** aerial bombardment for the purpose of frightening and demoralizing an enemy's civilian population.

terrorism • the calculated use of violence or threat of violence to inculcate fear. Terrorism is intended to coerce or intimidate governments or societies in the pursuit of goals that are generally political, religious, or ideological.

terrorism, state • the intimidation of citizens by a government by means of state resources such as the police, judiciary, and military, to quell domestic opposition to its policies.

terrorism, state-supported • the use of violence and intimidation in the pursuit of political aims, undertaken with the logistical, financial, and training support of a state.

terrorism, sub-state • the use of violence and intimidation in the pursuit of political aims by a private group with no support from governments.

Terry, Alfred Howe (1827–1890) • Union army officer. Born in Hartford, Connecticut, on November 10, 1827, Terry attended Yale University without graduating. He practiced law, served as clerk of the New Haven Superior Court (1854–1861), and rose to the rank of major in the militia by 1855. In 1861, he was commissioned as colonel of the 2nd Connecticut Infantry and later raised and commanded the 7th Connecticut. He fought at FIRST BULL RUN in 1861 and commanded at the regimental, brigade, and district level in North and South Carolina and Georgia until April 1864, being appointed brigadier general of volunteers in April 1862. In April 1864, he transferred to the Union ARMY OF THE JAMES and commanded a division in the Bermuda Hundred campaign (May–June 1864). He then led his division in operations against RICHMOND and PETERSBURG until rising to command the X Corps in late 1864. In January 1865, having been promoted to major general of volunteers, Terry led his corps to capture FORT FISHER, ending the usefulness of Wilmington, North Carolina, as a port for the Confederacy. Terry was then appointed brigadier general in the Regular Army and led troops in North Carolina until the end of the war. He remained in the Army after the Civil War and commanded U.S. troops in the South and in campaigns against the Plains Indians, notably as overall commander of the expedition against the Sioux in the summer of 1876 which led to disaster at the LITTLE BIGHORN (June 26, 1876). Terry was promoted to major general in 1886 and commanded the Division of the Missouri until his retirement from active service in 1888.

testing ground • an area or field of activity used for the testing of a product or an idea, especially a military site used for the testing of weapons.

Tet Offensive • the aggressive campaign by the North Vietnamese, beginning in January, 1968, the time of the local New Year celebrations, to attempt to win the VIETNAM WAR. Beginning on January 29th there were coordinated attacks in cities throughout South Vietnam. The fighting continued over most of the first half of the year and was an important factor in the escalation of the war: Gen. WILLIAM C. WESTMORELAND requested more than 200,000 more troops. Public opinion against the war in the United States also escalated, and President LYNDON B. JOHNSON began to see that the scope and duration of the war were beyond the control of the U.S. government.

Texas Army • the army of the TEXAS WAR OF INDEPENDENCE, led by SAM HOUSTON, that defeated ANTONIO LÓPEZ DE SANTA ANNA at the BATTLE OF SAN JACINTO in April 1836. The battle lasted only twenty minutes, but the Mexicans lost 630 men and 730 were taken prisoner.

Texas Rangers • established in the 1830s, a loosely organized militia that controlled law and order in the State of Texas until it was merged with the state highway patrol in 1935. After Texas had won its independence from Mexico, the Rangers also served as a border patrol. They were responsible for making the Colt revolver (six-shooter) the best-known weapon of the West, and now hold a prominent place in Texas legend.

Texas, Republic of • an independent nation established in 1836, after its people gained independence from Mexico, and annexed by the United States in 1845. Its first president was SAM HOUSTON. Until 1839 its capital was Houston, Texas, which was named in the president's honor. In 1839 the capital moved to Austin, named after Stephen F. Austin, who served as the republic's first secretary of state. Although Anglo-Americans dominated the top political posts, many of the leaders and armed settlers who fought for independence from Mexico were Mexicans. As early as 1836, Texans voted to ask for annexation by the United States, but it was resisted by the administrations of Presidents ANDREW JACKSON and MARTIN VAN BUREN. During the time of the Republic, the TEXAS RANGERS military force was established to protect against raids by Mexico and to maintain order. The U.S. annexation and other boundary disputes between Mexico and the United States triggered the MEXICAN WAR (1846–48).

Texas War of Independence • a war that arose over disputes concerning the governing of Texas. Local Mexican and Anglo residents resisted and resented the incompetent and remote administration from Mexico City. The right to import slaves was a key issue for the Texans and was opposed by the Mexican government. Fighting first broke out in October, 1835 between troops sent by the Mexican government and Texans. Forces of Texans were hastily organized and not very well prepared, but had admirable leadership under Stephen F. Austin and SAM HOUSTON. The battle of the ALAMO, in which the nearly 200 Texans defending were all killed, was the rallying point of the war. Tactical errors on the part of ANTONIO LÓPEZ DE SANTA ANNA led to his finally being defeated at San Jacinto. He was captured and signed a treaty pledging recognition of Texas as a republic, though the Mexican congress repudiated this. Eight years later, annexation of Texas by the United States led to the MEXICAN WAR (1846–48).

Thames, Battle of • a battle in the of WAR OF 1812, fought on October 5, 1813 along the Thames River in Ontario, Canada. Outnumbering American forces led by Gen. WILLIAM HENRY HARRISON attacked a combined force of British and Native American forces and defeated them decisively. It was the last battle of the war in the Northwest, and the Native American chief TECUMSEH was killed in it.

Thant, U (1909–1974) • a Myanmar educator, civil servant, and third secretary-general of the United Nations (1962–1971), Thant was born in Pantanaw, Burma (now Myanmar) and educated at the University of Yangôn (Rangoon). Because of the death of his father, however, he did not graduate, returning home, instead, to begin teaching at the National High School. In 1931 he became the school's headmaster, and, in 1942, became secretary to the educational reorganization committee of the Japanese government of occupied Burma. In 1943 he returned to Pantanaw and resumed his duties as headmaster at the high school there. At the end of WORLD WAR II, U Nu, who had met Thant when they were both students at the University of Yangôn, and Gen. U Aung San (leader of the Anti-Fascist People's Freedom League) recruited him for government service. Before he became the Myanmar (Burmese) delegate to the UNITED NATIONS (U.N.) in 1952, Thant served as his country's press director (1947), director of broadcasting (1948), and secretary of the Ministry of Information (1949). After serving as Burma's permanent representative to the U.N. (1957), Thant became vice president of the U.N.'s General Assembly in 1959, and, after the death of DAG HAMMARSKJÖLD, accepted the position of acting secretary general of the U.N. in 1961 when the Soviet Union and the United States failed to find a mutually acceptable candidate. In 1962, he was elected again to that position, which he held until his retirement in 1971. In 1974, he died of cancer in New York City. When his body was sent back to Yangôn, however, university students seized it on December 5 and buried it in a hastily constructed mausoleum at the Arts and Sciences University. On December 11, the police took Thant's body back by force, buried him in a secret place, and sealed the tomb with concrete. To quell the rioting that followed these events, the military regime declared martial law.

Thatcher, Henry Knox (1806–1880) • U.S. naval officer. Born in Maine, Henry Knox Thatcher entered WEST POINT in 1822. He soon left, however, and was appointed a midshipman in the Navy the next year. He worked his way through the ranks and when the CIVIL WAR began he commanded the corvette *Constellation*. In 1863 he took over the frigate *Colorado* in the North Atlantic Blockading Squadron. He commanded the first division of that squadron during Admiral DAVID D. PORTER's attacks on FORT FISHER. In January 1865 he succeeded Admiral DAVID FARRAGUT in command of the West Gulf Blockading Squadron. Thatcher assisted Gen. EDWARD R.S. CANBY in the capture of Mobile, Alabama in April and occupied Galveston, Texas in June. He was promoted to the rank of rear admiral in 1866, and retired two years later.

Thayer, Sylvanus (1785–1872) • U.S. military educator; "Father of the Military Academy." Born in Braintree, Massachusetts, Thayer attended Dartmouth College (1803–1807) before being graduated from WEST POINT and commissioned in the ARMY CORPS OF ENGINEERS in 1808. He performed engineering duties and rose to the rank of brevet major in the WAR OF 1812. In 1815, Thayer was sent to Europe to study European military doctrine, fortifications, and education. He returned to West Point in 1817 as superintendent and undertook a thorough reform of the administration and curriculum of the Military Academy, expanding both the liberal arts and the military training portions of the curriculum. His efforts made West Point the nation's premier engineering school and were largely responsible for the formation of the most prominent American military and civilian leaders of the mid-nineteenth century. In 1833, Thayer quarreled with President ANDREW JACKSON over the disciplining of cadets and resigned as superintendent. Promoted to lieutenant colonel of engineers in 1838, he spent the remainder of his military career on engineering duties, mainly in New England. He took a leave of absence for reasons of health in 1858 and was retired from active service in 1863 as a brevet brigadier general.

theater (also **theatre**) • *n.* **1** the area in which something happens: *a new **theater of war** has been opened up.* **2** denoting weapons for use in a particular region between tactical and strategic: *he was working on theater defense missiles.*

Theater High Altitude Area Defense • U.S. Army component of the U.S. theater missile defense system intended to complement the PATRIOT missile system.

theater missile defense • measures and weapons systems designed to intercept and defeat an enemy's theater ballistic missiles, such as the SCUD. The U.S. theater missile defense system includes the PATRIOT missile system, an enhanced U.S. Navy AEGIS air defense system, the U.S. Army THEATER HIGH

ALTITUDE AREA DEFENSE missile system, and the ground-based theater missile defense component of the GLOBAL PROTECTION AGAINST LIMITED STRIKES (GPALS) system.

theater of operations • a large geographical area designated for the conduct of military operations and for the administration of such operations.

theory of combat • a set of principles and procedures for the conduct of armed military operations.

thermal energy • the energy emitted from a fireball as thermal radiation.

The total amount of thermal energy received per unit area at a specified distance from a nuclear explosion is generally expressed in terms of calories per square centimeter.

thermal exposure • the total normal component of thermal radiation striking a given surface throughout the course of a detonation.

Thermal exposure is expressed in calories per square centimeter and/or megajoules per square meter.

thermal imagery • imagery produced by sensing and recording the thermal energy emitted or reflected from the objects that are imaged.

thermal radiation • **1** the heat and light produced by a nuclear explosion. **2** electromagnetic radiation emitted from a heat or light source as a consequence of its temperature. It consists essentially of ultraviolet, visible, and infrared radiations.

thermonuclear • *adj.* of, relating to, or involving weapons in which explosive force is produced by thermonuclear reactions.

thermonuclear weapon • a bomb in which very high temperatures are used to bring about the fusion of light nuclei such as those of hydrogen isotopes (e.g., deuterium and tritium) with the accompanying release of destructive energy. entry was plural; singularized

thimble • *n.* a metal ring, concave on the outside, around which a loop of rope is spliced.

think tank • a body of experts providing advice and ideas on specific political or economic problems: *a think tank devoted to the study of political and economic integration.*

DERIVATIVES: **think tanker**

Third Reich • term adopted by ADOLF HITLER in the 1920s to describe the thousand-year imperium he intended to create. The First Reich (or Empire) was the Holy Roman Empire which existed from the time of Charlemagne to 1806. The Second Reich was the German Empire of 1871–1918 created by Otto von Bismarck.

Third World • (usually **the Third World**) the developing countries of Asia, Africa, and Latin America.

ORIGIN: first applied in the 1950s by French commentators who used *tiers monde* to distinguish the developing countries from the capitalist and Communist blocs.

Thirteenth Amendment • an amendment to the U.S. Constitution, adopted in 1865. The Thirteenth Amendment abolished slavery within the United States.

thirty-eight • *n.* a revolver of .38 caliber.

38th parallel • the latitudinal line that approximately forms the boundary between North Korea and South Korea. Its use for the partition of Korea was proposed at the POTSDAM CONFERENCE in 1945. During the KOREAN WAR, each side temporarily controlled area beyond the line, but by the war's end the 38th parallel again was the dividing line between the countries.

Tho, Le Duc (1911–1990) • born Phan Dinh Khai in Nam Ha province, Vietnam, Le Duc Tho was a founder of the Indochinese Community Party (1930) and a leader of the VIETMINH (a group that sought Vietnamese independence from the French) and the Communist Party (revived as the Vietnam Workers' Party). Tho was the senior Viet Minh official in southern Vietnam until 1954, and a member of the Politburo of the Vietnam Workers' Party (the Communist Party ofVietnam after 1976) from 1955 on, overseeing the VIETCONG insurgency that began in the late 1950s. He is remembered in the West for his role in the cease-fire as special advisor to the North Vietnamese delegation to the PARIS PEACE CONFERENCES between 1968 and 1973, for which he was a corecipient of the Nobel Peace Prize in 1974 with HENRY KISSINGER. Tho, however, did not accept the honor. He remained a member of the Politburo until 1986.

thole pin • a pin, typically one of a pair, fitted to the gunwale of a rowboat to act as the fulcrum for an oar.

Thomas, David (1762–1831) • REVOLUTIONARY WAR soldier, state legislator, congressman. David Thomas was born in Pelham, Massachusetts. He joined an expedition to relieve Rhode Island in 1877, and served in the enlisted ranks in the Fifth and Third Massachusetts Regiments from 1781 to 1783. After the war he moved to New York, where he was commissioned a captain of the state militia in 1787. In 1805 he attained the rank of major general of the Northern Division of the New York Militia. He served four terms in the U.S. Congress representing the seventh district of New York, and then served in a number of state positions until his reputation was tarnished by a bribery charge in 1812. Though acquitted by a trial, he retired from political life and left the state.

Thomas, George Henry (1816–1870) • Union army officer. Born in Southampton County, Virginia, on July 31, 1816, Thomas studied law before attending WEST POINT. He was graduated from West Point and commissioned in the 3rd Artillery in 1840. Following service in the South, on the frontier, and in the MEXICAN WAR (1846–48) (in which he earned brevet promotions for gallantry at MONTERREY and BUENA VISTA), he fought the Seminoles in Florida (1840–1842, 1849–1850), taught tactics at West Point (1851–1854), and served as Lt. Col. of the 2nd U.S. Cavalry campaigning against the Indians in

Texas (1856–1860). One of the few Virginians to remain loyal to the Union at the beginning of the CIVIL WAR, Thomas served in the SHENANDOAH VALLEY campaign in 1861 and in Kentucky in 1862. He was appointed brigadier general of volunteers in 1861 and major general of volunteers in April 1862. Commanding the XIV Corps in the ARMY OF THE CUMBERLAND, his steadfast defense during the BATTLE OF CHICKAMAUGA (September 19–20, 1863) earned him the sobriquet "The Rock of Chickamauga," but, being a Virginian, he was suspect and did not receive subsequent promotions and commands commensurate with his abilities. Nevertheless, he eventually rose to command the Army of the Cumberland in the battles around CHATTANOOGA (1863) and in the ATLANTA campaign (1864). In late 1864, Thomas led his army north into Tennessee and gained a major victory over Confederate forces in the BATTLE OF NASHVILLE (December 15–16, 1864). Following the Civil War, he commanded in Tennessee and Kentucky and then the Military Division of the Pacific (1869–1870).

Thomas, Lorenzo (1804–1875) • Union army officer. Born in New Castle, Delaware, Lorenzo Thomas graduated from WEST POINT in 1823 with a commission in the infantry. He spent most of the next 17 years in Florida, and fought against the Seminole Indians there. During the MEXICAN WAR he won a brevet at MONTERREY while serving as chief of staff for Gen. WILLIAM O. BUTLER. In 1853 he became chief of staff to commanding general of the army WINFIELD SCOTT, and eight years later he was appointed adjutant general of the army, responsible for manning a force about to expand considerably for the CIVIL WAR. The demands were overwhelming, and in 1863 he was sent to Mississippi to recruit soldiers for black regiments. He stayed out of Washington the rest of the war, but in 1865 was brevetted major general for his services. President ANDREW JOHNSON recalled him to Washington from inspection duties in 1868, and then appointed Thomas interim Secretary of War to replace EDWIN M. STANTON. When Thomas tried to take the post, Stanton had him arrested for violation of the Tenure of Office Act, the same act over which Johnson was soon impeached. Thomas returned to his adjutant general duties for a year before retiring.

Thomas, William Holland (1805–1893) • the only white man to serve as chief of the North Carolina Cherokees, businessman, and Confederate army officer. Born in Haywood County, North Carolina, William Holland Thomas learned the customs and language of the local Cherokees as a boy. After successfully defending them in Washington from removal in 1836, he was named chief of the loosely organized tribe in 1839, a post he held for twenty-eight years. When the CIVIL WAR broke out he supported the Confederacy, and though having no military experience, he joined the army and raised and led a force of Indians and mountaineers called Thomas's Legion. They spent most of the war guarding railroad passes in eastern Tennessee, but Thomas still got court-martialed twice for disobeying orders. Once the charges were dropped and once JEFFERSON DAVIS pardoned Thomas before the trial began, so he managed to surrender with honor in May 1865. The war broke him, however, and he spent most of the rest of his life in mental hospitals.

Thompson, Robert George (1915–1965) • soldier and American Communist Party leader. Born in Fruitdale, Oregon, Robert George Thompson joined the Communist Party of the USA at the age of eighteen. In 1937 he joined the International Brigade fighting for Republican forces in the Spanish Civil War, and eventually rose to command a machine-gun battalion. He joined the U.S. Army shortly before PEARL HARBOR (1941), rising to the rank of staff sergeant and winning the DISTINGUISHED SERVICE CROSS for heroism in NEW GUINEA in January 1943. He was invalided out of the service later that year with malaria and tuberculosis. After the war Thompson held important Communist Party posts in New York and at the national level, but he also spent much time in prison. He suffered a fatal heart attack while organizing an anti- VIETNAM WAR demonstration in New York City. The secretary of the army, supported by the attorney general, ruled that Thompson's ashes could not be interred in Arlington National Cemetery, but his wife got that judgment overturned in federal court after a three-year battle.

Thompson, Samuel (1735–1798) • REVOLUTIONARY WAR army officer and politician. Samuel Thompson was born in Maine while it was still a part of Massachusetts. An ardent leader of the SONS OF LIBERTY, he was very active in the early days of the rebellion. In April 1775 he led a party to Falmouth in a fruitless attempt to capture the HMS *Canceaux*. His actions there were known locally as "Thompson's War" and the British retaliated by burning most of Falmouth. Later Thompson was appointed brigadier general, and he led Cumberland County's Second Regiment in the ill-fated Penobscot expedition in 1779. After the war he was instrumental in Maine's movement for statehood, and donated the land for Bowdoin College.

Thompson submachine gun • a .45 inch-caliber submachine gun developed in the late 1920s that became the most common Allied submachine gun in WORLD WAR II. It had a detachable box-type magazine holding 20 or 30 rounds and an effective range of 100 meters.

Thor • a nuclear-armed, intermediate-range ballistic missile that was developed in the 1960s and installed internationally as part of the nuclear deterrent strategy; it was the predecessor to the ICBM.

three-decker • *n.* a sailing warship with three gun decks.

three-fifths clause • formally known as the Three-Fifths Compromise, a clause to allow a slave to be counted as three-fifths of a person for the purposes of taxation and representation in the Congress. It was proposed in July 1787 during the drafting of the U.S. Constitution at the Constitutional Convention. It was negated by the THIRTEENTH AMENDMENT.

three-star • *adj.* having or denoting the rank of lieutenant general, the third-highest military rank in the U.S. armed forces, distinguished by three stars on the uniform.

Thresher • a U.S. Navy submarine that sank off the coast of New England in April, 1963, with the loss of nearly 130 crew. The probable cause was major leakage in the water pipe system that, through a series of events, caused the reactor to fail at a point when the sub was too deep to rise to the surface under the backup system. As a result of the incident, much stricter safety features were incorporated into future submarine design.

threshold • **1** the beginning of that portion of the runway usable for landing. **2** the point at which military operations transition from one level to another, for example, a nuclear threshold is that point at which the transition from the use of conventional weapons to the use of nuclear weapons takes place.

Threshold Test Ban Treaty • an agreement signed by the United States and the USSR on July 3, 1974 and enacted on December 11, 1990. Following the LIMITED TEST BAN TREATY, it prohibited underground nuclear weapons tests with a yield greater than 150 kilotons and called for on-site inspections and the exchange of nuclear weapons test program data.

thrust bearing • a bearing designed to take a load in the direction of the axis of a shaft, especially one transmitting the thrust of a propeller shaft to the hull of a ship.

thrust block • a casting or frame carrying or containing the bearings on which the collars of a propeller shaft press.

thruster |ˈTHrəstər| • *n.* **1** a small rocket engine on a spacecraft, used to make alterations in its flight path or altitude. **2** a secondary jet or propeller on a ship or offshore rig, used for accurate maneuvering and maintenance of position.

thrust reverser • a device for reversing the flow of gas from a jet engine so as to produce a retarding backward force.

Thunderbolt • (**P-47**) an extremely effective single-seat single-engine fighter aircraft that saw duty in both the European and Pacific Theaters of WORLD WAR II. It first entered service in 1943, and remained in service until 1955.

More P-47s were built for the Allied air forces than any other fighter.

Thunderbolt II • (**A-10**) a twin-engine, subsonic, turbofan, tactical fighter/bomber capable of using air-to-surface-launched weapons in a close air support role. Short fields with unimproved surfaces are its normal takeoff/landing areas, and it is capable of long-range operation in a target area and can be refueled in the air. It carries an internally mounted 30 mm cannon that can destroy a variety of armored vehicles. See also A-10A.

Thunderbolt, Operation • the first of five offensives launched by U.N. forces during the KOREAN WAR in early 1951. The success of these offensives led President HARRY S. TRUMAN to invite the Communists to negotiate a ceasefire. Gen. DOUGLAS MACARTHUR, however, broadcast an ultimatum to the enemy commander that undermined the president's plan. After Congressman Joseph Martin released a letter from MacArthur in which the general repeated his criticism of the administration, Truman began the process which was to end with MacArthur's being relieved from command on April 11, 1951.

Thunderchief • (**F-105**) A large fighter/bomber that proved very effective in the VIETNAM WAR in spite of early problems during its development.

thunderflash • *n.* a noisy but harmless pyrotechnic device used especially in military exercises.

ticket • *n.* **1** a certificate or warrant, in particular, especially a certificate of qualification as a ship's master, pilot, or other crew member. **2** Brit. a certificate of discharge from the army. **3** a list of candidates put forward by a party in an election: *his presence on the Republican ticket.* **4** a set of principles or policies supported by a party in an election: *he stood for office on a strong right-wing, no-nonsense ticket.*

DERIVATIVES: **ticketless** *adj.*

***Ticonderoga*, USS** • **1** (**CV-14**) a carrier commissioned in May 1944. After intensive training in the West Indies, the carrier loaded provisions, fuel, aviation gas, seventy-seven new planes, and the Marine Corps aviation and defense units to accompany them at San Diego, then departed for Pearl Harbor. The *Ticonderoga* made significant contributions in Pacific Theater battles against the Japanese during WORLD WAR II. **2** (**CG-47**) the first of the Ticonderoga-class cruisers, a U.S. Navy cruiser armed with the model 3 AEGIS weapons system, two MK 45 5"/54-caliber lightweight gun mounts, two MK 26 guided missile launchers, two HARPOON missile quad-canister launchers, two MK 32 MOD 14 torpedo tubes, one 15 MOD close-in weapons systems, one MK 36 MOD 2 super rapid-blooming off-board chaff system, and two 50-caliber machine guns. It was delivered to the Navy in December 1982. See also GUIDED MISSILE CRUISER.

tidal basin • a basin for boats that is accessible or navigable only at high tide.

tide • *n.* **1** the alternate rising and falling of the sea, usually twice in each lunar day at a particular place, due to the attraction of the moon and sun: *the changing patterns of the tides | they were driven on by wind and tide.* **2** the water as affected by this: *the rising tide covered the wharf.* • *v.* (of a ship) float or drift in or out of a harbor by taking advantage of favoring tides.

tidemark • *n.* a mark left or reached by the sea on a shore at the highest or lowest point of a tide.

tide table • a table indicating the times of high and low tides at a particular place.

tidewater • *n.* **1** water brought or affected by tides. **2** an area that is affected by tides: *a large area of tidewater country.*

tideway • *n.* a channel in which a tide runs, especially the tidal part of a river.

tie • *v.* (**tying**) attach or fasten (someone or something) with string or similar cord: *the downed pilot was tied to a chair and interrogated | the sailors tied down the loose rigging.*

tie-down • *n.* **1** the fastening or securing of a load to its carrier by use of ropes, cables, or other means to prevent shifting during transport. **2** the material employed to secure a load in such a manner.

tie-up • *n.* a place for mooring a boat.

Tiger • World War II-era German tank. See TANKS, GERMAN, WORLD WAR II-ERA.

Tiger I • see TANKS, GERMAN, WORLD WAR II-ERA.

Tilghman, Benjamin Chew |ˈtilmən| (1821–1901) • U.S. army officer, inventor, and manufacturer. Born in Philadelphia, Pennsylvania, Tilghman graduated from the University of Pennsylvania in 1839 and went into manufacturing with his brother. When the CIVIL WAR began, Tilghman joined the Twenty-sixth Regiment of Pennsylvania Volunteers and commanded a company. He participated in all the key eastern battles of the ARMY OF THE POTOMAC, rising in rank to regimental commander before he was wounded at CHANCELLORSVILLE in May 1863. While recuperating, Tilghman was offered command of the Third Regiment of COLORED TROOPS, recruited in Philadelphia. He took his new unit to FORT SUMTER and Jacksonville, Florida, eventually earning promotion by brevet to brigadier general of volunteers. After the war he invented a new sandblasting process upon which he based a thriving business.

Tilghman, Tench |ˈtilmən| (1744–1786) • REVOLUTIONARY WAR army officer. Born in Talbot County, Maryland, Tench Tilghman graduated from what would become the University of Pennsylvania in 1761. When the Revolutionary War began he sold his business and joined a local infantry company as a lieutenant. He became a captain before being appointed as military secretary and aide to Gen. GEORGE WASHINGTON. He served in that position throughout the war, mostly without pay. Washington obtained a promotion to lieutenant colonel for Tilghman in early 1781, and when Lord CHARLES CORNWALLIS surrendered at YORKTOWN, Washington gave his faithful secretary the honor of delivering the news to Congress. After the war, Tilghman pursued commercial interests in Baltimore until he died there.

tiller • *n.* a horizontal bar fitted to the head of a boat's rudder post and used for steering.

time bomb • a bomb designed to explode at a preset time.

time fuze • a fuze that contains a graduated time element to regulate the time interval after which the fuze will function.

time of attack • the hour at which an attack is to be launched. If a line of departure is prescribed, it is the hour at which the line is to be crossed by the leading elements of the attack.

time of flight • in artillery and naval gunfire support, the time in seconds from the instant a weapon is fired, launched, or released from the delivery vehicle or weapons system to the instant it strikes or detonates.

time-sensitive targets • targets requiring immediate response because they pose (or will soon pose) a clear and present danger to friendly forces or because they are highly lucrative, fleeting targets of opportunity.

tin hat • informal, chiefly Brit. a soldier's steel helmet.

Tinian • one of the Marianas Islands, first taken from the Japanese by the Marines in 1944 and thereafter developed as an airbase for bombing raids on Japan. The components of the "LITTLE BOY" bomb were assembled here.

tip-and-run • *n.* (of a military raid) executed swiftly and followed by immediate withdrawal.

Tippecanoe, Battle of • a battle fought November 7, 1811, on the Tippecanoe River in Indiana between Shawnee and U.S. forces. A tribal alliance organized by TECUMSEH and his brother threatened to impede the progress of white settlement of the area by undermining concessions made by other leaders. Both sides suffered equal losses but white settlement proceeded and the battle was seen as a victory for Gen. WILLIAM HENRY HARRISON, helping to establish him as a presidential contender later.

Titan II • a massive intercontinental ballistic missile with a nuclear warhead that was developed during the COLD WAR for nuclear deterrence. It was first installed at various locations in 1962, and decommissioned in the 1980s.

Tito, Marshall (1892–1980) • born Josip Broz near Zagreb, Croatia, and a locksmith by trade, Tito was a Yugoslav revolutionary and eventually occupied high-level political positions as a Communist, serving as the secretary-general of the Communist Party (League of Communists) and then its president (1939–1980). He was supreme commander of the Yugoslav Partisans during WORLD WAR II (1941–1945), and, after the war, of the Yugoslav People's Army (1945–1980). He was marshal (1943–1980), premier (1945–1953), and then the first president of the republic of Yugoslavia from 1953 to 1980. He was the prime mover in the Yugoslavian socialist federation that lasted until 1991, and the first Communist leader to challenge Soviet control in Eastern Europe.

TMD • *abbr.* theater missile defense.

TNT • *abbr.* the high explosive trinitrotoluene, commonly known as dynamite.

TNT equivalent • a measure of the energy released from the detonation of a nuclear weapon, or from the explosion of a given quantity of fissionable material, in terms of the amount of TNT (trinitrotoluene) that could release the same amount of energy when exploded.

toad stabber • slang (also **toad sticker**) (in the CIVIL WAR) a bayonet, sword, or knife. See also PIG-STICKER.

Tojo, Hideki (1884–1948) • a Japanese soldier and prime minister. After graduating from the Imperial Military Academy and the Military Staff College, Tojo was briefly a military attaché at the Japanese embassy in Berlin after WORLD WAR I, but, noted as a talented administrative and skilled field commander, he became commander of the 1st Infantry Regiment of the Japanese Army. Having served as chief of staff of the Kwantung Army in Manchuria during Japan's occupation, he returned to Japan to take up his duties as vice-minister of war in 1938 and actively supported Japan's Tripartite Pact with Germany and Italy (1940). Premier Prince Konoe Fumimaro appointed him to his cabinet as minister of war, and Tojo became prime minister in 1941. An efficient bureaucrat and committed militarist, Tojo led Japan's war effort after its attack on the U.S. military installation at PEARL HARBOR (1941), and, after initial victories in the Pacific arena, Japan's fortunes turned. and he became chief of the General Staff. He was removed from that position after the U.S. invasion of the MARIANAS ISLANDS in mid-July 1944, and his entire cabinet resigned only two days later. Having failed in a suicide attempt after Japan's surrender in September 1945, Tojo recovered and was then indicted and tried for war crimes in April 1946 by the INTERNATIONAL MILITARY TRIBUNAL FOR THE FAR EAST. He was found guilty as charged and hanged.

Tokyo Rose (1916–) • radio propagandist. born Ikuko Toguri in Los Angeles, California, Iva Toguri graduated from UCLA in 1941 and ended up stranded in Japan after the Japanese bombed PEARL HARBOR (1941) and the United States entered WORLD WAR II. The Japanese government regarded her as an "enemy alien" after she refused to become a Japanese citizen. Married to Felipe d'Aquino, Iva Toguri d'Aquino found a job as an announcer at Radio Tokyo, where she met two prisoners of war (one Australian, the other a U.S. citizen) who were forced to write Japanese propaganda intended to demoralize Allied soldiers. However, they planned to subvert the project and convinced her to work as the announcer and she made her first broadcast in November 1943. When she was able to return to the United States in 1947, people demanded she be put on trial, which began in 1949. Found guilty, she was sentenced to ten years in prison and fined $10,000, but she served only six years of her sentence and was released in 1956 for good behavior. Many years later, the truth of her circumstances during WORLD WAR II came to light, and she was pardoned by President GERALD FORD in January 1977.

Tokyo War Crimes Trials • an International War Crimes Tribunal for the Far East was established in Tokyo in January 1946 by the Supreme Commander Allied Powers Gen. DOUGLAS MACARTHUR. The tribunal consisted of judges from each of the eleven countries at war with Japan during WORLD WAR II. Twenty-eight major Japanese military and civilian leaders were tried between May 1946 and November 1948. All but two of the defendants were found guilty of conspiracy to wage aggressive war, and all were convicted on other charges of war crimes.

tolerance dose • the amount of radiation that may be received by an individual within a specified period with negligible results.

tomahawk |ˈtäməˌhôk| • *n.* a light ax used as a tool or weapon by American Indians. • *v.* strike or cut with or as if with a tomahawk.

Tomahawk • (**BGM-109**) a versatile, long-range cruise missile with surface or air launching capability, carrying a nuclear or conventional warhead. It has wings that protrude during flight after the initial rocket burn that extend its effective range.entry was Tomahawk cruise missile

Tomb of the Unknown Soldier (also **Tomb of the Unknowns**) • a memorial to soldiers killed in battle, located at ARLINGTON NATIONAL CEMETERY in Arlington, Virginia. It was originally established on March 4, 1921, when Congress approved the burial of an unidentified American soldier from WORLD WAR I to represent the sacrifice of the average soldier. The remains of unknown soldiers from WORLD WAR II, the KOREAN WAR, and the VIETNAM WAR have since been interred there. It has never officially been named.

Tomcat • (**F-14**) a large powerful two-seat shipboard fighter aircraft, produced in 1972 and one of the most effective heavy fighters. Its weapon system, combined with the PHOENIX missile, make it unrivaled for long-distance interceptions.

The F-14 is expensive and maintenance-intensive; the only export customer was Iran.

Tommy (also **tommy**) • *n.* (pl. **-ies**) informal a British private soldier. [ORIGIN: nickname for the given name *Thomas*; from a use of the name *Thomas Atkins* in examples of completed official forms in the British army during the 19th cent.]

tommy gun • informal a type of submachine gun.

ORIGIN: 1920s: contraction of *Thompson gun*, named by its designer after John T. *Thompson* (1860–1940), the American army officer who conceived the idea for it.

tompion |ˈtämpēən| • *n.* variant spelling of TAMPION.

ton (abbr.: **t** also **tn**) • *n.* **1** (also **short ton**) a unit of weight equal to 2,000 lb avoirdupois (907.19 kg). **2** (also **long ton**) a unit of weight equal to 2,240 lb avoirdupois (1016.05 kg). **3** short for metric ton. **4** (also **displacement ton**) a unit of measurement of a ship's weight representing the weight of water it displaces with the load line just immersed, equal to 2,240 lb or 35 cu. ft. (0.99 cubic meters).

Tonkin, Gulf of • see GULF OF TONKIN.

tonnage |ˈtənij| • *n.* **1** weight in tons, especially of cargo or freight: *road convoys carry more tonnage.* **2** the size or carrying capacity of a ship measured in tons. **3** shipping considered in terms of total carrying capacity: *the port's total tonnage.*

Toombs, Robert Augustus (1810–1885) • U.S. congressman, Confederate cabinet member, and Confederate general. Toombs was born in Wilkes County, Georgia, and graduated from Union College and the University of Virginia Law School. He built up a fortune based on slaves and real estate in Georgia, serving the state for four terms as a representative before being selected twice to be a senator. He became the first Confederate secretary of state, but served only a few months before resigning after securing a brigadier general's commission. He was the most prominent political general in the ARMY OF NORTHERN VIRGINIA, and handled his brigade of mostly Georgia troops poorly during the SEVEN DAYS' battles and SECOND BULL RUN (1862). He did, however, do very well holding Burnside's Bridge at ANTIETAM (1862) for many hours with only five hundred men against thousands of Union attackers. When he did not get the promotion he believed he had earned there he resigned, fulfilling a promise to his wife that he would leave the army after distinguishing himself in a big battle. He spent the rest of the war quarreling with the Confederate government, and fled to Europe for two years after the war. Though he never sought a pardon and could not vote or hold office, he still dominated Georgia's constitutional convention in 1877. He died in Washington, Georgia, suffering from alcoholism and blindness.

toothless • *adj.* lacking genuine force or effectiveness: *laws that are well intentioned but toothless.*

DERIVATIVES: **toothlessly** *adv.* **toothlessness** *n.*

toothpick • slang (World War I) a bayonet.

The French *cure-dent*, "toothpick," also means bayonet.

top • *n.* a platform at the head of a ship's mast, especially (in a sailing ship) a platform around the head of each of the lower masts, serving to extend the topmast shrouds.

topgallant |täp'gælənt; tə'gæl-| • *n.* **1** (also **topgallant mast**) the section of a square-rigged sailing ship's mast immediately above the topmast. **2** (also **topgallant sail**) a sail set on such a mast.

topmast |'täp,mæst; -məst| • *n.* the second section of a square-rigged sailing ship's mast, immediately above the lower mast.

topographic map • a map that presents the vertical position of features in measurable form as well as their horizontal positions.

topsail |'täpsəl; -,sāl| • *n.* **1** a sail set on a ship's topmast. **2** a fore-and-aft sail set above the gaff.

top secret • **1** of the highest secrecy; highly confidential: *the experiments were top secret | a top-secret mission.* **2** (of information or documents) given the highest security classification, above secret.

topside • *n.* (often **topsides**) the upper part of a ship's side, above the waterline. • *adv.* on or toward the upper decks of a ship: *we stayed topside.*

Torbert, Alfred Thomas Archimedes (1833–1880) • Union army officer and diplomat. Born in Delaware, Torbert graduated from WEST POINT in 1855 and went into the infantry. When the Civil War began he was ordered to New Jersey to recruit volunteers, and was appointed colonel of the 1st New Jersey Volunteer Infantry. He commanded that unit during the PENINSULAR CAMPAIGN in 1862 before getting a brigade in the VI Corps of the ARMY OF THE POTOMAC. He was promoted to brigadier general and fought in all the key eastern battles through GETTYSBURG (1863). In April 1864 he took command of the First Cavalry Division under PHILIP H. SHERIDAN. Torbert performed admirably with Sheridan, distinguishing himself on many occasions and rising to the rank of major general of regulars and command of the Army of the Shenandoah. After the war Torbert served in diplomatic posts in El Salvador, Cuba, and Paris. He was lost at sea off the coast of Florida sailing to visit business interests in Mexico.

Torch, Operation • the invasion of French North Africa by American and British forces in November 1942; the first major joint Allied offensive in WORLD WAR II. Beginning on Nov. 8, four days after the British stopped German general ERWIN ROMMEL in Egypt, the Anglo-American landings commenced with port assaults and nighttime beach landings. The Allies aided Free French rebels and overwhelmed VICHY French resistance. As a result of the invasion, ADOLF HITLER ordered the German Army to occupy Vichy France and rushed troops to Tunisia before the Americans could conquer it. By May 13, 1943, though, 250,000 German and Italian troops had surrendered to the Allied forces, ending the North Africa Campaign.

torpedo • *n.* (pl. **-oes**) a cigar-shaped self-propelled underwater missile designed to be fired from a ship or submarine or dropped into the water from an aircraft and to explode on reaching a target. • *v.* (**-oes, -oed**) attack or sink (a ship) with a torpedo or torpedoes.

DERIVATIVES: **torpedolike** *adj.*

torpedo boat • a small, fast, light warship armed with torpedoes. See PT BOAT.

torpedo bomber • an ordinary bomber reconfigured to carry small anti-ship torpedoes, allowing it to stand off from its target and attack from a greater range.

torpedo defense net • a net employed to close an inner harbor to torpedoes fired from the sea or to protect an individual ship that is at anchor or underway.

torpedo net • a net made of steel wire, hung in the water around an anchored ship to intercept torpedoes.

torpedo tube • a tube in a submarine or other ship from which torpedoes are fired by the use of compressed air or an explosive charge.

toss • *v.* move or cause to move from side to side or back and forth: *the yachts were tossed* *around in the harbor like toys* | (**-tossed**) *a storm-tossed sea.*

toss bombing • a method of bombing where an aircraft flies on a line toward the target, pulls up in a vertical plane, releasing the bomb at an angle that will compensate for the effect of gravity drop on the bomb. Compare with LOFT BOMBING, OVER-THE-SHOULDER BOMBING.

total dosage attack • a chemical operation that does not involve a time limit within which to produce the required toxic level.

totalitarianism • *n.* a system of government that is centralized and dictatorial and requires complete subservience to the state.

total war • (**total warfare**) a war that is unrestricted in terms of the weapons used, the territory or combatants involved, or the objectives pursued, especially one in which the laws of war are disregarded.

Totten, Joseph Gilbert (1788–1864) • U.S. army officer and engineer. Born in New Haven, Connecticut, Totten graduated from WEST POINT in 1805 with a commission as a second lieutenant of engineers. He served as the chief engineer of the army on the Niagara front during the WAR OF 1812, earning brevets to major and lieutenant colonel. For twenty-four years after the war he was engaged in coastal defense, river, and harbor works. In December 1838 he was promoted to colonel and named chief engineer of the army and inspector at West Point. He held those posts until his death, far longer than any other officer ever did. During the MEXICAN WAR (1846–48) he was WINFIELD SCOTT's chief engineer and won a brevet to brigadier general for planning the siege of VERACRUZ. He was still chief of engineers when the CIVIL WAR began, and received a permanent promotion to brigadier general in 1863 when the Corps of Engineers and Topographical Engineers were merged. He received another brevet, to major general, in April 1864, but died the next day in Washington, D.C.

touchdown • *n.* the contact, or moment of contact, of an aircraft or spacecraft with the landing surface.

touchhole • *n.* a small hole in early firearms through which the charge is ignited.

tour • *n.* (also **tour of duty**) a period of duty on military or diplomatic service: *he was haunted by his tour of duty in Vietnam.*

TOW |tō| • *abbr.* tube-launched, optically guided, wire-guided (missile).

towboat • *n.* see TUGBOAT.

Tower, John Henry (1885–1955) • U.S. naval officer and aviator. Born in Rome, Georgia, John Henry Tower graduated from the U.S. NAVAL ACADEMY in 1906. In 1911 he became only the third naval officer to qualify as a pilot. During his first ten years as an aviator he set up naval air stations, held key staff positions in Washington, and commanded the flight of three Navy-Curtis seaplanes that tried to fly the Atlantic in May 1919. He later served as captain of the carriers *Langley* and *Saratoga*, and by 1939 was a rear admiral and chief of the Bureau of Aeronautics. He oversaw a massive buildup in the naval air arm before becoming a vice admiral and commander of the Air Force, Pacific Fleet in 1942. Two years later he became deputy to Admiral CHESTER W. NIMITZ, commander of Pacific Ocean Areas and Pacific Fleet. Tower then commanded Task Force 38 and the Fifth Fleet before reaching the rank of full admiral and succeeding Admiral Raymond Spruance as the theater commander. Tower retired from the navy in 1947, serving as vice-president of Pan-American World Airways until 1953.

Townshend Acts • four acts of the British Parliament in 1767 that imposed duties on the import of paint, glass, paper, lead, and tea to the North American colonies. The acts also called for quartering of British troops in the colonies. Though eventually repealed (except for the tax on tea), the acts were the source of resentment and led to the famous charge of "taxation without representation" and directly to the BOSTON MASSACRE.

toxin agent • a poison formed as a specific secretion product in the metabolism of a vegetable or animal organism as distinguished from inorganic poisons. Such poisons can also be manufactured by synthetic processes.

Tpr • *abbr.* Trooper.

TRAC • see U.S. ARMY TRAINING AND DOCTRINE COMMAND ANALYSIS CENTER.

tracer • *n.* a bullet or shell whose course is made visible in flight by a trail of flames or smoke, used to assist in aiming.

track[1] • *n.* **1** (usually **tracks**) a mark or line of marks left by a person, animal, or vehicle in passing: *he followed the tracks made by the police cars in the snow.* **2** the course or route followed by someone or something (used especially in talking about their pursuit by others): *I didn't want the Russians* ***on my track.*** **3** a continuous line of rails on a railroad. **4** a continuous articulated metal band around the wheels of a heavy vehicle such as a tank or bulldozer, intended to facilitate movement over rough or soft ground. • *v.* follow the course or trail of (someone or something), typically in order to find them or note their location at various points: *secondary radars that track the aircraft in flight.*

track[2] • *v.* tow (a boat) along a waterway from the bank.

tracking • *n.* **1** the precise and continuous position-finding of targets by radar, optical, or other means. **2** in air intercept, a code meaning, "By my evaluation, target is steering true course indicated."

tractor group • in an amphibious operation, a group of landing ships that carries the amphibious vehicles of the landing force.

Tracy, Benjamin Franklin (1830–1915) • U.S. army officer, jurist, and secretary of the navy. Born in Tioga County, New York, Tracy earned a CONGRESSIONAL MEDAL OF HONOR commanding the 109th New York Regiment in the BATTLE OF THE WILDERNESS. Worn out after that campaign, he returned home to recuperate, and agreed to administer the draft rendezvous and prisoner-of-war camp at Elmira. He had to deal with riots and protests over the draft and overcrowding and malnourishment among the prisoners. After the war Southern Congressmen compared the conditions at Elmira to ANDERSONVILLE, but Tracy had tried to improve the situation as best he could. He went back to his legal career until he was chosen by President BENJAMIN HARRISON to be secretary of the navy in 1889. Tracy seized upon broad political support, new technology, and the seapower theories of ALFRED THAYER MAHAN to secure the first true battleships of the steel navy along with other vessels. Tracy became the administration's most prominent advocate for an expansionist foreign policy, which also benefited his navy. He also improved training and administration of the service before he left office in 1893. The press called him "the father of the fighting navy," and his fleet performed admirably in the SPANISH-AMERICAN WAR. He died in Brooklyn from complications after experiencing an automobile accident on his way to a GRAND ARMY OF THE REPUBLIC parade.

Tracy, Nathaniel (1751–1796) • REVOLUTIONARY WAR privateer and merchant. Born in Newbury (later Newburyport), Massachusetts, Nathaniel Tracy received his M.A. from Harvard in 1772. When the Revolution broke out, he owned and outfitted the first American privateer and received the first letter of marque from the Continental Congress. He sent twenty-four cruisers to sea that captured 120 vessels, and also owned 110 merchant ships. He made a great deal of money in the first two years of the war, but in 1777 he lost all but one of his privateers and 97 of his merchant ships. He also provided many donations to the American forces, and lost money dealing with the French and Spanish. He served in a number of posts in state government, and was a charter member of the American Academy of Arts and Sciences. He was ruined by the war, and died in genteel poverty in Newburyport.

trade • *n.* (usually **trades**) a trade wind: *the north-east trades.*

trader • *n.* a merchant ship.

Trading with the Enemies Act • an act passed by Congress in October 1917, after U.S. entry into WORLD WAR I, to restrict the content of foreign-language publications. It allowed censorship of mail and other communications with foreign countries and extended the power of the Postmaster General over the American foreign-language press.

TRADOC |ˈtrāˌdäk| • *abbr.* Training and Doctrine Command.

traffic density • the average number of vehicles that occupy one mile (or one kilometer) of road space, expressed in vehicles per mile (or per kilometer).

traffic flow • the total number of vehicles passing a given point in a given time, expressed in vehicles per hour.

traffic pattern • the traffic flow that is prescribed for aircraft landing at, taxiing on, and taking off from an airport. The usual components of a traffic pattern are upwind leg, crosswind leg, downwind leg, base leg, and final approach.

trail • *n.* the rear end of a gun carriage, resting or sliding on the ground when the gun is unlimbered. • *v.* follow (a person or animal), typically by using marks, signs, or scent left behind.

PHRASES: **at the trail** with a rifle hanging balanced in one hand and (in Britain) parallel to the ground. **trail arms** let a rifle hang in such a way.

Trail of Tears • the forced removal of nearly 20,000 Cherokee from their ancestral lands in Georgia and the Carolinas in 1838 and 1839, following the refusal of state and federal officials to honor their claim to the land; a small group of Cherokee had ceded the lands to the U.S., though the Supreme Court invalidated this cession. Nearly 4,000 Cherokee died en route to the new INDIAN TERRITORY (later, Oklahoma), owing to bad weather, poor planning, and the cruelty of the troops that escorted them.

train • *v.* **1** teach (a person or animal) a particular skill or type of behavior through practice and instruction over a period of time: *the recruits were trained to endure hardships far beyond the ordinary | the dogs are trained to sniff out illegal stowaways.* **2** (**trained**) cause (a mental or physical faculty) to be sharp, discerning, or developed as a result of instruction or practice: *an alert mind and trained eye give astute evaluations.* **3** (**train something on**) point or aim something, typically a gun: *the officer trained his gun on the side door.* • *n.* **1** a trail of gunpowder for firing an explosive charge. **2** a series of railroad cars moved as a unit by a locomotive or by integral motors: *a freight train | the journey took two hours **by train**.* **3** a succession of vehicles or pack animals traveling in the same direction: *a camel train.*

training • *n.* the action of teaching a person or animal a particular skill or type of behavior: *in-service training for staff.*

Training and Doctrine Command • (**TRADOC**) established in July 1973 as one of the final structural changes accomplished by a major reorganization of the U.S. Army, TRADOC assumed responsibility for the command and readiness of all divisions and corps in the continental United States and the installations they occupy. The TRADOC commander develops and manages the U.S. Army's training programs, develops training doctrine, and provides training support for individual and group training in units.

training ship • **1** a ship on which people are taught sailing and related skills. **2** any ship used by the U.S. Navy to train personnel.

tramp • *n.* a cargo vessel that carries goods among many different ports rather than sailing a fixed route: *a tramp steamer.*

Transcontinental Treaty • see ADAMS-ONÍS TREATY.

transient • *n.* **1** (usually **transients**) personnel, ships, or craft stopping temporarily at a post, station or port to which they are not assigned or attached, and having destination elsewhere. **2** an independent merchant ship calling at a port and sailing within 12 hours, and for which routing instructions to a further port have been promulgated. **3** an individual awaiting orders, transport, etc., at a post or station to which he or she is not attached or assigned.

transmission frequency • see PULSE REPETITION FREQUENCY.

Trans-Mississippi Department • an area of the southwestern United States west of the Mississippi, including Texas, Arizona, and New Mexico, that was under Confederate control during the last half of the CIVIL WAR. The Trans-Mississippi Department was headquartered at Houston, Texas, under the command of Gen. E. KIRBY SMITH, and was the last major Confederate force to surrender to Federal troops, on May 26, 1865.

transom |ˈtrænsəm| • *n.* **1** the flat surface forming the stern of a vessel. **2** a horizontal beam reinforcing the stern of a vessel.

transonic • *adj.* of or pertaining to the speed of a body in a surrounding fluid when the relative speed of the fluid is subsonic in some places and supersonic in others. This is encountered when passing from subsonic to supersonic speeds and vice versa.

transponder • *n.* a receiver-transmitter that will generate a reply signal, upon proper interrogation.

transport • *v.* |trænsˈpôrt| take or carry (people or goods) from one place to another by means of a vehicle, aircraft, or ship: *the bulk of freight was transported by truck.* • *n.* **1** a system or means of conveying people or goods from place to place by means of a vehicle, aircraft, or ship: *air transport.* **2** the action of transporting something or the state of being transported: *the transport of crude oil.* **3** a large vehicle, ship, or aircraft used to carry troops or stores.

transport aircraft • aircraft that are designed for transporting personnel or cargo. Such aircraft are classified on the basis of their range at normal cruising conditions: Short-range—not to exceed 1,200 nautical miles; medium-range—capable of operating between 1,200 and 3,500 nautical miles; long-range—able to operate at distances of more than 3,500 nautical miles. See also STRATEGIC TRANSPORT AIRCRAFT; TACTICAL TRANSPORT AIRCRAFT.

Transportation Command • see U.S. TRANSPORTATION COMMAND.

transportation component command • (**TCC**) the three component commands of the U.S. Transportation Command: Air Force Air Mobility Command, Navy Sealift Command, and Army Military Traffic Management Command. Each command is a major command of its Service and organizes, trains, and equips its forces as specified by law, and, in addition, continues to perform Service-unique missions. See also UNITED STATES TRANSPORTATION COMMAND.

Transportation Corps • the combat service support branch of the U.S. Army responsible for the movement of passengers and materiel.

transport capacity • the number of persons or the weight or volume of the load that can be carried by means of transport under given conditions.

transport plane • aircraft designed and used, without modification, to transport cargo and personnel. See also AIRCRAFT.

transport vehicle • a motor vehicle designed and used, without modification to its chassis, to transport cargo and personnel. See also VEHICLE.

transship (also **tranship**) • *v.* (**-shipped, -shipping**) transfer (cargo) from one ship or other form of transport to another.
DERIVATIVES: **transshipment** *n.*

Tran Van Tra (1918–1996) • Vietnamese military leader. Raised in southern Vietnam, Tra began his military career fighting against the French in the VIETMINH resistance movement during the 1930s. He occupied a variety of posts in the North Vietnamese Army after Vietnam was partitioned by the GENEVA AGREEMENT ON INDOCHINA in 1954, but was sent back to the south in 1963 to become the leader of the VIETCONG, the guerillas who fought the South Vietnamese military and their U.S. advisers. A highly successful commander on the battlefield, he was appointed the military head of the underground Communist government in South Vietnam. In spite of numerous disagreements with Party leaders about strategy, he was called back to North Vietnam for a brief time to assist with the planning of the final assault on Saigon in the mid-1970s.In 1982, Tra, surprised by how little credit he and other military leaders from South Vietnam were being given for their part in the victory, published a personal account of the war in 1982, but it was immediately censored. Out of favor in Hanoi, Tra joined with other former army officials to found a war veterans organization. The group, however, was extremely vocal in its criticism of the government and it was banned in 1990.

trapeze • *n.* a harness attached by a cable to a dinghy's mast, enabling a sailor to balance the boat by leaning backward out over the windward side.

traverse |trəˈvərs| • *v.* **1** travel across or through: *he traversed the forest.* **2** cross a hill or mountain by means of a series of sideways movements: *I often use this route, eventually traversing around the headwall.* **3** turn (a large gun or other device on a pivot) to face a different direction. **4** (of such a gun or device) be turned in this way. • *n.* **1** an act of traversing something. **2** a zigzag course followed by a ship because winds or currents prevent it from sailing directly toward its destination. **3** a mechanism enabling a large gun to be turned to face a different direction. **4** a pair of right-angled bends incorporated in a trench to avoid enfilading fire.

Travis, William Barrett (1809–1836) • Texan patriot and military leader. Born in Cambridge, South Carolina, Travis taught school and became a lawyer at age 20. In 1831, he immigrated to Texas and became involved in the Texas independence movement. In December 1835, he was appointed lieutenant colonel in the Army of the Republic of Texas and was sent to hold San Antonio for the Republic. He organized a force of some 180 volunteers to defend an old mission which became famous as the ALAMO. On February 23, 1836, Mexican forces under Gen. ANTONIO LÓPEZ DE SANTA ANNA laid siege to the Alamo and carried the stronghold by assault on March 6, 1836. Travis died with the other defenders.

treason • *n.* violation of the allegiance owed to one's sovereign or state; the betrayal of one's country.

Treason Act • an act passed on July 17, 1862 to prohibit the crime of treason against the U.S. government and to counter disloyalty as it was defined during the CIVIL WAR. An individual convicted could be sentenced to death as authorized in the 1790 Treason Act, but it also allowed for a lighter sentence that included imprisonment and a fine at the discretion of the court.

Treaty on Conventional Armed Forces in Europe • see CFE.

trebuchet |ˌtrebyəˈsHet| • *n.* a machine used in medieval siege warfare for hurling large stones or other missiles.

trench • *n.* **1** a long, narrow ditch. **2** such a ditch dug by troops to provide a place of shelter from enemy fire. **3** (**trenches**) a connected system of such ditches forming an army's line. **4** (**the trenches**) the battlefields of northern France and Belgium in WORLD WAR I: *the slaughter in the trenches created a new cynicism.* • *v.* dig a trench or trenches in (the ground): *the soldiers trenched a long line of defense.*

trench coat • **1** a loose, belted, double-breasted raincoat in a military style. **2** a lined or padded waterproof coat worn by soldiers.

trench fever • **1** in WORLD WAR I, a highly contagious rickettsial disease transmitted by lice that infested soldiers in the trenches. **2** fever, aches and pains, and homesickness suffered by soldiers.

trench foot • a disease of the feet caused by exposure to cold and damp, a scourge of soldiers in the trench warfare of WORLD WAR I. Called JUNGLE ROT in WORLD WAR II and PADDY FOOT in the VIETNAM WAR.

trench interment (also **trench burial**) • a method of interment in which remains are placed head-to-toe. It is used only for temporary multiple burials.

trench mortar • a light simple mortar designed to propel a bomb into enemy trenches.

trench mouth • ulcerative gingivitis, a disease that causes ulceration and bleeding of the gums, caused by adenoidal-pharyngeal-conjunctival viruses that result from poor oral hygiene.

trench warfare • a type of combat in which opposing troops fight from trenches facing each other.

Trent affair • the seizing of two Confederate commissioners from the British ship *Trent* by Captain CHARLES WILKES in the U.S. warship *San Jacinto*, while the men were enroute to Europe with the aim of raising support for the Confederacy. The seizure of the men, in November, 1861, without bringing the ship to port was seen as a violation of the laws of the sea, and applauded in the Union but the source of indignation in Britain, which threatened to side with and support the Confederacy. The conflict was resolved through diplomatic channels and the men were released in January 1862.

Trenton, Battle of • a battle of the REVOLUTIONARY WAR following a surprise attack of Continental troops under the command of GEORGE WASHINGTON on British and Hessian troops at Trenton, New Jersey. Washington and his men crossed the icy Delaware River on Christmas Day, 1776, and attacked the next day, completely surprising the British. It was the first American victory of the war, and helped to restore American morale.

trestle |ˈtresəl| • *n.* **1** a framework consisting of a horizontal beam supported by two pairs of sloping legs, used in pairs to support a flat surface such as a tabletop. **2** (also **trestlework**) an open braced framework used to support an elevated structure such as a bridge. **3** (also **trestletree**) each of a pair of horizontal pieces on a sailing ship's lower mast supporting the topmast.

triage |trēˈäzH; ˈtrēˌäzH| • *n.* the evaluation and classification of casualties for purposes of treatment and evacuation. It consists of the immediate sorting of patients according to type and seriousness of injury and likelihood of survival, and the establishment of priority for treatment and evacuation to assure medical care of the greatest benefit to the largest number.

triangulation • *n.* **1** (in surveying) the tracing and measurement of a series or network of triangles in order to determine the distances and relative positions of points spread over a territory or region, especially by measuring the length of one side of each triangle and deducing its angles and the length of the other two sides by observation from this baseline. **2** formation of or division into triangles. **3** (in navigation) the location of an unknown point by using a triangle with two known points and the unknown point as the vertices.

trick • *n.* a sailor's turn at the helm, usually lasting for two or four hours.

Trident • an Ohio-class submarine from which the Trident II solid-propellant ballistic missile can be launched.

Trident I • (**UGM-96A**) a submarine-launched ballistic missile designed for use in Trident submarines or retrofitted to POSEIDON submarines. It is equipped with advanced guidance, nuclear warheads, and a maneuverable bus that can deploy warheads to separate targets.

Trident II • (**UGM-133A**) a submarine-launched ballistic missile designed for a Trident submarine. It is larger than the Trident I and can be used against hard targets.

Trident submarine missile patrol • underwater patrols by U.S. Ohio-class and Royal Navy Vanguard-class submarines armed with

TRIDENT D-5 SLBMs. Such patrols can last several months.

Trilateral Commission • a nongovernmental organization for promoting world trade and economic stability, particularly in regard to North America, Europe, and Japan, the 'three sides' referred to in the group's name. It was founded in New York City in 1973 by David Rockefeller, chairman of the board of directors of Chase Manhattan Bank. The commission consists of about 325 influential people with backgrounds primarily in banking, business, politics, academics, and news media. The commission holds annual planning meetings and also issues several reports per year on topics of concern to its members. Because of its influential membership, the commission is able to play a significant role in shaping public policy.

Trilateral Negotiations • talks among the United States, the United Kingdom, and the Federal Republic of Germany in 1966–67 concerning the defense of the NATO alliance against the perceived threat of the Soviet Union. Specific topics included troop numbers and their funding, and the placement of strategic nuclear and conventional weapons.

trim • *v.* **1** adjust (sails) to take best advantage of the wind. **2** adjust the forward and after drafts of (a vessel) by changing the distribution of weight on board, especially cargo and ballast. **3** keep or adjust the degree to which (an aircraft) can be maintained at a constant altitude without any control forces being present. • *n.* **1** the degree to which an aircraft can be maintained at a constant altitude without any control forces being present: *the pilot's only problem was the need to constantly readjust the trim.* **2** the difference between a vessel's forward and after drafts, especially as it affects its navigability.

PHRASES: **in trim** in good order.

Trimble, Isaac Ridgway (1802–1888) • Confederate army officer. Born in Culpepper County, Virginia, Trimble graduated from WEST POINT in 1822. He left the army in 1832 and worked as the chief engineer for a number of railroads. In August 1861 he was appointed a brigadier general in command of a brigade in RICHARD S. EWELL's division. He rendered distinguished service under STONEWALL JACKSON in the SHENANDOAH VALLEY campaign, and Jackson called Trimble's action taking the Union supply base at Manassas Junction in the Second Bull Run campaign (1862) "the most brilliant that has come under my observation during the present war." In January 1863 Trimble, though recovering from a wound suffered at Groveton, was promoted to major general. He rejoined the ARMY OF NORTHERN VIRGINIA in June 1863 as a supernumerary with Ewell's Second Corps. Trimble was wounded and captured leading two brigades in GEORGE E. PICKETT's famous charge at GETTYSBURG (1863). Federal surgeons amputated his leg.

Trinity • code name for the U.S. atomic bomb tests at Alamogordo, New Mexico, in 1945.

Trinity Site • an area of the desert in New Mexico where the first atomic bomb was tested at 5:29:45 am on July 16, 1945. Trinity Site is located on the WHITE SANDS MISSILE RANGE, sixty miles (ninety-seven km) northwest of Alamogordo and 110 miles (177 km) south of Albuquerque.

trip • *v.* **1** release and raise (an anchor) from the seabed by means of a buoyed line attached to the anchor's crown. **2** turn (a yard or other object) from a horizontal to a vertical position for lowering.

triphibious • *adj.* capable of assaulting a hostile shore using air, naval, and landing (ground) forces.

triplane • *n.* an airplane that has three wings positioned at separate levels above each other.

tripod • *n.* a three-legged stand for supporting a gun, camera, or other apparatus.

DERIVATIVES: **tripodal** *adj.*

ORIGIN: early 17th cent.: via Latin from Greek *tripous, tripod-*, from *tri-* 'three' + *pous, pod-* 'foot.'

Tripolitan War • see BARBARY WARS.

tripwire |ˈtripˌwīr| • *n.* **1** a wire stretched close to the ground, working a trap, explosion, or alarm when disturbed and serving to detect or prevent people or animals entering an area. **2** a comparatively weak military force employed as a first line of defense, engagement with which will trigger the intervention of strong forces: *if these peacekeeping efforts fail, they should have the function of a tripwire | the placing of tripwire forces on disputed borders.*

triumph • *n.* **1** a great victory or achievement: *a garden built to celebrate Napoleon's many triumphs.* **2** the state of being victorious or successful: *the king returned home* ***in triumph.*** • *v.* achieve a victory; be successful: *capitalism seems to have* ***triumphed over*** *socialism.*

triumphalism |trīˈəmfəˌlizəm| • *n.* excessive exultation over one's success or achievements (used especially in a political context): *an air of triumphalism reigns in his administration | the poem lampoons the country's military triumphalism.*

DERIVATIVES: **triumphalist** *adj.* & *n.*

TROA • *abbr.* The Retired Officers Association.

Trobriand, Régis Dénis de |ˈtrōbrēˌænd; -ənd| (1816–1897) • French aristocrat, U.S. army officer, writer. Born near Tours, France to a general in the army of the Restoration, Régis Dénis de Trobriand trained to be a soldier and lawyer before becoming a writer. He married an American in 1841 and was writing for a French language newspaper in New York when the CIVIL WAR broke out. He accepted American citizenship and the colonelcy of the 55th New York Infantry in 1861, and fought in most of the key battles of the ARMY OF THE POTOMAC. His most famous service came while he commanded a brigade in the III Corps on the second day at GETTYSBURG, when his unit suffered heavy casualties. He finished the war as a division commander and brevet major general. His lively memoirs, published in France in 1868 and the United States in 1889, are among the most quoted from the war. He remained in the army, commanding western forts and military districts, executing winter campaigns against Indians, and supporting Reconstruction governments in Louisiana. After retirement in 1879, he maintained homes in New Orleans, Paris, and New York.

Trojan horse • **1** Greek mythology a hollow wooden statue of a horse in which the Greeks concealed themselves in order to enter Troy. **2** a person or thing intended secretly to undermine or bring about the downfall of an enemy or opponent: *the rebels may use this peace accord as a Trojan horse to try and take over.* **3** Computing a program designed to breach the security of a computer system while ostensibly performing some innocuous function.

troop • *n.* **1** (**troops**) soldiers or armed forces: *U.N. peacekeeping troops* | (**troop**) *troop withdrawals.* **2** a cavalry unit commanded by a captain. **3** a unit of artillery and armored formation.

troop carrier • a large aircraft or armored vehicle designed for transporting troops.

trooper • *n.* **1** a private soldier in a cavalry, armored, or airborne unit. **2** a cavalry horse.

troopship • *n.* a ship designed or used for transporting troops.

trophy |ˈtrōfē| • *n.* (pl. **-ies**) **1** a cup or other decorative object awarded as a prize for a victory or success. **2** a souvenir of an achievement, especially a part of an animal taken when hunting. **3** (in ancient Greece or Rome) the weapons and other spoils of a defeated army set up as a memorial of victory. **4** a representation of such a memorial; an ornamental group of symbolic objects arranged for display.

ORIGIN: late 15th cent. (sense 3, denoting a display of weapons): from French *trophée*, via Latin from Greek *tropaion*, from *tropē* 'a rout,' from *trepein* 'to turn.'

tropopause |ˈträpəˌpôz; ˈtrō-| • the interface between the troposphere and the stratosphere. In polar and temperate regions the tropopause usually occurs at an altitude of about 25,000 to 45,000 feet (eight to fifteen kilometers), while in the tropics it occurs at 55,000 feet (twenty kilometers).

troposhere |ˈträpəˌsfir; ˈtrō-| • *n.* the lower layers of atmosphere, in which clouds form and in which the change of temperature with height is relatively large. Clouds form and convection occurs in this layer. The troposphere extends from the earth's surface to a height of about 3.5-6 miles (6-10 kilometers) (the lower boundary of the stratosphere).

trough |trôf| • *n.* a hollow between two wave crests in the sea.

TRS • *abbr.* Tactical Reconnaissance Squadron.

truce • *n.* an agreement between enemies or opponents to stop fighting or arguing for a certain time: *the guerrillas called a three-day truce.*

DERIVATIVES: **truceless** *adj.*

truce supervision • the deployment of military and civilian personnel to observe and report violations of a truce agreement between two groups in conflict.

truck • *n.* **1** a large, heavy motor vehicle, used for transporting goods, materials, or troops. It can have anywhere from four to eighteen tires. **2** a wooden disk at the top of a ship's mast or flagstaff, with sheaves for signal halyards. • *v.* convey by truck: *the food was trucked to St. Petersburg.*

ORIGIN: Middle English (denoting a solid wooden wheel): perhaps short for truckle in the sense 'wheel, pulley.' The sense 'wheeled vehicle' dates from the late 18th cent.

truck bomb • a truck loaded with explosives and a detonation device that is typically used as a terrorist weapon.

true altitude • the height of an aircraft as measured from mean sea level.

true north • the direction from an observer's position to the geographic North Pole, or the north direction of any geographic meridian.

Truman Doctrine • a containment policy presented by President HARRY S. TRUMAN to Congress on March 12, 1947, during the COLD WAR, to protect Greece and Turkey from potential Soviet communist aggression. It proposed a military and economic aid program of $400 million. It was approved by Congress in May 1947, after much resistance and debate, and effectively stabilized Greece and Turkey.

Truman, Harry S. (1884–1972) • 33rd president of the United States (1949–1953), born in Lamar, Missouri, and raised in Independence, Missouri. Truman finished out the remainder of FRANKLIN D. ROOSEVELT's fourth term as president of the United States (1945–1948), then ran for president himself. Truman spent ten years (1906–1916) trying his hand at farming and investing, disliking the former and failing at the latter, he rejoined the National Guard in 1917. After the United States entered WORLD WAR I, he served as captain of 129th Field Artillery Regiment during World War I at ST. MIHIEL, the MEUSE-ARGONNE offensive, and METZ. He returned home to marry Bess Wallace (1919) and open a haberdashery shop in downtown Kansas City with an Army buddy. That, too, failed, and Truman, heavily in debt, decided to use his Democratic machine connections and good reputation to enter the political arena in 1922. His early political career was unsteady at best, but he had the support of the Kansas City Democratic machine run by Boss Tom Pendergast, and was eventually elected to the U.S. Senate in 1934. He served there for ten years, immersing himself in transportation issues, helping to create the Civil Aeronautics Act of 1938, and foreign policy, becoming a strong advocate for global involvement and the UNITED NATIONS. His popularity among liberal conservative Democrats made him the compromise choice as Roosevelt's vice presidential candidate in the 1944 presidential campaign. When Roosevelt suddenly died after less than four months in office, Truman became president. As president, Truman would face the difficulties of war and the uneasy peace that followed. After Germany's surrender in May 1945, he ordered the atomic bombing of HIROSHIMA and NAGASAKI, Japan in August. After his attempts to appease JOSEF STALIN failed, he announced the TRUMAN DOCTRINE of containment against Soviet expansion in 1947, and quickly followed that in 1948 with the MARSHALL PLAN, a comprehensive plan for rebuilding Europe. Invited to participate in the Plan, Stalin refused, and the next step in containment, the North Atlantic Treaty was overwhelmingly ratified by the U.S. Senate, and NATO was established in 1949. The intensification of the COLD WAR with the Soviets, and their alliance with the victorious Chinese Communists under the leadership of MAO ZEDONG, had focused the attention of the U.S. on Communist gains around the world. Amid the rising tide of anticommunist sentiment, U.S. intelligence analysts announced that the USSR had detonated its first atomic bomb. In 1950, Truman reluctantly approved the development of a thermonuclear "superbomb" (EDWARD TELLER's hydrogen bomb), as well as obtaining the support of the United Nations to defend South Korea against the invading North Korean Communists. In spite of Gen. DOUGLAS MACARTHUR's surprise victory over the North Koreans at INCHON, the war continued to drag on, and MacArthur pushed to extend the war into China, using atomic bombs, if necessary. When he learned that MacArthur had told Republican leaders how he thought the war in Korea should be carried out, using a method that neither the UNITED NATIONS nor our European allies would countenance, Truman relieved him of duty in 1951. At the same time that Truman was ordering U.S. occupation troops from Japan into Korea, JULIUS AND ETHEL ROSENBERG were arrested; earlier in 1950, ALGER HISS, a former assistant secretary of state, had been convicted of perjury for denying under oath that he had given classified information to the USSR. In March 1952, Truman announced that he would not seek reelection, and, although he campaigned strenuously on behalf of the Democratic candidate, Adlai Stevenson, Gen. DWIGHT D. EISENHOWER, the Republican candidate, won in a landslide. Truman retired to Independence, Missouri in 1953 to write his memoirs.

Trumbull, Henry Clay (1830–1903) • U.S. army chaplain, evangelist, and author. Born in Stonington, Connecticut, Trumbull is best known for his extensive religious writings. In 1862 he accepted the chaplaincy of the Tenth Connecticut Regiment, and after being ordained as a Congregationalist minister he reported to his unit in North Carolina. He was captured in 1863 while searching for wounded Union soldiers after the attack on FORT WAGNER (1863). Exchanged a few months later he rejoined his regiment in Florida. He was frequently under fire at the siege of PETERSBURG (1864–65), and memorialized many of his fellow soldiers in his later writings. After he war he became a popular speaker and prolific author. Trumbull was one of the officiating clergy at the funeral of ULYSSES S. GRANT.

Trumbull, Joseph (1737–1778) • REVOLUTIONARY WAR army officer. Born in Lebanon, Connecticut, Trumbull graduated from Harvard in 1756. His family was very involved with state politics, as his father and brother both served as governor and Joseph spent many years in the colonial assembly. His performance as commissary general for Connecticut troops around Boston so impressed GEORGE WASHINGTON that he persuaded Congress to appoint Trumbull to the same position for the Continental army in July 1775 with the rank of colonel. Once the army left Boston the logistics situation became much more complicated. Frustrated by recalcitrant state officials, some corrupt subordinates, and demanding generals, Trumbull retired back to Connecticut in late 1776. The next year Washington and Congress divided commissary functions into separate purchasing and issuing departments, and Trumbull returned to take charge of the latter. By then his health was deteriorating, and he resigned his post in November 1777 without fixing the chaotic supply system that made the ensuing winter at VALLEY FORGE so terrible. He died the next year back in Lebanon.

trumpeter • *n.* a cavalry or artillery soldier who gives signals with a trumpet.

trumpet major • the chief trumpeter of a cavalry regiment, typically a principal musician in a regimental band.

truncheon |ˈtrənCHən| • *n.* chiefly Brit. **1** a short, thick stick carried as a weapon by a police officer. **2** a staff or baton acting as a symbol of authority.

ORIGIN: Middle English (denoting a piece broken off (especially from a spear), also a cudgel): from Old French *tronchon* 'stump,' based on Latin *truncus* 'trunk.'

trunnion |ˈtrənyən| • *n.* **1** a pin or pivot forming one of a pair on which something is supported. **2** a supporting cylindrical projection on each side of a cannon or mortar.

truss |trəs| • *n.* a heavy metal ring securing the lower yards to a mast. • *v.* tie up (someone) with their arms at their sides: *I found him **trussed up** in his closet.*

DERIVATIVES: **trusser** *n.*

Truxton, Thomas (1755–1822) • U.S. naval officer. Born near Hempstead, New York, Thomas Truxton went to sea on a merchant ship when he was twelve. During the REVOLUTIONARY WAR he captured a number of prizes as captain of American privateers. In 1794 he was appointed a captain in the fledgling U.S. Navy. He supervised the construction of the frigate *Constellation* and commanded her during the undeclared naval war with France. He became a national hero for his victories over *Insurgente* and *La Vengeance*. Chosen to command a squadron bound for the Tripolitan War in 1801, his protest over a choice of captains was seized upon as a resignation by the administration of THOMAS JEFFERSON, probably because Truxton was a Federalist. After retirement he wrote noteworthy works on navigation and naval tactics. He served as sheriff of Philadelphia before he died there.

TRW • *abbr.* a Tactical Reconnaissance Wing, an airforce unit responsible for reconnaissance and containing one or more Tactical Reconnaissance Squadrons (TRS).

trysail |ˈtrīsəl; -ˌsāl| • *n.* a small, strong fore-and-aft sail set on the mainmast or other mast of a sailing vessel in heavy weather.

Tsetung, Mao • see MAO ZEDONG.

TSgt • *abbr.* Technical Sergeant.

tub • *n.* informal a short, broad boat that handles awkwardly.

Tucker, John Randolph (1812–1883) • Confederate naval officer. Born in Alexandria, Virginia, Tucker entered the navy as a midshipman in 1826. He cruised all over the world and commanded a bombship during the MEXICAN WAR (1846–48). He resigned from the navy when Virginia seceded from the Union, and soon was commissioned in the Confederate Navy with the rank of commander. Put in charge of the naval defense of the James River, Tucker commanded from the cruiser *Patrick Henry,* covering the Confederate flank during the PENINSULAR CAMPAIGN and assisting the *Virginia* in her attack on HAMPTON ROADS (1862). He adroitly extricated his flotilla when the Union captured Norfolk navy yard, before being transferred to Charleston. He was promoted to captain and given command of the naval forces there, but when the city fell in 1865 he returned to Richmond. He reformed his crews into a naval brigade that acted as a rearguard for the ARMY OF NORTHERN VIRGINIA when it evacuated the Confederate capital, and he was captured at the BATTLE OF SAILOR'S CREEK. In 1866 he accepted a commission as rear admiral in the Peruvian navy, and commanded the combined navies of Peru and Chile in their war with Spain. While he was in New York overseeing the making of charts from his hydrographic survey of the Amazon in 1877, Peru withdrew his commission.

Tucker, Samuel (1747–1833) • REVOLUTIONARY WAR naval officer. Born in Marblehead, Massachusetts, Tucker first went to sea at the age of eleven. As captain of a schooner in 1776 he aided GEORGE WASHINGTON by capturing many British vessels with valuable supplies. The next year he was commissioned captain in the Continental navy, and during the next three years he captured even more prizes with the frigate *Boston*. Tucker was taken prisoner at the fall of CHARLESTON in 1780. When he was exchanged he turned one of his earlier prizes into a privateer, and he captured seven more British vessels before being taken himself near the mouth of the St. Lawrence River. When his captors released him in an open boat to sail to Nova Scotia he went to Boston instead. He spent some time in the merchant service before becoming a farmer in 1792. When the British were harassing the coast of Maine in 1813, the feisty Tucker outfitted a schooner with improvised and borrowed armament and captured one of their privateers. He served in the state legislature before he died in Bremen, Maine.

Tudor, William (1750–1819) • lawyer and first judge advocate of the Continental army. William Tudor was born in Boston, Massachusetts and received his M.A. from Harvard in 1772 after studying law with JOHN ADAMS. Tudor established a law practice in Boston. After the BATTLE OF BUNKER HILL, GEORGE WASHINGTON appointed him a captain and judge advocate of the Continental army. Tudor's first task was to prosecute some officers accused of cowardice at the battle, and he accompanied Washington as one of his staff officers when the army moved to New York. Tudor persuaded Adams to get the Continental Congress to adopt a modified version of the British Articles of War. In August 1776 Tudor was promoted to lieutenant colonel and given the title judge advocate general, but he left the Army the next year to return to his law practice in Boston. He was active in civic and professional affairs there throughout the war, and afterwards served in a number of positions in the state government.

tug • *v.* (**tugged, tugging**) tow (a ship) by means of a tug or tugs. • *n.* **1** (also **tugboat**) a small, powerful boat used for towing larger boats and ships, especially in harbor. **2** an aircraft towing a glider.

tugboat • *n.* a small but very powerful boat used to tow or move larger ships. Also called TOWBOAT; TUG.

Tullahoma campaign • a CIVIL WAR campaign for Union control of central Tennessee in mid-1863, under the leadership of Gen. WILLIAM S. ROSECRANS. Though often overlooked because of more dramatic contemporaneous events at GETTYSBURG and VICKSBURG, it had important strategic consequences; the Confederate forces under Gen. BRAXTON BRAGG were completely routed from Tennessee, and nearly 2,000 prisoners as well as artillery and siege guns were captured.

tumbler • *n.* a notched pivoted plate in a gunlock.

tumbril |ˈtəmbrəl| (also **tumbrel**) • *n.* a two-wheeled covered cart that carried tools or ammunition for an army.

turbojet • *n.* an aircraft propelled by a turbojet engine.

turn • *v.* **1** move or cause to move in a circular direction wholly or partly around an axis or point: *the counteroffensive turned as though around an axis | I turned the key in the door and crept in.* **2** (of the tide) change from flood to ebb or vice versa. **3** pass around (the flank or defensive lines of an army) so as to attack it from the side or rear. • *n.* **1** an act of moving something in a circular direction around an axis or point: *a safety lock requiring four turns of the key.* **2** a change of direction when moving: *they made a left turn and picked up speed.* **3** one round in a coil of rope or other material.

▸**turn someone out** call a guard from the guardroom.

turnaround • the length of time between arriving at a point and being ready to depart from that point. Turnaround typically refers to the time necessary to complete such procedures as the loading, unloading, refueling, and rearming of vehicles, aircraft, and ships.

turnbuckle |ˈtərnˌbəkəl| • *n.* a coupling with internal screw threads used to connect two rods, lengths of boat's rigging, etc., lengthwise and to regulate their length or tension.

Turnbull, William (1801–1857) • U.S. army officer and military engineer. Born in Philadelphia, Pennsylvania, William Turnbull graduated from WEST POINT in 1819. Though commissioned in the artillery, his earliest assignments dealt mostly with topographic engineering, and he was promoted to brevet captain of that branch in 1831. The next year he was given the challenging assignment to build a canal aqueduct across the Potomac River near Georgetown, District of Columbia. Using innovative cofferdams and pumps, he completed the project in 1843 and gained an international reputation. During the MEXICAN WAR (1846–48) he was the chief topographical engineer on WINFIELD SCOTT's staff. His maps were critical for the march on MEXICO CITY, and Turnbull was brevetted to lieutenant colonel and colonel for his conduct at the battles around the city. He was recalled from Mexico at the request of the Secretary of the Treasury to build a new customhouse in New Orleans. He soon moved on to other projects, including harbor improvements on the Great Lakes. He died suddenly in Wilmington, North Carolina while supervising efforts to improve navigation on the Cape Fear River.

turncoat • *n.* a person who deserts one party or cause in order to join an opposing one: *they denounced him as a turncoat.*

Turner, John Wesley (1833–1899) • U.S. soldier and businessman. Born in Saratoga County, New York, John Wesley Turner graduated from WEST POINT in 1855 as a second lieutenant in the field artillery. He spent the first two years of the Civil War as a staff officer for Maj. Gens. DAVID HUNTER and BENJAMIN BUTLER, until Maj. Gen. Quincy Gilmore made Turner chief of staff and chief of artillery for the Department of the South. After helping force the evacuation of FORT WAGNER in Charleston Harbor (1863), Turner accompanied Gilmore to join the Army of the James. Turner ably commanded a division during the Bermuda Hundred campaign and the early months of the siege of PETERSBURG before falling deathly ill (1864–65). When he recovered in early 1865 he took command of the "Wild Cat" Division from West Virginia and Ohio. They won special notice for taking Fort Gregg, the key to the Petersburg defenses on April 2, and then doggedly pursued the fleeing Confederates to help force the surrender of the ARMY OF NORTHERN VIRGINIA. Turner was breveted a major general for his accomplishments. After the war he administered Richmond, earning considerable resentment there by preventing leading secessionists from holding municipal office. After the war he served as purchasing and depot commissary in St. Louis until he left the army in 1871. He managed companies, directed banks, and served as street commissioner in that city before he died.

Turner, Nat (1800–31) • a preacher, and the leader of a slave rebellion, born into slavery on October 2 on a plantation in Southampton county, Virginia. Turner learned to read from one of his master's sons and became a lay preacher, believing himself divinely inspired to lead his people out of bondage. On the night of August 31, 1831, Turner and several other slaves killed Joseph Travis, Turner's master at the time, and Travis' family. Turner then proceeded to Jerusalem, which was the county seat and where he planned to capture the armory, and in two days and nights with a force of some seventy-five followers, killed about sixty white people; more than in any other rebellion in the nation's history. Turner's rebellion was defeated a few miles from Jerusalem by armed resistance from local whites and the arrival of the state militia, a total force of 3,000 men. The Virginia militia captured Turner on October 30, and he was tried on November 5 and hanged on November11. In response to fears sparked by the insurrection, as many as 200 innocent blacks were killed by angry whites. The rebellion led to stringent legislation in several Southern states to prohibit the education, movement, and assembly of slaves.

Turner, Stansfield (1923–) • a native of Highland Park, Illinois, he completed two years at Amherst College in Massachusetts before transferring to the U.S. NAVAL ACADEMY at Annapolis, where he played football and earned a Bachelor of Science degree in 1946 (Class of 1947). Turner served one year at sea before going on to Oxford University as a Rhodes Scholar and earning a master's degree in philosophy, politics, and economics. He returned to the sea after graduation from Oxford, and served primarily on destroyers, commissioning the U.S.S. *Horne*, a guided missile cruiser. During the next two years, he served with the Seventh Fleet off Vietnam, served in the Navy's Office of Politico-Military Affairs, in the Office of Systems Analysis under then Secretary of Defense ROBERT S. MCNAMARA, and as Executive Assistant and Naval Aide to Paul Ignatius and JOHN CHAFEE, both secretaries of the Navy. In May 1970, Turner was promoted to Rear Admiral. He served as a flag officer in command of a Carrier Task Group of the Sixth Fleet in the Mediterranean, as the director of the Navy's Office of Systems Analysis, and as Commander, Second Fleet and as President of the NAVAL WAR COLLEGE at Newport, Rhode Island. Promoted to Admiral in 1975, he became commander in chief of NATO's southern flank, headquartered in Naples, Italy, where he served until President JIMMY CARTER nominated him to be Director of Central Intelligence. In this capacity, he worked to develop closer congressional and executive oversight procedures of the intelligence community, helped the intelligence community come to grips with the new age of real-time photographic satellites, and guided major managerial reforms in the CIA. When he left this position in 1981, President Carter awarded him the National Security Medal. Since then, Turner has taught at Yale University and at the U.S. MILITARY ACADEMY and, since 1991, on the faculty of the Graduate School of Public Affairs at the University of Maryland. In 1995, Adm. Turner was awarded a Senior Research Fellowship at the Norwegian Nobel Peace Institute in Oslo.

Turner, Thomas Caldwell (1882–1931) • U.S. Marine aviator. Born in Mare Island, California, Turner joined the Marine Corps in 1901. He was commissioned a second lieutenant the next year. While commanding the detachment at San Diego Marine Barracks in 1916, Turner took flight training with the U.S. Army Signal Corps Aviation School nearby. He remained attached to the U.S. Air Service throughout WORLD WAR I, in charge of flying at Ellington Field, Texas. In 1920 newly appointed Marine Corps commandant Maj. Gen. JOHN A. LEJEUNE appointed Turner head of aviation. He reorganized the service air arm during his five year tenure but few funds were being expended on defense at that peaceful time. He served in a ground assignment and flying in China before becoming head of marine aviation again in 1929. This time the onset of the Great Depression brought more shrinking defense budgets, and Turner continued to struggle to build up his component. When he flew to inspect Marine air units in Haiti in October 1931, his airplane rolled off the runway and sank into soft sand. When Turner jumped out to inspect the damage, he received a fatal injury when struck by a propeller. He was about to become the first marine aviator to be a brigadier general.

turnpike • *n.* **1** a toll gate. **2** (also **turnpike road**) a road on which a toll was collected at such a gate.

turret • *n.* a low, flat armored tower, typically one that revolves, for a gun and gunners in a ship, aircraft, fort, or tank.
DERIVATIVES: **turreted** *adj.*

turtle • **1** slang one's replacement. [ORIGIN: because they are always slow in arriving.] **2** in ancient and medieval siege warfare, a roofed structure, usually mounted on wheels, used to protect troops manning a ram, mouse, or other engine to breech a gate or wall.
PHRASES: **turn turtle** (chiefly of a boat) capsize.

Tuscarora War • a war fought in 1711–12 along the North Carolina coast between the Tuscarora tribe and colonists, over land, trade, and the treatment that the Tuscarora received from the colonials. The governor instituted a draft of all men between the ages of 16 and 20, and, with the help of the Yamasee of South Carolina, defeated the Tuscarora.

Tuxpan • a city on the Gulf Coast of Mexico that was the target of an attack and subsequent capture in April, 1847 by Com. MATTHEW C. PERRY. It was at the time one of the few Gulf ports not under U.S. control and was a particular prize, since a U.S. ship wrecked there earlier, the *Truxton*, had yielded guns to the Mexicans. The town was poorly defended and was easily taken by the invading forces.

'tween decks • the space between the decks of a ship, especially that above the lowest deck and below the upper deck.

twelve-bore • *n.* Brit. TWELVE-GAUGE.

twelve-gauge • *n.* a shotgun with a gauge corresponding to the diameter of a round bullet of which twelve constitute a pound in weight.

Twenty-Slave Law • an exemption to the CONSCRIPTION LAW passed by the Confederate Congress in April 1862. It excused slaveholders owning twenty or more slaves from being drafted for service in the CIVIL WAR.

Twiggs, David Emanuel (1790–1862) • U.S. and Confederate army officer. Born in Richmond County, Georgia, in 1790, Twiggs attend Franklin College in Athens, Georgia, and studied law before being commissioned a captain in the U.S. 8th Infantry at the beginning of the WAR OF 1812. After 1814, he served in infantry units in the southeast, in Wisconsin Territory, Georgia, and Louisiana. He became the first colonel of the 2nd U.S. Dragoons in 1836, fought against the Seminoles in Florida, and commanded divisions under both ZACHARY TAYLOR and WINFIELD SCOTT during the Mexican War, (1846–48) being promoted to brigadier general, Regular Army, and brevetted major general. In 1857, he was assigned to command the Department of Texas. Rather than resigning his commission at the outbreak of the CIVIL WAR and leaving to join the Confederacy, as did other Southern officers, Twiggs instead surrendered his command to the Confederates on February 18, 1861, becoming the only U.S. Army officer to actually commit treason at the start of the war. He was dismissed from the U.S. Army by President JAMES BUCHANAN on March 1, 1861. In May 1861, Twiggs was commissioned as a major general in the Confederate Army and held several commands in Louisiana and Alabama but was soon retired as too old for active service.

twilight • the periods of incomplete darkness following sunset and preceding sunrise. Twilight is designated as *civil*, *nautical*, or *astronomical*, as the darker limit occurs when the center of the sun is 6 degrees, 12 degrees, or 18 degrees, respectively, below the celestial horizon.

Twining, Nathan Farragut (1897–1982) • U.S. army and air force officer. Born in Monroe, Wisconsin, Nathan Farragut Twining initially graduated from the accelerated course at WEST POINT in November 1918, but was then among the half of his classmates brought back to continue their education as student officers for another year. He began his commissioned service as an infantry officer, but transferred to the Air Service in 1926. When WORLD WAR II began, he was an the air staff in Washington, but in August 1942 he became a temporary brigadier general and chief of staff of army forces in the South Pacific. He received another star and command of the Thirteenth Air Force in early 1943. He was responsible for supporting operations on

GUADALCANAL and BOUGAINVILLE. In January 1944 he transferred to the European theater, taking over the Fifteenth Air Force and Mediterranean Allied Strategic Air Forces. He supported operations in Italy while mounting strategic bombing raids on Germany. In mid-1945 he was promoted to lieutenant general and sent back to the Pacific to command the Twentieth Air Force, which carried out the last incendiary raids on the Japanese homeland and dropped the two atomic bombs. He held a number of key positions in the new independent air force, rising to full general and becoming chief of staff in 1953. President DWIGHT D. EISENHOWER appointed Twining chairman of the JOINT CHIEFS OF STAFF in 1957, a position he held until retiring in 1960.

twin-screw • *adj.* (of a ship) having two propellers on separate shafts that rotate in opposite directions.

twist • *n.* the rifling in the bore of a gun: *barrels with a 1:24 inch twist.*

Twitchell, Marshall Harvey (1840–1905) • U.S. soldier and Reconstruction politician. Born in Townsend, Vermont, Twitchell enlisted in the Fourth Vermont Regiment when the CIVIL WAR began. He rose to the rank of first sergeant and survived a near-fatal wound in the WILDERNESS. In 1864 he accepted a commission as a captain in the 109th U.S. COLORED TROOPS and served with them through the PETERSBURG and APPOMATTOX campaigns, as well as during the postwar buildup in Texas against Maximilian's regime in Mexico. In September 1865 Twitchell joined the Freedman's Bureau and was assigned to Louisiana, where he became a leader in the Republican party. After wielding much power there in the early 1870's he lost most of his family killed by the White League, who sought to redeem the state from the Republicans. Twitchell himself was seriously wounded, and was eventually rewarded by President RUTHERFORD B. HAYES in 1878 with the position of American consul in Kingston, Ontario.

two-person rule (also, especially formerly, **two-man rule**) • a system designed to prohibit access by an individual to nuclear weapons and certain designated components by requiring the presence at all times of at least two authorized persons, each capable of detecting incorrect or unauthorized procedures with respect to the task to be performed.

two-star • *adj.* having or denoting the rank of major general, distinguished by two stars on the uniform.

Tyler, John (1790–1862) • 10th president of the United States (1841–1845). Born in Greenway, Virginia, in 1790, Tyler practiced law before entering politics. He served in the U.S. House of Representatives (1817–1821), as governor of Virginia (1825–1827), and in the U.S. Senate (1827–1836). In 1840, Tyler was elected Vice President on the Whig ticket. When President WILLIAM HENRY HARRISON died in office on April 4, 1841, Tyler became President. He clashed with Senator HENRY CLAY, oversaw settlement of the boundary disputes with Great Britain, and ended the Second SEMINOLE WAR in 1842. In December 1845, shortly before leaving office, Tyler engineered a joint resolution of Congress annexing Texas. He subsequently presided over the 1861 Virginia Peace Convention but eventually went with the secessionists. He was elected to the Confederate House of Representatives but died in 1862 before taking his seat.

typhoid |ˈtīˌfoid| (also **typhoid fever**) • *n.* an infectious bacterial fever with an eruption of red spots on the chest and abdomen and severe intestinal irritation.

DERIVATIVES: **typhoidal** *adj.*

Uu

U-2 • a single-seat single-engine high-altitude reconnaissance aircraft, built by Lockheed in 1956. It was used as a spyplane above the Soviet Union, China, and Cuba, although the United States claimed that it had been restricted to meteorological and environment-control flights.

U-2 incident • the shooting down of a U.S. spy plane (named U-2) in the firsts week of May, 1960. The plane, flown by GARY POWERS, had departed from Peshawar, Pakistan on May 1st, bound for Bodo, Norway, where it never arrived. The Soviet government revealed that it had been shot down. The United States initially denied that it was on an intelligence mission, but later owned up and accepted responsibility, without apologizing. The tensions that the incident created led to NIKITA KHRUSHCHEV refusing to attend an already scheduled summit between the two countries, and diminished the standing of President DWIGHT D. EISENHOWER in the waning days of his administration.

UAV • *abbr.* unmanned aerial vehicle.

U-boat |ˈyo͞o ˌbōt| • *n.* a German submarine used in WORLD WAR I or WORLD WAR II.

ORIGIN: from German *U-Boot*, abbreviation of *Unterseeboot* 'undersea boat.'

UGM-27 • see POLARIS.

UGM-73A • see POSEIDON.

UGM-84A • see HARPOON.
UGM-96A • see TRIDENT I.
UGM-133A • see TRIDENT II.
UH-1 • see IROQUOIS.
UH-60 • see BLACK HAWK.
UIC • *abbr.* unit identification code.
ultimatum • *n.* (pl. **ultimatums** | or **ultimata**) a final demand or statement of terms, the rejection of which will result in retaliation or a breakdown in relations: *the U.N. Security Council ultimatum demanding Iraq's withdrawal from Kuwait.*
ULTRA • code name for WORLD WAR II signals intelligence derived by the Allies from the interception and decoding of German ENIGMA machine ciphers.
ultraviolet imagery • imagery produced as a result of sensing ultraviolet radiations reflected from a given target surface.
Um al-Mar'rik • the PERSIAN GULF WAR.
ORIGIN: Arabic, literally, the "mother of all battles."
umbrella • *n.* a protecting force or influence: *the American nuclear umbrella over the west.*
U.N. (or **UN**) • *abbr.* United Nations.
UNAAF • *abbr.* Unified Action Armed Forces.
unbend • *v.* (past and past part. **unbent**) **1** unfasten (sails) from yards and stays. **2** cast (a cable) loose. **3** untie (a rope).
UNC • *abbr.* United Nations Command.
unclassified matter • official matter that does not require the application of security safeguards, but the disclosure of which may be subject to control for other reasons.
UNCMAC • *abbr.* United Nations Command Military Armistice Commission.
unconditional surrender • the surrender of a military force or nation without being able to set any limits on the subsequent actions of the victorious power. Following the CASABLANCA CONFERENCE in January 1943, the Allies announced an unconditional surrender policy with respect to the Axis powers, that is, the Allies would fight on until such time as the Axis powers surrendered unconditionally. In fact, Italy was allowed to surrender in 1943 with some conditions, but German capitulated unconditionally in May 1945, and Japan surrendered unconditionally (saving the person and institution of the Emperor) in September 1945.
unconventional warfare • (**UW**) a broad spectrum of military and paramilitary operations, normally of long duration, predominantly conducted by indigenous or surrogate forces who are organized, trained, equipped, supported, and directed in varying degrees by an external source. Unconventional warfare includes guerrilla warfare and other direct offensive, low visibility, covert, or clandestine operations, as well as the indirect activities of subversion, sabotage, intelligence activities, and evasion and escape.
unconventional warfare forces • forces having an existing unconventional warfare capability.
undecorated • *adj.* (of a member of the armed forces) not honored with an award.
under • *prep.* lower in grade or rank than: *under him in the hierarchy.*
PHRASES: **under way 1** having started and making progress. **2** (of a boat) moving through the water: *no time was lost in **getting under way**.*
undercurrent • *n.* a current of water below the surface and moving in a different direction from any surface current.
Underhill, John (1597?–1672) • Colonial official and militia officer. Born in England, John Underhill grew up in the Netherlands, where he received some military training. He came to Massachusetts Bay in 1630 to organize the colonial militia. He was appointed captain of the militia and played a major role in the Pequot War in 1637. Afterwards he got in trouble with the Puritan administration for his religious beliefs and lost his position. He served the Dutch colony of New Netherland as an Indian fighter for a time, but when war broke out between the English and Dutch in 1652 he switched sides to help the British. During the ANGLO-DUTCH WARS of 1664–1665 he helped extend English rule over the Dutch possessions, and then performed various public duties for the newly-named colony of New York.
underlever • *n.* a lever behind the trigger guard on a rifle.
undermine • *v.* dig or excavate beneath (a building or fortification) so as to make it collapse.
undersecretary • *n.* (pl. **-ies**) a subordinate official, in particular (in the U.S.) the principal assistant to a member of the cabinet, or (in the UK) a junior minister or senior civil servant.
underslung • *adj.* **1** suspended from the underside of something: *helicopters hover to lift underslung loads.* **2** (of a vehicle chassis) hanging lower than the axles.
underslung load • in helicopter transport operations, any external load hanging under the helicopter fuselage.
understrength • not having the authorized number of personnel.
undertow • *n.* a current below the surface of the sea moving in the opposite direction to the surface current, especially away from the shore: *I was swept away by the undertow.*
underwater demolition • the destruction or neutralization of underwater obstacles. This is normally accomplished by underwater demolition teams.
underwater demolition team • a group specially trained and equipped for the following: making hydrographic reconnaissance of approaches to prospective landing beaches; effecting demolition of obstacles and clearing mines in certain areas; locating, improving, and marking useable channels; achieving channel and harbor clearance; acquiring pertinent data during pre-assault operations, including military information; making visual observation of the hinterland to gain information useful to the landing force; performing miscellaneous underwater and surface tasks within their capabilities.

underway replenishment, doctrine of • U.S. Navy doctrine for those operations required to make a transfer of personnel and/or supplies when at sea in order to keep naval forces on station and eliminate the necessity of returning to port to replenish fuel, ammunition, rations, personnel, etc. Also called REPLENISHMENT AT SEA.

underway replenishment force • a task force of fleet auxiliaries (consisting of oilers, ammunition ships, stores issue ships, etc.) adequately protected by escorts furnished by the responsible operational commander. The function of this force is to provide underway logistic support for naval forces.

undock • *v.* **1** separate (a spacecraft) from another in space: *Conrad undocked Gemini and used his thruster to back slowly away | Atlantis is scheduled to undock from Mir today.* **2** take (a ship) out of or away from a dock.

unexploded • *adj.* (of a bomb or other explosive device) not having exploded.

unexploded explosive ordnance • explosive ordnance that has been primed, fused, armed, or otherwise prepared for action, and that has been fired, dropped, launched, projected, or placed in such a manner as to constitute a hazard to operations, installations, personnel, or material, and that remains unexploded either by malfunction or design or for any other cause.

unguided • *adj.* (of a missile) not directed by remote control or internal equipment.

Unified Action Armed Forces • (**UNAAF**) a publication that describes the policies, principles, doctrines, and functions that govern the U.S. armed forces when two or more military departments (or service elements thereof) are working together.

Unified Combatant Command • a grouping of large forces from more than one branch of the military under a single command, typically assigned to a specific geographic area and identified by an acronym.

unified command • in the U.S. services the unified commands are those commands with broad continuing missions under a single commander and composed of forces from two or more military departments, and which are established by the President, through the Secretary of Defense with the advice and assistance of the Chairman of the JOINT CHIEFS OF STAFF (to whom the commanders of the various unified commands report). The number and designation of the unified commands change from time to time, but at present there are nine. The five unified area commands are: U.S. Atlantic Command (USLANTCOM aka USACOM); U.S. Pacific Command (USPACOM); U.S. European Command (USEUCOM); U.S. Southern Command (USSOUTHCOM); and U.S. Central Command (USCENTCOM). The four unified functional commands are: U.S. Transportation Command (USTRANSCOM); U.S. Special Operations Command (USSOCOM); U.S. Strategic Command (USSTRATCOM); and U.S. Space Command (USSPACECOM).

unified operation • a broad generic term that describes the wide scope of actions taking place within unified commands under the overall direction of the commanders of those commands.

uniform • *n.* the distinctive clothing worn by members of the same organization: *an officer in uniform.*

Uniform Code of Military Justice • a comprehensive federal statute enacted by Congress in May 1950 to establish procedures, policies, and penalties for the military justice system. U.S. Secretary of Defense JAMES V. FORRESTAL led a committee to create the code after the unification of the armed forces under the DEPARTMENT OF DEFENSE.

uniformed services • the U.S. Army, Navy, Air Force, Marine Corps, Coast Guard, National Oceanic and Atmospheric Administration, and Public Health Service.

Uniform Militia Act • see MILITIA ACT (1792)

unilateral |ˌyo͞onəˈlæt̬ərəl; -ˈlætrəl| • *adj.* (of an action or decision) performed by or affecting only one person, group, or country involved in a particular situation, without the agreement of another or the others: *unilateral nuclear disarmament.*

DERIVATIVES: **unilaterally** *adv.*

unilateral arms control measure • an arms control course of action taken by a nation without any compensating concession being required of other nations.

unilateral disarmament • the disarmament, selective or total, by one nation without reference to the actions of any other nation.

union • *n.* **1** (also **Union**) a political unit consisting of a number of states or provinces with the same central government, in particular: **a** the United States, especially from its founding by the original thirteen states in 1787–90 to the secession of the Confederate states in 1860–61. **b** (also **the Federal Union**) the northern states of the United States that opposed the seceding Confederate states in the CIVIL WAR. **2** a part of a flag with an emblem symbolizing national union, typically occupying the upper corner next to the staff.

Union Jack • **1** the national flag of the United Kingdom, consisting of red and white crosses on a blue background. [ORIGIN: originally a small British union flag flown as the jack of a ship.] **2** (**union jack**) a small flag consisting of the union from the national flag, flown at the bows of vessels in harbor.

Union Veteran Legion • an organization of Union veterans of the CIVIL WAR. Founded in Pittsburgh, Pennsylvania, in 1884, its membership was open only to those who had served in the Union forces for at least two years and those who had been wounded. Because of its limited membership, its political and cultural significance was secondary to the GRAND ARMY OF THE REPUBLIC, the largest Union veterans' group.

unit • *n.* **1** any military element whose structure is prescribed by competent authority, such as a table of organization and equipment; specifically, part of an organization. **2** an organization title of a subdivision of a group in a task force. **3** (also **unit of issue**) a standard or basic quantity into which an item of supply is divided, issued, or used. **4** (regarding reserve components of the armed forces) a selected reserve unit that is organized, equipped, and trained for mobilization to serve on active duty as a unit or to augment or be augmented by another unit. (Headquarters and support functions without wartime missions are not considered units.)

unit aircraft • aircraft grouped together as a unit in order to carry out a mission. See also AIRCRAFT.

United Confederate Veterans • the largest veterans' group made up of members of the Confederate forces of the CIVIL WAR. It was formed in 1889, and by 1903 it had an estimated 80,000 members.

United Defense, L.P. • a private company that provides everything necessary for war in six major markets: combat vehicle systems, fire support, combat support vehicle systems, weapons delivery systems, amphibious assault vehicles, and combat support services. It also supplies soldiers, sailors, airmen, and marines. It began as Food Machinery Corp. (FMC) and filled a U.S. military order for 1,000 amphibious landing craft. During WORLD WAR II, FMC produced more than 10,000 armored vehicles. In 1994, in response to the complex military-industrial base and a declining market, FMC merged with Harsco, another company that built tanks during World War II, becoming United Defense Limited Partnership. In 1997, The Carlyle Group bought United Defense, now located in Arlington, Virginia.

United Nations • (**U.N.** or **UN**) an international organization of countries set up in 1945, in succession to the LEAGUE OF NATIONS, to promote international peace, security, and cooperation. Its members, originally the countries that fought against the Axis Powers in WORLD WAR II, now number more than 150 and include most sovereign states of the world, the chief exceptions being Switzerland and North and South Korea. Administration is by a secretariat headed by the Secretary General. The chief deliberative body is the General Assembly. The Security Council bears the primary responsibility for the maintenance of peace and security. The headquarters of the United Nations are in New York. See UNITED NATIONS GENERAL ASSEMBLY; UNITED NATIONS SECURITY COUNCIL; and UNITED NATIONS TASK FORCE.

United Nations Command • (**UNC**) a command in Korea that was established on July 7, 1950, and is commanded by a U.S. Army four-star general (CINCUNC) from headquarters in Seoul, South Korea. CINCUNC serves concurrently as Commander, U.S. Forces Korea (USFK); Commander in Chief, ROK/U.S. Combined Forces Command (CINCCFC); and Commanding General, Eighth U.S. Army. CINCUNC is responsible for carrying out the terms and conditions of the July 27, 1953, Armistice agreement in Korea.

United Nations Command Military Armistice Commission • (**UNCMAC**) an organization of the UNITED NATIONS responsible for supervising the implementation of the armistice agreement between North and South Korea since 1953. Ten senior military officers from U.N. member nations serve in the Command on a rotational basis. Its headquarters is located in Seoul, Korea.

United Nations Declaration • a statement signed on January 1, 1942, during WORLD WAR II, at the ANGLO-AMERICAN ARCADIA CONFERENCE in Washington, D.C. A sequel to the ATLANTIC CHARTER, it expressed the Allies' war objectives. The United Nations was established in 1945.

United Nations General Assembly • the chief deliberative body of the United Nations, in which all U.N. members are represented. Each country has one vote, and substantive matters are decided by a majority or by a two-thirds vote, depending on the importance of the question. The Assembly holds an executive position within the United Nations since it has deliberative, administrative, fiscal, and elective powers. Of most importance are the Assembly's deliberative activities, during which global conflicts may be addressed. Recommendations are passed but are not binding on members, and in general have had little effect on world politics.

United Nations Participation Act • a measure passed by Congress in 1945 to implement the United Nations Charter and to determine the procedures for the use of force in United Nations operations. It required that the president receive congressional approval before committing armed forces to special agreements with the United Nations.

Presidents HARRY S. TRUMAN and GEORGE H. BUSH cited United Nations authorization for the use of force in the Korean and Iraq hostilities, but Truman used force prior to authorization and neither followed the procedures established by the act.

United Nations Protection Force • see UNPROFOR.

United Nations Security Council • a body of the United Nations tasked with keeping international peace. Located at U.N. headquarters in New York City, it was originally comprised of eleven members with five permanent members representing China, France, the Soviet Union, the United Kingdom, and the United States, and six nonpermanent representatives. In 1965 the body was amended to a fifteen-member council, composed of the same five permanent members and ten nonpermanent members. On substantive issues all five permanent members must be included in the affirmative vote, unless a member abstains, and permanent members have veto power. The Council may advise U.N. members to seek diplomatic or economic sanctions, and military action by U.N. forces may follow if sanctions prove inadequate.

United Nations Task Force • ad hoc and

other committees established by the United Nations' main bodies. Task force committees may conduct research and make reports, carry out recommendations and duties, or coordinate programs. Issues such as disarmament, outer-space exploration, peacekeeping, decolonization, and human rights are examples of the kinds of questions task force committees work on. Reports from task force committees are given at U.N.-sponsored international conferences.

United States • for entries beginning "United States," see U.S.

***United States*, USS** • the U.S. frigate, commanded by Capt. STEPHEN DECATUR, that defeated the HMS *Macedonian* in the battle off the coast of Africa on October 25, 1812.

unit identification code • (**UIC**) a six-character, alphanumeric code that uniquely identifies each active, reserve, and National Guard unit of the armed forces.

unit readiness • see MILITARY CAPABILITY.

unit reserves • the prescribed quantities of supplies carried by a unit as a reserve to cover emergencies.

unit rotation • the substitution of one military unit for another at a given station.

unit strength • as applied to a friendly or enemy unit, the number of personnel, amount of supplies, armament equipment and vehicles, and the total logistic capabilities.

unit type code • (**UTC**) a five-character, alphanumeric code that uniquely identifies each type unit of the armed forces.

Universal Military Training and Service Act • the name given to the SELECTIVE SERVICE ACT of 1948 when it was amended in 1951.

Universal Time • a measure of time that conforms, within a close approximation, to the mean diurnal rotation of the earth and serves as the basis of civil timekeeping. Universal Time (UT1) is determined from observations of the stars, radio sources, and also from ranging observations of the moon and artificial earth satellites. The scale determined directly from such observations is designated **Universal Time Observed** (UTO); it is slightly dependent on the place of observation. When UTO is corrected for the shift in longitude of the observing station caused by polar motion, the time scale UT1 is obtained. Also called ZULU TIME. Formerly called GREENWICH MEAN TIME.

unknown • *n.* **1** a code meaning "information not available." **2** an unidentified target. Compare with BOGEY.

Unknown Soldier • an unidentified representative member of a country's armed forces killed in war, given burial with special honors in a national memorial.

unlade |ˌənˈlād| • *v.* archaic unload (a ship or cargo).

unlay • *v.* (past and past part. **unlaid**) untwist (a rope) into separate strands.

unlimber • *v.* **1** detach (a gun) from its limber so that it can be used. **2** unpack or unfasten (something) ready for use: *we had to unlimber some of the gear.*

unmanned • *adj.* not having or needing a crew or staff: *an unmanned space flight.*

unmanned aerial vehicle • (**UAV**) an aerial vehicle that does not require a human operator and can fly independently or be operated remotely, is either recoverable or expendable, and is capable of carrying a lethal or nonlethal payload.

unmilitary • *adj.* not typical of, suitable for, or connected with the military.

unmoor • *v.* release the moorings of (a vessel).

unnavigable • *adj.* (of a waterway or sea) not able to be sailed on by ships or boats.

UNOSOM • two United Nations Operations in Somalia involving the deployment of soldiers. **UNOSOM I** sent unarmed soldiers as peace keepers in April 1992 in order to ease tensions among various warring factions that had arisen following the ouster if Siad Barre, the former dictator. **UNOSOM II** was a second peacekeeping force tasked with establishing a Somali government. It started in March 1993 and ended two years later. Civil strife in Somalia initially increased during this mission and the U.N. troops were attacked. The United States sent in DELTA FORCE commandos in a mission to capture one of the Somali warlords, without success. The events had a negative public relations impact for the U.N.'s ability to operate successful peacekeeping missions.

UNPROFOR • the United Nations Protection Force, mandated by the United Nations Security Council to protect Sarajevo in the Republic of Bosnia and Herzegovina, starting in 1992. It was replaced by IFOR.

unreeve |ˌənˈrēv| • *v.* (past **unrove**) withdraw (a rope) from a pulley block or other object.

unrig • *v.* (**unrigged, unrigging**) remove the rigging from (a ship).

unseaworthy • *adj.* (of a boat or ship) not in a good enough condition to sail on the sea.

unship • *v.* (**unshipped, unshipping**) **1** remove (an oar, mast, or other object) from its fixed or regular position: *they unshipped the oars.* **2** unload (a cargo) from a ship or boat.

unsinkable • *adj.* (of a ship or boat) unable to be sunk: *the supposedly unsinkable ship hit an iceberg.*

unsoldierly • *adj.* not characteristic of a good soldier.

unsounded • *adj.* unfathomed.

unstep • *v.* (**unstepped, unstepping**) remove (a mast) from its step.

Untersee boat • see U-BOAT.

up • *adv.* **1** [as exclam.] used as a command to a soldier or an animal to stand up and be ready to move or attack: *up, boys, and at 'em.* **2** (of sailing) against the current or the wind. **3** (of a ship's helm) moved around to windward so that the rudder is to leeward. • *prep.* to a higher part of (a river or stream), away from the sea: *a cruise up the Rhine.*

up-anchor • *v.* (of a ship) weigh anchor.

uphaul • *n.* a rope used for hauling up a boat's sail or centerboard.

Up, Out, and Down • the motto of the U.S. Navy surface forces.

upper works • the parts of a ship's hull that are above the water when it is fully laden.

uprising • *n.* an act of resistance or rebellion; a revolt: *an armed uprising.*

Upton, Emory (1839–1881) • U.S. army officer, military intellectual, and reformer. Born near Batavia, New York, on August 27, 1839, Upton attended Oberlin College (1854–1856) before entering WEST POINT from which he was graduated and commissioned in the artillery in 1861. He quickly rose to command an artillery brigade in the PENINSULAR CAMPAIGN and at ANTIETAM in 1862. In October 1862, he obtained the colonelcy of the 121st New York Infantry, and by July 1863 had become a brigade commander, serving in all the major battles in the East. A tactical innovator, Upton devised new tactics by which his troops penetrated the Confederate trench works at SPOTSYLVANIA (1864). He was subsequently promoted to brigadier general, led troops at COLD HARBOR (1864), and was seriously wounded while commanding a division of the VI Corps in the SHENANDOAH VALLEY in July 1864. He returned to active duty in December 1864 as a major general assigned to command a cavalry division in the western theater, participating in the taking of Selma, Alabama, and Columbus, Georgia. Having commanded forces in all three arms (artillery, infantry, and cavalry), after the Civil War Upton interested himself in military reform and the study of military history and the art of war. In 1867, he published *A New System of Infantry Tactics*, which became the standard U.S. Army tactical manual. He served as commandant of cadets at West Point (1870–1875) before undertaking a round-the-world tour to study foreign armies in 1875–1876. His resulting book, *The Armies of Asia and Europe* (1878), was very influential in promoting the adoption of certain aspects of the Prussian military system in the United States, particularly a national reserve system, a general staff for war planning, and a war college to train staff officers. In *The Military Policy of the United States* (completed in 1880; published in 1904), Upton argued against lack of military efficiency inherent in the state-dominated militia and volunteer system and for a well-trained, expansible, professional army. Upton also served as superintendent of the Artillery School at Fort Monroe (1877–1880) making it a model of modern officer education. Suffering from nasal tuberculosis and psychological depression, Upton, then commanding the 4th Artillery at the Presidio of San Francisco, California, resigned his commission and committed suicide on March 15, 1881.

urban warfare • warfare conducted in cities and other built-up areas.

URGENT FURY, Operation • code name for the invasion of Grenada by U.S. forces in 1983.

urgent priority • a category of immediate mission request which is lower than emergency priority but takes precedence over ordinary priority, e.g., enemy artillery or mortar fire which is falling on friendly troops and causing casualties or enemy troops or mechanized unites moving up in such force as to threaten a break-through.

Urrea, José de (1797–1849) • a Mexican general, born in the presidio of Tucson (now Arizona, who fought in numerous battles with Gen. ANTONIO LÓPEZ DE SANTA ANNA in the TEXAS WAR OF INDEPENDENCE. He was opposed to the withdrawal of Mexican troops after the battle of SAN JACINTO, and was later appointed commandant general of the departments of Sinaloa and Sonora. Passed over for appointment to governor in 1837, he initiated several revolts. He fought against the United States in the MEXICAN WAR (1846–48).

USA • *abbr.* **1** United States of America. **2** United States Army.

USACE • *abbr.* U.S. Army Corps of Engineers.

USAF • *abbr.* United States Air Force.

USAFLANT • *abbr.* U.S. Air Forces Atlantic.

USAFE • *abbr.* U.S. Air Forces in Europe.

U.S. Air Force • see AIR FORCE.

U.S. Air Forces in Europe • (**USAFE**) the Air Force component of the U.S. EUROPEAN COMMAND (USEUCOM) commanded by a U.S. Air Force four-star general (CINCUSAFE) from headquarters at Ramstein Air Base, Germany. CINCUSAFE also serves as the commander of NATO's Allied Air Forces Central Europe (CINCAAFCE) and is responsible for providing air force support to NATO in the European theater and U.S. forces in parts of Africa and the Middle East. See U.S. EUROPEAN COMMAND (USEUCOM).

USARCENT • *abbr.* U.S. Army Forces Central Command/Third U.S. Army.

USAREUR • *abbr.* U.S. Army Europe/Seventh U.S. Army.

USARLANT • *abbr.* U.S. Army Forces Atlantic Command.

U.S. Armed Forces • the regular components of the U.S. Air Force, Army, Marine Corps, and Navy.

U.S. Army • for schools, installations, groups, and divisions of the U.S. Army, see ARMY, U.S.GENERAL .

U.S. Army Corps of Engineers • see ARMY CORPS OF ENGINEERS.

U.S. Army Corps of Topographic Engineers • see ARMY CORPS OF TOPOGRAPHIC ENGINEERS.

U.S. Army Europe/Seventh U.S. Army • (USAREUR/Seventh Army) the Army component of the U.S. EUROPEAN COMMAND (USEUCOM) commanded by a U.S. Army four-star general (Commanding General, USAREUR/Seventh Army) from headquarters at Heidelberg, Germany. The mission of USAREUR/Seventh U.S. Army is to provide logistical and administrative support to U.S. Army forces in Europe and parts of Africa and the Middle East. The operational command of U.S. Army combat forces in Europe is held by CINCUSEUCOM/ SACEUR, but the Commanding General, USAREUR/Seventh Army also serves as the commander of NATO's Central Army Group (CENTAG).

U.S. Army Rangers • see ARMY RANGERS.

U.S. Asiatic Fleet • see ASIATIC FLEET.

USASSI • *abbr.* U.S. Army Soldier Support Institute.

U.S. Atlantic Command • (**USLANTCOM**; also **USACOM**) U.S. unified area command established on December 1, 1947, and commanded by a U.S. four-star flag officer (CINCUSLANTCOM) from headquarters in Norfolk, Virginia. CINCUSLANTCOM also serves as NATO's Supreme Allied Commander Atlantic (SACLANT) and in time of war USLANTCOM forces would come under NATO's Allied Command Atlantic. USCINCLANTCOM is responsible for operational command of all U.S. forces in the Atlantic from the North Pole to the South Pole, including the Norwegian, Greenland, and Barents Seas; the Caribbean Sea; the waters surrounding Africa to the Cape of Good Hope; and the Pacific Ocean east of 92o W. longitude. The subordinate component commands of USLANTCOM are: U.S. Atlantic Fleet (USLANTFLT with headquarters at Norfolk, Virginia); U.S. Army Forces Atlantic Command (USARLANT with headquarters at Fort McPherson, Georgia) (Normally, the Commanding General, U.S. Army Forces Command serves concurrently as CINCUSARLANT.); and U.S. Air Forces Atlantic (USAFLANT with headquarters at Langley Air Force Base, Virginia). The subordinate unified commands of USLANTCOM include: Iceland Defense Forces (IDF); U.S. Forces Azores; and Special Operations Command Atlantic (SOCLANT).

USCENTCOM • *abbr.* U.S. Central Command.

U.S. Central Command • (**USCENTCOM**) U.S. unified area command established on January 1, 1983, and commanded by a U.S. four-star flag officer (USCINCCENT) from headquarters at MacDill Air Force Base in Tampa, Florida. USCINCCENT exercises operational command of all U.S. forces in Southwest Asia, the Middle East, and East Africa. The subordinate component commands of USCENTCOM are: U.S. Army Forces Central Command/Third U.S. Army (USARCENT/Third Army); U.S. Naval Forces Central Command (USNAVCENT); and U.S. Air Forces Central Command (USCENTAF). USCENTCOM has one subordinate unified command, Special Operations Command Central (SOCCENT). The bulk of the forces assigned to USCENTCOM are based in the continental United States and are deployed overseas as necessary.

USCINCCENT • *abbr.* Commander in Chief, U.S. Central Command.

U.S. Civilian Internee Information Center • see CIVILIAN INTERNEE INFORMATION CENTER.

U.S. Colored Troops • see COLORED TROOPS.

U.S. controlled shipping • ships under the U.S. flag plus selected ships under foreign flags that are considered to be under "effective United States control," that is, ships that can reasonably be expected to be made available to the United States in time of national emergency.

U.S. Court of Appeals for the Armed Forces • see COURT OF APPEALS FOR THE ARMED FORCES.

USCT • *abbr.* United States Colored Troops.

U.S. Disciplinary Barracks • see DISCIPLINARY BARRACKS.

USEUCOM • *abbr.* U.S. European Command.

U.S. European Command • (**USEUCOM**) the U.S. unified area command in Europe established on August 1, 1952, and commanded by a U.S. four-star flag officer (CINCUSEUCOM) also known as U.S. Commander in Chief, Europe (CINCEUR) from headquarters at Patch Barracks in Stuttgart-Vaihingen, Germany. CINCUSEUCOM serves concurrently as Supreme Allied Commander Europe (SACEUR) and is responsible for operational command of all U.S. forces in Europe and parts of Africa and the Middle East. USEUCOM has the primary mission of supporting NATO in conventional and nuclear operations. Although in recent years the position of CINCUSEUCOM/CINCEUR/SACEUR has been held by an Army general, the assignment may go to a flag officer of any service. The subordinate component commands of USEUCOM are: U.S. Army Europe (USAREUR); U.S. Naval Forces Europe (USNAVEUR); and U.S. Air Forces in Europe (USAFE). USEUCOM also has one subordinate unified command: Special Operations Command Europe (SOCEUR).

U.S. High Command • the U.S. group that conferred with Allied nations and was responsible for initiating and planning strategy during WORLD WAR II. Its members were President FRANKLIN D. ROOSEVELT, Vice President HARRY S. TRUMAN, Secretary of War HENRY L. STIMSON, Harry Hopkins, former Secretary of Commerce and special advisor to Roosevelt, Secretary of State CORDELL HULL and his successor in November 1944, Edward R. Stettinius, Jr., Secretary of the Navy Frank Knox, Adm. ERNEST J. KING, Chief of Naval Operations, Gen. GEORGE C. MARSHALL, Army Chief of Staff, and Adm. WILLIAM D. LEAHY, then S to both Roosevelt and Truman.

Ushijima, Mitsuru (?–1945) • commander of Japan's Thirty-Second Army during the bloody battles at OKINAWA in the Pacific Theater during WORLD WAR II, successfully repulsing the U.S. attempts to break through the Machinato Line until late in April 1945. He committed hara-kiri seconds before one of his aides decapitated him when U.S. forces took Okinawa.

USIA • *abbr.* United States Information Agency.

U.S. Information Agency • (**USIA**) established as a separate U.S. government agency in 1953, the USIA, the purpose of which is to disseminate positive information (propaganda) about the United States in foreign countries, has subsequently been placed under the control of the State Department. USIA maintains libraries in various foreign cities and produces a variety of films and printed materials promoting democracy, capitalism, and the American way of life.

U.S. Institute of Peace • an independent, nonpartisan federal organization created by Congress in 1984 and responsible for improving the country's ability to promote the peaceful resolution of international conflicts. It does this through its numerous publications and library services, conferences and workshops, and other educational projects. Its fifteen-member board of directors are appointed by the president and confirmed by the Senate.

USJFCOM • *abbr.* United States Joint Forces Command.

U.S. Joint Forces Command • (**USJFCOM**) U.S. unified area command established in 2000 as the successor to the U.S. ATLANTIC COMMAND (USLANTCOM aka USACOM). USJFCOM is commanded by a U.S. four-star flag officer (CINCUSJFCOM; currently a U.S. Army general) from headquarters in Norfolk, Virginia. CINCUSJFCOM serves concurrently as NATO's Supreme Allied Commander Atlantic (SACLANT). As CINCUSJFCOM he is responsible for the preparation of more than one million U.S.-based military personnel for joint deployments around the world as well as the operational command of assigned U.S. forces in the largest of the unified commands.

USLANTCOM • *abbr.* United States Atlantic Command.

USLANTFLT • *abbr.* U.S. Atlantic Fleet.

U.S. Lifesaving Service • see LIFESAVING SERVICE, U.S.

USLSS • *abbr.* United States Lifesaving Service.

U.S. Marine Corps • see MARINE CORPS.

USMC • *abbr.* United States Marine Corps.

U.S. Midshipmen's School • a school begun at Smith College and the Hotel Northhampton in Northhampton, Massachusetts (later branching out to Mount Holyoke College in South Hadley, Massachusetts). It trained more than 9000 women for the WAVES officers program beginning in 1942.

U.S. Military Academy • (also known as **West Point**) an undergraduate army service school at West Point, New York. Founded in 1802, it is one of the oldest service academies in the world. Candidates are appointed by political nomination. It began admitting black cadets in the 1870s, and female cadets were first admitted in 1976. Eminent American military commanders who graduated from the academy include ULYSSES S. GRANT, ROBERT E. LEE, and DWIGHT D. EISENHOWER.

U.S. Military Airlift Command • see MILITARY AIRLIFT COMMAND.

USN • *abbr.* United States Navy.

U.S. Naval Academy • see NAVAL ACADEMY.

USNAVCENT • *abbr.* U.S. Naval Forces Central Command.

U.S. Naval Forces Europe • (**USNAVEUR**) the Navy component of the U.S. EUROPEAN COMMAND (USEUCOM) commanded by a U.S. Navy four-star admiral (CINCNAVEUR) from headquarters in London. CINCUSNAVEUR is responsible for the operation and management of all U.S. naval forces in Europe from the eastern shores of Greenland through the North Atlantic and the Mediterranean Sea and for providing U.S. naval forces and support to NATO in time of war.

U.S. Naval Gun Factory • see WASHINGTON NAVY YARD.

U.S. Naval Institute • see NAVAL INSTITUTE.

U.S. Naval Lyceum • see NAVAL LYCEUM.

U.S. Naval Observatory • see NAVAL OBSERVATORY.

U.S. Naval Reserve • see NAVAL RESERVE.

U.S. Naval Ship • (**USNS**) a public ship in the custody of the Navy that belongs to the United States. Such a ship can be in the service of the MILITARY SEALIFT COMMAND, but carry a civil service crew, or a commercial enterprise under contract to the Military Sealift Command and carrying a merchant marine crew.

USNAVEUR • *abbr.* United States Naval Forces Europe.

U.S. Navy • see NAVY.

USNO • *abbr.* United States Naval Observatory.

USNS • *abbr.* United States Naval Ship.

USNSWC • *abbr.* U.S. NAVY SPECIAL WARFARE COMMAND.

USO • (Also called **United Service Organizations**) a non-profit service organization that offers support to uniformed members of all the armed forces, particularly when they are traveling or stationed abroad.

USO tour • a tour of military bases by a group of entertainers sponsored by the United Service Organization. Such tours to entertain the troops were started during WORLD WAR II, and the most famous entertainer to participate was the comedian Bob Hope, who undertook such tours from 1942 until the 1990s.

U.S. Pacific Command • (**USPACOM**) the oldest of the U.S. unified commands and the unified command with the largest area of responsibility, U.S. Pacific Command (USPACOM) was established on January 1, 1947, and is commanded by a U.S. Navy four-star admiral (CINCUSPACOM) from headquarters at Pearl Harbor, Oahu, Hawaii. The area for which CINCUSPACOM is responsible covers over 100 million square miles from the U.S. west coast to the east coast of Africa and from the Arctic to the Antarctic (less a part of the Pacific Ocean off South America under U.S. Southern Command and a part of the Indian Ocean and Arabian Sea under U.S. Central Command) and over half the world's population. CINCUSPACOM commands four subordinate unified commands (U.S. Forces Korea [USFK]; U.S. Forces Japan [USFJ]; Alaskan Command; and Special Operations Command, Pacific [USSOCOMPAC]) and four component commands (U.S. Army Pacific [USARPAC]; U.S. Pacific Fleet [PACFLT]; U.S. Pacific Air Forces [PACAF]; and Marine Forces Pacific) as well as two joint task forces (Joint Interagency Task Force West and Joint Task Force Full Accounting).

USPACOM • *abbr.* United States Pacific Command.

U. S. Prisoner of War Information Center • see PRISONER OF WAR INFORMATION CENTER.

US Roland • a short range, low-altitude surface-to-air missile based on the Franco-German Roland III missile system, which was developed by EUROMISSILE in the 1970s. It operated from a tracked vehicle and was used to protect troops, airfields, supply depots and other targets.

USS • *abbr.* United States Ship, used in the names of ships in the U.S. Navy: *the USS* Maine *was launched in 1895.*

USSOCOM • *abbr.* United States Special Operations Command.

USSOUTHCOM • *abbr.* United States Southern Command.

U.S. Southern Command • (**USSOUTHCOM**) U.S. unified area command established June 6, 1963 as the successor to the U.S. Caribbean Command. USSOUTHCOM is commanded by a U.S. Army four-star general (USCINCSO) from headquarters in Miami, Florida. USCINCSO exercises operational command of all U.S. forces in South and Central America (less Mexico). The subordinate component commands of USSOUTHCOM are: U.S. Army South (USARSO); U.S. Naval Forces Southern Command (USNAVSO); and U.S. Air Forces Southern Command (USAFSO).

USSPACECOM • *abbr.* United States Space Command.

U.S. Space Command • (**USSPACECOM**) U.S. unified functional command established September 23, 1985, and commanded by a U.S. Air Force four-star general (CINCUSSPACECOM) from headquarters at Peterson AFB, Colorado. CINCUSSPACECOM serves concurrently as Commander in Chief, North American Aerospace Defense Command (CINCNORAD) and Commander, Air Force Space Command, and is responsible for operational command of all space, air, and ballistic missile defense operations by U.S. services. The subordinate component commands of USSPACECOM are: U.S. Army Space and Missile Defense Command; Naval Space Command (NAVSPACECOM); and Air Force Space Command (AFSPACECOM).

U.S. Special Operations Command • (**USSOCOM**) U.S. unified functional command established on April 16, 1987, and commanded by a U.S. Army four-star general (CINCUSSOCOM) from headquarters at MacDill Air Force Base, Tampa, Florida. CINCUSSOCOM exercises operational command of all CONUS-based special operations forces and activities and is responsible for providing special operations forces to reinforce the other unified commands as well as for the development of special operations strategy, doctrine, and tactics; the conduct of special operations training; special operations funding and budgeting; and management of special operations intelligence support. The subordinate component commands of USSOCOM are: First Special Operations Command (1st SOCOM); Naval Special Warfare Command (NAVSPECWARCOM); and assigned Air Force special operations units.

USSTRATCOM • *abbr.* United States Strategic Command.

U.S. Strategic Army Forces • see STRATEGIC ARMY FORCES.

U.S. Strategic Command • (**USSTRATCOM**) U.S. unified functional command established on June 1, 1992, and commanded by a U.S. four-star flag officer (CINCUSSTRATCOM; currently a U.S. Navy admiral) from headquarters at Offut Air Force Base, Omaha, Nebraska. USSTRATCOM is the successor to the Strategic Air Command (SAC), and CINCUSSTRATCOM is responsible for U.S. strategic nuclear forces assigned the mission of deterring a nuclear attack on the United States and its allies, and, if deterrence fails, of conducting strategic nuclear warfighting operations to achieve national objectives. CINCUSSTRATCOM controls U.S. Air Force and U.S. Navy elements of the U.S. nuclear triad, which includes manned strategic bombers, intercontinental ballistics missiles (ICBM), and ballistic missile submarines (SSBN), as well as the Joint Strategic Target Planning Staff which prepares the SINGLE INTEGRATED OPERATIONAL PLAN (SIOP).

USTRANSCOM • *abbr.* United States Transportation Command.

U.S. Transportation Command • (**USTRANSCOM**) U.S. unified functional command established on October 1, 1987, and operational from October 1, 1988. USTRANSCOM is commanded from headquarters at Scott Air Force Base, Illinois, by the Commander in Chief, U.S. Transportation Command (CINCUSTRANSCOM), a four-star billet which may be filled by a flag officer from any service. USTRANSCOM provides strategic land, sea, and air transport across the full range of military operations and serves as the U.S. Department of Defense worldwide manager for common user ports of embarkation and debarkation. The subordinate component commands of USTRANSCOM are: Military Traffic Management Command (MTMC); Military Sealift Command (MSC); and Air Mobility Command (AMC).

Utah Beach • one of the five beaches targeted for landing in the D-DAY operation and one of the two under U.S. control. It was the westernmost beach, on the eastern shore of the base of the Cotentin Peninsula. It was added late in the planning for Normandy, with the mission of capturing Cherbourg. The landing was off-target by more than a mile, which proved to be fortunate because it allowed the men to go ashore in a less defended area. See also OMAHA BEACH.

Utah Militia • the militia forces of the Mormon-led government in the Utah Territory. On September 15, 1857, the Mormon leader Brigham Young mobilized the Utah militia to resist United States troops under ALBERT SIDNEY JOHNSTON sent to quell Mormon opposition to the Federal government. The resulting MORMON WAR was ended in June 1858 without significant bloodshed when Young permitted Johnston's forces to march through Salt Lake City and encamp nearby.

UTC • *abbr.* unit type code.

utility helicopter • a multipurpose helicopter that transports troops but is also capable of performing other battle roles, including command and control, logistics, casualty evacuation, or firepower support, for example, the SEASPRITE.

Utrecht, Treaty of |ˈyo͞oˌtrekt; ˈNˌtreKHt| • (also called **Peace of Utrecht**) a treaty to end QUEEN ANNE'S WAR and that included agreements signed by France and Great Britain on April 11, 1713 and by Spain and Great Britain on July 13, 1713. France recognized the British claim to the Hudson Bay Territory, Acadia, and the island of Newfoundland, but it retained fishing rights to the island. French settlers in newly acquired British territory were permitted to practice the Roman Catholic faith. France also agreed to stop supporting James Edward, the son of the deposed James II, recognized Queen Anne as Britain's sovereign ruler. Spain pledged to keep in its possession all portions of Spanish America and to allow Britain to send an annual trade ship there.

UUM-44A • see SUBMARINE ROCKET.

UW • *abbr.* unconventional warfare.

Uzi |ˈo͝ozē| • *n.* a type of submachine gun of Israeli design.

ORIGIN: 1950s: from *Uziel* Gal, the Israeli army officer who designed it.

V-1 • *n.* a small flying bomb powered by a simple jet engine, used by the Germans in WORLD WAR II. Also called DOODLEBUG.

ORIGIN: abbreviation of German *Vergeltungswaffe* 'reprisal weapon.'

V-2 • *n.* a rocket-powered flying bomb, which was the first ballistic missile, used by the Germans in WORLD WAR II.

ORIGIN: see V-1.

V-22 • see OSPREY.

VA • *abbr.* **1** Veterans' Administration. **2** Vice Admiral.

Valcour Island, Battle of • an important battle in the REVOLUTIONARY WAR, fought on October 10, 1776 on Lake Champlain between rival fleets of British and American warships. The Americans were far outnumbered and seeing their desperate plight, commander BENEDICT ARNOLD made a daring nighttime retreat past the British. He managed to salvage a few ships, though the British were in hot pursuit and engaged him again the next day. The battle gave decisive control of Lake Champlain to the British.

Vallejo, Mariano Guadalupe |vəˈlā(h)ō| (1808–1890) • California provincial official and army officer. Born in Monterey, California, Vallejo became a soldier when he was fifteen. In the 1830s he supported revolts against authoritarian Mexican governors, and after his nephew became governor Vallejo was appointed commandant of the provincial military forces in 1838. He aided the many Americans coming to settle in California, but was repaid by being imprisoned for two months during the Bear Flag Revolt in 1846. Afterwards he served in the new state's legislature and spent much of his time occupied in lawsuits to help old Spanish-Mexican families salvage property from the newcomers. He died at his home in Sonoma.

Valley Campaign • see SHENANDOAH VALLEY.

Valley Forge • an area in Chester County, Pennsylvania, where Gen. GEORGE WASHINGTON, during the winter of 1777–78, established the headquarters of the Continental army in the REVOLUTIONARY WAR. Although the suffering of troops during that winter is part of American folklore, other winter ordeals were probably worse; Valley Forge is well known because Washington stressed his army's suffering in order to gain political support. However, the army's discipline and efficiency improved during the winter, which marked a turning point in the war, and the encampment became a symbol of endurance in adversity. Valley Forge became a Pennsylvania state park in 1893 and a U.S. national park on July 4, 1976.

***Valley Forge*, USS** • (**CV-45**) a Ticonderoga-class carrier constructed with money raised by Philadelphia citizens and commissioned early in November 1946. It delivered the first air strike of the KOREAN WAR on July 3, 1950. In 1952, after a return to the United States, the *Valley Forge* was reclassified as an attack carrier with the designation CVA-45 and, in 1953, began strikes against Communist supply dumps and troop billeting areas behind the front lines. Returning to San Diego early in the summer of 1953, the ship was again reclassified, this time as an antisubmarine warfare support carrier, redesignated CVS-45, and transferred to the Atlantic Fleet. After delivering U.S. Marines and CH-53 SEA STALLION helicopters in numerous assaults during the course of the VIETNAM WAR, the *Valley Forge* was decommissioned in 1970. Attempts to raise funds to convert the ship to a museum failed, and it was sold for scrap in 1971.

van • *n.* (**the van**) the foremost part of a company of people moving or preparing to move forward, especially the foremost division of an advancing military force: ***in the van*** *were the foremost chiefs and some of the warriors astride horses.*

Van Buren, Martin (1782–1862) • 8th President of the United States (1837–1841). Born in Kinderhook, New York, in 1782, Van Buren studied law and became active in Democratic Party politics in New York. He served in the New York Senate (1812–1816), as Attorney General (1816–1819), as U.S. Senator (1821–1828), and as governor of New York (1828–1829), from which office he resigned in to become Secretary of State (1829–1831) under President ANDREW JACKSON. He subsequently served as U.S. ambassador to Great Britain before being elected Vice President in 1832. In 1836, he was elected President of the United States. He was defeated for reelection by WILLIAM HENRY HARRISON in 1840 but remained active in politics and was the Free Soil candidate for President in 1848.

Van Cortlandt, Philip |væn 'kôrtlənt| (1749–1831) • Revolutionary army officer and New York politician. Born in New York City into one of the original Dutch land-owning families, Philip Van Cortlandt began his military career as a major in the Westchester militia in 1775. He soon was given command of a regiment by the Continental Congress. He served under Gen. HORATIO GATES during the SARATOGA campaign in 1777 and supervised the camp at VALLEY FORGE that winter as a member of GEORGE WASHINGTON's staff. Afterwards he accompanied Gen. JOHN SULLIVAN on his campaign against the Indians and participated in the American victory at YORKTOWN (1781). He was promoted to brevet brigadier general in 1782 for his courageous conduct under the MARQUIS DE LAFAYETTE. After the war he held a number of important state offices and served nine terms in the U.S. House of Representatives. When Lafayette visited the United States in 1824, Van Cortlandt had the honor to escort him as the ranking surviving officer of the Continental army.

Vandegrift, Alexander Archer |'vændə ˌgrift| (1887–1973) • U.S. marine officer. Born in Charlottesville, Virginia, Alexander Vandegrift enlisted in the marine corps in 1908 and was commissioned a second lieutenant the next year. He saw action in Nicaragua and Mexico before serving in the Haitian constabulary for most of the period from 1916 to 1923. He held a number of important assignments in China and Washington before being named assistant commander of the 1st Marine Division in 1941. The next year he was promoted to major general and given command of the division, just a few months before it landed on GUADALCANAL in the first big Allied amphibious assault on the road to Tokyo. The campaign there was one of the hardest-fought of the war. By the time Vandegrift's depleted division was relieved in December, the tide of battle on the island had swung decisively in the Americans' favor. In 1943 Vandegrift was awarded the CONGRESSIONAL MEDAL OF HONOR for his actions, and became only the second marine to reach the rank of lieutenant general. He commanded the 1st Marine Amphibious Corps in the landings on BOUGAINVILLE before leaving the theater to become commandant of the marine corps in January 1944. A year later he became the first marine on active duty ever to become a full general. He retired in 1949 and died in Bethesda, Maryland many years later.

Vandenberg, Hoyt Sanford (1899–1954) • U.S. army and air force officer. Born in Milwaukee, the nephew of U.S. senator Arthur H. Vandenberg, Hoyt Vandenberg graduated from WEST POINT in 1923. He went into the Air Service and followed a normal career pattern that found him on the Air Staff in Washington when American entered WORLD WAR II. In October 1942 he became Gen. JAMES H. DOOLITTLE's chief of staff, first for the Twelfth Air Force and then for the Northwest Africa Strategic Air Force. He flew many combat missions himself, and earned an appointment in 1944 as deputy commander of the Allied Expeditionary Air Forces for OPERATION OVERLORD. In August he took command of the Ninth Air Force that provided tactical air support for American ground forces in northwest Europe and flew escort missions for strategic bombers. He held a number of key posts in the new independent air force after the war, and became chief of staff in July 1948. He used his political connections and administrative skills to keep the service viable during a period of restricted defense budgets, and guided the air force through the Berlin airlift and its buildup during the KOREAN WAR. Worn out by his exertions and very ill, he retired in June 1953, and died in Washington, D.C. less than a year later.

Van Dorn, Earl |væn 'dôrn| (1820–1863) • U.S. and Confederate army officer. Born near Port Gibson, Mississippi, in 1820, Earl Van Dorn was graduated from West Point in 1842. He served in the MEXICAN WAR (1846–48)and with the 2nd U.S. Cavalry along the Mexican border fighting the Comanches. In 1861, Van Dorn resigned his U.S. commission and accepted appointment as a colonel in the Confederate army. In September 1861, he was promoted to major general and named to command the Trans-Mississippi Department. After defeats at PEA RIDGE (1862) and CORINTH (1862), Van Dorn was relieved of his command and reassigned to command a troop of cavalry. Although ill-suited to higher command, he was an energetic and successful small unit commander and achieved great success in an attack on the Union supply depot at Holly Springs, Mississippi (December 20, 1862), forcing Gen. ULYSSES S. GRANT to retreat to Memphis, Tennessee. While meeting with his staff on May 8, 1863, Van Dorn was shot and killed by a jealous husband.

vane • *n.* **1** a broad blade attached to a rotating axis or wheel that pushes or is pushed by wind or water and forms part of a machine or device such as a windmill, propeller, or turbine. **2** a broad, flat projecting surface designed to guide the motion of a projectile, such as a feather on an arrow or a fin on a torpedo.

Van Fleet, James Alward (1892–1992) • Born in Coytesville, New Jersey, James A. Van Fleet graduated with the renowned WEST POINT class of 1915. He joined the infantry branch and saw action in WORLD WAR I commanding a machine gun battalion in the MEUSE-ARGONNE OFFENSIVE. Most of his assignments before WORLD WAR II dealt with training reservists, and for the first three years of the conflict he commanded the 8th Infantry Regiment. His unit led the assault on UTAH BEACH in June 1944 and helped capture CHERBOURG. In October he took command of the 90th Division, and led it through the BATTLE OF THE BULGE. He then took over the XXIII Corps in England before moving to command the III Corps in March, where he spearheaded the First Army's advance out of the Remagen bridgehead. From 1948 to 1950 Van Fleet directed successful military adviser missions sent to defeat communist insurgencies in Greece and Turkey under the TRUMAN DOCTRINE. In April 1951 he succeeded Gen. MATTHEW B. RIDGWAY as commander of the Eighth Army in Korea. Promoted to full general, Van Fleet endured bitter fighting, frustrating negotiations, and the loss of his son on a bombing mission. He is recognized as "the father of the South Korean Army" for his work training Republic of Korea forces.

vanguard • *n.* the foremost part of an advancing army or naval force.

Van Lew, Elizabeth L. |væn 'lo͞o| (1818–1900) • Union spy. Born in Richmond, Virginia, Elizabeth Van Lew was educated in Philadelphia and developed strong antislavery views. During the CIVIL WAR she remained loyal to the Union, often visiting LIBBY PRISON to help prisoners and gather information that she could transmit by agents and relay stations to Union headquarters outside of Richmond. She hid escaped prisoners in her house, and after Gen. HUGH KILPATRICK's disastrous 1864 cavalry raid on the Confederate capital she spirited the body of his deputy Col. Ulric Dahlgren out of the city. She even had an agent in JEFFERSON DAVIS's home, and her intelligence gathering proved invaluable during the siege of PETERSBURG. After the fall of Richmond, Gen. ULYSSES S. GRANT personally thanked and protected Van Lew. She later served as the postmistress of Richmond and in the Post Office Department in Washington. She returned to Richmond in the late 1880s and lived as a social outcast in her family mansion until her death.

Van Schaick, Goose |væn 'skīk| (1736–1789) • REVOLUTIONARY WAR army officer. Born in Albany, New York into a wealthy family, GOOSE VAN SCHAICK picked up his first military experience as a militia officer during the FRENCH AND INDIAN WARS. He began the Revolutionary War as colonel of the Second New York Regiment, which saw limited service during Gen. Richard Montgomery's invasion of Canada. In 1776 Van Schaick took command of the First New York Regiment of the Continental army. He spent most of the war organizing state defenses against Indian and British incursions, though he did join GEORGE WASHINGTON's army for the Battles of MONMOUTH and YORKTOWN. Van Schaick's most notable military feat was his successful April 1779 raid against the Onondaga Indians, which was a precursor to Gen. JOHN SULLIVAN's Indian campaign and earned praise from Washington and Congress. Van Schaick was breveted brigadier general in October 1783 and retired from the army the next month.

Van Wyck, Charles Henry |væn 'wīk; 'wik| (1824–1895) • U.S. army officer and politician. Charles Henry Van Wyck was born in Poughkeepsie, New York to a distinguished Dutch family. He graduated from Rutgers in 1843 and beagan a law career. He served two terms representing his New York 11th district in Congress before the outbreak of the CIVIL WAR. He raised and commanded the Fifty-sixth New York Volunteer Regiment, which served under GEORGE B. MCCLELLAN in the PENINSULAR CAMPAIGN (1862) and later under Rufus Saxton in the Department of the South. Van Wyck stayed in service a year after the war ended as commander of the District ofWestern South Carolina. He then returned to his political career in New York, serving two more terms in Congress before moving to Nebraska. He was elected to the U.S. Senate from his new state in 1881.

variable • *adj.* **1** (of a wind) tending to change direction. **2** (**variables**) the region of light, variable winds to the north of the northeast trade winds or (in the southern hemisphere) between the southeast trade winds and the westerlies.

Varick, Richard (1753–1831) • REVOLUTIONARY WAR army officer and New York politician. Born in Hackensack, New Jersey, Richard Varick was a lawyer in New Yok City when the Revolutionary War broke out. He proved himself an able staff officer for Gens. PHILIP SCHUYLER and BENEDICT ARNOLD. Varick was Arnold's aide-de-camp when the treasonous general's plot was discovered to turn over WEST POINT to the British, and Varick appealed for help in restoring his own reputation to GEORGE WASHINGTON. With Congressional approval, Washington appointed Varick his private secretary, with the responsibility to preserve Washington's headquarters papers for posterity. Varick took two and a half years to produce forty-four bound volumes. After the war, he held a number of public offices in New York. He was also a founder of the American Bible Society, and was serving as its president when he died in Jersey City, New Jersey.

Varnum, James Mitchell (1748–1789) • REVOLUTIONARY WAR army officer and public official. Born in Dracut, Massachusetts, James Mitchell Varnum graduated from Rhode Island College (now Brown University) in 1769 and began practicing law in that state. In May 1775 he was appointed colonel of the 1st Rhode Island Infantry Regiment, which next year was mustered into Continental service and redesignated as the 9th Infantry. He led that unit throughout the siege of Boston and the battles around New York City. He became a brigadier general of the Continental army in 1777, and conducted operations to contain the British in Philadelphia. In 1779 he was named commander of the Rhode Island district, but after two months he resigned from the army and resumed his law practice, though he remained major general of Rhode Island militia. He was elected to the Continental Congress the next year. In October 1787 Congress appointed him a judge of the Northwest Territory. Varnum resigned as commander of the Rhode Island militia in May 1788 and moved to Marietta, Ohio to assume his new duties. He died there a few months later.

Varnum, Joseph Bradley (1750–1821) • U.S. militia officer and public servant. Born in Dracut, Massachusetts, Joseph Bradley Varnum served in a local militia company during the REVOLUTIONARY WAR. In 1776 he became its captain, and after the war he led it in the campaign to suppress SHAYS'S REBELLION. By 1805 he rose to the rank of major general of the Third Division, Massachusetts militia. By that time he was serving as a representative in Congress. In a noteworthy career in Washington, Varnum served as both Speaker of the House and president pro tempore of the Senate. He returned to Massachusetts in 1817 and was reelected to his old seat in the state Senate. He held that post until he died on the same Dracut farm where he had been born.

Vauban, Marshal Sébastien Le Prestre de • French military engineer, inventor of ricochet gunfire and the bayonet.

vaulting horse • a padded wooden block used for vaulting over by gymnasts and athletes.

VAW-133 • *abbr.* Carrier Airborne Early Warning Squadron 113.

VC • *abbr.* **1** Vietcong. **2** Victoria Cross.

vector • *n.* in air intercept, close air support, and air interdiction usage, a code meaning, "Alter heading to magnetic heading indicated." The heading ordered must be in three digits (e.g., "vector zero six zero").

vectored attack • attack in which a weapon carrier (air, surface, or subsurface), not holding contact on the target, is vectored to the weapon delivery point by a unit (air, surface, or subsurface) that holds contact on the target.

V-E Day • May 8, 1945, the day that marked victory in Europe for the Allies in WORLD WAR II. The defining events were the German's unconditional surrender to Gen. DWIGHT D. EISENHOWER at Rheims, France, and to the Soviets in Berlin on May 7. President HARRY S. TRUMAN announced the event over the radio in the United States at 9 am.

vedette |və'det| • *n.* a mounted sentry positioned beyond an army's outposts to observe the movements of the enemy.

veer[1] • *v.* **1** change direction suddenly: *an oil tanker that had veered off course.* **2** (of the wind) change direction clockwise around the points of the compass: *the wind veered southwest.* The opposite of BACK.

veer[2] • *v.* slacken or let out (a rope or cable) in a controlled way.

vehicle • *n.* any self-propelled device, for example, an aircraft or a car, tank, or truck, designed to transport people as well as cargo.

Vela Hotel • an early U.S. satellite program for detecting nuclear detonations in space; now absorbed by the Integrated Satellite system.

Venable, Charles Scott |'venəbəl| (1827–1900) • Confederate army officer and teacher. Born in Prince Edward County, Virginia, Charles Venable taught mathematics at Hampden-Sydney College, the University of Georgia, and South Carolina College in the years before the CIVIL WAR. He served as a second lieutenant in the militia at the bombardment of FORT SUMTER before enlisting in the Confederate army for the First Battle of BULL RUN in 1861. He rose to the rank of captain defending New Orleans and Vicksburg, before being selected as one of Gen. ROBERT E. LEE's aides during his staff reorganization of 1862. Venable served faithfully in that position until the surrender at Appomattox, finishing the war as a lieutenant colonel. In the spring of 1865 he accepted a teaching position at the University of Virginia, and was instrumental in reestablishing it as a leader in the South for higher education in both mathematics and astronomy.

vent • *n.* the touch hole of a gun.
DERIVATIVES: **ventless** *adj.*

Veracruz • a major Gulf Coast seaport in Mexico that was the site of the first U.S. amphibious landing by Gen. WINFIELD SCOTT on March 9, 1847, during a campaign of the MEXICAN WAR (1846–48). After landing unopposed, Scott's marines dragged naval guns ashore and besieged the city until it surrendered on March 20.

Veracruz incident • an ancillary incident in WORLD WAR I, in which the Mexican city of Veracruz was occupied by American forces dispatched by President WOODROW WILSON in April, 1914, in the wake of an American ship being detained near Tampico. Later the port was seized on the strength of a report that Germany had dispatched an arms shipment to the Mexican dictatorship then in power.

Verdun, Battle of • a long-running battle in WORLD WAR I between French and German forces at Verdun, France. Fighting began on February 21, 1916 with a German attack on the fortified citadel there, which the Germans had chosen with the aim of wearing down the French through attrition. Fighting continued for four months with casualties in the hundreds of thousands on both sides, but the French eventually prevailed in the wake of German focus being drawn to the battle of the SOMME. By December the French had regained much of their lost ground.

verification • *n.* **1** the process of establishing the truth, accuracy, or validity of something: *the verification of official documents.* **2** the process of ensuring that procedures laid down in weapons limitation agreements are followed.

Versailles, Treaty of • a peace treaty signed by Germany and the Allies on June 28, 1919 at the end of WORLD WAR I. Negotiated at the Paris Peace Conference, it approved most of the proposals in President WOODROW WILSON'S FOURTEEN POINTS and included the Covenant of the League of Nations, Wilson's fourteenth point. It altered boundaries of several European nations and forced Germany to pay financial reparations, undergo disarmament, and relinquish its colonies. The U.S. Senate opposed the treaty, instead signing the TREATY OF BERLIN with Germany in August 1921.

vertical and/or short takeoff and landing • the vertical and/or short takeoff and landing capability for aircraft.

vertical envelopment • a tactical maneuver in which troops, either air-dropped or air-landed, attack the rear and flanks of a force, in effect cutting off or encircling the force.

vertical replenishment • the use of a helicopter for the transfer of materiel to or from a ship.

vertical/short takeoff and landing aircraft • (**VTOL**) any aircraft capable of taking off and landing either horizontally, using a short runway, or vertically.

vertical/short takeoff and landing aircraft • (**V/STOL**) an aircraft capable of executing a vertical takeoff and landing, a short takeoff and landing, or any combination of these modes of operation.

vertical takeoff and landing • the capability of an aircraft to take off and land vertically and to transfer to or from forward motion at heights required to clear surrounding obstacles.

Very light |ˈverē; ˈvirē| • a flare fired into the air from a pistol for signaling or for temporary illumination.

ORIGIN: early 20th cent.: named after Edward W. *Very* (1847–1910), American naval officer.

Very pistol |ˈvi(ə)rē ˌpistl; ˈverē ˌpistl| • a hand-held gun used for firing a Very light.

vessel • *n.* a ship or large boat.

veteran • *n.* **1** a person who has had long experience in a particular field, especially military service: *a veteran of two world wars.* **2** an ex-serviceman or -servicewoman.

Veterans Administration • see VETERANS AFFAIRS, DEPARTMENT OF.

Veterans Affairs, Department of • (**VA**) a U.S. federal agency that provides information on programs, benefits, and facilities for the U.S. veteran worldwide. Benefits to veterans of American wars date back as far as 1636. During the wars that followed, the benefits established include medical care and centers, pensions, loans for education, insurance, and burial costs. In 1930 several organizations were combined to form the Veterans Administration, which was responsible for the administration of veterans' benefits. It is now called the Department of Veterans Affairs, and it serves the veteran, veterans' dependents, veterans' organizations, the military, the general public, and veteran employees.

Veterans Bureau • an organization for veterans of American wars established in 1921 under President WARREN G. HARDING. Given direct authority to construct veteran hospitals, the Bureau's first director, Charles R. Forbes, oversaw the building of veterans' hospitals that were free of safety hazards. In addition, he conceived of treating separate illnesses at separate facilities rather than caring for all patients together at one hospital. The Veterans Bureau, despite scandals, set a standard for veterans' hospitals built later. It was succeeded by the Veterans Administration. See VETERANS AFFAIRS, DEPARTMENT OF.

Veterans Day • (in the United States) a public holiday held on the anniversary of the end of WORLD WAR I (November 11) to honor U.S. veterans and victims of all wars. It replaced ARMISTICE DAY in 1954.

Veterans of Foreign Wars • (Also, **Veterans of Foreign Wars of the United States;** official name **VFW**) an association founded in Columbus, Ohio, in 1899 and chartered by Congress in 1936. To be eligible, members must have served in the U.S. military in a foreign country or in hostile waters during a campaign for which the U.S. government has authorized the awarding of a medal. The association, which is based in Kansas City, Missouri, helps members in dealing with the VETERANS ADMINISTRATION and works to secure benefits for veterans in areas such as job training and employment. Its local branches also sponsor patriotic and educational programs for communities and youth. Membership is nearly 1.75 million, making it the second-largest veterans' organization, after the AMERICAN LEGION.

Veterans Rights Union • (**VRU**) a veterans' group established by Union veterans of the CIVIL WAR. The organization lobbied for benefits on behalf of veterans.

"V for Victory" • a slogan and hand sign (formed by holding up the index and middle fingers of the right hand in a V-shape, palm out) popular among the allies in WORLD WAR II.

vice • *n.* informal short for VICE ADMIRAL, etc.

vice admiral • a naval officer of very high rank, in particular an officer in the U.S. Navy or Coast Guard ranking above rear admiral and below admiral.

Vichy Regime • the right-wing authoritarian government of Marshal Philippe Pétain which came to power in France following the defeat of France by Germany in 1941. Located in the spa town of Vichy in southern France, the collaborationist Pétain government controlled fully only that French territory not physically occupied by German forces. In the latter area, Vichy rule was subject to the German authorities in Paris. Although in some ways resistant to its German masters, the Vichy government did cooperate in various repressive measures and in both the round-up of French citizens for compulsory labor service in German and in the deportation of French Jews to the Nazi death camps in Eastern Europe. With the allied liberation of France in 1944 and the assumption of power by the Free French forces of Gen. CHARLES DE GAULLE, the Vichy government was spirited away under German protection and its members subsequently endured exile or returned to France to face trial as traitors. Vichy legislation and policies were voided by the post-war French government.

Vicksburg campaign • fighting in the CIVIL WAR in and around Vicksburg, Mississippi between October 1862 and July 1863, when the city finally fell to forces under Gen. ULYSSES S. GRANT. This gave control of the Mississippi to the Union and split the Confederacy in half. The city was under siege by Union forces for the last six weeks of the campaign; the surviving Confederate forces under Gen. JOHN PEMBERTON surrendered on July 4th.

victor • *n.* a person who defeats an enemy or opponent in a battle, game, or other competition.

Victoria Cross (VC) • a decoration awarded for conspicuous bravery in the British Commonwealth armed services, instituted by Queen Victoria in 1856.

Victory • **1** code name for U.S. XVIIIth Airborne Corps phase line in the PERSIAN GULF WAR (1991). **2** HMS *Victory*, Admiral Horatio Nelson's flagship in the Battle of Trafalgar.

victory • *n.* (pl. **-ies**) an act of defeating an enemy or opponent in a battle, game, or other competition: *an election victory | after six years of war, victory at last.*

Victory Program • the plan developed by the U.S. Army War Plans Division for the mobilization of the American manpower and materiel needed to defeat the Axis powers in WORLD WAR II. The principal architect of the "Jenkin Program" was Maj. (later Lt. Gen.) ALBERT C. WEDEMEYER, who calculated that the United States could mobilize a maximum of 8,75,658 men organized in 213 Army divisions. In the event, by May 31, 1945, the United States had mobilized 8,291,236 men, including U.S. Army Air Forces personnel, organized in only 90 divisions, a force barely sufficient, with the aid of our allies, to defeat first Germany and then Japan.

victualer |ˈvidlər| • *n.* a ship providing supplies for troops or other ships.

VIDOC • *abbr.* visual information documentation.

Vietcong • a derogatory contraction of the term *Viet Nam Cong San* ("Vietnamese Communists") used to refer to the Communist-led insurgents operating in the Republic of (South) Vietnam from the mid-1950s to 1975. The term was never used by Vietnamese Communists who preferred to identify themselves as the *National Front for the Liberation of South Vietnam.*

Vietminh • an abbreviation of *Vietnam Doc Lap Dong Minh Hoi* (League for the independence of Vietnam), the Communist-led nationalist organization formed in southern China in 1941 under the leadership of HO CHI MINH to combat the Japanese occupiers and French collaborationist administration in Indochina. In 1951, the Vietminh political apparatus was incorporated in the newly formed Workers' Party of Vietnam (*Dang Lao Dong Viet Nam*). The term Vietminh is also used to designate the military arm of the Vietnamese nationalist movement. Led by Gen. VO NGUYEN GIAP, the Vietminh guerrilla army evolved toward a conventional force after 1945 and led the fight to expel the French colonialist administration of Indochina. The Vietminh defeated the French-led forces at DIEN BIEN PHU in 1954 and brought about the withdrawal of the French from Indochina. Subsequently, the Vietminh forces were transformed into the People's Army of Vietnam (PAVN) and supported the Communist-led NATIONAL LIBERATION FRONT in its successful bid to unite Vietnam by conquering the Western-oriented Republic of (South) Vietnam.

Vietnamization program • U.S. policy developed during the Nixon administration after the United States election of 1968 which encompassed the withdrawal of United States troops from South Vietnam and the "turning over" of the war against the Communist insurgents and North Vietnamese forces in South Vietnam to the government of the Republic of (South) Vietnam and its armed forces.

Vietnam syndrome • in the United States, an exaggerated preference for a policy which precludes the use of U.S. military forces overseas unless in overwhelming numbers, with unambiguous public and Congressional support, and with an assurance of a quick victory. Likewise the policy preference for not becoming involved in protracted military operations abroad. So called because of the perception that the failures of the VIETNAM WAR could be attributed to the (inadequate) incremental application of force, lack of public and Congressional support, and the inability to achieve a quick victory with relatively low casualties.

Vietnam Veterans Against the War • see VIETNAM VETERANS OF AMERICA.

Vietnam Veterans of America • (**VVA**) the only national organization for Vietnam veterans that was chartered by Congress and is dedicated exclusively to Vietnam-era veterans and their families. Initially known as the Council of Vietnam Veterans, Vietnam Veterans of America was formed in 1978; it provides legal, social, and educational services to members, and lobbies Congress on their behalf in the areas of employment and health. National membership is approximately 50,000.

Vietnam Veterans War Memorial • a memorial to American military personnel killed or missing in the VIETNAM WAR, located on The Mall in Washington, D.C. Designed by a young architect, Maya Lin, the original memorial consisted of a semi-sunken black marble wall inscribed with the names of the killed or missing and was the center of considerable controversy in that many veterans considered it symbolically inappropriate ("a black hole in the ground"). A more traditional memorial statue grouping and an American flag have since been added, and even many early opponents of Ms. Lin's design have come to accept the memorial as a fitting tribute to the sacrifice of those whose names are inscribed upon it.

Vietnam War • (1965–75) the most domestically divisive and least militarily decisive overseas campaign ever fought by the U.S. Given the slow and hesitant commitment to the war, its ambiguous results may not be that surprising. From 1950 to 1965, U.S. presidents gradually increased military and economic aid, first to French Indochina and then to South Vietnam, Laos, and Cambodia in an effort to halt thespread of Communism. President HARRY S. TRUMAN first authorized aid in 1950 to help France maintain control of its colony. In 1954, the French were defeated at DIEN BIEN PHU by the Communist-led Vietnamese Nationalist Army, leading to the GENEVA AGREEMENT ON INDOCHINA, which set up terms and a timetable for Vietnamese independence. The U.S. did not sign the treaty and though it agreed to abide by its spirit, it quickly began to undermine it by sending military advisers and the CIA to help create South Vietnam, eventually installing a pro-U.S. leader, NGO DINH DIEM, who had little Vietnamese backing. And though President DWIGHT D. EISENHOWER's military experience made him reluctant to step up the involvement, President JOHN F. KENNEDY did increase it in 1961 by sending arms, military advisers, and GREEN BERET forces in order to equip and train the South Vietnamese for counterinsurgency tactics against Communist guerrillas. To justify these commitments, American foreign policymakers relied upon the DOMINO THEORY, which posited that if one country succumbed to Communism, the rest would fall too. Vietnam—that is, the VIETMINH (later the National Liberation Front) and HO CHI MINH's government—was seen as the domino in line after China, and thus had to be stopped. Of course, there were economic motives, too, as the U.S. hoped to widen its Pacific trade. But perhaps the most important factor was the commitment itself, as each president feared looking weak both at home and abroad. Democrats, under whose watch, the Republicans famously claimed, Americans hadlost China to Communism, were particularly vulnerable. And for Kennedy, the failure to stop Cuban Communism was an even more recent debacle. On an international level, all administrations from Truman's through Nixon's were concerned about the negative impression a de-escalation might make on other nations, considering that the U.S. had pledged its support to South Vietnam. It is quite certain that few policymakers, at least until the latter half of the 1960s, foresaw the extent of American involvement,let alone the possibility of failure.Not just the gradual escalation, but the lack of a formal declaration of war makes it hard to determine its precise beginning. Conventionally, it is dated to the GULF OF TONKIN RESOLUTION, issued by Congress at the behest of President LYNDON B. JOHNSON in August 1964, which authorized the U.S. military to retaliate against the North Vietnamese for what was most probably a nonexistent attack against U.S. ships. The resolution functioned as a legislative basis for all subsequent deployment, which was quickly heightened when Johnson authorized a bombing campaign of North Vietnam in early 1965. During the next three years, the number of ground deployments, air force sorties, and bombing tonnage rose dramatically, and the targets spread throughout North Vietnam and into Laos, as well. What Johnson had intended to be a limited war, particularly because he feared Soviet and Chinese involvement, was no longer so limited. In response, Hanoi began sending more units of the North Vietnamese Army into the South, launching a major offensive in the Central Highlands in October 1965. The U.S. won the ensuing Battle of the Ia Drang Valley, a campaign from which it concluded that airborne "search and destroy" tactics could win what appeared to be awar of attrition. But while U.S. estimations of enemy body counts, which were regularly reported to the media, continued to rise, the intensity of North Vietnamese military engagement was not waning. In early 1967, Gen. WILLIAM C. WESTMORELAND mounted OPERATION CEDAR FALLS near Saigon and OPERATION JUNCTION CITY in the Central Highlands in an attempt to win the war. These operations saw the introduction to Vietnam of carpet-bombing, which had originated in the Pacific theater in WORLD WAR II, and of AGENT ORANGE, the now-notorious toxic defoliant. Still, the enemy did not disappear, and with third-party negotiations rejected by both Hanoi and Washington, the war reached a stalemate.In January 1968, the Vietcong successfully launched the TET OFFENSIVE, a series of coordinated attacks on urban centers and military posts in South Vietnam that were intended to foment a widespread rebellion against Saigon and the U.S. Although no cities succumbed, both sides suffered heavy casualties, and the result was astrategic victory for the North and its Southern followers. Roughly at the same time, the North Vietnamese three-month siege of KHE SANH was rebuffed by the outnumbered Marines, but again, U.S. victory was ambiguous. In the face of the exacting casualtytoll, the inconclusive results, and increasingly intense public and political scrutiny, Johnson declared in March that bombing of North Vietnam would be restricted and policies would concentrate on a negotiated settlement. This was the same month in which U.S. soldiers committed numerous atrocities in the MY LAI MASSACRE, an incident that was covered up from the press and the public until late 1969. What Johnson's de-escalation policies meant was an increasing development of VIETNAMIZATION, an effort to train Saigon's army to take over the bulk of the fighting. President RICHARD M. NIXON elaborated upon this goal by mounting a campaign of secret bombings of Cambodia in early 1969, while also starting to withdraw U.S. troops. Soldier morale sapped further as the futilityof what was rapidly becoming limited ground action, such as was evident at HAMBURGER HILL, sank in. The public at home was no more satisfied with the slow-moving withdrawal, which still left over 150,000 troops in Vietnam by late 1971. American aircraft continued to strafe Laos and Cambodia in support of Saigon's ground forces, who were not so efficiently completing the process of Vietnamization. Indeed, by the final official bombing campaigns, which included the LINEBACKER and LINEBACKER II raids on North Vietnam in late 1972 and early 1973, total U.S. bomb tonnage had far exceeded the total dropped in World War II. On January 27, 1973, the U.S., North and South Vietnam, and the NLF's provisionary government signed the PARIS PEACE AGREEMENTS, confirming terms of a ceasefire agreed to but not enforced three months earlier. By April 1, almost all U.S. forces had left Vietnam. Shortly afterwards, Congress stopped funding the bombing campaign in Cambodia, and in November, it overcame Nixon's veto to pass the WAR POWERS RESOLUTION, which restricted the president's power to deploy forces without Congressional approval. This act culminated pressure to stop what had been labeled the "imperial presidency" since early in the war. Nixon, who had declared the treaty to be "peace with honor" was perhaps lucky to already be out of office when the VIETCONG captured Saigon in 1975, forcing a dramatic rooftop evacuation by the U.S. embassy staff. This episode underlines the notion that, on a military level, the motivations to fight the war were exaggerated and the military strategies ill-conceived. Some maintain that in the midst of the COLD WAR, U.S. global credibility was at stake, and that an increased number and efficiency of the attacks should have been formulated. Still, that would have probably drawn Chinese and Soviet involvement, and perhaps escalated the tragedy beyond its already significant proportions. Worse still was that the war not only severely damaged the American economy, but also appeared to have torn the even larger fabric of American society in two. War-related spending had produced high inflation, high unemployment, an unfavorable balance of trade, and insufficient tax increases. These factors contributed to the oil crisis in 1973, as well as to the speculation-driven real estate boom of the 1970s, and also led to the creation of variable interest rates. And during the war itself, the staggering economy did little to improve Johnson or Nixon's standing, most notably among the lower and lower-middle classes. Johnson's underselling of the war which stripped his more popular Great Society programs of necessary funding, quickly came back to haunt him. Not only did he fail to garner public support for the war, but the strength of the antiwar movement contributed considerably to running him out of office. In 1968, the bloody riots at the Democratic National Convention in Chicago maimed George McGovern's campaign, even if the protesters were not, in the final analysis, primarily responsible for the violence. Draft dodging, draft resistance and conscientious objectors pervaded the war effort, especially as the system seemed to discriminate in favor of the middle and upper class. While Nixon tried to placate resistance by instituting the lottery in December 1969, it did not cease until he terminated the draft in July 1973. Still, like Johnson, Nixon generally believed that the antiwar movement bolstered North Vietnamese hopes and thus considered the protesters treacherous. And while de-escalation quelled the protests, the 1970 revelation of the secret campaigns in Cambodia re-ignited them, including the tragedies at Kent State and Jackson State Universities. Further down the road, some of Nixon's extralegal and illegal inquiries into antiwar protesters became part of the WATERGATE scandal. On the whole, then, the war cost America dearly. A depressed economy, decreased global credibility, loss of faith in the government, and an overwhelming loss of pride were only some of the longer-term effects. A renewed commitment to isolationism, as well as a popular image of the deranged Vietnam Veteran, have combined to throw doubt on foreign policy commitments in the past three decades. And while scholarly and military interpretations of the war have continued to change over that same time, from soul-searching to anti-government to anti-liberal and back again, the consensus appears to remain that, in the sometimes mirage-making heat of the Cold War, the U.S. fatally mistook the ardency of Vietnamese nationalism for a fervent commitment to Communism.

vigilance committee • a body of vigilantes.

vigilante |ˌvijəˈlæntē| • *n.* a member of a self-appointed group of citizens who undertake law enforcement in their community without legal authority, typically because the legal agencies are thought to be inadequate.
DERIVATIVES: **vigilantism** |-ˌtizəm| *n.*
ORIGIN: mid 19th cent.: from Spanish, literally 'vigilant.'

Vigilante • an advanced twin-engine, supersonic all-weather attack aircraft designed to carry a free-fall nuclear bomb and optimized for low-level attacks at high speed. It is one of the largest aircraft flown from a carrier.

It proved unsuccessful as a nuclear bomber, perhaps because the bomb ejection mechanism was unsatisfactory.

Viking • (**S-3**) a multicrew antisubmarine aircraft propelled by twin turbofan engines that can operate from aircraft carriers. Using an integrated computer-controlled attack system, combined with a variety of conventional and/or nuclear ordnance, the S-3 can detect, locate, and destroy submarines or surface vessels.

Villa, Pancho (1878–1923) • a Mexican revolutionary and guerrilla leader. He was given the birth name Doroteo Arango (also called Francisco). Having killed the owner of the estate where he worked because he had assaulted Villa's sister, Villa was forced to flee to the mountains, spending his adolescence as a fugitive. He fought in the revolts against two dictators, Porfirio Díaz and Victoriano Huerta, and fled Mexico in 1912, but returned in 1913 and formed a military group of several thousand men, the famous División del Norte. In 1914, joining his force with that of Venustiano Carranza, they won a decisive victory over Huerta and entered Mexico City as the victorious leaders of a revolution. His relationship with Carranza was short-lived, however, and, after being defeated in several battles, Villa and Emiliano Zapata fled to the northern mountains of Mexico, where he engaged in rebellion and guerilla activities. In 1916, after he executed sixteen U.S. citizens at Santa Isabel, President WOODROW WILSON sent Gen. JOHN J. PERSHING after Villa. But the willingness of his comrades to help him and his knowledge of the geography of northern Mexico, in addition to the fact that Mexico didn't want Pershing on its soil, made it impossible to catch him. When Carranza's government was toppled in 1920, Villa was pardoned and given a ranch in Chihuahua after he promised to retire from political activities. He was assassinated on his ranch in 1923.

***Vincennes*, USS** • (**CA-44**) a Ticonderoga-class guided missile cruiser torpedoed and sunk by Japanese warships off Savo in the SOLOMON ISLANDS on August 8, 1942.

Vinson, Carl (1883–1981) • a congressman in the U.S. House of Representatives for more than fifty years (1914–1965), Vinson served on the House Naval Affairs Committee (1917–1948), chairing it from 1932–1946, and, after the Republican-instigated reorganization of Congress's committee infrastructure, became chairman of the HOUSE ARMED SERVICES COMMITTEE when Democrats regained control of the House in 1948. Throughout his career, Vinson was a staunch advocate for support and strengthening of the military, and, as well, a staunch opponent of civil rights legislation, desegregation, and implementation of the U.S. Supreme Court's decision in *Brown v. Board of Education* (1954). During his tenure, Speaker of the House Sam Rayburn called Vinson the "best legislative technician in the House," and his colleagues called him the "old swamp fox."

Vinson-Trammel Naval Act • an act cosponsored by Georgia Democrat CARL VINSON in 1934 as part of the naval expansion program of President FRANKLIN D. ROOSEVELT's administration during the Great Depression. It authorized the navy to construct 102 new warships over the next eight years to bring the U.S. Navy up to the strength authorized by the WASHINGTON NAVAL ARMS LIMITATIONS TREATY of 1922.

violence • *n.* behavior involving physical force intended to hurt, damage, or kill someone or something.

Viper • slang F-16. See FIGHTING FALCON.

***Virginia*, CSS** • originally built by the United States and christened the *Merrimack,* the Confederacy salvaged the conventional steam frigate, cut away the hull, and converted into it into an ironclad vessel rechristened the *Virginia.* On March 8, 1862, the *Virginia,* supported by several other Confederate vessels, destroyed an entire fleet of wooden Union warships off the coast of Newport News, Virginia, including both the *Congress* and the *Cumberland*; the *Minnesota,* a Union frigate, ran aground. When Confederate forces abandoned the GOSPORT NAVY YARD on May 11, 1862, the crew scuttled the ship so that Union forces could not capture it.

The success of the *Virginia* marked the end of wooden navies.

Virginia Military Institute • an undergraduate private military school in Lexington, Virginia. Founded in 1839 and modeled on WEST POINT's engineering program, it was the first military college in the U.S. to receive state support. In response to a 1996 U.S. Supreme Court ruling, it began admitting female cadets in 1997.

Union troops burned down the school in 1864, and it was reopened in 1865.

visit-and-search • *n.* the procedure employed by Navy and Coast Guard patrol vessels involving the boarding and systematic search of a suspect vessel for contraband.

visual information documentation • (**VIDOC**) motion media, still photography, and audio recording of technical and nontechnical events while they occur, usually not controlled by the recording crew. Visual information documentation encompasses combat camera, operational documentation, and technical documentation.

vital ground • ground of such importance that it must be retained or controlled for the success of the mission.

Vittles, Operation • see BERLIN AIRLIFT.

V-J Day • August 15, 1945, the day that Japan surrendered to terms proposed by the Allies at the POTSDAM CONFERENCE. The precipitating events were the dropping of atomic bombs on HIROSHIMA and NAGASAKI on August 6 and 9 respectively. The actual signing of the peace instruments was on September 2, 1945.

Vladivostok Agreement • an informal accord reached by President GERALD R. FORD and Soviet leader LEONID BREZHNEV in 1974 to limit the total number of each side's strategic launchers and bombers. It was negotiated during SALT II and established the framework for the SALT II Treaty.

VMI • *abbr.* Virginia Military Institute.

volley • *n.* (pl. **-eys**) a number of bullets, arrows, or other projectiles discharged at one time: *the infantry let off a couple of volleys.*

volley fire • a method of small arms or artillery fire in which all of a given units weapons are fired simultaneously so as to maximize the effect on the enemy.

voluntary training • training in a non-pay status for INDIVIDUAL READY RESERVISTS and active-status standby reservists. Participation in voluntary training is for retirement points only and may be achieved by any of the following: training with the SELECTED RESERVE or voluntary training units; completing authorized military correspondence courses; attending designated courses of instruction; performing equivalent duty; participating in special military and professional events designated by the military departments; participating in authorized civil-defense activities. Retirees may voluntarily train with organizations to which they are properly preassigned by orders for recall to active duty in a national emergency or declaration of war.

voluntary training unit • a unit formed by volunteers to provide reserve component training in a non-pay status for INDIVIDUAL READY RESERVISTS and active-status standby reservists attached under competent orders and participating in such units for retirement points. Also called REINFORCEMENT TRAINING UNIT.

volunteer • *n.* **1** a person who freely enrolls for military service rather than being conscripted, especially a member of a force formed by voluntary enrollment and distinct from the regular army. **2** a person who freely offers to take part in an enterprise or undertake a task. **3** a person who works for an organization without being paid. • *v.* **1** freely offer to do something: *he volunteered for the job.* **2** offer (help) in such a way: *he volunteered his services as a driver for the convoy.* **3** work for an organization without being paid. **4** commit (someone) to a particular undertaking, typically without consulting them: *he was volunteered for parachute training by friends.*

Volunteers, U.S. • any of many volunteer groups that have served in the U.S. armed forces in every major war, including the CIVIL WAR and the SPANISH-AMERICAN WAR.

Von Braun, Werner (1912–1977) • rocket engineer. Born in Wirsitz, Germany, Werner Von Braun became chief of rocket research for the German army in 1932. When ADOLF HITLER built a new research facility at Peenemünde, Von Braun's group took advantage of their improved resources to develop the liquid-fueled V-2 missile, jet-assisted takeoff units, and even preliminary work on an intercontinental ballistic missile. Over 3500 of the V-2s were fired at London and Antwerp. Shortly before the end of the war Von Braun and many of his colleagues fled the advancing Russians and surrendered to American forces. He came to the United States to direct the army's missile proving ground at White Sands, New Mexico, and in 1950 took over the missile research facility at Huntsville, Alabama, where he supervised the development of REDSTONE, JUPITER, JUNO, and PERSHING rockets. He became a U.S. citizen in 1955. Von Braun pressed for a program of space exploration and his group orbited the first U.S. satellite, *Explorer I*, in 1958. When his group became part of the National Aeronautics and Space Administration in 1960, they worked on developing new launch vehicles, most notably the Saturn V that sent men to the moon. From 1970–1972 he served as deputy administrator of NASA, before retiring to enter private industry. For all of his contributions to the U.S. space program, von Braun was never able to completely leave behind his life and the work he'd done in Germany. He had joined the Nazi Party in 1937, probably in order to advance his own career as well as the acceptability of his dream of space flight, and accepted an honorary commission from the SS in 1940. In fact, he was arrested by the GESTAPO in 1944 for having placed his enthusiasm for space travel above the development of an effective missile, but he was released two weeks later because he was indispensable to the success of the crucial V-2 program. But he accepted the use of forced labor at Peenemunde and certainly knew that workers were being beaten, starved, and killed at Nordhausen.

VRU • *abbr.* Veterans Rights Union.

V/STOL • *abbr.* vertical/short takeoff and landing aircraft.

VTOL • *abbr.* vertical takeoff and landing.

Vulcan • an antiaircraft artillery gun with a 6--barreled, air-cooled, 20 mm rotary-fired system, designed for mounting on an armored personnel carrier. It was developed in the 1960s.

vulnerability • *n.L* **1** the susceptibility of a nation or military force to any action by any means through which its war potential or combat effectiveness may be reduced or its will to fight diminished. **2** the characteristics of a system which cause it to suffer a definite degradation (incapability to perform the designated mission) as a result of having been subjected to a certain level of effects in an unnatural (manmade) hostile environment.

VVA • *abbr.* Vietnam Veterans of America.

Ww

WAAC • the Women's Army Auxiliary Corps, or a member of this; formed in World War II and the predecessor of the WAC.

WAC |wæk| • *abbr.* Women's Army Corps.

wad • *n.* a disk of felt or another material used to keep powder or shot in place in a gun barrel. • *v.* (**wadded, wadding**) stop up (an aperture or a gun barrel) with a bundle or lump of soft material.

wadcutter • *n.* a bullet designed to cut a neat hole in a paper range target.

Waddell, James Iredell (1824–1886) • U.S. and Confederate naval officer. Born in Pittsboro, North Carolina, in 1824, James Iredell Waddell entered the U.S. Navy as a midshipman in 1841. He saw action off Veracruz during the Mexican War (1846–48) and then attended Annapolis, from which he was graduated in 1847. Upon his return from the Far East in 1862, he resigned his U.S. commission and joined the Confederate navy, serving on the Mississippi and on the Atlantic coast. In October 1864, he took command of the Confederate raider CSS *Shenandoah* in England, and sailed to the Pacific where he destroyed most of the Union whaling fleet. Following the Civil War, Waddell captained commercial vessels.

Wadsworth, James (1730–1817) • Revolutionary War militia officer and Connecticut politician. Born in Durham, Connecticut, James Wadsworth commanded a militia company in the Ticonderoga campaigns of 1758 and 1759. When the Revolutionary War began he was colonel of the Tenth Connecticut Militia Regiment, and he led a detachment of militia sent to reinforce the siege of Boston. In 1777 he became Connecticut's second highest ranking military officer, with the rank of major general of the militia. He resigned his commission in 1779, but continued to serve in the general assembly and on the Committee of Safety. After the war he became Connecticut's leading opponent of the new federal Constitution, and he spent his last thirty years in relative seclusion before dying in Durham, Connecticut.

Wadsworth, James Samuel (1807–1864) • U.S. army officer and politician. Born in Geneseo, New York, James Samuel Wadsworth was active in the state Republican party before the outbreak of the Civil War. He gave up a political appointment as a major general and volunteered his services as an aide to Gen. Irvin McDowell. Wadsworth displayed great courage at the First Battle of Bull Run (1861) and earned a commission as a brigadier general. He caused great controversy as commander of the defenses of Washington in 1862 when he claimed that Gen. George B. McClellan had not left sufficient forces behind, and consequently President Abraham Lincoln held back a corps from the Peninsula campaign. McClellan never forgave Wadsworth, and he could only get field duty after McClellan's removal. He commanded a division in the Army of the Potomac that saw only limited action at Chancellorsville, but suffered heavy casualties buying time for the army to arrive at Gettysburg on the first day of that engagement (1863). Afterwards he asked to be relieved, but after he served a short tour in the Mississippi Valley, Ulysses S. Grant reassigned Wadsworth to command another division in the Army of the Potomac. He was mortally wounded heroically rallying his soldiers in the Battle of the Wilderness on May 6, 1864. He died in a Confederate hospital two days later. A soldier there who had been treated kindly while Wadsworth's prisoner had the general given a proper burial, and then wrote to his wife so she could arrange to retrieve the body and return it to Geneseo.

Wadsworth, Jeremiah (1743–1804) • Revolutionary War soldier, congressman, and businessman. Born in Hartford, Connecticut, Jeremiah Wadsworth earned a reputation as shrewd businessman in the years before the Revolutionary War. He began the war serving as a commissary for Connecticut forces, but by 1778 the Continental Congress had appointed him to be commissary general for the Continental army. His efforts to keep that force amply supplied despite a lack of money and limited support from the states earned accolades from Gen. George Washington. Wadsworth resigned his position in early 1780 to return to his own business interests, which included employment by the Comte de Rochambeau as commissary for his French army in America. After the war Wadsworth developed many pioneering practices in farming, banking, insurance, and manufacturing. He was elected to three terms in the U.S. House of Representatives until resigning in 1795. He then served on the Connecticut state executive council until a few years before his death in Hartford.

Wadsworth, Peleg (1748–1829) • Revolutionary militia officer and congressman. Born in Duxbury, Massachusetts, Peleg Wadsworth graduated from Harvard in 1769. As captain of a company of militiamen he responded immediately to news of the Battle of Lexington (1775), joining forces in Boston assisting in the fortification of Dorchester Heights. He took part in the campaigns around New York with George Washington in 1776 and in John Sullivan's expedition to Rhode Island in 1778. Wadsworth became adjutant general of Massachusetts militia in 1778 and a brigadier general the next year. He was involved in the disastrous expedition to Penobscot Bay, and took command of the eastern militia department of Massachusetts in 1780. He was captured by a British raiding party the next year, but escaped after a few months confinement in Fort George. After the war he served in the state legislature before beginning a tenure of seven terms in Congress. In 1807 he moved to what is now Maine and established the town of Hiram, where he eventually died.

Waesche, Russell Randolph |'wāshē| (1886–1946) • U.S. Coast Guard officer. Born in Thurmont, Maryland, Russell Randolph Waesche graduated from Revenue Cutter Cadet School in 1906. In 1915 the Revenue Cutter Service became part of the new U.S. Coast Guard, and he soon commanded a series of cutters and destroyers. In 1936, President FRANKLIN D. ROOSEVELT appointed Waesche commandant of the Coast Guard with the rank of rear admiral. He was reappointed twice, in 1940 and 1944, and commanded the service throughout WORLD WAR II, when the Coast Guard was transferred from the Treasury Department to the Department of the Navy and given vastly increased responsibilities. These included patrol of waters around Greenland, antisubmarine patrols which sank 12 U-BOATS, coastal defense, and sea rescue. During the war the Coast Guard expanded from a strength of about 10,000 to almost 172,000 men, with 10,000 women in a women's reserve. Waesche was the first Coast Guard officer to reach the ranks of vice admiral and admiral.

WAF |wæf| • *abbr.* Women in the Air Force. • *n.* a member of the WAF.

Waffen-SS |'väfən| • the part of German SS armed, trained, organized, and employed during WORLD WAR II as elite conventional ground forces. By the end of the war in May 1945 more than 800,000 men had served in the 38 division-size units of the Waffen-SS. Waffen-SS units, which included formations composed of foreign volunteers, participated in all the major campaigns fought by German forces in World War II and were often given priority for equipment and replacements and assigned the most difficult offensive or defensive missions.

ORIGIN: German *Waffen* 'arms, weapons.'

WAFS • the Women's Auxiliary Ferrying Squadron, a unit of the Air Transport Command that delivered U.S.-manufactured military aircraft to Great Britain in WORLD WAR II.

wagon soldier • slang an artilleryman, a light artilleryman, or a field artilleryman.

The term "wagon soldier" appears in some versions of the artillery-oriented "Caisson Song" by Brig. Gen. Edmund L. Gruber (1879–1941), an adaptation of which by JOHN PHILIP SOUSA was popular during WORLD WAR I.

Wainwright, Jonathan Mayhew (1883–1953) • U.S. army officer. Born at Fort Walla Walla, Washington, Jonathan Wainwright graduated from WEST POINT in 1906 with a commission in the cavalry. He served at western posts and in the Philippines fighting Moro rebels before filling a position on the staff of the first officers training camp at Plattsburg, New York in 1917. Early the next year he became assistant chief of staff for the 82d Infantry Division in France, participating in both the ST. MIHIEL and MEUSE-ARGONNE OFFENSIVES. After a series of routine postwar cavalry and school assignments, he reported back to the Philippines in 1940 to take command of the Philippines Division. When the Japanese invaded in December 1941, he served as senior field commander of American and Filipino forces under Gen. DOUGLAS MACARTHUR. The defenders retreated back into positions in the BATAAN peninsula and threw back many Japanese attacks, though supplies were dwindling. When MacArthur was ordered off Bataan in March, Wainwright was promoted to lieutenant general and succeeded to command of U.S. Army Forces in the Philippines. Bataan fell in April, while Wainwright and a small core of starving defenders held out on the island fortress of CORREGIDOR. The Japanese gained a foothold there on May 5, and Wainwright surrendered the next day. He was forced to broadcast orders for other local American commanders to surrender as well. He was held in a series of prison camps until the Russians liberated him in Manchuria in August 1945. He witnessed the surrender on the battleship *Missouri* the next month and then returned to the Philippines to receive the surrender of Japanese forces there. After the war he received the CONGRESSIONAL MEDAL OF HONOR, was promoted to full general, and took over Fourth Army. He retired in 1947 and died in San Antonio, Texas.

Wainwright, Richard (1849–1926) • U.S. naval officer. Born in Washington, D.C., Richard Wainwright graduated from the U.S. NAVAL ACADEMY in 1868. He had a series of routine assignments highlighted by a year as chief of the office of naval intelligence, before joining the battleship *Maine* as executive officer in 1897. He directed recovery efforts for that ship after it was blown up in Havana Harbor the next year, and received command of the converted yacht *Gloucester* in Admiral WILLIAM T. SAMPSON's squadron. During the sea battle off Santiago during the SPANISH-AMERICAN WAR (1898), Wainwright won recognition by sinking two enemy destroyers and rescuing the Spanish commander from his burning flagship. Afterwards the *Gloucester* led the ships bearing Gen. NELSON A. MILES and his troops to take Puerto Rico. Wainwright became superintendent of the Naval Academy in 1900, and later was given a number of fleet divisional commands. He retired as a rear admiral in 1911.

waist • *n.* the middle part of a ship, between the forecastle and the quarterdeck.

waiting position • any suitable position in which naval units can be kept ready for operations at immediate notice.

wake • *n.* a trail of disturbed water or air left by the passage of a ship or aircraft.

Wake Island • an island in the western Pacific that was claimed by the United States in 1899 and thereafter developed as an airbase. It was invaded by the Japanese in December 1941 and shortly afterwards surrendered to them, not being sufficiently manned for effective defense. The Japanese executed about 100 U.S. POWs on the island in October, 1943. They did not surrender the island until September, 4, 1945.

Waldo, Samuel (1696–1759) • Colonial militia officer and land speculator. Born in England, Samuel Waldo moved to Boston with his family in 1700. He became one of Massachusetts' greatest land proprietors, and was appointed colonel commanding one of the state's two militia regiments in 1742. During KING GEORGE'S WAR, Waldo was the third ranking officer of the New England militiamen that captured Louisbourg in 1745, a brilliant and surprising accomplishment for such a force. At the conclusion of that campaign he was a brigadier general. During the FRENCH AND INDIAN WAR (1754–63), Waldo proposed that a fort be built at the mouth of the Penobscot River. On a trip with the state governor to inspect the progress of that project, Waldo died suddenly of apoplexy.

wale knot • a knot made at the end of a rope by intertwining strands to prevent unraveling or act as a stopper.

Walke, Henry (1808–1896) • U.S. naval officer. Born in Virginia, Henry Walke entered the navy as a midshipman in 1827. He served on a bomb ketch during the MEXICAN WAR (1846–48), and was put on the reserve list in 1855. Recalled for the secession crisis, he was court-martialed in early 1861 for leaving his station in Pensacola, Florida to escort Union evacuees from that city. New Secretary of the Navy GIDEON WELLES rescued Walke from lighthouse inspections and assigned him to duty with river gunboats in St. Louis. There Walke earned command of the new ironclad *Carondelet*, and performed exemplary service supporting ULYSSES S. GRANT's attacks on FORTS HENRY and DONELSON and running Confederate batteries at Island Number Ten to enable JOHN POPE's army to outflank and capture that installation. Walke commanded the ironclad ram *Lafayette* in operations around VICKSBURG, and then too over the sloop of war *Sacramento*. Sent to European waters to find the Confederate raider *Alabama*, Walke instead helped blockade the raider *Rappahannock* in Calais. He rose to the rank of rear admiral before retiring in 1871 and moving to Brooklyn, New York, where he resided until his death.

Walker, Walton Harris (1889–1950) • U.S. army officer. Born in Belton, Texas, Walton Walker attended VIRGINIA MILITARY INSTITUTE for a year before entering WEST POINT. After graduating in 1912 with a commission in the infantry, he participated in the occupation of VERACRUZ before reporting to France in April 1918. He saw action in both the ST. MIHIEL and MEUSE-ARGONNE OFFENSIVES. After a series of postwar student and instructor assignments he took command of the 3rd Armored Division in January 1942. In September he took over the IV Armored Corps, and after it was redesignated the XX Corps it was ordered to England in early 1944. In July it landed in France as part of GEORGE S. PATTON's Third Army, and it earned the nickname "the Ghost Corps" for the speed of its advances across France and Germany. Walker earned promotion to lieutenant general, and in June 1946 took over Fifth Army in Chicago. Two years later he was transferred to Japan to command Eighth Army under Gen. DOUGLAS MACARTHUR's Far East Command. When the North Koreans attacked South Korea across the 38TH PARALLEL in June 1950, Walker organized a delaying withdrawal with demoralized Republic of Korea forces and understrength American units. He adroitly defended the "Pusan perimeter" in the southeast corner of Korea in August and September, and then broke out after MacArthur's amphibious turning movement at Inchon. Walker drove deep into North Korea before his forces were surprised and pummeled by heavy Chinese attacks in late November. He again retreated south, and established a new defense line at roughly the 38th Parallel. On December 23 he was killed in a jeep accident.

Walker, William (1824–1860) • U.S. adventurer. Born in Nashville, Tennessee, William Walker received a medical degree from the University of Pennsylvania in 1843. He practiced medicine in Nashville and law in New Orleans before heading for the California goldfields in 1850. Walker began his career of filibustering by trying to create the Republic of Lower California on the Baja Peninsula in Mexico, but Mexican troops drove him all the way back over the Colorado River. After being acquitted in California for violating American neutrality laws, Walker took a band of mercenaries to help a warring faction in Nicaragua. His forces were very successful and in 1856 he named himself president of the country and head of its army. Walker's ambitions in the region soon clashed with those of Cornelius Vanderbilt, who sent agents to help surrounding nations overthrow Walker's regime. The U.S. had recognized his government and evacuated him, but naval authorities prevented him from returning in 1857. Walker was again acquitted of violating neutrality laws, and tried to mount an expedition into Nicaragua from Honduras. He was captured there by the British Navy, who turned Walker over to local authorities. They executed him by firing squad in Trujillo, Honduras.

Walker, William Henry Talbot (1816–1864) • Confederate army officer. Born in Augusta, Georgia, Walker graduated from WEST POINT in 1837 with a commission in the infantry. He saw considerable action against the Seminoles in Florida before earning brevets for gallantry at CONTRERAS and MOLINO DEL REY during the MEXICAN WAR (1846–48). He resigned from the army in December 1860 and accepted an appointment as major general of Georgia volunteers four months later. In May he became a brigadier general in the Confederate army, but he had to resign for health reasons in October. He reentered Confederate service in March 1863 and commanded a division that year in Mississippi, Georgia, and Tennessee. He was promoted to major general in January 1864. Commanding a division in the ARMY OF TENNESSEE during the ATLANTA campaign, Walker led a sortie out of the city against besieging Union forces and was killed at PEACHTREE CREEK.

walkie-talkie • *n.* a portable two-way radio.

walking wounded • **1** (usually **the walking wounded**) people who have been injured in a battle but who are still able to walk. **2** people who have suffered emotional wounds.

Wallace, Lewis (1827–1905) • U.S. army officer and historical novelist. Born in Brookville, Indiana, Lew Wallace was largely self-educated. He served with Indiana militia units in the MEXICAN WAR (1846–1848) and thereafter remained active in the militia, being named Adjutant-General of Indiana at the start of the CIVIL WAR. He subsequently led the 11th Indiana Volunteer Infantry in the battles of Romney and HARPERS FERRY, West Virginia. He was promoted to brigadier general of volunteers in September 1861 and to major general of volunteers in March 1862. He commanded with distinction at FORT DONELSON (February 1862) and SHILOH (April 1862), prevented Confederate general E. KIRBY SMITH's raid on Cincinnati, Ohio (1863), and delayed Confederate general JUBAL EARLY's advance on Washington at the Monocacy River, Maryland (July 1864). After the war, Wallace served on the trial by court-martial of the assassins of ABRAHAM LINCOLN and was president of the court-martial which convicted the Confederate commandant of ANDERSONVILLE prison, Captain Henry Wirz, of war crimes. He became active in Republican politics and served as governor of New Mexico (1878–1881) and as U.S. minister to Turkey (1881–1885). In 1880, Wallace published the very successful historical novel, *Ben Hur, A Tale of the Christ.* He also published several less successful historical novels.

Walleye • a guided air-to-surface glide bomb for the destruction of large semi-hard targets such as fuel tanks, tunnels, bridges, radar sites, port facilities, and ammunition depots. It uses a contrast-tracking television system for guidance.

wall knot (also **wale knot**) • a knot made at the end of a rope by intertwining strands to prevent unraveling or act as a stopper.

Walter Reed Army Medical Center • the U.S. Army hospital named in honor of U.S. Army pathologist and bacteriologist WALTER REED, who proved that yellow fever is caused by a mosquito's bite. It is located in Washington, D.C.

Walthall, Edward Cary (1831–1898) • Confederate army officer and U.S. senator. Born in Richmond, Virginia, Edward Cary Walthall grew up in Mississippi, where he was elected first lieutenant of a local volunteer company at the outbreak of the CIVIL WAR. It became part of the 15th Mississippi Infantry, a unit Walthall commanded in the Battle of Mill Spring, Kentucky in January 1862. He was promoted to colonel of the 29th Mississippi Infantry in April, and advanced to brigadier general after a year of heavy campaigning. He led a brigade during the BATTLE OF CHICKAMAUGA and the siege of CHATTANOOGA, which conducted a heroic rearguard stand though depleted in numbers. Promoted to major general in June 1864, he served under JOHN B. HOOD in the ARMY OF TENNESSEE from the siege of Atlanta through the disastrous Nashville campaign. After the war Walthall resumed his law practice, and was elected to the U.S. Senate from Mississippi in 1885.

Walt, Lewis William (1913–1989) • U.S. marine officer. Born in Harleyville, Kansas, Lewis William Walt was a star football player at Colorado State University before being commissioned as a second lieutenant in the U.S. Marine Corps. He served in China before America's entry into WORLD WAR II, and then joined the First Marine Raider Battalion as a captain. He won a Silver Star on Tulagi, and then earned promotion to lieutenant colonel with the Fifth Marine Regiment on GUADALCANAL. He won one NAVY CROSS for heroism on New Britain as a battalion commander and another in the savagery on Peleliu. He added to his impressive list of awards by winning a LEGION OF MERIT and BRONZE STAR during the last year of the KOREAN WAR. By 1965 he was a major general commanding the III Marine Amphibious Force in South Vietnam. Walt disagreed with Gen. WILLIAM C. WESTMORELAND's search and destroy strategy and instead favored rural pacification with Combined Action Platoons. Walt was frustrated by disputes with Westmoreland and Washington, and left Vietnam in 1967. He became a full general and assistant commandant of the Marine Corps before retiring in 1971. He died in Gulfport, Mississippi and is buried in the Quantico National Cemetery.

WAMCATS • *abbr.* Washington-Alaska Military Cable and Telegraph System.

Wampanoag • an Indian tribe located in southern New England. Under their chief METACOM ("King Philip"), the Wampanoags joined with other tribes in a war against the English colonists in Massachusetts, Connecticut, and Rhode Island in 1675-1676 known as KING PHILIP'S WAR. The Wampanoags and their allies were defeated when the Mohawks sided with the colonists and most of the Indian land in New England was opened to English settlement.

Wappinger War • see KIEFT'S WAR.

war • *n.* **1** a state of armed conflict between different nations or states or different groups within a nation or state: *Britain **declared war** on Germany on August 4, 1914 | Iran and Iraq had been **at war** for six years.* **2** a particular armed conflict: *after the war, they emigrated to America.* • *v.* (**warred, warring**) engage in a war: *small states warred against each other.* PHRASES: **go to war** declare, begin, or see active service in a war. **war of attrition** a prolonged war or period of conflict during which each side seeks to gradually wear out the other by a series of small-scale actions.

war baby • **1** a child born in wartime, especially WORLD WAR II. **2** a child born in wartime, especially one fathered illegitimately by a serviceman.

War Between the States, the • see CIVIL WAR.

warbird • *n.* a vintage military aircraft.

war bride • a woman who marries a man whom she met while he was on active service.

War Cabinet (**War Council**) • a five-member council formed by the coalition government of British Prime Minister DAVID LLOYD GEORGE in 1916. The War Cabinet was meant to reform British policy regarding WORLD WAR I. One member was former Lord of the Admiralty WINSTON CHURCHILL, who would be Prime Minister during World War II.

war chest • a reserve of funds used for fighting a war.

war college • a senior service college where advanced instruction in military subjects is provided to experienced officers.

war correspondent • a newspaper or periodical writer or radio or television journalist assigned to report on a war or combat situation from direct observation.

war crime • an action carried out during the conduct of a war that violates accepted international rules of war.

DERIVATIVES: **war criminal**

war crimes tribunal • a court established to try cases of alleged criminal violations of the laws and customs of war.

war cry • a call made to rally soldiers for battle or to gather together participants in a campaign.

ward • *n.* **1** a separate room in a hospital, typically one allocated to a particular type of patient: *a children's ward | a ward nurse.* **2** archaic the action of keeping a lookout for danger: *I saw them keeping ward at one of those huge gates.* **3** an area of ground enclosed by the encircling walls of a fortress or castle. • *v.* archaic guard; protect: *it was his duty to ward the king.*

war damage • damage to equipment or property resulting from active combat operations.

war dance • a ceremonial dance performed before a battle or to celebrate victory.

Ward, Artemas (1727–1800) • American army officer. Born in Shrewsbury, Massachusetts, in 1727, Artemas Ward attended Harvard College and was soon elected to the colonial general assembly. He served in the militia during the FRENCH AND INDIAN WAR (1754–63), rising to the rank of lieutenant colonel. With the coming of the REVOLUTIONARY WAR, Ward was appointed brigadier general by the Massachusetts Provincial Congress (October 27, 1774) and nominally commanded American forces in the BATTLE OF BUNKER HILL. He served for a brief time as Gen. GEORGE WASHINGTON's second-in-command, but had to resign his commission due to ill health. He subsequently served in the U.S. Congress (1791–1795) and died in 1800.

Artemas Ward should not be confused with the American humorist, Artemus Ward (a pseudonym of Charles Farrar Browne, 1834–1867).

---

war, declaration of • see DECLARATION OF WAR.

War Department • organization established by Congress in August 1789 to oversee all elements of the conduct of war. In an effort to unify various military agencies under civilian control, Congress passed the NATIONAL SECURITY ACT in 1947, which set up the National Military Establishment, changed the War Department to the Department of the Army, and legalized the JOINT CHIEFS OF STAFF (set up during WORLD WAR II). In 1949, the National Military Establishment was renamed the DEPARTMENT OF DEFENSE.

Ward, Frederick Townsend (1831–1862) • U.S. adventurer and Chinese military leader. Born in Salem, Massachusetts, Frederick Townsend Ward wanted to serve in the MEXICAN WAR (1846–48), but his father persuaded him to begin traveling around the world instead. Ward participated in filibusterer WILLIAM WALKER's attempt to set up a Republic of Lower California in 1853, and served as a lieutenant in the French army during the Crimean War. In 1859 he got caught up in the Taiping Rebellion in China. Recruited by a Chinese merchant to drill and lead Chinese soldiers, Ward trained his men and outfitted them with Western weaponry, including repeating carbines. After winning a number of battles, his force became known as the "Ever Victorious Army," and Ward was made a Mandarin and allowed to display the button of the fourth rank, a recognition no other foreigner had achieved in Chinese service. He was mortally wounded leading his men in an attack on Tz'u-chi. He was buried in Sungchiang, and the Chinese built him a memorial hall there. The Communists later destroyed it.

war dog • a dog, usually a larger dog such as a German Shepherd or mastiff, trained to perform military duties such as sentry duty, scouting, the carrying of messages, or the direct attack of enemy personnel. War dogs have also been employed to find mines, booby traps, and other explosives and to carry explosive charges beneath enemy vehicles.

wardroom • *n.* a commissioned officers' mess on board a warship.

war drum • a drum beaten as a summons or an accompaniment to battle.

war economy • the organization of a nation's economic activities in such a way as to maximize its ability to sustain a war.

war establishment | • the level of equipment and manning laid down for a military unit in wartime.

warfare • *n.* engagement in or the activities involved in war or conflict: *guerrilla warfare.*

war game • **1** a simulation, by whatever means, of a military operation involving two or more opposing forces, using rules, data, and procedures designed to depict an actual or assumed real-life situation. **2** a simulated military conflict carried out as a game, leisure activity, or exercise in personal development.

war gaming • *n.* **1** the action of playing a war game as a leisure activity or exercise in personal development. **2** the action of engaging in a campaign or course of action using the strategies of a military exercise.

war grave • a grave of a serviceman who has died on active service, especially one among a number of graves in a site serving as a monument: *his is the only war grave in the churchyard | he had gone to visit the war graves in Flanders | the ships in Pearl Harbor were considered war graves.*

war hawk • **1** a person who supports the initiation or continuance of a war. **2** (**War Hawk**) a term used to describe members of the Twelfth Congress (1811–13) who supported war with Britain and whose bellicose attitudes contributed to the conflict. Chief among them were HENRY CLAY and JOHN C. CALHOUN, and most of them came from the west and the north, areas near the frontier that would benefit from a British defeat. Northerners hoped that the British would be forced from Canada and that the Native Americans would be more quiescent with the departure of their allies, while the westerners hoped to wrest Florida from Spain, an ally of Britain's at the time.

warhead • *n.* the part of a missile, projectile, torpedo, rocket, or other munition that contains either the nuclear or thermonuclear system, high-explosive system, chemical or biological agents, or inert materials intended to inflict damage.

warhead mating • the act of attaching a completely assembled warhead to a rocket or missile body, torpedo, airframe, motor, or guidance section.

warhead section • a completely assembled warhead including appropriate skin sections and related components.

warhorse • *n.* **1** (in historical contexts) a large, powerful horse ridden in a battle. **2** informal an elderly person such as a soldier, politician, or sports player who has fought many campaigns or contests.

War Industries Board • a committee created before WORLD WAR I whose task was to help mobilize the American economy for possible war. It began in 1916 as the Council on National Defense, a cabinet committee created by Congress. The committee functioned chaotically at first as a loose grouping of over 100 subcommittees, headed by various industrial executives who refused to work with each other, let alone the military. Wilson re-created it as the War Industries Board in the winter of 1917–18, but the Board did not become effective until prominent financier Bernard Baruch was appointed by the president to head the committee on March 4, 1918. Baruch delegated work efficiently and cajoled some measure of unified action between disparate groups of industry and the army. By ARMISTICE DAY, one quarter of industrial manufacturing had been converted to military use. The policies of the War Industries Board provided a template for the New Deal and the mobilization for WORLD WAR II.

warlike • *adj.* **1** disposed toward or threatening war; hostile: *a warlike clan.* **2** (of plans, preparations, or munitions) directed toward or prepared for war.

war loan • stock issued by the government to raise funds at a time of war.

warlord • *n.* a military commander, especially an aggressive regional commander with individual autonomy.

WARM • *abbr.* wartime reserve modes.

war machine • **1** the military resources of a country organized for waging war. **2** an instrument or weapon of war.

WARMAPS • *abbr.* wartime manpower planning system.

war memorial • a monument commemorating those killed in a war.

warmonger |ˈwôrˌməNGgər; -ˌmäNG-| • *n.* a sovereign or political leader or activist who encourages or advocates aggression or warfare toward other nations or groups.

DERIVATIVES: **warmongering** *n.* & *adj.*

Warner, Seth (1743–1784) • Revolutionary militia and army officer. Born in Woodbury, Connecticut, Seth Warner moved to the New Hampshire Grants (now Vermont) in 1763. Along with ETHAN ALLEN he became a leader in the "Green Mountain Boys." Warner was second-in-command at the capture of FORT TICONDEROGA on May 10, 1775, and led the storming of CROWN POINT two days later. When Allen was captured in September Warner took command of the Green Mountain Boys, and they participated in RICHARD MONTGOMERY's invasion of Canada. Congress appointed Warner a colonel in July 1776. During JOHN BURGOYNE's 1777 campaign, Warner commanded the rearguard for ARTHUR ST. CLAIR's army after it abandoned Fort Ticonderoga, and then brought his regiment to Bennington in time to secure JOHN STARK's victory there. He served under HORATIO GATES for the rest of the SARATOGA campaign. The newly organized Vermont legislature commissioned Warner to be a brigadier general of militia in 1778, but he saw little further action because of failing health.

warning • *n.* a communication and acknowledgment of dangers implicit in a wide spectrum of activities by potential opponents, ranging from routine defense measures to substantial increases in readiness and force preparedness and to acts of terrorism or political, economic, or military provocation.

warning net • a communication system established for the purpose of disseminating warning information of enemy movement or action to all interested commands.

warning of attack • a warning to national policymakers that an adversary is not only preparing its armed forces for war, but intends to launch an attack in the near future.

warning of war • a warning to national policymakers that a state or alliance intends war, or is on a course that substantially increases the risk of war and is taking steps to prepare for war.

warning red • an air defense warning condition in which attack by hostile aircraft and/or missiles is imminent or is in progress.

warning white • an air defense warning condition in which attack by hostile aircraft and/or missiles is improbable.

warning yellow • an air defense warning condition in which attack by hostile aircraft and/or missiles is probable.

War of 1812 • (1812–15) Often called the "second war of independence" because it, too, was fought against Great Britain, this war yielded no territorial gain, but it did carry sharp political and economic ramifications. Its origins were partly political but primarily economic. During the Napoleonic Wars (1793–1801, 1803–15), Great Britain impressed a considerable number of American seamen into the Royal Navy, claiming they were either deserters or British subjects and refusing to recognize their naturalized status. Equally offensive to U.S. sovereignty and more damaging to its economy was that its maritime neutrality was being repeatedly violated by both Great Britain and France. The administrations of THOMAS JEFFERSON and JAMES MADISON were particularly piqued by British orders of council in 1807 and 1809, which authorized the seizure of neutral vessels bound for the Continent if they did not pay duties and unload cargo at a British port. Jefferson's retaliatory embargoes in 1807 and 1809 not only failed to influence the British but also crippled the U.S. economy. Subsequent legislation issued under Madison demanded the end of antineutrality on the part of both European powers. In August 1810, Napoleon announced that he would repeal his Berlin and Milan decrees, to which the British had long been pointing as justification for their orders of council. But Great Britain did not follow suit and repeal their orders, and after months-long deliberation, Congress responded to Madison's request and declared war on June 18, 1812. Most of the fighting took place on the American-Canadian frontier between Detroit and Lake Champlain. This area was both the nearest British possessions that the U.S. army and navy could attack and a significant resource of timber for both countries. But in the opening months of the war, the U.S. lost every battle it waged there, due to poor preparation, inadequate leadership, and untrained soldiers, as well as to a staunch defense by the British aided by northwestern Indians who had been feeling the brunt of American westward expansion. The only battles the U.S. one were while protecting trade routes in the Atlantic, where its inferior navy managed to sink or capture three British ships. The U.S. was somewhat more successful in the middle months of 1813, capturing Fort George and York in Upper Canada in May, retaking Detroit in September, and from there embarking on the BATTLE OF THE THAMES, which destroyed the British-Indian alliance in November. But further incursions into Upper and Lower Canada were either thwarted or aborted. Moreover, the Royal Navy began to assert its superiority by extending its blockade of trade routes throughout the year, to the great frustration of coastal communities and overseas traders. In the South, meanwhile, "Redstick" factions of the Creek Nation took out their frustration on garrisons and settlements, but were eventually repelled by Maj. Gen. ANDREW JACKSON at HORSESHOE BEND in March, 1814. The improvement of both training and leadership led to greater military success in 1814. But Napoleon's defeat in the spring also meant that Britain could commit more troops to North America and thus stretch U.S. defenses. While Capt. Thomas Macdonough repelled the British on Lake Champlain, other British forces occupied northeastern Maine and still others torched Washington, including the White House and the Capitol. The Maryland militia and the Fort McHenry cannons managed to fend off an attempt to capture Baltimore, the battle in which Francis Scott Key composed "The Star-Spangled Banner." The last major battle was a U.S. victory in New Orleans, fought two weeks after peace had officially been reached with the signing of the TREATY OF GHENT on December 24, 1814. The treaty was long in the making. Though the British had repealed the orders of council as soon as Congress declared war, Madison wanted to use the war to settle larger grievances. Attempts at Russian mediation in 1813 were rebuffed by Britain, and then, after it opened separate negotiations in July, 1814, demanded a neutral independent buffer Indian state and to revise the American-Canadian border established by the 1783 TREATY OF PARIS. In the face of these exaggerated demands, the U.S. did not press its own for Canadian territory and an end to British maritime practices that were hurting American trade. Both sides eventually settled for the prewar status quo. Thus, while maritime rights were not finalized, nor were they threatened again until WORLD WAR I. And while Canadian territory was not gained, Indian opposition to westward expansion was considerably quelled in the north- and southwest. More troubling, however, were the increasing tensions between Federalists and Republicans and between northern and southern states. The Federalists had opposed the war, and after meeting to nullify the war in late 1814, appeared as disloyal, which greatly contributed to the party's demise after 1815. In the long term, the postwar economic recovery sharpened the rift between North and South, as federal expenditures rose, demand for domestic manufacturing grew, and large-scale industries, especially in New England, reaped the bulk of the rewards. And when the economy proved still unstable, it gradually became clearer that the war was an important stand against the British Empire, but not the final step toward cultural, economic, and political independence for the U.S.

War Office • a former department of the British government that was in charge of the army (incorporated into the MINISTRY OF DEFENCE in 1964).

War of Jenkins's Ear • (1739–41) part of the struggle between Spain and England that led to the WAR OF THE AUSTRIAN SUCCESSION. Robert Jenkins, master of the ship *Rebecca*, had his ear cut off by Spanish coast guards. Jenkins showed his carefully preserved ear in the British House of Commons in 1738, and England, already resentful at its exclusion from the Spanish colonial trade, declared war.

War of the Austrian Succession • (1740–48) a series of conflicts arising from the death of Charles VI, the Holy Roman Emperor and ruler of the Hapsburg lands. His daughter the Archduchess Maria Theresa succeeded him but there were counterclaimants. Fighting began when King Frederick II of Prussia invaded the Austrian-controlled province of Silesia in 1744. Other European powers were involved in complicated alliances, in which the New World colonies were occasionally viewed as possible prizes for a victor. The conflict ended in 1748 with the PEACE OF AIX-LA-CHAPELLE, which restored the status quo ante.

War of the Regulation • see NORTH CAROLINA REGULATORS.

War of the Spanish Succession • a war arising over succession to the Spanish throne after the death in 1701 of the childless Charles II. The principal contestants were the Grand Alliance, consisting of England, the Netherlands, Denmark, Portugal, and Austria, against France and Spain, aided by some minor principalities; the two sides favored different claimants in Spain. The main issues of the war ended in 1713 with the PEACE OF UTRECHT, which also signaled the end of the related QUEEN ANNE'S WAR.

War on Drugs • the efforts, including the use of military forces, of the United States government to suppress the illegal trade in narcotics worldwide.

War Order No. 1 • an order issued in January 1862 by President ABRAHAM LINCOLN, calling for a unified aggression by all Union forces against the Confederacy on February 22. It was impractical to implement and the order was ignored by Gen. GEORGE B. MCCLELLAN.

warp • *v.* **1** move (a ship) along by hauling on a rope attached to a stationary object on shore. **2** (of a ship) move in such a way. • *n.* a rope attached at one end to a fixed point and used for moving or mooring a ship.

warpaint • *n.* a pigment or paint traditionally used in some societies, especially those of North American Indians, to decorate the face and body before battle.

war party • **1** a band of warriors engaged in a raid or other combat action. **2** a political party urging a nation to embark upon or continue a war.

warpath • *n.* (in phrase **on the warpath**) **1** (of American Indians) heading toward a battle with an enemy. **2** in an angry and aggressive state about a conflict of dispute: *the party has been on the warpath, demanding devolution of power* | *he intends to go on the warpath with a national campaign to reverse the decision.*

war pension • a pension paid to someone who is disabled or bereaved by war.

warplane • *n.* an airplane designed and equipped to engage in air combat or to drop bombs.

War Powers Resolution • a law passed by Congress on November 7, 1973, overruling an October 23, 1973 veto by President RICHARD M. NIXON, to "insure that the collective judgment of both the Congress and the President" would apply to the use of armed forces in hostilities. Established after the VIETNAM WAR and during the WATERGATE crisis, it was widely disputed, and Congress abandoned it by the end President RONALD REAGAN's administration.

warrant | 'wôrənt; 'wä- | • *n.* an official certificate of appointment issued to an officer of lower rank than a commissioned officer.

warrant officer • an officer in the U.S. armed forces ranking below the commissioned officers and above the noncommissioned officers.

War Refugee Board • an interdepartmental committee established by President FRANKLIN D. ROOSEVELT on January 22, 1944, at the urging of Secretary of the Treasury Henry Morganthau, Jr. It was formed after two years of reports of Nazi mass murders of Jews and other minorities in Europe. The Board made diplomatic efforts on behalf of refugees in Nazi-occupied countries and helped to rescue and repatriate up to 200,000 Jews during WORLD WAR II. Jewish organizations criticized the efforts of the War Refugee Board as insufficient.

Warren, Gouverneur Kemble (1830–1882) • U.S. army officer and military engineer. Born in Cold Spring, New York, in 1830, Gouverneur K. Warren was graduated from WEST POINT in 1850 and was commissioned in the Corps of Topographical Engineers. Before the CIVIL WAR, he conducted surveys in the Mississippi delta, the Dakotas, and Nebraska. With Captain ANDREW A. HUMPHREYS, Warren studied possible routes for a transcontinental railroad. He was an assistant professor of mathematics at West Point when the Civil War began and left to accept a commission as lieutenant colonel of the 5th New York Volunteer Infantry. He later was assigned to military engineering duties and served as the chief engineer of the ARMY OF THE POTOMAC. He distinguished himself on the second day of the Battle of GETTYSBURG (1863) by organizing the defense of the key Union position on LITTLE ROUND TOP. He was then named to command the II Corps, and then the V Corps, of the Army of the Potomac, serving with distinction until the BATTLE OF FIVE FORKS (1865) where he was summarily relieved of command. Following the Civil War, Warren conducted various surveying projects and repeatedly sought rectification of his relief at Five Forks, which he received from a court of inquiry in December 1879. He died in 1882.

war reserve • nuclear weapons materiel stockpiled in the custody of the DEPARTMENT OF ENERGY or transferred to the custody of the DEPARTMENT OF DEFENSE and intended for employment in the event of war.

war reserves • stocks of materiel amassed in peacetime to meet the increase in military requirements consequent upon an outbreak of war. War reserves are intended to provide the interim support essential to sustain operations until resupply can be effected.

War Resisters League • a U.S. organization formed in 1923 by people who had opposed WORLD WAR I, many of whom had been jailed for refusing to serve in the military. Still active, with headquarters in New York City, it advocates nonviolent civil disobedience, offers assistance to conscientious objectors, and works toward eliminating war by focusing on issues of social justice in the United States and internationally.

warrior • *n.* (especially in former times) a brave or experienced soldier or fighter.

War Risk Insurance Act • a law passed in 1917 requiring that insurance against death or total permanent disability be granted to all enlisted personnel on the grounds that they were fit for service when inducted.

war room • a space set aside in a military or governmental headquarters and used for tracking the military situation, conducting briefings, and discussing the current military situation and planned actions.

Warsaw Pact • a treaty of mutual defense and military aid signed at Warsaw on May 14, 1955 by Communist states of Europe under Soviet influence, in response to the admission of West Germany to NATO; collectively, the group of states which signed the treaty. Following changes in eastern Europe and the collapse of the Communist system, the pact was dissolved in 1991.

warship • *n.* a ship equipped with weapons and designed to take part in warfare at sea.

war, state of • see STATE OF WAR.

warthog • *n.* slang the A-10 Thunderbolt II attack aircraft.

wartime • *n.* a period during which a war is taking place.

wartime load • the maximum quantity of supplies of all kinds that a ship can carry. The composition of the load is prescribed by proper authority.

wartime manpower planning system • (**WARMAPS**) a standardized DOD-wide procedure, structure, and database for computing, compiling, projecting, and portraying the time-phased wartime manpower requirements, demand, and supply of the DOD components.

wartime reserve modes • (**WARM**) the characteristics and operating procedures of sensor, communications, navigation aids, threat recognition, weapons, and countermeasures systems that will contribute to military effectiveness if unknown to or misunderstood by opposing commanders before they are used, but could be exploited or neutralized if known in advance. Wartime reserve modes are deliberately held in reserve for wartime or emergency use and seldom, if ever, applied or intercepted prior to such use.

war widow • a woman whose husband has been killed in war.

war zone • a designated area in which the rights of neutrals may not be respected by a belligerent at war, especially an ocean area so designated in which neutral vessels travel at their own risk.

War Zone C • an area of Vietnam targeted for assault in OPERATION JUNCTION CITY. It consisted of Tay Ninh and the surrounding area north of Saigon, which was the site of VIETCONG bases and the Vietcong military headquarters in South Vietnam.

wash • *n.* the disturbed water or air behind a moving boat or aircraft or the sound made by this: *the wash of a motorboat.*

Washington-Alaska Military Cable and Telegraph System • (**WAMCATS**) a system of cables and telegraph lines authorized by the U.S. Congress in 1900 and constructed by the U.S. Army SIGNAL CORPS, the purpose of which was to link the nation's capital with the military posts in Alaska, to connect the various military installations in Alaska, and to serve the commercial telegraph needs of the territory. Upon completion in 1904 the system comprised some 2,079 miles of undersea cable, 1,439 miles of land lines, and a wireless segment of some 107 miles across Norton Sound. A major role in the construction of WAMCATS was played by Signal Corps Captain BILLY MITCHELL, who later achieved fame as an advocate of miltiary aviation.

Washington, George (1732–1799) • Revolutionary army officer and U.S. president. Born in Westmoreland County, Virginia, George Washington got his first military experience during the FRENCH AND INDIAN WAR (1754–63). He won the conflict's first small engagement after he built FORT NECESSITY near FORT PITT in 1754, but soon had to surrender to a superior force. As an aide to Gen. EDWARD BRADDOCK the next year, Washington organized an orderly retreat after the general was killed in the ambush that decimated his force. Washington commanded all Virginia forces before resigning his commission in 1758. He began the REVOLUTIONARY WAR as a delegate to the Continental Congress, but in June 1775 they selected him unanimously to be commander of chief of the new Continental army. After managing a successful siege of Boston, Washington lost most of his army in a series of disastrous battles around the city of NEW YORK in 1776. He revived Patriot fortunes with winter victories at TRENTON and PRINCETON. In 1777 he lost battles at BRANDYWINE and GERMANTOWN, as well as the city of Philadelphia. His army dwindled during the hard winter of 1777–1778 at VALLEY FORGE, but BARON VON STEUBEN's training and the French alliance improved the American situation. Washington's forces performed much better at MONMOUTH in 1778 as the British withdrew from Philadelphia to New York. Activity in the northern theater quieted after the

British shifted their primary efforts to the South, but in 1781 Washington took a combined French-American army south to join with Gen. NATHANAEL GREENE's forces at YORKTOWN, and with the assistance of the French fleet they forced the capitulation of Lord CHARLES CORNWALLIS's army. Washington remained in command of American forces until late 1783, awaiting the peace and quelling discontent in his poorly-paid army. After the war he presided over the Constitutional Convention in 1787, and was elected the new nation's first president in 1789. He served wisely and well before leaving office in 1797. He had one last appointment to military service in 1798, when President JOHN ADAMS made Washington a lieutenant general in charge of a Provisional Army preparing for possible war with France, but the crisis passed and he never took the field. He died at his plantation at Mount Vernon.

Washington, John Macrae (1797–1853) • U.S. army officer. Born in Stafford County, Virginia, John Macrae Washington graduated from WEST POINT in 1817 with a commission in artillery. He fought against the Seminoles in Florida and served on Gen. WINFIELD SCOTT's staff during the removal of the Cherokee Indians in 1838–1839. During the MEXICAN WAR, Washington earned a brevet to lieutenant colonel in 1847 commanding a battery that anchored the American right wing at the BATTLE OF BUENA VISTA. After that engagement he served as the military governor of Saltillo before becoming chief of artillery of the army of occupation. The next year he was assigned to be the civil and military governor of New Mexico, filling that position from October 1848 to October 1849. While on a steamer heading for the Pacific Coast in 1853, he was swept off the deck in a violent storm and drowned.

Washington Naval Arms Limitation Treaty • an agreement established at the Washington Conference of 1921–22, after WORLD WAR I, and signed on February 6, 1922. It established numbers and tonnage ratios of battleships and aircraft carriers of the United States, Great Britain, Japan, France, and Italy. It was one of several treaties intended to end naval competition between the United States, Great Britain, and Japan and to stabilize the political situation in East Asia. It expired on December 31, 1936.

Washington Navy Yard • a U.S. naval facility established in 1799 in Washington, D.C. The Washington Navy Yard began as a shipbuilding facility. During the War of 1812, it was burned by U.S. forces to prevent its capture by the British. After the war the yard became a site for development of ordnance (weapons) technology. By World War II, the Washington Navy Yard was the largest naval ordnance plant in the world, and was renamed the U.S. Naval Gun Factory in December 1945. In 1964 the former name of Washington Navy Yard was restored, and it developed into an administrative and research center. Today it also houses the CHIEF OF NAVAL OPERATIONS, the Naval Historical Center, and the Marine Corps Historical Center.

WASP • a member of the Women's Airforce Service Pilots, formed in WORLD WAR II mainly owing to a shortage of suitable male pilots. About 1,000 in number, they undertook various air duties, particularly ferrying aircraft, starting in 1943. They were disbanded in 1944, shortly after the D-DAY LANDING. Just under forty died in training or in service. Though they were never officially militarized, they were the first women in history trained to fly U.S. military aircraft.

watch • *n.* **1** an act or instance of carefully observing someone or something over a period of time: *the security forces have been* ***keeping a close watch on*** *our activities.* **2** a fixed period of duty on a ship, usually lasting four hours. **3** (also **starboard** or **port watch**) the officers and crew on duty during one such period. **4** a body of soldiers making up a guard. **5** (usually **the watch**) a watchman or group of watchmen who patrolled and guarded the streets of a town before the introduction of the police force.

watchfire • *n.* a fire maintained during the night as a signal or for the use of someone who is on watch.

watching mine • a naval mine secured to a mooring but showing on the surface in certain tidal conditions.

watchkeeper • *n.* a person who keeps watch or acts as a lookout, especially on board a ship.

watchword • *n.* archaic a military password.

water • *n.* (**waters**) an area of sea regarded as under the jurisdiction of a particular country: *Japanese coastal waters.* • *v.* take a fresh supply of water on board (a ship or steam train): *the ship was watered and fresh livestock taken aboard.*

PHRASES: **by water** using a ship or boat for travel or transport: *at the end of the lake was a small gazebo, accessible only by water.* **make water** (of a ship or boat) take in water through a leak.

water cannon • a device that ejects a powerful jet of water, typically used to disperse a crowd.

watercraft • *n.* **1** a vessel designed to travel through water. **2** such vessels treated as a group.

waterfront • *n.* a part of a town that borders a body of water.

Watergate • an exclusive apartment complex along the Potomac River in Washington, D.C., which became infamous as the site of the June 17, 1972, break-in of the offices of the Democratic Party by operatives apparently working for Republican President RICHARD M. NIXON's reelection committee. Attempts by President Nixon and his staff to cover up their connection to the break-in led to Nixon's impeachment by the Judiciary Committee of the House of Representatives on July 30, 1974. Before the impeachment trial could begin in the Senate, President Nixon resigned on August 9, 1974, and Vice President GERALD R. FORD became President.

waterline • *n.* **1** the line to which a vessel's hull is immersed when loaded in a specified way. **2** any of various structural lines of a ship, parallel with the surface of the water, representing the contour of the hull at various heights above the keel.

water power • power that is derived from the weight or motion of water, used as a force to drive machinery.
DERIVATIVES: **water-powered** *adj.*

Waters, Daniel (1731–1816) • REVOLUTIONARY WAR naval officer. Born in Charlestown, Massachusetts, Daniel Waters began the Revolutionary War fighting in the BATTLE OF LEXINGTON (1775) with a company of militiamen. He commanded a gunboat in the siege of Boston in 1775 and took several prizes with a schooner in 1776. The next year he was commissioned a captain in the Continental navy, beginning a number of cruises on various sloops and privateers. In command of the Boston privateer *Thorn* in December 1779 he defeated two British privateers of equal armament. After the war he took up farming in Malden, Massachusetts, where he died.

water suit • a G-suit in which water is used in the interlining thereby automatically approximating the required hydrostatic pressure-gradient under G forces.

watertight compartment • a space on a ship which can be sealed so as to keep out water entering the vessel from a breech in the hull or other damage.

water torture • a form of torture in which the victim is exposed to the incessant dripping of water on the head or to the sound of dripping.

waterway • *n.* a river, canal, or other route for travel by water.

Watie, Stand |ˈwätē| (1806–1871) • Confederate army officer and Indian leader. Born near present-day Rome, Georgia, Stand Watie became a leader in the Cherokee Indian tribe. He was a signer of the Treaty of New Echota in 1835 that committed them to move to INDIAN TERRITORY (now part of Oklahoma), and he narrowly escaped assassination by those who disagreed. In August 1861 Chief John Ross reluctantly allied his Cherokees with the Confederacy, and Watie was commissioned a colonel and given command of the regiment of Mounted Rifles raised among the tribe. They fought in battles in Arkansas and Missouri, as well as in Indian Territory, before the majority of the Cherokees repudiated their Confederate alliance in 1863. Watie stayed in Southern service, however, and the next year was promoted to brigadier general in charge of a brigade of Cherokee, Seminole, and Osage Indians. He surrendered in June 1865 and later died in Indian Territory.

wave • *n.* a formation of forces, landing ships, craft, amphibious vehicles or aircraft, required to beach or land about the same time.

According to type, function, or order, a wave may be classified as an **assault wave, boat wave, helicopter wave, numbered wave, on-call wave,** or **scheduled wave**.

WAVES |wāvz| • *plural n.* the women's section of the U.S. Naval Reserve, established in 1942, or, since 1948, of the U.S. Navy.
ORIGIN: acronym from *Women Appointed* (later *Accepted*) *for Volunteer Emergency Service*.

Waxhaws, Battle of the • a battle on May 29, 1780 fought between the forces of Lt. Col. BANASTRE TARLETON and Col. ABRAHAM BUFORD. The result was a complete British victory: 300 American soldiers were killed. American survivors believed that Tarleton's men deliberately slaughtered men who were trying to capitulate. The Waxhaws battlefield joined the register of National Historic Places in 1990.

way • *n.* **1** forward or backward motion of a ship or boat through water: *the dinghy lost way and drifted toward the shore.* **2** (**ways**) a sloping structure down which a new ship is launched.

Wayne, Anthony (1745–1796) • U.S. army officer and Congressman. Born in Chester County, Pennsylvania, Anthony Wayne earned the nickname of "Mad Anthony" for his boldness and courage in battle during the REVOLUTIONARY WAR. He was commissioned colonel of the of the 4th Pennsylvania Regiment in January 1776. During that year he saw action at Three Rivers and commanded FORT TICONDEROGA. He took part as a brigadier general in the battles around Philadelphia in 1777, distinguishing himself at GERMANTOWN. He fought at MONMOUTH in June 1778, and was later given command of a new corps of light infantry. In July 1779 he took the British post at Stony Point in a brilliant night bayonet attack that boosted American spirits while demoralizing the British. In 1781 he was sent south to reinforce American forces there, participating in the YORKTOWN campaign and later liberating Georgia and Charleston. He served in the Pennsylvania assembly before moving to Georgia, where he was elected once to the U.S. House of Representatives. In April 1792 President GEORGE WASHINGTON recalled him to duty as the senior officer in the army. Wayne was given the mission to pacify Indians in the Ohio Valley who were being encouraged by the British and had already defeated two previous American expeditions. Wayne organized and trained his "Legion" well. They built a line of forts as they approached the Indian strongholds, and then won the decisive battle of the campaign at FALLEN TIMBERS in August 1794. The next year he dictated the TREATY OF GREENVILLE to the pacified chiefs, which opened much of the Old Northwest to settlement. In 1796 he was sent back to the region to take possession of British forts being relinquished according to the terms of Jay's Treaty. He died returning from that mission.

way point • in air operations, a point or a series of points in space to which an aircraft may be vectored.

W/Cdr • *abbr.* wing commander.

weapon • *n.* a thing designed or used for inflicting bodily harm or physical damage: *nuclear weapons.*

DERIVATIVES: **weaponed** *adj.* **weaponless** *adj.*

weaponization • *n.* the conversion of civilian technology to military purposes.

weaponry • *n.* weapons regarded collectively.

weapons free • another term for GUNS FREE.

weapons hold • in air defense, a weapon control order imposing a status whereby weapons systems may only be fired in self-defense or in response to a formal order.

weapons inspection • the examination of individual weapons, a weapons system, or a nation's entire stock of type weapons for the purpose of determining their number, condition, and availability for use.

weapons of mass destruction • in arms control usage, weapons that are capable of a high order of destruction and/or of being used in such a manner as to destroy large numbers of people. The term can be applied to nuclear, chemical, biological, and radiological weapons, but excludes the means of transporting or propelling the weapon where such means is a separable and divisible part of the weapon.

weapons readiness state • the degree of readiness of air defense weapons that can become airborne or be launched to carry out an assigned task.

Weapons readiness states are expressed in numbers of minutes or hours. For example: *2 minutes* means "weapons can be launched within two minutes"; *3 hours* means "weapons can be launched within three hours."

weapon(s) system • a combination of one or more weapons with all related equipment, materials, services, personnel, and means of delivery and deployment (if applicable) required for self-sufficiency.

weapons tight • another term for GUNS TIGHT.

wear[1] • *v.* (past **wore**; past part. **worn**) (of a ship) fly (a flag).

wear[2] • *v.* (past and past part. **wore**) bring (a ship) about by turning its head away from the wind: *Shannon gives the order to **wear ship**.* Compare with TACK (sense 1).

weather • *n.* denoting the side from which the wind is blowing, especially on board a ship; windward: *the weather side of the yacht.* Contrasted with LEE. • *v.* **1** come safely through (a storm). **2** (of a ship) get to the windward of (a cape or other obstacle).

weathercock • *v.* (of a boat or aircraft) tend to turn its head into the wind.

weather helm • a tendency in a sailing ship to head into the wind if the tiller is released.

weatherly • *adj.* (of a boat) able to sail close to the wind without drifting much to leeward.

weave • *v.* take evasive action in an aircraft, typically by moving it from side to side.

Weaver, James Baird (1833–1912) • U.S. soldier, congressman, and politician. Born in Dayton, Ohio, James Baird Weaver established a legal practice in Bloomfield, Iowa a few years before the CIVIL WAR. When it began he was elected a first lieutenant in the Second Iowa Infantry. He saw action at FORT DONELSON and SHILOH (both 1862) and earned a reputation for bravery in combat. He assumed command of the regiment during the BATTLE OF CORINTH and was promoted to colonel soon after. He carried out occupation duties in Tennessee before participating in the early stages of WILLIAM T. SHERMAN's drive on Atlanta. When Weaver's enlistment expired in May 1864 he left the army, though he was later retroactively brevetted brigadier general for his gallantry. After the war he was elected to Congress on the Greenback ticket, and he later became prominent in the Populist movement, winning twenty-two electoral votes as their presidential candidate in 1892.

webbing • *n.* the system of belts, pouches, and straps worn by a soldier as part of his combat uniform.

Webster-Ashburton Treaty • an 1842 agreement between the United States, represented by Daniel Webster, and Great Britain, represented by the first Baron Ashburton, that settled the Northwest Boundary Dispute and also fixed most of the border between the United States and Canada. Other clauses provided for cooperation in the suppression of the slave trade and for mutual extradition of criminals.

Webster, Joseph Dana (1811–1876) • U.S. army officer and engineer. Born in Hampton, New Hampshire, Joseph Dana Webster obtained a commission as a second lieutenant in the new Corps of Topographical Engineers in 1838. He rose to captain in 1853 after serving in the MEXICAN WAR (1846–48), but left the army a year later to do engineering work for Chicago. When the CIVIL WAR broke out he was appointed chief state engineer and began work on fortifications around Cairo. He became chief of staff for ULYSSES S. GRANT in late 1861, and received a colonel's commission early the next year. He served Grant at FORTS HENRY and DONELSON, and gathered the massed artillery together at SHILOH (1862) that stabilized the situation there at the end of the first day. By the spring of 1863 Webster was a brigadier general in charge of all the railroads supplying Grant's army for the VICKSBURG campaign. When Grant was transferred east Webster became chief of staff for WILLIAM T. SHERMAN. When the army moved out for ATLANTA, Webster supervised the railroads and insured a continuous flow of supplies. When Sherman abandoned his supply lines to march through Georgia, Webster assisted GEORGE THOMAS to gather and supply the forces which won the BATTLE OF NASHVILLE (1864). Webster then rejoined Sherman at Savannah for the campaign into the Carolinas. At the end of the war, Webster was brevetted major general of volunteers. He returned to Chicago after the war, serving in a number of financial positions there until he died.

Wedemeyer, Albert Coady (1897–1989) • U.S. Army officer. Born in Omaha, Nebraska, Albert C. Wedemeyer initially graduated from the war-shortened course at WEST POINT in 1918, but he was one of the half of that group recalled to serve another year there as student officers before officially becoming the Class of 1919. After a series of routine infantry assignments, in 1936 he became the first American officer to attend the Kriegsakademie, the German general staff school, since WORLD WAR I. In 1941 he was assigned to the War Plans Division of the General Staff, where he became the primary author of the "Victory Plan" predicting American requirements for the coming war. He served as an aide to Gen. GEORGE C. MARSHALL for the principal Allied strategy conferences until October 1943, when newly-promoted Maj. Gen. Wedemeyer was appointed deputy chief of staff to Lord LOUIS MOUNTBATTEN, supreme Allied commander in Southeast Asia. After Gen. JOSEPH STILWELL's recall a year later, Wedemeyer was named commander of the China theater and chief of staff to Nationalist Chinese leader CHIANG KAI-SHEK. After the war he commanded the Second and Sixth Armies, before retiring in July 1951. Three years later he was promoted to full general on the retired list.

Weedon, George |'wēdn| (1734–1793) • militia and REVOLUTIONARY WAR officer. Born in Westmoreland County, Virginia, George Weedon served as a junior officer in the Virginia militia during the FRENCH AND INDIAN WAR(1754–63). Virginia appointed Weedon colonel of the Third Virginia Regiment when the Revolutionary War began, and in 1776 Congress named him commander of the Third Virginia Continental Regiment. He joined GEORGE WASHINGTON's army just in time for the fight at Harlem Heights, and saw considerable action through the fall of 1777, particularly distinguishing himself at the battle of BRANDYWINE. Congress promoted Weedon to brigadier general in 1777, but he resigned from the army that winter in a dispute over seniority. Congress recalled him to command Virginia militia in 1781. Weedon supervised the supplying of the MARQUIS DE LAFAYETTE's army in Virginia and commanded 1,500 militiamen in the YORKTOWN campaign. Weedon died at his home in Fredericksburg after a long battle with gout.

weekend warrior • derogatory a National Guardsman or Reservist; so called because their training sessions often take place on weekends. See also CITIZEN-SOLDIER.

Wehrmacht |'ver,mäkt| the German armed forces, especially the army, from 1921 to 1945.

ORIGIN: German, literally 'defensive force.'

weigh anchor • see ANCHOR.

Weimar Republic • the German government in the post- WORLD WAR I period, so called because the REICHSTAG (national assembly) met in the town of Weimar. The republic was proclaimed on November 9, 1918, and its constitution was adopted on July 31, 1919. The Weimar Republic ended with the ascension of ADOLF HITLER as Chancellor on January 30, 1933, and the passage of the Enabling Act on March 23 of that year.

Weinberger, Caspar W. (1917–) • born in San Francisco, California, and educated at Harvard College (1938) and Harvard Law School (1941), he served in the Pacific theater on Gen. DOUGLAS MACARTHUR's intelligence staff. He worked as a law clerk to U.S. Court of Appeals Judge William E. Orr from 1945 to 1947, and then went into the private practice of law. In 1952, Weinberger was elected to the Assembly of the California State Legislature and was reelected in 1954 and 1956. He returned to his private practice for ten years after losing his bid to become the California Attorney General, until then Governor RONALD REAGAN appointed him to the position of California Director of Finance. In 1969, he was nominated for Chairman of the Federal Trade Commission (FTC) by President RICHARD M. NIXON, and held that position until Nixon promoted him to Director of the Office of Management and Budget (OMB). Nixon then appointed him Secretary of Health, Education, and Welfare, a position he held until 1975.

Weinberger doctrine • United States politico-military doctrine made public by Secretary of Defense CASPAR WEINBERGER in November 1984. The Weinberger doctrine has six main points: 1. U.S. forces should not be committed to combat unless the vital national interests of the U.S. or its allies are involved; 2. U.S. troops should only be committed abroad wholeheartedly and with the intention of winning; 3. U.S. troops should be committed abroad only to achieve clearly defined political and military objectives and with the means to achieve those objectives; 4. The relationship between the objectives sought and the size and composition of the forces committed should be constantly reassessed and adjusted as necessary; 5. U.S. troops should be committed to battle only with a "reasonable assurance" of the support of the Congress and the U.S. public; 6. The commitment of U.S. armed forces should be considered only as a last resort.

Weitzel, Godfrey |'wītsəl| (1835–1884) • U.S. army officer and engineer. Born in Cincinnati, Ohio, Godfrey Weitzel graduated from WEST POINT in 1855 with a commission in the engineers. Early in the war he served as chief engineer for the Department of the Ohio and then for BENJAMIN BUTLER's expedition that captured New Orleans. Weitzel was appointed brigadier general of volunteers in August 1862 and commanded a division in the assault on PORT HUDSON. He rejoined Butler in the ARMY OF THE JAMES in 1864, taking command of XVIII Corps and capturing Fort Harrison in September. In December he transferred to XXV Corps for the unsuccessful attack on FORT FISHER, North Carolina. He took part in the final campaigns around RICHMOND, taking possession of the city on April 3, 1865 and receiving a brevet to major general of regulars. After the war he resumed his engineer duties at a much reduced rank, building ship canals at Louisville and Sault Sainte Marie.

well deck • an open space on the main deck of a ship, lying at a lower level between the forecastle and poop.

Welles, Gideon (1802–1878) • U.S. politician and Secretary of the Navy. Born in Glastonbury, Connecticut, on July 1, 1802, Gideon Wells attended the academy at Norwich, Vermont (now Norwich University). In the 1820s he pursued a career in journalism, became prominent in Democratic politics, and was an active supporter of ANDREW JACKSON. In the 1830s he served at various times as comptroller of Connecticut, postmaster of Hartford, editor of the *Hartford Times*, and a Connecticut legislator. In 1846, he was appointed by President JAMES K. POLK as chief of the Naval Bureau of Provisions and Clothing, in which post he served until 1849 when he was removed by President ZACHARY TAYLOR, a Whig. Welles opposed slavery, and in 1855, he joined the newly-formed Republican Party and ran unsuccessfully for governor of Connecticut. From March 1861 to March 1869, he served as Secretary of the Navy under Presidents ABRAHAM LINCOLN and ANDREW JOHNSON, mobilizing and equipping the U.S. Navy for the CIVIL WAR and ensuring the efficient administration of his department and the measured introduction of new technology into the greatly expanded Navy.

well-found • (chiefly of a boat) well equipped and maintained.

Wentworth, Paul (?–1793) • REVOLUTIONARY WAR spy. Probably born on the island of Barbados, Paul Wentworth lived in Surinam and London before becoming involved in the turmoil in New Hampshire at the beginning of the Revolutionary War. Though not really related to the Royal Governor of New Hampshire, John Wentworth, Paul was accepted as a kinsman and used those connections to develop ties with many colonial leaders. These relationships proved very useful when he became a British spy in 1772. His primary asignment became to gather information at the French court and watch the American diplomatic delegation there. He developed a complicated plan to prevent the French-American alliance with a wholesale bribery of Congress, but his attempt to force American negotiations with England might have actually backfired into speeding the very coalition he was supposed to prevent. After the war Wentworth speculated on stocks in London and became a trustee of Dartmouth College in New Hampshire, before retiring to his plantation in Surinam, where he died.

Western Approaches • an area of the North Atlantic where ships traveling between the United States and Britain were attacked by German U-BOATS (submarines) during WORLD WAR II. Shipping convoys using escort carriers, radar, and aircraft helped defend the Western Approaches to Europe by 1943.

Western Front • the zone of fighting in western Europe in WORLD WAR I, in which the German army engaged the armies to its west, i.e., France, the UK (and its dominions), and, from 1917, the U.S. For most of the war the front line stretched from the Vosges mountains in eastern France through Amiens to Ostend in Belgium. Fighting began in August 1914: German forces attacking through Belgium were checked in the first battle of the MARNE and then at YPRES, both sides eventually engaged in TRENCH WARFARE, the distinctive feature of warfare on this front. Battles were inconclusive with heavy casualties on both sides, notably at VERDUN, the SOMME, and YPRES. Early in 1917 the Germans withdrew to the HINDENBURG LINE, a fortified line of trenches that was not breached for more than a year; U.S. forces in the region from 1917 helped to tip the balance in the Allies' favor.

Western Hemisphere Institute for Security Cooperation • see SCHOOL OF THE AMERICAS.

westing • *n.* **1** distance traveled or measured westward, especially at sea. **2** a figure or line representing westward distance on a map.

Westmoreland, William Childs (1914–) • U.S. Army officer. Born in Spartanburg County, South Carolina, William C. Westmoreland graduated from WEST POINT in 1936 with a commission in the field artillery. He had a distinguished combat record. In WORLD WAR II, he commanded a field artillery battalion in North Africa and Sicily, and became chief of staff of the 9th Infantry Division in NORMANDY. He commanded the 187th Regimental Combat Team in the KOREAN WAR, earning promotion to brigadier general there in 1952. He led the 101st Airborne Division before becoming superintendent of West Point in 1960. After that he took over the XVIII Airborne Corps and was promoted to lieutenant general. In 1964 he was designated to command U.S. MILITARY ASSISTANCE COMMAND in South Vietnam, and another star followed. For the next four years he supervised the expansion of American combat forces in Vietnam to a strength of over 500,000, relying on heavy firepower and "search and destroy" tactics to try to draw out and destroy an elusive guerrilla foe. After defeating the enemy's surprise TET OFFENSIVE in early 1968, Westmoreland became chief of staff of the army in July, a post he held until retiring four years later. He has spent much effort since then defending his reputation from critics who blame him for various aspects of American failure in Vietnam, including taking CBS to court for libel.

West Point • a U.S. military reservation on the Hudson River in Orange county, New York, United States. West Point Academy, also known as the U.S. MILITARY ACADEMY, has been on the site since 1802.

In 1779 GEORGE WASHINGTON established his headquarters at West Point while trying to defend the Hudson River Valley from the British, and in 1780 BENEDICT ARNOLD unsuccessfully tried to betray the land to the British.

Westwall • see SIEGFRIED LINE.

wet • *adj.* (of a ship) liable to take in water over its bows or sides.

wet dock • a dock in which water is maintained at a level that keeps a vessel afloat.

Wewak • a city on the coast of northern Papua New Guinea near the mouth of the Sepik River. Certain topographical features (crags, coves, and caves) made it a very defensible position, and its port facilities made it an attractive target for military occupation. The Japanese overran the city in early 1942, and successfully held it until May 1944. The battle for Wewak was part of the BOUGAINVILLE campaign and lasted from late 1944 until the following May.

Wg Cdr • *abbr.* Wing Commander.

whaleboat • *n.* **1** a long rowboat designed to be very maneuverable and used to pursue and kill whales. **2** a boat resembling a whaleboat in size and shape. Also called WHALER.

whaler • *n.* **1** a whaling ship. **2** See WHALEBOAT, def. 2.

wharf • *n.* (pl. **wharves** or **wharfs**) a level quayside area to which a ship may be moored to load and unload.

wharfage • *n.* accommodation provided at a wharf for the loading, unloading, or storage of goods.

Wheaton, Frank (1833–1903) • U.S. army officer. Born in Providence, Rhode Island, Frank Wheaton obtained a commission as a first lieutenant in the 1st Cavalry in 1855. When the CIVIL WAR began he joined the 2nd Rhode Island Volunteers, succeeding in command of that regiment after distinguishing himself at FIRST BULL RUN (1861). He fought in all the ARMY OF THE POTOMAC's battles from 1862 to June 1864, rising to command of a brigade. He was leading a division in the SHENANDOAH VALLEY in July when he rushed to defend Washington from JUBAL EARLY, repulsing him at Fort Stevens. Wheaton finished the war at Petersburg as a brevet major general. He served as commander of the Departments of Texas and Colorado before retiring as a major general in 1897.

wheel • *v.* (of an aircraft) fly in a wide circle or curve: *the plane wheeled and dived.*

Wheeler, Earle Gilmore (1908–1975) • U.S. Army officer. Born in Washington, D.C., Earle Wheeler graduated from WEST POINT in 1932 with a commission in the infantry. After various training assignments during the first half of WORLD WAR II, he finally got to Europe as chief of staff of the 63rd Infantry Division. During the 1950s he served on staffs in NATO and Washington, and commanded a division and a corps. In October 1962 he became chief of staff of the army, and two years later he was appointed chairman of the JOINT CHIEFS OF STAFF. He held that post during a tumultuous six years that covered the heaviest American involvement in the war in Southeast Asia. He has been criticized for not doing more to shape or restrain the U.S. commitment there.

Wheeler, George Montague (1842–1905) • U.S. army officer and explorer. Born in Hopkinton, Massachusetts, George Montague Wheeler graduated from West Point in 1866 with a commission in the engineers. He began his military career building harbor defenses in San Francisco, before taking charge of the survey of American territory west of the 100th meridian in 1871. He directed that huge project for the next eight years, taking fourteen long field trips that produced maps, as well as archaeological, biological, and geological data. He spent the rest of his time in military service writing the official report of his work. Failing health led to his retirement in 1888.

Wheeler, Joseph (1836–1906) • U.S. and Confederate army officer. Born in Augusta, Georgia, on September 10, 1836, Joseph Wheeler was graduated from WEST POINT and commissioned a lieutenant of dragoons in 1859. He served in New Mexico until April 1861 when he resigned and accepted a commission in the Confederate army. Assigned to Fort Barrancas, Florida, he was soon offered the colonelcy of the 19th Alabama Infantry. He rose to command an infantry brigade in 1862 before transferring to command the cavalry of the Army of Mississippi in July 1862. He subsequently earned a reputation as the leading Confederate cavalry commander in the western theater, conducting successful rearguard actions after the battles of SHILOH, PERRYVILLE, STONES RIVER (all 1862), and CHICKAMAUGA (1863). In 1864–1865, Wheeler's cavalry opposed Sherman's march to the sea and through the Carolinas. Wheeler was captured near Atlanta, Georgia, in May 1865, as he attempted to protect the fleeing Confederate President, JEFFERSON DAVIS. After the Civil War, he ran a hardware store, became a successful plantation owner, practiced law, and entered Democratic politics in Alabama, winning a seat in the U.S. House of Representatives in 1883. He served eight terms in Congress and was a member of the House Military Affairs Committee. Following the United States declaration of war on Spain in April 1898, President WILLIAM MCKINLEY offered Wheeler a commission as a major general of volunteers. He was placed in command of the cavalry forces for the invasion of Cuba, and he successfully attacked the Spaniards at Las Guasimas (June 24, 1898), urging his men to "Give them Yankees hell, boys!" He subsequently obtained an assignment as a brigadier general of volunteers in the Philippines in June 1899. There he proved able, at the advanced age of 63, to outmarch soldiers forty years his junior. He returned to the United States in January 1900, received promotion to brigadier general in the Regular Army, and commanded the Department of the Lakes until his retirement in September 1900.

wheelhouse • *n.* a part of a boat or ship serving as a shelter for the person at the wheel.

wheelman • *n.* (pl. **-men**) a person who takes the wheel of a boat.

wheelsman • *n.* (pl. **-men**) a person who steers a ship or boat.

When Johnny Comes Marching Home • a CIVIL WAR-era song attributed to Patrick S. Gilmore, written under the pseudonym Louis Lambert in 1863, after the Battle of Gettysburg. Gilmore was the bandmaster of BENJAMIN BUTLER's Union Army, and the song was popular with soldiers in both the North and South. The origin of the music is unclear.

whiffle |ˈ(h)wifəl| • *n.* **2** (also **whiffle cut**) informal a very short haircut worn by U.S. soldiers in WORLD WAR II.

Whig party • a 19th-century U.S. political party that favored loose interpretation of the Constitution and opposed the Democratic party. Active between 1834 and 1854, the Whig party promoted national development and opposed what it viewed as the executive tyranny of ANDREW JACKSON. In the late 1840s, the emergence of antislavery and proslavery factions spelled the end for the party.

Whipple, Abraham (1733–1819) • REVOLUTIONARY WAR naval officer. Born in Providence, Rhode Island, Abraham Whipple captured 23 French prizes in six months as a privateer during the FRENCH AND INDIAN WAR (1754–63). He led one of earliest overt acts of colonial rebellion when a group of rebels from Providence captured and burned the troublesome British revenue cutter *Gaspée* in June 1772. Three years later he captured the first British ship taken under an official commission while commanding a state coast defense vessel. In December 1775 he was commissioned a captain in the Continental navy. He took many British prizes as commander of the *Columbus* and then the *Providence*. The three ship squadron he led in the latter vessel captured 11 merchantmen out of one convoy in July 1779. The next year his reinforced squadron was sent to strengthen the defenses of Charleston, but when the city fell to the British Whipple was captured. He was paroled but saw no more action. After the war he farmed for a while in Rhode Island before moving to Marietta, Ohio, where he died.

whirlpool • *n.* a rapidly rotating mass of water in a river or sea into which objects may be drawn, typically caused by the meeting of conflicting currents.

whirlybird • *n.* informal a helicopter.

Whiskey Rebellion • the refusal of U.S. grain farmers and whiskey distillers to pay a new excise tax on spirits in 1794, and the subsequent government quashing of this rebellion, regarded as the first real test of the federal government's power to enforce laws. The conflict was largely confined to western Pennsylvania, where much whiskey was produced. President GEORGE WASHINGTON ordered a large militia to meet the resistance, which quickly disappeared. The Whiskey Tax was repealed under President THOMAS JEFFERSON.

White Army • the constitutionalist and monarchist armed forces which opposed the Bolshevik Red Army in the Russian civil war of 1917–20. Comprised of several different groups with varying objectives, the Whites, led by former officers of the Imperial Russian armed forces, were ultimately unsuccessful in stemming the expansion of Bolshevik control throughout the country, and the bedraggled remnants of the White Army were evacuated from the Crimean peninsula by the British and French navies in November 1920.

white ensign • a white British naval flag carrying a St. George's cross with the UNION JACK in the top corner next to the flagstaff, flown by the Royal and most Commonwealth naviesand the Royal Yacht Squadron.

white flag • a white flag or cloth used as a symbol of surrender, truce, or a desire to parley.

Whitehall • a complex of buildings on Whitehall Street in central London where a number of British government offices are located. Thus, by association, Whitehall has come to mean the British government itself.

Whitehorse (or **White Horse**) • an elevated site or outposted hill on the perimeter of the IRON TRIANGLE in North Korea.

white horses • white-crested waves at sea.

White House (also, **the White House**) • **1** the official residence of the president in Washington, D.C. **2** the U.S. president, presidency, or government: **3** the Russian parliament building.

White House, Burning of • a dramatic event in 1814, part of the WAR OF 1812, when British troops, having sailed up the Potomac, set fire to the 23-year-old presidential residence, after first marching inside and helping themselves to food. The fire was extinguished by a thunderstorm but only the shell of the building remained. It was immediately rebuilt.

whiteout • *n.* the loss of orientation with respect to the horizon, caused by the sun reflecting on snow and an overcast sky.

White Plains, Battle of • a battle in the REVOLUTIONARY WAR fought on October 28, 1776 at White Plains, New York. British and Hessian forces under Gen. Sir WILLIAM HOWE met American forces under Gen. GEORGE WASHINGTON after each had spent some days gathering. The Americans were outnumbered and eventually retreated.

white propaganda • information used purposefully by an acknowledged source to promote a biased point of view to a particular public.

White Sands Missile Range • (**WSMR**) a testing ground for U.S. Army missiles and other weapons technology since its establishment as the White Sands Proving Ground in July 1945, during WORLD WAR II. The White Sands Missile Range also includes TRINITY SITE, where the first atomic bomb was exploded on July 16, 1945. Because of the research and testing of rocket technology at White Sands Missile Range, it is known as the "Birthplace of the Race to Space." It oversees projects such as the recent high-energy laser systems testing, and research at the U.S. ARMY ELECTRONIC PROVING GROUND at Fort Huachuca, Arizona.

whiz-bang |ˈ(h)wiz ˌbæNG| • *n.* Brit. or informal (also **whizz-bang, whizbang**) (especially during World War I) a low-velocity shell.

WIA • *abbr.* wounded in action.

Wickes, Lambert (1735?-1777) • REVOLUTIONARY WAR naval officer. Born in Kent County, Maryland, Lambert Wickes attracted patriot attention in 1774 when he refused to accept a cargo of tea for his ship in London. In 1776 Congress gave him a commission as a captain in the Continental navy and command of the *Reprisal*. He took a number of prizes before ferrying Benjamin Franklin to France in November. Under Franklin's direction in 1777, Wickes captured many British ships and sold them in neutral French ports. He caused further British protests by refitting in St. Malo after barely escaping from a much larger British ship of the line. On his voyage back to America in October his ship foundered off Newfoundland, and only the cook survived.

Wilcox, Cadmus Marcellus (1824–1890) • Confederate army officer. Born in Wayne County, North Carolina, Cadmus Wilcox graduated from WEST POINT in 1846 and reached Mexico just in time for the BATTLE OF MONTERREY. He then joined the march on the Mexican capital, distinguishing himself several times in the battles around the city. After the war he served in routine frontier assignments and as an instructor at West Point, where he wrote the first American rifle manual. He resigned from the army in 1861 and took a commission as the colonel of the 9th Alabama Infantry. He served with the ARMY OF NORTHERN VIRGINIA throughout the war. He performed very well at FRAYSER'S FARM (1862), and commanded three brigades at SECOND BULL RUN (1862). He rendered important service at CHANCELLORSVILLE and GETTYSBURG (both 1863), including taking part in PICKETT'S CHARGE. In 1864 he was promoted to major general and given his own division, which he commanded from May 1864 until the end of the war. After the Confederate surrender he went to Mexico, but he soon returned to settle in Washington, D.C., where he eventually died.

Wildcat • (**F4F**) a single-seat single-engine shipboard fighter, the primary airplane used on carriers when the United States entered WORLD WAR II. It resembled a barrel in shape, but was well-armed and extremely reliable.

Wilderness, Battle of the • a CIVIL WAR battle fought on May 5–7, 1864 in densely wooded areas of Spotsylvania County, Virginia. Large forces under the commands of Gens. ULYSSES S. GRANT and ROBERT E. LEE exacted large numbers of casualties from each other in continuous attempts to outmaneuver. While the battle itself was a tactical draw, it did not stop Grant from continuing his campaign to take PETERSBURG, the rail center serving Richmond.

Wilderness to Petersburg Campaign • the name given to the series of battles from the BATTLE OF THE WILDERNESS to the siege of PETERSBURG (1864), during the CIVIL WAR. Initiated by Gen. ULYSSES S. GRANT with the Union's Army of the Potomac to defeat Gen. ROBERT E. LEE and the Confederate's ARMY OF NORTHERN VIRGINIA, the campaign began on May 4 when Grant crossed the Rapidian River west of Lee and stopped for the night in the Wilderness near Spotsylvania, Virginia. On May 5, Lee surprised Grant in the two-day indecisive Battle of the Wilderness, which cost 18,000 Federal and 11,000 Confederate casualties. Trying to draw the Confederates out of the Wilderness, Grant headed southeast toward Spotsylvania Court House, but a portion of the Confederate army arrived there first. On May 8, the BATTLE OF SPOTSYLVANIA began, which included combat at the bend in the Confederate earthworks called the "Bloody Angle," and after a repulse by Confederate artillery on May 18, Grant gave up and swung east and south. Lee divided Grant's army at North Anna Creek by deploying his own army into an inverted "V," and on May 26, as Grant advanced toward Richmond, Lee drew a strong line along Totopotomoy Creek. On May 30, Lee attacked part of Grant's army near Bethesda Church, and on June 1, the armies clashed in the BATTLE OF COLD HARBOR. On June 3, Grant launched a frontal attack to break Lee's line but was repulsed with 12,000 Union soldiers killed or wounded. On June 12–14, Grant marched to and crossed the James River, heading for Petersburg, the railroad center serving Richmond. The Federals repeatedly attempted to seize Petersburg on June 15–18, but the Confederates withstood the attacks. Grant subsequently initiated siege operations, which continued until April 2, 1865. The campaign, ending in June and strategically a Union success, cost 60,000 Union casualties and perhaps 35,000 Confederate losses.

wild weasel • **1** n. an aircraft that has been modified for the purposes of identifying, locating, and suppressing or destroying enemy air-defense systems on the ground. Such aircraft are equipped with sensors that radiate electromagnetic energy. **2** (**Wild Weasel**) (F-4G) an F-4 fighter aircraft used to detect and destroy enemy radar installations and missile batteries.

Wilkes, Charles (1798–1877) • U.S. naval officer, explorer, and scientist. Born in New York City on April 3, 1877, Charles Wilkes went to sea in his teens. In 1818, he entered the U.S. Navy as a midshipman and served in various positions at sea and on shore, gaining a reputation as a naval scientist. In 1838, Wilkes, a junior Lieutenant, was chosen to command the U.S. Exploring Expedition, which circled the globe between 1838 and 1842 collecting valuable scientific data. A quarrelsome martinet, Wilkes was convicted by a court-martial soon after his return to the United States in 1842, for improper punishment of several sailors on the expedition. Nevertheless, he was promoted to commander in 1843 and to captain in 1855, spending most of his time editing the journals of the expedition. On November 8, 1861, while commanding the USS *San Jacinto* in the Caribbean, Wilkes boarded the British mail steamer *Trent* and arrested James Mason and John Slidell, Confederate envoys enroute to England. His actions were clearly a violation of international law, and the "*Trent* Affair" aroused British indignation, but Wilkes was generally applauded in the North. He later commanded the James River Flotilla, the Potomac Flotilla, and the West India Squadron before being recalled in 1863 and court-martialed in April 1864 for insubordination and disobedience of orders. He was convicted and sentenced to a public reprimand and three year's suspension (later reduced to one year). Wilkes retired from the Navy in 1866.

Wilkinson, James (1757–1825) • U.S. army officer; Commanding General of the U.S. Army (1796–1812). Born in Benedict, Maryland, in 1757, James Wilkinson was educated by a private tutor and practiced medicine briefly before obtaining a commission as a captain in the Continental Army in 1776. He served at the siege of Boston and with BENEDICT ARNOLD's expedition to Montreal (1776), under Gen. GEORGE WASHINGTON at TRENTON and PRINCETON (1776–1777), and under Gen. HORATIO GATES at SARATOGA (1777). He then served as secretary to the BOARD OF WAR AND ORDNANCE in 1778 and earned promotion to brigadier general. From 1779 to 1783 he served as Clothier-General of the army. In 1783, Wilkinson moved to Kentucky, laid claim to large tracts of land near present-day Louisville and Lexington, and became involved in opening the Mississippi to American commerce. The latter endeavor entangled him with the Spanish governor of New Orleans, but in 1791 President Washington offered him a commission as colonel in the U.S. Army and he accepted. Critical of the Army's leadership, he nevertheless served successfully under MAD ANTHONY WAYNE at FALLEN TIMBERS (1794) and received promotion to brigadier general. In 1796, Wilkinson was named to the position of Commanding General of the Army, in which position he served until 1812. Wilkinson had a penchant for intrigue and once again took up questionable conducts with Spanish authorities in New Orleans and quarreled with other senior officers and politicians. AARON BURR attempted to implicate Wilkinson in his conspiracy (1805–1806), but Wilkinson apparently avoided the affair and remained loyal to President THOMAS JEFFERSON. During the WAR OF 1812, he commanded the unsuccessful second invasion of Canada (1813), and was subsequently shunted aside, retiring in 1815. He wrote a bitter memoir and settled near New Orleans as a sugar planter. In 1822, he went to Mexico to obtain a grant to colonize lands in Texas, an effort which was unsuccessful.

Wilkinson, John (1821–1891) • U.S. and Confederate naval officer. Born in Norfolk, Virginia, John Wilkinson entered the U.S. navy as a midshipman in 1837. He rose to the rank of lieutenant before resigning his commission in April 1861, and he then accepted the same rank in the Confederate service. He was captured in the fall of New Orleans but was exchanged in August 1862. He then went to England to buy and equip the blockade-runner *Robert E. Lee*, one of the most successful of the war. Many of his deceptive tactics were adopted by other blockade runners and became standard practice. He later commanded the raiders *Chickamauga* and *Chameleon*. He lived in Nova Scotia for a while after the war before returning to Virginia.

Willard, Simon (1605–1676) • colonial soldier, magistrate, and fur trader. Born in England, Simon Willard arrived in Boston in 1634. Because of his military training he was given special responsibilities by the Puritans. He drilled militia and set up a number of garrison towns while expanding his own fur trade with the Indians. He devoted much time to public service in the towns he founded and on the frontier, including leading expeditions against the Indians. His most demanding test came during KING PHILIP'S WAR , an Indian uprising in 1675. Willard tried to defend the long frontier throughout the winter and spring against attacks from west and north, patrolling with militia and shoring up garrison houses. Many settlements were burned before the Indians were defeated. His demanding duties eventually wore Willard out, and he died from exhaustion.

Willcox, Orlando Bolivar (1823–1907) • U.S. army officer. Born in Detroit, Michigan, Orlando Willcox graduated from WEST POINT in 1847. He served in a number of frontier assignments and fought the Seminoles before resigning from the army in 1857 and returning to Michigan. When the CIVIL WAR broke out he was appointed colonel of the First Michigan Volunteer Infantry, which he led at FIRST BULL RUN (1861). Wounded and captured there, he was imprisoned for over a year. After his release he was promoted to brigadier general and given a division in AMBROSE BURNSIDE's Ninth Corps. That is basically the level where Willcox stayed the whole war, except for a mediocre performance commanding the corps at FREDERICKSBURG (1862). He rarely distinguished himself in the many battles where he participated, and he finished the war as one of the most senior brigadier generals in the army. He did finally receive a brevet to the next rank, but he was mustered out of service in early 1866. By July, however, he obtained a regular appointment as colonel of the Twenty-ninth Infantry, and he served tours on RECONSTRUCTION duty in Virginia as well as commanding Alcatraz Island. Finally promoted to brigadier general, he retired in 1887.

Willett, Marinus (1740–1830) • REVOLUTIONARY WAR officer and New York politician. Born near Jamaica, New York, Marinus Willett served as a junior officer with New York militia during the FRENCH AND INDIAN WAR (1754–63). When the Revolutionary War began, he again took a commission as a militia officer, serving in the early phases of the invasion of Canada and in the battles around New York City. In late 1776 he joined the Third Continental Regiment as a lieutenant colonel. Ordered to FORT STANWIX in 1777, he performed so well against the Indians they were convinced he had supernatural powers. In 1779 he participated in GOOSE VAN SCHAICK's raids on the Onondagas and JOHN SULLIVAN's expedition against the Iroquois. He became colonel of the Fifth New York Regiment in 1780. After leaving the army briefly, he took over New York frontier defense, retaining his rank. He again excelled, routing a number of Tory-Indian forces. After the war, President GEORGE WASHINGTON used Willett as a special envoy to the Indians, and he secured the nation's first treaty under the new Constitution, with the Creeks in 1790. Willett also got involved in New York politics, serving as sheriff and mayor of New York City.

Williams, Alpheus Starkey (1810–1878) • U.S. army officer and congressman. Born in Deep River, Connecticut, Alpheus Williams graduated from Yale in 1831. He practiced law and rendered public service in Detroit, and was selected as the lieutenant colonel of the only Michigan regiment to serve Mexico during the MEXICAN WAR (1846–48). When the CIVIL WAR began, he was appointed brigadier general of state troops, and was soon given the same rank of volunteers by President ABRAHAM LINCOLN. He served in the SHENANDOAH VALLEY before distinguishing himself leading a division against STONEWALL JACKSON at CEDAR MOUNTAIN in August 1862. He served as an acting corps commander at ANTIETAM, and shored up the shattered Union flank at Chancellorsville on May 2, 1863, saving the Army from an even worse disaster. Still the acting corps commander of XII Corps at GETTYSBURG (1863), he stiffened the Union left against a Confederate breakthrough on the second day, then shifted back to the right to save CULP'S HILL. He reverted to division command in Tennessee later that year, distinguishing himself again during the WILLIAM T. SHERMAN's Atlanta campaign. Williams marched on to Savannah with the army, and into the Carolinas, earning a brevet to major general along the way and again serving as an acting corps commander. After the war he resigned his commission to become the U.S. minister to El Salvador. He was elected to Congress from Michigan in 1876, and died in Washington.

Williamsburg • the first battle of Union Maj. Gen. GEORGE B. MCCLELLAN's PENINSULAR CAMPAIGN, fought on May 5, 1862, during the CIVIL WAR. McClellan captured the town of Williamsburg, Virginia, after skirmishes with Confederate Maj. Gen. JAMES LONGSTREET's forces.

Williams, George Washington (1849–1891) • U.S. soldier, clergyman, and state legislator. Born in Bedford Springs, Pennsylvania, George Washington Williams lied about his age to join the U.S. COLORED TROOPS in 1864. He saw combat in operations around PETERSBURG and RICHMOND. He was stationed in Texas after the war, and slipped over the Rio Grande to fight with Mexican republican forces. He returned to the Tenth Cavalry, and was discharged in 1868 for disability after being shot through the lung. After the war he became a minister, served as the first African-American in the Ohio House of Representatives, and wrote a history of black soldiers in the Civil War. When he died in London he was crusading against King Leopold's exploitation of the Congo.

Williams, John Foster (1743–1814) • REVOLUTIONARY WAR naval officer. Born in Boston, John Foster Williams went to sea at an early age. When the Revolutionary War began he was commissioned captain of a sloop in the Massachusetts state navy. During the war he commanded a series of sloops and privateers, capturing many prizes with the *Hazard* and *Protector*, in particular. He participated in the ill-fated Penobscot expedition in 1779, and was captured by the British in early 1781. He returned to sea in 1783 after being exchanged. President Washington appointed Williams captain of the revenue cutter *Massachusetts* in 1790, and he held that post until his death in Boston.

Williamson, Andrew (1730?–1786) • REVOLUTIONARY WAR army officer. Born in Scotland,, Andrew Williamson was a leading businessman in the area around Ninety Six, South Carolina, when the Revolutionary War began. He built a small fort there and participated in many campaigns against Loyalists and British Florida. He also served as a member of the South Carolina General assembly, and was appointed brigadier general of the militia. After the fall of Charleston, Williamson tried to rally his troops, but had to surrender to the British. They treated him well, and he tried to persuade his neighbors to cease further resistance. Twice he was kidnapped by patriot forces, once to give him a chance to relent and then to hang him, but when liberated he returned to Charleston. He was branded a traitor after the war, but NATHANAEL GREENE later revealed Williamson had taken great risk to provide intelligence to the American army for some time. He remained a controversial figure until his death in St. Paul's Parish.

Williams, Otho Holland (1749–1794) • REVOLUTIONARY WAR army officer. Born in Prince Georges County, Maryland, Otho Williams started the Revolutionary War as a first lieutenant in a Maryland rifle company that served in the siege of Boston. He rose to become major of a combined Maryland-Virginia rifle regiment before getting captured at Fort Washington in 1776. He was appointed colonel of the 6th Maryland Regiment while still a prisoner, but was exchanged in early 1778 and saw action at MONMOUTH. Sent to the southern theater, Williams fought at CAMDEN and KINGS MOUNTAIN (both 1780) before NATHANAEL GREENE appointed him adjutant general of the southern army. Williams commanded a light corps as Greene's rearguard during much of the North Carolina campaign, and led a determined bayonet charge that cleared the field at EUTAW SPRINGS(1781). He was promoted to brigadier general in 1782. After the war he served as federal collector of the port of Baltimore.

Willich, August (1810–1878) • U.S. army officer and socialist. Born in East Prussia, Johann August Ernst von Willich became a socialist and led a unit in the Revolution of 1848. After a period with Friedrich Engals and Karl Marx in London, Willich emigrated to America. He became a newspaper editor and writer in Cincinnati. He enlisted in a German regiment as a private when the CIVIL WAR began, but after distinguished service at battles such as SHILOH (1862), CHICKAMAUGA, and MISSIONARY RIDGE (both 1863), he rose to the rank of brevet major general. He always addressed his troops as "citizen" and often lectured them on socialism. He was involved in Liberal Republican politics after the war, and was much beloved in St. Marys, Ohio when he died there.

"Will to Victory" program • a pacification plan implemented by the South Vietnamese and their American advisers in 1964 which was based on the so-called "oil spot concept." "Will to Victory" (CHIEN THANG in Vietnamese) called for the occupation and pacification of a central village by government troops and paramilitary personnel and the gradual expansion around the central village of the area free of Communist insurgents. Ultimately, Chien Thang was unsuccessful due to poor execution and a lack of support from conventional military units of the Army of the Republic of Vietnam.

Willys-Overland (also **Willys-Overland Motors**) • an automotive manufacturing company that produced approximately 360,000 of the 660,000 JEEPS made for the U.S. Army during WORLD WAR II.

Wilmot Proviso • an amendment presented on August 8, 1846 by Democratic congressman David Wilmot and supported by northern congressmen to prohibit the establishment of slavery in any territories gained in the MEXICAN WAR (1846–48). It passed in the House, where the North had a majority, but was defeated in the Senate and resulted in increased tensions between the national parties and between Northern and Southern states.

Wilson, James Harrison (1837–1925) • U.S. army officer. Born near Shawneetown, Illinois, on September 2, 1837, James H. Wilson was graduated from WEST POINT and commissioned in the Corps of Topographical Engineers in 1860. During 1861–1864, he served as a military engineer and an inspector general in the Union armies in both the eastern and western theaters. In 1864, Wilson was assigned to Washington to organize the Cavalry Bureau and its remount system. His success at that task led to his appointment to command a cavalry division in the ARMY OF THE POTOMAC and then the cavalry corps under Gen. WILLIAM T. SHERMAN. He played key roles at NASHVILLE (December 1864) and the capture of Selma, Alabama (April 1865). As Chief of the Cavalry Bureau, Wilson had championed the adoption of the Spencer repeating carbine for cavalrymen, and once in command of cavalry troops he developed the effective tactic of riding to battle and dismounting for the final assault, relying on the firepower of the Spencer. Following the Civil War, he supervised navigation improvements along the Mississippi River before resigning from the Army in December 1870 to enter private business. Wilson returned to active duty as a major general of volunteers in 1898 and saw service during the War with Spain in both Puerto Rico and Cuba. He also served as the second-in-command of U.S. troops in China during the BOXER REBELLION (July–November 1900), returning home in 1900 to retire as a brigadier general, Regular Army. He was advanced to major general on the retired list in 1915.

Wilson, Woodrow (1856–1924) • U.S. president. Born in Staunton, Virginia, Woodrow Wilson grew up in a South devastated by the CIVIL WAR. He graduated from Princeton and began a distinguished career of public service that included president of Princeton, governor of New Jersey, and finally president of the United States in 1912. Though reelected in 1916 with a slogan "He kept us out of war," Wilson did try to influence the political situation in Mexico by occupying VERACRUZ in 1914, and sent JOHN J. PERSHING into that country two years later to chase PANCHO VILLA. Wilson also could not keep the nation out of WORLD WAR I forever, and after the provocations of submarine attacks sinking American ships and the ZIMMERMAN TELEGRAM, Wilson declared "the world must be made safe for democracy" and got a Congressional declaration of war in April 1917. He exerted vigorous leadership at home, setting up Selective Service and establishing government agencies to support the war effort, and developed his famous FOURTEEN POINTS as a framework for the peace. He instructed John J. Pershing to resist amalgamation of the AMERICAN EXPEDITIONARY FORCES in France to strengthen the United States' position at a final settlement. American forces did not display any special brilliance on the battlefield, but their timely mass arrival in 1918 restored Allied morale and broke that of the Germans. Wilson was frustrated by his dealings with the Allies at the PARIS PEACE CONFERENCE, and the unsuccessful struggle to get U.S. Senate support for a LEAGUE OF NATIONS broke his health. He stayed in Washington preaching America's global mission until his death.

Winchester |ˈwinˌCHestər| • *n.* (also **Winchester rifle**) trademark a breech-loading side-action repeating rifle. [ORIGIN: named after Oliver F. *Winchester* (1810–80), the American manufacturer of the rifle.]

Winchester, James (1752–1826) • Revolutionary and U.S. army officer. Born in Carroll County, Maryland, James Shay was captured twice by the British during the REVOLUTIONARY WAR. He finished that conflict as a captain with NATHANAEL GREENE's army at Yorktown (1781). In 1785 he moved to Tennessee, where he eventually became a brigadier general of militia. When war with England loomed in 1812, he was appointed to the same rank in the U.S. army, and took several regiments to Cincinnati. After a dispute with WILLIAM HENRY HARRISON about command of the Army of the Northwest, Winchester took command of one wing. He was captured when a large British-Indian force attacked him at the River Raisin in January 1813, and Indians slaughtered many of his troops after they surrendered. The River Raisin Massacre became an American rallying cry for the rest of the war. Winchester was exchanged after a year of captivity and finished the conflict as commander of the District of Mobile.

Winchester Repeating Arms Company • a rifle, shotgun, and ammunition manufacturer that was founded in 1867 by Oliver Fisher Winchester. The company was a successor to a company he had bought in 1857. The Winchester lever-action Henry repeating rifle developed by B.T. Henry in 1860 was widely used during the CIVIL WAR. Today the company is called Winchester Rifles and Shotguns and is a part of the U.S. Repeating Arms Company.

windage • *n.* **1** the effect of the wind in deflecting a missile such as a bullet. **2** the air resistance of a moving object, such as a vessel or a rotating machine part, or the force of the wind on a stationary object.

windbound |'wind,bownd| • *adj.* (of a sailing ship) unable to sail because of extreme or contrary winds.

Winder, John Henry (1800–1865) • Confederate Army officer. Born in Somerset County, Maryland, John Henry Winder graduated from WEST POINT in 1820. He had reached the rank of captain by the time of MEXICAN WAR (1846–48), and earned brevets up to lieutenant colonel for bravery at CONTRERAS, CHURUBUSCO, and CHAPULTEPEC in 1847. In April 1861 he resigned his commission and joined the Confederate army. In July he was appointed provost marshal and commander of military prisons in Richmond, Virginia, with a rank of brigadier general. When the first Union prisoners arrived after FIRST BULL RUN (1861), Winder established the notorious LIBBY PRISON. In May 1864 most of the inmates were moved to Macon, Georgia and Winder was put in charge of all prisons in Georgia and Alabama. A few months later his responsibility was expanded to cover everything east of the Mississippi.

wind gauge |wind| • an anemometer.

windjammer |'wind,jæmər| • *n.* a merchant sailing ship.

windlass |'windləs| • *n.* a type of winch used especially on ships to hoist anchors and haul on mooring lines. • *v.* haul or lift (something) with a windlass.

window • *n.* **1** an interval or opportunity for action: *the window for rescuing the submarine crew was closing with each passing day.* **2** an interval during which atmospheric and astronomical circumstances are suitable for the launch of a spacecraft. **3** strips of metal foil or metal filings dispersed in the air to obstruct radar detection. [ORIGIN: military code word.]

PHRASES: **window of vulnerability** an opportunity to attack something that is at risk (especially as a COLD WAR claim that America's land-based missiles were easy targets for a Soviet first strike).

windsail |'wind,sāl| • *n.* a long wide tube or funnel of sailcloth used to convey air to the lower parts of a ship.

wind shear • a change of wind direction and magnitude.

windsock |'wind,säk| • *n.* a light, flexible cylinder or cone mounted on a mast to show the direction and strength of the wind, especially at an airfield.

windward • *adj. & adv.* facing the wind or on the side facing the wind: *the windward side of the boat.* Contrasted with LEEWARD. • *n.* the side or direction from which the wind is blowing: *he had beaten to windward across St Austell Bay.*

wing • *n.* **1** a rigid horizontal structure that projects from both sides of an aircraft and supports it in the air. **2** (**wings**) a pilot's certificate of ability to fly a plane, indicated by a badge representing a pair of wings. **3** a flank of a battle array. **4** an air force unit of several squadrons or groups.

Wingco • *abbr.* wing commander.

wing commander • a rank of officer in the RAF, above squadron leader and below group captain.

winglet • *n.* **1** a little wing. **2** a vertical projection on the tip of an aircraft wing for reducing drag.

wingman • *n.* **1** an aviator subordinate to and in support of the designated section leader. **2** the aircraft flown in this role.

wing sail • a rigid or semi-rigid structure similar to an aircraft wing fixed vertically on a boat to provide thrust from the action of the wind.

wingspan (also **wingspread**) • *n.* the maximum extent across the wings of an aircraft, bird, or other flying animal, measured from tip to tip.

Winn, Richard (1750?–1824?) • REVOLUTIONARY WAR soldier and congressman. Born in Fauquier County, Virginia, Richard Winn was a large land-holder in South Carolina when the Revolutionary War began. He served as a junior officer with militia units until captured at Fort McIntosh in southeast Georgia in early 1777. Though paroled he did not return to duty until 1780. He quickly rose to the rank of colonel serving under THOMAS SUMTER. Winn developed a fierce reputation in numerous engagements against Loyalist forces. In December 1780 the British captured his brother John and sentenced him to hang. Winn sent word that if his brother died so would the first 100 enemy soldiers he captured. John Winn was pardoned. After the war Richard Winn became a major general in the South Carolina militia. He served as superintendent of Indian affairs for the Southern District, as well as many terms in the U.S. House of Representatives.

Winslow, John (1703–1774) • colonial soldier. Born into a leading New England family in Marshfield, Massachusetts, John Winslow served as a captain in WILLIAM GOOCH's American Foot during the Cartagena expedition of 1741. He later served at the same rank in a succession of British regiments in North America before retiring on half-pay in 1751. At the beginning of the FRENCH AND INDIAN WAR (1754–63) he served as a lieutenant colonel commandant of a New England regiment that contributed to successful sieges of French forts in Nova Scotia. In late 1755 Winslow was appointed a major general of a 7000 man provincial force with a mission to take the French stronghold at CROWN POINT, but his army balked when they were told they would be incorporated into a larger regular force for the expedition. The militiamen feared their enlistment contracts would be violated and they were eventually disbanded. Winslow received some blame for their recalcitrance, and that failed campaign ended his military career.

Winslow, John Ancrum (1811–1873) • U.S. naval officer. Born in Wilmington, North Carolina, John Ancrum Winslow entered the navy as a midshipman in 1827. He had a number of routine assignments before seeing action under Commodore MATTHEW C. PERRY during the MEXICAN WAR (1846–48). In the years before the Civil War Winslow served primarily on shore, but in 1861 he was assigned to the Western River Squadron. He was promoted to captain there, but was placed on waiting orders in 1862 because of his outspoken criticism of Union strategy. He was finally given command of the sloop *Kearsarge* and sent out to seek Confederate raiders. He patrolled European waters through 1863 and into 1864, and his diligence was rewarded in June when he caught the *Alabama* in port at Cherbourg. Its captain, RAPHAEL SEMMES, accepted Winslow's challenge and sailed out to meet him on June 19. While thousands of spectators watched, the heavier armed *Kearsarge* sank its famous opponent. Winslow earned a promotion for his success. After the war, Winslow commanded the Gulf and Pacific Squadrons, and was promoted to rear admiral.

Winslow, Josiah (1629?–1680) • colonial military leader and governor. Born the son of the governor of Plymouth Colony, Josiah Winslow became its military commander in 1659. He became governor himself in 1673. When KING PHILIP'S WAR began in 1675, Winslow was chosen commander in chief of the militia forces of the United Colonies. He led more than 1000 men from Plymouth, Massachusetts Bay, and Connecticut in the Great Swamp Fight of December 19, 1675 which broke the power of the Narragansett tribe and virtually ended the war in that region. He served as governor until his death in Marshfield.

winter quarters • accommodations for the winter, especially for soldiers.

Winthrop, John (1638–1707) • colonial military leader and governor. Born the son of the governor of Connecticut, John Winthrop was also known as Fitz or Fitz-John. He reached the rank of captain in the English Army and helped restore King Charles II in 1660. Back in the colonies, he led militia on Long Island during the third ANGLO-DUTCH WAR (1673–1674), and in 1687 was appointed major general in charge of the combined militias of Connecticut and Massachusetts. During KING WILLIAM'S WAR in 1690 he led a colonial-Indian force from Albany in an unsuccessful campaign into Canada. In 1698 he was elected governor of Connecticut, a position he held until his death in Boston nine years later.

wire-guided • *adj.* (of a missile) directed by means of electrical signals transmitted along fine connecting wires that uncoil during the missile's flight.

Wirz, Henry (1823–1865) • Confederate army officer. Born in Zurich Switzerland, Hartmann Heinrich Wirz emigrated to the United States in 1849. He was overseeing a plantation when the CIVIL WAR began. He enlisted in the Fourth Louisiana Infantry in 1861, and was injured badly enough the next year to lose the use of his right arm. He was promoted to captain and assigned to the staff of Brig. Gen. JOHN HENRY WINDER, who put Wirz in command of the Richmond military prison, where he was actually popular with the inmates. When he was reassigned to Alabama, they petitioned to keep him. Wirz spent most of 1863 in Europe, and when he returned to the Confederacy in early 1864 Winder gave him command of the stockade at ANDERSONVILLE, Georgia. Prisoner exchanges had stopped, all supplies were scarce, and the prison was severely overcrowded, and as a result its Union inmates died by the thousands. Wirz was arrested in May 1865, still tending to the sick at Andersonville. By then Winder had died, and Wirz was left to bear sole responsibility for the horrors he had supervised. He was tried for the murder and abuse of prisoners and sentenced to hang in Washington, D.C. He was the only Confederate officer executed as a war criminal.

Wise, Henry Alexander (1806–1876) • Congressman, governor, and Confederate army officer. Born on Virginia's Eastern Shore, Henry Alexander Wise served six terms in Congress and also as minister to Brazil. He was the governor of Virginia when JOHN BROWN raided HARPERS FERRY, and signed the abolitionist's death warrant. Wise was appointed a brigadier general in the Confederate army in June 1861. His lack of military experience showed in his early failures in the Kanawha Valley campaign and at Roanoke Island, but later in the war he did better. He helped save PETERSBURG from the initial Union assault in June 1864, and performed well the next year on the retreat to APPOMATTOX. After the war he refused to seek a pardon, and often signed his letters "prisoner of war."

Wise, Henry Augustus (1819–1869) • born in Brooklyn, New York to a naval family, Henry Augustus Wise entered the navy himself as a midshipman in 1834. During the MEXICAN WAR (1846–48) he saw action in the Gulf of California, and after that conflict he became an expert on gunnery. When the CIVIL WAR began Wise was torn between staying in the U.S. Navy and serving Virginia, where he had grown up. He decided to retain his commission, and was almost immediately ordered to destroy the GOSPORT NAVY YARD, near his old home. After a few months on blockade duty he was assigned to the Bureau of Ordnance and Hydrography, becoming acting chief in 1863. President ABRAHAM LINCOLN appointed Wise chief of the bureau in 1864, a position he held until illness forced his resignation in 1868. He died in Naples, Italy while trying to regain his health.

wishbone • *n.* a boom in two halves that curve outward around a sail and meet aft of it.

withdrawal operation • a planned operation in which a force in contact disengages from an enemy force.

Withlacoochee, Battle of the • a battle in the second SEMINOLE WAR fought on December 30, 1835, along the Withlacoochee River in Citrus County, Florida. Though strongly outnumbered, the Seminoles held their position and prevented an attack on their villages, owing to poor preparation and confused leadership of a militia whose term of enlistment was about to expire.

WMD • *abbr.* weapons of mass destruction.

WO • *abbr.* Warrant Officer.

Wolfe, James (1727–1759) • British army officer. Born in Westerham, Kent, England, in 1727, James Wolfe entered the British military service as a lieutenant in his father's regiment of marines in 1741. He commanded a company in Flanders, was appointed brigade major in 1745, and served at the Battle of Culloden that same year. He then returned to fight in the Netherlands where he was wounded at Laeffelt. In January 1748, he obtained a majority in the 20th Regiment of Foot. Since the regiment's colonel, Lord CHARLES CORNWALLIS, was often absent, Wolfe, who was promoted to lieutenant colonel in 1749, frequently commanded the regiment and introduced a system of tactics which remained in use for some time. In June 1757, he was made quartermaster general of Newcastle's expedition against Rochefort, France, and was subsequently rewarded for his service with brevet promotion to colonel. In 1758, William Pitt offered Wolfe a brigade command in Sir JEFFREY AMHERST's expedition against LOUISBOURG. Wolfe subsequently distinguished himself during the landing and successful siege of the French fortress. After the capture of Louisbourg, Wolfe was sent to destroy French fishing camps in the Gulf of St. Lawrence, after which he returned to England. Although he had never held an independent command, in 1759 Wolfe was selected by Prime Minister William Pitt to command the British expedition against Quebec. Wolfe's initial assault on the MARQUIS DE MONTCALM's position at Montmorency (July 31, 1759) failed, but in August he moved his forces up the river to a point above the city, and in the early morning hours of September 13, 1759, seized the Plains of Abraham, forcing Montcalm into an attack which failed. Both Montcalm and Wolfe were mortally wounded during the brief engagement.

wolf pack • a group of people or things that operate as a hunting and attacking pack, in particular a group of attacking submarines or aircraft.

Women Reservists • a U.S. Army organization authorized when President HARRY S. TRUMAN signed the Women's Armed Services Act in June 1948, which allowed women to serve in the Organized Reserves, but their numbers were limited to 10 percent of the enlisted force. They were called to active duty for the first time in the KOREAN WAR. In 1972, there were 483 women reservists in the WOMEN'S ARMY CORPS; by 1999, there were 50,000 women reservists, 24.2 percent of the Army Reserve.

Women's Armed Services Integration Act • a law proposed by Gen. DWIGHT D. EISENHOWER and signed on June 12, 1948 by President HARRY S. TRUMAN to allow women to serve as full members of the U.S. armed forces. It permanently established the Women's Army Corps law, which had allowed women full status in the army since 1947, and extended it to all of the armed forces.

Women's Army Corps • (**WAC**) originally established as the Women's Army Auxiliary Corps (WAAC) because Congresswoman Edith Nourse Rogers of Massachusetts wanted to ensure that women who served in the U.S. armed forces would receive pay, pensions, and benefits equal to those provided to men in the military. With the support of Gen. GEORGE C. MARSHALL, the bill passed Congress and was signed by President FRANKLIN D. ROOSEVELT in 1941, after the bombing of PEARL HARBOR; OVETA CULP HOBBY was appointed the first director of the WAAC. In 1943, Congress authorized the conversion of the WAAC to the Women's Army Corps.

wonder • *n.* (usually **ninety-day** (or **thirty-day**) **wonder**) a person who has had intensive military training for the specified time.

Wonsan • a port and naval base on the Sea of Japan in southeastern North Korea. Gen. DOUGLAS MACARTHUR ordered an amphibious assault on the city in order to get a site offering a better chance at efficient logistical support than PUSAN or INCHON. The Tenth Corps landed and was scheduled to meet the Eighth Army inland as they marched north from Seoul. The assault was a success, but North Korean forces had sown the harbor with mines, and many minesweepers were lost in attempts to find and destroy them.

Woodford, William (1734–1780) • REVOLUTIONARY WAR army officer. Born in Caroline County, Virginia, William Woodford served in the Virginia militia during the FRENCH AND IN-

DIAN WAR (1754–63). He began the Revolutionary War in command of the 3rd Virginia Regiment, and was instrumental in defeating Lord Dunmore's Loyalists and compelling the royal governor to leave the state. In 1776 Woodford was appointed a colonel in Continental service, and he was promoted to brigadier general the next year. He fought at the battles at BRANDYWINE, GERMANTOWN (both 1777), and MONMOUTH (1778). In December 1779 GEORGE WASHINGTON ordered Woodford south with 700 soldiers to reinforce BENJAMIN LINCOLN in Charleston. Woodford arrived in April 1780, and was taken prisoner the next month when the city fell to the British. He died in captivity in New York City.

Woodhull, Alfred Alexander (1837–1921) • U.S. army medical officer. Born in Princeton, New Jersey, Alfred Alexander Woodhull earned his M.D. from the University of Pennsylvania in 1859. He entered the Union Army Medical Department as an assistant surgeon in 1861, serving in that capacity throughout the conflict. After the war he published a number of pioneering works on hygiene and sanitation. His ideas were taught throughout the army, and helped inform the growing public health movement in the United States and its territories. He left the army in 1901 as a colonel, but was promoted to brigadier general on the retired list by Congress three years later.

Woodhull, Nathaniel (1722–1776) • Revolutionary army officer. Born in Suffolk County, New York, Nathaniel Woodhull served in the New York militia during the FRENCH AND INDIAN WAR (1754–63). He commanded the Third New York Provincial Regiment in campaigns to capture Fort Frontenac and Montreal. In August 1776, the New York convention ordered him to lead the Long Island militia in driving livestock away from the invading British army. He was wounded and captured by some roving Light Dragoons. Though his gangrenous arm was amputated, he died in a hospital at New Utrecht on 20 September. In 1821 a patriotic ballad appeared that claimed Woodhull had been purposefully wounded after capture in retaliation for his refusal to say "God save the king." There is no good evidence to support this claim, but the historical dispute generated by the ballad has perpetuated Woodhull's memory.

Wood, John Taylor (1830–1904) • Confederate naval officer. Born at Fort Snelling, in what would become Minnesota, John Taylor Wood graduated from the NAVAL ACADEMY in 1853. He gave up his commission in April 1861, and accepted an appointment as a lieutenant in the Confederate States navy in October. He served on the *Virginia* during its battles in HAMPTON ROADS in 1862. In January 1863 Wood was appointed as the naval aide to his uncle, President JEFFERSON DAVIS. In August Wood led a daring raid in the Chesapeake that captured five federal schooners. A year later he ran the blockade in the raider *Tallahassee*, capturing 33 vessels in one 19 day cruise. In February 1865 he was promoted to captain, but two months later he had to flee Richmond. He made his way to Cuba and later to Halifax, Nova Scotia, where he engaged in business until his death.

Wood, Leonard (1860–1927) • U.S. army officer and military governor. Born in Winchester, New Hampshire, Leonard Wood received his M.D. degree from Harvard Medical School in 1884. Two years later he secured an army appointment as a lieutenant and assistant surgeon in Arizona Territory, and took part in the campaign against Geronimo and his Apaches. Wood was awarded a CONGRESSIONAL MEDAL OF HONOR for his performance as both a medical and line officer. In 1895 Wood became White House physician, eventually forming a close friendship with assistant secretary of the navy THEODORE ROOSEVELT. They organized the 1st Volunteer Cavalry Regiment, known as the "ROUGH RIDERS," for the SPANISH-AMERICAN WAR (1898). Wood was colonel in command, but in Cuba he quickly moved up to take over a brigade. He served as a military governor in both Cuba and the Philippines in the years after that conflict, accomplishing many needed reforms while earning promotions up to major general by 1903. In April 1910 he became chief of staff of the army. He firmly established that position by breaking the power of entrenched bureau chiefs, and was a strong advocate for preparedness. He worked around official channels to establish civilian training camps at Plattsburg, New York, which caused some friction with President WOODROW WILSON and the WAR DEPARTMENT. Though he was the senior officer in the army, Wood spent WORLD WAR I training units in the United States. After the war he dabbled in politics and was unsuccessful in his bid for the Republican presidential nomination. He accepted an appointment as governor-general of the Philippines in 1921, and was serving in that position when he died in Boston following surgery.

Woods, Charles Robert (1827–1885) • Born in Newark, Ohio, Charles Robert Woods graduated from WEST POINT in 1852. In January 1861 he commanded two hundred soldiers on the *Star of the West* sent to relieve Fort Sumter. When enemy ships came out in Charleston harbor to attack them Woods ordered the *Star of the West* to escape. In October he raised the Seventy-Sixth Ohio Volunteer Infantry and was elected its colonel. He led it at FORT DONELSON and SHILOH (both 1862). Later he commanded a brigade in operations around CORINTH (1862) and along the Mississippi River. After the Vicksburg campaign Woods was promoted to brigadier general of volunteers. He continued to lead his brigade through the battle of LOOKOUT MOUNTAIN (1863) and WILLIAM T. SHERMAN's march through Georgia and the Carolinas. Woods earned a brevet promotion to major general for meritorious service at Bentonville. After the war he rejoined the regular army as a lieutenant colonel and finished his career fighting Indians in Kansas. He retired in 1874 as a colonel.

Wood, Thomas John (1823–1906) • U.S. army officer. Born in Munfordville, Kentucky, Thomas John Wood graduated from WEST POINT in 1845 with a commission in the Corps of Engineers. He transferred to the cavalry during the MEXICAN WAR (1846–48) and distinguished himself at BUENA VISTA. When the CIVIL WAR began Wood was appointed brigadier general of volunteers and given command of an Indiana brigade he had helped raise. He commanded a division in the ARMY OF THE OHIO, later the ARMY OF THE CUMBERLAND, and was wounded at STONES RIVER (1862–63). At CHICKAMAUGA (1863) Wood obeyed orders to move his division and left a gap in the line that allowed a Confederate attack to cut the Union army in two. WILLIAM S. ROSECRANS blamed Woods for his defeat, but ULYSSES S. GRANT relieved Rosecrans and kept Wood. Grant's judgment paid off at MISSIONARY RIDGE (1863), where Wood's men disobeyed orders to halt and swept up over the top of the Confederate position in a spectacular attack that sent the enemy army reeling and broke the siege of Chattanooga. Wood served with WILLIAM T. SHERMAN in his ATLANTA campaign, and then helped GEORGE THOMAS shatter JOHN B. HOOD'S ARMY OF TENNESSEE at NASHVILLE. Wood finished the war as a major general, and was assigned to occupation duty in Mississippi. He did not like it, and retired from the army in 1868.

Wool, John Ellis (1784–1869) • U.S. army officer. Born in Newburgh, New York, on February 29, 1784, John E. Wool joined the militia in 1807 and raised a militia company in Troy, New York, at the beginning of the WAR OF 1812. He soon received a commission as a captain of the new 13th U.S. Infantry (April 1812), was badly wounded at Queenston Heights (September 1812), was promoted to major, and was brevetted lieutenant colonel for gallantry at the Battle of Plattsburgh (August 1814). He was appointed inspector general of the Northern Division in 1816 and subsequently served as Inspector General of the Army (1821–1841) and supervised the removal of the Cherokees to Oklahoma (1836–1837). Brevetted brigadier general for service in 1826, Wool was promoted to brigadier general in the Regular Army in June 1841 and took command of the Eastern Department. During the MEXICAN WAR (1846–48), he marched his troops 900 miles from San Antonio to Saltillo (September 1846–January 1847) in time to support Gen. ZACHARY TAYLOR's forces at the BATTLE OF BUENA VISTA (February 22–23, 1847). He became Taylor's second-in-command and was brevetted major general. Wool returned to command of the Department of the East from 1848 to 1854 when he was sent to command the Department of the Pacific. In 1857, he returned again to command the Eastern Department and was credited with securing FORT MONROE and reinforcing Washington at the outbreak of the CIVIL WAR. Wool was promoted to major general, Regular Army, in May 1862 and was sent to command the Middle Department at Baltimore, Maryland. His final duty before being retired for disability at age 79 on August 1, 1863, was to suppress the New York draft riots in July of that year.

Woolsey, R. James, Jr. (1941–) • born in Tulsa, Oklahoma, Woolsey was educated at Stanford (BA, 1963) and Oxford University as a Rhodes Scholar (BA, 1965), and returned to the United States and received his LLB from Yale in 1968. He went back to Oxford and earned an MA (1970) as well. From 1968–1970, he served as a Captain in the U.S. Army, working as a program analyst in the office of the secretary of defense, and was a delegate to the STRATEGIC ARMS LIMITATIONS TALKS (SALT I) in Helsinki and Vienna (1969–1970) before joining the NATIONAL SECURITY COUNCIL Staff in 1970. From 1970–1973, he was the general counsel to the U.S. Senate's Committee on the Armed Services, before going into private law practice (1973–1977). In 1977, he was appointed as Under Secretary of the Navy, but returned to private practice in 1979. Although he retained his position as a partner in the law firm of Shea Gardner for ten years, he also served as a delegate to the United States—Soviet STRATEGIC ARMS REDUCTION TALKS (START) and the Nuclear and Space Talks (NST) (1983–1986) and on several presidential commissions (1983–1989). He was appointed Director of the CENTRAL INTELLIGENCE AGENCY by President BILL CLINTON in 1993, and held that position until 1995, when he again took up his private law practice.

wooly-pully sweater • a heavy wool knit pullover sweater, usually reinforced at the shoulders and elbows, worn by military personnel.

Wooster, Charles Whiting (1780–1848) • U.S. and Chilean navy officer. Born in New Haven, Connecticut, Charles Whiting Wooster went to sea when he was only eleven. During the WAR OF 1812 he took 22 British prizes as the captain of the privateer *Saratoga*. He ended that conflict commanding a battalion of volunteer "sea fencibles" protecting New York Harbor. In October 1817 he accepted a commission in the newly-created Chilean Navy, serving there for most of the next 18 years and rising to the rank of rear admiral. He was named commander of the navy in 1822, and four years later led the joint land-sea assault on the island of Chiloé, the final Spanish stronghold in Chile. In 1835 he returned to the United States, and when the California Gold Rush began he decided to try mining.

Wooster, David (1711–1777) • colonial and REVOLUTIONARY WAR army officer. Born in Stratford, Connecticut, David Wooster graduated from Yale in 1738. He served as a captain of militia at the capture of Louisbourg in 1745, and afterwards was commissioned as a captain in a regiment of regulars. During the FRENCH AND INDIAN WAR (1754–63) he commanded the 3rd Connecticut Regiment of militia, earning a promotion to brigadier general in 1763. He began the Revolutionary War as major general of Connecticut militia, and was soon appointed a brigadier general in the Continental army. He took part in Gen. RICHARD MONTGOMERY's invasion of Canada, and succeeded to command of the force when Montgomery died in the failed assault on Quebec. He did not impress Congress with his performance, and was sent back to lead Connecticut militia in late 1776. When a large British raiding party attacked a Continental supply depot in Danbury in April the next year, Wooster assembled a small force of militiamen to harass the invaders as they returned to their ships. He was mortally wounded attacking the raiders, and died in Danbury.

Worden, John Lorimer (1818–1897) • U.S. naval officer. Born in Westchester County, New York, John Worden entered the navy as a midshipman in 1834. His career followed a normal pattern until the beginning of the CIVIL WAR. He was captured by Confederate authorities while returning from delivering secret dispatches to the naval squadron off Pensacola, and held prisoner for seven months. Shortly after his release in early 1862 he was given command of the new ironclad *Monitor* that was under construction in New York. He sailed the untried experimental vessel through heavy seas to HAMPTON ROADS, Virginia in time to save the Union fleet there from destruction by the Confederate ironclad *Virginia*. The two ships fought to a momentous draw on March 9, 1862. Worden was temporarily blinded by flying fragments late in the engagement, but he recovered to receive the thanks of Congress. In October he took command of the monitor *Montauk* in the South Atlantic Blockading Squadron, figuring prominently in a number of coastal actions and sinking the cruiser *Nashville*. From mid-1863 to the end of the war he was assigned to supervise the construction of new ironclads. He became superintendent of the NAVAL ACADEMY in 1869, and later commanded the European Squadron. He retired as a rear admiral in 1886.

work • *n.* (usually **works**) a defensive structure. • *v.* make progress to windward, with repeated tacking: *trying to work to windward in light airs.*

workboat • *n.* a boat used for work such as commercial fishing or transporting freight, rather than leisure or naval service.

working anchorage • a place where ships can lie while their cargoes are unloaded to coasters or lighters. See also EMERGENCY ANCHORAGE.

World Trade Organization • (**WTO**) an international organization that administers trade agreements among nations, handles trade disputes, and provides technical assistance and training for developing countries. It was established in 1995, bsaed on the GENERAL AGREEMENT ON TARIFFS AND TRADE.

Critics of the WTO contend that the organization hurts developing countries and weakens health and environmental safety standards in order to promote the interests of large corporations.

---

world war • a war involving many large nations in all different parts of the world. The name is commonly given to the wars of 1914–18 and 1939–45, although only the second of these was truly global. See WORLD WAR I, WORLD WAR II.

World War I • (1914–18) Essentially a civil war in Europe with global implications, World War I resulted in a shift of economic and cultural influences away from Europe, ultimately enabling new nations to emerge and encouraged others (notably the United States) to challenge Europe's international leadership. The fighting pitted Germany, the Austro-Hungarian Empire, and the Ottoman Empire (together styled the Central Powers) against an alliance of Britain, France, Russia, Italy and, eventually, the United States. With the mobilization of 65 million troops, World War I was ultimately most destructive military conflict in world history to that point. Triggered by the assassination of the heir to the Austro-Hungarian throne in Bosnia-Herzegovina's capital, Sarajevo (allegedly by Serbian nationalists), open warfare grew from a series of strategic alliances that drew in powers that seemingly had little interest in this immediate cause. The Austrians, given unequivocal support by their ally, Germany, decided to crush Serbia's perceived challenge. Russia, fearing domestic uprisings in support of Orthodox Serbia, gave notice that it would support its coreligionists against Catholic Austria-Hungary. German military leaders, particularly Gen. Alfred von Schlieffen, sought to advance their own goals by using the crisis as a justification for attacking Russia's ally, France. That all these nations had been steadily arming over the previous years only further exacerbated the crisis, pushing them toward war. By August 12, all major powers had declared war, and Germany, challenging Belgium's declarations of neutrality, began hostilities by marching through the smaller nation in order to launch an attack on France. France and Britain responded by meeting the German attack. Acting on its own declaration of war, Russia launched an attack on Germany's eastern front. Within three weeks the engaged armies had fought to a virtual standstill. German troops destroyed an entire Russian army at Tannenberg (August 26–30). A week later, British and French stopped Germany's own flanking maneuver through Belgium in the First Battle of the Marne (September 5–9). Soon the western armies had constructed an almost continuous parallel line of defensive systems stretching from Switzerland to the North Sea. Trench warfare, most prominent in France and Flanders, but existing in some areas of Russia, Italy, the Balkans, and Palestine as well, flouted attempts by Europe's military leaders to return to a war of maneuver by rupturing the enemy's front. To restore the offensive, both sides eventually introduced new weapons such as tanks and chemical warfare. High-explosive shells, recoilless carriages, optical sights, improved communications, and cannon ranges of 20 or more miles made indirect artillery bombardment the dominant force of the battlefield. The application of massive and increasingly sophisticated artillery fire proved to be the most effective means of reducing fortifications. But western defenses were so strong and thickly defended that, although it was possible to break into them, there remained severe limitations to any advance. In 1915, the Central Powers concentrated their resources on the eastern front. The vastness of that front, and the clear superiority of German artillery and leadership, made possible an advance of some 300 miles. Although Italy left its pre-war pact with Germany and Austro-Hungary to join the Allies in 1915, by the end of the year, Berlin dominated Central and southeastern Europe. British efforts to find a "way around" the western front ended in dismal failure in the Dardanelles and Gallipoli campaigns. In 1916, Germany sought to break the stalemate in the west in the ten-month BATTLE OF VERDUN, deliberately seeking a decisive battle of attrition and will. To relieve Verdun, a massive Anglo-French offensive was launched on the SOMME in July. Nevertheless, when winter ended the fighting, the western front had changed little. 1917 marked two important changes in the war. In October, Russian revolutionaries bolstered by public discontent over the country's dismal fortunes in the war overthrew the Tsar, and the new Soviet Union removed itself from the fighting. A perhaps more important shift occurred when the previously neutral United States joined the Allies against Germany. President WOODROW WILSON had attempted to keep the United States in a mediating position. Germany's attempt to quickly end the war by stopping U.S. shipments to the Allies through unlimited submarine warfare and secretly propositioning Mexico to attack (discovered when British code-breakers intercepted the ZIMMERMAN TELEGRAM) backfired and drew the United States into the conflict. Wilson's goals, however, differed from his allies' in that he advocated a plan for "peace without victory" he announced in January 1917 and further codified a year later in his FOURTEEN POINTS. United States troops, called the AMERICAN EXPEDITIONARY FORCES (AEF), did relatively little to alleviate the military stalemate when they arrived on European soil. AEF commander-in-chief JOHN J. PERSHING planned to launch a win-the-war campaign in 1919. Early AEF actions were less than successful, however. Logistical chaos, flawed tactics, and inexperienced men and officers contributed to a disastrous start to the MEUSE-ARGONNE offensive (September 26–November 11, 1918) and by the armistice Pershing's troops had moved just thirty-four miles. Nevertheless, although only involved in heavy fighting for 110 days, the AEF made vital contributions to Germany's defeat. With tens of thousands of "doughboys" crossing the Atlantic to reinforce the Allies, and with the AEF emerging as a superior fighting force, the exhausted and depleted German army appealed for peace based on Wilson's Fourteen Points in early October. As the Great War concluded with the armistice on November 11, 1918, the Allies were divided on how to construct the peace. American policy was directed toward the repudiation of power politics and the erection of a "permanent" peace. Wilsonianism promised an end to war primarily through democratic institutions, the end of secret diplomacy, self-determination for ethnic minorities, and most especially through a LEAGUE OF NATIONS. The war had destroyed the old balance of power in Europe, and the peace settlement made revisionist nations out of the two states that would soon dominate the continent, Germany and the Soviet Union. Yet, the peace settlement did not prove satisfactory. British and French insistence on reparations created lingering animosity within Germany. Likewise, the division of colonies and former Central Powers territories aggravated tensions in areas such as North Africa, the Balkans, Palestine and the Arabian Peninsula. The United States, the greatest economic beneficiary of the war, helped make the peace, but with its rejection of the TREATY OF VERSAILLES refused responsibility for maintaining it. The war ended in a twenty-year truce instead of a "permanent peace." The failure to achieve Wilson's unrealistic though desirable goal was hardly surprising, but another general war was not inevitable. WORLD WAR II was caused by many factors, including the flawed peace settlement of 1919, the great Depression of the 1930s, and the psychological scars of World War I, which enfeebled the democracies. But the inability of the victorious powers, especially Great Britain and the United States, to work together to prevent the resurgence of German military power, was certainly one of the most important reasons for the resumption of war in 1939.

World War II • (1939–1945) The Second World War was a truly global conflict which pitted the forces of democracy and liberalism against the forces of fascism and nationalistic militarism. On one side stood the Western democracies, led by Britain, France, and the United States, together with two regimes themselves essentially totalitarian in nature, the Soviet Union and the Republic of China. On the other side crouched ADOLF HITLER's Nazi Germany, BENITO MUSSOLINI's Fascist Italy, a Japanese Empire dominated by militarists, and right-wing authoritarian regimes in Hungary, Romania, and Bulgaria. Although an enormously complex affair in which events in one hemisphere impacted upon events half a world away, World War II can be conveniently divided into two parts: the war in Europe, North Africa, the Middle East, Russia, and the Atlantic Ocean and the war in Asia and the Pacific. Motivated by the desire to expand the territory of the German Reich, gather in ethnic Germans in Eastern Europe, and dominate Central Europe, German forces invaded Poland on September 1, 1939, thereby provoking the British and French to declare war on Germany on September 3. Hitler's well-trained and well-equipped forces quickly conquered Poland, which was also attacked simultaneously from the east by the Soviet Union, and turned to the west where a standoff, known as the SITZKRIEG or the "Phony War," lasted until the Germans invaded Norway in April 1940. On May 10, 1940, the Nazis mounted a strong offensive which took the Netherlands, Belgium, and Luxembourg in short order and drove across the French border on May 12, quickly defeating the French and their British allies. The remaining British forces were withdrawn under fire from the beaches of Dunkirk (May 26–June 3), and the German forces entered Paris (June 14). On June 10, Italy declared war on Britain and France and invaded French territory. The demoralized French subsequently signed an armistice at Compiégne (where German forces had surrendered to end WORLD WAR I) on June 22, and France was divided into a northern zone occupied by the Germans and a southern area which, for the time being, was controlled by the authoritarian, pro-Nazi VICHY regime led by Marshal Henri Pétain. Unable to proceed directly to an amphibious invasion of England, Hitler launched an air campaign against Britain accompanied by unrestricted submarine warfare in the Atlantic designed to isolate Britain from the resources of her empire and America. By dint of organizational skill and raw courage, the British ROYAL AIR FORCE prevailed over the German LUFTWAFFE in the aerial campaign known as the BATTLE OF BRITAIN in the summer and early fall of 1940. Meanwhile, the German Afrika Korps under Gen. ERWIN ROMMEL reinforced Italian forces in North Africa and drove toward Egypt and the Suez Canal, engaging the defending British Commonwealth forces in a see-saw battle in the Western Desert. The British were defeated at Tobruk (June 1942) but won a substantial victory at El Alamein under British Gen. BERNARD LAW MONTGOMERY (October 23–November 4, 1942), preventing the loss of Egypt. In 1941, the Germans conquered Yugoslavia (April 17) and then Greece (April 27) thus securing their flanks for their most ambitious project, the invasion of the Soviet Union on June 22, 1941. At first the Germans encountered only weak resistance from the stunned Soviet forces, but the Red Army rallied to establish a successful defense before Leningrad in the north and Moscow in the center. In the south, the Germans seized the Crimea and pushed on into the Caucasus, but Soviet resistance stiffened at STALINGRAD on the Volga. The war in the East was enormous in scope and magnitude, and the Germans found themselves stymied as much by the vast spaces and inclement climate as by the Soviet armed forces. Eventually the Soviet forces went over to the offensive (November 1942), and the German Sixth Army surrendered at Stalingrad (February 1–2, 1943), marking the turning point of the war in the East. Thereafter, the Soviet force inexorably pushed the Germans back toward Berlin. The largest tank battle of the war was fought at Kursk in July 1943, and the Germans never recovered from the loss of armored forces in that battle. From September 1939 to December 1941, the United States followed a policy of neutrality with respect to the war raging in Europe. However, Britain and the United States discussed possible mutual action against the Axis powers, and in March 1941 Congress passed the LEND-LEASE ACT legitimizing the flow of war materials to Britain which had been going on for some time. Following the Japanese attack on PEARL HARBOR (1941), both Germany and Italy declared war on the United States, and Congress reciprocated with a declaration of war on them on December 11, 1941. Allied strategy and policy were subsequently coordinated in a series of meetings of the various Allied heads of state (U.S. President FRANKLIN D. ROOSEVELT, and after his death on April 12, 1945, President HARRY S. TRUMAN; British Prime Minister WINSTON CHURCHILL; Soviet Premier JOSEF STALIN; and Nationalist Chinese Generalissimo CHIANG KAI-SHEK) at the ANGLO-AMERICAN ARCADIA CONFERENCE (December 1941); CASABLANCA (January 1943); QUEBEC (August 1943); CAIRO (November 1943); TEHRAN (November-December 1943); and YALTA (February 1945). The strategic decision was made to defeat the Axis forces in Europe first before turning to deal with the Japanese in Asia and the Pacific, and U.S. air and ground forces were rushed to England in anticipation of an early invasion of Continental Europe. First, however, U.S. and British forces mounted an invasion of French North Africa at Casablanca, Oran, and Algiers (November 8, 1942) and, following a galling American defeat by the Germans at the KASSERINE PASS (February 1943), proceeded to roll up the German and Italian forces in Tunisia and Libya, pushing them against Montgomery's British 8th Army moving westward from Egypt. The remnants of the vaunted Afrika Korps surrendered at Cap Bon, Tunisia, on May 12, 1943, ending the war in North Africa. In July, U.S. and British forces invaded SICILY and completed the defeat of its German and Italian defenders by September 3. On July 25, 1943, Mussolini was deposed and Marshal Badoglio was named premier, and on September 8, 1943, Italy surrendered to the Allies. However, strong German forces remained in Italy, and on September 9, 1943, the Allies landed at Salerno south of Naples and began the long, arduous drive toward Rome, a drive stalled for some time in the winter of 1943–1944 along the line of the RAPIDO RIVER south of CASSINO. On January 22, 1944, the U.S. and British forces conducted another amphibious landing at ANZIO on the west coast of Italy just below Rome. Although heavily pounded by the German defenders, the Allies managed to break out of the Anzio beachhead as well as cross the Rapido River line, and on June 4, 1944, the Allies entered Rome and subsequently continued the tough fight up the Italian peninsula lasting until the end of the war in May 1945. The news of the taking of Rome was overshadowed by the most massive and elaborate amphibious operation of the war, the Allied landings in NORMANDY on June 6, 1944. Bogged down for a time in the beachhead and the hedgerow country of Normandy, the Allies broke out in July 1944, and the Germans quickly retreated behind the Rhine River pursued closely by the Allied forces. A second Allied landing was made in the south of France on August 15, and Paris was liberated on August 25. In far-off Greece, Athens was freed by the Allies on October 13. During the fall and early winter of 1944, the Allies focused on closing up to the Rhine and securing the logistical bases necessary for carrying the war into Germany. On December 16, 1944, the Germans launched a last ditch counterattack against the Allied forces in Belgium, and the resulting BATTLE OF THE BULGE, although a near-run thing, ultimately resulted in an Allied victory. On March 9, 1945, U.S. forces crossed the Rhine at Remagen and a few weeks later joined with Field Marshal Montgomery's forces to trap some 350,000 German troops in the Ruhr. Thereafter, the Allies quickly drove deep into Germany. Meanwhile, on May 2, 1945, Soviet forces took Berlin, and on May 7, 1945, the Germans signed an unconditional surrender to the Allies at Rheims. Benito Mussolini was killed by Italian partisans at Lake Como on April 28, and Adolf Hitler took his own life on May 1, as did other Nazi leaders. The remaining Nazi leaders were rounded up by Allied forces and put on trial for war crimes and crimes against humanity at Nuremberg in 1945–1946. Air and naval forces also played an important role in the war in the West. Although the Germans neglected the development of long-range strategic bombers, the Stuka dive-bombers, light bombers, and fighters of the Luftwaffe were an integral part of the successful German *blitzkrieg* tactics. After failing to destroy the British Royal Air Force in the Battle of Britain in the summer and fall of 1940, the Luftwaffe turned to the bombing of British cities and industrial facilities, and the RAF BOMBER COMMAND retaliated in kind. With the American entry into the war, the U.S. 8th Air Force in England (on August 17, 1942) and the U.S. 15th Air Force in the Mediterranean took up the strategic bombing of Germany and her allies, and American light bombers and fighters took on the task of gaining air superiority over Germany and supporting Allied ground forces with reconnaissance, interdiction strikes and close air support. Air transport also played a role in supporting the rapid movement of critical supplies, air evacuation of casualties, liaison flights, and troop carriers for airborne operations. Allied air forces also performed coastal surveillance and convoy security duties. In England, the RAF Bomber Command and U.S. 8th Air Force worked out a plan (the Combined Bomber Offensive) for the round-the-clock bombing of Germany, with 8th Air Force taking on the daylight precision bombing task and Bomber Command that of night area bombing of German cities. Lacking a strategic bomber force and increasingly dominated by Allied air power, the Germans resorted to new technology and attacked Britain with rocket-powered flying bombs (the V-1 "buzzbomb") and the more powerful V-2 rocket. At sea, German surface forces were rendered impotent after the successful British attacks against German capital ships in the Norwegian fjords and the North Sea (April-June 1940) and the sinking of the German battleship *Bismarck* by the Royal Navy (May 27, 1941). However, the greatest threatcame from German submarine operations in the so-called Battle of the Atlantic. By mid-1943, German submarines threatened to isolate Britain as they had in World War I, and Allied shipping losses were surpassing the capacity of British and American shipyards to produce new vessels. However, the tide turned in the spring of 1943 as the Allies capitalized on their intelligence advantages (such as ULTRA intercepts of German communications), introduced more effective convoy protection methods (such as the escort carrier and land-based air cover), and new technology (such as better radar and sonar and improved depth charges) became available for the detection and destruction of German submarines. By the end of the war, the German submarine fleet commanded by Admiral Karl Doenitz, having lost 800 U-BOATS and 28,000 sailors in sinking some 2,700 Allied ships, was all but driven from the seas, and a massive stream of men and supplies flowed from America to Britain. Japan had long sought to expand her economic hegemony in Asia in order to obtain the raw materials necessary for her industries. Accordingly, Japan had invaded China in 1937. The principal obstacle to the establishment of the Japanese "East Asia Co-Prosperity Sphere" was the United States, and in 1941 the Japanese decided to take action. The war in the Pacific began with the Japanese attack on Pearl Harbor, Hawaii, on December 7, 1941, accompanied by coordinated attacks on U.S. forces in the Philippines; on British Commonwealth forces in Hong Kong, Malaya, and New Guinea; and on the Dutch in the East Indies. The British surrendered Singapore on February 15, 1942, and the U.S. forces in the Philippines surrendered on May 6, 1942, following a desperate defense of BATAAN and the fortified island of CORREGIDOR in Manila Bay. The U.S. Pacific Fleet was severely damaged by the Japanese attack at Pearl Harbor, but the U.S. aircraft carriers were unharmed. The U.S. Navy thus immediate took the offensive and blunted the Japanese offensive in the indecisive BATTLE OF THE CORAL SEA (May 7–8,

1942) and the BATTLE OF MIDWAY (June 4, 1942) in which the Japanese lost four carriers and 253 aircraft, losses from which the Japanese carrier forces never recovered. A token attack on Tokyo was also carried out on April 18, 1942, by sixteen U.S. Army Air Corps B-25 bombers launched from the aircraft carrier USS *Hornet*. The bombers under the command of Lt. Col. JAMES H. DOOLITTLE did only minor damage but greatly shocked the Japanese. Following the fall of the Philippines, the American commander in the Southwest Pacific, Gen. DOUGLAS MACARTHUR, established U.S. forces in Australia and began the long island-hopping drive back to liberate the Philippines. Japanese forces invaded New Guinea and took Tulagi and GUADALCANAL in the SOLOMON ISLANDS, but Australian and American forces halted the Japanese advance in New Guinea and held against six months of Japanese counterattacks. On August 7, 1942, U.S. Marines landed on Guadalcanal and, later aided by U.S. Army forces, fought three major land battles on Guadalcanal and six major naval engagements in nearby waters before securing the island on February 9, 1943. While MacArthur's forces fought the Japanese in New Guinea and the Solomons, U.S. air, naval, and amphibious forces under Admiral CHESTER W. NIMITZ began a drive in the Central Pacific westward toward Formosa (Taiwan), taking TARAWA and Makin in the Gilbert Islands in 1943 and the MARSHALL ISLANDS and Saipan, Tinian, and GUAM in the MARIANAS in 1944 and destroying the remaining Japanese carrier forces in the BATTLE OF THE PHILIPPINE SEA (June 19–20, 1944). Meanwhile, MacArthur's Southwest Pacific forces returned to the Philippines, landing on Leyte (October 20, 1944) and destroying the Japanese surface fleet in the BATTLE OF LEYTE GULF (October 23–26, 1944), the largest naval engagement in history. American forces subsequently landed on LUZON (January 9, 1945), and Manila was liberated on March 3. While MacArthur's forces secured the Philippines and began preparations for the invasion of the Japanese home islands, Nimitz' forces cleared key islands necessary for forward airbases for the strategic bombing of Japan. The U.S. Army Air Forces had begun the strategic bombing of Japan from bases in China in 1944 but transferred operations to the Marianas Islands after they were secured in November 1944. To secure an additional forward base, primarily for the recovery of bombers damaged over Japan, the island of Iwo Jima was invaded on February 19, 1945, and fell to American forces after 36 days of terrible fighting. On April 1, 1945, U.S. forces invaded OKINAWA, where the battle raged until June 22, again with heavy losses, including several ships to Japanese kamikaze attacks, which became common over the American fleet off Okinawa. Elsewhere Nationalist Chinese forces continued to oppose Japanese advances in China, and British Commonwealth, Nationalist Chinese, and a small contingent of American ground troops fought in Burma to prevent a Japanese invasion of India. The Dutch and other Allied forces were overwhelmed in the East Indies in early 1942, and the retaking of the East Indies was largely delegated to British Commonwealth forces who also bore the brunt of the defense of New Guinea. By the summer of 1945, Allied forces had retaken most of the areas earlier conquered by the Japanese and were closing in on the Japanese homeland, which had already been effectively isolated by Allied airpower. Facing the possibility of terrible casualties on both sides in a massive amphibious invasion of the Japanese home islands, U.S. President Harry S. Truman authorized the use of America's newest and most powerful weapon, the atomic bomb. The U.S. B-29 " ENOLA GAY" dropped the first atomic bomb on the Japanese city of HIROSHIMA on August 6, 1945, and three days later a second bomb was dropped on NAGASAKI. On August 8, the Soviet Union declared war on Japan. Japanese military leaders still hesitated to surrender, but the Japanese Emperor HIROHITO prevailed upon them, and Japanese authorities surrendered on to the Allies unconditionally on August 14. Formal surrender ceremonies presided over by Gen. Douglas MacArthur, attended by many of the Allied commanders who had surrendered at the beginning of the war and had been prisoners of the Japanese, were held aboard the battleship USS *Missouri* in Tokyo Bay on September 2, 1945, thus ending the Second World War. Japan, like Germany, was subsequently occupied by Allied forces, and her leaders were put on trial for war crimes, although the Emperor was spared and left in place as a figurehead. The commitment of resources and the destruction brought about by the Second World War far exceeded anything seen before or since as did the scope and magnitude of the war itself. The human toll of the Second World War was frightful. As many as 50 million military personnel and civilians were killed, some 14 million in the Soviet Union alone. Military casualties were heavy on both sides. The Germans lost 3.25 million combatants dead and another 7.25 million wounded; the Italians 149,496 dead and 66,716 wounded; and the Japanese 1.27 million dead and 140,000 wounded. Allied casualties were equally heavy. The Soviet Union lost at least 6.2 million killed and over 14 million wounded. Nationalist China lost 1.33 million killed and 1.76 million wounded, and Great Britain lost 357,116 killed and 369,267 wounded *not* counting Commonwealth forces. U.S. military casualties totaled 291,557 battle deaths, 113,842 deaths from other causes, and 670,846 wounded. The civilian death toll included over 6 million Jews and other "undesirables" murdered by the Nazis in the death camps and during the campaigns in Eastern Europe and Russia. The outcome of the war shaped the remaining half of the twentieth century and continues to have an important impact well into the twenty-first century. Although the totalitarian regimes in

Germany, Italy, and Japan were defeated, the war left many unresolved political, social, and economic problems in its wake and brought the Western democracies into direct confrontation with their erstwhile ally, the Soviet Union under Josef Stalin, thereby initiating a period of nearly half a century of skirmishing and nervous watchfulness as two blocs, each armed with nuclear weapons, faced each other probing for any sign of weakness.

World War Veterans Adjusted Compensation Act • an act passed by Congress on May 19, 1924, over a veto by President Calvin Coolidge, to grant veterans a cash payment for the loss of wages due to wartime service. It was achieved by the political efforts of the Veterans of Foreign Wars. (Also known as **"the Soldier's Bonus."**)

wounded in action • (**WIA**) a casualty category applicable to a hostile casualty, other than the victim of a terrorist activity, who has incurred an injury due to an external agent or cause. The term encompasses all kinds of wounds and other injuries incurred in action, whether there is a piercing of the body (as in a penetration or perforated wound) or none (as in a contused wound). These wounds include fractures, burns, blast concussions, all effects of biological and chemical warfare agents, and the effects of an exposure to ionizing radiation or any other destructive weapon or agent. The hostile casualty's status may be very seriously ill or injured, seriously ill or injured, incapacitatingly ill or injured, or not seriously injured.

Wounded Knee, Battle of • a battle fought on December 29, 1890 at Wounded Knee, South Dakota that was the last major encounter between Native Americans and the U.S. Army. The Army had surrounded a village of LAKOTA SIOUX while attempting to disarm a party of them who had been captured. The accidental discharge of a firearm led to panic, and the Army opened fire on the village, massacring nearly all its inhabitants. The battle is remembered today as one of the great injustices perpetrated against Native Americans by the U.S. government.

WRAC |ræk| • *abbr.* Women's Royal Army Corps (in the UK, until 1993).

WRAF |ræf| • *abbr.* Women's Royal Air Force (in the UK, until 1994).

wreck • *n.* **1** the destruction of a ship at sea; a shipwreck: *the survivors of the wreck.* **2** a ship destroyed in such a way: *the salvaging of treasure from wrecks.* • *v.* **1** (usually **be wrecked**) cause the destruction of (a ship) by sinking or breaking up: *he was drowned when his ship was wrecked.* **2** involve (someone) in such a wreck: *sailors who had the misfortune to be wrecked on these coasts.* **3** (**wrecking**) cause the destruction of a ship in order to steal the cargo: *the locals reverted to the age-old practice of wrecking.* **4** suffer or undergo shipwreck.

wrecker • *n.* a person employed in recovering a wrecked ship or its contents.

Wren • *n.* (in the UK) a member of the former Women's Royal Naval Service.

ORIGIN: early 20th cent.: originally in the plural, from the abbreviation WRNS.

Wright, Horatio Gouverneur (1820–1899) • U.S. army officer and engineer. Born in Clinton, Connecticut, Horatio Gouverneur Wright graduated from WEST POINT in 1841 with a commission in the engineers. He helped destroy the Norfolk Navy Yard when the CIVIL WAR began, and then worked on fortifications around Washington. He was appointed brigadier general of volunteers in September 1861, and during the next year commanded some landing forces in coastal operations before moving on to command the Department of the Ohio. He took over a division in the VI Corps of the ARMY OF THE POTOMAC in May 1863. When JOHN SEDGWICK was killed during the battle of SPOTSYLVANIA in May 1864, Wright became the corps commander. He led that organization through the terrible combat at the "Bloody Angle" and was promoted major general of volunteers. In July he defended Washington from JUBAL EARLY, and then served under PHILIP H. SHERIDAN in the SHENANDOAH VALLEY. The VI Corps was the first to break the Confederate line at PETERSBURG in April 1864, and led the attack at SAILOR'S CREEK that forced the surrender of RICHARD S. EWELL. Afterwards Wright was brevetted a major general of regulars. After the war Wright resumed his regular engineering duties as a lieutenant colonel, helping to build the East River Bridge and the Washington Monument. In June 1879 he became the chief of engineers with a rank of brigadier general. He retired from the army in 1884.

Wright, Joseph Jefferson Burr (1801–1878) • U.S. army medical officer. Born in Wilkes-Barre, Pennsylvania, attended the University of Pennsylvania School of Medicine. In 1833 he joined the army as as assistant surgeon, and served the next seven years at frontier outposts. During the second SEMINOLE WAR he developed new techiques to use quinine to combat malaria. Wright skillfully administered hospitals for both ZACHARY TAYLOR and WINFIELD SCOTT in Mexico, contributing significantly to American success there. During the first year of the CIVIL WAR, Wright served as the medical director for the Departments of the Ohio and of the Missouri, but he spent most of the conflict as the surgeon at CARLISLE BARRACKS in Pennsylvania. After the war the post became a training center for the Army Hospital Corps, and he became one of its instructors. Wright retired as a colonel in 1876 and died in Carlisle.

Wright-Patterson Air Force Base • located in Dayton, Ohio, where it is home to more than seventy units from seven different Air Force commands and numerous DEPARTMENT OF DEFENSE organizations, Wright-Patterson AFB is a major center for aviation research and development. First established in 1917 as McCook Field, it was joined by Wilbur Wright Field in 1924, located on land donated by the local community. In 1931,

Wright Field was renamed Patterson Field for Lt. Frank Patterson, and the two fields, McCook and Patterson, became a single installation, renamed Wright-Patterson AFB. Wright-Patterson AFB is responsible for researching and developing weapon systems of the future, and is the headquarters of a worldwide logistics system that supports the entire U.S. Air Force.

Wright, Wilbur (1867–1912) and **Orville (1871–1948)** • born, respectively in Indiana (near Millville) and Dayton, Ohio, the two brothers who invented the airplane in December 1903. Although they dated their interest in flight to 1878, when their father, Milton Wright, gave them a toy helicopter, they opened a printing business 1889 together and were moderately successful. In 1896, their interest in flight was renewed by the death of the German gliding pioneer Otto Lilienthal in a glider crash. After learning all they could about aeronautics and determining that Kitty Hawk, North Carolina had the best weather conditions for testing aircraft, in 1900 they began testing a kite/glider large enough to carry a human being aloft. Although their early experiments proved disappointing, the Wright brothers realized that the results of their experiments had to be traced to erroneous information they were using from their predecessors and set out to collect accurate information. They were finally successful in December 1903, and demonstrated that a heavier-than-air craft could take off from level ground and fly far enough to show that it was operating under a pilot's control. By October 1905, they were able to remain airborne for as long as thirty-nine minutes, but decided to suspend their experiments until they had secured patents for their invention. In 1908, the Wrights secured a U.S. Army contract for $25,000 to deliver the first airplane, and did so in 1909. Wilbur began to concentrate his energies on business and legal disputes. Returning exhausted to Dayton from a series of legal meetings and court appearances, he died in 1912, and Orville assumed the position of president of the Wright Company (founded in 1909). In 1915, Orville sold his shares in the company, and worked as an aeronautical engineer and consultant during WORLD WAR I, and played a major role in the development of a pilotless aircraft bomb. After the war, he retired from the aircraft industry. In 1925, he loaned the 1903 Wright airplane to the London Science Museum, refusing to bring it back to the United States until the Smithsonian Institution accepted the Wright Brothers' claim that they had invented the first aircraft. The Smithsonian finally acceded to Orville's conditions in 1944.

writ |rit| • *n.* a form of written command in the name of a court or other legal authority to act, or abstain from acting, in some way: *the two reinstated officers* ***issued a writ for*** *libel* ***against*** *the applicants.*

writ of habeas corpus • see HABEAS CORPUS.

WRNS historical • *abbr.* (in the UK) Women's Royal Naval Service.

WSMR • *abbr.* White Sands Missile Range.

WTO • *abbr.* World Trade Organization.

WWI • *abbr.* World War I.

WWII • *abbr.* World War II.

Wye Accord • an agreement signed at Maryland's Wye Plantation on October 23, 1998 by Israeli Prime Minister Benjamin Netanyahu and Palestinian Authority chairman Yasir Arafat. Mediated by U.S. President BILL CLINTON, it was an attempt to establish a new framework for peace in the Israel-Palestinian conflict. Israel pledged to withdraw from territory on the West Bank, thereby allowing Palestine more land in the region and security control over it. In turn, Palestine accepted monitoring by the CENTRAL INTELLIGENCE AGENCY to ensure active efforts of the control of terrorist actions. It succeeded the Oslo peace accords.

Xx

XYZ Affair • a diplomatic incident in 1798 between the United States and France during a period when French privateers were regularly seizing U.S. merchant ships and the U.S. government was contemplating a naval war. President JOHN ADAMS dispatched envoys to negotiate with France's foreign minister, who refused to meet them but instead had his own envoys approach the Americans, inviting them to pay tribute and extend a loan to France in order to stop the privateering. This offer was refused; the anonymous French agents, referred to as X, Y, and Z in Adams' report to Congress, were vilified, and public outcry led to the Congress authorizing 1,000 privateers to capture or repel French vessels.

Yy

yacht |yät| • *n.* **1** a medium-sized sailboat equipped for cruising or racing. **2** a powered boat or small ship equipped for cruising, typically for private or official use: *a steam yacht.*

Yakima War • a war between Anglo settlers and the Native American Yakima tribe in Pacific Northwest in 1855. A government agent, sent to the newly created reservation to investigate reports of Yakima violence against miners who were attempting to settle on and work their lands, was himself killed by the Yakima. A military force made up mostly of local volunteers was formed to punish the Yakima for this action. Fighting continued for about three years, until the combined forces of the Spokane, Palouse, Coeur d'Alene, and Yakima were finally defeated.

Yalta Conference • a WORLD WAR II peace conference held on February 4–11, 1945, at Yalta in the Crimea, between President FRANKLIN D. ROOSEVELT, British Prime Minister WINSTON CHURCHILL, and Soviet premier JOSEF STALIN. Issues they discussed included the occupation of Germany, the establishment of a government and borders in Poland, Soviet entry into the war against Japan, and voting procedures for the UNITED NATIONS. In the aftermath of the war, the agreements reached by the leaders proved largely unsuccessful.

It was held in Yalta because Stalin refused to leave the Soviet Union.

Yalu • a river that forms the border between North Korea and China and marks the high tide of the United States and South Korean troops in the North. On September 27, 1950, President HARRY S. TRUMAN authorized Gen. DOUGLAS MACARTHUR to take troops north of the 38TH PARALLEL, and the combined forces swiftly swept north to the banks of the Yalu River and the border with Red China. This so alarmed Communist China that it sent a large force across the river, undetected by the United States and South Korea, and launched a major counteroffensive in conjunction with the North Koreans on November 25, pushing the invaders back to the 38th Parallel. Most of the action during the rest of the war would be involved in holding this line.

Yamamoto, Isoroku (1884–1943) • Japan's greatest naval strategist in WORLD WAR II, and the naval officer who conceived of the surprise attack on the U.S. naval base at PEARL HARBOR in 1941. He graduated from the naval academy in 1904, fought in the Russo-Japanese War, and served as naval attaché in the Japanese embassy in Washington, D.C. (1926–1927). In little more than ten years he rose quickly through the ranks, becoming vice minister of the Japanese navy in 1936, commander of Japan's First Fleet in 1938, and commander in chief of Japan's Combined Fleet in August 1941. Yamamoto opposed war with the United States, but, once the decision had been made, he argued that the only way to win such a war was a surprise attack that would completely disable the U.S. naval forces in the Pacific. (He also predicted that, should the war with the United States last longer than a year, Japan would lose.) After the successful attack on Pearl Harbor, Yamamoto wanted a decisive battle with the remainder of the U.S.'s Pacific forces (its aircraft carriers), but Japan lost that battle, at MIDWAY in June 1942. His next campaign, in the SOLOMON ISLANDS, was also unsuccessful, and he died when the U.S. forces shot down his plane over Bougainville Island in the Solomons.

Yamasee War • a war fought sporadically from 1715 to 1728 in South Carolina between the Yamasee tribe and Colonial settlers. Conflict arose initially over trade abuses by the colonists, such as the selling into slavery of Native wives and children for the settlement of debts. The settlers received some aid from northern colonies and also conscripted their slaves to fight for them. Several colonial forts fell at first, but the colonists, with help from the Cherokee, then brutally repressed the revolt. Many small Carolina tribes disappeared completely in this conflict. Some of the Yamasee fled south with runaway slaves to join the Seminoles in Florida.

Yamashita, Tomoyuki (1885–1946) • Japanese general known for his successful attacks on Malaya and Singapore during WORLD WAR II. He became the highest ranking general in the Japanese Imperial Army's air force. He helped plan Japan's invasion of the Thai and Malay peninsulas in 1941–1942, and his Twenty-fifth Army overran all of Malaya and defeated the British naval base at Singapore in a ten-week campaign. Retired to Manchuria by Prime Minister TOJO HIDEKI, he was militarily inactive until Tojo's fall in 1944, when he was sent to command the defense of the Philippines. In spite of the fact that his forces were defeated in both the LEYTE and LUZON campaigns, he held on until Japan surrendered in August 1945. He was tried for war crimes and, in spite of his denials of knowledge concerning atrocities committed under his command, was eventually convicted and hanged.

Yank • *abbr.* Yankee.

Yankee • *n.* **1** an inhabitant of New England or one of the northern states. **2** a Union soldier in the Civil War. **3** (also **Yankee jib**) a large jib set forward of a staysail in light winds.

Yankee Doodle • a song composed in the 1750s during the FRENCH AND INDIAN WAR (1754–63), and one of the most popular during the REVOLUTIONARY WAR. The lyrics are of British origin and were written to ridicule American colonists and the attire of American soldiers. The Americans adopted the song as one of their own, which led to the development of many different versions and parodies, both British and American. It is believed the Americans played it when the British surrendered at YORKTOWN (1781). The tune is believed to be of American origin.

Yankee Station • a base of U.S. naval operations in the Gulf of Tonkin, South China Sea, during the VIETNAM WAR.

***Yank* magazine** • a popular publication for servicemen during WORLD WAR II, and officially titled *YANK, The Army Weekly*. It published editions in every major theater of combat during the war; and it included coverage of the war and special features, such as cartoon characters, Mail Call, and the YANK Pinup Girl.

The first permanent feature of the magazine was Sad Sack, a cartoon creation of Sgt. George Baker.

---

yard • *n.* a cylindrical spar, tapering to each end, slung across a ship's mast for a sail to hang from.

yardarm |ˈyärdˌärm| • *n.* the outer extremity of a ship's yard.

Yardley, Herbert Osborne (1889–1958) • born in Worthington, Indiana, the cryptographer responsible for the U.S.'s first official code-breaking activities during and following WORLD WAR I. He entered the U.S. State Department at 23 as a coding clerk, but was soon recommending ways to improve and protect U.S. codes. By 1917, he was in charge of MI8, the code-breaking group of the MILITARY INTELLIGENCE DIVISION. When the war ended, he suggested a permanent code-breaking organization, and, in 1919, a joint agency of the State Department and the military was created, with Yardley at its head. In spite of its successful breaking of the Japanese diplomatic code in 1921, the group was generally ignored or attacked by government officials, and was disbanded after several years. Unable to find work, Yardley published *The American Black Chamber* (1931), a best-seller, and nineteen nations changed their diplomatic codes. At the request of CHIANG KAI-SHEK, the Chinese Nationalist leader, he went to China to break the Japanese army's codes and remained there until 1940, when he went to Canada and established his own cryptology service.

yare • *adj.* (of a ship) moving lightly and easily; easily manageable.

yaw • *v.* (of a moving ship or aircraft) twist or oscillate about a vertical axis: *the jet yawed sharply to the right.* • *n.* a twisting or oscillation of a moving ship or aircraft about a vertical axis.

yawl • *n.* **1** a two-masted fore-and-aft-rigged sailboat with the mizzenmast stepped far aft so that the mizzen boom overhangs the stern. **2** a ship's jolly boat with four or six oars.

Yazoo River • a river joining the Mississippi River at the town of VICKSBURG, Mississippi, which was a Confederate stronghold during the CIVIL WAR. Union Gen. ULYSSES S. GRANT fought to capture Vicksburg by land and water from mid October 1862. Several attempts to seize Vicksburg, which was well-defended and surrounded by high river bluffs, involved use of gunboats in the Yazoo and Mississippi Rivers. The U.S.S. *Cairo* was the first vessel torpedoed and sunk by Confederate forces on December 12, 1862, in the Yazoo River. Maj. Gen. WILLIAM T. SHERMAN continued to challenge Confederate forces from the water. Bombings from mortar boats on the Yazoo River May 24–31, 1863, aided the siege of Vicksburg by land. Confederate troops at Vicksburg surrendered on July 3, 1863.

yellow fever • a tropical viral disease affecting the liver and kidneys, causing fever and jaundice and often fatal. It is transmitted by mosquitoes.

Yellow Fever Commission • U.S. Army commission, ca. 1899–1902, formed to investigate the causes of yellow fever among Army personnel in Havana, Cuba. Under the direction of Maj. WALTER REED the commission identified the *Aëdes aegypti* mosquito as the vector of the disease, thereby making possible the eradication of the disease in Cuba by controlling its vector.

yellow flag • a ship's yellow flag, denoting the letter Q for 'quarantine.' When flown with another flag, it indicates disease on board; when flown alone, it indicates the absence of disease and signifies a request for customs clearance.

yellow jack • archaic term for YELLOW FEVER.

yeoman |ˈyōmən| • *n.* (pl. **-men**) a petty officer in the US Navy performing clerical duties on board ship.

yeomanry |ˈyōmənrē| • *n.* historical a volunteer cavalry force raised from men who held and cultivated small landed estates (1794–1908).

yield • see NUCLEAR YIELD.

yoke • *n.* **1** the crossbar of a rudder, to whose ends ropes are fastened. **2** a control lever in an aircraft.

Yom Kippur War • a war in the Middle East that started during the Yom Kippur holiday in 1973 when combined forces from Egypt and Syria attacked Israel with the aim of regaining territory lost to Israel in 1967. They made initial gains, capturing part of the Sinai and occupying part of the Golan Heights, until the United States airlifted massive quantities of materiel to Tel Aviv. When the Soviet Union threatened to intervene militarily in the conflict, the United States brokered a ceasefire that brought military hostilities to an end. Some remaining issues were settled at the CAMP DAVID ACCORDS a few years later.

York, Alvin Cullum (1887–1964) • U.S. soldier, born in Pall Mall, Tennessee. York declared himself a conscientious objector at the beginning of WORLD WAR I. Despite his deep religious beliefs, his petition for draft exemption was denied twice, and he was inducted into the army and sent to France with the 328th Regiment of the 82nd Division. York won a CONGRESSIONAL MEDAL OF HONOR and a CROIX DE GUERRE during the MEUSE-ARGONNE offensive (1918) for one of the most remarkable individual performances of any war. On October 8, 1918, York, then only a private first class, led a seventeen-man patrol in an attack on a German machine gun nest. Before the day was done, he had single-handedly killed twenty-five enemy soldiers and was credited with capturing 132 more. He was promoted to sergeant and became one of the most celebrated heroes of the war, but he preferred to live out the rest of his life quietly on a farm granted to him by a grateful state of Tennessee.

Yorktown, Battle of • a REVOLUTIONARY WAR battle at Yorktown, Virginia starting in August, 1781, when British troops under Gen. CHARLES CORNWALLIS were attacked by American land forces. The Americans were later joined by forces approaching by sea and in early October began a formal siege. On October 17th Cornwallis surrendered along with his 8,000 men. It was a turning point in the war since Cornwallis's army was the only British force that was surplus to garrison requirements in North America and British popular opinion began to suspect that there were not adequate resources available to win the war.

***Yorktown*, USS** • **1** (**CV-5**) the third ship with the name, a carrier commissioned at Norfolk, Virginia on September 30, 1937. After participating in Fleet Problems XX and XXI—wargames that would characterize future warfare in the Pacific Theater, the carrier remained off the west coast of the United States until U-BOAT depredations on British merchant vessels in the Atlantic required the United States to transfer a large force to the Atlantic, including the *Yorktown*, a division of battleships, and cruisers and destroyers. After the Japanese bombing of the U.S. fleet at PEARL HARBOR (1941), the *Yorktown* was transferred back to the Pacific as the flagship for the newly created Task Force (TF) 17, where it participated in the first U.S. attack on the Marshall and Gilbert Island groups. It was lost at the BATTLE OF MIDWAY in 1942. **2** an Essex-class aircraft carrier commissioned in 1943. The second of its class, it replaced its namesake, lost in 1942, and its aircraft inflicted heavy losses on the Japanese at Truk and the Marianas, and supported U.S. troops in the Philippines and at IWO JIMA and OKINAWA (1944). After serving in the KOREAN WAR, the ship was modified for antisubmarine warfare and sent to Vietnam. It was decommissioned in 1970 and is now part of a fleet of ships at Patriots Point and serves as host to several carrier memorials. **3** a Ticonderoga-class guided missile cruiser that carries two SH-2 Seasprite multipurpose helicopters instead of the SH-60s carried on ships of this class built later.

You, Dominique |yoo| (1770?–1830) • buccaneer and artillerist. Little is known of Dominique You's early life except that he became a skilled seaman and gunner before joining JEAN LAFFITE's pirates at Barataria, near New Orleans, around 1810. You and his comrades preyed on Spanish and American ships, until they were captured in a U.S. Navy raid on their stronghold in September 1814. All pirate vessels were captured and You, second-in-command, was the highest ranking prisoner. When the British threatened New Orleans later that year, Jean Laffite offered Gen. ANDREW JACKSON the services of the surviving buccaneers. All the captives were released and armed, and You commanded one of two cannons manned by Baratarian crews that took part in the battles around the city in December and January. The gunners were commended in Jackson's dispatches, and in February President JAMES MADISON pardoned all of Laffite's men. After the war You served as an example for lawless elements of the local populace to be loyal to the United States, and was involved in a plot to rescue Napoleon from St. Helena. When he died in New Orleans he was given a military funeral at state expense.

Young, Charles (1864–1922) • U.S. army officer. Born to former slaves in Mayslick, Kentucky, Young became only the third African-American graduate of WEST POINT in 1889. Officers of his race had few opportunities for assignment, and he spent most of his service with the Ninth or Tenth Cavalry Regiments and teaching military science at Wilberforce University. He was the only black commissioned officer in the army during the SPANISH-AMERICAN WAR (1898). Though he missed action in Cuba because he was training black volunteers in Ohio, he did serve with the Ninth Cavalry helping to quell the PHILIPPINE WAR. After that conflict he served as a military attaché in Haiti and Liberia. In 1916 he was promoted to lieutenant colonel while leading elements of the Tenth Cavalry as part of JOHN J. PERSHING's PUNITIVE EXPEDITION into Mexico. When the U.S. entered WORLD WAR I the prospect that Young might advance to command that regiment brought protests from white officers and U.S. senators, resulting in Young's forced retirement for health reasons. He rode on horseback from Ohio to Washington to protest and demonstrate his vigor, but to no avail. He was retired at the rank of colonel, the highest level achieved by an African-American officer to that date. Young was recalled late in the war to train troops, and then sent to Liberia again as military attaché in 1919. While visiting Lagos, Nigeria he fell ill and died. He was buried with full military honors at ARLINGTON NATIONAL CEMETERY.

Young, Pierce Manning Butler (1836–1896) • Confederate army officer, U.S. congressman, and diplomat. Born in Spartenburg, South Carolina, Young entered WEST POINT in 1857. However, he resigned in March 1861 to become a second lieutenant in the Confederate army. He quickly rose to the rank of lieutenant colonel in Cobb's Legion of WADE HAMPTON's brigade. By November 1862 he had been wounded twice and promoted to colonel. He led a cavalry brigade in the ARMY OF NORTHERN VIRGINIA in 1863. He was promoted to major general in 1864 and commanded a division under Hampton that fought WILLIAM T. SHERMAN in the Carolinas. After the war, Young was elected to the U.S. House of Representatives from Georgia, and was allowed to take his seat because of strong letters of recommendation from the military governor of Georgia, Gen. GEORGE G. MEADE. Young became a symbol of national reconciliation, later serving in diplomatic posts in Russia, Guatemala, and Honduras.

Young, Samuel Baldwin Marks (1840–1924) • U.S. army officer. Born in Pittsburgh, Pennsylvania, Young enlisted as a private in a Pennsylvania volunteer unit when the CIVIL WAR began. He served in the ARMY OF THE POTOMAC throughout the conflict, rising to the rank of brevet brigadier general of volunteers for his service in the final campaign. After the war he accepted a regular appointment as a second lieutenant, and by 1897 was the colonel of the 3rd Cavalry Regiment. When the SPANISH-AMERICAN WAR (1898) began, he was made a brigadier general of volunteers and given a brigade in JOSEPH WHEELER's division for the Santiago campaign. After service in Cuba, Young saw action in the PHILIPPINE WAR and served as military governor of northern Luzon. He was promoted to major general of regulars in 1901, going on to command the Department of California. In July 1902 he became the first president of the ARMY WAR COLLEGE. The next year he was promoted to lieutenant general and appointed the first chief of staff of the army under the new GENERAL STAFF system. He held that post until his retirement in 1904. In 1909–1910 he was president of a board of inquiry that upheld President THEODORE ROOSEVELT's harsh punishments for black soldiers involved in the 1906 Brownsville riot. In 1910, Young became the governor of the SOLDIERS HOME in Washington, D.C., a position he held for ten years.

Ypres • |ˈēpr(ə)| a town in northwest Belgium near the border with France, in the province of West Flanders. Ypres was the scene of some of the bitterest fighting of WORLD WAR I.

Ypres, Battles of • three battles in World War I fought near Ypres, western Belgium, which was a key point of an Allied salient that blocked the Germans from approaching the English Channel. Mainly British and some Canadian forces were engaged against the Germans in all of the battles. The first battle, in late 1914, stopped a German march toward the sea but resulted in the Allied forces being surrounded. The second battle, in the spring of 1915, marked the first occasion on which poison gas (chlorine, by the Germans) was used as a weapon, against the rules of the HAGUE CONVENTION. Casualties were in the tens of thousands on both sides. The last battle in July to November of 1917, also called the battle of Passchendaele, was the longest and bloodiest. It was fought in torrential rains with a quarter of a million casualties on both sides, and an effective pushback of the German line of only five miles.

Yuma Proving Ground • a testing site in the Sonoran Desert 26 miles northeast of Yuma, Arizona, used by the U.S. Army since 1942. It was built initially to test bridging and engineering equipment on the Colorado River. Covering 1,300 square miles (3,367 square kilometers), it is used today for ordnance testing and training, including extreme weather conditions testing of materials and technology. The 1 million acre installation employs some 300 military and 1,400 civilian personnel.

Zz

Zane, Betty (1766?–1831?) • patriot. Except for the fact that she was born Elizabeth Zane in the Potomac River Valley of western Virginia, little about Betty Zane's life can be confirmed with much accuracy. She attained legendary status for heroism during the British and Indian siege of FORT HENRY, near what is now Wheeling, West Virginia, though the chroniclers disagree about the exact details of her exploits, as well as whether they occurred during sieges in 1777 or 1782. When the fort ran low on ammunition, Betty volunteered to run a sixty-yard gauntlet to her home to retrieve gunpowder stored there. Whether she ran or walked, whether she was shot at or not, and how she carried back the powder are all disputed, but the ammunition she brought back enabled the fort's defenders to hold out until relief arrived. The date of her death on a farm in Ohio is also uncertain, but a memorial statue marks her grave in Walnut Grove Cemetery in Martin's Ferry, Ohio.

Zedong, Mao • see MAO ZEDONG.

Zeke • (in World War II), the Allies' code name for the Japanese A6m built by Mitsubishi. Also called ZERO.

zero • short for ZERO HOUR. • *v.* (**-oes**, **-oed**) set the sights of (a gun) for firing.

▸**zero in** take aim with a gun or missile: *jet fighters* ***zeroed in on*** *the rebel positions.*

Zero • the Mitsubishi fighter aircraft, a single-seat monoplane deployed from carriers and used by the Japanese Air Force with great success during WORLD WAR II. The Allies were unable to build a comparable fighter plane until 1943. Although the Allies code-named it "ZEKE," it was known more generally as the Zero, a name derived from one of its original names, *Reisen Kanjikisen* (Zero Celebration Carrier-based Fighter Airplane): 1940, the first year it was produced, was also the 2,600th anniversary of Jimmu's, Japan's first emperor, ascent to the throne, and so the "zero-year" celebration.

In the final months of World War II, many of the surviving Zeros were used as kamikaze aircraft.

zero hour • the time at which a planned operation, typically a military one, is set to begin.

zero point • the location of the center of a burst of a nuclear weapon at the instant of detonation. The zero point may be in the air, or on or beneath the surface of land or water, dependent upon the type of burst, and it is thus to be distinguished from ground zero.

Zhou Enlai (1898–1976) • born into the Chinese gentry, a leading figure in the Chinese Communist Party (CCP), premier of China (1949–1976), and foreign minister of the People's Republic of China (1949–1958). He played a significant role in the Chinese revolution and one of the great negotiators of the twentieth century. Arrested in 1920 for dissent and political agitation, he went to France when he was released and, while there, made his commitment to Communism. He returned to China in 1924 and participated in the National Revolution, led by Sun Yat-sen's Nationalist Party (KUOMINTANG) with the collaboration of the CCP and Russian assisstance. He was appointed deputy director of the political department at the Whampoa Military Academy and, in 1927, became director of the military department of the CCP. After organizing the workers of Shanghai for CHIANG KAI-SHEK's Nationalists, he fled to Wu-han, the center of Communist power, when Chiang purged his Communist allies. He was elected to the CCP Central Committee and its Politburo during the Party's Fifth National Congress, and helped organize the Nan-ch'ang Uprising, a Communist insurrection, in August 1927. He retreated again, this time to Shanghai via Hong Kong, after the Nationalists recaptured Nan-ch'ang. He returned to China in 1928, and eventually left Shanghai for Kiangsi province, where he Zhu De and MAO ZEDONG had been working to develop Communist rural bases (soviets). In 1932, Zhou succeeded Mao as the political commissar of the Red Army, commanded by Zhu De. The success of Chiang's campaigns finally forced a Communist retreat in 1934, and the Long March to the north of China began. Although Zhou had earlier sided with the CCP leaders who took control of the Kiangsi soviet from Mao, they became close associates. When the Long March ended in 1935 at the Communist base in Shensi province, Zhou became the CCP's chief negotiator and succeeded in forming an alliance with the Nationalists to resist Japan's aggression. When Chiang's generals arrested him in order to stop the CCP-Nationalist civil war, Zhou negotiated Chiang's release on the condition that he cease attacking the Communists and support the United Front. From the outbreak of the SINO-JAPANESE WAR in 1937, Zhou became the CCP's chief representative to the Nationalist government, a position he held until 1943. After Japan surrendered in 1945, he accompanied Mao Zedong to peace talks arranged with Chiang Kai-shek. He was also an important figure in the negotiations with the Nationalists in 1946, and was a major factor in Chiang's eventual downfall in 1947. Zhou became the first premier of the Republic of China in October 1949, and served as the chief administrator of its huge civil bureaucracy. Between 1950 and 1964, he continued in his role as negotiator and traveled widely. He was also responsible for arranging and carrying out plans for the historic meeting between Mao Zedong and President RICHARD M. NIXON in 1972.

Ziegler, David |ˈzēglər| (1748–1811) • Revolutionary and U.S. army officer and public servant. Born in Heidelberg, Germany, David Ziegler had already served six years in the Russian army before emigrating to Pennsylvania in 1774. He joined the army the next year and became a second lieutenant in the First Regiment of Continental Infantry in 1776. His military experience proved very useful training soldiers at VALLEY FORGE, and he earned promotion to captain for distinguished performance at MONMOUTH (1778). Ziegler retired briefly from the army after the war, but in 1784 he accepted a captaincy in Pennsylvania's First American Regiment. He and his well-trained company provided some dependable troops for Gens. ARTHUR ST. CLAIR and JOSIAH HARMAR in their unsuccessful campaigns to subjugate the Indians in the Ohio country. Ziegler rose to the rank of major before resigning his commission in 1792. Afterwards he served in a number of elected and appointed political positions in Ohio.

Zimmerman telegram • a coded message written by German foreign secretary Arthur Zimmerman and sent to Mexican president Venustiano Carranza on January 16, 1917 during WORLD WAR I. It proposed a German-Mexican alliance and suggested Mexico reclaim its former territory by starting a war with the United States, thereby distracting the United States from the overseas war. It was published by President WOODROW WILSON on March 1, 1917, and the U.S. entered the war five weeks later.

zip gun • informal a cheap homemade or makeshift gun.

Zippo • **1** (in the Vietnam War) a flamethrower. **2** a popular brand of cigarette lighter, with a flip-top and nearly wind-resistant flame, that American soldiers in Vietnam could buy at PX stores.

It was customary among soldiers to have a motto or slogan engraved on their Zippos. One from the early 1970s read, "If I had been at Kent State there would have been one hell of a body count."

Zippo job • (in the Vietnam War) a mission or raid, especially a search-and-destroy mission against VIETCONG-occupied hamlets in which hooches and villages were burned with flamethrowers or set afire with cigarette lighters.

zone of action • (generally applied to an offensive action) a tactical subdivision of a larger area, the responsibility for which is assigned to a tactical unit.

zone of fire • an area into which a designated ground unit or fire support ship delivers, or is prepared to deliver, fire support. Fire may or may not be observed.

Zouave |zōō'äv; zwäv| • a member of one of several CIVIL WAR era Union and Confederate military formations attired in the colorful uniforms based on Algerian designs made popular by the French Army in the mid-19th Century. The uniform of each Zouave unit varied according to the taste and imagination of its leaders and members, but all Zouave units generally adopted such identifiable items as baggy trousers, short jackets, white leggings, and a form of the fez as headgear.

Zulu time • **1** (also **Universal Time**) formerly Greenwich Mean Time—a measure of time that conforms, within a close approximation, to the mean diurnal rotation of the Earth and serves as the basis of civil timekeeping. **2** more commonly, the time at 0° longitude (the meridian of Greenwich), expressed thus, 0950Z, meaning 9:50 A.M. at the meridian of Greenwich.

Zumwalt, Elmo Russell, Jr. (1920–2000) • U.S. naval officer. Born in San Francisco, California, Elmo Russell Zumwalt, Jr. graduated from the U.S. NAVAL ACADEMY in 1942. During WORLD WAR II he served on a destroyer that saw action at the decisive BATTLE OF LEYTE GULF (1944). He commanded a destroyer escort at the beginning of the KOREAN WAR, and saw combat as navigator for the battleship *Wisconsin*. He served in a series of command and staff assignments before becoming a vice admiral and Commander Naval Forces, Vietnam, in 1968. After two years there, he was appointed CHIEF OF NAVAL OPERATIONS, and became the youngest four-star admiral in American history. In that position he instituted a wide range of reforms to revitalize the Navy, many initiated by his famous "Z-grams." After retirement in 1974, he handled a number of senior corporate positions, and also was associated with many foundations dealing with service-connected diseases. He was awarded the Presidential Medal of Freedom in 1998.

Special Reference Sections

Ranks

Pay Grade	Army	Navy/ Coast Guard	Air Force	Marine Corps
E-1	Private (PV1)	Seaman Recruit (SR)	Airman Basic (AB)	Private (PVT)
E-2	Private (PV2)	Seaman Apprentice (SA)	Airman (Amn)	Private First Class (PFC)
E-3	Private First Class (PFC)	Seaman (SN)	Airman First Class (A1C)	Lance Corporal (LCpl)
E-4	Corporal (CPL) Specialist (SPC)	Petty Officer Third Class (PO3)	Senior Airman (SrA)	Corporal (Cpl)
E-5	Sergeant (SGT)	Petty Officer Second Class (PO2)	Staff Sergeant (SSgt)	Sergeant (Sgt)
E-6	Staff Sergeant (SSG)	Petty Officer First Class (PO1)	Technical Sergeant (TSgt)	Staff Sergeant (SSgt)
E-7	Sergeant First Class (SFC)	Chief Petty Officer (CPO)	Master Sergeant First Sergeant (Master Sergeant)	Gunnery Sergeant (GySgt)
E-8	Master Sergeant (MSG) First Sergeant (1SG)	Senior Chief Petty Officer (SCPO)	Senior Master Sergeant (SMSgt) First Sergeant (Senior Master Sergeant)	Master Sergeant (MSgt) First Sergeant (1stSgt)
E-9	Sergeant Major (SGM) Command Sergeant Major	Master Chief Petty Officer (MCPO)	Chief Master Sergeant (CMSgt) First Sergeant (Chief Master Sergeant) Command Chief Master Sergeant	Master Gunnery (MGySgt) Sergeant Major (SgtMaj)
Special Pay Grade	Sgt. Major of the Army (SMA)	Master Chief Petty Officer of the Navy (MCPON)	Chief Master Sergeant of the Air Force (CMAF)	Sgt. Major of the Marine Corps. (SgtMajMC)

Pay Grade	Army	Navy/Coast Guard	Marines
W-1	Warrant Officer One (WO1)	Warrant Officer (WO1)	Warrant Officer (WO1)
W-2	Chief Warrant Officer Two (CW2)	Chief Warrant Officer Two (CW2)	Warrant Officer 2 (WO2)
W-2	Chief Warrant Officer Three (CW3)	Chief Warrant Officer Three (CW3)	Warrant Officer 3 (WO3)
W-4	Chief Warrant Officer Four (CW4)	Chief Warrant Officer Four (CW4)	Warrant Officer 4 (WO4)
W-5	Master Warrant Officer (CW5)		Warrant Officer 5 (WO5)

Note: The Air Force does not have Warrant Officers.

Pay Grade	Army/Air Force/Marines	Navy/Coast Guard
O-1	Second Lieutenant (2LT)	Ensign (ENS)
O-2	First Lieutenant (1LT)	Lieutenant Junior Grade (LTJG)
O-3	Captain (CPT)	Lieutenant (LT)
O-4	Major (MAJ)	Lieutenant Commander (LCDR)
O-5	Lieutenant Colonel (LTC)	Commander (CDR)
O-6	Colonel (COL)	Captain (CAPT)
O-7	Brigadier General (BG)	Real Admiral (lower half) (RDML)
O-8	Major General (MG)	Rear Admiral (upper half) (RADM)
O-9	Lieutenant General (LTG)	Vice Admiral (VADM)
O-10	General (GEN)	Admiral (ADM)

Ranks and Insignia by Branch of Service

OFFICERS

USAF, USMC, USARMY:

O-1: 2nd Lieutenant	single gold bar
O-2: 1st Lieutenant	two silver bars
O-3: Captain	two silver bars
O-4: Major	gold oak leaf
O-5: Lt. Colonel	silver oak leaf
O-6: Colonel	silver eagle
O-7: Brigadier General	single silver star
O-8: Major General	two silver stars
O-9: Lt. General	three silver stars
O-10: General	four silver stars
O-11: General of the service	(only in wartime) five silver stars in a circle

USN:

O-1: Ensign	single gold bar or, on sleeve or epaulette, single thin stripe
O-2: Lieutenant J.G.	single silver bar or, on sleeve or epaulette, one thin and one broad stripe
O-3: Lieutenant	two silver bars or, on sleeve or epaulette, two broad stripes
O-4: Lt. Commander	gold oak leaf or, on sleeve or epaulette, two broad stripes with one narrow between
O-5: Commander	silver oak leaf or, on sleeve or epaulette, three broad stripes
O-6: Captain	silver eagle or, on sleeve or epaulette, four broad stripes
O-7: Rear Admiral (lower half)	silver star or, on sleeve or epaulette, single wide stripe
O-8: Rear Admiral (upper half)	two silver stars, or, on sleeve or epaulette, one wide and one narrow stripe
O-9: Vice Admiral	three silver stars, or, on sleeve or epaulette, one wide stripe and two narrow stripes
O-10: Admiral	four silver stars, or, on sleeve or epaulette, one wide stripe and three narrow stripes
O-11: Fleet Admiral	five stars in a circle or, on sleeve or epaulette, one wide stripe and three narrow stripes

ENLISTED

U.S. ARMY

E-1: Private (recruit)	no chevron
E-2: Private (after basic)	one chevron
E-3: Private 1st Class	one full chevron
E-4: Corporal	two chevrons (Specialist 4 wears black patch with gold eagle)
E-5: Sergeant	three chevrons
E-6: Staff Sergeant	two chevrons above one full chevron
E-7: Sergeant First Class	two chevrons above one full chevron and one below
E-8: Master Sergeant	two chevrons above one full chevron and two below
E-8: First Sergeant	two chevrons above one full chevron and two below, with a center diamond
E-9: Sergeant Major	two chevrons above one full chevron and two below, with a center star
E-9: Command Sergeant Major	two chevrons above one full chevron and two below, with a center star-and-wreath
E-9: Sergeant Major of the Army	two chevrons above full chevron and two below, with center eagle and side stars

Ranks and Insignia by Branch of Service *(cont.)*

ENLISTED

U.S. Marines

Rank	Insignia
E-1: Private (recruit)	no chevron
E-2: Private First Class	one chevron
E-3: Lance Corporal	one chevron with crossed rifles
E-4: Corporal	two chevrons with crossed rifles
E-5: Sergeant	three chevrons with crossed rifles
E-6: Staff Sergeant	two chevrons above crossed rifles and one below
E-7: Gunnery Sergeant	two chevrons above crossed rifles and two below
E-8: Master Sergeant	two chevrons above crossed rifles and two below
E-8: First Sergeant	two chevrons above full chevron and two below, with center diamond
E-9: Sergeant Major	two chevrons above full chevron and three below, with center star
E-9: Master Gunnery Sergeant	two chevrons above full chevron and three below, with center USMC insignia
E-9: Master Sergeant of the Marine Corps	two chevrons above full chevron and three below, with center USMC insignia and side stars

U.S. Navy

Rank	Insignia
E-1: Seaman Recruit	no insignia
E-2: Seaman Apprentice	two diagonal stripes
E-3: Seaman	three diagonal stripes
E-4: Petty Officer Third Class	eagle, crossed anchors, and one red stripe
E-5: Petty Officer Second Class	eagle, crossed anchors, and two red stripes
E-6: Petty Officer First Class	eagle, crossed anchors, and three red stripes
E-7: Chief Petty Officer	eagle, full chevron, and two gold chevrons
E-8: Senior Chief Petty Officer	star, eagle, full chevron, and two gold chevrons
E-9: Master Chief Petty Officer	two silver stars, eagle, full chevron, and two gold chevrons
E-9: Fleet/Command Master Chief Petty Officer	two gold stars, eagle, full chevron, and two gold chevrons
E-9: Master Chief Petty Officer of the Navy	three gold stars, eagle, full chevron with center star, and two gold chevrons

Coast Guard rank is the same as the U.S. Navy except for color and the seaman recruit rank, which has one stripe.

U.S. Air Force

Rank	Insignia
E-1: Airman Basic (boot camp)	
E-2: Airman	one star-in-circle chevron
E-3: Airman First Class	two star-in-circle chevrons
E-4: Senior Airman	three star-in-circle chevrons
E-5: Staff Sergeant	three star-in-circle chevrons and one chevron below
E-6: Technical Sergeant	three star-in-circle chevrons and two chevrons below
E-7: Master Sergeant	one full chevron, three star-in-circle chevrons and two chevrons below
E-7: First Sergeant	one full chevron with center diamond, three star-in-circle chevrons and two chevrons below
E-8: Senior Master Sergeant	two chevrons over one full chevron, three star-in-circle chevrons and two chevrons below
E-8: First Sergeant	two chevrons over one full chevron with center diamond, three star-in-circle chevrons and two chevrons below
E-9: Chief Master Sergeant	three chevrons over one full chevron, three star-in-circle chevrons and two chevrons below
E-9: First Sergeant	three chevrons over one full chevron with center diamond, three star-in-circle chevrons and two chevrons below
E-9: Command Master Sergeant	three chevrons over one full chevron with center star, three star-in-circle chevrons and two chevrons below
E-9: Chief Master Sergeant of the Air Force	three chevrons over one full chevron, three center-laurel chevrons and two chevrons below

Table of Casualties by Battle

Battle	Total Estimated Casualties	US-Federal-Allied	Confederate, Axis, German, North Vietnamese, or other opponents	Notes
Alamance, Battle of the	26	26		(Many wounded.)
Alamo, Battle of the	1,715	115	1,600	
An Loc, Vietnam	2,600	800	1,800	
Antietam, Battle of	22,000			
Antwerp, liberation of				
Anzio, Battle of	25,000			(25,000 lost in related advance.)
Argonne Forest	217,000	117,000	100,000	(26,000 taken prisoner.)
Arnhem, capture of	4,430	1,130	3,300	
Atlanta, Battle of		3,722	7,000	(est.)
Balls (or Ball's) Bluff, Battle of	1255	1,100	155	(700 Federal prisoners taken.)
Baltimore Affair	456	110	346	
Bataan Death March	10,000	10,000		(est.)
Bataan, Battle of		600 U.S., 5-10,000 Filipino		
Bay of Pigs invasion	300	300		(est.)
Belleau Wood, Battle of		5,200	unknown	
Bismarck Sea, Battle of the			6,000	
Black Hawk War	2,000			
Bleeding Kansas	201			
Bosnian Crisis	250,000			(as of 12/14/95.)
Boston Massacre	5			
Braddock's Defeat	1,016			
Brandy Station, Battle of	1,351	866	485	
Brandywine, Battle of the	1,490	900	590	
Buena Vista, Battle of	4,100	600	3,500	
Bulge, Battle of the	277,000	77,000	200,000	
Bull Run, First Battle of	4,878	2,896	1,982	
Bull Run, Second Battle of	24,000	14,500	9,500	
Bunker Hill, Battle of	1,400	400	1,000	
Cambodia, invasion of	500,000			
Camden, Battle of			312	
Cassino, Battle of	21,000			
Cedar Creek, Battle of	8,685	5685	3,000	
Cerro Gordo, Battle of	1,100	400	700	
Chancellorsville, Battle of	30,000	17,000	13,000	
Chapultepec, Battle of	2,360	860	1,500	
Chickamauga, Battle of	34,000	16,000	18,000	
Chickasaw Bayou, Battle of	1,983	1,776	207	
Chilean Crisis	19	19		
Chosin Reservoir, Battle of the	29,400	4,400	25,000	
Cold Harbor, Battle of	95,000	60,000	35,000	(est.)
Contreras, Battle of	7,600	1,100	6,500	(est.)
Corregidor, Battle of	3,300		3,300	
Cowpens, Battle of	401	72	329	
Crater, Battle of the	4,975	3,793	1,182	
Custer's Last Stand	225	225		
D-day	296,549	140,549	156,000	(within two weeks of Normandy.)
D-Day Landing		4,900		(German is considerably higher.)
Desert Shield, Operation *see* PERSIAN GULF WAR.				
Desert Storm, Operation *see* PERSIAN GULF WAR.				
Dien Bien Phu, Vietnam	24,600	2,600	22,000	
Easter Offensive			100,000	(est. Vietnamese)
El Alamein, Battle of	38,500	13,500	25,000	

Table of Casualties by Battle *(cont.)*

Battle	*Total Estimated Casualties*	*US-Federal-Allied*	*Confederate, Axis, German, North Vietnamese, or other opponents*	*Notes*
Fallen Timbers, Battle of		133		(No Indian casualty estimate available.)
Fort Fisher, capture of		955		(No Confederate casualty estimate available.)
Fort Henry, capture of	176			
Fort Pillow, Battle of	431	331	100	
Fort Wagner, seige of	1,689	1,515	174	
France, Liberation of	925,000	225,000	700,000	(Allied casualties include 20,000 missing.)
Franklin, Battle of	8,573	2,326	6,247	
Fredericksburg, Battle of	18,000	13,000	5,000	
Gettysburg, Battle of	44,049	23,049	21,000	
Guadalcanal, Battle of	37,500	7,500	30,000	(est.)
Guam	15,000	3,000	12,000	
Guilford Courthouse, Battle of	793	261	532	
Gulf of Tonkin Incidents				
Hamburger Hill, Battle of	1,076	476	600	(High South Vietnamese casualties; many wounded North Vietnamese not included.)
Hampton Roads, Battle of	270	260	10	
Hiroshima, bombing of	120,000			
Horseshoe Bend, Battle of	1,099	199	900	
Huè, Vietnam	5,600	600	5,000	
Ia Drang Valley, Battle of the	234			
Inchon landing		6,000		(opposition unknown)
Italy, invasion of	746,646	312,000	434,646	
Iwo Jima, Battle of		23,303		(No Korean casualty estimate available.)
Jutland, Battle of	8,819	6,274	2,545	
Kasserine Pass, Battle of	2,816	2,816		
Kettle Hill, Battle of	1,976	1,385	591	
Khe Sanh, Siege of	15,828	3,328	12,500	
Kings Mountain, Battle of	410	90	320	
Korean War	3,459,360	459,360	3,000,000	
Kosovo Crisis	6200			
Kwajalein, Battle of	11,187	2,187	9,000	
Lake Erie, Battle of	257	123	134	
Lexington, Battle of	100			
Leyte Gulf, Battle for	85,500	15,500	70,000	
Little Bighorn, Battle of the *see* CUSTER'S LAST STAND.				
Lundy's Lane, Battle of	1,700	850	850	
Lusitania, Sinking of the	1,128			
Luzon, Philippines		39,851		(Japanese casualties were much higher.)
Maine, USS, Sinking of the		260	260	
Manila Bay, Battle of	389	8	381	
Marne, Second Battle of the	160,000	60,000	100,000	
Mayaguez incident	88	88		
Meuse-Argonne Offensive	217,000	117,000	100,000	(est.)
Midway, Battle of	5,307	307	5,000	
Missionary Ridge, Battle of	12,491	5,824	6,667	
Mobile Bay, Battle of	631	319	312	
Molino del Rey, Battle of	3,488	788	2,700	
Monmouth, Battle of	720	360	360	
Mons, Battle of	4,600	1,600	3,000	(est.)

Table of Casualties by Battle *(cont.)*

Battle	*Total Estimated Casualties*	*US-Federal-Allied*	*Confederate, Axis, German, North Vietnamese, or other opponents*	*Notes*
Monterey, Battle of	835	468	367	
Murfreesboro, Battle of	16,000	8,000	8,000	
My Lai Massacre	300			(est. is 175-400)
Nagasaki	75,000			
Nashville, Battle of	9,061	3,061	6,000	
New Guinea campaign	156,850	33,850	123,000	
New Market Heights, Battle of	888	831	57	
New York, Battle of		5,000		(British casualties unknown.)
Newport, Battle of	571	311	260	
Normandy, Invasion of *see* D-DAY				
North Africa campaign		18,500		(No data on Germany casualties.)
Okinawa, Battle of	186,413	44,413	142,000	
Omaha Beach	2,500	2,500		(est.)
Operation Market Garden	3,500	3,500		
Panay Incident	33	33		
Paris, liberation of	4,160	960	3,200	
Pea Ridge, Battle of	3,384	1,384	2,000	
Pearl Harbor, attack on	3,522	3,522		
Peleliu, Battle of	21,519	7,919	13,600	
Perryville, Battle of	7,000	4,000	3,000	
Persian Gulf War	40,565	565	40,000	(Iraqi casualties est. between 25-65,000)
Petersburg, Siege of	70,000	42,000	28,000	
Philippine Sea, Battle of	1,749	49	1,700	
Philippine War		4,374		(No Filipino data.)
Philippines, Invasion of	312,425	62,425	250,000	
Pickett's Charge	8,500			(est. 7-10,000)
Pontiac's Rebellion			450	(Indian and settler casualties unknown.)
Port Hudson, battle of			1,700	(Federal casualties were higher.)
Pueblo incident	1	1		(1 dead, several wounded.)
Quèbec, Battle of		658	644	
Queenston Heights, Battle of		600		(British casualties unknown.)
San Jacinto, Battle of	39	39	0	
San Juan Hill (Cuba), Battle of	1,572	1,572		
Santiago Bay, Battle of	300		300	
Saratoga, Battles of	1,640	443	1,197	
Seven Days' Battle	37,000	16,500	20,500	
Seven Pines, Battle of	11,000	5,000	6,000	
Shays's Rebellion	4			
Shiloh, Battle of	23,741	13,047	10,694	
Sicily Campaign	196,383	22,383	174,000	
Solomon Islands	22,654	7,654	15,000	
Somme, Battle of the	1,575,000	775,000	800,000	(Both phases together.)
Spotsylvania, Battle of	27,000	9,600	17,400	
St. Lô, capture of	755	600	155	
St. Mihiel offensive		7,000		(15,000 Germans captured.)
Stalingrad, Battle of	200,000		200,000	(German only.)
Stones River, Battle of	26,000	13,000	13,000	
Tarawa, Battle of	3,381	3,381		
Tinian	11,098	2,098	9,000	
Trail of Tears	4,000			

Table of Casualties by Battle *(cont.)*

Battle	*Total Estimated Casualties*	*US-Federal-Allied*	*Confederate, Axis, German, North Vietnamese, or other opponents*	*Notes*
Vera Cruz, capture of	262	82	180	
Verdun, Battle of	977,000	543,000	434,000	
Vicksburg, siege of		9,000	10,000	
Vietnam War	2,798,000	361,000	2,437,000	
Wadke				
Wake Island	1,295	120	1,175	
White Plains, New York	600	300	300	
Wilderness to Petersburg Campaign		12,000		(Confederate casualties unknown.)
Wilderness, Battle of the	29,000	18,000	11,000	
World War I		116,516		(U.S. only.)
World War II	400,000	400,000		(uniformed U.S. personnel only)
Wounded Knee, Battle of	284	84	200	
Yorktown, Battle of	744			
Ypres, Battle(s) of	830,155	600,155	230,000	

Secretaries of War and Defense

President	*Years*	*Secretaries of Defense*
Washington	1789-97	Henry Knox
		Timothy Pickerson
		James McHenry
Adams	1797-1801	James McHenry
		Samuel Dexter
Jefferson	1801-9	Henry Dearborn
Madison	1809-17	William Eustis
		John Armstrong
		James Monroe
		William H. Crawford
Monroe	1817-25	George Graham
		John C. Calhoun
Adams	1825-9	James Barbour
		Peter B. Porter
Jackson	1829-37	John Henry Earon
		Lewis Cass
		Benjamin Butler
Van Buren	1837-41	Joel R. Poinsett
Harrison	1841	John Bell
Tyler	1841-5	John Bell
		John C. Spencer
		James M. Porter
		William Wilkins
Polk	1845-9	William L. Marcy
Taylor	1849-50	George W. Crawford
Fillmore	1850-3	Charles M. Conrad
Pierce	1853-7	Jefferson Davis
Buchanan	1857-61	John Floyd
		Joseph Holt
Lincoln	1861-5	Simon Cameron
		Edwin M. Stanton
Johnson	1865-9	Edwin M. Stanton
		Ulysses S. Grant
		John M. Schofield
Grant	1869-77	John A. Rawlins
		William Tecumseh Sherman
		WW Belknap
		Alphonso Taft
		James D. Cameron
Hayes	1877-81	George M. McCrary
		Alexander Ramsey
Garfield	1881	Robert Todd Lincoln
Arthur	1881-5	Robert Todd Lincoln
Cleveland	1885-9	William M. Endicott
Harrison	1889-93	Redfield Procter
		Stephen B. Elkins
Cleveland	1893-7	Daniel S. Lamont
McKinley	1897-1901	Russell A. Alger
		Elihu Root
Roosevelt	1901-09	Elihu Root
		William H. Taft
		Luke E. Wright
Taft	1909-13	Jacob M. Dickinson
		Henry L. Stimson
Wilson	193-21	Lindley M. Garrison
		Newton D. Baker
Harding	1921-3	John W. Weeks
Coolidge	1923-9	John W. Weeks
		Dwight F. Davis
Hoover	1929-33	James W. Good
		Patrick J. Hurley
Roosevelt	1933-45	George H. Derns
		Harry H. Woodring
		Henry L. Stimson

Secretaries of War and Defense *(cont.)*

President	*Years*	*Secretaries of Defense*
Truman	1945-53	Robert P. Patterson
		Kenneth C. Royall
Eisenhower	1953-61	Charles E. Wilson
		Neil H. McElroy
		Thomas S. Gates
Kennedy	1961-63	Robert McNamara
Johnson	1963-69	Robert McNamara
		Clark Clifford
Nixon	1969-74	Melvin Laird
		Elliot Richardson
		James R. Schlesinger
Ford	1974-77	James R. Schlesinger
		Donald H. Rumsfeld
Carter	1977-81	Harold Brown
Reagan	1981-89	Caspar Weinberger
		Frank C. Carlucci
Bush	1989-93	Dick Cheney
Clinton	1993-2001	Les Aspin
		William J. Perry
		William Cohen
Bush	2001-	Donald H. Rumsfeld

Four- and Five-Star Generals

1789–2001

Four-Star Generals

Downing, Wayne A.
Franks, Frederick M.
Grant, Ulysses S.
Hartzog, William W.
Joulwan, George A.
Luck, Gary E.
Maddox, David M.
Peay, J. H. Binford, III
Pershing, John J.
Reimer, Dennis J.
Ross, Jimmy D.
Shalikashvili, John M.
Sheridan, Philip
Sherman, William T.
Sullivan, Gordon R.

Five-Star Generals

George C. Marshall
Douglas MacArthur
Dwight D. Eisenhower
Henry H. Arnold
Omar N. Bradley
William D. Leahy
Ernest J. King
Chester W. Nimitz
William F. Halsey

Leahy, King, Nimitz, and Halsey are Admirals (the equivalent rank).

Arnold held this title in the army and then later in the Air Force. He was the only person in the Air Force to ever hold that title.